The Solicitor's H
2011

C000152253

Gain 1 hour's CPD with this book

As part of your purchase of *The Solicitor's Handbook 2011*, you are entitled to one hour's CPD, which you can gain by taking an online assessment consisting of 15 questions based on the content of the book.

In order to take the assessment you will need to do the following:

1. Register and log in at the Law Society's CPD Centre at **www.lawsociety.org.uk/ cpdcentre**.
2. Select 'The Solicitor's Handbook 2011' in the list of Law Society Online Learning.
3. Click on 'Add to record'
4. Access the assessment through the 'Record' area of the CPD Centre. In order to claim your hour you must achieve a pass mark of 80%. Upon adding the assessment to your 'Record' area you will have 90 days in which to complete the questions.

For further details contact cpdcentre@lawsociety.org.uk.

THE SOLICITOR'S HANDBOOK 2011

By

Andrew Hopper QC

and

Gregory Treverton-Jones QC

The Law Society

© The Law Society 2011

ISBN 978-1-85328-988-0

Crown copyright material in the Appendices is reproduced with the permission of the Controller of Her Majesty's Stationery Office.

First edition published in 2008
Second edition published in 2009

This third edition published in 2011 by the Law Society
113 Chancery Lane, London WC2A 1PL

Typeset by Columns Design XML Ltd, Reading
Printed and bound in the UK by Hobbs the Printers Ltd, Totton, Hants

The paper used for the text pages of this book is FSC certified. FSC (The Forest Stewardship Council) is an international network to promote responsible management of the world's forests.

Contents

Foreword to the 2008 edition

The authors have asked me to write a short foreword to this book. I am delighted to do so because I entirely agree with the views expressed in the Preface. Although I quite understand that it may be necessary to use the Internet in order for practitioners to be fully up to date at any given moment, many people (and not only the very old like me) like to have a book which sets out the basic principles and which they can readily consult. *The Solicitor's Handbook* is precisely that. It concisely sets out the relevant position under a number of different headings and is very user friendly.

The authors express the hope that the book will prove to be a valuable resource for regulator and regulated alike and that it will contribute to good regulation by identifying and explaining areas of particular concern and risk, especially where practitioners have, in the past, made innocent mistakes which have nevertheless had serious consequences.

I know that hope springs eternal, but in this case I am confident that the authors' hopes will be fulfilled. I wish it well.

Sir Anthony Clarke

Master of the Rolls
Royal Courts of Justice
October 2007

Preface to the 2008 edition

For generations of solicitors *The Guide to the Professional Conduct of Solicitors* (first published in 1960 and always provided free of charge) was the source of all knowledge in relation to the rules that controlled the profession. If you could not find it in the Guide, or if the available published guidance still left you in a quandary, you could always 'ring Redditch' – the Law Society's ethics helpline. Looking it up in the Guide and seeking the Law Society's advice was a total solution. After all; how could you be criticised for following the Law Society's own advice?

The Guide is no more. The eighth edition, published in 1999, was the last. We have moved into the modern era; the paperless age. The Solicitors' Code of Conduct 2007 (which henceforth we will refer to as 'the Code') appears on the website of the Solicitors Regulation Authority (SRA); so do the Solicitors' Accounts Rules 1998, and the Financial Services Rules and other rules. Diligent searching on the Law Society website will reveal much in the way of published guidance, pronunciations and edicts. Information about how clients can complain about you, and what will happen when they do, can be found on the website of the Legal Complaints Service (LCS).

Only in the two thick volumes of the mighty *Cordery on Solicitors* will practitioners find in written form all the law and professional rules relating to solicitors.

But the paperless age and rapidly changing regulatory rules carry with them real dangers for practitioners who may find it difficult or impossible to discover what rules were in force when they did things which later become the subject of regulatory concern. This Handbook, which will be updated annually, seeks to remove those problems.

This Handbook brings together all the professional rules governing the conduct and regulation of solicitors in a manner that is convenient and inexpensive. We hope that we have added much more of value, by drawing upon our professional experience to explain how the rules and the regulatory machinery work in practice.

We have addressed our book to 'you' the practitioner: it has been written from the perspective of the practitioner, to whom it is intended to provide information and guidance. We have included material that we consider relevant and important to the practitioner but which is not included within the formal rules (for example, how money laundering, mortgage fraud and investment scams work), so that independently of the published guidance you can spot problems before they develop into loss to clients and others, damage to reputation, and regulatory interest.

We have included guidance on the workings of the Solicitors Disciplinary Tribunal, on the powers of intervention available to the SRA and the regime for the imposition of conditions on practising certificates.

And we have included a section on where you can obtain further specialist advice and help if all else fails.

It is unlikely that any practitioner currently feels that the profession is under-regulated; the weight of regulation, and dealings with the SRA, can be daunting. The Solicitors' Practice Rules 1936 (made by virtue of section 1 of the Solicitors Act 1933) comprised seven rules (in reality only four) and could be printed on one page.[1] The latest Code, if printed on A4, occupies 253 pages (and 190 pages of this book). We also live in a rapidly changing regulatory environment. The Code came into force on 1 July 2007: one month later it was amended for the first time. An updated version of the Accounts Rules to be incorporated into the Code by amendment is already in contemplation. We now have two regulators – the LCS, dealing with client complaints and redress for poor service, and the SRA, dealing with everything else. Under the previous system, if a complaint engaged both conduct and service issues it was a 'hybrid' and both aspects were dealt with together. Now, all consumer complaints and redress will be dealt with first by the LCS and if any conduct issues are considered to arise they will be referred to the SRA to be dealt with subsequently (although, if very serious concerns are raised and the interests of the public require it, more urgent action will no doubt be taken).

You can still 'ring Redditch' for advice on issues of professional conduct, but the official and published position of the SRA is that for the purpose of any investigation or adjudication it is 'not bound' by any opinion or advice given by its own staff on the ethics helpline. In other words, you can follow the advice of the regulator, but – in theory at least – the regulator can nevertheless find you guilty of misconduct and impose sanctions. It is also not clear to what extent, if at all, information provided for the purposes of seeking such advice will be regarded as confidential, as opposed to being useful intelligence for regulatory purposes about the person making the enquiry.

The Legal Services Act 2007 maintains the division between conduct and service, hiving off consumer complaints and redress to the independent Office for Legal Complaints, which will succeed the LCS. The Act grants significant new powers to the SRA (which we have touched upon in **CHAPTER 2**) and sweeps away significant parts of the current statutory regime, for example in relation to conditions on practising certificates. Where changes will occur, we explain what the future holds.

We hope that this book will prove to be a valuable resource for regulator and regulated alike, and that it will contribute to good regulation in identifying and explaining areas of particular concern and risk – especially where practitioners have in the past made innocent mistakes that have nevertheless had serious consequences.

We would welcome feedback from practitioners, and particularly any requests and recommendations for the inclusion of material in areas we have not covered in this first edition.

We are grateful to the following for their drafting and other suggestions: Euros Jones of James Saunders & Co., who conducted extensive research and provided consider-able input for the money laundering chapter; Mike Calvert of the SRA and Che Odlum of the Law Society, who shared their practical experience of money laundering and investment fraud issues; Iain Miller of Bevan Brittan for his substantial contributions to the chapter on the Code; and Geoffrey Williams QC for reviewing and suggesting amendments to Chapter 14. Many other members of the SRA and SDT, notably Sue Elson and Liz Aldred, answered our queries construc-tively and with unfailing courtesy. All provided invaluable assistance, although the responsibility for any errors and omissions is ours alone. Others deserve particular thanks. Michael Hoyle was the inspiration for Andrew Hopper's original interest in solicitors' regulatory law and practice. When legal complications arose after we finished the writing, we received matchless assistance from Nick Gardner and David Mayhew at Herbert Smith, and valuable advice from Tony Grabiner at 1 Essex Court, and Sean Wilken and Ben Williams at 39 Essex Street. Finally, we are both deeply grateful to our respective wives, Ros and Tamsin, for their support and forbearance while their otherwise apparently sane husbands buried themselves in some of the more esoteric material contained in this book.

1   In brief – Rule 1: no touting; Rule 2: no charging under the published scale fees; Rule 3: no fee sharing; Rule 4: no association with ambulance chasers; Rule 5: provision for waivers; Rule 6: definitions; Rule 7: commencement.

Preface to the 2011 edition

When we embarked on *The Solicitor's Handbook 2008* we were driven principally by the absence of a single convenient source of information to which solicitors could turn to know and interpret the volume of regulation they faced.

The adoption of the Solicitors' Code of Conduct in July 2007, coupled with the absence of any updated equivalent of *The Guide to the Professional Conduct of Solicitors*, persuaded us that the Handbook was needed to plug that gap.

At the time, the Legal Services Bill was making its rapid passage through Parliament and was obviously going to change legal practice in fundamental ways that could not be wholly predicted. We had not anticipated that there would be even greater change than was then expected from the arrival of alternative business structures – true external ownership of law firms – and the replacement of the Legal Complaints Service with the Legal Ombudsman (see **CHAPTER 2** and **CHAPTER 12**).

In the event, a second and contemporaneous revolution is also now taking place. The sparkling new all-embracing, fully codified set of professional rules established by the Solicitors' Code of Conduct 2007 will be consigned to the history books before the end of 2011. It will have lasted just over four years, about the same amount of time that it took to draft it and obtain all the necessary approvals (the process started in 2003). There will be a new Code, and another accompanying new set of rules to deal with specialist areas, such as property selling and cross-border practice. Ironically, this will be part of what the Solicitors Regulation Authority (SRA) refers to as its *Handbook* (we are honoured by this nomenclature, of course), although it is understood that only the Code will be printed and sold and in other respects the profession will have to consult the SRA website. The new Code is in advanced draft form, not anticipated to be the subject of major further change, and we seek to anticipate the major consequences of its adoption in this edition.

In parallel with the development of the new Code, which will come into force in late 2011, probably 6 October, other changes are already taking place. There is to be a wholesale change in the relationship between the SRA and those it regulates. It would be fair to say that we are probably recognised to be not the greatest admirers of the style of regulation adopted by the SRA from its inception in 2007. We have lost count of the number of times we have made or endorsed comments or submissions directed to lack of proportionality.

It is therefore enormously heartening to learn that the SRA recognises that its approach hitherto has been wrong, and insufficiently targeted at what matters: at where the risks really are. The nit-picking, box-ticking approach is to go, and the whole culture of the SRA is to change. Dozens of pages of prescriptive rules will disappear. Instead of reading the rules and ticking the boxes, solicitors will have greater freedom of action in how to run their practices and safeguard the best interests of their clients. The relationship between regulator and regulated will be more adult, more focused on education and problem avoidance than disciplinary action (when, by definition, it is too late). It is equally heartening to know that although this change will involve a radical adjustment in attitude from both the SRA and the profession, the SRA accepts that it must take the lead and show that it has changed, so engendering the essential level of trust between the regulated and the regulator.

All of this is the consequence of a shift to outcomes-focused regulation or OFR, which we discuss in more detail in **CHAPTER 3**.

Other profound changes have occurred since the 2009 edition was published. From 1 June 2010, the SRA acquired statutory powers to fine (up to £2,000) or administer a written rebuke to a solicitor, and to publicise the decision. Gone are the days, therefore, when reprimands were treated as confidential between the SRA and the solicitor. The publication of a rebuke on the SRA website could have far-reaching consequences for the affected solicitor, and we can expect controversy to develop. In the courts, as we note in **CHAPTER 15**, the SRA has successfully appealed two decisions in which solicitors found to have been dishonest had not been struck off by the Tribunal. A third such appeal is pending.

The 2008 edition of this book ran to 947 pages (excluding preliminary pages), but for complicated reasons much of the Code of Conduct appeared in it twice. At 1173 pages, the 2009 edition was in real terms more than 300 pages longer, and was starting to resemble not so much a handbook as a doorstep. We were determined to keep the book manageable despite the avalanche of new material, and so we have taken the pruning shears to the present edition. We have removed the Law Society Practice Note on money laundering and incorporated its most important contents in **CHAPTER 11**. We have trimmed other material without, we hope, losing anything of value. The result is a return to what we had originally envisaged – a volume of convenient size for practitioners to carry around. We believe that it is more needed than ever before.

We continue to be indebted to Iain Miller of Bevan Brittan LLP (in all respects), Euros Jones of Weightmans LLP in relation to the chapter on money laundering and to Mike Calvert, former head of forensic investigations at the SRA, for his invaluable contributions to the chapters on fraud.

The law is stated as at 30 November 2010.

Table of Cases

Table of Statutes

Paragraph references printed in **bold type** indicate where the Enactment is set out in part or in full.

Table of Statutory Instruments

Paragraph references printed in **bold type** indicate where the Enactment is set out in part or in full.

Table of European Legislation and Other International Materials

Table of Other Enactments

Paragraph references printed in **bold** type indicate where the Enactment is set out in part or in full.

PART I
Overview

CHAPTER I

The regulatory and disciplinary landscape

1.1

In the earliest times only the courts exercised disciplinary jurisdiction over solicitors, as officers of the court. When Mr Brounsall was struck off the roll of attorneys in 1778, having been convicted of stealing a guinea, for which he had been sentenced 'to be branded on the hand, and to be confined to the house of correction for nine months' the question was raised as to whether the striking off would amount to a second, and unlawful, penalty. Lord Mansfield announced that as this raised issues concerning the dignity of the profession, 'a solemn opinion should be given' and that the matter should be mentioned 'to all the judges'. On 27 June 1778, a Saturday, Lord Mansfield announced:

> 'We have consulted all the judges upon this case, and they are unanimously of opinion, that the defendant's having been burnt in the hand, is no objection to his being struck off the roll. And it is on this principle; that he is an unfit person to practise as an attorney.'[1]

By the nineteenth century, and by virtue of the Solicitors Act 1888, applications against solicitors were made to a Committee of the Incorporated Law Society, whose members were appointed by the Master of the Rolls. The Committee made findings which were embodied in a report to the court, but the court continued to exercise the disciplinary jurisdiction. No report from the Society's Committee was necessary however; the court could still act on its own motion.[2]

1   *Ex Parte Brounsall* [1778] 2 Cowp 829.
2   Sections 12, 13 and 19 of the Solicitors Act 1888; and see *Re Weare* [1893] 2 QB 439.

1.2

The Solicitors Act 1919 granted the powers of the court, to strike solicitors from the roll and to impose other penalties, to the Disciplinary Committee of the Law Society, but preserved the court's inherent jurisdiction. The Disciplinary Committee was not a committee of the Council of the Law Society, but a separate statutory body whose members continued to be appointed by the Master of the Rolls. The Disciplinary Committee was replaced by the Solicitors Disciplinary Tribunal in 1975, by the Solicitors Act 1974. Section 50 of that Act continues to preserve the court's parallel and inherent jurisdiction. The functions of the investigator and prosecutor have remained with the Law Society throughout, as they still do (in the sense that although the Solicitors Regulation Authority (SRA) operates independently of the Society through its own Board, it has no separate legal existence).

In 1990 an additional regulatory layer was added by the appointment of the Legal Services Ombudsman.[1] The Ombudsman was given the power to investigate complaints about solicitors that had already been made to the Law Society and could, optionally, investigate or re-investigate the original complaint. In practice this was rarely done and the Ombudsman generally confined her investigation to the manner in which the Law Society had itself investigated the complaint and could direct or recommend reconsideration by the Society (the SRA or Legal Complaints Service (LCS)).[2]

The office of Legal Services Ombudsman (LSO) is abolished by section 159 of the Legal Services Act 2007 (LSA 2007) and, allowing for the possibility of a trickle of matters from the Legal Complaints Service during its remaining life (see below), her office is expected to close in about April 2011, although the Legal Ombudsman (see **CHAPTER 12**) may continue to fulfil the statutory function for a short while after that until no further matters could be referred to the LSO in relation to decisions of LCS.

1   Section 21 of the Courts and Legal Services Act 1990.
2   Sections 22(2) and 23(2) and (2A) of the Courts and Legal Services Act 1990.

1.3

In January 2007 the Law Society split into three organisations:

(1)   the Society itself, based in Chancery Lane, which remains the representative body for solicitors; their 'trade union' – though not in the fullest sense of that phrase. It remains impossible, for example, for the Law Society to assist directly in the defence of any individual solicitor in dealings with the SRA;

(2)   the Solicitors Regulation Authority (SRA), based in Redditch and Leamington Spa, which is the professional regulator; and

(3)   the Legal Complaints Service (LCS), based in Leamington Spa, which dealt with client complaints (including complaints from persons with interests in the administration of estates where the solicitor may, as executor, be his own client).

All functions of LCS have now been taken over by the Legal Ombudsman (based in Birmingham) in respect of all complaints made on and after 6 October 2010 (see below and **CHAPTER 12**). LCS continues to exist, at the time of publication of this volume, but is in 'run off' dealing with complaints that were in progress or made before 6 October 2010. It is expected to close finally before the middle of 2011. The SRA and LCS are run by their own Boards. As the statutory powers remain vested in the Council of the Law Society, under the Solicitors Act 1974 as amended, those powers are delegated by the Council to and through the Boards, to enable the SRA and LCS to operate independently of the Law Society.

1.4

Under LSA 2007, the Legal Services Board is established to promote and maintain regulatory objectives relating to the provision of legal services, namely:

(1)   protecting and promoting public interest;

(2)   supporting the constitutional principle of the rule of law;

(3)   improving access to justice;

(4)   protecting and promoting the interests of consumers;

(5)   promoting competition in the provision of legal services;

(6)   encouraging an independent, strong, diverse and effective legal profession;

(7)   increasing public understanding of the citizen's legal rights and duties; and

(8)   promoting and maintaining adherence to professional principles.[1]

The professional principles are:

(1)   acting with independence and integrity;

(2)   maintaining proper standards of work;

(3)   acting in the best interests of clients;

(4)   complying with the duty to the court to act with independence in the interests of justice in relation to litigation and advocacy; and

(5)   keeping the affairs of clients confidential.[2]

The Legal Services Board regulates the regulators, delegating the primary role to approved regulators (including the Law Society/SRA) but maintaining oversight. A detailed consideration of the Board's powers is outside the parameters of this book.

Consumer or client complaints are removed by LSA 2007 from the existing regulators altogether[3] and vested in the Office for Legal Complaints (which uses the title of Legal Ombudsman). Part 6 of LSA 2007 establishes a comprehensive ombudsman scheme for the handling of complaints by consumers.

1   Section 1(1) of LSA 2007.
2   Section 1(3).
3   Section 157.

1.5

Part 5 of LSA 2007 is concerned with alternative business structures (ABSs) – the licensing of bodies, not owned or controlled by lawyers, to provide legal services (the so-called 'Tesco law'). At the time of publication the target for the first grant of licences to ABSs remains 6 October 2011 and draft licensing rules have yet to be published by the Legal Services Board. Nevertheless, the SRA – which has declared its ambition to be the lead licensing authority for ABSs – has consulted on draft rules that anticipate the way in which it will regulate these new forms of law practice, which we consider in **CHAPTER 2**.

Interest is already being shown in external ownership of law firms. This will not be possible before ABSs are authorised, which can only occur when the regulatory regime for them is in place. Practitioners and firms should be extremely careful not to 'jump the gun' as the SRA is likely to look keenly at any non-compliant practice structure.[1] On the other hand, there is a clear need for guidance from the SRA as to what is permitted in the interim, as solicitors try, in an extremely difficult financial climate, to develop their businesses, acquire new income streams and innovate where they can (see para **13.22**).

When the ABS regime is in force, any legal disciplinary partnership with a non-lawyer manager (see **CHAPTER 2**) will have to re-register as an ABS.

1   In this respect the SRA has plainly laid down a marker by the new guidance on 'independence': see para **3.6**.

Duties of approved regulators

1.6

Under section 28 of LSA 2007, approved regulators are under a statutory duty to act in a way that is compatible with the regulatory objectives (see para **1.4**) and in a way most appropriate for the purpose of meeting those objectives. Those objectives require, of course, regulation in the public interest, but a strong and independent profession is in the view of Parliament an essential requirement in the public interest. It is therefore part of the function of the SRA to work towards improving access to justice, promoting competition in the provision of legal services, encouraging an independent, strong, diverse and effective legal profession, and increasing public understanding of the citizen's legal rights and duties, all of which involve support for the profession.

Approved regulators must also have regard to the principles under which regulatory activities should be transparent, accountable, proportionate, consistent and targeted only at cases in which action is needed.[1] It has not always been the case (so it has seemed to informed commentators and so it may have seemed to the profession following encounters with the SRA) that these principles have been rigorously applied in practice, although they are officially adopted as SRA policy. As we discussed in the preface to this edition the SRA is committed to change which may see these aspirations fulfilled.

1   Section 28(3) of LSA 2007.

CHAPTER 2

The regulation of business entities

2.1

The year 2009 saw the beginning of a revolution in the way that the profession is regulated. The Solicitors Regulation Authority (SRA) moved to firm-based regulation, although the first signs of this happening in practice did not emerge until the third quarter of 2010. The focus of investigation and regulatory action is more frequently to be the business within which solicitors practise, rather than individual practitioners. Explanations will be sought from the firm, in relation to matters perceived to have gone wrong, and less from individual solicitors. The business entity has become liable to rebukes, fines and controls on the way it will be permitted to operate, although individual solicitors, or other managers or employees of the business, may also be targeted.

Secondly, the Legal Services Act 2007 (LSA 2007) has created an environment in which businesses that provide legal services may have a choice as to which of the available approved regulators is to regulate the firm. For example, the Council for Licensed Conveyancers (CLC) can regulate those who supply conveyancing and probate services, and the Institute of Chartered Accountants of Scotland has successfully applied to the Legal Services Board to be approved to regulate the supply of probate services in England and Wales. Furthermore, it is evident that the CLC proposes to expand its role so as to be able to regulate the supply of all legal services and, if that expectation becomes reality, it will become a direct rival to the SRA. The regulatory arm of the Institute of Legal Executives (ILEX Professional Standards or IPS) also intends to expand its role.

Since 31 March 2009, firms of solicitors have been able to become legal disciplinary partnerships and, if they limit the services they provide to conveyancing and probate, may choose to be regulated by the CLC in place of the SRA. Anecdotally, it appears that specialist and bulk conveyancing solicitors' practices have shown considerable interest in doing so.

In consequence, solicitors may find themselves subject to two different regulatory regimes simultaneously. For example, the business by which they are employed may be an entity regulated by the CLC, while the solicitors as individuals may be regulated by the SRA. The LSA 2007 provides[1] that if a conflict arises between the regulations that apply to the entity and those that apply to an employee or manager of the entity, the regulations applying to the entity prevail. Thus, a solicitor who is a manager of or employed by a business regulated by the CLC must comply with the rules of the CLC in relation to, for example, referral fees and deposit interest. These rules are different from those of the SRA; the CLC rules about referral fees are less onerous than those contained in the Solicitors' Code of Conduct 2007, whereas the rules about deposit interest are somewhat tighter than their equivalents in the Solicitors' Accounts Rules. In substance, the only direct bearing SRA regulation will have on the individual in those circumstances will be in respect of the core duties of rule 1 of the Solicitors' Code of Conduct and the practising certificate require-ments.[2]

For these reasons a publication concerned with the regulation of solicitors can no longer focus exclusively on the rules promulgated by the SRA. Therefore, a brief consideration of the differences between the CLC rules and the rules of the SRA is contained in **CHAPTER** 9.

1   Section 52(4) of LSA 2007.
2   By rule 23.01(2) of the Solicitors' Code of Conduct 2007, the only rules that apply to a solicitor in these circumstances are rules 1, 12 (Framework of practice), 20 (Rights and obligations of practice), 21 (Separate businesses), 23 (Application of the Rules) and 24 (Interpretation).

Entity- or firm-based regulation by the SRA

2.2

The LSA 2007 refers to entities, the Solicitors' Code of Conduct 2007, as amended, refers to firms, and the SRA refers to the concept of firm-based regulation, which we will adopt. A number of substantial changes came into effect on 31 March 2009. All the SRA's existing rules, including the Code of Conduct, the Solicitors' Accounts Rules 1998 and the other rules considered in subsequent chapters, were amended to ensure that the rules applied not only to solicitors (and registered European lawyers (RELs) and registered foreign lawyers (RFLs)) but also to recognised bodies, and all managers and employees of recognised bodies and employees of solicitors. A manager is a partner in a partnership, a member of a limited liability partnership or a director of a company.[1]

At the same time, the SRA Recognised Bodies Regulations 2009, which regulate the procedures for recognition, the imposition of conditions on recognition, revocation of recognition, and the process for approval of non-lawyers as managers of legal disciplinary partnerships (LDPs), came into force.

The SRA Practising Regulations 2009 became effective from 1 July 2009 and introduced the concept of the recognised sole practitioner, with similar provisions as to the process of recognition and revocation. By this means all solicitors, if they work within businesses regulated by the SRA, practise through a 'recognised' entity, either a recognised body or a recognised sole practitioner. All individuals working in entities regulated by the SRA are therefore controlled by a form of licensing system applicable to the business entity through the recognition process, and the application of professional rules to the business entity and everyone managing and employed by it, and through the issue of practising certificates to individuals, and the professional rules applicable to them as individuals.

In one sense, this is not wholly new regulatory territory; from the point at which it became possible to practise through a corporate structure as a recognised body, since 1986,[2] the regulator has been able to exercise direct control over the business entity. Disciplinary action could be taken against the recognised body by the revocation of recognition and applications could be made to the Solicitors Disciplinary Tribunal for disciplinary sanctions, but in practice these powers were not used. In the two decades and more since the Administration of Justice Act 1985 (AJA 1985) created the ability to practise through a recognised body, until 31 March 2009 only two applications were made to the Tribunal against such a body as a respondent.[3] In both cases the company was a respondent to proceedings which were primarily directed at individuals, and in one of those two cases the Tribunal accepted a submission that any sanction on the company would simply be a second sanction against the individual who owned it, for the same offence, and declined to impose any separate sanction.[4]

1   See the definition in rule 24 of the Solicitors' Code of Conduct 2007; **APPENDIX 21**.
2   Section 9 of and Schedule 2 to AJA 1985.
3   *Atikpakpa and others*, 8913–2004, SDT and *Le Moine and others*, 9048–2004, SDT.
4   *Le Moine and others*, 9048–2004, SDT.

2.3

However, the SRA has signalled a cultural change, stimulated by the LSA 2007, and it has adopted guidelines as to the circumstances in which the focus for enforcement and disciplinary action will be on the firm, as opposed to the individual.

If the subject matter arises from a criminal conviction of an individual or behaviour outside legal practice, the focus will be on the individual and the firm need not be involved at all. In all other cases, the firm's position will be considered. The question as to whether only the firm is to be the focus of action or whether the conduct of both firm and individual are considered will depend on whether there are any issues which bear on the fitness to practise of the individual.

Examples of issues affecting the fitness to practise of an individual would be criminality, dishonesty, personal gain, recklessness, carelessness, incompetence or the personal professional history of the individual (this is not intended to be an exhaustive list). If there are no such issues present, then the firm will be the only focus for regulatory action. Of course, an initial decision one way or the other could be reviewed, possibly several times, as an investigation progresses.

Process of recognition of bodies and sole practitioners

2.4

As a consequence of the SRA Recognised Bodies Regulations 2009[1] and the SRA Practising Regulations 2009[2] from 31 March 2009 (for new firms) or 1 July 2009 (for new sole practitioners) or 31 October 2009 (for all practices on annual renewal), the process of recognition has applied and applications for recognition must be made and granted before the business can provide regulated legal services. The new regulations require the provision of more information than was formerly required from existing recognised bodies (see further below). The Recognised Bodies Regulations apply to all partnerships; that is, traditional partnerships as well as limited liability partnerships. Previously, only corporate bodies needed to be recognised – companies or LLPs – but all existing firms and sole practitioners were 'passported' into recognition provided they were lawfully in practice on 31 March and 1 July 2009 respectively.[3]

An applicant for recognition as a recognised body must be in compliance with rule 14 of the Solicitors' Code of Conduct 2007 in terms of its formation, composition, structure and practising address, with rule 5.02 of the Code in relation to the requirements for supervision, and with the Solicitors' Indemnity Insurance Rules.[4] A partnership must adopt a suitable name under which it is to be registered.[5] The SRA may refuse an application for initial recognition if:

'(a) the SRA is not satisfied that a manager or a person with an interest in the body is a suitable person to be engaged in the management or ownership of a recognised body, taking into account that person's history, character, conduct or associations;

(b) the SRA is not satisfied that the body's managers or owners are suitable, as a group, to operate or control a business providing regulated legal services; or

(c) for any other reason the SRA reasonably considers that it would be against the public interest to grant recognition.'[6]

1   See **APPENDIX 1**.
2   See **APPENDIX 2**.
3   Regulation 8.4 of the SRA Recognised Bodies Regulations 2009 and regulation 4.4 of the SRA Practising Regulations 2009.
4   Regulation 2.1 of the SRA Recognised Bodies Regulations 2009.
5   Regulation 2.1(d) of the SRA Recognised Bodies Regulations 2009.
6   Regulation 2.2 of the SRA Recognised Bodies Regulations 2009.

2.5

In reaching a decision, the SRA may take into account: any event listed in regulation 3.1 of the SRA Practising Regulations applying to a manager of the applicant body;[1] any other conduct on the part of a manager of the applicant body which calls into question his or her honesty, integrity or respect for law; failure or refusal to disclose, or attempts to conceal, any such matter in relation to the application; that the SRA is not satisfied that the managers of the applicant body, taken together, have sufficient skills and knowledge to run and manage a business which provides regulated legal services; and any other facts which the SRA reasonably considers should be taken into account.[2]

When considering an application for renewal of recognition, if the SRA is not satisfied that the body's managers, taken together, are suitable to run and manage a business providing regulated legal services; or considers that for any other reason it would not be in the public interest to renew the body's recognition, the SRA may defer renewal of recognition pending a decision whether the body's recognition should be revoked.[3]

When granting an application for recognition or for renewal of recognition, the SRA may impose a condition, and the granting of recognition free of conditions does not prevent the SRA subsequently imposing a condition.[4]

1   That is, the circumstances in which practising certificate conditions are likely to be considered; see para **14.5**.
2   Regulation 2.3 of the SRA Recognised Bodies Regulations 2009.
3   Regulation 2.5; for revocation see para **2.17**.
4   Regulation 2.7.

2.6

The process of recognition for sole practitioners is very similar. An applicant must be practising or intending to practise from an office in England and Wales; must not be subject, or about to be subject, to a practising certificate condition preventing practice as a sole practitioner; must comply with the supervision requirements of rule 5.02 of the Solicitors' Code of Conduct 2007; and must adopt a suitable name under which to be recognised.[1] The SRA may refuse an application if it is not satisfied that the applicant is suitable to run and manage the business, or if for any other reason the SRA reasonably considers that it would be against the public interest to grant recognition.[2] When reaching a decision the SRA may take into account: any event listed in regulation 3.1 of the SRA Practising Regulations applying to the applicant; any other conduct on the part of the applicant which calls into question his or her honesty, integrity or respect for law; failure or refusal to disclose, or an attempt to conceal, any such matter in relation to the application; or that the SRA is not satisfied that the applicant has sufficient skills or knowledge in relation to the running and management of a business which provides regulated legal services.[3] When granting an application the SRA may impose a condition on the applicant's practising certificate.[4]

1   Regulation 4.2(a) of the SRA Practising Regulations 2009.
2   Regulation 4.2(b).
3   Regulation 4.2(c).
4   Regulation 4.2(d).

Legal disciplinary partnerships

2.7

Legal disciplinary partnerships (LDPs) are not statutorily defined but the term has become a well recognised shorthand to describe, initially, a firm in which lawyers of different disciplines may be principals, and latterly, a firm in which there may be either a mixture of legal disciplines or non-lawyer participation in ownership and management, or both.

The statutory mechanism by which this has been achieved for firms regulated by the SRA[1] is by redefining a 'legal services body', through amendment of AJA 1985[2] by LSA 2007, and by permitting a legal services body to be regulated by the SRA for the supply of reserved legal activities. Reference should be made to sections 9 and 9A of AJA 1985[3] to identify all the various permutations that are possible, including the extent to which another incorporated or unincorporated body may be a manager of a legal services body, but in essence LDPs may be owned and managed by any combination of individual lawyers who are authorised persons for the purposes of the LSA 2007 (solicitors, barristers, notaries, licensed conveyancers, patent and trade mark agents, legal executives and law costs draftsman), RELs, RFLs, and exempt European lawyers,[4] provided at least one manager is a solicitor, REL or 'qualifying body' (meaning a body in which at least one manager is a solicitor with a current practising certificate or REL and which satisfies other conditions).[5]

Non-lawyers may also participate in LDPs provided that qualified lawyers comprise at least 75 per cent of the managers of the firm and hold at least 75 per cent of the shares[6] and exercise or control the exercise of at least 75 per cent of the voting rights, and all those who are not legally qualified who have an interest in the firm are managers, and are approved by the SRA as suitable to be managers.[7] It follows that participation by non-lawyers in LDPs cannot be through the equivalent of shareholding only. Outside investment in law firms in the fullest sense will only be permitted with the advent of the alternative business structure (ABS) regime in late 2011. Non-lawyers with an interest in LDPs must be managers of the firm.

1   LDPs and a form of alternative business structure (ABS) have been permitted and regulated by the Council for Licensed Conveyancers for some years. There is no restriction on outside non-lawyer ownership of a licensed conveyancing practice, provided the majority of directors or members are qualified as licensed conveyancers. This is considered further in **CHAPTER 9**.
2   Sections 9 and 9A of AJA 1985; see **APPENDIX 18**.
3   See **APPENDIX 18**.
4   Exempt European lawyers are those who are not lawyers of England and Wales but who are entitled to practise as a member of an Establishment Directive profession (Directive 98/5/EC of the European Parliament and the Council) by being registered as the equivalent of an REL with another regulator such as the Bar Standards Board, or who are based entirely outside England and Wales.
5   Section 9A(4), (5) and (6) of AJA 1985.
6   Shares for this purpose are defined by the LSA 2007 and include allotted shares in a company, rights to share in the capital of a company, if the body has capital but no share capital, and if the body has no capital, interests conferring the right to share in profits or liability to contribute to losses, or obligation to contribute to debts and expenses in the event of a winding up; see section 79 of LSA 2007.
7   Section 9A(2) of AJA 1985.

2.8

For regulatory purposes, LDPs are simply a form of recognised body and the provisions as to recognition, and the other regulations applicable to recognised bodies considered in this chapter apply equally to them if they are regulated by the SRA. They are no different from any other recognised body if the principals, the managers, are all legally qualified and regulated for the purposes of the LSA 2007 by one or other of the approved regulators.

Additional rules apply if there is a need to approve managers who are non-lawyers (or who are otherwise outside the definition of 'legally qualified' for the purposes of section 9A of AJA 1985). There are three possible categories: non-lawyers in the normal sense that this would be understood; members of a foreign legal profession whose members are not eligible to become RFLs; and non-practising barristers and non-practising members of other legal professions who are prevented by professional rules or training regulations from changing status so as to be able to seek approval as practising lawyers. Any such individual must be approved by the SRA in order to be a manager or owner of a recognised body or a manager of a body corporate which is a manager of a recognised body.[1]

1   Regulation 3(1) of the SRA Recognised Bodies Regulations 2009.

Non-lawyers – the approval process

2.9

The character and suitability of the individual will be assessed against standards comparable to those which are applied for the admission of solicitors: that there is confidence that the individual is honest and trustworthy, willing to comply with regulatory requirements, and able responsibly to manage financial affairs for him- or herself and clients; and that there is no reasonable risk that the approval of the individual as a non-lawyer manager will diminish the public's confidence in the profession or be harmful to members of the public, the profession or him- or herself. The approval process involves a Criminal Records Bureau check.

The application for approval must be made by the recognised body or prospective recognised body concerned and may be made when applying for initial recognition or at any time after recognition has been granted. It is for the applicant body to demonstrate that the individual concerned meets the criteria for approval. The applicant body must co-operate, and secure the co-operation of the individual concerned, to assist the SRA to obtain all information and documentation the SRA requires in order to determine the application; must obtain all other information and documentation in relation to that individual which the prescribed form[1] requires the body to obtain; and keep all information and documentation for a period of not less than six years after the individual concerned has ceased to be a manager of the body. The individual concerned must confirm in writing on the face of the application that the information supplied about him or her is correct and complete.[2]

1   The SRA form is an NL1.
2   Regulation 3.4 of the SRA Recognised Bodies Regulations 2009.

2.10

The SRA has a discretion to reject an application for approval if it is not satisfied that the individual is suitable to be involved in the provision of legal services, and to exercise influence over the conduct of the recognised body concerned because the applicant, the individual or any recognised body or authorised non-SRA firm in which that individual has previously been a manager or employee has been:

'(i)   reprimanded, made the subject of a disciplinary sanction or ordered to pay costs by the Solicitors Disciplinary Tribunal, or struck off or suspended by the Court;

(ii)   rebuked or fined by the SRA under section 44D of the Solicitors Act 1974 or paragraph 14B of Schedule 2 to AJA 1985;

(iii) intervened in by the SRA (or previously by the Law Society);

(iv) notified in writing by the SRA (or previously by the Law Society) that it does not regard as satisfactory an explanation given at the SRA's (or the Law Society's) request; or

(v)   made the subject of disciplinary sanction by, or refused registration with or authorisation by, another approved regulator, professional or regulatory tribunal, or regulatory authority, whether in England and Wales or elsewhere,

in respect of a matter involving the individual;'[1]

or if the individual:

'(i)   has been committed to prison in civil or criminal proceedings;

(ii)   has been disqualified from being a company director;

(iii) has been removed from the office of charity trustee or trustee for a charity by an order within the terms of section 72(1)(d) of the Charities Act 1993;

(iv) is an undischarged bankrupt;

(v)   has been adjudged bankrupt and discharged;

(vi) has entered into an individual voluntary arrangement or a partnership voluntary arrangement under the Insolvency Act 1986;

(vii) has been a manager of a recognised body which has entered into a voluntary arrangement under the Insolvency Act 1986;

(viii) has been a director of a company or member of an LLP which has been the subject of a winding up order, an administration order or administrative receivership; or has entered into a voluntary arrangement under the Insolvency Act 1986; or has been otherwise wound up or put into administration in circumstances of insolvency;

(ix) lacks capacity (within the meaning of the Mental Capacity Act 2005) and powers under sections 15 to 20 or section 48 of that Act are exercisable in relation to that individual;

(x) is the subject of outstanding judgments involving the payment of money;

(xi) is currently charged with an indictable offence, or has been convicted of an indictable offence or any offence under the Solicitors Act 1974, the Financial Services and Markets Act 2000, the Immigration and Asylum Act 1999 or the Compensation Act 2006;

(xii) has been the subject of an order under section 43 of the Solicitors Act 1974; or

(xiii) has been the subject of an equivalent circumstance in another jurisdiction to those listed in (i) to (xi);

(xiv) has been involved in other conduct which calls into question his or her honesty, integrity or respect for law;'[2]

or if the applicant or the individual fails to disclose, refuses to disclose or seeks to conceal any such matter in relation to the application.[3]

1   Regulation 3.3(a) of the SRA Recognised Bodies Regulations 2009.
2   Regulation 3.3(b).
3   Regulation 3.3(c).

2.11

Approval takes effect from the date of the decision unless otherwise stated. The SRA's decision to approve or refuse approval must be notified in writing to the applicant body and, separately, to the individual concerned. If the applicant body is a recognised body it must not allow the individual to become a manager until it has received written notice that the individual has been approved. Approval continues until it is withdrawn, or until two years have elapsed during which the individual has not been a manager of a recognised body.[1] The SRA may at any time require the production of information or documentation from an approved individual, a recognised body in which an approved individual is a manager, or the body which originally obtained approval for that individual and which holds the information and documentation required to be retained,[2] in order to satisfy the SRA that the individual met the criteria for approval or continues to meet the criteria for approval.[3]

The SRA may decide to withdraw approval if it is not satisfied that an approved individual met the criteria for approval or continues to meet the criteria for approval or if information or documentation is not promptly supplied in response to a request. Withdrawal of approval takes effect on expiry of the notice (usually 28 days)[4] or on such later date as may be stated in the notice but if an appeal is made before the withdrawal of approval takes effect, the withdrawal of approval is suspended pending determination or discontinuance of the appeal, unless in the opinion of the

SRA the proceedings on that appeal have been unduly protracted by the appellant or are unlikely to be successful.[5] Where withdrawal of approval relates to a director of a company, the SRA may set separate dates for that individual ceasing to be a director and disposing of his or her shares.[6]

1 Regulation 3.5 of the SRA Recognised Bodies Regulations 2009.
2 Regulation 3.4(c); see para **2.9**.
3 Regulation 3.6.
4 Regulation 6.2.
5 Regulation 3.7.
6 Regulation 3.8.

Provision of information

2.12

Applications for recognition of bodies or sole practitioners require the provision of more information about the business than has previously been the case. So far, information comparable to that required by professional indemnity insurers has been required to be provided to the SRA as part of the recognition process; that is, information as to turnover, the number of non-solicitor fee earners, a breakdown of the types of work undertaken as a percentage of turnover, and a record of any negligence claims. It is very likely that future requests will be rather more targeted and sophisticated.

2.13

Furthermore, the Practising Regulations contain new requirements to give notice to the SRA of certain specific events in addition to the obligation to notify any change of practice address (under section 84 of the Solicitors Act 1974 (SA 1974)). A solicitor, REL or RFL must inform the SRA within 14 days if he or she:

'(a) is committed to prison in civil or criminal proceedings;

(b) is charged with or convicted of an indictable offence;

(c) is made the subject of bankruptcy proceedings;

(d) makes a proposal for an individual voluntary arrangement or is a manager of a firm which makes a proposal for a company voluntary arrangement or a partnership voluntary arrangement under the Insolvency Act 1986;

(e) is admitted as:

   (i) a member of a legal profession of a jurisdiction other than England and Wales; or

   (ii) as a lawyer of England and Wales other than a solicitor;

(f) is made subject to disciplinary proceedings:

   (i) as a member of a legal profession of a jurisdiction other than England and Wales; or

   (ii) as a lawyer of England and Wales other than a solicitor;

(g) becomes a manager of or acquires an ownership interest in a firm which is a recognised body or an authorised non-SRA firm;

(h) sets up a sole practice as a member of a legal profession of a jurisdiction other than England and Wales, or as a lawyer of England and Wales other than a solicitor.'[1]

A solicitor, registered European lawyer or registered foreign lawyer who ceases to practise must inform the SRA within 14 days and supply the SRA with a contact address.[2]

1   Regulation 14.1 of the SRA Practising Regulations 2009.
2   Regulation 14.2.

Conditions on recognition

2.14

The SRA may impose one or more conditions on a recognised body's recognition: when granting initial recognition; when granting renewal of recognition; when granting approval of a non-lawyer manager; when deciding to withdraw approval of a non-lawyer manager; or at any other time.[1]

The SRA may impose a condition if:

- the condition would limit, restrict, halt or prevent an activity or activities on the part of the body, or of a manager or employee of the body, which is putting or is likely to put at risk the interests of clients, third parties or the public, and it is in the public interest to impose the condition;

- the condition would limit the activities of a manager or employee of the body who is considered unsuitable to undertake a particular activity, either at all or save as specified in the condition, and it is in the public interest to impose the condition;

- the condition would limit, halt or prevent a risk to clients, third parties or the public arising from a business agreement or association which the body has or is likely to enter into, or a business practice which the body has or is likely to adopt, and it is in the public interest to impose the condition;

- a relevant insolvency event[2] has occurred in relation to a recognised body, and the event has not triggered expiry of recognition,[3] and the SRA considers that it is in the public interest to impose the condition;

- the condition will, in the public interest, facilitate closer monitoring by the SRA of compliance with rules and regulations on the part of the body;

- the condition will, in the public interest, require the body concerned to take specified steps conducive to the carrying on of efficient practice by that body;

- in any other case concerning a body which is currently recognised, it would be in the public interest to impose the condition.[4]

A condition imposed under this regulation takes effect from the date on which the condition is imposed unless a later date is specified in the condition.[5]

The SRA must give 28 days' written notice with reasons to the recognised body concerned, when the SRA decides to impose a condition on the body's recognition, or revoke the body's recognition. The SRA may shorten or dispense with the 28-day period in imposing a condition if it is satisfied on reasonable grounds that it is in the public interest to do so.[6]

There are no comparable provisions in relation to conditions on the recognition of a sole practitioner; controls would be applied through conditions on the practising certificate of the individual principal (see para **2.6** and **CHAPTER 14**).

There is a substantial body of case-law as to the principles to be applied when considering the imposition of conditions on practising certificates (see **CHAP-TER 14**). As has been noted, the mechanism for the imposition of the equivalent of conditions on the recognition of a sole practitioner is by means of practising certificate conditions; the concepts of conditions on practising certificates and conditions on recognition are thus logically and contextually very close if not identical. The same tests and principles as those which have historically applied to practising certificate conditions can therefore be expected to be applied to issues of recognition.

1   Regulation 4.1 of the SRA Recognised Bodies Regulations 2009.
2   Within the meaning of paragraph 32(1A) of Schedule 2 to AJA 1985; see **APPENDIX 18**.
3   Under regulation 10 of the SRA Recognised Bodies Regulations 2009, which occurs automatically if the body is wound up or for any other reason ceases to exist.
4   Regulation 4.2 of the SRA Recognised Bodies Regulations 2009.
5   Regulation 4.3.
6   Regulations 6.2 and 6.3.

Temporary emergency recognition

2.15

As has been seen, the process by which all firms regulated by the SRA must be recognised, either as bodies or sole practitioners, operates as a form of licensing system so that a firm or sole practitioner cannot begin practice until recognition has been granted. No solicitor or firm can simply 'put up a plate' and start a new business, without obtaining recognition. It is appreciated, however, that as a result of a partnership split, one or more new partnerships may be formed; or that the change in the structure of a partnership (e g by the resignation, retirement or death of one of two partners) may result in a solicitor becoming a sole practitioner, and that such events could occur with little or no notice. This situation is managed by the mechanism of temporary emergency recognition under regulation 5 of the SRA Recognised Bodies Regulations 2009 for recognised bodies and under regulations 4.5 and 4.6 of the SRA Practising Regulations 2009 for sole practitioners.

2.16

The provisions are nearly identical. If such a situation occurs, the SRA must be notified within seven days.

An application for temporary emergency recognition may be made by telephone, provided that details given by telephone are confirmed in writing the same day; and must be made (or confirmed) on the prescribed form at the earliest possible opportunity, and accompanied by all information and documentation that the SRA may reasonably require. The SRA must be satisfied that the applicant sole practitioner or partners could not reasonably have commenced an application for recognition in advance of the change. If the new body is a partnership it must otherwise comply with rule 14 of the Solicitors' Code of Conduct 2007 in relation to its composition and structure and its practising address in England and Wales; the applicant sole practitioner or partners must comply with the Solicitors' Indemnity Insurance Rules, and must have adopted a suitable name under which the applicant is to be registered.[1]

Temporary emergency recognition may be granted initially for 28 days; may be extended in response to a reasonable request by the applicant; must be extended pending determination of a substantive application for initial recognition commenced during the currency of a temporary emergency recognition (unless for exceptional reasons it is revoked);[2] may be granted or extended subject to such conditions as the SRA thinks fit, in circumstances in which a condition could be imposed on the recognition of a recognised body or on the practising certificate of a sole practitioner; is to be treated as initial recognition for the purpose of the regulations; if granted, cannot prejudice the discretion of the SRA to refuse a substantive application for recognition; and in exceptional circumstances, and for reasonable cause, may be revoked at any time.[3]

It is notable that the procedure is available only if the applicant is able to demonstrate to the satisfaction of the SRA that the circumstances could not have been anticipated and that an application could not have been made in advance of the change.

1   Regulations 5.1 to 5.3 of the SRA Recognised Bodies Regulations 2009; regulations 4.5 and 4.6(a), (b) of the SRA Practising Regulations 2009.
2   Regulation 5.4(g) of the SRA Recognised Bodies Regulations 2009; regulation 4.6(c)(vii) of the SRA Practising Regulations 2009.
3   Regulation 5.4 of the SRA Recognised Bodies Regulations 2009; regulation 4.6(c) of the SRA Practising Regulations 2009.

Revocation of recognition

2.17

The SRA must give 28 days' written notice, with reasons, to the recognised body concerned, when the SRA decides to revoke the body's recognition.[1] The SRA may revoke a body's recognition, if:

- recognition was granted as a result of error or fraud;

- the body would not be eligible to be recognised if it were at that time applying for initial recognition;

- the renewal date has passed and the SRA has not received an application for renewal of recognition and all required fees, information and documentation;

- the body has a temporary emergency recognition but has not within the initial 28-day period or any extension of that period commenced a substantive application for recognition;

- the body has ceased to practise;

- an approved regulator other than the SRA has authorised the body;

- the SRA has decided not to renew the body's recognition; or

- a relevant insolvency event[2] has occurred in relation to the recognised body which has not triggered expiry of recognition[3] and (in any and all cases) if the SRA is satisfied that revocation would not present a risk to clients, to the protection of client money or to any investigative process.[4]

Revocation takes effect on expiry of the notice period or on such later date as may be stated in the notice, but if an appeal is made before the revocation takes effect, the revocation is suspended pending determination or discontinuance of the appeal, unless in the opinion of the SRA the proceedings on that appeal have been unduly protracted by the appellant or are unlikely to be successful.[5]

1   Regulation 6.2 of the SRA Recognised Bodies Regulations 2009.
2   Within the meaning of paragraph 32(1A) of Schedule 2 to AJA 1985; see **APPENDIX 18**.
3   Under regulation 10 of the SRA Recognised Bodies Regulations 2009, which occurs automatically if the body is wound up or for any other reason ceases to exist.
4   Regulation 9.1 of the SRA Recognised Bodies Regulations 2009.
5   Regulation 9.2.

2.18

Authorisation as a recognised sole practitioner expires on the expiry or revocation of the solicitor's practising certificate or the imposition of a condition on the solicitor's practising certificate which prohibits practice as a sole practitioner.[1] The SRA may revoke a practising certificate at any time, if the SRA is satisfied that the practising certificate was granted as a result of error or fraud; if the replacement or renewal date has passed and the SRA has not received an application for replacement of the practising certificate which complies with the Regulations; or if the SRA refuses to replace a practising certificate on annual renewal.[2]

The SRA may revoke authorisation as a recognised sole practitioner at any time if:

- the authorisation as a recognised sole practitioner was granted as a result of error or fraud;

- the solicitor is not practising from an office in England and Wales;

- the SRA is not satisfied that the recognised sole practitioner continues to meet the criteria for authorisation as a recognised sole practitioner;

- the recognised sole practitioner has a temporary emergency recognition but has not within the initial 28-day period or any extension of that period commenced a substantive application for recognition; or

- the SRA has decided not to renew authorisation as a recognised sole practitioner.[3]

The SRA may also revoke a practising certificate or authorisation as a recognised sole practitioner on the application of the person concerned, but there is no discretion to refund any part of the fee paid for that practising year and the SRA may refuse the application if there is an outstanding complaint against the applicant or for any other reason relating to the public interest.[4]

When the SRA decides to revoke a practising certificate or authorisation as a recognised sole practitioner it must give the person concerned 28 days' notice, with reasons. The notice may be given together with notification of refusal of an application to replace a practising certificate or renew an authorisation.[5] Revocation takes effect on expiry of the notice or on such later date as may be stated in the notice, except that if an appeal is made during the period of notice the revocation does not take effect until determination or discontinuance of any appeal.[6]

1   Regulation 9.1(d) of the SRA Practising Regulations 2009.
2   Regulation 9.2(a).
3   Regulation 9.2(b).
4   Regulation 9.2(c).
5   Regulation 9.3(a).
6   Regulation 9.3(b).

Appeals

2.19

Appeals should[1] first be pursued within the SRA's own appeals procedure, but thereafter appeal lies to the High Court. Appeals within the SRA's appeals procedure must be commenced within 28 days of notification of the relevant decision, and appeals to the High Court within 28 days of notification of the relevant decision or of notification of the refusal of the internal appeal.[2] An application for a practising certificate is deemed to have been refused at the end of the ninetieth day if regulation 3 of the Practising Regulations does not apply, and at the end of the 180th day if regulation 3 applies to the application, and notice of the decision is deemed to have been given on that day.[3] Similarly, applications for recognition of a body and for approval of a non-lawyer manager are deemed to have been refused if by the end of the ninetieth day the SRA has not notified a decision to the applicant body and the individual concerned, and notice of the decision is deemed to have been given on that day.[4]

Those whose applications encounter considerable delay must therefore be alive to the fact that, on a particular date in the calendar, without actual notice of any kind, they will be deemed to have been given notice of refusal, so that time automatically starts to run for the purposes of any appeal.

1   When appeal lay to the Master of the Rolls he always encouraged appellants first to exhaust any internal appeal process, and the High Court can be expected to take the same view. Some appeals must first employ the SRA's internal procedure: against a decision to revoke recognition of a body, against a refusal to approve a non-lawyer manager, and against the withdrawal of approval of a non-lawyer manager; see regulations 7.2 and 7.3 of the SRA Recognised Bodies Regulations 2009.
2   Regulation 7.5 of the SRA Recognised Bodies Regulations 2009; regulation 7.6 of the SRA Practising Regulations 2009.
3   Regulation 7.5 of the SRA Practising Regulations 2009.
4   Regulation 7.4 of the SRA Recognised Bodies Regulations 2009.

Alternative business structures: an overview

2.20

Although the Legal Services Board (LSB) has yet (at the time of publication) to make or approve licensing rules, LSA 2007 contains the regulatory framework and the SRA has begun the consultation process as to how it will regulate ABSs if it becomes a licensing authority; it is therefore possible to predict how the regulatory regime will operate.

Part 5 (sections 71 to 111) of LSA 2007 and Schedules 10 to 14 create the statutory framework for ABSs; that is the regulatory structure for bodies which are not themselves authorised persons[1] who wish to carry out reserved legal activities, The statutory term for an ABS is a 'licensable body' or a 'licensed body'. A licensable body may be in one or other or both of two forms (section 72(1) and/or section 72(2) of LSA 2007). It may be a body in which a non-authorised person is a manager or has an interest.[2] Alternatively, it may be a body ('B') of which another body ('A') is a manager or which has an interest in B where non-authorised persons are entitled to exercise or control the exercise of at least 10 per cent of the voting rights in A. One consequence of the statutory definition is that existing LDPs with a non-lawyer manager will have to become licensed as ABSs.

Draft rules providing for the expected form and content of applications for licences are not available at the time of publication, but it can be expected that the requirements will be fairly exacting. The SRA has published draft Authorisation Rules, an updated version of the present SRA Recognised Bodies Regulations 2009 (see **APPENDIX 1**) designed to accommodate applications by licensable bodies. All applications for authorisation, whether in the form of the grant of a licence to a licensable body, or in the form of the grant of recognition to a more traditional legal services body, will follow the same procedure, which is broadly that set out in the current Recognised Bodies Regulations. However, the draft rules show an intention on the part of the SRA to extend the concept of heads of legal practice (HoLPs) and heads of finance and administration (HoFAs) to all firms and sole practitioners, not just to ABSs: they are intended to be renamed as compliance officers for legal practice (CoLPs) and for finance and administration (CoFAs), and they will have to go through a process of approval. The logic underlying this, other than that of convenience in dealing with all applications in the same way, is not particularly evident. However, a consequence will be that the withdrawal of approval by the SRA of the appointed CoLP or CoFA will have the effect of threatening the existence of the firm, as it would not be able to continue lawfully without approved persons in each of those roles.

1   That is, not a person authorised by an approved regulator, such as a solicitor or recognised body.
2   A manager is a member of a limited liability partnership, a director of a company, a partner in a partnership or the member of a governing body of an unincorporated association (section 207 of LSA 2007). An interest involves either the holding of shares or an entitlement to exercise or control the exercise of voting rights in the body (section 72(3)).

2.21

The regulatory structure for ABSs is entirely different from that for traditional law firms. This has already led the SRA to indicate a desire to 'harmonise' the two schemes of regulation. Traditional law firms are regulated by an approved regulator; ABSs are regulated by a licensing authority. The LSB is itself a licensing authority and may designate any approved regulator, including the Law Society/SRA, to be a licensing authority.

A pivotally important difference in regulation is that in relation to traditional law firms and individual solicitors (and other regulated persons) the SRA can take regulatory action, but its disciplinary powers are modest, and before 1 June 2010, non-existent. In proceedings before the Solicitors Disciplinary Tribunal the SRA always has been and still is the prosecuting authority, not the decision-maker. It cannot strike off solicitors: only the Tribunal (and the High Court) can do that. From 1 June 2010, in respect of actions and defaults occurring or continuing after that date, it may impose low level fines and rebukes, and publish them, subject to appeal to the Tribunal (see **CHAPTER 13**). But in relation to ABSs, and all managers and employees of ABSs, the licensing authority has the power to impose unlimited fines, and to disqualify individuals from participating in an ABS, as well as the power to revoke or suspend licences.

In relation to ABSs as a licensing authority, the SRA will therefore have all the equivalent powers of the Solicitors Disciplinary Tribunal itself; it will be the investigator, prosecutor and judge, with a right of appeal to an external body (which might or might not be the Solicitors Disciplinary Tribunal). The SRA consultations that have been published to date strongly suggest a desire to apply the ABS form of regulation to all it regulates. It is regarded by the SRA to be anomalous that it will be able, on acquiring the status of a licensing authority, to fine an ABS or the manager of an ABS an unlimited amount, but fine a recognised body or a manager of a recognised body only £2,000 (with an option to refer to the SDT); and that it will be able to disqualify a solicitor from ever working in an ABS, but will not be able to suspend or strike off a solicitor who is practising through a traditional law firm.

Ownership

2.22

Schedule 13 to LSA 2007 makes detailed provisions as to the ownership of ABSs. Ownership of an ABS by non-authorised persons is subject to regulation where a non-authorised person has a 'restricted interest' in an ABS. The definition of a restricted interest depends to some extent on licensing rules yet to be made. A restricted interest includes a 'material interest' and a 'controlled interest' if rules are made in relation to, and with a view to defining, controlled interests. A controlled interest is a larger interest than a material interest and may be subject to increased levels of regulatory control. A material interest is defined in paragraph 3 of Schedule 13 and amounts to at least 10 per cent[1] of the shares in the ABS or of a parent company, or equivalent voting rights, or an ability to exercise significant influence over the management of the ABS or its parent by virtue of the shareholding. A 'person' may include the individual and any associates. Licensing rules may provide for different levels of control for different levels of interest.

Any holding of a restricted interest by a non-authorised person must be approved by the licensing authority.[2] The approval requirements are that the person's holding of a restricted interest does not compromise the regulatory objectives (see **CHAPTER 1**); does not compromise the duty of the ABS or any employee or manager of the ABS to comply with regulatory obligations; and that the person is otherwise a fit and proper person to hold that interest.[3] The licensing authority must have particular regard to the person's probity and financial position; whether the person has been disqualified under section 99 of LSA 2007 and the disqualification remains in force or is included on the LSB's list of persons subject to objections and conditions; the person's associates; and any other matter specified in licensing rules.[4]

A person's associates are widely defined by paragraph 5 of Schedule 13 to include various family relationships, corporate connections and arrangements to act in concert.

Approval of a person's restricted interest may be subject to conditions.[5] The licensing authority may impose restrictions on shares, for example that no voting rights in relation to them are exercisable, and may apply to the High Court for an order of divestiture; that is, a requirement that shares be sold, in certain circumstances of default.[6]

It will be noted that this form of regulation applies if a person or body, with or without associates, owns or controls at least 10 per cent of the ABS or otherwise through share ownership exercises 'significant influence over the management' of the ABS. If that threshold is not met (and if licensing rules do not change the percentage), those with a financial interest in an ABS are not subject to direct control, nor is there any requirement to notify lesser interests or the identity of investors (at least under the provisions of Schedule 13; one can envisage that the SRA could well specify this as information it requires for general regulatory purposes).

1   Unless licensing rules make any different provision reducing the percentage.
2   Paragraph 1(1) of Schedule 13 to LSA 2007.
3   Paragraph 6(1) and (2).
4   Paragraph 6(3).
5   Paragraph 17 and 18.
6   Paragraphs 41 to 45.

Structure

2.23

Part 2 of Schedule 11 to LSA 2007 sets out the structural requirements for ABSs. At least one of the ABS's managers must be an authorised person in relation to the ABS's licensed activity who is not disqualified from acting as a manager of a licensed body.[1]

An ABS must also have at all times an individual who is designated as the HoLP and an individual who is designated as the HoFA and whose designation as such is approved by the licensing authority.[2] The HoLP must be an authorised person in relation to one or more of the licensed activities of the ABS and who is not disqualified from holding that position. A person will only be approved as HoLP if the licensing authority is satisfied that the person is a fit and proper person to carry out the duties imposed upon him or her by section 91 of LSA 2007, which are to take all reasonable steps to ensure compliance with the terms of the body's licence; to report any failure to comply to the licensing authority; to take all reasonable steps to ensure that all authorised persons who are managers or employees, and all non-authorised persons who are managers or employees or who have an interest in the ABS comply with their regulatory obligations, and to report any failure to comply to the licensing authority.[3]

It is plainly envisaged that HoLPs will be required to show some enhanced level of fitness and capacity, beyond that already demonstrated by being a member of a regulated profession, because HoLPs must be authorised persons to be qualified to fulfil the role. Probably some form of management training will be involved.

The HoFA is responsible for ensuring compliance with accounts rules; that is licensing rules made by virtue of paragraph 20 of Schedule 11 as to the treatment of money received, held or dealt with by the licensed body, its managers and employees for clients and other persons, and for the keeping of accounts, and for reporting any failure to the licensing authority.[4] HoFAs do not have to be authorised persons.

1   Paragraph 9(2) and (3) of Schedule 11.
2   Paragraphs 11 and 13 of Schedule 11.
3   Section 91.
4   Section 92.

Regulation and discipline

2.24

Although none of the relevant rules are yet available for analysis, both the framework and likely procedures can be deduced. Regulatory control over ABSs will take the form of:

- the licensing process; the grant or refusal of and the imposition of conditions upon licences;

- the approval or non-approval of non-lawyer managers;

- the approval or non-approval of HoLPs and HoFAs;

- the control of ownership where there are restricted interests, by means of the approval process, the imposition of conditions and restriction notices and divestiture orders;

- the imposition of fines, in unlimited amounts, on the licensed body and on any manager or employee;[1]

- the disqualification of HoLPs, HoFAs and any manager or employee from holding the relevant position or from employment in any licensed body;[2]

- the revocation or suspension of a licence;[3] and

- the exercise of powers of intervention.[4]

Fines historically imposed on solicitors have been 'forfeit to Her Majesty The Queen' and paid to the Treasury, which is responsible for any enforcement action, but fines imposed on ABSs and their managers and employees are payable in the first instance to the licensing authority, which recovers the sum as a debt, and accounts for it to the Consolidated Fund.[5]

Disqualification may follow where an individual, intentionally or through neglect, breaches a relevant duty to which the individual is subject, or causes or materially contributes to a significant breach of the terms of the body's licence.

A licence may be suspended or revoked in seven sets of circumstances set out in paragraph 24 of Schedule 11. These are in brief:

(1)   the ABS ceases to be a body capable of being a licensable body;

(2)   it fails to comply with licensing rules;

(3)   there is a breach of the requirements on shareholding or voting rights;

(4)   a non-authorised person within the ABS fails to comply with regulatory obligations;

(5)   an authorised person within the ABS fails to comply with regulatory obligations;

(6)   the ABS has employed a disqualified person; or

(7)   it is unable to comply with its duties relating to having an HoLP and HoFA.

The powers of intervention, contained in Schedule 14, are for all practical purposes the same as are available to the SRA in relation to traditional law firms.

1   Section 95.
2   Section 99.
3   Section 101.
4   Section 102 and Schedule 14.
5   Section 97.

2.25

The SRA has published draft Disciplinary Procedure Rules setting out how it would deal with decision-making in relation to its powers as a licensing authority. These are drawn heavily from the existing SRA (Disciplinary Procedure) Rules 2010 (**APPEN-DIX 12**) which in turn were drawn from existing but non-codified practice (see **CHAPTER 13**). In consequence it seems that the SRA proposes to use existing procedures, which were designed for the most part to deal with relatively low level regulatory activity such as in-house reprimands and practising certificate conditions (and referring more serious matters for decision by the Tribunal), for more serious matters such as disqualification, which could have equivalent consequences for the individual to being struck off or suspended.

It is questionable whether that is wholly appropriate, but at this stage these are draft rules for consultation and no more.

2.26

Section 80 of LSA 2007 provides that the Lord Chancellor may establish a body to hear and determine appeals from decisions of a licensing authority and may modify the functions of existing bodies for this purpose, specifically referring to the Solicitors Disciplinary Tribunal and the Discipline and Appeals Committee of the Council for Licensed Conveyancers.

The LSB has indicated its preference for there to be one appellate body to hear all ABS-related appeals from all licensing authorities and that this should be within the Tribunal Service under the aegis of the First-tier Tribunal. Consultations are continuing in this respect at the time of publication.

PART 2
The Rules

The Solicitors' Code of Conduct 2007

Introduction

3.1

The rather modest regulatory impact of the 1936 Solicitors' Practice Rules has been mentioned in the Preface to the 2008 edition. The Practice Rules changed very little in subsequent decades. A new rule was made in 1967, requiring that only solicitors with practising certificates should be listed on notepaper and the office nameplate. Rule 2 (which prohibited the sin of charging less than scale fees) was replaced in 1972 with a rule against acting for both parties in conveyancing transactions subject to familiar exceptions. A comprehensive new set of Rules was made in 1987, which are recognisably the precursor to the Solicitors' Practice Rules 1990 and very little different from the 1990 Rules in their original form. The 1990 Rules were amended and supplemented extensively after they were implemented; not all the changes were readily accessible.

The Law Society embarked on the preparation of a new comprehensive set of rules in and before 2004, and the resulting Solicitors' Code of Conduct 2007 ('the Code') came into force on 1 July 2007. This affects not only solicitors in private practice but also employed and non-practising solicitors (as well as registered European lawyers (RELs), registered foreign lawyers (RFLs) and recognised bodies) and, with effect from 31 March 2009, all managers and employees of recognised bodies and employees of solicitors.

Historically, the conduct of solicitors has been analysed as being either statutory or non-statutory misconduct. Statutory misconduct is a breach of the Solicitors Act 1974 (SA 1974) or of rules made by the Law Society pursuant to statute (such as the Solicitors' Accounts Rules 1998 and the former Solicitors' Practice Rules). Non-statutory misconduct is any act or failure that is considered by the Solicitors Disciplinary Tribunal to amount to conduct unbefitting a solicitor. This is the common law of conduct that has developed over time.[1]

The question as to how a solicitor should behave (in relation to both statutory and non-statutory matters) was historically addressed by guidance provided by the Law Society – primarily by means of successive editions of *The Guide to the Professional Conduct of Solicitors*. The last of these, the eighth edition, was published in 1999 and was subsequently made available in an updated form on the Law Society's website. The published guidance on non-statutory misconduct has never purported to be complete and comprehensive. It has never been possible to say, 'It isn't in the Guide so I must be able to do it' – although this argument has been advanced, and on one occasion, remarkably, as far as the Divisional Court.[2]

1   See generally, **CHAPTER 8**.
2   *Henneberry v Law Society* [2000] Transcript CO/1858/99.

3.2

The Solicitors' Code of Conduct 2007 (see **APPENDIX 21**) abandons the historical approach of relatively narrow practice rules and wider but non-exclusive (official and published) guidance. Instead, it creates a comprehensive regulatory framework for all aspects of a solicitor's conduct. The Code comprises 25 individual rules and is supplemented by guidance produced by the SRA which amplifies and explains its provisions. The guidance is not mandatory and does not form part of the Code; however, the SRA added a note to the preamble to the Code with effect from 31 March 2009 to the effect that if solicitors do not follow the guidance they may be required to demonstrate (ie, prove) how they nevertheless complied with the rules. The Code, as has been mentioned, is a form of delegated legislation, required to undergo a process of statutory approval, formerly involving the concurrence or approval of the Master of the Rolls and/or the Lord Chancellor and/or the Secretary of State, and currently of the Legal Services Board. The guidance is subject to no such independent scrutiny and can be changed at will by the SRA (and has been; see para **3.6**). It is important therefore that it is wholly reliable, and not employed as a means of altering the meaning of the rules. The guidance has not proved to be wholly reliable in all respects (see para **3.10**).

In order to stay up to date with the rules, practitioners have to monitor the SRA website on a regular basis, and no other method of ensuring up-to-date knowledge on the part of those regulated is in contemplation.

The advent of the Code created a situation in which there was no such thing as non-statutory misconduct. This has obvious benefits in that the whole of the law is in one place (or it would be if the other codified rules such as the Solicitors' Accounts Rules 1998, the Financial Services Rules, the Indemnity Insurance Rules, the Recognised Bodies Regulations and the Practising Regulations were to be added to it). The disadvantage is that non-statutory misconduct can be developed by the Tribunal and the courts over time. This may be more problematic with an all encompassing Code. In fact this has already been proved to be so, rather graphically: precisely one month after it came into force, and after the printed version of it had gone on sale to the profession, the Code was amended because the regulations concerning the provision of home information packs had come into force, making it necessary to change rule 18 to record the additional obligations that those regulations imposed. It can therefore be seen that sequential changes to the Code might become necessary as a result of changes in the general law, because the Code has to cover everything.

A solicitor's personal life has been brought within the Code and therefore within the concept of statutory misconduct (a solicitor's misconduct in his or her private life was always capable of being non-statutory misconduct). Further, a breach of the Code is a breach. It is only necessary that the words apply: no specific intent or mental element will be required (although invariably there was some such element in anything that historically has been alleged to be unbefitting conduct).

It has always been recognised that liability for breaches of the Solicitors' Accounts Rules is absolute, and falls on all principals, partners and (in the current terminology) managers of firms, but the same has never been true of any other rule of conduct. The Code contains no indication of any need on the part of the regulator to demonstrate any specific intent or level of knowledge and the SRA treats any breach of the Code as a matter of strict or absolute liability; that a breach is a breach regardless of any other considerations, such as the degree to which it is technical as opposed to substantive or has no adverse consequence. It needs to be recognised that this represents a seismic movement away from the former position, when a large part of the ambit of regulatory action related to non-statutory misconduct, which necessarily involved a consideration of the level of personal fault, and the degree of mischief caused (if any), and thus whether objectively it involved behaviour which no reasonable solicitor would regard to be acceptable.

It is also the case that if the SRA carries out an investigation and finds a breach, it may direct the individual or firm to pay the costs of the investigation or a contribution to them.

It is plainly right that neither disciplinary action nor costs consequences should follow a breach of the Code on the basis simply and solely of absolute liability, but only when it is both proportionate and necessary. This must necessarily involve consideration of factors which would have been considered if non-statutory misconduct was still a live concept.

An apparent lacuna, so far as the Code is concerned, is the position of a solicitor who misbehaved badly, in a manner that would be relevant to the reputation of the profession and risks to the public, but who was not a solicitor at the time of his offences. There would seem to be no scope to allege any breach of the Code, even of the core values, which are addressed to solicitors. However, the Tribunal would still have jurisdiction to impose sanctions.[1]

1   *Re a Solicitor (Ofosuhene)* [1997] Transcript CO/2860/96.

3.3

A major change effective from 31 March 2009 has already been highlighted in **CHAPTER 2**; the Code no longer applies only to solicitors, RELs, RFLs and recognised bodies. The arrival of firm-based regulation means that the Code applies also to all employees of solicitors and recognised bodies and to all managers of recognised bodies, whether or not they are solicitors or otherwise legally qualified.

However, having highlighted that fact, as this is *The Solicitor's Handbook*, principally directed to and intended to be for the benefit of solicitors, we will continue to refer to solicitors and firms when considering the Code and other obligations.

It should not be overlooked that the Code has implications beyond the personal conduct of an individual solicitor. The Code is delegated legislation and as such has the force of statute.[1] This means that the Code takes precedence over existing common law. This has proved a real problem in the areas of costs and referral fees, where contractual arrangements entered into by solicitors in breach of the then Practice Rules were held to be unenforceable.[2] It appears that the SRA would prefer that the Code should not have, or always have, this effect (see, for example, the guidance in relation to rule 2 and the commentary on that point at para **3.9**), but there is a real question as to whether the SRA can – by non-binding guidance – derogate from the effect of a rule that has to be interpreted as subordinate legislation. It is not known whether, for example, there have been unreported disputes and challenges to the recovery of fees based on non-compliance with rule 2.

1   *Swain v Law Society* [1983] 2 All ER 827; *Mohammed v Alaga & Co (a firm)* [1999] All ER (D) 205; *Hughes v Kingston upon Hull District Council* [1992] 2 All ER 49; and *Awwad v Geraghty* [2000] 1 All ER 608.
2   See e g *Mastercigars Direct Ltd v Withers LLP (No 2)* (25 April 2007, unreported), where the previous Client Care Code was relied upon in respect of a decision to disallow costs claimed by solicitors from their client over and above a written costs estimate. This has been reversed on appeal ([2007] EWHC 2733 (Ch)) but future comparable challenges relying on the Code's requirements can be expected.

The future: the new approach to regulation

3.4

As mentioned in the Preface to this edition, we are again in the midst of change: the Solicitors' Code of Conduct 2007 will be replaced, probably on 6 October 2011, with a new Code, the latest draft of which is in **APPENDIX 22** and which is considered later in this Chapter. But we are emphatically being told by the SRA that another change is already happening – the SRA is adopting outcomes-focused regulation (OFR). This is designed to move away, both in the form of rules and the way in which they are policed, from the tick-box, strict liability, 'every breach is a breach' approach described above, and which has seriously damaged the relationship between the profession and the regulator. The problem with that approach has been that it has been too easy to hit the wrong target: the solicitor trying to get it right but making mistakes, as opposed to the one who does not care, or deliberately breaks the rules.

In an open and healthy manner the SRA has announced that:

> 'We know that the current rule book is too prescriptive. OFR will give firms the flexibility to do new and better things for consumers. It will lead to a more grown-up relationship between the SRA and the regulated community.'

and:

> 'The introduction of OFR will give a simplified rulebook and freedom to practise innovatively, which will be good for consumers and providers of legal services alike. OFR is risk-based regulation; firms will have to comply with broad principles rather than detailed rules. Firms will be able to comply with the principles in the ways which best suit their businesses. Formal rules will still apply in important areas including accounts and indemnity, where they are necessary. …

> The SRA's enforcement of OFR will be effective, fair and proportionate. We will focus on the things which really matter to consumers; for example risks which may lead to a loss of their money, justice, or social or economic wellbeing.'[1]

This is profoundly welcome as it turns the clock back to a time when the consequence of something going wrong – whether there was in fact any mischief or prejudice caused, as opposed to being a 'bare breach' – was an important if not determinative factor in how the regulator treated the solicitor concerned.

Accordingly, we should see a different approach to enforcement of the present rules and Code, despite the fact that the new Code – drafted to be consistent with the concept of OFR – is not yet in force. A new, different and more adult approach to regulation by the regulator does not need to wait for a new rule book.

The present Code will continue to be relevant for some time to come as it will apply to all matters; all actions and defaults, between 1 July 2007 and (probably) 6 October 2011 and therefore still needs to be considered in detail. The next edition of this Handbook is intended to be published shortly after the date upon which the new Code will come into force, with a more comprehensive analysis of the new regime, which at present is in draft form and subject to ongoing consultation.

1   Extracts from 'A Passport to regulatory reform' issued by the SRA as part of its Freedom in Practice: Better Outcomes for Consumers campaign in April 2010.

Rule 1 – Core duties

3.5

The core duties of rule 1 require solicitors to uphold the rule of law and the proper administration of justice, to act with integrity, not to allow professional independence to be compromised, to act in the best interests of each client, to provide a good standard of service to clients, and not to behave in a way that is likely to diminish the trust the public places in the individual or the legal profession.

3.6

Rule 1 covers all aspects of a solicitor's practice, but also impacts on the private lives of solicitors. The former Practice Rule 1, which contained comparable core principles of professional conduct, imposed obligations 'in the course of practising as a solicitor'. Rule 1 in the Code is not limited by those words.

The former Practice Rule, in imposing standards of competence, required only a 'proper standard of work'. Anything short of a 'good' standard constitutes a breach of the present rule 1. There is no exception to this obligation. The associated guidance only states that, 'Disciplinary action will not always follow where breaches of this duty are minor and isolated'.

Where two or more of the core duties encompassed by rule 1 come into conflict the factor determining precedence will be the public interest, not the client's interest.

The duty to act in the best interests of the client is occasionally misguidedly quoted by solicitors in defence of actions which are improper. A better way of considering that particular obligation is to emphasise that the client's interests are paramount as between the solicitor and the client (the solicitor must not prefer his own interests to those of the client), and as between a client and any other party, but the duty of a solicitor to place his client's interests first is subject to his other professional obligations – and in particular the due administration of justice.

New guidance effective from 31 March 2009 radically changed the interpretation of the rule that solicitors may not allow their independence to be compromised. The former guidance focused exclusively on the independence of advice to clients, by providing a cross-reference to rules 3 (Conflict of interest) and 9 (Referrals), and on avoiding situations in which solicitors could be constrained in the advice they might give. The emphasis has now wholly changed to assert that 'independence means your own and your firm's independence, and not merely your ability to give independent advice to a client' and examples are given:

- finance agreements/loans to the firm with particular strings attached;

- finance arrangements which suggest dependency upon an outside body, such as arrangements which could, at that body's discretion, effectively put the firm out of business;

- contractual conditions in agreements with referrers of business or funders which effectively cede control of the firm to the outside body;

- granting options to purchase an interest in the firm for nominal value;

- allowing a third party access to confidential information concerning clients;

- a relationship with an outside body which is not at arm's length, and/or which suggests that the firm is more akin to a part of or subsidiary of that body, rather than an independent law firm;

- fee sharing arrangements which go beyond what is allowed under rule 8.02;

- any arrangement for a third party to fund legal action which lays constraints on the conduct of the matter which go beyond the legitimate interests of a funder.

A number of these provisions can be seen to be aimed at preventing any course which 'jumps the gun' in relation to the regulation of alternative business structures (ABSs).

Rule 2 – Client relations

3.7

Rule 2 covers the principles involved in taking on clients, client care, the provision of information about costs, contingency fees in contentious proceedings, complaints handling, commissions, and the restriction on the limitation of civil liability to clients by contract.

3.8

The rule brings together under the heading 'Client relations' the previous Practice Rules 8 (contingency fees), 10 (receipt of commission from third parties) and 15 (costs information and client care). In addition, it incorporates some of the guidance provided by the Law Society in Chapter 12 of *The Guide to the Professional Conduct of Solicitors* (8th edn) (retainer) and the Solicitors' Costs Information and Client Care Code 1999.

All practitioners will be familiar with client care and costs information requirements, which have achieved ever greater regulatory prominence. Rule 2 does not add significantly to the former obligations in this regard but does provide further detail, particularly in rule 2.02, in giving emphasis as to the need to agree service levels with the client and to explain what responsibilities fall respectively on solicitor and client.

Failure to comply with rule 2 can be used to support an allegation of inadequate professional service by a solicitor under Schedule 1A to SA 1974, in so far as matters were already in the hands of the Legal Complaints Service (LCS) before that body ceased to receive complaints on 6 October 2010. Such a rule breach is significantly less likely to be regarded as material by the Legal Ombudsman (see **CHAPTER 12**). More serious or persistent failures in client care can lead to regulatory sanctions or result in proceedings before the Solicitors Disciplinary Tribunal.

Rule 2 also covers matters concerned with retainers, such as when instructions can or should be refused, and limitation of liability by contract.

It is not permissible to exclude or to attempt to exclude all liability to clients, but liability may be limited to the minimum level of cover required by the Solicitors' Indemnity Insurance Rules if this is clearly brought to the client's attention in writing.

Solicitors are generally free to decide whether or not to accept instructions, but must refuse to act or cease to act when acting for the client would involve a breach of the law or professional rules, or when the solicitor has insufficient resources or competence; and the solicitor must be satisfied that instructions given by a third party, or by one client on behalf of others, represent the true intentions of the client or all clients, and that instructions are not affected by undue influence or duress.

Rule 2.01(1)(b), which requires solicitors to decline to act or to cease to act when they have insufficient resources or lack the competence to deal with the matter, was considered by the Court of Appeal in *R v Ulcay*.[1] In a criminal trial the judge had refused an adjournment for the amount of time requested by defence counsel and solicitors who had been instructed in place of the original defence team at the end of the prosecution case. The (new) solicitors had withdrawn on the basis that the time allowed did not enable them to prepare their client's case to the necessary standard. It was held that they were wrong to do so and that the rule does not allow a solicitor to refuse to act or to cease to act where an order of the court creates difficulties and makes it harder for him to discharge his professional duties. Those difficulties arose because of the judge's ruling, and not as a result of the absence of appropriate resources or competence.

The familiar requirement in rule 2.01 (reproducing the common law position) that solicitors must not cease acting for a client except for good cause and on reasonable notice was considered in *Richard Buxton (Solicitors) v Mills-Owen*[2] in a situation in which the client was persisting in a course that his solicitors and counsel considered unwise. He insisted on points being advanced and argued on his behalf that his lawyers considered to be wholly unarguable. They considered their position to be untenable, obtained supportive advice to this effect from the Law Society and ceased to act on reasonable notice. It was held at first instance that they were not entitled to do so:

> 'if a client who is prepared to pay for a case to be advanced, and who wants the claim advanced on a particular basis, which does not involve impropriety on the part of the solicitor or counsel, then it is no answer for the solicitor to say that he believes it is bound to fail therefore he will not do it.'

In consequence, a claim for costs by the solicitor for the work done up to the date the retainer was terminated was disallowed on the basis that he was required to complete the retainer: to carry on the action to the end. This was (fortunately) reversed by the Court of Appeal[3] which held that the solicitors had good reason to terminate the retainer, and were entitled to be paid their costs to date. The Law Society intervened in the appeal in support of the firm. The court noted that rule 11.01(3) of the Code provides:

> 'you must not construct facts supporting your client's case or draft any documents relating to any proceedings containing:
>
> (a)   any contention which you do not consider to be properly arguable'

Dyson LJ (with whom Sir Mark Potter P and Maurice Kay LJ agreed) stated:

> 'There is no comprehensive definition of what amounts to a good reason to terminate in the Solicitors' Practice Rules or the Code of Conduct (although examples are given in both documents), or in any of the authorities that have been cited to us. That is not surprising, since whether there is a good reason to terminate is a fact-sensitive question. I accept the submission of Mr Drabble [*for the Law Society*] that it is wrong to restrict the circumstances in which a solicitor can lawfully terminate his retainer to those in which he is instructed to do something improper – I am in no doubt that even before the point was spelt out in the 2007 Code, it would have been understood by all solicitors that, as officers of the court, they were under a professional duty (i) not to include in the court documents that they drafted any contention which they did not consider to be properly arguable and (ii) not to instruct counsel to advance contentions which they did not consider to be properly arguable. That duty was reinforced by CPR 1.3.'

Rule 2, in so far as it relates to the provision of information about costs and in relation to complaints handling, underwent two additional changes in August 2009 and March 2010 as a result of the revocation of the Solicitors' (Non-Contentious Business) Remuneration Order 1994 and its replacement by the 2009 Order of the same name (SI 2009/1931) with effect from 11 August 2009. This abolished the remuneration certificate procedure. In August 2009 an emergency rule was introduced to require solicitors, before bringing any action on a bill or immediately on deducting sums for costs from funds held on behalf of clients, to inform clients of their entitlement to seek detailed assessment of costs. After a proper consultation process this was replaced on 1 March 2010 with a rather more proportionate requirement that, when clients are given the information required by rule 2.05 about complaints handling, they also have to be informed that any issue raised with the firm could include a complaint about the firm's bill; that there may also be a right to object to the bill by making a complaint to the LCS or (now) the Legal Ombudsman (LeO), and/or by applying to the court for detailed assessment; and that if all or part of a bill remains unpaid, the firm may be entitled to charge interest. It needs to be borne in mind that the LeO provides a service only to individuals and small businesses (see **CHAPTER 12**) so that telling all clients including large corporate clients that there 'may' be an opportunity to complain to the LeO is unhelpful.

Rule 5.01(1)(e), which is concerned with the management of a practice (see further para **3.21**), imposes an express obligation on principals to make effective arrangements to ensure compliance with rule 2.

In one material respect the rule changes the common law and curtails the right of solicitors to exercise a lien for their unpaid fees. Rule 2.03(1)(e) requires that clients are notified of circumstances in which a lien may be exercised. A failure to do so will seemingly remove the right.

1   [2007] EWCA Crim 2379.
2   [2008] EWHC 1831 (QB).
3   [2010] EWCA Civ 122.

3.9

The guidance to rule 2 states that 'it is not envisaged or intended that a breach of 2.02, 2.03 or 2.05 should invariably render a retainer unenforceable'. This is clearly a reference to the fact that, because the Code is subordinate legislation, any agreement which would constitute a breach of the Code is prima facie unenforceable.[1]

Rule 2.04 restates the former Practice Rule 8 in that it provides that a solicitor cannot enter into an arrangement to receive a contingency fee in contentious proceedings, *except as permitted by statute or the common law*. The italicised words were introduced into Practice Rule 8 in January 1999 in response to *Thai Trading & Co (a firm) v Taylor*[2] as it was thought that it might be possible for solicitors to enter into some forms of contingency or conditional fee arrangements at common law because public policy no longer required a complete prohibition of such arrangements. However, subsequent cases reaffirmed the common law's objection to contingency arrangements in relation to contentious proceedings (at least at the time that the fee agreement was made in *Awwad*,[3] that is in 1993) and, pending a review of the law and the impact of public policy as at some later date by the Court of Appeal or the Supreme Court, the only arrangement that is permitted as an exception to the rule is statutory (that is, by means of a lawful conditional fee agreement).

1   See *Swain v Law Society* [1983] 1 AC 598; *Hughes v Kingston upon Hull District Council* [1992] 2 All ER 49; *Mohammed v Alaga & Co (a firm)* [1999] All ER (D) 205; and *Awwad v Geraghty* [2000] 1 All ER 608.
2   [1998] QB 781, [1998] 3 All ER 63.
3   *Awwad v Geraghty* [2000] 1 All ER 608.

3.10

By reason of rule 2.06 solicitors are required to account to their clients for any commission received of more than £20, a figure unchanged since 1990 and designed to provide a de minimis threshold. The de minimis provision does not apply to commissions attributable to regulated activities as defined by the Financial Services and Markets Act 2000 (Regulated Activities) Order 2001.[1] In this respect solicitors must comply with rule 2.06 regardless of the amount involved.

A commission is a financial benefit received by reason of, and in the course of, a solicitor/client relationship as a consequence of an introduction of a client to a third party or vice versa.

Rule 2.06 is concerned with commission and not with other commercial arrangements, however they may be described; the granting of a rebate on the price of a service (for example a conveyancing search service) is a discount and not commission, and the rule therefore provides no basis on which solicitors can retain such a rebate of £20 or less in reliance on its de minimis provision.[2] It has to be noted however that this distinction is somewhat artificial, in that the rule is based on the

CHAPTER 3
THE SOLICITORS' CODE OF
CONDUCT 2007

equitable duty of a fiduciary to make no secret profit. The mischief is secrecy, not the making of a profit if the client gives fully informed consent.

Paragraph 57 of the official guidance to rule 2.06 (see **APPENDIX 21**) states that even if the provisions of the rule are met in all respects commission may, in effect, only be retained by the solicitor if the client receives a direct benefit, by the commission being set off against, or otherwise used to reduce, the amount of the solicitor's costs. That would have the literal effect of giving the benefit of the commission to the client so that the solicitor would not retain it at all. The guidance thus has the effect of negating the rule. In such circumstances the terms of the rule must prevail. It is understood that consideration was being given to amending the guidance but this has yet to happen, and it can now be assumed that no further resources will be devoted to possible changes in the current rules or guidance, having regard to the concentrated effort involved in finalising the new Code. It is to be hoped, however, that this anomaly is recognised by those concerned in investigation and enforcement. Relevantly and enlighteningly, the equivalent of rule 2.06 in the new draft Code is an 'outcome' that: 'you properly account to your clients for any financial benefit you receive as a result of your instructions'. A financial benefit includes any commission, discount or rebate but does not include fees or interest earned on any client account. The significance is that the de minimis provision will go, but so will any artificial distinction between commission and discounts, and the regulatory requirement will simply reflect the position at law. Although the associated indicative behaviours require solicitors to 'justify' retaining commission even if clients have consented, there is no indication as to how such justification is to be measured.

1   SI 2001/544. See **CHAPTER 5**.
2   *Law Society v Adcock* [2006] EWHC 3212 (Admin). The court nevertheless upheld the Tribunal's decision to dismiss the case against the solicitors on a summary basis in view of the obvious confusion which had existed within the Law Society as to the proper interpretation of the rule at that time.

The Provision of Services Regulations 2009

3.11

It is convenient to deal with these Regulations (SI 2009/2999) at this point because, like rule 2, they require certain information to be provided to clients, but these requirements go beyond what is required by the Code: specifically, the firm's VAT number, details of compulsory professional indemnity insurance cover, details as to how to access professional rules and details of complaint resolution procedures.[1] Not all the information has to be provided in the same way. The VAT number and insurance information – which must include the contact details of the insurers and the territorial coverage of the insurance – may optionally be given in writing at the outset, in a client care letter or terms of business, or made easily accessible to clients in hard copy at the firm's offices or on the firm's website.

Information about professional rules, which requires a reference to the Solicitors' Code of Conduct 2007 and a link to the Code on the SRA website, must be provided in a clear and unambiguous manner in good time before the conclusion of the contract or, if there is no written contract, before the service is provided. It must also be provided on request. Making the information and link available on the firm's website and including a reference to where the information could be found (or including the information itself) within the client care letter would suffice.

Information about complaint resolution procedures involves telling clients about the role of the Legal Ombudsman and where further information can be obtained. Similarly, this must be provided in a clear and unambiguous manner in good time before the conclusion of the contract or, if there is no written contract, before the service is provided, but must also be provided in any information document in which the firm gives a detailed description of the service provided. This could therefore also be provided through a website and/or the client care letter. However, the LeO provides a service only to individuals and small businesses (see **CHAPTER 12**), so that telling all clients including large corporate clients that there is a complaint resolution service through the LeO when they will not, in fact, be able to take advantage of it would be misleading and unhelpful.

1   Regulation 8(1)(g) covers VAT; 8(1)(n), insurance; 9(1)(d), professional rules; 10(1), complaint resolution; and 11, manner of providing information.

Rule 3 – Conflict of interests

3.12

Rule 3 deals with conflicts of interest, both in general terms, and by reference to such things as gifts and bequests from clients; the possibilities of conflicts arising from public appointments (such as a coroner) and from involvement in alternative dispute resolution; the circumstances in which firms may act despite a conflict of interests between clients in strictly controlled circumstances; and the detailed requirements when acting for more than one party in a conveyancing transaction (whether or not in strict terms a true conflict of interests exists).

3.13

The rule replaced Practice Rule 16D, which came into force on 25 April 2006. Prior to that date conflicts of interest were not covered by a Practice Rule but were the subject of guidance in *The Guide to the Professional Conduct of Solicitors*, and to the common law.

The Code separates conflict of *interests* – conflicts between the interests of solicitors and their clients, and between the interests of two existing or potential clients – from the conflict of *duties* a solicitor may have where he or she is in possession of confidential information as a result of a retainer. This latter circumstance is now dealt with under rule 4.

Rules 3 and 4 should be considered together because even if solicitors are satisfied that no conflict exists (or a rule 3 exception applies), there may remain problems associated with the possession of confidential information.

Rule 3 defines a conflict as arising when:

> 'you owe, or your firm owes, separate duties to act in the best interests of two or more clients in relation to the same or related matters, and those duties conflict, or there is a significant risk that those duties may conflict.'[1]

It follows that for the purposes of the rule a conflict is only relevant if the situation arises 'in relation to the same or related matters'. The associated guidance deals with this in some detail. As with many aspects of the rules in relation to conflict, a solicitor may be required to form a judgement – in this respect as to whether matters are related. However, this does not mean that a solicitor's professional obligations are discharged merely by giving careful thought to the matter. If a solicitor does not honestly and genuinely address the matter he may be guilty of a disciplinary offence. And if his decision is one that no reasonably competent solicitor could have made, it may be inferred that he had not (or could not have) properly addressed the issue. This inference may well be appropriate where the reason given for the solicitor's professional decision is manifestly unsustainable.[2] Even if matters are not 'related' within the rule in the opinion of the solicitor, it will be prudent to consider the clients' views on the matter.

Although the rule does now define conflict of interest, it may be thought that to define it as a situation in which relevant interests are or may be in conflict does not add very much. *The Guide to the Professional Conduct of Solicitors* (8th edn) contained a valuable commentary which remains valid and the substance of which is reproduced here: where a solicitor is acting for two or more clients, whether they are husband and wife, business partners or companies embarking on a joint venture, the solicitor always owes a duty to each individual person or body and he or she must advise each individual in accordance with that individual's interests. A practical initial test to apply to assist in identifying whether a conflict exists is to ask: what would occur if the solicitor was only acting for one of the parties? In particular, would any advice be different?

The prohibition against a solicitor acting where his or her personal interests actually conflict with those of a client is absolute. Many solicitors continue to believe that merely informing a client that independent advice should be taken is sufficient to discharge his or her duties to the client. This is not so and normally, if the client does not in fact take independent advice, the solicitor must not proceed with the transaction (whether it be the purchase of an asset from the client, the drafting of a will containing a significant bequest in favour of the solicitor, or as the case may be).

1   Rule 3.01(2)(a).
2   See *Connolly v Law Society* [2007] EWHC 1175 (Admin).

3.14

Notwithstanding the general rule set out above, rule 3 specifies situations of conflict between clients where a solicitor may still act provided he has obtained the clients' consent. The situations are defined in rule 3.02(1) and rule 3.02(2).

Rule 3.02(1) provides that the solicitor may act if the different clients have a substantially common interest in relation to the matter (or a particular aspect of it). The circumstances where a common interest can arise and the requirements that must be met are dealt with in the guidance.

Rule 3.02(2) provides a separate exception where clients are competing for the same asset which, if attained by one client, will make that asset unattainable to the other client(s).

At first sight, both of these exceptions seem to allow solicitors to act in circumstances in which they were previously precluded from acting. However, this should be approached with caution. These exceptions exist for the benefit of clients and not solicitors. This should always be borne in mind when solicitors contemplate acting in these circumstances. It would be very rare for the exceptions to be applied where the clients are not sophisticated users of legal services. The rule and guidance set out the strict conditions that need to be satisfied. Solicitors should ensure that all clients give informed consent and that the terms of the arrangement are properly set out in writing. Solicitors must also comply with any relevant obligations under rule 4 in relation to confidential information held on behalf of any affected client.

3.15

Rule 3 does not permit a client to consent to a solicitor acting in a conflict of interest situation unless one of the specified exceptions applies. It is not possible to erect an information barrier (or Chinese wall) to 'cure' a rule 3 conflict.

A conflict between clients must involve current retainers from two or more relevant clients. Rule 3 does not prohibit a solicitor from acting for a client against a former client. In this situation, rule 4 will be in play in relation to any confidential information that may be held about the former client.

The rules enabling solicitors to act despite the existence of a conflict of interests between clients, in limited circumstances, continue to be (almost constantly) reviewed and the SRA is, at the time of publication, still consulting on the choice of three different possible models for the rule in the new Code.

The former Practice Rule 6 (avoiding conflicts in conveyancing) is replaced by rules 3.07 to 3.22 of the Code. In this respect the regulatory requirements have remained settled and unchanged for many years. These rules concern the circumstances in which a solicitor may act for seller and buyer or borrower and lender in property transactions. They restrict a solicitor's freedom to act even if there is no conflict of interest. Unless specified exceptions apply, even where there is no conflict of interest a solicitor, his or her practice or any associated practice, may not act for more than one party to a transfer of land for value at arm's length, for the grant or assignment of a lease or some other interest in land, for value at arm's length, or for the grant of a mortgage of land.

The new draft rule on conflict of interest would have a substantial impact on the way in which conveyancing is undertaken, but this was only released for consultation at the end of October 2010 and could well be changed; it is premature to consider these potential developments in this edition.

Rule 4 – Confidentiality and disclosure

3.16

Rule 4 deals with the duties to keep confidential the affairs of clients and former clients, save where disclosure is required or permitted by law, or by the client; the duty to disclose to your client all information of which you are aware material to that client's matter, and the rules that apply should those duties conflict.

3.17

The rule replaced Practice Rule 16E, which came into force on 25 April 2006. Before that date there had been no specific Practice Rule dealing with the duty of confidentiality – although such a duty had long been recognised by the courts and in the guidance provided by the Law Society. As emphasised in the commentary on rule 3, compliance issues that arise in relation to conflicts of interest and confidentiality are closely linked and rules 3 and 4 should be considered together.

Rule 4 creates three obligations:

(1)   the duty to keep clients' affairs confidential, except where disclosure is required or permitted by law (rule 4.01);

(2)   the duty to disclose to a client all information of which a solicitor is aware which is material to a client's matter regardless of the source of the information (rule 4.02);

(3)   the duty not to put a client's confidential information at risk by acting for another client where the information is material and that other client's interests are adverse to the client or former client to whom the duty of confidentiality is owed (rule 4.03).

The duty of confidentiality continues beyond the end of the retainer.

The obligation to disclose material information to a client is limited to the individual lawyer or fee earner concerned and information known to him or her in relation to a matter in which that lawyer or fee earner is personally acting or supervising; it does not extend to other information within his firm of which he or she is not personally aware.

3.18

Practical issues in relation to rule 4 are likely to occur when a firm intends to take on a matter under one of the exceptions specified in rule 3, or where a firm holds confidential information in relation to a former client and wishes to consider whether it can properly act on behalf of a client whose interests are adverse to the former client on behalf of whom the information is held, and where such information could be material to the new client.

Rule 4.04 provides that a solicitor or his firm may act in these circumstances where both clients consent to the arrangement. Both clients must give their informed consent and it must in all the circumstances be reasonable for the matter to proceed in this way. Solicitors will need to justify their approach should questions be raised by the SRA or the courts. A detailed written record of all aspects of the matter, including the informed consent of the clients, will therefore be all but essential. Particular caution should be exercised where the clients or former clients are not sophisticated users of legal services.

3.19

Rule 4.05 provides that where it is not possible to obtain the consent of the person on behalf of whom the confidential information is held, the firm may nevertheless act if an information barrier is put in place – if the current client consents and if it is reasonable in all the circumstances to act in this way. An amendment to rule 4.05 effective from 13 July 2010 enables firms to apply this exception when taking on clients, if all the conditions are satisfied, and not only when the situation develops after instructions have been accepted.

Any information barrier must comply with the requirements of the guidance[1] and with existing case law. Few such arrangements have found favour with the courts. If the arrangement is challenged the solicitor will have the burden of demonstrating that there is no risk of disclosure. Such a risk must be real as opposed to fanciful or theoretical, but the starting point is that, unless special measures are taken, information moves within a firm.[2]

1   Rule 4 guidance, paragraphs 41 to 45.
2   See *Bolkiah v KPMG* [1999] 2 AC 222; *Marks & Spencer plc v Freshfields* [2004] EWCA Civ 741; and, for an example of an arrangement that was approved, *Koch Shipping Inc v Richards Butler* [2003] PNLR 11.

Rule 5 – Business management in England and Wales

3.20

Rule 5 deals with the supervision and management of firms and of in-house practice and is concerned with the overall framework for supervision and management, the requirement for a person 'qualified to supervise' and the minimum standards for supervision of client matters and business arrangements.

3.21

The rule replaced and extensively changed and extended the former Practice Rule 13. Rule 5.01(1) sets out 12 aspects of practice and imposes obligations on recognised bodies, managers of recognised bodies and on recognised sole practitioners to make arrangements so that all such aspects are effectively managed within the firm:

- appropriate supervision of all staff and the proper supervision and direction of clients' matters;

- compliance with money laundering regulations;

- compliance with key regulatory requirements (such as recognition, practising certificates, insurance, accountants' reports and reporting information);

- identification of conflicts of interest;

- compliance with rule 2 (client relations);

- control of undertakings;

- safekeeping of documents and assets entrusted to the firm;

- compliance with rule 6 (equality and diversity);

- training to maintain competence;

- financial controls;

- continuation of the practice in the event of absences or emergencies; and

- the management of risk.

This list is more extensive than the former requirements of Practice Rule 13. It will be seen that many items are concerned with business and risk management relating to the practice as a whole, in addition to the familiar requirements as to the proper handling and supervision of individual client matters. This is a shift in focus.

CHAPTER 3
THE SOLICITORS' CODE OF CONDUCT 2007

Successive editions of *The Guide to the Professional Conduct of Solicitors* (the last of which was published in 1999) contained express guidance encouraging sole practitioners to make arrangements for the running of the practice after his or her death, by the appointment of one or more solicitor executors able to manage the practice, or by clear instructions for the appointment of a suitable solicitor manager.[1] There is no comparable current guidance, but it is strongly arguable that the obligation imposed by rule 5.01(1)(k) to make arrangements for 'the continuation of the practice of the firm in the event of absences and emergencies' would include such a requirement, which could be enforced against sole practitioners while they are still in practice.

A solicitor who is head of an in-house legal department must make effective arrangements for supervision and management of the department to include adequate supervision of assistants, the control of undertakings and identification of conflicts of interest.

1   See paragraph 3.14 of *The Guide to the Professional Conduct of Solicitors 1999* (8th edition).

3.22

Each firm (irrespective of size) needs one person who is 'qualified to supervise' – but only one.[1] To be qualified a person needs to have been entitled to practise as a lawyer for at least 36 months in the last ten years. In addition he or she must have undertaken a management skills course of at least 12 hours.[2]

There is no longer a need for each office of a firm to be supervised by someone who is qualified to supervise and for whom that office is his or her normal place of work, as was the position under the former Practice Rule 13. However, this does not obviate the need to ensure that all client work is properly supervised and checked by experienced and competent persons within the firm.[3] In essence rule 5 requires one person to be suitably trained and qualified in management skills, and the implementation by the firm of proper and adequate systems of supervision, proportionate to the individual practice, its size and complexity.

1   Rule 5.02.
2   Rule 5 guidance, paragraph 44.
3   Rule 5.03; and in the case of an in-house solicitor in, eg, a law centre, the comparable need for proper supervision of work undertaken for members of the public.

Rule 6 – Equality and diversity

3.23

Rule 6 replaces the Solicitors' Anti-Discrimination Rules 2004. Its scope is wider than the Rules it replaces as it includes age discrimination and discrimination on the basis of civil partnership status, gender reassignment, pregnancy, maternity and paternity. The duties imposed by the rule are in addition to and not in substitution for statutory obligations.

All firms must have a written policy for promoting equality, preventing discrimination and dealing with instances of discrimination.[1] The SRA has not published a model policy and each firm must devise its own.

By virtue of rule 5.01(1)(h) a principal in private practice must ensure arrangements are in place to ensure compliance with rule 6.

1   Rule 6.03 and guidance, paragraph 22.

Rule 7 – Publicity

3.24

This rule imposes requirements that publicity must not be misleading or inaccurate, and that professional charges must be clear; it imposes limitations on the manner in which work may be attracted (cold calling) and contains detailed requirements for the content of letterheads websites and e-mails. The first two items involve no change in the professional obligations that have existed for many years and need no elucidation.

3.25

Rule 7.03, formerly entitled 'Unsolicited visits or telephone calls' was amended with effect from 14 January 2009 to read 'Unsolicited approaches in person or by telephone'.

The background to this change is that firms have received introductions and referrals of work through companies registered with the Compensation Act 2006 regulator whose method of obtaining client contacts involves approaching members of the public in the street to complete lifestyle questionnaires and the like. It was difficult to maintain that this amounted to an unsolicited 'visit', which has connotations of knocking on doors. Nevertheless it was a practice of which the Compensation Act regulator disapproved. The Code of Conduct was therefore amended to bring the regulation of claims management companies and solicitors into closer alignment. Firms are not able to accept referrals of work from companies using that method of marketing (see further below in relation to rule 9, para **3.33**).

3.26

Letterheads (including fax headings) websites and e-mails must comply with rule 7.07. All must show the words 'regulated by the Solicitors Regulation Authority' as well as the firm's registered name and number if it is a company or LLP, or the name and number under which it is registered with the SRA if it is a partnership or sole practitioner.

The letterhead of a recognised sole practitioner must include the name of the sole practitioner. The letterhead of a recognised body which is a partnership of 20 or fewer partners must include a list of the partners. The letterhead of a recognised body which is a partnership of more than 20 partners must include either a list of the partners, or a statement that a list of the partners is open to inspection at the office. The letterhead of a recognised body which is an LLP must include either a list of the members, identified as members, or a statement that a list of the members is open to inspection at the office, unless the LLP is practising under a name other than its corporate name and has 20 or fewer members, in which case the list must be on the letterhead. The letterhead of a recognised body which is a company with a sole director must include the name of the director, identified as director. The letterhead of a recognised body which is a company with more than one director must include either a list of the directors, identified as directors, or a statement that a list of the directors is open to inspection at the office.

In a recognised body, if the managers include persons other than solicitors, *any* list must identify any solicitor as a solicitor, in the case of any lawyer or notary of an Establishment Directive state other than the United Kingdom, identify the jurisdiction(s) (local or national as appropriate) under whose professional title the lawyer or notary is practising, give the professional title(s), expressed in an official language of the Establishment Directive state(s) concerned, and if the lawyer is an REL, refer to that lawyer's registration with the SRA, and indicate the professional qualification(s) of any other lawyer and the country or jurisdiction of qualification of any RFL. The list must also identify any individual non-lawyer as a non-lawyer and identify the nature of any body corporate, if this is not clear from its name.

Rule 8 – Fee sharing

3.27

The rule restricts the persons and businesses with whom fees can be shared, for the purpose of protecting independence.

3.28

The provisions of rule 8 are substantively in the same form as the former Practice Rule 7 (as amended in 2004 and 2006), save that the involvement of non-lawyers in LDPs has caused necessary consequential amendments to permit the sharing of fees with non-lawyers who are owners or managers of the firm, and the like. However, it should be noted that because the former Practice Rules (and therefore the Solicitors' Code of Conduct 2007) had (and has) the effect of subordinate legislation enacted for the protection of the public,[1] the rule against fee sharing with non-solicitors is not merely for the purpose of professional regulation: it renders an agreement to share fees in breach of the rule illegal and unenforceable.[2] This is of major importance if an arrangement is made for the provision of capital in the form of investment or loan finance in exchange for a share of profits, in a way that is not permitted by the rule (see para **3.30**) because in that event the agreement would be unenforceable by either party. The current guidance on 'independence' is highly relevant in this respect: see para **3.6**.

1   *Swain v Law Society* [1983] 1 AC 598.
2   *Mohammed v Alaga & Co (a firm)* [1999] All ER (D) 205; *Westlaw Services Limited and anor v Boddy* [2010] EWCA Civ 929.

3.29

This rule has taken on a new significance because of the way in which its near identical predecessor was relaxed in March 2004 to permit the sharing of fees with providers of capital and services. Historically, breaches of the rule (and its predecessor) have been mostly associated with unlawful partnerships or 'fronting' operations in which a solicitor nominally owned and ran the firm but non-qualified 'employees' took a substantial share of the profits, or where an old-style managing clerk or more modern financial director received income which exactly matched a profit share such as a partner might receive.

Currently, the rule is engaged in two further problematic areas. First, it is not uncommon to have a referral arrangement which also has a fee sharing element, where the referral fee may be expressed as a percentage of costs, or where a wider fee sharing arrangement is part of the financial relationship between firm and introducer. It thus becomes primarily an issue to be considered in relation to rule 9, in terms of independence and disclosure (see paras **3.6** and **3.33**).

3.30

Also, the rule has been seen by some as a kind of transition or move towards outside investment in law firms, which will be permitted when the LSA 2007 is fully implemented in this respect and ABSs are authorised. That is misconceived.

In ordinary commercial terms, the investment of capital (in particular) and a return based on a share of income, amounts to or would be perceived as equity participation, but this is not envisaged or permitted by the rule. If it were so, there would have been no need for a regulatory regime for ABSs as provided by LSA 2007.

The rule in this respect permits only more flexible arrangements to deal with debt obligations, not shareholding and the payment of dividends.

The main risk is that a fee sharing arrangement may be perceived as a disguised partnership or a form of external ownership of the firm. Firms must be prepared to justify the arrangement in commercial terms and to demonstrate that it is not capable of criticism on those grounds. It should also be possible to show that the arrangement is wholly reasonable on ordinary business principles and a sound business decision for the firm to have made. If there is anything which suggests that the fee sharer is getting an element of bonus, something better than a realistic return for the services it provides, the suspicion will be that the arrangement is not what it is said to be.

3.31

The rule also enables fees to be shared with a registered charity, provided this does not amount to a partnership, and the arrangement does not offend any other rule, such as the requirement for independence or the rules relating to referrals. As details of any such arrangement must be produced to the SRA on request, it is desirable, if not in practice essential, that any such agreement is in writing.

Rule 9 – Referrals of business

3.32

Rule 9 replaced Practice Rule 3 and the Solicitors' Introduction and Referral Code 1990. The rule is directed at ensuring that a solicitor's duties to his client are not impaired by his relationship with an introducer of work.

Until March 2004, the Solicitors' Introduction and Referral Code prevented a solicitor from rewarding an introducer by the payment of commission or otherwise (the only exception being 'normal hospitality'). In March 2004 the Code was changed to allow such payments, but only if certain conditions were met. These are now contained in rules 9.01 and 9.02 without material change, save that agreements

CHAPTER 3
THE SOLICITORS' CODE OF
CONDUCT 2007

with introducers have to be in writing (formerly this was the subject of non-binding guidance), and the information required to be given by way of disclosure to clients by solicitors must also be in writing.

Referral fees are probably most prevalent in claimant personal injury work. Businesses dealing with or having an understanding of solicitors' practices, and indeed individual claimants, have not been slow to recognise that there is a value in every case on which a solicitor can make a profit, and that the profession is therefore prepared to pay for the introduction of potentially profitable cases, and in particular to pay for a guaranteed flow of work. The payment of referral fees to organisations which either have a natural capacity to refer claims to solicitors, or which can act as a marketing facility for the profession to acquire potential claims, is not so much commonplace, as a fundamental part of much of personal injury practice. The rule also permits, for example, the payment of introduction fees by conveyancing solicitors to estate agents.

It seems that referral fees are rarely out of the headlines. The profession itself is sharply divided over the concept, and there is even disagreement about who 'wins' the argument in numerical terms. One part of the profession regards the whole idea of buying work, and thereby increasing the basic overhead cost of conducting a client's case, to be distasteful, and damaging in tending to increase costs. The other maintains that solicitors' practices are businesses, that the payment of commissions for the introduction of work is a common and inevitable feature of business life, and that a return to more restrictive practices would defy the marketplace, which never really works, and in any event it would probably be unlawful as being anti-competitive. (For completeness, there is probably a third part of the profession which regards the whole debate as arid and irrelevant to them, and wishes people would stop talking about it.) The Law Society's official position is that referral fees should be banned across the legal services market. However, based on research for and views expressed by the Legal Services Consumer Panel, the Legal Services Board has indicated that it would not support a ban, but would encourage greater transparency.

3.33

The rule is primarily about independence, disclosure and informed consent. A client needs to know, at the outset and before instructions are confirmed, that his or her case has been 'bought'. That requires proper disclosure of the financial arrangements between solicitor and introducer, and both the introducer and the solicitor have obligations in this respect. Secondly, solicitors have to satisfy themselves that introducers have conducted their own businesses properly, and have not, for example, acquired clients by cold calling, so that it is necessary to ensure that introducers are contractually committed to certain principles, and that solicitors can monitor the situation to check that introducers continue to be compliant. Thirdly, nothing in the arrangement may constrain the solicitor's professional judgement in advising the client. Introducers must not therefore be able to interfere in the solicitor/client relationship.

It would be wise to resolve all questions as to how much information to give in favour of more, not less. The rule requires that 'all relevant information' about the referral arrangements must be given, and one could expect the SRA to ask, if a particular aspect of the relationship was not disclosed or fully disclosed, why that was regarded as *not* to be relevant. The information must be given at the first opportunity, at the outset, before accepting instructions. And the information must be given in writing. It follows that it is not sufficient to see a client in interview, agree to act, and then send the required information as part of the solicitor's standard client care material or terms of business. That is too late and the need for disclosure at the very beginning of any potential solicitor/client relationship may be inconvenient in administrative terms.

There is, in our view, a reason that solicitors appear to be struggling with these particular compliance issues. The rule has detailed specific requirements. Most solicitors do not have an encyclopaedic understanding of the rules, but have a very good understanding of what they think matters, in terms of their relationship with their clients. They are driven by the need to serve their clients, and are acutely aware of anything which, in their perception, could be prejudicial to their clients. They tend to regard rules which, in their opinion, are technical requirements having no material impact on clients, as of lesser importance.

In contrast, to the SRA a rule is a rule and a breach is a breach. Non-compliance, any non-compliance, is a breach. It does not matter if no client has complained, or that no client has apparently been caused any prejudice, because the rules are there for a reason, and a failure to comply has the potential to cause prejudice. At least this has been its position until now; the move to OFR discussed above (see para **3.4**) may cause a change. It is right that the SRA has tended to find relatively high levels of non-compliance in relation to the minutiae of the rules relating to referral arrangements, but has also found, generally, that the non-compliance has caused no prejudice to clients.

To satisfy the demands of the regulator, the profession (or at least the part of it that cannot afford a compliance department) has had to adapt away from the approach that if a breach of a rule does not really matter, or can be seen to have had no adverse consequence, the rule can be safely disregarded, or at least that the SRA will not take such a breach seriously. Even if it can be argued that historically the SRA approach has been heavy-handed and disproportionate, this is not an argument that individual members of the profession can win, when they are under investigation. It is a fact that ordinary decent solicitors, who have never done anything worse than make mistakes while trying to get it right, are still being investigated and prosecuted in unprecedented numbers although there are signs over recent months of a more proportionate policy. To avoid becoming such a statistic, the profession has to adapt to the regulator's attitudes and demands, particularly as the requirements of the rule can be managed without major difficulty. It is to be hoped that the same changes forecast for OFR will bring a better and healthier relationship between regulator and regulated.

3.34

For the time being however there are four elements that need to be addressed:

(1) the contractual requirements to be imposed on the introducer, as part of the necessary written agreement;

(2) the obligations of the introducer to make disclosure to clients;

(3) the solicitor's disclosure obligations; and

(4) the solicitor's obligation to monitor compliance by the introducer and him- or herself.

These can all be addressed by standard documents or procedures.

With relatively little effort, a standard set of clauses can be designed for insertion in every agreement with introducers, recording the obligations and commitments of the introducer, to ensure regulatory compliance, particularly with rules 7 and 9; a flexible template could be drafted for use by introducers for disclosure of a financial arrangement to their customers, which could be used in leaflets and brochures or as a script in a call centre, and which the agreement would require the introducer to submit to the firm for approval; and a similar template could be designed for use by solicitors in making disclosure.

The fourth element is a protocol for monitoring the arrangement, for example, by adding a procedure to the office manual or the like to prompt the compliance partner to undertake a periodic check on the introducer's publicity material and website, on the degree of the firm's dependence on the introducer, and a review of the independence of advice, and for records of this to be kept; and by adding items to a client care checklist as to how clients came to be contacted by the introducer and what information has been given by the introducer.

These would, of course, have to be refined to reflect the firm's particular arrangements and circumstances.

3.35

Any firm reviewing its arrangements with introducers, or considering a new arrangement, should examine it with a view to identifying any element which could possibly prejudice the interests of clients. The SRA will not be slow (a) in identifying such a factor or (b) in asserting that in making the arrangement you had therefore preferred your own commercial interests to those of your clients.

A good way of ensuring the objectivity of any such appraisal is to imagine that you have discovered that a competing firm has just such an arrangement, and how you might object to it or complain about it.

3.36

The comparable rule in the new draft Code is substantially less prescriptive. The required outcomes are: that the solicitor's independence and professional judgment are not prejudiced by virtue of any arrangements with another person; that clients' interests are always protected regardless of the interests of an introducer or the solicitor's interests in receiving referrals; that clients are in a position to make an informed decision about how to pursue their legal matter; that clients are fully informed of any financial or other interest which an introducer has in referring the client to the solicitor; and that payments are not made to an introducer where clients are subject to criminal proceedings or have the benefit of public funding.

3.37

In November 2009, not without controversy, and with little consultation, the guidance to rule 9 was changed with immediate effect (though not the rule itself). In particular two new requirements were added (rule 9 guidance, paragraphs 1 and 3):

'You should not enter into a referral arrangement with an introducer whose overall scheme or arrangement will not be in the best interests of the clients referred to you'

and:

'If a client is entering into or has already entered into a scheme or arrangement with an introducer which is not in their best interests then you must advise the client accordingly. Schemes or arrangements which involve the client paying unnecessary or unreasonable fees will not normally be in the client's best interests'.

This additional guidance requires in substance that solicitors police the business models of introducers, their charging structures and policies. There is no guidance as to what is an unnecessary or unreasonable fee.

The new draft Code does contain comparable provisions, but rather more positively phrased. Included in the positive indicative behaviours in relation to referrals are: entering into referral and fee sharing arrangements with third parties that are reputable and monitoring the outcome of those arrangements for the purposes of ensuring that clients are treated fairly; in any case where a client has entered into, or is proposing to enter into, an arrangement with introducer in connection with the client's legal matter which is not in his best interests, advising the client that this is the case; and amongst the negative indicators: facilitating or participating in a scheme or arrangement that is not in the best interests of the clients referred.

3.38

Where the referral is in the other direction – that is, where there is a referral by the solicitor of a client to another firm, agency or business – the decision and recommendations must be made in the best interests of the client and in good faith, and no agreement may be made by a solicitor which would restrict the solicitor's freedom to make recommendations in accordance with those requirements.[1] This means that solicitors may not make an agreement binding themselves to recommend clients to a particular third party, and may not enter into an agreement, for example, with an introducer of work, that would require solicitors to instruct a sister company or commercial contact of the introducer for particular purposes, or engage only the introducer's 'preferred' service provider. To do so would interfere with the firm's independence, which it is the primary purpose of the rule to avoid.

1   Rule 9.03.

Rule 10 – Relations with third parties

3.39

Rule 10 brings together seven separate matters which were not previously the subject of a Practice Rule but were dealt with in *The Guide to the Professional Conduct of Solicitors*.

Undertakings are now the subject of a specific rule (rule 10.05) and professional obligations are thus given the force of law. Undertakings are now defined in rule 24. An undertaking is:

'a statement made by you or your firm to someone who reasonably relies upon it, that you or your firm will do something or cause something to be done, or refrain from doing something. The undertaking can be given orally or in writing and need not include the words "undertake" or "undertaking".'

Other matters covered are:

(1)   the duty not to take unfair advantage of others (rule 10.01);

(2)   an obligation to give sufficient information about your costs when they are payable by a third party (rule 10.02);

(3)   the entitlement to administer oaths and affirmations (rule 10.03);

(4)   restrictions on contacting directly the client of another lawyer (rule 10.04);

(5)   dealing with more than one prospective buyer in a conveyancing transaction ('contract races', the former Practice Rule 6A; now rule 10.06); and

(6)   the obligation to pay the fees of foreign lawyers if such lawyers have been instructed in the course of a solicitor's practice (rule 10.07).

Rule 11 – Litigation and advocacy

3.40

Rule 11 replaced the Law Society's Code for Advocacy and those principles that were previously contained in Chapter 21 of *The Guide to the Professional Conduct of Solicitors* (8th edn). Rule 11 imposes on all solicitors who conduct litigation some of the obligations that were previously only imposed on advocates. For example, a solicitor cannot draft documents containing any allegation that he or she does not consider properly arguable.[1]

This rule was considered by the Court of Appeal in *Richard Buxton (Solicitors) v Mills-Owen*[2] in which it was held that solicitors could lawfully determine their retainer when required by a client to advance an argument which they considered to be untenable.

The rule imposes duties in conduct not to deceive or mislead the court (including obligations to draw relevant cases and statutory provisions as well as any material procedural irregularity to the court's attention); a duty to comply with court orders; a provision making a finding of contempt of court a specific breach of the Code; limitations on refusing instructions as an advocate; and a restriction on accepting instructions if the advocate or anyone in the firm will be called as a witness, unless that will not cause any prejudice to the client or the interests of justice. No payment may be made to a witness dependent on the nature of the evidence given or the outcome of the case.

1   Rule 11.01(3)(a).
2   [2010] EWCA Civ 122.

3.41

If you are appearing as an advocate, you:

- must not say anything which is merely scandalous or intended only to insult a witness or any other person;

- must avoid naming in open court any third party whose character would thereby be called into question, unless it is necessary for the proper conduct of the case;

- must not call into question the character of a witness you have cross-examined unless the witness has had the opportunity to answer the allegations during cross-examination; and

- must not suggest that any person is guilty of a crime, fraud or misconduct unless such allegations go to a matter in issue which is material to your client's case; and appear to you to be supported by reasonable grounds.[1]

If you are acting in the defence or prosecution of an accused and you have in your possession a copy of an audio or video recording of a child witness which has been identified as having been prepared to be admitted in evidence at a criminal trial in accordance with the relevant provisions of the Criminal Justice Act 1991 or the Youth Justice and Criminal Evidence Act 1999, you must not make or permit any person to make a copy of the recording, must not release the recording to the accused, must not make or permit any disclosure of the recording or its contents to any person except when, in your opinion, it is necessary in the course of preparing the prosecution, defence or appeal against conviction and/or sentence, must ensure that the recording is always kept in a locked, secure container when not in use; and must return the recording when you are no longer instructed in the matter.[2]

1   Rule 11.05.
2   Rule 11.08.

Rule 12 – Framework of practice

3.42

The rule sets out the manner in which solicitors and recognised bodies (as well as RELs and RFLs) may practise.

A solicitor may practise from an office in England and Wales:

- as a recognised sole practitioner or the employee of a recognised sole practitioner;

- as a solicitor exempted from the obligation to be a recognised sole practitioner;[1]

- as a manager, employee, member or owner of a recognised body or a body corporate which is a manager, member or owner of a recognised body;

- as a manager, employee, member or owner of an authorised non-SRA firm[2] or a body corporate which is a manager, member or owner of an authorised non-SRA firm provided that all work done is either of a sort authorised by the firm's approved regulator, or done for the firm itself, or within rules 13.02 (Work colleagues), 13.03 (Related bodies) or 13.04 (Pro bono work);

- as the employee of another person, business or organisation, provided that the work is undertaken only for the employer, or as permitted by rule 13 (In-house practice, etc).[3]

A solicitor may practise outside England and Wales:

- as a sole practitioner (including a recognised sole practitioner);

- as the employee of a sole principal who is a lawyer;

- as a manager, employee, member or owner of a recognised body, provided that if any of the body's managers or owners are non-lawyers and the office is in an Establishment Directive state other than the United Kingdom, the rules for local lawyers would permit a local lawyer to practise through a business of that composition and structure;

- as the employee of another person, business or organisation, provided that the work undertaken is for the employer, or as permitted by rule 15.13 (In-house practice overseas); or

- as a manager, employee, member or owner of a business which has no office in England and Wales and meets all the following conditions:

  - the business carries on the practice of law;

  - a controlling majority of the managers and the owners are lawyers and/or bodies corporate in which lawyers constitute a controlling majority of the managers and owners;

  - if any of the business's managers or owners are non-lawyers and any manager or owner is subject to the rules for local lawyers, the composition and structure of the business complies with those rules, and if any of the business's managers or owners are non-lawyers and the office is in an Establishment Directive state, the rules for local lawyers would permit a local lawyer to practise through a business of that composition and structure.[4]

Recognised bodies may practise in England and Wales:

- as a stand-alone firm;

- as a manager, member or owner of another recognised body; or

- as a manager, member or owner of an authorised non-SRA firm, in which case the services provided must all fall within the scope of the firm's authorisation;

- as an executor, trustee or nominee company, or a company providing company secretarial services, owned and operated by another recognised body or by a recognised sole practitioner.[5]

Recognised bodies may practise outside England and Wales:

- as a stand-alone firm, provided that if any of the body's managers or owners are non-lawyers and the office is in an Establishment Directive state other than the United Kingdom, the rules for local lawyers would permit a local lawyer to practise through a business of that composition and structure;

- as an executor, trustee or nominee company, or a company providing company secretarial services, owned and operated by another recognised body or by a recognised sole practitioner; or

- as a manager, member or owner of a business which has no office in England and Wales and meets all the following conditions:

  - the business carries on the practice of law;

  - a controlling majority of the managers and the owners are lawyers and/or bodies corporate in which lawyers constitute a controlling majority of the managers and owners;

  - if any of the business's managers or owners are non-lawyers and any manager or owner is subject to the rules for local lawyers, the composition and structure of the business complies with those rules; and

  - if any of the business's managers or owners are non-lawyers and the office is in an Establishment Directive state other than the United Kingdom, the rules for local lawyers would permit a local lawyer to practise through a business of that composition and structure.[6]

1   See rule 20.03(2).
2   A firm regulated by another regulator such as the Council for Licensed Conveyancers.
3   Rule 12.01(1).
4   Rule 12.01(2).
5   Rule 12.04(1).
6   Rule 12.04(2).

Rule 13 – In-house practice

3.43

Rule 13 replaced the former Practice Rule 4 and the Employed Solicitors Code.

The regulatory requirements imposed on in-house lawyers may be divided into two categories:

(1)   those relating to in-house solicitors who provide legal services to their employer only; and

(2)   those relating to in-house solicitors providing legal services to persons other than their employer, including members of the public. In-house solicitors in this latter category are subject to more extensive obligations under rule 13.

In-house solicitors may only provide legal services to persons other than their employers within one or other of the categories specified in, and subject to the requirements of, this rule.

3.44

In addition to rule 13, the following apply to all in-house solicitors:

- Rule 1 – Core duties.

- Rule 3 – Conflicts of interest. A solicitor who acts only for his or her employer is likely only to be concerned with possible conflicts between the interests of the employer and the solicitor's own personal interests. The principal issues likely to affect in-house solicitors are set out in the guidance to that rule at paragraphs 17 to 22.

- Rule 4 – Confidentiality. A solicitor who acts only for his or her employer is likely only to be affected by the normal duty of confidentiality to the employer.

- Rule 5 – Business management in England and Wales. In-house solicitors are specifically required under rule 5.01(2) to have in place management arrangements for supervision, control of undertakings and the identification of conflicts of interest. The rule 5 guidance makes clear at paragraph 41 that this obligation falls on the head of an in-house legal department.

- Rule 6 – Equality and diversity. The requirement on in-house solicitors is upon those who have management responsibilities and is to 'use all reasonable endeavours to secure the adoption' of an appropriate equality and diversity policy.[1]

- Rule 10 – Relations with third parties. Rule 10 contains a number of provisions, including those relating to undertakings which are of application to in-house solicitors.

- Rule 11 – Litigation and advocacy. Rule 11 will apply to in-house solicitors in so far as they conduct litigation.

- Rule 20 – Rights and obligations of practice. In particular, all in-house solicitors will need a practising certificate if they are held out as, or employed as, a solicitor or lawyer, carry out reserved work, supervise in accordance with rule 5.02, or authorise withdrawal of money from client account.[2] This is an extension of the former requirements: in-house solicitors did not formerly need a practising certificate unless they were held out as solicitors, administered oaths or appeared before a court or tribunal. Even then, no practising certificate was required if the solicitor was supervised by a solicitor with a practising certificate.[3] The guidance to rule 20.01 states that it puts into rule form the underlying requirements of section 1 of SA 1974. This is not strictly correct in our view and the effect of the rule is to widen the categories of solicitors who are required to hold practising certificates. There remain now only a limited number of statutory exceptions to the need to hold a practising certificate in favour of solicitors working for certain public bodies.

1   Rule 6.04.
2   Rule 20 guidance, paragraphs 10 to 14.
3   *The Guide to the Professional Conduct of Solicitors* (8th edn), pp 145 to 146.

3.45

Rule 13 sets out 11 sets of circumstances in which an in-house solicitor can act for persons other than his or her employer.

These are:

- for work colleagues in the specific and limited circumstances set out in rule 13.02;

- for bodies related to the employer as provided in rule 13.03;

- pro bono work, subject to limitations and the requirement for insurance (rule 13.04);

- for members of an association if employed by the association (rule 13.05);

- for insured parties if employed by an insurer, subject to the limitations of rule 13.06;

- providing telephone legal advice for a commercial legal advice service subject to satisfactory insurance arrangements (rule 13.07);

- in the course of employment in local government subject to the limitations of rule 13.08;

- through law centres, charities or other non-commercial advice services as provided in rule 13.09, subject to satisfactory insurance arrangements;

- through employment by the Crown, non-departmental public body or the Legal Services Commission (rule 13.10);

- through foreign law firms as provided by rule 13.11; and

- through regulatory bodies (rule 13.12).

In all circumstances in which work is undertaken for a client other than an employer under rule 13, solicitors may not act if to do so would compromise their professional independence or integrity, their duty to act in the best interests of that client, their duty to comply with rule 3 (Conflict of interests), their duty to keep information about that client's affairs confidential from the employer (unless the other client consents to disclosure, or the solicitor is the employee of a foreign law firm), or the solicitor's ability to discharge any other duty owed to that client under the Code.[1]

In all cases the solicitor must either have professional indemnity insurance (for acting under the provisions of rules 13.04, 13.07, 13.09 and 13.11) or must consider whether the employer has appropriate indemnity insurance or funds to meet any award made as a result of a claim in professional negligence against the solicitor for which the employer might be liable. If there is no appropriate indemnity insurance, the solicitor must inform the client in writing that the solicitor is not covered by the compulsory insurance scheme.[2]

1   Rule 13.01(1)(a).
2   Rule 13.01(1)(b).

Rule 14 – Recognised bodies

3.46

Rule 14 governs the composition and structure of a recognised body and much of the rule reproduces the statutory requirements a body has to meet in order to be regulated by the SRA to provide reserved legal activities, as required by sections 9 and 9A of the Administration of Justice Act 1985. These are the services requirement, the relevant lawyer requirement and the management and control requirement; see **CHAPTER 2** in relation to LDPs and **APPENDIX 18**.

The rule provides that a recognised body which becomes unable to meet the relevant lawyer requirement or management and control requirement in unforeseen circumstances has a period of 28 days in which to remedy the situation and will be deemed to have remained in compliance if that is done.[1]

1   Rules 14.01(2)(b) and 14.01(3)(f).

3.47

Rule 14 imposes an obligation to comply with the rule on the recognised body itself, its managers and employees. A recognised body must comply with rule 14 and so far as possible ensure that its managers, members and owners comply with rule 14. A recognised body must not take on a new manager without first being satisfied of that manager's eligibility, by making necessary enquiries, obtaining written confirmation and retaining the record for production to the SRA if required.[1]

A manager of a recognised body must so far as possible ensure that the body complies with rule 14; must ensure that the body complies with any condition imposed on its recognition; and must not cause, instigate or connive at any breach of these rules by the recognised body or any of its managers or employees.[2]

A solicitor who is a member of, or the owner of a share in, a recognised body which is a company must not cause, instigate or connive at any breach of these rules by the recognised body or any of its managers or employees.[3]

A person employed to work in the practice of a recognised body must not cause, instigate or connive at any breach of these rules.[4]

The partners in a recognised body which is a partnership are responsible not only as managers but also, jointly and severally, as the recognised body.[5]

1 Rule 14.02(1)(a), (b) and (c).
2 Rule 14.02(2).
3 Rule 14.02(3).
4 Rule 14.02(4).
5 Rule 14.02(5).

3.48

The rule regulates who may be a partner in a recognised body which is a partnership, who may be a member of a recognised body that is an LLP, and who may be a director, member or share owner of a recognised body that is a company,[1] in a manner consistent with the Recognised Bodies Regulations (see **CHAPTER 2**), and provides for the consequences of a partnership split or other change in composition.[2]

The creation of any charge or third party interest by a partner in a partnership over his or her interest in the partnership, by a member of an LLP over the member's interest in the LLP, and by a member or share owner over his or her interest in a company is prohibited.[3]

There are requirements for the supply to the SRA of specified information, such as regarding a change in composition, structure or membership, and of any insolvency event.[4]

1 Rules 14.04(1), 14.05(1) and (2) and 14.06(1) and (2).
2 Rule 14.04(2) to (10) and 14.06(5) to (8).
3 Rule 14.04(11), 14.05(3) and 14.06(3).
4 Rule 14.07.

Rule 15 – Overseas practice

3.49

Rule 15 applies to overseas practice by solicitors and recognised bodies, as well as RELs and RFLs in some circumstances.

The rule explains which of the other rules in the Code apply to such practices, which do not, and which are modified in their effect. Rule 1 (Core duties) applies to overseas practice. Even if not practising as a solicitor, but in any other activity, either as a lawyer, or in other business or private capacity, rules 1.06 (Public confidence), 10.01 (Not taking unfair advantage) and 15.10(2) (Undertakings) apply to a solicitor.[1]

It also imposes obligations that, for firms practising in England and Wales, are imposed by other rules and regulations, but to a more limited extent. There is an obligation to pay interest on client money if it is fair to do so,[2] to have appropriate professional indemnity insurance,[3] and to comply with core elements of the duties imposed on solicitors practising in England and Wales by the Solicitors' Accounts Rules 1998[4] (in particular as to the proper keeping of accounts, the circumstances in which client money may be withdrawn from client account, and the provision of accountants' reports).

1   Rule 15.01(1)(a) and (b).
2   Rule 15.15.
3   Rule 15.26.
4   Rule 15.27.

Rule 16 – European cross-border practice

3.50

CCBE is the recognised abbreviation for the Council of the Bars and Law Societies of Europe and was originally the Commission Consultative des Barreaux d'Europe. Its correct current French title is 'Conseil des Barreaux Européens'. The Council's principal object is to study all questions affecting the legal profession in the Member States of the European Union and the European Economic Area and to formulate solutions designed to co-ordinate and harmonise professional practice. It has set up a Council for Advice and Arbitration to assist in resolving complaints between lawyers in different Member States.

The CCBE has published a Code of Conduct for Lawyers in the European Community (in October 1988; most recently updated in May 2006) for the purposes of regulating the conduct of lawyers within the Community concerned in cross-border activities.

3.51

The purpose of rule 16 is to bring together in one place the requirements imposed by the CCBE Code of Conduct for Lawyers in the European Community to the extent that those requirements are not replicated in other rules within the Solicitors' Code of Conduct 2007.

The consequence is that if solicitors comply with the Solicitors' Code of Conduct 2007 generally in relation to their practices, and with rule 16 in relation to any cross-border practice, they will comply in all respects with the CCBE Code of Conduct. The CCBE Code is nevertheless for completeness included at **APPENDIX 7**.

Cross-border practice is any professional activity in a CCBE state other than the United Kingdom (whether or not the solicitor is physically present) and any professional contact with a lawyer of a CCBE state other than in the United Kingdom, unless the professional contacts or activities are taking place within a firm or in-house practice.

3.52

Rule 16 deals with occupations incompatible with legal practice (an issue to be determined by reference to the rules of the CCBE state in question),[1] and imposes a prohibition on fee sharing with non-lawyers other than in specified circumstances.[2] It also requires co-operation between lawyers of CCBE states and deals with disputes and their resolution.[3]

The rule has a specific requirement in relation to correspondence. Because professional practices vary in the CCBE states as to communications which may be intended to be confidential or 'without prejudice', firms must express their intention *before* sending such a letter and establish whether the communication can be accepted on that basis. Solicitors must similarly inform those intending to send such correspondence to them whether it can be received on the intended basis.[4]

Although referral fees may be paid by solicitors to non-lawyer introducers of work in England and Wales, subject to the requirements of rule 9, referral fees may not be paid to non-lawyers in consideration for the referral of work if the introducer is situated in a CCBE state other than the United Kingdom or if the solicitor is practising from an office in such a CCBE state (whether physically present or not).[5]

1   Rule 16.02.
2   Rule 16.03.
3   Rules 16.04 and 16.07.
4   Rule 16.05.
5   Rule 16.06.

Rule 17 – Insolvency practice

3.53

Rule 17 requires solicitors who accept appointments as, or who act as, insolvency practitioners to comply with *The Insolvency Joint Code of Ethics* produced by the Joint Insolvency Committee, the fundamental principles of which are integrity, objectivity, professional competence and due care, confidentiality and professional behaviour.

Rule 18 – Property selling

3.54

Rule 18 is only concerned with property selling, that is, estate agency services provided through a solicitor's firm. (If the property-selling service is provided through a separate business, rule 21 applies.)

Rule 18 imposes standards of competency and service,[1] requires the prompt provision of clear information, in writing, as to the basis of the retainer and the fees to be charged,[2] and provides for the avoidance of conflicts of interest.[3]

The requirements in relation to avoidance of conflicts of interest are additional to those imposed by rule 3.

As a result of the introduction of home information packs (and during the short lifetime of that scheme), solicitors who were acting for a buyer in marketing a property were under a duty to have such a pack for the property as required by the relevant regulations.[4]

1   Rule 18.01.
2   Rule 18.02.
3   Rule 18.03.
4   Rule 18.01(2) and the Home Information Pack Regulations (No 2) 2007 (SI 2007/1667).

Rule 19 – Financial services

3.55

Rule 19 is concerned with the provision by solicitors of financial services of any kind. Solicitors who provide 'mainstream' financial services must be regulated by the Financial Services Authority (FSA), but if the financial services offered are incidental to other legal work and are within the limits set by the Solicitors' Financial Services (Scope) Rules 2001, solicitors will be engaged in 'exempt regulated activities' and can be regulated by the SRA. Solicitors regulated by the SRA (as opposed to the FSA) must comply with the Solicitors' Financial Services (Conduct of Business) Rules 2001.

Rule 19 applies in relation to the provision of financial services by solicitors whether they are regulated by the FSA or SRA, and prohibits solicitors engaged in regulated activities[1] (whether exempt or 'mainstream', and whether supplied through a firm regulated by the SRA or a separate business) from being an appointed representative (that is, a tied agent who is necessarily limited as to the products and services that can be offered to clients). It also prevents solicitors, subject to limited exceptions, from being constrained in the advice that may be given to clients or in the choice of those to whom clients may be referred.[2]

In short, the rule requires solicitors, as in all other things, to be independent.

1   As defined by the Financial Services and Markets Act 2000 (Regulated Activities) Order 2001 (SI 2001/544).
2   Rule 19.01(1) and (2).

Rule 20 – Rights and obligations of practice

3.56

Rule 20, as a consequence of the LSA 2007, specifies that solicitors are authorised by the SRA to undertake reserved legal activities provided they comply with rule 20.02(1), by holding a practising certificate or being exempt from that requirement under section 88 of SA 1974.

The reserved and other regulated activities which solicitors may undertake are:

- the exercise of any right of audience which solicitors had immediately before 7 December 1989;

- the exercise of any additional right of audience if the individual has a relevant higher courts advocacy qualification awarded by the SRA or another approved regulator;

- the conduct of, and the preparation of documents in, court and immigration tribunal proceedings;

- the preparation of instruments and the lodging of documents relating to the transfer or charge of land;

- the preparation of trust deeds disposing of capital;

- the preparation of papers on which to found or oppose a grant of probate or a grant of letters of administration;

- the administration of oaths and statutory declarations; and

- immigration services not otherwise provided for above and the provision of immigration advice.[1]

1   Rule 20.01(1).

3.57

The rule sets out in rule form an interpretation of sections 1, 1A and the former sections 20 to 23 of SA 1974 in relation to practising certificates and reserved work (sections 20 to 23 of SA 1974 have been replaced with effectively identical provisions in LSA 2007, in defining reserved legal activities). The interpretation provided by rule 20.02 in relation to the requirement to have a practising certificate is wide and is likely to cover all solicitors who offer services to members of the public and the vast majority of in-house solicitors, save for those who fall within certain statutory exceptions. The rule also deals with the obligations of solicitors to co-operate with the regulator.

Rule 20.03 prohibits solicitors from practising as sole practitioners unless they are recognised by the SRA or exempt, and provides for the consequences of the death of a recognised sole practitioner.

Rule 20.04 is a mechanism to ensure that all solicitors involved in the supply of legal services, whether through a business entity regulated by the SRA or by another regulator require a practising certificate. There is one exception as a result of a quirk of drafting in the amendment of section 1A of SA 1974 by the LSA 2007. If you are a director or employee of a firm providing regulated legal services under the auspices of a non-SRA regulator, such as the CLC, you are deemed to be doing so as a solicitor and require a practising certificate, but if you are a manager, member or owner of an authorised non-SRA firm you may practise as an individual authorised by another approved regulator.

3.58

Rule 20.05 imposes an obligation to co-operate with the SRA and LCS by dealing with those organisations in an open, prompt and co-operative way, and to provide information necessary for the SRA to deal with practising certificates and recognition, and to inform the SRA of any relevant changes to that information.

It also imposes a new obligation with effect from 31 March 2009 that enables the SRA to direct firms to investigate themselves as if complaints had been made by a particular class of client; see para **13.7**.

3.59

Rule 20.06 imposes an obligation on solicitors to report to the SRA 'serious misconduct' by a solicitor, RFL or REL, recognised body, a manager of a recognised body or an employee of a recognised body or recognised sole practitioner; reason to doubt the integrity of a solicitor, REL, RFL, manager or employee; or reason to believe that a recognised body, manager or firm is in serious financial difficulty that would put the public at risk. Not all perceived misconduct gives rise to a duty to report and careful thought may often need to be given to the matter. A consideration of the guidance in *The Guide to the Professional Conduct of Solicitors* (8th edn), and the examples there given,[1] implies that 'serious' means dishonesty or lack of integrity. The current guidance is slightly more narrow and restrictive,[2] and refers only to conduct involving dishonesty or deception or a serious criminal offence. It will be noted that there is a second category where a report is required, where there is reason to doubt integrity. The obligation in relation to 'serious financial difficulty' arises where the solicitor judges that this poses a risk to clients or others. However, bearing in mind that a failure to report could (if the exercise of judgement is later found to be badly mistaken) result in sanctions on the solicitor who failed to report, it is suggested that practitioners should err on the side of caution.

Rule 20.08 imposes an obligation to provide information and explanations, as well as documents, to the SRA to assist any investigation into compliance by the solicitor with the Code or other professional rules currently in force. Rule 20.08 overlaps with the procedure under sections 44B and 44BA of SA 1974, which allows the SRA to require the production by a solicitor of files, documents, information and explanations. The solicitor may also be required to give permission for information to be provided by third parties.

Rule 20.09 requires firms to deal properly with claims and circumstances likely to give rise to a claim. Rule 20.10 imposes an obligation to comply with conditions on a practising certificate or recognition.

---

1   See at pp 361 to 362.
2   Rule 20 guidance, paragraph 36.

CHAPTER 3
THE SOLICITORS' CODE OF CONDUCT 2007

Rule 21 – Separate businesses

3.60

As the nature of legal practice develops and expands, the restriction on separate businesses in which solicitors have a substantial interest or active participation assumes greater significance. Rule 21 replaced Practice Rule 5 and the Solicitors' Separate Business Code and eased some of the former restrictions.

The philosophy of the rule is that clients should not be confused into believing that they are dealing with a firm regulated by the SRA (which is highly controlled and provides them with the benefit of minimum levels of insurance and the Compensation Fund) when they are not. It is also designed to ensure that core legal services are only provided through a properly regulated firm and by properly regulated individuals, and to prevent part of a case or matter being severed so as to remove statutory protections available to the client.

3.61

The rule deals with three situations. First, it sets out in rule 21.02 the core legal activities which cannot be hived off to a separate business. A solicitor is precluded from providing these services other than through a solicitors' practice and is prohibited from involvement in a separate business that provides those services. The definition of 'involvement' is a broad one[1] and one element of that – 'active participation' – has been construed widely by the Solicitors Disciplinary Tribunal in the context of the former Practice Rule 5 (the wording of which was not materially different in this respect).[2]

1   See 'providing a service through a separate business' in rule 24.
2   *Nixon,* 9393–2005, SDT, where the writing of letters on behalf of a separate business in which the solicitor had no beneficial interest or other involvement was, on the particular facts, deemed sufficient to fall within the definition of 'active participation'.

3.62

Secondly, certain activities that may be carried out by a solicitor in a separate business or within a solicitors' firm or in-house practice are subject to safeguards. These include management consultancy services, alternative dispute resolution services and the provision of any other business, advisory or agency services which could be provided by a solicitors' firm but which do not fall within the core activities set out in rule 21.02.

It is not uncommon for firms to want to provide non-legal advisory services to clients or prospective clients. If they are provided by a solicitors' firm they are subject to the full range of other regulatory requirements, including rules 2 and 5, which may mean that the firm cannot provide these services economically. The firm would also need to consider whether such work fell within the terms of its professional indemnity insurance policy.

One of the practical difficulties under the former Separate Business Code was that these 'either way'[1] services could not be carried out by a business that had a name that had a 'substantial element' in common with the name of the solicitors' practice. This phrase was undefined. The new rule does not repeat the phrase and states the position more widely.[2] This is confirmed by the guidance, which states that while the same name cannot be used there is no objection to using a similar or related name or 'brand'.[3] There is therefore much greater potential for solicitors to run a separate business with the benefit of the goodwill and reputation associated with the 'brand', as represented by the firm's name and style of practice, provided that the other conditions set out in rule 21.05 are met.

1   This phrase was used in the guidance to the former Separate Business Code.
2   Rule 21.05(2)(a).
3   Rule 21 guidance, paragraph 16(a).

3.63

The third situation covered by rule 21, and which is expressly permitted without additional safeguards, involves the provision of services that fall outside the scope of a solicitors' practice but which can be provided in conjunction with a solicitors' firm or in-house practice. These are qualified notary public services, educational activities, and authorship, journalism and publishing.

Rule 22 – Waivers

3.64

Rule 22 enables the Board of the SRA to grant waivers in writing in relation to rules within the Code, to impose conditions on any such waiver and to revoke waivers. Waivers are not available in respect of rules that establish core principles (such as rule 1, most of rule 3, rules 4 and 6), as opposed to those concerned with practical arrangements (such as rules 2, 5 and 7 to 14). Rule 22 provides a comprehensive list.

Any waiver granted in relation to the Practice Rules and remaining valid will continue to apply for a period of two years from 1 July 2007, unless an earlier date is specified in the waiver.

Rule 23 – Application of these rules

3.65

Rule 23 specifies those to whom the Code applies – namely solicitors, RELs, RFLs, recognised bodies and the managers and employees of recognised bodies and employees of recognised sole practitioners – and makes it clear that relevant rules apply to solicitors outside their professional practices, in their private lives (the duty to maintain public confidence, rule 1.06; the duty not to take unfair advantage of others, rule 10.01; the duty to comply with undertakings if given as a solicitor, rule 10.05).

Rule 24 – Interpretation

3.66

Rule 24 contains the definitions of words and phrases used in the Code. Items of particular significance have been mentioned in the analysis of individual rules. It is, however, an indication of the complexity of current regulation that the list of words and phrases that have specific meanings and which require to be defined for the purposes of the rule covers 9 pages of this book and contains 75 items.

Rule 25 – Commencement and repeals

3.67

The Code became effective on 1 July 2007. It has been amended several times, most extensively on 31 March 2009 and most recently on 6 October 2010.

The Solicitors' Practice Rules 1990 and all six of their associated Codes, as well as the Anti-Discrimination Rules 2004, the Overseas Practice Rules 1990, the Incorporated Practice Rules 2004, and *The Guide to the Professional Conduct of Solicitors* (and the updated version of that which was on the Law Society's website, the 'Guide Online'), are all repealed.

The Solicitors' Accounts Rules 1998 were unaffected, as were the Solicitors' Indemnity Insurance Rules, the Solicitors' Financial Services (Scope) Rules 2001, the Solicitors' Financial Services (Conduct of Business) Rules 2001 and the Solicitors' Compensation Fund Rules 1995. However, all these rules have since been amended, as indicated in later chapters.

The Practice Rules, in their final form before the introduction of the Code, can be found archived on the SRA website.

A glimpse of the future: the new draft Code

3.68

Consultations about the new Code and all the associated sets of rules will close on 13 January 2011, and the final form of the Code to be effective from October 2011 is not yet known. However the structure is likely to be settled and there are some clear indications of a change in approach. The new Code in the latest available draft form is in **APPENDIX 22**. It is built around ten core principles (as drafted at present); four more than the core duties set out in rule 1 of the present Code; they are addressed to the regulated person as 'you must':

'1   uphold the rule of law and the proper administration of justice;

2   act with integrity;

3   not allow your independence to be compromised;

4   act in the best interests of each client;

5   provide a proper standard of service to your clients;

6   behave in a way that maintains the trust the public places in you and in the provision of legal services;

7   comply with your legal and regulatory obligations and deal with your regulators and ombudsmen in an open, timely and co-operative manner;

8   run your business or carry out your role in the business effectively and in accordance with proper governance and sound financial and risk management principles;

9   run your business or carry out your role in the business in a way that encourages equality of opportunity and respect for diversity;

10   protect client money and assets.'

The new Code is divided into five sections comprising 15 chapters in all (with Chapters 13 to 15 dealing with the application of the rules, waivers, interpretation, commencement and repeals). The section 'You and your client' contains client care, equality and diversity, conflicts, confidentiality and disclosure, the client and the court, and introductions of clients to third parties. 'You and your business' contains business management, publicity, and fee sharing and referrals. 'You and your regulator' is Section 3 and Chapter 10. 'You and others' covers relations with third parties and separate businesses.

Each chapter contains mandatory 'outcomes' rather than prescriptive rules, and non-mandatory 'indicative behaviours', both positive – consistent with compliance, and negative – indicative of non-compliance. Examples of specified outcomes have been given above in relation to the successor to rule 9 (para **3.36**).

Generally the impression is of a trend to deregulation, omitting rules when there is no need for them. An example has been given above in relation to the future rule on accounting for commissions and the like, which appears simply to adopt the position in law (para **3.10**). Another example is that there is to be no rule dealing with contingency fees, which are currently prohibited only in narrow and (arguably) historical and anomalous circumstances. The future equivalent is Outcome 6 of Chapter 1 'Client care': 'you only enter into fee agreements that are legal, and which you consider are suitable for the client's needs and take accounts of the client's best interests.

There is much that is positive about these anticipated changes, but the most crucial need is for a change in the SRA culture which will create a measure of trust between practitioners and their regulator. Possibly the most optimistic indication is that the SRA clearly and openly recognises the need for it to change. All staff are being trained/retrained and judged for their fitness for the new OFR world.

CHAPTER 4

The Solicitors' Accounts Rules 1998

4.1

The Solicitors' Accounts Rules 1998 ('the Accounts Rules'), which have been in force since 2000, are in seven parts (for the Accounts Rules themselves see **APPENDIX 3**).

Part A, comprising rules 1 to 13, is concerned with general matters, definitions, persons governed by and exempt from the Accounts Rules and, importantly, an explanation of the categories of money handled by solicitors (rule 13) – all money held or received in the course of practice is 'client money' or 'office money'. Further comment will be made about this subject, which is of crucial importance. The former third category, 'controlled trust money', has been removed by amendments to the Rules effective on 31 March 2009.

Part B, rules 14 to 23, concerns the proper handling of client money and the correct operation of client account. Part C, rules 24 to 28, sets out the requirements as to accounting for interest.

Part D, rules 29 to 33, is concerned with the proper maintenance of accounting systems. Part E, rule 34, provides the monitoring and investigation powers of the Law Society. Part F, rules 35 to 49, regulates the provision of accountants' reports.[1] Part G, rule 50, covers the commencement of the Accounts Rules and transitional provisions.

1   Section 34 of the Solicitors Act 1974.

4.2

The Accounts Rules are accompanied by guidance notes. The guidance associated with the Solicitors' Code of Conduct 2007 is not part of the Code and is not binding, but in the Accounts Rules the guidance forms part of the Rules themselves – the notes form part of the Rules and are mandatory.[1]

Failure to comply with any of the Accounts Rules may be the subject of a complaint to the Solicitors Disciplinary Tribunal.[2] Compliance with the Rules is an absolute requirement, and a breach of the Rules is one of absolute liability. Indeed it is commonplace for solicitors to be unaware that breaches have occurred until well after the event, but still to be liable for the breaches and to disciplinary sanctions. The lack of knowledge or complicity does not mean that a breach has not occurred on the part of the ignorant individual: he or she had an obligation to ensure it did not happen. That is why sound systems, and hands-on involvement and oversight at partnership or management level are essential (more of which later).

1   Rule 2(1).
2   Section 32(3) of the Solicitors Act 1974.

4.3

Although the Accounts Rules are lengthy, and in some respects complex, the underlying principles are straightforward, and are well known to all practitioners – even if they may not claim to be familiar with all the detail.

The Accounts Rules apply to solicitors and their employees, registered European lawyers (RELs) and their employees, registered foreign lawyers (RFLs), and recognised bodies and their managers and employees in respect of their practice in England and Wales.[1]

The principles underlying the Accounts Rules are set out in rule 1 (see **APPENDIX 3**). Effective compliance with the Accounts Rules involves an understanding of relatively few principles:

(1)   have a proper accounts system and keep it up to date;

(2)   keep your own money separate from other people's money;

(3)   use only each client's or trust's money for that client's or trust's matters;

(4)   pay interest when required;

(5)   deliver your annual accountant's reports on time; and

(6)   co-operate with regulatory checks and inspections by the SRA.

1   Rule 4(1).

Proper accounting systems

4.4

The obligation to have and to maintain proper accounting systems needs no explanation. One issue, however, deserves special mention: it is accepted that errors will occur in the best ordered systems and one of the most effective controls in ensuring that mistakes are identified is a bank reconciliation that satisfies rule 32(7). This compares the total of all individual client ledger balances with the client cashbook and the amount shown on the bank statement or statements, shows any difference between any one of those three components and any other, and reconciles that difference. If this is done properly most significant errors will be identified – certainly any client account shortage should be immediately spotted. The bank reconciliation is important; it is not a tedious bureaucratic requirement, but an essential management tool designed to enable principals who are not concerned with the day-to-day minutiae of the accounts to be informed of any serious underlying problems.

All of the principals in a firm have an obligation to ensure compliance with the Accounts Rules; that is, compliance not only by the principals themselves but by everyone employed in the practice.[1] Any breach of the Accounts Rules must be remedied promptly upon discovery. This includes the replacement of any money improperly withheld or withdrawn from client account[2] using the principal's own money if necessary. This duty falls on all principals in the practice, and not just on the individual causing the breach or who was, for example, the partner responsible for supervising the person at fault.[3]

For this reason all principals should know what is going on in their own accounts department; they will be personally responsible for putting right any problem, with their own money. While accounting functions are invariably delegated to non-solicitors in all but the tiniest practices, there must be effective oversight at management level, for example in checking client balances; that the five-weekly (monthly in practice) reconciliation has been carried out, and is understood; and that any information given by it which prompts action is acted upon.

1 Rule 6.
2 Rule 7(1).
3 Rule 7(2).

Client money or office money?

4.5

Keeping your own money and that of other people separate should create no problems of interpretation, but solicitors still appear to have problems with this issue from time to time. All money held or received in the course of practice is 'client money' (held or received for a client or as trustee) or 'office money' (which belongs to the solicitor or the practice).[1]

The simplest approach is to ask the question: does this money belong, now, unconditionally and exclusively, to me or to my firm? If the answer is 'yes', the money must be paid into office account. If the answer is 'no', it must be paid into client account (or trust account, if relevant).

The word 'unconditionally' is used to emphasise the fact that if a condition has to be satisfied in order for the solicitor or firm to be entitled (such as the delivery of a bill), it is client money. The word 'exclusively' is used to emphasise that if someone else has an interest in the money, even the solicitor's wife, if she is not a partner in the firm, it is client money.

1 Rule 13.

Costs

4.6

Particular issues arise over costs. When a firm is paid on account of costs for work that has not yet been done, that money still belongs to the client and must be paid into client account. In contrast, where a firm agrees a fee which cannot be varied upwards or downwards and receives funds in payment of that fixed fee, it is the solicitor's or firm's money and must be paid into office account.[1]

Firms may legitimately transfer money from client account to office account for the payment of their fees, *but only if a bill or other written notification of costs has been sent to the client*.[2] The Tribunal's records are packed with cases involving solicitors who transferred money to which they considered they were fully entitled, because they had done the work, but where they had 'not got around to sending a bill'. Similar numbers of cases have involved 'tidying up the accounts' by sweeping old and small balances from client to office account on the basis of 'dummy bills' or 'accounts only bills' (meaning pieces of paper that were never intended to be delivered to the clients whose money was being taken).

1   Rule 19(4) and (5).
2   Rule 19(2); an agreed fee must be evidenced in writing.

Teeming and lading

4.7

Using a client's money only for that client's purposes is a fundamental requirement. The Tribunal's caseload is materially increased by those solicitors who, when something goes wrong (either by miscalculation or through a transactional problem) and more money is needed for the client than is available, simply overdraw that client's individual ledger, using the substantial balance available in the general client bank account. This invariably means that the funds of one or more clients are being used, without their knowledge, for someone else's benefit. Transfers may be effected between the clients' ledgers in these circumstances to 'cover' the shortage. If the client whose money was wrongly used needs it, a third client's funds may need to be moved. This is teeming and lading – robbing Peter to pay Paul. It does not overcome the fundamental problem – that there is an overall shortage of client funds. Rule 30 was introduced in an attempt to inhibit this practice: it is not permissible to make a private (ie non-institutional) loan of one client's funds to another, even by means of a paper transfer between ledgers, except with the prior written authority of both clients.

Professional disbursements

4.8

Another problem area is the treatment of professional disbursements, which are defined as the fees of counsel or other lawyer or of a professional or other agent or expert instructed by the solicitor, and will include interpreters, translators, process servers, surveyors and the like.[1] It is common and proper to bill a client for costs and disbursements, including professional disbursements that are yet to be paid. It is permissible to pay the whole sum received in payment of such a bill into office account *provided* that the element relating to unpaid professional disbursements is paid either into client account or to the professionals entitled to the money *by the end of the second working day following receipt.*[2] Alternatively, the whole sum may be paid into client account and the part of the payment which is office money transferred to office account within 14 days.

It is a well-known but wholly improper practice in such circumstances to credit the whole sum to office account and to withhold payment of the unpaid disbursements so that the office overdraft is reduced by the amount owed to counsel and others, possibly many thousands or tens of thousands of pounds. A slightly more sophisticated version of this practice is to write cheques to those entitled, which when entered on the accounts appear to show a compliant picture, but the cheques are not sent and, rather, accumulate in the top left-hand drawer of the principal's or bookkeeper's desk, or comparable location. This would be regarded very seriously.

Special rules apply to the treatment of payments from the Legal Services Commission.[3] Though complex the advantage is that they are contained within one rule to which legal aid practitioners can readily refer.

1   Rule 2(2)(s) and note (v).

2   Rule 19(1)(b).
3   Rule 21.

Withdrawals from client account

4.9

Money may only be withdrawn from client account in favour of the solicitor or firm by cheque or transfer, never in cash.[1] Money may only be withdrawn from client account on the specific authority of a solicitor with a current practising certificate; an REL; a Fellow of the Institute of Legal Executives or a licensed conveyancer who is a manager of the practice, where the practice is a recognised body; a Fellow of the Institute of Legal Executives or licensed conveyancer who is an employee of the practice, where the practice is a recognised body or recognised sole practitioner; an RFL who is a manager of the practice, where the practice is a recognised body, or any other individual who is a manager of the practice.[2]

1   Rule 23(3).
2   Rule 23(1).

Interest

4.10

The interest requirements, which are not unduly burdensome, are set out in rules 24 to 27 and are self-explanatory. The option that was formerly available for a client or other person funding the firm's fees to seek a deposit interest certificate from the Law Society has been removed with effect from 31 March 2009 by the repeal of the former rule 28. Clients are now encouraged to attempt to resolve the issue with the firm and failing that to complain to the Legal Complaints Service.[1]

1   Note (xa) to rule 24.

Compliance

4.11

When required to do so, you must make available all relevant documents to any person appointed by the SRA and must be prepared to explain any departures from the SRA's published guidelines for accounting procedures and systems.[1]

A solicitor who has held or received client money during an accounting period must deliver to the SRA an accountant's report for that accounting period within six months of the end of the period.[2] In addition, the SRA may (with effect from 31 March 2009) require the delivery of an accountant's report in any other circumstances 'if the SRA has reason to believe that it is in the public interest to do so'.[3] Examples of such circumstances are:

- when no report has been delivered but the SRA has reason to believe that a report should have been delivered;

- when a report has been delivered but the SRA has reason to believe that it may be inaccurate;

- when the conduct of the solicitor gives the SRA reason to believe that it would be appropriate to require earlier delivery of a report (eg three months after the end of the accounting period);

- when the conduct of the solicitor gives the SRA reason to believe that it would be appropriate to require more frequent delivery of reports (eg every six months);

- when the SRA has reason to believe that the regulatory risk justifies the imposition on a category of solicitors of a requirement to deliver reports earlier or at more frequent intervals;

- when a condition on a solicitor's practising certificate requires earlier delivery of reports or the delivery of reports at more frequent intervals.[4]

The Accounts Rules restrict those who may prepare such reports to members of various accountants' professional bodies who are also registered auditors, or their employees.[5] Stringent provisions govern the terms upon which the accountant can be retained.[6] The accountant must request, and the firm must provide, details of all accounts held at banks, building societies and other financial institutions operated by the firm during the relevant accounting period,[7] and the accountant is duty-bound to carry out detailed and specified tests to ensure the compliance of the firm's accounting systems with the Accounts Rules.[8]

A waiver from the requirement to deliver accountant's reports may be obtained from the SRA if only a small number of transactions is undertaken or a small volume of client money is held in an accounting period.[9] This is the only form of waiver of the Accounts Rules that is permitted.

If there is a genuine difficulty in providing the required report by the specified date, an application can be made for an extension of time, but this must be done before the deadline in question. It is too late to apply for an extension when the six-month period has already expired, and every principal will in that event be in default. Section 12 of the Solicitors Act 1974, and an obligation to pay additional fees when applying for a practising certificate (at least), will automatically apply.[10]

1   Rule 34.
2   Rule 35.
3   Rule 35(2).
4   Note (i) to rule 35.
5   Rule 37.
6   Rule 38.
7   Rule 41.
8   Rule 42.
9   Rule 49 and note (ix) to rule 35.
10 Sections 12(1)(ee) and 12A of the Solicitors Act 1974. With effect from 1 July 2009, regulation 3 of the SRA Practising Regulations 2009 will apply.

Dormant balances

4.12

New rules were introduced with effect from 14 July 2008 to deal with the substantial problem caused by dormant accounts or 'residual balances'. There is an obligation to return funds to the client or other person entitled promptly, as soon as there is no longer any proper reason to retain them. If money is received after the firm has accounted to the client, for example a refund of some kind, it must be paid to the client promptly.[1] If money is retained after the end of a matter or the substantial conclusion of a matter, the firm must promptly inform the client (or other person entitled) in writing of the amount held and the reason for retaining it, and must provide a written report every 12 months, again as to the amount and the reason for retaining it, for so long as the fund is held.[2]

It is now permissible to dispose of minor residual balances without obtaining the specific consent of the SRA[3] by paying such sums to charity if:

- the amount does not exceed £50 for any one client or trust;

- the firm establishes the identity of the owner of the money, or makes reasonable attempts to do so;

- the firm makes adequate attempts to ascertain the proper destination of the money and to return it to the rightful owner, unless the reasonable costs of doing so are likely to be excessive in relation to the amount held;

- the firm records the steps taken and retains the records, including all relevant documentation such as receipts from the charity (like most other accounting information, for six years); and

- the firm keeps a central register of all such withdrawals, detailing the name of the client, trust or other person entitled (if established), the amount, the name of the recipient charity and the date.

Applications may also be made to the SRA (through the Professional Ethics Guidance Team) for authorisation to withdraw funds from client account when it would not otherwise be permitted, either if the amount is greater than £50, or if it is not intended to pay the amount to charity (as could occur if the amount is genuinely owed to the firm but it is not possible to deliver a bill because the client is untraceable). Firms may also choose to apply for authorisation in all cases rather than use the procedure permitted by rule 22(1)(ga) and (2A).[4]

1   Rule 15(3).
2   Rule 15(4).
3   Rule 22(1)(ga).
4   Rule 22(1)(h).

Draft new rules

4.13

As part of its consultation on the new Code and all other professional rules intended to become effective from 6 October 2011, the SRA has published draft new SRA Accounts Rules. These are rather complicated in appearance in that they have been drafted to provide not only for alternative business structures but also for multi-disciplinary practices (MDPs): ABSs, which might provide a range of services only some of which might be regulated by the SRA. There are rules about 'out-of-scope' money which is money held or received by an MDP in relation to its non-regulated activities. It is intended that the next edition of this book will deal with the new Accounts Rules, in their final form as they will be applied.

In the meantime, there are two particular pointers to the consequences of the move to outcomes-focused regulation (OFR). It will be for the firm to design procedures and to select suitable people to be authorised to withdraw money from client account: there is no prescriptive list. The rule in relation to client account interest is simply that interest should be paid when it is fair and reasonable to do so in all the circumstances, but the firm must have a written policy on the payment of interest which seeks to provide a fair outcome. There is no de minimis 'less than £20' provision, but firms are free to decide as a matter of policy to set a minimum figure, which would need to be kept under review.

One new draft rule may be mentioned – rule 15(5):

> 'You must not provide banking facilities through a client account. Payments into, and transfers or withdrawals from, a client account must be in respect of instructions relating to an underlying transaction (and the funds arising therefrom) or to a service forming part of your normal regulated activities'.

There is an existing guidance note broadly to this effect, but less firmly expressed. It is designed to discourage activities which could assist money laundering.

CHAPTER 5

Financial services regulation

5.1

The statutory framework for financial services regulation is provided by the Financial Services and Markets Act 2000 (FSMA 2000). Section 19(1) of FSMA 2000 provides that no person may carry on a regulated activity in the United Kingdom or purport to do so unless he is (a) an authorised person or (b) an exempt person. This is referred to as the general prohibition. A breach of this requirement is a criminal offence with a maximum penalty of two years' imprisonment.

Regulated activities are defined by the Financial Services and Markets Act 2000 (Regulated Activities) Order 2001 (RAO 2001).[1] Activities are regulated if an *activity* of a specified kind is carried on *by way of business* in relation to an *investment* of a specified kind. The Financial Services and Markets Act 2000 (Carrying on Regulated Activities by Way of Business) Order 2001[2] makes provision as to when a person is or is not to be regarded as carrying on a regulated activity by way of business. We are dealing with solicitors acting in the course of their professional practice and will assume that this requirement will be met.

1   SI 2001/544.
2   SI 2001/1177.

'Activities'

5.2

The specified *activities* are:

- accepting deposits;[1]

- issuing electronic money;

- effecting and carrying out contracts of insurance;

- dealing or arranging deals in investments;

- managing investments;

- assisting in the administration and performance of a contract of insurance;

- safeguarding and administering investments;

- sending dematerialised instructions;[2]

- specified involvement in collective investment schemes;

- the like involvement in pension schemes;

- providing basic advice on stakeholder products;

- advising on investments;

- various forms of activity at Lloyd's;

- providing funeral plan contracts; and

- specified involvement in regulated mortgage contracts, regulated home reversion plans, and regulated home purchase plans.

There are exclusions applicable to the various categories of activity.

1   A sum is not a deposit for these purposes if it is received by a practising solicitor acting in the course of his profession: article 7 of RAO 2001. A 'practising solicitor' includes recognised bodies, registered European lawyers and registered foreign lawyers.
2   See the Uncertificated Securities Regulations 2001 (SI 2001/3755) – essentially the process whereby shares and other investments can be held in electronic form on computer systems.

'Investments'

5.3

The specified *investments* are:

- deposits;

- electronic money;

- rights under a contract of insurance;

- shares;

- debt instruments (debentures, loan stock, bonds, certificates of deposit);

- government and public securities (gilts);

- warrants and other instruments giving entitlement to investments;

- certificates representing certain securities (conferring contractual or property rights in shares, debentures, etc);

- units in a collective investment scheme;

- rights under a pension scheme;

- options;

- futures;

- contracts for differences (for example trading on the expected performance of a share or other index);

- Lloyd's syndicate capacity and syndicate membership; and

- rights under a funeral plan contract, regulated mortgage contract, regulated home reversion plan or regulated home purchase plan.

5.4

This book does not attempt to deal with the requirements imposed by the Financial Services Authority (FSA) on those authorised and regulated by that Authority. Solicitors and their practices may become involved in mainstream investment business and be required to be authorised by the FSA, but the vast majority of the profession take advantage of Part XX of FSMA 2000 which allows persons who are regulated by designated professional bodies (of which the Law Society/SRA is one) to undertake regulated activities without being authorised by the FSA, provided that they comply with rules made by their own professional body. Solicitors and others regulated by the SRA complying with their own professional rules will be carrying on 'exempt regulated activities'.[1]

The Rules applicable to solicitors and their practices are the Solicitors' Financial Services (Scope) Rules 2001 and the Solicitors' Financial Services (Conduct of Business) Rules 2001, which in this chapter will be referred to as the 'Scope Rules' and the 'COB Rules' (for the Rules themselves, see **APPENDIX 4** and **APPENDIX 5**).

The Scope Rules specify the regulated activities which solicitors and others regulated by the SRA may and may not undertake if they are to take advantage of the Part XX exemption, and the conditions that must be satisfied. The COB Rules regulate the manner in which exempt regulated activities may be carried on by solicitors and their practices.

1   Section 327 of FSMA 2000.

The Scope Rules

5.5

The Scope Rules require that certain basic conditions be met. These are primarily:

(1)   that the regulated activities arise out of, or are complementary to, the provision of a particular professional service to a particular client;

(2)   that the provision of any service relating to regulated activities is incidental to the provision of professional services (this would, for example, therefore cover the arrangement of after the event insurance which is incidental to the main purpose of the retainer, i e the pursuit of a claim for damages);

(3)   that the firm accounts to the client for any pecuniary reward or other advantage which the firm receives from a third party (so that in relation to commission earned through regulated activities a firm does not have the benefit of the £20 de minimis provision in rule 2.06 of the Solicitors' Code of Conduct 2007); and

(4)   that the firm does not carry on or hold itself out as carrying on any regulated activity that is not permitted under the Scope Rules.[1]

1   Rule 4 of the Scope Rules.

Prohibited activities

5.6

Activities from which solicitors are prohibited under the Scope Rules are:

●   market-making in investments;

●   buying, selling, subscribing for or underwriting investments as principal where the firm holds itself out as engaging in the business of buying with a view to selling, or as engaging in the business of underwriting such investments or where the firm regularly solicits members of the public to enter into such transactions;

- buying or selling investments with a view to stabilising or maintaining the market price;

- acting as a stakeholder pension scheme manager;

- entering into a broker funds arrangement;

- effecting and carrying out contracts of insurance as principal;

- establishing, operating or winding up a collective investment scheme or a stakeholder pension scheme;

- managing underwriting capacity of a syndicate as a managing agent at Lloyd's;

- advising a person to become a member of a particular Lloyd's syndicate;

- entering as provider into a funeral plan contract; and

- entering into a regulated mortgage contract as lender or administering a regulated mortgage contract unless this is in the firm's capacity as a trustee or personal representative and the borrower is a beneficiary of the trust, will or intestacy.[1]

All relevant definitions are contained in the Scope Rules or RAO 2001.

1   Rule 3 of the Scope Rules.

5.7

There are other restrictions depending on the kind of investment.

- Firms must not recommend or make arrangements for a client to buy a packaged product (typically a life policy with an investment element such as an endowment or pension policy, or units or shares in a unit trust or investment trust savings scheme) unless the proposed purchase is by way of assignment, or where the firm is managing assets in accordance with advice from someone authorised for that purpose by the FSA or who is exempt from the general prohibition, or where the firm only arranges the transaction on the basis that the client is not relying on the firm for advice.[1]

- Firms must not recommend that a client buys or disposes of rights or interests in a personal pension scheme.[2]

- Firms must not make arrangements for a client to buy any rights or interests in a personal pension scheme unless it is on the basis that the client is not relying on the firm for advice. However, the benefit of this exception is not available where the transaction involves a pension transfer or opt-out.[3]

- Firms must not recommend that a client buys or subscribes for investments that are not packaged products where the transaction would be:

    – made with a person acting in the course of the business of buying, selling, subscribing or underwriting the investment (whether as principal or agent);

    – made on an investment exchange or market to which the investment is admitted for dealing; or

—   made in response to an invitation to subscribe for an investment which is or is to be admitted for dealing on an investment exchange or market.

This prohibition does not apply if the client is not an individual, or is an individual who is the controller of a business or an individual acting in his or her capacity as trustee of an occupational pension scheme.[4]

- Firms must not engage in discretionary management of investments unless the firm (or a partner, officer or employee of the firm) is a trustee, personal representative, donee of a power of attorney or receiver appointed by the Court of Protection *and* all decisions are taken by, or in accordance with, the advice of a person authorised for that purpose by the FSA or who is exempt from the general prohibition.[5]

- Firms must not act as a sponsor to an issue of securities to be admitted for dealing on the London Stock Exchange or as nominated adviser to an issue of securities to be admitted for dealing on the Alternative Investment Market of the London Stock Exchange.[6]

1   Rule 5(1) of the Scope Rules.
2   Rule 5(2)(a).
3   Rule 5(2)(b).
4   Rule 5(3).
5   Rule 5(4).
6   Rule 5(5).

Insurance mediation

5.8

Firms must not carry on any insurance mediation activities unless they are registered in the FSA register and have appointed a compliance officer who will be responsible for those activities.[1]

The phrase 'insurance mediation' has caused much confusion, not least because of the use of the word 'mediation'. This is a term of art used in the Scope Rules and involves dealing as an agent in contracts of insurance, making arrangements with a view to a person entering into a contract of insurance, assisting in the administration or performance of a contract of insurance, advising on the merits of buying or selling a contract of insurance, or agreeing to do any of the above.

Most insurance contracts are now regulated investments, including life and pension policies, defective title and missing beneficiary indemnity policies, household and building insurance, long-term care insurance and after the event legal expenses insurance.

In practice, therefore, most of the profession will be likely to become involved in insurance mediation activities, even if only by advising on or arranging a title indemnity policy or after the event insurance. The process of being registered with the FSA for these purposes is arranged through the SRA (by completing the question on the annual application for practising certificates to confirm that the firm does carry out this activity) or by informing the SRA separately if this has not been done or if the circumstances have changed since certificates were renewed.

It seems that many firms have made mistakes in this respect. All that is required is that the person filling in the firm's application for renewal of the practising certificates for partners and employees does not appreciate that 'insurance mediation' has a special meaning and ticks the box for 'No' as to whether the firm engages in that activity. In consequence the firm will not be registered with the FSA and there will be criminal offences committed every time the firm arranges an after the event legal expenses policy or title indemnity insurance.

1   Rule 5(6) of the Scope Rules.

Regulated mortgages

5.9

Firms must not recommend that a client enters into a regulated mortgage contract as a borrower, but can endorse a recommendation given by a person who is regulated by the FSA for this purpose or who is exempt from the general prohibition.[1]

A regulated mortgage contract is one where the borrower is an individual or trust, the lender takes a first legal charge over property in the United Kingdom and at least 40 per cent of the property is occupied or intended to be occupied by the borrower as a dwelling or, in the case of a trust, by a beneficiary, or (in either case) by that person's spouse (or someone, whether or not of the opposite sex, whose relationship with the borrower or beneficiary has the characteristics of the relationship between husband and wife) or that person's parent, brother, sister, child, grandparent or grandchild.

1   Rule 5(7) of the Scope Rules.

The COB Rules

5.10

As explained above, these Rules govern the manner in which solicitors' firms may carry out regulated activities that they are permitted to carry out under the Scope Rules. They apply, with one exception, to firms that are not regulated by the FSA and to firms that are regulated by the FSA but only in relation to non-mainstream regulated activities.

Status disclosure

5.11

The exception is rule 3, which relates to status disclosure and which applies only to firms that are *not* regulated by the FSA. Before such a firm provides any service which includes a regulated activity it must give the client the following information in writing, in a manner that is clear, fair and not misleading:

- a statement that the firm is not regulated by the FSA;
- the name and address of the firm;
- the nature of the regulated activities carried on by the firm and the fact that they are limited in scope;

- a statement that the firm is regulated by the SRA; and

- a statement explaining that complaints and redress mechanisms are provided through the SRA and the Legal Ombudsman (LeO).[1]

The following words are not compulsory but are in an acceptable form when combined with the other specific requirements listed above:

'The Law Society is a designated professional body for the purposes of the Financial Services and Markets Act 2000 but responsibility for regulation and complaints handling has been separated from the Law Society's representative functions. The Solicitors Regulation Authority is the independent regulatory body of the Law Society.'

The following specific written disclosure, in these precise words, must be provided to the client before any service is provided that includes an insurance mediation activity:

'[This firm is] [We are] not authorised by the Financial Services Authority. However, we are included on the register maintained by the Financial Services Authority so that we can carry on insurance mediation activity, which is broadly the advising on, selling and administration of insurance contracts. This part of our business, including arrangements for complaints or redress if something goes wrong, is regulated by the Solicitors Regulation Authority. The register can be accessed via the Financial Services Authority website at www.fsa.gov.uk/register.'

There is no reason why the required disclosures cannot be incorporated in the firm's standard client care material, but they can be provided separately. It is not necessary to tailor the disclosure to the needs of the specific client.[2] However, the LeO's service is not available to all clients, but only to individuals and small businesses (see **CHAPTER 12**) and care should be used in making reference to the availability of a redress mechanism.

1   Rule 3(2) of the COB Rules.
2   Rule 3(3) of the COB Rules, and associated guidance notes.

Other requirements

5.12

Firms must ensure that when it has been decided or agreed to effect a transaction they must do so as soon as possible, unless it is reasonably believed that it is not in the best interests of the client to do so.[1]

The COB Rules contain provisions requiring specified records to be kept of transactions, commissions received, and as to the safekeeping of clients' investments.[2]

If a firm arranges any transaction for a client involving a packaged product on an execution–only basis, the firm must send written confirmation to the client, as the case may be, that no advice had been sought from or given by the firm or that advice had been given but that the client nevertheless persisted in requiring the transaction to be effected – and in either case that the transaction is effected on express instructions.[3]

There are additional detailed requirements where firms engage in insurance mediation activities. These are primarily concerned with the disclosure of information and the extent to which a comparative market analysis has been carried out, with the need to establish by reasonable steps that the recommended policy is suitable for the client's demands and needs, and with the obligation to provide a 'demands and needs statement' before the contract is finalised (amongst other things explaining any recommendation made).[4]

1   Rule 4 of the COB Rules.
2   Rules 5, 6, 7 and 9.
3   Rule 8.
4   Rule 8A and Appendix 1.

Financial promotions

5.13

There is a second separate strand of regulation under the FSMA 2000 of which practitioners should be aware. Under section 21 of FSMA 2000, you are prohibited from, in the course of business, communicating an invitation or inducement to engage in investment activity unless this is done by an authorised person, or the content of the communication is approved by an authorised person. Solicitors' practices are not authorised persons but can take advantage of an exemption to undertake exempt regulated activities as explained above, for the purposes of the RAO 2001. This regime does not, however, apply to financial promotions, which are covered by the Financial Services and Markets Act 2000 (Financial Promotion) Order 2005 (FPO 2005).[1] Regulated activities for the purposes of the RAO 2001 are not precisely the same as (though very similar to) controlled activities for the purposes of the FPO 2005.

If a firm, therefore, does communicate invitations or inducements to engage in an investment activity, it must, if it is regulated by the SRA rather than the FSA, be able to rely on an exemption within the FPO 2005. Fortunately, there are exemptions specifically in favour of members of professions. Under article 55 of FPO 2005, the financial promotion restriction does not apply to a real time communication (whether solicited or unsolicited) which is made by a person who carries on a regulated activity to which the general prohibition does not apply by virtue of section 327 of FSMA 2000 (in other words those carrying out exempt regulated activities and who are regulated by their own professional body); and which is made to a recipient who has, prior to the communication being made, engaged that person to provide professional services, and where the activity to which the communication relates is (in short) for the purposes of, and incidental to, the provision of professional services to or at the request of the recipient.

A real time communication is any communication made in the course of a personal visit, telephone conversation or other interactive dialogue.[2] Note that this exemption applies to communications with existing clients, but can be solicited or unsolicited.

The article 55 exemption does not apply to non-real time communications, including letters, e-mails and material in a publication such as a brochure. Article 55A provides an exemption for members of a profession in relation to non-real time communications if the stated conditions are satisfied. The financial promotion restriction does not apply to a non-real time communication which is made by a person who carries on Part XX activities (that is, again, those who are carrying out exempt regulated activities and who are regulated by their own professional body) and which is limited to a communication expressly provided for in article 55A; that is, one that promotes an activity that is within Part XX of FSMA 2000 (in other words, one that is not prohibited by the Scope Rules. The communication must contain the following:

> 'This [firm/company] is not authorised under the Financial Services and Markets Act 2000 but we are able in certain circumstances to offer a limited range of investment services to clients because we are members of [*relevant designated professional body*]. We can provide these investment services if they are an incidental part of the professional services we have been engaged to provide.'[3]

Note that this is similar to but not identical with the notice that is required by the COB Rules for insurance mediation activities (para **5.11**).

Firms can therefore communicate an invitation or inducement in writing provided the promoted activities fall within the scope of exempt regulated activities and the invitation or inducement is accompanied by the specified notice.

1   SI 2005/1529.
2   Article 7 of FPO 2005.
3   Article 55A(2) of FPO 2005.

CHAPTER 6

Professional indemnity insurance

6.1

The compulsory requirement that solicitors should be insured against professional risks dates from 1976, when the Law Society made indemnity rules under the powers provided by section 37 of the Solicitors Act 1974. From then until 1987 the Law Society negotiated the terms of a master policy with the insurance industry year by year. In 1987 the Solicitors Indemnity Fund (SIF) was established to replace the master policy scheme.

In 2000 the requirement that all solicitors be insured through the SIF was abolished and solicitors became free to negotiate their professional indemnity insurance on the open market. There were and remain two stipulations:

(1)   the insurer must be a qualifying insurer, that is an authorised insurer (essentially any insurer authorised to carry out that class of business under the Financial Services and Markets Act 2000)[1] which has entered into a qualifying insurer's agreement with the Law Society which remains in force for the purposes of underwriting new business at the date of the insurance contract; and

(2)   the terms of the insurance cover must meet the 'Minimum Terms and Conditions' set by the current indemnity insurance rules.[2]

Qualifying insurance may be underwritten by more than one insurer provided that, collectively, the minimum terms and conditions are satisfied and that one insurer is identified as the lead insurer.[3] A list of qualifying insurers can be found on the Law Society website at www.sra.org.uk/indemnity.

1   See the definition in rule 3.1 of the Solicitors' Indemnity Insurance Rules 2010.
2   Appendix 1 to the Solicitors' Indemnity Insurance Rules 2010.
3   Appendix 1, clause 2.6.

6.2

The SIF remains relevant to current regulatory requirements in that it will provide run-off cover for new claims against principals who retired before 1 September 2000 in circumstances where there is no successor practice, and will also provide run-off cover for claims where the run-off cover provided by qualifying insurers has expired. Qualifying insurers provide run-off cover for a period of six years under the minimum terms and conditions. The SIF will provide cover between 1 September 2007 and 1 September 2017 for claims notified after the six-year period of commercial run-off cover has expired (and has arranged reinsurance in respect of those risks).

Solicitors are currently subject to two sets of indemnity rules – the Solicitors' Indemnity Rules 2007, which regulate the relationship between the profession and the SIF, and the Solicitors' Indemnity Insurance Rules 2010 (SIIR 2010), which set out the requirements for qualifying insurance obtained on the open market (for the SIIR 2010 see **APPENDIX 6**).

The SIF is in substantial surplus, in spite of the fact that contributions made to the Fund for the indemnity periods 2001/02 and 2002/03 have been repaid to those who made them or their estates. It is therefore expected that the Solicitors' Indemnity Rules 2007 will only be relevant in practice to the mechanisms for dealing with an increasingly small number of potential claims capable of being indemnified under the run-off arrangements. These issues are likely to be of minimal significance and will therefore not be considered.

The Solicitors' Indemnity Insurance Rules 2010 – the basic requirements

6.3

Solicitors are not entitled to practise without having qualifying insurance in force. It is necessary to produce evidence of qualifying insurance when an application is made for a practising certificate. The SRA may refuse, and arguably has to refuse, an application for a practising certificate if it is not satisfied that the solicitor is complying with current indemnity rules.[1] The SIIR 2010 enable the SRA to require the production of information and evidence that qualifying insurance is in place.[2]

Every practice regulated by the SRA must arrange insurance with one or more qualifying insurers that must comply with the minimum terms and conditions set out in Appendix 1 to the SIIR 2010 or be admitted to the Assigned Risks Pool (see further below).[3]

The SIIR 2010 do not apply to overseas practice. In respect of overseas practice, rule 15.26 of the Solicitors' Code of Conduct 2007 requires that professional indemnity insurance be in force at all times, and that it must be reasonable in extent and amount having regard the risks associated with the practice, the local conditions and the terms on which indemnity is available. It does not have to exceed the minimum requirements of the SIIR 2010 (but local conditions and laws may in practice require this).

The minimum level of cover is £2 million, or £3 million if the firm is a recognised body, with narrow exceptions.[4] Firms are free to arrange cover in excess of the minimum levels and may do so with insurers which are not qualifying insurers, and are also free to negotiate the level of any excess which the firm may elect to meet in respect of claims. The minimum terms and conditions require that if the excess is not paid by the insured the insurer must meet the full amount of the claim and recover the amount due from the firm.

A minimum of six years' run-off cover is required if the firm ceases to practise during an indemnity period. Run-off cover is not required if there is a successor practice. In that event the qualifying insurance will be that of the successor practice.

---

1   Section 10 of the Solicitors Act 1974. See also *Hidveghy v Law Society (No 9 of 2003)* (unreported), where the solicitor was a former partner in a firm which had been dissolved, but which remained in default of the requirements to pay insurance contributions. Neither he nor the other partner was in a position to meet these liabilities. The petitioning solicitor was insolvent and had become employed by

an unconnected firm which was not in default. Lord Phillips MR held that section 10 had to be given a purposive construction and that the solicitor was no longer a member of a firm which was in default, and the Society was obliged to issue a practising certificate.
2   Rule 7 of SIIR 2010.
3   Rules 4 and 5.
4   The exceptions are unlimited companies, companies acting in a purely nominee capacity and 'ordinary' partnerships where no partner is an LLP or corporate body with limited liability; see the definition of 'relevant recognised body' in clause 8.2 of Appendix 1 to SIIR 2010.

The Assigned Risks Pool

6.4

Some firms may not be able to negotiate indemnity insurance on the open market, perhaps because of a poor claims record. The Assigned Risks Pool (ARP) is designed to ensure that, at least in the short term, firms can continue to operate with the required level of cover. Insurance through the ARP is provided by all qualifying insurers in the proportions that their premium income bears to the total premium income in the period in question.

Firms seeking to enter the ARP on or after 1 October 2010 may not do so if they have been insured through the ARP for more than 12 months in a four-year period, that is, during the four indemnity periods immediately prior to the date from which cover is sought. Further, no new start-up firm may enter the ARP; any applicant to the ARP must have previously had in place qualifying insurance in the open market.[1] If a firm in either of these categories is unable to obtain insurance on the open market it must cease to practise. There is a provision to apply to the SRA to relax this requirement, but it is envisaged that the discretion will be exercised only in the most exceptional of circumstances.[2] Any application for this form of relief should be made at least three months before the firm would cease to be eligible to enter or remain in the ARP.

A firm is free to leave the ARP at any time if it can negotiate insurance with a qualifying insurer for the remainder of the relevant indemnity period.[3]

The premium payable is designed to be substantially more expensive than commercially available insurance and is calculated by reference to a percentage of a firm's gross fee income. For firms with annual gross fees of up to £500,000 the premium is set at 27.5 per cent of gross fees (30 per cent for relevant recognised bodies), and the percentage gradually reduces thereafter for firms with higher gross fees.[4] The uninsured excess is set at £4,500 per principal, with a maximum of £225,000 for each claim.[5]

1   See the definition of 'eligible firm' in rule 3 of SIIR 2010.
2   Rule 12.7.
3   Rule 12.1.
4   Appendix 2, clause 1.
5   Appendix 2, clause 1.14.

6.5

It is necessary to apply to enter the ARP – firms do not automatically acquire qualifying insurance through the ARP if they are unable to obtain cover elsewhere. Application must be made *before* the start of the relevant indemnity period if qualifying insurance cannot otherwise be obtained (or before commencing practice if the firm is starting up after the beginning of the indemnity period).[1] Application must be made on the specified proposal form.[2] It is the firm's responsibility to ensure that the application has been safely received.[3] If application is made late the firm is 'in default' and liable to a 'default premium', which is 20 per cent more than the standard ARP premium.[4]

A firm will be issued with an ARP policy only if it discharges the premium or, as the case may be, the default premium, in full within 30 days of being notified of it (or such longer period as the SRA may allow).[5]

By applying to enter the ARP a firm agrees to, and is required to pay, the relevant premium, to submit to investigation and monitoring by the SRA at the firm's expense, and to implement any steps, referred to as 'special measures', that may be required as a result of that investigation to reduce the firm's risk profile or to address issues that caused the firm to enter the ARP (such as attending training courses or implementing specified practice management measures). These special measures will also be at the firm's expense.[6]

It is a disciplinary offence to fail to implement special measures that the firm has been directed to take.[7]

Firms which fail to obtain qualifying insurance and fail to apply to enter the ARP remain liable to pay the whole of the default premium for the indemnity period in question, the premium being calculated by the ARP manager by making an assumption as to the firm's gross fees.[8]

1 Rules 10.1 and 10.2 of SIIR 2010.
2 Rules 10.5 to 10.8.
3 Rules 10.8 to 10.11.
4 Appendix 2, clause 2.
5 Rules 10.12 and 13.2(c).
6 Rules 10.3 and 11.
7 Rule 16.2.
8 Rule 14.

The minimum terms and conditions

6.6

The minimum terms and conditions are set out in Appendix 1 to SIIR 2010. Some aspects have already been mentioned, namely the minimum level of cover at £2 million or £3 million for relevant recognised bodies for each claim.[1] The insurance must indemnify against civil liability to the extent that it arises from private legal practice in connection with the insured firm's practice, on a 'claims made' basis; that is, claims are covered if made within the period of insurance, or after it in respect of an occurrence notified during the period of insurance.

The insurance must indemnify against any amount paid or payable in accordance with the recommendation of the Legal Services Ombudsman, the Legal Complaints Service, the Office for Legal Complaints/Legal Ombudsman or any other regulatory authority to the same extent as it indemnifies the insured against civil liability, but not in respect of any determination requiring the firm to refund fees.

Defence costs must also be covered without limit.[2] Where a claim exceeds the sum insured, the insurer may limit its liability for costs to the proportion that the sum insured bears to the total amount paid or payable to dispose of the claim.[3]

The insurance may make provision as to the meaning of 'one claim' for the purposes of determining the limit of indemnity and, in particular, may provide that all claims against any one or more insured will be regarded as one claim when arising from:

(1)   one act or omission;

(2)   one series of related acts or omissions;

(3)   the same act or omission in a series of related matters or transactions; or

(4)   similar acts or omissions in a series of related matters or transactions; and

(5)   all claims against one or more insured arising from one matter or transaction.[4]

As already mentioned, firms are free to negotiate the level of excess to be applied – meaning firms can elect to self-insure to a substantial extent without regard to the minimum terms.[5] Protection for the public is maintained as, if the insured fails to pay the amount of any excess to the claimant, the insurer must make good the sum, reclaiming it from the insured as necessary.[6] Any excess may not reduce the total limit of liability.[7] The excess must not apply to defence costs.[8] The insurance may provide for multiple claims to be treated as one claim for the purpose of calculating any excess, on terms that may be agreed between insurer and insured.[9]

The most important element of the minimum terms and conditions comprises the restrictions they impose on insurers for the purpose of ensuring that members of the public are not deprived of the benefits of compulsory professional indemnity insurance as a result of matters which, in other circumstances, might enable an insurer to disclaim or avoid liability. These are referred to in Appendix 1 to SIIR 2010 as 'special conditions'.[10]

1   Appendix 1, clause 2.1 to SIIR 2010.
2   Appendix 1, clause 2.2.
3   Appendix 1, clause 2.3.
4   Appendix 1, clause 2.5. See also *Lloyds TSB General Insurance Holdings Ltd v Lloyds Bank Group Insurance Co Ltd* [2003] UKHL 48, [2003] 4 All ER 43. Clause 2.5 has been drafted to overcome the difficulties in aggregating claims caused by the manner in which policies were drafted prior to that decision.
5   Appendix 1, clause 3.1.
6   Appendix 1, clause 3.4.
7   Appendix 1, clause 3.2.
8   Appendix 1, clause 3.3.
9   Appendix 1, clause 3.5.
10   Appendix 1, clause 4.

Restrictions on insurers – the 'special conditions'

6.7

Insurers are not entitled to avoid or repudiate insurance on any grounds whatsoever, including non-disclosure or misrepresentation (fraudulent or otherwise). They are not entitled to reduce or deny their liability on any grounds whatsoever, including any breach of any term or condition of the insurance, other than if one of the specified exclusions apply (see further below). They are not entitled to cancel the insurance unless alternative qualifying insurance is in place (for example in the event of a merger of firms), and cancellation must not affect rights and obligations that accrued prior to the cancellation. Insurers cannot set off any amounts due from the insured, such as any premium or reimbursement that may be due, against any amount payable to a claimant; they cannot reduce or exclude liability by reason of the existence or availability of other insurance (except other qualifying insurance in respect of an earlier period or cover by the SIF), although insurers are not prevented from seeking an appropriate contribution from that other insurer; and they cannot exclude or limit liability because relevant matters occurred before a specified date.

Insurers must meet defence costs as and when they are incurred unless and until the insured admits that he or she has committed or condoned dishonesty or a fraudulent act or omission, or a court or other judicial body finds that the insured was guilty of such dishonesty or fraudulent act or omission.

The parties are required to take all reasonable steps to resolve disputes about coverage as between potentially liable insurers and there is a provision entitling the Law Society to give directions as to how the claim should be conducted and, if necessary, compromised and paid in the meantime.[1]

The insurance must provide that it is to be construed or rectified so as to comply with the requirements of the minimum terms and conditions, and that any inconsistent provision must be severed or rectified to be compliant.

1   Paragraphs 4.9 and 4.10 of Appendix 1 to SIIR 2010.

Run-off and successor practices

6.8

Clause 5 of Appendix 1 to SIIR 2010 deals with run-off cover, which must be for a minimum period of six years from the end of the indemnity period, if the practice ceases during the indemnity period *without* a successor practice. As explained above claims may be made on the SIF if they are made later than six years after the end of the primary indemnity period.

What is or is not a successor practice is a very material consideration, and not just in this respect, because the insurers of a successor practice will become liable for any claims against the former practice that have not already been discovered and notified. This term has its own definition in clause 8 of Appendix 1 to SIIR 2010 (see **APPENDIX 6**), to which reference should be made. In brief, most circumstances involving the partners or other owners of a practice (or a majority of them) being absorbed into another firm – or even a minority in certain circumstances, or anything done or said which holds out expressly or impliedly that the second firm is succeeding to or incorporating the first firm – will result in the second firm being a successor practice. The definition focuses on people and ownership, rather than on cases and clients, so that if a firm does not hold itself out as a successor practice and acquires the clients and files of a firm that closes (for example) but does not take on its owners, either as principals or employees, it will not be a successor practice.

However, a firm which is about to close and to which there would be a successor practice for the purpose of the SIIR now has an option. It may allow that situation to occur, or it may, before the cessation of its business, elect to trigger its own run-off cover and pay the premium. Notice must be given to the SRA within seven days of receipt of notice of the election, by the insurer, to which the firm must irrevocably agree. In that event, there is no successor practice. If the election is not made, or if the run-off premium is not paid, the option is lost and the normal rules on succession will apply.[1]

1   Clause 5.3 of Appendix 1 to SIIR 2010.

Permitted exclusions

6.9

The minimum terms and conditions specify the permitted exclusions from liability in clause 6 of Appendix 1 to SIIR 2010. They are:

- claims where cover is provided by the SIF or under insurance for a prior period;

- claims for death or bodily injury, except psychological injury and emotional distress arising from an insured breach of duty (that is, in the performance of or failure to perform legal work);

- claims for damage or loss to, or destruction of, property – unless it is property in the care of the insured or where the damage or loss arises from an insured breach of duty;

- claims arising from partnership disputes within the firm or the like;

- claims in the nature of employment disputes about dismissal, harassment or discrimination and the like;

- personal debts and trading disputes;

- claims in relation to guarantees, indemnities or undertakings in connection with the provision of financial or other benefits for the personal advantage of the insured;

- any fine or penalty or order for costs in relation to a professional conduct complaint; and

- punitive or exemplary damages awarded under US or Canadian law, other than in defamation.

Insurers may also exclude liability (and always do) for dishonesty or a fraudulent act or omission committed or condoned by an individual insured, but insurance must nonetheless cover each other insured and no dishonesty can be imputed to a body corporate unless it was committed or condoned by all directors of a company or members of a limited liability partnership.

Cover may also be excluded for company directors' or officers' liability, in that capacity (unless it arises from an insured breach of duty) and for claims arising from terrorism, war and other hostilities, and asbestos-related injury or damage (unless arising from an insured breach of duty).

Defence costs

6.10

Defence costs include costs and disbursements reasonably and necessarily incurred with the consent of the insurer in:

- defending any proceedings relating to a claim;

- conducting any proceedings for indemnity, contribution or recovery relating to a claim;

- investigating, reducing, avoiding or compromising any actual or potential claim; and

- acting for any insured in connection with any investigation or inquiry (save in respect of any disciplinary proceeding under the authority of the Law Society (including, without limitation, the SRA and the Solicitors Disciplinary Tribunal)).

The costs of disciplinary proceedings were formerly covered, with some limitations, but this aspect of cover was removed from 1 October 2010.

A claim includes any civil claim for damages or compensation or an intimation of the same, and also includes an obligation on the insured to remedy any breach of the Solicitors' Accounts Rules 1998 – even if no individual has made any claim or given any intimation of a claim in relation to such breach.

Other regulatory obligations

6.11

The disciplinary consequences for any failure to carry out 'special measures' as directed has already been mentioned, and any other breach of the SIIR 2010 will also be a disciplinary matter.[1]

Any qualifying insurer, including the ARP manager, may bring to the attention of the SRA:

- any failure on the part of a firm to pay any sum by the date specified in the SIIR 2010;

- any failure to reimburse any payment made by the insurer which is within a policy excess;

- any material inaccuracy in a proposal form;

- the fact that a firm is in run-off;

- any matter or circumstances which would entitle the insurer to avoid or repudiate the insurance were it not for the provisions of clause 4 of Appendix 1 to SIIR 2010;

- any suspected dishonesty or fraud on the part of an insured; or

- any claim of inadequate professional services against the firm,

at any time and without notice to the firm concerned.[2]

A firm, and any principal, is required to provide details of its qualifying insurance to any person who asserts a claim apparently covered by the policy, and to anyone who is insured under the policy, upon request.[3]

Any accountant's report provided under section 34 of the Solicitors Act 1974 must contain a statement certifying whether the firm has qualifying insurance for the whole of the period covered by the report and whether insurance has been provided by the ARP.[4]

1   Rule 16 of SIIR 2010.
2   Rule 17.
3   Rule 18.
4   Rule 20.

CHAPTER 7

Registered European lawyers and registered foreign lawyers

7.1

A registered European lawyer (REL) is an individual registered with the SRA under regulation 17 of the European Communities (Lawyer's Practice) Regulations 2000[1] ('the 2000 Regulations'): see **APPENDIX 9**.

A registered foreign lawyer (RFL) is an individual registered with the SRA under section 89 of the Courts and Legal Services Act 1990 (CLSA 1990): see **APPENDIX 19**.

By virtue of their registration, both RELs and RFLs become subject to regulation by the SRA and are subject to the same rules of professional conduct and the whole regulatory and disciplinary regime that is in place for solicitors, with very little modification or exception. Further, as a result of the move to entity-based regulation, RELs and RFLs will be liable for compliance with all relevant professional rules, including the Solicitors' Code of Conduct 2007, as managers or employees of regulated practices (see **CHAPTER 2**).

1   SI 2000/1119.

7.2

RELs may practise, for all practical purposes, as if they are solicitors, and subject to the same restrictions, in that they can practise on their own account (but only if they are authorised as recognised sole practitioners), with other RELs, with non-registered European lawyers, and with RFLs, as well as with solicitors and recognised bodies and in any combination.[1]

RELs may carry out under their home professional titles any professional activity that may be carried out by solicitors,[2] with only three exceptions:

(1)   In any proceedings before a court, tribunal or public authority where the professional activities in question may only be carried out by a solicitor, barrister or other qualified person an REL must act in conjunction with a solicitor or barrister who is entitled to practise in that forum and who could lawfully provide those professional activities, and the solicitor or barrister in question is answerable to the court or tribunal as the case may be.[3]

(2)   In property transactions RELs are not entitled to prepare for remuneration any instrument creating or transferring an interest in land unless their home professional titles were obtained in Denmark, the Republic of Ireland, Finland, Sweden, Iceland, Liechtenstein, Norway, the Czech Republic, Cyprus, Hungary or Slovakia.[4]

(3)   In relation to probate matters RELs are not entitled to prepare for remuneration any instrument for obtaining title to administer the estate of a deceased person unless their home professional titles were obtained in Denmark, Germany, the Republic of Ireland, Austria, Finland, Sweden, Iceland, Liechtenstein, Norway, Cyprus or Slovakia.[5]

1   Rule 12.02 of the Solicitors' Code of Conduct 2007.
2   Regulation 6 of the 2000 Regulations.
3   Regulation 11.
4   Regulation 12.
5   Regulation 13.

7.3

RFLs, in contrast, are more restricted in the way they can practise. The sole purpose of being registered as an RFL is to enable the individual to practise in a recognised body with a solicitor or solicitors, or an REL or RELs or a combination of the two – that is, as a manager, member or owner of a recognised body.[1] There is no requirement on a foreign lawyer to become an RFL for the purposes of being employed by a recognised body or a recognised sole practitioner. Registration does not permit an RFL to practise as a sole practitioner or an in-house RFL.

A foreign lawyer practising as a sole principal, or as a manager, member or owner of any business or organisation other than a recognised body or an authorised non-SRA firm (or with a comparable interest in a body which is a manager, member or owner of such a firm), or as an employee of such a firm, is not practising as an RFL and must not be held out or described as an RFL or as registered with or regulated by the Law Society or the SRA.[2] If an RFL is involved in this kind of business as well as one which may properly include an RFL, the former will be a separate business for the purpose of rule 21 of the Solicitors' Code of Conduct 2007.[3]

Further, an RFL may not be held out in any way which suggests that he or she is, or is entitled to practise as, a lawyer of England and Wales, and is prohibited from undertaking certain reserved activities, such as advocacy, the conduct of litigation and the preparation of documents relating to court proceedings, transfer or charging of land and probate papers, subject to certain exceptions.[4] There are also restrictions on the provision of immigration advice and immigration services.[5]

1   Rule 12.03(1) of the Solicitors' Code of Conduct 2007.
2   Rule 12.03(2).
3   Rule 12.03(3).
4   Rule 12.03(4).
5   Rule 12.03(5).

7.4

Under Schedule 4 to the 2000 Regulations most of the statutory regime applying to solicitors through the Solicitors Act 1974 is extended to RELs, including provisions relating to:

●   the suspension of practising certificates in certain circumstances (as if references to such certificates were references to registration as an REL – sections 13B and 15);

●   the whole of the regime concerning inadequate professional services (section 37A and Schedule 1A);

- the control of remuneration (sections 57 to 75);

- the control of the employment of disqualified persons, equally applicable to RELs as employers and employees (sections 41 to 44) and the powers of investigation and intervention (sections 35, 44B, 44C and Schedule 1); and

- the powers of the Solicitors Disciplinary Tribunal and the High Court (sections 46 to 53).

This is not intended to be an exhaustive list.

The statutory regime governing RFLs is to be found in Schedule 14 to CLSA 1990 (see **APPENDIX 19**). This makes provision for applications for registration, registration subject to conditions, the renewal of registration, and for appeals to the Master of the Rolls against a refusal to register, refusal to renew registration, and the imposition of conditions. This part of the regulatory system, concerned with the process of registration, is also largely applied to RELs by virtue of the 2000 Regulations.

The Schedule also provides for contributions to the Compensation Fund (and this also is extended to RELs in the same way), imposes a requirement to provide accountants' reports, provides for the effect of bankruptcy and for the effect of disciplinary action leading to the RFL being dealt with in his or her home jurisdiction in a way that is equivalent to being struck off or suspended, and extends the jurisdiction of the Solicitors Disciplinary Tribunal to RFLs.

CHAPTER 7
REGISTERED EUROPEAN /
FOREIGN LAWYERS

CHAPTER 8

Conduct unbefitting a solicitor

8.1

Historically, there have been two types of professional misconduct by solicitors:

(1)   statutory misconduct, consisting of breaches of provisions of the Solicitors Act 1974 (for example in relation to the obligation to deliver accountants' reports) or of rules made by virtue of that Act (such as the Solicitors' Accounts Rules 1998); and

(2)   non-statutory misconduct – what could be called the common law of conduct, which covered anything and everything that could bring the individual or the profession into sufficient disrepute so as to engage the risk of disciplinary sanction, but which was not covered by any specific rule.

In the Solicitors Disciplinary Tribunal any action, failing or course of conduct that offended the common law of conduct was alleged to be 'professional misconduct', until the late 1950s when the phrase 'conduct unbefitting a solicitor' was substituted. The latter formulation enabled the point to be made as necessary that misconduct outside a solicitor's professional practice, in his or her private life, could have disciplinary consequences.

On 1 July 2007 the Solicitors' Code of Conduct 2007 came into force. The Code has been considered to be an all-embracing and codified system of professional regulation. Accordingly, it seemed as though the concept of non-statutory misconduct would fade away, and prosecutors in the Tribunal started to allege a breach of a rule *simpliciter* (rather than conduct unbefitting) against solicitors whose conduct had been referred to the Tribunal. This presupposed that any breach of any rule could amount to a disciplinary offence – a controversial proposition. This debate will however become largely academic, as the Code of Conduct will be swept away and replaced by far less prescriptive rules under the system of 'outcomes-focused regulation' to be adopted by the SRA with effect from October 2011. Under such a system of regulation, the concept of conduct unbefitting a solicitor, or non-statutory professional misconduct, may again take centre stage in disciplinary proceedings.

8.2

Although rule 1 of the Code can be seen to be the successor to rule 1 of the Solicitors' Practice Rules 1990, it differs from its predecessor in one material way. The Practice Rule applied to anything done by a solicitor 'in the course of practising as a solicitor' and therefore did not address issues that arose outside professional practice, such as criminal convictions for drink driving offences, assault or even murder. Rule 1.06 of the Code ('You must not behave in a way that is likely to diminish the trust the public places in you or the legal profession') is not subject to the same limitation.

8.3

'Professional misconduct' and 'conduct unbefitting a solicitor' are not defined; there is no reference to either phrase in the Solicitors Act 1974 and 'misconduct' is that which the Tribunal and the judges from time to time consider it to be. Thus, 'conduct which would be regarded as improper according to the consensus of professional, including judicial, opinion could be fairly stigmatised as such whether it violated the letter of a professional code or not'.[1] On the other hand, it has always been the case that solicitors were not penalised for making mistakes – 'generally the honest and genuine decision of a solicitor on a question of professional judgment does not give rise to a disciplinary offence'.[2] Negligence may, however, amount to misconduct if it is sufficiently reprehensible or 'inexcusable and such as to be regarded as deplorable by his fellows in the profession'.[3]

1   *Ridehalgh v Horsefield* [1994] Ch 205, [1994] 3 All ER 848.
2   *Connolly v Law Society* [2007] EWHC 1175 (Admin).
3   *Re A Solicitor* [1972] 2 All ER 811 at 815.

8.4

It is in fact undesirable to attempt a comprehensive definition:

> 'The suggestion was that the phrase "moral turpitude" is analogous to conduct unbefitting. My response to that is that it may be in some circumstances, but not in all. Allegations against professional men vary infinitely in gravity. What constitutes conduct unbefitting a solicitor is best judged, in my view, by his professional colleagues, applying their undoubted experience of what is to be properly expected of a solicitor in his practice, when they are sitting formally as part of a disciplinary tribunal in judgment of one of them. I should be most reluctant to attempt to provide any kind of definition of a term which is used, the words being slightly different here and there, in many professions, including the armed forces'.[1]

It has been argued that only conduct specifically referred to and prohibited in *The Guide to the Professional Conduct of Solicitors* current at that time or specific rules is capable of being treated as conduct which is conduct unbefitting a solicitor. This was, unsurprisingly, rejected:

> 'The purpose of Professional Conduct Rules ... is to identify in particular those areas of conduct in respect of which there should be specific prohibitions or requirements because they are likely to represent the most prevalent situations and the most prevalent conduct then in the profession. The fact that such a particular area of conduct is specifically dealt with does not mean that all other conduct is permissible or within the standards of the profession. It is thus ordinarily open to professional disciplinary tribunals to apply sanctions for professional misconduct generally, regardless of whether it is conduct singled out for mention in the rules. Were it otherwise, professional people might be permitted to conduct themselves in plainly deplorable ways without any disciplinary control'.[2]

1   *Re A Solicitor* (1991, unreported), per Watkins LJ; cited with approval in *Re A Solicitor* (1995, unreported), per Lord Taylor CJ.
2   *Henneberry v Law Society* (2000, unreported).

CHAPTER 9

Regulation by other approved regulators

9.1

As pointed out in **CHAPTER 2**, in any analysis of the regulation of solicitors it is no longer possible to consider only the rules and regulations promulgated by the SRA. From 31 March 2009, a solicitor could be individually regulated by the SRA, but employed by or a manager of a business entity supplying legal services that is regulated by another approved regulator. In that situation, the solicitor, in his professional dealings, must comply with the rules of the business's regulator, because the Legal Services Act 2007 (LSA 2007) specifies that if there is a conflict between the regulation of the entity and the regulation of the individual, the regulation of the entity takes precedence.[1]

Currently, the only other approved regulator likely to be relevant in this context is the Council for Licensed Conveyancers (CLC) (though others may enter the market in the future). Other current regulators have shown less interest in regulating business entities, as opposed to their own members. The CLC may at present only regulate the supply of conveyancing and probate services, but is consulting on the possibility of widening its remit to regulate other reserved legal activities. In the meantime, the number of solicitors likely to find themselves in this position can be expected to be a very small minority. Therefore, while a brief consideration of the CLC rules is justified, this is not intended to be exhaustive.

1   Section 52(4) of LSA 2007.

Recognition and regulatory controls

9.2

In order to be eligible for recognition as a body regulated by the CLC, at least one of the managers of the body must be a licensed conveyancer.[1] A manager is a member of a company, if the company is run by its members; or a director of a company, a partner in a partnership, a member of an LLP, a member of an unincorporated body other than a partnership, or a licensed conveyancer if none of those situations applies and the body is not managed by another licensed conveyancer.[2] Recognition may be refused on the grounds of past disciplinary action against the applicant, or any manager or employee who is or was a licensed conveyancer, or if a manager, employee or shareholder has been convicted of a criminal offence involving fraud, dishonesty, deception or violence, or any other indictable offence, or on the grounds that any manager is not a suitable person by reason of that person's character, conduct or associations, or for any other reason in the public interest.[3] Every manager is under a duty to ensure that he is informed promptly of any matter which could have justified a refusal of recognition and must notify the CLC of any such event within 14 days.[4]

A manager of a recognised body must produce all records, papers, files and accounts of the recognised body to an appointee of the CLC at the time and place fixed, that are reasonably required to enable a report to be made as to compliance with the CLC's rules.[5]

Recognition will generally be for 12 months, and on application for renewal within the period of the recognition the existing recognition continues in force until a new certificate is issued, and .f refused will continue in force during the time for any appeal, and if appealed until determination of the appeal.[6] An application for recognition is deemed to be refused if no decision is notified within 42 days.[7] Appeals against refusal or deemed refusal lie to the Discipline and Appeals Committee of the CLC within one month.[8]

The Discipline and Appeals Committee has the power to revoke recognition and to impose other penalties on a recognised body.[9] Appeal lies to the High Court.[10]

1 Rule 4.4 of the CLC Regulation of Practices (Recognised Bodies) Rules 2009.
2 Rule 2.1.
3 Rule 5.1.
4 Rule 6.
5 Rule 16.1.
6 Rule 10.
7 Rule 9.2.
8 Paragraph 8(1) of Schedule 6 to the Administration of Justice Act 1985 (AJA 1985).
9 Paragraphs 4(2) and 5(1) of Schedule 6.
10 Paragraph 6(1) of Schedule 6.

9.3

Just as the SRA and the Solicitors Disciplinary Tribunal have jurisdiction over the managers and employees of solicitors and of bodies recognised by the SRA, even if they are not solicitors, so the CLC and the Discipline and Appeals Committee have jurisdiction over the managers and employees of recognised bodies regulated by the CLC, even if they are not licensed conveyancers. Thus solicitors who are managers or employees of such bodies may be fined by the Investigation Committee of the CLC and ordered to pay costs,[1] or referred to the Discipline and Appeals Committee, which may also impose a fine, make an order for costs, or an order requiring the CLC to take such steps in relation to the individual as the Committee may specify, or an order requiring the CLC to refer the conduct of the individual to his own regulator.[2]

1 Paragraph 3A of Schedule 6 to AJA 1985.
2 Paragraph 4(2A) and (2B) of Schedule 6.

Conduct rules

9.4

The latest version of the Solicitors' Code of Conduct 2007 and its associated guidance occupies 212 pages of this book.[1] The Licensed Conveyancers' Conduct Rules 2009 occupy 10 pages of A4 and there are 14 guidance notes in addition. The guidance notes deal with practice location (enabling the foreign outsourcing of operations); guidance on undertakings; supervision of staff; management arrangements; conflicts of interest; disclosure in relation to introductions and referrals; ownership of file contents and the retention of records; costs estimates and terms of engagement; complaints procedures; money laundering; dealing with unqualified third parties; home information packs; acting for lenders and mortgage fraud.

A manager of a practice licensed by the CLC is treated as a licensed conveyancer.[2] The core duties are to act with honesty and integrity; to act with reasonable care, skill and diligence; not to bring the profession into disrepute; to comply with directions of the CLC; and not to discriminate on prohibited grounds.[3]

1   See **APPENDIX 21**.
2   Rule 3.5 of the Licensed Conveyancers' Conduct Rules 2009.
3   Rule 4.1.

9.5

A manager must:

- ensure that all the managers and employees of the recognised body comply with the CLC's rules;

- immediately notify the CLC in writing of any breach of the CLC's rules by him or by any of the managers or employees of the recognised body;

- not conduct himself in a manner which he knows or has reasonable grounds for suspecting will result in a breach of the law or of the CLC's rules;

- comply fully with any undertaking given by him, the recognised body or any employee;

- never give false or misleading information relating to the provision of regulated services to any person;

- promptly comply with any request for information made by the CLC as authorised by statute or by the CLC's rules;

- promptly notify the CLC in writing of any facts or matters which may give rise to a claim under the CLC's Compensation Fund;

- promptly notify his insurers in writing of any facts or matters which may give rise to a claim under the CLC's Indemnity Policy; and cease to provide regulated services for any period for which the current evidence of insurance issued to the recognised body has been avoided.[1]

With the exception of unsolicited telephone calls or unsolicited visits, a licensed conveyancer or a manager may promote the firm's regulated services through any means provided that a person may freely choose a practitioner to act on his behalf.[2]

A licensed conveyancer (and thus any manager of a CLC regulated firm) must:

- at all times keep paramount the interests of the client except as required by law or by the CLC's rules;

- keep confidential all information about the client except as authorised by the client or as required by law or the CLC's rules;

- not accept instructions from a person nor continue to act for any client whose interests conflict directly or indirectly with his own or those of the recognised body, or with those of any other client; and cease acting in any matter if the client so instructs.[3]

CHAPTER 9
REGULATION BY OTHER
APPROVED REGULATORS

The firm must, except as permitted in guidance issued by the CLC, act only for one client in a matter unless each client is informed in writing in advance that the firm has been asked to act for another client, each client is at all times represented by different qualified persons, and those qualified persons conduct themselves in the matter as though they were members of different entities.[4]

The guidance note on conflicts of interest adds an obligation to obtain informed consent in writing from each client, but permits one qualified person to act for more than one party if the matter is not an arm's length transaction or one of the clients is an institutional lender.

On the granting or redemption of a mortgage, a licensed conveyancer or manager must not act for himself nor for any client prohibited by the instructions of any lender. A licensed conveyancer or manager must only accept instructions and undertake matters within his professional competence; must advise a client to seek legal or other advice where a matter is beyond his professional competence; must only seek to exclude or limit liability with the informed written consent of the client; and ensure that all communications are clear, fair and not misleading.[5]

There must be disclosed to a client in writing, as soon as it is known, the existence and amount of any sum payable by or to the firm arising, whether directly or indirectly, from the client's instructions; client information and records must be kept safe on a durable medium until delivered to the client or disposed of in accordance with guidance issued by the CLC.[6]

It will be seen, therefore, that there is a specific requirement to report immediately to clients on the financial situation whenever any money is owed by or to the client.

The firm must:

- before or when accepting instructions, set out in writing to the client the terms on which instructions are accepted, an estimate of costs and the firm's complaints procedure;

- where a complaint is received, comply with the complaints procedure;

- keep the client properly informed;

- not delay completion because fees are outstanding (for this purpose fees do not include disbursements);

- with the authority of the seller client, at once disclose in writing to all prospective buyers any instruction to submit contracts to more than one prospective buyer: if the seller client refuses to give such authority the firm must immediately cease to act.[7]

After giving its client reasonable notice in writing, with reasons, a recognised body may cease acting in any matter where it is reasonable for it to do so.[8]

1   Rule 4.4 of the Licensed Conveyancers' Conduct Rules 2009.
2   Rule 4.5.
3   Rule 5.1.
4   Rule 5.2.1.
5   Rules 5.2.2 to 5.2.7.
6   Rules 5.2.8 and 5.2.9.
7   Rules 5.2.10 to 5.2.14.
8   Rule 5.3.

9.6

A recognised body must not, except with the written permission of the CLC, employ or pay or continue to employ or pay any person to provide regulated services who is known to have been convicted of a relevant criminal offence or who is disqualified on other specified bases. A manager must immediately notify the CLC in writing if to his knowledge he or any manager in the recognised body becomes so disqualified or has been the subject of other specified events involving debt, insolvency, regulatory action or mental incapacity.[1]

1   Rules 6.2 and 6.3 of the Licensed Conveyancers' Conduct Rules 2009.

Accounts and financial services

9.7

Solicitors familiar with the Solicitors' Accounts Rules 1998 will not encounter any difficulties in complying with the Council for Licensed Conveyancers' Accounts Rules 2008. The latter are a rather less complex set of rules but directed to the same ends.

A licensed conveyancer or manager must:

- comply with the Accounts Rules;

- ensure that all his partners, employees and directors (including partners, employees and directors who are not licensed conveyancers) comply with the Rules;

- comply with the Accounts Guidance Notes (which are the italicised guidance notes within the Rules) unless he has good reason not to do so in the particular circumstances;

- use each client's money only for that client's matters;

- establish and maintain proper accounting systems, procedures, processes and internal controls, to ensure compliance with the Rules and the Accounts Guidance Notes;

- ensure there is no debit balance on the client side of a client ledger account nor a credit balance on the office side of a client ledger account;

- remedy any breach of the rules without delay (which means normally the same day or the next working day); and

- account to the client as soon as possible after completion of any transaction or after a retainer has been terminated.[1]

Money held on account of costs and disbursements must be withdrawn from client account within 28 days of the date on which a bill of costs is sent to a client, provided it is made clear to the client or the paying party either before or at the time the bill of costs is sent that such money will be applied towards or in payment of that bill of costs.[2] Undrawn costs or disbursements must not remain in client account, either in anticipation of future errors which could result in a shortage on that account or any current shortage on that account, and are not available as a set-off against any general shortage on client account.[3] The CLC must be notified without delay upon discovery of any misappropriation of client money.[4]

When client money is held in a separate designated account, a reasonable rate of interest must be sought on money held in that account and the firm must account to the client for all interest earned on that account. When money is held for a client in a client account other than in a separate designated account, or if money should have been held in a client account but was not so held, the firm must account to the client for a sum in lieu of interest calculated at the sole expense of the firm for such period as the CLC may determine. There is no requirement to pay to a client a sum in lieu of interest if the amount calculated is £20 or less.[5] The effect of these rules is that, unlike the SRA rules, there is no schedule or table specifying minimum amounts and periods of time. Interest is always payable unless it falls within the de minimis exception.

1   Rule 3 of the Council for Licensed Conveyancers' Accounts Rules 2008.
2   Rule 6.1.4.
3   Rule 6.6.
4   Rule 7.16.
5   Rule 9.

9.8

The CLC has issued the Licensed Conveyancers' Designated Professional Body Rules 2004 and an associated Code of Practice to regulate the supply of services under Part XX of the Financial Services and Markets Act 2000 by licensed conveyancing practices, enabling CLC regulated firms to provide specified financial services that are incidental to conveyancing or other services regulated by the CLC.

PART 3
Fraud and money laundering

CHAPTER 10

The risks of fraud

10.1

In this section it is intended to highlight certain danger areas which have resulted in guidance being given to the profession but which are not reflected in any specific rule.

Mortgage fraud

10.2

The Law Society has issued successive warnings on mortgage fraud (the 'Green Cards') and the SRA has recently updated this guidance (see **APPENDIX 10**)[1] but the significance of this is more easily understood when the basics of mortgage fraud are themselves understood.

The involvement, innocent or otherwise, of solicitors or licensed conveyancers is essential to all mortgage fraud, in the sense that they are required to enable the transaction to occur.

There have historically been four basic types of 'traditional' mortgage fraud, with a potentially endless selection of variations on the basic theme:

(1)   exaggeration of the borrower's income to obtain a mortgage that would otherwise be declined;

(2)   multiple purchases, where a fraudster uses false names or nominees to build up a portfolio of property through residential rather than commercial borrowing;

(3)   identity theft, where money is borrowed in the name of the proprietor on a remortgage, and diverted to the fraudsters; and

(4)   exaggeration of price or value, to obtain a higher mortgage than would properly be justified.

Of course, sometimes more than one element can feature in a fraudulent scheme.

Recently, identity theft as a mortgage fraud device has been extended to situations in which property is sold from under the genuine proprietor by a fraudster using the proprietor's name.

Solicitors will not generally expect to encounter false employers' references, for example, although there could well arise circumstances to put any reasonable solicitor on notice that the borrower client's means do not appear to match the lender's requirements for the amount being loaned. Furthermore, the obligations under the Money Laundering Regulations 2007[2] of due diligence and enhanced due diligence, and the obligation to monitor business relationships and transactions as they develop (considered in detail in **CHAPTER 11**) now have a direct relevance to these issues and should result in such patterns being detected. Regrettably, there have been solicitors who have been prepared to provide false references for their own employees or even to indulge in this kind of fraud for their own benefit.[3]

Solicitors are well placed to detect and prevent frauds of the second and third kinds and in some cases their active complicity, or determinedly deliberate Nelsonian blindness, is essential to the success of the frauds.

1 Recently extensively revised and updated, see: www.sra.org.uk/solicitors/scams/fraud-dishonesty.page.
2 SI 2007/2157.
3 *Re A Solicitor (Maharaj)* (1999, unreported).

10.3

In a rising market fraud can frequently remain undetected as, if questions are asked or arrears develop, the property can be sold at a profit and the lender's concerns assuaged. It is when a sudden drop in prices occurs and there is no escape route that frauds become particularly apparent. It is for that reason that following the recession that started in about 1989 and continued into the 1990s the profession was caught up in one of its greatest scandals as the extent of widespread mortgage fraud became known, and the extent to which the negligence of solicitors, or worse, had contributed to it.

The recent recession is having the same effect in disclosing mortgage fraud and, as expected, extensive fraudulent activities have been and are being uncovered. The adverse effects on the buy-to-let market caused by the economic downturn have provided opportunities for fraudsters in relation to the bulk refinancing/remortgaging of such borrowing. Lenders and the SRA, as well as other regulators, are becoming ever more proactive in policing and detecting trends and risks.

Multiple purchases

10.4

When it was the norm to meet your client in routine domestic conveyancing it was easier to spot warning signs. Now, despite the requirement for identity checks imposed by money laundering legislation, because of the development of commoditised conveyancing and online dealings, the conveyancing environment remains relatively friendly to frauds of this kind.

Individual buyers may be real people, but nominees. A common feature of this kind of fraud is a central figure through whom communications are required to be channelled. This could be a broker or a senior family member. All or most instructions are given by the key individual; solicitors may be encouraged to correspond with clients through that individual, and to send money and documents to that individual. Documents are sent to him or her to be signed by others and come back signed and witnessed. It all seems very efficient.

10.5

Solicitors should be alive to the fact that commercial pressures exist, and that fraudsters are highly attuned to the business community. They may be attracted to your practice, not because it has the best local reputation for efficient conveyancing, but because it is new or not apparently very wealthy, so that offers of substantial work might encourage the turning of a blind eye. Fraudsters will have their own intelligence network and will seek out those perceived to be vulnerable or susceptible to financial pressures, flattery, or occasionally coercion and blackmail. Coercion and blackmail sound like extreme scenarios, but you need to bear in mind that if a solicitor bends or breaks a rule as a 'favour' he also gives any person with knowledge of his wrongdoing power over him, including the person to whom he gave the favour ('We are now in this together …').

A more sophisticated version of this fraud involves the fraudster instructing a panel of solicitors, without disclosing to any firm that he is using more than one. Multiple transactions become more difficult to detect. If you become aware that an individual has more than one firm acting for him in such circumstances or for unexplained reasons, be suspicious.

Mules

10.6

Experienced conveyancers are very familiar with the patterns of behaviour of purchaser clients. To most, buying a new home is a very substantial, serious and potentially stressful transaction; they will ask questions, be concerned about matters of detail, be anxious about dates and progress. If clients introduced by Mr X show a pattern of near indifference, and contact is limited and amounts to virtually no more than an exchange of documents, there are likely to be grounds for suspicion. If the attitude of Mr X appears to be that of a businessman asking questions that are consistent with a businessman's outlook, rather than the questions clients could be expected to ask, it is more likely that it is he who has the true interest in the transaction, rather than those he purports to represent.

Mules – nominees or people with false identification used as buyers of property to facilitate fraud – have none of the normal interest that buyers of property will display. They may sometimes be exposed by even casual questioning.

Identity theft

10.7

Fraudsters can steal the identity of property owners, either to remortgage the property or to sell it to a genuine buyer or a co-conspirator. Ensure you know with whom you are dealing, Be concerned if it is said that there are reasons why the seller cannot be contacted. Common features are:

- a central figure, usually a broker introducing multiple transactions to the practice. He will be the only point of contact and will deal with clients on your behalf. He will reassure you that all regulatory and professional obligations have already been attended to. You may rarely if ever meet or have direct dealings with the client;

- rushed transactions; there will be an explanation such as a family crisis or other reason for urgency;

- the only money changing hands being the mortgage advance;
- instructions to remit funds to the client account of a named firm of solicitors (possibly the funds are urgently needed for mother's nursing home fees). The destination account may involve a bogus firm of solicitors or a ghost branch office of a genuine firm.

Exaggerated price or value

10.8

At its most basic this involves a friendly valuer putting too high a figure on the property and some private arrangement between buyer and seller, but in this type of fraud it is more often than not the case that the manipulation of the price is apparent to a watchful solicitor.

A solicitor should be alive to anything which could artificially inflate the price to be paid so that the amount of money that changes hands is less than the stated purchase price. Historically this has been done by such things as mythical 'deposits paid direct' or an 'allowance on completion' operating as a substantial discount on the stated price.

Another mechanism is to introduce a third party into the chain so that the transaction proceeds as a sale and sub-sale, or a 'back-to-back' sale and resale – the first half of the transaction being at the correct price agreed to be paid to the seller and the second half involving a sale to the real buyer at the inflated price declared to the mortgagee.

The purpose is to achieve a situation in which the mortgagee lends more than 100 per cent of the true value or price so that the fraudulent buyer acquires the property and a cash bonus.

Another warning sign is a client instructing a solicitor geographically distant from the property for no good apparent reason; this limits the opportunities for personal dealing and avoids local knowledge of the housing market.

The current flat property market offers limited opportunities for price leverage but sale and leaseback can be used for this purpose, for example where there is a distressed vendor (facing repossession), genuine or impersonated. A firm may be approached by a broker and offered a package of such transactions, all pre-agreed and pre-arranged.

10.9

Solicitors can become complicit by failing to identify the relevant features of the transaction for what they are, or occasionally by more active assistance. One solicitor, when faced with solicitors acting for the seller who refused to co-operate by agreeing, as requested, to an inflated contract price and an 'allowance on completion' amounting to more than 25 per cent of the true price, solved his fraudulent client's problem by acquiring an off the shelf Isle of Man company and arranging the sale to the company at the true price and immediate sale on by the company to his client at the inflated price declared to the mortgagee. He charged for both conveyancing transactions, and the services involved in arranging the company and its involvement.[1]

Solicitors will face not only civil claims from mortgagees if fraud has occurred, but also disciplinary proceedings with serious consequences – even if it is ultimately established that the solicitor was not actively complicit as a co-conspirator, but only insufficiently alert to the danger signs.

1   *Levinson*, 6942–1995 SDT. Mr Levinson explained to the Tribunal that this was not his own idea; he had copied it from his former partner, a Mr Nathan, who had in the meantime been struck off and sent to prison. Mr Levinson was struck off.

Fraud factories

10.10

Another relatively recent development involves the acquisition of law practices by fraudsters. Genuine firms facing difficulties or under financial pressure may be offered the opportunity of being taken over by a team which offers to introduce a portfolio of transactions, and conveyancing clerks to manage it. The purchaser may purport to be a solicitor, impersonating a genuine solicitor. Alternatively it may be a non-solicitor who makes the same offer, on the basis that he will become a financial controller or office manager. All such new arrivals, and their support teams, will be heavily resistant to supervision.

These arrangements are not designed to last for long, and the new owners have no interest in the success of the business; they are simply designed to obtain mortgage advances which are stolen. These 'fraud factories' may have a life of only three months, but those who control them can steal millions in that time.

Investment fraud

10.11

This is another serious issue for the profession because, in relation to the kinds of fraud that are discussed here, solicitors are essential to their success.

The broad nature of these frauds is that they offer to be highly profitable – to the point of absurdity – while being at the same time wholly secure. The justification for this investment paradox, which defies all normal rules, is that they are reserved to the few insiders who know about them. They are also targeted at those who can afford, or can at least find, large sums to invest – commonly $1 million or more (the medium is usually US dollars) – so that the victim may think that it is his wealth that enables him to engage in business ventures unavailable to others.

The trap

10.12

These frauds are more successful than would otherwise be expected because of the involvement of solicitors. The necessity for the involvement of solicitors is explained by an understanding of the different attitudes of the three participants – fraudster, victim and solicitor – which the fraudster exploits.

The victim will think, 'This is new to me; I have not heard of this form of investment before, but I am sure that if it was not genuine no solicitor would permit himself to be involved.'

The solicitor's attitude is, 'I do not truly understand what is going on here, but I do not have to. All I am being asked to do is to confirm that this copy document is a true copy of an original, or that I have received a particular document or a document of a particular description, or that I have received a specific sum of money. I do not have to go beyond that and I am not required to.'

The fraudster's position is, 'If I can get a solicitor involved the victim will be reassured, and the scheme given a credibility that it would not otherwise have. I am prepared to pay substantial sums for that involvement; it will be money well spent.'

The solicitor may be offered generous fees for doing very little, or the opportunity to earn interest on very large sums of money that pass through his or her client account.

The test

10.13

It is not considered to be particularly helpful to attempt to describe the range of possible kinds of fraud or the (usually highly complex and turgid) details of those that have been attempted in the past. They change and become more sophisticated as time passes. The one thing they have in common is that if they are carefully considered they do not make sense. They were often referred to as 'Prime Bank Instrument' frauds, by reference to the kind of document that was used to perpetrate them; they have also been termed 'High Yield Investment Programmes'. They were described by Neuberger J in *Dooley v Law Society*[1] in these words:

> 'Bank instrument frauds are based on documents which are full of impressive phrases, which on analysis make little sense, and which promise returns which are fantastic in both senses in which that word is used, namely fictitious and enormous. They are used by unscrupulous rogues to encourage the badly advised, the ignorant, the gullible and the greedy to part with their money, tempted by promises of the fantastically high returns. Once these investors part with their money, they are lucky if they see any of it again. Generally speaking, a man may as well burn his money for all the good it would do him. At least it would remove the false hopes and subsequent agony that such so-called investments involve.'

1   (2000, unreported).

10.14

The Tribunal has dealt with many such cases. The following comments made by the Tribunal help to identify the pattern, and particularly the kind of mistake, that solicitors make:

> 'Members of the solicitors' profession had been warned about the dangers of becoming involved in prime bank instrument fraud or money launder-ing. The matter in which the Respondent had become involved demon-strated many of the notified hallmarks of fraud; it was entirely clear that the Respondent himself had no understanding of the investment scheme and had simply done what he was told and allowed his client account to be a repository for a huge sum of money.

The Tribunal has had cause in the past to make the observation which it again makes. A solicitor is not a bank. A solicitor can have no business simply in receiving and paying out money with no purpose attached to it. If a solicitor is not more knowledgeable about the subject matter of the cases of which he has conduct than his clients then he should not be handling such cases. A solicitor's stock-in-trade is his knowledge and expertise. If his clients are not utilising such knowledge and expertise it is likely that the solicitor is being involved in order that a spurious scheme be given a cloak of respectability.[1]

It is not for a client to explain the nature of a transaction to a solicitor but rather the solicitor's role is to explain the nature of a transaction to the client. It can be described as nothing other than crass stupidity to accept a role as, for example, an "escrow agent" when the solicitor cannot know what that means as, indeed, that expression has no meaning in English law. It is, in any event, serious professional misconduct for a solicitor to accept instructions to undertake work in connection with which he has no knowledge, expertise or experience and where the only reason for his involvement is to add a "cloak of respectability" and thereby induce the victims of fraud to take part. The Respondent himself accepts that he should have known or suspected that the transactions in which he became involved were not viable commercial transactions ...[2]

The Respondent had ensured that scurrilous transactions were given a cloak of respectability by allowing his firm's name to be used in connection with what was on its face a transaction of the type against which the Law Society had issued warnings. It is in the Tribunal's opinion perhaps the most important aspect of this case that the Respondent was prepared to write letters regarding a matter in which he played no part as a solicitor. He had no knowledge of the type of transactions involved, he had no relevant experience and he did not, and indeed could not, give anybody any advice as to the legal aspects. A solicitor becomes involved in acting for a client when the client needs the solicitor's advice and expertise in the relevant area of law. The Tribunal accepts that there are rogues and fraudsters who are extremely plausible. A solicitor is unlikely to be taken in by such a person if he asks himself the question "why am I invited to become involved in this matter?" If the answer is not "because the client seeks to rely upon my legal expertise, knowledge and experience", he should not be playing any part in the matter.[3]

The Respondent at the relevant time had been an experienced practitioner. He had stated that he had not seen the yellow warning card issued by the Law Society. The warning card had however not changed the then existing duties on solicitors but had provided clarificatory guidance. The Respondent had clearly been asked to become involved in something which was out of his ordinary line of business involving overseas countries and huge sums of money. The Respondent had put his name to unintelligible documents and to documents drafted by his client which he had not questioned. He had distributed funds received from third parties at the direction of his client and had produced no evidence of proper authority to do so. He had written letters of comfort to banks and solicitors. He had involved himself in the transactions over a period of time. The transactions had never completed. The Respondent had expected significant personal gain from his involvement.[4]

The Respondent himself had come to recognise that he should not have been involved in the dubious HYI [High Yield Investment] transactions details of which had been placed before the Tribunal. The attention of members of the profession had been drawn to the proliferation of fraudulent investment schemes purporting to produce extraordinarily high returns on investments. It was recognised that a number of fraudsters sought to deprive potential investors of large sums of money by the production of bizarre schemes, spurious documentation and promises of very high returns indeed, often with the added incentive to invest provided by an assurance that monies would be used for charitable causes or humanitarian projects. It ill behoves a solicitor to use phrases and expressions that have no meaning in English law. It beggars belief that a solicitor should employ such phrases in letters that he himself has written. The question has to be asked, "how can a solicitor offer advice to any client or third party upon a scheme which is so nonsensical that he himself cannot have any useful knowledge of it?" It is well recognised that the fraudsters customarily seek to involve a member of the solicitors' profession in order that a cloak of respectability may be achieved and those defrauded are encouraged to part with large sums of money because of the comfort they derive from the fact that a solicitor is involved in the transaction. In becoming involved in the fraudulent schemes, as the Respondent did, he falsely allowed his own status and the good reputation of the solicitors' profession to be used improperly to persuade potential "investors" to make substantial investment of money. The only proper way for a solicitor to behave when invited to participate in one of these schemes, in whatever capacity, is to refuse to do so and report the approach made to him to the appropriate authorities. For a solicitor to become involved in dubious and/or fraudulent transactions of this type was not compatible with his continued membership of the profession.'[5]

1   *Wayne*, 8189–2000, SDT.
2   *Wilson-Smith*, 8772–2003, SDT.
3   *Rose*, 9067–2004, SDT.
4   *Rosling*, 9242–2005, SDT.
5   *Heath*, 9502–2006, SDT.

10.15

It will have been noted that the single strand of logical concern that permeates these cases is that the client knows more about the subject matter than the solicitor: he is not seeking legal advice and assistance; he is directing the solicitor in what he is required to do and explaining matters to the solicitor, not seeking guidance. In fact, many such schemes are constructed purely for the purposes of money laundering between individuals with a common interest, serving only to move large amounts of money into and out of a solicitor's client account. Compliance with the Money Laundering Regulations 2007 considered in **CHAPTER 11** is vital, and would be effective to prevent involvement in such schemes if faithfully followed.

Further, if solicitors ask themselves the questions identified by the Tribunal in *Rose* and *Heath* the precise nature of the fraudulent scheme will not matter. However much fraudsters change the language and apparent structure, and even if the consequence of such changes is that every 'common characteristic' or 'typical phrase' appearing in the Law Society's warning card[1] is avoided, it will be a straightforward matter for solicitors to identify dubious transactions and avoid involvement.

In *Bryant and Bench v Law Society*,[2] solicitors who had acted for clients in a series of 'dubious' transactions, even though not themselves dishonest, were both suspended. 'Dubious' in this context meant that the transactions bore the indicia of fraud or possible fraud, and that it was professional misconduct for the appellants to act or to continue to act in relation to them without carrying out sufficient enquiries to satisfy themselves that the transactions were not, in fact, fraudulent. The Divisional Court stated at paragraphs 199 and 244 of its judgment:

> 'In our view the appellants should have concluded that these transactions involving NIC and Mr Alonso were "dubious" in the sense described above at the very latest by the end of August 2003. But they never did so. They appeared to be naïve, uncommercial and unwilling to question matters; whereas we would have expected solicitors who had considerable experience of international clients and transactions to have developed a healthy scepticism.
>
> In the case of Mr Bryant, the incompetence displayed was considerable and continued for approximately a year. In the case of Mr Bench, his culpability was far less, but, on our findings, remains significant. We accept the submission on behalf of the Law Society that such incompetence threatens the reputation of the profession for prudence as well as competence and that it puts the public at risk.'

1   See **APPENDIX 10**.
2   [2007] EWHC 3043 (Admin).

Money laundering

11.1

This chapter provides a brief introduction to this important and complex subject, specific guidance on the Money Laundering Regulations 2007,[1] and some commentary on the principal elements of the criminal law that are engaged. It does not provide an all-encompassing guide to the subject, which derives from the criminal law and is beyond the scope of this book. The focus in this chapter is on the regulation of practitioners and the warning signs.

1   SI 2007/2157.

What is money laundering?

11.2

To quote the Financial Action Task Force of the Organisation for Economic Co-operation and Development:

> 'The goal of a large number of criminal acts is to generate a profit for the individual or group that carries out the act. Money laundering is the processing of these criminal proceeds to disguise their illegal origin. This process is of critical importance, as it enables the criminal to enjoy these profits without jeopardising their source.'

Money laundering is the process by which assets illegally obtained are 'cleaned' to give them apparent legitimacy to enable their subsequent use. It involves the purported legitimisation of *any asset* that is illegitimately obtained. An accumulation of small amounts obtained or retained by tax evasion would be criminal property for these purposes. Money laundering is designed to disguise the true origin of criminal proceeds. The process typically involves three stages – placement, layering and integration – but these are not clear cut distinctions and money laundering may become a seamless blend of all three.

Placement

11.3

The placement stage involves the placing in the financial/banking system of the proceeds of crime. The intention is to change the identity of the illegitimate asset. A solicitor's client account will serve this purpose.

Layering

11.4

The layering stage involves moving the asset through the financial system. The intention is to hide the origins of the illegitimate asset, making it difficult to trace and recover. Complex transactions may be used to disguise the source of funds. Sometimes the transactions may have no legitimate economic purpose, but simply result in money moving around (see the commentary on investment frauds at para **10.11**).

Integration

11.5

The integration stage involves the translation of the laundered funds into a legitimate asset, such as the purchase of property through a conveyancing solicitor.

Solicitors as 'gatekeepers'

11.6

According to the Serious Organised Crime Agency:

> 'Serious organised criminals have a number of options when looking to realise the proceeds of their criminal activities. These include smuggling cash or assets out of the UK; laundering the money themselves; employing "gatekeepers", such as solicitors and accountants, with access to financial facilities; corrupting or coercing bank employees; or using professional launderers.'[1]

Professionals including solicitors may have a lack of awareness or lack of curiosity, so allowing themselves to be used by criminals to access the banking system and to enable the conversion of criminal funds into legitimate assets.

Solicitors may assist by becoming involved in normal transactions, such as a property purchase, but in circumstances where the client's true identity or status as nominee are disguised, and/or where the source of funds cannot be ascertained or is suspicious. Solicitors may also become involved in unusual transactions with no obvious logic where large amounts of money move about without any apparent aim. Investment frauds of the kind considered in **CHAPTER 10** invariably 'fail' in the sense that nothing comes of the 'investment' but it can be that all parties to the scheme are colluding and that the only real purpose is to move money in and out of a solicitor's client account.

A derivative of investment frauds is sham litigation. Here the fraudsters collude to litigate over an original scheme which, on close analysis, may make little sense. Signs to watch for will include clients with an unusual lack of interest in the risks of litigation, and who seem reluctant to engage in the detail. Another indicator is that one party to the litigation will suddenly capitulate, submitting to judgment for the full amount, without material effort to achieve a compromise solution.

1   The Serious Organised Crime Agency, *United Kingdom Threat Assessment of Serious Organised Crime 2006/07.*

Six key questions for solicitors

11.7

There is no substitute for understanding and following the Money Laundering Regulations 2007 (see para **11.9**), but solicitors should always ask themselves:

- Am I confident I know who this person is and that I understand with whom I am really dealing?

- Am I confident that I know and understand the source of funds?

- Am I confident that I know and understand the transaction?

- Is there anything about the transaction which is unusual or financially illogical?

- Is the client showing an appropriate degree of interest in the transaction?

- Do I understand why this client has chosen to instruct me?

These are issues of which solicitors should be aware at the beginning of a business relationship or transaction, *and* which they should also continue to have in mind and to monitor as relationships and transactions develop.

Law Society guidance and assistance

11.8

The Law Society has published a Practice Note aimed at assisting solicitors to understand the current anti-money laundering legislation. Treasury approval has been given to this guidance. Therefore in assessing whether any solicitor has committed an offence, took all reasonable steps or exercised all due diligence to avoid committing the offence, the court must consider whether there has been compliance with the Society's guidance.

The SRA will also take the Practice Note into account when exercising its regulatory and supervisory functions.

The full guidance, which runs to more than 100 pages, can be found at www.lawsociety.org.uk/productsandservices/practicenotes/aml.page. In addition the Society's Practice Advice Service will assist in understanding the Practice Note and by talking through any problems (Tel: 0870 606 2522). There is also a list[1] of solicitors with relevant expertise willing to give other solicitors 30 minutes' free advice on legal issues relating to compliance.

1   See www.lawsociety.org.uk/choosingandusing/findasolicitor/moneylaunderingdirectory.page.

The Money Laundering Regulations 2007

11.9

The Money Laundering Regulations 2007 ('the 2007 Regulations')[1] were implemented to ensure compliance with the Third Money Laundering Directive.[2] They came into force on 15 December 2007.

1   SI 2007/2157.
2   Directive 2005/60/EC of the European Parliament and of the Council on the prevention of the use
    of the financial system for the purposes of money laundering and terrorist financing.

Relevant persons

11.10

The 2007 Regulations impose obligations on 'relevant persons'[1] to implement management systems that will enable the detection of money laundering and terrorist funding activities by imposing a duty to apply 'customer due diligence measures'.[2]

Relevant persons include 'independent legal professionals' acting in the course of business carried on in the United Kingdom.

An independent legal professional, for the purposes of the 2007 Regulations, is:

> '... a firm or sole practitioner who by way of business provides legal or notarial services to other persons, when participating in financial or real property transactions concerning –
>
> (a)   the buying and selling of real property or business entities;
>
> (b)   the managing of client money, securities or other assets;
>
> (c)   the opening or management of bank, savings or securities accounts;
>
> (d)   the organisation of contributions necessary for the creation, operation or management of companies; or
>
> (e)   the creation, operation or management of trusts, companies or similar structures,
>
> and, for this purpose, a person participates in a transaction by assisting in the planning or execution of the transaction or otherwise acting for or on behalf of a client in the transaction.'[3]

Most solicitors fall within the definition of a relevant person (save those working in-house or for a public authority) and have to adopt procedures to comply with the provisions of the 2007 Regulations as a result, but it is to be noted that part of the requirement is involvement in financial or real property transactions so that, for example, a firm conducting exclusively claimant litigation would not be within the definition of a relevant person.

The Treasury has confirmed that a solicitor does not generally become a relevant person only by receiving a payment on account of costs or payment of a bill, or by giving legal advice. Paragraph 1.4.5 of the Practice Note sets out a list of activities that would not generally be viewed as participation in financial transactions:

- preparing a home information pack or any document or information for inclusion in a HIP – it is specifically excluded under Regulation 4(1)(f)

- payment on account of costs to a solicitor or payment of a solicitor's bill

- provision of legal advice

- participation in litigation or a form of alternative dispute resolution

- will-writing, although you should consider whether any accompanying taxation advice is covered

- work funded by the Legal Services Commission.

It adds: 'If you are uncertain whether the regulations apply to your work, seek legal advice on the individual circumstances of your practice or simply take the broadest of the possible approaches to compliance with the regulations.'

1   Defined in regulation 3 of the 2007 Regulations. Regulation 4 provides for exclusions.
2   Regulations 5 and 7.
3   Regulation 3(9).

Customer due diligence and ongoing monitoring

11.11

Subject to certain exceptions a relevant person must apply customer due diligence measures when he or she:

- establishes a business relationship;[1]

- carries out an occasional transaction;[2] or

- suspects money laundering or terrorist financing; or

- doubts the veracity or adequacy of documents, data or information previously obtained for the purposes of client identification or verification.[3]

A relevant person 'must also apply customer due diligence measures at other appropriate times to existing customers on a risk-sensitive basis'.[4]

Customer due diligence measures are defined by regulation 5 of the 2007 Regulations and are:

'(a) identifying the customer and verifying the customer's identity on the basis of documents, data or information obtained from a reliable and independent source;

(b) identifying, where there is a beneficial owner who is not the customer, the beneficial owner and taking adequate measures, on a risk-sensitive basis, to verify his identity so that the relevant person is satisfied that he knows who the beneficial owner is, including, in the case of a legal person, trust or similar legal arrangement, measures to understand the ownership and control structure of the person, trust or arrangement; and

(c) obtaining information on the purpose and intended nature of the business relationship.'

A relevant person must 'determine the extent of customer due diligence measures on a risk-sensitive basis depending on the type of customer, business relationship, product or transaction', and 'be able to demonstrate to his supervisory authority that the extent of the measures is appropriate in view of the risks of money laundering and terrorist financing'.[5] This is required as part of both customer due diligence measures, and ongoing monitoring. Where a relevant person has to apply customer

CHAPTER 11
MONEY LAUNDERING

due diligence in the case of a trust or similar arrangement and the beneficial owner consists of a class of persons, it is not necessary to identify all members of the class.[6]

A relevant person must keep under review every business relationship and conduct 'ongoing monitoring'. This means:

'(a) scrutiny of transactions undertaken throughout the course of the relationship (including, where necessary, the source of funds) to ensure that the transactions are consistent with the relevant person's knowledge of the customer, his business and risk profile; and

(b) keeping the documents, data or information obtained for the purpose of applying customer due diligence measures up to date.'[7]

1   A 'business relationship' means a business, professional or commercial relationship between a relevant person and a customer, which is expected by the relevant person, at the time when contact is established, to have an element of duration: regulation 2 of the 2007 Regulations.
2   Regulation 2 of the 2007 Regulations. An 'occasional transaction' means a transaction (carried out other than as part of a business relationship) amounting to 15,000 Euro or more, whether the transaction is carried out in a single operation or several operations which appear to be linked.
3   Regulation 7(1)(a) to (d).
4   Regulation 7(2).
5   Regulation 7(3)(a) and (b).
6   Regulation 7(4).
7   Regulation 8(2)(a) and (b).

11.12

It is important to note that, by requiring a risk-based assessment of the needs of due diligence and a full and proper understanding of transactions, the 2007 Regulations impose obligations actively to police and monitor the way that business relationships and transactions develop, with an understanding of the aims of money laundering. This is not a box-ticking exercise so that, having obtained a copy passport and a utility bill (for example), a solicitor can consider the money laundering requirements to have been satisfied. There is an ongoing obligation for relevant persons in relation to all clients and all transactions. Many will involve minimal risk and commensurate monitoring, but the Regulations require relevant persons to be watchful and thoughtful.

A client's identity must be verified before a business relationship is established or an occasional transaction is carried out[1] but the verification process may be completed during the establishment of a business relationship, if it is 'necessary not to interrupt the normal conduct of business' and 'there is little risk of money laundering or terrorist financing occurring' provided that the verification is completed as soon as practicable after contact is first established.[2]

A solicitor unable to establish a client's identity must not carry out any transaction with or for the client through a bank account, must not establish a business relationship or carry out an occasional transaction with the client, must terminate any existing business relationship with the client and must consider whether he or she is required to make a disclosure (under Part 7 of the Proceeds of Crime Act 2002 or Part 3 of the Terrorism Act 2000).[3] There is an important exception in favour of a solicitor where he is 'in the course of establishing the legal position for his client or performing his task of defending or representing that client in, or concerning, legal proceedings, including advice on the institution or avoidance of proceedings'.[4]

This enables a solicitor to undertake preparatory work in litigation matters subject to subsequent client identity verification being achieved.

1   Regulation 9(2) of the 2007 Regulations.
2   Regulation 9(3).
3   Regulation 11(1)(a) to (d). For matters concerning disclosure under the Acts of 2000 and 2002, see para **11.24**.
4   Regulation 11(2) of the 2007 Regulations.

Enhanced customer due diligence

11.13

There are requirements for 'enhanced customer due diligence and ongoing monitoring' where the customer has not been physically present for identification purposes,[1] where the client is a 'politically exposed person'[2] or in any other situation which by its nature can present a higher risk of money laundering or terrorist financing.[3] A politically exposed person is an individual who is or has at any time in the preceding year been entrusted with a prominent public function by a state other than the United Kingdom, by a European Community institution or by an international body, or who is an immediate family member or known close associate of such a person.[4]

Enhanced due diligence in the case of clients who are not physically present for identification purposes requires additional specific and adequate measures to compensate for the higher risk, for example by obtaining additional documents, data or information verifying identity, by taking supplementary measures to verify documents supplied, by obtaining confirmation by a bank or other financial institution, or by ensuring that the first payment is carried out through a bank or other financial institution.

Enhanced due diligence in the case of politically exposed persons requires measures to be taken to establish the source of wealth and source of funds involved in the proposed business relationship or occasional transaction.

1   Regulation 14(2) of the 2007 Regulations.
2   Regulation 14(4).
3   Regulation 14(1)(b).
4   Regulation 14(5). The phrases 'immediate family member' and 'known close associate' are defined in Schedule 2 to the 2007 Regulations.

Law Society guidance on customer due diligence

11.14

Chapter 4 of the Law Society Practice Note contains comprehensive guidance on customer due diligence. It provides detailed advice as to how to deal with the verification of UK residents; persons not resident in the UK; clients unable to produce standard documentation; other professionals; partnerships and LLPs; public companies listed in the UK; private and unlisted companies in the UK; public overseas companies; and private and unlisted overseas companies. It also explains how to approach money-laundering issues concerning other legal or quasi-legal entities such as trusts, foundations, charities, deceased persons' estates, churches, schools, clubs and pension funds.

CHAPTER 11
MONEY LAUNDERING

As for ongoing monitoring, the Note states:

'Regulation 8 requires that you conduct ongoing monitoring of a business relationship on a risk-sensitive and appropriate basis. Ongoing monitoring is defined as:

- scrutiny of transactions undertaken throughout the course of the relationship (including where necessary, the source of funds), to ensure that the transactions are consistent with your knowledge of the client, their business and the risk profile;

- keeping the documents, data or information obtained for the purpose of applying CDD up to date. You must also be aware of obligations to keep clients' personal data updated under the Data Protection Act.

You are not required to:

- conduct the whole CDD process again every few years;

- conduct random audits of files;

- suspend or terminate a business relationship until you have updated data, information or documents, as long as you are still satisfied you know who your client is, and keep under review any request for further verification material or processes to get that material;

- use sophisticated computer analysis packages to review each new retainer for anomalies.

Ongoing monitoring will normally be conducted by fee earners handling the retainer, and involves staying alert to suspicious circumstances which may suggest money laundering, terrorist financing, or the provision of false CDD material.'

Financial Action Task Force counter-measures

11.15

Customer due diligence systems must enable identification of persons from a country subject to Financial Action Task Force counter-measures, where the Treasury has imposed financial sanctions.[1] The full list can be accessed at: www.hm-treasury.gov.uk/financialsanctions.

1   Under regulation 18 of the 2007 Regulations the Treasury 'may direct any relevant person (a) not to enter into a business relationship; (b) not to carry out an occasional transaction; or (c) not to proceed any further with a business relationship or occasional transaction, with a person who is situated or incorporated in a non-EEA state to which the Financial Action Task Force has decided to apply counter-measures.'

Reliance on third parties and outsourcing

11.16

Solicitors may rely on a third party to conduct customer due diligence on their behalf, provided the third party consents to be relied upon[1] and the third party is a bank or other financial institution, a professionally regulated auditor, insolvency practitioner, external accountant, tax adviser or independent legal professional.[2] A solicitor may also outsource customer due diligence but whether the solicitor relies on a consenting third party or outsources the service, he or she, as the relevant person, remains liable for any default by the third party or agent.[3] That being so, these options are unlikely to be practicable or attractive to solicitors.

1   Regulation 17(1)(a) of the 2007 Regulations.
2   Regulation 17(2).
3   Regulation 17(1)(b) and (4).

Record-keeping

11.17

Relevant persons must keep records to demonstrate compliance with the 2007 Regulations. In substance this requires you to keep evidence of identity and other file records of a relationship or transaction for five years from the completion of the transaction or the end of the relationship.[1]

1   Regulation 19 of the 2007 Regulations.

Systems and training

11.18

Relevant persons must establish and maintain appropriate risk-sensitive policies and procedures to prevent activities relating to money laundering or terrorist financing. These must address:

- customer due diligence measures and ongoing monitoring;
- reporting;
- record-keeping;
- internal control;
- risk assessment and management; and
- the monitoring and management of compliance with, and the internal communication of, such policies and procedures.[1]

Solicitors' firms must have a money laundering reporting officer (MLRO) – a 'nominated officer' for the purpose of the 2007 Regulations to receive and to make disclosures.[2]

Policies and procedures must include those which provide for the identification and scrutiny of:

- complex or unusually large transactions;
- unusual patterns of transactions which have no apparent economic or visible lawful purpose; and
- any other activity which the relevant person regards as particularly likely by its nature to be related to money laundering or terrorist financing.[3]

As mentioned above, the requirement to have a full and proper understanding of transactions is reinforced, and it will be seen that a responsible application of regulation 20 will avoid the involvement of solicitors in the kind of investment frauds considered in **CHAPTER 10**.

Relevant persons must take appropriate measures to ensure that 'all relevant employees' are 'made aware of the law relating to money laundering and terrorist financing', and are 'regularly given training in how to recognise and deal with transactions and other activities which may be related to money laundering and terrorist financing.'[4]

For the Law Society's guidance on training see paragraphs 3.9.1 to 3.9.4 of the Practice Note. Paragraph 3.9.2 contains the following advice:

'When setting up a training and communication system you should consider:

- which staff require training;

- what form the training will take;

- how often training should take place;

- how staff will be kept up to date with emerging risk factors for the firm.

Assessments of who should receive training should include who deals with clients in areas of practice within the regulated sector, handles funds or otherwise assists with compliance. Consider fee earners, reception staff, administration staff and finance staff, because they will each be differently involved in compliance and so have different training requirements.

Training can take many forms and may include:

- face-to-face training seminars;

- completion of online training sessions;

- attendance at AML/CTF conferences;

- participation in dedicated AML/CTF forums;

- review of publications on current AML/CTF issues;

- firm or practice group meetings for discussion of AML/CTF issues and risk factors.

Providing an AML/CTF policy manual is useful to raise staff awareness and can be a continual reference source between training sessions.'

1   Regulation 20(1)(a) to (f) of the 2007 Regulations.
2   Regulation 20(2)(d)(i).
3   Regulation 20(2)(a)(i) to (iii).
4   Regulation 21(a) and (b).

Compliance

11.19

The Law Society, through the SRA, is a supervisory authority with responsibility to monitor those it regulates and to take necessary measures for the purposes of securing compliance with the 2007 Regulations.[1] Powers are also given to other authorities to obtain information from individuals and corporate bodies, to search and enter properties with and without warrants, and to question individuals.[2]

A failure to comply with any of the requirements of the 2007 Regulations listed above is a criminal offence punishable by a term of imprisonment of up to two years.[3] No offence is committed if all reasonable steps were taken and all due diligence was exercised to avoid committing the offence.[4]

Civil penalties may also be imposed (primarily in practice by the Financial Services Authority, but also by the Office of Fair Trading and HM Revenue and Customs) of any amount sufficient to be effective, proportionate and dissuasive.[5] The same defence is available.[6]

1   Regulation 23(1)(c), Schedule 3 Part 1, and regulation 24 of the 2007 Regulations.
2   Regulations 37 to 41.
3   Regulation 45.
4   Regulation 45(4).
5   Regulation 42(1).
6   Regulation 42(2).

Communications with clients

11.20

Although not required by the 2007 Regulations, it may be regarded as good practice and good client relations to explain the statutory obligations to which solicitors are subject, in terms of customer due diligence and reporting, in client care material and/or terms of business.

The criminal law – primary offences

11.21

The primary money laundering offences are currently found in Part 7 of the Proceeds of Crime Act 2002 (PCA 2002). There are also separate offences aimed at preventing the laundering of and dealing with terrorist property in Part 3 of the Terrorism Act 2000 (TA 2000).

The three primary money laundering offences are those contained in sections 327, 328 and 329 of PCA 2002. These are:

- concealing criminal property (section 327);

- arrangements involving criminal property (section 328); and

- acquiring criminal property (section 329).

Of these, that which is most relevant to solicitors is the offence under section 328. It is an offence if a person 'enters into or becomes concerned in an arrangement which he knows or suspects facilitates (by whatever means) the acquisition, retention, use or control of criminal property by or on behalf of another person'.[1]

Knowledge or suspicion that the property is criminal property is required for an offence to be committed. The Crown must show that the offender knew or suspected that the arrangement was an arrangement which facilitated the acquisition, retention or control of criminal property. For property to be 'criminal property' the offender must be proved to have known or suspected that the property constituted a person's benefit from criminal conduct, or that it represented such a benefit (in whole or in part, directly or indirectly).[2]

There is no statutory definition of an arrangement; the courts have only been called upon to rule as to what 'arrangements' do *not* include. In *Bowman v Fels*[3] the Court of Appeal held that an arrangement does not include action undertaken in the context of litigation:

'... the issue or pursuit of ordinary legal proceedings with a view to obtaining the court's adjudication upon the parties' rights and duties is not to be regarded as an arrangement or a prohibited act within ss 327–9'.[4]

The Law Society's views as to whether and in what circumstances solicitors are involved in an 'arrangement' in the light of *Bowman v Fels* are set out in the Practice Note at paragraph 5.4.3 in the following terms:

'*Bowman v Fels* [2005] EWCA Civ 226 held that s.328 does not cover or affect the ordinary conduct of litigation by legal professionals, including any step taken in litigation from the issue of proceedings and the securing of injunctive relief or a freezing order up to its final disposal by judgment.

Our view, supported by Counsel's opinion, is that dividing assets in accordance with the judgment, including the handling of the assets which are criminal property, is not an arrangement. Further, settlements, negotiations, out of court settlements, alternative dispute resolution and tribunal representation are not arrangements. However, the property will generally still remain criminal property and you may need to consider referring your client for specialist advice regarding possible offences they may commit once they come into possession of the property after completion of the settlement.

The recovery of property by a victim of an acquisitive offence will not be committing an offence under either s.328 or s.329 of the Act.'

1   Section 328(1) of PCA 2002.
2   Section 340.
3   [2005] EWCA Civ 226, [2005] 1 WLR 3083, [2005] 4 All ER 609.
4   [2005] EWCA Civ 226, [2005] 1 WLR 3083, [2005] 4 All ER 609 at para 95.

11.22

There are broadly comparable offences under TA 2000. Those most likely to be of concern to solicitors are contained in sections 17 and 18 of TA 2000. A person commits an offence if he 'enters into or becomes concerned in an arrangement as a result of which money or other property is made available or is to be made available to another', and he 'knows or has reasonable cause to suspect that it will or may be used for the purposes of terrorism';[1] and a person commits an offence if he 'enters into or becomes involved in an arrangement which facilitates the retention or control by or on behalf of another person of terrorist property' by concealment, removal from the jurisdiction, transfer to nominees or in any other way.

It is a defence to prove that the person accused did not know and had no reasonable cause to suspect that the arrangement related to terrorist property.[2]

Although, as has been seen, the Money Laundering Regulations 2007 encourage and require a proportionate risk-based approach, this is not the test applied to the primary and secondary criminal offences, where the obligations not to engage in prohibited activities and to make disclosure when required are mandatory.

1   Section 17 of TA 2000.
2   Section 18.

Disclosure

11.23

The concept of 'disclosure' in relation to this area of the law is relevant in two respects.

The offence of non-disclosure

11.24

Section 330 of PCA 2002 applies to information received in the course of business in the regulated sector, and therefore applies to solicitors who are relevant persons for the purposes of the Money Laundering Regulations 2007. The corresponding non-disclosure offence in respect of terrorist funding is found in section 21A of TA 2000. It is a criminal offence for a person to fail to disclose information received in those circumstances where that person knows or suspects or has reasonable grounds to know or suspect that another person is involved in money laundering or terrorist funding, and is either able to identify the person concerned, or the whereabouts of any of the laundered property, or believes (or can reasonably be expected to believe) that the information will or may assist in identifying the person or the whereabouts of laundered property.

The information required to be disclosed is the identity of the person concerned if known, the whereabouts of the laundered property, so far as known, and any information leading to the identification of the person or location of the property.

Non-disclosure, tipping-off or otherwise prejudicing the course of an investigation (see further at paras **11.32–11.34**) are referred to as secondary offences.

It will have been noted that by introducing the concept of having 'reasonable grounds for knowing or suspecting', a negligence test is applied. This is on the basis that a higher standard of understanding and diligence can be expected of those in the regulated sector.

CHAPTER 11
MONEY LAUNDERING

Authorised disclosure – a defence

11.25

If a person is involved in an arrangement such as would be caught by section 328 of PCA 2002 (or the related sections), it is a defence to make an authorised disclosure, and a solicitor in this position commits no offence despite carrying through the transaction to completion if, having made proper disclosure, he or she is given 'appropriate consent' to continue to act. It is essential that all the statutory requirements are met.

The relevance of an authorised disclosure is that a solicitor may be under an obligation to carry through a transaction to completion and it might not be practicable either to prevent the transaction continuing or to attempt to interfere with its course. Further, this might serve to tip-off the money launderer. The authorised disclosure regime enables the crime prevention agencies to take appropriate steps and divests the reporting professional of criminal responsibility for any continuing involvement in the suspect transaction. The future course of the transaction is then decided by others – those to whom disclosure is made.

Timing

11.26

To constitute an authorised disclosure sufficient to amount to a defence for someone who has become involved in an activity prohibited by sections 327 to 329 of PCA 2002, disclosure must be made as soon as practicable after the information or other matter on which his or her knowledge or suspicion (or reasonable grounds for such knowledge or suspicion) was acquired.

Disclosure should be made *before* a prohibited act takes place.[1]

If disclosure is made *during* the prohibited act the solicitor must have had no relevant knowledge or suspicion when the act was started; the disclosure must be made as soon as practicable after relevant knowledge or suspicion was acquired, and the disclosure must be made on the solicitor's own initiative (that is, not for example prompted by the realisation of imminent discovery or the encouragement of another). The burden of proof will be on the accused to satisfy the court that these conditions are met, otherwise the disclosure is not an authorised disclosure and no defence is available.[2]

If disclosure is made *after* the prohibited act has taken place there must have been good reason why a disclosure was not made before the prohibited act was carried out; the disclosure must have been made as soon as practicable after the prohibited act has taken place, and the disclosure must have been made on the solicitor's own initiative. Again, the burden of proof will be on the accused to satisfy the court that these conditions are met, otherwise the disclosure is not an authorised disclosure and no defence is available.[3]

1   Section 338(2) of PCA 2002.
2   Section 338(2A).
3   Section 338(3).

Form

11.27

There are two forms of disclosure for individual solicitors. An internal report may be made in any form and manner designed by the firm (there is no statutory requirement as to this) to the firm's money laundering reporting officer (MLRO). Once such a report is made the reporting solicitor has no further responsibility and the onus is on the MLRO to consider the information and, if required, to make disclosure to the Serious Organised Crime Agency (SOCA). It is the MLRO who will commit the offence of non-disclosure if, on the facts, there is a requirement to report and the MLRO fails to do so.[1]

There is no reason why an individual solicitor cannot make disclosure direct to SOCA, and in a small firm where one partner may have responsibility for the work and another is the MLRO, the practical and all important requirement is an external report to SOCA where the facts so require. The form and manner of such a report is prescribed and the SOCA form, called a suspicious activity report, must be used. It is an offence not to report in the prescribed manner.[2]

The preferred method of reporting is online by completing the form at: www.soca.gov.uk/financialIntel/suspectActivity.html#forms.

The SOCA Financial Intelligence Helpdesk (Tel: 020 7238 8282) will give assistance on completing the form, on issues concerning consent, and in relation to the risks of tipping-off.

Otherwise, the more onerous responsibilities falling on MLROs are beyond the scope of this chapter.

1   Section 331 of PCA 2002.
2   See generally sections 337 to 338 and 339.

'Appropriate consent' to further action

11.28

In general terms, once a disclosure has been made, the disclosing party can take no further action until consent is obtained. An MLRO may give consent, but only if he or she has obtained consent from SOCA or certain time limits have expired. In reality, in a firm of solicitors, further action is determined exclusively by the reaction of SOCA.[1]

There are three possibilities:

(1)   SOCA may give consent to the transaction continuing.

(2)   If SOCA does not reply refusing consent within seven working days starting with the first working day after disclosure is made, this is treated as appropriate consent.

(3)   SOCA may reply within the same period refusing consent. This imposes a moratorium on further action which lasts for 31 days starting with the day on which notice of refusal of consent is given. If the moratorium expires without any further action being taken by SOCA this is treated as appropriate consent.

CHAPTER 11
MONEY LAUNDERING

The delay could of course cause prejudice to clients, and although compliance with the statutory obligation would be a defence to any claim solicitors may be required ultimately to justify the suspicion that prompted the report and caused the delay.[2]

1   Sections 335 and 336 of PCA 2002.
2   *Shah v HSBC Private Bank (UK) Ltd* [2010] EWCA Civ 31.

Disclosure, confidentiality and privilege

11.29

The disclosure offences under sections 330 to 332 of PCA 2002 and section 21A of TA 2000 specifically exclude any obligation to disclose information received in privileged circumstances.[1] The phrase 'privileged circumstances' is a term of art defined in section 330(10) of PCA 2002 and section 21A(8) of TA 2000 and is not identical with legal professional privilege. However the two are closely linked concepts.

As noted above, the Court of Appeal held in *Bowman v Fels* that litigation did not involve an arrangement for the purposes of sections 327 to 329 of PCA 2002. It was also held that the giving of legal advice (other than in circumstances making the legal adviser a co-conspirator or accessory to any other offence) did not constitute an arrangement and did not itself give rise to any duty of disclosure.[2]

1   Section 330(6), (7B), (10) of PCA 2002; section 21A(5) of TA 2000.
2   *Bowman v Fels* [2005] EWCA Civ 226, [2005] 1 WLR 3083, [2005] 4 All ER 609 at para 63.

11.30

Solicitors must keep the affairs of clients and former clients confidential except where disclosure is required or permitted by law,[1] but confidentiality and privilege are not synonymous, and confidentiality is overridden by the statutory duties of disclosure here being considered. The duties of disclosure are express duties imposed by statute and 'An authorised disclosure is not to be taken to breach any restriction on the disclosure of information (however imposed)'.[2]

Not all confidential information is covered by legal professional privilege, the ambit of which is quite narrow. Legal advice privilege covers all communications made in confidence between solicitors and their clients for the purpose of giving or obtaining legal advice. It does not matter whether the communication is directly between the client and his legal adviser or is made through an intermediate agent of either.[3]

Litigation privilege covers oral or written communications between a person or his lawyer (on the one hand) and third parties (on the other) or other documents created by or on behalf of the client or his lawyer, which came into existence once litigation is in contemplation or has commenced, and which came into existence for the dominant purpose of obtaining information or advice in connection with, or of conducting or aiding in the conduct of, such litigation (for example, obtaining evidence to be used in litigation or information which might lead to such evidence).[4]

A characteristic of litigation privilege is that it involves dealings between a lawyer and a third party (such as a potential witness). The characteristic of legal advice privilege is that it always relates to dealings between solicitor and client.

As has already been seen, litigation will not be likely to engage any of the primary offences.

Legal advice privilege is, expressly, limited to communications 'for the purposes of giving or obtaining legal advice'. Privilege does not attach to documents which are the products of legal advice. If one considers a typical property purchase (something that could readily engage money laundering concerns), the conveyancing documents and records of the financing of the transaction are not the subject of legal professional privilege, whereas correspondence between solicitor and client is privileged if directly related to the performance of the solicitor's professional duties as legal adviser.[5]

1   Rule 4.01 of the Solicitors' Code of Conduct 2007: see para **3.17**.
2   Sections 337(4A) and 338(4) of PCA 2002; see also section 21B(1) of TA 2000.
3   *Three Rivers District Council and others v Governor and Company of the Bank of England (No 6)* [2005] 1 AC 610 at para 50.
4   *Three Rivers District Council and others v Governor and Company of the Bank of England (No 6)* [2005] 1 AC 610 at para 102.
5   *R v Inner London Crown Court, ex p Baines* [1988] 1 QB 579, [1987] 2 WLR 549, [1987] 3 All ER 1025; and see *Three Rivers District Council and others v Governor and Company of the Bank of England (No 6)* [2005] 1 AC 610 at para 111.

Law Society guidance on disclosure

11.31

In short, legal professional privilege in both its limbs – litigation privilege and legal advice privilege – overrides the duty to disclose. The Law Society Practice Note offers valuable further guidance at paragraph 6.4 in the following terms:

'6.4.2 Advice privilege

Principle

Communications between a lawyer, acting in his capacity as a lawyer, and a client, are privileged if they are both:

● confidential;

● for the purpose of seeking legal advice from a solicitor or providing it to a client.

Scope

Communications are not privileged merely because a client is speaking or writing to you. The protection applies only to those communications which directly seek or provide advice or which are given in a legal context, that involve the lawyer using his legal skills and which are directly related to the performance of the lawyer's professional duties (*Passmore on Privilege* 2nd edition 2006).

Case law helps define what advice privilege covers.

Communications subject to advice privilege:

● a solicitor's bill of costs and statement of account (*Chant v Brown* (1852) 9 Hare 790);

CHAPTER 11
MONEY LAUNDERING

- information imparted by prospective clients in advance of a retainer will attract LPP if the communications were made for the purpose of indicating the advice required (*Minster v Priest* [1930] AC 558 per Lord Atkin at 584).

Communications not subject to advice privilege:

- notes of open court proceedings (*Parry v News Group Newspapers* (1990) 140 New Law Journal 1719) are not privileged, as the content of the communication is not confidential;

- conversations, correspondence or meetings with opposing lawyers (*Parry v News Group Newspapers* (1990) 140 New Law Journal 1719) are not privileged, as the content of the communication is not confidential;

- a client account ledger maintained in relation to the client's money (*Nationwide Building Society v Various Solicitors* [1999] PNLR 53);

- an appointments diary or time record on an attendance note, time sheet or fee record relating to a client (*R v Manchester Crown Court, ex p. Rogers* [1999] 1 WLR 832;

- conveyancing documents are not communications so not subject to advice privilege (*R v Inner London Crown Court, ex p. Baines & Baines* [1988] QB 579).

Advice within a transaction

All communications between a lawyer and his client relating to a transaction in which the lawyer has been instructed for the purpose of obtaining legal advice are covered by advice privilege, notwithstanding that they do not contain advice on matters of law and construction, provided that they are directly related to the performance by the solicitor of his professional duty as legal adviser of his client (*Three Rivers District Council and Others v Bank of England* [2004] UKHL 48 at 111).

This will mean that where you are providing legal advice in a transactional matter (such as a conveyance) the advice privilege will cover all:

- communications with;
- instructions from; and
- advice given to

the client, including any working papers and drafts prepared, as long as they are directly related to your performance of your professional duties as a legal adviser.

6.4.3 Litigation privilege

Principle

This privilege, which is wider than advice privilege, protects confidential communications made after litigation has started, or is reasonably in prospect, between either:

- a lawyer and a client;

- a lawyer and an agent, whether or not that agent is a lawyer;
- a lawyer and a third party.

These communications must be for the sole or dominant purpose of litigation, either:

- for seeking or giving advice in relation to it;
- for obtaining evidence to be used in it;
- for obtaining information leading to obtaining such evidence.

6.4.4 Important points to consider

An original document not brought into existence for these privileged purposes and so not already privileged, does not become privileged merely by being given to a lawyer for advice or other privileged purpose.

Further, where you have a corporate client, communication between you and the employees of a corporate client may not be protected by LPP if the employee cannot be considered to be 'the client' for the purposes of the retainer. As such some employees will be clients, while others will not (*Three Rivers District Council v The Governor and Company of the Bank of England (No.5)* [2003] QB 1556).

It is not a breach of LPP to discuss a matter with your nominated officer for the purposes of receiving advice on whether to make a disclosure.

6.4.5 Crime/fraud exception

LPP protects advice you give to a client on avoiding committing a crime (*Bullivant v Att-Gen of Victoria* [1901] AC 196) or warning them that proposed actions could attract prosecution (*Butler v Board of Trade* [1971] Ch 680). LPP does not extend to documents which themselves form part of a criminal or fraudulent act, or communications which take place in order to obtain advice with the intention of carrying out an offence (*R v Cox & Railton* (1884) 14 QBD 153). It is irrelevant whether or not you are aware that you are being used for that purpose (*Banque Keyser Ullman v Skandia* [1986] 1 Lloyd's Rep 336).

Intention of furthering a criminal purpose

It is not just your client's intention which is relevant for the purpose of ascertaining whether information was communicated for the furtherance of a criminal purpose. It is also sufficient that a third party intends the lawyer/client communication to be made with that purpose (e.g. where the innocent client is being used by a third party) (*R v Central Criminal Court, ex p. Francis & Francis* [1989] 1 AC 346).

Knowing a transaction constitutes an offence

If you **know** the transaction you're working on is a principal offence, you risk committing an offence yourself. In these circumstances, communications relating to such a transaction are not privileged and should be disclosed.

Suspecting a transaction constitutes an offence

If you merely suspect a transaction might constitute a money laundering offence, the position is more complex. If the suspicions are correct, communications with the client are not privileged. If the suspicions are unfounded, the communications should remain privileged and are therefore non-disclosable.

Prima facie evidence

If you suspect you are unwittingly being involved by your client in a fraud, the courts require prima facie evidence before LPP can be displaced (*O'Rourke v Darbishire* [1920] AC 581). The sufficiency of that evidence depends on the circumstances: it is easier to infer a prima facie case where there is substantial material available to support an inference of fraud. While you may decide yourself if prima facie evidence exists, you may also ask the court for directions (*Finers v Miro* [1991] 1 WLR 35).

The Crown Prosecution Service guidance for prosecutors indicates that if a solicitor forms a genuine, but mistaken, belief that the privileged circumstances exemption (see 6.5 below) applies (for example, the client misleads the solicitor and uses the advice received for a criminal purpose) the solicitor will be able to rely on the reasonable excuse defence. It is likely that a similar approach would be taken with respect to a genuine, but mistaken, belief that LPP applies.

We believe you should not make a disclosure unless you know of prima facie evidence that you are being used in the furtherance of a crime.'

Further, information obtained on disclosure of documents in litigation which gives rise to a relevant suspicion about the opposing party, but which is subject to the implied undertaking that the documents may not be used for any purpose other than the conduct of the litigation, is not subject to any duty of disclosure.[1]

But as privileged material is excluded from the duty of disclosure it is important to understand what is, and what is not, covered by legal professional privilege.

1   *Bowman v Fels* [2005] 4 All ER 609 at para 89.

Other offences

11.32

Other secondary offences relevant to solicitors involve tipping-off or otherwise prejudicing the course of an investigation.

Tipping-off

11.33

It is an offence if a person discloses (other than in strictly limited circumstances) that a disclosure has been made under section 337 or 338 if it is likely to prejudice any investigation that might be conducted following the disclosure, and if the information came to the person in the course of business in the regulated sector.[1]

It is an offence if a person discloses that an investigation into allegations that an offence has been committed under Part 7 of PCA 2002 is being contemplated or carried out, if the disclosure is likely to prejudice that investigation and the information came to the person in the course of business in the regulated sector.[2]

It is *not* an offence if a professional legal adviser makes the disclosure to a client and it is made for the purposes of dissuading the client from committing an offence.[3] It is a defence if the person making the disclosure does not know or suspect that disclosure is likely to prejudice any investigation.[4]

1 Section 333A(1) and (2) of PCA 2002. The circumstances in which disclosure may be made are set out in sections 333B, 333C and 333D of PCA 2002 and relate, in summary, to disclosures within the same organisation; between financial organisations and legal professionals in relation to a client or transaction common to both parties, if the purpose is only to prevent an offence being committed; and to disclosures to the authorities with a view to the detection, investigation or prosecution of offences.
2 Section 333A(3) of PCA 2002.
3 Section 333D(2).
4 Section 333D(3) and (4).

Prejudicing an investigation

11.34

It is an offence if a person who knows or suspects that a relevant investigation[1] is being conducted or is about to be conducted makes a disclosure that is likely to prejudice an investigation, or if that person falsifies, conceals, destroys or otherwise disposes of documents that are relevant to any investigation, or causes any of the above to take place. An investigation for these purposes is a confiscation investigation, a civil recovery investigation or a money laundering investigation.[2]

The defences are effectively identical to those in respect of the offence of tipping-off.

1 Section 342(1). The various kinds of investigations are defined in section 341.
2 Section 342(2)(a) and (b) of PCA 2002.

Law Society guidance on tipping-off and prejudicing an investigation

11.35

The Law Society's Practice Note contains helpful guidance at paragraphs 5.8.1 and 5.8.2:

'5.8.1 Offences

Tipping off – in the regulated sector

There are two tipping off offences in S333A of POCA. They apply only to business in the regulated sector.

S333A(1) – disclosing a suspicious activity report (SAR). It is an offence to disclose to a third person that a SAR has been made by any person to the police, HM Revenue and Customs, SOCA or a nominated officer, if that disclosure might prejudice any investigation that might be carried out as a result of the SAR. This offence can only be committed:

- **after** a disclosure to SOCA or a nominated officer

- if you know or suspect that by disclosing this information, you are likely to prejudice any investigation related to that SAR

- the information upon which the disclosure is based came to you in the course of business in the regulated sector.

S333A(3) – disclosing an investigation. It is an offence to disclose that an investigation into a money laundering offence is being contemplated or carried out if that disclosure is likely to prejudice that investigation. The offence can only be committed if the information on which the disclosure is based came to the person in the course of business in the regulated sector. The key point is that you can commit this offence, even where you are unaware that a SAR was submitted

Prejudicing an investigation – outside the regulated sector

Section 342(1) contains an offence of prejudicing a confiscation, civil recovery or money laundering investigation, if the person making the disclosure knows or suspects that an investigation is being, or is about to be conducted. Section 342(1) was amended by paragraph 8 of the TACT and POCA Regulations 2007. The offence in s342 (2) (a) only applies to those outside the regulated sector. The offence in s342 (2) (b) applies to everyone.

You only commit the offence in s342 (2) (a) if you knew or suspected that the disclosure would, or would be likely to prejudice any investigation.

5.8.2 Defences

Tipping off

The following disclosures are permitted:

S333B – disclosures within an undertaking or group, including disclosures to a professional legal adviser or relevant professional adviser

S333C – disclosures between institutions, including disclosures from a professional legal adviser to another professional legal adviser

S333D – disclosures to your supervisory authority

S333D(2) – disclosures made by professional legal advisers to their clients for the purpose of dissuading them from engaging in criminal conduct

A person does not commit the main tipping off offence if he does not know or suspect that a disclosure is likely to prejudice an investigation.

s333B – Disclosures within an undertaking or group etc

It is not an offence if an employee, officer or partner of a firm discloses that a SAR has been made if it is to an employee, officer or partner of the same undertaking.

A solicitor will not commit a tipping off offence if a disclosure is made to another lawyer either:

- within a different undertaking, if both parties carry on business in an EEA state

- in a country or territory that imposes money laundering requirements equivalent to the EU and both parties share common ownership, management or control.

s333C – disclosures between institutions etc

A solicitor will not commit a tipping off offence if **all** the following criteria are met:

- The disclosure is made to another lawyer in an EEA state, or one with an equivalent AML regime.

- The disclosure relates to a client or former client of both parties, or a transaction involving them both, or the provision of a service involving them both.

- The disclosure is made for the purpose of preventing a money laundering offence.

- Both parties have equivalent professional duties of confidentiality and protection of personal data.

S333D(2) – limited exception for professional legal advisers

A solicitor will not commit a tipping off offence if the disclosure is to a client and it is made for the purpose of dissuading the client from engaging in conduct amounting to an offence. This exception and the tipping off offence in s333A apply to those carrying on activities in the regulated sector.

Prejudicing an investigation

S342(4) – professional legal adviser exemption

It is a defence to a s342(1) offence that a disclosure is made by a legal adviser to a client, or a client's representative, in connection with the giving of legal advice or to any person in connection with legal proceedings or contemplated legal proceedings.

Such a disclosure will not be exempt if it is made with the intention of furthering a criminal purpose (s342(5)).'

PART 4

The regulatory and disciplinary system in practice

The Legal Ombudsman

12.1

The date 6 October 2010 was another major milestone on the road to the transformation of the regulation of legal services brought about by the Legal Services Act 2007 (LSA 2007): the Legal Ombudsman opened for business. The Legal Ombudsman (LeO), is the brand adopted by the Office for Legal Complaints, a body corporate established by section 114 of LSA 2007.

All consumer complaints about the quality of service provided by any regulated legal professional (or 'authorised person' to use the terminology of LSA 2007), are now made to the LeO. The previous fragmented system, whereby complaints about barristers went to the Bar Standards Board, those about solicitors went to the Legal Complaints Service (LCS) of the Law Society, and those about licensed conveyancers went to the Council for Licensed Conveyancers, has been swept away. A typical consequence will be that a litigation client who knows or believes that something has gone wrong, but does not know whether it is the fault of his solicitor or barrister, will not have to guess to whom he should complain, in the expectation of choosing the wrong one first. The LeO will have the task of establishing whether anything did go wrong, and, if so, who should provide redress.

The LeO starts with a clean slate; it does not take over any complaints which were already in the hands of the former organisations, which will take them to a conclusion.

The LCS will therefore continue to be relevant to solicitors for a short time but any complaints unresolved by the LCS by 31 March 2011 pass from its control (see **12.19**). For the practices and procedures of the LCS, please see Chapter 12 of the Solicitor's Handbook 2009.

The new approach

12.2

In no sense should the LeO be seen as a seamless successor to the LCS. This is no rebranding exercise. If anything the LeO is keen to distance itself as far as possible from the approach of the LCS. Aspects of the latter which will happily be consigned to history are: a determination to identify anything the client might have complained about but did not; an adversarial approach which encouraged a ping-pong of rebuttals and rejoinders; over-lengthy and often bewilderingly complex analyses unlikely to assist the average complainant; and an over-emphasis on the presence or absence of any breach of a rule.

LSA 2007 does not contain any words which are the equivalent of 'inadequate professional service' as used in Schedule 1A to the Solicitors Act 1974. The LeO has jurisdiction in relation to complaints made by clients (and limited other categories) about acts or omissions of authorised persons; the only threshold or test to be satisfied for an award or direction to be made is that it is fair and reasonable in all the circumstances of the case.[1]

The LeO will concentrate on what the client is actually complaining about, and in particular what would put it right (not for example what the client would like to happen to the solicitor). This could be as simple as an acknowledgement that something had gone wrong, and an apology or a modest amount of money to recognise non-economic or non-quantifiable loss for inconvenience, annoyance and distress, but could also be the equivalent of common law damages (in amount) for real financial loss.

The investigative approach will be inquisitorial, not adversarial; a fact-gathering exercise. The LeO will examine what happened, and what if anything went wrong; to establish this it will request information and documents from the parties. The flow of information will be to the LeO pursuant to targeted requests, and the ping-pong of charge and counter-charge will be avoided so far as possible.

The existence or otherwise of rule breaches will not be a central consideration; after all, a clear, helpful and comprehensive client care letter may be followed by appalling service, and an excellent service might be provided despite muddled initial correspondence. Rule breaches are primarily matters for the regulator, not the LeO.

Nor will the degree of fault be the measure of compensation – a very bad error could have negligible consequences, and a small mistake could be very costly; redress will relate to the consequence of the failing, and is designed to put the complainant so far as possible in the position he or she should have been in; but it is not a penalty imposed on the professional for a more or less serious mistake.

1   Section 137(1) of LSA 2007.

Structure and process in outline

12.3

Based on the experience of ombudsman schemes generally, and purely to enable sensible planning, the LeO expects that it may receive about 100,000 contacts a year, in the sense of enquiries and expressions of interest, of which about 20,000 will become legitimate complaints within the LeO's jurisdiction. Experience of other ombudsman schemes suggests that only 10 per cent of that figure will reach the point of formal adjudication, the remainder being resolved by agreement or abandonment. There are currently eight ombudsmen. The organisation is determinedly 'lay-led', though four of the appointed ombudsmen have legal qualifications; others have experience in the public sector and in consumer services. Staff numbers are expected to be about 120 initially, growing to about 350 at full strength (the full staff complement of the Legal Complaints Service was about 400).

12.4

LeO caseworkers will first determine exactly what the complaint is about and what is sought by way of redress. Assuming that the complaint is not premature because the complainant has not used the solicitors' own complaints procedures, is not out of time and is not obviously without merit (more of which below), the caseworker investigates in the manner described above and, having given both parties the opportunity to make representations, will come to a provisional decision. However, the LeO is committed to resolving complaints at the earliest possible stage, so that the process of investigation should not prevent an agreed resolution at any time.

If both parties accept the provisional decision, the matter is resolved on that basis; if either party demurs, the matter is referred to an ombudsman for final determination. Only information and documentation to be considered by the ombudsman will be disclosed to the parties, not necessarily everything gathered by the caseworker in the course of the investigation. The ombudsman may require further information and, for example, may conduct an oral hearing, although it is envisaged that these will be exceedingly rare and only justified by compelling and exceptional circumstances (particularly in the case of solicitors whose actions are generally heavily documented).

If the ombudsman comes to a conclusion which is materially different from that of the caseworker's provisional decision, it can be expected that the ombudsman would provide an opportunity to both parties to make further representations.

It is open to the complainant (only) to accept or reject an ombudsman's determination. If it is accepted by the complainant, it is binding on all parties and final.[1] If it is rejected, the role of the LeO is concluded and the complainant is free to pursue other remedies.

There is no appeal from an ombudsman's determination, so that judicial review is the only available mechanism for challenge. However, it is envisaged that if an obvious mistake has been made, an ombudsman would be prepared voluntarily to reconsider the matter.

Provisional decisions and ombudsman determinations are narrative in form and seek to avoid the black and white concepts which involve 'upholding' the complaint or the opposite. It may be difficult or inappropriate to say whether a multiple complaint, of which one element was found to justify criticism, was 'upheld'. Rather, the decision recites what the caseworker or ombudsman has considered to have gone wrong and what the redress should be.

Compensation for non-financial loss is in modest amounts: the low hundreds of pounds.

1   Section 140(4) of LSA 2007.

The overlap with negligence

12.5

The limit of compensation available through the LeO is £30,000 (considered in more detail below). This is sufficiently large to attract many cases which might otherwise have been pursued as negligence claims. A complaint to the LeO involves no expense and no adverse costs risk for a complainant.

The LeO will not reject complaints simply because they could be pursued as negligence claims. However, neither will they be considered as if they were negligence claims. As in all matters, the question will be whether it is fair and reasonable for redress to be provided in all the circumstances, in consequence of an act or omission by an authorised person. Awards may be made by the LeO whether or not the complainant may have a cause of action against the authorised person in negligence.[1]

It must follow that there could be circumstances in which complainants might achieve a higher award of damages by court action than could be directed by the LeO, and in accepting an award capped at £30,000, might lose what might have been available in another jurisdiction. If an LeO award is accepted and becomes binding, it is full satisfaction; no further proceedings may be taken in relation to the subject matter (see **12.17**) and the potential for a higher award of damages will be lost. On the other hand, litigation is risky and expensive. It is essentially a choice for the consumer. It can be expected that in appropriate cases the LeO may consider it prudent to remind the complainant of the options available where obviously high levels of loss are claimed to have been sustained, but the complaint will not be rejected; nor can it be expected that the complainant will, for example, be required to take advice before pursuing a complaint or accepting a determination.

1   Section 137(5) of LSA 2007.

Fee structure

12.6

No fee is payable by the complainant to the LeO. No fee is payable by the authorised person who is the subject of complaint if the complaint is abandoned or withdrawn. If the complaint is resolved by any other means, the authorised person is normally liable to pay a fee, called a case fee, but will not be liable if both of two conditions are satisfied: first, that the complaint is settled, resolved or determined in favour of the authorised person; and, second, that the LeO is satisfied that the authorised person took all reasonable steps to try to resolve the complaint under his or her own complaints handling system.

In all other cases, the authorised person is liable to pay the case fee, currently £400 for each complaint. However, in each financial year of the LeO two complaints may be made against an authorised person without a fee being payable. The £400 (if it is payable in principle by reference to the manner in which the complaint is resolved) is only payable for the third and any subsequent complaints made in the same year against the same authorised person, and a matter is only a 'complaint' in this sense if it is within the jurisdiction of the LeO.[1]

1   Rules 6.1 to 6.4 of the LeO Scheme Rules 2010.

Publicity

12.7

The LeO has published what is described as the first stage in its consultation process about its policy for publishing its decisions, with a deadline for responses of 23 December 2010. This will be followed by a second consultation with specific options being put forward. At present the LeO has no firm proposals; it also intends to commission its own research. It is thus impracticable to address this subject in this edition. It can only be said with confidence that there will certainly be some level of publicity, and the crucial question for practitioners is the extent to which individual firms or lawyers may be named. It is clear from the consultation that LeO is alive to the right issues, including the danger of disproportionate consequences of publicity, and that some areas of legal practice may be more vulnerable to complaints than others. It remains a possibility that authorised persons will only be 'named and shamed' if a certain level of justified complaint is encountered, and not, perhaps, for an isolated failing.

The scheme rules in more detail

Who can complain[1]

12.8

A complainant must be an individual, or any of the following:

- a small business: a micro-enterprise as defined in European Recommendation 2003/361/EC of 6 May 2003 (broadly, an enterprise with fewer than 10 staff and a turnover or balance sheet value not exceeding €2 million);

- a charity with an annual income less than £1 million;

- a club, association or society with an annual income less than £1 million;

- a trustee of a trust with a net asset value less than £1 million;

- a personal representative or the residuary beneficiaries of an estate where a person with a complaint died before referring it to the ombudsman scheme.

If a complainant who has referred a complaint to the LeO dies or is otherwise unable to act, the complaint may be continued by anyone authorised by law (for example the executor of a complainant who has died or someone with a lasting power of attorney from a complainant who is incapable or the residuary beneficiaries of the estate of a complainant who has died).

A complainant must not have been, at the time of the act or omission to which the complaint relates, a public body (or acting for a public body) in relation to the services complained about, or an authorised person who procured the services complained about on behalf of someone else. For example, where the complaint is about a barrister who was instructed by a solicitor on behalf of a consumer, the consumer may complain but the solicitor may not.

A complainant may authorise someone else in writing (including an authorised person) to act on behalf of the complainant in pursuing a complaint, but the LeO remains free to contact the complainant direct where it considers that to be appropriate.

1   See rules 2.1 to 2.5 of the LeO Scheme Rules 2010.

What can be complained about[1]

12.9

There are no categories of complaint that are excluded. The complaint must relate to an act or omission by someone who was an authorised person at the relevant time.

CHAPTER 12
THE LEGAL OMBUDSMAN

An act or omission by an employee is usually treated as an act or omission by the employer, whether or not the employer knew or approved. An act or omission by a partner is usually treated as an act or omission by the partnership, unless the complainant knew (at the time of the act or omission) that the partner had no authority to act for the partnership.[2]

The act or omission does not have to relate to a reserved legal activity; nor to have occurred after LSA 2007 came into force. The complaint must relate to services which the authorised person provided to the complainant or to another authorised person who procured them on behalf of the complainant, or to – or as – a personal representative or trustee where the complainant is a beneficiary of the estate or trust.

A complaint is not affected by any change in the composition of a partnership or other unincorporated body. Where a firm or business closes and another business succeeds to the whole of it, or substantially the whole of it, the successor body becomes responsible for the acts and omissions of and complaints against the original firm.[3]

1   Rules 2.6 to 2.10 of the LeO Scheme Rules 2010.
2   Section 131 of LSA 2007.
3   Section 132 of LSA 2007.

Jurisdiction and time limits

12.10

Ordinarily, a complainant cannot complain to the LeO unless the complainant has first used the authorised person's complaints procedure.[1] However, this does not apply if the complaint has not been resolved to the complainant's satisfaction within eight weeks of being made to the authorised person, or if an ombudsman considers that there are exceptional reasons to consider the complaint sooner, or without it having been made first to the authorised person, or where in-house resolution is not possible due to irretrievable breakdown in the relationship between the lawyer and the person making the complaint. For example, an ombudsman may decide that the ombudsman service should consider the complaint where the authorised person has refused to consider it, or where delay would harm the complainant.[2]

Ordinarily, a complainant must refer a complaint to the LeO within six months of the date of the authorised person's written response (within the firm's complaints handling system), but only if that written response prominently included an explanation that the LeO service was available if the complainant remained dissatisfied and full contact details for the LeO were given, together with a warning that the complaint must be referred to the LeO within six months.[3]

A complainant must also generally refer a complaint to the LeO within one year from the act or omission complained of, or within one year from the point at which the complainant should reasonably have known that there was cause for complaint without taking advice from a third party, whichever is later.[4]

If an ombudsman considers that there are exceptional circumstances (for example a delay caused by illness), he or she may extend any of these time limits to the extent that he or she considers fair.[5]

1   Section 126 of LSA 2007.

2   Rules 4.1 to 4.3 and 5.3 of the LeO Scheme Rules 2010.
3   Rule 4.4.
4   Rule 4.5.
5   Rules 4.7 and 4.8.

Preliminary consideration and summary dismissal

12.11

If an ombudsman considers that all or part of the complaint is not within the LeO's jurisdiction, or is out of time, or may be one that should be dismissed without considering its merits, the ombudsman will give the complainant an opportunity to make representations before deciding. If an authorised person challenges the complaint on the same grounds, the ombudsman will give all parties an opportunity to make representations. In either case, the ombudsman will then make a decision and give reasons.[1]

An ombudsman may (but does not have to) dismiss all or part of a complaint without considering its merits if, in his or her opinion:

- the complaint does not have any reasonable prospect of success, or is frivolous or vexatious;

- the complainant has not suffered (and is unlikely to suffer) financial loss, distress, inconvenience or other detriment;

- the authorised person has already offered fair and reasonable redress in relation to the circumstances alleged by the complainant and the offer is still open for acceptance;

- the complainant has previously complained about the same issue to the LeO or a predecessor complaints scheme (unless the ombudsman considers that material new evidence, likely to affect the outcome, only became available to the complainant afterwards);

- a comparable independent complaints (or costs-assessment) scheme or a court has already dealt with the same issue;

- a comparable independent complaints (or costs-assessment) scheme or a court is dealing with the same issue, unless those proceedings are first stayed, by the agreement of all parties or by a court order, so that the LeO can deal with the issue;

- it would be more suitable for the issue to be dealt with by a court, by arbitration or by another complaints (or costs-assessment) scheme;

- the issue concerns an authorised person's decision when exercising a discretion under a will or trust;

- the issue concerns an authorised person's failure to consult a beneficiary before exercising a discretion under a will or trust, where there is no legal obligation to consult;

- the issue involves someone else who has not complained and the ombudsman considers that it would not be appropriate to deal with the issue without that person's consent;

- it is not practicable to investigate the issue fairly because of the time which has elapsed since the act or omission;

- the issue concerns an act or omission outside England and Wales and the circumstances do not have a sufficient connection with England and Wales;

- there are other compelling reasons why it is inappropriate for the issue to be dealt with under the ombudsman scheme.[2]

Exceptionally, an ombudsman may refer a discrete legal question to a court if the resolution of the question is necessary to resolve the matter, but it is not more suitable for the court to deal with the whole dispute. The authorised person may request that a matter be considered as a test case by a court and an ombudsman may accommodate that request by dismissing the complaint to enable proceedings to be taken, but only on an undertaking that the authorised person will pay the complainant's costs and on such other terms as the ombudsman considers appropriate.[3]

An ombudsman may also refer the complaint to another complaints scheme in appropriate circumstances.[4]

1   Rules 5.4 to 5.6 of the LeO Scheme Rules 2010.
2   Rule 5.7.
3   Rules 5.8 to 5.11.
4   Rule 5.12.

Procedure, evidence and hearings

12.12

The LeO may request the assistance of others, including approved regulators, in the investigation and consideration of complaints.[1] The LeO is not restricted by the terms of the complaint as to who is investigated. If appropriate the LeO will investigate another authorised person as a joint respondent.[2]

Efforts will be made to resolve all complaints at the earliest possible stage by any appropriate means, including informal resolution.[3] If an investigation is necessary, a caseworker will make a provisional decision after the parties have been given an opportunity to make representations, and will set a time limit for response. If no party disagrees within the specified time limit, the complaint may be treated as resolved by the provisional decision. If any party disagrees, the matter is referred to an ombudsman for final determination.[4]

1   Rule 5.14 of the LeO Scheme Rules 2010.
2   Rules 5.15 and 5.16.
3   Rule 5.17.
4   Rules 5.19 and 5.20.

12.13

An apology will not of itself be treated as an admission of liability. An ombudsman cannot require anyone to produce any information or document which that person could not be compelled to produce in High Court civil proceedings. An ombudsman may:

- give directions as to the issues on which evidence is required and the way in which evidence should be given; may take into account evidence from approved regulators or the Legal Services Board or from other third parties;

- treat any finding of fact in disciplinary proceedings against the authorised person as conclusive;

- include or exclude evidence that would be inadmissible or admissible in court;

- accept information in confidence where he or she considers that this is both necessary and fair;

- make a determination on the basis of what has been supplied;

- draw inferences from any party's failure to provide information requested; and

- dismiss a complaint if the complainant fails to provide information that has been requested.[1]

An ombudsman may require a party to attend to give evidence and produce documents at a specified time and place. An ombudsman may require a party to produce any information or document that the ombudsman considers necessary for the determination of a complaint; may specify the time within which this must be done; may specify the manner or form in which the information is to be provided; and may require the person producing the document to explain it. If the document is not produced, an ombudsman may require the relevant party to say, to the best of his or her knowledge and belief, where the document is.

If an authorised person fails to comply with a requirement to produce information or a document, the ombudsman will tell the relevant approved regulator and may require that approved regulator to tell the ombudsman what action it will take (and may report any failure by the approved regulator to the Legal Services Board). If any party fails to comply with a requirement to produce information or a document, the ombudsman may also enforce the requirement through the High Court.[2]

An ombudsman may fix (and may extend) a time limit for any stage of the investigation, consideration and determination of a complaint. If any party fails to comply with such a time limit, the ombudsman may proceed with the investigation, consideration and determination; and draw inferences from the failure. Where the failure is by the complainant, the ombudsman may dismiss the complaint; or where the failure is by the authorised person, may include compensation for any inconvenience caused to the complainant in any award.[3]

1 Rules 5.21 to 5.24 of the LeO Scheme Rules 2010.
2 Sections 147 to 149 of LSA 2007; rules 5.25 to 5.30 of the LeO Scheme Rules 2010.
3 Rules 5.31 and 5.32 of the LeO Scheme Rules 2010.

12.14

An ombudsman will only hold an oral hearing where he or she considers that the complaint cannot be fairly determined without one. In deciding whether (and how) to hold a hearing, the ombudsman will take account of article 6 of the European Convention on Human Rights. A party who wishes to request a hearing must do so in writing setting out the issues he or she wishes to raise and (if appropriate) any reasons why the hearing should be in private. The ombudsman will consider whether the issues are material, whether a hearing should take place and whether any hearing should be in public or private. A hearing may be held by any means the ombudsman considers appropriate in the circumstances, including (for example) by telephone.[1]

1 Rules 5.33 to 5.35 of the LeO Scheme Rules 2010.

Determinations and awards

12.15

An ombudsman will determine a complaint by reference to what is, in his or her opinion, fair and reasonable in all the circumstances of the case. In determining what is fair and reasonable, the ombudsman will take into account (but is not bound by) what a court might decide, the relevant approved regulator's rules of conduct at the time of the act or omission, and what the ombudsman considers to have been good practice at the time.[1]

Awards and determinations may include any one or more of the following directions to the authorised person in favour of the complainant:

- to apologise;
- to pay compensation of a specified amount for loss suffered;
- to pay interest on that compensation from a specified time;
- to pay compensation of a specified amount for inconvenience or distress caused;
- to ensure (and pay for) putting right any specified error, omission or other deficiency;
- to take (and pay for) any specified action in the interests of the complainant;
- to pay a specified amount for costs incurred by the complainant in pursuing the complaint (however, as a complainant does not usually need assistance to pursue a complaint with the LeO, awards of costs are likely to be rare);
- to limit the authorised person's fees to a specified amount.[2]

If the determination contains a direction to limit fees to a specified amount, it may also require the authorised person to ensure that: all or part of any amount paid is refunded; interest is paid on that refund from a specified time; all or part of the fees are remitted; the right to recover the fees is waived, wholly or to a specified extent; or any combination of these.[3]

An ombudsman may set a time limit for the authorised person to comply with a determination, and may set different time limits for different parts of a determination. Any interest payable under the determination will be at the rate specified in the determination or, if not specified, at the rate payable on High Court judgment debts.[4]

1 Section 137 of LSA 2007; rules 5.36 and 5.37 of the LeO Scheme Rules 2010.
2 Rules 5.38 and 5.39 of the LeO Scheme Rules 2010.
3 Rule 5.40.
4 Rules 5.41 and 5.42.

12.16

There is a limit of £30,000 on the total value that can be awarded on the determination of a complaint in respect of the total of: compensation for loss suffered; compensation for inconvenience or distress caused; the reasonable cost of putting right any error, omission or other deficiency; and the reasonable cost of any specified action in the interests of the complainant. If (before or after the determination is issued) it appears that the total value will exceed £30,000, an ombudsman may direct which part or parts of the award are to take preference.[1]

The £30,000 limit does not apply to: an apology; interest on specified compensation for loss suffered; any specified amount for costs the complainant incurred in pursuing the complaint; the financial consequences of limiting fees to a specified amount; or interest on fees to be refunded.[2]

1   Section 138 of LSA 2007; rules 5.43 and 5.44 of the LeO Scheme Rules 2010.
2   Rule 5.45 of the LeO Scheme Rules 2010.

12.17

The determination is in writing, signed by the ombudsman. It must give reasons and require the complainant to notify the ombudsman, before a specified time, whether the complainant accepts or rejects the determination. The ombudsman may require any acceptance or rejection to be in writing, but will have regard to any reason why the complainant may be unable to communicate in writing. The ombudsman will send copies of the determination to the parties and the relevant approved regulator. If the complainant tells the ombudsman that he or she accepts the determination it is binding on the parties and final.[1]

Once a determination becomes binding and final, neither party may start or continue legal proceedings in respect of the subject matter of the complaint.[2]

If the complainant does not tell the ombudsman, before the specified time, that he or she accepts the determination, it is treated as rejected. But if the complainant later tells the ombudsman that he or she accepts the determination, and the complainant has not previously told the ombudsman that he or she rejects the determination, and if the ombudsman is satisfied that there are sufficient reasons why the complainant did not respond in time, the determination will be treated as accepted, final and binding. If the complainant does not respond before the specified time, the ombudsman will notify the parties and the relevant approved regulator of the outcome, describing the provisions concerning late acceptance. Whether the complainant accepts or rejects the determination, the ombudsman will notify the parties and the relevant approved regulator of the outcome.[3]

If a determination is rejected (or treated as rejected) by the complainant, it has no effect on the legal rights of any party.[4]

1   Section 140(1) to (4) of LSA 2007; rules 5.46 to 5.49 of the LeO Scheme Rules 2010.
2   Section 140(11) of LSA 2007; rule 5.50 of the LeO Scheme Rules 2010.
3   Rules 5.51 to 5.53 of the LeO Scheme Rules 2010.
4   Rule 5.54 of the LeO Scheme Rules 2010.

Enforcement and misconduct

12.18

A binding and final determination can be enforced through the High Court or a county court by the complainant. The LeO may also enforce a determination through the courts if the complainant agrees and the LeO considers it appropriate in all the circumstances. A court which makes an enforcement order must inform the LeO and the LeO will then inform the relevant approved regulator, may require the approved regulator to tell the LeO what action it will take, and may report any failure by the approved regulator to the LSB.[1]

At any stage after the LeO receives a complaint, if the LeO considers that the complaint discloses any alleged misconduct about which the relevant approved regulator should consider action against the authorised person, or if the LeO considers that an authorised person has failed to cooperate with the LeO, the LeO will tell the relevant approved regulator, may require the approved regulator to tell the LeO what action it will take, and may report any failure by the approved regulator to the LSB. If an approved regulator is informed about a matter involving potential misconduct, the LeO will tell the complainant that this has been done.[2] The duty to report potential misconduct is not affected by any withdrawal or abandonment of the complaint.

The LeO will disclose to an approved regulator any information that the regulator requests to enable it to investigate alleged misconduct or to fulfil its regulatory functions, if the LeO considers that the information is reasonably required, and the approved regulator has regard to any right of privacy of any complainant involved.[3]

1   Sections 141 and 142 of LSA 2007; rules 5.56 to 5.58 of the LeO Scheme Rules 2010.
2   Sections 143 and 146 of LSA 2007; rules 5.59 and 5.60 of the LeO Scheme Rules 2010.
3   Rule 5.61 of the LeO Scheme Rules 2010.

The Legal Services Ombudsman

12.19

The Legal Services Ombudsman (LSO), is not to be confused with the Office for Legal Complaints or the Legal Ombudsman previously described in this Chapter. By section 159 of LSA 2007 the office of the LSO is abolished. For the historical role and procedures of the LSO, please refer to Chapter 12 of the Solicitor's Handbook 2009.

In the same way that the Legal Complaints Service will continue in existence for some months (see **12.1**) to resolve any matters still in the system at 6 October 2010, so the LSO will continue to have a reviewing role for a short while. With effect from 1 January 2011, the LSO ceases to have the power to recommend or require the Legal Complaints Service (or the Solicitors Regulation Authority) to reconsider a complaint.

Any matter that was referred to the LCS before 6 October 2010 which is still unresolved on 1 April 2011 is treated as if a valid referral had been made to the LSO and is investigated to a conclusion by that office, so that 31 March 2011 is the final day for the LCS, even if there are still matters that have not been concluded.

Any matter still unresolved in the hands of the LSO on 31 December 2011 must be treated as if it is a complaint within the jurisdiction of the LeO and will be taken over and investigated by the LeO accordingly.

It is understood that the offices and infrastructure of the LSO will be closed in about April 2011, and that an ombudsman of the LeO may be appointed to fulfil the LSO's residual functions, so that in practice the LeO's systems and policies are likely to be influential in any matter that was in the hands of the LCS but remains unresolved on 1 April 2011.

CHAPTER 13

The Solicitors Regulation Authority – conduct investigations and SRA-imposed sanctions

The new landscape

13.1

At the date of publication of this edition, the SRA is in the middle of a period of intense and fundamental change. A complete new rule book incorporating a new Code of Conduct is expected to be published in its final form in April 2011, to come into force in October 2011. Major changes are being made to the organisational structure; IT systems are being completely modernised, one consequence of which will be that the profession will have most of its administrative dealings with the SRA online: practising certificate and recognition applications will be made online from July 2011. Because outcomes-focused regulation (OFR) has been embraced, the whole manner in which the SRA will interface with and supervise the regulated community will change. And in addition to all of that, the SRA has new powers to impose sanctions (see **13.2**).

Because these changes have by no means been completed, the future cannot be predicted with certainty, in particular how exactly OFR will affect the manner in which the profession experiences contact with its regulator. In the successive editions of *The Solicitor's Handbook* this chapter has been intended to explain to solicitors what they are likely to experience in regulatory and disciplinary investigations undertaken by the SRA. We explain here the present systems, and how they may be expected to change over the course of 2011.

13.2

Until the summer of 2010 the only regulatory 'sanction' that the SRA could impose upon a solicitor was a reprimand or severe reprimand. This was kept confidential between the solicitor and the SRA. The Legal Services (LSA) 2007 introduced a new section 44D into the SA 1974. This provided a statutory power for the SRA to impose fines of up to £2,000, or a written rebuke, upon solicitors. Parliament's intention was to remove the less serious cases from the Tribunal, and to allow the SRA to deal with them more speedily and cheaply instead. The worrying feature for solicitors is that the confidentiality of the process has been swept away. The SRA may publish details of any action it has taken under section 44D if it considers this to be in the public interest.

The new statutory powers could not be exercised until the SRA had made Rules in accordance with the terms of section 44D, which also required consultation with the Tribunal about the content of the Rules. There was considerable delay in the promulgation of the Rules, caused largely by disagreement over the standard of proof to be adopted by the SRA in making disciplinary decisions. Eventually the SRA (which wanted to use the civil standard against the wishes of the Tribunal and the Master of the Rolls) prevailed, and the LSB approved the SRA (Disciplinary Procedure) Rules 2010 (2010 Rules), which commenced on 1 June 2010. The Rules do not apply to any matters where the relevant act or omission occurred before that date.[1] Accordingly, it is necessary to describe both the pre- and post-June 2010 regimes.

The importance of the new statutory powers cannot be over-stated. By section 44D(10), the Lord Chancellor may by order increase the £2,000 limit to such other amount as may be specified in the order. Furthermore, the SRA has a power to impose an unlimited fine upon alternative business structures (ABSs) when they become licensed as from October 2011. These are undoubtedly powerful new regulatory weapons in the armoury of the SRA.

The issue of publicity is a vexed one. On the one hand, as a statutory regulator, regulating in the public interest, the SRA wishes to operate in an open and transparent manner. On the other, the effect of publicity for the individual solicitor may be wholly disproportionate to the regulatory breach that occurred. In the internet age, such information is easily obtained by a prospective client, and is bound to have a deterrent effect upon the prospective client's intention to instruct the solicitor in question. It is to be hoped that the Law Society on behalf of the profession, and the SRA, can agree ground rules or protocols as to what decisions should be published, and for how long. It would make good sense for low-level disciplinary sanctions to be removed from a solicitor's regulatory record after a specified period.

Section 44E of SA 1974 confers a right of appeal upon a solicitor who is fined or rebuked under section 44D, if a decision has been made to publish the rebuke. The appeal lies to the Tribunal. It remains to be seen whether such protection proves to be popular with the profession. An appeal to the Tribunal itself carries the risk of unwelcome publicity, and the current costs practice in the Tribunal, summarised at paras **15.40** to **15.42**, may provide an additional deterrent. There is a compelling case for the Tribunal to depart from the *Baxendale-Walker* approach when sitting as a court of appeal, and to adopt the general principle that the successful solicitor-appellant should ordinarily be awarded costs.

Before dealing with the new statutory regime, it is necessary to describe the investigatory processes of the SRA.

1   Rule 12 of the SRA (Disciplinary Procedure) Rules 2010.

SRA investigations generally

13.3

From the perception of the solicitor an SRA investigation is likely to commence in one of three ways:

(1)   as a result of a complaint by a client or other party (for example a client's complaint dealt with by the Legal Ombudsman (LeO), which includes a

conduct element such as delay or conflict of interest, or a complaint by other solicitors of a failure to comply with an undertaking, or misconduct in litigation[1]);

(2)   as a consequence of a visit by the Practice Standards Unit; or

(3)   by notice of a forensic investigation by the SRA.

Only the first of these options involves a third party; in the other two situations only the SRA as the regulator is involved.

In the case of third party complaints the current practice is to treat the source of the complaint as an informant, rather than a complainant. It is a matter for the caseworker to decide whether and to what extent the informant is kept advised and informed. This will usually be done only where the informant can continue to contribute to the investigation by providing further information (for example) or where the informant has a legitimate personal interest in the outcome, as where the informant is complaining about non-compliance with an undertaking which is causing him prejudice.

The Practice Standards Unit (PSU) of the SRA has historically carried out 'monitoring visits' to firms which are targeted on the basis of risk assessment. These visits could be made as a result of the firm's profile or complaints history, but could also be genuinely random. They have been, broadly speaking, pastoral in nature as the practice standards adviser engages in a dialogue with the firm to encourage good practice and the improvement of office systems as well as, more directly, regulatory compliance. The purpose of the visit is not expressly to investigate the firm, in a hostile sense, but to maintain standards and give advice. Nevertheless, if any issues of professional conduct arise that are considered to merit a more formal investigation, that will inevitably follow.

The role of the PSU is likely to change dramatically, as a consequence of OFR. The historic approach has been to 'tick the boxes' in relation to the firm's systems; for example in relation to arrangements with introducers, client care issues, and accounts and business management. A 'tick-box' approach is alien to the concept of OFR and a risk-based approach to regulation. The probability is that while something akin to historic PSU visits will continue to occur, they will be specifically targeted on identified problem areas that represent perceived risks to the public: for example, in a firm heavily involved in conveyancing, the manner in which mortgage fraud risks are monitored and managed.

---

1   Such complaints are sometimes made by judges who have tried cases in which a solicitor has apparently misconducted him- or herself.

Forensic investigations

13.4

A forensic investigation is not pastoral in character: whereas monitoring visits have typically taken a few days, a forensic investigation can take weeks or months, with investigators staying for many days at a time. A forensic investigation is never random; the investigators will have specific concerns or specific reasons for their visit. Until quite recently (2009–10) reasons were never given (although they could usually be deduced). Now some reason for the inquiry will usually be given, unless it is believed that this will prejudice the investigation.

Solicitors are under an obligation to deal with the SRA in an open, prompt and co-operative way.[1] They must also promptly comply with any notice from the SRA in writing requiring the production of documents and 'all information and explanations requested' or the provision of consents and permissions necessary for investigators to obtain information from clients, staff, banks or other financial institutions, or the supply of copies of documents or documents in electronic form.[2]

Refusal to co-operate either generally or in relation to specific requests is most unwise, at least in the absence of strong expert advice that the investigators are exceeding their powers or otherwise acting unlawfully. The SRA has the ultimate deterrent that if there is a failure to comply with rule 20.08 (and/or the comparable rule 34 of the Solicitors' Accounts Rules 1998) the powers of intervention will have arisen. No solicitor could prudently take that risk.

However, an obligation to provide information promptly is not an obligation to do so instantly, or without proper consideration or advice (if appropriate); nor is it unreasonable in a situation of complexity or apparent seriousness to obtain clarification of requests by seeking them in writing. Investigators are fully aware of this and should not object.

1 Rule 20.05 of the Solicitors' Code of Conduct 2007.
2 Rule 20.08.

13.5

Approximately half of all forensic investigations result in no action, but, at the other extreme, when the public interest requires, they can result in intervention into the solicitor's practice without notice (as where apparent dishonesty is revealed).

Other than in the most extreme case of obvious dishonesty, when an urgent intervention will occur after a very brief inspection, forensic investigations will begin with an initial fact-finding exercise concerned with basic details about the practice and partners (questionnaires are provided for completion in advance). Then will come investigations into accounts, office systems and business arrangements (such as agreements with introducers) and client files over a period of time, requests being made for further information and explanation as matters arise. The investigation concludes with a final interview at which the investigators summarise all matters identified as causing apparent concern (and on which they require a more formal response).

That interview is not under caution, and there is no obligation to give a caution, as this is not a criminal investigation. However, it has some of the characteristics of a police interview in that it can be expected to be searching, challenging and potentially hostile in terms of the style of questioning. Admissions that rules have been broken may be expressly required or invited. The preferred option is to record the whole interview on a digital medium, but this is not compulsory (and can result in large and potentially unwieldy transcripts).

The investigators are unlikely to be drawn on the question that virtually every solicitor will ask: 'What is going to happen?'. They ordinarily say that they will submit a report that will be disclosed to you and you will be given an opportunity to comment, but are unlikely to be persuaded to go further. In the case of an urgent intervention the report will not be disclosed until after the intervention has occurred.

The caseworker's investigation

13.6

Whether a matter arrives in a caseworker's hands as a direct complaint, as a referral from the Practice Standards Unit or as a result of a Forensic Investigations Report (an FI Report), the procedure that follows is the same. The process, which has largely been unchanged for a period of years, is now regulated by rules 4 to 6 of the 2010 Rules.

The caseworker, who may or may not be legally qualified, writes to the individual solicitor, or to the senior partner or an equivalent person if a number of individuals are affected (in which case the request will be made that it be confirmed that the response is on behalf of all), requesting a formal explanation of the matters which the caseworker has identified as requiring an explanation. The letter will contain warnings that any reply may be used in disciplinary proceedings, and that a failure to provide a sufficient and satisfactory explanation may result in regulation 3 of the SRA Practising Regulations 2009 and the regime relating to conditional practising certificates coming into force (see para **14.3**). Information concerning the Solicitors' Assistance Scheme is provided with the standard letter.

The letter will usually require a reply within 14 days. Some leeway is likely to be available, but it is wise to make progress as best you can, and then to explain that there are specific reasons why more time is needed, rather than to complain that the deadline is impossible and that you need (for example) a minimum of three months.

There is no doubt that regulatory investigations can be exceptionally demanding and stressful, and may well interfere materially with your ability to carry on your practice. Specialist advice and assistance can assist, both in ensuring that efforts are appropriately targeted, and in ensuring balance and objectivity.

The process of interrogation by correspondence may continue with further requests for clarification or supplementary questions. The caseworker may consult with the forensic investigators or seek further information from the informant.

Hitherto, having carried out a further investigation, the caseworker has produced a report (see **13.8**). The SRA is currently experimenting with an alternative to the present system whereby a forensic investigator produces a report, which is handed to a caseworker, who then conducts a further investigation by correspondence. The process, described as the 'single report', involves the forensic investigator carrying the whole process through to adjudication, if necessary with the benefit of advice from the SRA's legal department – a process not unlike that of the police and CPS and likely to owe something to it.

In this process solicitors may encounter a combination of personal visits, on-site investigations and interviews, and subsequent correspondence in which specific matters of concern may be raised or allegations made by the same investigator or investigators. However, this is not intended to result in any change in the opportunities for regulated persons to make representations in the course of the investigation and adjudication process.

Investigatory powers

13.7

The SRA has the power to require production of the full file or files, and other information from any person or body it regulates. If this is not volunteered, it can use statutory powers to compel the production of files and use the powers of intervention to enforce that requirement.[1]

If a notice has been given under section 44B of SA 1974, the SRA may by notice under section 44BA require the person notified to attend at a specified time and place to provide an explanation of any information provided or document produced pursuant to the notice. Because this also involves the use of intervention powers, non-compliance is a criminal offence and the costs of the process are a debt due from the individual to the SRA, unless the court orders otherwise.[2] It is a criminal offence deliberately to interfere in this investigation process, or deliberately or recklessly to give false or misleading information.[3]

This is a powerful and potentially oppressive weapon. A solicitor may be required to attend the SRA's offices at his own expense, to be subjected to interrogation and under an obligation to answer questions, with criminal sanctions for failing to cooperate or for providing inaccurate answers. The investigators are likely to be accompanied by their own legal adviser. While a solicitor (or other regulated person) is entitled to be accompanied by, for example, a specialist adviser, the latter may be excluded at the discretion of the SRA investigators if they conclude that the adviser's presence is obstructing the inquiry. And the solicitor may be required to pay the costs of the SRA (including its legal costs) incurred in the section 44BA investigation.

It is devoutly to be hoped that this process will be used sparingly and only in exceptional circumstances. It is understood that at the time of going to press it has only been used twice.

The SRA may apply to the High Court for an order directing the provision of information and documents material to a regulatory investigation held by a person or body that is not regulated by the SRA.[4]

The SRA may also in effect require solicitors and law firms to investigate themselves. Under rule 20.05(3) of the Solicitors' Code of Conduct 2007 (as amended), if the SRA gives notice requiring such action to be taken in relation to a matter specified in the notice, you must act promptly to:

- investigate whether any person may have a claim for redress resulting from an act or omission of yours;

- provide the SRA with a report on the outcome of such an investigation, identifying persons who may have such a claim;

- notify such persons that they may have a right of redress against you, providing them with information as to the nature of the possible claim, about the firm's complaints procedures and about the LeO; and

- where you have identified a person who may have a claim for redress, ensure that the matter is dealt with under the firm's complaints procedures as if that person had made a complaint. This somewhat remarkable provision was designed, during the course of the Legal Services Bill through Parliament, to give the SRA additional powers to deal with firms caught up in the miners' compensation scheme in a manner thought to justify criticism. It enables the SRA to direct firms to act in a way likely to lead to an identified class of client being compensated en masse.

1   Section 44B of SA 1974. See also 'limited intervention' at para **16.22**. Rule 20.08 of the Solicitors' Code of Conduct 2007 imposes a duty to co-operate in this process.
2   Section 44BA(3) and paragraphs 9(3) and 13 of Schedule 1 to SA 1974.
3   Section 44BC.
4   Section 44BB.

The report stage

13.8

At the conclusion of the investigation process the caseworker has several options. He or she may decide that there are no grounds for action, or that although there have been errors or rule breaches they are not such as to justify a referral to an adjudicator. In this event a 'letter of advice' will be sent, which identifies the fault found and advises against repetition, but confirms that there is no sanction. Such a result will however remain on the 'record' of the individuals affected in case it should ever be relevant in the future.

Items on a solicitor's record are never 'spent'; they remain forever, but can of course become irrelevant in practice due to lapse of time.

If the matter is to go forward to adjudication the caseworker prepares a report which is disclosed to the affected solicitor(s)[1] and (optionally) to the informant, if any, at the caseworker's discretion. This will set out the facts in summary, identify the relevant issues, state the caseworker's conclusions and make recommendations to the adjudicator. This does not in any way bind the adjudicator but gives a clear indication to the solicitor as to what he or she faces so that focused representations can be made on the report. The solicitor might of course agree with the recommendations.

The caseworker may recommend that some or all issues should be resolved in favour of the solicitor and no action taken. In respect of investigations into matters occurring before 1 June 2010, the option remains of an in-house sanction consisting of a reprimand or severe reprimand, if fault is found but the matter does not warrant disciplinary proceedings. This is informal in character in that such sanctions are not in pursuance of any statutory power and amount to an expression of opinion by the regulator. With effect from 1 June 2010, in respect of regulatory breaches on or after that date, the SRA acquired new powers to impose a statutory rebuke, to require the payment of a fine not exceeding £2,000 to be forfeit to the Crown, and to publicise such decisions.

Yet more seriously for the solicitor, the recommendation may be that he or she should be referred to the Tribunal, and/or that practising certificate conditions and/or intervention should be considered.

The solicitor will have 14 days to respond, with some leeway unless intervention is in contemplation.

There is a procedure whereby the formal process of adjudication, following disclosure of the caseworker's report with recommendations, can be bypassed, with the result that a decision to refer the solicitor's conduct to the Solicitors Disciplinary Tribunal can be made after a solicitor's explanation is received, but otherwise without notice and without any right of appeal (see para **13.13**).[2] The decision may be taken by the SRA's in-house advocates or their managers if they are satisfied that the evidential and public interest tests are satisfied (see para **13.10**). There is no published guidance as to when this 'fast track' system may be employed or as to the criteria to be applied in making that choice. However, it appears likely that the SRA will seek to streamline the process of decision-making (consistently with the 'single report' process described at **13.6**), and that in any case in which it is felt that the evidential and public interest tests for referral to the Tribunal are likely to be met, the fast track system, involving a dialogue between the caseworker and/or investigator and the legal department, may become the norm.

Bearing in mind the absence of notice, the absence of any right of appeal, and the absence of any available guidance as to when this system could be expected to be used, it is to be hoped that it would only be used in the clearest cases where, for example, there is nothing more that the solicitor could say that could possibly affect the outcome; that is, where a referral to the Tribunal is absolutely inevitable. Many cases historically involved a fine judgement as to whether the matter requires referral to the Tribunal or can proportionately be dealt with by a severe reprimand, and the same will apply to the new regime of in-house rebukes and fines. It would be most unfortunate if in any such case a solicitor was deprived of the opportunity to make submissions on that issue at a time when he or she understood that a referral to the Tribunal was clearly in prospect.

At present, the dialogue between caseworker and the legal department involves an exchange of internal memoranda without disclosure to the regulated person. There is accordingly scope for human error, for example in misunderstanding the facts or misinterpreting the explanations provided, without the solicitor having an opportunity to correct any such fault. If indeed this system is to become the norm, it is to be hoped that this will change and that solicitors will at least be given an opportunity to comment on the investigator's or caseworker's conclusions so as to avoid the possibility of such errors influencing the decision.

Less sensitively, this fast track system may also be employed to add further matters to a case to be considered by the Tribunal, after the conduct of a solicitor has already been the subject of a referral on other matters.

1   See now Rule 6 of the SRA (Disciplinary Procedure) Rules 2010.
2   Rule 8.

Publicity during investigations – prior to 1 June 2010

13.9

Generally, no publicity is given to investigations and matters remain confidential as between the solicitor and the SRA, but the SRA has a discretion to publish information if it considers that it is in the public interest to do so, for example where there is an investigation giving rise to significant public concern. The SRA may disclose how the investigation is progressing or that it has been concluded without an adverse finding against the solicitor. This policy applies to investigations which commenced on or after 1 January 2008. The new regime for publication of SRA-imposed fines and rebukes is described below.

The powers of the adjudicator and adjudication panels – prior to 1 June 2010

13.10

Very nearly all decisions are taken by adjudicators, some of whom are Law Society employees whose independence from casework management has been guaranteed by the Council of the Law Society[1] and some of whom are external appointments and independent of the SRA. With limited exceptions irrelevant for present purposes, the only decisions now required to be taken by an adjudication panel are to authorise interventions. An adjudication panel can consist of two or three individual adjudicators, but a single adjudicator can in an emergency authorise an intervention.

1   By resolution in December 1999.

13.11

Adjudication panels can take any one of the following steps, in descending order of gravity; adjudicators can take any one of these steps, other than the first, but a single adjudicator can authorise an intervention in an emergency, as mentioned above:

- Resolve to intervene – see generally **CHAPTER 16**, and in particular para **16.4**.

- Refer the matter to the police. If the matter is serious enough to involve the police, it is most unlikely that this will be the only action taken by the adjudicator or panel.

- Refer the matter to the Solicitors Disciplinary Tribunal. There is a two-stage test in deciding to refer – an evidential test (is it more likely than not that a finding of misconduct will be made by the Tribunal?) and a public interest test (is a prosecution justified in the public interest, or are the allegations too trivial, old, etc?). There is no right of appeal where the adjudicator or adjudication panel decides to refer a case to the Tribunal (the same applies in relation to a fast track decision made by a member of the legal department). Although in theory such a decision is susceptible to judicial review, the court will only intervene 'in exceptional circumstances where the facts cry out for that intervention, for example where irreparable harm or unfairness is likely to occur or justice could only be met by intervention'.[1] The affected solicitor has the opportunity to state his case and have the allegations against him dismissed at the Tribunal itself.[2]

A decision to refer a solicitor's conduct to the Tribunal does not engage the solicitor's civil rights for the purposes of Article 6 of the European Convention on Human Rights.[3] There is therefore little prospect of the solicitor being able to overturn a reference through the courts, but the decision to refer can be, and sometimes is, reconsidered and rescinded in the light of fresh information or further representations on behalf of the affected solicitor.

Unless there are exceptional reasons not to do so, the SRA will publish on its website decisions to refer a solicitor's conduct to the Tribunal and a short statement as to the basis of the referral, once the Tribunal has certified a prima facie case (see para **15.12**).

• Impose a reprimand or a severe reprimand. This becomes part of the solicitor's regulatory record, and so may be taken into account when any future regulatory action is taken or contemplated. Reprimands and severe reprimands are disclosed to the Ministry of Justice if the solicitor applies for a judicial appointment, but at present are otherwise confidential as between the SRA and the solicitor (and his senior partner if relevant) and (optionally) the informant. A reprimand or severe reprimand may also have to be disclosed to the Financial Services Authority (FSA) if the solicitor wishes to be appointed as a director of an FSA authorised organisation carrying out controlled functions under the financial services legislation.[4] These 'sanctions' similarly do not determine any civil rights of the solicitor.[5]

• Make directions as to the payment of the costs of the investigation[6] (see below).

• Take no further action. A decision to take no further action may, however, be accompanied by a 'finding and warning' that the solicitor has been at fault, and that this will remain on his regulatory record, and may be taken into account in the future.

1   *R (Aurangzeb) v Law Society* [2003] EWHC 1286 (Admin).
2   *R (Aurangzeb) v Law Society* [2003] EWHC 1286 (Admin).
3   *R (Thompson) v Law Society* [2004] 1 WLR 2522.
4   Approval is only to be granted to persons who satisfy the fit and proper person test (see the FSA Handbook *The Fit and Proper Test for Approved Persons*, Chapter 1 and 2). In determining a person's honesty, integrity and reputation the FSA will have regard to: 'whether the person or any business with which the person has been involved, has been investigated, disciplined, censured or suspended or criticised by a regulatory or professional body, a court or tribunal whether publicly or *privately*' (paragraph 2.1.3(10) – emphasis added).
5   *R (Thompson) v Law Society* [2004] 1 WLR 2522.
6   Section 44C of SA 1974.

The new powers of the adjudicator and adjudication panels – after 1 June 2010

13.12

By Rule 3 of the 2010 Rules, three conditions must be met before a rebuke or fine can be imposed:

• The first condition is that the SRA must be satisfied that the relevant act or omission by the solicitor fulfils one or more of the following:

– it was deliberate or reckless;

– it caused or had the potential to cause loss or significant inconvenience to another;

– it was or was related to a failure or refusal to ascertain, recognise or comply with the regulated person's professional or regulatory obligations such as, but not limited to, compliance with requirements imposed by legislation or rules made pursuant to legislation, the SRA, the Law Society, the LeO, the Tribunal or the court;

- it continued for an unreasonable period taking into account its seriousness;

- it persisted after the regulated person realised or should have realised that it was improper;

- it misled or had the potential to mislead clients, the court or other persons, whether or not that was appreciated by the regulated person;

- it affected or had the potential to affect a vulnerable person or child;

- it affected or had the potential to affect a substantial, high-value or high-profile matter;

- it formed or forms part of a pattern of misconduct or other regulatory failure by the regulated person.

- The second condition is that a fine or rebuke represents a proportionate outcome.

- The third condition is that the relevant act or omission was neither trivial nor justifiably inadvertent.

The third element of the first condition is nonsensical. All other elements of the first condition have the character of exacerbating features; in other words, a factor which makes a 'bare' breach of a rule more serious. However, the third element simply requires there to have been a rule breach, As sanctions could only ever be imposed in circumstances where there had been a rule breach of some kind, that particular provision adds nothing and makes no sense. The entire thrust of the rule conveys the impression that something beyond a bare breach of a rule is required before a sanction would be considered appropriate. If the third element of the first condition is to be taken at face value, this impression is wholly misleading, and no exacerbating feature is required.

As yet there has been insufficient opportunity to observe how the rule is used in practice and how this anomaly is resolved.

13.13

The decision may be made by an Adjudicator or an Adjudication Panel consisting of at least two members. The strict rules of evidence do not apply. The standard of proof adopted will be the civil standard, in contrast to the Tribunal which operates on the criminal standard (see para **15.25**). Any fine is payable to the Treasury, but is not payable until the time for appealing has expired.

With effect from 1 June 2010, any decision other than an intervention can also be taken by 'a person duly authorised by the SRA'; that is, a person employed by the SRA in some capacity other than as an adjudicator, whose independence from the investigation process is not subject to any guarantee. Any decision may also be taken by agreement with the regulated person.

Publication of decisions made under the new statutory regime

13.14

The criteria for publication are included as an Appendix to the 2010 Rules. This lists a series of factors supporting a decision to publish and a (smaller) series of factors supporting a decision not to publish. The most important of the latter is '(e) in all the circumstances the impact of publication on the individual or the firm would be disproportionate'. According to paragraph 7 of the Appendix, the SRA will from time to time publish indicative guidance about the application of these criteria.

Oral hearings

13.15

It is theoretically open to a solicitor to request an oral hearing, but such hearings are rarely if ever granted, and attempts to obtain such hearings via judicial review in the past in relation to comparable Law Society systems have invariably foundered.[1] In order to have any prospect of persuading the adjudicator to grant an oral hearing, the solicitor will have to explain why such a hearing is necessary, and why the matter cannot be adequately considered on paper. In order to have any prospect of success in judicial review proceedings based upon the failure to have an oral hearing, it will be essential for the solicitor to have requested such a hearing; failure to have done so will be fatal to the application.[2]

The rarity of oral hearings is likely to continue under the new regime, although now that the SRA has powers to impose sanctions that have a material consequence in financial and reputational terms it is probable that pressure for oral hearings will increase.

1   *R v Law Society, ex p Curtin* (1993) Times, 3 December, CA.
2   *R (Thompson) v Law Society* [2004] 1 WLR 2522. See also *R (Smith) v Parole Board (No 2)* [2004] 1 WLR 421.

Costs of the investigation

13.16

Where the SRA investigates possible professional misconduct by a solicitor, or a failure or apprehended failure by a solicitor to comply with any regulatory requirement, the solicitor may be directed to pay an amount which is calculated to be the cost of investigating and dealing with the matter – or a reasonable contribution towards that cost.[1] The current practice is to charge on a time basis in bands. If an investigation takes less than two hours' work (which would be unusual), the costs are a fixed figure of £300. If the time spent is between two and seven hours, the charge is £600. Between eight and 16 hours' work results in a charge of £1,350 and longer investigations are charged at £1,350 plus £75 for each hour over the sixteenth. With effect from 31 March 2009, this has been put on a formal basis by the SRA (Costs of Investigations) Regulations 2009.[2]

1   Section 44C of SA 1974.
2   See **APPENDIX 13**.

Internal appeals

13.17

The current policy on internal appeals from first instance decisions came into force in May 2005. There is a right of appeal in relation to the imposition of reprimands and severe reprimands, and in respect of practising certificate decisions, but not in relation to a decision to refer to the Tribunal. The new powers to rebuke, fine and publicise the sanction are subject to a right of appeal. If the decision was made by an authorised person, the appeal is to an adjudicator; if it was made by an adjudicator the appeal is to an adjudication panel (two or three adjudicators).[1] The appeal must be launched within 14 days and is dealt with on paper, and it is important for the appellant to provide properly reasoned arguments in support of the appeal.

Importantly, the SRA itself can 'appeal' a decision by seeking a reconsideration of it if it appears, to one of a number of specified senior officials of the SRA, to be fundamentally wrong, whether or not the decision has been disclosed to any person. This is a matter for the absolute discretion of the decision-maker, without any right of appeal. Therefore, despite the apparent independence of the adjudication process (the freedom of adjudicators from influence by those concerned with casework management being guaranteed by the Council of the Law Society in 1999 – as mentioned at para **13.10**) there is a theoretical possibility that senior staff of the SRA could keep putting a matter back to an adjudicator or successive adjudicators until a 'satisfactory' decision was reached. The policy statement does not make any particular provision as to the extent to which affected solicitors are to be kept informed of such steps when they are taken.

1   Rule 9 of the SRA (Disciplinary Procedure) Rules 2010.

Appeals to the Tribunal

13.18

In respect of regulatory breaches occurring after 1 June 2010, there is a free-standing right of appeal to the Tribunal against a fine, against any direction for publicity, and against a rebuke only if there is a direction to publicise.[1]

1   Section 44E of SA 1974.

Judicial review

13.19

The existing power to reprimand from which there is no right of independent appeal will, however, continue to be relevant for some time because, as has been noted, the new powers are only available in respect of acts and omissions after 1 June 2010. Judicial review will continue thereafter to be theoretically available in respect of (1) decisions made about acts and omissions occurring before 1 June 2010 and (2) decisions by an adjudicator or an adjudication panel to impose a reprimand or rebuke without publication. Ordinary public law principles would apply to such applications. Judicial review is often seen as a disproportionate response in circum-stances where the decision, even if challengeable, makes little difference to the solicitor in practice, and permission can be refused on that basis alone.

As for decisions in respect of which a statutory right of appeal to the Tribunal exists, these cannot be challenged in judicial review proceedings due to the existence of this alternative remedy.

Consistency of decision-making

13.20

In reaching their decisions, neither the adjudicators nor the adjudication panels have any database of earlier decisions to which to refer. They rely upon their individual and collective experience. The adjudication panel made 404 decisions in 2009. Individual adjudicators make many more. In 2009, the adjudicators made 2,839 casework decisions – this gives some idea of the number and breadth of the in-house decision-making process. These figures include pre-admission and post-intervention matters, including applications to the Compensation Fund. In the light of the more formal process introduced with effect from 1 June 2010, it is to be hoped that a database of SRA decisions will be created, and greater consistency achieved.

Regulatory settlements

13.21

The SRA is now prepared to enter into agreements to settle regulatory and disciplinary cases. The agreement may take two forms: a settlement agreement, which will resolve the whole matter, or an issue agreement, which will resolve a particular issue within an investigation without concluding the investigation.

There is no requirement or compulsion on the SRA to consider a regulatory settlement of either kind or to enter into negotiations. If negotiations are conducted they will be on a without prejudice basis, and will not be referred to in any investigations or proceedings unless the court or the Solicitors Disciplinary Tribunal orders otherwise. Agreements may be rescinded if there proves to have been material misrepresentation.

It is understood that agreements will only be contemplated if the solicitor's integrity is not in issue and if compliance with the agreement by the solicitor can be assured.

Agreements will be in writing, state the relevant facts, identify any failings admitted by the solicitor, identify the action the solicitor has taken or intends to take, identify any sanction imposed (such as a reprimand) and will be published by the SRA unless expressly agreed otherwise.

Any agreed course of action will be supported by professional undertakings and a breach of the agreement will be considered to be misconduct.

The investigation will be reopened if the solicitor fails to comply with the agreement or acts inconsistently with it (for example by denying misconduct that has been admitted for the purposes of the agreement).

Examples of regulatory settlements are:

- agreed public statements, whereby a solicitor publicly acknowledges a failure and states what has been and will be done to avoid repetition, where the publicity, in conjunction with any other sanction, is considered to be a proportionate result; and

- schemes for correction, improvement and restitution (for example where failings have impacted on clients), whereby relevant faults can be properly and proportionately addressed by identifying and contacting all affected clients, refunding money to them, reporting periodically to the SRA and submitting to the scheme being monitored.

13.22

As business models become more complex, as firms contemplate legal disciplinary partnerships and ABSs, and as innovative fee sharing schemes are developed, it is becoming increasingly apparent that there is a need for some form of positive vetting service, so that firms can obtain reassurance, rather than take the risk of regulatory or disciplinary action, having done their best to get it right.

There are currently some signs that guidance will be offered as to the kind of provisional agreements that might be possible – in relation to potential ABS arrangements – without offending the current rules.

The future

13.23

As indicated above (para **13.1**) the SRA's approach to regulation is changing. We are likely to find that although some aspects of the current styles of investigation may continue as before, the SRA may begin to work with the profession in unfamiliar ways. Whereas forensic investigation may remain largely unchanged, to be used when there is a perceived high level of risk, a more risk-based approach by PSU can be expected; although the pattern of quasi-pastoral visits may well continue in a slightly different form, as will caseworker investigations, particularly into regulatory issues such as practising certificates and recognition issues.

There will be relationship management, either on a permanent basis with large or commercial firms including ABSs, or on a temporary basis for example with firms in the Assigned Risk Pool (see **CHAPTER 6**). This will involve maintaining regular contact with the firm through dedicated supervisors.

There will be desk-based supervision, involving the assessment of risks based on information from a variety of sources. This could lead, for example, to the identification of particular trends or business models about which warnings should be given, but this may not necessarily result in an inspection of a firm; it might result in general information, by means of 'Dear Senior Partner' letters, or other forms of publicity intending to warn practitioners of the identified risks. Firms might be asked to provide information, if they are believed to be affected by particular risks, as to the extent to which they are aware of them and are responding to them.

We are assured that disciplinary action will only be taken if it is the only correct way of dealing with the situation (although this could involve taking exemplary action in an appropriate case) and that there will be a major change of focus towards encouraging practitioners into good behaviour, rather than punishing those who have made mistakes.

CHAPTER 14

Practising certificate controls

14.1

Every solicitor must at all times hold a valid practising certificate in order to practise as such.[1] Very few solicitors outside government service can escape the requirement to hold a practising certificate.[2] Accordingly, the power to impose conditions on a solicitor's practising certificate represents a very powerful regulatory control in the hands of the SRA. Indeed, the high cost of interventions has led recently to an increased use of practising certificate conditions as a means of protecting the public where otherwise the SRA might have intervened in a solicitor's practice.

An additional control, with effect from 1 July 2009, is the requirement on sole practitioners to have a sole solicitor endorsement on their practising certificates to enable them to practise as such. Existing sole practitioners were 'passported' into compliance with the new regulations provided they were currently lawfully practising in that capacity.[3] From November 2009, however, a sole practitioner has to satisfy the SRA, as part of the process for renewing the practising certificate and sole solicitor endorsement, that he or she may properly practise as a sole practitioner by showing, amongst other things, that he or she has sufficient skills or knowledge in relation to the running and management of a business which provides regulated legal services[4] (see **CHAPTER 2**).

1   Section 1 of the Solicitors Act 1974 (SA 1974).
2   See rule 20 of the Solicitors' Code of Conduct 2007 and commentary at para **3.56**.
3   Regulation 4.4 of the SRA Practising Regulations 2009.
4   Regulation 4.2.

14.2

The whole regulatory system in relation to practising certificates changed on 1 July 2009, when section 12 of SA 1974 and associated provisions were repealed and replaced by a rule-based system, comprised principally in the SRA Practising Regulations 2009. Although the statutory basis of regulation has changed, there are only modest changes of substance (the list of circumstances in which conditions can be applied is somewhat longer). There are unlikely to be any material changes in the processes of investigation and adjudication, or in the principles to apply: Past decisions by the Master of the Rolls will therefore remain relevant.

14.3

The equivalent of section 12 of SA 1974 as from 1 July 2009 is regulation 3.1 of the SRA Practising Regulations 2009. On an initial application for a practising certificate or on an application for its renewal, the SRA has a discretion to impose conditions on the certificate, or to refuse the application 'following certain events' which are listed:

'(a) The applicant has been:

    (i)   reprimanded, fined or made the subject of an order under section 43 of the Solicitors Act 1974, ordered to pay costs or made the subject of a recommendation to the SRA to consider imposing a condition, by the Solicitors Disciplinary Tribunal;

    (ii)   made the subject of an order under section 43 of the Solicitors Act 1974 or rebuked or fined under section 44D of that Act by the SRA;

    (iii)   made the subject of, or been a manager of a recognised body which has been the subject of, an intervention by the SRA; or

    (iv)   made the subject of a disciplinary sanction by, or refused registration with or authorisation by, another approved regulator, professional or regulatory tribunal, or regulatory authority, whether in England and Wales or elsewhere.

(b)   The SRA has requested an explanation from the applicant in respect of a matter relating to the applicant's conduct and has notified the applicant in writing that it does not regard the applicant's response, or lack of response, as satisfactory.

(c)   The applicant has failed to deliver within the period allowed an accountant's report required by rules made under section 34 of the Solicitors Act 1974.

(d)   The applicant's practising certificate or registration has been suspended and the suspension:

    (i)   has come to an end;

    (ii)   was continuing when the applicant's last practising certificate or previous registration expired or was revoked; or

    (iii)   is continuing.

(e)   The applicant has been suspended from practice and the suspension has come to an end.

(f)   The applicant's last practising certificate or previous registration expired or was revoked whilst subject to a condition.

(g)   The applicant's practising certificate or registration is currently subject to a condition.

(h)   The applicant's right to practise as a lawyer of another jurisdiction or as a lawyer of England and Wales (other than as a solicitor) is subject to a condition or restriction.

(i)   The applicant has been restored to the roll or register, having previously been struck off.

(j)   The applicant is an undischarged bankrupt.

(k)   The applicant:

    (i)   has been adjudged bankrupt and discharged;

    (ii)   has entered into an individual voluntary arrangement or a partnership voluntary arrangement under the Insolvency Act 1986;

(iii) has been a manager of a recognised body which has entered into a voluntary arrangement under the Insolvency Act 1986;

(iv) has been a director of a company or a member of an LLP which has been the subject of a winding up order, an administration order or administrative receivership; or has entered into a voluntary arrangement under the Insolvency Act 1986.

(l) The applicant lacks capacity (within the meaning of the Mental Capacity Act 2005) and powers under sections 15 to 20 or section 48 of that Act are exercisable in relation to the applicant.

(m) The applicant has been committed to prison in civil or criminal proceedings and:

(i) has been released; or

(ii) has not been released.

(n) The applicant has been made subject to a judgment which involves the payment of money, other than one:

(i) which is limited to the payment of costs; or

(ii) in respect of which the applicant is entitled to indemnity or relief from another person as to the whole sum; or

(iii) which the applicant has paid, and supplied evidence of payment to the SRA.

(o) The applicant is currently charged with an indictable offence.

(p) The applicant has been convicted of an indictable offence or any offence under the Solicitors Act 1974, the Financial Services and Markets Act 2000, the Immigration and Asylum Act 1999 or the Compensation Act 2006.

(q) The applicant has been disqualified from being a company director.

(r) The applicant has been removed from the office of charity trustee or trustee for a charity by an order within the terms of section 72(1)(d) of the Charities Act 1993.

(s) The applicant has been the subject in another jurisdiction of any circumstance equivalent to those listed in (j) to (r).'

If any of these circumstances applies, an application for replacement of a practising certificate must be commenced at least six weeks before the replacement or renewal date.[1] If regulation 3 applies by reason of paragraphs (j) (bankruptcy), (m) (committal to prison), (n) (money judgment) or (p) (conviction of a relevant criminal offence) and the judgment or order is subject to appeal, the application for a practising certificate must not be refused before the determination of the appeal, unless in the opinion of the SRA the appeal proceedings have been unduly protracted by the appellant or (again in the opinion of the SRA) they are unlikely to be successful, but the SRA may in the meantime postpone a decision on the application and may impose a condition on the applicant's practising certificate.[2]

If regulation 3 applies by reason of paragraph (o) (the applicant is currently charged with an indictable offence), the application may not be refused unless the applicant is convicted, but the SRA may postpone a decision on the application and may impose a condition on the applicant's practising certificate in the meantime.[3]

If the SRA has decided to impose a condition, it may postpone the issue of the certificate pending determination or discontinuance of any appeal against the decision; but the postponement may be rescinded if in its opinion proceedings on appeal have been unduly protracted by an appellant or (again in the SRA's opinion) are unlikely to be successful.

1   Regulation 3.2 of the SRA Practising Regulations 2009.
2   Regulation 3.3(b).
3   Regulation 3.3(c).

Immediate imposition of conditions

14.4

The SRA may impose one or more conditions on a practising certificate at any time during the practising year.[1] The SRA Practising Regulations 2009 do not specify that the power to do so is only exercisable if one or more of the circumstances set out in regulation 3.1 applies. Section 13A of SA 1974 (as amended by the LSA 2007) provides that conditions may be imposed on a current practising certificate if it appears to the SRA that the case is of a 'prescribed description' and 'prescribed' means prescribed by the relevant regulations.[2] It is possible that the SRA Practising Regulations 2009 are intended to be read so as to mean that the prescribed circumstances for the imposition of immediate conditions are those set out in regulation 3.1.

If a condition is to be imposed on a current certificate, the SRA must give 28 days' written notice, with reasons, to the individual concerned, but may shorten or dispense with the 28-day period if it is satisfied on reasonable grounds that it is in the public interest to do so.[3]

1   Regulation 6.1 of the SRA Practising Regulations 2009.
2   Sections 13A and 28 of SA 1974.
3   Regulation 6.4 of the SRA Practising Regulations 2009.

The specified purposes

14.5

The purposes for which the SRA may impose conditions, either on renewal or on a current certificate, are now spelled out in regulation 6.1 of the SRA Practising Regulations 2009:

> '(a) The SRA considers the individual concerned unsuitable to undertake certain activities in relation to a legal practice, either at all or save as specified in the condition, and that imposing the condition will, in the public interest, limit, restrict, halt or prevent the involvement of the individual concerned in those activities.
>
> (b) The SRA considers that the individual concerned is putting or is likely to put at risk the interests of clients, third parties or the public by taking certain steps in relation to a legal practice, and that imposing the

condition will, in the public interest, limit, restrict, halt or prevent the taking of such steps by the individual concerned.

(c) The SRA considers the individual concerned unsuitable to engage in certain business agreements, business associations or practising arrangements and that imposing a condition requiring the applicant to obtain the SRA's written approval before taking certain steps will, in the public interest, limit, halt or prevent a risk to clients, third parties or the public.

(d) The SRA considers that imposing the condition will, in the public interest, require the individual concerned to take specified steps conducive to the carrying on of efficient practice by the individual concerned.

(e) The SRA considers that imposing the condition will, in the public interest, facilitate closer monitoring by the SRA of compliance by the individual concerned with rules and regulations.

(f) The SRA considers that it would be in the public interest to impose the condition in any other case during the currency of a practising certificate or registration.'

Paragraph (f) would seem to be sufficiently broad that the other stated purposes are scarcely required to be listed, but it remains, as affirmed by the Master of the Rolls (see para **14.12**) a question as to what is necessarily and proportionately required for the protection of the public. The other paragraphs, however, do give some indication as to the nature of the conditions that will be considered.

Revocation of practising certificates and sole solicitor endorsements

14.6

The SRA may revoke a practising certificate at any time, if it is satisfied that it was granted as a result of error or fraud, if the replacement or renewal date has passed and the SRA has not received an application for renewal of the certificate, or as a result of a decision to refuse to renew a practising certificate.[1]

The SRA may revoke authorisation as a recognised sole practitioner at any time:

- if the authorisation was granted as a result of error or fraud;

- if the solicitor is not practising from an office in England and Wales;

- if the SRA is not satisfied that the recognised sole practitioner continues to meet the criteria for authorisation as a recognised sole practitioner;

- if the recognised sole practitioner has a temporary emergency recognition but has not within the initial 28-day period or any extension of that period commenced a substantive application for recognition;[2] or

- if the SRA has decided not to renew authorisation as a recognised sole practitioner.[3]

The SRA may revoke a practising certificate or authorisation as a recognised sole practitioner on the application of the person concerned but there is no discretion to refund any part of the fee paid for that practising year, and the SRA may refuse the application if there is an outstanding complaint against the applicant, or for any other reason relating to the public interest.[4]

If the SRA decides to revoke a practising certificate or authorisation as a recognised sole practitioner, it must give the person concerned 28 days' notice, with reasons. The notice may be given together with notification of refusal of an application to replace a practising certificate or renew an authorisation. Revocation takes effect on expiry of the notice or on such later date as may be stated in the notice, except that if an appeal is made during the period of notice the revocation does not take effect until determination or discontinuance of any appeal, whether under the SRA's own procedure, or to the High Court.[5]

1 Regulation 9.2(a) of the SRA Practising Regulations 2009.
2 For 'temporary emergency recognition' see para **2.15**.
3 Regulation 9.2(b) of the SRA Practising Regulations 2009.
4 Regulation 9.2(c).
5 Regulation 9.3.

Suspension of practising certificate

14.7

A practising certificate may also be suspended with immediate effect in the following circumstances:

- Where the solicitor has been convicted of an offence involving dishonesty or deception, or an indictable offence, *and* the SRA has referred his conduct to the Solicitors Disciplinary Tribunal, the SRA may suspend his practising certificate for up to six months, and may renew that suspension once for a maximum of a further six months.[1]

- Where an order has been made for the suspension of a solicitor from practice by a court or the Tribunal, or on a solicitor's bankruptcy. These operate as an automatic suspension of the practising certificate[2] – from any date specified by the court or Tribunal in the case of a suspension from practice, and immediately on an adjudication of bankruptcy.

- Where there is an intervention on the grounds of suspected dishonesty, or breaches of the Solicitors' Accounts Rules 1998, or breaches of any rules made under section 31 of SA 1974 (which include the Solicitors' Code of Conduct 2007), or because the solicitor has been committed to prison in criminal or civil proceedings. This also automatically suspends the solicitor's practising certificate, unless the adjudicator or adjudication panel which resolves to intervene directs otherwise.[3] The additional provision relating to breaches of practice rules, effected by amendment of the SA 1974 by the LSA 2007, means that in practical terms the practising certificate will be suspended on every intervention unless the decision-maker directs otherwise.

1 Section 13B of SA 1974.
2 Section 15(1).
3 Section 15(1A) and (1B).

14.8

When a practising certificate is suspended on intervention or by reason of bankruptcy the solicitor may apply to the SRA to terminate the suspension.[1]

It is a common and erroneous belief that bankruptcy is the equivalent of being struck off. It is not; indeed, when a solicitor knows that he or she will be made bankrupt, or is very likely to be, it is possible to apply to the SRA in advance of the date on which the adjudication is expected for the inevitable and automatic suspension to be terminated on acceptable conditions. In the case of bankruptcy the usual conditions will require the solicitor to practise only in employment that has been expressly approved by the SRA and that the solicitor has no access to client funds.

If an insolvent solicitor is already in employment or has a willing potential employer it is possible to apply for the suspension to be terminated and for the employment to be approved in advance in one adjudication process, and it is possible to arrange all this so that the adjudicator's decision becomes effective immediately the bankruptcy order is made, so that the solicitor can continue to practise seamlessly.

For the situation that arises following interventions, see para **16.10**.

1   Section 16(3) and (4) of SA 1974.

Common conditions on practising certificates – the test to apply

14.9

Practising certificate conditions are imposed solely to protect the public, primarily the solicitor's clients, by managing risk. The 'certain events' listed in regulation 3.1 of the SRA Practising Regulations 2009, are situations in which a solicitor may be regarded as representing an increased risk. Conditions are not imposed for the purposes of punishing solicitors, although conditions may be expensive for the solicitor, or even drive him or her out of business (for example a condition of approved employment upon a sole practitioner who cannot or does not wish to find such employment).

The correct approach to the imposition of conditions is:

(1)   to identify the risk;

(2)   to identify a mechanism to manage and control the risk to minimise its consequences; and

(3)   to determine whether the proposed mechanism is necessary and proportionate to the risk. As conditions are not intended to be penal, the control mechanism should be no more than is necessary to manage the risk.

Thus in cases of accounts that have been badly kept, resulting in substantial accounting errors and breaches of the Solicitors' Accounts Rules 1998, the imposition of a condition requiring more frequent accountant's reports (usually half-yearly rather than annually) would be the obvious course. Where serious errors of judgement have occurred, and there is a risk of repetition, or where there have been serious administrative failings, a condition requiring a solicitor to practise only in approved partnership or, in extreme cases, approved employment, could be appropriate.

In *Razeen (No 15 of 2008)*[1] the Master of the Rolls stated:

'Mr Goodwin [for the SRA] submits that regulatory conditions are imposed either to protect the public interest or the reputation of the profession or both. It appears to me that the essential point is whether conditions are necessary and proportionate to protect the public interest. Reference to reputation of the profession is really an incident of the protection of the public interest … I am also unable, however, to accept what I think may be Mr Goodwin's submission, that the SRA does not have to identify a specific risk. Absent identification of the risk, it appears to me that the SRA cannot properly assess the reasonableness or proportionality of any conditions that it seeks to impose.'

1   *Razeen (No 15 of 2008)* [2008] EWCA Civ 1220 at paras 12 and 13. See also *Lebow (No 13 of 2007)* [2008] EWCA Civ 411 at para 23: 'Conditions, however, if they are to be imposed, must be both necessary and proportionate'.

14.10

The precise content of conditions will depend upon the regulatory concerns of the SRA, and as to how the public can best be protected. For instance, the solicitor may be excluded from carrying out specified work of a particular kind, such as probate, or may be required to attend a particular type of training course on solicitors' accounting procedures or practice management. The SRA may take into account, when imposing conditions, that an application has been made against the solicitor to the Solicitors Disciplinary Tribunal if the allegations are sufficiently serious, even though those allegations have not yet been adjudicated upon.[1]

Conditions, once imposed, are likely to be re-imposed from year to year, although it is open to the solicitor upon renewal to apply for a certificate free from conditions. If the condition was imposed by reason of a set of circumstances which by their nature continue (for example the existence of judgment debts), the solicitor can expect the condition to continue until the underlying cause is removed (for example by the discharge of those debts).[2]

If the cause of the condition was a particular event, such as the imposition of a penalty by the Tribunal, or a return to practice after suspension, conditions are likely to be imposed for at least three or four years. There is, however, no hard rule to this effect and it may well be possible for the solicitor to secure an unconditional certificate if it can clearly be demonstrated that the problem period is over, and there is no continuing cause for concern or the need for any additional safeguard.

If an unconditional certificate is granted to a solicitor upon whom conditions were previously imposed by reason of regulation 3.1(a), (b), (c), (d)(i), (e), (j), (k), (m)(i), (n), (o), (p), (q), (r) or (s) of the SRA Practising Regulations 2009, then conditions cannot be re-imposed by reason of the same facts. In effect, the cause of the problem becomes 'spent' for regulatory purposes. However, this does not apply where the decision to grant an unconditional certificate was made by the SRA in ignorance of the relevant circumstances.[3]

1   *Burdett (No 8 of 2002)* [2002] EWCA Civ 1194; *Awan v Law Society* [2003] EWCA 1969; *Walker (No 13 of 2002)* [2002] EWCA Civ 1596.
2   Comments by Lord Donaldson MR in *No 6 of 1990* (unreported).
3   Regulation 3.3(a) of the SRA Practising Regulations 2009.

Procedure

14.11

The procedure followed is similar to that used for adjudication on matters of conduct (see para **13.6**), by the production of a caseworker's report which contains recommendations on which the solicitor has the opportunity to comment, usually within 14 days. If the solicitor does not oppose the recommended course or does not respond the provisional decision becomes final (subject to appeal). To that extent the power to make decisions rests with the individual caseworker.

If the proposed course is not accepted and representations are made, the matter is adjudicated upon, but the level and seniority of the decision-maker can vary. The matter may be referred to an adjudicator, but increasingly decisions at first instance are being taken by caseworkers or their managers.

Similar procedures are followed where, for example, there is an existing practising certificate condition requiring approval of any proposed partnership or employment, and application is made for approval.

Appeals

14.12

All the decisions of the SRA set out above can be contested by way of appeal to the High Court rather than to the Master of the Rolls as was the case prior to LSA 2007.[1] Previous decisions of successive Masters of the Rolls will continue to be highly persuasive, as the High Court comes to grips with this new jurisdiction. In *Akodu v SRA*[2] Moses LJ candidly accepted the inexperience of the High Court in dealing with such issues, and remitted the issue of practising certificate conditions to the Adjudicator, stating:[3]

> 'I would for my part underline what Mr. Barton [for the SRA] urged, namely, that in the normal case, this court should deal with these questions rather than remitting them. No doubt, as the body of experience expands, confined as it will be to a body of nominated judges as we were told, it will not be necessary to adopt the course I have reluctantly decided should be adopted.'

Although the High Court has an unfettered discretion in hearing such appeals, appropriate weight will be accorded to the professional expertise of the SRA decision-makers who imposed the conditions.[4] When such appeals were heard by the Master of the Rolls costs were in the discretion of the Master of the Rolls by virtue of his inherent power when exercising his quasi-visitorial jurisdiction over solicitors.[5] The High Court can be expected to apply traditional costs principles to practising certificate appeals, so that costs will ordinarily follow the event.

The SRA also operates an in-house appeals system, which it encourages solicitors to utilise before exercising their statutory rights of appeal (historically the Master of the

Rolls took the same view).[6] If the first instance decision is by a decision-maker other than an adjudicator, the appeal lies to an adjudicator; if it was by an adjudicator, appeal lies to an adjudication panel.

Appeals under the SRA's own appeals procedure must be commenced within 28 days of notification of the relevant decision.[7]

If and when the SRA makes rules to this effect, appeals may lie to the Tribunal rather than the High Court.[8] It is understood that such rules are not immediately in prospect.

The Tribunal has no power itself to impose conditions on a practising certificate when imposing a penalty upon a solicitor, but it can make recommendations to the SRA and, because it can make 'such order as it may think fit',[9] it can also make orders requiring solicitors not to practise in particular ways (such as a sole practitioner) either for a finite period or indefinitely with liberty to apply. The Divisional Court has encouraged the Tribunal to use such a power, where it considers it to be in the public interest to do so, rather than to leave such future considerations to the SRA.[10] In *Olufeku (No 7 of 2007)* and *Brandon (No 12 of 2008)*,[11] the Master of the Rolls considered the overlapping jurisdictions of the SRA and Tribunal in such matters. The decisions of the Tribunal are punitive and disciplinary; those of the SRA are regulatory and not punitive.

Inevitably, if the Tribunal were to make such orders, the SRA would impose matching or more restrictive practising certificate conditions.

1   Sections 13, 13A(6), 13B(7) and 16(5) of SA 1974.
2   [2009] EWHC 3588 (Admin).
3   Paragraph 14.
4   See *Lebow (No 13 of 2007)* [2008] EWCA Civ 411 at 23: 'This appeal is by way of re-hearing, although one of the factors which successive Masters of the Rolls and I myself have taken into account in the past is the importance of the judgment of the adjudicator and the appeal panel'. It may be noted, however, that the policy of the SRA is to have decisions made at the lowest practicable level of staff within the organisation and it remains to be seen whether this degree of confidence will continue to be held when all decisions are, for all practical purposes, made by individuals employed by the SRA, with no consideration by independent practitioners. It was the case that adjudication panels comprised representatives of the profession and the public, rather than employed adjudicators as is now mostly the case.
5   Sir Thomas Bingham MR gave this as his opinion when requested for a ruling on 20 September 1993.
6   Regulation 7 of the SRA Practising Regulations 2009.
7   Regulation 7.6(a) of the SRA Practising Regulations 2009.
8   Section 49A of SA 1974.
9   Section 47(2) of SA 1974.
10   *Camacho v Law Society* [2004] 33 LS Gaz R 37; *Taylor v Law Society* [2005] EWCA Civ 1473.
11   [2007] EWCA Civ 840 and [2008] EWCA Civ 967, respectively.

Publicity

14.13

The SRA now intends to publish regulatory decisions on its website unless there are exceptional reasons not to do so. All decisions to impose practising certificate conditions, where the investigation that led to the decision commenced on or after 1 January 2008, will be published when conditions are first imposed or materially varied. Decisions will not generally be published when they are the subject of an appeal (either internally or to the High Court). Published information will usually be limited to a short statement as to the decision and the reasons for it. The Master of the Rolls has emphasised the importance of appeals to him being held in public save in exceptional circumstances.[1]

1   *L v Law Society (No 13 of 2008)* [2008] EWCA Civ 811. This appeal concerned the revocation of a student's membership on the grounds of fitness for admission to the roll, but considered the principles of public and private hearings generally.

Agreements

14.14

The SRA may be prepared to enter into a regulatory settlement as an alternative to the imposition of practising certificate conditions (for regulatory settlements generally, see para **13.21**). Such agreements may enable undertakings to be given, for example:

- not to engage in a particular form of work, such as conveyancing, acting for lenders or litigation;

- to practise only as an employee after a specified date, pending the outcome of an investigation; or

- to provide independent evidence that accounts are in compliance, or of a return to medical or psychiatric good health.

The roll

14.15

A solicitor may keep his or her name on the roll without holding a practising certificate on payment of an annual fee of £20 (which is waived if a solicitor has been on the roll for 50 years or more),[1] but as explained above the circumstances in which a solicitor may practise or be held out as a solicitor without a practising certificate are now very few. A solicitor without a practising certificate may nevertheless be described as a 'solicitor – not practising'.

Every year the SRA writes to every solicitor whose name is on the roll but who does not have a practising certificate enquiring whether he or she wants to remain on the roll.[2] Anyone who either replies asking to be removed from the roll, or who fails to reply or to pay the required fee, may have his or her name removed from the roll. A solicitor may also apply to have his or her name removed from the roll at any time.[3]

A person whose name has been removed from the roll in this way may apply to the SRA for it to be restored.[4] The SRA may refuse to restore the name of a solicitor to the roll if there are outstanding complaints, and may refuse to remove the solicitor from the roll in the same circumstances.[5]

The SRA will not remove a solicitor's name from the roll when there are proceedings pending before the Tribunal.[6] There is provision for appeal to the High Court for persons aggrieved by decisions of the SRA to remove a name from the roll, or refuse to restore a name to the roll, after first exhausting the SRA internal appeal process.[7]

Arrangements for the change of name of a solicitor on the roll are covered by the same Regulations.

1   Regulation 13 of the Solicitors (Keeping of the Roll) Regulations 1999: see **APPENDIX 15**.
2   Regulation 4.
3   Regulation 5.
4   Regulation 6. This does not, of course, apply if the solicitor has been struck off or the Tribunal has ordered that the solicitor may not be restored to the roll other than by order of the Tribunal.
5   Regulation 8.
6   Regulation 9.
7   Regulation 14 of the Solicitors (Keeping of the Roll) Regulations 1999. Appeals must be made within four weeks of the relevant decision.

Removal from the roll by consent

14.16

The SRA can, where it is in the interests of the public to do so, agree to the removal from the roll of a solicitor where that would not otherwise be done under the Solicitors (Keeping of the Roll) Regulations 1999 because proceedings are pending in the Solicitors Disciplinary Tribunal or there are outstanding complaints (for the circumstances in which regulatory settlements may or may not be contemplated, see para **13.21**).

Such an agreement will be associated with a witness statement from the solicitor containing a statement of truth and which makes relevant admissions as to the facts, the allegations of misconduct and any previous relevant disciplinary history. It will record that a serious sanction from the Tribunal could be expected in the light of the admissions and will request removal from the roll to avoid costs, distress and further risk to the public. The statement will acknowledge that the statement itself and the agreement will be publicised by the SRA. Undertakings will be required not to apply to be restored to the roll, not to work in a solicitors' practice without the written permission of the SRA, and to make full and frank disclosure to any prospective employer of the agreement that had been reached.

CHAPTER 15

The Solicitors Disciplinary Tribunal

Membership and constitution

15.1

Members of the Solicitors Disciplinary Tribunal are appointed by the Master of the Rolls. The Tribunal consists of solicitor members, who are practising solicitors of not less than ten years' standing, and lay members, who are neither solicitors nor barristers. Lay members are paid a daily stipend by the Ministry of Justice; until 2009 solicitor members were unpaid but can now be paid from the Tribunal's annual budget met by the Law Society. The President of the Tribunal is elected to the post, and must be a solicitor member.[1] The members also appoint one solicitor member and one lay member to be vice-presidents. The Tribunal has been held to be an independent and impartial tribunal for the purposes of Article 6 of the European Convention on Human Rights.[2]

1   Rule 3 of the Solicitors (Disciplinary Proceedings) Rules 2007 (SI 2007/3588).
2   *Pine v Law Society* [2000] DC Transcript CO 1385/2000.

The Tribunal's statutory powers

15.2

On the hearing of an application, the Tribunal has the power, in relation to solicitors, to make such order as it thinks fit, and any such order may in particular include provision for any of the following matters:[1]

'(a) the striking off the roll of the name of the solicitor to whom the application or complaint relates;

(b) the suspension of that solicitor from practice indefinitely or for a specified period;

(ba) the revocation of that solicitor's sole solicitor's endorsement (if any);

(bb) the suspension of that solicitor from practice as a sole solicitor indefinitely or for a specified period;

(c) the payment by that solicitor or former solicitor of an unlimited penalty, which shall be forfeit to Her Majesty;[2]

(d) the exclusion of that solicitor from providing representation funded by the Legal Services Commission as part of the Criminal Defence Service (either permanently or for a specified period);

(e) the termination of that solicitor's unspecified period of suspension from practice;

(f) the restoration to the roll of the name of a former solicitor whose name has been struck off the roll and to whom the application relates;

(g)   in the case of a former solicitor whose name has been removed from the roll, a direction prohibiting the restoration of his name to the roll except by order of the Tribunal;

(h)   in the case of an application under subsection (1)(f) [of the Solicitors Act 1974], the restoration of the applicant's name to the roll; and

(i)   the payment by any party of costs or a contribution towards costs of such amount as the Tribunal may consider reasonable.'

1   Section 47(2) of SA 1974.
2   The former limit of £5,000 for each offence has been removed by the Legal Services Act 2007 (LSA 2007) with effect from 31 March 2009. It can be expected that much higher fines may be levied on recognised bodies in the context of firm-based regulation (see **CHAPTER 2**) if the offence has led to material financial gain.

Suspensions

15.3

Suspensions are normally imposed for one year or more. Where they are for a period of months (or less) it is important to note that the expiry of the suspension does not enable an automatic return to practice. The solicitor's practising certificate is not automatically restored; rather it remains suspended until the SRA terminates the suspension on the application of the solicitor (although an application may be made before the suspension expires, so minimising the consequences).[1] The termination of the suspension may be accompanied by the imposition of conditions on the practising certificate[2] and almost certainly will.

1   Section 16(3) of SA 1974.
2   Section 16(4) of SA 1974.

Practising restrictions

15.4

The Tribunal has no power itself to impose conditions on a practising certificate when imposing a penalty upon a solicitor, but can make recommendations to the SRA and, because it can make 'such order as it may think fit', it can also make orders requiring a solicitor not to practise in particular ways, for example as a sole practitioner.

In *Camacho v Law Society*[1] the Tribunal had ordered the indefinite suspension of a solicitor. On the solicitor's appeal, the Divisional Court substituted a finite period of suspension but identified five conditions which it considered should be imposed in relation to the way in which the solicitor might practise. The court held that the terms of section 47(2) of SA 1974 were sufficiently wide to give the Tribunal itself power to impose restrictions on the manner in which a solicitor might practise, and that if the Tribunal considered that a period of complete suspension followed by a period of restricted practice was the appropriate sanction to protect the public, that was part of the decision it had made and – unless there were exceptional reasons – it should be for the Tribunal to make that order, rather than to make recommendations to the SRA as had been the former practice.

Where the Tribunal makes such an order for an indefinite period it should grant liberty to apply, as there is otherwise no mechanism for a solicitor subject to such an order to apply for it to be varied or reviewed.[2]

The Tribunal has on one occasion refined this approach by imposing a suspension from practice for one year, but suspending that order for so long as the solicitor practised only (in substance) in employment expressly approved by the SRA without access to clients' money. The Tribunal gave guidance as to the circumstances in which an application might be made to the Tribunal to vary or revoke the terms of the restriction.[3]

Inevitably when the Tribunal makes such orders the SRA can be expected to impose matching or more restrictive practising certificate conditions.

1 [2004] EWHC 1675 (Admin), [2004] 1 WLR 3037.
2 *Taylor v Law Society* [2005] EWCA Civ 1473. The formula substituted on appeal to the Master of the Rolls in *Taylor* was: 'In the future the petitioner may not practise as a sole practitioner but only in employment or partnership. When employed he must not operate a client account. The petitioner to have liberty to apply to the Tribunal to vary these conditions'.
3 *Bajela and Fonkwo*, 9543–2006, SDT.

Reprimands

15.5

Although it has no express statutory power to do so, the Tribunal frequently issues a reprimand to a solicitor. It has also censured a solicitor, stating that this was a more serious order than a reprimand and has directed a solicitor to pay counsels' fees (thereby making an unenforceable obligation enforceable as a High Court order).[1]

1 *Prince*, 6578–1994, SDT, unsuccessfully appealed as *Re a Solicitor*, CO 1324–1995. See also section 48(4) of SA 1974.

Other powers and jurisdictions

15.6

The Tribunal has jurisdiction over recognised bodies (incorporated practices registered with the SRA),[1] registered European lawyers,[2] registered foreign lawyers[3] and in respect of non-solicitors involved in legal practice.[4] The Tribunal has the jurisdiction to direct that an award for inadequate professional services made by the Legal Complaints Service be enforceable as an order of the High Court.[5] The Tribunal also has jurisdiction to disqualify solicitors from undertaking legal aid work,[6] but so far as can be established the power has never been used.

The Tribunal has jurisdiction to consider the conduct of and to impose sanctions on an individual who was not a solicitor at the time of the actions complained of but who had since been admitted a solicitor.[7]

The Tribunal has jurisdiction over former solicitors in respect of conduct while they were solicitors.[8]

Appeal lies to the Tribunal from the imposition of fines by the SRA under section 44D of SA 1974 and/or under paragraph 14B of Schedule 2 to the

Administration of Justice Act 1985 (AJA 1985) and in respect of written rebukes by the SRA (under the same provisions) if a decision is made that the rebuke should be published, and also against any decision to publish the details of any action taken by the SRA under section 44D of SA 1974.[9] On such an appeal the Tribunal may affirm or revoke the SRA's decision, vary the amount of any fine, and also may exercise its normal jurisdiction over the appellant (to strike off, suspend, revoke a sole solicitor endorsement, fine, and so forth) as if an application had been made against that person.[10]

The SRA may also make rules, with the approval of the Tribunal, providing for appeals to the Tribunal from certain decisions of the SRA where appeal would otherwise lie to the High Court. These relate primarily to practising certificate conditions, and no such rules have yet been made.[11] It is understood that these are not in immediate contemplation.

1   Paragraphs 16 to 18 of Schedule 2 to AJA 1985.
2   Regulation 26 of the European Communities (Lawyer's Practice) Regulations 2000 (SI 2000/1119).
3   Paragraphs 15 to 17 of Schedule 14 to the Courts and Legal Services Act 1990 (CLSA 1990).
4   Sections 43 and 47(2E) of SA 1974: see paras **18.4–18.9**.
5   Paragraph 5 of Schedule 1A to SA 1974.
6   Section 47(2A), (2B), (2C) and (2D) of SA 1974. These sub-sections were introduced by the AJA 1985, granting the Tribunal the powers formerly vested in the Legal Aid (Complaints) Tribunal (established by the Legal Aid Act 1974, and which had dealt with two cases in its lifetime) and the Legal Aid in Criminal Cases (Complaints) Tribunal (established under the Criminal Justice Act 1967, which had dealt with one).
7   *Re a Solicitor (Ofosuhene)* (21 February 1997, unreported).
8   Section 41(1)(c) of SA 1974.
9   Section 44E(1) of SA 1974; paragraph 14C of Schedule 2 to AJA 1985.
10 Section 44E(4) of SA 1974; paragraph 14C of Schedule 2 to AJA 1985.
11 Section 49A of SA 1974. The matters which, subject to the rules if and when they are made, may be appealed to the Tribunal are: decisions under the Solicitors (Keeping of the Roll) Regulations 1999 as to restoring the name of a solicitor removed from the roll under those Regulations (section 8(4) of SA 1974); the imposition of conditions on practising certificates or refusal to issue practising certificates or sole solicitor endorsements (sections 13A(6) and 28(3D)); decisions relating to the termination of the suspension of practising certificates (section 16(5)); decisions relating to the grant of permission to employ a struck off or suspended solicitor (section 41(3)); and decisions under the parallel jurisdiction in relation to conditions on the registration of foreign lawyers (paragraph 14 of Schedule 14 to CLSA 1990).

The Solicitors (Disciplinary Proceedings) Rules 2007

15.7

The Tribunal's procedures are currently governed by either the Solicitors (Disciplinary Proceedings) Rules 1994 ('the 1994 Rules'),[1] which came into force on 1 March 1994 (having replaced the 1985 Rules of the same name), or by the Solicitors (Disciplinary Proceedings) Rules 2007 ('the 2007 Rules'),[2] which came into force on 14 January 2008, depending on the date that the proceedings were commenced. The 1994 Rules are only relevant to proceedings commenced before 14 January 2008 and will not be considered. The 2007 Rules are set out in full in **APPENDIX 16**.

1   SI 1994/288.
2   SI 2007/3588.

Commencement of proceedings and the allegations

15.8

When an adjudicator or adjudication panel or other authorised person of the SRA resolves to refer the conduct of a solicitor to the Tribunal, the case is allocated by the Legal Directorate of the SRA either to an in-house advocate in that department or to a solicitor member of the panel of solicitors instructed by the SRA to prosecute cases. That individual, referred to in the proceedings as the applicant, is responsible for drafting the originating process, which is known as the rule 5 statement (so named from rule 5 of the 2007 Rules[1]). This sets out the allegations and facts relied upon against the solicitor, who is termed the respondent.

1   Under the 1994 Rules regime it was the rule 4 statement.

Alleging dishonesty

15.9

If dishonesty is to be alleged against a solicitor, this must be made clear – ideally in the rule 5 statement. Failure expressly to allege or particularise dishonesty in a document in advance of the Tribunal hearing is likely to amount to a serious procedural flaw, which may well result in any finding of dishonesty by the Tribunal being overturned.[1]

The test for dishonesty is that set out in *Twinsectra v Yardley*.[2] This requires both objective and subjective elements. It was expressed thus by Lord Hutton at paragraph 27:

> '... before there can be a finding of dishonesty it must be established that the defendant's conduct was dishonest by the standards of reasonable and honest people *and* that he himself realised that by those standards his conduct was dishonest.' (*Emphasis added.*)

The words before the highlighted 'and' can be referred to as the objective test and those after it as the subjective element of the combined test.

Lord Hutton went on at paragraph 36:

> '... dishonesty requires knowledge by the defendant that what he was doing would be regarded as dishonest by honest people, although he should not escape a finding of dishonesty because he set his own standards of honesty and does not regard as dishonest what he knows would offend the normally accepted standard of honest conduct.'

In *Twinsectra*, Lord Millett delivered a powerful dissenting speech, advocating a purely objective test in respect of dishonesty in the context of accessory liability for breach of trust. Two subsequent cases suggested that the courts were moving away from the twin subjective/objective test enunciated by Lord Hutton in *Twinsectra*, towards a predominantly objective test.[3] In the context of disciplinary proceedings, however, the Divisional Court has emphatically held in *Bryant and Bench v Law Society*[4] that the *Twinsectra* test, as previously understood, should continue to determine whether a solicitor has been dishonest.

> 'In our judgment, the decision of the Court of Appeal in *Bultitude* stands as binding authority that the test to be applied in the context of solicitors' disciplinary proceedings is the *Twinsectra* test as it was widely understood before *Barlow Clowes*, that is a test that includes the separate subjective element. The fact that the Privy Council in *Barlow Clowes* has subsequently placed a different interpretation on *Twinsectra* for the purposes of the accessory liability principle does not alter the substance of the test accepted in *Bultitude* and does not call for any departure from that test.

> In any event there are strong reasons for adopting such a test in the disciplinary context and for declining to follow in that context the approach in *Barlow Clowes*. As we have observed earlier, the test corresponds closely to that laid down in the criminal context by *R v Ghosh*; and in our view it is more appropriate that the test for dishonesty in the context of solicitors' disciplinary proceedings should be aligned with the criminal test than with the test for determining civil liability for assisting in a breach of a trust. It is true, as Mr Williams [leading counsel for the Law Society] submitted, that disciplinary proceedings are not themselves criminal in character and that they may involve issues of dishonesty that could not give rise to any criminal liability (e.g. lying to a client as to whether a step had been taken on his behalf). But the tribunal's finding of dishonesty against a solicitor is likely to have extremely serious consequences for him both professionally (it will normally lead to an order striking him off) and personally. It is just as appropriate to require a finding that the defendant had a subjectively dishonest state of mind in this context as the court in *R v Ghosh* considered it to be in the criminal context.'

The Tribunal is regularly called upon to consider whether the failings of a solicitor amount to dishonesty, with an understanding that if that is found to be the correct description, the solicitor will almost inevitably be struck off (see paras **15.32** and **15.33** below).

1   *Singleton v Law Society* [2005] EWHC 2915 (Admin); *Constantinides v Law Society* [2006] EWHC 725 (Admin); *Onibudo v Law Society* [2002] EWHC 2030 (Admin).
2   [2002] UKHL 12, [2002] 2 All ER 377.
3   See *Barlow Clowes International Ltd (In liquidation) v Eurotrust International Ltd* [2005] UKPC 37, [2006] 1 WLR 1476, [2006] 1 All ER 333; *Abou-Rahmah v Abacha* [2006] EWCA Civ 1492, [2007] 1 Lloyd's Rep 115.
4   [2007] EWHC 3043 (Admin) at paras 153–154.

Conduct unbefitting a solicitor and rule breaches

15.10

Traditionally, allegations have been of two kinds – either of specific breaches of rules, such as the Solicitors' Accounts Rules 1998, or conduct unbefitting a solicitor in specified circumstances (which can vary infinitely). There is no all-embracing definition of conduct unbefitting a solicitor. In essence, conduct unbefitting is conduct which is regarded as professional misconduct by the Solicitors Disciplinary Tribunal as supervised by the courts. There is no need to prove intention or recklessness; conduct may be conduct unbefitting even though the solicitor attempted to conform to the highest professional standards. Negligent conduct may amount to conduct unbefitting a solicitor.[1] The issues are discussed in greater detail in **CHAPTER 8**.

During the life of the Solicitors' Code of Conduct 2007 – now drawing to its close – the practice gradually grew up of alleging specific breaches of the rules in the Code, including rule 1, in place of unbefitting conduct. We may see in future a similar pattern of allegations being made of breach of the core principles of the new draft Code, where those breaches are sufficiently serious as to warrant proceedings before the Tribunal.

A breach of the Solicitors' Accounts Rules 1998 is effectively a disciplinary offence of absolute liability due to the terms of rule 6 of those Rules, which requires all the principals in a practice to ensure compliance with the Rules by themselves and by everyone else working in the practice.

1   *Re a Solicitor* [1972] 2 All ER 811 and *Connolly v Law Society* [2007] EWHC 1175 (Admin) at para 62.
    See also **CHAPTER 8**, where this subject is discussed in greater detail.
2   See generally **CHAPTER 8**.

Liability of 'innocent' partners

15.11

In recent years there has been some confusion as to whether partners who have not known of or directly participated in a decision that breached a regulatory rule should face disciplinary action as a result. It was felt by the SRA that if, for instance, an equity partner benefitted financially from a breach of the prohibition against referral fees, that partner should face disciplinary proceedings. It is submitted that the better view is that unless a disciplinary offence is one of strict liability (such as an Accounts Rule breach), a solicitor should only face disciplinary consequences if he or she is in some way culpable.

This had been the general approach of the Tribunal. The concept of conduct unbefitting a solicitor carries with it some degree of moral culpability: the Tribunal had held that partners should not be required to supervise or monitor the work of other partners, and that a partner is not guilty of professional misconduct merely because he is the partner of a solicitor who is guilty of professional misconduct.[1]

This general approach has been approved by the Divisional Court in *Akodu v SRA* [2009] EWHC 3588 (Admin) per Moses LJ:

> '… there is no other reasonable conclusion that can be reached other than that the basis upon which he had been found guilty was merely on the basis that he was a partner of the firm. If that was the only basis, then there has been no argument advanced on behalf of the Law Society to suggest that that was a lawful basis upon which any solicitor can be found guilty of conduct unbefitting the profession. If any authority is needed for the proposition, it can be found in Cordery on Solicitors at J 2225. Some degree of personal fault is required.'

1 *Ali and Shabir*, 9339–2005, SDT, *Aziz and Saunders*, 9032–2004, SDT, *Ross and others*, 10002–2008; and *Bagri and others*, 10229–2009.
2 See para **3.2**.

The Tribunal's procedures

15.12

The Tribunal's procedures are governed, as mentioned, by the Solicitors (Disciplinary Proceedings) Rules 1994 and 2007, depending upon whether proceedings were commenced before or after 14 January 2008. Often, however, the Rules play little overt part in the disciplinary proceedings, as the parties are able to agree case management decisions between themselves. The following points from the Rules are highlighted.

Certification of a case to answer

15.13

When the rule 5 statement and supporting documents are filed with the Tribunal, the papers are considered by a solicitor member of the Tribunal, who certifies whether a 'case to answer' is made out against the respondent.[1] If no such case is revealed, the papers are considered by another solicitor member and a lay member, and, if all agree, the case will be dismissed without hearing any party. Under the 1994 Rules, the Tribunal could invite representations from the parties at this stage, but if they were received uninvited they were unlikely to be entertained. The 2007 Rules contain no comparable provision.

1 See generally rule 6 of the 2007 Rules.

Defence material

15.14

There is no specific obligation in the Rules upon the respondent to provide a defence case statement. However, a Tribunal Clerk may give any directions deemed necessary or appropriate for the hearing of any matter brought before the Tribunal, including as to documentation, inspection, statements, skeleton arguments and the place and time of any hearing, and the Tribunal itself may give directions to secure the timely hearing of the matter, so that in suitable cases directions may be given requiring the position of the respondent to be stated and clarified.[1] Four copies will be required of any document filed with the Tribunal – one for each of the members and one for the Clerk.

No witness may be called to give evidence unless a witness statement or proof of evidence is provided to the Tribunal and the other parties at least ten days in advance of the hearing.[2] In the case of the respondent him- or herself it is usually accepted that the representations made to the SRA at the investigation stage can stand as his or her evidence.

Despite the absence of any specific requirement for the provision of a defence submission or statement it should be borne in mind that the rule 5 statement and allegations may be framed quite differently from the case the solicitor was invited to meet at the SRA investigation stage, and although all representations previously made should – without fail – be included in the documentation annexed to the rule 5 statement,[3] these may not meet the case in its refined form. Moreover, the Tribunal members read the papers in advance of the hearing. If the respondent wishes the members to have an understanding of his or her case in advance of the hearing, this will only be achieved by filing and serving some indication of the defence position.

The respondent has the option whether or not to give evidence, although it is unusual for him or her to elect not to do so in a contested case.

It is common to produce, without undue formality, bundles of testimonials as to the respondent's good character. This can be by way of pure mitigation but can also be directly relevant to issues of honesty and integrity. Such evidence is relevant and admissible where the disciplinary allegations brought against the solicitor impugn his or her honesty.[4]

1   Rule 11(1), (2) and (4) of the 2007 Rules.
2   Rule 14(6) of the 2007 Rules. Historically the Tribunal has generally taken an emollient view of breaches of this rule and its predecessor and has permitted evidence to be given despite the absence of formal witness statements, but this should not be relied upon, either in principle or as an indication of future practice.
3   See *Bluett*, 8221–2000, SDT, where a failure to do this was severely criticised.
4   *Donkin v Law Society* [2007] EWHC 414 (Admin) and *Bryant and Bench v Law Society* [2007] EWHC 3043 (Admin).

Public hearings

15.15

The 2007 Rules provide that hearings should be held in public but that a party, or any person affected by the application, may seek an order from the Tribunal that all or part of the hearing be conducted in private on the grounds of exceptional hardship or exceptional prejudice.[1] Applications have been granted for the purposes of protecting members of the public (such as former clients of the respondent) but not for the protection of the respondent from the consequences of publicity.[2] In any event, the usual practice in the Tribunal is to refer to clients only by their initials.

In *L v Law Society* (a case concerned with an appeal against a decision of the SRA to revoke student membership, but which canvassed wider issues concerning public and private hearings), the Master of the Rolls emphasised the importance of public hearings in the Tribunal in maintaining the confidence of the public in the disciplinary process.[3]

1   Rules 11(5) and 12(4) to (6) of the 2007 Rules.
2   Though in one case, which did not in fact proceed to a final hearing for the same reason, a hearing in private was contemplated where medical and psychiatric evidence showed that there was a serious and credible risk of the respondent self-harming to the extent that his life might have been threatened if the hearing took place in public.
3   [2008] EWCA Civ 811 at para 41.

Adjournments

15.16

The Tribunal has published a practice direction on the subject of adjournments (see **APPENDIX 16**). It is generally not prepared to adjourn the disciplinary proceedings pending completion of a criminal investigation or prosecution.[1] The same applies in relation to civil proceedings.[2] The only exception is where there is a risk of 'muddying the waters of justice' but in practice this is usually either an illusory or a manageable risk.

1   *R v Solicitors Disciplinary Tribunal, ex p Gallagher* (1991, unreported).
2   *Lipman Bray v Hillhouse and Jacob* [1987] NLJR 171, CA.

Disputed facts

15.17

Not less than 28 days before the date of the hearing, the applicant may require the respondent to indicate within 14 days which of the facts set out in the rule 5 statement are in dispute. This is invariably done in a standard form letter at an early stage. There is no sanction for any failure to co-operate in this way (other than in costs), but if there is a defence to be argued, as has already been explained, it is generally in the interests of the respondent to state what it is.

The absence of such co-operation will usually mean that the applicant will serve notices to admit documents under the Civil Evidence Act 1995, and witness statements if required, so that in the absence of a constructive response the case can be proved on documents without the attendance of witnesses.

The nature of legal practice means that normally the case against the solicitor is wholly documented. The primary evidence against the respondent in most cases is likely to be the content of his or her own files. Serious disputes of fact as to the prosecution case are comparatively rare, and often it is unnecessary for the applicant to call any oral evidence. The outcome of the case will usually depend upon the respondent's evidence.

Witness summonses

15.18

Either party may compel the attendance of witnesses and the production by witnesses of documents by means of witness summonses.[1] Although a form of subpoena is contained in the Rules, witness summonses are not issued by the Tribunal itself but by the Administrative Court under CPR 34.4 and the form must be compliant with the Civil Procedure Rules 1998.

The 2007 Rules as drafted also imply that an application may be made to the Tribunal to set aside any witness summons. The reference in the form to the Tribunal should be a reference to the court. This has now been corrected.[2]

1   Section 46(11) of SA 1974.
2   Form 5 in the Schedule to the 2007 Rules.

Absence of the respondent

15.19

The Tribunal may proceed in the absence of the respondent upon proof of service of the notice of hearing.[1] This regularly occurs. Where a respondent was neither present nor represented, and the Tribunal decided the case in his absence, he may apply for a re-hearing within 14 days of the filing of the order (in practice therefore within 14 days of the hearing) – which the Tribunal may grant upon such terms as it thinks fit.[2] A solicitor who voluntarily absents himself from the hearing will ordinarily, however, receive little sympathy from the Tribunal, and is unlikely to obtain a re-hearing. In *R (Elliott) v Solicitors Disciplinary Tribunal*[3] the applicant applied for an adjournment of the substantive hearing, and then walked out when the adjournment was refused. The Tribunal heard the remainder of the case in his absence, and subsequently refused an application for a re-hearing. It was held in judicial review proceedings that the rule (then rule 25 of the 1994 Rules) did not apply to such a situation.

1   Rule 16(2) of the 2007 Rules.
2   Rule 19(1) of the 2007 Rules.
3   [2004] EWHC 1176 (Admin).

Findings of another court or tribunal

15.20

Findings of fact by another court or tribunal are admissible as prima facie proof of those facts. Accordingly, civil judgments relevant to issues before the Tribunal can be admitted into evidence but may be rebutted. The Tribunal is free to depart from findings in civil proceedings and has done so in several cases,[1] although it will be slow to do so.[2] The situation in relation to criminal convictions is otherwise: it has been held that the Tribunal was right to refuse to hear evidence intended to show a wrongful conviction, as public policy required that, save in exceptional circumstances, a challenge to a criminal conviction should not be entertained by a disciplinary tribunal.[3] Rule 15 of the 2007 Rules makes more explicit provision as to these matters than did rule 30 of the 1994 Rules: findings of fact upon which a criminal conviction was based are admissible as conclusive proof of those facts save in exceptional circumstances, whereas a civil court judgment is admissible as proof but not conclusive proof of the findings of fact upon which the judgment was based.

1   See *Gold,* 6050–1991, SDT; *Brebner,* 8805–2003, SDT; *Slater,* 9619–2006, SDT; and, for the general approach, *Choudry v Law Society* [2001] EWHC Admin 633.
2   See *General Medical Council v Spackman* [1943] AC 627.
3   *Re a Solicitor* (1996) Times, 18 March.

Power to regulate its own procedure

15.21

Rule 21(1) and (2) of the 2007 Rules confers the all-important powers on the Tribunal to regulate its own procedure subject to the Rules, and to dispense with any requirements of the Rules in respect of notices, statements, witnesses, service or time in any case where it appears to be just to do so. At the discretion of the Tribunal, the strict rules of evidence do not apply.[1]

1   Rule 13(10) of the 2007 Rules.

Interlocutory orders

15.22

Because it can regulate its own procedure, although there is no specific provision in the Rules for interlocutory processes the Tribunal will entertain applications for interlocutory relief, such as disclosure or further particularisation, and will direct the exchange of skeleton arguments in appropriate circumstances. There is a practice direction on the position of the Tribunal on disclosure of documents: see **APPENDIX 16**.

There is no statutory appeal against an interlocutory order of the Tribunal, and the only avenue of challenge is therefore an application for judicial review. In *Stokes v Law Society*[1] Kennedy LJ observed that relief would be given only in exceptional circumstances 'and never where, as here, the error relied upon has been rectified'.

1   [2001] EWHC 1101 (Admin).

Abuse of process

15.23

The Tribunal may strike out proceedings if it considers that the prosecution amounts to an abuse of process. In the criminal courts, it has long been held that applications to stay proceedings for abuse of process should only rarely be granted, and that the threshold to be surmounted by the applicant is a high one.[1] The Tribunal takes a similar approach, and successful abuse of process applications are rare.

One particular area in which such applications have succeeded is where there has been inordinate delay in bringing the case before the Tribunal.[2] This may amount to an abuse of process on a traditional common law analysis, or it may breach the 'reasonable time' requirement in Article 6(1) of the European Convention on Human Rights. The Tribunal has held that time starts for this purpose when the decision to refer the solicitor to the Tribunal is made, and has struck out cases which have been inordinately delayed.[3]

The Tribunal has ruled that proceedings should generally be issued within three months of the decision to refer a respondent to the Tribunal, and that if necessary an application for further time (if needed before the matter was listed for hearing) could be considered by the Tribunal.[4]

1   The leading cases are *Connelly v DPP* [1964] AC 1254; *DPP v Humphrys* [1977] AC 1; and *R v Horseferry Road Magistrates' Court, ex p Bennett* [1994] 1 AC 42.
2   For the general approach of the courts, see *Attorney-General's Reference (No 2 of 2001)* [2004] 2 AC 72; *Porter v Magill* [2002] 2 AC 357; and *Dyer v Watson* [2004] 1 AC 379.
3   See generally *Loomba and Loomba*, 9022–2004, SDT; *Davis*, 9017–2004, SDT; *Judge and Stanger*, 9028–2004, SDT; *Rutherford*, 9074–2004, SDT; *Fallon*, 9154–2004, SDT and *Sancheti and others*, 7976–2007, SDT.
4   *Nulty and Trotter*, 9871–2008, SDT – memorandum of preliminary hearing, 1 July 2008.

Summary disposal

15.24

If the respondent considers that there is a fatal flaw in the applicant's case against him, the Tribunal may be willing to consider that as a preliminary issue with a view to saving time and expense. Accordingly, cases can be disposed of summarily at the start of the substantive hearing, and there would seem to be no reason in principle in an appropriate case why the respondent should not seek an early listing of the case to ascertain whether it can be summarily disposed of in this way.[1] It must be accepted that these situations are likely to be rare.

1   *Law Society v Adcock and Mocroft* [2006] EWHC 3212 (Admin) at para 30. In *Maddocks*, 9536–2006, SDT seven of eight partners against whom proceedings had been commenced sought summary dismissal of the case on the ground that the Law Society had adduced no evidence against them. The Law Society argued that the Tribunal did not have jurisdiction summarily to dismiss charges in this way. The case was ultimately compromised, the proceedings against the affected partners were dismissed by consent, and the Tribunal was not called upon to rule on the point. However, it is submitted that basic principles of pragmatism and fairness should lead to the conclusion that the Tribunal has power in an appropriate case to conclude at an early stage that the applicant's case is unsustainable. Certainly that jurisdiction has in fact been exercised, and not only in *Adcock and Mocroft*: see *Burchnall*, 9030–2004, SDT.

Standard of proof

15.25

It has been held by the Privy Council that the standard of proof in deciding facts against a respondent solicitor in disciplinary proceedings should be the criminal standard, irrespective of whether dishonesty is alleged.[1] The SRA is resistant to application of the criminal standard, and in *Richards v Law Society*[2] sought to argue for the civil standard: the Divisional Court held that on the particular facts of the case, the issue was academic, but strongly implied that the Tribunal was bound to apply the criminal standard unless and until the Supreme Court ruled otherwise.[3]

1   *Campbell v Hamlet* [2005] UKPC 19, [2005] 3 All ER 1116, interpreting *Re A Solicitor* [1993] QB 69. The adoption of the criminal standard is of long standing, is supported by high authority, and mirrors the practice in disciplinary proceedings against barristers. The Tribunal has regularly asserted that it will consistently employ the criminal standard, most recently in *Beresford and Smith*, 9666–2007, SDT (a case in which the SRA sought to argue the contrary), and has ruled that this should also be applied in cases involving orders against employees of solicitors; see *Ahmed*, 8645–2002, SDT.
2   [2009] EWHC 2087 (Admin). The case was remarkable, in that the two component parts of the Law Society (SRA and representative body) argued on opposite sides for opposite conclusions.
3   [2009] EWHC 2087 (Admin) at paragraph 22.

Pre-trial procedure – what happens in practice

15.26

Following a decision to refer a solicitor to the Tribunal the solicitor will receive, after an interval, confirmation that the papers have been referred to an external panel solicitor or to an in-house advocate. On the assumption that the Tribunal determines that there is a case to answer, the next development will be service of the papers. It is not unusual for there to be a delay of several months before proceedings are issued.

Service is arranged by the Tribunal by special delivery mail. It is possible to inform the applicant in advance that papers can be served on a nominated representative. The documents served will include the rule 5 statement and any documents annexed or exhibited to it, a full set of the current Solicitors (Disciplinary Proceedings) Rules, copies of the Tribunal's published practice directions, a list of those most regularly appearing in the Tribunal as advocates, and documents concerned with listing.

Notice will be given of a Pre-Listing Day, usually some two months ahead. This is not a hearing in the true sense; the Tribunal does not convene. The Tribunal's Clerk sits to receive information and make listing decisions. There is no requirement to attend and it is not usual to do so. The only requirement in practice is to give to the Tribunal before that date the information it needs to make a decision as to listing. For this purpose a questionnaire is provided, and the respondent is encouraged to contact the applicant to clarify issues.

That requirement is reinforced by a letter in standard form from the applicant requiring the respondent to identify issues of fact, which will arrive usually within days of the papers being served.

Essentially the Tribunal needs to know what level of dispute there is likely to be and how long will be required for the hearing.

15.27

The Tribunal generally sits between two and three days a week, in addition to any court time needed for multi-day cases, and has three courtrooms so that long cases can be accommodated in one court while routine matters occupy the other courts in greater numbers. A typical list of routine matters will have three to five applications listed for hearing. Because the Tribunal members pre-read the papers and most cases are well documented (see above), even quite substantial contests can be disposed of in less than a day.

A normal case with an expected duration of one to two hours will generally be listed some five months after proceedings are issued.

The Tribunal expects the parties to have a sensible dialogue to refine issues and avoid unnecessary contention. The overwhelming majority of cases proceed on the basis of admissions and mitigation, or on the basis of admitted facts with argument limited to the proper interpretation of those facts and the inferences that it is proper to draw. Only infrequently, in very substantial or complex cases, is there any need to consider interlocutory applications. For example, even if there is a perceived need for the applicant to clarify the case the respondent has to meet, one would expect that clarification to be volunteered without the need for any formal intervention by the Tribunal. Most cases therefore proceed directly from the service of papers, and a brief dialogue between the parties in which issues and pleas are identified, to a final hearing.

Shortly before the hearing the applicant can be expected to provide a schedule of his or her costs for possible agreement, on the basis that a fixed costs order can be made by the Tribunal if the amount can be agreed.

The hearing

15.28

Hearings in the Tribunal are a mixture of the formal and informal; evidence is taken on oath but, as has been seen, the strict rules of evidence do not apply. The parties conduct their advocacy seated. No pleas to the allegations are formally taken. The applicant is expected to have established the position in this respect and will inform the Tribunal which allegations are admitted and which require to be resolved by the Tribunal. The respondent is required to do no more at this stage, hopefully, than give a monosyllabic confirmation.

The applicant will then open the case and call his or her evidence. As has been said, only rarely is it necessary for the applicant to rely on oral evidence, and usually the applicant's case can be presented entirely by reference to documents, including the written explanations and submissions of the respondent at the investigation stage. The one witness most frequently called by applicants will be the investigating officer of the SRA's Forensic Investigation Unit who undertook the original investigation of, for example, the respondent's accounts.

Examination, cross-examination and re-examination of witnesses proceed as normal, following the pattern of the civil courts as to the use of any witness statement as primary evidence-in-chief.

Following the conclusion of the applicant's case the respondent may make a submission of no case to answer,[1] and then will open his or her case, give evidence and call witnesses, and may make a closing submission. In contested cases it tends to be assumed that the respondent will give evidence; in cases where the respondent is accused of and denies dishonesty it would be an exceptional course to fail to do so.

It is not usual for the applicant to make a closing speech, but he or she may do so in a lengthy or complex case where evidence can helpfully be summarised and commented upon. The applicant does not have a right of reply save in relation to points of law or to correct mistakes.[2]

---

1   The Tribunal has frequently demonstrated a reluctance to accede to such a submission. There is at this stage in a contested application an understandable interest in hearing what the respondent has to say. For an exceptional case in which the Tribunal acceded to such a submission see *Cohen and Others*, 9942–2008.
2   This should be taken to reflect current practice; there is no formal rule as to this.

Decision, mitigation and penalty

15.29

The Tribunal invariably announces its findings, together with brief reasons, at the conclusion of the hearing. If it finds any of the allegations against the respondent substantiated, the Chairman asks the Tribunal Clerk whether there have been previous findings against the respondent. The respondent is permitted to make a plea in mitigation (possibly at this stage adducing testimonials as to character) and the Tribunal then determines penalty.[1] If the Tribunal decides to suspend a solicitor, it may be prepared to delay the start of that suspension to enable the solicitor to make appropriate arrangements for running his practice during the period of suspension. The Tribunal is noticeably more reluctant to delay the effect of a striking-off order although this does occasionally happen.[2] Respondents seeking a stay pending appeal must, if the Tribunal does not grant a stay, appeal and apply to the Administrative Court for a stay pending a hearing of the substantive appeal. The appeal does not operate as a stay. For further guidance on appeals, see paras **15.46–15.49**.

The full written findings of the Tribunal are ordinarily delivered some weeks after the hearing. In *Virdi v Law Society*[3] a full scale attack was made on the Tribunal's process for production of the findings, on the basis that the clerk had a role in producing a first draft of the document based, inter alia, on the oral findings and reasons given by the chairman at the conclusion of the hearing. Although the (exceptional) delay in producing the findings in that case was the subject of criticism, the process was held to be entirely proper by both the Divisional Court and the Court of Appeal.

1   This summary of the current practice is now enshrined in rule 16 of the 2007 Rules.
2   *Aaronson* 10099–2008.
3   [2009] EWHC 918 (Admin) (Divisional Court); [2010] EWCA Civ 100 (Court of Appeal).

Penalties – the approach in practice

15.30

Cases before the Tribunal vary infinitely and no analytical consideration of particular facts, individual cases or individual penalties is of material assistance. There are, however, some general principles and typical classes of case that can usefully be considered.

The general approach – Bolton v Law Society

15.31

In *Bolton v Law Society*[1] the Master of the Rolls, Sir Thomas Bingham, made a general and oft-cited statement of the rationale for and purpose of punishment by the Tribunal. It merits citation here, as it provides the logical cornerstone for much of what both the Tribunal and appellate courts decide:

> 'It is required of lawyers practising in this country that they should discharge their professional duties with integrity, probity and complete trustworthiness …
>
> Any solicitor who is shown to have discharged his professional duties with anything less than complete integrity, probity and trustworthiness must expect severe sanctions to be imposed upon him by the Solicitors Disciplinary Tribunal. Lapses from the required high standard may, of course, take different forms and be of varying degrees. The most serious involves proven dishonesty, whether or not leading to criminal proceedings and criminal penalties. In such cases the tribunal has almost invariably, no matter how strong the mitigation advanced for the solicitor, ordered that he be struck off the Roll of Solicitors … If a solicitor is not shown to have acted dishonestly, but is shown to have fallen below the required standards of integrity, probity and trustworthiness, his lapse is less serious but it remains very serious indeed in a member of a profession whose reputation

depends upon trust. A striking off order will not necessarily follow in such a case, but it may well. The decision whether to strike off or to suspend will often involve a fine and difficult exercise of judgment, to be made by the tribunal as an informed and expert body on all the facts of the case. Only in a very unusual and venial case of this kind would the tribunal be likely to regard as appropriate any order less severe than one of suspension.'

The Master of the Rolls explained in addition to the need to punish in appropriate cases, there was an additional purpose in imposing sanctions, and that this was:

'... the most fundamental of all: to maintain the reputation of the solicitors' profession as one in which every member, of whatever standing, may be trusted to the ends of the earth. To maintain this reputation and sustain public confidence in the integrity of the profession it is often necessary that those guilty of serious lapses are not only expelled but denied re-admission. If a member of the public sells his house, very often his largest asset, and entrusts the proceeds to his solicitor, pending re-investment in another house, he is ordinarily entitled to expect that the solicitor will be a person whose trustworthiness is not, and never has been, seriously in question. Otherwise, the whole profession, and the public as a whole, is injured. A profession's most valuable asset is its collective reputation and the confidence which that inspires.'

1   [1994] 1 WLR 512.

Dishonesty in connection with client account

15.32

Such is the importance of the principle that clients' money must be held separately from a solicitor's own funds, that any dishonest misappropriation of clients' moneys will lead inevitably to a striking-off order, whether or not the misappropriation also amounts to theft. This is now seen as all but automatic.[1] In *Bultitude v Law Society*[2] the Law Society appealed against the reduction of a striking–off order to a suspension by the Divisional Court. The appeal was allowed by the Court of Appeal, and the Court was informed that there was only one known instance of dishonesty in connection with client account that had not resulted in a striking off.

1   See *Bolton v Law Society* [1994] 1 WLR 512; *Weston v Law Society* (1998) Times, 15 July.
2   [2004] EWCA Civ 1853.

Other forms of dishonesty

15.33

Historically, a solicitor found guilty of any form of dishonesty could be expected to be struck off, and as a general proposition this undoubtedly remains the position.[1] Indeed, any solicitor who is dishonestly involved in a mortgage fraud, investment fraud or money laundering will inevitably be struck off. Even without dishonesty, solicitors who become caught up in the criminal activity or dubious commercial practices of others are likely to be struck off or suspended for a considerable period.[2]

Very occasionally, the Tribunal permits a solicitor found guilty of dishonesty to remain on the Roll. This may be because in recent times, the SRA has alleged dishonesty in circumstances where the solicitor has not personally profited (other than by way of fee income charged at a reasonable rate) from improper acts which are alleged to have been carried out dishonestly.[3] In such cases, the Tribunal may consider that even if dishonesty or conscious impropriety has been established, the public interest can be served by a period of suspension, and thereafter by regulatory controls such as practising certificate conditions being imposed upon the solicitor. Moreover, in some cases which could reasonably have attracted the label of dishonesty, but where the failing is isolated and plainly out of character, the Tribunal and/or the Divisional Court has on occasion taken a merciful approach,[4] recognising that honest people can do very strange and irrational things in circumstances of acute stress. It should be emphasised however, that these are exceptional cases, and in *SRA v Sharma* the Divisional Court allowed an appeal by the SRA against a 3-year suspension imposed upon a solicitor who had forged documents, and sent them as 'duly signed' under cover of a letter written on his firm's notepaper. The Court imposed a striking-off order in place of the suspension, and Coulson J. stated at [13]:

'(a) Save in exceptional circumstances, a finding of dishonesty will lead to the solicitor being struck off the roll, see *Bolton*[6] and *Salsbury*.[7] That is the normal and necessary penalty in cases of dishonesty: see *Bultitude*.[8]

(b) There will be a small residual category where striking off will be a disproportionate sentence in all the circumstances: see *Salsbury*.

(c) In deciding whether or not a particular case falls into that category, relevant factors will include the nature, scope and extent of the dishonesty itself; whether it was momentary, such as *Burrowes*,[9] or over a lengthy period of time, such as *Bultitude*; whether it was a benefit to the solicitor (*Burrowes*), and whether it had an adverse effect on others.'

And also (at [26]):

'The question for this court is whether in the light of the principles outlined above, the Tribunal's decision can be described as excessively lenient. If it can, then this court should substitute for the Tribunal's sentence, the sentence that it considers to be commensurate with these offences. If the sentence cannot be regarded as excessively lenient, even if it is not necessarily the sentence which this court would itself have imposed, the sentence should remain unchanged.'

A similar approach was taken by the Divisional Court in *SRA v Tilsiter*[10] in which an indefinite suspension was increased on appeal to a striking-off order.

1   *Law Society v Salsbury* [2008] EWCA Civ 1285.
2   See *Bryant and Bench v Law Society* [2007] EWHC 3043 (Admin).
3   *Pitts-Tucker*, 9722–2007, SDT.
4   See *Burrowes v Law Society* and the cases referred to in the judgment: [2002] EWHC 2900 (Admin) at paras 6, 10–13, 17 and 20.
5   [2010] EWHC 2022 (Admin)
6   *Bolton v Law Society* [1994] 1 WLR 512.
7   *Law Society v Salsbury* [2008] EWCA Civ 1285.
8   *Bultitude v Law Society* [2004] EWCA Civ 1853.
9   *Burrowes v Law Society* [2002] EWHC 2900 (Admin).
10 [2009] EWHC 3787 (Admin).

Breaches of the Solicitors' Accounts Rules 1998

15.34

Breaches of the Accounts Rules can range from the serious to the trivial. Improper transfers from client accounts to office accounts falling short of dishonesty may merit a striking-off order or suspension, as may a chaotic accounting system which creates risk to clients and to the public. The importance of regular reconciliations and submission of accountants' reports cannot be overestimated, as these are the mechanisms by which problems can be detected at a relatively early stage. Other administrative failings and errors, including failure to carry out reconciliations timeously or to submit accountants' reports at the correct time, if standing alone, are likely to be visited with a fine.

Culpable or dishonest overcharging

15.35

There is potentially a wide spectrum of 'overcharging' by a solicitor. The reduction of a solicitor/own client bill at a detailed assessment is an everyday experience for solicitors and implies no professional misconduct of any sort. Where such a reduction is very substantial, however, the solicitor may be open to a charge of 'culpable overcharging'. As a rule of thumb, if a bill is reduced by more than 50 per cent on assessment, this may give cause for regulatory concern, and may lead to further investigation (and possible disciplinary proceedings).[1] The concept of culpable overcharging does not incorporate within it any allegation of dishonesty.

At the most serious end of the spectrum is dishonest overcharging, where the solicitor has no honest belief that the sum charged is a reasonable sum for the work done. As with any form of dishonesty, a solicitor found guilty of dishonest overcharging can expect to be struck off.

Unsurprisingly, therefore, penalties imposed by the Tribunal on this subject vary considerably. Particular care may be required in probate cases, where a solicitor may be the sole executor of the estate and there may be no independent scrutiny of his or her charges.[2] In *Sheikh v Law Society*, Chadwick LJ observed that evidence from a costs draftsman with suitable experience as to what he would expect to see in such cases provides a useful starting point in evaluating the issue as to whether there has been not merely culpable but possibly dishonest overcharging, in the sense that significant deviation from the norm may require explanation.[3]

1   This is consistent with article 5(1) of the Solicitors' (Non-Contentious Business) Remuneration Order 1994 (SI 1994/2616) which required any costs judge who reduces a solicitor/client non-contentious bill by more than half on detailed assessment to report the matter to the SRA.
2   See, eg, *Sheikh v Law Society* [2006] EWCA Civ 1577, [2007] 3 All ER 183 at para 45.
3   *Sheikh v Law Society* [2006] EWCA Civ 1577, [2007] 3 All ER 183 at para 64.

Conflicts of interest

15.36

Actual or potential conflicts of interest may arise in a variety of ways and those of a relatively innocent nature, such as those due to an error of judgement, will merit no more than a fine.[1] Some conflicts are infinitely more serious and involve solicitors deliberately or recklessly preferring their own interests to those of their clients, for example by obtaining unsecured loans from clients without ensuring that the clients receive independent advice. These are likely to be regarded very seriously and to result in the solicitor being struck off.[2]

1   For example *O'Brien, 9574–2006,* SDT (the 'Freshfields Two' case).
2   Unhappily there have been very many cases in this category – over 100 in the last ten years. Examples are *Predko, 7099–1996,* SDT and *Austin-Olsen, 9361–2005,* SDT.

Payment of referral fees

15.37

Until 2004, there was an outright ban on the payment of referral fees by solicitors to introducers of work. This proved difficult to enforce, and there were concerns that it might offend competition law. In 2004 the ban was abolished. Instead, the Law Society required that solicitors be transparent about the fact and amount of referral fees in a new section 2A of the Solicitors' Introduction and Referral Code. This has been replicated in substance in the Solicitors' Code of Conduct 2007, rule 9.

The issue of referral fees has continued to cause controversy within the profession, and in 2006 the SRA carried out a major investigation into firms which had arrangements with introducers of work in the fields of personal injury and conveyancing. In February 2007 the SRA published a warning to every firm in the country, stating that it was 'cracking down' on solicitors 'whose referral arrangements compromise their clients' interests and who undermine public confidence in solicitors'.

More recently it has transpired that while there was a high level of non-compliance because the rules were complex, there had rarely been any material prejudice to clients. The Tribunal has recognised that regulation in this area has been problematic and in the past has dealt with such cases by way of a fine.[1]

1   For example, *Mendelson, 9212–2005,* SDT.

Failure to reply to correspondence from clients and/or the SRA and LCS

15.38

Failures to reply to correspondence are regarded seriously by the Tribunal, as they damage the reputation of the profession. Standing alone, such failures will merit a fine – even if the original complaint, to which the respondent failed to respond, was in fact without merit.

Regulatory settlements[1]

15.39

The Tribunal is prepared in an appropriate case to adopt a process akin to a *Carecraft* procedure,[2] whereby the matter can be dealt with on agreed facts and with an agreed result, subject always to the Tribunal's permission and discretion.[3]

1   See also para **13.21**.
2   *Re Carecraft Construction Co Ltd* [1994] 1 WLR 172.
3   *Wilson-Smith,* 8772–2003, SDT.

Costs

Costs orders against the Law Society/SRA

15.40

Until relatively recently, those appearing in the Tribunal could expect, and advise their clients to expect, that costs would probably follow the event. If a respondent were to be acquitted of all charges in the Tribunal, he could generally expect an order that his costs should be paid by the Law Society.

This state of affairs altered with the decision of the Divisional Court in *Baxendale-Walker v Law Society*,[1] which has been upheld by the Court of Appeal.[2] The rationale is that the Law Society is a statutory regulator, exercising its powers in the public interest; when the Law Society/SRA is addressing the question whether there is sufficient evidence to justify an application to the Tribunal, the ambit of its responsibility is far greater than it would be for a litigant deciding whether to bring civil proceedings.

The normal approach to costs decisions in ordinary civil litigation, that costs should follow the event, accordingly has no direct application to disciplinary proceedings against solicitors. What will be considered just and reasonable will depend on all the relevant facts and circumstances. The Tribunal may consider it just that costs should follow the event, but need not think so in all cases. Where the regulatory authority has acted reasonably, properly and on grounds that reasonably appear to be sound in the exercise of its public duty, the Tribunal should consider – in addition to any other relevant fact or circumstance – the financial prejudice to the particular respondent if an order for costs is not made in his favour and the need to encourage public authorities to make and stand by honest, reasonable and apparently sound decisions made in the public interest without fear of exposure to undue financial prejudice if the decision is successfully challenged.

Success by a respondent is a factor in his favour, but is not decisive; it is not the starting point but simply one factor for consideration.

However, where for example disciplinary proceedings are held to amount to an abuse of process, have been inefficiently prosecuted or have been mounted upon inadequate evidence, the respondent solicitor will ordinarily have a powerful argument that costs should follow the event.

The principles set out in *Baxendale-Walker* do not apply directly to appeals from the Solicitors Disciplinary Tribunal. On such appeals, the costs provisions of the Civil Procedure Rules are applied. An appellant who successfully challenges findings against him or her can ordinarily expect to be awarded the costs of the appeal.[3]

1   [2006] EWHC 643 (Admin), [2006] 3 All ER 675.
2   [2007] EWCA Civ 233, [2007] 3 All ER 330.
3   See *Bryant and Bench v Law Society* [2007] EWHC 3043 (Admin) at para 251.

Costs against a successful respondent solicitor

15.41

Rule 22 of the 1994 Rules specifically provided that an order for costs may be made by the Tribunal against the respondent without finding any allegation proved – and even if no other order is made if, having regard to his or her conduct or to all the circumstances (or both), the Tribunal shall think it fit.[1] In *Rowe v Lindsay* the Divisional Court indicated that this rule did not justify an order for costs against a successful respondent who had been acquitted of misconduct and whose conduct in relation to the questions before the Tribunal, and since the commencement of proceedings against him, had not in the event been criticised.[2]

If intending to impose a costs sanction (either an order under rule 22 or an order depriving a successful respondent solicitor of his costs) by reason of any fault found against the solicitor, the Tribunal is bound to consider what impact the conduct of the solicitor, of which it is critical, has had on the costs incurred. The calculation need not be exact, but there must be a reasonable and just balance between the order made and what has occurred in the proceedings. There must be a causal connection between the fault found by the Tribunal and the incurring of costs.[3]

1   This provision is not replicated in the 2007 Rules, rule 18 of which gives the Tribunal a wide discretion as to costs orders.
2   [2001] DC Transcript CO/4737/2000.
3   *Hayes v Law Society* [2004] EWHC 1165 (Admin). In referring to depriving the successful respondent of his costs (as distinct from the possibility of an order under rule 22) this decision should now be considered to have been overruled by *Baxendale-Walker v Law Society* [2007] EWCA Civ 233, [2007] 3 All ER 330.

Costs against the unsuccessful respondent

15.42

A very high percentage of applications against solicitors are successful in whole or in part and the respondent in those cases will be ordered to pay the costs of the SRA. Even if not all allegations are found proved it is the Tribunal's practice to award all the costs against the respondent if, on the facts, it was reasonable to make those allegations. If there has been a substantial contest over part of the case in which the respondent has been successful, the order may be to pay a reduced percentage of the SRA's costs.

The normal order for costs in a case where there has been a forensic investigation is an order for the payment of costs 'of and incidental to the application and enquiry' to include the costs of the forensic investigation. These are usually considerable – several thousands of pounds – and can exceed the applicant's legal costs.

The Tribunal can endorse an agreement between the parties and make an order for fixed costs, can summarily assess the costs in appropriate circumstances, or can order that the costs be subject to detailed assessment if not agreed – with or without an interim payment of costs being directed. As orders made by the Tribunal are enforceable as orders of the High Court,[1] detailed assessment is dealt with by the Supreme Court Costs Office and the Civil Procedure Rules 1998 apply to that assessment in the usual way.

In imposing fines and making costs orders the Tribunal should take into account the means of the respondent. In particular, where a solicitor is suspended or struck off, enquiry as to the solicitor's means must be made before any decision is made.[2]

1 Section 48(4) of SA 1974.
2 See *Merrick v Law Society* [2007] EWHC 2997 (Admin) at paras 60–66, in which an order for costs in the sum of £45,000 against a suspended solicitor, who did not have the means or ability to pay, was quashed on appeal. The Tribunal regularly makes orders for costs, not to be enforced without leave of the Tribunal, where the respondent's financial circumstances are such as to merit this course.

Restoration to the Roll

15.43

The Tribunal has a statutory power under s.47(1)(e) of SA 1974 to restore struck off solicitors to the Roll. However, the guidance provided by the Court of Appeal in *Bolton v Law Society*[1] as to the purposes of imposing disciplinary sanctions and summarised at **15.30** above, applies to applications to restore to the Roll:

> '... the most fundamental [purpose] of all: to maintain the reputation of the solicitors' profession as one in which every member, of whatever standing, may be trusted to the ends of the earth. To maintain this reputation and sustain public confidence in the integrity of the profession it is often necessary that those guilty of serious lapses are not only expelled but denied re-admission.'

1 [1994] 1 WLR 512.

15.44

As a result, it has hitherto proved all but impossible for former solicitors who have been struck off for disciplinary offences including dishonesty, to persuade the Tribunal to permit restoration to the roll. The former Master of the Rolls, Lord Donaldson of Lymington said in one case[1]:

> '... however sympathetic one may be towards an individual member of either branch of the legal profession, if you fall very seriously below the standards of that profession and are expelled from it, there is a public interest in the profession itself in hardening its heart if any question arises of your rejoining it. Neither branch of the profession is short of people who have never fallen from grace. There is considerable public interest in the public as a whole being able to deal with members of those professions knowing that, save in the most exceptional circumstances, they can be sure that none of them have ever been guilty of any dishonesty at all.'

In his final decision as Master of the Rolls, Lord Donaldson went further, and wondered whether Parliament had ever contemplated that a solicitor who had been guilty of fraud could be restored to the roll, although he continued:[2]

> 'It may be that in a very exceptional case it did – something which really could be described as a momentary aberration under quite exceptional strain, the sort of strain which not everybody meets but some people do meet in the course of their everyday lives.'

To date in the modern era (that is for some three decades at least), only one solicitor who has been struck off for dishonesty has successfully applied for restoration to the roll.[3]

1   No. 5 of 1987, unreported.
2   No. 11 of 1990, unreported.
3   *Vane*, 8607–2002.

15.45

A former solicitor who has been struck off for less serious disciplinary offences, not involving dishonesty, may be more fortunate. In order to contemplate making an order of restoration, the Tribunal will need to be satisfied firstly that the former solicitor has demonstrated his or her complete rehabilitation, and secondly that restoration to the roll would not involve any damage to the reputation of the profession. Lord Donaldson encouraged the Tribunal to ask:[1]

'If this was the sort of case where, even if the back history was known (that is whatever explanation and mitigation was available to explain why the solicitor committed the original offence), and without the explanation as to what has happened subsequently, the members of the public would say "that does not shake my faith in solicitors as a whole".'

These hurdles, particularly the second, remain very difficult to surmount. Even if they are overcome, it is unlikely that the Tribunal, or the SRA, would contemplate permitting the solicitor, once restored to the roll, to practice without any form of restriction upon his or her practising certificate.

1   No. 11 of 1990, unreported.

Appeals from the Tribunal

Statutory provisions

15.46

Either party may appeal to the High Court without permission and are governed by CPR Part 52.[1]

Until 6 April 2010, paragraph 22.6B of the Practice Direction to Part 52 provided that the time within which appeals should be brought in respect of decisions of the Solicitors Disciplinary Tribunal was 14 days from the filing of the Tribunal's findings (the full written reasons for its decision). With effect from 6 April 2010 the Practice Direction was amended and appeals from the Tribunal are now governed by CPR rule 52.4 as modified by paragraphs 17.3 and 17.4 of the Practice Direction, so that the appellant's notice must be filed within 28 days after the statement of reasons (the findings) is received by the appellant.

The court has power to make such order on an appeal as they may think fit.[2] Appeals to the High Court are heard in the Administrative Court, usually by a two- or three-judge Divisional Court.

1   Section 49 of SA 1974. The one exception, which will only be relevant when rules are made to permit appeals to the Tribunal from decisions of the SRA in relation to practising certificate and comparable issues, is that the decision of the Tribunal on such appeals will be final; see section 49A(3) of SA 1974. See para **15.6 FN 11**.
2   Section 49(4) of SA 1974.

Stay pending appeal

15.47

As has been said (see para **15.29**), the Tribunal does not readily grant a stay pending appeal, or any other period of grace, in cases where an order for striking off is made, still less when there has been a finding of dishonesty, and an appeal does not in itself operate as a stay.[1] It is necessary to lodge an appeal and to apply within that appeal for interlocutory relief. The test that will be applied is set out in *Re A Solicitor.*[2]

> 'For such a submission to succeed, it would be necessary to establish not only that the applicant's appeal against striking off would have a reasonable prospect of success, but, further, that this Court would be likely to impose in substitution for the order of the Tribunal a penalty no greater than suspension from practice for some three or four months [being the period within which the substantive appeal could be expected to be heard].'

In that case, in which the application was heard in November 1998, the appeal was expected to be heard in February 1999.

It will be seen that an application for a stay pending appeal would be more likely to succeed in a case of a suspension from practice where the suspension would substantially have been served by the time the appeal came to be heard. Successful applications for a stay pending appeal where the solicitor has been struck off can be expected to be rare.

Where the Tribunal has directed that inadequate professional services (IPS) awards are enforceable as orders of the High Court, and there is an appeal, it would similarly be necessary to seek a stay pending appeal if the enforcement of the awards is intended to be avoided or postponed in the meantime.

1   CPR Pt 52.7.
2   16 November 1998, unreported, transcript CO/4359/98, per Rose LJ.

Approach of the courts

15.48

Until the advent of the Human Rights Act 1998, the courts were reluctant to interfere with the decisions of the Tribunal as an expert professional disciplinary tribunal. It was stated that it would require a very strong case to interfere with sentence, because the Tribunal was best placed to weigh the seriousness of professional misconduct.[1] The modern approach of the courts in the light of the Human Rights Act 1998 has altered in this respect, and was first determined in *Langford v Law Society*.[2] The following extracts from Lord Millett's speech in *Ghosh v General Medical Council*[3] were cited by Rose LJ in *Langford*:

'... their Lordships wish to emphasise that their powers are not as limited as may be suggested by some of the observations which have been made in the past ...

... the Board will accord an appropriate measure of respect to the judgment of the committee whether the practitioner's failings amount to serious professional misconduct and on the measures necessary to maintain professional standards and provide adequate protection to the public. But the Board will not defer to the committee's judgment more than is warranted by the circumstances. The council conceded, and their Lordships accept, that it is open to them to ... decide whether the sanction of erasure was appropriate and necessary in the public interest or was excessive and disproportionate; and in the latter event either to substitute some other penalty or to remit the case to the committee for reconsideration.'

The correct approach of the courts to appeals from the Tribunal was comprehensively reviewed in *Law Society v Salsbury:*[4]

'The correct analysis is that the Solicitors Disciplinary Tribunal comprises an expert and informed tribunal, which is particularly well placed in any case to assess what measures are required to deal with defaulting solicitors and to protect the public interest. Absent any error of law, the High Court must pay considerable respect to the sentencing decisions of the tribunal. Nevertheless if the High Court, despite paying such respect, is satisfied that the sentencing decision was clearly inappropriate, then the court will interfere. It should also be noted that an appeal from the Solicitors Disciplinary Tribunal to the High Court normally proceeds by way of review; see CPR rule 52.11(1).'

1   See *McCoan v General Medical Council* [1964] 1 WLR 1007; and *Bolton v Law Society* [1994] 1 WLR 512.
2   [2002] EWHC 2802; see particularly at paras 14 and 15.
3   [2001] 1 WLR 1915.
4   [2008] EWCA Civ 1285 at para 30.

Further appeal to the Court of Appeal

15.49

Further appeals require the permission of the Court of Appeal, as a second appeal governed by CPR 52.13, and are rarely mounted. The Law Society has appealed to the Court of Appeal on only three occasions, in each case to establish important points of principle.[1]

1   *Bolton v Law Society* [1994] 1 WLR 512; *Bultitude v Law Society* [2004] EWCA Civ 1853, (2005) *Times*, 14 January; and *Law Society v Salsbury* [2008] EWCA Civ 1285.

CHAPTER 16

Intervention

16.1

The intervention regime was introduced in the Solicitors Act 1941 as a necessary adjunct to the creation in the same statute of the Law Society Compensation Fund: if a solicitor's conduct might give rise to a claim on the Compensation Fund (which would then have to be met by the profession as a whole), it was felt that a power to intervene could operate to prevent or minimise such a claim. The Law Society has been described as the guardian not only of the profession, but also of the public in their dealings with the profession. The power to intervene provides (now) the SRA with the opportunity to nip dishonesty in the bud, to preserve public confidence in the profession and to reduce claims on the Compensation Fund.[1]

Intervention represents the most powerful regulatory weapon available to the SRA, as it involves the effective destruction of a solicitor's practice (see paras **16.11–16.14**). In the many decades since the introduction of the intervention regime, there have been only two successful statutory challenges to interventions,[2] and in both cases the Law Society did not oppose the withdrawal of the intervention. The claimant in *Sheikh v Law Society* succeeded in a contested challenge at first instance,[3] but the decision was reversed by the Court of Appeal.[4]

The statutory provisions are draconian. They have been described as such, and as potentially striking a mortal blow to the solicitor's practice.[5]

1   See *Buckley v Law Society (No 2)* [1984] 1 WLR 1101 at 1105–1106, per Sir Robert Megarry VC; *Sritharan v Law Society* [2005] EWCA Civ 476 at paras 17 and 18, [2005] 1 WLR 2708 at 2714A-D; and *Sheikh v Law Society* [2006] EWCA Civ 1577, [2007] 3 All ER 183.
2   See *Yogarajah v Law Society* [1982] 126 Sol Jo 430 and *Patel v Law Society* (December 2008, unreported).
3   [2005] EWHC 1409 (Ch), [2005] 4 All ER 7177.
4   [2006] EWCA Civ 1577, [2007] 3 All ER 183.
5   See *Buckley v Law Society (No 2)* [1984] All ER 313; *Giles v Law Society* [1995] 8 Admin LR 105 at 116D–E, CA, per Ward LJ.

Grounds for action

16.2

The grounds upon which the SRA is entitled to intervene in a solicitor's practice are contained in Schedule 1 to the Solicitors Act 1974 (SA 1974) as amended by the Legal Services Act 2007 (LSA 2007). Essentially, these are designed to permit intervention when a solicitor cannot run (through ill health, imprisonment, bankruptcy and the like), or alternatively cannot be trusted to run, a solicitor's practice so as to ensure that clients' moneys are secure. The statutory grounds are the following:[1]

- The SRA has reason to suspect dishonesty on the part of the solicitor, an employee of the solicitor or the personal representatives of a deceased solicitor, in connection with that solicitor's practice or former practice, or in connection with any trust of which that solicitor is or formerly was a trustee or that employee is or was a trustee in his capacity as such an employee (paragraph 1(1)(a) of Schedule 1).

- The SRA has reason to suspect dishonesty on the part of a solicitor in connection with (i) the business of any body of which the solicitor is or was a manager or (ii) any business carried on by the solicitor as a sole trader (paragraph 1(1)(aa) of Schedule 1).

- The SRA considers that there has been undue delay on the part of the personal representatives of a deceased solicitor who immediately before his death was practising as a sole solicitor, in connection with that solicitor's practice or in connection with any trust (paragraph 1(1)(b) of Schedule 1).

- The SRA is satisfied that the solicitor has failed to comply with rules made by virtue of sections 31, 32 or 37(2)(c) of SA 1974, namely the Solicitors' Practice Rules, the Solicitors' Accounts Rules 1998, the Solicitors' Indemnity Insurance Rules and the Solicitors' Code of Conduct 2007 (paragraph 1(1)(c) of Schedule 1).

- The solicitor has been adjudged bankrupt or has made a composition or arrangement with his creditors (paragraph 1(1)(d) of Schedule 1).

- The solicitor has been committed to prison in any civil or criminal proceedings (paragraph 1(1)(e) of Schedule 1).

- The SRA is satisfied that a sole solicitor is incapacitated by illness, injury or accident to such an extent as to be unable to attend to his practice (paragraph 1(1)(ee) of Schedule 1).

- The solicitor lacks capacity within the meaning of the Mental Capacity Act 2005 to act as a solicitor and powers under sections 15 to 20 or section 48 of that Act are exercisable in relation to him (paragraph 1(1)(f)) of Schedule 1).

- The name of a solicitor has been removed from or struck off the roll or a solicitor has been suspended from practice (paragraph 1(1)(g) of Schedule 1).

- The SRA is satisfied that a sole solicitor has abandoned his practice (paragraph 1(1)(h) of Schedule 1).

- The SRA is satisfied that a sole solicitor is incapacitated by age to such an extent as to be unable to attend to his practice (paragraph 1(1)(i) of Schedule 1).

- Any power conferred by Schedule 1 to SA 1974 has been exercised in relation to a sole solicitor by virtue of sub-paragraph (1)(a) (reason to suspect dishonesty) and he has acted as a sole solicitor within the period of 18 months beginning with the date on which it was so exercised (paragraph 1(1)(j) of Schedule 1).[2]

- The SRA is satisfied that a person has acted as a solicitor at a time when he did not have a practising certificate which was in force (paragraph 1(1)(k) of Schedule 1).

- The SRA is satisfied that the solicitor has failed to comply with any condition, subject to which his practising certificate was granted or otherwise has effect, to the effect that he may act as a solicitor only in employment which is approved by the SRA in connection with the imposition of that condition, or as a member of a partnership which is so approved, or as a manager of a body recognised by the SRA under section 9 of the Administration of Justice Act 1985 and so approved – or in any specified combination of those ways (paragraph 1(1)(l) of Schedule 1). The word 'manager' has the same meaning as in the LSA 2007 (see section 207 of LSA 2007).[3]

- The SRA is satisfied that it is necessary to exercise the powers of intervention, or any of them, to protect the interests of clients, or former or potential clients, of the solicitor or his firm, or the interests of the beneficiaries of any trust of which the solicitor is or was a trustee (paragraph 1(1)(m) of Schedule 1).

1   The statute refers to 'the Society' but in practice the powers are exercised by the SRA.
2   This is an anachronism – it has been superseded by the provision for the automatic suspension of the solicitor's practising certificate when an intervention occurs by reason of a suspicion of dishonesty. Before this power was acquired (by section 15(1A) of SA 1974, inserted by the Courts and Legal Services Act 1990) a solicitor who was the subject of an intervention could theoretically immediately set himself up in practice again and encourage all his clients to reinstruct him.
3   Paragraph 1(1A) of Schedule 1 to SA 1974.

16.3

It is arguable that the new ground for intervention, paragraph 1(1)(m) of Schedule 1, introduced by LSA 2007, is so widely drawn that all other grounds are obsolete, but it is anticipated that reliance will continue to be placed on the traditional grounds, if only because there will be an obligation to explain why the SRA considered it 'necessary' to intervene.

Another new ground added by the LSA 2007 is paragraph 1(1)(aa) of Schedule 1, which envisages intervention when there is suspected dishonesty on the part of a solicitor in connection with a business that is not a solicitor's practice; that is, a business (not being a solicitor's practice or trust) of which the solicitor is the sole proprietor, or of which he or she is an employee or manager. This is intended to deal with the situation in which a solicitor has a legal practice but is also involved in another business, for example one that provides financial services, where there is reason to suspect dishonesty in relation to that separate business. One could see that if the Financial Services Authority (using the same example) took action against such a business in circumstances where a suspicion of dishonesty arose, there could be a need to intervene in the solicitor's practice, as the same person could be seen to pose a risk to clients.

It was the case that the powers of intervention could only be exercised after specific notice had been given to the solicitor if they were to be exercised under sub-paragraph 1(c) – breaches of specified rules including the Solicitors' Code of Conduct 2007.[1] The solicitor had to be given notice in writing that he had failed to comply with the rules specified in the notice and also (at the same or any later time) notice that the powers of intervention were accordingly exercisable, but this provision was repealed by the LSA 2007.

Intervention can therefore occur with no notice at all, and the solicitor may have no opportunity to make any representations on his or her own behalf before the decision to intervene is made.

1   Paragraph 1(2) of Schedule 1 to SA 1974 was repealed by paragraph 77(2)(k) of Schedule 16 to LSA 2007.

The adjudication process

16.4

The resolution to intervene may be made by two adjudicators, including members of the adjudication panel and employed adjudicators, save that one adjudicator may do so in cases of urgency. Accordingly, an intervention into a solicitor's practice can be authorised by a single employee of the SRA. Typically the adjudicators will consider a Forensic Investigation Report, any representations the solicitor may have made in answer to that report, and the recommendations of a caseworker contained in his or her own report which will summarise the facts and issues. The recommendation of a caseworker is in no sense binding upon the panel; in *Sheikh v Law Society*,[1] the caseworker had recommended against intervention but the adjudication panel nevertheless resolved to intervene.

In cases of clear suspected dishonesty or where it is intended that the intervention should occur without notice, the caseworker's report will not be disclosed to the solicitor. Indeed, in the most serious cases, usually involving an obvious and substantial client account shortfall in circumstances amounting to theft, the procedure may involve a brief visit from an investigating officer, a report by way of a one-page memorandum and an intervention as soon as the necessary practical arrangements have been made.

1   [2006] EWCA Civ 1577, [2007] 3 All ER 183.

Natural justice and Human Rights Act 1998 implications

16.5

Solicitors who are the subject of interventions have challenged the exercise of this powerful and terminally damaging regulatory weapon without any requirement for notice, on the grounds that it is in breach of the principles of natural justice and that it is incompatible with the rights protected by the Human Rights Act 1998 (HRA 1998). All such challenges have failed. The natural justice arguments were rejected in *Giles v Law Society*,[1] and the HRA 1998 arguments failed in *Holder v Law Society*.[2] In the latter case, the Court of Appeal held that the statutory regime as a whole did not offend HRA 1998, although it remained open to a solicitor to assert that an intervention in a particular case breached the rights protected by the European Convention.

1   [1996] Admin LR 105, CA. See also *Yogarajah v Law Society* (1982) 126 Sol Jo 430; and *Buckley v Law Society* (9 October 1985, unreported).
2   [2003] EWCA Civ 39, [2003] 3 All ER 62, [2003] 1 WLR 1059.

The extent of the powers

16.6

The mechanism selected by Parliament to permit the Law Society to achieve intervention in a solicitor's practice is, in essence, to vest the solicitor's practice moneys in the Society, and to require the solicitor to yield up the practice documents.

Money

16.7

The intervention resolution vests all sums of money held by or on behalf of a solicitor or his firm in connection with his practice, and the right to recover or receive those sums, in the SRA.[1] In short, the SRA takes control of office and client accounts. Where the intervention is solely by reason of the death of a sole practitioner, only client account is affected.[2]

The SRA holds the money on trust for the purposes of the intervention and 'subject thereto [...] upon trust for the persons beneficially entitled to them'.[3] What this means in practice is that the SRA holds client money on trust for the clients, and office money (if any) in circumstances where the solicitor is likely to be in substantial debt (a) to his clients in the event of any client account shortfall and (b) to the SRA in respect of the intervention costs (more of which below: see para **16.13**). While the solicitor is 'beneficially entitled' to anything that might be left, it is unlikely that there will be anything. Sums recovered by the solicitor after the intervention in connection with his practice, such as payment of outstanding bills of costs, also vest in the SRA.[4]

Schedule 1 to SA 1974 provides the court with specific powers to assist the SRA in gaining control of the practice moneys. The court may order that no payment shall be made without the leave of the court by any person (whether or not named in the order) of any money held by him (in whatever manner and whether it was received before or after the making of the order) on behalf of the solicitor or his firm.[5] The court may require a person suspected of holding money on behalf of the solicitor or his firm to provide information to the SRA as to such money and the accounts in which it is held.[6]

The SRA may also resolve to vest in itself the right to recover or receive debts due to the solicitor or his firm in connection with his practice or former practice.[7]

1 Paragraph 6 of Schedule 1 to SA 1974.
2 Paragraphs 2 and 6(2)(b) of Schedule 1.
3 Paragraph 6(1) of Schedule 1.
4 *Dooley v Law Society (No 2)* [2001] All ER (D) 362, (2002) Times, 16 January.
5 Paragraph 5(1) of Schedule 1 to SA 1974.
6 Paragraph 8 of Schedule 1.
7 Paragraph 6A of Schedule 1. This was added by LSA 2007 and puts on an express statutory footing that which had been held in *Dooley* (above) to be the case as a matter of proper interpretation of the statute prior to its amendment.

Practice documents

16.8

The intervention resolution results in a notice to the solicitor or his firm requiring the production or delivery to any person appointed by the SRA of all documents in the possession of the solicitor or his firm in connection with his practice.[1] Failure or refusal to comply with the notice is a criminal offence.[2] The High Court has power to order the production or delivery of documents by the solicitor and/or by any person suspected of being in possession of relevant documents.[3] Once possession has been taken of the documents, the SRA must serve on the solicitor a notice that possession has been taken by the person appointed on its behalf.[4]

1 Paragraph 9 of Schedule 1 to SA 1974.
2 Paragraph 9(3) of Schedule 1.
3 Paragraph 9(4) and (5) of Schedule 1.
4 Paragraph 9(7) of Schedule 1.

Other powers

16.9

The SRA's intervention costs, which can easily amount to £100,000 or more, are a debt due from the solicitor or his estate, unless the High Court orders otherwise.[1] The High Court may also make orders permitting forcible entry to premises to search for and seize documents,[2] for the re-direction of mail, telephone and electronic communications[3] and for the appointment of a new trustee in substitution for the solicitor as trustee of any trust.[4]

The High Court may, on the application of the SRA, order a former partner of the solicitor to pay a specified proportion of the intervention costs otherwise payable by the solicitor if it is satisfied that the conduct of the solicitor that led to the intervention was carried on with the consent or connivance of, or attributable to any neglect on the part of the former partner.[5]

The SRA's statutory powers in relation to money and documents take precedence over any lien or other right to possession in any other person.[6] These powers continue to be exercisable after a solicitor's death, or after his name has been removed from or struck off the roll.

1 Paragraph 13 of Schedule 1 to SA 1974.
2 Paragraph 9(6) of Schedule 1.
3 Paragraph 10 of Schedule 1.
4 Paragraph 11 of Schedule 1.
5 Paragraph 13A of Schedule 1.
6 Paragraph 12 of Schedule 1.

Practising certificate

16.10

Where an intervention is authorised because of a suspicion of dishonesty on the part of the solicitor, breaches of the Solicitors' Accounts Rules 1998, breaches of any other rule made under section 31 of SA 1974, including the Solicitors' Code of

Conduct 2007, or the solicitor's committal to prison, any practising certificate of the solicitor then in force is immediately suspended[1] – unless the adjudicator or adjudication panel authorising the intervention directs otherwise.[2]

The solicitor may (at any time before the certificate expires) apply to the SRA to terminate the suspension and the SRA may terminate the suspension conditionally or unconditionally or refuse the application.[3] If the SRA refuses the application, or the solicitor is aggrieved at the conditions imposed he or she may appeal to the High Court.[4]

In practice, the SRA is usually prepared to restore a solicitor's practising certificate subject to stringent conditions, commonly a requirement that the solicitor may only practise in employment approved by the SRA, and on condition that he or she has no access to clients' money.

1   Section 15(1A) of SA 1974, inserted by section 91(2) of the Courts and Legal Services Act 1990.
2   Section 15(1B) of SA 1974.
3   Section 16(3) and (4).
4   Section 16(5).

The practical reality

16.11

The legal department of the SRA, which manages interventions, appoints an intervening agent, a solicitor who is a member of the SRA's Intervention Panel practising in the relevant area, who will take direct responsibility for (in particular) client files. Provisional arrangements may be made in advance of the intervention resolution when it can reasonably be expected to occur. Notice of the intervention will not be given to the solicitor (even if the Panel has resolved on the intervention some days before) until the agents are ready to act and the solicitor's bank has received notice. The solicitor will therefore not know of the intervention until after his or her bank accounts are frozen. The first that a solicitor will typically hear of the decision will be by a cryptic telephone call from the SRA requesting him to stand by his fax machine to receive an important communication. This is likely to be in the late afternoon when the agents and representative of the SRA are due to arrive at the firm's offices the following morning.

The intervening agents attend at the solicitor's address and take possession of the practice documents which in most cases are removed without delay. Matters which are urgent and require prompt action are identified and (hopefully, assuming the solicitor's co-operation) discussed. Practice moneys are transferred to a bank account under the control of the intervening agents. The intervening agents attempt to bring the practice's accounting records into proper order.

Clients will receive a standard letter informing them that the SRA has been obliged to exercise its statutory powers and inviting them to nominate successor solicitors or, if appropriate, to accept delivery of their papers themselves.

If claims in professional negligence or breach of fiduciary duty are made against the solicitor, the solicitor's professional indemnity insurers may wish to see the files seized by the Law Society to seek to discover grounds for declining indemnity cover. However, the SRA refuses to provide insurers with the files in those circumstances unless the lay client has provided consent, and this refusal was upheld by the Court of Appeal in *Quinn Direct Insurance Ltd v Law Society*[1] on the ground that privilege and confidentiality in the documents remains after intervention, and there is no room for implying into the statutory scheme any entitlement in insurers to see the documents.[2]

1   [2010] EWCA Civ 805.
2   Paragraph 29.

16.12

The intervening agents do not in any sense take over or run the practice. They seek to ensure that all clients are informed of the intervention and find alternative solicitors, and that the practice moneys are distributed properly; they may have to seek directions from the court to achieve this. They are likely to have to take urgent and protective steps in circumstances where it is necessary to guard the interests of clients, but it is not their function to take over client matters in any other sense or for any other purpose.

The description of intervention as striking a mortal blow to the practice[1] is, if anything, an understatement. Quite apart from the automatic suspension of the practising certificate, the solicitor loses control of the practice's bank accounts and the practice's documentation. It instantly becomes impossible to service any bank overdraft. Unless the intervention is rapidly reversed by the court, the solicitor's practice is lost without any compensation, and the solicitor faces almost inevitable financial ruin.

1   *Giles v Law Society* [1995] 8 Admin LR 105, CA.

16.13

Many practices have little in the way of measurable assets – offices are rented, equipment and cars leased, and the office account is likely to be in substantial overdraft. Assets represented by goodwill and work in progress suddenly become worthless. In addition, as has been said, the solicitor is liable for the costs of intervention, recoverable as a debt due to the SRA.[1] As already indicated, these costs can be very substantial. Unless the solicitor has private wealth there will be nothing left. Intervention and subsequent bankruptcy commonly go hand in hand.

Although, in theory, a solicitor subject to an intervention is entitled to payment for work in progress at the time of the intervention, this entitlement is more apparent than real. The successor solicitor taking over an individual file will have to extract such payment from the client, and will often doubtless be met by an argument from the lay client that he or she should not be liable for two sets of fees in respect of the same legal work. The intervened solicitor has no means of compelling anyone to recover outstanding costs. The SRA is under no obligation to do so.[2] Any payments recovered in respect of work in progress will first be set off against the solicitor's liability for the intervention costs.[3] Further, the SRA may have vested in itself the right to recover debts due to the practice, including outstanding bills and the value of work in progress.

Ownership of the solicitor's other assets, such as office furniture, computer equipment and the like is not affected by the intervention. Only practice moneys and documents are affected (save that the SRA may require possession of computer equipment necessary to access documents held only in electronic form[4]). Similarly, the solicitor's contractual obligations are unaffected – the intervention does not have the effect of dismissing employees or in itself making them redundant.[5]

1   Paragraph 13 of Schedule 1 to SA 1974. The solicitor may require the detailed assessment of the costs: *Pine v Law Society (No 2)* [2002] EWCA Civ 175, [2002] 2 All ER 658.
2   *Dooley v Law Society (No 2)* [2001] All ER (D) 362, (2002) Times, 16 January. Under the LSA 2007, the SRA will acquire the right to recover sums due to the solicitor and may therefore elect to pursue outstanding costs and work in progress to meet client liabilities or intervention costs.
3   *Dooley v Law Society (No 2)* [2001] All ER (D) 362, (2002) Times, 16 January.
4   Paragraphs 9(5A) and (6)(b) of Schedule 1 to SA 1974.
5   *Rose v Dodd* [2005] EWCA Civ 957, [2006] 1 All ER 464.

16.14

Essentially, therefore, an intervention means the total destruction of a solicitor's practice. The solicitor is unable to sell that practice to a willing purchaser. The practice's clients have to find new solicitors. The practice's employees have to find new jobs. And the solicitor has to apply for the suspension of the practising certificate to be lifted if he or she is to resume any sort of practice as a solicitor. The solicitor will only be able to practise at all by finding a willing employer.

Ordinarily, at the time of making the resolution to intervene, the adjudication panel will also refer the solicitor's conduct to the Solicitors Disciplinary Tribunal.

Because all the statutory provisions refer to a solicitor, and a solicitor's practice, it is possible (and it does occur) that interventions are authorised into the practice of a solicitor who may be a partner in a firm. In that event only the client funds, client documents and any practice funds and papers personal to that solicitor are subject to the intervention. Inevitably this has the potential to be highly disruptive for the remaining partners, but they are not directly affected by the exercise of the statutory powers.

Challenging an intervention[1]

16.15

The SRA must serve on the solicitor or his or her firm, and on any other person having possession of sums of money caught by the intervention, a certified copy of the intervention resolution and a notice prohibiting the payment out of any such sums of money.[2] Within eight days of the service of that notice, the solicitor, on giving not less than 48 hours' notice in writing to the SRA, may apply to the High Court for an order directing the SRA to withdraw the notice.[3]

Likewise, where the SRA has taken possession of practice documents, the solicitor may apply to the High Court (again, within eight days of the service of the notice) for an order directing the SRA to deliver the documents to such person as the solicitor claimant may require.[4]

If the court makes an order in favour of the solicitor, it shall have power also to make such other order as it may think fit.[5]

The eight-day time limit is mandatory, and cannot be extended by the court or by the consent of the parties.[6] The proceedings are assigned to the Chancery Division and are governed by CPR Pt 8 and 67.4. If the proceedings are not litigated expeditiously by the solicitor, so that they eventually become academic due to the destruction of his practice, they may be struck out as an abuse of process.[7]

There is no power for the SRA to withdraw an intervention once it has been put in place. If it is rapidly concluded that the decision was lawful but not justified or was ill advised, the solution is a consent order of the High Court.[8]

1 This term is used as there is no 'appeal' against an intervention – the remedy is an application to the High Court for an order directing the withdrawal of the intervention.
2 Paragraph 6(3) of Schedule 1 to SA 1974.
3 Paragraph 6(4) of Schedule 1.
4 Paragraph 9(8) and (9) of Schedule 1.
5 Paragraphs 6(5) and 9(11) of Schedule 1.
6 *Re a Solicitor* [1994] Ch 1994 B 4973.
7 *Virdi v Law Society* [1999] 29 LS Gaz R 29. Mr Virdi's appeal to the Court of Appeal was dismissed, but this is unreported.
8 *Patel v Law Society* [2008] EWHC 3564 (Ch). Norris J commented in approving a consent order that the parties were right to seek such an order as there was no power provided to the SRA by the statute to reverse its own decision.

16.16

As has been seen, it has proved to be almost impossible to challenge an intervention successfully. This is at least in part because of the financial consequences of an intervention described above. The solicitor is in a quandary – does he or she recognise the likely reality that the only way in which family and personal financial commitments can be met is if he or she finds a job with a willing employer? If so, the solicitor must recognise also that the original practice will not survive; the conditions on his or her practising certificate will prevent recovery of the remnants of that practice, even if the challenge is successful. There is the additional risk that the proceedings will be struck out as an abuse as they will no longer have any practical purpose.

Alternatively, does the solicitor fight on, without employment or other income, with mounting and unserviceable debts, probably without funds to pay for the needed specialist assistance, and with no prospect of obtaining public funding,[1] against an opponent with unlimited resources?

If a solicitor believes that he or she is at risk of intervention, it is wise to take precautions (such as putting another solicitor in funds) to ensure that a rapid statutory challenge can be mounted if so advised. Once the intervention has commenced, it will be impossible to draw upon office account. Any attempt to put funds beyond the reach of the SRA after the intervention has commenced may well be taken into account against the solicitor at the High Court hearing.[2]

It is highly doubtful whether the courts have jurisdiction to provide interim relief by 'unscrambling' the intervention and/or reversing the suspension of the solicitor's practising certificate pending the full hearing. Where the solicitor challenges the intervention, the SRA will ordinarily be prepared to co-operate in slowing down the practical effect of the intervention (ie by not informing clients of the intervention unless the particular matter is urgent).

However, the problem will remain as to what is to be done for those clients whose matters are not particularly pressing but who cannot be ignored. The solicitor who is the subject of the intervention cannot continue to act; he or she has no practising certificate. It is possible, if there is a suitable and willing person and the solicitor can afford to remunerate him or her (allowing for the fact that money coming in to the practice will vest in the SRA), for the solicitor to appoint another solicitor with an unconditional practising certificate as practice manager; this might be an existing employee or someone brought in for the purpose. Such arrangements will in practice require the co-operation of the SRA but will provide a mechanism for maintaining the status quo where a challenge is credibly made and expeditiously pursued.

1   Intervention challenges relate to 'matters arising out of the carrying on of a business' and are thus excluded from public funding: section 6 of and paragraph 1 of Schedule 2 to the Access to Justice Act 1999.
2   See *Sheikh v Law Society* [2006] EWCA Civ 1577, [2007] 3 All ER 183.

16.17

The solicitor mounting a statutory challenge will be well advised to make an early application for directions to ensure that the case is brought on speedily for trial, and that the essential issues are identified at the outset.

The statutory challenge provided by paragraphs 6 and 9 of Schedule 1 to SA 1974 is the only manner in which an intervention can be challenged.[1] Any issues under the HRA 1998 can be considered within the statutory proceedings.

1   *Hedworth v Law Society* (1994, unreported); *Miller v Law Society* [2002] EWHC 1453 (Ch), [2002] 4 All ER 312.

The proceedings and the test to be applied

16.18

In providing an extremely short mandatory limitation period (see para **16.15**), Parliament clearly envisaged a swift summary procedure. One reason for the lack of successful challenges to interventions may be that this laudable aim has become lost in the complexities of High Court litigation. The tortuous course of the proceedings in *Sheikh v Law Society*[1] indicated that the statutory remedy was not working efficiently. The claimant's application to set aside the intervention did not come on for hearing for four months, and occupied eight days of court time. The judgments at first instance and of the Court of Appeal each ran to 70 pages of single-spaced typescript.

In most cases, the reasons for intervention will be obvious to all. However, this is not invariably so, and unless the reasons are properly identified at an early stage, there is a danger that the solicitor will be denied the effective summary remedy that Parliament intended to provide.

The burden of proof to justify the continuation of the intervention rests on the SRA – the solicitor, though nominally the claimant, is in reality the defendant.[2] Accordingly, unless the parties agree otherwise, the SRA will present its case first.

The traditional approach to the statutory challenge was the 'two-stage test' propounded by Neuberger J in *Dooley v Law Society*[3] approved by the Court of Appeal in *Holder v Law Society*:[4]

'The court's decision is a two-stage process. First it must decide whether the grounds under paragraph 1 are made out; in this case, primarily, whether there are grounds for suspecting dishonesty. Secondly, if the court is so satisfied, then it must consider whether in the light of all the evidence before it the intervention should continue. In deciding the second question, the court must carry out a balancing exercise between the need in the public interest to protect the public from dishonest solicitors and the inevitably very serious consequences to the solicitor if the intervention continues.'

1   [2006] EWCA Civ 1577, [2007] 3 All ER 183.
2   See *Giles v Law Society* [1995] 8 Admin LR 105 at 114F–G, CA, per Nourse LJ.
3   [2000] HC Transcript 0002868.
4   [2003] EWCA Civ 39, [2003] 3 All ER 62.

16.19

That must now be considered in the light of the more subtle approach suggested by the Court of Appeal in *Sheikh v Law Society*.[1] The court may need to decide whether, at the time of the resolution to intervene, the statutory ground relied upon by the Law Society actually existed – for example whether there was, at that time, reason to suspect dishonesty on the basis of the information available to the SRA. It has not been conclusively decided whether, if no such ground existed, the solicitor is entitled to have the notices of intervention withdrawn for that reason alone, but it seems likely that in that event the resolution will have been fundamentally flawed and liable to be set aside. On the other hand, such a circumstance is likely to be very rare.

If there is no challenge to the validity of the resolution or to the service of the intervention notices, the single issue for the court is whether the notices should be withdrawn. In considering this, the court is exercising its own judgment and is entitled to take into account material that was not available to the SRA when resolving to intervene, but which is available to the court. Moreover, the court will also take into account the views of the SRA as a relevant evidential factor, although it is unclear how these views are ascertained in practice – save through the mouths of the advocates representing the SRA at the hearing of the application to withdraw the intervention notices. This is an unsatisfactory 'evidential' basis upon which to ask a court to make decisions.

As noted above, the intervention regime is in principle compliant with the requirements of natural justice and the HRA 1998, but is capable of being operated unfairly in an individual case.

1   [2006] EWCA Civ 1577, [2007] 3 All ER 183.

16.20

If the challenge is successful the statute envisages an order requiring the withdrawal of the paragraph 6(3) notice[1] so as to return control of practice moneys to the solicitor, and an order directing the SRA to deliver the practice documents to such person as the solicitor claimant may require. In addition, the court probably has jurisdiction to restore the suspended practising certificate to the solicitor,[2] and in *Sheikh v Law Society*,[3] the judge at first instance imposed a condition on the successful claimant's practising certificate.

The statutory scheme set out in Schedule 1 to SA 1974 cannot be replaced by a judge-made scheme. There is no 'half-way house': the court must either direct or decline to direct withdrawal of the intervention[4] (although the court's power to make consequential orders should enable it to ensure that the SRA is able to exercise proper regulatory control over the solicitor in the light of the facts found by the court).

There is no statutory entitlement to damages at the suit of the successful solicitor if the challenge succeeds. Whether damages may be awarded at common law, under the statute or under the Human Rights Act 1998, has not been decided and may well depend upon the court's view as to whether the decision to intervene was justified at the time it was made.

1   *Holder v Law Society* [2003] EWCA Civ 39, [2003] 3 All ER 62; *Sritharan v Law Society* [2005] EWCA Civ 476, [2005] 4 All ER 1105.
2   *Sritharan v Law Society* [2005] EWCA Civ 476, [2005] 4 All ER 1105.
3   [2006] EWCA Civ 1577, [2007] 3 All ER 183.
4   *Sritharan v Law Society* [2005] EWCA Civ 476, [2005] 4 All ER 1105.

Alternatives to intervention

16.21

In recent years the Law Society has increasingly sought to find alternatives to intervention, principally because the cost of intervention is high and recovery of this from the solicitor is uncertain. The SRA is more willing than hitherto to achieve tight regulatory control over a solicitor who would otherwise have been subject to an intervention by means of the imposition of stringent conditions on his practising certificate. Alternatively, the SRA may permit the orderly disposal of the practice. The SRA may be prepared to enter into a regulatory settlement whereby the solicitor agrees to close his firm within a set period, or to correct errors in the firm's accounts and provide independent evidence of the accounts being compliant, or to seek medical treatment and provide independent evidence, for example as to an addiction being overcome (see para **13.21** as to regulatory settlements generally).

Despite these initiatives, because a credit squeeze or a downturn in the economy puts solicitors under pressure, the current economic trends continue to cause increasing numbers of interventions. In 2009 (the last year for which there are available figures) there were 97 interventions, compared with 71 in 2008. Of these, 33 involved a suspicion of dishonesty, as compared to 30 in 2008.

Limited intervention

16.22

This form of intervention is of a very different character and for very different purposes and is almost entirely unrelated to the matters discussed above.

It is designed solely to recover from a solicitor a file or files relating to specific matters, either for the purposes of their being handed to clients or for the purposes of inspection by the SRA to assist in the investigation of complaints or regulatory concerns respectively.

CHAPTER 16
INTERVENTION

It may occur in two circumstances. The first is concerned exclusively with delay, and is somewhat convoluted. If the SRA is satisfied that there has been undue delay in connection with any matter in which the solicitor or his firm is or was acting on behalf of a client or with any trust, or by any employee of a solicitor in connection with a trust of which the employee is or was a trustee in his capacity as such an employee, and the solicitor has been invited to give an explanation in answer to the complaint within a specified period[1] and:

- the solicitor fails within that period to give an explanation which is regarded as satisfactory;

- notice has been given to the solicitor of the fact that he has failed to give a satisfactory explanation; and

- either then or later a notice is given that the powers of intervention are exercisable for those reasons,

the SRA may 'intervene' in the solicitor's practice for the limited purpose of recovering the file or files in question, and for that purpose only.[2] In this event the file will be obtained and handed to the client or to successor solicitors appointed by the client, so that the problems encountered as a result of the unexplained delays are overcome.

The second circumstance arises if a decision is made to require the solicitor to produce a file or files for inspection by the SRA for the purposes of an investigation,[3] the powers of intervention can be employed to compel the delivery up of such files.[4] The documents required in these circumstances will be all the documents in the possession of the solicitor or his firm relevant to the matter under investigation.

In either event the procedure is the same: an agent of the SRA is appointed, usually a solicitor on the SRA's Intervention Panel or a member of the staff of the SRA. The solicitor is given notice of the time and date on which the agent will attend at his offices for the purposes of collecting the file or files, and the agent is instructed to collect the file or files accordingly. Such limited interventions generally occur only after an unsuccessful attempt has been made to persuade the solicitor to deliver up the files voluntarily.

Because these powers are part of the intervention regime the statutory powers of the High Court are available and in the event of non-co-operation on the part of the solicitor an application could be made by the SRA for an order to compel delivery. One would naturally expect this to be an extremely rare occurrence, and it is understood only to have been necessary once.[5]

---

1 Paragraph 3 of Schedule 1 to SA 1974 requires not less than eight days' notice. In practice invariably 14 days' notice is given.
2 Paragraph 3 of Schedule 1 to SA 1974.
3 Section 44B(1) of SA 1974.
4 Section 44B(6) of SA 1974.
5 *Stevenson*, 7814–1999, SDT.

CHAPTER 17

The High Court

17.1

Solicitors are officers of the Senior Courts: the court itself can discipline solicitors, and may order that a solicitor's name be struck off the roll of solicitors, rather than referring the matter to the SRA. This power is available to the High Court, the Crown Court and the Court of Appeal, or any division or judge of those courts.[1] This jurisdiction is only rarely exercised.

A claimant applying to the High Court to exercise this jurisdiction, rather than making an application to the Tribunal, would need to show that it was reasonable to follow this exceptional course. This has been done only once successfully in modern times.[2] The power has also been used in the course of other litigation, on the application of the Law Society.[3]

Applications of this kind made by litigants in person will not be entertained because the Solicitors Act 1974 preserves the court's inherent jurisdiction as it had been prior to the Supreme Court of Judicature Act 1873, and both before and after that Act it was settled law that the jurisdiction was limited in practice, in that an application could only be made if supported by counsel.[4]

Ordinarily, if a judge is concerned that a solicitor may have been guilty of professional misconduct, he will order that the matter be referred to the SRA, and a transcript made of the relevant part of the proceedings.

1   Section 50 of the Solicitors Act 1974; the procedure is set out in section 51.
2   *Parsons v Davies* (1983, unreported), CA.
3   *Penna v Law Society (No 3)* (1999, unreported); and *Law Society v Young* [2002] EWHC 2962 Admin. In each case the solicitor had been the subject of an intervention on the grounds of a suspicion of dishonesty. In *Penna*, in the subsequent proceedings by which he sought to challenge the intervention the solicitor so misconducted himself in defiance of court orders that the court on the Law Society's application used its inherent powers to strike him off, taking the facts that led to the intervention and his subsequent conduct into account. In *Young* the solicitor continued to practise as a solicitor and to hold himself out as a solicitor in court proceedings, so that there was contempt as well as continuing misconduct.
4   *Re Solicitors, ex p Peasegood* [1994] 1 All ER 298.

CHAPTER 18

Control of solicitors' employees

18.1

Parliament originally, through the Solicitors Act 1974 (SA 1974) and its predecessors, provided regulatory powers to the Law Society and the Solicitors Disciplinary Tribunal to enable the control of non-solicitors who work in solicitors' firms, and who may abuse their position. The rationale for the existence of these powers is the need to protect those who deal with solicitors, and to safeguard the reputation of the profession. The Legal Services Act 2007 (LSA 2007) promotes the concept of firm- or business entity-based regulation so that all managers and employees of regulated practices are now subject to personal regulation by virtue of their employment, whether or not they are legally qualified. In consequence, regulation of solicitors' employees now takes three forms: (1) statutory restrictions on the employment of certain disqualified persons, for example former solicitors who have been struck off; (2) the making of orders that control the employment of non-solicitors guilty of material misconduct; and (3) direct disciplinary control of employees of regulated practices (see paras **2.2**, **2.9** and **3.3**, and paras **18.8** and **18.9**).

Restriction on employment of persons struck off or suspended

18.2

A solicitor may not, in connection with his practice as a solicitor, employ or remunerate persons who to his knowledge have been disqualified from acting as solicitors through being struck off or suspended from practice, save with the written permission of the SRA. The SRA may grant permission for such period and subject to such conditions as it thinks fit.[1]

Until 31 March 2009, section 41(4) of SA 1974 provided a mandatory penalty of suspension or striking off for any solicitor found to have acted in breach of this prohibition. There were originally two offences attracting a mandatory penalty: acting as an agent for an unqualified person in court proceedings (section 39 of SA 1974 which was repealed in full in 1991, so removing the statutory offence as well as the mandatory penalty); and employing or remunerating a struck off or suspended solicitor without written permission. The LSA 2007 retains the statutory offence but removes the mandatory penalty. In *Re a Solicitor (Rosen)*[2] the Divisional Court requested and was provided with a schedule of penalties imposed upon solicitors for breaches of section 41. There was a wide range, some suspensions being for a few days only, sometimes being timed to coincide with holidays already arranged by the solicitor concerned or (in the case of a number of partners all requiring to be sentenced) being staggered so as to minimise disruption to the practice concerned.[3] In these instances, the Tribunal had plainly felt that little or no moral blame attached to the solicitors in question, and would not have suspended them in the absence of the mandatory provision. At the other end of the spectrum were solicitors who had been struck off for deliberately flouting the statutory provisions. The removal of the mandatory penalty enables the Tribunal more effectively to tailor the penalty to the breach.

It is important to appreciate that a breach of section 41 is a strict liability offence. All that is required is (1) that the solicitor knows the true status of the employee, namely that he or she has been struck off or suspended; and (2) that, as a matter of fact, the written permission of the Law Society/SRA has not been obtained (or that conditions imposed on the grant of permission have not been met). It does not provide a defence, for example, to show that one partner had responsibility for making the employment arrangements and reassured all other partners that there was no compliance issue, and they reasonably relied on that reassurance.[4] It has even happened that a struck off solicitor has forged the permission; the employing solicitor was still guilty of the offence.[5] Indeed, this serves to reinforce the point that the employer, and not the proposed employee, must obtain the necessary SRA permission.

1   Section 41 of SA 1974.
2   [2004] EWHC 907 (Admin).
3   Cases in which this sort of leniency was shown include *McMillan*, 5740–1989, SDT; *Cunnew*, 6134–1992, SDT; and *Coxall*, 8401–2001, SDT.
4   *Coxall*, 8401–2001, SDT.
5   *Awoloye-Kio*, 8940–2003, SDT.

18.3

The Tribunal has also emphasised that wilful ignorance of the true status of the employee could lead to a breach of this provision:

> 'The Tribunal take the view that a solicitor can only claim not to have knowledge of a striking off order if he has first made appropriate enquiries. Total ignorance as a result of a total failure to make the enquiries which a prudent solicitor employer would make is not a state of knowledge but a state of deliberate ignorance.'[1]

As this is a statutory offence to be construed by reference to the precise words of the section this conclusion must be open to some doubt. Nevertheless, it is apparent that the Tribunal will strive to give a purposive construction to the section to meet the perceived mischief:

> 'The Tribunal accept that the mischief which section 41 seeks to avert is the handling of clients' affairs in a solicitors office by a struck off solicitor except in circumstances where he is subject to strict controls. It is clear that the constraints are imposed to protect the interests of the public and maintain the good name of the solicitors' profession.'[2]

The words 'employ or remunerate' have been construed widely, to include even the payment of expenses:

> 'The Tribunal consider that "employment" should be construed in the wider sense of "keeping busy" or "keeping occupied". It follows from that that payment of a wage is not essential to establish employment. The intention of section 41 is that struck off solicitors be kept out of solicitors offices save in exceptional and closely regulated cases. Although not argued before them, the Tribunal believe it is useful to add that in its view the word

"remunerate" should also be interpreted in its widest sense so that it not only means "to reward" or "to pay for services" but also "to provide recompense for". The payment of out of pocket expenses by the respondent was therefore remuneration.'[3]

1 *Cunnew,* 6134–1992, SDT.
2 *Cunnew,* 6134–1992, SDT.
3 *Cunnew,* 6134–1992, SDT.

Control of solicitors' employees and consultants

18.4

The SRA may act to prevent or control the employment in legal practice of those individuals whom it considers to be undesirable.[1] Both the SRA and the Tribunal have the power to make the relevant order preventing all solicitors from employing or remunerating, in connection with their practice as solicitors, the individual in question (except in accordance with permission in writing granted by the SRA for such period and subject to such conditions as the SRA may think fit). The order can also prevent any employee of a solicitor from employing or remunerating the individual in relation to legal practice, and can prevent an individual being a manager of or having an interest in a legal practice. It seems that the SRA will consider it appropriate to make the order itself at the adjudication stage if there has been a conviction or there is no dispute as to the facts, and will make an application to the Tribunal for an order when there is likely to be a dispute of fact or other factor justifying an oral hearing, or when the employing solicitor also faces Tribunal proceedings arising from the same facts.

The standard of proof in either event is the criminal standard.[2]

There are two statutory grounds for making this order, (a) criminal convictions, and (b) certain acts or defaults while working in a legal practice.

1 Section 43 of SA 1974.
2 *Ahmed,* 8645/2002, SDT

Criminal convictions

18.5

The order may be made when the person concerned has been convicted of a criminal offence which is such that, in the opinion of the SRA, it would be undesirable for him to be involved in legal practice.[1]

1 Section 43(1)(a) of SA 1974.

Acts or defaults while working in a legal practice

18.6

The order may also be made when the person concerned has 'occasioned or been a party to, with or without the connivance of a solicitor, an act or default in relation to a legal practice which involved conduct on his part of such a nature that, in the opinion of the SRA, it would be undesirable for him to be involved in a legal practice'.[1]

This somewhat convoluted sub-section requires the SRA or the Tribunal to answer two essential questions:

(1) Has the person concerned occasioned an act or default which involved conduct on his part of such a nature that it would be undesirable for him to be involved in a legal practice?

(2) If so, was that act or default occasioned in relation to a legal practice?

The two sub-sections must be construed independently of each other. Sub-section (a) requires there to have been a criminal conviction, but sub-section (b) does not require similar or equivalent conduct. An order under section 43(1)(b) can be founded upon foolishness, recklessness or errors of judgement if the consequence is that it is undesirable for the individual concerned to work in a legal practice.[2]

The statutory jurisdiction did not (as originally enacted) extend to or cover a situation in which the party alleged to be at fault remunerated himself, purporting to be an employee of a solicitor but in fact being his own employer in a sham arrangement;[3] however, the section as amended by the LSA 2007 is probably sufficiently wide to overcome this difficulty.

The SRA and the Tribunal have, respectively, the power to make orders for costs when exercising this jurisdiction.[4]

1 Section 43(1)(b) of SA 1974.
2 See *Ojelade v Law Society* [2006] EWHC 2210 (Admin); and, particularly, *Gregory v Law Society* [2007] EWHC 1724 (Admin).
3 *Izegbu and Okoronkwo v Law Society* [2008] EWHC 1043 (Admin).
4 Section 43(2A) and (4) of SA 1974.

Appeals and reviews

18.7

Both the SRA and the Tribunal can revoke section 43 orders. If the SRA makes the order an application can be made to it to revoke it, for example because it is no longer required as the individual has been employed in the profession without further fault for a period of years. If the order was made by the Tribunal any application for revocation is made to the Tribunal.[1] A person aggrieved by an order made by the SRA can apply to the Tribunal for a review of that order and the Tribunal can quash it, vary it or confirm it.[2] An order made by the Tribunal can be appealed to the High Court.[3] The High Court has power to make such order on an appeal as it thinks fit.

1 Section 43(3) of SA 1974.
2 Section 43(3A).
3 Section 49(1).

Disciplinary control of employees

18.8

The LSA 2007 amended the SA 1974 by adding sections 34A and sub-section 47(2E). Section 34A enables the SRA to provide that the rules of professional conduct: 'have effect in relation to employees of solicitors with such additions, omissions or other modifications as appear to the [SRA] to be necessary or expedient'. The SRA has amended the Solicitors' Code of Conduct 2007 and other professional rules (including the Solicitors' Accounts Rules 1998) to make clear that it regulates not only solicitors but also the employees of solicitors, registered European lawyers and their employees, registered foreign lawyers, recognised bodies (including recognised sole practitioners) and their managers and employees. Section 47(2E) of SA 1974 extends the Tribunal's jurisdiction to the employees of solicitors. LSA 2007 also amended Schedule 2 to the Administration of Justice Act 1985 (AJA 1985) (which relates to incorporated practices or 'recognised bodies') to give the same powers to the Tribunal in relation to managers and employees of recognised bodies.

18.9

In relation to managers and employees, the Tribunal may:

- impose a fine, unlimited in amount, payable to the Treasury;[1]

- require the SRA to take such steps in relation to the relevant person as the Tribunal may specify;[2] and/or

- order the SRA to refer the conduct of the relevant person to an appropriate regulator,[3] as well as being able to make an order controlling the employment of the relevant person under section 43 of SA 1974.[4] An 'appropriate regulator' would be the relevant approved regulator authorised under the LSA 2007 if the manager or employee is an authorised person in relation to a reserved legal activity (eg, a barrister or licensed conveyancer) or any body which regulates the activities actually undertaken by the person concerned, if he or she was not an authorised person for LSA 2007 purposes.[5]

---

1   Section 47(2E)(a) of SA 1974; paragraph 18A(2)(a) of Schedule 2 to AJA 1985.
2   Section 47(2E)(b) of SA 1974; paragraph 18A(2)(b) of Schedule 2 to AJA1985.
3   Section 47(2E)(d) of SA 1974; paragraph 18A(2)(d) of Schedule 2 to AJA 1985.
4   Section 47(2E)(c) of SA 1974; paragraph 18A(2)(c) of Schedule 2 to AJA 1985.
5   Section 47(2H) of SA 1974; paragraph 18A(7) of Schedule 2 to AJA 1985.

CHAPTER 19

Sources of help

19.1

What do you do when a letter arrives from the Solicitors Regulation Authority or Legal Ombudsman (LeO) with some kind of complaint, or if you are subject to a forensic investigation by the SRA, or if you face disciplinary proceedings? Where do you turn for assistance?

The first point to make is that doing nothing is not an option. Both the LeO and the SRA apply strict time limits; adjudications will be adverse if you do not provide your explanations – your side of the story – for the benefit of the adjudicator or ombudsman. Do not assume that you will be given extensions of time – any request for more time will have to be fully justified and will be considered on the premise that complying with the requirements of the regulator will be a matter of priority. At the other extreme, failing to appear at the Solicitors Disciplinary Tribunal in your own defence may be a terminal mistake.

19.2

In any matter of complexity or apparent seriousness it is desirable to obtain specialist assistance, and there are relatively few with the requisite expertise.

The ethics helpline formerly operated by the Law Society is now under the jurisdiction of the SRA. It is not known to what extent information received as a result of advice being sought will be treated as information about the person enquiring, for the purposes of regulatory action.

The Solicitors' Assistance Scheme is independent of the Law Society and SRA. Established in 1972, it now has some 80 members around the country available to give advice and assistance, not only on matters of professional regulation but also on partnership and employment issues, financial concerns and stress-related problems. The initial interview is without charge. They can be contacted via the helpline number on 020 7117 8811 and at www.thesas.org.uk.

Professional indemnity insurance no longer provides cover for the costs of defending disciplinary or regulatory proceedings.

LawCare is a confidential advisory and support service to help lawyers, their staff and their immediate families to deal with health problems, such as depression and addiction, and related emotional difficulties. The contact number for solicitors, law students and legal executives in England and Wales is 0800 279 6888. Their website is www.lawcare.org.uk.

The Law Society's Practice Advice Service is a dedicated support-line for solicitors, trainees and employees of law firms. It is staffed by a team of experienced solicitors who deal with enquiries using their own knowledge and a variety of information sources, as well as the experience of other specialists within the Law Society. They are able to assist with enquiries on legal practice in many areas including anti-money laundering; solicitors' costs; multi-party actions; conveyancing; conditional fee agreements; probate; and rights of audience in the Crown Court. Advice by the Practice Advice Service does not constitute legal advice and cannot be relied upon as such. The contact number is 0870 606 2522 and e-mail lib-pas@lawsociety.org.uk.

19.3

Less relevant to the regulatory context, but a potential source of financial assistance for those in need, is the Solicitors Benevolent Association (SBA) which is the principal nationwide charity for solicitors in England and Wales. The aim of the Association is to assist solicitors and their dependants who are in need. The SBA helps those suffering ill-health (typical examples are debilitating diseases such as multiple sclerosis, and mental conditions such as bipolar disorder and schizophrenia), accident victims, and those without work – for whatever reason. Most applicants are in receipt of state benefits. The Association's telephone number is 020 8675 6440, or see its website: www.sba.org.uk.

PART 5
Appendices

The SRA Recognised Bodies Regulations 2009

[Law Society copyright. For the latest updates to the material, please see www.sra.org.uk.]

[Last amended 1 October 2010]

SRA Recognised Bodies Regulations 2009

[Professional Ethics]

Contents

Rules dated 31 March 2009 and commencing 31 March 2009, made by the Solicitors Regulation Authority Board under sections 79 and 80 of the Solicitors Act 1974 and sections 9 and 9A of the Administration of Justice Act 1985, with the concurrence of the Master of the Rolls and the Lord Chancellor under paragraph 16 of Schedule 22 to the Legal Services Act 2007, making provision as to:

- the procedures for, and the circumstances in which, bodies may be recognised by the SRA as suitable to undertake the provision of legal services, the duration of recognition and the circumstances in which recognition will expire or may be revoked;

- the procedures for, and the circumstances in which, individuals who are not legally qualified may be approved by the SRA as suitable to be managers of recognised bodies, and the circumstances in which such approval may be withdrawn;

- the form and manner of applications relating to the recognition of a body, the approval of an individual, and other applications under rules applying to recognised bodies, their managers and employees, and the fees to accompany such applications;

- the circumstances in which a body's recognition may be made subject to a condition;

- appeals relating to recognition of a body, conditions on recognition, or approval of an individual;

- the names used by recognised bodies; and

- the register of recognised bodies.

Part 1 – Applications, conditions and appeals

Regulation 1 – Form, timing and fees for applications

1.1   Applications under these regulations, or under any other rule which applies to a recognised body, its manager or employee, must comprise:

(a)   the prescribed form, correctly completed;

(b)   the fee or fees for the application, as determined from time to time by the SRA Board;

(c)   if the application is for recognition or for renewal of recognition, any prescribed contribution to the Solicitors' Compensation Fund;

(d)   such additional information, documents and references as may be specified by the SRA; and

(e)   any additional information and documentation which the SRA may reasonably require.

It is not necessary to submit all documents, information and payments simultaneously, but an application will only have been made once the SRA has received all of the documentation, information and payments comprising that application.

1.2   An application for renewal of recognition must be sent to the SRA so as to arrive on or before the renewal date.

1.3   A recognised body must notify the SRA on or before the renewal date if it does not intend to apply for renewal of recognition.

1.4   The SRA shall determine the amount of any fees required under these regulations and the SRA's decision shall be final.

1.5   The SRA may prescribe from time to time a fee moderation process under which a recognised body may make an application for the fee for renewal of recognition to be varied. A decision under this process shall be final.

Regulation 2 – Initial recognition and renewal of recognition

2.1   The SRA may grant an application for initial recognition or renewal of recognition, if it is satisfied that the applicant body is a partnership, LLP or company which meets the conditions in (a) to (d) below:

(a)   the body complies with rule 14 of the Solicitors' Code of Conduct in relation to:

(i)   its formation as a body corporate or partnership;

(ii)   its composition and structure, including any necessary approval of a participant under Regulation 3; and

(iii)   its practising address (and if appropriate, its registered office) in England and Wales;

(b)   the body complies with the Solicitors' Indemnity Insurance Rules;

(c)   the body complies with (or has a waiver of) rule 5.02 of the Solicitors' Code of Conduct; and

(d)   if the body is a partnership, it has adopted a name under which it is to be registered, and which complies with rule 7 of the Solicitors' Code of Conduct.

2.2   The SRA may refuse an application for initial recognition if:

(a)   the SRA is not satisfied that a manager or a person with an interest in the body is a suitable person to be engaged in the management or ownership of a recognised body, taking into account that person's history, character, conduct or associations;

(b)   the SRA is not satisfied that the body's managers or owners are suitable, as a group, to operate or control a business providing regulated legal services; or

(c)   for any other reason the SRA reasonably considers that it would be against the public interest to grant recognition.

2.3   In reaching a decision under 2.2 the SRA may take into account:

(a)   any event listed in regulation 3.1 of the SRA Practising Regulations applying to a manager of the applicant body;

(b)   any other conduct on the part of a manager of the applicant body which calls into question his or her honesty, integrity or respect for law;

(c)   failure or refusal to disclose, or attempts to conceal, any matter within (a) or (b) above in relation to the application;

(d)   that the SRA is not satisfied that the managers of the applicant body, taken together, have sufficient skills and knowledge to run and manage a business which provides regulated legal services,

and any other facts which the SRA reasonably considers should be taken into account.

2.4   An application for initial recognition of a body which will not comply with 2.1(c) will be treated as including an application for a waiver of rule 5.02 of the Solicitors' Code of Conduct.

2.5   If, when considering an application for renewal of recognition, the SRA:

(a)   is not satisfied that the body's managers, taken together, are suitable to run and manage a business providing regulated legal services; or

(b)   considers that for any other reason it would not be in the public interest to renew the body's recognition, the SRA may defer renewal of recognition pending a decision whether the body's recognition should be revoked under regulation 9.

2.6   A grant of initial recognition takes effect from the date of the decision unless otherwise stated.

2.7   (a)   When granting an application for recognition or for renewal of recognition the SRA may impose a condition in accordance with regulation 4.

        (b)   The granting of recognition free of conditions under regulation 2 does not prevent the SRA subsequently imposing a condition under regulation 4.

Regulation 2A – Fee determinations for acquisitions, mergers and splits

The turnover of a recognised body for the purpose of determining the fee for renewal of recognition is based on a historic turnover figure submitted to the SRA. Where in the 12 months following the submission of that figure a recognised body merges or splits, a notice of succession identifying all recognised bodies and recognised sole practitioners affected by the merger or split and any resulting apportionment of the historic turnover figures for those firms will enable the SRA to ensure that the turnover figure on which the fee is based reflects the impact of the merger or split.

2A.1   A recognised body which has succeeded to the whole or a part of one or more recognised bodies or recognised sole practitioners must within 28 days of the change taking place deliver to the SRA a notice of succession in the prescribed form.

2A.2   For the purposes of regulation 2A.1, 'succeeded' includes any taking over of the whole or any part of a recognised body or recognised sole practitioner, for value or otherwise.

2A.3   A recognised body which:

        (a)   has split or ceded part of the practice to a recognised body or recognised sole practitioner; and

        (b)   wishes this change to be considered by the SRA when determining the recognised body's next fee for renewal of recognition

        must within 28 days of the change taking place deliver to the SRA a notice of succession in the prescribed form.

2A.4   A notice of succession delivered under these regulations must;

        (a)   identify all recognised bodies and recognised sole practitioners affected by the succession; and

        (b)   provide details of any resulting apportionment of the turnover figures for those recognised bodies and recognised sole practitioners.

2A.5   A recognised body delivering a notice of succession under these regulations must seek the agreement of all affected recognised bodies or recognised sole practitioners to the contents of the notice of succession.

2A.6   Where a notice of succession is delivered to the SRA which has not been agreed by all affected recognised bodies or recognised sole practitioners, the recognised body delivering the notice of succession shall be treated as having made an application for the SRA to apportion the turnover figures of the affected recognised bodies or recognised sole practitioners for the purposes of determining the fee for renewal of recognition.

2A.7   Before apportioning the turnover figures under regulation 2A.6, the SRA will contact any affected recognised body or recognised sole practitioner identified in the notice of succession who has not agreed with the notice of succession and may require the production of additional information.

Regulation 3 – Approval of an individual as suitable to be a manager

3.1   An individual who is not a lawyer of England and Wales, an REL, an RFL or an exempt European lawyer must be approved by the SRA under this regulation in order to be:

(a)   a manager or owner of a recognised body; or

(b)   a manager of a body corporate which is a manager of a recognised body.

3.2   The following are not eligible for approval under this regulation:

(a)   a member (practising or non-practising) of any profession coming within the meaning of lawyer of England and Wales (including a solicitor);

(b)   an REL;

(c)   an RFL;

(d)   an exempt European lawyer; and

(e)   a member (practising or non-practising) of any profession eligible for approval by the SRA under paragraph 2(2) of Schedule 14 to the Courts and Legal Services Act 1990;

except that an individual who is not a solicitor or a practising member of any profession of lawyers, but is a non-practising barrister or a non-practising member of another profession of lawyers, and who is prevented by his or her professional rules or training regulations from changing status so as to able to practise through the recognised body as a practising lawyer, may apply for approval under this regulation.

3.3   The SRA has a discretion to reject an application under regulation 3 if it is not satisfied that the individual concerned is suitable to be involved in the provision of legal services, and to exercise influence over the conduct of the recognised body concerned because:

(a)   the applicant, the individual concerned or any recognised body or authorised non-SRA firm in which that individual has previously been a manager or employee, has been:

    (i)   reprimanded, made the subject of disciplinary sanction or ordered to pay costs by the Solicitors Disciplinary Tribunal, or struck off or suspended by the Court;

    (ii)   rebuked or fined by the SRA under section 44D of the Solicitors Act 1974 or paragraph 14B of Schedule 2 to the Administration of Justice Act 1985;

    (iii)   intervened in by the SRA (or previously by the Law Society);

    (iv)   notified in writing by the SRA (or previously by the Law Society) that it does not regard as satisfactory an explanation given at the SRA's (or the Society's) request; or

    (v)   made the subject of disciplinary sanction by, or refused registration with or authorisation by, another approved regulator, professional or regulatory tribunal, or regulatory authority, whether in England and Wales or elsewhere,

in respect of a matter involving the individual concerned;

(b)   the individual concerned:

    (i)   has been committed to prison in civil or criminal proceedings;

    (ii)   has been disqualified from being a company director;

(iii) has been removed from the office of charity trustee or trustee for a charity by an order within the terms of section 72(1)(d) of the Charities Act 1993;

(iv) is an undischarged bankrupt;

(v) has been adjudged bankrupt and discharged;

(vi) has entered into an individual voluntary arrangement or a partnership voluntary arrangement under the Insolvency Act 1986;

(vii) has been a manager of a recognised body which has entered into a voluntary arrangement under the Insolvency Act 1986;

(viii) has been a director of a company or a member of an LLP which has been the subject of a winding up order, an administration order or administrative receivership; or has entered into a voluntary arrangement under the Insolvency Act 1986; or has been otherwise wound up or put into administration in circumstances of insolvency;

(ix) lacks capacity (within the meaning of the Mental Capacity Act 2005) and powers under sections 15 to 20 or section 48 of that Act are exercisable in relation to that individual;

(x) is the subject of outstanding judgments involving the payment of money;

(xi) is currently charged with an indictable offence, or has been convicted of an indictable offence or any offence under the Solicitors Act 1974, the Financial Services and Markets Act 2000, the Immigration and Asylum Act 1999 or the Compensation Act 2006;

(xii) has been the subject of an order under section 43 of the Solicitors Act 1974;

(xiii) has been the subject of an equivalent circumstance in another jurisdiction to those listed in (i) to (xi); or

(xiv) has been involved in other conduct which calls into question his or her honesty, integrity or respect for law;

(c) the applicant or the individual concerned fails to disclose, refuses to disclose or seeks to conceal any matter within (a) or (b) above in relation to the application.

3.4 (a) The application for approval must be made by the recognised body or prospective recognised body concerned and may be made:

(i) when applying for initial recognition; or

(ii) at any time after recognition has been granted.

(b) It is for the applicant body to demonstrate that the individual concerned meets the criteria for approval.

(c) The applicant body must:

(i) co-operate, and secure the co-operation of the individual concerned, to assist the SRA to obtain all information and documentation the SRA requires in order to determine the application;

(ii) obtain all other information and documentation in relation to that individual which the prescribed form requires the body to obtain and keep; and

(iii) keep all information and documentation under (ii) above for a period of not less than 6 years after the individual concerned has ceased to be a manager of the body.

(d) The individual concerned must confirm in writing on the face of the application that the information supplied about him or her is correct and complete.

3.5 (a) Approval takes effect from the date of the decision unless otherwise stated.

 (b) The SRA's decision to approve or refuse approval must be notified in writing to the applicant body and, separately, to the individual concerned.

 (c) If the applicant body is a recognised body it must not allow the individual concerned to become a manager until it has received written notice that the individual has been approved.

 (d) Approval continues until:

  (i) it is withdrawn; or

  (ii) two years have elapsed during which the individual has not been a manager of a recognised body.

3.6 The SRA may at any time require the production of information or documentation from:

 (a) an approved individual;

 (b) a recognised body in which an approved individual is a manager; or

 (c) the body which originally obtained approval for that individual and holds information and documentation under 3.4(c)(iii) above;

in order to satisfy the SRA that the individual met the criteria for approval or continues to meet the criteria for approval.

3.7 (a) The SRA may decide to withdraw approval if it is not satisfied that an approved individual met the criteria for approval or continues to meet the criteria for approval or if information or documentation is not promptly supplied in response to a request made under regulation 3.6.

 (b) Subject to (c) below, withdrawal of approval takes effect on expiry of the notice period under regulation 6.2(b) or on such later date as may be stated in the notice.

 (c) If an appeal is made before the withdrawal of approval takes effect, the withdrawal of approval is suspended pending determination or discontinuance of the appeal, unless in the opinion of the SRA the proceedings on that appeal have been unduly protracted by the appellant or are unlikely to be successful.

3.8 Where withdrawal of approval relates to a director of a company, the SRA may set separate dates for that individual ceasing to be a director and disposing of his or her shares.

Regulation 4 – Conditions on recognition

4.1 The SRA may impose one or more conditions on a recognised body's recognition:

 (a) when granting initial recognition;

 (b) when granting renewal of recognition;

 (c) when granting approval of an individual under regulation 3;

 (d) when deciding to withdraw approval of an individual under regulation 3; or

 (e) at any other time.

4.2 The purposes for which the SRA may impose a condition are set out in (a) to (g) below.

 (a) The SRA considers that:

(i) the condition would limit, restrict, halt or prevent an activity or activities on the part of the body, or of a manager or employee of the body, which is putting or is likely to put at risk the interests of clients, third parties or the public, and

(ii) it is in the public interest to impose the condition.

(b) The SRA considers that:

(i) the condition would limit the activities of a manager or employee of the body who is considered unsuitable to undertake a particular activity, either at all or save as specified in the condition, and

(ii) it is in the public interest to impose the condition.

(c) The SRA considers that:

(i) the condition would limit, halt or prevent a risk to clients, third parties or the public arising from a business agreement or association which the body has or is likely to enter into, or a business practice which the body has or is likely to adopt, and

(ii) it is in the public interest to impose the condition.

(d) A relevant insolvency event within the meaning of paragraph 32(1A) of Schedule 2 to the Administration of Justice Act 1985 has occurred in relation to a recognised body, and:

(i) the event has not triggered expiry of recognition under regulation 10, and

(ii) the SRA considers that it is in the public interest to impose the condition.

(e) The SRA considers that imposing the condition will, in the public interest, facilitate closer monitoring by the SRA of compliance with rules and regulations on the part of the body.

(f) The SRA considers that imposing the condition will, in the public interest, require the body concerned to take specified steps conducive to the carrying on of efficient practice by that body.

(g) The SRA considers, in any other case concerning a body which is currently recognised, that it would be in the public interest to impose the condition.

4.3 A condition imposed under this regulation takes effect from the date on which the condition is imposed unless a later date is specified in the condition.

Regulation 5 – Temporary emergency recognition following a partnership split

5.1 If a partnership split brings into being a new partnership which is not a recognised body:

(a) the SRA must be notified within 7 days; and

(b) temporary emergency recognition may be granted, subject to 5.2 to 5.4 below, so as to enable the partners in the new partnership to practise through the new partnership for a limited period without breach of the law.

5.2 An application for temporary emergency recognition may be made by telephone, provided that details given by telephone are confirmed in writing the same day; and must be made (or confirmed) on the prescribed form at the earliest possible opportunity, and accompanied by all information and documentation the SRA may reasonably require.

5.3   The SRA may grant an application for temporary emergency recognition if the following conditions are met.

(a)   The SRA must be satisfied that the partners could not reasonably have commenced an application for recognition in advance of the change.

(b)   The partnership must otherwise comply with rule 14 of the Solicitors' Code of Conduct in relation to its composition and structure and its practising address in England and Wales.

(c)   The partnership must comply with the Solicitors' Indemnity Insurance Rules, and must have adopted a name under which it is to be registered and which complies with rule 7 of the Solicitors' Code of Conduct.

5.4   Temporary emergency recognition:

(a)   may be granted initially for 28 days;

(b)   may be extended in response to a reasonable request by the applicant;

(c)   must be extended (subject to (g) below) pending determination of a substantive application for initial recognition commenced during the currency of a temporary emergency recognition;

(d)   may be granted or extended subject to such conditions as the SRA thinks fit, in circumstances falling within regulation 4;

(e)   is to be treated as initial recognition for the purpose of these regulations;

(f)   if granted, cannot prejudice the discretion of the SRA to refuse a substantive application for recognition of the body under regulation 2 (which is also, for the purpose of these regulations, to be treated as initial recognition); and

(g)   in exceptional circumstances, and for reasonable cause, may be revoked at any time.

Regulation 6 – Notification of decisions by the SRA

6.1   (a)   The SRA must notify its reasons in writing when it:

(i)   refuses an application;

(ii)   grants an application subject to a condition; or

(iii)   refuses a permission required under a condition on a body's recognition.

(b)   The reasons must be given to the applicant body and to the individual concerned, when refusing approval of an individual under regulation 3.

6.2   The SRA must give 28 days written notice, with reasons:

(a)   to the recognised body concerned, when the SRA decides to impose a condition on the body's recognition, or revoke the body's recognition;

(b)   to the body and the individual concerned, when the SRA decides to withdraw an approval granted under regulation 3.

6.3   The SRA may shorten or dispense with the 28 day period under 6.2 in imposing a condition if it is satisfied on reasonable grounds that it is in the public interest to do so.

Regulation 7 – Appeals

7.1   Before exercising its right of appeal to the High Court:

(a)   under paragraph 2(1)(a) of Schedule 2 to the Administration of Justice Act 1985, against refusal of initial recognition;

(b)   under paragraph 2(1)(b) or (c) of that Schedule, against the imposition of a condition; or

(c)   under paragraph 2(2) of that Schedule, against refusal by the SRA to approve a step which, under a condition on the body's recognition, requires such prior approval,

a body may invoke the SRA's own appeals procedure.

7.2   A body may appeal to the High Court against the SRA's decision to revoke the body's recognition, but must first invoke the SRA's own appeals procedure.

7.3   A body, and/or the individual concerned, may appeal to the High Court against the SRA's decision:

(a)   not to approve the individual under regulation 3; or

(b)   to withdraw its approval of the individual under regulation 3,

but must first invoke the SRA's own appeals procedure.

7.4   (a)   An application for initial recognition under regulation 2 is deemed, for the purpose of any appeal under 7.1(a) above, to be refused on the 90th day after the SRA has received the application and all additional information and documentation required, and duly notified to the applicant on that day, if by the end of that day the SRA has not notified the applicant body of its decision.

(b)   An application for approval of an individual under regulation 3 is deemed, for the purpose of any appeal under 7.3(a) above, to be refused on the 90th day after the SRA has received the application and all additional information and documentation required, and duly notified to the applicant on that day, if by the end of that day the SRA has not notified the applicant body, and the individual concerned, of its decision.

7.5   (a)   Appeals under the SRA's own appeals procedure must be made within 28 days of notification of the SRA's reasons for its decision, or within 28 days of deemed refusal under 7.4 above.

(b)   Unless otherwise provided in rules of Court, an appeal to the High Court must be made:

(i)   within 28 days of notification of the relevant decision; or

(ii)   within 28 days of notification of refusal of an appeal under the SRA's own appeals procedure,

as appropriate.

7.6   An appeal under the SRA's own appeals procedure under 7.3(a) above shall be treated as an application for the purpose of these regulations.

Part 2 – Duration of recognition, renewal date, revocation and expiry

Regulation 8 – Duration of recognition and renewal date

8.1   Except where transitional provisions in 8.5 to 8.7 apply, recognition is renewable yearly and the renewal date is 31 October in each successive year.

8.2   Recognition continues in force unless it is revoked, or unless it expires under regulation 10 or is suspended by the High Court.

8.3   Renewal of recognition commences on the day following the renewal date.

Passporting

8.4   (a)   All partnerships carrying on the practice of solicitors and/or RELs on 31 March 2009 will be recognised as recognised bodies on 31 March 2009 provided that:

(i)   the composition and structure of the partnership complies with rule 14 of the Solicitors' Code of Conduct; and

(ii)   the partnership is practising from an office in England and Wales.

(b)   The first renewal date for partnerships recognised under this provision is 31 October 2009.

Transitional provisions

8.5   If a body's recognition commenced on or before 1 November 2006, recognition lasts for three years and the renewal date is that stated on the certificate of recognition.

8.6   If a body's recognition commenced after 1 November 2006 but before 31 March 2009:

(a)   recognition lasts until 31 October 2009 and the renewal date is not that stated on the certificate of recognition but 31 October 2009; and

(b)   when applying for renewal of recognition the body will be given credit for fees and contributions already paid in respect of the cancelled period of recognition after 31 October 2009.

8.7   If a body's recognition commenced on or after 31 March 2009 but before 1 November 2009, the renewal date will be 31 October 2009.

Regulation 9 – Revocation of recognition

9.1   The SRA may revoke a body's recognition, if:

(a)   recognition was granted as a result of error or fraud;

(b)   the body would not be eligible to be recognised if it were at that time applying for initial recognition;

(c)   the renewal date has passed and the SRA has not received an application for renewal of recognition and all required fees, information and documentation;

(d)   the body has a temporary emergency recognition but has not within the initial 28 day period or any extension of that period commenced a substantive application for recognition;

(e)   the body has ceased to practise;

(f)   an approved regulator other than the SRA has authorised the body;

(g)   the SRA has decided under regulation 2.5 not to renew the body's recognition; or

(h)   a relevant insolvency event within the meaning of paragraph 32(1A) of Schedule 2 to the Administration of Justice Act 1985 has occurred in relation to the recognised body which has not triggered expiry of recognition under regulation 10,

and the SRA is satisfied that revocation would not present a risk to clients, to the protection of client money or to any investigative process.

9.2   (a)   Subject to (b) below, revocation takes effect on expiry of the notice period under regulation 6.2(a) or on such later date as may be stated in the notice.

(b)   If an appeal is made before the revocation takes effect, the revocation is suspended pending determination or discontinuance of the appeal, unless in the opinion of the SRA the proceedings on that appeal have been unduly protracted by the appellant or are unlikely to be successful.

Regulation 10 – Expiry of recognition

Subject to 14.04(2) of the Solicitors' Code of Conduct, a body's recognition will automatically expire if the body is wound up or for any other reason ceases to exist.

Part 3 – Name, the register and certificate of recognition

Regulation 11 – Name of a recognised body

11.1   A body corporate will be recognised under its corporate name.

11.2   A partnership must elect to have a name under which it is to be recognised.

Regulation 12 – The register of recognised bodies

12.1   The SRA must keep a register of recognised bodies, which may be kept in electronic form.

12.2   The register of recognised bodies must contain, for each recognised body:

(a)   the name and number under which the body is recognised;

(b)   any other practising styles used by the body;

(c)   the recognised body's registered office and registered number, if it is an LLP or company;

(d)   the recognised body's principal practising address in England and Wales;

(e)   all the recognised body's other practising addresses;

(f)   whether the recognised body is a partnership, an LLP or a company; and

(g)   if the recognised body is a company, whether it is:

    (i)   a company limited by shares;

    (ii)   a company limited by guarantee;

    (iii)   an unlimited company;

    (iv)   an overseas company registered in England and Wales;

    (v)   an overseas company registered in Scotland or Northern Ireland; or

    (vi)   a societas Europaea;

(h)   a list of the body's managers, and in respect of each manager, whether that manager is:

    (i) a lawyer of England and Wales, and if so the nature of his or her qualification;

    (ii) an REL, and if so his or her professional title and jurisdiction of qualification;

    (iii) an exempt European lawyer registered with the Bar Standards Board, and if so his or her professional title and jurisdiction of qualification;

(iv) an exempt European lawyer based entirely at an office or offices outside England and Wales, and if so his or her professional title and jurisdiction of qualification;

(v) an RFL, and if so his or her professional title and jurisdiction of qualification;

(vi) an individual approved under regulation 3;

(vii) a company, and if so whether it is a recognised body, a European corporate practice or an authorised non-SRA firm;

(viii) an LLP, and if so whether it is a recognised body, a European corporate practice or an authorised non-SRA firm; and

(ix) a partnership with separate legal personality, and if so whether it is a recognised body, a European corporate practice or an authorised non-SRA firm;

(i) any condition to which the body's recognition is subject; and

(j) any other reasonable information, necessary for carrying out the SRA's statutory objectives, from time to time prescribed by the SRA.

12.3 (a) Entries in the register must be available for inspection by any member of the public, except that the SRA may withhold an address in exceptional circumstances where the SRA considers that to do so would be in the public interest.

(b) The date on which, and the circumstances in which, a recognised body's recognition expired or was revoked must be made available to a member of the public on request.

Regulation 13 – Certificates of recognition

13.1 When a body is granted initial recognition or its recognition is renewed, the SRA must issue a certificate of recognition.

13.2 Each certificate of recognition must state, in respect of the recognised body:

(a) the name and number under which the body is recognised;

(b) its registered office, if it is an LLP or company;

(c) its principal practising address in England and Wales;

(d) whether it is a partnership, an LLP or a company; and if it is a company, whether it is:

(i) a company limited by shares;

(ii) a company limited by guarantee;

(iii) an unlimited company;

(iv) an overseas company registered in England and Wales;

(v) an overseas company registered in Scotland or Northern Ireland; or

(vi) a societas Europaea;

(e) the date from which recognition is granted or renewed;

(f) the next renewal date; and

(g) any condition to which the body's recognition is subject.

Part 4 – Interpretation, waivers and reconsideration

Regulation 14 – Interpretation

In these regulations:

(a) commencing an application means submitting a completed application form, together with the prescribed fee and any Compensation Fund contribution required;

(b) all terms are to be interpreted in accordance with rule 24 of the Solicitors' Code of Conduct;

(c) "prescribed form" means a form prescribed from time to time by the SRA;

(d) "prescribed fee" means the fee prescribed from time to time by the SRA;

(e) "Solicitors' Code of Conduct" means the Solicitors' Code of Conduct 2007;

(f) "SRA Practising Regulations" means the SRA Practising Regulations 2009; and

(ff) "turnover figure" means as prescribed from time to time by the SRA; and

(g) the date of any notification or notice given under these regulations is deemed to be:

(i) the date on which the communication is delivered to or left at the recipient's address or is sent electronically to the recipient's e-mail or fax address; or

(ii) seven days after the communication has been sent by post or document exchange to the recipient's last notified contact address.

Regulation 15 – Waivers

In any particular case or cases the SRA shall have power to waive in writing the provisions of these regulations for a particular purpose or purposes expressed in such waiver, and to revoke such waiver.

Regulation 16 – Reconsideration

16.1 The SRA may reconsider or rescind a decision made under these regulations when it appears that the decision maker:

(a) was not provided with material evidence that was available to the SRA;

(b) was materially misled;

(c) failed to take proper account of material facts or evidence;

(d) took into account immaterial facts or evidence;

(e) made a material error of law;

(f) made a decision which was otherwise irrational or procedurally unfair;

(g) made a decision which was otherwise ultra vires; or

(h) failed to give sufficient reasons.

16.2 (a) A decision may be reconsidered under 16.1 only on the initiative of the SRA and if a person duly authorised by the SRA gives a direction to that effect.

(b)   That person may also give directions:

    (i)   for further investigations to be undertaken;

    (ii)   for further information or explanation to be obtained; and

    (iii)   for the reconsideration to be undertaken by the original decision maker or by a different decision maker or panel.

Regulation 17 – Notifying third parties of decisions

The SRA may, if it considers it in the public interest to do so, notify any or all of the following persons of a decision made under these regulations:

(a)   a recognised body or authorised non-SRA firm of which the body or individual concerned is a manager or has an ownership interest;

(b)   a recognised sole practitioner, recognised body or authorised non-SRA firm of which the individual concerned is an employee;

(c)   any approved regulator;

(d)   the Legal Services Board;

(e)   the Legal Complaints Service or the Office for Legal Complaints;

(f)   the regulatory body for any profession of which the individual concerned is a member or which regulates the body concerned;

(g)   any law enforcement agency.

Regulation 18 – Commencement and repeal

These regulations come into force on 31 March 2009 and repeal the Solicitors' Recognised Bodies Regulations 2007.

The SRA Practising Regulations 2009

[Last amended 14 July 2010]

SRA Practising Regulations 2009

[Professional Ethics]

Contents

Regulation 15 – Notifying third parties of decisions

Regulation 16 – Reconsideration

Part 5 – Interpretation, commencement and repeals

Regulation 17 – Interpretation

Regulation 18 – Commencement and repeals

Regulations and rules about:

- applications for practising certificates by solicitors and for registration by European lawyers and foreign lawyers;

- applications for authorisation to practise as sole practitioners, by solicitors and registered European lawyers;

- applications for renewal of practising certificates and registration;

- the issue of practising certificates to solicitors and the issue of certificates of registration to European lawyers and foreign lawyers; and

- the keeping of the register of solicitors who hold practising certificates, the register of European lawyers and the register of foreign lawyers,

dated 1 JULY 2009 and commencing 1 JULY 2009

made by the Master of the Rolls under section 28 of the Solicitors Act 1974 and article 3 of the Legal Services Act 2007 (Commencement No. 5, Transitory and Transitional Provisions) Order 2009

with the concurrence of the Secretary of State and the Lord Chief Justice under article 3 of the Legal Services Act 2007 (Commencement No. 5, Transitory and Transitional Provisions) Order 2009, and

made by the Solicitors Regulation Authority Board under sections 13, 13ZA, 31, 79 and 80 of the Solicitors Act 1974 and paragraphs 2 and 3 of Schedule 14 to the Courts and Legal Services Act 1990

with the concurrence of the Master of the Rolls under section 31 of the Solicitors Act 1974 and paragraph 2 of Schedule 14 to the Courts and Legal Services Act 1990 and article 3 of the Legal Services Act 2007 (Commencement No. 5, Transitory and Transitional Provisions) Order 2009

and the concurrence of the Secretary of State under article 3 of the Legal Services Act 2007 (Commencement No. 5, Transitory and Transitional Provisions) Order 2009.

Part 1 – Applications, conditions and appeals

Regulation 1 – General requirements for applications under these regulations

1.1   An application under these regulations must comprise:

(a)   the prescribed form, correctly completed;

(b)   the prescribed fee or fees;

(c)   if the application is for a practising certificate, for replacement of a practising certificate, for registration or for renewal of registration, any prescribed contribution to the Solicitors' Compensation Fund;

(d)   such additional information, documents and references as may be specified by the SRA; and

(e)   any additional information and documentation which the SRA may reasonably require.

It is not necessary to submit all documents, information and payments simultaneously, but an application will only have been made once the SRA has received all of the documentation, information and payments comprising that application.

1.2   Every applicant must ensure that all details relating to him or her given on any form prescribed under these regulations are correct and complete.

1.3   Every form submitted under these regulations must be personally signed by the applicant unless:

(a)   a solicitor or registered European lawyer has been given written permission by the SRA, in exceptional circumstances, to sign on the applicant's behalf; or

(b)   the application is made wholly or partly on a prescribed form which is designed to be completed and signed on behalf of a number of applicants in one firm or organisation. In that case, the form must be signed by a solicitor or registered European lawyer who:

(i)   is authorised to sign the form by the firm or organisation;

(ii)   has the consent of all the persons named in the form to sign the form on their behalf; and

(iii) has taken reasonable steps to ensure that all details given on the form are correct and complete.

1.4   The SRA must notify its reasons in writing to the applicant when it:

(a)   refuses an application;

(b)   grants an application subject to a condition; or

(c)   refuses a permission required under a condition on a practising certificate or registration.

1.5   The SRA shall determine the amount of any fees required under these regulations and the SRA's decision shall be final.

1.6   The SRA may prescribe from time to time a fee moderation process under which a recognised sole practitioner may make an application for the fee for renewal of authorisation as a recognised sole practitioner to be varied. A decision under this process shall be final.

Regulation 2 – Applications for practising certificates and registration

2.1   The following applications may be made under regulation 2:

(a)   unless regulation 3 applies, initial applications for practising certificates and applications for replacement of practising certificates under section 9 of the Solicitors Act 1974;

(b)   unless regulation 3 applies, initial applications for registration in the register of European lawyers and applications for renewal of registration in the register of European lawyers under regulation 17 of the European Communities (Lawyer's Practice) Regulations 2000; and

(c)   initial applications for registration in the register of foreign lawyers and applications for renewal of registration in the register of foreign lawyers under section 89 of the Courts and Legal Services Act 1990.

2.2   Where application is made under regulation 2 for a practising certificate or for replacement of a practising certificate the SRA must grant the application if:

(a)   the applicant's name is on the roll of solicitors;

(b)   the applicant is not suspended from practice as a solicitor;

(c)   the applicant has supplied satisfactory evidence that he or she will comply with or be exempt from the Solicitors' Indemnity Insurance Rules; and

(d)   the application is made in accordance with these Regulations,

and the SRA must not grant the application unless conditions (a) to (c) are met.

2.3   (a)   Where application is made under regulation 2 for initial registration or for renewal of registration in the register of European lawyers the SRA must grant the application if:

(i)   the applicant is not (subject to (c) below) a solicitor, barrister or advocate of any of the UK jurisdictions, a barrister of the Irish Republic, or registered under the Establishment Directive with the Bar Standards Board, the Faculty of Advocates or the Bar Council of Northern Ireland;

(ii)   the applicant is a member, and entitled to practise as such, of an Establishment Directive profession;

(iii)   the applicant is a national of an Establishment Directive state;

(iv)   the applicant applies with the intention of practising on a permanent basis in the UK and is legally entitled to do so;

(v)   the applicant is not struck off the register, suspended from the register, or subject to a direction of the Tribunal prohibiting his or her restoration to the register;

(vi)   the applicant has supplied satisfactory evidence that he or she will comply with or be exempt from the Solicitors' Indemnity Insurance Rules; and

(vii)   the application is made in accordance with these Regulations,

except that if the SRA has reasonable cause to believe that the applicant is not a fit and proper person to practise in the UK it may refuse an application for initial registration.

(b)   The SRA must not grant the application unless the conditions in (a)(i) to (vi) are met.

(c)   The provisions of (a)(i) above will not apply to prevent the renewal of the registration of a European lawyer who has become a solicitor of Scotland or Northern Ireland at a time when he or she was registered both with the SRA and with the Law Society of Scotland and/or the Law Society of Northern Ireland.

2.4   Where application is made under regulation 2 for initial registration or for renewal of registration in the register of foreign lawyers, the following provisions apply.

(a)   The SRA may grant the application (subject to such conditions as it may think fit) if:

(i)   the applicant is not a solicitor, registered European lawyer or barrister;

(ii)   the applicant is a member, and entitled to practise as such, of a legal profession which is regulated within a jurisdiction outside England and Wales and is approved by the SRA in accordance with paragraph 2(2) of Schedule 14 to the Courts and Legal Services Act 1990;

(iii) the applicant is not struck off the register, subject to an order of the Solicitors Disciplinary Tribunal suspending his or her registration or subject to a direction of the Tribunal prohibiting his or her restoration to the register; and

(iv) the application is made in accordance with these Regulations.

(b) The SRA may (without prejudice to its general discretion under paragraph 2 of Schedule 14 to the Courts and Legal Services Act 1990) reject the application if:

(i) the SRA is not satisfied that the applicant is eligible for registration;

(ii) the applicant is prohibited by the rules of his or her profession from practising as a manager of a recognised body;

(iii) the SRA is not satisfied that the applicant will be in compliance with the Solicitors' Indemnity Insurance Rules;

(iv) the SRA is not satisfied that the applicant intends to become a manager or employee of a recognised body; or

(v) the SRA is not satisfied that the applicant is a fit and proper person to practise as a manager of a recognised body.

(c) A person who has been reinstated to the register under paragraph 12 of Schedule 14 to the Courts and Legal Services Act 1990 is to be treated as entitled to practise as a member of his or her home legal profession.

2.5 The granting of a practising certificate or registration free of conditions under regulation 2 does not prevent the SRA subsequently imposing a condition in accordance with regulation 6.

Regulation 3 – Application following certain events

3.1 Regulation 3 applies (subject to 3.3 below) to an initial application for a practising certificate, an application for replacement of a practising certificate, an initial application for registration in the register of European lawyers and an application for renewal of registration in the register of European lawyers, in any of the following circumstances.

(a) The applicant has been:

(i) reprimanded, made the subject of disciplinary sanction or made the subject of an order under section 43 of the Solicitors Act 1974, ordered to pay costs or made the subject of a recommendation to the Law Society or the SRA to consider imposing a condition, by the Solicitors Disciplinary Tribunal, or struck off or suspended by the Court;

(ii) made the subject of an order under section 43 of the Solicitors Act 1974 by the Law Society or the SRA or rebuked or fined under section 44D of that Act by the SRA;

(iii) made the subject of, or been a manager of a recognised body which has been the subject of, an intervention by the Law Society or the SRA; or

(iv) made the subject of a disciplinary sanction by, or refused registration with or authorisation by, another approved regulator, professional or regulatory tribunal, or regulatory authority, whether in England and Wales or elsewhere.

(b) The SRA (or previously the Law Society) has requested an explanation from the

APPENDIX 2

applicant in respect of a matter relating to the applicant's conduct and has notified the applicant in writing that it does not regard the applicant's response, or lack of response, as satisfactory.

(c) The applicant has failed to deliver within the period allowed an accountant's report required by rules made under section 34 of the Solicitors Act 1974.

(d) The applicant's practising certificate or registration has been suspended and the suspension:

    (i) has come to an end;

    (ii) was continuing when the applicant's last practising certificate or previous registration expired or was revoked; or

    (iii) is continuing.

(e) The applicant has been suspended from practice (or suspended from the register, if the applicant is a European lawyer), and the suspension has come to an end.

(f) The applicant's last practising certificate or previous registration expired or was revoked whilst subject to a condition.

(g) The applicant's practising certificate or registration is currently subject to a condition.

(h) The applicant's right to practise as a lawyer of another jurisdiction or as a lawyer of England and Wales (other than as a solicitor) is subject to a condition or restriction.

(i) The applicant has been restored to the roll or register, having previously been struck off.

(j) The applicant is an undischarged bankrupt.

(k) The applicant:

    (i) has been adjudged bankrupt and discharged;

    (ii) has entered into an individual voluntary arrangement or a partnership voluntary arrangement under the Insolvency Act 1986;

    (iii) has been a manager of a recognised body which has entered into a voluntary arrangement under the Insolvency Act 1986;

    (iv) has been a director of a company or a member of an LLP which has been the subject of a winding up order, an administration order or administrative receivership; or has entered into a voluntary arrangement under the Insolvency Act 1986; or has been voluntarily wound up in circumstances of insolvency.

(l) The applicant lacks capacity (within the meaning of the Mental Capacity Act 2005) and powers under sections 15 to 20 or section 48 of that Act are exercisable in relation to the applicant.

(m) The applicant has been committed to prison in civil or criminal proceedings and:

    (i) has been released; or

    (ii) has not been released.

(n) The applicant has been made subject to a judgment which involves the payment of money, other than one:

    (i) which is limited to the payment of costs; or

    (ii) in respect of which the applicant is entitled to indemnity or relief from another person as to the whole sum; or

     (iii)   which the applicant has paid, and supplied evidence of payment to the SRA (or previously to the Law Society).

(o)   The applicant is currently charged with an indictable offence.

(p)   The applicant has been convicted of an indictable offence or any offence under the Solicitors Act 1974, the Financial Services and Markets Act 2000, the Immigration and Asylum Act 1999 or the Compensation Act 2006.

(q)   The applicant has been disqualified from being a company director.

(r)   The applicant has been removed from the office of charity trustee or trustee for a charity by an order within the terms of section 72(1)(d) of the Charities Act 1993.

(s)   The applicant has been the subject in another jurisdiction of any circumstance equivalent to those listed in (j) to (r).

3.2   If regulation 3 applies:

(a)   an application for replacement of a practising certificate or for renewal of registration in the register of European lawyers must be commenced at least six weeks before the replacement or renewal date; and

(b)   the SRA:

     (i)   has no discretion under regulation 3 to grant the application if the applicant does not meet the conditions in regulation 2.2(a) to (c) or 2.3(a)(i) to (vi);

     (ii)   has discretion to impose a condition or conditions in accordance with regulation 6; and

     (iii)   has discretion to refuse the application.

3.3   The provisions of 3.1 and 3.2 above are subject to the following exceptions.

(a)   Regulation 3 does not apply by virtue of 3.1(a), (b), (c), (d)(i), (e), (j), (k), (m)(i), (n), (o), (p), (q), (r) or (s) if the applicant has previously applied for and obtained a practising certificate or registration, provided that:

     (i)   the applicant's practising certificate or registration is not subject to a condition relating to any of those provisions;

     (ii)   the SRA (or previously the Law Society) was aware, when granting that application, of all the relevant facts; and

     (iii)   no new circumstances have arisen which would bring the application within any of those provisions.

(b)   If regulation 3 applies only by virtue of 3.1(j), (m), (n) or (p) and an appeal has been made to the appropriate court against the order or judgment in question, the following provisions apply.

     (i)   The application must not be refused before the determination of that appeal, unless in the opinion of the SRA the proceedings on that appeal have been unduly protracted by the appellant or are unlikely to be successful.

     (ii)   The SRA may in the meantime postpone a decision on the application and may impose a condition on the applicant's practising certificate or registration.

(c)   If regulation 3 applies only by virtue of 3.1(o), the application may not be refused unless the applicant is convicted, but the SRA may postpone a decision on the application and may impose a condition on the applicant's practising certificate or registration.

Regulation 4 – Application to be a recognised sole practitioner

4.1   An application may be made under regulation 4 by a solicitor or European lawyer:

(a)   for initial authorisation as a recognised sole practitioner:

(i)   when making an initial application for a practising certificate or for registration in the register of European lawyers;

(ii)   when applying for replacement of a practising certificate or for renewal of registration in the register of European lawyers; or

(iii)   at any time during the currency of a solicitor's practising certificate or a registered European lawyer's registration; or

(b)   for renewal of an existing authorisation as a recognised sole practitioner when applying for replacement of a practising certificate or for renewal of registration in the register of European lawyers.

4.2   (a)   The SRA may grant an application under regulation 4 if the applicant:

(i)   will be practising as a sole practitioner from an office in England and Wales;

(ii)   is not, and is not about to be made, subject to a condition on his or her practising certificate or registration which would prohibit practice as a sole practitioner;

(iii)   has adopted a name under which his or her firm is to be recognised, and which complies with rule 7 of the Solicitors' Code of Conduct; and

(iv)   complies with (or has a waiver of) rule 5.02 of the Solicitors' Code of Conduct; and

(v)   complies with the Solicitors' Indemnity Insurance Rules in respect of his or her firm.

(b)   The SRA may refuse an application under regulation 4 if it is not satisfied that the applicant is suitable to run and manage a business providing regulated legal services or if for any other reason the SRA reasonably considers that it would be against the public interest to grant recognition.

(c)   In reaching a decision on an application under regulation 4 the SRA may take into account:

(i)   any event listed in regulation 3.1 applying to the applicant;

(ii)   any other conduct on the part of the applicant which calls into question his or her honesty, integrity or respect for law;

(iii)   failure or refusal to disclose, or an attempt to conceal, any matter within (i) or (ii) above in relation to the application; or

(iv)   that the SRA is not satisfied that the applicant has sufficient skills or knowledge in relation to the running and management of a business which provides regulated legal services.

(d)   When granting an application under regulation 4 the SRA may impose a condition on the applicant's practising certificate or registration in accordance with regulation 6.

4.3   An application for initial authorisation of a solicitor or European lawyer who will not comply with 4.2(a)(iv) will be treated as including an application for a waiver of rule 5.02 of the Solicitors' Code of Conduct.

4.4   A solicitor or registered European lawyer who is practising as a sole practitioner from an office in England and Wales immediately before 1 JULY 2009 will be authorised as a recognised sole practitioner on 1 July 2009 provided that the sole practitioner concerned:

(a)   has in place professional indemnity cover under the Solicitors' Indemnity Insurance Rules; and

(b)   is not on that date practising as a sole practitioner in breach of a condition on his or her practising certificate or registration.

4.5   If a change to the composition of a recognised body which was a partnership results in a solicitor or REL becoming its sole principal:

(a)   the SRA must be notified within seven days; and

(b)   temporary emergency recognition may be granted, subject to 4.6 below, so as to enable that sole principal to continue in practice without breach of rule 12 of the Solicitors' Code of Conduct.

4.6   (a)   An application for temporary emergency recognition:

    (i)   may be made by telephone, provided that details given by telephone are confirmed in writing the same day; and

    (ii)   must be made (or confirmed) on the prescribed form at the earliest possible opportunity, and accompanied by all information and documentation the SRA reasonably require.

(b)   The SRA may grant an application for temporary emergency recognition if the following conditions are met:

    (i)   the SRA must be satisfied that the applicant could not reasonably have commenced an application for recognition as a sole practitioner in advance of the change; and

    (ii)   the sole practitioner must comply with the Solicitors' Indemnity Insurance Rules, and must have adopted a name under which the firm is to be registered and which complies with rule 7 of the Solicitors' Code of Conduct.

(c)   Temporary emergency recognition:

    (i)   may be granted initially for 28 days;

    (ii)   may be extended for a further specified period or periods in response to a reasonable request by the applicant;

    (iii)   must be extended (subject to (vii) below) pending determination of a substantive application for initial recognition commenced during the currency of a temporary emergency recognition;

    (iv)   may be granted or extended subject to such conditions as the SRA thinks fit, in circumstances falling within regulation 6;

    (v)   is to be treated as initial recognition for the purpose of these regulations;

    (vi)   if granted, cannot prejudice the discretion of the SRA to refuse a substantive application for recognition under this regulation (which is also, for the purpose of these regulations, to be treated as initial recognition); and

    (vii)   in exceptional circumstances, and for reasonable cause, may be revoked at any time.

APPENDIX 2

Regulation 4A – Fee determinations for acquisitions, mergers and splits

The turnover of a recognised sole practitioner for the purpose of determining the fee for renewal of authorisation as a recognised sole practitioner is based on a historic turnover figure submitted to the SRA. Where in the 12 months following the submission of that figure a recognised sole practitioner merges or splits, a notice of succession identifying all recognised bodies and recognised sole practitioners affected by the merger or split and any resulting apportionment of histor c turnover figures for those firms will enable the SRA to ensure that the turnover figure on which the fee is based reflects the impact of the merger or split.

4A.1 A recognised sole practitioner who has succeeded to the whole or a part of one or more recognised bodies or recognised sole practitioners must within 28 days of the change taking place deliver to the SRA a notice of succession in the prescribed form.

4A.2 For the purposes of regulation 4A.1, "succeeded" includes any taking over of the whole or any part of a recognised body or recognised sole practitioner, for value or otherwise

4A.3 A recognised sole practitioner who:

(a) has split or ceded part of the practice to a recognised body or recognised sole practitioner; and

(b) wishes this change to be considered by the SRA when determining the recognised sole practitioner's next fee for renewal of authorisation as a recognised sole practitioner

must within 28 days of the change taking place deliver to the SRA a notice of succession in the prescribed form.

4A.4 A notice of succession delivered under these regulations must;

(a) identify all recognised bodies and recognised sole practitioners affected by the succession; and

(b) provide details of any resulting apportionment of the turnover figures for those recognised bodies and recognised sole practitioners.

4A.5 A recognised sole practitioner delivering a notice of succession under these regulations must seek the agreement of all affected recognised bodies or recognised sole practitioners to the contents of the notice of succession.

4A.6 Where a notice of succession is delivered to the SRA which has not been agreed by all affected recognised bodies or recognised sole practitioners, the recognised sole practitioner delivering the notice of succession shall be treated as having made an application for the SRA to apportion the turnover figures of the affected recognised bodies or recognised sole practitioners for the purposes of determining the fee for renewal of recognition.

4A.7 Before apportioning the turnover figures under regulation 4A.6, the SRA will contact any affected recognised body or recognised sole practitioner identified in the notice of succession who has not agreed with the notice of succession and may require the production of additional information.

Regulation 5 – Applications for reinstatement

The following applications are to be treated as made under these regulations:

(a) an application for reinstatement of a suspended practising certificate or suspended registration in the register of European lawyers under section 16(3) of the Solicitors Act 1974; and

(b) an application for reinstatement of a suspended registration in the register of foreign lawyers under paragraph 12(2) of Schedule 14 to the Courts and Legal Services Act 1990 or under section 16(3)(b) of the Solicitors Act 1974.

Regulation 6 – Conditions

6.1 The SRA may impose one or more conditions on a practising certificate or on the registration of a European lawyer when granting an application under regulation 3 to 5, or at any time during the practising year, for the following purposes.

(a) The SRA considers the individual concerned unsuitable to undertake certain activities in relation to a legal practice, either at all or save as specified in the condition, and that imposing the condition will, in the public interest, limit, restrict, halt or prevent the involvement of the individual concerned in those activities.

(b) The SRA considers that the individual concerned is putting or is likely to put at risk the interests of clients, third parties or the public by taking certain steps in relation to a legal practice, and that imposing the condition will, in the public interest, limit, restrict, halt or prevent the taking of such steps by the individual concerned.

(c) The SRA considers the individual concerned unsuitable to engage in certain business agreements, business associations or practising arrangements and that imposing a condition requiring the applicant to obtain the SRA's written approval before taking certain steps will, in the public interest, limit, halt or prevent a risk to clients, third parties or the public.

(d) The SRA considers that imposing the condition will, in the public interest, require the individual concerned to take specified steps conducive to the carrying on of efficient practice by the individual concerned.

(e) The SRA considers that imposing the condition will, in the public interest, facilitate closer monitoring by the SRA of compliance by the individual concerned with rules and regulations.

(f) The SRA considers that it would be in the public interest to impose the condition in any other case during the currency of a practising certificate or registration.

6.2 Without prejudice to the powers of the SRA under paragraph 2A, 12 or 13 of Schedule 14 to the Courts and Legal Services Act 1990, the SRA may when granting an application under regulation 2.1(c) or at any time during the currency of a registration, impose such conditions on a foreign lawyer's registration as it sees fit:

(a) if any event listed in regulation 3.1 applies to the individual concerned;

(b) for a purpose within regulation 6.1(a) to (f); or

(c) where the SRA considers in any other case that imposing the condition would be in the public interest.

6.3 When the SRA decides, on an initial application for a practising certificate or registration or on an application for replacement of a practising certificate or renewal of registration, to grant the application subject to a condition:

(a) the SRA may postpone the issue of the certificate or the registration pending determination or discontinuance of any appeal; but

(b) the postponement may be rescinded if in the SRA's opinion proceedings on appeal have been unduly protracted by an appellant or are unlikely to be successful.

6.4 (a) The SRA must, subject to (b) below, give 28 days written notice, with reasons, to the individual concerned, when the SRA decides to impose a condition during the currency of a practising certificate or registration.

(b) The SRA may shorten or dispense with the 28 day period under (a) if it is satisfied on reasonable grounds that it is in the public interest to do so.

(c) A condition is effective from the date on which the condition is imposed unless a later date is specified in the condition.

Regulation 7 – Appeals

7.1 The rights of appeal conferred by regulation 7 supplement the statutory rights of appeal referred to in 7.4.

7.2 A person who is the subject of any of the following decisions has a right of appeal to the High Court against:

(a) revocation, under regulation 9.2(a)(i), (ii) or (v), of a solicitor's practising certificate;

(b) revocation, under regulation 9.2(b), of a solicitor's or European lawyer's authorisation as a recognised sole practitioner.

7.3 A solicitor, registered European lawyer or registered foreign lawyer may appeal under the SRA's own appeals procedure against:

(a) refusal to revoke a practising certificate or registration under regulation 9.2(c);

(b) refusal to withhold a solicitor's, European lawyer's or foreign lawyer's place of business from the relevant register under regulation 10, 11 or 12.

7.4 A solicitor, European lawyer of foreign lawyer may invoke the SRA's own appeals procedure before exercising a right of appeal to the High Court:

(a) under section 13(1) the Solicitors Act 1974, against refusal to issue or replace a practising certificate or refusal to renew registration in the register of European lawyers;

(b) under Regulation 20 of the European Communities (Lawyer's Practice) Regulations 2000 (S.I. 2000 No. 1119), against refusal to grant initial registration in the register of European lawyers;

(c) under paragraph 14 of Schedule 14 to the Courts and Legal Services Act 1990, against refusal to grant or renew registration in the register of foreign lawyers, or against a decision of the SRA to revoke his or her registration;

(d) under section 13(1) or 13ZA(6) of the Solicitors Act 1974 or regulation 20 of the European Communities (Lawyer's Practice) Regulations 2000, against refusal to grant or renew authorisation of a solicitor or registered European lawyer as a recognised sole practitioner;

(e) under section 13(1), 13ZA(6), 13A(6) or 16(5) of the Solicitors Act 1974, regulation 20 of the European Communities (Lawyer's Practice) Regulations 2000 or paragraph 14 of Schedule 14 to the Courts and Legal Services Act 1990, against the imposition of a condition on a practising certificate or the registration of a European lawyer or foreign lawyer;

(f) under section 13(2) or 13A(9) of the Solicitors Act 1974, against refusal of permission to take a step for which the SRA's permission is required under a condition on a practising certificate or the registration of a European lawyer or foreign lawyer;

(g) under section 13B(7) of the Solicitors Act 1974, against suspension of a practising certificate or suspension of registration in the register of foreign lawyers;

(h)   under regulation 20 of the European Communities (Lawyer's Practice) Regulations 2000, against suspension of registration in the register of European lawyers;

(i)   under section 13B(7) of the Solicitors Act 1974, against extension of suspension of a practising certificate or suspension of the registration of a European lawyer or foreign lawyer;

(j)   under section 13B(7) of the Solicitors Act 1974, against suspension of authorisation of a solicitor or registered European lawyer as a recognised sole practitioner;

(k)   under section 16(5) of the Solicitors Act 1974 or paragraph 14 of Schedule 14 to the Courts and Legal Services Act 1990, against refusal to reinstate a suspended practising certificate or the suspended registration of a European lawyer or foreign lawyer;

(l)   under section 16(5) of the Solicitors Act 1974, against refusal to reinstate a suspended authorisation as a recognised sole practitioner;

(m)   under regulation 20 of the European Communities (Lawyer's Practice) Regulations 2000 against revocation of registration in the register of European lawyers;

(n)   under regulation 19 and 20 of the European Communities (Lawyer's Practice) Regulations 2000 against failure to determine, within four months, an application for initial registration in the register of European lawyers;

(o)   under paragraph 14 of Schedule 14 to the Courts and Legal Services Act 1990, against failure to determine, within a reasonable time, an application for registration, renewal of registration or reinstatement of a suspended registration in the register of foreign lawyers;

(p)   against a decision mentioned in regulation 7.2(a) or (b).

7.5   (a)   If an application is made in accordance with regulation 1.1, and the SRA has not notified the applicant of its decision:

        (i)   by the end of the 90th day, in the case of any application except an application for renewal of a practising certificate or registration which is made under regulation 3; or

        (ii)   by the end of the 180th day, in the case of an application for renewal of a practising certificate or registration which is made under regulation 3,

the application is to be treated as having been refused and the refusal having been duly notified to the applicant on that day.

    (b)   The provisions of (a) above do not apply to an application from which an appeal lies under 7.4(n) or (o).

7.6   (a)   Appeals under the SRA's own appeals procedure must be commenced within 28 days of notification of the relevant decision.

    (b)   Unless otherwise provided in the relevant statute, regulations or rules of Court, an appeal to the High Court must be commenced:

        (i)   within 28 days of notification of the relevant decision; or

        (ii)   within 28 days of notification of refusal of an appeal under the SRA's own appeals procedure, as appropriate.

Part 2 – Duration, expiry and revocation of practising certificates and registrations

Regulation 8 – Commencement, replacement and renewal dates

8.1 (a) The commencement date for a practising certificate is the day on which it is entered in the register of holders of practising certificates.

(b) The commencement date for registration in the register of European lawyers is the day on which the lawyer's name is entered in the register.

(c) The commencement date for registration in the register of foreign lawyers is the day on which the lawyer's name is entered in the register.

(d) The commencement date for authorisation as a recognised sole practitioner is the day on which the authorisation is entered in the register of holders of practising certificates or the register of European lawyers.

8.2 (a) The replacement date for a practising certificate is the 31 October following the issue of the certificate.

(b) The renewal date for registration in the register of European lawyers is the first 31 October following initial registration, and 31 October in each successive year.

(c) The renewal date for registration in the register of foreign lawyers is the first 31 October following initial registration, and 31 October in each successive year.

(d) The renewal date for authorisation as a recognised sole practitioner is the first 31 October following the initial authorisation, and 31 October in each successive year.

Regulation 9 – Expiry and revocation

9.1 (a) A practising certificate expires:

(i) when a replacement certificate is issued;

(ii) on the death of the solicitor;

(iii) if the solicitor is removed from or struck off the roll;

(iv) in the case of a practising certificate which is suspended, on its replacement date, or if its replacement date has passed, 14 days after the suspension took effect.

(b) The registration of a registered European lawyer expires:

(i) if the lawyer becomes a solicitor, barrister or advocate of any of the UK jurisdictions or a barrister of the Irish Republic;

(ii) if the lawyer ceases to be a member, and entitled to practise as such, of an Establishment Directive profession;

(iii) if the lawyer ceases to be a national of an Establishment Directive state;

(iv) on the death of the lawyer;

(v) if the lawyer is removed from or struck off the register; or

(vi) in the case of a registration which is suspended, on its renewal date, or if its renewal date has passed, 14 days after the suspension took effect,

except that the registration of a European lawyer will not expire by virtue of the lawyer becoming a solicitor of Scotland or Northern Ireland at a time when he or she is registered both with the SRA and with the Law Society of Scotland and/or the Law Society of Northern Ireland.

(c) The registration of a registered foreign lawyer expires:

    (i) if the lawyer becomes a solicitor, registered European lawyer or barrister;

    (ii) if the lawyer ceases to be a member, and entitled to practise as such, of a legal profession which is regulated within a jurisdiction outside England and Wales and is approved by the SRA in accordance with paragraph 2(2) of Schedule 14 to the Courts and Legal Services Act 1990;

    (iii) on the death of the lawyer;

    (iv) if the lawyer is removed from or struck off the register; or

    (v) in the case of a registration which is suspended, on its renewal date or if its renewal date has passed, 14 days after the suspension took effect.

(d) Authorisation as a recognised sole practitioner expires on:

    (i) the expiry or revocation of the solicitor's practising certificate or the European lawyer's registration; or

    (ii) the imposition of a condition on the solicitor's practising certificate or the European lawyer's registration which prohibits practice as a sole practitioner.

9.2 (a) The SRA may revoke a practising certificate, registration in the register of European lawyers or registration in the register of foreign lawyers:

    (i) at any time, if the SRA is satisfied that the practising certificate or registration was granted as a result of error or fraud;

    (ii) on a date chosen by the SRA, if the replacement or renewal date has passed and the SRA has not received an application for replacement of the practising certificate or renewal of the registration made in accordance with regulation 1;

    (iii) at any time, if the SRA is satisfied, in the case a registered European lawyer, that the lawyer has no intention of practising on a permanent basis in the United Kingdom;

    (iv) at any time, if the SRA is satisfied, in the case a registered foreign lawyer, that the lawyer has no intention of practising in a recognised body or an authorised non-SRA firm or as the employee of a recognised sole practitioner; or

    (v) on refusing, under regulation 2 or 3, to replace a practising certificate or to renew a registration.

(b) The SRA may revoke authorisation as a recognised sole practitioner at any time if:

    (i) the authorisation as a recognised sole practitioner was granted as a result of error or fraud;

    (ii) the solicitor or registered European lawyer is not practising from an office in England and Wales;

    (iii) the SRA is not satisfied that the recognised sole practitioner continues to meet the criteria for authorisation as a recognised sole practitioner;

    (iv) the recognised sole practitioner has a temporary emergency recognition but has not within the initial 28 day period or any extension of that period commenced a substantive application for recognition; or

(v)   the SRA has decided under regulation 4 not to renew authorisation as a recognised sole practitioner.

(c)   The SRA may revoke a practising certificate, registration, or authorisation as a recognised sole practitioner on the application of the person concerned but:

(i)   there is no discretion to refund any part of the fee paid for that practising year; and

(ii)   the SRA may refuse the application if there is an outstanding complaint against the applicant or for any other reason relating to the public interest.

9.3   (a)   When the SRA decides to revoke a practising certificate, registration, or authorisation as a recognised sole practitioner under 9.2(a) or (b) it must give the person concerned 28 days notice, with reasons. The notice may be given together with notification of refusal of an application to replace a practising certificate, renew a registration or renew an authorisation.

(b)   Revocation takes effect on expiry of the notice under (a), or on such later date as may be stated in the notice, except that if an appeal is made during the period of notice the revocation does not take effect until determination or discontinuance of any appeal, whether under the SRA's own procedure, or to the High Court under statutory provisions, or to the High Court under regulation 7.6(b).

Part 3 – The registers, practising certificates and certificates of registration

Regulation 10 – The register of holders of practising certificates

10.1   The SRA must keep a register of solicitors who hold practising certificates, which may be kept in electronic form.

10.2   The register must contain, in respect of each solicitor who holds a practising certificate, the following information:

(a)   full name as shown on the roll;

(b)   date of birth;

(c)   registration number;

(d)   any other legal profession of which the solicitor is a member and whether the solicitor is entitled to practise as a member of that profession;

(e)   date of admission as a solicitor;

(f)   the commencement and replacement dates for the solicitor's current practising certificate;

(g)   whether the solicitor is a recognised sole practitioner, and if so:

(i)   the registered name of the solicitor's sole practice; and

(ii)   any other practising styles used by the solicitor as a sole practitioner;

(h)   the solicitor's place or places of business, except in the case of a non-practising solicitor;

(i)   an address for correspondence in the case of a non-practising solicitor;

(j)   any condition to which the solicitor's practising certificate is subject;

(k)   a note about any suspension of the solicitor from practice, or suspension of the solicitor's practising certificate, or suspension of the solicitor from practice as a sole practitioner, or suspension of the solicitor's authorisation as a recognised sole practitioner, or the termination of any such suspension;

(l)   a note of any order of the Solicitors Disciplinary Tribunal under section 47 of the Solicitors Act 1974 in respect of the solicitor (or former solicitor), and a note of any order of the High Court or the Court of Appeal striking the solicitor off the roll; and

(m)   any other reasonable information, necessary for carrying out the SRA's statutory objectives, from time to time prescribed by the SRA.

10.3 (a)   Entries in the register under 10.2(a), (c) to (h) and (j) to (m) must be available for inspection by any member of the public, except that the SRA may in exceptional circumstances and if it considers that to do so would be in the public interest, withhold:

(i)   the address of any or all a solicitor's places of business; or

(ii)   all information about a condition to which a solicitor's practising certificate is subject, or details of the condition.

(b)   The date on which a solicitor's practising certificate or authorisation as a recognised sole practitioner expired or was revoked must be made available to a member of the public on request.

Regulation 11 – The register of European lawyers

11.1 The SRA must keep a register of European lawyers, which may be kept in electronic form.

11.2 The register must contain, in respect of each registered European lawyer, the following information:

(a)   full name;

(b)   date of birth;

(c)   registration number;

(d)   in relation to each Establishment Directive profession of which the lawyer is a member:

(i)   the professional title;

(ii)   the professional body; and

(iii)   whether the lawyer is entitled to practise as a member of that profession;

(e)   any other legal profession of which the lawyer is a member and whether the lawyer is entitled to practise as a member of that profession;

(f)   the date of initial registration;

(g)   the commencement and renewal dates for the current period of registration;

(h)   whether the lawyer is a recognised sole practitioner, and if so:

(i)   the registered name of the lawyer's sole practice; and

(ii)   any other practising styles used by the lawyer as a sole practitioner in the United Kingdom;

(i)   the lawyer's place or places of business in the United Kingdom;

(j)   any condition to which the lawyer's registration is subject;

APPENDIX 2

(k)   a note about any suspension of the lawyer's registration, or suspension of the lawyer's authorisation as a recognised sole practitioner, or the termination of any such suspension;

(l)   a note of any order of the Solicitors Disciplinary Tribunal under section 47 of the Solicitors Act 1974 in respect of the lawyer, and a note of any order of the High Court or the Court of Appeal striking the lawyer off the register; and

(m)   any other reasonable information, necessary for carrying out the SRA's statutory objectives, from time to time prescribed by the SRA.

11.3   (a)   Entries in the register under 11.2(a) and (c) to (m) must be available for inspection by any member of the public, except that the SRA may in exceptional circumstances and if it considers that to do so would be in the public interest, withhold:

(i)   the address of any or all an REL's places of business; or

(ii)   all information about a condition to which an REL's registration is subject or details of the condition.

(b)   The date on which a registered European lawyer's registration or authorisation as a recognised sole practitioner expired or was revoked must be made available to a member of the public on request.

11.4   A registered European lawyer whose name has changed may apply to the SRA to change his or her name on the register.

Regulation 12 – The register of foreign lawyers

12.1   The SRA must keep a register of foreign lawyers, which may be kept in electronic form.

12.2   The register must contain, in respect of each registered foreign lawyer, the following information:

(a)   full name;

(b)   date of birth;

(c)   registration number;

(d)   in relation to each legal profession of which the lawyer is a member:

(i)   the professional title;

(ii)   the professional body; and

(iii)   whether the lawyer is entitled to practise as a member of that profession;

(e)   the date of initial registration;

(f)   the commencement and renewal dates for the current period of registration;

(g)   the registered name and place or places of business of any recognised body or authorised non-SRA firm of which the lawyer is a manager or in which the lawyer has an ownership interest;

(h)   the registered name of any recognised sole practitioner, recognised body or authorised non-SRA firm who or which is the lawyer's employer, and the address of the lawyer's place of employment;

(i)   any condition to which the lawyer's registration is subject;

(j)   a note about any suspension of the lawyer's registration, or the termination of such suspension;

(k)   a note of any order of the Solicitors Disciplinary Tribunal in respect of the lawyer; and

(l)   any other reasonable information, necessary for carrying out the SRA's statutory objectives, from time to time prescribed by the SRA.

12.3 (a)   Entries in the register under 12.2(a) and (c) to (l) must be available for inspection by any member of the public, except that the SRA may in exceptional circumstances and if it considers that to do so would be in the public interest, withhold:

  (i)   the address of any or all an RFL's places of business; or

  (ii)   all information about a condition to which an RFL's registration is subject or details of the condition.

(b)   The date on which a registered foreign lawyer's registration expired or was revoked must be made available to a member of the public on request.

12.4 A registered foreign lawyer whose name has changed may apply to the SRA to change his or her name on the register.

Regulation 13 – Practising certificates and certificates of registration

13.1 Each practising certificate and each certificate of registration must specify:

(a)   the individual's full name;

(b)   its commencement date;

(c)   its replacement date;

(d)   in the case of a solicitor or registered European lawyer who is authorised as a recognised sole practitioner, a statement to that effect; and

(e)   any condition to which the practising certificate or registration is subject, to the extent that it is public information under regulation 10, 11 or 12.

13.2 Every practising certificate or certificate of registration must be delivered to the applicant at the applicant's principal place of business or to such other address as may be specified by or on behalf of the applicant in writing, and may be delivered by post or electronically.

Part 4 – Information requirements, notifying third parties and review of decisions

Regulation 14 – Information requirements

14.1 In addition to any requirements under section 84 of the Solicitors Act 1974 or any other rules applicable by virtue of that Act, a solicitor, registered European lawyer or registered foreign lawyer must inform the SRA within 14 days if he or she:

(a)   is committed to prison in civil or criminal proceedings;

(b)   is charged with or convicted of an indictable offence;

(c)   is made the subject of bankruptcy proceedings;

(d)   makes a proposal for an individual voluntary arrangement or is a manager of a firm which makes a proposal for a company voluntary arrangement or a partnership voluntary arrangement under the Insolvency Act 1986;

(e)   is admitted as:

APPENDIX 2

 (i) a member of a legal profession of a jurisdiction other than England and Wales;

 (ii) a lawyer of England and Wales other than a solicitor;

(f) is made subject to disciplinary proceedings as:

 (i) a member of a legal profession of a jurisdiction other than England and Wales; or

 (ii) a lawyer of England and Wales other than a solicitor;

(g) becomes a manager of or acquires an ownership interest in a firm which is a recognised body or an authorised non-SRA firm;

(h) sets up a sole practice as:

 (i) a member of a legal profession of a jurisdiction other than England and Wales; or

 (ii) a lawyer of England and Wales other than a solicitor.

14.2 A solicitor, registered European lawyer or registered foreign lawyer who ceases to practise must inform the SRA within 14 days and supply the SRA with a contact address.

Regulation 15 – Notifying third parties of decisions

The SRA may, if it considers it in the public interest to do so, notify any or all of the following persons of a decision made under these regulations:

(a) a recognised body or an authorised non-SRA firm of which the solicitor, registered European lawyer or registered foreign lawyer concerned is a manager, or in which he or she has an ownership interest;

(b) a recognised sole practitioner, recognised body or authorised non-SRA firm of which the solicitor, registered European lawyer or registered foreign lawyer concerned is an employee;

(c) any approved regulator;

(d) the Legal Services Board;

(e) the Legal Complaints Service or the Office for Legal Complaints;

(f) the regulatory body for any profession of which the solicitor, registered European lawyer or registered foreign lawyer concerned is a member;

(g) any law enforcement agency.

Regulation 16 – Reconsideration

16.1 The SRA may reconsider or rescind a decision made under these regulations when it appears that the decision maker:

(a) was not provided with material evidence that was available to the SRA;

(b) was materially misled;

(c) failed to take proper account of material facts or evidence;

(d) took into account immaterial facts or evidence;

(e) made a material error of law;

(f) made a decision which was otherwise irrational or procedurally unfair;

(g)   made a decision which was otherwise ultra vires; or

(h)   failed to give sufficient reasons.

16.2   (a)   A decision may be reconsidered under 16.1 only on the initiative of the SRA
              and if a person duly authorised by the SRA gives a direction to that effect.

       (b)   That person may also give directions:

              (i)   for further investigations to be undertaken;

              (ii)   for further information or explanation to be obtained; and

              (iii) for the reconsideration to be undertaken by the original decision maker
                     or by a different decision maker or panel.

Part 5 – Interpretation, commencement and repeals

Regulation 17 – Interpretation

17.1   All terms in these regulations are to be interpreted in accordance with rule 24 of the
       Solicitors' Code of Conduct.

17.2   The Interpretation Act 1978 shall apply to the interpretation of these regulations as it
       applies to the interpretation of an Act of Parliament.

17.3   The date of any notification or notice given under these regulations is deemed to be:

       (a)   the date on which the communication is delivered to or left at the recipient's
              address or is sent electronically to the recipient's e-mail or fax address;

       (b)   if the recipient is practising, seven days after the communication has been sent by
              post or document exchange to the recipient's last notified practising address; or

       (c)   if the recipient is not practising, seven days after the communication has been
              sent by post to the recipient's last notified contact address.

17.4   In these regulations:

       (a)   commencing an application under these regulations means submitting a com-
              pleted application form, together with the prescribed fee and any Compensation
              Fund contribution required;

       (b)   "prescribed form" means the form prescribed by the SRA;

       (c)   "prescribed fee" means a fee prescribed:

              (i)   under section 11 of the Solicitors Act 1974 for a practising certificate or
                     registration in the register of European lawyers;

              (ii)   under section 13ZB of the Solicitors Act 1974 for authorisation as a sole
                     practitioner; or

              (iii) under paragraph 2 of Schedule 14 to the Courts and Legal Services
                     Act 1990 or section 11 of the Solicitors Act 1974 for registration in the
                     register of foreign lawyers;

       (d)   revocation of a practising certificate or registration includes withdrawal of a
              practising certificate or registration for the purposes of the Solicitors Act 1974
              and cancellation of registration for the purposes of Schedule 14 to the Courts
              and Legal Services Act 1990;

       (e)   "Solicitors' Code of Conduct" means the Solicitors' Code of Conduct 2007;

APPENDIX 2

(f)   "SRA" means the Solicitors Regulation Authority; and

(g)   "turnover figure" means as prescribed from time to time by the SRA

Regulation 18 – Commencement and repeals

These regulations commence on 1 July 2009 and replace:

(a)   the Practising Certificate Regulations 1995;

(b)   the European Lawyers Registration Regulations 2000; and

(c)   the Foreign Lawyers Registration Regulations 1995, in relation to the issue and replacement of practising certificates and initial registration of and renewal of registration of European and foreign lawyers for any period commencing on or after 1 JULY 2009.

The Solicitors' Accounts Rules 1998

[Law Society copyright. For the latest updates to the material, please see www.sra.org.uk.]

[Solicitors' Accounts Rules last amended 31 March 2009; Appendix 5 amended May 2009.]

Solicitors' Accounts Rules 1998

Authority: Made under sections 32, 33A, 34 and 37 of the Solicitors Act 1974 and section 9 of the Administration of Justice Act 1985 with the concurrence, where requisite, of the Master of the Rolls under those sections and of the Lord Chancellor under paragraph 16 of Schedule 22 to the Legal Services Act 2007;

date: 22nd July 1998;

replacing: the Solicitors' Accounts Rules 1991, the Solicitors' Accounts (Legal Aid Temporary Provision) Rule 1992 and the Accountant's Report Rules 1991;

regulating: the accounts of solicitors and their employees, registered European lawyers and their employees, registered foreign lawyers, and recognised bodies and their managers and employees, in respect of practice in England and Wales.

Contents

Solicitors' Accounts Rules 1998

Part A – General

Rule 12 – Solicitor's rights not affected

Rule 13 – Categories of money

Part B – Client money and operation of a client account

Rule 14 – Client accounts

Rule 15 – Use of a client account

Rule 16 – Client money withheld from client account on client's instructions

Rule 17 – Other client money withheld from a client account

Rule 18 – [*repealed*]

Rule 19 – Receipt and transfer of costs

Rule 20 – Receipt of mixed payments

Rule 21 – Treatment of payments to legal aid practitioners

Rule 22 – Withdrawals from a client account

Rule 23 – Method of and authority for withdrawals from client account

Part C – Interest

Rule 24 – When interest must be paid

Rule 25 – Amount of interest

Rule 26 – Interest on stakeholder money

Rule 27 – Contracting out

Rule 28 – [*repealed*]

Part D – Accounting systems and records

Rule 29 – Guidelines for accounting procedures and systems

Rule 30 – Restrictions on transfers between clients

Rule 31 – Executor, trustee or nominee companies

Rule 32 – Accounting records for client accounts, etc.

Rule 33 – Accounting records for clients' own accounts

Part E – Monitoring and investigation by the SRA

Rule 34 – Production of records

Part F – Accountants' reports

Rule 35 – Delivery of accountants' reports

Rule 36 – Accounting periods

Rule 37 – Qualifications for making a report

Rule 38 – Reporting accountant's rights and duties – letter of engagement

Rule 39 – Change of accountant

Rule 40 – Place of examination

Rule 41 – Provision of details of bank accounts, etc.

Rule 42 – Test procedures

Rule 43 – Departures from guidelines for accounting procedures and systems

Rule 44 – Matters outside the accountant's remit

Rule 45 – Privileged documents

Rule 46 – Completion of checklist

Rule 47 – Form of accountant's report

Rule 48 – Practices with two or more places of business

Rule 49 – Waivers

Part G – Commencement

Rule 50 – Commencement

Appendices

Appendix 1 – Flowchart – effect of Solicitors' Accounts Rules 1998

Appendix 2 – Chart – special situations

Appendix 3 – SRA guidelines – accounting procedures and systems

Appendix 4 – Reporting accountant's checklist

Appendix 5 – Accountant's report form

For the definition of words in italics see rule 2 – Interpretation.

Part A – General

Rule 1 – Principles

A *solicitor* must comply with the requirements of rule 1 of the Solicitors' Code of Conduct 2007, and in particular must:

(a) keep other people's money separate from money belonging to the *solicitor* or the practice;

(b)   keep other people's money safely in a *bank* or *building society* account identifiable as a *client account* (except when the rules specifically provide otherwise);

(c)   use each *client's* money for that *client's* matters only;

(d)   use money held as *trustee* of a *trust* for the purposes of that *trust* only;

(e)   establish and maintain proper accounting systems, and proper internal controls over those systems, to ensure compliance with the rules;

(f)   keep proper accounting records to show accurately the position with regard to the money held for each *client* and *trust*;

(g)   account for interest on other people's money in accordance with the rules;

(h)   co-operate with the *SRA* in checking compliance with the rules; and

(i)   deliver annual accountant's reports as required by the rules.

Rule 2 – Interpretation

(1)   The notes form part of the rules and are mandatory.

(2)   In the rules, unless the context otherwise requires:

(a)   "accounting period" has the meaning given in rule 36;

(b)   "agreed fee" has the meaning given in rule 19(5);

(ba)   "approved regulator" means any body listed as an approved regulator in paragraph 1 of Schedule 4 to the Legal Services Act 2007 (whether or not that paragraph has been brought into force), or designated as an approved regulator by an order under paragraph 17 of that Schedule;

(bb)   "authorised non-SRA firm" means a *firm* which is not authorised to practise by the *SRA* but is authorised to practise by another *approved regulator*;

(c)   "bank" has the meaning given in section 87(1) of the Solicitors Act 1974;

(d)   "building society" means a building society within the meaning of the Building Societies Act 1986;

(e)   "client" means the person for whom a *solicitor* acts;

(f)   "client account" has the meaning given in rule 14(2);

(g)   "client money" has the meaning given in rule 13;

(h)   [deleted]

(i)   [deleted]

(j)   "costs" means a *solicitor's fees* and *disbursements*;

(ja)   "Court of Protection deputy" includes a deputy who was appointed by the Court of Protection as a receiver under the Mental Health Act 1983 before the commencement day of the Mental Capacity Act 2005;

(k)   "disbursement" means any sum spent or to be spent by a *solicitor* on behalf of the *client* or *trust* (including any VAT element);

(l)   "fees" of a *solicitor* means the *solicitor's* own charges or profit costs (including any VAT element);

(la)   "firm" means a sole practitioner, *partnership*, *LLP* or company operating as a legal practice;

(m)   "general client account" has the meaning given in rule 14(5)(b);

(ma)   "lawyer" includes a barrister, notary, legal executive, licensed conveyancer, patent agent, trade mark agent or costs draftsman;

(mb) "LLP" means a limited liability partnership incorporated under the Limited Liability Partnerships Act 2000;

(mc) "manager" means:

    (i) a *partner* in a *partnership*;

    (ii) a member of an *LLP*; or

    (iii) a director of a company;

(n) "mixed payment" has the meaning given in rule 20(1);

(o) "non-solicitor employer" means any employer other than a *solicitor* or *authorised non-SRA firm*;

(p) "office account" means an account of the *solicitor* or the practice for holding *office money*, or other means of holding *office money* (for example, the office cash box);

(q) "office money" has the meaning given in rule 13;

(qa) "partner" means a person who is or is held out as a partner in an unincorporated practice;

(qb) "partnership" means an unincorporated partnership, and includes any unincorporated practice in which persons are or are held out as partners, but does not include an *LLP*;

(r) "principal" means:

    (i) a sole practitioner;

    (ii) a *partner* in a *partnership*;

    (iia) in the case of a *recognised body* which is an *LLP* or company, the *recognised body* itself;

    (iii) the principal *solicitor of the Supreme Court* or *registered European lawyer* (or any one of them) employed by a *non-solicitor employer* (for example, in a law centre or in commerce and industry);

(s) "professional disbursement" means the fees of counsel or other lawyer, or of a professional or other agent or expert instructed by the *solicitor*;

(t) "recognised body" means a *partnership*, company or *LLP* recognised by the *SRA* under section 9 of the Administration of Justice Act 1985;

(ta) "recognised sole practitioner" means a *solicitor of the Supreme Court* or *registered European lawyer* authorised by the *SRA* under section 1B of the Solicitors Act 1974 to practise as a sole practitioner;

(tb) "registered European lawyer" means a person registered by the *SRA* under regulation 17 of the European Communities (Lawyer's Practice) Regulations 2000;

(u) "registered foreign lawyer" means a person registered by the *SRA* under section 89 of the Courts and Legal Services Act 1990;

(ua) "regular payment" has the meaning given in rule 21;

(v) "separate designated client account" has the meaning given in rule 14(5)(a);

(w) [deleted]

(x) "solicitor" means:

    (i) a *solicitor of the Supreme Court*;

    (ii) a *registered European lawyer*;

    (iii) a *registered foreign lawyer* practising:

(A) as a *partner* in a *partnership* which is a *recognised body* or *authorised non-SRA firm*; or in a *partnership* which should be a *recognised body* but has not been recognised by the *SRA*;

(B) as the director of a company which is a *recognised body* or *authorised non-SRA firm*, or as the director of a company which is a *manager* of a *recognised body* or *authorised non-SRA firm*;

(C) as a member of an *LLP* which is a *recognised body* or *authorised non-SRA firm*, or as a member of an *LLP* which is a *manager* of a *recognised body* or *authorised non-SRA firm*;

(D) as a *partner* in a *partnership* with separate legal personality which is a *manager* of a *recognised body* or *authorised non-SRA firm*;

(E) as an employee of a *recognised body* or *recognised sole practitioner*; or

(F) as an employee of a *partnership* which should be a *recognised body* but has not been authorised by the *SRA*, or of a sole practitioner who should be a *recognised sole practitioner* but has not been authorised by the *SRA*;

   (iv) a *recognised body*;

   (v) a *manager* of a *recognised* body;

   (vi) an employee of a *recognised body* or *recognised sole practitioner*; or

   (vii) an employee of a *partnership* which should be a *recognised body* but has not been authorised by the *SRA*, or of a sole practitioner who should be a *recognised sole practitioner* but has not been authorised by the *SRA*;

(xa) "solicitor–manager", in rule 22(8)(b), means a *solicitor of the Supreme Court* (or *registered European lawyer*) appointed by the personal representatives of a deceased sole practitioner to carry on the practice;

(xb) "solicitor of the Supreme Court" means an individual who is a solicitor of the Supreme Court of England and Wales; and, with effect from the coming into force of section 59(1) of the Constitutional Reform Act 2005, all references to a solicitor of the Supreme Court are to be replaced by references to a solicitor of the Senior Courts;

(xc) "SRA" means the Solicitors Regulation Authority, and reference to the SRA as an *approved regulator* means the SRA carrying out regulatory functions assigned to the Law Society as an *approved regulator*;

(y) "trustee" includes a personal representative (i.e. an executor or an administrator), and "trust" includes the duties of a personal representative;

(z) "without delay" means, in normal circumstances, either on the day of receipt or on the next working day; and

(za) the singular includes the plural and vice versa, and references to the masculine or feminine include the neuter.

NOTES

(i) Although many of the rules are expressed as applying to an individual solicitor, the effect of the definition of "solicitor" in rule 2(2)(x) is that the rules apply equally to all those who carry on or work in a practice and to the practice itself. See also rule 4 (persons governed by the rules) and rule 5 (persons exempt from the rules). Note however that, until 1 July 2009, rules which are stated to apply to a recognised sole practitioner, or the employee of a recognised sole practitioner, will apply to a sole practitioner or the employee of a sole practitioner.

(ii) A client account must be at a bank or building society's branch in England and Wales – see rule 14(4).

(iii) For the full definition of a "European authorised institution" (rule 2(2)(c)), see the Banking Co-ordination (Second Council Directive) Regulations 1992 (S.I. 1992 no. 3218).

(iv) [deleted]

(v) The fees of interpreters, translators, process servers, surveyors, estate agents, etc., instructed by the solicitor are professional disbursements (see rule 2(2)(s)). Travel agents' charges are not professional disbursements.

(vi) The general definition of "office account" is wide (see rule 2(2)(p)). However, rule 19(1)(b) (receipt and transfer of costs) and rule 21(1)(b) and 21(2)(b) (payments from the Legal Services Commission) specify that certain money is to be placed in an office account at a bank or building society.

(vii) An index is attached to the rules but it does not form part of the rules. For the status of the flowchart (Appendix 1) and the chart dealing with special situations (Appendix 2), see note (xiii) to rule 13.

Rule 3 – Geographical scope

The rules apply to practice carried on from an office in England and Wales.

NOTE

Accounts of a practice carried on from an office outside England and Wales are governed by the Solicitors' Code of Conduct 2007 rule 15.27 (accounts), rule 15.15 (deposit interest) and rule 20.08 (production of documents and information).

Rule 4 – Persons governed by the rules

(1) The rules apply to:

    (a) *solicitors of the Supreme Court* or *registered European lawyers* who are:

        (i) sole practitioners;

        (ii) *partners* in a *partnership* which is a *recognised body* or *authorised non-SRA firm*, or in a *partnership* which should be a *recognised body* but has not been recognised by the *SRA*;

        (iii) assistants, associates, professional support lawyers, consultants, locums or persons otherwise employed in the practice of a *recognised body*, *recognised sole practitioner* or *authorised non-SRA firm*; or of a *partnership* which should be a *recognised body* but has not been recognised by the *SRA*, or of a sole practitioner who should be a *recognised sole practitioner* but has not been authorised by the *SRA*;

        (iv) employed as in-house lawyers by a *non-solicitor employer* (for example, in a law centre or in commerce and industry);

        (v) directors of companies which are *recognised bodies* or *authorised non-SRA firms*, or of companies which are *managers* of *recognised bodies* or *authorised non-SRA firms*;

        (vi) members of *LLPs* which are *recognised bodies* or *authorised non-SRA firms*, or of *LLPs* which are *managers* of *recognised bodies* or *authorised non-SRA firms*; or

        (vii) *partners* in a *partnership* with separate legal personality which is a *manager* of a *recognised body* or *authorised non-SRA firm*;

(b) *registered foreign lawyers* who are practising in any of the ways set out in rule 2(2)(x)(iii);

(c) *recognised bodies*;

(d) *managers* and employees of a *recognised body*, or of a *partnership* which should be a *recognised body* but has not been authorised by the *SRA*; and

(e) employees of a *recognised sole practitioner*, or of a sole practitioner who should be a *recognised sole practitioner* but has not been authorised by the *SRA*.

(2) Part F of the rules (accountants' reports) also applies to reporting accountants.

NOTES

(i) All employees of a recognised body are directly subject to the rules, following the amendment of section 9 of the Administration of Justice Act 1985 by the Legal Services Act 2007. All employees of a recognised sole practitioner are also directly subject to the rules as from the coming into force of new sections 1B and 34A of the Solicitors Act 1974. Non-compliance by any member of staff will also lead to the principals being in breach of the rules – see rule 6. Misconduct by an employee can also lead to an order of the SRA or the Solicitors Disciplinary Tribunal under section 43 of the Solicitors Act 1974 imposing restrictions on his or her employment.

(ii) Solicitors who have held or received client money, but no longer do so, whether or not they continue in practice, continue to be bound by some of the rules – for instance:

- rule 7 (duty to remedy breaches);

- rule 19(2), and note (xi) to rule 19, rule 32(8) to (15) and rule 33 (retention of records);

- rule 34 (production of records);

- Part F (accountants' reports), and in particular rule 35 and rule 36(5) (delivery of final report), and rule 38(2) and rule 46 (completion of checklist).

(iii) The rules do not cover a solicitor's trusteeships carried on in a purely personal capacity outside any legal practice. It will normally be clear from the terms of the appointment whether the solicitor is being appointed trustee in a purely personal capacity or in his or her professional capacity. If a solicitor is charging for the work, it is clearly being done as solicitor. Use of professional stationery may also indicate that the work is being done in a professional capacity.

(iv) A solicitor who wishes to retire from private practice must make a decision about any professional trusteeship. There are three possibilities:

(a) continue to act as a professional trustee (as evidenced by, for instance, charging for work done, or by continuing to use the title "solicitor" in connection with the trust). In this case, the solicitor must continue to hold a practising certificate, and money subject to the trust must continue to be dealt with in accordance with the rules.

(b) continue to act as trustee, but in a purely personal capacity. In this case, the solicitor must stop charging for the work, and must not be held out as a solicitor (unless this is qualified by words such as "non-practising" or "retired") in connection with the trust.

(c) cease to be a trustee.

Rule 5 – Persons exempt from the rules

The rules do not apply to:

(a) a *solicitor* when practising as an employee of:

(i)   a local authority;

(ii)   statutory undertakers;

(iii) a body whose accounts are audited by the Comptroller and Auditor General;

(iv)   the Duchy of Lancaster;

(v)   the Duchy of Cornwall; or

(vi)   the Church Commissioners; or

(b)   a *solicitor* who practises as the Solicitor of the City of London; or

(c)   a *solicitor* when carrying out the functions of:

(i)   a coroner or other judicial office; or

(ii)   a sheriff or under-sheriff; or

(d)   a *solicitor* when practising as a *manager* or employee of an *authorised non-SRA firm* and acting within the scope of that *firm's* authorisation to practise.

NOTES

(i)   "Statutory undertakers" means:

(a)   any persons authorised by any enactment to carry on any railway, light railway, tramway, road transport, water transport, canal, inland navigation, dock, harbour, pier or lighthouse undertaking or any undertaking for the supply of hydraulic power; and

(b)   any licence holder within the meaning of the Electricity Act 1989, any public gas supplier, any water or sewerage undertaker, the Environment Agency, any public telecommunications operator, the Post Office, the Civil Aviation Authority and any relevant airport operator within the meaning of Part V of the Airports Act 1986.

(ii)   "Local authority" means any of those bodies which are listed in section 270 of the Local Government Act 1972 or in section 21(1) of the Local Government and Housing Act 1989.

(iii) A solicitor practising as a manager or employee of an authorised non-SRA firm is exempt from the Solicitors' Accounts Rules when the solicitor is acting within the scope of the firm's authorisation. Thus if a solicitor is a partner or employee in a firm authorised by the Council for Licensed Conveyancers, the rules will not apply to any money received by the solicitor in connection with conveyancing work. However if the solicitor does in-house litigation work – say collecting money owed to the firm – the Solicitors' Accounts Rules will apply to any money received by the solicitor in that context. This is because, whilst in-house litigation work is within the scope of the solicitor's authorisation as an individual, it is outside the scope of authorisation of the firm.

Rule 6 – Principals' responsibility for compliance

All the *principals* in a practice must ensure compliance with the rules by the *principals* themselves and by everyone employed in the practice. This duty also extends to the directors of a *recognised body* which is a company, or to the members of a *recognised body* which is an *LLP*.

Rule 7 – Duty to remedy breaches

(1)   Any breach of the rules must be remedied promptly upon discovery. This includes the replacement of any money improperly withheld or withdrawn from a *client account*.

APPENDIX 3

(2)   In a private practice, the duty to remedy breaches rests not only on the person causing the breach, but also on all the *principals* in the practice. This duty extends to replacing missing *client money* from the *principals'* own resources, even if the money has been misappropriated by an employee or another *principal*, and whether or not a claim is subsequently made on the Solicitors' Indemnity or Compensation Funds or on the *firm's* insurance.

NOTE

For payment of interest when money should have been held in a client account but was not, see rule 24(2).

Rule 8 – [repealed]

Rule 9 – Liquidators, trustees in bankruptcy, Court of Protection deputies and trustees of occupational pension schemes

(1)   A *solicitor* who in the course of practice acts as

*   a liquidator,

*   a trustee in bankruptcy,

*   a *Court of Protection deputy*, or

*   a trustee of an occupational pension scheme which is subject to section 47(1)(a) of the Pensions Act 1995 (appointment of an auditor) **and** section 49(1) (separate bank account) **and** regulations under section 49(2)(b) (books and records),

must comply with:

(a)   the appropriate statutory rules or regulations;

(b)   the principles set out in rule 1; and

(c)   the requirements of paragraphs (2) to (4) below;

and will then be deemed to have satisfactorily complied with the Solicitors' Accounts Rules.

(2)   In respect of any records kept under the appropriate statutory rules, there must also be compliance with:

(a)   rule 32(8) – bills and notifications of costs;

(b)   rule 32(9)(c) – retention of records;

(c)   rule 32(12) – centrally kept records;

(d)   rule 34 – production of records; and

(e)   rule 42(1)(l) and (p) – reporting accountant to check compliance.

(3)   If a liquidator or trustee in bankruptcy uses any of the practice's *client accounts* for holding money pending transfer to the Insolvency Services Account or to a local bank account authorised by the Secretary of State, he or she must comply with the Solicitors' Accounts Rules in all respects whilst the money is held in the *client account*.

(4)   If the appropriate statutory rules or regulations do not govern the holding or receipt of *client money* in a particular situation (for example, money below a certain limit), the *solicitor* must comply with the Solicitors' Accounts Rules in all respects in relation to that money.

NOTES

(i)   The Insolvency Regulations 1994 (S.I. 1994 no. 2507) regulate liquidators and trustees in bankruptcy.

(ii) The Court of Protection Rules 2007 (S.I. 2007 no. 1744 (L.12)) regulate Court of Protection deputies (see rule 2(2)(ja)).

(iii) Money held or received by solicitor liquidators, trustees in bankruptcy, Court of Protection deputies and trustees of occupational pension schemes is client money but, because of the statutory rules and rule 9(1), it will not normally be kept in a client account. If for any reason it is held in a client account, the Solicitors' Accounts Rules apply to that money for the time it is so held (see rule 9(3) and (4)).

Rule 10 – Joint accounts

(1)   If a *solicitor* acting in a *client's* matter holds or receives money jointly with the *client*, another *solicitors'* practice or another third party, the rules in general do not apply, but the following must be complied with:

    (a)   rule 32(8) – bills and notifications of costs;

    (b)   rule 32(9)(b)(ii) – retention of statements and passbooks;

    (c)   rule 32(13) – centrally kept records;

    (d)   rule 34 – production of records; and

    (e)   rule 42(1)(m) and (p) – reporting accountant to check compliance.

Operation of the joint account by the solicitor only

(2)   If the joint account is operated only by the *solicitor*, the *solicitor* must ensure that he or she receives the statements from the *bank, building society* or other financial institution, and has possession of any passbooks.

Shared operation of the joint account

(3)   If the *solicitor* shares the operation of the joint account with the *client,* another *solicitor's* practice or another third party, the *solicitor* must:

    (a)   ensure that he or she receives the statements or duplicate statements from the *bank, building society* or other financial institution and retains them in accordance with rule 32(9)(b)(ii); and

    (b)   ensure that he or she either has possession of any passbooks, or takes copies of the passbook entries before handing any passbook to the other signatory, and retains them in accordance with rule 32(9)(b)(ii).

Operation of the joint account by the other account holder

(4)   If the joint account is operated solely by the other account holder, the *solicitor* must ensure that he or she receives the statements or duplicate statements from the *bank, building society* or other financial institution and retains them in accordance with rule 32(9)(b)(ii).

NOTE

Although a joint account is not a client account, money held in a joint account is client money.

Rule 11 – Operation of a client's own account

(1)   If a *solicitor* in the course of practice operates a *client's* own account as signatory (for example, as donee under a power of attorney), the rules in general do not apply, but the following must be complied with:

    (a)   rule 33(1) to (3) – accounting records for clients' own accounts;

    (b)   rule 34 – production of records; and

    (c)   rule 42(1)(n) and (p) – reporting accountant to check compliance.

Operation by the solicitor only

(2)   If the account is operated by the *solicitor* only, the *solicitor* must ensure that he or she receives the statements from the *bank*, *building society* or other financial institution, and has possession of any passbooks.

Shared operation of the account

(3)   If the *solicitor* shares the operation of the account with the *client* or a co-attorney outside the *solicitor's* practice, the *solicitor* must:

    (a)   ensure that he or she receives the statements or duplicate statements from the *bank*, *building society* or other financial institution and retains them in accordance with rule 33(1) to (3); and

    (b)   ensure that he or she either has possession of any passbooks, or takes copies of the passbook entries before handing any passbook to the *client* or co-attorney, and retains them in accordance with rule 33(1) to (3).

Operation of the account for a limited purpose

(4)   If the *solicitor* is given authority (whether as attorney or otherwise) to operate the account for a limited purpose only, such as the taking up of a share rights issue during the *client's* temporary absence, the *solicitor* need not receive statements or possess passbooks, provided that he or she retains details of all cheques drawn or paid in, and retains copies of all passbook entries, relating to the transaction, and retains them in accordance with rule 33(1) and (2).

Application

(5)   This rule applies only to *solicitors* in private practice.

NOTES

    (i)   Money held in a client's own account (under a power of attorney or otherwise) is not "client money" for the purpose of the rules because it is not "held or received" by the solicitor. If the solicitor closes the account and receives the closing balance, this becomes client money and must be paid into a client account, unless the client instructs to the contrary in accordance with rule 16(1)(a).

    (ii)   A solicitor who merely pays money into a client's own account, or helps the client to complete forms in relation to such an account, is not "operating" the account.

    (iii) A solicitor executor who operates the deceased's account (whether before or after the grant of probate) will be subject to the limited requirements of rule 11. If the account is subsequently transferred into the solicitor's name, or a new account is opened in the solicitor's name, the solicitor will have "held or received" client money and is then subject to all the rules.

(iv) The rules do not cover money held or received by a solicitor attorney acting in a purely personal capacity outside any legal practice. If a solicitor is charging for the work, it is clearly being done in the course of legal practice. See rule 4, note (iv) for the choices which can be made on retirement from private practice.

(v) "A client's own account" covers all accounts in a client's own name, whether opened by the client himself or herself, or by the solicitor on the client's instructions under rule 16(1)(b).

(vi) "A client's own account" also includes an account opened in the name of a person designated by the client under rule 16(1)(b).

(vii) Solicitors should also remember the requirements of rule 32(8) – bills and notifications of costs.

(viii) For payment of interest, see rule 24, note (iii).

Rule 12 – Solicitor's rights not affected

Nothing in these rules deprives a *solicitor* of any recourse or right, whether by way of lien, set off, counterclaim, charge or otherwise, against money standing to the credit of a *client account*.

Rule 13 – Categories of money

All money held or received in the course of practice falls into one or other of the following categories:

(a) "client money" – money held or received for a *client* or as *trustee*, and all other money which is not *office money*; or

(b) "office money" – money which belongs to the *solicitor* or the practice.

NOTES

(i) "Client money" includes money held or received:

  (aa) as trustee;

  (a) as agent, bailee, stakeholder, or as the donee of a power of attorney, or as a liquidator, trustee in bankruptcy, Court of Protection deputy or trustee of an occupational pension scheme;

  (b) for payment of unpaid professional disbursements (for definition of "professional disbursement" see rule 2(2)(s));

  (c) for payment of stamp duty land tax, Land Registry registration fees, telegraphic transfer fees and court fees; this is not office money because the solicitor has not incurred an obligation to the Inland Revenue, the Land Registry, the bank or the court to pay the duty or fee (contrast with note (xi)(c)(C) below); (on the other hand, if the solicitor has already paid the duty or fee out of his or her own resources, or has received the service on credit, payment subsequently received from the client will be office money – see note (xi)(c)(B) below);

  (d) as a payment on account of costs generally;

  (e) as commission paid in respect of a solicitor's client, unless the client has given the solicitor prior authority to retain it in accordance with rule 2.06 of the Solicitors' Code of Conduct 2007, or unless it falls within the £20 de minimis figure specified in that rule.

(ii)   A solicitor to whom a cheque or draft is made out, and who in the course of practice endorses it over to a client or employer, has received client money. Even if no other client money is held or received, the solicitor will be subject to some provisions of the rules, e.g.:

- rule 7 (duty to remedy breaches);

- rule 32 (accounting records for client money);

- rule 34 (production of records);

- rule 35 (delivery of accountants' reports).

(iii)   Money held by solicitor liquidators, trustees in bankruptcy, Court of Protection deputies and trustees of occupational pension schemes is client money, subject to a limited application of the rules – see rule 9.

(iv)   Money held jointly with another person outside the practice (for example, with a lay trustee, or with another firm of solicitors) is client money subject to a limited application of the rules – see rule 10.

(v)   Money held to the sender's order is client money.

    (a)   If money is accepted on such terms, it must be held in a client account.

    (b)   However, a cheque or draft sent to a solicitor on terms that the cheque or draft (as opposed to the money) is held to the sender's order must not be presented for payment without the sender's consent.

    (c)   The recipient is always subject to a professional obligation to return the money, or the cheque or draft, to the sender on demand.

(vi)   An advance to a client from the solicitor which is paid into a client account under rule 15(2)(b) becomes client money. For interest, see rule 24(3)(e).

(vii)   [deleted]

(viii)   If the SRA intervenes in a practice, money from the practice is held or received by the SRA's intervention agent subject to a trust under Schedule 1 paragraph 7(1) of the Solicitors Act 1974, and is therefore client money. The same provision requires the agent to pay the money into a client account.

(ix)   A solicitor who, as the donee of a power of attorney, operates the donor's own account is subject to a limited application of these rules – see rule 11. Money kept in the donor's own account is not "client money", because it is not "held or received" by the solicitor.

(x)   Money held or received by a solicitor in the course of his or her employment when practising in one of the capacities listed in rule 5 (persons exempt from the rules) is not "client money" for the purpose of the rules, because the rules do not apply at all.

(xi)   Office money includes:

    (a)   money held or received in connection with running the practice; for example, PAYE, or VAT on the firm's fees;

    (b)   interest on general client accounts; the bank or building society should be instructed to credit such interest to the office account – but see also rule 15(2)(d); and

    (c)   payments received in respect of:

        (A)   fees due to the practice against a bill or written notification of costs incurred, which has been given or sent in accordance with rule 19(2);

        (B)   disbursements already paid by the practice (for definition of "disbursement" see rule 2(2)(k));

        (C)   disbursements incurred but not yet paid by the practice, but excluding unpaid professional disbursements (for definition of "professional disbursement" see rule 2(2)(s), and note (v) to rule 2);

(D) money paid for or towards an agreed fee – see rule 19(5); and

(d) money held in a client account and earmarked for costs under rule 19(3) (transfer of costs from client account to office account); and

(e) money held or received from the Legal Services Commission as a regular payment (see rule 21(2)).

(xii) A solicitor cannot be his or her own client for the purpose of the rules, so that if a practice conducts a personal or office transaction – for instance, conveyancing – for a principal (or for a number of principals), money held or received on behalf of the principal(s) is office money. However, other circumstances may mean that the money is client money, for example:

(a) If the practice also acts for a lender, money held or received on behalf of the lender is client money.

(b) If the practice acts for a principal and, for example, his or her spouse jointly (assuming the spouse is not a partner in the practice), money received on their joint behalf is client money.

(c) If the practice acts for an assistant solicitor, consultant or non-solicitor employee, or (if it is a company) a director, or (if it is an LLP) a member, he or she is regarded as a client of the practice, and money received for him or her is client money – even if he or she conducts the matter personally.

(xiii) For a flowchart summarising the effect of the rules, see Appendix 1. For more details of the treatment of different types of money, see the chart "Special situations – what applies" at Appendix 2. These two appendices are included to help solicitors and their staff find their way about the rules. Unlike the notes, they are not intended to affect the meaning of the rules.

Part B – Client money and operation of a client account

Rule 14 – Client accounts

(1) A *solicitor* who holds or receives *client money* must keep one or more *client accounts* (unless all the *client money* is always dealt with outside any *client account* in accordance with rule 9, rule 10, rule 16 or rule 17).

(2) A "client account" is an account of a practice kept at a *bank* or *building society* for holding *client money*, in accordance with the requirements of this part of the rules.

(3) The client account(s) of:

(a) a sole practitioner must be either in the *solicitor's* own name or in the practice name;

(b) a *partnership* must be in the *firm* name;

(c) an incorporated practice must be in the company name, or the name of the *LLP*;

(d) in-house *solicitors* must be in the name of the current *principal solicitor* or *solicitors*;

(e) *trustees*, where all the *trustees* of a *trust* are *managers* and/or employees of the same *recognised body*, must be either in the name of the *recognised body* or in the name of the *trustee(s)*;

and the name of the account must also include the word "client".

(4)   A *client account* must be:

    (a)   a *bank* account at a branch (or a *bank's* head office) in England and Wales; or

    (b)   a *building society* deposit or share account at a branch (or a society's head office) in England and Wales.

(5)   There are two types of *client account*:

    (a)   a "separate designated client account", which is a deposit or share account for money relating to a single *client*, other person or *trust*, and which includes in its title, in addition to the requirements of rule 14(3) above, a reference to the identity of the *client*, other person or *trust*; and

    (b)   a "general client account", which is any other *client account*.

NOTES

  (i)   For the client accounts of an executor, trustee or nominee company owned by a practice, see rule 31.

 (ii)   In the case of in-house solicitors, any client account should include the names of all solicitors of the Supreme Court or registered European lawyers held out on the notepaper as principals. The names of other employees who are solicitors of the Supreme Court or registered European lawyers may also be included if so desired. Any person whose name is included will be subject to the full Compensation Fund contribution and his or her name will have to be included on the accountant's report.

(iii)   "Bank" and "building society" are defined in rule 2(2)(c) and (d) respectively.

(iv)   A practice may have any number of separate designated client accounts and general client accounts.

 (v)   The word "client" must appear in full; an abbreviation is not acceptable.

(vi)   Compliance with rule 14(1) to (4) ensures that clients, as well as the bank or building society, have the protection afforded by section 85 of the Solicitors Act 1974.

(vii)   Money held in a client account must be immediately available, even at the sacrifice of interest, unless the client otherwise instructs, or the circumstances clearly indicate otherwise.

Rule 15 – Use of a client account

(1)   *Client money* must *without delay* be paid into a *client account*, and must be held in a *client account*, except when the rules provide to the contrary (see rules 9, 10, 16, 17, 19 and 21).

(2)   Only *client money* may be paid into or held in a *client account*, except:

    (a)   an amount of the *solicitor's* own money required to open or maintain the account;

    (b)   an advance from the *solicitor* to fund a payment on behalf of a *client* or *trust* in excess of funds held for that *client* or *trust*; the sum becomes *client money* on payment into the account (for interest on *client money*, see rule 24(3)(e));

    (c)   money to replace any sum which for any reason has been drawn from the account in breach of rule 22; the replacement money becomes *client money* on payment into the account; and

    (d)   a sum in lieu of interest which is paid into a *client account* to enable the *solicitor* to make payment from the *client account* of all money owed to the *client* as an alternative to making separate payments from the *office* and *client accounts*;

and except when the rules provide to the contrary (see note (iv) below).

(3)   *Client money* must be returned to the *client* (or other person on whose behalf the money is held) promptly, as soon as there is no longer any proper reason to retain those funds. Payments received after the *solicitor* has already accounted to the *client*, for example by way of a refund, must be paid to the *client* promptly.

(4)   A *solicitor* must promptly inform a *client* (or other person on whose behalf the money is held) in writing of the amount of any *client money* retained at the end of a matter (or the substantial conclusion of a matter), and the reason for that retention. The *solicitor* must inform the *client* (or other person) in writing at least once every twelve months thereafter of the amount of *client money* still held and the reason for the retention, for as long as the *solicitor* continues to hold that money.

NOTES

(i)   See rule 13 and notes for the definition and examples of client money.

(ii)   "Without delay" is defined in rule 2(2)(z).

(iii) Exceptions to rule 15(1) (client money must be paid into a client account) can be found in:

- rule 9 – liquidators, trustees in bankruptcy, Court of Protection deputies and trustees of occupational pension schemes;

- rule 10 – joint accounts;

- rule 16 – client's instructions;

- rule 17 – cash paid straight to client, beneficiary or third party;

    - cheque endorsed to client, beneficiary or third party;

    - money withheld from client account on the SRA's authority;

    - money withheld from client account in accordance with a trustee's powers;

- rule 19(1)(b) – receipt and transfer of costs;

- rule 21(1) – payments by the Legal Services Commission.

(iv)   Rule 15(2)(a) to (d) provides for exceptions to the principle that only client money may be paid into a client account. Additional exceptions can be found in:

- rule 19(1)(c) – receipt and transfer of costs;

- rule 20(2)(b) – receipt of mixed payments;

- rule 21(2)(c)(ii) – transfer to client account of a sum for unpaid professional disbursements, where the solicitor receives regular payments from the Legal Services Commission.

(v)   Only a nominal sum will be required to open or maintain an account. In practice, banks will usually open (and, if instructed, keep open) accounts with nil balances.

(vi)   [deleted]

(vii) If client money is invested in the purchase of assets other than money – such as stocks or shares – it ceases to be client money, because it is no longer money held by the solicitor. If the investment is subsequently sold, the money received is, again, client money. The records kept under rule 32 must include entries to show the purchase or sale of investments.

(viii) Some schemes proposed by banks would aggregate the sums held in a number of client accounts, including one or more separate designated client accounts, in order to maximise the interest payable. This is acceptable only if:

- each client account remains a separate account;

- the rate of interest applied by the bank is the same for each client account; and

APPENDIX 3

- the bank credits the total amount of the interest earned in respect of each separate designated client account to that account (see rule 24(1)), and credits the interest earned on any general client account to the office account (see note (xi)(b) to rule 13).

(ix) In the case of Wood and Burdett (case number 8669/2002 filed on 13 January 2004), the Solicitors Disciplinary Tribunal said that it is not a proper part of a solicitor's everyday business or practice to operate a banking facility for third parties, whether they are clients of the firm or not. Solicitors should not, therefore, provide banking facilities through a client account. Further, solicitors are likely to lose the exemption under the Financial Services and Markets Act 2000 if a deposit is taken in circumstances which do not form part of a solicitor's practice. It should also be borne in mind that there are criminal sanctions against assisting money launderers.

(x) As with rule 7 (Duty to remedy breaches), "promptly" in rule 15(3) and (4) is not defined but should be given its natural meaning in the particular circumstances. Accounting to a client for any surplus funds will often fall naturally at the end of a matter. Other retainers may be more protracted and, even when the principal work has been completed, funds may still be needed, for example, to cover outstanding work in a conveyancing transaction or to meet a tax liability.

(xi) There may be some instances when, during the course of a retainer, the specific purpose for which particular funds were paid no longer exists, for example, the need to instruct counsel or a medical expert. Rule 15(3) is concerned with returning funds to clients at the end of a matter (or the substantial conclusion of a matter) and is not intended to apply to ongoing retainers. However, solicitors must always act in the best interests of their clients and may need to take instructions in such circumstances to ascertain, for instance, whether the money should be returned to the client or retained to cover the general funding or other aspects of the case.

(xii) (See rule 22(1)(ga)–(h) for withdrawals from a client account when the rightful owner of funds cannot be traced.)

Rule 16 – Client money withheld from client account on client's instructions

(1) Client money may be:

(a) held by the solicitor outside a client account by, for example, retaining it in the solicitor's safe in the form of cash, or placing it in an account in the solicitor's name which is not a client account, such as an account outside England and Wales; or

(b) paid into an account at a bank, building society or other financial institution opened in the name of the client or of a person designated by the client;

but only if the client instructs the solicitor to that effect for the client's own convenience, and only if the instructions are given in writing, or are given by other means and confirmed by the solicitor to the client in writing.

(2) It is improper to seek blanket agreements, through standard terms of business or otherwise, to hold client money outside a client account.

NOTES

(i) For advance payments from the Legal Services Commission, withheld from a client account on the Commission's instructions, see rule 21(1)(a).

(ii) If a client instructs the solicitor to hold part only of a payment in accordance with rule 16(1)(a) or (b), the entire payment must first be placed in a client account. The relevant part can then be transferred out and dealt with in accordance with the client's instructions.

(iii)   Money withheld from a client account under rule 16(1)(a) remains client money, and the record-keeping provisions of rule 32, including monthly reconciliations, must be complied with.

(iv)   Once money has been paid into an account set up under rule 16(1)(b), it ceases to be client money. Until that time, the money is client money and a record must therefore be kept of the solicitor's receipt of the money, and its payment into the account in the name of the client or designated person, in accordance with rule 32. If the solicitor can operate the account, the solicitor must comply with rule 11 (operating a client's own account) and rule 33 (accounting records for clients' own accounts). In the absence of instructions to the contrary, any money withdrawn must be paid into a client account – see rule 15(1).

(v)   Clients' instructions under rule 16(1) must be kept for at least six years – see rule 32(9)(d).

(vi)   A payment on account of costs received from a person who is funding all or part of the solicitor's fees may be withheld from a client account on the instructions of that person given in accordance with rule 16(1) and (2).

(vii)   For payment of interest, see rule 24(6) and notes (ii) and (iii) to rule 24.

Rule 17 – Other client money withheld from a client account

The following categories of *client money* may be withheld from a *client account*:

(a)   cash received and *without delay* paid in cash in the ordinary course of business to the *client* or, on the *client's* behalf, to a third party, or paid in cash in the execution of a *trust* to a beneficiary or third party;

(b)   a cheque or draft received and endorsed over in the ordinary course of business to the *client* or, on the *client's* behalf, to a third party, or *without delay* endorsed over in the execution of a *trust* to a beneficiary or third party;

(c)   money withheld from a *client account* on instructions under rule 16;

(ca)   money which, in accordance with a *trustee's* powers, is paid into or retained in an account of the *trustee* which is not a *client account* (for example, an account outside England and Wales), or properly retained in cash in the performance of the *trustee's* duties;

(d)   unpaid *professional disbursements* included in a payment of *costs* dealt with under rule 19(1)(b);

(e)   (i)   advance payments from the Legal Services Commission withheld from *client account* (see rule 21(1)(a)); and

   (ii)   unpaid *professional disbursements* included in a payment of *costs* from the Legal Services Commission (see rule 21(1)(b)); and

(f)   money withheld from a *client account* on the written authorisation of the *SRA*. The *SRA* may impose a condition that the *solicitor* pay the money to a charity which gives an indemnity against any legitimate claim subsequently made for the sum received.

NOTES

(i)   "Without delay" is defined in rule 2(2)(z).

(ii)   If money is withheld from a client account under rule 17(a) or (b), rule 32 requires records to be kept of the receipt of the money and the payment out.

(iia)   If money is withheld from a client account under rule 17(ca), rule 32 requires a record to be kept of the receipt of the money, and requires the inclusion of the money in the monthly reconciliations.

(iii)   It makes no difference, for the purpose of the rules, whether an endorsement is effected by signature in the normal way or by some other arrangement with the bank.

(iv)   The circumstances in which authorisation would be given under rule 17(f) must be extremely rare. Applications for authorisation should be made to the Professional Ethics Guidance Team.

Rule 18 – [repealed]

Rule 19 – Receipt and transfer of costs

(1)   A *solicitor* who receives money paid in full or part settlement of the *solicitor's* bill (or other notification of *costs*) **must follow one of the following four options:**

(a)   **determine the composition of the payment *without delay*, and deal with the money accordingly:**

(i)   if the sum comprises *office money* only, it must be placed in an *office account*;

(ii)   if the sum comprises only *client money* (for example an unpaid *professional disbursement* – see rule 2(2)(s), and note (v) to rule 2), the entire sum must be placed in a *client account*;

(iii)   if the sum includes both *office money* and *client money* (such as unpaid *professional disbursements*; purchase money; or payments in advance for court fees, stamp duty land tax, Land Registry registration fees or telegraphic transfer fees), the *solicitor* must follow rule 20 (receipt of mixed payments); **or**

(b)   **ascertain that the payment comprises only *office money*, and/or *client money* in the form of *professional disbursements* incurred but not yet paid, and deal with the payment as follows:**

(i)   place the entire sum in an *office account* at a *bank* or *building society* branch (or head office) in England and Wales; and

(ii)   by the end of the second working day following receipt, either pay any unpaid *professional disbursement*, or transfer a sum for its settlement to a *client account*; **or**

(c)   **pay the entire sum into a *client account* (regardless of its composition), and transfer any *office money* out of the *client account* within 14 days of receipt; or**

(d)   **on receipt of *costs* from the Legal Services Commission, follow the option in rule 21(1)(b).**

(2)   A *solicitor* who properly requires payment of his or her *fees* from money held for a *client* or *trust* in a *client account* must first give or send a bill of *costs*, or other written notification of the *costs* incurred, to the *client* or the paying party.

(3)   Once the *solicitor* has complied with paragraph (2) above, the money earmarked for *costs* becomes *office money* and must be transferred out of the *client account* within 14 days.

(4)   A payment on account of *costs* generally is *client money*, and must be held in a *client account* until the *solicitor* has complied with paragraph (2) above. (For an exception in the case of legal aid payments, see rule 21(1)(a).)

(5)   A payment for an *agreed fee* must be paid into an *office account*. An "agreed fee" is one

that is fixed – not a *fee* that can be varied upwards, nor a *fee* that is dependent on the transaction being completed. An *agreed fee* must be evidenced in writing.

NOTES

(i) For the definition and further examples of office and client money, see rule 13 and notes.

(ii) • Money received for paid disbursements is office money.

• Money received for unpaid professional disbursements is client money.

• Money received for other unpaid disbursements for which the solicitor has incurred a liability to the payee (for example, travel agents' charges, taxi fares, courier charges or Land Registry search fees, payable on credit) is office money.

• Money received for disbursements anticipated but not yet incurred is a payment on account, and is therefore client money.

(iii) The option in rule 19(1)(a) allows a solicitor to place all payments in the correct account in the first instance. The option in rule 19(1)(b) allows the prompt banking into an office account of an invoice payment when the only uncertainty is whether or not the payment includes some client money in the form of unpaid professional disbursements. The option in rule 19(1)(c) allows the prompt banking into a client account of any invoice payment in advance of determining whether the payment is a mixture of office and client money (of whatever description) or is only office money.

(iv) A solicitor who is not in a position to comply with the requirements of rule 19(1)(b) cannot take advantage of that option.

(v) The option in rule 19(1)(b) cannot be used if the money received includes a payment on account – for example, a payment for a professional disbursement anticipated but not yet incurred.

(vi) In order to be able to use the option in rule 19(1)(b) for electronic payments or other direct transfers from clients, a solicitor may choose to establish a system whereby clients are given an office account number for payment of costs. The system must be capable of ensuring that, when invoices are sent to the client, no request is made for any client money, with the sole exception of money for professional disbursements already incurred but not yet paid.

(vii) Rule 19(1)(c) allows clients to be given a single account number for making direct payments by electronic or other means – under this option, it has to be a client account.

(viii) A solicitor will not be in breach of rule 19 as a result of a misdirected electronic payment or other direct transfer, provided:

(A) appropriate systems are in place to ensure compliance;

(B) appropriate instructions were given to the client;

(C) the client's mistake is remedied promptly upon discovery; and

(D) appropriate steps are taken to avoid future errors by the client.

(ix) "Properly" in rule 19(2) implies that the work has actually been done, whether at the end of the matter or at an interim stage, and that the solicitor is entitled to appropriate the money for costs.

(x) Costs transferred out of a client account in accordance with rule 19(2) and (3) must be specific sums relating to the bill or other written notification of costs, and covered by the amount held for the particular client or trust. Round sum withdrawals on account of costs will be a breach of the rules.

(xi) In the case of a trust of which the only trustee(s) are within the firm, the paying party will be the trustee(s) themselves. The solicitor must keep the original bill or notification of costs on the file, in addition to complying with rule 32(8) (central record or file of copy bills, etc.).

(xii) Undrawn costs must not remain in a client account as a "cushion" against any future errors which could result in a shortage on that account, and cannot be regarded as available to set off against any general shortage on client account.

(xiii) The rules do not require a bill of costs for an agreed fee, although a solicitor's VAT position may mean that in practice a bill is needed. If there is no bill, the written evidence of the agreement must be filed as a written notification of costs under rule 32(8)(b).

Rule 20 – Receipt of mixed payments

(1)   A "mixed payment" is one which includes *client money* as well as *office money*.

(2)   A *mixed payment* must either:

   (a)   be split between a *client account* and *office account* as appropriate; or

   (b)   be placed *without delay* in a *client account*.

(3)   If the entire payment is placed in a *client account*, all *office money* must be transferred out of the *client account* within 14 days of receipt.

(4)   See rule 19(1)(b) and (c) for additional ways of dealing with (among other things) *mixed payments* received in response to a bill or other notification of *costs*.

(5)   See rule 21(1)(b) for (among other things) *mixed payments* received from the Legal Services Commission.

NOTE

"Without delay" is defined in rule 2(2)(z).

Rule 21 – Treatment of payments to legal aid practitioners

Payments from the Legal Services Commission

(1)   Two special dispensations apply to payments (other than *regular payments*) from the Legal Services Commission:

   (a)   An advance payment in anticipation of work to be carried out, although *client money*, may be placed in an *office account*, provided the Commission instructs in writing that this may be done.

   (b)   A payment for *costs* (interim and/or final) may be paid into an *office account* at a *bank* or *building society* branch (or head office) in England and Wales, regardless of whether it consists wholly of *office money*, or is mixed with *client money* in the form of:

      (i)   advance payments for *fees* or *disbursements*; or

      (ii)   money for unpaid *professional disbursements*;

      provided all money for payment of *disbursements* is transferred to a *client account* (or the *disbursements* paid) within 14 days of receipt.

(2)   The following provisions apply to *regular payments* from the Legal Services Commission:

(a)   "Regular payments" (which are *office money*) are:

    (i)   standard monthly payments paid by the Commission under the civil legal aid contracting arrangements;

    (ii)   monthly payments paid by the Commission under the criminal legal aid contracting arrangements; and

    (iii) any other payments for work done or to be done received from the Commission under an arrangement for payments on a regular basis.

(b)   *Regular payments* must be paid into an *office account* at a *bank* or *building society* branch (or head office) in England and Wales.

(c)   A *solicitor* must within 28 days of submitting a report to the Commission, notifying completion of a matter, either:

    (i)   pay any unpaid *professional disbursement(s)*, or

    (ii)   transfer to a *client account* a sum equivalent to the amount of any unpaid *professional disbursement(s)*,

relating to that matter.

(d)   In cases where the Commission permits *solicitors* to submit reports at various stages during a matter rather than only at the end of a matter, the requirement in paragraph (c) above applies to any unpaid *professional disbursement(s)* included in each report so submitted.

Payments from a third party

(3)   If the Legal Services Commission has paid any *costs* to a *solicitor* or a previously nominated *solicitor* in a matter (advice and assistance or legal help *costs*, advance payments or interim *costs*), or has paid *professional disbursements* direct, and *costs* are subsequently settled by a third party:

(a)   The entire third party payment must be paid into a *client account*.

(b)   A sum representing the payments made by the Commission must be retained in the *client account*.

(c)   Any balance belonging to the *solicitor* must be transferred to an *office account* within 14 days of the *solicitor* sending a report to the Commission containing details of the third party payment.

(d)   The sum retained in the *client account* as representing payments made by the Commission must be:

    (i)   **either** recorded in the individual *client's* ledger account, and identified as the Commission's money;

    (ii)   **or** recorded in a ledger account in the Commission's name, and identified by reference to the *client* or matter;

and kept in the *client account* until notification from the Commission that it has recouped an equivalent sum from subsequent payments due to the *solicitor*. The retained sum must be transferred to an *office account* within 14 days of notification.

NOTES

(i)   This rule deals with matters which specifically affect legal aid practitioners. It should not be read in isolation from the remainder of the rules which apply to all solicitors, including legal aid practitioners.

(ii)   Franchised firms can apply for advance payments on the issue of a certificate. The Legal

Services Commission has issued instructions that these payments may be placed in office account. For regular payments, see notes (vii)–(x) below.

(iii)   Rule 21(1)(b) deals with the specific problems of legal aid practitioners by allowing a mixed or indeterminate payment of costs (or even a payment consisting entirely of unpaid professional disbursements) to be paid into an office account, which for the purpose of rule 21(1)(b) must be an account at a bank or building society. However, it is always open to the solicitor to comply with rule 19(1)(a) to (c), which are the options for all solicitors for the receipt of costs. For regular payments, see notes (vii)–(x) below.

(iv)   Solicitors are required by the Legal Services Commission to report promptly to the Commission on receipt of costs from a third party. It is advisable to keep a copy of the report on the file as proof of compliance with the Commission's requirements, as well as to demonstrate compliance with the rule.

(v)   A third party payment may also include unpaid professional disbursements or outstanding costs of the client's previous solicitor. This part of the payment is client money and must be kept in a client account until the solicitor pays the professional disbursement or outstanding costs.

(vi)   In rule 21, and elsewhere in the rules, references to the Legal Services Commission are to be read, where appropriate, as including the Legal Aid Board.

(vii)   Regular payments are office money and are defined as such in the rules (rule 13, note (xi)(e)). They are neither advance payments nor payments of costs for the purposes of the rules. Regular payments must be paid into an office account which for the purpose of rule 21(2)(b) must be an account at a bank or building society.

(viii)   Firms in receipt of regular payments must deal with unpaid professional disbursements in the way prescribed by rule 21(2)(c). The rule permits a solicitor who is required to transfer an amount to cover unpaid professional disbursements into a client account to make the transfer from his or her own resources if the regular payments are insufficient.

(ix)   The 28 day time limit for paying, or transferring an amount to a client account for, unpaid professional disbursements is for the purposes of these rules only. An earlier deadline may be imposed by contract with the Commission or with counsel, agents or experts. On the other hand, a solicitor may have agreed to pay later than 28 days from the submission of the report notifying completion of a matter, in which case rule 21(2)(c) will require a transfer of the appropriate amount to a client account (but not payment) within 28 days. Solicitors are reminded of their professional obligation to pay the fees of foreign lawyers (see rule 10.07 of the Solicitors' Code of Conduct).

(x)   For the appropriate accounting records for regular payments, see note (v) to rule 32.

Rule 22 – Withdrawals from a client account

(1)   *Client money* may only be withdrawn from a *client account* when it is:

(a)   properly required for a payment to or on behalf of the *client* (or other person on whose behalf the money is being held);

(aa)   properly required for a payment in the execution of a particular *trust*, including the purchase of an investment (other than money) in accordance with the *trustee's* powers;

(b)   properly required for payment of a *disbursement* on behalf of the *client* or *trust*;

(c)   properly required in full or partial reimbursement of money spent by the *solicitor* on behalf of the *client* or *trust*;

(d)   transferred to another *client account*;

(e)   withdrawn on the *client's* instructions, provided the instructions are for the *client's* convenience and are given in writing, or are given by other means and confirmed by the *solicitor* to the *client* in writing;

(ea)   transferred to an account other than a *client account* (such as an account outside England and Wales), or retained in cash, by a *trustee* in the proper performance of his or her duties;

(f)   a refund to the *solicitor* of an advance no longer required to fund a payment on behalf of a *client* or *trust* (see rule 15(2)(b));

(g)   money which has been paid into the account in breach of the rules (for example, money paid into the wrong *separate designated client account*) – see paragraph (4) below;

(ga)   money not covered by (a) to (g) above, where the *solicitor* complies with the conditions set out in rule 22(2A); or

(h)   money not covered by (a) to (g) above, withdrawn from the account on the written authorisation of the *SRA*. The *SRA* may impose a condition that the *solicitor* pay the money to a charity which gives an indemnity against any legitimate claim subsequently made for the sum received.

(2)   [deleted]

(2A)   A withdrawal of *client money* under paragraph (1)(ga) above may be made only where the amount withdrawn does not exceed £50 in relation to any one individual *client* or *trust* matter and the *solicitor*:

(a)   establishes the identity of the owner of the money, or makes reasonable attempts to do so;

(b)   makes adequate attempts to ascertain the proper destination of the money, and to return it to the rightful owner, unless the reasonable costs of doing so are likely to be excessive in relation to the amount held;

(c)   pays the funds to a charity;

(d)   records the steps taken in accordance with paragraphs (a)–(c) above and retains those records, together with all relevant documentation (including receipts from the charity), in accordance with rule 32(8A) and (9)(a); and

(e)   keeps a central register in accordance with rule 32(13A).

(3)   *Office money* may only be withdrawn from a *client account* when it is:

(a)   money properly paid into the account to open or maintain it under rule 15(2)(a);

(b)   properly required for payment of the *solicitor's costs* under rule 19(2) and (3);

(c)   the whole or part of a payment into a *client account* under rule 19(1)(c);

(d)   part of a *mixed payment* placed in a *client account* under rule 20(2)(b); or

(e)   money which has been paid into a *client account* in breach of the rules (for example, interest wrongly credited to a *general client account*) – see paragraph (4) below.

(4)   Money which has been paid into a *client account* in breach of the rules must be withdrawn from the *client account* promptly upon discovery.

(5)   Money withdrawn in relation to a particular *client* or *trust* from a *general client account* must not exceed the money held on behalf of that *client* or *trust* in all the *solicitor's general client accounts* (except as provided in paragraph (6) below).

(6)   A *solicitor* may make a payment in respect of a particular *client* or *trust* out of a *general client account*, even if no money (or insufficient money) is held for that *client* or *trust* in the *solicitor's general client account(s)*, provided:

(a)   sufficient money is held for that *client* or *trust* in a *separate designated client account*; and

(b)   the appropriate transfer from the *separate designated client account* to a *general client account* is made immediately.

(7)   Money held for a *client* or *trust* in a *separate designated client account* must not be used for payments for another *client* or *trust*.

(8)   A *client account* must not be overdrawn, except in the following circumstances:

(a)   A *separate designated client account* of *solicitor-trustee(s)* can be overdrawn if the *trustee(s)* make payments on behalf of the *trust* (for example, inheritance tax) before realising sufficient assets to cover the payments.

(b)   If a sole practitioner dies and his or her *client accounts* are frozen, the *solicitor-manager* can operate *client accounts* which are overdrawn to the extent of the money held in the frozen accounts.

NOTES

Withdrawals in favour of solicitor, and for payment of disbursements

(i)   Disbursements to be paid direct from a client account, or already paid out of the solicitor's own money, can be withdrawn under rule 22(1)(b) or (c) (or rule 22(2)(b) or (c)) in advance of preparing a bill of costs. Money to be withdrawn from a client account for the payment of costs (fees and disbursements) under rule 19(2) and (3) becomes office money and is dealt with under rule 22(3)(b).

(ii)   Money is "spent" under rule 22(1)(c) (or rule 22(2)(c)) at the time when the solicitor despatches a cheque, unless the cheque is to be held to the solicitor's order. Money is also regarded as "spent" by the use of a credit account, so that, for example, search fees, taxi fares and courier charges incurred in this way may be transferred to the solicitor's office account.

(iii)   See rule 23(3) for the way in which a withdrawal from a client account in favour of the solicitor must be effected.

Cheques payable to banks, building societies, etc.

(iv)   In order to protect client money against misappropriation when cheques are made payable to banks, building societies or other large institutions, it is strongly recommended that solicitors add the name and number of the account after the payee's name.

Drawing against uncleared cheques

(v)   A solicitor should use discretion in drawing against a cheque received from or on behalf of a client before it has been cleared. If the cheque is not met, other clients' money will have been used to make the payment in breach of the rules. See rule 7 (duty to remedy breaches). A solicitor may be able to avoid a breach of the rules by instructing the bank or building society to charge all unpaid credits to the solicitor's office or personal account.

Non-receipt of telegraphic transfer

(vi)   If a solicitor acting for a client withdraws money from a general client account on the strength of information that a telegraphic transfer is on its way, but the telegraphic transfer does not arrive, the solicitor will have used other clients' money in breach of the rules. See also rule 7 (duty to remedy breaches).

Withdrawals on instructions

(vii)   One of the reasons why a client might authorise a withdrawal under rule 22(1)(e) might be to have the money transferred to a type of account other than a client account. If so, the requirements of rule 16 must be complied with.

Withdrawals where the rightful owner cannot be traced, on the SRA's authorisation and without SRA authorisation

(viii)   Applications for authorisation under rule 22(1)(h) should be made to the Professional

Ethics Guidance Team, who can advise on the criteria which must normally be met for authorisation to be given. Solicitors may under rule 22(1)(ga) pay to a charity sums of £50 or less per client or trust matter without the SRA's authorisation, provided the safeguards set out in rule 22(2A) are followed. Solicitors may, however, if they prefer, apply to the SRA for prior authorisation in all cases.

(viiia) Solicitors will need to apply to the SRA, whatever the amount involved, if the money to be withdrawn is not to be paid to a charity. This situation might arise, for example, if a solicitor has been unable to deliver a bill of costs because the client has become untraceable and so cannot make a transfer from client account to office account in accordance with rule 19(2)–(3).

(ix) After a practice has been wound up, banks sometimes discover unclaimed balances in an old client account. This money remains subject to rule 22 and rule 23. An application can be made to the SRA under rule 22(1)(h).

(x) See rule 15(3) and notes (x)–(xi) to rule 15 on the return of client money when there is no longer any reason for its continued retention. See also rule 15(4) on reporting to the client when client money is retained at the end of a matter.

Rule 23 – Method of and authority for withdrawals from client account

(1) A withdrawal from a *client account* may be made only after a specific authority in respect of that withdrawal has been signed by at least one of the following:

(a) a *solicitor* who holds a current practising certificate or a *registered European lawyer*;

(b) a Fellow of the Institute of Legal Executives or licensed conveyancer who is a *manager* of the practice, where the practice is a *recognised body*;

(c) a Fellow of the Institute of Legal Executives or licensed conveyancer who is an employee of the practice, where the practice is a *recognised body* or *recognised sole practitioner*;

(d) a *registered foreign lawyer* who is a *manager* of the practice, where the practice is a *recognised body*; or

(e) any other individual who is a *manager* of the practice.

(2) There is no need to comply with paragraph (1) above when transferring money from one *general client account* to another *general client account* at the same *bank* or *building society*.

(3) A withdrawal from a *client account* in favour of the *solicitor* or the practice must be either by way of a cheque to the *solicitor* or practice, or by way of a transfer to the *office account* or to the *solicitor's* personal account. The withdrawal must not be made in cash.

NOTES

(a) Reference should also be made to paragraph 4.1.A of the Guidelines for accounting procedures and systems at Appendix 3.

(i) Instructions to the bank or building society to withdraw money from a client account (rule 23(1)) may be given over the telephone, provided a specific authority has been signed in accordance with this rule before the instructions are given. If a solicitor decides to take advantage of this arrangement, it is of paramount importance that the scheme has appropriate in-built safeguards, such as passwords, to give the greatest protection possible for client money. Suitable safeguards will also be needed for practices which operate a CHAPS terminal.

(ii) In the case of a withdrawal by cheque, the specific authority (rule 23(1)) is usually a signature on the cheque itself. Signing a blank cheque is not a specific authority.

(iii) A withdrawal from a client account by way of a private loan from one client to another can only be made if the provisions of rule 30(2) are complied with.

APPENDIX 3

(iv)   It is advisable that a withdrawal for payment to or on behalf of a client (or on behalf of a trust) be made by way of a crossed cheque whenever possible.

(v)   Solicitor-trustees who instruct an outside administrator to run, or continue to run, on a day to day basis, the business or property portfolio of an estate or trust will not need to comply with rule 23(1), provided all cheques are retained in accordance with rule 32(10). (See also rule 32, note (ii)(d).)

(vi)   Where the sum due to the client is sufficiently large, the solicitor should consider whether it should not appropriately be transferred to the client by direct bank transfer. For doing this, the solicitor would be entitled to make a modest administrative charge in addition to any charge made by the bank in connection with the transfer.

Land Registry application fees paid by direct debit

(vii)   Solicitors may set up a direct debit system of payment for Land Registry application fees on either the office account or a client account. If a direct debit payment is to be taken from a client account for the payment of Land Registry application fees, the signature of a person, within one of the categories listed in rule 23(1), on the application for registration will constitute the specific authority required by rule 23(1). As with any other payment method, care must be taken to ensure that sufficient uncommitted funds are held in the client account for the particular client before signing the authority. Solicitors should also bear in mind that should the Land Registry take an incorrect amount in error from a firm's client account (for example, a duplicate payment), the firm will be in breach of the rules if other clients' money has been used as a result.

(viii) If a solicitor fails to specify the correct Land Registry fee on the application for registration (either by specifying a lesser amount than that actually due, or failing to specify any fee at all), the solicitor will be in breach of rule 23(1) if the Land Registry takes a sum from the solicitor's client account greater than that specified on the application, without a specific authority for the revised sum being in place as required by rule 23. In order that the solicitor can comply with the rules, the Land Registry will need to contact the solicitor before taking the revised amount, so that the necessary authority may be signed prior to the revised amount being taken.

(ix)   Where the Land Registry contacts the solicitor by telephone, and the solicitor wishes to authorise an immediate payment by direct debit over the telephone, the solicitor will first need to check that there is sufficient money held in client account for the client and, if there is, that it is not committed to some other purpose.

(x)   The specific authority required by rule 23(1) can be signed after the telephone call has ended but must be signed before the additional payment (or correct full payment) is taken by the Land Registry. It is advisable to sign the authority promptly and, in any event, on the same day as the telephone instruction is given to the Land Registry to take the additional (or correct full) amount. If the solicitor decides to fund any extra amount from the office account, the transfer of office money to the client account would need to be made, preferably on the same day but, in any event, before the direct debit is taken. The solicitor's internal procedures would need to make it clear to unqualified staff how to deal with such situations; for example, who they should consult before a direct debit for an amount other than that specified on the application can be authorised, and the mechanism for ensuring the new authority is signed by a person within one of the categories listed in rule 23(1).

(xi)   A solicitor may decide to set up a direct debit system of payment on the office account because, for example, he or she does not wish to allow the Land Registry to have access to the firm's client account. Provided the solicitor is in funds, a transfer from the client account to the office account may be made under rule 22(1)(c) to reimburse the solicitor as soon as the direct debit has been taken.

Part C – Interest

Rule 24 – When interest must be paid

(1) When a *solicitor* holds money in a *separate designated client account* for a *client*, or for a person funding all or part of the *solicitor's fees*, or for a *trust*, the *solicitor* must account to the *client* or that person or *trust* for all interest earned on the account.

(2) When a *solicitor* holds money in a *general client account* for a *client*, or for a person funding all or part of the *solicitor's fees*, or for a *trust* (or if money should have been held for a *client* or such other person or *trust* in a *client account* but was not), the *solicitor* must account to the *client* or that person or *trust* for a sum in lieu of interest calculated in accordance with rule 25.

(3) A *solicitor* is not required to pay a sum in lieu of interest under paragraph (2) above:

   (a) if the amount calculated is £20 or less;

   (b) (i) if the *solicitor* holds a sum of money not exceeding the amount shown in the left hand column below for a time not exceeding the period indicated in the right hand column:

Amount	Time
£1,000	8 weeks
£2,000	4 weeks
£10,000	2 weeks
£20,000	1 week

   (ii) if the *solicitor* holds a sum of money exceeding £20,000 for one week or less, unless it is fair and reasonable to account for a sum in lieu of interest having regard to all the circumstances;

   (c) on money held for the payment of counsel's fees, once counsel has requested a delay in settlement;

   (d) on money held for the Legal Services Commission;

   (e) on an advance from the *solicitor* under rule 15(2)(b) to fund a payment on behalf of the *client* or *trust* in excess of funds held for that *client* or *trust*; or

   (f) if there is an agreement to contract out of the provisions of this rule under rule 27.

(4) If sums of money are held intermittently during the course of acting, and the sum in lieu of interest calculated under rule 25 for any period is £20 or less, a sum in lieu of interest should still be paid if it is fair and reasonable in the circumstances to aggregate the sums in respect of the individual periods.

(5) If money is held for a continuous period, and for part of that period it is held in a *separate designated client account*, the sum in lieu of interest for the rest of the period when the money was held in a *general client account* may as a result be £20 or less. A sum in lieu of interest should, however, be paid if it is fair and reasonable in the circumstances to do so.

(6) (a) If a *solicitor* holds money for a *client* (or person funding all or part of the *solicitor's fees*) in an account opened on the instructions of the *client* (or that person) under rule 16(1)(a), the *solicitor* must account to the *client* (or that person) for all interest earned on the account.

(aa)   If a *solicitor-trustee*, whether or not in strict accordance with rule 17(ca), holds money for a *trust* in an account of the *solicitor-trustee* which is not a *client account*, the *solicitor-trustee* must account to the *trust* for all interest earned on the account.

(b)   If a *solicitor* has failed to comply with instructions to open an account under rule 16(f)(a), the *solicitor* must account to the *client* (or the person funding all or part of the *solicitor's fees*) for a sum in lieu of any net loss of interest suffered by the *client* (or that person) as a result.

(7)   [deleted]

NOTES

Requirement to pay interest

(i)   The whole of the interest earned on a separate designated client account must be credited to the account. However, the obligation to pay a sum in lieu of interest for amounts held in a general client account is subject to the de minimis provisions in rule 24(3)(a) and (b). Section 33(3) of the Solicitors Act 1974 permits solicitors to retain any interest earned on client money held in a general client account over and above that which they have to pay under these rules. (See also note (viii) to rule 15 on aggregation of accounts.)

(ii)   There is no requirement to pay a sum in lieu of interest on money held on instructions under rule 16(1)(a) in a manner which attracts no interest.

(iii)   Accounts opened in the client's name under rule 16(1)(b) (whether operated by the solicitor or not) are not subject to rule 24, as the money is not held by the solicitor. All interest earned belongs to the client. The same applies to any account in the client's own name operated by the solicitor as signatory under rule 11.

(iv)   Money subject to a trust is client money (see rule 13), and rule 24 therefore applies to it.

De minimis provisions (rule 24(3)(a) and (b))

(v)   The sum in lieu of interest is calculated over the whole period for which money is held (see rule 25(2)); if this sum is £20 or less, the solicitor need not account to the client, other person or trust. If sums of money are held in relation to separate matters for the same client, other person or trust, it is normally appropriate to treat the money relating to the different matters separately, so that, if any of the sums calculated is £20 or less, no sum in lieu of interest is payable. There will, however, be cases when the matters are so closely related that they ought to be considered together – for example, when a solicitor is acting for a client in connection with numerous debt collection matters.

Administrative charges

(vi)   It is not improper to charge a reasonable fee for the handling of client money when the service provided is out of the ordinary.

Unpresented cheques

(vii)   A client may fail to present a cheque to his or her bank for payment. Whether or not it is reasonable to recalculate the amount due will depend on all the circumstances of the case. A reasonable charge may be made for any extra work carried out if the solicitor is legally entitled to make such a charge.

Liquidators, trustees in bankruptcy, Court of Protection deputies and trustees of occupational pension schemes

(viii)   Under rule 9, Part C of the rules does not normally apply to solicitors who are liquidators, etc. Solicitors must comply with the appropriate statutory rules and regulations, and rules 9(3) and (4) as appropriate.

Joint accounts

(ix) Under rule 10, Part C of the rules does not apply to joint accounts. If a solicitor holds money jointly with a client, interest earned on the account will be for the benefit of the client unless otherwise agreed. If money is held jointly with another solicitors' practice, the allocation of interest earned will depend on the agreement reached.

(x) [deleted]

Failure to pay interest

(xa) A client, including one of joint clients, or a person funding all or part of a solicitor's fees, may complain to the Legal Complaints Service if he or she believes that interest, or a sum in lieu of interest, was due and has not been paid, or that the amount paid was insufficient. It is advisable for the client (or other person) to try to resolve the matter with the solicitor before approaching the Legal Complaints Service.

Rule 25 – Amount of interest

(1) *Solicitors* must aim to obtain a reasonable rate of interest on money held in a *separate designated client account*, and must account for a fair sum in lieu of interest on money held in a *general client account* (or on money which should have been held in a *client account* but was not). The sum in lieu of interest need not necessarily reflect the highest rate of interest obtainable but it is not acceptable to look only at the lowest rate of interest obtainable.

(2) **The sum in lieu of interest** for money held in a *general client account* (or on money which should have been held in a *client account* but was not) **must be calculated**

- **on the balance or balances held over the whole period for which cleared funds are held**

- **at a rate not less than (whichever is the higher of) the following**

  (i) the rate of interest payable on a *separate designated client account* for the amount or amounts held, or

  (ii) the rate of interest payable on the relevant amount or amounts if placed on deposit on similar terms by a member of the business community

- **at the *bank* or *building society* where the money is held.**

(3) If the money, or part of it, is held successively or concurrently in accounts at different *banks* or *building societies*, the relevant *bank* or *building society* for the purpose of paragraph (2) will be whichever of those *banks* or *building societies* offered the best rate on the date when the money was first held.

(4) If, contrary to the rules, the money held for a *client* or other person is not held in a *client account*, the relevant *bank* or *building society* for the purpose of paragraph (2) will be a clearing *bank* or *building society* nominated by the *client* (or other person).

(5) If, contrary to the rules, money held by a *solicitor-trustee* is not held in a *client account*, the *solicitor-trustee* has a particular obligation to comply with the requirement in paragraph (1) to account for a fair sum in lieu of interest.

NOTES

(i) The sum in lieu of interest has to be calculated over the whole period for which money is held – see rule 25(2). The solicitor will usually account to the client at the conclusion of the client's matter, but might in some cases consider it appropriate to account to the client at intervals throughout.

(ii) When looking at the period over which the sum in lieu of interest must be calculated, it will usually be unnecessary to check on actual clearance dates. When money is received by cheque and paid out by cheque, the normal clearance periods will usually cancel each other out, so that it will be satisfactory to look at the period between the dates when the incoming cheque is banked and the outgoing cheque is drawn.

(iii)   Different considerations apply when payments in and out are not both made by cheque. So, for example, the relevant periods would normally be:

- from the date when a solicitor receives incoming money in cash until the date when the outgoing cheque is sent;

- from the date when an incoming telegraphic transfer begins to earn interest until the date when the outgoing cheque is sent;

- from the date when an incoming cheque or banker's draft is or would normally be cleared until the date when the outgoing telegraphic transfer is made or banker's draft is obtained.

(iv)   The sum in lieu of interest is calculated by reference to the rates paid by the appropriate bank or building society (see rule 25(2) to (5)). Solicitors will therefore follow the practice of that bank or building society in determining how often interest is compounded over the period for which the cleared funds are held.

(v)   Money held in a client account must be immediately available, even at the sacrifice of interest, unless the client otherwise instructs, or the circumstances clearly indicate otherwise. The need for access can be taken into account in assessing the appropriate rate for calculating the sum to be paid in lieu of interest, or in assessing whether a reasonable rate of interest has been obtained for a separate designated client account.

(vi)   For failure by the solicitor to pay a sufficient sum by way of interest, or in lieu of interest, see note (xa) to rule 24.

Rule 26 – Interest on stakeholder money

When a *solicitor* holds money as stakeholder, the *solicitor* must pay interest, or a sum in lieu of interest, on the basis set out in rule 24 to the person to whom the stake is paid.

NOTE

For contracting out of this provision, see rule 27(2) and the notes to rule 27.

Rule 27 – Contracting out

(1)   In appropriate circumstances a *client* and his or her *solicitor* may by a written agreement come to a different arrangement as to the matters dealt with in rule 24 (payment of interest).

(2)   A *solicitor* acting as stakeholder may, by a written agreement with his or her own *client* and the other party to the transaction, come to a different arrangement as to the matters dealt with in rule 24.

NOTES

(i)   Solicitors should act fairly towards their clients and provide sufficient information to enable them to give informed consent if it is felt appropriate to depart from the interest provisions. Whether it is appropriate to contract out depends on all the circumstances, for example, the size of the sum involved or the nature, status or bargaining position of the client. It might, for instance, be appropriate to contract out by standard terms of business if the client is a substantial commercial entity and the interest involved is modest in relation to the size of the transaction. The larger the sum of interest involved, the more there would be an onus on the solicitor to show that a client who had accepted a contracting out provision was properly informed and had been treated fairly. Contracting out is never appropriate if it is against the client's interests.

(ii)   In principle, a solicitor-stakeholder is entitled to make a reasonable charge to the client for acting as stakeholder in the client's matter.

(iii)   Alternatively, it may be appropriate to include a special provision in the contract that the solicitor-stakeholder retains the interest on the deposit to cover his or her charges for acting as stakeholder. This is only acceptable if it will provide a fair and reasonable payment for the work and risk involved in holding a stake. The contract could stipulate a maximum charge, with any interest earned above that figure being paid to the recipient of the stake.

(iv)   Any right to charge the client, or to stipulate for a charge which may fall on the client, would be excluded by, for instance, a prior agreement with the client for a fixed fee for the client's matter, or for an estimated fee which cannot be varied upwards in the absence of special circumstances. It is therefore not normal practice for a stakeholder in conveyancing transactions to receive a separate payment for holding the stake.

(v)   A solicitor-stakeholder who seeks an agreement to exclude the operation of rule 26 should be particularly careful not to take unfair advantage either of the client, or of the other party if unrepresented.

Rule 28 – [repealed]

Part D – Accounting systems and records

Rule 29 – Guidelines for accounting procedures and systems

The *SRA* may from time to time publish guidelines for accounting procedures and systems to assist *solicitors* to comply with Parts A to D of the rules, and *solicitors* may be required to justify any departure from the guidelines.

NOTES

(i)   The current guidelines appear at Appendix 3.

(ii)   The reporting accountant does not carry out a detailed check for compliance, but has a duty to report on any substantial departures from the guidelines discovered whilst carrying out work in preparation of his or her report (see rules 43 and 44(e)).

Rule 30 – Restrictions on transfers between clients

(1)   A paper transfer of money held in a *general client account* from the ledger of one *client* to the ledger of another *client* may only be made if:

    (a)   it would have been permissible to withdraw that sum from the account under rule 22(1); and

    (b)   it would have been permissible to pay that sum into the account under rule 15;

    (but there is no requirement in the case of a paper transfer for the written authority of a *solicitor*, etc., under rule 23(1)).

(2)   No sum in respect of a private loan from one *client* to another can be paid out of funds held for the lender either:

(a)   by a payment from one *client account* to another;

(b)   by a paper transfer from the ledger of the lender to that of the borrower; or

(c)   to the borrower directly,

except with the prior written authority of both *clients*.

NOTES

(i)   "Private loan" means a loan other than one provided by an institution which provides loans on standard terms in the normal course of its activities – rule 30(2) does not apply to loans made by an institutional lender. See also the Solicitors' Code of Conduct 2007 rule 3.16(2)(b), which prohibits a solicitor from acting for both lender and borrower in an individual mortgage at arm's length.

(ii)   If the loan is to be made by (or to) joint clients, the consent of each client must be obtained.

Rule 31 – Executor, trustee or nominee companies

(1)   If a *solicitors'* practice owns all the shares in a *recognised body* which is an executor, trustee or nominee company, the practice and the *recognised body* must not operate shared *client accounts*, but may:

(a)   use one set of accounting records for money held, received or paid by the practice and the *recognised body*; and/or

(b)   deliver a single accountant's report for both the practice and the *recognised body*.

(2)   If such a *recognised body* as nominee receives a dividend cheque made out to the *recognised body*, and forwards the cheque, either endorsed or subject to equivalent instructions, to the share-owner's *bank* or *building society*, etc., the *recognised body* will have received (and paid) *client money*. One way of complying with rule 32 (accounting records) is to keep a copy of the letter to the share-owner's *bank* or *building society*, etc., on the file, and, in accordance with rule 32(14), to keep another copy in a central book of such letters. (See also rule 32(9)(f) (retention of records for six years).)

NOTES [DELETED]

Rule 32 – Accounting records for client accounts, etc.

Accounting records which must be kept

(1)   A *solicitor* must at all times keep accounting records properly written up to show the *solicitor's* dealings with:

(a)   *client money* received, held or paid by the *solicitor*, including *client money* held outside a *client account* under rule 16(1)(a) or rule 17(ca); and

(b)   [deleted]

(c)   any *office money* relating to any *client* or *trust* matter.

(2)   All dealings with *client money* must be appropriately recorded:

(a)   in a client cash account or in a record of sums transferred from one client ledger account to another; and

(b)   on the client side of a separate client ledger account for each *client* (or other person, or *trust*).

No other entries may be made in these records.

(3)   If *separate designated client accounts* are used:

    (a)   a combined cash account must be kept in order to show the total amount held in *separate designated client accounts*; and

    (b)   a record of the amount held for each *client* (or other person, or *trust*) must be made either in a deposit column of a client ledger account, or on the client side of a client ledger account kept specifically for a *separate designated client account*, for each *client* (or other person, or *trust*).

(4)   All dealings with *office money* relating to any *client* matter, or to any *trust* matter, must be appropriately recorded in an office cash account and on the office side of the appropriate client ledger account.

Current balance

(5)   The current balance on each client ledger account must always be shown, or be readily ascertainable, from the records kept in accordance with paragraphs (2) and (3) above.

Acting for both lender and borrower

(6)   When acting for both lender and borrower on a mortgage advance, separate client ledger accounts for both *clients* need not be opened, provided that:

    (a)   the funds belonging to each *client* are clearly identifiable; and

    (b)   the lender is an institutional lender which provides mortgages on standard terms in the normal course of its activities.

Reconciliations

(7)   The *solicitor* must, at least once every fourteen weeks in the case of money held by *solicitor-trustees* in passbook-operated *separate designated client accounts*, and at least once every five weeks in all other cases:

    (a)   compare the balance on the client cash account(s) with the balances shown on the statements and passbooks (after allowing for all unpresented items) of all *general client accounts* and *separate designated client accounts*, and of any account which is not a *client account* but in which the *solicitor* holds *client money* under rule 16(1)(a) or rule 17(ca), and any *client money* held by the *solicitor* in cash; and

    (b)   as at the same date prepare a listing of all the balances shown by the client ledger accounts of the liabilities to *clients* (and other persons, and *trusts*) and compare the total of those balances with the balance on the client cash account; and also

    (c)   prepare a reconciliation statement; this statement must show the cause of the difference, if any, shown by each of the above comparisons.

Bills and notifications of costs

(8)   The *solicitor* must keep readily accessible a central record or file of copies of:

    (a)   all bills given or sent by the *solicitor*; and

    (b)   all other written notifications of *costs* given or sent by the *solicitor*;

in both cases distinguishing between *fees*, *disbursements* not yet paid at the date of the bill, and paid *disbursements*.

Withdrawals under rule 22(1)(ga)

(8A) A *solicitor* who withdraws *client money* under rule 22(1)(ga) must keep a record of the steps taken in accordance with rule 22(2A)(a)–(c), together with all relevant documentation (including receipts from the charity).

Retention of records

(9) The *solicitor* must retain for at least six years from the date of the last entry:

    (a) all documents or other records required by paragraphs (1) to (8A) above;

    (b) all statements and passbooks, as printed and issued by the *bank*, *building society* or other financial institution, and/or all duplicate statements and copies of passbook entries permitted in lieu of the originals by rule 10(3) or (4), for:

        (i) any *general client account* or *separate designated client account*;

        (ii) any joint account held under rule 10;

        (iii) any account which is not a *client account* but in which the *solicitor* holds *client money* under rule 16(1)(a) or rule 17(ca); and

        (iv) [deleted]

        (v) any *office account* maintained in relation to the practice;

    (c) any records kept under rule 9 (liquidators, trustees in bankruptcy, *Court of Protection deputies* and trustees of occupational pension schemes) including, as printed or otherwise issued, any statements, passbooks and other accounting records originating outside the *solicitor's* office;

    (d) any written instructions to withhold *client money* from a *client account* (or a copy of the *solicitor's* confirmation of oral instructions) in accordance with rule 16;

    (e) any central registers kept under paragraphs (11) to (13A) below; and

    (f) any copy letters kept centrally under rule 31(2) (dividend cheques endorsed over by nominee company).

(10) The *solicitor* must retain for at least two years:

    (a) originals or copies of all authorities, other than cheques, for the withdrawal of money from a *client account*; and

    (b) all original paid cheques (or digital images of the front and back of all original paid cheques), unless there is a written arrangement with the *bank*, *building society* or other financial institution that:

        (i) it will retain the original cheques on the *solicitor's* behalf for that period; or

        (ii) in the event of destruction of any original cheques, it will retain digital images of the front and back of those cheques on the *solicitor's* behalf for that period and will, on demand by the *solicitor*, the *solicitor's* reporting accountant or the *SRA*, produce copies of the digital images accompanied, when requested, by a certificate of verification signed by an authorised officer.

Centrally kept records for certain accounts, etc.

(11) Statements and passbooks for *client money* held outside a *client account* under rule 16(1)(a) or rule 17(ca) must be kept together centrally, or the *solicitor* must maintain a central register of these accounts.

(12) Any records kept under rule 9 (liquidators, trustees in bankruptcy, *Court of Protection deputies* and trustees of occupational pension schemes) must be kept together centrally, or the *solicitor* must maintain a central register of the appointments.

(13) The statements, passbooks, duplicate statements and copies of passbook entries relating to any joint account held under rule 10 must be kept together centrally, or the *solicitor* must maintain a central register of all joint accounts.

(13A) A central register of all withdrawals made under rule 22(1)(ga) must be kept, detailing the name of the *client*, other person or *trust* on whose behalf the money is held (if known), the amount, the name of the recipient charity and the date of the payment.

(14) If a nominee company follows the option in rule 31(2) (keeping instruction letters for dividend payments), a central book must be kept of all instruction letters to the share-owner's *bank* or *building society*, etc.

Computerisation

(15) Records required by this rule may be kept on a computerised system, apart from the following documents, which must be retained as printed or otherwise issued:

(a) original statements and passbooks retained under paragraph (9)(b) above;

(b) original statements, passbooks and other accounting records retained under paragraph (9)(c) above; and

(c) original cheques and copy authorities retained under paragraph (10) above.

There is no obligation to keep a hard copy of computerised records. However, if no hard copy is kept, the information recorded must be capable of being reproduced reasonably quickly in printed form for at least six years, or for at least two years in the case of digital images of paid cheques retained under paragraph (10) above.

Suspense ledger accounts

(16) Suspense client ledger accounts may be used only when the *solicitor* can justify their use; for instance, for temporary use on receipt of an unidentified payment, if time is needed to establish the nature of the payment or the identity of the *client*.

NOTES

(i) It is strongly recommended that accounting records are written up at least weekly, even in the smallest practice, and daily in the case of larger firms.

(ii) Rule 32(1) to (6) (general record-keeping requirements) and rule 32(7) (reconciliations) do not apply to:

(a) solicitor liquidators, trustees in bankruptcy, Court of Protection deputies and trustees of occupational pension schemes operating in accordance with statutory rules or regulations under rule 9(1)(a);

(b) joint accounts operated under rule 10;

(c) a client's own account operated under rule 11; the record-keeping requirements for this type of account are set out in rule 33;

(d) solicitor-trustees who instruct an outside administrator to run, or continue to run, on a day to day basis, the business or property portfolio of an estate or trust, provided the administrator keeps and retains appropriate accounting records, which are available for inspection by the SRA in accordance with rule 34. (See also note (v) to rule 23.)

(iii) When a cheque or draft is received on behalf of a client and is endorsed over, not passing through a client account, it must be recorded in the books of account as a

APPENDIX 3

receipt and payment on behalf of the client. The same applies to cash received and not deposited in a client account but paid out to or on behalf of a client. A cheque made payable to a client, which is forwarded to the client by the solicitor, is not client money and falls outside the rules, although it is advisable to record the action taken.

(iv)   For the purpose of rule 32, money which has been paid into a client account under rule 19(1)(c) (receipt of costs), or under rule 20(2)(b) (mixed money), and for the time being remains in a client account, is to be treated as client money; it should be recorded on the client side of the client ledger account, but must be appropriately identified.

(v)   For the purpose of rule 32, money which has been paid into an office account under rule 19(1)(b) (receipt of costs), rule 21(1)(a) (advance payments from the Legal Services Commission), or under rule 21(1)(b) (payment of costs from the Legal Services Commission), and for the time being remains in an office account without breaching the rules, is to be treated as office money. Money paid into an office account under rule 21(2)(b) (regular payments) is office money. All these payments should be recorded on the office side of the client ledger account (for the individual client or for the Legal Services Commission), and must be appropriately identified.

(vi)   Some accounting systems do not retain a record of past daily balances. This does not put the solicitor in breach of rule 32(5).

(vii)   "Clearly identifiable" in rule 32(6) means that by looking at the ledger account the nature and owner of the mortgage advance are unambiguously stated. For example, if a mortgage advance of £100,000 is received from the ABC Building Society, the entry should be recorded as "£100,000, mortgage advance, ABC Building Society". It is not enough to state that the money was received from the ABC Building Society without specifying the nature of the payment, or vice versa.

(viii)   Although the solicitor does not open a separate ledger account for the lender, the mortgage advance credited to that account belongs to the lender, not to the borrower, until completion takes place. Improper removal of these mortgage funds from a client account would be a breach of rule 22.

(ix)   Reconciliations should be carried out as they fall due, and in any event no later than the due date for the next reconciliation. In the case of a separate designated client account operated with a passbook, there is no need to ask the bank, building society or other financial institution for confirmation of the balance held. In the case of other separate designated client accounts, the solicitor should either obtain statements at least monthly, or should obtain written confirmation of the balance direct from the bank, building society or other financial institution. There is no requirement to check that interest has been credited since the last statement, or the last entry in the passbook.

(x)   In making the comparisons under rule 32(7)(a) and (b), some solicitors use credits of one client against debits of another when checking total client liabilities. This is improper because it fails to show up the shortage.

(xi)   The effect of rule 32(9)(b) is that the solicitor must ensure that the bank issues hard copy statements. Statements sent from the bank to its solicitor customer by means of electronic mail, even if capable of being printed off as hard copies, will not suffice.

(xii)   Rule 32(9)(d) – retention of client's instructions to withhold money from a client account – does not require records to be kept centrally; however this may be prudent, to avoid losing the instructions if the file is passed to the client.

(xiii)   A solicitor who holds client money in a currency other than sterling should hold that money in a separate account for the appropriate currency. Separate books of account should be kept for that currency.

(xiv)   The requirement to keep paid cheques under rule 32(10)(b) extends to all cheques drawn on a client account, or on an account in which client money is held outside a client account under rule 16(1)(a) or rule 17(ca).

(xv)   Solicitors may enter into an arrangement whereby the bank keeps digital images of paid cheques in place of the originals. The bank should take an electronic image of the front and back of each cheque in black and white and agree to hold such images, and to make printed copies available on request, for at least two years. Alternatively, solicitors may take and keep their own digital images of paid cheques.

(xvi)   Microfilmed copies of paid cheques are not acceptable for the purposes of rule 32(10)(b). If a bank is able to provide microfilmed copies only, the solicitor must obtain the original paid cheques from the bank and retain them for at least two years.

(xvii)   Certificates of verification in relation to digital images of cheques may on occasion be required by the SRA when exercising its investigative and enforcement powers. The reporting accountant will not need to ask for a certificate of verification but will be able to rely on the printed copy of the digital image as if it were the original.

Rule 33 – Accounting records for clients' own accounts

(1)   When a *solicitor* operates a *client's* own account as signatory under rule 11, the *solicitor* must retain, for at least six years from the date of the last entry, the statements or passbooks as printed and issued by the *bank, building society* or other financial institution, and/or the duplicate statements, copies of passbook entries and cheque details permitted in lieu of the originals by rule 11(3) or (4); and any central register kept under paragraph (2) below.

(2)   The *solicitor* must either keep these records together centrally, or maintain a central register of the accounts operated under rule 11.

(3)   If, when the *solicitor* ceases to operate the account, the *client* requests the original statements or passbooks, the *solicitor* must take photocopies and keep them in lieu of the originals.

(4)   This rule applies only to *solicitors* in private practice.

NOTE

Solicitors should remember the requirements of rule 32(8) (central record of bills, etc.).

Part E – Monitoring and investigation by the SRA

Rule 34 – Production of records

(1)   Any *solicitor* must at the time and place fixed by the SRA produce to any person appointed by the SRA any records, papers, *client* and *trust* matter files, financial accounts and other documents, and any other information, necessary to enable preparation of a report on compliance with the rules.

(2)   A requirement for production under paragraph (1) above must be in writing, and left at or sent by the "recorded signed for" or "special delivery next day" service to the most recent address held by the SRA's Information Directorate, or delivered by the SRA's appointee. If sent through the post, receipt will be deemed 48 hours (excluding Saturdays, Sundays and Bank Holidays) after posting.

(3)   Material kept electronically must be produced in the form required by the SRA's appointee.

APPENDIX 3

(4)   The *SRA's* appointee is entitled to seek verification from *clients* and staff, and from the *banks, building societies* and other financial institutions used by the *solicitor*. The *solicitor* must, if necessary, provide written permission for the information to be given.

(5)   The *SRA's* appointee is not entitled to take original documents away but must be provided with photocopies on request.

(6)   A *solicitor* must be prepared to explain and justify any departures from the guidelines for accounting procedures and systems published by the *SRA* (see rule 29).

(7)   Any report made by the *SRA's* appointee may, if appropriate, be sent to the Crown Prosecution Service or the Serious Fraud Office and/or used in proceedings before the Solicitors Disciplinary Tribunal. In the case of a *registered European lawyer* or *registered foreign lawyer*, the report may also be sent to the competent authority in that lawyer's home state or states. In the case of a *solicitor of the Supreme Court* who is established in another state under the Establishment of Lawyers Directive 98/5/EC, the report may also be sent to the competent authority in the host state. The report may also be sent to any of the accountancy bodies set out in rule 37(1)(a) and/or taken into account by the *SRA* in relation to a possible disqualification of a reporting accountant under rule 37(3).

(8)   Without prejudice to paragraph (1) above, any *solicitor* must produce documents relating to any account kept by the *solicitor* at a *bank* or with a *building society*:

(a)   in connection with the *solicitor's* practice; or

(b)   in connection with any *trust* of which the *solicitor* is or formerly was a *trustee*,

for inspection by a person appointed by the *SRA* for the purpose of preparing a report on compliance with the rules or on whether the account has been used for or in connection with a breach of any other rules, codes or mandatory guidance made or issued by the *SRA*. Paragraphs (2)–(7) above apply in relation to this paragraph in the same way as to paragraph (1).

NOTES

(i)   "Solicitor" in rule 34 (as elsewhere in the rules) includes any person to whom the rules apply – see rule 2(2)(x), rule 4 and note (ii) to rule 4.

(ii)   The SRA's powers override any confidence or privilege between solicitor and client.

(iii) The SRA's monitoring and investigation powers are exercised by Forensic Investigations.

(iv)   Reasons are never given for a visit by Forensic Investigations, so as:

(a)   to safeguard the SRA's sources of information; and

(b)   not to alert a defaulting manager or employee to conceal or compound his or her misappropriations.

(v)   [deleted]

Part F – Accountants' reports

Rule 35 – Delivery of accountants' reports

(1)   A *solicitor* who or which has, at any time during an *accounting period*, held or received *client money*, or operated a *client's* own account as signatory, must deliver to the *SRA* an accountant's report for that *accounting period* within six months of the end of the *accounting period*. This duty extends to the directors of a company, or the members of an *LLP*, which is subject to this rule.

(2)   In addition the *SRA* may require the delivery of an accountant's report in circumstances other than those set out in paragraph (1) above if the *SRA* has reason to believe that it is in the public interest to do so.

NOTES

(i)   Examples of situations under rule 35(2) include:

- when no report has been delivered but the SRA has reason to believe that a report should have been delivered;

- when a report has been delivered but the SRA has reason to believe that it may be inaccurate;

- when the conduct of the solicitor gives the SRA reason to believe that it would be appropriate to require earlier delivery of a report (for instance three months after the end of the accounting period);

- when the conduct of the solicitor gives the SRA reason to believe that it would be appropriate to require more frequent delivery of reports (for instance every six months);

- when the SRA has reason to believe that the regulatory risk justifies the imposition on a category of solicitors of a requirement to deliver reports earlier or at more frequent intervals;

- when a condition on a solicitor's practising certificate requires earlier delivery of reports or the delivery of reports at more frequent intervals.

(ii)   For accountant's reports of limited scope see rule 9 (liquidators, trustees in bankruptcy, Court of Protection deputies and trustees of occupational pension schemes), rule 10 (joint accounts) and rule 11 (operation of a client's own account). For exemption from the obligation to deliver a report, see rule 5 (persons exempt from the rules).

(iii)   The requirement in rule 35 for a registered foreign lawyer to deliver an accountant's report applies only to a registered foreign lawyer practising in one of the ways set out in rule 2(2)(x)(iii).

(iv)   The form of report is dealt with in rule 47.

(v)   When client money is held or received by an unincorporated practice, the principals in the practice will have held or received client money. A salaried partner whose name appears in the list of partners on a firm's letterhead, even if the name appears under a separate heading of "salaried partners" or "associate partners", is a principal.

(va)   In the case of an incorporated practice, it is the company or LLP (i.e. the recognised body) which will have held or received client money. The recognised body and its directors (in the case of a company) or members (in the case of an LLP) will have the duty to deliver an accountant's report, although the directors or members will not usually have held client money.

(vi)   Assistant solicitors, consultants and other employees do not normally hold client money. An assistant solicitor or consultant might be a signatory for a firm's client account, but this does not constitute holding or receiving client money. If a client or third party hands cash to an assistant solicitor, consultant or other employee, it is the sole principal or the partners (rather than the assistant solicitor, consultant or other employee) who are regarded as having received and held the money. In the case of an incorporated practice, whether a company or an LLP, it would be the recognised body itself which would be regarded as having held or received the money.

(vii)   If, exceptionally, an assistant solicitor, consultant or other employee has a client account (as a trustee), or operates a client's own account as signatory, the assistant solicitor, consultant or other employee will have to deliver an accountant's report. The assistant solicitor, consultant or other employee can be included in the report of the practice, but must ensure that his or her name is added, and an explanation given.

(viii) A solicitor to whom a cheque or draft is made out, and who in the course of practice endorses it over to a client or employer, has received (and paid) client money. That solicitor will have to deliver an accountant's report, even if no other client money has been held or received.

(ix) When only a small number of transactions is undertaken or a small volume of client money is handled in an accounting period, a waiver of the obligation to deliver a report may sometimes be granted. Applications should be made to the Information Directorate.

(x) If a solicitors' practice owns all the shares in a recognised body which is an executor, trustee or nominee company, the practice and the recognised body may deliver a single accountant's report (see rule 31(1)(b)).

Rule 36 – Accounting periods

The norm

(1) An "accounting period" means the period for which the accounts of the *solicitor* are ordinarily made up, except that it must:

(a) begin at the end of the previous *accounting period*; and

(b) cover twelve months.

Paragraphs (2) to (5) below set out exceptions.

First and resumed reports

(2) For a *solicitor* who is under a duty to deliver his or her first report, the *accounting period* must begin on the date when the *solicitor* first held or received *client money* (or operated a *client's* own account as signatory), and may cover less than twelve months.

(3) For a *solicitor* who is under a duty to deliver his or her first report after a break, the *accounting period* must begin on the date when the *solicitor* for the first time after the break held or received *client money* (or operated a *client's* own account as signatory), and may cover less than twelve months.

Change of accounting period

(4) If a practice changes the period for which its accounts are made up (for example, on a merger, or simply for convenience), the *accounting period* immediately preceding the change may be shorter than twelve months, or longer than twelve months up to a maximum of 18 months, provided that the *accounting period* shall not be changed to a period longer than twelve months unless the *SRA* receives written notice of the change before expiry of the deadline for delivery of the accountant's report which would have been expected on the basis of the *firm's* old *accounting period*.

Final reports

(5) A *solicitor* who for any reason stops holding or receiving *client money* (and operating any *client's* own account as signatory) must deliver a final report. The *accounting period* must end on the date upon which the *solicitor* stopped holding or receiving *client money* (and operating any *client's* own account as signatory), and may cover less than twelve months.

NOTES

(i)   In the case of solicitors joining or leaving a continuing partnership, any accountant's report for the practice as a whole will show the names and dates of the principals joining or leaving. For a solicitor who did not previously hold or receive client money, etc., and has become a principal in the firm, the report for the practice will represent, from the date of joining, the solicitor's first report for the purpose of rule 36(2). For a solicitor who was a principal in the firm and, on leaving, stops holding or receiving client money, etc., the report for the practice will represent, up to the date of leaving, the solicitor's final report for the purpose of rule 36(5) above.

(ii)   When a partnership splits up, it is usually appropriate for the books to be made up as at the date of dissolution, and for an accountant's report to be delivered within six months of that date. If, however, the old partnership continues to hold or receive client money, etc., in connection with outstanding matters, accountant's reports will continue to be required for those matters; the books should then be made up on completion of the last of those matters and a report delivered within six months of that date. The same would be true for a sole practitioner winding up matters on retirement.

(iii)   When a practice is being wound up, the solicitor may be left with money which is unattributable, or belongs to a client who cannot be traced. It may be appropriate to apply to the SRA for authority to withdraw this money from the solicitor's client account – see rule 22(1)(h) and note (viii) to rule 22.

Rule 37 – Qualifications for making a report

(1)   A report must be prepared and signed by an accountant

    (a)   who is a member of:

        (i)   the Institute of Chartered Accountants in England and Wales;

        (ii)   the Institute of Chartered Accountants of Scotland;

        (iii)   the Association of Chartered Certified Accountants;

        (iv)   the Institute of Chartered Accountants in Ireland; or

        (v)   the Association of Authorised Public Accountants; **and**

    (b)   who is also:

        (i)   an individual who is a registered auditor within the terms of section 35(1)(a) of the Companies Act 1989; or

        (ii)   an employee of such an individual; or

        (iii)   a *partner* in or employee of a *partnership* which is a registered auditor within the terms of section 35(1)(a) of the Companies Act 1989; or

        (iv)   a director or employee of a company which is a registered auditor within the terms of section 35(1)(a) of the Companies Act 1989; or

        (v)   a member or employee of an *LLP* which is a registered auditor within the terms of section 35(1)(a) of the Companies Act 1989.

(2)   An accountant is not qualified to make a report if:

    (a)   at any time between the beginning of the *accounting period* to which the report relates, and the completion of the report:

        (i)   he or she was a *partner* or employee, or an officer or employee (in the case of a company), or a member or employee (in the case of an *LLP*) in the practice to which the report relates; or

        (ii)   he or she was employed by the same *non-solicitor employer* as the *solicitor* for whom the report is being made; or

(b) he or she has been disqualified under paragraph (3) below and notice of disqualification has been given under paragraph (4) (and has not subsequently been withdrawn).

(3) The *SRA* may disqualify an accountant from making any accountant's report if:

(a) the accountant has been found guilty by his or her professional body of professional misconduct or discreditable conduct; or

(b) the *SRA* is satisfied that a *solicitor* has not complied with the rules in respect of matters which the accountant has negligently failed to specify in a report.

In coming to a decision, the *SRA* will take into account any representations made by the accountant or his or her professional body.

(4) Written notice of disqualification must be left at or sent by recorded delivery to the address of the accountant shown on an accountant's report or in the records of the accountant's professional body. If sent through the post, receipt will be deemed 48 hours (excluding Saturdays, Sundays and Bank Holidays) after posting.

(5) An accountant's disqualification may be notified to any *solicitor* likely to be affected and may be printed in the Law Society's Gazette or other publication.

NOTE

It is not a breach of the rules for a solicitor to retain an outside accountant to write up the books of account and to instruct the same accountant to prepare the accountant's report. However, the accountant will have to disclose these circumstances in the report – see the form of report in Appendix 5.

Rule 38 – Reporting accountant's rights and duties – letter of engagement

(1) The *solicitor* must ensure that the reporting accountant's rights and duties are stated in a letter of engagement incorporating the following terms:

"In accordance with rule 38 of the Solicitors' Accounts Rules 1998, you are instructed as follows:

(i) I/this firm/this company/this limited liability partnership recognises that, if during the course of preparing an accountant's report:

(a) you discover evidence of fraud or theft in relation to money

- held by a solicitor (or registered European lawyer, or registered foreign lawyer, or recognised body, or employee of a solicitor or registered European lawyer, or manager or employee of a recognised body) for a client or any other person (including money held on trust), or

- held in an account of a client, or an account of another person, which is operated by a solicitor (or registered European lawyer, registered foreign lawyer, recognised body, employee of a solicitor or registered European lawyer, or manager or employee of a recognised body); or

(b) you obtain information which you have reasonable cause to believe is likely to be of material significance in determining whether a solicitor (or registered European lawyer, or registered foreign lawyer, or recognised body, or employee of a solicitor or registered European lawyer, or manager or employee of a recognised body) is a fit and proper person

- to hold money for clients or other persons (including money held on trust), or

- to operate an account of a client or an account of another person,

you must immediately give a report of the matter to the Solicitors Regulation Authority in accordance with section 34(9) of the Solicitors Act 1974;

(ii) you may, and are encouraged to, make that report without prior reference to me/this firm/this company/this limited liability partnership;

(iii) you are to report directly to the Solicitors Regulation Authority should your appointment be terminated following the issue of, or indication of intention to issue, a qualified accountant's report, or following the raising of concerns prior to the preparation of an accountant's report;

(iv) you are to deliver to me/this firm/this company/this limited liability partnership with your report the completed checklist required by rule 46 of the Solicitors' Accounts Rules 1998; to retain for at least three years from the date of signature a copy of the completed checklist; and to produce the copy to the Solicitors Regulation Authority on request;

(v) you are to retain these terms of engagement for at least three years after the termination of the retainer and to produce them to the Solicitors Regulation Authority on request; and

(vi) following any direct report made to the Solicitors Regulation Authority under (i) or (iii) above, you are to provide to the Solicitors Regulation Authority on request any further relevant information in your possession or in the possession of your firm.

To the extent necessary to enable you to comply with (i) to (vi) above, I/we waive my/the firm's/the company's/the limited liability partnership's right of confidentiality. This waiver extends to any report made, document produced or information disclosed to the Solicitors Regulation Authority in good faith pursuant to these instructions, even though it may subsequently transpire that you were mistaken in your belief that there was cause for concern."

(2) The letter of engagement and a copy must be signed by the *solicitor* (or by a *partner*, or in the case of a company by a director, or in the case of an *LLP* by a member) and by the accountant. The *solicitor* must keep the copy of the signed letter of engagement for at least three years after the termination of the retainer and produce it to the *SRA* on request.

NOTES

(i) Any direct report by the accountant to the SRA under rule 38(1)(i) or (iii) should be made to the Fraud and Confidential Intelligence Bureau.

(ii) Rule 38(1) envisages that the specified terms are incorporated in a letter from the solicitor to the accountant. Instead, the specified terms may be included in a letter from the accountant to the solicitor setting out the terms of the engagement. If so, the text must be adapted appropriately. The letter must be signed in duplicate by both parties – the solicitor will keep the original, and the accountant the copy.

Rule 39 – Change of accountant

On instructing an accountancy practice to replace that previously instructed to produce accountant's reports, the *solicitor* must immediately notify the *SRA* of the change and provide the name and business address of the new accountancy practice.

Rule 40 – Place of examination

Unless there are exceptional circumstances, the place of examination of a *solicitor's* accounting records, files and other relevant documents must be the *solicitor's* office and not the office of the accountant. This does not prevent an initial electronic transmission of data to the accountant for examination at the accountant's office with a view to reducing the time which needs to be spent at the *solicitor's* office.

Rule 41 – Provision of details of bank accounts, etc.

The accountant must request, and the *solicitor* must provide, details of all accounts kept or operated by the *solicitor* in connection with the *solicitor's* practice at any *bank*, *building society* or other financial institution at any time during the *accounting period* to which the report relates. This includes *client accounts*, *office accounts*, accounts which are not *client accounts* but which contain *client money*, and *clients'* own accounts operated by the *solicitor* as signatory.

Rule 42 – Test procedures

(1)   The accountant must examine the accounting records (including statements and passbooks), *client* and *trust* matter files selected by the accountant as and when appropriate, and other relevant documents of the *solicitor*, and make the following checks and tests:

(a)   confirm that the accounting system in every office of the *solicitor* complies with:

- rule 32 – accounting records for *client accounts*, etc;

- rule 33 – accounting records for clients' own accounts;

and is so designed that:

(i)   an appropriate client ledger account is kept for each *client* (or other person for whom *client money* is received, held or paid) or *trust*;

(ii)   the client ledger accounts show separately from other information details of all *client money* received, held or paid on account of each *client* (or other person for whom *client money* is received, held or paid) or *trust*; and

(iii)   transactions relating to *client money* and any other money dealt with through a *client account* are recorded in the accounting records in a way which distinguishes them from transactions relating to any other money received, held or paid by the *solicitor;*

(b)   make test checks of postings to the client ledger accounts from records of receipts and payments of *client money*, and make test checks of the casts of these accounts and records;

(c)   compare a sample of payments into and from the *client accounts* as shown in *bank* and *building society* statements or passbooks with the *solicitor's* records of receipts and payments of *client money;*

(d)   test check the system of recording *costs* and of making transfers in respect of *costs* from the *client accounts;*

(e)   make a test examination of a selection of documents requested from the *solicitor* in order to confirm:

(i)   that the financial transactions (including those giving rise to transfers from one client ledger account to another) evidenced by such documents comply with Parts A and B of the rules, rule 30 (restrictions on transfers between clients) and rule 31 (executor, trustee or nominee companies); and

(ii)   that the entries in the accounting records reflect those transactions in a manner complying with rule 32;

(f)   subject to paragraph (2) below, extract (or check extractions of) balances on the client ledger accounts during the *accounting period* under review at not fewer than two dates selected by the accountant (one of which may be the last day of the *accounting period*), and at each date:

    (i)   compare the total shown by the client ledger accounts of the liabilities to the *clients* (and other persons for whom *client money* is held) and *trusts* with the cash account balance; and

    (ii)   reconcile that cash account balance with the balances held in the *client accounts*, and accounts which are not *client accounts* but in which *client money* is held, as confirmed direct to the accountant by the relevant *banks*, *building societies* and other financial institutions;

(g)   confirm that reconciliation statements have been made and kept in accordance with rule 32(7) and (9)(a);

(h)   make a test examination of the client ledger accounts to see whether payments from the *client account* have been made on any individual account in excess of money held on behalf of that *client* (or other person for whom *client money* is held) or *trust*;

(i)   check the office ledgers, office cash accounts and the statements provided by the *bank*, *building society* or other financial institution for any *office account* maintained by the *solicitor* in connection with the practice, to see whether any *client money* has been improperly paid into an *office account* or, if properly paid into an *office account* under rule 19(1)(b) or rule 21(1), has been kept there in breach of the rules;

(j)   check the accounting records kept under rule 32(9)(d) and (11) for *client money* held outside a *client account* to ascertain what transactions have been effected in respect of this money and to confirm that the *client* has given appropriate instructions under rule 16(1)(a);

(k)   make a test examination of the client ledger accounts to see whether rule 32(6) (accounting records when acting for both lender and borrower) has been complied with;

(l)   for liquidators, trustees in bankruptcy, *Court of Protection deputies* and trustees of occupational pension schemes, check that records are being kept in accordance with rule 32(8), (9)(c) and (12), and cross-check transactions with *client* or *trust* matter files when appropriate;

(m)   check that statements and passbooks and/or duplicate statements and copies of passbook entries are being kept in accordance with rule 32(9)(b)(ii) and (13) (record-keeping requirements for joint accounts), and cross-check transactions with *client* matter files when appropriate;

(n)   check that statements and passbooks and/or duplicate statements, copies of passbook entries and cheque details are being kept in accordance with rule 33 (record-keeping requirements for clients' own accounts), and cross-check transactions with *client* matter files when appropriate;

(na)   for money withdrawn from *client account* under rule 22(1)(ga), check that records are being kept in accordance with rule 32(8A), (9)(a) and (13A), and cross-check with *client* or *trust* matter files when appropriate;

(o)   check that interest earned on *separate designated client accounts*, and in accounts opened on *clients'* instructions under rule 16(1)(a), is credited in accordance with rule 24(1) and (6)(a), and note (i) to rule 24;

(p)   in the case of private practice only, check that for the period which will be covered by the accountant's report the practice was covered for the purposes of the Solicitors' Indemnity Insurance Rules in respect of its offices in England and Wales by:

- certificates of qualifying insurance outside the assigned risks pool; or

- a policy issued by the assigned risks pool manager; or

- certificates of indemnity cover under the professional requirements of a *registered European lawyer's* home jurisdiction in accordance with paragraph 1 of Appendix 3 to those Rules, together with the *SRA's* written grant of full exemption; or

- certificates of indemnity cover under the professional requirements of a *registered European lawyer's* home jurisdiction plus certificates of a difference in conditions policy with a qualifying insurer under paragraph 2 of Appendix 3 to those Rules, together with the *SRA's* written grant of partial exemption; and

(q)   ask for any information and explanations required as a result of making the above checks and tests.

Extracting balances

(2)   For the purposes of paragraph (1)(f) above, if a *solicitor* uses a computerised or mechanised system of accounting which automatically produces an extraction of all client ledger balances, the accountant need not check all client ledger balances extracted on the list produced by the computer or machine against the individual records of client ledger accounts, provided the accountant:

(a)   confirms that a satisfactory system of control is in operation and the accounting records are in balance;

(b)   carries out a test check of the extraction against the individual records; and

(c)   states in the report that he or she has relied on this exception.

NOTES

(i)   The rules do not require a complete audit of the solicitor's accounts nor do they require the preparation of a profit and loss account or balance sheet.

(ii)   In making the comparisons under rule 42(1)(f), some accountants improperly use credits of one client against debits of another when checking total client liabilities, thus failing to disclose a shortage. A debit balance on a client account when no funds are held for that client results in a shortage which must be disclosed as a result of the comparison.

(iii)   The main purpose of confirming balances direct with banks, etc., under rule 42(1)(f)(ii) is to ensure that the solicitor's records accurately reflect the sums held at the bank. The accountant is not expected to conduct an active search for undisclosed accounts.

(iv)   In checking compliance with rule 22(1)(ga), the accountant should check on a sample basis that the solicitor has complied with rule 22(2A) and is keeping appropriate records in accordance with rules 32(8A), (9)(a) and (13A). The accountant is not expected to judge the adequacy of the steps taken to establish the identity of, and to trace, the rightful owner of the money.

Rule 43 – Departures from guidelines for accounting procedures and systems

The accountant should be aware of the *SRA's* guidelines for accounting procedures and systems (see rule 29), and must note in the accountant's report any substantial departures from the guidelines discovered whilst carrying out work in preparation of the report. (See also rule 44(e).)

Rule 44 – Matters outside the accountant's remit

The accountant is not required:

(a)   to extend his or her enquiries beyond the information contained in the documents produced, supplemented by any information and explanations given by the *solicitor*;

(b)   to enquire into the stocks, shares, other securities or documents of title held by the *solicitor* on behalf of the *solicitor's clients*;

(c)   to consider whether the accounting records of the *solicitor* have been properly written up at any time other than the time at which his or her examination of the accounting records takes place;

(d)   to check compliance with the provisions in rule 24(2) to (5) and (6)(b) on payment of sums in lieu of interest;

(e)   to make a detailed check on compliance with the guidelines for accounting procedures and systems (see rules 29 and 43); or

(f)   to determine the adequacy of the steps taken under paragraphs (a) and (b) of rule 22(2A).

Rule 45 – Privileged documents

A *solicitor*, acting on a *client's* instructions, will normally have the right on the grounds of privilege as between *solicitor* and *client* to decline to produce any document requested by the accountant for the purposes of his or her examination. In these circumstances, the accountant must qualify the report and set out the circumstances.

NOTE

In a recognised body with one or more managers who are not legally qualified, legal professional privilege may not attach to work which is neither done nor supervised by a legally qualified individual – see Legal Services Act 2007, section 190(3) to (7), and Schedule 22, paragraph 17.

Rule 46 – Completion of checklist

The accountant should exercise his or her professional judgment in adopting a suitable "audit" programme, but must also complete and sign a checklist in the form published from time to time by the *SRA*. The *solicitor* must obtain the completed checklist, retain it for at least three years from the date of signature and produce it to the *SRA* on request.

NOTES

(i)   The current checklist appears at Appendix 4. It is issued by the SRA to solicitors at the appropriate time for completion by their reporting accountants.

(ii)   The letter of engagement required by rule 38 imposes a duty on the accountant to hand the completed checklist to the solicitor, to keep a copy for three years and to produce the copy to the SRA on request.

Rule 47 – Form of accountant's report

The accountant must complete and sign his or her report in the form published from time to time by the *SRA*.

NOTES

(i) The current form of accountant's report appears at Appendix 5.

(ii) The form of report is prepared and issued by the SRA to solicitors at the appropriate time for completion by their reporting accountants. Separate reports can be delivered for each principal in a partnership but most firms deliver one report in the name of all the principals. For assistant solicitors, consultants and other employees, see rule 35, notes (vi) and (vii).

(iia) An incorporated practice will deliver only one report, on behalf of the company and its directors, or on behalf of the LLP and its members – see rule 35(1).

(iii) Although it may be agreed that the accountant send the report direct to the SRA, the responsibility for delivery is that of the solicitor. The form of report requires the accountant to confirm that either a copy of the report has been sent to each of the persons (including bodies corporate) to whom the report relates, or a copy of the report has been sent to a named partner on behalf of all the partners in the firm. A similar confirmation is required in respect of the directors of a recognised body which is a company, or the members of a recognised body which is an LLP.

(iv) A reporting accountant is not required to report on trivial breaches due to clerical errors or mistakes in book-keeping, provided that they have been rectified on discovery and the accountant is satisfied that no client suffered any loss as a result.

(v) In many practices, clerical and book-keeping errors will arise. In the majority of cases these may be classified by the reporting accountant as trivial breaches. However, a "trivial breach" cannot be precisely defined. The amount involved, the nature of the breach, whether the breach is deliberate or accidental, how often the same breach has occurred, and the time outstanding before correction (especially the replacement of any shortage) are all factors which should be considered by the accountant before deciding whether a breach is trivial.

(vi) The SRA receives a number of reports which are qualified only by reference to trivial breaches, but which show a significant difference between liabilities to clients and client money held in client and other accounts. An explanation for this difference, from either the accountant or the solicitor, must be given.

(vii) Accountants' reports should be sent to the Information Directorate.

(viii) For direct reporting by the accountant to the SRA in cases of concern, see rule 38 and note (i) to that rule.

Rule 48 – Practices with two or more places of business

If a practice has two or more offices:

(a) separate reports may be delivered in respect of the different offices; and

(b) separate *accounting periods* may be adopted for different offices, provided that:

    (i) separate reports are delivered;

    (ii) every office is covered by a report delivered within six months of the end of its *accounting period*; and

    (iii) there are no gaps between the *accounting periods* covered by successive reports for any particular office or offices.

Rule 49 – Waivers

The *SRA* may waive in writing in any particular case or cases any of the provisions of Part F of the rules, and may revoke any waiver.

NOTE

Applications for waivers should be made to the Information Directorate. In appropriate cases, solicitors may be granted a waiver of the obligation to deliver an accountant's report (see rule 35, and note (ix) to that rule). The circumstances in which a waiver of any other provision of Part F would be given must be extremely rare.

Part G – Commencement

Rule 50 – Commencement

The Solicitors' Accounts Rules 1998 took effect on 22 July 1998 and had to be implemented by 1 May 2000. They replaced the Solicitors' Accounts Rules 1991, the Solicitors' Accounts (Legal Aid Temporary Provision) Rule 1992 and the Accountant's Report Rules 1991.

Appendix 1 – Flowchart – effect of Solicitors' Accounts Rules 1998

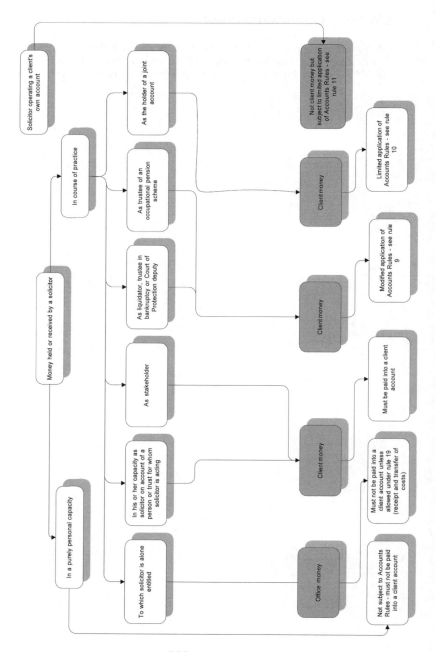

Appendix 2 – Special situations – what applies

		Is it client money?	Subject to reconciliations?	Keep books?	Retain statements?	Subject to accountant's report?	Produce records to SRA?	Interest?	Retain records generally?	Central records?	Subject to reporting accountant's comparisons?
1	R.16(1)(a) a/cs in solicitor's name (not client a/c)	Yes	Yes	Yes – r.32(1)(a) and 32(2)	Yes – r.32(9)	Yes	Yes	Yes – r.24	Yes – r.32(9)	Statements or register – r.32(11), bills – r.32(8)	Yes – r.42(1)(f)
2	R.16(1)(b) a/cs in name of client – not operated by solicitor	No	No	No – record solicitor's receipt and payment only	No	No	No	No – all interest earned for client – r.24, note (iii)	No – except record of solicitor's receipt and payment	Bills – r.32(8)	No
3	R.16(1)(b) a/cs in name of client – operated by solicitor	No	No	No – record solicitor's receipt and payment only	Yes – r.33	Limited – r.42(1)(n)	Yes – r.11	No – all interest earned for client – r.24, note (iii)	No – except record of solicitor's receipt and payment	Statements – r.33, Bills – r.32(8)	No

4	Liquidators, trustees in bankruptcy and Court of Protection deputies	Yes – r.9	No – r.9	Modified – statutory records – r.9	Yes – r.9 and r.32(9)(c)	Limited – r.42(1)(l)	Yes – r.9	No – r.9 – comply with statutory rules	Yes – modified r.32(9)(c)	Yes – r.32(12) Bills – r.32(8)	No – r.9
5	Trustees of occupational pension schemes	Yes – r.9	No – r.9	Modified – statutory records – r.9	Yes – r.9 and r.32(9)(c)	Limited – r.42(1)(l)	Yes – r.9	No – r.9 – comply with statutory rules	Yes – modified r.32(9)(c)	Yes – r.32(12) Bills – r.32(8)	No – r.9
6	Joint accounts – r.10	Yes – r.10	No – r.10	No – r.10	Yes – r.10 and r.32(9)(b)(ii)	Limited – r.42(1)(m)	Yes – r.10	No. For joint a/c with client, all interest to client (r.24, note (ix)); for joint a/c with sol. depends on agreement	No – r.10	Statements – r.32(13) Bills – r.32(8)	No – r.10
7	Solicitor acting under power of attorney	Yes	Yes	Yes	Yes	Yes	Yes	Yes	Yes	Bills – r.32(8)	Yes

8	Solicitor operates client's own a/c e.g. under power of attorney – r.11	No	No	No	Yes – r.33	Limited – r.42(1)(n)	Yes – r.11	No – all interest earned for client (r.24, note (iii))	No – r.11	Statements – r.33 Bills – r.32(8)	No
9	Exempt solicitors under r.5	No	No	No	No	No	No	No	No	No	No

Appendix 3 – SRA guidelines – accounting procedures and systems

1. Introduction

1.1 These guidelines, published under rule 29 of the Solicitors' Accounts Rules 1998, are intended to be a benchmark or broad statement of good practice requirements which should be present in an effective regime for the proper control of client money. They should therefore be of positive assistance to firms in establishing or reviewing appropriate procedures and systems. They do not override, or detract from the need to comply fully with, the Accounts Rules.

1.2 References to partners or firms in the guidelines are intended to include sole practitioners, and recognised bodies and their managers.

2. General

2.1 Compliance with the Accounts Rules is the equal responsibility of all partners in a firm. They should establish policies and systems to ensure that the firm complies fully with the rules. Responsibility for day to day supervision may be delegated to one or more partners to enable effective control to be exercised. Delegation of total responsibility to a cashier or book-keeper is not acceptable.

2.2 The firm should hold a copy of the current version of the Solicitors' Accounts Rules and/or have ready access to the current on-line version. The person who maintains the books of account must have a full knowledge of the requirements of the rules and the accounting requirements of solicitors' firms.

2.3 Proper books of account should be maintained on the double-entry principle. They should be legible, up to date and contain narratives with the entries which identify and/or provide adequate information about the transaction. Entries should be made in chronological order and the current balance should be shown on client ledger accounts, or be readily ascertainable, in accordance with rule 32(5).

2.4 Ledger accounts for clients, other persons or trusts should include the name of the client or other person or trust and contain a heading which provides a description of the matter or transaction.

2.5 Separate designated client accounts should be brought within the ambit of the systems and procedures for the control of client money, including reconciliations (see 5.4 below).

2.6 Manual systems for recording client money are capable of complying with these guidelines and there is no requirement on firms to adopt computerised systems. A computer system, with suitable support procedures will, however, usually provide an efficient means of producing the accounts and associated control information.

2.7 If a computer system is introduced care must be taken to ensure:

(1) that balances transferred from the old books of account are reconciled with the opening balances held on the new system before day to day operation commences;

(2) that the new system operates correctly before the old system is abandoned. This may require a period of parallel running of the old and new systems and the satisfactory reconciliation of the two sets of records before the old system ceases.

2.8 The firm should ensure that office account entries in relation to each client or trust matter are maintained up to date as well as the client account entries. Credit balances on office account in respect of client or trust matters should be fully investigated.

2.9   The firm should operate a system to identify promptly situations which may require the payment of interest to clients.

3. Receipt of client money

3.1   The firm should have procedures for identifying client money, including cash, when received in the firm, and for promptly recording the receipt of the money either in the books of account or a register for later posting to the client cash book and ledger accounts. The procedures should cover money received through the post, electronically or direct by fee earners or other personnel. They should also cover the safekeeping of money prior to payment to bank.

3.2   The firm should have a system which ensures that client money is paid promptly into a client account.

3.3   The firm should have a system for identifying money which should not be in a client account and for transferring it without delay.

3.4   The firm should determine a policy and operate a system for dealing with money which is a mixture of office money and client money, in compliance with rules 19–21.

4. Payments from client account

4.1   The firm should have clear procedures for ensuring that all withdrawals from client accounts are properly authorised. In particular, suitable persons, consistent with rule 23(1), should be named for the following purposes:

(1)   authorisation of internal payment vouchers;

(2)   signing client account cheques;

(3)   authorising telegraphic or electronic transfers.

No other personnel should be allowed to authorise or sign the documents.

4.1A   The firm should establish clear procedures and systems for ensuring that persons permitted to authorise the withdrawal of client money from a client account have an appropriate understanding of the requirements of the rules, including rules 22 and 23 which set out when and how a withdrawal from client account may properly be made.

4.2   Persons nominated for the purpose of authorising internal payment vouchers should, for each payment, ensure there is supporting evidence showing clearly the reason for the payment, and the date of it. Similarly, persons signing cheques and authorising transfers should ensure there is a suitable voucher or other supporting evidence to support the payment.

4.3   The firm should have a system for checking the balances on client ledger accounts to ensure no debit balances occur. Where payments are to be made other than out of cleared funds, clear policies and procedures must be in place to ensure that adequate risk assessment is applied.

N.B. If incoming payments are ultimately dishonoured, a debit balance will arise, in breach of the rules, and full replacement of the shortfall will be required under rule 7. See also rule 22, notes (v) and (vi).

4.4   The firm should establish systems for the transfer of costs from client account to office account in accordance with rule 19(2) and (3). Normally transfers should be made only on the basis of rendering a bill or written notification. The payment from the client account should be by way of a cheque or transfer in favour of the firm or sole principal – see rule 23(3).

4.5   The firm should establish policies and operate systems to control and record accurately any transfers between clients of the firm. Where these arise as a result of loans between clients, the written authority of both the lender and borrower must be obtained in accordance with rule 30(2).

APPENDIX 3

4.6   The firm should establish policies and operate systems for the timely closure of files and the prompt accounting for surplus balances in accordance with rule 15(3).

4.7   The firm should establish systems in accordance with rule 15(4) to keep clients (or other people on whose behalf money is held) regularly informed when funds are retained for a specified reason at the end of a matter or the substantial conclusion of a matter.

5. Overall control of client accounts

5.1   The firm should maintain control of all its bank and building society accounts opened for the purpose of holding client money. In the case of a joint account, a suitable degree of control should be exercised.

5.2   Central records or central registers must be kept in respect of:

(1)   accounts held for client money, which are not client accounts (rules 16(1)(a), 17(ca) and 32(11));

(2)   practice as a liquidator, trustee in bankruptcy, Court of Protection deputy or trustee of an occupational pension scheme (rules 9 and 32(12));

(3)   joint accounts (rules 10 and 32(13));

(4)   dividend payments received by an executor, trustee or nominee company as nominee (rules 31(2) and 32(14)); and

(5)   clients' own accounts (rules 11, 16(1)(b) and 33(2)).

5.3   In addition, there should be a master list of all:

●   general client accounts;

●   separate designated client accounts;

●   accounts held in respect of 5.2 above; and

●   office accounts.

The master list should show the current status of each account; e.g. currently in operation or closed with date of closure.

5.4   The firm should operate a system to ensure that accurate reconciliations of the client accounts are carried out at least every five weeks or, in the case of passbook-operated separate designated client accounts for money held by solicitor-trustees, every 14 weeks. In particular it should ensure that:

(1)   a full list of client ledger balances is produced. Any debit balances should be listed, fully investigated and rectified immediately. The total of any debit balances cannot be "netted off" against the total of credit balances;

(2)   a full list of unpresented cheques is produced;

(3)   a list of outstanding lodgements is produced;

(4)   formal statements are produced reconciling the client account cash book balances, aggregate client ledger balances and the client bank accounts. All unresolved differences must be investigated and, where appropriate, corrective action taken;

(5)   a partner checks the reconciliation statement and any corrective action, and ensures that enquiries are made into any unusual or apparently unsatisfactory items or still unresolved matters.

5.5   Where a computerised system is used, the firm should have clear policies, systems and procedures to control access to client accounts by determining the personnel who should have "write to" and "read only" access. Passwords should be held confidentially by designated personnel and changed regularly to maintain security. Access to the system should not unreasonably be restricted to a single person nor should more people than necessary be given access.

5.6 The firm should establish policies and systems for the retention of the accounting records to ensure:

- books of account, reconciliations, bills, bank statements and passbooks are kept for at least 6 years;

- paid cheques, digital images of paid cheques and other authorities for the withdrawal of money from a client account are kept for at least 2 years;

- other vouchers and internal expenditure authorisation documents relating directly to entries in the client account books are kept for at least 2 years.

5.7 The firm should ensure that unused client account cheques are stored securely to prevent unauthorised access. Blank cheques should not be pre-signed. Any cancelled cheques should be retained.

Appendix 4 – Reporting Accountant's Checklist

The following items have been tested to satisfy the examination requirements under rules 41–43, with the results as indicated. Where the position has been found to be unsatisfactory as a result of these tests, further details have been reported in section 6 of this checklist or reported by separate appendix.

Name of practice

Results of test checks:

1. For all client money	Were any breaches discovered? (Tick the appropriate column.)		If "yes" should breaches be noted in the accountant's report?		Cross reference to audit file documentation.
(a) **Book-keeping system for every office:**	Yes	No	Yes	No	
(i) The accounting records satisfactorily distinguish client money from all other money dealt with by the firm.					
(ii) A separate ledger account is maintained for each client and trust (excepting section (l) below) and the particulars of all client money received, held or paid on account of each client and trust, including funds held on separate designated deposits, or elsewhere, are recorded.					
(iii) The client ledgers for clients and trusts show a current balance at all times, or the current balance is readily ascertainable.					
(iv) A record of all bills of costs and written notifications has been maintained, which distinguishes profit costs from disbursements, either in the form of a central record or a file of copies of such bills.					
(b) **Postings to ledger accounts and casts:**	Yes	No	Yes	No	
(i) Postings to ledger accounts for clients and trusts from records of receipts and payments are correct.					
(ii) Casts of ledger accounts for clients and trusts and receipts and payments records are correct.					
(iii) Postings have been recorded in chronological sequence with the date being that of the initiation of the transaction.					
(c) **Receipts and payments of client money:**	Yes	No	Yes	No	
(i) Sample receipts and payments of client money as shown in bank and building society statements have been compared with the firm's records of receipts and payments of client money, and are correct.					

1. continued.....		Were any breaches discovered? (Tick the appropriate column.)		If "yes" should breaches be noted in the accountant;'s report?		Cross reference to audit file documentation.
(ii)	Sample paid cheques, or digital images of the front and back of sample paid cheques, have been obtained and details agreed to receipts and payment records.					
(d)	**System of recording costs and making transfers:**	Yes	No	Yes	No	
(i)	The firm's system of recording costs has been ascertained and is suitable.					
(ii)	Costs have been drawn only where required for or towards payment of the firm's costs where there has been sent to the client a bill of costs or other written notification of the amount of the costs.					
(e)	**Examination of documents for verification of transactions and entries in accounting records:**	Yes	No	Yes	No	
(i)	Make a test examination of a number of client and trust files.					
(ii)	All client and trust files requested for examination were made available.					
(iii)	The financial transactions as detailed on client and trust files and other documentation (including transfers from one ledger account to another) were valid and appropriately authorised in accordance with Parts A and B of the Solicitors' Accounts Rules 1998 (SAR).					
(iv)	The financial transactions evidenced by documents on the client and trust files were correctly recorded in the books of account in a manner complying with Part D SAR.					
(f)	**Extraction of client ledger balances for clients and trusts:**	Yes	No	Yes	No	
(i)	The extraction of client ledger balances for clients and trusts has been checked for no fewer than two separate dates in the period subject to this report.					
(ii)	The total liabilities to clients and trusts as shown by such ledger accounts has been compared to the cash account balance(s) at each of the separate dates selected in (f)(i) above and agreed.					
(iii)	The cash account balance(s) at each of the dates selected has/have been reconciled to the balance(s) in client bank account and elsewhere as confirmed directly by the relevant banks and building societies.					
(g)	**Reconciliations:**	Yes	No	Yes	No	
(i)	During the accounting year under review, reconciliations have been carried out at least every five weeks or, in the case of passbook-operated separate designated client accounts for money held by solicitor-trustees, every fourteen weeks.					
(ii)	Each reconciliation is in the form of a statement set out in a logical format which is likely to reveal any discrepancies.					
(iii)	Reconciliation statements have been retained.					
(iv)	On entries in an appropriate sample of reconciliation statements:	Yes	No	Yes	No	
	(A) All accounts containing client money have been included.					
	(B) All ledger account balances for clients and trusts as at the reconciliation date have been listed and totalled.					
	(C) No debit balances on ledger accounts for clients and trusts have been included in the total.					

1. continued.......	Were any breaches discovered? (Tick the appropriate column.)		If "yes" should breaches be noted in the accountant,'s report?		Cross reference to audit file documentation.
(D) The cash account balance(s) for clients and trusts is/are correctly calculated by the accurate and up to date recording of transactions.					
(E) The client bank account totals for clients and trusts are complete and correct being calculated by:					
the closing balance **plus** an accurate and complete list of outstanding lodgements **less** an accurate and complete list of unpresented cheques.					
(v) Each reconciliation selected under paragraph (iv) above has been achieved by the comparison and agreement **without adjusting or balancing entries** of:					
total of ledger balances for clients and trusts;					
total of cash account balances for clients and trusts;					
total of client bank accounts.					
(vi) In the event of debit balances existing on ledger accounts for clients and trusts, the firm has investigated promptly and corrected the position satisfactorily.					
(vii) In the event of the reconciliations selected under paragraph (iv) above not being in agreement, the differences have been investigated and corrected promptly.					
(h) Payments of client money:	Yes	No	Yes	No	
Make a test examination of the ledger accounts for clients and trusts in order to ascertain whether payments have been made on any individual account in excess of money held on behalf of that client or trust.					
(i) Office accounts – client money:	Yes	No	Yes	No	
(i) Check such office ledger and cash account and bank and building society statements as the firm maintains with a view to ascertaining whether any client money has not been paid into a client account.					
(ii) Investigate office ledger credit balances and ensure that such balances do not include client money incorrectly held in office account.					
(j) Client money not held in client account:	Yes	No	Yes	No	
(i) Have sums not held on client account been identified?					
(ii) Has the reason for holding such sums outside client account been established?					
(iii) Has a written client agreement been made if appropriate?					
(iv) Are central records or a central register kept for client money held outside client account on the client's instructions?					
(k) Rule 30 – inter-client transfers:	Yes	No	Yes	No	
Make test checks of inter-client transfers to ensure that rule 30 has been complied with.					
(l) Rule 32(6) – acting for borrower and lender:	Yes	No	Yes	No	
Make a test examination of the client ledger accounts in order to ascertain whether rule 32(6) SAR has been complied with, where the firm acts for both borrower and lender in a conveyancing transaction.					
(m) Rule 32(14) – executor, trustee or nominee companies:	Yes	No	Yes	No	
Is a central book of dividend instruction letters kept?					

1. continued.......	Were any breaches discovered? (Tick the appropriate column.)		If 'yes' should breaches be noted in the accountant;'s report?		Cross reference to audit file documentation.
(n) **Information and explanations:**	Yes	No	Yes	No	
All information and explanations required have been received and satisfactorily cleared.					

2. Liquidators, trustees in bankruptcy, Court of Protection deputies and trustees of occupational pension schemes (rule 9).	Were any breaches discovered? (Tick the appropriate column.)		If 'yes' should breaches be noted in the accountant's report?		Cross reference to audit file documentation
	Yes	No	Yes	No	
(a) A record of all bills of costs and written notifications has been maintained which distinguishes profit costs from disbursements, either in the form of a central record or a file of copies of such bills or notifications.					
(b) Records kept under rule 9 including any statements, passbooks and other accounting records originating outside the firm's office have been retained.					
(c) Records kept under rule 9 are kept together centrally, or a central register is kept of the appointments.					

3. Joint accounts (rule 10)	Were any breaches discovered? (Tick the appropriate column.)		If 'yes' should breaches be noted in the accountant's report?		Cross reference to audit file documentation
	Yes	No	Yes	No	
(a) A record of all bills of costs and written notifications has been maintained which distinguishes profit costs from disbursements, either in the form of a central record or a file of copies of such bills or notifications.					
(b) Statements and passbooks and/or duplicate statements or copies of passbook entries have been retained.					
(c) Statements, passbooks, duplicate statements and copies of passbook entries are kept together centrally, or a central register of all joint accounts is kept.					

4. Clients' own accounts (rule 11)	Were any breaches discovered? (Tick the appropriate column.)		If 'yes' should breaches be noted in the accountant's report?		Cross reference to audit file documentation
	Yes	No	Yes	No	
(a) Statements and passbooks and/or duplicate statements, copies of passbook entries and cheque details have been retained.					
(b) Statements and passbooks and/or duplicate statements, copies of passbook entries and cheque details are kept together centrally, or a central register of clients' own accounts is kept.					

5.	SRA guidelines – accounting procedures and systems		Yes	No
	Discovery of substantial departures from the guidelines? *If "yes" please give details below.*			

6. Please give further details of unsatisfactory items below. (Please attach additional schedules as required.)

Signature	Date
Reporting Accountant	Print Name

Appendix 5 – Accountant's Report Form

AR1

Accountant's Report Form

Under rule 35 of the Solicitors' Accounts Rules 1998 (SAR) an annual accountant's report is required from:

◆ a sole practitioner, if the practitioner or any of his or her employees have held or received client money, or operated a client's own account as signatory;

◆ a recognised body and its managers, if the recognised body or any of its managers or employees have held or received client money, or operated a client's own account as signatory;

◆ a solicitor or registered European lawyer (REL) in in-house practice who has held or received client money, or operated a client's own account as signatory, unless exempt under rule 5;

◆ a solicitor, REL or registered foreign lawyer (RFL) who was a manager or employee of a partnership which should have been a recognised body but was not, if the partnership or any of those managers or employees held or received client money, or operated a client's own account as signatory.

"Client money" in these notes and in the form includes controlled trust money held or received before 31 March 2009. As from 31 March 2009, that type of money is included in the definition of "client money".

A "recognised body" is a partnership, limited liability partnership (LLP) or company recognised by the SRA under section 9 of the Administration of Justice Act 1985. A "manager" is a partner in a partnership, a member of an LLP or a director of a company. In the case of a partnership, "manager" includes any person held out as a partner, including a "salaried partner", "associate partner" or "local partner". As from 1 July 2009 a sole practitioner has to be recognised by the SRA as a "recognised sole practitioner".

The managers and employees who, along with the recognised body, must be named on a recognised body's report, are those who are managers as at the date the report is signed by the accountant (or were managers as at the last date on which the report should have been delivered under rule 35, if the report is signed after that date) and, in addition:

◆ in the case of a partnership, any person who was a manager at any time during the report period, and any person who, as an employee during that period, held or received client money (e.g. as a named trustee) or operated a client's own account as signatory;

◆ in the case of an LLP or company, any person who, as a manager or employee during the report period, held or received client money (e.g. as a named trustee) or operated a client's own account as signatory.

The accountant who prepares the report must be qualified under rule 37 of the SAR and is required to report on compliance with Parts A and B, rule 24(1) of Part C, and Part D of the SAR.

When a practice ceases to hold and/or receive client money (and/or to operate any client's own account as signatory), either on closure of the practice or for any other reason, the practice must deliver a final report within six months of ceasing to hold and/or receive client money (and/or to operate any client's own account as signatory), unless the SRA requires earlier delivery.

When a practice closes but the ceased practice continues to hold or receive client money during the process of dealing with outstanding costs and unattributable or unreturnable funds, the SAR, including the obligation to deliver accountant's reports, will continue to apply. On ceasing to hold or receive client money, the ceased practice must deliver a final report within six months of ceasing to hold and/or receive client money, unless the SRA requires earlier delivery.

If you need any assistance completing this form please contact Information Services on 0870 606 2555 or by email at **contactcentre@sra.org.uk**. Our lines are open from 09.00 to 17.00 Monday to Friday. Please note calls may be monitored/recorded for training purposes.

If you are calling from overseas please use +44 (0) 1527 504450. Note that reports in respect of practice from an office outside England and Wales are submitted under rule 15.27 of the Solicitors' Code of Conduct 2007, and not under the SAR. Specimen form **AR2** may be used for such reports.

1

1 Firm details Insert here all names used by the firm or in-house practice in respect of practice from the offices covered by this report. This must include the registered name of a recognised body which is an LLP or company, and the name under which a partnership or sole practitioner is recognised.

Firm name(s) during the reporting period		SRA no	

Report Period from		to	

Is this the practice's final report?	Yes		No	

2 Firm's address(es) covered by this report All address(es) of the practice during the reporting period must be covered by an accountant's report, except those offices outside England and Wales not required under rule 15 of the Solicitors' Code of Conduct 2007 to deliver a report.

Address(es)

Office Type (Head office / branch office)		Office Type (Head office / branch office)	

PLEASE COMPLETE ONE ONLY OF SECTIONS 3A, 3B, 3C AND 3D AS APPROPRIATE.

3A Sole practice. Please list the name of the sole practitioner and any consultant or employee who held or received client money, or operated a client's own account as signatory, during the report period.

Surname	Initials	SRA No.	Category – sole solicitor, sole REL, consultant, employee

2

3B **Recognised body (partnership).** Please list the names of all the "managers", whether individuals or bodies corporate, at the relevant date (date report is signed or due date for delivery); and any person who was a "manager" at any time during the report period; and any consultant or employee who held or received client money (e.g. as a named trustee), or operated a client's own account as signatory, during the report period; (see introductory notes).

Surname or corporate name	Initials	SRA No.	Category – manager, corporate manager, consultant, employee	Quote date if ceased to hold or receive client money

3

3C **Recognised body (LLP or company).** Please list the names of all the "managers", whether individuals or bodies corporate, at the relevant date (date report is signed or due date for delivery); and any "manager", consultant or employee who held or received client money (e.g. as a named trustee), or operated a client's own account as signatory, during the report period; (see introductory notes).

Surname or corporate name	Initials	SRA No.	Category – manager, corporate manager, consultant, employee

3D **In-house practice.** Please list the name of every principal solicitor / REL who held or received client money at any time during the report period.

Surname	Initials	SRA No.	Category – solicitor, REL	Quote date if ceased to hold or receive client money

4

4 Comparison dates

The results of the comparisons required under rule 42(1)(f) of the Solicitors' Accounts Rules 1998, at the dates selected by me/us were:

(a) at _____ *(insert date 1)*

 (i) Liabilities to clients and trusts (and other persons for whom client money is held) as shown by ledger accounts for client and trust matters. £ _____

 (ii) Cash held in client account, and client money held in any account other than a client account, after allowances for lodgments cleared after date and for outstanding cheques. £ _____

 (iii) Difference between (i) and (ii) (if any). £ _____

(b) at _____ *(insert date 2)*

 (i) Liabilities to clients and trusts (and other persons for whom client money is held) as shown by ledger accounts for client and trust matters. £ _____

 (ii) Cash held in client account, and client money held in any account other than a client account, after allowances for lodgments cleared after date and for outstanding cheques. £ _____

 (iii) Difference between (i) and (ii) (if any). £ _____

Notes:

The figure to be shown in 4(a)(i) and 4(b)(i) above is the total of credit balances, without adjustment for debit balances (unless capable of proper set off, i.e. being in respect of the same client), or for receipts and payments not capable of allocation to individual ledger accounts.

An explanation must be given for any significant difference shown at 4(a)(iii) or 4(b)(iii) - see note (vi) to rule 47 of Solicitors' Accounts Rules 1998. If appropriate, it would be helpful if the explanation is given here.

5

5 Qualified report

Have you found it necessary to make this report 'Qualified'?   No ☐   If "No" proceed to section 6

Yes ☐   If "Yes" please complete the
relevant boxes

(a)   Please indicate in the space provided any matters (other than trivial breaches) in respect of which it appears to you that there has been
a failure to comply with the provisions of Parts A and B, rule 24(1) of Part C, and Part D of the Solicitors' Accounts Rules 1998 and, in
the case of private practice only, any part of the period covered by this report for which the practice does not appear to have been
covered in respect of its offices in England and Wales by the insurance/indemnity documents referred to in rule 42(1)(p) of the Solicitors'
Accounts Rules 1998 *(continue on an additional sheet if necessary)*:

(b)   Please indicate in the space provided any matters in respect of which you have been unable to satisfy yourself and the reasons for
that inability, e.g. because a client's file is not available *(continue on an additional sheet if necessary)*.

6 Accountant details   The reporting accountant must be qualified in accordance with rule 37 of the Solicitors' Accounts Rules 1998.

Name of accountant	Professional body
	Accountant membership/ registration number
Recognised Supervisory Body under which individual/firm is a registered auditor	Reference number of individual/firm audit registration(s)
Firm name	
Firm address	

7 Declaration

In compliance with Part F of the Solicitors' Accounts Rules 1998, I/we have examined to the extent required by rule 42 of those rules, the accounting records, files and other documents produced to me/us in respect of the above practice.

In so far as an opinion can be based on this limited examination, I am/we are satisfied that during the above mentioned period the practice has complied with the provisions of Parts A and B, rule 24(1) of Part C, and Part D of the Solicitors' Accounts Rules 1998 except so far as concerns:

    (i)   certain trivial breaches due to clerical errors or mistakes in book-keeping, all of which were rectified on discovery and none of which, I am/we are satisfied, resulted in any loss to any client or trust; and/or

    (ii)   any matters detailed in section 5 of this report.

In the case of private practice only, I/we certify that, in so far as can be ascertained from a limited examination of the insurance/indemnity documents produced to me/us, the practice was covered in respect of its offices in England and Wales for the period covered by this report by the insurance/indemnity documents referred to in rule 42(1)(p) of the Solicitors' Accounts Rules 1998, except as stated in section 5 of this report.

I/we have relied on the exception contained in rule 42(2) of the Solicitors' Accounts Rules 1998.   <u>Yes</u>

Rule 42(2) of the Solicitors' Accounts Rules 1998 states: "For the purposes of paragraph(1)(f) above [extraction of balances] if a solicitor uses a computerised or mechanised system of accounting which automatically produces an extraction of all client ledger balances, the accountant need not check all client ledger balances extracted on the list produced by the computer or machine against the individual records of client ledger accounts, provided the accountant:

(a)   confirms that a satisfactory system of control is in operation and the accounting records are in balance;

(b)   carries out a test check of the extraction against the individual records; and

(c)   specifies in the report that he or she has relied on this exception."

In carrying out work in preparation of this report, I/we have discovered the following substantial departures from the SRA's current Guidelines for Accounting Procedures and Systems (*continue on an additional sheet if necessary*):

7

346

Please tick the "Yes" or "No" box for the following items (i) to (v) to show whether, so far as you are aware, the relevant statement applies in respect of yourself or any principal, director (in the case of a company), member (in the case of an LLP) or employee of your accountancy practice. *Give details if appropriate.*

		Yes	No
(i)	Any of the parties mentioned above is related to any solicitor(s)/REL(s)/RFL(s) or other manager(s) to whom this report relates.		

		Yes	No
(ii)	Any of the parties mentioned above normally maintained, on a regular basis, the accounting records to which this report relates.		

		Yes	No
(iii)	Any of the parties mentioned above, or the practice, places substantial reliance for referral of clients on the practice to which this report relates.		

		Yes	No
(iv)	Any of the parties mentioned above, or the practice, is a client or former client of the practice to which this report relates.		

		Yes	No
(v)	There are other circumstances which might affect my independence in preparing this report.		

The information is intended to help the SRA to identify circumstances which might make it difficult to give an independent report. Answering "Yes" to any part of this section does not disqualify the accountant from making the report.

Information within the accountant's personal knowledge should always be disclosed. Detailed investigations are not necessary but reasonable enquiries should be made of those directly involved in the work.

8

I/we have completed and signed the checklist and retained a copy. The original checklist has been sent to either each of the persons listed in Section 3 or to one of them on behalf of them all.

I/we confirm that a copy of this report has been sent to (* delete as appropriate):

(a)   * Each of the persons listed in Section 3; or

(b)   * The following manager in the recognised body, on behalf of all the managers in the recognised body:

The form should then be signed and dated. The report can be signed in the name of the firm of accountants of which the accountant is a partner (in the case of a partnership) or director (in the case of a company) or member (in the case of an LLP) or employee. Particulars of the individual accountant signing the report must be given in section 6.

Please note that if this report is not completed by an accountant with the qualifications required under rule 37 of the Solicitors' Accounts Rules 1998 it will not be accepted and will be returned to the firm for which the report has been submitted.

Date	
Signature	
Name (Block Capitals)	

Please return this form to: Information Directorate
Solicitors Regulation Authority
Ipsley Court
Berrington Close
Redditch
Worcestershire
B98 0TD

OR   DX 19114 Redditch

The reporting accountant's checklist should be retained by the legal practice for at least three years, and not submitted with this report.

9

The Solicitors' Financial Services (Scope) Rules 2001

[Law Society copyright. For the latest updates to the material, please see www.sra.org.uk.]

The Solicitors' Financial Services (Scope) Rules 2001

[Last amended 20 January 2010]

Contents

1. Purpose

2. Application

3. Prohibited activities

4. Basic conditions

5. Other restrictions

6. Effect of a breach of these rules

7. Repeal and commencement

8. Interpretation

These rules, dated 18 July 2001, are made under section 31 of the Solicitors Act 1974 and section 9 of the Administration of Justice Act 1985 with the concurrence of the Master of the Rolls under those sections and the concurrence, where requisite, of the Lord Chancellor under paragraph 16 of Schedule 22 to the Legal Services Act 2007, regulating the practices of:

- solicitors and recognised bodies in any part of the world,

- registered European lawyers in any part of the United Kingdom, and

- registered foreign lawyers in England and Wales,

in carrying out "regulated activities" in, into or from the United Kingdom.

1. Purpose

(1) The Law Society is a designated professional body under Part XX of *the Act*, and *firms* may therefore carry on certain *regulated activities* without being regulated by the *FSA*, if they can meet the conditions specified in section 327 of *the Act*. As a designated professional body the Law Society is required to make rules governing the carrying on by *firms* of *regulated activities*. The purpose of these rules is to set out the scope of the *regulated activities* which may be undertaken by *firms* which are not regulated by the *FSA*.

(2) These rules:

- prohibit *firms* which are not regulated by the *FSA* from carrying on certain *regulated activities*;

- set out the basic conditions which those *firms* must satisfy when carrying on any *regulated activities*;

- set out other restrictions on *regulated activities* carried on by those *firms*.

2. Application

These rules apply only to *firms* which are not regulated by the *FSA*.

3. Prohibited activities

A *firm* must not carry on, or agree to carry on, any of the following activities:

(a)   *market making* in *investments*;

(b)   *buying*, selling, subscribing for or underwriting *investments* as principal where the *firm*:

   (i)   holds itself out as engaging in the business of *buying* such *investments* with a view to selling them;

   (ii)   holds itself out as engaging in the business of underwriting *investments* of the kind to which the *transaction* relates; or

   (iii)   regularly solicits members of the public with the purpose of inducing them, as principals or agents, to enter into *transactions* and the *transaction* is entered into as a result of the *firm* having solicited members of the public in that manner.

(c)   *buying* or selling *investments* with a view to stabilising or maintaining the market price of the *investments*;

(d)   acting as a *stakeholder pension scheme manager*;

(e)   entering into a *broker funds arrangement*;

(f)   effecting and carrying out *contracts of insurance* as principal;

(g)   establishing, operating or winding up a collective investment scheme;

(h)   establishing, operating or winding up a *stakeholder pension scheme* or a *personal pension scheme*;

(i)   managing the underwriting capacity of a Lloyds syndicate as a managing agent at Lloyds;

(j)   advising a person to become a member of a particular Lloyd's syndicate;

(k)   entering as provider into a *funeral plan contract*;

(l)   entering into a *regulated mortgage contract* as lender or administering a *regulated mortgage contract* (unless this is in the *firm's* capacity as a trustee or personal representative and the borrower is a beneficiary under the trust, will or intestacy);

(m)   entering into a *regulated home purchase plan* as provider or administering a *regulated home purchase plan* (unless this is in the *firm's* capacity as a trustee or personal representative and the *home purchaser* is a beneficiary under the trust, will or intestacy);

(n)   entering into a *regulated home reversion plan* as a provider or administering a *regulated home reversion plan* (unless this is in the *firm's* capacity as a trustee or personal representative and the *reversion seller* is a beneficiary under the trust, will or intestacy); or

(o)   entering into a *regulated sale and rent back agreement* as an *agreement provider* or administering a *regulated sale and rent back agreement* (unless this is in the *firm's* capacity as a trustee or personal representative and the *agreement seller* is a beneficiary under the trust, will or intestacy).

4. Basic conditions

A *firm* which carries on any *regulated activities* must ensure that:

(a) the activities arise out of, or are complementary to, the provision of a particular *professional service* to a particular client;

(b) the manner of the provision by the *firm* of any service in the course of carrying on the activities is incidental to the provision by the *firm* of *professional services*;

(c) the *firm* accounts to the *client* for any pecuniary reward or other advantage which the *firm* receives from a third party;

(d) the activities are not of a description, nor do they relate to an *investment* of a description, specified in any order made by the Treasury under section 327(6) of *the Act*;

(e) the *firm* does not carry on, or hold itself out as carrying on, a *regulated activity* other than one which is allowed by these rules or one in relation to which the *firm* is an *exempt person*;

(f) there is not in force any order or direction of the *FSA* under sections 328 or 329 of *the Act* which prevents the *firm* from carrying on the activities; and

(g) the activities are not otherwise prohibited by these rules.

5. Other restrictions

(1) **Packaged products (except personal pension schemes)**

A *firm* must not recommend, or make arrangements for, a *client* to *buy* a *packaged product* except where:

(a) recommending, or arranging for, a *client* to *buy* a *packaged product* by means of an assignment;

(b) the arrangements are made as a result of a *firm* managing assets within the exception to rule 5(4) below; or

(c) arranging a *transaction* for a *client* where the *firm* assumes on reasonable grounds that the *client* is not relying on the *firm* as to the merits or suitability of that *transaction*.

(2) **Personal pension schemes**

(a) A *firm* must not recommend a *client* to buy or dispose of any rights or interests in a *personal pension scheme*.

(b) A *firm* must not make arrangements for a *client* to buy any rights or interests in a *personal pension scheme* **except where** the *firm* assumes on reasonable grounds that the *client* is not relying on the *firm* as to the merits or suitability of that *transaction* but this exception does not apply where the *transaction* involves:

(i) a *pension transfer*; or

(ii) an *opt-out*.

(3) **Securities and contractually based investments (except packaged products)**

(a) A *firm* must not recommend a *client* to buy or subscribe for a *security* or a *contractually based investment* where the *transaction* would be made:

> (i) with a person acting in the course of carrying on the business of *buying*, selling, subscribing for or underwriting the *investment*, whether as principal or agent;
>
> (ii) on an investment exchange or any other market to which that *investment* is admitted for dealing; or
>
> (iii) in response to an invitation to subscribe for an *investment* which is, or is to be, admitted for dealing on an *investment* exchange or any other market.

(b) This rule does not apply where the *client* is:-

> (i) not an individual;
>
> (ii) an individual who acts in connection with the carrying on of a business of any kind by himself or by an undertaking of which the *client* is, or would become as a result of the *transaction* to which the recommendation relates, a *controller*; or
>
> (iii) acting in his capacity as a trustee of an *occupational pension scheme*.

(4) Discretionary management

A *firm* must not manage assets belonging to another person in circumstances which involve the exercise of discretion **except where** the *firm* or a *manager* or *employee* of the *firm* is a trustee, personal representative, donee of a power of attorney, or deputy or receiver appointed by the Court of Protection, and either:

(a) all routine or day to day decisions, so far as relating to that activity, are taken by an *authorised person* with permission to carry on that activity or an *exempt person*; or

(b) any decision to enter into a *transaction*, which involves *buying* or subscribing for an *investment*, is undertaken in accordance with the advice of an *authorised person* with permission to give advice in relation to such an activity or an *exempt person*.

(5) Corporate finance

A *firm* must not act as any of the following:

(a) sponsor to an issue in respect of *securities* to be admitted for dealing on the London Stock Exchange; or

(b) nominated adviser to an issue in respect of *securities* to be admitted for dealing on the Alternative Investment Market of the London Stock Exchange; or

(c) corporate adviser to an issue in respect of *securities* to be admitted for dealing on the PLUS Market.

(6) Insurance mediation activities

(a) Unless a *firm* is registered in the *FSA Register* it must not carry on any *insurance mediation activities*.

(b) Any *firm* undertaking *insurance mediation activities* must appoint a *compliance officer* whose details will be made known to the *FSA* and who will be responsible for the *firm*'s *insurance mediation activities*.

(7) Regulated mortgage contracts

A *firm* must not recommend a *client* to enter as borrower into a *regulated mortgage contract* but can endorse a recommendation given by an *authorised person* with permission to advise on *regulated mortgage contracts* or an *exempt person* in relation to the giving of such advice.

(8) **Regulated home purchase plans**

A *firm* must not recommend a *client* to enter as *home purchaser* into a *regulated home purchase plan* with a particular person but can endorse a recommendation given by an *authorised person* with permission to advise on *regulated home purchase plans* or an *exempt person* in relation to the giving of such advice.

(9) **Regulated home reversion plans**

A *firm* must not recommend a *client* to enter as *reversion seller* or *plan provider* into a *regulated home reversion plan* with a particular person but can endorse a recommendation given by an *authorised person* with permission to advise on *regulated home reversion plans* or an *exempt person* in relation to the giving of such advice.

(10) **Regulated sale and rent back agreements**

A *firm* must not recommend a *client* to enter as *agreement seller* or *agreement provider* into a *regulated sale and rent back agreement* with a particular person but can endorse a recommendation given by an *authorised person* with permission to advise on *regulated sale and rent back agreements* or an *exempt person* in relation to the giving of such advice.

6. Effect of a breach of these rules

(1) The Solicitors Regulation Authority may exercise its statutory powers in respect of any *firm* which breaches these rules.

(2) In determining whether or not there has been a breach of these rules the Solicitors Regulation Authority will take account of whether the *firm* has given due regard to the guidance issued by the Law Society or the Solicitors Regulation Authority on how to determine whether *regulated activities* are carried on in accordance with these rules.

(3) A *firm* which breaches these rules may:

(a) be committing a criminal offence under section 23 of *the Act*; and

(b) be made subject to an order by the *FSA* under section 329 of *the Act* which could prevent the *firm* from carrying on any *regulated activities*.

7. Repeal and commencement

(1) These rules repeal the Solicitors' Investment Business Rules 1995.

(2) These rules come into force on 1 December 2001.

8. Interpretation

(1) In these rules unless the context otherwise requires:

the Act means the Financial Services and Markets Act 2000;

agreement provider has the meaning given by article 63J(3) of the Regulated Activities Order read with paragraphs (6) and (7) of that article;

agreement seller has the meaning given by article 63J(3) of the Regulated Activities Order;

asset means an *investment*;

authorised person has the meaning given in section 31 of *the Act*;

broker funds arrangement means an arrangement between a *firm* and a *life office* (or operator of a *regulated collective investment scheme*) under which the *life office* (or operator of the *regulated collective investment scheme*) agrees to establish a separate fund whose composition may be determined by instructions from the *firm* and in which it is possible for more than one *client* to invest;

buy or *buying* includes acquiring for valuable consideration;

client, in relation to any *regulated activities* carried on by a *firm* for a trust or the estate of a deceased person (including a controlled trust), means the trustees or personal representatives in their capacity as such and not any person who is a beneficiary under the trust or interested in the estate;

collective investment scheme means (in accordance with section 235 of *the Act* (Collective Investment Schemes)) any arrangements with respect to property of any description, including money, the purpose or effect of which is to enable persons taking part in the arrangements (whether by becoming owners of the property or any part of it or otherwise) to participate in or receive profits or income arising from the acquisition, holding, management or disposal of the property or sums paid out of such profits or income, which are not excluded by the Financial Services and Markets Act (Collective Investment Schemes) Order 2001 (SI 2001/1062);

compliance officer means the individual within the management structure of the *firm* who is responsible for an *insurance mediation activity*;

contract of insurance means (in accordance with article 3(1) of the *Regulated Activities Order*) any *contract of insurance* which is a *long-term insurance contract* or a *general insurance contract*;

contractually based investment has the meaning given by article 3(1) of the *Regulated Activities Order* but does not include an *investment* which falls within the definition of a *packaged product*;

controller has the meaning given in section 422 of *the Act*;

employee means an individual who is employed in connection with the *firm's regulated activities* under a contract of service or under a contract for services such that he or she is held out as an employee or consultant of the *firm*;

exempt person means a person who is exempt from the *general prohibition* as a result of an exemption order made under section 38(1) or as a result of section 39(1) or 285(2) or (3) of *the Act* and who, in engaging in the activity in question, is acting in the course of business in respect of which that person is exempt;

FSA Register means the record maintained by the *FSA* as required by section 347 of *the Act* and including those persons that carry on, or are proposing to carry on, *insurance mediation activities*;

FSA means the Financial Services Authority;

firm means:

(a)   in England and Wales, a sole solicitor or *registered European lawyer*, or a *partnership* consisting of solicitors, *registered European lawyers* and/or *recognised bodies* with or without *registered foreign lawyers* and/or *non-registered European lawyers*;

(b)   in Scotland or Northern Ireland, a sole solicitor or *registered European lawyer*, or a *partnership* consisting of solicitors, *registered European lawyers* and/or *recognised bodies* with or without *non-registered European lawyers*;

(c)   outside the United Kingdom, a sole solicitor, or a *partnership* consisting of solicitors and/or *recognised bodies*;

(d)   a *recognised body*;

funeral plan contract has the meaning given in article 59 of the *Regulated Activities Order*;

general insurance contract is any *contract of insurance* within Part 1 of Schedule 1 to the *Regulated Activities Order*;

general prohibition has the meaning given in section 19(2) of *the Act*;

home purchaser has the meaning given by article 63F(3) of the *Regulated Activities Order*;

individual pension contract means a *pension policy* or *pension contract* under which contributions are paid to:

(a)   a *personal pension scheme* approved under section 630 of the Income and Corporation Taxes Act 1988, whose sole purpose is the provision of annuities or lump sums under arrangements made by individuals in accordance with the scheme; or

(b)   a retirement benefits scheme approved under section 591(2)(g) of the Income and Corporation Taxes Act 1988, for the provision of relevant benefits by means of an annuity contract made with an insurance company of the *employee*'s choice;

Individual Savings Account means an account which is a scheme of *investment* satisfying the conditions prescribed in the Individual Savings Account Regulations 1998 (S.I. 1998/1870);

insurance mediation activity means any of the following activities specified in the *Regulated Activities Order* which is carried on in relation to a contract of insurance or rights to or interests in a *life policy*:

(a)   dealing in *investments* as agent;

(b)   arranging (bringing about) deals in *investments*;

(c)   making arrangements with a view to *transactions* in *investments*;

(d)   assisting in the administration and performance of a *contract of insurance*;

(e)   advising on *investments*;

(f)   agreeing to carry on a regulated activity in (a) to (e) above;

investment means any of the investments specified in Part III of the *Regulated Activities Order*;

investment trust means a closed-ended company which is listed in the United Kingdom or another member state and:

(a)   is approved by the Inland Revenue under section 842 of the Income and Corporation Taxes Act 1988 (or, in the case of a newly formed company, has declared its intention to conduct its affairs so as to obtain approval); or

(b)   is resident in another member state and would qualify for approval if resident and listed in the United Kingdom;

investment trust savings scheme means a dedicated service for *investment* in the securities of one or more *investment trusts* within a particular marketing group (and references to an *investment trust savings scheme* include references to securities to be acquired through that scheme);

ISA means an *Individual Savings Account*;

life office means a person with permission to effect or carry out *long-term insurance contracts*;

life policy means a *long-term insurance contract* other than a *pure protection contract* or a reinsurance contract, but including a *pension policy*;

LLP means a limited liability partnership incorporated under the Limited Liability Partnership Act 2000;

long-term care insurance contract has the meaning given in article 1 of the Financial Services and Markets Act 2000 (Regulated Activities) (Amendment)(No 2) Order 2003;

long-term insurance contract has the meaning given in Part II of Schedule 1 to the *Regulated Activities Order*;

manager means:

(i)   a *partner* in a *partnership*;

(ii)   a member of an *LLP*; or

(iii)   a director of a company;

market making means where a *firm* holds itself out as willing, as principal, to *buy*, sell or subscribe for *investments* of the kind to which the *transaction* relates at prices determined by the *firm* generally and continuously rather than in respect of each particular *transaction*;

non-registered European lawyer means a member of a profession covered by the Establishment of Lawyers Directive 98/5/EC who is based entirely at an office or offices outside England and Wales and who is not a solicitor, *registered European lawyer* or *registered foreign lawyer*;

occupational pension scheme means any scheme or arrangement which is comprised in one or more documents or agreements and which has, or is capable of having, effect in relation to one or more descriptions or categories of employment so as to provide benefits, in the form of pensions or otherwise, payable on termination of service, or on death or retirement, to or in respect of earners with qualifying service in an employment of any such description or category;

opt-out means a *transaction* resulting from a decision by an individual to opt out of or decline to join a final salary or money-purchase *occupational pension scheme* of which he or she is a current member, or which he or she is, or at the end of a waiting period will become, eligible to join, in favour of an *individual pension contract* or contracts;

packaged product means a *life policy*, a unit or share in a *regulated collective investment scheme*, or an *investment trust savings scheme* whether or not held within an ISA or PEP, or a *stakeholder pension scheme*;

partner and *partnership* refer only to an unincorporated *firm* and not to a *firm* which is incorporated as a limited liability partnership;

pension contract means a right to benefits obtained by the making of contributions to an *occupational pension scheme* or to a *personal pension scheme*, where the contributions are paid to a *regulated collective investment scheme*;

pension policy means a right to benefits obtained by the making of contributions to an *occupational pension scheme* or to a *personal pension scheme*, where the contributions are paid to a *life office*;

pension transfer means a *transaction* resulting from a decision by an individual to transfer deferred benefits from a final salary *occupational pension scheme*, or from a money-purchase *occupational pension scheme*, in favour of an *individual pension contract* or contracts;

PEP means a personal equity plan within the Personal Equity Plan Regulations 1989;

personal pension scheme means any scheme or arrangement which is not an *occupational pension scheme* or a *stakeholder pension scheme* and which is comprised in one or more instruments or agreements, having or capable of having effect so as to provide benefits to or in respect of people on retirement, or on having reached a particular age, or on termination of service in an employment;

plan provider has the meaning given by article 63B(3) of the *Regulated Activities Order* read with paragraphs (7) and (8) of that article;

professional services means services provided by a *firm* in the course of its practice and which do not constitute carrying on a *regulated activity*;

pure protection contract means:

(1)   a *long-term insurance contract*:

      (a)   under which the benefits are payable only in respect of death or of incapacity due to injury, sickness or *infirmity*;

> (b) which has no surrender value or the consideration consists of a single premium and the surrender value does not exceed that premium; and
>
> (c) which makes no provision for its conversion or extension in a manner which would result in its ceasing to comply with (a), or (b); or

(2) a *reinsurance contract* covering all or part of a risk to which a person is exposed under a *long-term insurance contract*;

recognised body means a *partnership*, company or *LLP* recognised by the Solicitors Regulation Authority under section 9 of the Administration of Justice Act 1985;

registered European lawyer means a person registered by the Solicitors Regulation Authority under regulation 17 of the European Communities (Lawyer's Practice) Regulations 2000;

registered foreign lawyer means a person registered under section 89 of the Courts and Legal Services Act 1990;

Regulated Activities Order means the Financial Services and Markets Act 2000 (Regulated Activities) Order 2001;

regulated activity means an activity which is specified in the *Regulated Activities Order*;

regulated collective investment scheme means:

(a) an investment company with variable capital;

(b) an authorised unit trust scheme as defined in section 237(3) of *the Act*; or

(c) a scheme recognised under sections 264, 270 or 272 of *the Act*;

regulated home purchase plan has the meaning given by article 63F(3) of the *Regulated Activities Order*;

regulated home reversion plan has the meaning given by article 63B(3) of the *Regulated Activities Order*;

regulated mortgage contract has the meaning given by article 61(3) of the *Regulated Activities Order*;

regulated sale and rent back agreement has the meaning given by article 63J(3) of the *Regulated Activities Order*;

reinsurance contract means a *contract of insurance* covering all or part of a risk to which a person is exposed under a *contract of insurance*;

reversion seller has the meaning given by article 63B(3) of the *Regulated Activities Order*;

security has the meaning given by article 3(1) of the *Regulated Activities Order* but does not include an *investment* which falls within the definition of a *packaged product*;

stakeholder pension scheme means a scheme established in accordance with Part I of the Welfare and Pensions Reform Act 1999 and the Stakeholder Pension Scheme Regulations 2000; and

transaction means the purchase, sale, subscription or underwriting of a particular *investment*.

(2) In these rules references to statutes, rules, codes or regulations, statements or principles etc. other than these rules include any modification or replacement thereof.

(3) As the context requires, other words and expressions shall have the meanings assigned to them by the Interpretation Act 1978, *the Act* and the Solicitors Act 1974.

(4) References in these rules to activities carried on by a *firm* include activities carried on by an individual as sole principal, *manager* or *employee* of the *firm*.

APPENDIX 5

The Solicitors' Financial Services (Conduct of Business) Rules 2001

[Law Society copyright. For the latest updates to the material, please see www.sra.org.uk.]

The Solicitors' Financial Services (Conduct of Business) Rules 2001

[Last amended 6 October 2010]

Contents

These rules, dated 18 July 2001, are made by the Council of the Law Society with the concurrence of the Master of the Rolls under section 31 of the Solicitors Act 1974 and section 9 of the Administration of Justice Act 1985, regulating the practices of:

- solicitors and recognised bodies in any part of the world,

- registered European lawyers in any part of the United Kingdom, and

- registered foreign lawyers in England and Wales,

in carrying out "regulated activities" in, into or from the United Kingdom.

1. **Purpose**

(1) The Law Society is a designated professional body under Part XX of *the Act*, and *firms* may therefore carry on certain *regulated activities* without being regulated by the *FSA*.

(2) The Solicitors Financial Services (Scope) Rules 2001 set out the scope of the *regulated activities* which may be undertaken by *firms* which are not regulated by the *FSA*. These rules regulate the way in which *firms* carry on such exempt *regulated activities*.

2. **Application**

Apart from rule 3 (status disclosure), these rules apply to:

(a) *firms* which are not regulated by the *FSA*; and

(b) *firms* which are regulated by the *FSA* but these rules only apply to such firms in respect of their *non-mainstream regulated activities*.

3. **Status disclosure**

(1) This rule applies only to *firms* which are not regulated by the *FSA*.

(2) A *firm* shall give the *client* the following information in writing in a manner that is clear, fair and not misleading before the *firm* provides a service which includes the carrying on of a *regulated activity*

    (a) a statement that the *firm* is not authorised by the *FSA*;

    (aa) the name and address of the *firm*;

    (b) the nature of the *regulated activities* carried on by the *firm*, and the fact that they are limited in scope;

    (c) a statement that the *firm* is regulated by the Solicitors Regulation Authority; and

    (d) a statement explaining that complaints and redress mechanisms are provided through the Solicitors Regulation Authority and the Legal Ombudsman.

(3) Before a *firm* provides a service which includes the carrying on of an *insurance mediation activity* with or for a *client*, it must make the following statement in writing to the *client* in a way that is clear, fair and not misleading

"[This firm is]/[We are] not authorised by the Financial Services Authority. However, we are included on the register maintained by the Financial Services Authority so that we can carry on insurance mediation activity, which is broadly the advising on, selling and administration of insurance contracts. This part of our business, including arrangements for complaints or redress if something goes wrong, is regulated by Solicitors Regulation Authority. The register can be accessed via the Financial Services Authority website at www.fsa.gov.uk/register."

GUIDANCE NOTES

1. Where the status disclosure relates to insurance mediation activities then the statement in rule 3(3) must be used. The status disclosure need not be tailored to the needs of the individual client. The disclosures may be provided alongside or integrated with other material provided to the client. These disclosures may be made in the firm's client care letter or in a separate letter.

2.   Rule 7.07(1) of the Solicitors' Code of Conduct 2007 states that the letterhead of a firm must bear the words "regulated by the Solicitors Regulation Authority" which will assist in meeting the requirements of rule 3(2).

3.   The provisions of rule 3(2)(d) and rule 3(3) reflect the requirements of rule 2.05 of the Solicitors' Code of Conduct 2007 in respect of complaints handling. Rule 2.05 states that a firm must have a written complaints handling procedure and that complaints are handled promptly, fairly and effectively in accordance with it. It also requires firms to tell clients about their right to complain, including their right to refer their complaint to the Legal Ombudsman. If a client makes a complaint about an exempt regulated activity, the firm will need to be able to demonstrate that there has been an investigation in accordance with rule 2.05. If the client is not satisfied with the results of the investigation the client must be told that they can refer their complaint to the Legal Ombudsman, the timescale for doing so and full contact details of the Ombudsman. (See www.legalombudsman.org.uk). The Legal Complaints Service will investigate and consider whether redress is appropriate and/or whether the complaint raises conduct issues which will be considered by the Solicitors Regulation Authority.

4. Execution of transactions

A *firm* shall ensure that where it has agreed or decided in its discretion to effect a *transaction*, it shall do so as soon as possible, unless it reasonably believes that it is in the *client's* best interests not to do so.

GUIDANCE NOTES

1.   Rule 1.04 of the Solicitors' Code of Conduct 2007 emphasises a solicitor's duty to act in the best interests of the client. Accordingly, in cases where there is any doubt on the point, firms should ensure that transactions are effected on the best terms reasonably available.

2.   Rule 2.02 of the Solicitors' Code of Conduct 2007 provides that clients should be kept fully informed of transactions effected on their behalf, unless clients have indicated to the contrary.

5. Records of transactions

(1)   Where a *firm* receives instructions from a *client* to effect a *transaction*, or makes a decision to effect a *transaction* in its discretion, it shall keep a record of:

   (a)   the name of the *client*;

   (b)   the terms of the instructions or decision; and

   (c)   in the case of instructions, the date when they were received.

(2)   Where a *firm* gives instructions to another person to effect a *transaction*, it shall keep a record of:

   (a)   the name of the *client*;

   (b)   the terms of the instructions;

   (c)   the date when the instructions were given; and

   (d)   the name of the other person instructed.

GUIDANCE NOTE

It is not necessary for the firm to make a separate record. Normal file notes or letters on the file will meet the requirements of this rule provided that they include the appropriate information. If instructions are given or received over the telephone, an appropriate attendance note would satisfy this rule.

6. Record of commissions

Where a *firm* receives commission which is attributable to *regulated activities* carried on by the *firm*, it shall keep a record of:

(a)   the amount of the commission; and

(b)   how the *firm* has accounted to the *client*.

GUIDANCE NOTES

1.   Any commission received by the firm has to be dealt with in accordance with rule 2.06 of the Solicitors' Code of Conduct 2007. However, firms should bear in mind that in the case of commissions attributable to regulated activities, the exception for commissions received of £20 or less, does not apply because it is overridden by the condition in section 327(3) of the Act.

2.   The record could be a letter or bill of costs provided the information is clear.

7. Safekeeping of clients' investments

(1)   Where a *firm* undertakes the *regulated activity* of safeguarding and administering investments, the *firm* must operate appropriate systems, including the keeping of appropriate records, which provide for the safekeeping of *assets* entrusted to the *firm* by *clients* and others.

(2)   Where such *assets* are passed to a third party:

(a)   an acknowledgement of receipt of the property should be obtained; and

(b)   if they have been passed to a third party on the *client's* instructions, such instructions should be obtained in writing.

8. Packaged products – execution-only business

If a *firm* arranges for a *client* on an *execution-only* basis any *transaction* involving a *packaged product*, the *firm* shall send the *client* written confirmation to the effect that:

(a)   the *client* had not sought and was not given any advice from the *firm* in connection with the transaction; or

(b)   the *client* was given advice from the *firm* in connection with that *transaction* but nevertheless persisted in wishing the *transaction* to be effected;

and in either case the *transaction* is effected on the *client's* explicit instructions.

8A. Insurance mediation activities

Where a *firm* undertakes *insurance mediation activities* for a *client*, it must comply with appendix 1 to these rules.

9. Retention of records

Each record made under these rules shall be kept for at least six years.

GUIDANCE NOTE

The six years shall run from the date on which the relevant record has been made.

10. Waivers

(1)   In any particular case or cases the Council shall have power to waive in writing any of the provisions of these rules, but shall not do so unless it appears that:

    (a)   compliance with them would be unduly burdensome having regard to the benefit which compliance would confer on investors; and

    (b)   the exercise of the power would not result in any undue risk to investors.

(2)   The Council shall have power to revoke any waiver.

11. Commencement

These rules come into force on 1 December 2001.

12. Interpretation

(1)   The interpretation of these rules is governed by rule 8(1)–(4) of the Solicitors' Financial Services (Scope) Rules 2001.

(2)   In these rules:

execution-only (*transaction*) means a *transaction* which is effected by a *firm* for a *client* where the *firm* assumes on reasonable grounds that the *client* is not relying on the *firm* as to the merits or suitability of that *transaction*;

GUIDANCE NOTES

1.   Whether a transaction is "execution-only" will depend on the existing relationship between the client and the firm and the circumstances surrounding that transaction. Generally, a transaction will be "execution-only" if the client instructs the firm to effect it without having received advice from the firm. Even though this is the case, however, the transaction may still not qualify as "execution-only" because, in view of the relationship, the client may reasonably expect the firm to indicate if the transaction is inappropriate. In any event, a firm may be negligent (and possibly in breach of rule 1.04 of the Solicitors' Code of Conduct 2007) if it fails to advise on the appropriateness or otherwise.

2.   A transaction will also be "execution-only" if the firm has advised the client that the transaction is unsuitable, but the client persists in wishing the transaction to be carried out. In those circumstances it is good practice (and in some cases a requirement) for the firm to confirm in writing that its advice has not been accepted, and that the transaction is being effected on an "execution-only" basis.

3.   Where the transaction involves a packaged product, there is a specific requirement to confirm in writing the "execution-only" nature of a transaction (see Rule 8 above).

insurance undertaking means an undertaking, whether or not an insurer, which carries on insurance business.

Insurer means a firm with permission to effect or carry out *contracts of insurance* (other than a bank)

non-mainstream regulated activity means a *regulated activity* of a *firm* regulated by the FSA in relation to which the conditions in the Professional Firms Sourcebook (5.2.1R) are satisfied.

(3)   These rules are to be interpreted in the light of the guidance notes.

APPENDIX 1 – Insurance Mediation Activities

1. Disclosure of information

(1) Where a *firm* undertakes *insurance mediation activities* for a *client*, it must take reasonable steps to communicate information to the *client* in a way that is clear, fair and not misleading.

(2) Where a *firm* recommends a *contract of insurance* (other than a *life policy*) to a *client*, the *firm* must inform the *client* whether the *firm* has given advice on the basis of a fair analysis of a sufficiently large number of *insurance contracts* available on the market to enable the *firm* to make a recommendation in accordance with professional criteria regarding which *contract of insurance* would be adequate to meet the *client's* needs.

(3) If the *firm* does not conduct a fair analysis of the market, the *firm* must:

   (a) advise the *client* whether the *firm* is contractually obliged to conduct *insurance mediation activities* only with one or more *insurance undertakings*;

   (b) advise the *client* that the *client* can request details of the *insurance undertakings* with which the *firm* conducts business; and

   (c) provide the *client* with such details on request.

(4) The information referred to in paragraphs 1(2) and 1(3) above must be provided to the client on paper or on any other durable medium available and accessible to the client.

GUIDANCE NOTES

1. Paragraph 1(1) covers all communications with the client, including oral statements and telephone calls.

2. Rule 19.01(1)(b) and (c) of the Solicitors' Code of Conduct 2007 provides that solicitors must not in connection with regulated activities have any arrangement with other persons under which the solicitors could be constrained to recommend to clients or effect for them (or refrain from doing so) transactions in some investments but not others, or with some persons but not others, or through the agency of some persons but not others. However, the provisions of rule 19.01(1)(b) and (c) do not apply to arrangements in connection with regulated mortgage contracts, general insurance contracts or pure protection contracts.

3. Paragraphs 1(2) and 1(3) apply to contracts of insurance other than life policies. Solicitors who are not authorised by the FSA are not allowed to recommend the buying of life policies, but they can make recommendations and advise on other contracts of insurance.

4. Reference to a durable medium in paragraph 1(4) is to a form that allows for the storage of information to be reproduced without changes. This includes floppy disks, CD-roms, DVDs and hard drives where emails are stored.

2. Suitability

(1) Before a *firm* recommends a *contract of insurance* (other than a *life policy*) the *firm* must take reasonable steps to ensure that the recommendation is suitable to the *client's* demands and needs by:

   (a) considering relevant information already held;

   (b) obtaining details of any relevant existing insurance;

   (c) identifying the *client's* requirements and explaining to the *client* what the *client* needs to disclose;

(d)   assessing whether the level of cover is sufficient for the risks that the *client* wishes to insure; and

(e)   considering the relevance of any exclusions, excesses, limitations or conditions.

(2)   Where the *firm* recommends a *contract of insurance* that does not meet the needs of the *client* because there is no such contract available in the market, this should be disclosed to the *client*.

3. Demands and needs statement

(1)   Where a *firm* recommends a *contract of insurance* (other than a *life policy*) or arranges a *contract of insurance*, the *firm* must, before the *contract* is finalised, provide the *client* with a written demands and needs statement that:

(a)   sets out the *client's* demands and needs on the basis of the information provided by the *client*;

(b)   where a recommendation has been made, explains the reason for recommending that *contract of insurance*;

(c)   reflects the complexity of the *insurance contract* being proposed; and

(d)   is on paper or on any other durable medium available and accessible to the *client*.

(2)   Where a *firm* arranges a *contract of insurance* on an execution-only basis, the demands and needs statement need only identify the *contract of insurance* requested by the *client*, confirm that no advice has been given and state that the *firm* is undertaking the arrangement at the *client's* specific request.

(3)   The requirement in paragraph 3(1) to provide the *client* with a written demands and needs statement before the contract is finalised will not apply in the following circumstances:

(a)   where the *firm* acts on the renewal or amendment of a *contract of insurance* other than a *life policy* if the information given to the *client* in relation to the initial contract is still accurate and up-to-date. If the information previously disclosed has changed, the *firm* must draw the attention of the *client* to the matters which have changed before the renewal or amendment takes place;

(b)   where the information is provided orally at the request of the *client*;

(c)   where immediate cover is required;

(d)   where the *contract* is concluded by telephone; or

(e)   where the *firm* is introducing the *client* to an *authorised person* or an *exempt person* and taking no further part in arranging the *contract of insurance*.

save that in (b), (c) and (d) above the information contained in the written demands and needs statement must be provided to the *client* immediately after the conclusion of the *contract of insurance*.

GUIDANCE NOTES

1.   Reference to a durable medium in paragraph 3(I)(d) is to a form that allows for the storage of information and allows the information to be reproduced without changes. This includes floppy disks, CD-Roms, DVDs and hard drives where emails are stored.

2.   Paragraph 2 and 3(I) apply to contracts of insurance other than life policies. Solicitors who are not authorised by the FSA are not allowed to recommend the buying of life policies, but they can make recommendations and advise on other contracts of insurance.

APPENDIX 5

4. Exclusion for large risks

Paragraphs 1 – 3 above do not apply where a *firm* carries on insurance mediation activities for commercial *clients* in relation to *contracts of insurance* covering risks within the following categories:

(a)   railway rolling stock, aircraft, ships (sea, lake, river and canal vessels), goods in transit, aircraft liability and liability of ships (sea, lake, river and canal vessels);

(b)   credit and suretyship, where the policyholder is engaged professionally in an industrial or commercial activity or in one of the liberal professions, and the risks relate to such activity;

(c)   land vehicles (other than railway rolling stock), fire and natural forces, other damage to property, motor vehicle liability, general liability, and miscellaneous financial loss, in so far as the policyholder exceeds the limits of at least two of the following three criteria:

  (i)   balance sheet total: €6.2 million;

  (ii)   net turnover: €12.8 million;

  (iii)   average number of employees during the financial year: 250.

5. Notification of establishment and services in other Member States

If a *firm* wishes to exercise the right conferred by Article 6 of the Insurance Mediation Directive to establish a branch or provide cross-border services in another EEA state an appropriate application must be made directly to the FSA. The Rules under the FSA's Supervision Manual, SUP 13, Exercise of Passport Rights by UK firms, contain details of the applicable process. A *firm* proposing to provide such services must comply with the applicable provisions of the Act, as laid down in the FSA's Professional Firms' Sourcebook Chapter 7 as amended from time to time.

The Solicitors' Indemnity Insurance Rules 2010

Solicitors' Indemnity Insurance Rules 2010

[Rules in force from 1 October 2010. Last updated 1 October 2010]

Contents

Introductory commentary

Solicitors' Indemnity Insurance Rules 2010

Introductory commentary

1 Introduction

1.1   The Law Society introduced arrangements for solicitors' professional indemnity insurance with effect from 1 September 2000 which achieved broad coverage for the profession and its clients, whilst at the same time allowing the profession access to a competitive, commercial insurance market.

1.2   At its meeting on 13 April 2000, the Council of the Law Society resolved, among other matters, that:

    1   With effect from 1 September 2000, the regulated profession in private practice

will be required under the Solicitors' Indemnity Insurance Rules 2000 to secure professional indemnity insurance complying with certain Minimum Terms and Conditions, from any of the Qualifying Insurers.

2   Each Qualifying Insurer will be required to enter into a Qualifying Insurer's Agreement with the Law Society.

1.3   The Solicitors' Indemnity Insurance Rules 2010 were approved by the Board of the Solicitors Regulation Authority (SRA) with the concurrence of the Legal Services Board. They apply in respect of the indemnity period beginning on 1 October 2010.

2 Summary of the arrangements

2.1   Principals in private practice are free to secure professional indemnity insurance either by dealing direct with Qualifying Insurers or via their insurance brokers or other intermediaries. The Solicitors Indemnity Fund (**SIF**) has not underwritten new risks since 1 September 2000 but continues to run off the existing claims account. Since 1 September 2007, it has also provided cover in respect of firms which ceased to practise on or after 1 September 2000 without a successor practice (as defined in clause 8.2 of the Minimum Terms and Conditions), after the six-year run-off cover provided under their qualifying insurance has expired.

2.2   Evidence of professional indemnity insurance that complies with the Minimum Terms and Conditions is a requirement for obtaining a practising certificate. Solicitors are not permitted to practise without current professional indemnity insurance in force.

2.3   Each firm is obliged to arrange its professional indemnity insurance with one or more Qualifying Insurers, or to be admitted to the Assigned Risks Pool (see paragraph 4 below). That insurance must comply with the Minimum Terms and Conditions set out in Appendix 1 to the Rules.

2.4   The Rules require firms to take out a policy which includes cover in accordance with the Minimum Terms and Conditions for that part of their practice carried on from offices located in England and Wales. They do not apply to any part of the practice of the firm carried on from offices located outside England and Wales (although rule 15 of the Solicitors' Code of Conduct 2007 does apply in such cases). However, the cover in relation to the practice carried on from offices located in England and Wales must extend to acts or omissions wherever in the world they occur, and wherever in the world the claim is brought.

2.5   Each firm which is not a body corporate is required to secure professional indemnity insurance with Qualifying Insurer(s) to a limit of indemnity of £2,000,000 any one claim. Most bodies corporate, such as LLPs, are required to obtain such insurance with Qualifying Insurer(s) to a limit of indemnity of £3,000,000 any one claim.

2.6   Cover in excess of these amounts (**top-up cover**) is not subject to the Rules, and firms are free to make whatever arrangements they wish. Firms should always consider whether the minimum level of cover is adequate for their needs. Arrangements for top-up cover may be made with any insurer, not just a Qualifying Insurer.

2.7   Firms are free to negotiate with Qualifying Insurer(s) the level of excess – i.e., the amount of each claim that the firm itself would have to meet – that applies to their policy. The Minimum Terms and Conditions provide that, if a firm does not pay the part of any claim covered by the excess, the insurer will pay that part of the claim, but recover that amount from the Principals of the firm.

2.8   The Minimum Terms and Conditions require that a policy of Qualifying Insurance must provide at least 6 years' run-off cover if the firm's practice ceases during an indemnity period. However, if there is a "successor practice" (as defined in clause 8.2 of the Minimum Terms and Conditions) to that firm's practice, no run-off cover will be triggered. Instead, the Qualifying Insurance of the successor practice will be required to cover claims against the ceased practice. Under Rule 12.6, the Council may determine the eligibility of any successor firm for the purposes of the Assigned Risks Pool (see paragraph 4 below).

3 Minimum Terms and Conditions

3.1 In exercising its statutory functions the Law Society must act in such manner as it reasonably believes to be in the public interest. To this end the Council resolved on 23 June 1999 that the Society would, so far as possible, seek to replicate in the current arrangements the breadth of cover formerly provided by SIF.

3.2 The Minimum Terms and Conditions are not drafted as a policy, but rather as an expression of the scope of minimum coverage to be afforded to firms in respect of their regulated business. Qualifying Insurers are free to issue their own policy so long as they provide at least the coverage set out in the Minimum Terms and Conditions. As a safety net for both the public and for firms, Qualifying Insurers have committed that the coverage set out in the Minimum Terms and Conditions will apply as a minimum, regardless of the wording of the policy actually issued. The Minimum Terms and Conditions appear as Appendix 1 to the Rules.

4 The Assigned Risks Pool

4.1 It is recognised that some firms may not be able to secure terms from Qualifying Insurers, or may not be able reasonably to afford those terms which are available to them. This might be as a result of a poor claims record, a major claim being outstanding but not yet decided, or other risk factors. It is not the intention for such firms to be left without cover, at least in the short term. To this end, an Assigned Risks Pool (**ARP**) has been established to accept those risks which fall into this category.

4.2 Firms may not be insured through the ARP for more than, in aggregate, 12 months in any four consecutive indemnity periods. Those firms receiving cover under the ARP will be required to pay a high premium, will be inspected and monitored (at the firm's expense), and may be required to attend approved courses and to implement specified practice management measures. It is envisaged that firms will apply for cover in the ARP only if they are unable to obtain insurance from a Qualifying Insurer in the open market. If a firm which has been insured through the ARP is unable to obtain cover with a Qualifying Insurer in the open market by the end of the maximum permitted period, the firm will have to cease practice.

4.3 The cover provided through the ARP is underwritten by each Qualifying Insurer in the same proportion as its proportion of premium income from underwriting the compulsory cover bears to the total of all premium income written by all the Qualifying Insurers for the compulsory cover in the indemnity period in question.

4.4 The premium for entry into the ARP is calculated in accordance with a formula set out in Appendix 2 to the Rules, and is based on a firm's gross fees. An additional premium is payable in the event that run-off cover is triggered.

4.5 In certain circumstances (for example, where a firm without Qualifying Insurance fails to apply to be insured through the ARP within the time period specified in the Rules), a default premium, 20% higher than the normal ARP premium, will be payable for the whole of the indemnity period in question.

4.6 In addition, in keeping with the duty to safeguard the interests of the public, the ARP will cover claims against firms which do not, for whatever reason, secure their own insurance arrangements in accordance with the Rules, including run-off cover in the case of firms which have no policy of qualifying insurance in place when they cease practice. Where firms fail to effect cover, however, the ARP Manager is entitled to recover the amount of any claims and any associated costs, plus interest, from the principals of the firm concerned.

4.7   The ARP is managed by a manager appointed by the SRA. The functions of the ARP manager are currently carried out by Capita Commercial Insurance Services Limited on behalf of the SRA.

5 Arrangements with Travelers

5.1   The Law Society has entered into a joint venture with Travelers. The purpose of these arrangements is to ensure that cover is offered to all sectors of the profession, alongside the commercial market. That does not mean that every firm will necessarily receive a quotation. Travelers – like any other individual Qualifying Insurer – is free to reject firms for reasons particular to that firm such as a poor premium payment record. But it will not exclude firms because of the type of firm that they are, or the type of work that they do.

6 Changes for the 2010–2011 Indemnity Period

6.1   A number of small amendments to the Rules have been made this year. As well as the normal annual date changes, the following changes have been made:

6.1.1   The definition of "Eligible Firm" at Rule 3 has been amended to make it clear that a Firm is not eligible for cover from the Assigned Risks Pool indefinitely, to set out the new maximum time that a Firm may obtain cover in the Assigned Risks Pool and to prevent Firms which are unable to obtain cover outside of the Assigned Risks Pool from commencing business;

6.1.2   The commentary to Rule 6, in relation to the insolvency of a Qualifying Insurer, has been amended to make it clear that it ceases to be a Qualifying Insurer for the purposes of writing new policies and the Firms insured by that Insurer must seek alternative cover;

6.1.3   The Rules (in particular, Rule 10.2) relating to applying to the Assigned Risks Pool have been amended to make it clear that a Firm wishing to commence Practice may not do so without first obtaining Qualifying Insurance outside the Assigned Risks Pool;

6.1.4   The Rules and the Minimum Terms and Conditions have been updated to incorporate references to the Office for Legal Complaints (including the Legal Ombudsman) where appropriate; and

6.1.5   The Minimum Terms and Conditions contained in Appendix 1 to the Rules have been amended:

   (a)   for the establishment of the new office of the Legal Ombudsman to provide that an Insurer is liable for certain awards made by the Legal Ombudsman but that an Insurer will have no liability in respect of a determination by the Legal Ombudsman for a Firm to refund any fees paid to an Insured;

   (b)   to allow Firms that would normally be the subject of a Succession to elect to be either insured under the run-off cover set out in paragraph 5.1 of the Minimum Terms and Conditions, or insured as a Prior Practice (provided there is appropriate insurance in place in relation to that Successor Practice). The definition of "Prior Practice" has been amended accordingly; and

   (c)   to permit the exclusion of cover in respect of Firm's legal liability arising in the course of the Firm's practice from its use of or access to the HM Land Registry network under a Network Access Agreement (save for the payment of fees to HM Land Registry in the ordinary course).

7 Legal Services Act 2007

7.1   As a result of changes brought about by the Legal Services Act 2007 (the LSA), the

Rules were amended with effect from 31 March 2009 to take account of legal disciplinary practices and other new regulatory arrangements, such as the requirement for partnerships to become recognised bodies.

7.2   The Rules apply in respect of firms which are recognised by the SRA, or partnerships or sole practitioners which are not recognised by the SRA, but where the SRA is the only approved regulator which could grant them recognition.

7.3   Firms which are considering taking advantage of the new structures permitted under the LSA should consider the indemnity insurance implications.

8 About the Rules

8.1   The Solicitors' Indemnity Insurance Rules 2010 were approved by the SRA Board, with the concurrence of the Legal Services Board. They apply in respect of the indemnity period beginning on 1 October 2010.

8.2   Commentary is provided after a number of provisions of the Rules where it is thought that this might be helpful, and is printed in italics. However, the commentary does not form part of the Rules, is provided for guidance only, and does not affect the meaning or interpretation of the Rules in any way. The Solicitors Regulation Authority reserves the right to amend or supplement the commentary at any time. The Appendices to the Rules appear in normal type.

8.3   References in the Rules to the Council include any committee or person to whom any of the functions of the Council may be delegated by virtue of section 79 of the Solicitors Act 1974.

9 Contact details for further information

9.1   If you are in doubt about any aspect of the indemnity insurance arrangements, you may contact the Client Protection Policy Unit of the Solicitors Regulation Authority on 01527 504487. Information about the arrangements, including a list of Qualifying Insurers, is provided on the website of the Solicitors Regulation Authority, at www.sra.org.uk.

Solicitors' Indemnity Insurance Rules 2010

The commentary provided with these Rules does not form part of the Rules, is provided for guidance only, and does not affect the meaning or interpretation of the Rules in any way.

Part 1: General

1 Authority and commencement

1.1   These Rules are made by the Solicitors Regulation Authority Board under sections 31, 37, 79 and 80 of the Solicitors Act 1974 (as amended by the Legal Services Act 2007) and section 9 of the Administration of Justice Act 1985 (as amended by the Legal Services Act 2007) with the approval of the Legal Services Board under Schedule 4 Part 3 of the Legal Services Act 2007.

1.2   These Rules come into force on 1 October 2010.

1.3   These Rules require Solicitors, Registered European Lawyers, Registered Foreign Lawyers and Recognised Bodies and their managers in Private Practice in England and Wales to take out and maintain professional indemnity insurance with Qualifying Insurers with effect from 1 October 2010.

APPENDIX 6

Commentary:

These Rules apply to:

- *Solicitors*

- *Registered European Lawyers*

- *Registered Foreign Lawyers and*

- *Recognised Bodies and their managers*

carrying on Private Practice in England and Wales as a Firm at any time after 1 October 2010. Refer to the definitions in Rule 3 for guidance on the exact meanings of these terms.

1.4   These Rules will apply to any Indemnity Period beginning on or after 1 October 2010.

Commentary:

Before 1 September 2000, Firms were required to take out insurance with the Solicitors Indemnity Fund. Since 1 September 2000, Firms have been required to take out insurance in accordance with the Solicitors' Indemnity Insurance Rules. From 1 October 2010, Firms must take out insurance in accordance with these Rules with one or more Qualifying Insurers. Continuing arrangements dealing with past claims on the Solicitors Indemnity Fund are covered in the Solicitors' Indemnity Rules.

1.5   The Solicitors Indemnity Insurance Rules 2009 shall not apply in respect of any Indemnity Period beginning on or after 1 October 2010, but they shall remain in force in respect of the Indemnity Period from 1 October 2008 to 30 September 2009 inclusive (as amended by the Solicitors' Indemnity Insurance (Amendment) Rules with effect from 31 March 2009) subject to the provisions of Rules 19.1(a), 19.1(b), 19.1(c) and 19.1(d) below.

Commentary:

You should refer to previous Solicitors' Indemnity Insurance Rules in relation to earlier Indemnity Periods since 1 September 2000. However, you should refer to Rules 19.1(a) to 19.1(d) in relation to time limits in respect of an application for a waiver of the provisions of the Solicitors' Indemnity Insurance Rules 2000 to 2010.

2 Citation

2.1   These Rules may be cited as the Solicitors' Indemnity Insurance Rules [2010].

3 Definitions and interpretation

3.1   In these Rules, unless the context otherwise requires:

Appointed Person means any person who is designated as a fee-earner in accordance with any arrangements made from time to time between the Firm and the Legal Services Commission pursuant to the provisions of the Access to Justice Act 1999, regardless of whether the services performed for the Firm by that person in accordance with Rule 4.1 are performed pursuant to such arrangements or otherwise, and who is engaged by the Firm under a contract for services in the course of the Private Practice of the Firm.

Commentary:

Under Rule 4, work carried out by a designated fee-earner may be covered under the Qualifying Insurance of the Firm for which they do that work.

Approved Regulator means a body listed in the first column of the table in paragraph 1 of Schedule 4 to the Legal Services Act 2007 (whether or not that paragraph has been brought into force), or designated as an approved regulator by an order under Part 2 of that Schedule.

Assigned Risks Pool means the arrangements by which an Eligible Firm may obtain professional indemnity insurance against civil liability by means of an ARP Policy on the terms set out in Part 3 of these Rules.

Commentary:

The Assigned Risks Pool is designed to ensure that professional indemnity insurance will be available to all Eligible Firms. However, it is important to note that premiums payable to the Assigned Risks Pool are intended to be high. Refer to Appendix 2 to the Rules for the method of calculation of the ARP Premium.

ARP Manager means the manager of the Assigned Risks Pool being any person from time to time appointed by the Society to carry out all or any particular functions of the ARP Manager or the Society and any such person.

ARP Policy means a contract of professional indemnity insurance issued by the ARP Manager on behalf of Qualifying Insurers to an Eligible Firm in the Assigned Risks Pool including where the context permits a Policy provided to a Firm in Default.

Commentary:

A copy of the standard-form ARP Policy is available on the website of the Solicitors Regulation Authority at www.sra.org.uk, and is also available from the Solicitors Regulation Authority. Contact details appear at the end of the introductory commentary.

ARP Premium means the premium calculated in accordance with Part 1 of Appendix 2 to these Rules, **ARP Default Premium** means the premium calculated in accordance with Part 2 of Appendix 2 to these Rules and **ARP Run-off Premium** means the premium calculated in accordance with Part 3 of Appendix 2 to these Rules.

ARP Run-off Policy means a contract of professional indemnity insurance issued by the ARP Manager on behalf of Qualifying Insurers to a Run-off Firm in the Assigned Risks Pool.

Authorised Insurer means:

(a) a person who has permission under Part IV of the Financial Services and Markets Act 2000 to effect or carry out contracts of insurance of a relevant class;

(b) a person who carries on an insurance market activity, within the meaning of section 316(3) of that Act;

(c) an EEA Firm of the kind mentioned in paragraph 5(d) of Schedule 3 to that Act, which has permission under paragraph 15 of that Schedule (as a result of qualifying for authorisation under paragraph 12 of that Schedule) to effect or carry out contracts of insurance of a relevant class; or

(d) a person who does not fall within paragraph (a), (b) or (c) and who may lawfully effect or carry out contracts of insurance of a relevant class in a member state other than the United Kingdom

where relevant class has the meaning set out in section 87(1B) of the Solicitors Act 1974 and provided that this definition must be read with section 22 of the Financial Services and Markets Act 2000, any relevant order under that section and Schedule 2 to that Act.

Commentary:

Under the Solicitors Act 1974, it is only permitted to enter into arrangements with authorised insurers (including relevant Lloyd's syndicates), as defined under section 87(1A) of that Act. A Qualifying Insurer must be authorised to write new business on the date on which a Policy incepts, but the Policy will remain a Policy of Qualifying Insurance until it expires, even if the Qualifying Insurer then ceases to write, or be authorised to write, new insurance business.

Council means the Council of the Society.

Difference In Conditions Policy means a contract of professional indemnity insurance, made between one or more Qualifying Insurers and a Firm, which provides cover including the Minimum Terms and Conditions as modified in accordance with paragraph 2 of Appendix 3 to these Rules.

Eligible Firm means any Firm which is eligible to be in the Assigned Risks Pool, being any Firm other than:

(a) a Firm that has been in the Assigned Risks Pool for twelve months or more in the four Indemnity Periods immediately prior to the date from which cover is sought, without the prior written approval of the Council unless:

   (i) the date from which cover is sought is on or before 1 October 2010; and

   (ii) immediately prior to that date the Firm is in the Assigned Risks Pool, without the prior written approval of the Council, for less than twenty four months (or twenty five months in the case of a Firm which was in the Assigned Risks Pool for the whole of the Indemnity Period from 1 September 2003 to 30 September 2004) in the four Indemnity Periods immediately prior to that date, in which case the Firm is eligible to be in the Assigned Risks Pool only for any unexpired part of the twenty four or twenty five month period (as the case may be);

(b) a Firm determined by the Council not to be an Eligible Firm by reason of its being treated as one single Firm with one or more other Firms already in the Assigned Risks Pool for the purposes of Rule 12.5 or Rule 12.6; or

(c) subject to Rule 12.3, a Firm that at the end of any Indemnity Period to which these Rules apply is in Policy Default; or

(d) a Firm which, at the time it applies to enter the Assigned Risks Pool, already has in place Qualifying Insurance outside the Assigned Risks Pool for the Indemnity Period in which that Firm requests cover through the Assigned Risks Pool to commence; [or]

(e) a Firm that has never had in place Qualifying Insurance except through the Assigned Risks Pool.

Commentary:

Firms cannot remain insured through the Assigned Risks Pool indefinitely. A Firm which at 1 October 2010 has been in the Assigned Risks Pool during the previous four indemnity periods is eligible for cover through the Assigned Risks Pool for a maximum of twenty four months (or twenty five months in the specified circumstances) less the aggregate number of months in which that Firm was insured through the Assigned Risks Pool during those previous four indemnity periods. For example, a Firm which has been insured through the Assigned Risks Pool for the 2007/08 and 2008/09 Indemnity Periods will not be eligible to be insured through the Assigned Risks Pool for the 2010/11 Indemnity Period. Additionally, for the 2010/2011 indemnity year, a Firm which has not been insured through the Assigned Risks Pool in any of the four indemnity periods expiring on 1 October 2010 will, as from that date be entitled to be insured through the Assigned Risks Pool for a maximum of twelve months during the four indemnity years prior to the date from which cover is sought.

Subject to any waiver granted under Rule 19, any Firm which no longer fulfils the definition of an Eligible Firm is therefore required to obtain Qualifying Insurance from a Qualifying Insurer outside the Assigned Risks Pool, or to cease Practice.

A newly created Firm not previously regulated by the Solicitors Regulation Authority or a Non-SRA Firm which elects (and is accepted) to become regulated by the Solicitors Regulation Authority must obtain Qualifying Insurance in the open market outside the Assigned Risks Pool.

In addition, a Firm is not eligible to join the Assigned Risks Pool if it has already obtained Qualifying Insurance from a Qualifying Insurer outside the Assigned Risks Pool for the relevant Indemnity Period.

Firm means:

(a)   Recognised Sole Practitioner; or

(b)   any Recognised Body (as constituted from time to time); or

(c)   any solicitor or Registered European Lawyer who is a sole practitioner, unless that sole practitioner is a Non-SRA Firm; or

(d)   any Partnership (as constituted from time to time) which is eligible to become a Recognised Body and which meets the requirements applicable to Recognised Bodies set out in rules 14.01, 14.03 and 14.04 of the Solicitors' Code of Conduct 2007, unless that Partnership is a Non-SRA Firm,

whether before or during any relevant Indemnity Period.

Commentary:

If you are unsure whether you or your business fall within this definition, you should consult the Solicitors Regulation Authority. Contact details appear at the end of the introductory commentary.

Firm in Default means a Firm that has failed to obtain Qualifying Insurance outside the Assigned Risks Pool and which,

(a)   in the case of an Eligible Firm, has failed to apply in accordance with these Rules to be admitted into the Assigned Risks Pool before either the start of any Indemnity Period to which these Rules apply or the start of its Practice, whichever is the later; or

(b)   in the case of a Firm which is not an Eligible Firm, is a Firm which is carrying on or continuing to carry on a Practice without Qualifying Insurance outside the Assigned Risks Pool; or

(c)   in the case of a Run-off Firm, is a Run-off Firm which has failed to make an application in manner prescribed by these Rules to be issued with an ARP Run-off Policy; or

(d)   is a Firm which is a Firm in Default by virtue of Rule 10.4,

or a Firm which, having previously obtained Qualifying Insurance, has failed to obtain alternative Qualifying Insurance when required to do so in accordance with Rule 6.

Commentary:

A Firm In Default, and each Principal in that Firm, will be required to pay the ARP Default Premium, and/or the ARP Run-Off Premium to the Assigned Risks Pool, and each Principal in that Firm will have committed a disciplinary offence by having breached these Rules. Refer to Part 4 of these Rules for the provisions that apply to a Firm In Default.

Indemnity Period means the period of one year starting on 1 September 2000, 2001 or 2002, the period of 13 calendar months starting on 1 September 2003, or the period of one year starting on 1 October in any subsequent calendar year.

Commentary:

Under the Qualifying Insurer's Agreement, each Policy is required to expire at the end of an Indemnity Period. It is envisaged that any change to these Rules or to the Minimum Terms and Conditions would take effect from the start of an Indemnity Period, so that at any one time, all Policies in force comply with the same version of these Rules and the Minimum Terms and Conditions.

Qualifying Insurers are permitted under the Qualifying Insurer's Agreement to issue a Policy covering more than one Indemnity Period, provided that the Policy expires at the end of a subsequent Indemnity Period, and provided that the terms of the Policy are amended if required to reflect any change in the Rules or the Minimum Terms and Conditions while the Policy is in force.

Insolvency Event means in relation to a Qualifying Insurer:

(a)   the appointment of a provisional liquidator, administrator, receiver or an administrative receiver; or

(b)   the approval of a voluntary arrangement under Part 1 of the Insolvency Act 1986 or the making of any other form of arrangement, composition or compounding with its creditors generally; or

(c)   the passing of a resolution for voluntary winding up where the winding up is or becomes a creditors' voluntary winding up under Part IV of the Insolvency Act 1986; or

(d)   the making of a winding up order by the court; or

(e)   the making of an order by the court reducing the value of one or more of the Qualifying Insurer's contracts under section 377 of the Financial Services and Markets Act 2000; or

(f)   the occurrence of any event analogous to any of the foregoing insolvency events in any jurisdiction outside England and Wales.

Limited Liability Partnership means a limited liability partnership incorporated under the Limited Liability Partnerships Act 2000.

Manager means:

(a)   a Partner in a Partnership;

(b)   a member of a Limited Liability Partnership; or

(c)   a director of a company.

Minimum Terms and Conditions means the minimum terms and conditions with which a Policy of Qualifying Insurance is required by these Rules to comply a copy of which is annexed as Appendix 1 to these Rules.

Commentary:

All Qualifying Insurers agree under the Qualifying Insurer's Agreement to issue Policies which comply with the Minimum Terms and Conditions. However, under Rule 4 it remains the duty of each Firm and each Principal within that Firm to ensure that the Policy issued to it is issued by an insurer which is a Qualifying Insurer for the Indemnity Period in question, and that it complies with the Minimum Terms and Conditions. The SRA does not approve Qualifying Insurers, nor does it review their policy terms.

The standard form ARP Policy does comply with the Minimum Terms and Conditions.

In addition, each Firm should satisfy itself that the professional indemnity insurance that it has in place is sufficient. This may mean that the Firm takes out additional insurance over and above that provided under the Minimum Terms and Conditions. Any such "top-up" cover is outside the scope of these Rules, and does not have to be taken out with a Qualifying Insurer.

Most recognised bodies are required to obtain cover complying with the minimum terms and conditions and with a sum insured of £3 million, rather than £2 million for other Firms. The definition of "Relevant Recognised Body" in clause 8.2 of the Minimum Terms and Conditions indicates which recognised bodies this requirement applies to.

Non-SRA Firm means a sole practitioner, Partnership, Limited Liability Partnership or company which is not authorised to practise by the Solicitors Regulation Authority, and which is either:

(a)   authorised or capable of being authorised to practise by another Approved Regulator; or

(b)   not capable of being authorised to practise by any Approved Regulator.

Partnership means an unincorporated Firm in which persons are or are held out as partners and does not include a Firm incorporated as a Limited Liability Partnership and **Partner** means a person who is or is held out to be a partner in a Partnership.

Commentary:

A limited liability partnership is treated for these purposes as a Recognised Body, rather than as a partnership.

Period Of Default means in relation to a Firm in Default the period starting with the date when such Firm first became a Firm in Default and ending with the date when it ceased to be a Firm in Default.

Policy means a contract of professional indemnity insurance made between one or more persons, each of which is a Qualifying Insurer, and a Firm, including where the context permits an ARP Policy and an ARP Run-off Policy.

Policy Default means a failure on the part of a Firm or any Principal of that Firm:

(a)   to pay for more than two months after the due date for payment all or any part of the premium or any other sum due in respect of a Policy (including without limitation any payment due under Rule 14.1); or

(b)   to pay for more than two months after the due date for payment all or any part of any ARP Premium, any ARP Default Premium, or any ARP Run-Off Premium, or any instalment payable in relation thereto whether payable to the ARP Manager or otherwise; or

(c)   to reimburse within two months a Qualifying Insurer (including the ARP Manager on behalf of Qualifying Insurers) in respect of any amount falling within a Firm's Policy excess which has been paid on an insured's behalf to a claimant by a Qualifying Insurer or by the ARP Manager.

For the purposes of this definition, the due date for payment means, in respect of any Policy or any payment to be made under any Policy:

(i)   the date on which such payment fell due under the terms of the Policy or any related agreement or arrangement; or

(ii)   if a Firm was first required under these or any previous Rules to effect such a Policy prior to the date on which it did so, the date if earlier on which such payment would have fallen due had such Policy been effected by the Firm when it was first required to do so under these Rules or any previous rules.

Commentary:

Principals are committing a disciplinary offence if they or their Firm is in Policy Default, whether as a result of failing to pay premium when demanded or as a result of failing to take out a Policy when required to do so. In addition, their Firm will cease to be an Eligible Firm for the purpose of taking out or renewing an ARP Policy.

Practice means the whole or such part of the Private Practice of a Firm as is carried on from one or more offices in England and Wales.

Commentary:

The Rules require Firms to take out Policies which include cover in accordance with the Minimum Terms and Conditions for that part of their Practice carried on from offices located in England and Wales. They do not apply to any part of the Practice of the Firm carried on from offices outside England and Wales (although rule 15.26 of the Solicitors' Code of Conduct 2007 does apply in such cases). However, the cover in relation to the Practice carried on from offices located in England and Wales must extend to acts or omissions wherever in the world they occur, and would therefore include, for example, a Principal based in a Firm's London office who travels to Paris to advise a client.

If you are unsure whether you or your business fall within this definition, you should consult the Solicitors Regulation Authority. Contact details appear at the end of the introductory commentary.

Principal means:

(a) where the Firm is or was:

    (i) a sole practitioner – that practitioner;

    (ii) a Partnership – each Partner;

    (iii) a company with a share capital – each director of that company and any solicitor, Registered European Lawyer or Registered Foreign Lawyer who:

        (A) is held out as a director; or

        (B) beneficially owns the whole or any part of a share in the company; or

        (C) is the ultimate beneficial owner of the whole or any part of a share in the company.

    (iv) a company without a share capital – each director of that company and any solicitor, Registered European Lawyer or Registered Foreign Lawyer who:

        (A) is held out as a director; or

        (B) is a member of the company; or

        (C) is the ultimate owner of the whole or any part of a body corporate or other legal person which is a member of the company;

    (v) a Limited Liability Partnership – each member of that Limited Liability Partnership, and any solicitor, Registered European Lawyer or Registered Foreign Lawyer who is the ultimate owner of the whole or any part of a body corporate or other legal person which is member of the Limited Liability Partnership.

(b) where a body corporate or other legal person is a Partner in the Firm, all solicitors, Registered European Lawyers or Registered Foreign Lawyers who are within paragraph (a)(iii) of this definition (including sub paragraphs (A) and (C) thereof), paragraph (a)(iv) of this definition (including sub paragraphs (A) and (C) thereof), or paragraph (a)(v) of this definition.

Commentary:

It is the duty of each Principal, under Rule 4, to ensure that the Firm has Qualifying Insurance at all times.

Private Practice includes without limitation all the professional services provided by a Firm including acting as a personal representative, trustee, attorney, notary, insolvency practitioner or in any other role in conjunction with a Practice, and includes services provided pro bono publico, but does not include:

(a)   Practice carried on by a Solicitor or Registered European Lawyer in the course of employment with an employer other than a Firm; or

(b)   Practice carried on through a Non-SRA Firm; or

(c)   discharging the functions of any of the following offices or appointments:

   (i)   judicial office;

   (ii)   Under Sheriffs;

   (iii)   members and clerks of such tribunals, committees, panels and boards as the Council may from time to time designate but including those subject to the Tribunals and Inquiries Act 1992, the Competition Commission, Legal Services Commission Review Panels and Parole Boards;

   (iv)   Justices' Clerks;

   (v)   Superintendent Registrars and Deputy Superintendent Registrars of Births, Marriages and Deaths and Registrars of Local Crematoria;

   (vi)   such other offices as the Council may from time to time designate; or

(d)   Practice consisting only of:

   (i)   providing professional services without remuneration for friends, relatives, or companies wholly owned by the solicitor or Registered European Lawyer's family, or registered charities; or

   (ii)   administering oaths and taking affidavits.

Commentary:

If you are unsure whether you or your Practice fall within this definition, you should consult the Solicitors Regulation Authority. Contact details appear at the end of the introductory commentary.

Qualifying Insurance means a single Policy which includes the Minimum Terms and Conditions, or more than one Policy which, taken together, include the Minimum Terms and Conditions, and each of which includes the Minimum Terms and Conditions except only in relation to the Sum Insured (as defined in the Minimum Terms and Conditions).

Commentary:

All Firms are required to take out and maintain, as a minimum, Qualifying Insurance. This may take the form of a single policy, or policies written by more than one Qualifying Insurer which together provide the minimum cover required under these Rules.

Qualifying Insurer means an Authorised Insurer which has entered into a Qualifying Insurer's agreement with the Society which remains in force for the purposes of underwriting new business at the date on which the relevant contract of Qualifying Insurance is made.

Commentary:

A list of all Qualifying Insurers appears on the website of the Solicitors Regulation Authority at www.sra.org.uk, and is also available from the Solicitors Regulation Authority. Contact details appear at the end of the introductory commentary.

Qualifying Insurer's Agreement means an agreement in such terms as the Society may from time to time prescribe setting out the terms and conditions on which a Qualifying Insurer may provide professional indemnity insurance to solicitors and others in Private Practice in England and Wales.

Commentary:

A copy of this standard form agreement, which each Qualifying Insurer is required to enter into, is available on request from the Solicitors Regulation Authority. Contact details appear at the end of the introductory commentary.

Recognised Body means a body for the time being recognised by the Solicitors Regulation Authority under section 9 of the Administration of Justice Act 1985 and the SRA Recognised Bodies Regulations 2009.

Recognised Sole Practitioner means a solicitor or Registered European Lawyer authorised by the Solicitors Regulation Authority under section 1B of the Solicitors Act 1974 to practise as a sole practitioner.

Registered European Lawyer means an individual registered with the Society under regulation 17 of the European Communities (Lawyer's Practice) Regulations 2000.

Registered Foreign Lawyer means an individual registered with the Society under section 89 of the Courts and Legal Services Act 1990.

Rules means these rules as from time to time modified or amended.

Run-off Firm means a Firm or former Firm which has ceased to practise in circumstances where, in accordance with paragraph 5.1 of the Minimum Terms and Conditions, run-off cover is not required to be provided by any Qualifying Insurer.

Society means the Law Society of England and Wales.

Solicitor means a person who has been admitted as a solicitor and whose name is on the roll (within the meaning of the Solicitors Act 1974) and who practises as a solicitor whether or not he or she has in force a practising certificate as referred to in that Act and also includes practice under home title of a former Registered European Lawyer who has become a solicitor.

Solicitors Regulation Authority means the Solicitors Regulation Authority carrying out regulatory functions assigned to the Law Society as an Approved Regulator.

Special Measures means such measures as the Council may from time to time require with a view to reducing the risk of claims being made against a Firm in the future or with a view to enabling a Firm in the future to obtain Qualifying Insurance outside the Assigned Risks Pool.

Supplementary Run-off Cover means run-off cover provided by the Solicitors Indemnity Fund following the expiry of run-off cover provided to a Firm in accordance with these Rules or otherwise under a Policy (but subject to compliance with the Minimum Terms and Conditions).

3.2 **Interpretation**

In these Rules, unless the context otherwise requires:

(a)   the singular includes the plural, and vice versa;

(b)   a reference to a person includes a body corporate, partnerships, and other unincorporated associations or bodies of persons;

(c)   a reference to a Rule is to a Rule forming part of these Rules;

(d)   a reference to any statute, statutory provision, code or regulation includes:

> (i)   any subordinate legislation (as defined by section 21(1) of the Interpretation Act 1978) made under it; and
>
> (ii)   any provision which it has superseded or re-enacted (with or without modification) or amended, and any provision superseding it or re-enacting it (with or without modification) or amending it either before, or at the date of the commencement of these Rules, or after the date of the commencement of these Rules;

(e)   references to the Society and to the Council include the Solicitors Regulation Authority and the Legal Complaints Service, and any body or person which succeeds in whole or in part to the functions of the Society, the Council, the Solicitors Regulation Authority or the Legal Complaints Service, and any delegate of the Society, the Council, the Solicitors Regulation Authority, the Legal Complaints Service or any such body or person;

(f)   headings are for ease of reference only and shall not affect the interpretation of these Rules;

(g)   explanatory notes and commentary shall be ignored in interpreting these Rules; and

(h)   the appendices to these Rules form part of these Rules.

These Rules will be governed by and interpreted in accordance with English law.

Part 2: Responsibility and monitoring

4 Obligation to effect insurance

4.1   All Firms carrying on a Practice during any Indemnity Period beginning on or after 1 October 2010 must take out and maintain Qualifying Insurance under these Rules.

4.2   A solicitor or Registered European Lawyer is not required to take out and maintain Qualifying Insurance under these Rules in respect of work done as an employee or whilst otherwise directly engaged in the Practice of another Firm (including without limitation as an Appointed Person), where that Firm is required by these Rules to take out and maintain Qualifying Insurance.

4.3   A Run-off Firm must apply in accordance with these Rules to be issued with an ARP Run-off Policy.

Commentary:

Under these Rules, Firms have a continuing obligation to ensure that they have Qualifying Insurance in place at all times with effect from 1 October 2010. Refer to the definitions of Practice, amongst others, to establish whether a Firm falls within the scope of these Rules. Firms should also check that any insurance that they take out in order to comply with these Rules (as opposed to any "top-up" cover) is taken out with a Qualifying Insurer. A list of Qualifying Insurers appears on the website of the Solicitors Regulation Authority at www.sra.org.uk, and is also available from the Solicitors Regulation Authority. Contact details appear at the end of the introductory commentary.

Firms should note in particular that work carried out by an Appointed Person for that Firm may be covered by the Firm's Policy, whether that person is engaged as an employee or on a contract for services.

APPENDIX 6

If a Firm cannot obtain a Policy from a Qualifying Insurer it should apply to join the Assigned Risks Pool in accordance with Part 3 of the Rules, if it is an Eligible Firm. If it is not an Eligible Firm, it must cease Practice.

Note that, under the Minimum Terms and Conditions, a Policy, once taken out, cannot be cancelled before the end of an Indemnity Period unless:

(1)   *the Policy is an ARP Policy and the Firm has replaced it with a Policy of Qualifying Insurance outside the Assigned Risks Pool; or*

(2)   *the Firm merges with another Firm and a Policy of Qualifying Insurance is in place for the merged Firm; or*

(3)   *it subsequently transpires that the Firm was not in fact required to take out and maintain a Policy under these Rules; or*

(4)   *in the case of an ARP Policy, it subsequently transpires that the Firm was not, or has ceased to be, an Eligible Firm; or*

(5)   *the Qualifying Insurer which issues the Policy becomes the subject of an Insolvency Event, and the Firm has replaced the Policy with another Policy of Qualifying Insurance.*

The effect of cancellation in the circumstances described in (3) or (4) above is that the Firm ceases to have Qualifying Insurance in place with effect from the cancellation, and would therefore be in breach of Rule 4.1 if it were to carry on a Practice thereafter without taking out a new Policy.

Most Recognised Bodies are required to obtain cover complying with the Minimum Terms and Conditions and with a sum insured of £3 million, rather than £2 million for other Firms. The definition of "Relevant Recognised Body" in clause 8.2 of the Minimum Terms and Conditions indicates which Recognised Bodies this requirement applies to.

4.4   The provisions of this Rule 4 shall be without prejudice to the ability of Firms to include as insureds on a Policy persons not required under these Rules to be insured.

5 Responsibility

5.1   Each Firm carrying on a Practice during any Indemnity Period beginning on or after 1 October 2010, and any person who is a Principal of such a Firm, must ensure that:

(a)   that the Firm has in place and maintains Qualifying Insurance outside the Assigned Risks Pool during any such Indemnity Period;

or, in the case of an Eligible Firm,

(b)   that the Firm has applied to enter the Assigned Risks Pool in accordance with the procedure set out in Rule 10;

in either case before the start of any relevant Indemnity Period or the start of Practice whichever is later.

Commentary:

Note that the duty to ensure that Qualifying Insurance is in place rests not just on the Firm as a whole, but also on every Principal within that Firm.

5.2   A Run-off Firm, and any person who was a Principal of that Run-off Firm immediately prior to it becoming a Run-off Firm, must ensure that the Run-off Firm has applied to enter the Assigned Risks Pool in accordance with the procedure set out in Rule 13.4(a). Making such an application does not absolve any Firm or person from any breach of Rule 5.1.

Commentary:

A Firm which has continued to practise without Qualifying Insurance immediately prior to closing down is required to apply for Run-Off Cover through the Assigned Risks Pool, but the Firm and any Principal of the Firm may still face action for a breach of Rule 5.1 for practising without Qualifying Insurance.

6 Insolvency of Qualifying Insurer

6.1   If a Firm is carrying on a Practice which is being provided with Qualifying Insurance by a Qualifying Insurer (whether alone or together with other Qualifying Insurers) and that Qualifying Insurer is the subject of an Insolvency Event then, subject to any waiver under Rule 19.1, the Firm and any person who is a Principal of the Firm must ensure:

(a)   that the Firm has in place Qualifying Insurance with another Qualifying Insurer which must be arranged as soon as may be reasonably practicable and in any event within four weeks of such an Insolvency Event;

or, in the case of an Eligible Firm,

(b)   that the Firm applies within that period of four weeks to enter the Assigned Risks Pool in accordance with the procedure set out in Rule 10.4.

Commentary:

It is important to be aware that the arrangements for professional indemnity insurance put in place by the Solicitors Regulation Authority do not seek to protect Firms against the insolvency of a Qualifying Insurer. If an Insolvency Event occurs in respect of an insurer, that insurer will cease to be a Qualifying Insurer for the purposes of writing new policies and Firms insured by that insurer must effect alternative insurance in accordance with these Rules. This is because, in such circumstances, the insurer may not be in a position to pay claims in full. Any Firm which has qualifying insurance with a Qualifying Insurer which is the subject of an Insolvency Event is required therefore to obtain replacement cover as soon as possible, and in any event within four weeks of the Insolvency Event occurring. Having done so, a Firm should cancel the policy with the insolvent insurer and, if entitled to do so, seek a return of the premium relating to the balance of the Indemnity Period from the insurer which has become the subject of the Insolvency Event.

7 Monitoring

The Council may require from a Firm or any Principal in a Firm carrying on, or reasonably believed by the Council to be carrying on, a Practice such information and evidence as it may reasonably require to satisfy itself that such a Firm has in place Qualifying Insurance.

8 Registered European Lawyers

8.1   The special provisions contained in Appendix 3 to these Rules shall apply to a Firm that has at least one Principal who is a Registered European Lawyer.

Part 3: The Assigned Risks Pool

9 Operation of the Assigned Risks Pool

The Assigned Risks Pool shall be managed by the ARP Manager.

10 Applying to the Assigned Risks Pool

10.1 Where a Firm carrying on a Practice has not obtained Qualifying Insurance outside the Assigned Risks Pool in respect of any Indemnity Period or part thereof to which these Rules apply it must, if an Eligible Firm apply in accordance with the procedure set out in this Rule 10 to enter the Assigned Risks Pool, subject to Rule 10.2, before the start of the relevant Indemnity Period.

Commentary:

A Firm which for any reason does not have Qualifying Insurance in place should apply to the Assigned Risks Pool before the start of the relevant Indemnity Period if it is an Eligible Firm. However, it is important to note that premiums payable to the Assigned Risks Pool are intended to be high, and Firms would therefore be prudent to seek quotations from Qualifying Insurers outside the Assigned Risks Pool before the start of an Indemnity Period.

An ARP Policy can be cancelled if it is replaced by a Policy with a Qualifying Insurer. A return premium may be payable to a Firm which cancels an ARP Policy in these circumstances – refer to Appendix 2 for the basis on which the ARP Premium and any return premium is calculated.

Firms should also be aware of the other consequences of being insured through the Assigned Risks Pool set out in this part of the Rules, including the need to comply with any Special Measures under Rule 10, and the limitations on eligibility set out in the definition of "Eligible Firm".

10.2 A Firm must not start carrying on a Practice without having obtained Qualifying Insurance outside the Assigned Risks Pool.

Commentary:

Any Firm wishing to start up a new Practice must obtain Qualifying Insurance with a Qualifying Insurer other than the Assigned Risks Pool, before starting Practice. For the avoidance of doubt, a Firm which has not previously been regulated by the Solicitors Regulation Authority or a Non-SRA Firm that elects (and is accepted) for regulation by the SRA must also arrange Qualifying Insurance outside the Assigned Risks Pool in order to commence carrying on a Practice. Subject to this requirement, a new Firm may start Practice at any time during an Indemnity Period.

10.3 By applying to enter the Assigned Risks Pool, the Firm and any person who is a Principal of that Firm agrees to, and (if the Firm is admitted to the Assigned Risks Pool) the Firm and any person who is a Principal of that Firm shall be jointly and severally liable to:

(a) pay the ARP Premium in accordance with these Rules, together with any other sums due to the ARP Manager under the ARP Policy; and

(b) submit to such investigation and monitoring and to pay the Society's costs and expenses as referred to in Rule 11.2; and

(c) pay any costs and expenses incurred by the Society or the ARP Manager incurred as a result of any failure or delay by the Firm in complying with these Rules;

and shall be required to implement at the expense of the Firm any Special Measures.

Commentary:

Firms within the Assigned Risks Pool may be subject to a range of Special Measures. The appointed inspectors (in the first instance, the Forensic Investigations Unit of the Compliance Directorate) will visit a Firm insured through the Assigned Risks Pool to carry out investigation and monitoring of the Firm. This is in order to determine what Special Measures are appropriate for that Firm, and to ensure that those measures are fully implemented. It should be noted that the costs of investigation and monitoring by the Inspection & Investigation Directorate, costs and expenses incurred through any failure or delay by the Firm to comply, and the implementation of the Special Measures will be payable by the Firm concerned (and by any Principal of that Firm), in addition to paying the ARP Premium.

10.4   Any material misrepresentation made in an application for admission to the Assigned Risks Pool shall, subject to any waiver under Rule 19.1, render the Firm a Firm in Default for the purposes of Part 4 of these Rules. The provisions of that Part shall apply to the Firm as if that Firm had not been admitted to the Assigned Risks Pool but neither the Firm nor any Principal of the Firm shall be entitled to the refund of any ARP Premium paid to the ARP Manager. Any amount so paid shall be credited against any sums payable under Part 4 of these Rules.

Commentary:

Although an ARP Policy, once issued, cannot be cancelled (unless and until a replacement Policy with a Qualifying Insurer is issued to that Firm), a Firm which makes a material misrepresentation in its application to be admitted to the Assigned Risks Pool will be nevertheless treated in the same way as a Firm in Default.

10.5   The application for admission to the Assigned Risks Pool must be made to the ARP Manager on the proposal form provided by the ARP Manager.

10.6   The applicant must state on the proposal form the date from which cover is sought. This date must not be earlier than the date on which the application is made for admission to the Assigned Risks Pool. The applicant must also provide such other information as the ARP Manager requires for the purposes of setting a premium.

10.7   If the applicant is a Firm in Default it must state on the proposal form that it is a Firm in Default and give the date of the start of the Period of Default from which retrospective cover is sought.

Commentary:

The ARP Premium is calculated in accordance with a formula set out in Appendix 2, and is linked to the gross fees of the Firm concerned. It is important to note that, under Rule 15, any material misrepresentation in an application will result in the Firm being treated in the same way as a Firm In Default, including being liable to pay the ARP Default Premium.

10.8   The Firm, together with each Principal of the Firm, must ensure that the Firm's application has been made and must provide the ARP Manager with all information it reasonably requires to process the application.

Commentary:

It is in the interests of the Firm and each of the Principals of that Firm to verify that the application to enter the Assigned Risks Pool has been received and that the Firm is insured. An application should be made before the start of an Indemnity Period. Failure to comply with the requirements of this Rule and Rules 13 to 15 will result in the Firm becoming a Firm in Default.

10.9   If a Firm has not received a written acknowledgement of its application from the ARP Manager 30 days after making the application, or within such other period as is stated on the proposal form, the Firm and any person who is a Principal of the Firm must seek written confirmation that the Firm's application has been received by the ARP Manager. If that written confirmation is not obtained within seven days after the end of the 30 days, or within seven days after such other period specified on the proposal form, the application shall be deemed not to have been made.

10.10   An applicant whose first application is deemed under Rule 10.9 not to have been made must, within seven days of the day when under Rule 10.9 the first application is deemed not to have been made, make a fresh application. The Firm and any person who is a Principal of the Firm must ensure that the Firm is in a position to prove to the reasonable satisfaction of the Society that the Firm's fresh application was delivered within those seven days to the ARP Manager at the address specified on the proposal form. Provided the Firm's fresh application was so delivered, the application shall be treated as having been made at the date when the Firm's first application was made. A Firm that is not in a position to prove to the reasonable satisfaction of the Society that its fresh application was so delivered shall be deemed not to have made any application.

10.11 Provided that an application or, if necessary, a fresh application, has been made in accordance with Rules 10.5 to 10.10, a Firm which is an Eligible Firm will be covered in the terms of the ARP Policy to be issued to it from the start of the relevant Indemnity Period or, in the case of a Firm to which Rule 10.2 applies, the date specified in the application, being the date specified in accordance with Rule 10.6, until whichever is the earlier of:

(a)   the end of the relevant Indemnity Period; or

(b)   the date on which the Firm obtains Qualifying Insurance outside the Assigned Risks Pool; or

(c)   the date when the Firm ceases to be an Eligible Firm.

Commentary:

An Eligible Firm which should have applied to the Assigned Risks Pool before the start of an Indemnity Period but fails to do so will have breached these Rules by failing to take out a Policy from the start of the Indemnity Period. It may make a later application, but will be liable to pay the ARP Default Premium for the Indemnity Period in question. Each Principal in an Eligible Firm which fails to make an application in time commits a disciplinary offence.

10.12 Any Firm in the Assigned Risks Pool, and any person who is a Principal of that Firm, is liable to pay to the ARP Manager the ARP Premium in respect of that Firm within thirty days of such premium being notified to it by the ARP Manager.

Commentary:

It is a disciplinary offence for a Firm and for any Principal of that Firm to fail to pay the ARP Premium (including the ARP Run-off Premium) to the ARP Manager within the required 30 day period. A Firm may enter into arrangements with, for example, a premium funding company (whether offered by the ARP Manager or arranged independently) to enable it to make payments by instalments, provided that the premium is received in full by the ARP Manager from the premium funding company within the required 30 day period.

11   Special Measures

11.1   An Eligible Firm that has applied to enter the Assigned Risks Pool in accordance with the procedure set out in Rule 10 will be issued with an ARP Policy by the ARP Manager.

Commentary:

A copy of the standard-form ARP Policy is available on the website of the Solicitors Regulation Authority at www.sra.org.uk and is also available from the Solicitors Regulation Authority. Contact details appear at the end of the introductory commentary.

11.2 A Firm in the Assigned Risks Pool must if and to the extent required by the Council submit to investigation and monitoring by the Society and/or its agents, including investigation and monitoring:

(a) to determine the reasons why Qualifying Insurance outside the Assigned Risks Pool was not obtained;

(b) to ascertain what Special Measures should be taken by the Firm.

The Society's costs and expenses of the investigation and monitoring and the Society's costs and expenses of ascertaining what Special Measures should be taken and of monitoring them shall be met by the Firm and by any person who is a Principal of that Firm. The amount of such costs and expenses shall be determined by the Society which shall not be required to give any detailed breakdown thereof.

Commentary:

The appointed inspectors (in the first instance, the Forensic Investigations Department of the Inspection & Investigation Directorate) will visit a Firm insured through the Assigned Risks Pool to carry out investigation and monitoring. This is in order to determine what Special Measures should be taken and are appropriate for that Firm, and to ensure that those measures are fully implemented. It should be noted that the costs and expenses of investigation and monitoring by the Inspection & Investigation Directorate and the implementation of the Special Measures (together with VAT if applicable) will be payable by the Firm concerned (including each Principal of that Firm), in addition to paying the ARP Premium.

12 Time in the Assigned Risks Pool

12.1 A Firm may leave the Assigned Risks Pool at any time after it has satisfied the ARP Manager that the Firm has obtained Qualifying Insurance outside the Assigned Risks Pool at least until the expiry of the relevant Indemnity Period.

Commentary:

Refer to Appendix 2 to determine whether any return premium will be payable on leaving the Assigned Risks Pool.

12.2 Subject to Rule 12.7, a Firm may only remain in the Assigned Risks Pool so long as it is an Eligible Firm, or if it becomes a Run-off Firm.

Commentary:

Firms cannot remain insured through the Assigned Risks Pool for more than 12 months in any four consecutive Indemnity Periods, and should therefore seek insurance in the open market with a Qualifying Insurer as soon as practicable. A Firm which is no longer an Eligible Firm (because, for example, it has already been insured through the Assigned Risks Pool for 12 months in the last four Indemnity Periods) must either obtain Qualifying Insurance on the open market or cease carrying on Practice.

12.3 Subject to Rule 12.7(b), a Firm in Policy Default at the end of an Indemnity Period shall be deemed to be a Firm in Default for the purposes of Part 4 of these Rules and shall not be an Eligible Firm. This Rule shall not apply in any case where the Council is satisfied that there exists a genuine dispute between the Firm and a Qualifying Insurer or the ARP Manager which makes it unreasonable for the Firm to be deemed to be a Firm in Default pending the resolution of that dispute.

Commentary:

A Firm in Policy Default must remedy that default before the start of an Indemnity Period if it wishes to obtain insurance through the Assigned Risks Pool at any time during that Indemnity Period.

APPENDIX 6

Alternatively, it must either obtain Qualifying Insurance in the open market, or cease carrying on Practice. If a Firm believes that there is a genuine dispute which justifies that Firm not being deemed to be a Firm in Default, it should apply to the Solicitors Regulation Authority as soon as possible before the start of the next Indemnity Period. Contact details appear at the end of the introductory commentary.

12.4   A Firm that is no longer an Eligible Firm must either have Qualifying Insurance outside the Assigned Risks Pool or forthwith cease carrying on Practice.

12.5   Where the Practice of a Firm (the **Original Firm**) which has at any time been in the Assigned Risks Pool is split between two or more Firms (the **Successor Firms**), the Council may in its absolute discretion treat the Successor Firms or any of them and the Original Firm as being a single Firm for the purposes of determining whether the Successor Firms or any of them are or remain an Eligible Firm.

12.6   Where the Practice of a Firm (the **Original Firm**) which has at any time been in the Assigned Risks Pool is merged with, acquired, absorbed, or by any other means taken over by a Firm (the **Successor Firm**) the Council may in its absolute discretion treat the Successor Firm and the Original Firm as being a Single Firm for the purposes of determining whether the Successor Firm is or remains an Eligible Firm.

Commentary:

The purpose of this Rule is to ensure that the time limit on participation in the Assigned Risks Pool cannot be avoided by a merger or reconstitution of that Firm. A Firm which was not previously eligible to join the Assigned Risks Pool will not necessarily become an Eligible Firm by virtue of changes in the composition of a Firm. Firms which are unsure about their eligibility following any such change should consult the Solicitors Regulation Authority. Contact details appear at the end of the introductory commentary.

12.7   The Council shall have power in any particular case or cases:

(a)   to allow a Firm to remain in or to re-enter the Assigned Risks Pool after any date when the Firm would otherwise cease to be an Eligible Firm; and

(b)   to permit a Firm to be admitted into or remain in or to re-enter the Assigned Risks Pool notwithstanding that the Firm is in Policy Default on such terms and conditions as the Council may prescribe including the taking of steps by the Firm by a specified date or dates to remedy the Policy Default;

and when such power is exercised the Firm shall continue to be an Eligible Firm for so long as the Council may from time to time permit and provided that it complies with any such terms and conditions.

Commentary:

It is envisaged that these powers would be exercised only in exceptional circumstances. Any application seeking the exercise of this power should be made to the Solicitors Regulation Authority at least three months before the Firm in question would otherwise cease to be an Eligible Firm.

Part 4: Firms in default

13 Eligibility of Firms in Default

13.1   At any time during the Period of Default a Firm in Default is entitled to be admitted to the Assigned Risks Pool and to be issued with an ARP Policy in accordance with Rule 13.2, subject to the provisions of this Rule 13.

13.2   A Firm in Default is entitled to be admitted to the Assigned Risks Pool if:

(a)   it was an Eligible Firm at the start of the Period of Default;

(b)   had it been admitted to the Assigned Risks Pool at the start of the Period of Default, its admission at that time would not have rendered it ineligible to be admitted to the Assigned Risks Pool for any part of any subsequent Indemnity Period in which it was in fact admitted to the Assigned Risks Pool;

(c)   it has applied to join the Assigned Risks Pool in accordance with Rule 10;

(d)   the Firm discharges in full the ARP Default Premium calculated for the whole of the Indemnity Period or Indemnity Periods for which cover is sought within 30 days of such premium being notified to it by the ARP Manager or such longer period as the Council may allow;

(e)   the Firm will be subject to and [comply] with Rules 10.3(b) (other than Rule 10.3(a)) and 11.2.

Commentary:

If a Firm fails to make an application to the Assigned Risks Pool at the start of an Indemnity Period, and does not have any other Policy of Qualifying Insurance in force for that Indemnity Period, it may still be eligible to be issued with an ARP Policy provided that it meets all of the requirements of Rule 13.1. However, each Principal of the Firm will have committed a disciplinary offence, and the Firm and each Principal of that Firm will be liable to pay the ARP Default Premium under any ARP Policy issued.

13.3   An ARP Policy issued under this Rule may afford cover retrospectively from the start of the Period of Default until the earlier of:

(a)   the end of the then current Indemnity Period; or

(b)   the date on which the Firm in Default would have ceased to be an Eligible Firm, ignoring for these purposes any failure to pay the ARP Premium or the ARP Default Premium; or

(c)   the date on which, had the Firm in Default been admitted to the Assigned Risks Pool at the start of the Period of Default, its being covered by the Assigned Risks Pool from that time would have first caused it to have been ineligible to be admitted to the Assigned Risks Pool for any part of any subsequent Indemnity Period in which it was in fact admitted to the Assigned Risks Pool.

13.4   A Run-off Firm shall be entitled at any time following the date on which it first becomes a Run-off Firm to be admitted to the Assigned Risks Pool and to be issued with an ARP Run-off Policy, subject to the following conditions:

(a)   the Run-off Firm has made an application to join the Assigned Risks Pool in manner provided by Rule 10.5 stating on the proposal form that it is a Run-off Firm and giving the date from which cover under an ARP Run-off Policy is sought;

(b)   the ARP Run-off Premium is discharged in full within thirty days of such premium being notified by the ARP Manager to the Firm or such longer period as the Council may allow; and

(c)   the Firm, and any person who is a Principal of that Firm, will be subject to and comply with Rule 10.3(c).

Commentary:

A Run-off Firm will be eligible to be issued with an ARP Policy if it meets all of the requirements of Rule 13.4. However, each Principal of the Firm will have committed a disciplinary offence for failing to make an application to the Assigned Risks Pool for run-off cover in accordance with Rule 5.2, and the Firm and each Principal of the Firm will be required to pay the ARP Run-off Premium under any ARP Run-off Policy issued.

APPENDIX 6

13.5   An ARP Run-off Policy shall provide run-off cover to a Run-off Firm retrospectively from the date on which it became a Run-off Firm until the end of the day immediately prior to the sixth anniversary of:

(a)   the start of the Indemnity Period in which it became a Run-off Firm; or

(b)   if applicable, the start of the last Indemnity Period, prior to it becoming a Run-off Firm, in which it both ceased to be an Eligible Firm and was a Firm in Default and continued as such until the date on which it became a Run-off Firm,

whichever is the earlier.

Commentary:

Run-off Firms which are issued with an ARP Run-off Policy obtain six years' run-off cover either from the start of the Indemnity Period in which their Practice ceased, or the date on which they ceased to be eligible to apply for an ARP Policy while practising uninsured.

13.6   Rule 12.7 shall apply so as to enable the Council to extend the period in Rule 13.3 for which a Firm in Default may be issued with an ARP Policy.

Commentary:

It is envisaged that this power would be exercised only in exceptional circumstances.

13.7   Any Firm that has been admitted to the Assigned Risks Pool under Rule 13.1 shall for the purposes of computing its continuing eligibility to remain in the Assigned Risks Pool be deemed to have been admitted to the Assigned Risks Pool at start of the Period of Default and to have remained continuously in the Assigned Risks Pool until the end of the Indemnity Period current at the date of its application.

13.8   Rule 15.2 shall not apply to a Firm which has under Rule 13 been admitted to the Assigned Risks Pool and which has been issued with an ARP Policy or an ARP Run-off Policy, the liability of the Firm and of any person who is a Principal of that Firm being limited in those circumstances to the excess payable under the terms of the Policy.

Commentary:

If a Firm is eligible to be issued with an ARP Policy under Rule 13.1, or an ARP Run-off Policy under Rule 13.4 then, provided that it complies with the relevant requirements under Rule 13 and is issued with an ARP Policy or an ARP Run-off Policy, the Firm and the Principals of that Firm will be required to pay to the ARP Manager only the relevant premium and the excess in the event of any claim.

14 Firms which fail to apply to the Assigned Risks Pool

14.1   A Firm in Default which is entitled to be admitted to the Assigned Risks Pool and to be issued with an ARP Policy in accordance with Rule 13.1 but which does not make an application to join the Assigned Risks Pool shall, notwithstanding, be liable, together with any person who is a Principal of that Firm, to pay to the Society an amount equivalent to the ARP Default Premium calculated for the whole of the Period of Default.

14.2   A Firm in Default which is entitled to be admitted to the Assigned Risks Pool and to be issued with an ARP Run-off Policy in accordance with Rules 13.4 and 13.5 but which does not make an application to join the Assigned Risks Pool shall, notwithstanding, be liable, together with any person who is a Principal of that Firm, to pay to the Society an amount equivalent to the ARP Run-off Premium calculated for the whole of the period equivalent to that which would be provided by an ARP Run-off Policy in accordance with Rule 13.5, or, if shorter and if it can be ascertained, the Period of Default.

14.3 Any amount payable in accordance with Rules 14.1 or 14.2 shall be determined by the ARP Manager on the basis of such assumption as to the Firm's gross fees and other matters as the ARP Manager shall in its absolute discretion determine, and may be reviewed from time to time by the ARP Manager in its absolute discretion on the basis of any further information provided to it. Any such amount paid under Rule 14.1 or 14.2 shall be deducted from any amount payable pursuant to Rule 15.2. The ARP Manager may and is hereby authorised to recover all sums due under Rules 14.1 or 14.2 on behalf of the Society.

Commentary:

If a Firm fails to make an application to the Assigned Risks Pool, but carries on Practice without having obtained Qualifying Insurance, each Principal in that Firm will have committed a disciplinary offence. The same is true if a Run-off Firm fails to apply to be issued with an ARP Run-off Policy. In each case, that Firm, and each Principal in that Firm, will also be liable under these Rules to:

- *pay an amount to the Society equivalent to the ARP Default Premium calculated for the whole of the Period of Default; and*

- *reimburse to the Society in full under Rule 15 the amount of any claim (together with defence costs) made against the Firm and relating to the period when it did not have Qualifying Insurance in force, less any amount due under this Rule.*

15 Arrangements in relation to uninsured Firms

15.1 The ARP Manager on behalf of the Society shall make arrangements with Qualifying Insurers to cover any Claim (as defined in the Minimum Terms and Conditions) against:

(a)   a Firm in Default; and

(b)   a Run-off Firm

including any Defence Costs (as defined in the Minimum Terms and Conditions) relating to a Claim, in like manner and to the like extent as the Claim and the Defence Costs would have been covered had that Firm during the Period of Default been in the Assigned Risks Pool and been issued with an ARP Policy and/or, as the case may require, an ARP Run-off Policy.

15.2 Subject to Rule 13.8, Rule 14.1 and Rule 14.2, the Society on behalf of Qualifying Insurers shall be entitled to recover from each and every Principal in the Firm in Default during the Period of Default all amounts paid in or towards the discharge of a Claim and Defence Costs pursuant to Rule 15 together with interest thereon at Barclays Bank Plc base rate plus three per cent from the date when such amounts were respectively paid. The ARP Manager may and is hereby authorised to recover all sums due under this Rule on behalf of the Society.

15.3 A Firm shall not be deemed to have been admitted to the Assigned Risks Pool or to be covered in accordance with Rule 15 solely by virtue of the fact that the ARP Manager may conduct or settle any claim made against that Firm under the terms of any agreement between the Society and any Qualifying Insurer.

Commentary:

If a Firm fails to make an application to the Assigned Risks Pool, but carries on Practice without having obtained Qualifying Insurance, each Principal in that Firm will have committed a disciplinary offence. The same is true if a Run-off Firm fails to apply to be issued with an ARP Run-off Policy. In each case, that Firm, and each Principal in that Firm, will also be liable under these Rules to:

APPENDIX 6

- *reimburse to the Society in full the amount paid pursuant to Rule 15.1 in respect of any claim (together with defence costs) made against the Firm and relating to the period when it did not have Qualifying Insurance in force, less any amount due under Rule 14 (where applicable); and*

- *pay an amount under Rule 14 (where applicable) to the Society equivalent to the ARP Default Premium calculated for the whole of the Period of Default.*

However, if a Firm in these circumstances is eligible under Rule 13.1 to be issued with an ARP Policy, then, provided that it complies with Rule 13.1 and is issued with an ARP Policy, the liability of the Firm and the Principals of that Firm will be limited, from that point on, to the ARP Default Premium and the excess payable under the terms of the ARP Policy.

Part 5: Disciplinary offences and reporting

16 Disciplinary consequences of failure to comply with these Rules

16.1 The provisions in Part 4 of the Rules are made without prejudice to the powers of the Council or the Society under the Solicitors Act 1974, the Administration of Justice Act 1985, the Courts and Legal Services Act 1990 or the European Communities (Lawyer's Practice) Regulations 2000, or rules made under any of them, to bring disciplinary proceedings against any Firm that has failed to comply with these Rules or any person who is or was a Principal in such a Firm or to intervene in a Practice carried on by such a Firm.

Commentary:

Payment of the ARP Default Premium and/or the ARP Run-off Premium does not detract from the fact that the Firm in question, and each Principal of that Firm, has committed a breach of these Rules as a result of the Firm being a Firm in Default. If a Firm in Default is not an Eligible Firm, it must either obtain Qualifying Insurance in the open market, or cease carrying on Practice and make an application to the Assigned Risks Pool for run-off cover in accordance with Rule 5.2.

16.2 Without prejudice to any other disciplinary offence which may arise under these Rules, it shall be a disciplinary offence for any Firm or any person who is at the relevant time a Principal in a Firm to be in Policy Default, or to fail to implement any Special Measures to the satisfaction of the Society.

Commentary:

Policy Default and Special Measures are defined in Rule 3.1. Note that a Firm that is carrying on a Practice while in Policy Default will also not be an Eligible Firm for the purpose of seeking further cover through the Assigned Risks Pool.

17 Use of information

17.1 Any Qualifying Insurer (including the ARP Manager) may, in relation to any Firm which applies to it for Qualifying Insurance, and in the case of the ARP Manager any Run-off Firm or Firm in Default, whether or not that Firm applies to enter the Assigned Risks Pool, bring to the attention of the Society (including, in the case of the matters referred to in Rule 17.1(f), the Legal Complaints Service and/or the Office for Legal Complaints (including the Legal Ombudsman)) at any time and without notice to the Firm concerned:

    (a)   any failure on the part of the Firm or any person who is a Principal of that Firm to pay any sum, including an ARP Premium, ARP Default Premium or ARP

Run-off Premium, on or before the date specified in these Rules or to reimburse any amount falling within a Policy excess which has been paid out by a Qualifying Insurer to a claimant;

(b) a material inaccuracy in any proposal form submitted by or on behalf of the Firm;

(c) the fact that the Firm has become or is believed to have become a Run-off Firm;

(d) any matter or circumstances that would entitle the Firm's Qualifying Insurer to avoid or repudiate a Policy but for the provisions of clause 4.1 of the Minimum Terms and Conditions (and/or the corresponding of the Policy);

(e) any dishonesty or fraud suspected by a Qualifying Insurer on the part of any Insured as defined in the Minimum Terms and Conditions; and

(f) any claim of inadequate professional services made against the Firm or any Insured of that Firm of which it becomes aware.

Commentary:

All Firms, whether they obtain their Qualifying Insurance on the open market or through the Assigned Risks Pool, or whether, having failed to obtain Qualifying Insurance, they are subject to the provisions of Part 4 of these Rules, are deemed to have consented to their Qualifying Insurer or the ARP Manager bringing to the attention of the Solicitors Regulation Authority any of the matters referred to Rule 17.1 that may be applicable to the Firm. Any such information is subject to the confidentiality provisions of Rule 17.4.

17.2 The Legal Complaints Service of the Society and/or the Office for Legal Complaints (including the Legal Ombudsman) may pass such information as it in its absolute discretion sees fit to any other department or office of the Society, and to any Qualifying Insurer, including the ARP Manager, in relation to any complaint of inadequate professional services against a Firm of which it becomes aware.

17.3 The Council may require any Qualifying Insurer or the ARP Manager to bring to the attention of the Society any of the matters referred to in Rule 17.1 where it reasonably believes there are matters which ought to be brought to the attention of the Society in accordance with Rule 17.1.

17.4 In respect of any information that may be brought to the attention of the Society in accordance with Rules 17.1 to 17.3:

(a) the Society shall keep all such information confidential;

(b) the Society shall not (except where and to the extent required by law or in the proper performance by the Society of its regulatory functions) at any time reveal any such information to any person other than a duly authorised employee of the Society or any of its subsidiaries; and

(c) any privilege attaching to such information shall not be regarded as having been waived whether by virtue of such information having been provided to the Society or otherwise.

17.5 The provisions of Rule 17.4 shall not prevent the Society from:

(a) making use of any information referred to in that Rule for the purpose of bringing disciplinary proceedings against any person; or

(b) in relation to information about a Firm's Policy under Rule 18, disclosing that information, where and to the extent that the Society in its absolute discretion considers it appropriate, to any person entitled to such information, and to any other department or office of the Society, including without limitation to the Legal Complaints Service and/or the Office for Legal Complaints (including the Legal Ombudsman).

18 Details of Qualifying Insurer

18.1 If a person (a **Claimant**) asserts a claim against a Firm or any person insured under that Firm's Policy, and where such claim relates to any matter within the scope of cover of the Minimum Terms and Conditions (whether or not such claim would or may be upheld), the Firm and any person who is at the relevant time (or, in the case of a Firm which has ceased Practice, any person who was immediately before that Firm ceased Practice) a Principal in that Firm shall be required, upon being so requested by that Claimant, by any person insured under that Firm's Policy, or by any other person with a legitimate interest, to provide to that person the following details in relation to that Firm's Policy:

(a)   the name of the Qualifying Insurer(s) who issued the policy; and

(b)   the policy number; and

(c)   the address and contact details of the Qualifying Insurer(s) for the purpose of making a claim under the policy;

in each case in respect of the Policy which it is reasonably believed to be the relevant Policy to respond to the claim, or, if applicable, the fact that the Firm or person against whom the claim is asserted is covered by Supplementary Run-off Cover.

Commentary:

A Firm, and each Principal in that Firm, is required to provide details of that Firm's policy of Qualifying Insurance to any person who asserts a claim against anyone insured under that Firm's Policy. Under Rule 17, the Solicitors Regulation Authority has the power to disclose information regarding a Firm's Qualifying Insurer where it considers it appropriate to do so.

Part 6: General powers of the Council

19 Waiver powers

19.1 The Council shall have power on such terms and conditions as it shall think fit to waive any Rule or part of any Rule in a particular case or cases including extending the time, either prospectively or retrospectively, for the doing of any act under any Rule.

(a)   Any application by any person for a waiver of any Rule or part of any Rule under the Solicitors' Indemnity Insurance Rules 2001 to 2010 must be made in writing to the Society as soon as reasonably practicable, and in any event no later than the relevant date set out below:

Solicitors' Indemnity Insurance Rules	Relevant date whichever is the later of:		
2001	30 November 2001		30 November 2002
2002	30 November 2002	or 3 calendar months from the occurrence of any event or circumstances first giving rise to the obligation on that person under the relevant Rule or part of any Rule in respect of which the waiver application is or was made, but in any event no later than:	30 November 2003
2003	30 November 2003		31 December 2004
2004	31 December 2004		31 December 2005
2005	31 December 2005		31 December 2006
2006	31 December 2006		31 December 2007
2007	31 December 2007		31 December 2008
2008	31 December 2008		31 December 2009
2009	31 December 2009		31 December 2010
2010	31 December 2010		31 December 2011

(b) No application by any person for a waiver of any Rule or part of any Rule under the Solicitors' Indemnity Insurance Rules 2000 may be considered unless it was made in writing to the Society as soon as reasonably practicable and in any event no later than 28 February 2002.

(c) Any appeal against any decision made by the Society in respect of any application for a waiver of any Rule or part of any Rule under the Solicitors' Indemnity Insurance Rules 2000 to 2010) must be made in writing to the Society within 21 days from the date of the decision.

(d) An application for a waiver as contemplated by this Rule 19.1 or the making of an appeal against any decision made by the Society in respect of such application shall not relieve any person from any obligation under the Solicitors' Indemnity Insurance Rules 2000 to 2010 pending the determination of any such application or appeal.

Commentary:

It is envisaged that Rules will be waived only in exceptional circumstances. Anyone who wishes to apply for a waiver, or to appeal against an initial decision, must do so in accordance with the time limits set out in this Rule. Contact details appear at the end of the introductory commentary. The Panel of Adjudicators Sub Committee has adopted a waiver policy, which is available on request. Unless and until any waiver is granted, the person concerned must comply with the requirements of these Rules in full. A waiver may be granted subject to conditions, and may be revoked without notice.

19.2 The Council shall have power to treat any Firm as complying with any Rule or Rules for the purposes of the Solicitors Act 1974 notwithstanding that the Firm has failed to comply with a Rule or Rules where such non-compliance is regarded by the Council in a particular case or cases as being insignificant.

19.3 For the purposes of the Solicitors Act 1974 (including without limitation section 10 of that Act), any person who is in breach of any Rule or part of any Rule under the

APPENDIX 6

Solicitors' Indemnity Insurance Rules 2000 to 2010 shall be deemed, for so long as he remains in breach, not to be complying with these Rules.

Commentary:

The effect of this general power is that, for example, a practising certificate may be issued to a person notwithstanding a technical and insignificant breach by that person or a Firm of any provision of these Rules.

Part 7: Other obligations

20 Accountants' reports

Any accountant's report which a solicitor or Registered European Lawyer or registered foreign lawyer who is a Principal in a Practice or a Recognised Body is required to deliver to the Society under section 34 of the Solicitors Act 1974 or paragraph 8 of Schedule 14 to the Courts and Legal Services Act 1990 containing such information as is prescribed by rule 35 of the Solicitors' Accounts Rules 1998 must contain a statement certifying (if it is the case) for the whole period covered by the report (excluding any part of that period falling before 1 September 2000) either that the Firm has one or more certificates of Qualifying Insurance outside the Assigned Risks Pool or that the Firm has been issued with one or more policies by the ARP Manager.

Commentary:

Firms are required to provide evidence to their accountants that a Policy of Qualifying Insurance is in place. Each Qualifying Insurer is required under the Qualifying Insurer's agreement to provide a certificate of Qualifying Insurance to each Firm within 20 working days of the start of the period covered by the Policy. Producing the relevant certificate(s) to the reporting accountant will satisfy the requirement of this Rule.

Appendix I

Minimum Terms and Conditions of Professional Indemnity Insurance for Solicitors and Registered European Lawyers in England and Wales

I Scope of cover

1.1 Civil liability

The insurance must indemnify each Insured against civil liability to the extent that it arises from Private Legal Practice in connection with the Insured Firm's Practice, provided that a Claim in respect of such liability:

(a)   is first made against an Insured during the Period of Insurance; or

(b)   is made against an Insured during or after the Period of Insurance and arising from Circumstances first notified to the Insurer during the Period of Insurance.

1.2 Defence Costs

The insurance must also indemnify the Insured against Defence Costs in relation to:

(a)   any Claim referred to in clause 1.1, 1.4 or 1.6; or

(b)   any Circumstances first notified to the Insurer during the Period of Insurance; or

(c)   any investigation or inquiry (save in respect of any disciplinary proceeding under the authority of The Law Society of England and Wales (including, without limitation, the Solicitors Regulation Authority and the Solicitors Disciplinary Tribunal)) during or after the Period of Insurance arising from any Claim referred to in clause 1.1, 1.4 or 1.6 or from Circumstances first notified to the Insurer during the Period of Insurance.

1.3   The Insured

For the purposes of the cover contemplated by clause 1.1, the Insured must include:

(a)   the Insured Firm; and

(b)   each service, administration, trustee or nominee company owned as at the date of occurrence of relevant Circumstances by the Insured Firm and/or the Principals of the Insured Firm; and

(c)   each Principal, each former Principal and each person who becomes a Principal during the Period of Insurance of the Insured Firm or a company referred to in paragraph (b); and

(d)   each Employee, each former Employee and each person who becomes during the Period of Insurance an Employee of the Insured Firm or a company referred to in paragraph (b); and

(e)   the estate or legal personal representative of any deceased or legally incapacitated person referred to in paragraph (c) or (d).

1.4   Prior Practice

The insurance must indemnify each Insured against civil liability to the extent that it arises from Private Legal Practice in connection with a Prior Practice, provided that a Claim in respect of such liability is first made against an Insured:

(a)   during the Period of Insurance; or

(b)   during or after the Period of Insurance and arising from Circumstances first notified to the Insurer during the Period of Insurance.

1.5   The Insured – Prior Practice

For the purposes of the cover contemplated by clause 1.4, the Insured must include:

(a)   each Partnership or Recognised Body which, or Sole Practitioner who, carried on the Prior Practice; and

(b)   each service, administration, trustee or nominee company owned as at the date of occurrence of relevant Circumstances by the Partnership or Recognised Body which, or Sole Practitioner who, carried on the Prior Practice and/or the Principals of such Partnership or Recognised Body; and

(c)   each Principal and former Principal of each Partnership or Recognised Body referred to in paragraph (a) or company referred to in paragraph (b); and

(d)   each Employee and former Employee of the Partnership, Recognised Body or Sole Practitioner referred to in paragraph (a) or company referred to in paragraph (b); and

(e)   the estate or legal personal representative of any deceased or legally incapacitated Sole Practitioner referred to in paragraph (a) or person referred to in paragraph (c) or (d).

1.6   Successor Practice

The insurance must indemnify each Insured against civil liability to the extent that it arises from Private Legal Practice in connection with a Successor Practice to the Insured Firm's Practice (where succession is as a result of one or more separate mergers, acquisitions, absorptions or other transitions), provided that a Claim in respect of such liability is first made against an Insured:

(a)   during the Period of Insurance; or

(b)   during or after the Period of Insurance and arising from Circumstances first notified to the Insurer during the Period of Insurance,

unless run-off cover is provided in accordance with clause 5.3.

1.7   The Insured – Successor Practice

For the purposes of the cover contemplated by clause 1.6, the Insured must include:

(a)   each Partnership or Recognised Body which, or Sole Practitioner who, carries on the Successor Practice during the Period of Insurance; and

(b)   each service, administration, trustee or nominee company owned as at the date of occurrence of relevant Circumstances by the Partnership or Recognised Body which, or Sole Practitioner who, carries on the Successor Practice and/or the Principals of such Partnership or Recognised Body; and

(c)   each Principal, each former Principal and each person who becomes during the Period of Insurance a Principal of any Partnership or Recognised Body referred to in paragraph (a) or company referred to in paragraph (b); and

(d)   each Employee, each former Employee and each person who becomes during the Period of Insurance an Employee of the Partnership, Recognised Body or Sole Practitioner referred to in paragraph (a) or company referred to in paragraph (b); and

(e)   the estate or legal personal representative of any deceased or legally incapacitated Sole Practitioner referred to in paragraph (a) or person referred to in paragraph (c) or (d).

1.8   Award by regulatory authority

The insurance must indemnify each Insured against any amount paid or payable in accordance with the recommendation of the Legal Services Ombudsman, the Legal Complaints Service, the Office for Legal Complaints (including the Legal Ombudsman pursuant to sections 137(2)(c) and section 137(4)(b) of the Legal Services Act 2007) or any other regulatory authority to the same extent as it indemnifies the Insured against civil liability provided that the Insurer will have no liability in respect of any determination by the Legal Ombudsman pursuant to section 137(2)(b) of the Legal Services Act 2007 to refund any fees paid to the Insured.

2 Limit of insurance cover

2.1   Any one Claim

The Sum Insured for any one Claim (exclusive of Defence Costs) must be, where the Insured Firm is a Relevant Recognised Body, at least £3 million, and in all other cases, at least £2 million.

2.2   No limit on Defence Costs

There must be no monetary limit on the cover for Defence Costs.

2.3   Proportionate limit on Defence Costs

Notwithstanding clauses 2.1 and 2.2, the insurance may provide that liability for Defence Costs in relation to a Claim which exceeds the Sum Insured is limited to the proportion that the Sum Insured bears to the total amount paid or payable to dispose of the Claim.

2.4   No other limit

The insurance must not limit liability to any monetary amount (whether by way of an aggregate limit or otherwise) except as contemplated by clauses 2.1 and 2.3.

2.5   One Claim

The insurance may provide that, when considering what may be regarded as one Claim for the purposes of the limits contemplated by clauses 2.1 and 2.3:

(a)   all Claims against any one or more Insured arising from:

    (i)   one act or omission;

    (ii)   one series of related acts or omissions;

    (iii)   the same act or omission in a series of related matters or transactions;

    (iv)   similar acts or omissions in a series of related matters or transactions

and

(b)   all Claims against one or more Insured arising from one matter or transaction

will be regarded as one Claim.

2.6   Multiple underwriters

2.6.1   The insurance may be underwritten by more than one insurer, each of which must be a Qualifying Insurer, provided that the insurance may provide that the Insurer shall be severally liable only for its respective proportion of liability in accordance with the terms of the insurance.

2.6.2   Where the insurance is underwritten jointly by more than one insurer:

    (a)   the insurance must state which Qualifying Insurer shall be the Lead Insurer; and

    (b)   in addition to any proportionate limit on Defence Costs in accordance with clause 2.3, the insurance may provide that each Insurer's liability for Defence Costs is further limited to the extent or the proportion of that Insurer's liability (if any) in relation to the relevant Claim.

[Note: under clause 2.6 of the Qualifying Insurer's Agreement, a Policy may be issued on an excess of loss basis only in the layers set out in that clause.]

3 Excesses

3.1   The Excess

The insurance may be subject to an Excess of such monetary amount and on such terms as the Insurer and the Insured Firm agree. Subject to clause 3.4, the Excess may be "self-insured" or partly or wholly insured without regard to these minimum terms and conditions.

3.2   No deductibles

The insurance must provide that the Excess does not reduce the limit of liability contemplated by clause 2.1.

3.3   Excess not to apply to Defence Costs

The Excess must not apply to Defence Costs.

3.4   Funding of the Excess

The insurance must provide that, if an Insured fails to pay to a Claimant any amount which is within the Excess within 30 days of it becoming due for payment, the Claimant may give notice of the Insured's default to the Insurer, whereupon the Insurer is liable to remedy the default on the Insured's behalf. The insurance may provide that any amount paid by the Insurer to remedy such a default erodes the Sum Insured.

3.5   One Claim

The insurance may provide for multiple Claims to be treated as one Claim for the purposes of an Excess contemplated by clause 3.1 on such terms as the Insured Firm and the Insurer agree.

3.6   Excess layers

In the case of insurance written on an excess of loss basis, there shall be no Excess except in relation to the primary layer.

4 Special conditions

4.1   No avoidance or repudiation

The insurance must provide that the Insurer is not entitled to avoid or repudiate the insurance on any grounds whatsoever including, without limitation, non-disclosure or misrepresentation, whether fraudulent or not.

4.2   No adjustment or denial

The insurance must provide that the Insurer is not entitled to reduce or deny its liability under the insurance on any grounds whatsoever including, without limitation, any breach of any term or condition of the insurance, except to the extent that one of the exclusions contemplated by clause 6 applies.

4.3   No cancellation

The insurance must provide that it cannot be cancelled except (in the case of (a), (b) or (c) below) by the agreement of both the Insured Firm and the Insurer, and in any event only in circumstances where:

(a)   the Insured Firm's Practice is merged into a Successor Practice, provided that there is insurance complying with these minimum terms and conditions in relation to that Successor Practice, in which case cancellation shall have effect no earlier than the date of such merger; or

(b)   replacement insurance complying with these minimum terms and conditions commences, but only where, in the case of insurance not provided wholly or partly by the Assigned Risks Pool, the replacement insurance is not provided wholly or partly by the Assigned Risks Pool.

(c)   it subsequently transpires that the Insured Firm is not required under the Solicitors Indemnity Insurance Rules 2010 to effect a policy of Qualifying Insurance, in which case cancellation shall have effect from the later of (a) the start of the relevant Indemnity Period and (b) the date on which the Insured Firm ceased to be required to effect a policy of Qualifying Insurance, or such later date as the Insured Firm and the Insurer may agree; or

(d)   in the case of an ARP Policy, it subsequently transpires that the Insured Firm was not or has ceased to be an Eligible Firm, in which case cancellation shall have effect from the date on which it ceased to be an Eligible Firm.

Cancellation must not affect the rights and obligations of the parties accrued under the insurance prior to the date from which cancellation has effect.

4.4   No setoff

The insurance must provide that any amount payable by the Insurer to indemnify an Insured against civil liability to a Claimant will be paid only to the Claimant, or at the Claimant's direction, and that the Insurer is not entitled to set-off against any such amount any payment due to it by any Insured including, without limitation, any payment of premium or to reimburse the Insurer.

4.5   No "other insurance" provision

The insurance must not provide that the liability of the Insurer is reduced or excluded by reason of the existence or availability of any other insurance other than as contemplated by clause 6.1. For the avoidance of doubt, this requirement is not intended to affect any right of the Insurer to claim contribution from any other insurer which is also liable to indemnify any Insured.

4.6   No retroactive date

The insurance must not exclude or limit the liability of the Insurer in respect of Claims arising from incidents, occurrences, facts, matters, acts and/or omissions which occurred prior to a specified date.

4.7   Successor Practice – "double insurance"

The insurance may provide that, if the Insured Firm's Practice is succeeded during the Period of Insurance and, as a result, a situation of 'double insurance' exists between two or more insurers of the Successor Practice, contribution between insurers is to be determined in accordance with the relative numbers of Principals of the owners of the constituent Practices immediately prior to succession.

4.8   Advancement of Defence Costs

The insurance must provide that the Insurer will meet Defence Costs as and when they are incurred, including Defence Costs incurred on behalf of an Insured who is alleged to have committed or condoned dishonesty or a fraudulent act or omission, provided that the Insurer is not liable for Defence Costs incurred on behalf of that Insured after the earlier of:

(a)   that Insured admitting to the Insurer the commission or condoning of such dishonesty, act or omission; or

(b)   a court or other judicial body finding that that Insured was in fact guilty of such dishonesty, act or omission.

4.9   Resolution of disputes

The insurance must provide that, if there is a dispute as to whether a Practice is a Successor Practice for the purposes of clauses 1.4, 1.6 or 5.3, the Insured and the Insurer will take all reasonable steps (including, if appropriate, referring the dispute to arbitration) to resolve the dispute in conjunction with any related dispute between any other party which has insurance complying with these minimum terms and conditions and that party's insurer.

4.10   Conduct of a Claim pending dispute resolution

The insurance must provide that, pending resolution of any coverage dispute and without prejudice to any issue in dispute, the Insurer will, if so directed by the Society, conduct any Claim, advance Defence Costs and, if appropriate, compromise and pay the Claim. If the Society is satisfied that:

(a)   the party requesting the direction has taken all reasonable steps to resolve the dispute with the other party/ies; and

(b)   there is a reasonable prospect that the coverage dispute will be resolved or determined in the Insured's favour; and

(c)   it is fair and equitable in all the circumstances for such direction to be given;

it may in its absolute discretion make such a direction.

4.11 Minimum terms and conditions to prevail

The insurance must provide that:

(a)   the insurance is to be construed or rectified so as to comply with the requirements of these minimum terms and conditions; and

(b)   any provision which is inconsistent with these minimum terms and conditions is to be severed or rectified to comply.

4.12 Period of Insurance

The Period of Insurance must not expire prior to 30 September 2011.

5 Run-off cover

5.1 Cessation of the Insured Firm's Practice

The insurance must provide that, if the Insured Firm's Practice ceases during or on expiry of the Period of Insurance and the Insured Firm has not obtained succeeding insurance in compliance with these minimum terms and conditions (a **Cessation**), the insurance will provide run-off cover.

For these purposes, an Insured Firm's Practice shall (without limitation) be regarded as ceasing if (and with effect from the date upon which) the Insured Firm becomes a Non-SRA Firm.

5.2 Scope of run-off cover

The run-off cover referred to in clause 5.1 must indemnify each Insured in accordance with clauses 1.1 to 1.8 (but subject to the limits, exclusions and conditions of the insurance which are in accordance with these minimum terms and conditions) on the basis that the Period of Insurance extends for an additional six years (ending on the sixth anniversary of the date upon which, but for this requirement, it would have ended).

5.3 Succession

The insurance must provide that, if there is a Successor Practice to the ceased Practice, the Insured Firm may elect before its Cessation, whether it wishes the ceased Practice:

(a)   to be insured under the run-off cover referred to in clause 5.1; or

(b)   provided that there is insurance complying with these minimum terms and conditions in relation to that Successor Practice, to be insured as a Prior Practice under such insurance.

If the Insured Firm fails to make an election and/or fails to pay any premium due under the terms of the Policy, before its Cessation, clause 5.3(b) above shall apply.

The insurance must also provide that where an Insured Firm makes an election pursuant to this clause 5.3, the Insurer shall give notice to the Society in writing of the election not later than seven days following the receipt by the Insurer of the Insured Firm's election and that election has become effective and the Insured Firm shall irrevocably consent to that notification.

5.4 Suspended Practices

The insurance must provide that, where run-off cover has been activated in accordance with this clause 5, but where the Insured Firm's Practice restarts, the Insurer may (but shall not be obliged to) cancel such run-off cover, on such terms as may be agreed, provided that:

(a)   there is insurance complying with these minimum terms and conditions in relation to that Insured Firm in force on the date of cancellation;

(b)   the Qualifying Insurer providing such insurance confirms in writing to the Insured Firm and the Insurer (if different) that:

(i)   it is providing insurance complying with these minimum terms and conditions in relation to that Insured Firm for the then current Indemnity Period; and

(ii)   it is doing so on the basis that the Insured Firm's Practice is regarded as being a continuation of the Insured Firm's Practice prior to Cessation and that accordingly it is liable for Claims against the Insured Firm arising from incidents, occurrences, facts, matters, acts and/or omissions which occurred prior to Cessation.

6 Exclusions

The insurance must not exclude or limit the liability of the Insurer except to the extent that any Claim or related Defence Costs arise from the matters set out in this clause 6.

6.1   Prior cover

Any Claim in respect of which the Insured is entitled to be indemnified by the Solicitors Indemnity Fund (**SIF**) or under a professional indemnity insurance contract for a period earlier than the Period of Insurance, whether by reason of notification of Circumstances to SIF or under the earlier contract or otherwise.

6.2   Death or bodily injury

Any liability of any Insured for causing or contributing to death or bodily injury, except that the insurance must nonetheless cover liability for psychological injury or emotional distress which arises from a breach of duty in the performance of (or failure to perform) legal work.

6.3   Property damage

Any liability of any Insured for causing or contributing to damage to, or destruction or physical loss of, any property (other than property in the care, custody or control of any Insured in connection with the Insured Firm's Practice and not occupied or used in the course of the Insured Firm's Practice), except that the insurance must nonetheless cover liability for such damage, destruction or loss which arises from breach of duty in the performance of (or failure to perform) legal work.

6.4   Partnership disputes

Any actual or alleged breach of the Insured Firm's Partnership or shareholder agreement or arrangements, including any equivalent agreement or arrangement where the Insured Firm is a Limited Liability Partnership or a company without a share capital.

6.5   Employment breaches, discrimination, etc.

Wrongful dismissal, repudiation or breach of an employment contract or arrangement, termination of a training contract, harassment, discrimination or like conduct in relation to any Partnership or shareholder agreement or arrangement or the equivalent where the Insured Firm is a Limited Liability Partnership or a company without a share capital, or in relation to any employment or training agreement or arrangement.

6.6   Debts and trading liabilities

Any:

(a)   trading or personal debt of any Insured; or

(b)   legal liability assumed or accepted by an Insured or an Insured Firm under any contract or agreement for the supply to, or use by, the Insured or Insured Firm of goods or services in the course of the Insured Firm's Practice, save that this exclusion 6.6(b) will not apply to any legal liability arising in the course of an Insured Firm's Practice in connection with its or any Insured's use of or access to the HM Land Registry network (including, without limitation, access under a Network Access Agreement made under the Land Registration (Network Access) Rules and the Land Registration (Electronic Communications) Order 2007) other than an obligation to pay search fees or other charges for searches or services provided by HM Land Registry to the Insured Firm; or

(c)   guarantee, indemnity or undertaking by any particular Insured in connection with the provision of finance, property, assistance or other benefit or advantage directly or indirectly to that Insured.

6.7   Fines, penalties, etc

Any:

(a)   fine or penalty; or

(b)   award of punitive, exemplary or like damages under the law of the United States of America or Canada, other than in respect of defamation; or

(c)   order or agreement to pay the costs of a complainant, regulator, investigator or prosecutor of any professional conduct complaint against, or investigation into the professional conduct of, any Insured.

6.8   Fraud or dishonesty

The insurance may exclude liability of the Insurer to indemnify any particular person to the extent that any civil liability or related Defence Costs arise from dishonesty or a fraudulent act or omission committed or condoned by that person, except that:

(a)   the insurance must nonetheless cover each other Insured; and

(b)   the insurance must provide that no dishonesty, act or omission will be imputed to a body corporate unless it was committed or condoned by, in the case of a company, all directors of that company, or, in the case of a Limited Liability Partnership, all members of that Limited Liability Partnership.

6.9   Directors' or officers' liability

The insurance may exclude liability of the Insurer to indemnify any natural person in their capacity as a director or officer of a body corporate (other than a Recognised Body or a service, administration, trustee or nominee company referred to in clauses 1.3(b), 1.5(b) or 1.7(b)) except that:

(a)   the insurance must nonetheless cover any liability of that person which arises from a breach of duty in the performance of (or failure to perform) legal work; and

(b)   the insurance must nonetheless cover each other Insured against any vicarious or joint liability.

6.10   War and Terrorism, and Asbestos

The Insurance may exclude, by way of an exclusion or endorsement, liability of the Insurer to indemnify any Insured in respect of, or in any way in connection with:

(a)   terrorism, war or other hostilities; and/or

(b)   asbestos, or any actual or alleged asbestos-related injury or damage involving the use, presence, existence, detection, removal, elimination or avoidance of asbestos or exposure to asbestos,

provided that any such exclusion or endorsement does not exclude or limit any liability of the Insurer to indemnify any Insured against civil liability or related Defence Costs arising from any actual or alleged breach of duty in the performance of (or failure to perform) legal work or failure to discharge or fulfil any duty incidental to the Insured Firm's Practice or to the conduct of Private Legal Practice.

7 General conditions

7.1 As agreed

The insurance may contain such general conditions as are agreed between the Insurer and the Insured Firm, but the insurance must provide that the special conditions required by clause 4 prevail to the extent of any inconsistency.

7.2 Reimbursement

The insurance may provide that each Insured who:

(a) committed; or

(b) condoned (whether knowingly or recklessly):

    (i) non-disclosure or misrepresentation; or

    (ii) any breach of the terms or conditions of the insurance; or

    (iii) dishonesty or any fraudulent act or omission,

will reimburse the Insurer to the extent that is just and equitable having regard to the prejudice caused to the Insurer's interests by such non-disclosure, misrepresentation, breach, dishonesty, act or omission, provided that no Insured shall be required to make any such reimbursement to the extent that any such breach of the terms or conditions of the insurance was in order to comply with any applicable rules or codes laid down from time to time by the Society, or in the Society publication *Your Clients – Your Business*, as amended from time to time.

The insurance must provide that no non-disclosure, misrepresentation, breach, dishonesty, act or omission will be imputed to a body corporate unless it was committed or condoned by, in the case of a company, all directors of that company, or, in the case of a Limited Liability Partnership, all members of that Limited Liability Partnership. The insurance must provide further that any right of reimbursement contemplated by this clause 7.2 against any person referred to in clauses 1.3(d), 1.5(d) or 1.7(d) (or against the estate or legal personal representative of any such person if they die or become legally incapacitated) is limited to the extent that is just and equitable having regard to the prejudice caused to the Insurer's interests by that person having committed or condoned (whether knowingly or recklessly) dishonesty or any fraudulent act or omission.

7.3 Reimbursement of Defence Costs

The insurance may provide that each Insured will reimburse the Insurer for Defence Costs advanced on that Insured's behalf which the Insurer is not ultimately liable to pay.

7.4 Reimbursement of the Excess

The insurance may provide for those persons who are at any time during the Period of Insurance Principals of the Insured Firm, together with, in relation to a Sole Practitioner, any person held out as a Partner of that practitioner, to reimburse the Insurer for any Excess paid by the Insurer on an Insured's behalf. The Sum Insured must be reinstated to the extent of reimbursement of any amount which eroded it as contemplated by clause 3.4.

7.5 Reimbursement of moneys paid pending dispute resolution

The insurance may provide that each Insured will reimburse the Insurer following resolution of any coverage dispute for any amount paid by the Insurer on that Insured's behalf which, on the basis of the resolution of the dispute, the Insurer is not ultimately liable to pay.

APPENDIX 6

7.6   Withholding assets or entitlements

The insurance may require the Insured Firm to account to the Insurer for any asset or entitlement of any person who committed or condoned any dishonesty or fraudulent act or omission, provided that the Insured Firm is legally entitled to withhold that asset or entitlement from that person.

7.7   Premium

The premium may be calculated on such basis as the Insurer determines and the Insured Firm accepts including, without limitation, a basis which recognises Claims history, categories of work performed by the Insured Firm, numbers of Principals and Employees, revenue derived from the Insured Firm's Practice and other risk factors determined by the Insurer.

7.8   Co-operation and assistance

The insurance (except in the case of an ARP Policy) must provide that, if the ARP Manager is appointed to conduct any Claim, each Insured will give the ARP Manager and any investigators or solicitors appointed by it all information and documents they reasonably require, and full co-operation and assistance in the investigation, defence, settlement, avoidance or reduction of any actual or possible Claim or any related proceeding.

8   Definitions and interpretation

8.1   General

    8.1.1   In these minimum terms and conditions, unless the context otherwise requires:

        (a)   the singular includes the plural, and vice versa; and

        (b)   the male gender includes the female and neuter genders; and

        (c)   a reference to a person includes a body corporate, partnerships, and other unincorporated associations or bodies of persons;

        (d)   a reference to any statute, statutory provision, code or regulation includes:

           (i) any subordinate legislation (as defined by section 21(1) of the Interpretation Act 1978) made under it; and

           (ii) any provision which it has superseded or re-enacted (with or without modification) or amended, and any provision superseding it or re-enacting it (with or without modification) or amending it either before, or at or after the date of these minimum terms and conditions;

        (e)   references to the Society include the Solicitors Regulation Authority and the Legal Complaints Service and the Office for Legal Complaints (including the Legal Ombudsman) and any body or person which succeeds in whole or in part to the functions of the Society, the Solicitors Regulation Authority, the Legal Complaints Service or the Office for Legal Complaints (including the Legal Ombudsman) and any delegate of the Society, the Solicitors Regulation Authority, the Legal Complaints Service, the Office for Legal Complaints (including the Legal Ombudsman) or any such body or person;

        (f)   headings are for ease of reference only and shall not affect the interpretation of these minimum terms and conditions;

        (g)   explanatory notes and commentary shall be ignored in interpreting these minimum terms and conditions;

(h) a reference to a director includes a member of a Limited Liability Partnership;

(i) words and expressions which begin with a capital letter in these minimum terms and conditions have the meaning set out in this clause 8; and

(j) words and expressions in these minimum terms and conditions are to be construed consistently with the same or similar words or expressions in the Solicitors' Indemnity Insurance Rules 2010.

8.1.2 These minimum terms and conditions shall be, and the insurance shall be expressed to be, governed by and interpreted in accordance with English law.

8.2 Defined terms

In these minimum terms and conditions:

Circumstances means an incident, occurrence, fact, matter, act or omission which may give rise to a Claim in respect of civil liability

Claim means a demand for, or an assertion of a right to, civil compensation or civil damages or an intimation of an intention to seek such compensation or damages. For these purposes, an obligation on an Insured Firm and/or any Insured to remedy a breach of the Solicitors' Accounts Rules 1998 (as amended from time to time), or any rules which replace the Solicitors' Accounts Rules 1998 in whole or in part, shall be treated as a Claim, and the obligation to remedy such breach shall be treated as a civil liability for the purposes of clause 1, whether or not any person makes a demand for, or an assertion of a right to, civil compensation or civil damages or an intimation of an intention to seek such compensation or damages as a result of such breach, except where any such obligation may arise as a result of the insolvency of a bank (as defined in section 87 of the Solicitors Act 1974) or a building society (within the meaning of the Building Societies Act 1986) which holds client money in a client account of the Insured Firm or the failure of such bank or building society generally to repay monies on demand.

Claimant means a person or entity which has made or may make a Claim including a Claim for contribution or indemnity.

Defence Costs means legal costs and disbursements and investigative and related expenses reasonably and necessarily incurred with the consent of the Insurer in:

(a) defending any proceedings relating to a Claim; or

(b) conducting any proceedings for indemnity, contribution or recovery relating to a Claim; or

(c) investigating, reducing, avoiding or compromising any actual or potential Claim; or

(d) acting for any Insured in connection with any investigation, inquiry or disciplinary proceeding (save in respect of any disciplinary proceeding under the authority of The Law Society of England and Wales (including, without limitation, the Solicitors Regulation Authority and the Solicitors Disciplinary Tribunal)).

Defence Costs do not include any internal or overhead expenses of the Insured Firm or the Insurer or the cost of any Insured's time.

Employee means any person other than a Principal:

(a) employed or otherwise engaged in the Insured Firm's Practice (including under a contract for services) including, without limitation, as a solicitor, lawyer, trainee solicitor or lawyer, consultant, associate, locum tenens, agent, appointed person (as defined in the Solicitors' Indemnity Insurance Rules 2010), office or clerical staff member or otherwise;

(b)   seconded to work in the Insured Firm's Practice; or

(c)   seconded by the Insured Firm to work elsewhere.

Employee does not include any person who is engaged by the Insured Firm under a contract for services in respect of any work where that person is required, whether under the Solicitors' Indemnity Insurance Rules 2010 or under the rules of any other professional body, to take out or to be insured under separate professional indemnity insurance in respect of that work.

Excess means the first amount of a Claim which is not covered by the insurance.

Insured means each person and entity named or described as a person to whom the insurance extends and includes, without limitation, those referred to in clause 1.3 and, in relation to Prior and Successor Practices respectively, those referred to in clauses 1.5 and 1.7.

Insured Firm means the Firm (as defined for the purposes of the Solicitors Indemnity Insurance Rules 2010) which contracted with the Insurer to provide the insurance.

Insured Firm's Practice means:

(a)   the legal Practice carried on by the Insured Firm as at the commencement of the Period of Insurance; and

(b)   the continuous legal Practice preceding and succeeding the Practice referred to in paragraph (a) (irrespective of changes in ownership of the Practice or in the composition of any Partnership which owns or owned the Practice).

Insurer means the underwriter(s) of the insurance.

Lead Insurer means the insurer named as such in the contract of insurance, or, if no Lead Insurer is named as such, the first-named insurer on the relevant certificate of insurance.

Limited Liability Partnership means a limited liability partnership incorporated under the Limited Liability Partnerships Act 2000.

Partnership means an unincorporated Insured Firm in which persons are or are held out as partners and does not include an Insured Firm incorporated as a Limited Liability Partnership, and Partner means a person who is or is held out to be a partner in a Partnership.

Period of Insurance means the period for which the insurance operates.

Principal means:

(a)   where the Insured Firm is or was:

    (i)   a sole practitioner – that practitioner;

    (ii)   a Partnership – each Partner;

    (iii)   a company with a share capital each director of that company and any solicitor, Registered European Lawyer or Registered Foreign Lawyer who:

        (A) is held out as a director; or

        (B) beneficially owns the whole or any part of a share in the company; or

        (C) is the ultimate beneficial owner of the whole or any part of a share in the company.

    (iv)   a company without a share capital – each director of that company and any solicitor, Registered European Lawyer or Registered Foreign Lawyer who:

> (A) is held out as a director; or
>
> (B) is a member of the company; or
>
> (C) is the ultimate owner of the whole or any part of a body corporate or other legal person which is a member of the company;

(v) a Limited Liability Partnership – each member of that Limited Liability Partnership, and any solicitor, Registered European Lawyer or Registered Foreign Lawyer who is the ultimate owner of the whole or any part of a body corporate or other legal person which is member of the Limited Liability Partnership.

(b) where a body corporate or other legal person is a Partner in the Insured Firm, all solicitors, Registered European Lawyers or Registered Foreign Lawyers who are within paragraph (a)(iii) of this definition (including sub paragraphs (A) and (C) thereof), paragraph (a)(iv) of this definition (including sub paragraphs (A) and (C) thereof), or paragraph (a)(v) of this definition.

Prior Practice means each Practice to which the Insured Firm's Practice is ultimately a Successor Practice by way of one or more mergers, acquisitions, absorptions or other transitions, but does not include any such Practice which has elected to be insured under run-off cover in accordance with clause 5.3(a) of these minimum terms and conditions.

Private Legal Practice means the provision of services in private Practice as a solicitor or Registered European Lawyer including, without limitation:

(a) providing such services in England, Wales or anywhere in the world, whether alone or with other lawyers in a Partnership permitted to practise in England and Wales by rule 12 of the Solicitors' Code of Conduct 2007; and

(b) the provision of such services as a secondee of the Insured Firm; and

(c) any Insured acting as a personal representative, trustee, attorney, notary, insolvency practitioner or in any role in conjunction with a Practice; and

(d) the provision of such services by any Employee; and

(e) the provision of such services pro bono publico.

Private Legal Practice does not include:

(i) practising as an Employee of an employer other than a solicitor, a registered European lawyer, a Partnership permitted to practise in England and Wales by rule 12 of the Solicitors' Code of Conduct 2007, or a Recognised Body; or

(ii) discharging the functions of any of the following offices or appointments:

(A) judicial office;

(B) Under Sheriffs;

(C) members and clerks of such tribunals, committees, panels and boards as the Council may from time to time designate but including those subject to the Tribunals and Inquiries Act 1992, the Competition Commission, Legal Services Commission Review Panels and Parole Boards;

(D) Justices' Clerks; or

(E) Superintendent Registrars and Deputy Superintendent Registrars of Births, Marriages and Deaths and Registrars of Local Crematoria.

Recognised Body means a body for the time being recognised by the Solicitors Regulation Authority under Section 9 of the Administration of Justice Act 1985 and the SRA Recognised Bodies Regulations 2009.

APPENDIX 6

Relevant Recognised Body means a Recognised Body other than:

(a) an unlimited company, or an overseas company whose members' liability for the company's debts is not limited by its constitution or by the law of its country of incorporation; or

(b) a nominee company only, holding assets for clients of another Practice; and

    (i) it can act only as agent for the other Practice; and

    (ii) all the individuals who are Principals of the Recognised Body are also Principals of the other Practice; and

    (iii) any fee or other income arising out of the Recognised Body accrues to the benefit of the other Practice; or

(c) a partnership in which none of the partners is a limited company, a Limited Liability Partnership or a legal person whose members have limited liability.

Sole Practitioner means a solicitor or registered European lawyer who is a sole practitioner, and includes a Recognised Sole Practitioner.

Successor Practice means a Practice identified in this definition as 'B', where:

(a) "A" is the Practice to which B succeeds; and

(b) "A's owner" is the owner of A immediately prior to transition; and

(c) "B's owner" is the owner of B immediately following transition; and

(d) "transition" means merger, acquisition, absorption or other transition which results in A no longer being carried on as a discrete legal Practice.

B is a Successor Practice to A where:

(i) B is or was held out, expressly or by implication, by B's owner as being the successor of A or as incorporating A, whether such holding out is contained in notepaper, business cards, form of electronic communications, publications, promotional material or otherwise, or is contained in any statement or declaration by B's owner to any regulatory or taxation authority; and/or

(ii) (where A's owner was a Sole Practitioner and the transition occurred on or before 31 August 2000) – the Sole Practitioner is a Principal of B's owner; and/or

(iii) (where A's owner was a Sole Practitioner and the transition occurred on or after 1 September 2000) – the Sole Practitioner is a Principal or Employee of B's owner; and/or

(iv) (where A's owner was a Recognised Body) – that body is a Principal of B's owner; and/or

(v) (where A's owner was a Partnership) – the majority of the Principals of A's owner have become Principals of B's owner; and/or

(vi) (where A's owner was a Partnership and the majority of Principals of A's owner did not become Principals of the owner of another legal Practice as a result of the transition) – one or more of the Principals of A's owner have become Principals of B's owner and:

    (A) B is carried on under the same name as A or a name which substantially incorporates the name of A (or a substantial part of the name of A); and/or

    (B) B is carried on from the same premises as A; and/or

    (C) the owner of B acquired the goodwill and/or assets of A; and/or

    (D) the owner of B assumed the liabilities of A; and/or

    (E) the majority of staff employed by A's owner became employees of B's owner.

Notwithstanding the foregoing, B is not a Successor Practice to A under paragraph (ii), (iii), (iv) (v) or (vi) if another Practice is or was held out by the owner of that other Practice as the successor of A or as incorporating A, provided that there is insurance complying with these minimum terms and conditions in relation to that other Practice.

Sum Insured means the aggregate limit of liability of each Insurer under the insurance.

Appendix 2

Rating schedule for 2010/2011

1   Method for calculation of the ARP Premium

1.1   The annual ARP Premium is calculated by identifying the fee band appropriate to the Gross Fees (as defined below) of the Insured Firm. For a £2 million primary policy (£3 million in the case of Relevant Recognised Bodies), where the Gross Fees are £500,000 or less, the ARP Premium is calculated at a rate of 27½% of the fees declared (30% in the case of Relevant Recognised Bodies). Where the Gross Fees of the Insured Firm are £500,001 or more, the ARP Premium is the sum of:

- the Maximum Premium for the previous Fee Band; plus

- the Marginal Rate on Fees applied to the amount of fees that exceed the ceiling of the previous Fee Band.

There is a minimum premium of £1,500 irrespective of the level of Gross Fees, or the period of time spent in the Assigned Risks Pool during an Indemnity Period.

1.2   Firms other than Relevant Recognised Bodies (£2 million indemnity limit)

Fee bands	Marginal rate on fees	Calculation of maximum premium for fee band (Calculation of example premium)	Maximum premium for fee band	Minimum rate on fee for fee band
1 £0 to £500,000	27.5%	27.5% × £500,000 = £137,500	£137,500	27.50%
2 £500,001 to £1,500,000	22%	£137,500 (maximum premium for fee band 1) plus 22% × £1,000,000 = £220,000 = £357,000	£357,000	23.826%
e.g. if fees £1,000,000		*£137,500 plus (22% × £500,000 = £110,000) = £247,500*		
3 £1,500,001 to £3,000,000	16.5%	16.5% × £1,500,000 = £247,500 plus £357,000 (maximum premium for fee band 2) = £605,000	£605,000	20.163%
e.g. if fees £2,250,000		*£357,000 plus (16.5% × £750,000 = £123,750) = £481,250*		
4 £3,000,001 to £5,000,000	13.2%	13.2% × £2,000,000 = £264,000 plus £605,000 (maximum premium for fee band 3) = £869,000	£869,000	17.38%
e.g. if fees £4,000,000		*£605,000 plus (13.2% × £1,000,000 = £132,000) = £737,000*		

411

Fee bands	Marginal rate on fees	Calculation of maximum premium for fee band (Calculation of example premium)	Maximum premium for fee band	Minimum rate on fee for fee band
5 £5,000,001 to £20,000,000	11%	11% × £15,000,000 = £1,650,000 plus £869,000 (maximum premium for fee band 4) = £2,519,000	£2,519,000	12.595%
e.g. if fees £10,000,000		*£869,000 plus (11% × £5,000,000 = £550,000) = £1,419,000*		
6 £20,000,001 +	5.5%	5.5% × (actual fees − £20,000,000) plus £2,519,000 (maximum premium for fee band 5) = (annual premium)	—	—
e.g. if fees £30,000,000		*£2,519,000 plus (5.5% × £10,000,000) = £550,000 = £3,069,000*		
or if fees £50,000,000		*£2,519,000 plus (5.5% × £30,000,000 = £1,650,000) = £4,169,000*		

1.3   Relevant Recognised Bodies (£3 million indemnity limit)

Fee bands	Marginal rate on fees	Calculation of maximum premium for fee band (Calculation of example premium)	Maximum premium for fee band	Minimum rate on fee for fee band
1 £0 to £500,000	30%	30% × £500,000 = £150,000	£150,000	30.00%
2 £500,001 to £1,500,000	24%	£150,000 (maximum premium for fee band 1) plus 24% × £1,000,000 = £200,000 = £390,000	£390,000	25.992%
e.g. if fees £1,000,000		*£150,000 plus (24% × £500,000 = £120,000) = £270,000*		
3 £1,500,001 to £3,000,000	18%	18% × £1,500,000 = £270,000 plus £390,000 (maximum premium for fee band 2) = £660,000	£660,000	24.196%
e.g. if fees £2,250,000		*£390,000 plus (18% × £750,000 = £135,000) = £525,000*		
4 £3,000,001 to £5,000,000	14.4%	14.4% × £2,000,000 = £288,000 plus £660,000 (maximum premium for fee band 3) = £948,000	£948,000	18.96%
e.g. if fees £4,000,000		*£660,000 plus (14.4% × £1,000,000 = £144,000) = £804,000*		

Fee bands	Marginal rate on fees	Calculation of maximum premium for fee band (Calculation of example premium)	Maximum premium for fee band	Minimum rate on fee for fee band
5 £5,000,001 to £20,000,000	12%	12% × £15,000,000 = £1,800,000 plus £948,000 (maximum premium for fee band 4) = £2,748,000	£2,748,000	13.74%
e.g. if fees £10,000,000		*£948,000 plus (12% × £5,000,000 = £600,000) = £1,548,000*		
6 £20,000,001 +	6%	6% × (actual fees − £20,000,000) plus £2,748,000 (maximum premium for fee band 5) = (annual premium)	—	—
e.g. if fees £30,000,000		*£2,748,000 plus (6% × £10,000,000 = £600,000) = £3,348,000*		
or if fees £50,000,000		*£2,748,000 plus (6% × £30,000,000 = £1,800,000) = £4,548,000*		

1.4   Primary layer rates

Where an ARP Policy is written as a primary layer of £1 million, with excess layer(s) provided by a Qualifying Insurer, the premium due to the Assigned Risks Pool in respect of that policy shall be an amount calculated in accordance with the table below:

Fee bands	Marginal rate on fees	Calculation of maximum premium for fee band (Calculation of example premium)	Maximum premium for fee band	Minimum rate on fee for fee band
1 £0 to £500,000	25%	25% × £500,000 = £125,000	£125,000	25.00%
2 £500,001 to £1,500,000	20%	£125,000 (Maximum Premium for fee band 1) plus 20% × £1,000,000 = £200,000 = £325,000	£325,000	21.66%
e.g. if fees £1,000,000		*£125,000 plus (20% × £500,000 = £100,000) = £225,000*		
3 £1,500,001 to £3,000,000	15%	15% × £1,500,000 = £225,000 plus £325,000 (Maximum Premium for fee band 2) = £550,000	£550,000	18.33%
e.g. if fees £2,250,000		*£325,000 plus (15% × £750,000 = £112,500) = £437,500*		
4 £3,000,001 to £5,000,000	12%	12% × £2,000,000 = £240,000 plus £550,000 (Maximum Premium for fee band 3) = £790,000	£790,000	15.80%
e.g. if fees £4,000,000		*£550,000 plus (12% × £1,000,000 = £120,000) = £670,000*		

Fee bands	Marginal rate on fees	Calculation of maximum premium for fee band (Calculation of example premium)	Maximum premium for fee band	Minimum rate on fee for fee band
5 £5,000,001 to £20,000,000	10%	10% × £15,000,000 = £1,500,000 plus £790,000 (Maximum Premium for fee band 4) = £2,290,000	£2,290,000	11.45%
e.g. if fees £10,000,000		*£790,000 plus (10% × £5,000,000 = £500,000) = £1,290,000*		
6 £20,000,001 +	5%	5% × (actual fees − £20,000,000) plus £2,290,000 (Maximum Premium for fee band 5) = (annual premium)	—	—
e.g. if fees £30,000,000		*£2,290,000 plus (5% × £10,000,000 = £500,000 = £2,790,000*		
or if fees £50,000,000		*£2,290,000 plus (5% × £30,000,000 = £1,500,000) = £3,790,000*		

1.5 Excess layer rates

Where an ARP Policy is written as an excess layer and the primary layer is provided by a Qualifying Insurer, the premium due to the Assigned Risks Pool in respect of that policy shall be an amount equal to the percentage set out below of the primary layer rate calculated in accordance with the information above:

Excess layer	Percentage of primary layer rate
£1 million excess of £1 million (or any part thereof)	10%
£2 million excess of £1 million (or any part thereof)	20%
£1 million excess of £2 million (or any part thereof)	10%

1.6 Co-insurance

Where an ARP Policy is written as co-insurance, on the basis that one or more other Qualifying Insurers are liable in respect of a proportion only of the Sum Insured, the premium due to the Assigned Risks Pool in respect of that policy shall be an amount equal to **T × P**, where:

T = the total premium (including any default charge in accordance with Part 2) that would have been due to the Assigned Risks Pool in relation to that policy if the Assigned Risks Pool was the only insurer

P = the proportion, expressed as a percentage, in respect of which the Assigned Risks Pool is liable in relation to that policy

1.7 Definition of Gross Fees

For the purposes of the Assigned Risks Pool rating, Gross Fees means all professional fees of the Insured Firm for the latest complete financial year including remuneration, retained commission, and income of any sort whatsoever of the Insured Firm and notarial fees where a solicitor notary operates a notarial Practice in conjunction with a solicitor's Practice, but excluding only:

(a)   interest;

(b)   the reimbursement of disbursements;

(c)   any amount charged in respect of value added tax;

(d)   remuneration derived from any office excluded from the definition of private Practice by these Rules;

(e)   dividends;

(f)   rents received by the Insured Firm;

(g)   income and capital profits from reserved funds established or other investments made by the Insured Firm.

Where the Insured Firm has been in existence for less than 12 months, the Gross Fees for ARP rating purposes shall be the Insured Firm's best estimate of the Gross Fees likely to be received during its first 12 months of trading. However, where the expiry date of the Indemnity Period precedes the completion date of the first 12 months of trading, the Gross Fees for Assigned Risks Pool rating purposes shall be the Insured Firm's best estimate of the Gross Fees likely to be received during the period commencing with the starting date of the Practice and ending with the expiry date of the Indemnity Period.

In the event that the estimated amount of Gross Fees differs from the actual amount of Gross Fees for the relevant period, the Assigned Risks Pool premium shall be adjusted by reference to the actual amount of Gross Fees.

1.8   New Firms

In the case of a new Firm which commences Practice during the course of an Indemnity Period, the ARP Premium payable in relation to that Insured Firm shall be reduced pro rata according to the number of days elapsed in the relevant Indemnity Period prior to that Insured Firm commencing Practice.

1.9   Firms with limited eligibility

In the case of a Firm which will cease to be an Eligible Firm during the course of an Indemnity Period, the ARP Premium or ARP Default Premium (but not any ARP Run-off Premium) which would otherwise be payable in relation to that Insured Firm shall be reduced in accordance with the table below:

Point in Indemnity Period when Firm ceases to be an Eligible Firm	Reduction applied to ARP Premium payable
First calendar month	80%
Second or third calendar month	60%
Fourth, fifth or sixth calendar month	30%
Seventh, eighth or ninth calendar month	15%
Tenth, eleventh or twelfth calendar month	Nil

1.10   Premium payment

The ARP Premium shall be paid to the ARP Manager within 30 days of such premium being notified to the Insured Firm by the ARP Manager.

1.11   Cancellation

Where a Firm enters the Assigned Risks Pool during any Indemnity Period, but subsequently arranges Qualifying Insurance outside the Assigned Risks Pool before the end of that Indemnity Period, a return premium shall become due to the Insured Firm concerned. The return premium shall be calculated in accordance with the Short Period Scale shown below.

APPENDIX 6

1.12 Short Period Scale

Cancellation effective in which calendar month of the Indemnity Period	Percentage of ARP Premium to be returned
First calendar month	80%
Second or third calendar month	60%
Fourth, fifth or sixth calendar month	30%
Seventh, eighth or ninth calendar month	15%
Tenth, eleventh or twelfth calendar month	Nil

However, there shall be no return premium due to the Insured Firm in the event that any claims, or circumstances that may give rise to claims, have been notified to the ARP Manager during the Indemnity Period concerned. Furthermore, in the event that the Assigned Risks Pool insurers are called upon to deal with a claim that was first made against the Insured Firm during the Indemnity Period concerned, but which claim the Insured Firm failed to notify to the ARP Manager, the amount of the return premium shall be repaid to the ARP Manager. The ARP Manager may set off any return premium due to the Insured Firm against any part of the ARP Premium which is due in respect of that Insured Firm but which remains unpaid.

1.13 Run-off premium

If an Insured Firm ceases to carry on a Practice during the course of any Indemnity Period in circumstances where the Assigned Risks Pool is required to provide run-off cover in respect of that Insured Firm under the terms of an ARP Policy issued to that Insured Firm, no return premium shall be payable to that Insured Firm in respect of that ARP Policy.

In addition, in such circumstances the Insured Firm and every Principal of that Insured Firm (including, for these purposes, every person held out as a partner of a sole practitioner) shall be required to pay to the Assigned Risks Pool an additional premium equal to:

- 12/13 of the full annual ARP Premium (or, if applicable, the full annual ARP Default Premium and, for the avoidance of doubt, prior to any reduction applied under paragraph 1.9 above) payable in respect of that Insured Firm in relation to the last Indemnity Period for which such premium was payable, where such Indemnity Period was the period from 1 September 2003 to 30 September 2004; or

- 100 per cent of the full annual ARP premium (or, if applicable, the full annual ARP Default Premium and, for the avoidance of doubt, prior to any reduction applied under paragraph 1.9 above) payable in respect of that Insured Firm in relation to the last Indemnity Period for which such premium was payable, in the case of any other Indemnity Period.

Such additional premium shall be payable to the ARP Manager within 30 days of such premium being notified to the Insured nFirm by the ARP Manager.

1.14 Suspended Practices

If:

- an Insured Firm ceases to carry on a Practice during the course of any Indemnity Period in circumstances where the Assigned Risks Pool is required to provide run-off cover in respect of that Insured Firm under the terms of an ARP Policy issued to that Insured Firm; and

- that Insured Firm's Practice subsequently restarts; and

- the ARP Manager agrees to cancel such run-off cover

the Insured Firm shall be entitled to such reimbursement of premium (if any), as the ARP Manager considers appropriate.

If, in addition, the ARP Manager agrees to provide continuing cover in accordance with paragraph 5.4(b)(ii) of the Minimum Terms and Conditions, the Insured Firm and every Principal of that Insured Firm (including, for these purposes, every person held out as a partner of a Sole Practitioner) shall be liable to pay such additional premium (if any) as the ARP Manager considers appropriate.

1.15 Self-Insured excesses for 20010/2011

The Self-Insured excess for each and every claim shall be calculated by multiplying the relevant number of Principals by £4,500, subject to a maximum of £225,000 each claim. The relevant number of Principals is the number of Principals (including, for these purposes, every person held out as a partner of a Sole Practitioner) as at the inception date of the Policy.

2 Method for calculation of the ARP Default Premium

The ARP Default Premium shall be an amount equal to the ARP Premium calculated in accordance with Part 1 above, plus an additional default charge of 20% of the amount concerned.

3 Method for calculation of the ARP Run-off Premium

The ARP Run-off Premium shall be an amount equal to $\mathbf{A} + \mathbf{B} - \mathbf{C}$, where:

$\mathbf{A} =$ The amount that would have been payable as the ARP Default Premium calculated in accordance with Part 2 above in relation to each Indemnity Period in which the Firm has failed to obtain Qualifying Insurance prior to it becoming a Run-off Firm (including the Indemnity Period in which it ceased to practise)

$\mathbf{B} =$ A further amount equal to that which would have been payable as the ARP Default Premium calculated in accordance with Part 2 above in relation to the Indemnity Period during which the Firm ceased to practise

$\mathbf{C} =$ Any sum due under Rule 14.2

Appendix 3

Special provisions for Registered European Lawyers

1 If:

(a) one or more of the Principals of an Insured Firm are Registered European Lawyers who claim that professional indemnity insurance, or a professional indemnity fund, under their home professional rules provides the Insured Firm's Practice with professional indemnity cover in all respects equivalent in its conditions and extent to that which would be provided under the Minimum Terms and Conditions (**Full Home State Cover**); and

(b) the Council is so satisfied, (including, without limitation, by reason of any provider of the Full Home State Cover entering into such agreement as the Council may require from time to time but provided that the Council shall not be so satisfied if more than 25% of the Principals are Solicitors),

the Insured Firm and its Principals shall for so long as such cover continues (and, where the Council has required such agreement, for so long as such agreement remains in force and its requirements are complied with by the provider(s) of the Full Home State Cover that are party to it) be exempted from the obligation to take out and maintain Qualifying Insurance.

2   If on an application by one or more Registered European Lawyers who are Principals in an Insured Firm, the Council is satisfied that the Insured Firm's Practice has professional indemnity cover under home professional rules but that the equivalence is only partial (**Partial Home State Cover**) (including, without limitation, by reason of the provider of the Partial Home State Cover entering into such agreement as the Council may require from time to time), the Insured Firm and its Principals shall for so long as such cover continues (and, where the Council has required such agreement, for so long as such agreement remains in force and its requirements are complied with by the provider(s) of the Partial Home State Cover that are party to it) be exempted from the obligation to take out and maintain Qualifying Insurance, on condition that they take out and maintain a Difference In Conditions Policy, which shall provide cover including the Minimum Terms and Conditions as modified by the following changes (but not otherwise):

(a)   Clause 4.5 shall be deleted and replaced with the following:

4.5   No "other insurance" provision

The insurance must not provide that the liability of the Insurer is reduced or excluded by reason of the existence or availability of any other insurance other than as contemplated by clauses 6.2 or 6.12. For the avoidance of doubt, this requirement is not intended to affect any right of the Insurer to claim contribution from any other insurer which is also liable to indemnify any Insured.

(b)   Clause 4.9 shall be deleted and replaced with the following:

4.9   Resolution of disputes

The insurance must provide that, if there is a dispute as to whether a Practice is a Successor Practice for the purposes of clauses 1.4, 1.6 or 5.3, the Insured and the Insurer will take all reasonable steps (including, if appropriate, referring the dispute to arbitration) to resolve the dispute in conjunction with any related dispute between any other party which has insurance complying with these minimum terms and conditions and that party's insurer, and in conjunction with the provider of the Partial Home State Cover.

(c)   Clause 4.10 shall be deleted and replaced with the following:

4.10   Conduct of a Claim pending dispute resolution

The insurance must provide that, pending resolution of any coverage dispute and without prejudice to any issue in dispute, the Insurer will, if so directed by the Society, conduct any Claim, advance Defence Costs and, if appropriate, compromise and pay the Claim (whether alone or in conjunction with the provider of the Partial Home State Cover). If the Society is satisfied that:

(a)   the party requesting the direction has taken all reasonable steps to resolve the dispute with the other party/ies; and

(b)   there is a reasonable prospect that the coverage dispute will be resolved or determined in the Insured's favour; and

(c)   it is fair and equitable in all the circumstances for such direction to be given;

it may in its absolute discretion make such a direction.

(d)   Clause 4.12 shall be deleted and replaced with the following:

4.12   Period of Insurance

The Period of Insurance must not expire prior to the earlier of:

(a) 30 September 2011; or

(b) the date with effect on which the Partial Home State Cover expires or is avoided.

(e) The following clause shall be added:

6.11 Partial Home State Cover

The insurance may exclude any liability of the Insurer to the extent that any such liability is covered under the terms of the Partial Home State Cover irrespective of whether recovery is actually made in respect of such liability.

and in clause 8.2 the following definition shall be added:

Partial Home State Cover has the meaning given in Appendix 3 to the Solicitors' Indemnity Insurance Rules 2010.

3   In the event of an Insured Firm which has the benefit of an exemption under paragraph 1 or paragraph 2 of this Appendix ceasing for whatever reason to enjoy that exemption but continuing to carry on a Practice it shall be treated for all the purposes of these Rules as though it had commenced the Practice on the date when such exemption ceased.

4   Rule 6 (Insolvency Event) shall apply to an Insured Firm which has the benefit of an exemption under paragraph 1 or paragraph 2 of this Appendix in like manner as though the insurance company or entity or fund providing professional indemnity cover under its home professional rules, on the basis of which exemption or partial exemption was granted, was a Qualifying Insurer.

5   In the case of an Insured Firm which has the benefit of an exemption under paragraph 2 of this Appendix all the provisions of these Rules shall apply to the additional professional indemnity insurance required under that paragraph to be taken out with a Qualifying Insurer.

CCBE Code of Conduct

[The Code is reproduced with the kind permission of the CCBE. For the latest updates to the material, please see www.ccbe.org.]

Code of Conduct for European Lawyers

This Code of Conduct for European Lawyers was originally adopted at the CCBE Plenary Session held on 28 October 1988, and subsequently amended during the CCBE Plenary Sessions on 28 November 1998, 6 December 2002 and 19 May 2006. The Code includes an Explanatory Memorandum which was updated during the CCBE Plenary Session on 19 May 2006.

Editor: CCBE

Avenue de la Joyeuse Entrée, 1–5 – B-1040 Brussels
Tél. : +32 (0)2 234 65 10 – Fax : +32 (0)2 234 65 11/12
E-mail : ccbe@ccbe.org – http://www.ccbe.org

Contents

EXPLANATORY MEMORANDUM

1. Preamble

1.1. The Function of the Lawyer in Society

In a society founded on respect for the rule of law the lawyer fulfils a special role. The lawyer's duties do not begin and end with the faithful performance of what he or she is instructed to do so far as the law permits. A lawyer must serve the interests of justice as well as those whose rights and liberties he or she is trusted to assert and defend and it is the lawyer's duty not only to plead the client's cause but to be the client's adviser. Respect for the lawyer's professional function is an essential condition for the rule of law and democracy in society.

A lawyer's function therefore lays on him or her a variety of legal and moral obligations (sometimes appearing to be in conflict with each other) towards:

—   the client;

—   the courts and other authorities before whom the lawyer pleads the client's cause or acts on the client's behalf;

—   the legal profession in general and each fellow member of it in particular;

— the public for whom the existence of a free and independent profession, bound together by respect for rules made by the profession itself, is an essential means of safeguarding human rights in face of the power of the state and other interests in society.

1.2. The Nature of Rules of Professional Conduct

1.2.1. Rules of professional conduct are designed through their willing acceptance by those to whom they apply to ensure the proper performance by the lawyer of a function which is recognised as essential in all civilised societies. The failure of the lawyer to observe these rules may result in disciplinary sanctions.

1.2.2. The particular rules of each Bar or Law Society arise from its own traditions. They are adapted to the organisation and sphere of activity of the profession in the Member State concerned and to its judicial and administrative procedures and to its national legislation. It is neither possible nor desirable that they should be taken out of their context nor that an attempt should be made to give general application to rules which are inherently incapable of such application.

The particular rules of each Bar and Law Society nevertheless are based on the same values and in most cases demonstrate a common foundation.

1.3. The Purpose of the Code

1.3.1. The continued integration of the European Union and European Economic Area and the increasing frequency of the cross-border activities of lawyers within the European Economic Area have made necessary in the public interest the statement of common rules which apply to all lawyers from the European Economic Area whatever Bar or Law Society they belong to in relation to their cross-border practice. A particular purpose of the statement of those rules is to mitigate the difficulties which result from the application of "double deontology", notably as set out in Articles 4 and 7.2 of Directive 77/249/EEC and Articles 6 and 7 of Directive 98/5/EC.

1.3.2. The organisations representing the legal profession through the CCBE propose that the rules codified in the following articles:

— be recognised at the present time as the expression of a consensus of all the Bars and Law Societies of the European Union and European Economic Area;

— be adopted as enforceable rules as soon as possible in accordance with national or EEA procedures in relation to the cross-border activities of the lawyer in the European Union and European Economic Area;

— be taken into account in all revisions of national rules of deontology or professional practice with a view to their progressive harmonisation.

They further express the wish that the national rules of deontology or professional practice be interpreted and applied whenever possible in a way consistent with the rules in this Code.

After the rules in this Code have been adopted as enforceable rules in relation to a lawyer's cross-border activities the lawyer will remain bound to observe the rules of the Bar or Law Society to which he or she belongs to the extent that they are consistent with the rules in this Code.

1.4. Field of Application Ratione Personae

This Code shall apply to lawyers as they are defined by Directive 77/249/EEC and by Directive 98/5/EC and to lawyers of the Observer Members of the CCBE.

APPENDIX 7

1.5. Field of Application Ratione Materiae

Without prejudice to the pursuit of a progressive harmonisation of rules of deontology or professional practice which apply only internally within a Member State, the following rules shall apply to the cross-border activities of the lawyer within the European Union and the European Economic Area. Cross-border activities shall mean:

(a)   all professional contacts with lawyers of Member States other than the lawyer's own;

(b)   the professional activities of the lawyer in a Member State other than his or her own, whether or not the lawyer is physically present in that Member State.

1.6. Definitions

In this Code:

"Member State" means a member state of the European Union or any other state whose legal profession is included in Article 1.4.

"Home Member State" means the Member State where the lawyer acquired the right to bear his or her professional title.

"Host Member State" means any other Member State where the lawyer carries on cross-border activities.

"Competent Authority" means the professional organisation(s) or authority(ies) of the Member State concerned responsible for the laying down of rules of professional conduct and the administration of discipline of lawyers.

"Directive 77/249/EEC" means Council Directive 77/249/EEC of 22 March 1977 to facilitate the effective exercise by lawyers of freedom to provide services.

"Directive 98/5/EC" means Directive 98/5/EC of the European Parliament and of the Council of 16 February 1998 to facilitate practice of the profession of lawyer on a permanent basis in a Member State other than that in which the qualification was obtained.

2. General Principles

2.1. Independence

2.1.1. The many duties to which a lawyer is subject require the lawyer's absolute independence, free from all other influence, especially such as may arise from his or her personal interests or external pressure. Such independence is as necessary to trust in the process of justice as the impartiality of the judge. A lawyer must therefore avoid any impairment of his or her independence and be careful not to compromise his or her professional standards in order to please the client, the court or third parties.

2.1.2. This independence is necessary in non-contentious matters as well as in litigation. Advice given by a lawyer to the client has no value if the lawyer gives it only to ingratiate him- or herself, to serve his or her personal interests or in response to outside pressure.

2.2. Trust and Personal Integrity

Relationships of trust can only exist if a lawyer's personal honour, honesty and integrity are beyond doubt. For the lawyer these traditional virtues are professional obligations.

2.3. Confidentiality

2.3.1. It is of the essence of a lawyer's function that the lawyer should be told by his or her client things which the client would not tell to others, and that the lawyer should be the recipient of other information on a basis of confidence. Without the certainty of confidentiality there cannot be trust. Confidentiality is therefore a primary and fundamental right and duty of the lawyer.

The lawyer's obligation of confidentiality serves the interest of the administration of justice as well as the interest of the client. It is therefore entitled to special protection by the State.

2.3.2. A lawyer shall respect the confidentiality of all information that becomes known to the lawyer in the course of his or her professional activity.

2.3.3. The obligation of confidentiality is not limited in time.

2.3.4. A lawyer shall require his or her associates and staff and anyone engaged by him or her in the course of providing professional services to observe the same obligation of confidentiality.

2.4. Respect for the Rules of Other Bars and Law Societies

When practising cross-border, a lawyer from another Member State may be bound to comply with the professional rules of the Host Member State. Lawyers have a duty to inform themselves as to the rules which will affect them in the performance of any particular activity.

Member organisations of the CCBE are obliged to deposit their codes of conduct at the Secretariat of the CCBE so that any lawyer can get hold of the copy of the current code from the Secretariat.

2.5. Incompatible Occupations

2.5.1. In order to perform his or her functions with due independence and in a manner which is consistent with his or her duty to participate in the administration of justice a lawyer may be prohibited from undertaking certain occupations.

2.5.2. A lawyer who acts in the representation or the defence of a client in legal proceedings or before any public authorities in a Host Member State shall there observe the rules regarding incompatible occupations as they are applied to lawyers of the Host Member State.

2.5.3. A lawyer established in a Host Member State in which he or she wishes to participate directly in commercial or other activities not connected with the practice of the law shall respect the rules regarding forbidden or incompatible occupations as they are applied to lawyers of that Member State.

2.6. Personal Publicity

2.6.1. A lawyer is entitled to inform the public about his or her services provided that the information is accurate and not misleading, and respectful of the obligation of confidentiality and other core values of the profession.

2.6.2. Personal publicity by a lawyer in any form of media such as by press, radio, television, by electronic commercial communications or otherwise is permitted to the extent it complies with the requirements of 2.6.1.

2.7. The Client's Interest

Subject to due observance of all rules of law and professional conduct, a lawyer must always act in the best interests of the client and must put those interests before the lawyer's own interests or those of fellow members of the legal profession.

2.8. Limitation of Lawyer's Liability towards the Client

To the extent permitted by the law of the Home Member State and the Host Member State, the lawyer may limit his or her liabilities towards the client in accordance with the professional rules to which the lawyer is subject.

3. Relations with Clients

3.1. Acceptance and Termination of Instructions

3.1.1. A lawyer shall not handle a case for a party except on that party's instructions. The lawyer may, however, act in a case in which he or she has been instructed by another lawyer acting for the party or where the case has been assigned to him or her by a competent body.

The lawyer should make reasonable efforts to ascertain the identity, competence and authority of the person or body who instructs him or her when the specific circumstances show that the identity, competence and authority are uncertain.

3.1.2. A lawyer shall advise and represent the client promptly, conscientiously and diligently. The lawyer shall undertake personal responsibility for the discharge of the client's instructions and shall keep the client informed as to the progress of the matter with which the lawyer has been entrusted.

3.1.3. A lawyer shall not handle a matter which the lawyer knows or ought to know he or she is not competent to handle, without co-operating with a lawyer who is competent to handle it.

A lawyer shall not accept instructions unless he or she can discharge those instructions promptly having regard to the pressure of other work.

3.1.4. A lawyer shall not be entitled to exercise his or her right to withdraw from a case in such a way or in such circumstances that the client may be unable to find other legal assistance in time to prevent prejudice being suffered by the client.

3.2. Conflict of Interest

3.2.1. A lawyer may not advise, represent or act on behalf of two or more clients in the same matter if there is a conflict, or a significant risk of a conflict, between the interests of those clients.

3.2.2. A lawyer must cease to act for both or all of the clients concerned when a conflict of interests arises between those clients and also whenever there is a risk of a breach of confidence or where the lawyer's independence may be impaired.

3.2.3. A lawyer must also refrain from acting for a new client if there is a risk of breach of a confidence entrusted to the lawyer by a former client or if the knowledge which the lawyer possesses of the affairs of the former client would give an undue advantage to the new client.

3.2.4. Where lawyers are practising in association, paragraphs 3.2.1 to 3.2.3 above shall apply to the association and all its members.

3.3. Pactum de Quota Litis

3.3.1. A lawyer shall not be entitled to make a *pactum de quota litis*.

3.3.2. By "*pactum de quota litis*" is meant an agreement between a lawyer and the client entered into prior to final conclusion of a matter to which the client is a party, by virtue of which the client undertakes to pay the lawyer a share of the result regardless of whether this is represented by a sum of money or by any other benefit achieved by the client upon the conclusion of the matter.

3.3.3. "*Pactum de quota litis*" does not include an agreement that fees be charged in proportion to the value of a matter handled by the lawyer if this is in accordance with an officially approved fee scale or under the control of the Competent Authority having jurisdiction over the lawyer.

3.4. Regulation of Fees

A fee charged by a lawyer shall be fully disclosed to the client, shall be fair and reasonable, and shall comply with the law and professional rules to which the lawyer is subject.

3.5. Payment on Account

If a lawyer requires a payment on account of his or her fees and/or disbursements such payment should not exceed a reasonable estimate of the fees and probable disbursements involved.

Failing such payment, a lawyer may withdraw from the case or refuse to handle it, but subject always to paragraph 3.1.4 above.

3.6. Fee Sharing with Non-Lawyers

3.6.1. A lawyer may not share his or her fees with a person who is not a lawyer except where an association between the lawyer and the other person is permitted by the laws and the professional rules to which the lawyer is subject.

3.6.2. The provisions of 3.6.1 above shall not preclude a lawyer from paying a fee, commission or other compensation to a deceased lawyer's heirs or to a retired lawyer in respect of taking over the deceased or retired lawyer's practice.

3.7. Cost of Litigation and Availability of Legal Aid

3.7.1. The lawyer should at all times strive to achieve the most cost effective resolution of the client's dispute and should advise the client at appropriate stages as to the desirability of attempting a settlement and/or a reference to alternative dispute resolution.

3.7.2. A lawyer shall inform the client of the availability of legal aid where applicable.

3.8. Client Funds

3.8.1. Lawyers who come into possession of funds on behalf of their clients or third parties (hereinafter called "client funds") have to deposit such money into an account of a bank or similar institution subject to supervision by a public authority (hereinafter called a "client account"). A client account shall be separate from any other account of the lawyer. All client funds received by a lawyer should be deposited into such an account unless the owner of such funds agrees that the funds should be dealt with otherwise.

3.8.2. The lawyer shall maintain full and accurate records showing all the lawyer's dealings with client funds and distinguishing client funds from other funds held by the lawyer. Records may have to be kept for a certain period of time according to national rules.

3.8.3. A client account cannot be in debit except in exceptional circumstances as expressly permitted in national rules or due to bank charges, which cannot be influenced by the lawyer. Such an account cannot be given as a guarantee or be used as a security for any reason. There shall not be any set-off or merger between a client account and any other bank account, nor shall the client funds in a client account be available to defray money owed by the lawyer to the bank.

3.8.4. Client funds shall be transferred to the owners of such funds in the shortest period of time or under such conditions as are authorised by them.

3.8.5. The lawyer cannot transfer funds from a client account into the lawyer's own account for payment of fees without informing the client in writing.

3.8.6. The Competent Authorities in Member States shall have the power to verify and examine any document regarding client funds, whilst respecting the confidentiality or legal professional privilege to which it may be subject.

3.9. Professional Indemnity Insurance

3.9.1. Lawyers shall be insured against civil legal liability arising out of their legal practice to an extent which is reasonable having regard to the nature and extent of the risks incurred by their professional activities.

3.9.2. Should this prove impossible, the lawyer must inform the client of this situation and its consequences.

4. Relations with the Courts

4.1. Rules of Conduct in Court

A lawyer who appears, or takes part in a case, before a court or tribunal must comply with the rules of conduct applied before that court or tribunal.

4.2. Fair Conduct of Proceedings

A lawyer must always have due regard for the fair conduct of proceedings.

4.3. Demeanour in Court

A lawyer shall while maintaining due respect and courtesy towards the court defend the interests of the client honourably and fearlessly without regard to the lawyer's own interests or to any consequences to him- or herself or to any other person.

4.4. False or Misleading Information

A lawyer shall never knowingly give false or misleading information to the court.

4.5. Extension to Arbitrators etc.

The rules governing a lawyer's relations with the courts apply also to the lawyer's relations with arbitrators and any other persons exercising judicial or quasi-judicial functions, even on an occasional basis.

5. Relations between Lawyers

5.1. Corporate Spirit of the Profession

5.1.1. The corporate spirit of the profession requires a relationship of trust and co-operation between lawyers for the benefit of their clients and in order to avoid unnecessary litigation and other behaviour harmful to the reputation of the profession. It can, however, never justify setting the interests of the profession against those of the client.

5.1.2. A lawyer should recognise all other lawyers of Member States as professional colleagues and act fairly and courteously towards them.

5.2. Co-operation among Lawyers of Different Member States

5.2.1. It is the duty of a lawyer who is approached by a colleague from another Member State not to accept instructions in a matter which the lawyer is not competent to undertake. The lawyer should in such case be prepared to help that colleague to obtain the information necessary to enable him or her to instruct a lawyer who is capable of providing the service asked for.

5.2.2. Where a lawyer of a Member State co-operates with a lawyer from another Member State, both have a general duty to take into account the differences which may exist between their respective legal systems and the professional organisations, competences and obligations of lawyers in the Member States concerned.

5.3. Correspondence between Lawyers

5.3.1. If a lawyer intends to send communications to a lawyer in another Member State, which the sender wishes to remain confidential or without prejudice he or she should clearly express this intention prior to communicating the documents.

5.3.2. If the prospective recipient of the communications is unable to ensure their status as confidential or without prejudice he or she should inform the sender accordingly without delay.

5.4. Referral Fees

5.4.1. A lawyer may not demand or accept from another lawyer or any other person a fee, commission or any other compensation for referring or recommending the lawyer to a client.

5.4.2. A lawyer may not pay anyone a fee, commission or any other compensation as a consideration for referring a client to him- or herself.

5.5. Communication with Opposing Parties

A lawyer shall not communicate about a particular case or matter directly with any person whom he or she knows to be represented or advised in the case or matter by another lawyer, without the consent of that other lawyer (and shall keep the other lawyer informed of any such communications).

5.6.

(Deleted by decision of the Plenary Session in Dublin on 6 December 2002)

5.7. Responsibility for Fees

In professional relations between members of Bars of different Member States, where a lawyer does not confine him- or herself to recommending another lawyer or introducing that other lawyer to the client but instead him- or herself entrusts a correspondent with a particular matter or seeks the correspondent's advice, the instructing lawyer is personally bound, even if the client is insolvent, to pay the fees, costs and outlays which are due to the foreign correspondent. The lawyers concerned may, however, at the outset of the relationship between them make special arrangements on this matter. Further, the instructing lawyer may at any time limit his or her personal responsibility to the amount of the fees, costs and outlays incurred before intimation to the foreign lawyer of the instructing lawyer's disclaimer of responsibility for the future.

5.8. Continuing Professional Development

Lawyers should maintain and develop their professional knowledge and skills taking proper account of the European dimension of their profession.

5.9. Disputes amongst Lawyers in Different Member States

5.9.1. If a lawyer considers that a colleague in another Member State has acted in breach of a rule of professional conduct the lawyer shall draw the matter to the attention of that colleague.

5.9.2. If any personal dispute of a professional nature arises amongst lawyers in different Member States they should if possible first try to settle it in a friendly way.

5.9.3. A lawyer shall not commence any form of proceedings against a colleague in another Member State on matters referred to in 5.9.1 or 5.9.2 above without first informing the Bars or Law Societies to which they both belong for the purpose of allowing both Bars or Law Societies concerned an opportunity to assist in reaching a settlement.

Explanatory Memorandum

This Explanatory Memorandum was prepared at the request of the CCBE Standing Committee by the CCBE's deontology working party, who were responsible for drafting the first version of the Code of Conduct itself. It seeks to explain the origin of the provisions of the Code, to illustrate the problems which they are designed to resolve, particularly in relation to cross-border activities, and to provide assistance to the Competent Authorities in the Member States in the application of the Code. It is not intended to have any binding force in the interpretation of the Code. The Explanatory Memorandum was updated on the occasion of the CCBE Plenary Session on 19 May 2006.

The original versions of the Code are in the French and English languages. Translations into other Community languages are prepared under the authority of the national delegations.

Commentary on Article 1.1 – The Function of the Lawyer in Society

The Declaration of Perugia, adopted by the CCBE in 1977, laid down the fundamental principles of professional conduct applicable to lawyers throughout the EC. The provisions of Article 1.1 reaffirm the statement in the Declaration of Perugia of the function of the lawyer in society which forms the basis for the rules governing the performance of that function.

Commentary on Article 1.2 – The Nature of Rules of Professional Conduct

These provisions substantially restate the explanation in the Declaration of Perugia of the nature of rules of professional conduct and how particular rules depend on particular local circumstances but are nevertheless based on common values.

Commentary on Article 1.3 – The Purpose of the Code

These provisions introduce the development of the principles in the Declaration of Perugia into a specific Code of Conduct for lawyers throughout the EU and the EEA, and lawyers of the Observer Members of the CCBE, with particular reference to their cross-border activities (defined in Article 1.5). The provisions of Article 1.3.2 lay down the specific intentions of the CCBE with regard to the substantive provisions in the Code.

Commentary on Article 1.4 – Field of Application Ratione Personae

The rules are stated to apply to all lawyers as defined in the Lawyers Services Directive of 1977 and the Lawyers Establishment Directive of 1998, and lawyers of the Observer Members of the CCBE. This includes lawyers of the states which subsequently acceded to the Directives, whose names have been added by amendment to the Directives. The Code accordingly applies to all the lawyers represented on the CCBE, whether as full Members or as Observer Members, namely:

Austria	Rechtsanwalt;
Belgium	avocat / advocaat / Rechtsanwalt;
Bulgaria	advokat;
Croatia	odvjetnik;
Cyprus	dikegóros;
Czech Republic	advokát;
Denmark	advokat;
Estonia	vandeadvokaat;
Finland	asianajaja / advokat;
FYROMacedonia	advokat;
France	avocat;
Germany	Rechtsanwalt;
Greece	dikegóros;
Hungary	ügyvéd;
Iceland	lögmaður;
Ireland	barrister, solicitor;
Italy	avvocato;
Latvia	zvērināts advokāts;
Liechtenstein	Rechtsanwalt;
Lithuania	advokatas;
Luxembourg	avocat / Rechtsanwalt;
Malta	avukat, prokuratur legali;
Netherlands	advocaat;

Norway	advokat;
Poland	adwokat, radca prawny;
Portugal	advogado;
Romania	avocat;
Slovakia	advokát / advokátka;
Slovenia	odvetnik / odvetnica;
Spain	abogado / advocat / abokatu / avogado;
Sweden	advokat;
Switzerland	Rechtsanwalt / Anwalt / Fürsprech / Fürsprecher /avocat / avvocato /advokat;
Turkey	avukat;
Ukraine	advocate;
United Kingdom	advocate, barrister, solicitor.

It is also hoped that the Code will be acceptable to the legal professions of other non-member states in Europe and elsewhere so that it could also be applied by appropriate conventions between them and the Member States.

Commentary on Article 1.5 – Field of Application Ratione Materiae

The rules are here given direct application only to "cross-border activities", as defined, of lawyers within the EU and the EEA and lawyers of the Observer Members of the CCBE – see above on Article 1.4, and the definition of "Member State" in Article 1.6. (See also above as to possible extensions in the future to lawyers of other states.) The definition of cross-border activities would, for example, include contacts in state A even on a matter of law internal to state A between a lawyer of state A and a lawyer of state B; it would exclude contacts between lawyers of state A in state A of a matter arising in state B, provided that none of their professional activities takes place in state B; it would include any activities of lawyers of state A in state B, even if only in the form of communications sent from state A to state B.

Commentary on Article 1.6 – Definitions

This provision defines a number of terms used in the Code, "Member State", "Home Member State", "Host Member State", "Competent Authority", "Directive 77/249/EEC" and "Directive 98/5/EC".

The reference to "where the lawyer carries on cross-border activities" should be interpreted in the light of the definition of "cross-border activities" in Article 1.5.

Commentary on Article 2.1 – Independence

This provision substantially reaffirms the general statement of principle in the Declaration of Perugia.

Commentary on Article 2.2 – Trust and Personal Integrity

This provision also restates a general principle contained in the Declaration of Perugia.

Commentary on Article 2.3 – Confidentiality

This provision first restates, in Article 2.3.1, general principles laid down in the Declaration of Perugia and recognised by the ECJ in the *AM&S* case (157/79). It then, in Articles 2.3.2 to 4, develops them into a specific rule relating to the protection of confidentiality. Article 2.3.2 contains the basic rule requiring respect for confidentiality. Article 2.3.3 confirms that the obligation remains binding on the lawyer even if he or she ceases to act for the client in question. Article 2.3.4 confirms that the lawyer must not only respect the obligation of confidentiality him- or herself but must require all members and employees of his or her firm to do likewise.

Commentary on Article 2.4 – Respect for the Rules of Other Bars and Law Societies

Article 4 of the Lawyers Services Directive contains the provisions with regard to the rules to be observed by a lawyer from one Member State providing services on an occasional or temporary basis in another Member State by virtue of Article 49 of the consolidated EC treaty, as follows:

(a)   activities relating to the representation of a client in legal proceedings or before public authorities shall be pursued in each Host Member State under the conditions laid down for lawyers established in that state, with the exception of any conditions requiring residence, or registration with a professional organisation, in that state;

(b)   a lawyer pursuing these activities shall observe the rules of professional conduct of the Host Member State, without prejudice to the lawyer's obligations in the Member State from which he or she comes;

(c)   when these activities are pursued in the UK, "rules of professional conduct of the Host Member State" means the rules of professional conduct applicable to solicitors, where such activities are not reserved for barristers and advocates. Otherwise the rules of professional conduct applicable to the latter shall apply. However, barristers from Ireland shall always be subject to the rules of professional conduct applicable in the UK to barristers and advocates. When these activities are pursued in Ireland "rules of professional conduct of the Host Member State" means, in so far as they govern the oral presentation of a case in court, the rules of professional conduct applicable to barristers. In all other cases the rules of professional conduct applicable to solicitors shall apply. However, barristers and advocates from the UK shall always be subject to the rules of professional conduct applicable in Ireland to barristers; and

(d)   a lawyer pursuing activities other than those referred to in (a) above shall remain subject to the conditions and rules of professional conduct of the Member State from which he or she comes without prejudice to respect for the rules, whatever their source, which govern the profession in the Host Member State, especially those concerning the incompatibility of the exercise of the activities of a lawyer with the exercise of other activities in that state, professional secrecy, relations with other lawyers, the prohibition on the same lawyer acting for parties with mutually conflicting interests, and publicity. The latter rules are applicable only if they are capable of being observed by a lawyer who is not established in the Host Member State and to the extent to which their observance is objectively justified to ensure, in that state, the proper exercise of a lawyer's activities, the standing of the profession and respect for the rules concerning incompatibility.

The Lawyers Establishment Directive contains the provisions with regard to the rules to be observed by a lawyer from one Member State practising on a permanent basis in another Member State by virtue of Article 43 of the consolidated EC treaty, as follows:

(a)   irrespective of the rules of professional conduct to which he or she is subject in his or her Home Member State, a lawyer practising under his home-country professional title shall be subject to the same rules of professional conduct as lawyers practising under the relevant professional title of the Host Member State in respect of all the activities the lawyer pursues in its territory (Article 6.1);

(b) the Host Member State may require a lawyer practising under his or her home-country professional title either to take out professional indemnity insurance or to become a member of a professional guarantee fund in accordance with the rules which that state lays down for professional activities pursued in its territory. Nevertheless, a lawyer practising under his or her home-country professional title shall be exempted from that requirement if the lawyer can prove that he or she is covered by insurance taken out or a guarantee provided in accordance with the rules of the Home Member State, insofar as such insurance or guarantee is equivalent in terms of the conditions and extent of cover. Where the equivalence is only partial, the Competent Authority in the Host Member State may require that additional insurance or an additional guarantee be contracted to cover the elements which are not already covered by the insurance or guarantee contracted in accordance with the rules of the Home Member State (Article 6.3); and

(c) a lawyer registered in a Host Member State under his or her home-country professional title may practise as a salaried lawyer in the employ of another lawyer, an association or firm of lawyers, or a public or private enterprise to the extent that the Host Member State so permits for lawyers registered under the professional title used in that state (Article 8).

In cases not covered by either of these Directives, or over and above the requirements of these Directives, the obligations of a lawyer under Community law to observe the rules of other Bars and Law Societies are a matter of interpretation of any relevant provision, such as the Directive on Electronic Commerce (2000/31/EC). A major purpose of the Code is to minimise, and if possible eliminate altogether, the problems which may arise from "double deontology", that is the application of more than one set of potentially conflicting national rules to a particular situation (see Article 1.3.1).

Commentary on Article 2.5 – Incompatible Occupations

There are differences both between and within Member States on the extent to which lawyers are permitted to engage in other occupations, for example in commercial activities. The general purpose of rules excluding a lawyer from other occupations is to protect the lawyer from influences which might impair the lawyer's independence or his or her role in the administration of justice. The variations in these rules reflect different local conditions, different perceptions of the proper function of lawyers and different techniques of rule-making. For instance in some cases there is a complete prohibition of engagement in certain named occupations, whereas in other cases engagement in other occupations is generally permitted, subject to observance of specific safeguards for the lawyer's independence.

Articles 2.5.2 and 3 make provision for different circumstances in which a lawyer of one Member State is engaging in cross-border activities (as defined in Article 1.5) in a Host Member State when he or she is not a member of the Host State legal profession.

Article 2.5.2 imposes full observation of Host State rules regarding incompatible occupations on the lawyer acting in national legal proceedings or before national public authorities in the Host State. This applies whether the lawyer is established in the Host State or not.

Article 2.5.3, on the other hand, imposes "respect" for the rules of the Host State regarding forbidden or incompatible occupations in other cases, but only where the lawyer who is established in the Host Member State wishes to participate directly in commercial or other activities not connected with the practice of the law.

Commentary on Article 2.6 – Personal Publicity

The term "personal publicity" covers publicity by firms of lawyers, as well as individual lawyers, as opposed to corporate publicity organised by Bars and Law Societies for their members as a whole. The rules governing personal publicity by lawyers vary considerably in the Member States. Article 2.6 makes it clear that there is no overriding objection to personal publicity in cross-border practice. However, lawyers are nevertheless subject to prohibitions or restrictions laid down by their home professional rules, and a lawyer will still be subject to prohibitions or restrictions laid down by Host State rules when these are binding on the lawyer by virtue of the Lawyers Services Directive or the Lawyers Establishment Directive.

Commentary on Article 2.7 – The Client's Interest

This provision emphasises the general principle that the lawyer must always place the client's interests before the lawyer's own interests or those of fellow members of the legal profession.

Commentary on Article 2.8 – Limitation of Lawyer's Liability towards the Client

This provision makes clear that there is no overriding objection to limiting a lawyer's liability towards his or her client in cross-border practice, whether by contract or by use of a limited company, limited partnership or limited liability partnership. However it points out that this can only be contemplated where the relevant law and the relevant rules of conduct permit – and in a number of jurisdictions the law or the professional rules prohibit or restrict such limitation of liability.

Commentary on Article 3.1 – Acceptance and Termination of Instructions

The provisions of Article 3.1.1 are designed to ensure that a relationship is maintained between lawyer and client and that the lawyer in fact receives instructions from the client, even though these may be transmitted through a duly authorised intermediary. It is the responsibility of the lawyer to satisfy him- or herself as to the authority of the intermediary and the wishes of the client.

Article 3.1.2 deals with the manner in which the lawyer should carry out his or her duties. The provision that the lawyer shall undertake personal responsibility for the discharge of the instructions given to him or her means that the lawyer cannot avoid responsibility by delegation to others. It does not prevent the lawyer from seeking to limit his or her legal liability to the extent that this is permitted by the relevant law or professional rules – see Article 2.8.

Article 3.1.3 states a principle which is of particular relevance in cross-border activities, for example when a lawyer is asked to handle a matter on behalf of a lawyer or client from another state who may be unfamiliar with the relevant law and practice, or when a lawyer is asked to handle a matter relating to the law of another state with which he or she is unfamiliar.

A lawyer generally has the right to refuse to accept instructions in the first place, but Article 3.1.4 states that, having once accepted them, the lawyer has an obligation not to withdraw without ensuring that the client's interests are safeguarded.

Commentary on Article 3.2 – Conflict of Interest

The provisions of Article 3.2.1 do not prevent a lawyer acting for two or more clients in the same matter provided that their interests are not in fact in conflict and that there is no significant risk of such a conflict arising. Where a lawyer is already acting for two or more clients in this way and subsequently there arises a conflict of interests between those clients or a risk of a breach of confidence or other circumstances where the lawyer's independence may be impaired, then the lawyer must cease to act for both or all of them.

There may, however, be circumstances in which differences arise between two or more clients for whom the same lawyer is acting where it may be appropriate for the lawyer to attempt to act as a mediator. It is for the lawyer in such cases to use his or her own judgement on whether or not there is such a conflict of interest between them as to require the lawyer to cease to act. If not, the lawyer may consider whether it would be appropriate to explain the position to the clients, obtain their agreement and attempt to act as mediator to resolve the difference between them, and only if this attempt to mediate should fail, to cease to act for them.

Article 3.2.4 applies the foregoing provisions of Article 3 to lawyers practising in association. For example a firm of lawyers should cease to act when there is a conflict of interest between two clients of the firm, even if different lawyers in the firm are acting for each client. On the other hand, exceptionally, in the "chambers" form of association used by English barristers, where each lawyer acts for clients individually, it is possible for different lawyers in the association to act for clients with opposing interests.

Commentary on Article 3.3 – Pactum de Quota Litis

These provisions reflect the common position in all Member States that an unregulated agreement for contingency fees (*pactum de quota litis*) is contrary to the proper administration of justice because it encourages speculative litigation and is liable to be abused. The provisions are not, however, intended to prevent the maintenance or introduction of arrangements under which lawyers are paid according to results or only if the action or matter is successful, provided that these arrangements are under sufficient regulation and control for the protection of the client and the proper administration of justice.

Commentary on Article 3.4 – Regulation of Fees

Article 3.4 lays down three requirements: a general standard of disclosure of a lawyer's fees to the client, a requirement that they should be fair and reasonable in amount, and a requirement to comply with the applicable law and professional rules.

In many Member States machinery exists for regulating lawyers' fees under national law or rules of conduct, whether by reference to a power of adjudication by the Bar authorities or otherwise. In situations governed by the Lawyers Establishment Directive, where the lawyer is subject to Host State rules as well as the rules of the Home State, the basis of charging may have to comply with both sets of rules.

Commentary on Article 3.5 – Payment on Account

Article 3.5 assumes that a lawyer may require a payment on account of the lawyer's fees and/or disbursements, but sets a limit by reference to a reasonable estimate of them. See also on Article 3.1.4 regarding the right to withdraw.

Commentary on Article 3.6 – Fee Sharing with Non-Lawyers

In some Member States lawyers are permitted to practise in association with members of certain other approved professions, whether legal professions or not. The provisions of

Article 3.6.1 are not designed to prevent fee sharing within such an approved form of association. Nor are the provisions designed to prevent fee sharing by the lawyers to whom the Code applies (see on Article 1.4 above) with other "lawyers", for example lawyers from non-Member States or members of other legal professions in the Member States such as notaries.

Commentary on Article 3.7 – Cost of Litigation and Availability of Legal Aid

Article 3.7.1 stresses the importance of attempting to resolve disputes in a way which is cost-effective for the client, including advising on whether to attempt to negotiate a settlement, and whether to propose referring the dispute to some form of alternative dispute resolution.

Article 3.7.2 requires a lawyer to inform the client of the availability of legal aid where applicable. There are widely differing provisions in the Member States on the availability of legal aid. In cross-border activities a lawyer should have in mind the possibility that the legal aid provisions of a national law with which the lawyer is unfamiliar may be applicable.

Commentary on Article 3.8 – Client Funds

The provisions of Article 3.8 reflect the recommendation adopted by the CCBE in Brussels in November 1985 on the need for minimum regulations to be made and enforced governing the proper control and disposal of clients' funds held by lawyers within the Community. Article 3.8 lays down minimum standards to be observed, while not interfering with the details of national systems which provide fuller or more stringent protection for clients' funds.

The lawyer who holds clients' funds, even in the course of a cross-border activity, has to observe the rules of his or her home Bar. The lawyer needs to be aware of questions which arise where the rules of more than one Member State may be applicable, especially where the lawyer is established in a Host State under the Lawyers Establishment Directive.

Commentary on Article 3.9 – Professional Indemnity Insurance

Article 3.9.1 reflects a recommendation, also adopted by the CCBE in Brussels in November 1985, on the need for all lawyers in the Community to be insured against the risks arising from professional negligence claims against them.

Article 3.9.2 deals with the situation where insurance cannot be obtained on the basis set out in Article 3.9.1.

Commentary on Article 4.1 – Rules of Conduct in Court

This provision applies the principle that a lawyer is bound to comply with the rules of the court or tribunal before which the lawyer practises or appears.

Commentary on Article 4.2 – Fair Conduct of Proceedings

This provision applies the general principle that in adversarial proceedings a lawyer must not attempt to take unfair advantage of his or her opponent. The lawyer must not, for example, make contact with the judge without first informing the lawyer acting for the opposing party or submit exhibits, notes or documents to the judge without communicating them in good time to the lawyer on the other side unless such steps are permitted under the relevant rules of procedure. To the extent not prohibited by law a lawyer must not divulge or submit to the court any proposals for settlement of the case made by the other party or its lawyer without the express consent of the other party's lawyer. See also on Article 4.5 below.

Commentary on Article 4.3 – Demeanour in Court

This provision reflects the necessary balance between respect for the court and for the law on the one hand and the pursuit of the client's best interest on the other.

Commentary on Article 4.4 – False or Misleading Information

This provision applies the principle that the lawyer must never knowingly mislead the court. This is necessary if there is to be trust between the courts and the legal profession.

Commentary on Article 4.5 – Extension to Arbitrators etc.

This provision extends the preceding provisions relating to courts and other bodies exercising judicial or quasi-judicial functions.

Commentary on Article 5.1 – Corporate Spirit of the Profession

These provisions, which are based on statements in the Declaration of Perugia, emphasise that it is in the public interest for the legal profession to maintain a relationship of trust and cooperation between its members. However, this cannot be used to justify setting the interests of the profession against those of justice or of clients (see also on Article 2.7).

Commentary on Article 5.2 – Co-operation among Lawyers of Different Member States

This provision also develops a principle stated in the Declaration of Perugia with a view to avoiding misunderstandings in dealings between lawyers of different Member States.

Commentary on Article 5.3 – Correspondence between Lawyers

In certain Member States communications between lawyers (written or by word of mouth) are normally regarded as to be kept confidential as between the lawyers. This means that the content of these communications cannot be disclosed to others, cannot normally be passed to the lawyers' clients, and at any event cannot be produced in court. In other Member States, such consequences will not follow unless the correspondence is marked as "confidential".

In yet other Member States, the lawyer has to keep the client fully informed of all relevant communications from a professional colleague acting for another party, and marking a letter as "confidential" only means that it is a legal matter intended for the recipient lawyer and his or her client, and not to be misused by third parties.

In some states, if a lawyer wishes to indicate that a letter is sent in an attempt to settle a dispute, and is not to be produced in a court, the lawyer should mark the letter as "without prejudice".

These important national differences give rise to many misunderstandings. That is why lawyers must be very careful in conducting cross-border correspondence.

Whenever a lawyer wants to send a letter to a professional colleague in another Member State on the basis that it is to be kept confidential as between the lawyers, or that it is "without prejudice", the lawyer should ask in advance whether the letter can be accepted on that basis. A lawyer wishing that a communication should be accepted on such a basis must express that clearly at the head of the communication or in a covering letter.

A lawyer who is the intended recipient of such a communication, but who is not in a position to respect, or to ensure respect for, the basis on which it is to be sent, must inform the sender immediately so that the communication is not sent. If the communication has already been received, the recipient must return it to the sender without revealing its contents or referring to it in any way; if the recipient's national law or rules prevent the recipient from complying with this requirement, he or she must inform the sender immediately.

Commentary on Article 5.4 – Referral Fees

This provision reflects the principle that a lawyer should not pay or receive payment purely for the reference of a client, which would risk impairing the client's free choice of lawyer or the client's interest in being referred to the best available service. It does not prevent fee-sharing arrangements between lawyers on a proper basis (see also on Article 3.6 above).

In some Member States lawyers are permitted to accept and retain commissions in certain cases provided the client's best interests are served, there is full disclosure to the client and the client has consented to the retention of the commission. In such cases the retention of the commission by the lawyer represents part of the lawyer's remuneration for the service provided to the client and is not within the scope of the prohibition on referral fees which is designed to prevent lawyers making a secret profit.

Commentary on Article 5.5 – Communication with Opposing Parties

This provision reflects a generally accepted principle, and is designed both to promote the smooth conduct of business between lawyers and to prevent any attempt to take advantage of the client of another lawyer.

Commentary on Article 5.6 – Change of Lawyer

Article 5.6 dealt with change of lawyer. It was deleted from the Code on 6 December 2002.

Commentary on Article 5.7 – Responsibility for Fees

These provisions substantially reaffirm provisions contained in the Declaration of Perugia. Since misunderstandings about responsibility for unpaid fees are a common cause of difference between lawyers of different Member States, it is important that a lawyer who wishes to exclude or limit his or her personal obligation to be responsible for the fees of a foreign colleague should reach a clear agreement on this at the outset of the transaction.

Commentary on Article 5.8 – Continuing Professional Development

Keeping abreast of developments in the law is a professional obligation. In particular it is essential that lawyers are aware of the growing impact of European law on their field of practice.

Commentary on Article 5.9 – Disputes amongst Lawyers in Different Member States

A lawyer has the right to pursue any legal or other remedy to which he or she is entitled against a colleague in another Member State. Nevertheless it is desirable that, where a breach of a rule of professional conduct or a dispute of a professional nature is involved, the possibilities of friendly settlement should be exhausted, if necessary with the assistance of the Bars or Law Societies concerned, before such remedies are exercised.

The European Communities (Services of Lawyers) Order 1978

European Communities (Services of Lawyers) Order 1978

SI 1978/1910

Made 20th December 1978

Authority: European Communities Act 1972, s 2(2)

Citation and commencement

1

This Order may be cited as the European Communities (Services of Lawyers) Order 1978 and shall come into operation on 1st March 1979.

Interpretation

2

In this Order, unless the context otherwise requires—

"advocate", "barrister" and "solicitor" mean, in relation to any part of the United Kingdom, a person practising in that part as an advocate, barrister or solicitor as the case may be;

"country of origin", in relation to a European lawyer, means the country or countries in which he is established;

"the Directive" means the European Communities Council Directive No. 77/249/EEC to facilitate the effective exercise by lawyers of freedom to provide services;

"European lawyer" means a person entitled to pursue his professional activities in a state in column 1 under the designation referred to in column 2—

State	Designation(s)
Austria	Rechtsanwalt
Belgium	Avocat/Advocaat
Bulgaria	Адвокат
Cyprus	Δικηγόρος
Czech Republic	Advokát
Denmark	Advokat
Estonia	Vandeadvokaat
Finland	Asianajaja/Advokat
France	Avocat
Germany	Rechtsanwalt
Hellenic Republic	Δικηγόρος
Hungary	Ügyvéd

Iceland	Lögmaður
Republic of Ireland	Barrister/solicitor
Italy	Avvocato
Latvia	Zverināts advokāts
Liechtenstein	Rechtsanwalt
Lithuania	Advokatas
Luxembourg	Avocat
Malta	Avukat/Prokuratur Legali
Netherlands	Advocaat
Norway	Advokat
Poland	Adwokat/Radca prawny
Portugal	Advogado
Romania	Avocat
Slovakia	Advokát/Komercný právnik
Slovenia	Odvetnik/Odvetnica
Spain	Abogado/Advocat/Avogado/Abokatu
Sweden	Advokat
Switzerland	Avocat/Advokat/Rechtsanwalt/Anwalt/Fürsprecher/Fürsprech/Avvocato

...

"own professional authority", in relation to a European lawyer, means an authority entitled to exercise disciplinary authority over him in his member State of origin.

3

(1) The Interpretation Act 1978 shall apply to this Order as it applies to subordinate legislation made after the commencement of that Act.

(2) Unless the context otherwise requires, any reference in this Order to a numbered article or to the Schedule is a reference to an article of, or the Schedule to, this Order.

Purpose of Order

4

The provisions of this Order shall have effect for the purpose of enabling a European lawyer to pursue his professional activities in any part of the United Kingdom by providing, under the conditions specified in or permitted by the Directive, services otherwise reserved to advocates, barristers and solicitors; and services which may be so provided are hereafter in this Order referred to as services.

Representation in legal proceedings

5

No enactment or rule of law or practice shall prevent a European lawyer from providing any service in relation to any proceedings, whether civil or criminal, before any court, tribunal or public authority (including appearing before and addressing the court, tribunal or public authority) by reason only that he is not an advocate, barrister or solicitor; provided that throughout he is instructed with, and acts in conjunction with, an advocate, barrister or solicitor who is entitled to practise before the court, tribunal or public authority concerned and who could properly provide the service in question.

6

Nothing in this Order shall enable a European lawyer:—

(a) if he is established in practice as a barrister in the Republic of Ireland, to provide in the course of any proceedings any service which could not properly be provided by an advocate or barrister;

(b) if he is instructed with and acts in conjunction with an advocate or barrister in any proceedings, to provide in the course of those proceedings, or of any related proceedings, any service which an advocate or barrister could not properly provide;

(c) if he is instructed with and acts in conjunction with a solicitor in any proceedings, to provide in the course of those proceedings, or of any related proceedings, any service which a solicitor could not properly provide.

7

A European lawyer in salaried employment who is instructed with and acts in conjunction with an advocate or barrister in any proceedings may provide a service on behalf of his employer in those proceedings only in so far as an advocate or barrister in such employment could properly do so.

Drawing of documents, etc not related to legal proceedings

8

No enactment or rule of law or practice shall prevent a European lawyer from drawing or preparing for remuneration:—

(i)   in England, Wales or Northern Ireland, an instrument relating to personal estate, or

(ii) in Scotland, a writ relating to moveable property,

by reason only that he is not an advocate, barrister or solicitor.

9

Nothing in this Order shall entitle a European lawyer to draw or prepare for remuneration any instrument, or in Scotland any writ:—

(i)   creating or transferring an interest in land; or

(ii) for obtaining title to administer the estate of a deceased person.

Legal aid

10

Services may be provided by a European lawyer by way of legal advice and assistance or legal aid under the enactments specified in Part 1 of the Schedule; and references to counsel and solicitors in those and any other enactments relating to legal advice and assistance or legal aid shall be construed accordingly.

Title and description to be used by European lawyers

11

In providing any services, a European lawyer shall use the professional title and description applicable to him in his ... country of origin, expressed in the language or one of the languages of that country, together with the name of the professional organisation by which he is authorised to practise or the court of law before which he is entitled to practise in that country.

APPENDIX 8

Power to require a European lawyer to verify his status

12

A competent authority may at any time request a person seeking to provide any services to verify his status as a European lawyer.

13

Where a request has been made under article 12, the person to whom it is made shall not, except to the extent (if any) allowed by the competent authority making the request, be entitled to provide services in the United Kingdom until he has verified his status as a European lawyer to the satisfaction of that authority.

14

For the purposes of articles 12 and 13, a competent authority is:—

    (a)   where the services which the person concerned seeks to provide are reserved to advocates or barristers, or in any case where the person concerned claims to be a barrister established in practice in the Republic of Ireland, the Senate of the Inns of Court and the Bar, the Faculty of Advocates, or the Benchers of the Inn of Court of Northern Ireland, according to the part of the United Kingdom concerned; or

    (b)   where sub-paragraph (a) does not apply, the Law Society, the Law Society of Scotland, or the Incorporated Law Society of Northern Ireland, according to the part of the United Kingdom concerned; or

    (c)   in any case, any court, tribunal or public authority before which the person concerned seeks to provide services.

Professional misconduct

15

(1)   A complaint may be made to a disciplinary authority that a European lawyer providing any services has failed to observe a condition or rule of professional conduct referred to in article 4 of the Directive and applicable to him.

(2)   Where a complaint is made under paragraph (1), the disciplinary authority concerned shall consider and adjudicate upon it in accordance with the same procedure, and subject to the same rights of appeal, as apply in relation to an advocate, barrister or solicitor (as the case may be) over whom that authority has jurisdiction.

(3)   For the purposes of this article and article 16, a disciplinary authority is:—

    (a)   where the services in question are reserved to advocates or barristers, or in any case where the person whose conduct is in question is established in practice as a barrister in the Republic of Ireland, an authority having disciplinary jurisdiction over advocates or barristers (as the case may be) in the part of the United Kingdom concerned;

    (b)   where sub-paragraph (a) does not apply, an authority having disciplinary jurisdiction over solicitors in the part of the United Kingdom concerned.

16

(1)   Where a disciplinary authority finds that a European lawyer against whom a complaint has been made under article 15(1) has committed a breach of a condition or a rule of professional conduct mentioned in that article, that authority:—

    (a)   shall report that finding to the European lawyer's own professional authority; and

(b)   may, if it thinks fit, direct him not to provide services in the United Kingdom, except to such extent and under such conditions (if any) as the disciplinary authority may specify in the direction.

(2)   A disciplinary authority may at any time, if it thinks fit, vary, cancel or suspend the operation of a direction given by it under paragraph (1)(b).

17

A European lawyer in respect of whom a direction is made under article 16(1)(b) shall not be entitled to provide services in the United Kingdom except as allowed by the direction.

Modification of enactments

18

(1)   Without prejudice to the generality of articles 5 and 8, the enactments specified in Part 2 of the Schedule (being enactments which reserve the provision of certain services to advocates, barristers, solicitors and other qualified persons) shall be construed subject to those articles.

(2)   Notwithstanding anything in the Solicitors (Scotland) Act 1980, the Solicitors Act 1974 or the Solicitors (Northern Ireland) Order 1976, references to unqualified persons, however expressed, in the enactments specified in Part 3 of the Schedule (being enactments relating to unqualified persons acting as solicitors) shall not include a European lawyer providing services within the meaning of this Order.

(3)   Nothing in section 33 of the Solicitors (Scotland) Act 1980 shall prevent a European lawyer from recovering any remuneration or expenses to which that section applies by reason only that he is not qualified as a solicitor.

SCHEDULE

Article 10

PART 1
ENACTMENTS RELATING TO THE PROVISION OF LEGAL ADVICE
AND ASSISTANCE AND LEGAL AID

...

Legal Advice and Assistance Act 1972 (c. 50).

...

Access to Justice Act 1999 (c 22).

Financial Services and Markets Act 2000 (c 8).

PART 2
ENACTMENTS RESERVING THE PROVISION OF SERVICES TO
ADVOCATES, BARRISTERS, SOLICITORS, ETC

Article 18(1)

...

Solicitors Act 1974 (c. 47), sections 20, 22 and 23.

APPENDIX 8

PART 3
ENACTMENTS RELATING TO UNQUALIFIED PERSONS ACTING
AS SOLICITORS

Article 18(2)

...

Solicitors Act 1974 (c. 47), section 25(1).

...

The European Communities (Lawyer's Practice) Regulations 2000

European Communities (Lawyer's Practice) Regulations 2000

SI 2000/1119

Made 8th April 2000

Laid 19th April 2000

Coming into force in accordance with regulation 1

The Lord Chancellor, being a Minister designated for the purposes of section 2(2) of the European Communities Act 1972 in relation to matters relating to the practice of the profession of lawyer, in exercise of the powers conferred on him by that section, makes the following Regulations—

PART 1
INTRODUCTORY

1 Citation, commencement and transitional provisions

(1) These Regulations may be cited as the European Communities (Lawyer's Practice) Regulations 2000 and shall come into force on 22nd May 2000, except for regulations 21 and 22, which shall come into force on 22nd November 2000.

(2) Where, on 22nd May 2000 [16th September 2004/11th February 2008★], a European lawyer is practising professional activities under his home professional title on a permanent basis in England and Wales or Northern Ireland or commences such practice by 21st November 2000 [15th March 2005/10th August 2008★], he shall apply to be registered in accordance with regulation 16 by 21st November 2000 [15th March 2005/10th August 2008★] where he intends to continue to practise those activities on a permanent basis after that date.

(3) On or after 22nd November 2000 [16th March 2005/11th August 2008★], a European lawyer shall not practise as referred to in paragraph (2) without being registered in accordance with regulation 16, unless he was already practising before that date and has made an application for registration which has not been determined.

(4) In paragraphs (3) and (5), an application for registration shall, as at a particular date, be taken not to have been determined if as at that date the applicant—

(a) has not received a rejection of his application and the period for such a rejection or a deemed rejection has not yet expired; or

(b) is appealing against a rejection of the application (including a deemed rejection) and the appeal has not been determined.

(5) Regulations 21(1)(b) and 22 shall not apply to a European lawyer who satisfies all the following conditions—

(a) immediately before 22nd November 2000 [16th March 2005/11th August 2008★] he was practising on a permanent basis in any part of the United Kingdom;

(b) before 22nd November 2000 [16th March 2005/11th August 2008★] he applied for registration to any of the barristers' professional bodies or solicitors' professional bodies, or to the Faculty of Advocates or the Law Society of Scotland; and

(c)   as at the date in question his application for registration had not been determined.

[NOTES

Modification

*As from 16 September 2004 the Regulations were extended to cover lawyers qualified in Cyprus, the Czech Republic, Estonia, Hungary, Iceland, Latvia, Liechtenstein, Lithuania, Malta, Norway, Poland, Slovenia, Slovakia or Switzerland who were nationals of one of those states, or of the United Kingdom, or of one of the states already covered by the Regulations.

As from 11 February 2008 the Regulations were extended to cover lawyers qualified in Bulgaria or Romania who were nationals of one of those states, or of the United Kingdom, or of one of the states already covered by the Regulations.]

2   Interpretation

(1)   In these Regulations, unless the context otherwise requires—

"appeal body" means the body or person specified in relation to that profession in Schedule 1;

"barrister" means, in relation to England and Wales or Northern Ireland, a person who is a barrister of England and Wales or Northern Ireland, as the case may be;

"barristers' professional bodies" means the Inns of Court and the General Council of the Bar of England and Wales and the Executive Council of the Inn of Court of Northern Ireland;

"competent authority", in relation to England and Wales and Northern Ireland, means any of the bodies designated as competent authorities by regulation 4 to undertake the activities required by the Directive set out in that regulation;

"the Directive" means the European Communities Parliament and Council Directive No 98/5/EC to facilitate practice of the profession of lawyer on a permanent basis in certain States other than the State in which the professional qualification was obtained;

"European lawyer" has the meaning given in paragraphs (2) and (3);

"home State" means the State in paragraph (4) in which a European lawyer acquired his authorisation to pursue professional activities and, if he is authorised in more than one of those States, it shall mean any of those States;

"home professional title" means, in relation to a European lawyer, the professional title or any of the professional titles specified in relation to his home State in paragraph (4) under which he is authorised in his home State to pursue professional activities;

"Irish barrister" means a European lawyer who is authorised in the Republic of Ireland to pursue professional activities under the professional title of barrister and whose home State is the Republic of Ireland;

"Irish solicitor" means a European lawyer who is authorised in the Republic of Ireland to pursue professional activities under the professional title of solicitor and whose home State is the Republic of Ireland;

"limited liability partnership" has the meaning given by section 1(2) of the Limited Liability Partnerships Act 2000;

"member of a limited liability partnership" shall be construed in accordance with section 4 of the Limited Liability Partnerships Act 2000;

"member of the professional body" means a practising solicitor or barrister, as the case may be;

"Qualification Regulations" means the European Communities (Recognition of Professional Qualifications) Regulations 2007;

"registered European lawyer" means a European lawyer who is registered with a professional body in accordance with regulation 17 and whose registration has not been withdrawn or suspended;

"professional body" means, subject to regulation 16, any of the solicitors' professional bodies or the barristers' professional bodies;

"solicitor" means, in relation to England and Wales or Northern Ireland, a person who is a solicitor of England and Wales or Northern Ireland, as the case may be;

"solicitors' professional bodies" means the Law Society and the Law Society of Northern Ireland;

"the 1974 Act" means the Solicitors Act 1974.

(2) In these Regulations, "European lawyer" means a person who is—

(a)   a national of the United Kingdom or of a State listed in paragraph (4);

(b)   authorised in any of the States listed in paragraph (4) to pursue professional activities under any of the professional titles appearing in that paragraph; and

(c)   subject to paragraph (3), not a solicitor or barrister or, under the law of Scotland, a solicitor or advocate.

(3) Where a person is a European lawyer registered with more than one of the following—

(a)   the solicitors' professional bodies or the barristers' professional bodies, or

(b)   the Law Society of Scotland or the Faculty of Advocates,

and subsequently acquires the title used by members of one of those bodies, then notwithstanding paragraph (2)(c), that person shall continue to fall within the definition of a European lawyer in relation to that other professional body for the period that he remains registered with that other professional body.

(4) The States and professional titles referred to in the definition of European lawyer in paragraph (2) are as follows—

State	Professional title(s)
Belgium	Avocat/Advocaat/Rechtsanwalt
Denmark	Advokat
Germany	Rechtsanwalt
Greece	Δικηγόρος
Spain	Abogado/Advocat/Avogado/Abokatu
France	Avocat
Republic of Ireland	Barrister/Solicitor
Italy	Avvocato
Luxembourg	Avocat/Rechtsanwalt
Netherlands	Advocaat
Austria	Rechtsanwalt
Portugal	Advogado

Finland	Asianajaja/Advokat
Sweden	Advokat
Switzerland	Avocat/Advokat/Rechtsanwalt/Anwalt/Fürsprecher/ Fürsprech/Avvocato
Iceland	Lögmaður
Liechtenstein	Rechtsanwalt
Norway	Advokat
Czech Republic	Advokát
Estonia	Vandeadvokaat
Cyprus	Δικηγόρος
Latvia	Zverināts advokāts
Lithuania	Advokatas
Hungary	Ügyvéd
Malta	Avukat/Prokuratur Legali
Poland	Adwokat/Radca prawny
Slovenia	Odvetnik/Odvetnica
Slovakia	Advokát/Komercný právnik
Bulgaria	Адвокат
Romania	Avocat

(5)   Unless the context otherwise requires, any reference in these Regulations to a numbered regulation, Part or Schedule is a reference to a regulation or Part of, or a Schedule to, these Regulations.

3   Purpose of Regulations

(1)   The purpose of these Regulations is to implement the Directive in England and Wales and Northern Ireland.

(2)   The provisions of these Regulations shall have effect for the purposes of facilitating the practice of the profession of lawyer on a permanent basis by a European lawyer in England and Wales and Northern Ireland.

(3)   The provisions of these Regulations shall not affect the provision of services by lawyers within the meaning of the European Communities (Services of Lawyers) Order 1978.

4   Competent authorities

The bodies listed in column 2 of Schedule 2 shall be designated as the competent authorities for the purposes of—

(a)   receiving applications for registration by European lawyers under Part III of these Regulations;

(b)   receiving applications from registered European lawyers for entry into the profession of solicitor or barrister;

(c)   the regulation of registered European lawyers registered with them; and

(d)   the provision of certificates attesting to the registration of Solicitors or barristers registered with them.

5   Exchange of information

(1)   In order to facilitate the application of the Directive and to prevent its provisions from being misapplied, a professional body may supply to or receive from—

(a)   another professional body;

(b)   the Faculty of Advocates or the Law Society of Scotland; or

(c)   an authority in any of the States listed in regulation 2(4) which has been designated by that State under the Directive as a competent authority in that State,

any information relating to a European lawyer or to any person with whom he jointly practises.

(2)   Subject to paragraph (1), a professional body shall preserve the confidentiality of any information received in accordance with paragraph (1) relating to a European lawyer or to any person with whom he jointly practises.

(3)   A competent authority in England and Wales or Northern Ireland shall provide a certificate attesting to the registration of a solicitor or barrister registered with it and his authorisation to practise when requested to do so by that solicitor or barrister or by a competent authority in a State listed in regulation 2(4).

PART II
PRACTICE OF PROFESSIONAL ACTIVITIES BY A REGISTERED EUROPEAN LAWYER

6 Practice of professional activities

(1)   Subject to the provisions of these Regulations, a registered European lawyer shall be entitled to carry out under his home professional title any professional activity that may lawfully be carried out by a member of the professional body with which he is registered and any enactment or rule of law or practice with regard to the carrying out of professional activities by members of that professional body shall be interpreted and applied accordingly.

(2)   A registered European lawyer who is in salaried employment may carry out professional activities under his home professional title to the same extent that an employed member of the professional body with which he is registered may do so.

7 Title and description to be used by a registered European lawyer

(1)   Where a registered European lawyer is engaged in—

(a)   any professional activity authorised by the professional organisation in his home State which gave him the authorisation to practise; or

(b)   any professional activity that may be carried out by a member of the professional body with which he is registered,

he shall comply with the requirements set out in paragraph (2).

(2)   The requirements referred to in paragraph (1) are that a registered European lawyer shall—

(a)   use his home professional title expressed in an official language of his home State in a manner which avoids confusion with the title of solicitor, barrister or advocate;

(b)   indicate the professional organisation by which he is authorised to practise or the court of law before which he is entitled to practise in that State; and

(c)   indicate the professional body with which he is registered in the United Kingdom.

8 Joint practice

A registered European lawyer may carry out professional activities under his home professional title as part of a joint practice—

(a)   to the same extent and in the same manner as a member of the professional body with which he is registered may do so, with—

      (i)   a member of the professional body with which he is registered;

      (ii)   a registered European lawyer who is registered with the same professional body; or

      (iii) any other person permitted by the professional body with which he is registered; or

(b)   with another European lawyer who is practising on a permanent basis under his home professional title in that registered European lawyer's home State.

9 Name of joint practice

(1) Subject to paragraph (2), where a registered European lawyer is a member of a joint practice in his home State, he may use the name of that practice with his home professional title when practising as a registered European lawyer.

(2) Rules of conduct of the professional body with which a registered European lawyer is registered may prohibit the use by him of the name of a joint practice to the extent that—

(a)   that name is also used by persons who are not European lawyers or solicitors of any part of the United Kingdom; and

(b)   those rules prohibit members of that professional body from using that name.

10 Notification of joint practice

(1) Where a European lawyer is a member of a joint practice in his home State, he shall inform the professional body with which he intends to register and provide it with the following information—

(a)   the name of the joint practice;

(b)   his place of business;

(c)   the name and place of business of any member of his joint practice;

(d)   any other information about the joint practice requested by the professional body.

(2) A European lawyer shall notify that professional body of any changes in the information whether before or after registration.

11 Representation in legal proceedings

(1) Subject to paragraph (2), no enactment or rule of law or practice shall prevent a registered European lawyer from pursuing professional activities relating to the representation of a client in any proceedings before any court, tribunal or public authority (including addressing the court, tribunal or public authority) only because he is not a solicitor or barrister.

(2) In proceedings referred to in paragraph (1), where the professional activities in question may (but for these Regulations) be lawfully provided only by a solicitor, barrister or other qualified person, a registered European lawyer shall act in conjunction with a solicitor or barrister who is entitled to practise before the court, tribunal or public authority concerned and who could lawfully provide those professional activities.

(3) The solicitor or barrister referred to in paragraph (2) shall, where necessary, be answerable to the court, tribunal or public authority concerned.

(4) Paragraph (2) does not apply to professional activities relating to the representation of a client in proceedings before the Asylum and Immigration Tribunal or the Asylum Support Tribunal, or any tribunal hearing an appeal from those tribunals.

12 Property transactions

A registered European lawyer is not entitled, by virtue of regulation 6(1), to prepare for remuneration any instrument creating or transferring an interest in land unless he has a home professional title obtained in Denmark, the Republic of Ireland, Finland, Sweden, Iceland, Liechtenstein, Norway, the Czech Republic, Cyprus, Hungary or Slovakia.

13 Probate

A registered European lawyer is not entitled, by virtue of regulation 6(1), to prepare for remuneration any instrument for obtaining title to administer the estate of a deceased person unless he has a home professional title obtained in Denmark, Germany, the Republic of Ireland, Austria, Finland, Sweden, Iceland, Liechtenstein, Norway, Cyprus or Slovakia.

14 Legal aid

A registered European lawyer may provide professional activities by way of legal advice and assistance or legal aid under the enactments specified in Part 1 of Schedule 3 and references to a solicitor, counsel or legal representative in those and any other enactments relating to legal advice and assistance or legal aid shall be interpreted accordingly.

PART III
REGISTRATION

15 Establishment and maintenance of registers of European lawyers

Each professional body shall establish and maintain a register of registered European lawyers.

16 Application to be entered on a register

(1) Subject to regulation 18, a European lawyer who wishes to pursue professional activities under his home professional title on a permanent basis in England and Wales or Northern Ireland shall apply to be entered on the register maintained by a professional body.

(2) A European lawyer who wishes to register with a professional body in accordance with paragraph (1) shall provide the professional body with a certificate confirming his registration with the competent authority in each home State under whose home professional title he intends to practise.

(3) A professional body may require that the certificate referred to in paragraph (2) shall not have been issued more than three months before the date of the application under this regulation.

(4) An application for registration under this regulation shall comply with any applicable regulations made by the relevant professional body and be accompanied by the appropriate fee.

(5) Subject to regulation 18, a European lawyer may apply to be entered on the registers maintained by more than one professional body.

(6) In this regulation, "professional body" includes the Law Society of Scotland and the Faculty of Advocates.

17 Registration by professional body

(1) Subject to regulation 18, a professional body shall enter on its register the name of a European lawyer who applies to it in accordance with regulation 16.

(2) Where a professional body registers a European lawyer in accordance with paragraph (1), it shall inform the competent authority in the home State of the registration.

18 Restrictions on registration

(1) A European lawyer shall not be registered at the same time both with one of the solicitors' professional bodies and with one of the barristers' professional bodies.

(2) An Irish solicitor shall not be entered on a register maintained under regulation 15 by any of the barristers' professional bodies.

(3)   An Irish barrister shall not be entered on a register maintained under regulation 15 by any of the solicitors' professional bodies.

(4)   A European lawyer registered with the Law Society of Scotland shall not be entered on a register maintained under regulation 15 by any of the barristers' professional bodies.

(5)   A European lawyer registered with the Faculty of Advocates shall not be entered on a register maintained under regulation 15 by any of the solicitors' professional bodies.

19   Time limit for decision and notification by professional body

(1)   A professional body shall consider an application for registration under regulation 16 as soon as is reasonably practicable, and shall notify the European lawyer of its decision, and if the application is rejected or granted subject to conditions, the reasons upon which the rejection or the imposition of conditions is based, within four months of receipt of an application complying with regulation 16(2) and (4).

(2)   Where the professional body fails to take a decision and notify the European lawyer within four months in accordance with paragraph (1), it shall be deemed to have taken a decision to reject his application and to have notified it to him on the last day of that period.

(3)   Where a professional body withdraws or suspends a registration, it shall notify the European lawyer of its decision and of the reasons upon which the withdrawal or suspension is based.

20   Appeal by European lawyer

(1)   Within three months of the notification to him of the professional body's decision, or later with the permission of the appeal body, the European lawyer may appeal against the decision to the appeal body specified in Schedule 1.

(2)   An appeal body may, for the purpose of determining any appeal under this Part—

(a)   order the professional body to register the European lawyer;

(b)   refuse the appeal; or

(c)   remit the matter to the professional body with such directions as the appeal body sees fit.

(3)   The appeal body shall give reasons for its decision.

21   Offence of pretending to be a registered European lawyer

(1)   A person who is not registered as a European lawyer in any part of the United Kingdom (including a person whose registration has been suspended) and—

(a)   wilfully pretends to be a registered European lawyer or takes or uses any name, title, designation or description implying that he is a registered European lawyer; or

(b)   subject to paragraph (2), carries on professional activities under one of the professional titles listed in regulation 2(4) or under any name, designation or description implying that he is entitled to pursue those activities under one of those professional titles;

shall be guilty of an offence and liable on summary conviction to a fine not exceeding the fourth level on the standard scale.

(2)   Paragraph (1)(b) shall not apply to a person who satisfies any of the following conditions—

(a)   he is not a national of the United Kingdom or of any of the States listed in regulation 2(4);

(b)   he is a solicitor or barrister or, under the law of Scotland, a solicitor or advocate; or

(c)   he is providing services within the meaning of the European Communities (Services of Lawyers) Order 1978 at the time his activities fall within paragraph (1)(b).

22   Costs and fees of an unregistered European lawyer

Where a European lawyer is carrying on professional activities under his home professional title in England and Wales or Northern Ireland but is not registered as a European lawyer in any part of the United Kingdom (including a person whose registration has been suspended), any costs or fees in respect of those activities shall not be recoverable by him or any other person.

[NOTES

Modification

In relation to a person who became a relevant lawyer by virtue of being a national of, or qualified in, Cyprus, the Czech Republic, Estonia, Hungary, Iceland, Latvia, Liechtenstein, Lithuania, Malta, Norway, Poland, Slovenia, Slovakia or Switzerland, regulations 21 and 22 shall apply only as from 16 March 2005. (See S.I. 2004/1628, regulation 2)

In relation to a person who became a relevant lawyer by virtue of being a national of, or qualified in, Bulgaria or Romania, regulations 21(1)(b) and (2) and 22 shall apply only as from 11 August 2008. (See S.I. 2008/81, regulation 4)]

23   Evidence of registration

Any certificate purporting to be signed by an officer of a professional body and stating that a person—

(a)   is, or is not, registered with that professional body; or

(b)   was, or was not, registered with that professional body during a period specified in the certificate,

shall, unless the contrary is proved, be evidence of that fact and be taken to have been so signed.

24   Publication of names of registered European lawyers

(1)   Where a professional body publishes the names of solicitors or barristers registered with it, it shall also publish the names of any European lawyers registered with it.

(2)   In this regulation, "publishes" or "publish" includes the provision of information to a legal publisher.

PART IV
REGULATION AND DISCIPLINE

25   Rules of professional conduct applicable

Where a registered European lawyer is practising under his home professional title in the United Kingdom, he shall be subject to the same rules of professional conduct as a member of the professional body with which he is registered, and if he is registered with more than one, he shall be subject to the rules of professional conduct of all the professional bodies with which he is registered.

26   Disciplinary proceedings applicable

(1)   Where a registered European lawyer fails to comply with the rules of professional conduct to which he is subject under regulation 25, he shall be subject to the same rules of procedure, penalties and remedies as a member of the professional body with which the European lawyer is registered and shall, if appropriate, be subject to disciplinary proceedings brought by an appropriate authority.

(2)   Any sanction against a registered European lawyer in relation to disciplinary proceedings may include withdrawal or suspension of his registration.

(3)   The appropriate authority shall give reasons for its decision.

(4)   In this regulation, an appropriate authority means—

(a)   where the registered European lawyer is registered with one of the solicitors' professional bodies, an authority having disciplinary jurisdiction over solicitors in England and Wales or Northern Ireland, as the case may be;

(b)   where the registered European lawyer is registered with one of the barristers' professional bodies, an authority having disciplinary jurisdiction over barristers in England and Wales or Northern Ireland, as the case may be;

(c)   where the registered European lawyer is registered with more than one of the solicitors' professional bodies or the barristers' professional bodies, an authority having disciplinary jurisdiction over solicitors or barristers, as the case may be, in England and Wales or Northern Ireland.

27   Disciplinary proceedings against a registered European lawyer

(1)   Where a professional body intends to begin disciplinary proceedings against a registered European lawyer, it shall—

(a)   inform the competent authority in his home State of the intention to begin those proceedings and furnish it with all the relevant details;

(b)   co-operate with that authority throughout those proceedings; and

(c)   inform that authority of the decision reached in those proceedings, including the decision in any appeal, as soon as practicable after the decision is given.

(2)   Subject to paragraph (3), where the competent authority in the registered European lawyer's home State withdraws his authorisation to practise under the home professional title either temporarily or permanently, his registration with the professional body shall be automatically withdrawn to the same extent.

(3)   Where a registered European lawyer is authorised to practise under a home professional title in two or more home States, his registration shall be withdrawn in accordance with paragraph (2) only if his authorisation to practise under a home professional title has been withdrawn in all those home States.

(4)   Where there is an appeal against a decision in disciplinary proceedings against a registered European lawyer, the body responsible for hearing the appeal shall afford the competent authority in the registered European lawyer's home State an opportunity to make representations in relation to that appeal.

28   Disciplinary proceedings against a solicitor or barrister

Where a professional body intends to begin disciplinary proceedings against a solicitor or barrister practising in a State listed in regulation 2(4), it shall inform the competent authority in that State of—

(a)   the intention to begin those proceedings and furnish it with all the relevant details; and

(b)   the decision reached in those proceedings, including the decision in any appeal, as soon as practicable after the decision is given.

PART V
ENTRY INTO THE PROFESSION OF SOLICITOR OR BARRISTER

29 Application by registered European lawyer

(1)   Where a registered European lawyer applies to the professional body where he has been registered to become a solicitor or barrister, as the case may be, and that professional body requires him to pass an aptitude test under regulation 26(a) of the Qualification Regulations, he may apply to the professional body for an exemption from that requirement on the grounds that he falls within paragraph (2) or (3) of this regulation.

(2)   A person falls within this paragraph if—

   (a)   he is a European lawyer and has been registered with that professional body for at least three years; and

   (b)   he has for a period of at least three years effectively and regularly pursued in England and Wales or Northern Ireland, professional activities under his home professional title in the law of England and Wales or Northern Ireland, as the case may be.

(3)   A person falls within this paragraph if—

   (a)   he is a European lawyer and has been registered with that professional body for at least three years; and

   (b)   he has for a period of at least three years effectively and regularly pursued in England and Wales or Northern Ireland professional activities under his home professional title; and

   (c)   he has for a period of less than three years effectively and regularly pursued in England and Wales or Northern Ireland, professional activities under his home professional title in the law of England and Wales or Northern Ireland, as the case may be.

30 Decision by professional body

(1)   Subject to paragraph (3), the professional body shall grant an exemption applied for under regulation 29 if it considers that the requirements under paragraph (2) or (3) of regulation 29 have been met.

(2)   The registration of a registered European lawyer shall cease from the date he is granted entry into the profession of solicitor or barrister.

(3)   The professional body may refuse to grant an exemption if it considers that the registered European lawyer would be unfit to practise as a solicitor or barrister.

31 Evidence in support of application for exemption under regulation 29(2)

(1)   Where a registered European lawyer makes an application under paragraph (2) of regulation 29, he shall provide the professional body with any relevant information and documents which it may reasonably require.

(2)   The professional body may verify the effective and regular nature of the professional activity pursued and may, if necessary, request the registered European lawyer to provide, orally or in writing, clarification of, or further details on, the information and documents referred to in paragraph (1).

32 Evidence in support of application for exemption under regulation 29(3)

(1)   Where a registered European lawyer makes an application under paragraph (3) of regulation 29, he shall provide the professional body with any relevant information and documents it may reasonably require.

(2)   When deciding whether to grant an application under paragraph (3) of regulation 29, the professional body shall take into account the professional activities the registered European lawyer has pursued during the period he has been registered and any knowledge and professional experience he has gained of, and any training he has received in, the law of any part of the United Kingdom and the rules of professional conduct of the profession concerned.

(3)   Subject to paragraph (4), in the case of an application under paragraph (3) of regulation 29, the professional body shall assess and verify the registered European lawyer's effective and regular professional activity and his capacity to continue the activity he has pursued at an interview.

(4)   Where a professional body believes that an interview is unnecessary and intends to grant an application under paragraph (3) of regulation 29, it may dispense with that requirement.

33   Meaning of "effectively and regularly pursued"

For the purposes of regulations 29 to 32 activities shall be regarded as effectively and regularly pursued if they are actually exercised without any interruption other than those resulting from the events of everyday life.

34   Time limit for decision and notification by professional body

(1)   A professional body shall consider an application under regulation 29 as soon as is reasonably practicable, and shall notify the applicant of its decision and, if the application is rejected, the reasons for the rejection, within four months of receipt of all the relevant documents.

(2)   Where the professional body fails to take a decision and notify the registered European lawyer within four months in accordance with paragraph (1), it shall be deemed to have taken a decision to reject his application and to have notified it to him on the last day of that period.

35   Appeal by registered European lawyer

(1)   Within three months of the notification to him of the professional body's decision, or later with the permission of the appeal body, the registered European lawyer may appeal against the decision to the appeal body specified in Schedule 1.

(2)   An appeal body may, for the purpose of determining any appeal under this Part—

  (a)   give the exemption and the authorisation to enter into the profession of solicitor or barrister, as the case may be;

  (b)   refuse the appeal; or

  (c)   remit the matter to the professional body with such directions as the appeal body sees fit.

(3)   The appeal body shall give reasons for its decision.

36   Practice under the title of solicitor or barrister

(1)   This regulation applies where a registered European lawyer ("the lawyer") is granted entry into the profession of solicitor or barrister.

(2)   Subject to paragraph (3), the lawyer shall be entitled to continue to practise in England and Wales or Northern Ireland, as the case may be, under his home professional title, and to use his home professional title, expressed in an official language of his home State, alongside the title of solicitor or barrister, provided that he continues to be authorised in his home State to pursue professional activities under that title.

(3)   For the purposes of rules of professional conduct, including those relating to disciplinary and complaints procedures, the lawyer's continuing practice in the United Kingdom under his

home professional title shall be deemed to form part of his practice as a solicitor or barrister, and those rules shall apply to his practice under his home professional title as they do to his practice as a solicitor or barrister.

(4)   Where this regulation applies, a lawyer's registration in accordance with regulation 17 with the professional body whose title he has acquired shall cease from the date he is entitled to use that title.

(5)   Paragraph (4) shall not affect any registration the lawyer may have in another part of the United Kingdom.

PART VI
SUPPLEMENTARY PROVISIONS

37   Modification of enactments

(1)   The enactments specified in Part 2 of Schedule 3 (being enactments which reserve certain activities to solicitors, barristers and other qualified persons) shall be interpreted subject to regulations 6, 11, 12 and 13.

(2)   References to unqualified persons, however expressed, in the enactments specified in Part 3 of Schedule 3 (being enactments relating to unqualified persons acting as solicitors) shall not include a registered European lawyer pursuing professional activities within the meaning of these Regulations.

(3)   Schedule 4 (extension of enactments (England and Wales)) shall apply in relation to the registration of European lawyers with the Law Society.

(4)   Schedule 5 (extension of enactments (Northern Ireland)) shall apply in relation to the registration of European lawyers with the Law Society of Northern Ireland.

Irvine of Lairg, C

Dated 8th April 2000

SCHEDULE 1
Appeals Concerning Registration as a European Lawyer, Exemption from Regulation 26(a) of the Qualification Regulations and Entry into the Profession of Solicitor or Barrister

Regulations 2, 20 and 35

Column 1 **Profession**	*Column 2* **Appeal Body**
Solicitor (England and Wales)	The High Court
Solicitor (Northern Ireland)	The Lord Chief Justice of Northern Ireland
Barrister (England and Wales)	The Visitors to the Inns of Court
Barrister (Northern Ireland)	The Executive Council of the Inn of Court of Northern Ireland

SCHEDULE 2
Competent Authorities

Regulation 4

Column 1	Column 2
Profession	**Professional Body**
Solicitor (England and Wales)	The Law Society
Solicitor (Northern Ireland)	The Law Society of Northern Ireland
Barrister (England and Wales)	The Inns of Court and the General Council of the Bar of England and Wales
Barrister (Northern Ireland)	The Executive Council of the Inn of Court of Northern Ireland

SCHEDULE 3
Modification of Enactments

PART 1
ENACTMENTS RELATING TO THE PROVISION OF LEGAL ADVICE
AND ASSISTANCE AND LEGAL AID

Regulation 14

Legal Aid Act 1988.

Access to Justice Act 1999.

Financial Services and Markets Act 2000.

PART 2
ENACTMENTS RESERVING CERTAIN ACTIVITIES TO SOLICITORS,
BARRISTERS AND OTHER QUALIFIED PERSONS

Regulation 37(1)

Solicitors Act 1974, sections 20, 22 and 23.

PART 3
ENACTMENTS RELATING TO UNQUALIFIED PERSONS ACTING
AS SOLICITORS

Regulation 37(2)

Solicitors Act 1974, section 25(1).

SCHEDULE 4
Extension of Enactments in Relation to the Registration of European Lawyers with the
Law Society

Regulation 37(3)

1 (1) The power to make regulations under section 2 of the Solicitors Act 1974 shall also
be exercisable in relation to registered European lawyers.

(2) The power to make regulations under section 28(1)(c) to (d) of that Act shall also be exercisable in relation to registered European lawyers as it is in relation to solicitors, subject to the modifications specified in the Table and subject to paragraph 7(1A).

(2A) Section 28(3B) to (3G) of the 1974 Act has effect with respect to registered European lawyers as it has effect with respect to solicitors, subject to the modifications specified in the Table and subject to paragraph 7(1A).

(3) The power to make rules under—

(a) sections 31, 32, 33A, 34, 36 and 37 of the Solicitors Act 1974; and

(b) section 9 of the Administration of Justice Act 1985,

shall also be exercisable in relation to registered European lawyers.

...

2 Any of the powers referred to in paragraph 1 may be exercised so as to make different provision with respect to registered European lawyers.

3 ...

4 ...

5 ...

6 ...

7 (1) Subject to sub-paragraph (1A), the provisions of sections 1B, 9, 10, 10A, 11, 13, 13ZA, 13ZB, 13A, 13B, 15, 16, 17, 17A, 17B, 18 and 84 of the 1974 Act shall apply to registered European lawyers as they apply to solicitors subject to the modifications specified in the Table.

(1A) An appeal by a European lawyer in respect of the following decisions of the Law Society is to be made under regulation 20 and not under section 13 or 13B(7) of the 1974 Act or under regulations made under section 28(3D) of the 1974 Act—

(a) refusal of initial registration;.

(b) grant of initial registration whilst refusing sole practitioner endorsement;.

(c) grant of initial registration subject to a condition;.

(d) refusal to renew a registration;.

(e) failure to take a decision on an application for initial registration within the statutory time limit;.

(f) withdrawal or revocation of a registration;.

(g) suspension of a registration.

(2) Sections 31(2), 32(3) and (4), 33, 33A, 34(6) and (9), 34A, 34B, 38, 40, 44B, 44BA, 44BC, 44C, 44D, 44E, 56(1)(f), (2) and (4) to (7), 57 to 75, 81, 81A and 83 of the 1974 Act shall also apply to registered European lawyers as they apply to solicitors subject to the modifications specified in the Table.

(2A) The following provisions of the 1974 Act have effect as follows—

(a) in section 34(10) the reference to subsection (9) is to be read as including a reference to that subsection as it has effect by virtue of sub-paragraph (2);

(b) section 56(1)(a) to (e) to the extent necessary to give effect to section 56(1)(f) as it has effect by virtue of sub-paragraph (2).

(3)   Sections 41, 42, 43 and 44 of the 1974 Act shall apply to registered European lawyers as they apply to solicitors subject to the modifications specified in the Table.

(4)   Section 85 of the 1974 Act (bank accounts) shall apply to a registered European lawyer and to the partner of a registered European lawyer as it applies to a solicitor.

8   (1)   Subject to sub-paragraph (1A), sections 36 and 36A of the 1974 Act shall apply to registered European lawyers as they apply to solicitors.

(1A)   The Society may make different provision with respect to registered European lawyers, and European lawyers making an application for initial registration, from the provision made with respect to solicitors.

(2)   ...

(3)   ...

(4)   ...

9   Section 35 of, and Schedule 1 to, the Solicitors Act 1974 shall apply to registered European lawyers as they apply to solicitors, and for that purpose—

   (aa)   reference to the roll is to be read as a reference to the register of European lawyers;.

   (ab)   reference to a solicitor suspended from practice is to be read as a reference to a European lawyer whose registration is suspended;

   (ac)   in paragraph 1(1)(k) of Schedule 1 to the 1974 Act, reference to a person acting as a solicitor when he did not have a practising certificate which was in force is to be read as a reference to a European lawyer or registered European lawyer who has committed an offence under regulation 21 of these Regulations;

   (b)   references to a solicitor's practising certificate shall be interpreted as references to a registered European lawyer's registration;

   (c)   reference to a sole solicitor is to be read as a reference to a sole practitioner.

   (d)   ...

10   Sections 46(10)(c), 47, 48, 49, 50(2), 50(3), 51, 52, 53 and 55 of the Solicitors Act 1974 shall apply to registered European lawyers as they apply to solicitors subject to the modifications specified in the Table.

11   Part XX of the Financial Services and Markets Act 2000, including the definition of "members" in section 325(2), has effect in relation to registered European lawyers as it has in relation to solicitors.

12   For the purposes of section 391 of the Insolvency Act 1986 and the Insolvency Practitioners (Recognised Professional Bodies) Order 1986, registered European lawyers and their partners shall be deemed to be—

   (a)   part of the solicitors' profession; and

   (b)   subject to the Law Society's rules in the practice of their profession.

13   Section 142 of the County Courts Act 1984 shall apply to registered European lawyers as it applies to solicitors.

14   (1)   Section 89 of the Courts and Legal Services Act 1990 shall be amended as follows.

(2)   In subsection (9), the following shall be substituted for the definition of "multi-national partnership"—

""multi-national partnership" means a partnership whose members consist of one or more registered foreign lawyers and one or more other lawyers as permitted by rules made under section 31 of the Solicitors Act 1974;"

15 ...

16 Registered European lawyers shall be authorised advocates and authorised litigators, for the purposes of the Courts and Legal Services Act 1990 and for the purposes of other enactments where either of those terms is defined by reference to the meaning in that Act.

17 In the Estate Agents Act 1979 the reference to a practising solicitor in section 1(2)(a) (which exempts solicitors from that Act) shall be interpreted as including a reference to a registered European lawyer and the partner of a registered European lawyer, providing professional services in accordance with rules made under section 31 of the Solicitors Act 1974 or section 9 of the Administration of Justice Act 1985.

18 ...

19 In the Rehabilitation of Offenders Act 1974 (Exceptions) Order 1975 the reference to "solicitor" in Part I of Schedule 1 to the Order shall be interpreted as including reference to a registered European lawyer.

20 The Solicitors (Non-Contentious Business) Remuneration Order 1994 and any other order made under section 56 of the 1974 Act shall apply to registered European lawyers as it applies to solicitors.

21 Registered European lawyers shall be treated as if they were officers of the Supreme Court and shall be subject to the inherent jurisdiction of that court in like manner and to the same extent as if they were solicitors.

22 (1) References in the Charter to solicitors shall be deemed to include references to registered European lawyers.

(2) In this paragraph "the Charter" has the same meaning as it has in section 87(1) of the Solicitors Act 1974.

23 ...

24 (1) The provisions of sections 40 and 43 of the Administration of Justice Act 1985 apply to registered European lawyers as they apply to solicitors, and for this purpose the reference to a person's solicitor in section 40(1) is to be read as a reference to a registered European lawyer acting for a person.

(2) In Schedule 2 to that Act the provisions of paragraphs 7, 9(3), 10(3), 18A(2), 18A(3), 20, 21(1) and 25(1) apply to registered European lawyers as they apply to solicitors, subject to the following modifications—

(a) in paragraphs 9(3), 10(3) and 21(1) reference to the roll is to be read as a reference to the register of European lawyers;

(b) in paragraph 18A(2)(c) reference to a person who is not a solicitor is to be read as a reference to a person who is neither a solicitor nor a registered European lawyer;.

(c) in paragraph 21(1)(b) reference to suspension from practice as a solicitor is to be read as a reference to a European lawyer's suspension from the register of European lawyers.

Provision of the 1974 Act	Modification
Section 1B	Reference to a sole solicitor is to be read as a reference to a sole practitioner.
Section 1B(1)(a)	Reference to a practising certificate in force is to be read as a reference to a European lawyer's registration.
Section 1B(1)(b)	Reference to a certificate is to be read as a reference to a European lawyer's registration.
	Reference to a sole solicitor endorsement is to be read as a reference to a sole practitioner endorsement.
Section 9(1)	Reference to a person whose name is on the roll is to be read as a reference to a European lawyer, as defined by regulation 2(1) to (4) of these Regulations.
	Reference to the issuing of a practising certificate is to be read as a reference to initial registration or renewal of registration in the register of European lawyers.
Section 9(2)	Reference to a sole solicitor endorsement is to be read as a reference to a sole practitioner endorsement.
Section 9(4)(a)	Reference to a practising certificate is to be read as a reference to a European lawyer's registration.
Section 10(1) to (4)	Reference to the issuing of a practising certificate is to be read as a reference to initial registration or renewal of registration in the register of European lawyers.
	Reference to suspension from practice is to be read as a reference to suspension from the register of European lawyers.
Section 10(4)(a)	Reference to a sole solicitor endorsement is to be read as a reference to a sole practitioner endorsement.
	Reference to a sole solicitor is to be read as a reference to a sole practitioner.
Section 10(5)	Reference to a practising certificate is to be read as a reference to a European lawyer's registration.
Section 10A	Reference to solicitors who hold practising certificates is to be read as a reference to registered European lawyers.
Section 10A(2)(b)	Reference to a sole solicitor endorsement is to be read as a reference to a sole practitioner endorsement.
Section 11(1)	Reference to the issuing of a practising certificate is to be read as a reference to initial registration or renewal of registration.
Section 11(3)	Reference to a practising certificate is to be read as a reference to a European lawyer's registration.
Section 11(3)(b)	Reference to a practising certificate not having been issued since the Society became aware of the failure is to be read as a reference to a registration in the register of European lawyers not having been entered or renewed since the Society became aware of the failure.
Section 13	Section 13 is to be read as if subsection (1)(a) were omitted.

Section 13(1)(b) and (4)(b) and (f)	Reference to a sole solicitor endorsement or endorsement is to be read as a reference to a sole practitioner endorsement.
	Reference in section 13(1)(b) to an application for a solicitor endorsement being refused is not to be read as a reference to an application for initial registration including a sole solicitor endorsement.
Section 13(1)(c) and (4)(b) to (f)	Reference to the issuing of a practising certificate is to be read as a reference to renewal of registration.
	Reference to a practising certificate or certificate is to be read as a reference to a registration in the register of European lawyers.
Section 13(2)	Reference to a person who holds a practising certificate is to be read as a person who is registered in the register of European lawyers.
Section 13(3)	Reference to any application under section 9 is to be read as any application for renewal of registration in the register of European lawyers.
Section 13ZA(1)	Reference to a practising certificate being in force (a "current certificate") is to be read as a reference to a registered European lawyer's registration.
Section 13ZA(1), (2), (5) and (8)(b)	Reference to a sole solicitor endorsement or endorsement is to be read as a reference to a sole practitioner endorsement.
Section 13ZA(3)	Reference to suspension from practice as a sole solicitor is to be read as a reference to suspension of a sole practitioner endorsement.
Section 13ZA(2), (5), (6)(b) and (8)(c)	Reference to a practising certificate is to be read as a reference to a registered European lawyer's registration.
Section 13ZB	Reference to a sole solicitor endorsement or endorsement is to be read as a reference to a sole practitioner endorsement.
Section 13A(1), (2) and (7)(b)	Reference to a practising certificate being in force (a "current certificate") is to be read as a reference to a European lawyer's registration.
Section 13A(2)(a)	Reference to a sole solicitor endorsement is to be read as a reference to a sole practitioner endorsement.
Section 13A(9)	Reference to a solicitor who holds a practising certificate is to be read as a European lawyer who is registered in the register of European lawyers.
Section 13B(1) and (8)(b)	References to a practising certificate or the appellant's certificate are to be read as references to a registered European lawyer's registration.
	Reference to a sole solicitor endorsement is to be read as a reference to a sole practitioner endorsement.
Section 13B(6)	Reference to a solicitor's suspension from practice or from practice as a sole solicitor is to be read as a reference to a European lawyer's suspension from the register of European lawyers or suspension of a sole practitioner endorsement.

Section 15	Reference to a practising certificate is to be read as a reference to a European lawyer's registration.
	Reference in subsection (1) to suspension from practice is to be read as a reference to a European lawyer's suspension from the register of European lawyers.
Section 16	Reference to a practising certificate or certificate is to be read as a reference to a registration in the register of European lawyers.
	Reference to a solicitor's suspension from practice or suspension is to be read as reference to the suspension of a European lawyer's registration.
	Reference in subsections (1) and (3) to expiry of a certificate is to be read as expiry of a European lawyer's registration.
Section 17	Reference to suspension of a solicitor's practising certificate is to be read as reference to the suspension of a European lawyer's registration.
	Reference to a note against a solicitor's name on the roll is to be read as reference to a note against a European lawyer's name on the register of European lawyers.
Section 17A	Reference to a sole solicitor endorsement is to be read as a reference to a sole practitioner endorsement.
	Reference to suspension from practice as a sole solicitor is to be read as a reference to a European lawyer's suspension from practice as a sole practitioner.
Section 17B	Reference to suspension of a sole solicitor endorsement is to be read as a reference to suspension of a sole practitioner endorsement.
	Reference to a note against a solicitor's name on the roll is to be read as reference to a note against a European lawyer's name on the register of European lawyers.
Section 18	References to the register kept under section 10A are to be read as a reference to the register of European lawyers.
	Subsection (1) is to be read as if reference to an extract from the roll were omitted.
	Section 18 is to be read as if subsection (2)(a) were omitted.
Section 28(1)(c) to (d)	Reference in subsection (1)(c) to a practising certificate is to be read as a reference to a European lawyer's registration.
	Reference in subsection (1)(ca) to a sole solicitor endorsement is to be read as a reference to a sole practitioner endorsement.
	Reference in subsection (1)(d) to the register kept under section 10A is to be read as a reference to the register of European lawyers.

Section 28(3B) to (3G)	Reference to a practising certificate is to be read as a reference to a European lawyer's registration.
	Reference to a sole solicitor endorsement is to be read as a reference to a sole practitioner endorsement.
	Reference in subsection (3B)(d) and (e) to the issuing of a practising certificate is to be read as a reference to initial registration or renewal of registration.
	Reference in subsection (3B)(f) to a sole solicitor endorsement being made after a practising certificate was issued is to be read as a reference to a sole practitioner endorsement being made after registration in the register of European lawyers.
	Subsection (3B)(i) is to be read as if reference to replacement were omitted.
	Reference in subsection (3B)(k) to solicitors who hold practising certificates is to be read as reference to registered European lawyers.
	Reference in subsection (3C) to the register under section 10A is to be read as a reference to the register of European lawyers.
Section 41	Reference to a solicitor is to be read as to include a reference to a registered European lawyer.
	Reference in subsections (1)(a) and (4)(a) to the roll is to be read as to include a reference to the register of European lawyers.
	Reference in subsections (1)(b) and (4)(b) to suspension from practising as a solicitor is to be read as to include a reference to suspension from the register of European lawyers.
	Reference in subsection (1)(c) to a practising certificate being suspended is to be read as to include a reference to a European lawyer's registration being suspended.
	Reference in subsection (1B) to the "employed solicitor" is not to be read as a reference to an employed European lawyer.
Section 42	In subsection (1) reference to a person who is disqualified from practising as a solicitor by reason of a fact mentioned in paragraphs (a) to (c) is to be read as to include a reference to a European lawyer whose name has been struck off the register of European lawyers or whose registration in that register is suspended.
Section 43	In section 43(1) reference to a person who is not a solicitor is to be read as a reference to a person who is neither a solicitor nor a registered European lawyer.
Section 44	Reference to section 43(2) is to be read as to include a reference to that section as it has effect by virtue of these Regulations.

APPENDIX 9

Section 47	Reference to the roll is to be read as reference to the register of European lawyers.
	Reference in section 47(1)(d) and (2)(b) and (e) to suspension from practice is to be read as a reference to suspension from the register of European lawyers.
	Reference in section 47(1)(ea) and (2)(bb) and (ea) to suspension from practice as a sole solicitor is to be read as a reference to a European lawyer's suspension from practice as a sole practitioner.
	Reference in section 47(2)(ba) to a sole solicitor endorsement is to be read as a reference to a sole practitioner endorsement.
	Reference in section 47(2A)(a) to another solicitor is to be read as to include a reference to a solicitor or a registered European lawyer.
	Reference in section 47(2B) to a firm of solicitors is to be read as a reference to a firm of solicitors and/or registered European lawyers.
	Reference to an employee who is not a solicitor is to be read as a reference to an employee who is neither a solicitor nor a registered European lawyer
Section 51	Reference in section 51(1) and (3)(b) to the striking off of a name from the roll is to be read as reference to striking a European lawyer's name from the register of European lawyers.
Section 52	Reference to the striking off of a name from the roll is to be read as reference to striking a European lawyer's name from the register of European lawyers.
Section 53	Reference to the striking off of a name from the roll is to be read as reference to striking a European lawyer's name from the register of European lawyers.
	Reference to suspension from practice is to be read as a reference to suspension from the register of European lawyers.
	Reference to a note of the order on the roll is to be read as reference to a note on the register of European lawyers.
Section 55	Reference to the striking off of a name from the roll is to be read as reference to striking a European lawyer's name from the register of European lawyers.
Section 84	Reference to a solicitor who has in force, or who has applied for, a practising certificate is to be read as a reference to a European lawyer who is registered or who has applied for registration in the register of European lawyers.
	Reference in subsection (3) to a practising solicitor is to be read as a reference to a registered European lawyer.

SCHEDULE 5
Extension of Enactments in Relation to the Registration of European Lawyers with the
Law Society of Northern Ireland

Regulation 37(4)

1 (1) The power to make rules and regulations under article 75 of the Solicitors
(Northern Ireland) Order 1976 shall also be exercisable in relation to registered European
lawyers.

(2) The power to make regulations under articles 6, 26, 26A, 33, 34, 35, 61 and 63 shall also
be exercisable in relation to registered European lawyers.

2 The provisions of articles 7, 8, 10, 11, 13 and 14 to 18 of that Order shall apply to
registered European lawyers as they apply to solicitors, except that—

(a) references to a solicitor's practising certificate shall be interpreted as references to a
registered European lawyer's registration; and

(b) references to the roll shall be interpreted as references to the register of European
lawyers.

3 Articles 27, 28, 29, 32, 36 to 60, 62, 64A to 71H, 72A, 77 and 78 of, and Schedules 1,
1A and 2 to, that Order shall apply to registered European lawyers as they apply to solicitors
except that—

(a) references to a solicitor's practising certificate shall be interpreted as references to a
registered European lawyer's registration; and

(b) references to the roll shall be interpreted as references to the register of European
lawyers.

4 Article 51 of the County Courts (Northern Ireland) Order 1980 shall apply to registered
European lawyers as it applies to solicitors.

5 In the Estate Agents Act 1979 the reference to a practising solicitor in section 1(2)(a)
(which exempts solicitors from that Act) shall be interpreted as including a reference to a
registered European lawyer, and the partner of a registered European lawyer providing
professional services in accordance with article 26 of the Solicitors (Northern Ireland)
Order 1976.

6 In the Rehabilitation of Offenders (Northern Ireland) Order 1978 the references to
"solicitor" in the Order shall be interpreted as including reference to a registered European
lawyer.

7 The Solicitors Remuneration Order (Northern Ireland) 1977 shall apply to registered
European lawyers as it applies to solicitors.

8 Registered European lawyers shall be treated as if they were officers of the Supreme
Court of Northern Ireland and shall be subject to the inherent jurisdiction of that court in like
manner and to the same extent as if they were solicitors.

SRA Warning Cards

[Law Society copyright.]

Fraudulent financial arrangements

[Issued by the Solicitors Regulation Authority. Last updated April 2009]

The Solicitors Regulation Authority takes strong action against those it regulates who appear to facilitate fraud.

Your obligations are set out in rule 1 of the Solicitors' Code of Conduct 2007.

Avoid dubious financial arrangements

You must ensure that you do not become involved in dubious financial arrangements or investment schemes. Failure to observe our warnings could lead to disciplinary action, criminal prosecution or both.

Schemes are formulated by fraudsters to prey upon the wealthy, greedy or vulnerable. They often sound "too good to be true" and almost always are.

Warning signs

- The promise of unrealistically high returns

- Deals forming part of larger deals involving millions, or billions of pounds, dollars or other currencies

- Any advance fee payable to secure future lending or to buy into an "investment" process

- Trading in apparent banking instruments such as Promissory Notes or Standby Letters of Credit to provide returns for non banking investors

- Confusing and complex transactions involving misleading descriptions or ill defined terminology, such as "grand master collateral commitment"

- Vague reference to humanitarian or charitable aims

- The need for secrecy to protect the scheme, particularly to prevent proper checks

- Use of faxed or easily forged documents often from offshore companies or from financial institutions abroad

Why involve you?

The fraudster wants to be associated with the legitimacy and respectability which, as a person or firm regulated by the SRA, you provide by:

- endorsing the arrangements by acting as the fraudster's legal adviser or banker

- providing correspondence to the fraudster's company or third parties
- "securing" the transaction with an undertaking from you
- opening bank accounts, awaiting receipt of funds or using your client account
- referring to your insurance or to the Compensation Fund.

If you do not understand the documents or a transaction in which you are involved, you must ask questions to satisfy yourself that it is proper for you to act. Why have you been approached? Do you have any expertise in this area of law? If you are not wholly satisfied as to the propriety of the transaction, you must refuse to act.

To report to us on a confidential basis, contact our Fraud and Confidential Intelligence Bureau on 01926 439673 or 0845 850 0999 or email redalert@sra.org.uk.

For advice, contact our Professional Ethics helpline [see **www.sra.org.uk/contact-us**].

Money laundering

[Issued by the Solicitors Regulation Authority. Last updated April 2009]

The Solicitors Regulation Authority is determined to pursue those it regulates who are involved in money laundering.

Your obligations are set out in the Solicitors' Code of Conduct 2007, particularly rules 1 and 4, the Solicitors' Accounts Rules, the Proceeds of Crime Act 2002, the Terrorism Act 2000, and the Money Laundering Regulations 2007.

You must ensure that you do not facilitate laundering even when money does not pass through your firm's accounts. Failure to observe our warnings can lead to disciplinary action, criminal prosecution, or both.

Warning Signs

Unusual payment requests

- Payments from a third party where you cannot verify the source of the funds
- Receipts of cash and requests for payments by cash
- Money transfers where there is a variation between the account holder/signatory
- Payments to unrelated third parties
- Litigation settlements which are reached too easily.

Unusual instructions

- Instructions outside the normal pattern of your business
- Instructions changed without a reasonable explanation
- Transactions that take an unusual turn
- Movement of funds between accounts, institutions or jurisdictions without reason.

Use of your client account

- Never accept instructions to act as a banking facility, particularly if you do not undertake any related legal work – be aware of note (ix) to rule 15 of the Solicitors' Accounts Rules 1998

- Be wary if you are instructed to do legal work, receive substantial funds into your client account, but the instructions are later cancelled and you are asked to send the money to a third party or perhaps to your client.

Suspect territory

- Check official sources about suspect territories and sanctions
- Be wary of funds moved around without a logical explanation.

Loss making transaction

- Instructions potentially leading to financial loss without logical explanation, particularly where your client seems unconcerned.

Legislation may require you to make an official disclosure to the Serious Organised Crime Agency (SOCA), PO Box 8000, London, SE11 5EN, call **020 7238 8282**, or send an email by registering on the secure site at www.ukciu.gov.uk/saroline.aspx. You will not commit the offence of "tipping off" by reporting a matter to the SRA. To report to us on a confidential basis, contact our Fraud and Confidential Intelligence Bureau on **01926 439673 or 0845 850 0999** or email **redalert@sra.org.uk**.

For conduct advice, contact our Professional Ethics helpline.

For general queries about good-practice anti-money laundering compliance, contact the Law Society's Practice Advice Service on 0870 606 2522 (9:00–17:00 Monday to Friday) or refer to www.lawsociety.org.uk/moneylaundering.

Property fraud

[Issued by the Solicitors Regulation Authority. Last updated April 2009]

The Solicitors Regulation Authority will not tolerate property fraud.

Your obligations are set out in rules 1, 2, 3, 4 and 18 of the Solicitors' Code of Conduct 2007 and its guidance.

If in doubt – refuse to act

You must ensure that you do not facilitate dubious property transactions. Failure to observe our warnings could lead to disciplinary action or criminal prosecution.

If you doubt the propriety of a transaction you should refuse to act. Ensure you verify and question instructions to satisfy yourself that you are not facilitating a dubious transaction.

What is property fraud?

Mortgage fraud occurs when a loan is obtained on the basis of untrue statements to the lender, such as when a lender is led to believe that a property is worth more than its true value and therefore lends more than it would if it knew the true position. Always focus on informing the lender of the true price and other relevant facts, while taking into account confidentiality and legal professional privilege.

Some frauds do not involve a mortgage – only the deception of buyers.

Warning signs

- Back to back transactions where a property is bought and then sold quickly, apparently at a higher price. The lender advances money based on the higher price

- Misrepresentation or changes to the purchase price including sellers or developers providing incentives, allowances or discounts unless these are clearly and fully disclosed to the lender

- A representation to you that a deposit or part of the purchase price is paid direct

- "Gifted deposit" or "deposit paid" by the seller amounting to a reduction in the price paid by the buyer but distorting the value disclosed to the lender

- Unusual or suspicious instructions such as transactions controlled or funded by a third party; a client using an alias; sales and purchases between associates; parties using the same legal adviser; a request that net proceeds be sent to a third party

- Properties sold between related offshore or corporate companies that are commonly controlled by the same individuals, particularly where the properties are mortgaged at an inflated value

Be aware that variations of these warning signs exist and fraudsters change their methods. You do not need to act for the lender to become implicated. If you are not satisfied of the propriety of the transaction you should refuse to act.

Money laundering

Bear in mind that you may also have legal obligations to report your suspicions to the Serious Organised Crime Agency.

For good-practice advice, refer to www.lawsociety.org.uk/mortgagefraud.

To report to us on a confidential basis, contact our Fraud and Confidential Intelligence Bureau on 01926 439673 or 0845 850 0999 or email redalert@sra.org.uk.

For conduct advice, contact our Professional Ethics helpline.

Undertakings

[Issued by the Solicitors Regulation Authority. Last updated April 2009]

The SRA takes breaches of undertakings very seriously.

Your obligations are set out in rules 1, 5.01 and 10.05 of the Solicitors' Code of Conduct 2007 and its guidance.

Many transactions depend on the use of undertakings enabling you to negotiate and conduct your client's business successfully.

Where you give an undertaking

Those placing reliance on it will expect you to fulfil it. Ensure your undertakings are:

- Specific
- Measurable

- Agreed
- Realistic
- Timed

A breach of undertaking can lead to a disciplinary finding and costs direction.

Undertakings you give are also summarily enforceable by the High Court. Be aware that you do not become exposed to a liability within the excess of your firm's insurance.

Where you accept an undertaking

Ensure that in doing so your client's position is protected and you are not exposed to a breach.

If you are a regulated person or firm

- Be clear about who can give undertakings
- Ensure all staff understand they need your client's agreement
- Be clear about how compliance will be monitored
- Maintain a central record to ensure and monitor compliance
- Prescribe the manner in which undertakings may be given
- Prepare standard undertakings, where possible, with clear instructions that any departure be authorised in accordance with supervision and management responsibilities
- Adopt a system that ensures terms are checked by another fee-earner
- Confirm oral undertakings (given or received) in writing
- Copy each undertaking and attach it to the relevant file; label the file itself
- Ensure all staff understand the undertakings they give when using the Law Society's formulae for exchange of contracts and its code for completion by post.

To report to us on a confidential basis, contact our Fraud and Confidential Intelligence Bureau on **01926 439673 or 0845 850 0999** or email redalert@sra.org.uk.

For advice, contact our Professional Ethics helpline.

Equality and diversity

[Issued by the Solicitors Regulation Authority May 2010]

The SRA takes compliance with the principles of equality and diversity very seriously.

Rule 6 of the Solicitors' Code of Conduct 2007 and general law lay down your equality and diversity obligations. The SRA expects you to meet those obligations. You must treat everyone fairly and must not breach your conduct or legal duties.

When we visit your firm, we expect you to demonstrate this by

- having arrangements in place to demonstrate your compliance with the principles of equality and diversity (as currently set out in rule 6),

- making your policy available for consideration by the SRA,
- providing examples of how your policy is implemented.

What you need to do

If you are a regulated person or firm

- Ensure that you do not discriminate on the grounds of race, sex, sexual orientation, religion or belief, age or disability.
- Ensure that disabled employees or clients are not placed at a substantial disadvantage in comparison with others and make reasonable adjustments.
- Adopt and implement a policy that ensures a safe working environment, free from harassment and bullying.
- Provide training and challenge discriminatory behaviour.
- Ensure your management systems comply with rule 6.
- Ensure all staff are aware of your policy and comply with it.
- Challenge inappropriate behaviour.

If you are recruiting or interviewing

- Remember your obligations not to discriminate either in the process or when interviewing for any position.
- Ensure your processes are fair, transparent and comply with your obligations, even when using agencies.

Complying with the law

If a court or tribunal finds you have committed an unlawful act of discrimination, that is likely to lead to an SRA investigation and could lead to disciplinary proceedings before the Solicitors Disciplinary Tribunal.

Your obligations are set out in rules 1, 5.01 and 6 of the Solicitors' Code of Conduct and its guidance and in legislation including, but not confined to, the Sex Discrimination Act 1975, the Race Relations Act 1976 and the Disability Discrimination Acts 1995 and 2005

The Equality Act 2010 which comes into force in October 2010 prohibits unlawful discrimination on the grounds of age, disability, gender reassignment, marriage and civil partnership, pregnancy and maternity, race, religion or belief, sex or sexual orientation.

For conduct advice, contact our Professional Ethics helpline.

The Money Laundering Regulations 2007

[With consolidated amendments to 15 December 2007]

Money Laundering Regulations 2007

SI 2007/2157

Made 24th July 2007

Laid before Parliament 25th July 2007

Coming into force 15th December 2007

The Treasury are a government department designated for the purposes of section 2(2) of the European Communities Act 1972 in relation to measures relating to preventing the use of the financial system for the purpose of money laundering;

The Treasury, in exercise of the powers conferred on them by section 2(2) of the European Communities Act 1972 and by sections 168(4)(b), 402(1)(b), 417(1) and 428(3) of the Financial Services and Markets Act 2000, make the following Regulations:

PART 1
GENERAL

1 Citation, commencement etc

(1)   These Regulations may be cited as the Money Laundering Regulations 2007 and come into force on 15th December 2007.

(2)   These Regulations are prescribed for the purposes of sections 168(4)(b) (appointment of persons to carry out investigations in particular cases) and 402(1)(b) (power of the Authority to institute proceedings for certain other offences) of the 2000 Act.

(3)   The Money Laundering Regulations 2003 are revoked.

2 Interpretation

(1)   In these Regulations—

"the 2000 Act" means the Financial Services and Markets Act 2000;

"Annex I financial institution" has the meaning given by regulation 22(1);

"auditor", except in regulation 17(2)(c) and (d), has the meaning given by regulation 3(4) and (5);

"authorised person" means a person who is authorised for the purposes of the 2000 Act;

"the Authority" means the Financial Services Authority;

"the banking consolidation directive" means Directive 2006/48/EC of the European Parliament and of the Council of 14th June 2006 relating to the taking up and pursuit of the business of credit institutions;

"beneficial owner" has the meaning given by regulation 6;

"business relationship" means a business, professional or commercial relationship between a relevant person and a customer, which is expected by the relevant person, at the time when contact is established, to have an element of duration;

"cash" means notes, coins or travellers' cheques in any currency;

"casino" has the meaning given by regulation 3(13);

"the Commissioners" means the Commissioners for Her Majesty's Revenue and Customs;

"consumer credit financial institution" has the meaning given by regulation 22(1);

"credit institution" has the meaning given by regulation 3(2);

"customer due diligence measures" has the meaning given by regulation 5;

"DETI" means the Department of Enterprise, Trade and Investment in Northern Ireland;

"the electronic money directive" means Directive 2000/46/EC of the European Parliament and of the Council of 18th September 2000 on the taking up, pursuit and prudential supervision of the business of electronic money institutions;

"estate agent" has the meaning given by regulation 3(11);

"external accountant" has the meaning given by regulation 3(7);

"financial institution" has the meaning given by regulation 3(3);

"firm" means any entity, whether or not a legal person, that is not an individual and includes a body corporate and a partnership or other unincorporated association;

"high value dealer" has the meaning given by regulation 3(12);

"the implementing measures directive" means Commission Directive 2006/70/EC of 1st August 2006 laying down implementing measures for the money laundering directive;

"independent legal professional" has the meaning given by regulation 3(9);

"insolvency practitioner", except in regulation 17(2)(c) and (d), has the meaning given by regulation 3(6);

"the life assurance consolidation directive" means Directive 2002/83/EC of the European Parliament and of the Council of 5th November 2002 concerning life assurance;

"local weights and measures authority" has the meaning given by section 69 of the Weights and Measures Act 1985 (local weights and measures authorities);

"the markets in financial instruments directive" means Directive 2004/39/EC of the European Parliament and of the Council of 12th April 2004 on markets in financial instruments;

"money laundering" means an act which falls within section 340(11) of the Proceeds of Crime Act 2002;

"the money laundering directive" means Directive 2005/60/EC of the European Parliament and of the Council of 26th October 2005 on the prevention of the use of the financial system for the purpose of money laundering and terrorist financing;

"money service business" means an undertaking which by way of business operates a currency exchange office, transmits money (or any representations of monetary value) by any means or cashes cheques which are made payable to customers;

"nominated officer" means a person who is nominated to receive disclosures under Part 7 of the Proceeds of Crime Act 2002 (money laundering) or Part 3 of the Terrorism Act 2000 (terrorist property);

"non–EEA state" means a state that is not an EEA state;

"notice" means a notice in writing;

"occasional transaction" means a transaction (carried out other than as part of a business relationship) amounting to 15,000 euro or more, whether the transaction is carried out in a single operation or several operations which appear to be linked;

"the OFT" means the Office of Fair Trading;

"ongoing monitoring" has the meaning given by regulation 8(2);

"regulated market"—

(a) within the EEA, has the meaning given by point 14 of Article 4(1) of the markets in financial instruments directive; and

(b) outside the EEA, means a regulated financial market which subjects companies whose securities are admitted to trading to disclosure obligations which are contained in international standards and are equivalent to the specified disclosure obligations;

"relevant person" means a person to whom, in accordance with regulations 3 and 4, these Regulations apply;

"the specified disclosure obligations" means disclosure requirements consistent with—

(a) Article 6(1) to (4) of Directive 2003/6/EC of the European Parliament and of the Council of 28th January 2003 on insider dealing and market manipulation;

(b) Articles 3, 5, 7, 8, 10, 14 and 16 of Directive 2003/71/EC of the European Parliament and of the Council of 4th November 2003 on the prospectuses to be published when securities are offered to the public or admitted to trading;

(c) Articles 4 to 6, 14, 16 to 19 and 30 of Directive 2004/109/EC of the European Parliament and of the Council of 15th December 2004 relating to the harmonisation of transparency requirements in relation to information about issuers whose securities are admitted to trading on a regulated market; or

(d) Community legislation made under the provisions mentioned in sub-paragraphs (a) to (c);

"supervisory authority" in relation to any relevant person means the supervisory authority specified for such a person by regulation 23;

"tax adviser" (except in regulation 11(3)) has the meaning given by regulation 3(8);

"terrorist financing" means an offence under—

(a) section 15 (fund-raising), 16 (use and possession), 17 (funding arrangements), 18 (money laundering) or 63 (terrorist finance: jurisdiction) of the Terrorism Act 2000;

(b) paragraph 7(2) or (3) of Schedule 3 to the Anti-Terrorism, Crime and Security Act 2001 (freezing orders);

(c) article 7, 8 or 10 of the Terrorism (United Nations Measures) Order 2006; or

(d) article 7, 8 or 10 of the Al-Qaida and Taliban (United Nations Measures) Order 2006;

"trust or company service provider" has the meaning given by regulation 3(10).

(2)   In these Regulations, references to amounts in euro include references to equivalent amounts in another currency.

(3)   Unless otherwise defined, expressions used in these Regulations and the money laundering directive have the same meaning as in the money laundering directive and expressions used in these Regulations and in the implementing measures directive have the same meaning as in the implementing measures directive.

3   Application of the Regulations

(1)   Subject to regulation 4, these Regulations apply to the following persons acting in the course of business carried on by them in the United Kingdom ("relevant persons")—

(a)   credit institutions;

(b)   financial institutions;

(c)   auditors, insolvency practitioners, external accountants and tax advisers;

(d)   independent legal professionals;

(e)   trust or company service providers;

(f)   estate agents;

(g)   high value dealers;

(h)   casinos.

(2)   "Credit institution" means—

(a)   a credit institution as defined in Article 4(1)(a) of the banking consolidation directive; or

(b)   a branch (within the meaning of Article 4(3) of that directive) located in an EEA state of an institution falling within sub-paragraph (a) (or an equivalent institution whose head office is located in a non-EEA state) wherever its head office is located,

when it accepts deposits or other repayable funds from the public or grants credits for its own account (within the meaning of the banking consolidation directive).

(3)   "Financial institution" means—

(a)   an undertaking, including a money service business, when it carries out one or more of the activities listed in points 2 to 12 and 14 of Annex 1 to the banking consolidation directive (the relevant text of which is set out in Schedule 1 to these Regulations), other than—

    (i)   a credit institution;

    (ii)   an undertaking whose only listed activity is trading for own account in one or more of the products listed in point 7 of Annex 1 to the banking consolidation directive where the undertaking does not have a customer,

    and, for this purpose, "customer" means a third party which is not a member of the same group as the undertaking;

(b)   an insurance company duly authorised in accordance with the life assurance consolidation directive, when it carries out activities covered by that directive;

(c)   a person whose regular occupation or business is the provision to other persons of an investment service or the performance of an investment activity on a professional basis, when providing or performing investment services or activities (within the meaning of the markets in financial instruments directive), other than a person falling within Article 2 of that directive;

(d)   a collective investment undertaking, when marketing or otherwise offering its units or shares;

(e)   an insurance intermediary as defined in Article 2(5) of Directive 2002/92/EC of the European Parliament and of the Council of 9th December 2002 on insurance mediation, with the exception of a tied insurance intermediary as mentioned in Article 2(7) of that Directive, when it acts in respect of contracts of long-term insurance within the meaning given by article 3(1) of, and Part II of Schedule 1 to, the Financial Services and Markets Act 2000 (Regulated Activities) Order 2001;

(f)   a branch located in an EEA state of a person referred to in sub-paragraphs (a) to (e) (or an equivalent person whose head office is located in a non-EEA state), wherever its head office is located, when carrying out any activity mentioned in sub-paragraphs (a) to (e);

(g)   the National Savings Bank;

(h)   the Director of Savings, when money is raised under the auspices of the Director under the National Loans Act 1968.

(4) "Auditor" means any firm or individual who is a statutory auditor within the meaning of Part 42 of the Companies Act 2006 (statutory auditors), when carrying out statutory audit work within the meaning of section 1210 of that Act.

(5) Before the entry into force of Part 42 of the Companies Act 2006 the reference in paragraph (4) to—

(a)   a person who is a statutory auditor shall be treated as a reference to a person who is eligible for appointment as a company auditor under section 25 of the Companies Act 1989 (eligibility for appointment) or article 28 of the Companies (Northern Ireland) Order 1990; and

(b)   the carrying out of statutory audit work shall be treated as a reference to the provision of audit services.

(6) "Insolvency practitioner" means any person who acts as an insolvency practitioner within the meaning of section 388 of the Insolvency Act 1986 (meaning of "act as insolvency practitioner") or article 3 of the Insolvency (Northern Ireland) Order 1989.

(7) "External accountant" means a firm or sole practitioner who by way of business provides accountancy services to other persons, when providing such services.

(8) "Tax adviser" means a firm or sole practitioner who by way of business provides advice about the tax affairs of other persons, when providing such services.

(9) "Independent legal professional" means a firm or sole practitioner who by way of business provides legal or notarial services to other persons, when participating in financial or real property transactions concerning—

(a)   the buying and selling of real property or business entities;

(b)   the managing of client money, securities or other assets;

(c)   the opening or management of bank, savings or securities accounts;

(d)   the organisation of contributions necessary for the creation, operation or management of companies; or

(e)   the creation, operation or management of trusts, companies or similar structures,

and, for this purpose, a person participates in a transaction by assisting in the planning or execution of the transaction or otherwise acting for or on behalf of a client in the transaction.

(10) "Trust or company service provider" means a firm or sole practitioner who by way of business provides any of the following services to other persons—

    (a)   forming companies or other legal persons;

    (b)   acting, or arranging for another person to act—

        (i)   as a director or secretary of a company;

        (ii)   as a partner of a partnership; or

        (iii)   in a similar position in relation to other legal persons;

    (c)   providing a registered office, business address, correspondence or administrative address or other related services for a company, partnership or any other legal person or arrangement;

    (d)   acting, or arranging for another person to act, as—

        (i)   a trustee of an express trust or similar legal arrangement; or

        (ii)   a nominee shareholder for a person other than a company whose securities are listed on a regulated market,

    when providing such services.

(11) "Estate agent" means—

    (a)   a firm; or

    (b)   sole practitioner,

who, or whose employees, carry out estate agency work (within the meaning given by section 1 of the Estate Agents Act 1979 (estate agency work)), when in the course of carrying out such work.

(12) "High value dealer" means a firm or sole trader who by way of business trades in goods (including an auctioneer dealing in goods), when he receives, in respect of any transaction, a payment or payments in cash of at least 15,000 euros in total, whether the transaction is executed in a single operation or in several operations which appear to be linked.

(13) "Casino" means the holder of a casino operating licence and, for this purpose, a "casino operating licence" has the meaning given by section 65(2) of the Gambling Act 2005 (nature of licence).

(14) In the application of this regulation to Scotland, for "real property" in paragraph (9) substitute "heritable property".

4 Exclusions

(1) These Regulations do not apply to the following persons when carrying out any of the following activities—

    (a)   a society registered under the Industrial and Provident Societies Act 1965, when it—

        (i)   issues withdrawable share capital within the limit set by section 6 of that Act (maximum shareholding in society); or

        (ii)   accepts deposits from the public within the limit set by section 7(3) of that Act (carrying on of banking by societies);

    (b)   a society registered under the Industrial and Provident Societies Act (Northern Ireland) 1969, when it—

        (i)   issues withdrawable share capital within the limit set by section 6 of that Act (maximum shareholding in society); or

        (ii)   accepts deposits from the public within the limit set by section 7(3) of that Act (carrying on of banking by societies);

(c)   a person who is (or falls within a class of persons) specified in any of paragraphs 2 to 23, 25 to 38 or 40 to 49 of the Schedule to the Financial Services and Markets Act 2000 (Exemption) Order 2001, when carrying out any activity in respect of which he is exempt;

(d)   a person who was an exempted person for the purposes of section 45 of the Financial Services Act 1986 (miscellaneous exemptions) immediately before its repeal, when exercising the functions specified in that section;

(e)   a person whose main activity is that of a high value dealer, when he engages in financial activity on an occasional or very limited basis as set out in paragraph 1 of Schedule 2 to these Regulations; or

(f)   a person, when he prepares a home information pack or a document or information for inclusion in a home information pack.

(2)   These Regulations do not apply to a person who falls within regulation 3 solely as a result of his engaging in financial activity on an occasional or very limited basis as set out in paragraph 1 of Schedule 2 to these Regulations.

(3)   Parts 2 to 5 of these Regulations do not apply to—

(a)   the Auditor General for Scotland;

(b)   the Auditor General for Wales;

(c)   the Bank of England;

(d)   the Comptroller and Auditor General;

(e)   the Comptroller and Auditor General for Northern Ireland;

(f)   the Official Solicitor to the Supreme Court, when acting as trustee in his official capacity;

(g)   the Treasury Solicitor.

(4)   In paragraph (1)(f), "home information pack" has the same meaning as in Part 5 of the Housing Act 2004 (home information packs).

PART 2
CUSTOMER DUE DILIGENCE

5   Meaning of customer due diligence measures

"Customer due diligence measures" means—

(a)   identifying the customer and verifying the customer's identity on the basis of documents, data or information obtained from a reliable and independent source;

(b)   identifying, where there is a beneficial owner who is not the customer, the beneficial owner and taking adequate measures, on a risk-sensitive basis, to verify his identity so that the relevant person is satisfied that he knows who the beneficial owner is, including, in the case of a legal person, trust or similar legal arrangement, measures to understand the ownership and control structure of the person, trust or arrangement; and

(c)   obtaining information on the purpose and intended nature of the business relationship.

6   Meaning of beneficial owner

(1)   In the case of a body corporate, "beneficial owner" means any individual who—

(a)   as respects any body other than a company whose securities are listed on a regulated

APPENDIX 11

market, ultimately owns or controls (whether through direct or indirect ownership or control, including through bearer share holdings) more than 25% of the shares or voting rights in the body; or

(b) as respects any body corporate, otherwise exercises control over the management of the body.

(2) In the case of a partnership (other than a limited liability partnership), "beneficial owner" means any individual who—

(a) ultimately is entitled to or controls (whether the entitlement or control is direct or indirect) more than a 25% share of the capital or profits of the partnership or more than 25% of the voting rights in the partnership; or

(b) otherwise exercises control over the management of the partnership.

(3) In the case of a trust, "beneficial owner" means—

(a) any individual who is entitled to a specified interest in at least 25% of the capital of the trust property;

(b) as respects any trust other than one which is set up or operates entirely for the benefit of individuals falling within sub-paragraph (a), the class of persons in whose main interest the trust is set up or operates;

(c) any individual who has control over the trust.

(4) In paragraph (3)—

"specified interest" means a vested interest which is—

(a) in possession or in remainder or reversion (or, in Scotland, in fee); and

(b) defeasible or indefeasible;

"control" means a power (whether exercisable alone, jointly with another person or with the consent of another person) under the trust instrument or by law to—

(a) dispose of, advance, lend, invest, pay or apply trust property;

(b) vary the trust;

(c) add or remove a person as a beneficiary or to or from a class of beneficiaries;

(d) appoint or remove trustees;

(e) direct, withhold consent to or veto the exercise of a power such as is mentioned in sub-paragraph (a), (b), (c) or (d).

(5) For the purposes of paragraph (3)—

(a) where an individual is the beneficial owner of a body corporate which is entitled to a specified interest in the capital of the trust property or which has control over the trust, the individual is to be regarded as entitled to the interest or having control over the trust; and

(b) an individual does not have control solely as a result of—

(i) his consent being required in accordance with section 32(1)(c) of the Trustee Act 1925 (power of advancement);

(ii) any discretion delegated to him under section 34 of the Pensions Act 1995 (power of investment and delegation);

(iii) the power to give a direction conferred on him by section 19(2) of the Trusts of Land and Appointment of Trustees Act 1996 (appointment and retirement of trustee at instance of beneficiaries); or

(iv)   the power exercisable collectively at common law to vary or extinguish a trust where the beneficiaries under the trust are of full age and capacity and (taken together) absolutely entitled to the property subject to the trust (or, in Scotland, have a full and unqualified right to the fee).

(6)   In the case of a legal entity or legal arrangement which does not fall within paragraph (1), (2) or (3), "beneficial owner" means—

(a)   where the individuals who benefit from the entity or arrangement have been determined, any individual who benefits from at least 25% of the property of the entity or arrangement;

(b)   where the individuals who benefit from the entity or arrangement have yet to be determined, the class of persons in whose main interest the entity or arrangement is set up or operates;

(c)   any individual who exercises control over at least 25% of the property of the entity or arrangement.

(7)   For the purposes of paragraph (6), where an individual is the beneficial owner of a body corporate which benefits from or exercises control over the property of the entity or arrangement, the individual is to be regarded as benefiting from or exercising control over the property of the entity or arrangement.

(8)   In the case of an estate of a deceased person in the course of administration, "beneficial owner" means—

(a)   in England and Wales and Northern Ireland, the executor, original or by representation, or administrator for the time being of a deceased person;

(b)   in Scotland, the executor for the purposes of the Executors (Scotland) Act 1900.

(9)   In any other case, "beneficial owner" means the individual who ultimately owns or controls the customer or on whose behalf a transaction is being conducted.

(10)   In this regulation—

"arrangement", "entity" and "trust" means an arrangement, entity or trust which administers and distributes funds;

"limited liability partnership" has the meaning given by the Limited Liability Partnerships Act 2000.

7 Application of customer due diligence measures

(1)   Subject to regulations 9, 10, 12, 13, 14, 16(4) and 17, a relevant person must apply customer due diligence measures when he—

(a)   establishes a business relationship;

(b)   carries out an occasional transaction;

(c)   suspects money laundering or terrorist financing;

(d)   doubts the veracity or adequacy of documents, data or information previously obtained for the purposes of identification or verification.

(2)   Subject to regulation 16(4), a relevant person must also apply customer due diligence measures at other appropriate times to existing customers on a risk-sensitive basis.

(3)   A relevant person must—

(a)   determine the extent of customer due diligence measures on a risk-sensitive basis depending on the type of customer, business relationship, product or transaction; and

    (b)   be able to demonstrate to his supervisory authority that the extent of the measures is appropriate in view of the risks of money laundering and terrorist financing.

(4) Where—

    (a)   a relevant person is required to apply customer due diligence measures in the case of a trust, legal entity (other than a body corporate) or a legal arrangement (other than a trust); and

    (b)   the class of persons in whose main interest the trust, entity or arrangement is set up or operates is identified as a beneficial owner,

the relevant person is not required to identify all the members of the class.

(5) Paragraph (3)(b) does not apply to the National Savings Bank or the Director of Savings.

8 Ongoing monitoring

(1) A relevant person must conduct ongoing monitoring of a business relationship.

(2) "Ongoing monitoring" of a business relationship means—

    (a)   scrutiny of transactions undertaken throughout the course of the relationship (including, where necessary, the source of funds) to ensure that the transactions are consistent with the relevant person's knowledge of the customer, his business and risk profile; and

    (b)   keeping the documents, data or information obtained for the purpose of applying customer due diligence measures up-to-date.

(3) Regulation 7(3) applies to the duty to conduct ongoing monitoring under paragraph (1) as it applies to customer due diligence measures.

9 Timing of verification

(1) This regulation applies in respect of the duty under regulation 7(1)(a) and (b) to apply the customer due diligence measures referred to in regulation 5(a) and (b).

(2) Subject to paragraphs (3) to (5) and regulation 10, a relevant person must verify the identity of the customer (and any beneficial owner) before the establishment of a business relationship or the carrying out of an occasional transaction.

(3) Such verification may be completed during the establishment of a business relationship if—

    (a)   this is necessary not to interrupt the normal conduct of business; and

    (b)   there is little risk of money laundering or terrorist financing occurring,

provided that the verification is completed as soon as practicable after contact is first established.

(4) The verification of the identity of the beneficiary under a life insurance policy may take place after the business relationship has been established provided that it takes place at or before the time of payout or at or before the time the beneficiary exercises a right vested under the policy.

(5) The verification of the identity of a bank account holder may take place after the bank account has been opened provided that there are adequate safeguards in place to ensure that—

    (a)   the account is not closed; and

    (b)   transactions are not carried out by or on behalf of the account holder (including any payment from the account to the account holder),

before verification has been completed.

10 Casinos

(1)   A casino must establish and verify the identity of—

(a)   all customers to whom the casino makes facilities for gaming available—

(i)   before entry to any premises where such facilities are provided; or

(ii)   where the facilities are for remote gaming, before access is given to such facilities; or

(b)   if the specified conditions are met, all customers who, in the course of any period of 24 hours—

(i)   purchase from, or exchange with, the casino chips with a total value of 2,000 euro or more;

(ii)   pay the casino 2,000 euro or more for the use of gaming machines; or

(iii) pay to, or stake with, the casino 2,000 euro or more in connection with facilities for remote gaming.

(2)   The specified conditions are—

(a)   the casino verifies the identity of each customer before or immediately after such purchase, exchange, payment or stake takes place, and

(b)   the Gambling Commission is satisfied that the casino has appropriate procedures in place to monitor and record—

(i)   the total value of chips purchased from or exchanged with the casino;

(ii)   the total money paid for the use of gaming machines; or

(iii) the total money paid or staked in connection with facilities for remote gaming,

by each customer.

(3)   In this regulation—

"gaming", "gaming machine", "remote operating licence" and "stake" have the meanings given by, respectively, sections 6(1) (gaming & game of chance), 235 (gaming machine), 67 (remote gambling) and 353(1) (interpretation) of the Gambling Act 2005;

"premises" means premises subject to—

(a)   a casino premises licence within the meaning of section 150(1)(a) of the Gambling Act 2005 (nature of licence); or

(b)   a converted casino premises licence within the meaning of paragraph 65 of Part 7 of Schedule 4 to the Gambling Act 2005 (Commencement No 6 and Transitional Provisions) Order 2006;

"remote gaming" means gaming provided pursuant to a remote operating licence.

11 Requirement to cease transactions etc

(1)   Where, in relation to any customer, a relevant person is unable to apply customer due diligence measures in accordance with the provisions of this Part, he—

(a)   must not carry out a transaction with or for the customer through a bank account;

(b)   must not establish a business relationship or carry out an occasional transaction with the customer;

(c)   must terminate any existing business relationship with the customer;

(d)   must consider whether he is required to make a disclosure by Part 7 of the Proceeds of Crime Act 2002 or Part 3 of the Terrorism Act 2000.

(2)   Paragraph (1) does not apply where a lawyer or other professional adviser is in the course of ascertaining the legal position for his client or performing his task of defending or representing that client in, or concerning, legal proceedings, including advice on the institution or avoidance of proceedings.

(3)   In paragraph (2), "other professional adviser" means an auditor, accountant or tax adviser who is a member of a professional body which is established for any such persons and which makes provision for—

(a)   testing the competence of those seeking admission to membership of such a body as a condition for such admission; and

(b)   imposing and maintaining professional and ethical standards for its members, as well as imposing sanctions for non-compliance with those standards.

12   Exception for trustees of debt issues

(1)   A relevant person—

(a)   who is appointed by the issuer of instruments or securities specified in paragraph (2) as trustee of an issue of such instruments or securities; or

(b)   whose customer is a trustee of an issue of such instruments or securities,

is not required to apply the customer due diligence measure referred to in regulation 5(b) in respect of the holders of such instruments or securities.

(2)   The specified instruments and securities are—

(a)   instruments which fall within article 77 of the Financial Services and Markets Act 2000 (Regulated Activities) Order 2001; and

(b)   securities which fall within article 78 of that Order.

13   Simplified due diligence

(1)   A relevant person is not required to apply customer due diligence measures in the circumstances mentioned in regulation 7(1)(a), (b) or (d) where he has reasonable grounds for believing that the customer, transaction or product related to such transaction, falls within any of the following paragraphs.

(2)   The customer is—

(a)   a credit or financial institution which is subject to the requirements of the money laundering directive; or

(b)   a credit or financial institution (or equivalent institution) which—

(i)   is situated in a non-EEA state which imposes requirements equivalent to those laid down in the money laundering directive; and

(ii)   is supervised for compliance with those requirements.

(3)   The customer is a company whose securities are listed on a regulated market subject to specified disclosure obligations.

(4)   The customer is an independent legal professional and the product is an account into which monies are pooled, provided that—

(a)   where the pooled account is held in a non-EEA state—

(i)   that state imposes requirements to combat money laundering and terrorist financing which are consistent with international standards; and

> > (ii)   the independent legal professional is supervised in that state for compliance with those requirements; and

> (b)   information on the identity of the persons on whose behalf monies are held in the pooled account is available, on request, to the institution which acts as a depository institution for the account.

(5)   The customer is a public authority in the United Kingdom.

(6)   The customer is a public authority which fulfils all the conditions set out in paragraph 2 of Schedule 2 to these Regulations.

(7)   The product is—

> (a)   a life insurance contract where the annual premium is no more than 1,000 euro or where a single premium of no more than 2,500 euro is paid;

> (b)   an insurance contract for the purposes of a pension scheme where the contract contains no surrender clause and cannot be used as collateral;

> (c)   a pension, superannuation or similar scheme which provides retirement benefits to employees, where contributions are made by an employer or by way of deduction from an employee's wages and the scheme rules do not permit the assignment of a member's interest under the scheme (other than an assignment permitted by section 44 of the Welfare Reform and Pensions Act 1999 (disapplication of restrictions on alienation) or section 91(5)(a) of the Pensions Act 1995 (inalienability of occupational pension)); or

> (d)   electronic money, within the meaning of Article 1(3)(b) of the electronic money directive, where—

> > (i)   if the device cannot be recharged, the maximum amount stored in the device is no more than 150 euro; or

> > (ii)   if the device can be recharged, a limit of 2,500 euro is imposed on the total amount transacted in a calendar year, except when an amount of 1,000 euro or more is redeemed in the same calendar year by the bearer (within the meaning of Article 3 of the electronic money directive).

(8)   The product and any transaction related to such product fulfils all the conditions set out in paragraph 3 of Schedule 2 to these Regulations.

(9)   The product is a child trust fund within the meaning given by section 1(2) of the Child Trust Funds Act 2004.

14   Enhanced customer due diligence and ongoing monitoring

(1)   A relevant person must apply on a risk-sensitive basis enhanced customer due diligence measures and enhanced ongoing monitoring—

> (a)   in accordance with paragraphs (2) to (4);

> (b)   in any other situation which by its nature can present a higher risk of money laundering or terrorist financing.

(2)   Where the customer has not been physically present for identification purposes, a relevant person must take specific and adequate measures to compensate for the higher risk, for example, by applying one or more of the following measures—

> (a)   ensuring that the customer's identity is established by additional documents, data or information;

> (b)   supplementary measures to verify or certify the documents supplied, or requiring confirmatory certification by a credit or financial institution which is subject to the money laundering directive;

APPENDIX 11

    (c)   ensuring that the first payment is carried out through an account opened in the customer's name with a credit institution.

(3) A credit institution ("the correspondent") which has or proposes to have a correspondent banking relationship with a respondent institution ("the respondent") from a non-EEA state must—

    (a)   gather sufficient information about the respondent to understand fully the nature of its business;

    (b)   determine from publicly-available information the reputation of the respondent and the quality of its supervision;

    (c)   assess the respondent's anti-money laundering and anti-terrorist financing controls;

    (d)   obtain approval from senior management before establishing a new correspondent banking relationship;

    (e)   document the respective responsibilities of the respondent and correspondent; and

    (f)   be satisfied that, in respect of those of the respondent's customers who have direct access to accounts of the correspondent, the respondent—

        (i)   has verified the identity of, and conducts ongoing monitoring in respect of, such customers; and

        (ii)   is able to provide to the correspondent, upon request, the documents, data or information obtained when applying customer due diligence measures and ongoing monitoring.

(4) A relevant person who proposes to have a business relationship or carry out an occasional transaction with a politically exposed person must—

    (a)   have approval from senior management for establishing the business relationship with that person;

    (b)   take adequate measures to establish the source of wealth and source of funds which are involved in the proposed business relationship or occasional transaction; and

    (c)   where the business relationship is entered into, conduct enhanced ongoing monitoring of the relationship.

(5) In paragraph (4), "a politically exposed person" means a person who is—

    (a)   an individual who is or has, at any time in the preceding year, been entrusted with a prominent public function by—

        (i)   a state other than the United Kingdom;

        (ii)   a Community institution; or

        (iii)   an international body,

    including a person who falls in any of the categories listed in paragraph 4(1)(a) of Schedule 2;

    (b)   an immediate family member of a person referred to in sub-paragraph (a), including a person who falls in any of the categories listed in paragraph 4(1)(c) of Schedule 2; or

    (c)   a known close associate of a person referred to in sub-paragraph (a), including a person who falls in either of the categories listed in paragraph 4(1)(d) of Schedule 2.

(6) For the purpose of deciding whether a person is a known close associate of a person referred to in paragraph (5)(a), a relevant person need only have regard to information which is in his possession or is publicly known.

15 Branches and subsidiaries

(1)   A credit or financial institution must require its branches and subsidiary undertakings which are located in a non–EEA state to apply, to the extent permitted by the law of that state, measures at least equivalent to those set out in these Regulations with regard to customer due diligence measures, ongoing monitoring and record-keeping.

(2)   Where the law of a non–EEA state does not permit the application of such equivalent measures by the branch or subsidiary undertaking located in that state, the credit or financial institution must—

(a)   inform its supervisory authority accordingly; and

(b)   take additional measures to handle effectively the risk of money laundering and terrorist financing.

(3)   In this regulation "subsidiary undertaking"—

(a)   except in relation to an incorporated friendly society, has the meaning given by section 1162 of the Companies Act 2006 (parent and subsidiary undertakings) and, in relation to a body corporate in or formed under the law of an EEA state other than the United Kingdom, includes an undertaking which is a subsidiary undertaking within the meaning of any rule of law in force in that state for purposes connected with implementation of the European Council Seventh Company Law Directive 83/349/EEC of 13th June 1983 on consolidated accounts;

(b)   in relation to an incorporated friendly society, means a body corporate of which the society has control within the meaning of section 13(9)(a) or (aa) of the Friendly Societies Act 1992 (control of subsidiaries and other bodies corporate).

(4)   Before the entry into force of section 1162 of the Companies Act 2006 the reference to that section in paragraph (3)(a) shall be treated as a reference to section 258 of the Companies Act 1985 (parent and subsidiary undertakings).

16 Shell banks, anonymous accounts etc

(1)   A credit institution must not enter into, or continue, a correspondent banking relationship with a shell bank.

(2)   A credit institution must take appropriate measures to ensure that it does not enter into, or continue, a corresponding banking relationship with a bank which is known to permit its accounts to be used by a shell bank.

(3)   A credit or financial institution carrying on business in the United Kingdom must not set up an anonymous account or an anonymous passbook for any new or existing customer.

(4)   As soon as reasonably practicable on or after 15th December 2007 all credit and financial institutions carrying on business in the United Kingdom must apply customer due diligence measures to, and conduct ongoing monitoring of, all anonymous accounts and passbooks in existence on that date and in any event before such accounts or passbooks are used.

(5)   A "shell bank" means a credit institution, or an institution engaged in equivalent activities, incorporated in a jurisdiction in which it has no physical presence involving meaningful decision-making and management, and which is not part of a financial conglomerate or third-country financial conglomerate.

(6)   In this regulation, "financial conglomerate" and "third-country financial conglomerate" have the meanings given by regulations 1(2) and 7(1) respectively of the Financial Conglomerates and Other Financial Groups Regulations 2004.

17 Reliance

(1)   A relevant person may rely on a person who falls within paragraph (2) (or who the relevant person has reasonable grounds to believe falls within paragraph (2)) to apply any customer due diligence measures provided that—

(a)   the other person consents to being relied on; and

(b)   notwithstanding the relevant person's reliance on the other person, the relevant person remains liable for any failure to apply such measures.

(2)   The persons are—

(a)   a credit or financial institution which is an authorised person;

(b)   a relevant person who is—

    (i)   an auditor, insolvency practitioner, external accountant, tax adviser or independent legal professional; and

    (ii)   supervised for the purposes of these Regulations by one of the bodies listed in Part 1 of Schedule 3;

(c)   a person who carries on business in another EEA state who is—

    (i)   a credit or financial institution, auditor, insolvency practitioner, external accountant, tax adviser or independent legal professional;

    (ii)   subject to mandatory professional registration recognised by law; and

    (iii)   supervised for compliance with the requirements laid down in the money laundering directive in accordance with section 2 of Chapter V of that directive; or

(d)   a person who carries on business in a non-EEA state who is—

    (i)   a credit or financial institution (or equivalent institution), auditor, insolvency practitioner, external accountant, tax adviser or independent legal professional;

    (ii)   subject to mandatory professional registration recognised by law;

    (iii)   subject to requirements equivalent to those laid down in the money laundering directive; and

    (iv)   supervised for compliance with those requirements in a manner equivalent to section 2 of Chapter V of the money laundering directive.

(3)   In paragraph (2)(c)(i) and (d)(i), "auditor" and "insolvency practitioner" includes a person situated in another EEA state or a non-EEA state who provides services equivalent to the services provided by an auditor or insolvency practitioner.

(4)   Nothing in this regulation prevents a relevant person applying customer due diligence measures by means of an outsourcing service provider or agent provided that the relevant person remains liable for any failure to apply such measures.

(5)   In this regulation, "financial institution" excludes money service businesses.

18   Directions where Financial Action Task Force applies counter-measures

The Treasury may direct any relevant person—

(a)   not to enter into a business relationship;

(b)   not to carry out an occasional transaction; or

(c)   not to proceed any further with a business relationship or occasional transaction,

with a person who is situated or incorporated in a non-EEA state to which the Financial Action Task Force has decided to apply counter-measures.

PART 3
RECORD-KEEPING, PROCEDURES AND TRAINING

19 Record-keeping

(1) Subject to paragraph (4), a relevant person must keep the records specified in paragraph (2) for at least the period specified in paragraph (3).

(2) The records are—

   (a) a copy of, or the references to, the evidence of the customer's identity obtained pursuant to regulation 7, 8, 10, 14 or 16(4);

   (b) the supporting records (consisting of the original documents or copies) in respect of a business relationship or occasional transaction which is the subject of customer due diligence measures or ongoing monitoring.

(3) The period is five years beginning on—

   (a) in the case of the records specified in paragraph (2)(a), the date on which—

      (i)   the occasional transaction is completed; or

      (ii) the business relationship ends; or

   (b) in the case of the records specified in paragraph (2)(b)—

      (i)   where the records relate to a particular transaction, the date on which the transaction is completed;

      (ii) for all other records, the date on which the business relationship ends.

(4) A relevant person who is relied on by another person must keep the records specified in paragraph (2)(a) for five years beginning on the date on which he is relied on for the purposes of regulation 7, 10, 14 or 16(4) in relation to any business relationship or occasional transaction.

(5) A person referred to in regulation 17(2)(a) or (b) who is relied on by a relevant person must, if requested by the person relying on him within the period referred to in paragraph (4)—

   (a) as soon as reasonably practicable make available to the person who is relying on him any information about the customer (and any beneficial owner) which he obtained when applying customer due diligence measures; and

   (b) as soon as reasonably practicable forward to the person who is relying on him copies of any identification and verification data and other relevant documents on the identity of the customer (and any beneficial owner) which he obtained when applying those measures.

(6) A relevant person who relies on a person referred to in regulation 17(2)(c) or (d) (a "third party") to apply customer due diligence measures must take steps to ensure that the third party will, if requested by the relevant person within the period referred to in paragraph (4)—

   (a) as soon as reasonably practicable make available to him any information about the customer (and any beneficial owner) which the third party obtained when applying customer due diligence measures; and

   (b) as soon as reasonably practicable forward to him copies of any identification and verification data and other relevant documents on the identity of the customer (and any beneficial owner) which the third party obtained when applying those measures.

(7) Paragraphs (5) and (6) do not apply where a relevant person applies customer due diligence measures by means of an outsourcing service provider or agent.

(8)   For the purposes of this regulation, a person relies on another person where he does so in accordance with regulation 17(1).

20   Policies and procedures

(1)   A relevant person must establish and maintain appropriate and risk-sensitive policies and procedures relating to—

(a)   customer due diligence measures and ongoing monitoring;

(b)   reporting;

(c)   record-keeping;

(d)   internal control;

(e)   risk assessment and management;

(f)   the monitoring and management of compliance with, and the internal communication of, such policies and procedures,

in order to prevent activities related to money laundering and terrorist financing.

(2)   The policies and procedures referred to in paragraph (1) include policies and procedures—

(a)   which provide for the identification and scrutiny of—

(i)   complex or unusually large transactions;

(ii)   unusual patterns of transactions which have no apparent economic or visible lawful purpose; and

(iii)   any other activity which the relevant person regards as particularly likely by its nature to be related to money laundering or terrorist financing;

(b)   which specify the taking of additional measures, where appropriate, to prevent the use for money laundering or terrorist financing of products and transactions which might favour anonymity;

(c)   to determine whether a customer is a politically exposed person;

(d)   under which—

(i)   an individual in the relevant person's organisation is a nominated officer under Part 7 of the Proceeds of Crime Act 2002 and Part 3 of the Terrorism Act 2000;

(ii)   anyone in the organisation to whom information or other matter comes in the course of the business as a result of which he knows or suspects or has reasonable grounds for knowing or suspecting that a person is engaged in money laundering or terrorist financing is required to comply with Part 7 of the Proceeds of Crime Act 2002 or, as the case may be, Part 3 of the Terrorism Act 2000; and

(iii)   where a disclosure is made to the nominated officer, he must consider it in the light of any relevant information which is available to the relevant person and determine whether it gives rise to knowledge or suspicion or reasonable grounds for knowledge or suspicion that a person is engaged in money laundering or terrorist financing.

(3)   Paragraph (2)(d) does not apply where the relevant person is an individual who neither employs nor acts in association with any other person.

(4)   A credit or financial institution must establish and maintain systems which enable it to respond fully and rapidly to enquiries from financial investigators accredited under section 3 of

the Proceeds of Crime Act 2002 (accreditation and training), persons acting on behalf of the Scottish Ministers in their capacity as an enforcement authority under that Act, officers of Revenue and Customs or constables as to—

(a) whether it maintains, or has maintained during the previous five years, a business relationship with any person; and

(b) the nature of that relationship.

(5) A credit or financial institution must communicate where relevant the policies and procedures which it establishes and maintains in accordance with this regulation to its branches and subsidiary undertakings which are located outside the United Kingdom.

(6) In this regulation—

"politically exposed person" has the same meaning as in regulation 14(4);

"subsidiary undertaking" has the same meaning as in regulation 15.

21 Training

A relevant person must take appropriate measures so that all relevant employees of his are—

(a) made aware of the law relating to money laundering and terrorist financing; and

(b) regularly given training in how to recognise and deal with transactions and other activities which may be related to money laundering or terrorist financing.

PART 4
SUPERVISION AND REGISTRATION

Interpretation

22 Interpretation

(1) In this Part—

"Annex I financial institution" means any undertaking which falls within regulation 3(3)(a) other than—

(a) a consumer credit financial institution;

(b) a money service business; or

(c) an authorised person;

"consumer credit financial institution" means any undertaking which falls within regulation 3(3)(a) and which requires, under section 21 of the Consumer Credit Act 1974 (businesses needing a licence), a licence to carry on a consumer credit business, other than—

(a) a person covered by a group licence issued by the OFT under section 22 of that Act (standard and group licences);

(b) a money service business; or

(c) an authorised person.

(2) In paragraph (1), "consumer credit business" has the meaning given by section 189(1) of the Consumer Credit Act 1974 (definitions) and, on the entry into force of section 23(a) of the Consumer Credit Act 2006 (definitions of "consumer credit business" and "consumer hire business"), has the meaning given by section 189(1) of the Consumer Credit Act 1974 as amended by section 23(a) of the Consumer Credit Act 2006.

Supervision

23 Supervisory authorities

(1) Subject to paragraph (2), the following bodies are supervisory authorities—

 (a) the Authority is the supervisory authority for—

  (i) credit and financial institutions which are authorised persons;

  (ii) trust or company service providers which are authorised persons;

  (iii) Annex I financial institutions;

 (b) the OFT is the supervisory authority for—

  (i) consumer credit financial institutions;

  (ii) estate agents;

 (c) each of the professional bodies listed in Schedule 3 is the supervisory authority for relevant persons who are regulated by it;

 (d) the Commissioners are the supervisory authority for—

  (i) high value dealers;

  (ii) money service businesses which are not supervised by the Authority;

  (iii) trust or company service providers which are not supervised by the Authority or one of the bodies listed in Schedule 3;

  (iv) auditors, external accountants and tax advisers who are not supervised by one of the bodies listed in Schedule 3.

 (e) the Gambling Commission is the supervisory authority for casinos;

 (f) DETI is the supervisory authority for—

  (i) credit unions in Northern Ireland;

  (ii) insolvency practitioners authorised by it under article 351 of the Insolvency (Northern Ireland) Order 1989;

 (g) the Secretary of State is the supervisory authority for insolvency practitioners authorised by him under section 393 of the Insolvency Act 1986 (grant, refusal and withdrawal of authorisation).

(2) Where under paragraph (1) there is more than one supervisory authority for a relevant person, the supervisory authorities may agree that one of them will act as the supervisory authority for that person.

(3) Where an agreement has been made under paragraph (2), the authority which has agreed to act as the supervisory authority must notify the relevant person or publish the agreement in such manner as it considers appropriate.

(4) Where no agreement has been made under paragraph (2), the supervisory authorities for a relevant person must cooperate in the performance of their functions under these Regulations.

24 Duties of supervisory authorities

(1) A supervisory authority must effectively monitor the relevant persons for whom it is the supervisory authority and take necessary measures for the purpose of securing compliance by such persons with the requirements of these Regulations.

(2)   A supervisory authority which, in the course of carrying out any of its functions under these Regulations, knows or suspects that a person is or has engaged in money laundering or terrorist financing must promptly inform the Serious Organised Crime Agency.

(3)   A disclosure made under paragraph (2) is not to be taken to breach any restriction, however imposed, on the disclosure of information.

(4)   The functions of the Authority under these Regulations shall be treated for the purposes of Parts 1, 2 and 4 of Schedule 1 to the 2000 Act (the Financial Services Authority) as functions conferred on the Authority under that Act.

Registration of high value dealers, money service businesses and trust or company service providers

25   Duty to maintain registers

(1)   The Commissioners must maintain registers of—

   (a)   high value dealers;

   (b)   money service businesses for which they are the supervisory authority; and

   (c)   trust or company service providers for which they are the supervisory authority.

(2)   The Commissioners may keep the registers in any form they think fit.

(3)   The Commissioners may publish or make available for public inspection all or part of a register maintained under this regulation.

26   Requirement to be registered

(1)   A person in respect of whom the Commissioners are required to maintain a register under regulation 25 must not act as a—

   (a)   high value dealer;

   (b)   money service business; or

   (c)   trust or company service provider,

unless he is included in the register.

(2)   Paragraph (1) and regulation 29 are subject to the transitional provisions set out in regulation 50.

27   Applications for registration in a register maintained under regulation 25

(1)   An applicant for registration in a register maintained under regulation 25 must make an application in such manner and provide such information as the Commissioners may specify.

(2)   The information which the Commissioners may specify includes—

   (a)   the applicant's name and (if different) the name of the business;

   (b)   the nature of the business;

   (c)   the name of the nominated officer (if any);

   (d)   in relation to a money service business or trust or company service provider—

      (i)   the name of any person who effectively directs or will direct the business and any beneficial owner of the business; and

      (ii)   information needed by the Commissioners to decide whether they must refuse the application pursuant to regulation 28.

(3)   At any time after receiving an application and before determining it, the Commissioners may require the applicant to provide, within 21 days beginning with the date of being requested to do so, such further information as they reasonably consider necessary to enable them to determine the application.

(4)   If at any time after the applicant has provided the Commissioners with any information under paragraph (1) or (3)—

(a)   there is a material change affecting any matter contained in that information; or

(b)   it becomes apparent to that person that the information contains a significant inaccuracy,

he must provide the Commissioners with details of the change or, as the case may be, a correction of the inaccuracy within 30 days beginning with the date of the occurrence of the change (or the discovery of the inaccuracy) or within such later time as may be agreed with the Commissioners.

(5)   The obligation in paragraph (4) applies also to material changes or significant inaccuracies affecting any matter contained in any supplementary information provided pursuant to that paragraph.

(6)   Any information to be provided to the Commissioners under this regulation must be in such form or verified in such manner as they may specify.

28   Fit and proper test

(1)   The Commissioners must refuse to register an applicant as a money service business or trust or company service provider if they are satisfied that—

(a)   the applicant;

(b)   a person who effectively directs, or will effectively direct, the business or service provider;

(c)   a beneficial owner of the business or service provider; or

(d)   the nominated officer of the business or service provider,

is not a fit and proper person.

(2)   For the purposes of paragraph (1), a person is not a fit and proper person if he—

(a)   has been convicted of—

(i)   an offence under the Terrorism Act 2000;

(ii)   an offence under paragraph 7(2) or (3) of Schedule 3 to the Anti-Terrorism, Crime and Security Act 2001 (offences);

(iii) an offence under the Terrorism Act 2006;

(iv)   an offence under Part 7 (money laundering) of, or listed in Schedule 2 (lifestyle offences: England and Wales), 4 (lifestyle offences: Scotland) or 5 (lifestyle offences: Northern Ireland) to, the Proceeds of Crime Act 2002;

(v)   an offence under the Fraud Act 2006 or, in Scotland, the common law offence of fraud;

(vi)   an offence under section 72(1), (3) or (8) of the Value Added Tax Act 1994 (offences); or

(vii) the common law offence of cheating the public revenue;

(b)   has been adjudged bankrupt or sequestration of his estate has been awarded and (in either case) he has not been discharged;

(c)   is subject to a disqualification order under the Company Directors Disqualification Act 1986;

(d)   is or has been subject to a confiscation order under the Proceeds of Crime Act 2002;

(e)   has consistently failed to comply with the requirements of these Regulations, the Money Laundering Regulations 2003 or the Money Laundering Regulations 2001;

(f)   has consistently failed to comply with the requirements of regulation 2006/1781/EC of the European Parliament and of the Council of 15th November 2006 on information on the payer accompanying the transfer of funds;

(g)   has effectively directed a business which falls within sub-paragraph (e) or (f);

(h)   is otherwise not a fit and proper person with regard to the risk of money laundering or terrorist financing.

(3)   For the purposes of this regulation, a conviction for an offence listed in paragraph (2)(a) is to be disregarded if it is spent for the purposes of the Rehabilitation of Offenders Act 1974.

29   Determination of applications under regulation 27

(1)   Subject to regulation 28, the Commissioners may refuse to register an applicant for registration in a register maintained under regulation 25 only if—

(a)   any requirement of, or imposed under, regulation 27 has not been complied with;

(b)   it appears to the Commissioners that any information provided pursuant to regulation 27 is false or misleading in a material particular; or

(c)   the applicant has failed to pay a charge imposed by them under regulation 35(1).

(2)   The Commissioners must within 45 days beginning either with the date on which they receive the application or, where applicable, with the date on which they receive any further information required under regulation 27(3), give the applicant notice of—

(a)   their decision to register the applicant; or

(b)   the following matters—

   (i)   their decision not to register the applicant;

   (ii)   the reasons for their decision;

   (iii)   the right to require a review under regulation 43; and

   (iv)   the right to appeal under regulation 44(1)(a).

(3)   The Commissioners must, as soon as practicable after deciding to register a person, include him in the relevant register.

30   Cancellation of registration in a register maintained under regulation 25

(1)   The Commissioners must cancel the registration of a money service business or trust or company service provider in a register maintained under regulation 25(1) if, at any time after registration, they are satisfied that he or any person mentioned in regulation 28(1)(b), (c) or (d) is not a fit and proper person within the meaning of regulation 28(2).

(2)   The Commissioners may cancel a person's registration in a register maintained by them under regulation 25 if, at any time after registration, it appears to them that they would have had grounds to refuse registration under regulation 29(1).

(3)   Where the Commissioners decide to cancel a person's registration they must give him notice of—

(a)   their decision and, subject to paragraph (4), the date from which the cancellation takes effect;

(b)   the reasons for their decision;

(c)   the right to require a review under regulation 43; and

(d)   the right to appeal under regulation 44(1)(a).

(4)   If the Commissioners—

(a)   consider that the interests of the public require the cancellation of a person's registration to have immediate effect; and

(b)   include a statement to that effect and the reasons for it in the notice given under paragraph (3),

the cancellation takes effect when the notice is given to the person.

Requirement to inform the authority

31   Requirement on authorised person to inform the Authority

(1)   An authorised person whose supervisory authority is the Authority must, before acting as a money service business or a trust or company service provider or within 28 days of so doing, inform the Authority that he intends, or has begun, to act as such.

(2)   Paragraph (1) does not apply to an authorised person who—

(a)   immediately before 15th December 2007 was acting as a money service business or a trust or company service provider and continues to act as such after that date; and

(b)   before 15th January 2008 informs the Authority that he is or was acting as such.

(3)   Where an authorised person whose supervisory authority is the Authority ceases to act as a money service business or a trust or company service provider, he must immediately inform the Authority.

(4)   Any requirement imposed by this regulation is to be treated as if it were a requirement imposed by or under the 2000 Act.

(5)   Any information to be provided to the Authority under this regulation must be in such form or verified in such manner as it may specify.

Registration of Annex I financial institutions, estate agents etc

32   Power to maintain registers

(1)   The supervisory authorities mentioned in paragraph (2), (3) or (4) may, in order to fulfil their duties under regulation 24, maintain a register under this regulation.

(2)   The Authority may maintain a register of Annex I financial institutions.

(3)   The OFT may maintain registers of—

(a)   consumer credit financial institutions; and

(b)   estate agents.

(4)   The Commissioners may maintain registers of—

(a)   auditors;

(b)   external accountants; and

(c)   tax advisers,

who are not supervised by the Secretary of State, DETI or any of the professional bodies listed in Schedule 3.

(5) Where a supervisory authority decides to maintain a register under this regulation, it must take reasonable steps to bring its decision to the attention of those relevant persons in respect of whom the register is to be established.

(6) A supervisory authority may keep a register under this regulation in any form it thinks fit.

(7) A supervisory authority may publish or make available to public inspection all or part of a register maintained by it under this regulation.

33 Requirement to be registered

Where a supervisory authority decides to maintain a register under regulation 32 in respect of any description of relevant persons and establishes a register for that purpose, a relevant person of that description may not carry on the business or profession in question for a period of more than six months beginning on the date on which the supervisory authority establishes the register unless he is included in the register.

34 Applications for and cancellation of registration in a register maintained under regulation 32

(1) Regulations 27, 29 (with the omission of the words "Subject to regulation 28" in regulation 29(1)) and 30(2), (3) and (4) apply to registration in a register maintained by the Commissioners under regulation 32 as they apply to registration in a register maintained under regulation 25.

(2) Regulation 27 applies to registration in a register maintained by the Authority or the OFT under regulation 32 as it applies to registration in a register maintained under regulation 25 and, for this purpose, references to the Commissioners are to be treated as references to the Authority or the OFT, as the case may be.

(3) The Authority and the OFT may refuse to register an applicant for registration in a register maintained under regulation 32 only if—

  (a)   any requirement of, or imposed under, regulation 27 has not been complied with;

  (b)   it appears to the Authority or the OFT, as the case may be, that any information provided pursuant to regulation 27 is false or misleading in a material particular; or

  (c)   the applicant has failed to pay a charge imposed by the Authority or the OFT, as the case may be, under regulation 35(1).

(4) The Authority or the OFT, as the case may be, must, within 45 days beginning either with the date on which it receives an application or, where applicable, with the date on which it receives any further information required under regulation 27(3), give the applicant notice of—

  (a)   its decision to register the applicant; or

  (b)   the following matters—

      (i)   that it is minded not to register the applicant;

      (ii)   the reasons for being minded not to register him; and

      (iii)   the right to make representations to it within a specified period (which may not be less than 28 days).

(5) The Authority or the OFT, as the case may be, must then decide, within a reasonable period, whether to register the applicant and it must give the applicant notice of—

  (a)   its decision to register the applicant; or

  (b)   the following matters—

      (i)   its decision not to register the applicant;

    (ii)   the reasons for its decision; and

    (iii)   the right to appeal under regulation 44(1)(b).

(6)   The Authority or the OFT, as the case may be, must, as soon as reasonably practicable after deciding to register a person, include him in the relevant register.

(7)   The Authority or the OFT may cancel a person's registration in a register maintained by them under regulation 32 if, at any time after registration, it appears to them that they would have had grounds to refuse registration under paragraph (3).

(8)   Where the Authority or the OFT proposes to cancel a person's registration, it must give him notice of—

    (a)   its proposal to cancel his registration;

    (b)   the reasons for the proposed cancellation; and

    (c)   the right to make representations to it within a specified period (which may not be less than 28 days).

(9)   The Authority or the OFT, as the case may be, must then decide, within a reasonable period, whether to cancel the person's registration and it must give him notice of—

    (a)   its decision not to cancel his registration; or

    (b)   the following matters—

        (i)   its decision to cancel his registration and, subject to paragraph (10), the date from which cancellation takes effect;

        (ii)   the reasons for its decision; and

        (iii)   the right to appeal under regulation 44(1)(b).

(10)   If the Authority or the OFT, as the case may be—

    (a)   considers that the interests of the public require the cancellation of a person's registration to have immediate effect; and

    (b)   includes a statement to that effect and the reasons for it in the notice given under paragraph (9)(b),

the cancellation takes effect when the notice is given to the person.

(11)   In paragraphs (3) and (4), references to regulation 27 are to be treated as references to that paragraph as applied by paragraph (2) of this regulation.

Financial provisions

35 Costs of supervision

(1)   The Authority, the OFT and the Commissioners may impose charges—

    (a)   on applicants for registration;

    (b)   on relevant persons supervised by them.

(2)   Charges levied under paragraph (1) must not exceed such amount as the Authority, the OFT or the Commissioners (as the case may be) consider will enable them to meet any expenses reasonably incurred by them in carrying out their functions under these Regulations or for any incidental purpose.

(3)   Without prejudice to the generality of paragraph (2), a charge may be levied in respect of each of the premises at which a person carries on (or proposes to carry on) business.

(4) The Authority must apply amounts paid to it by way of penalties imposed under regulation 42 towards expenses incurred in carrying out its functions under these Regulations or for any incidental purpose.

(5) In paragraph (2), "expenses" in relation to the OFT includes expenses incurred by a local weights and measures authority or DETI pursuant to arrangements made for the purposes of these Regulations with the OFT—

(a)   by or on behalf of the authority; or

(b)   by DETI.

PART 5
ENFORCEMENT

Powers of designated authorities

36   Interpretation

In this Part—

"designated authority" means—

(a)   the Authority;

(b)   the Commissioners;

(c)   the OFT; and

(d)   in relation to credit unions in Northern Ireland, DETI;

"officer", except in regulations 40(3), 41 and 47 means—

(a)   an officer of the Authority, including a member of the Authority's staff or an agent of the Authority;

(b)   an officer of Revenue and Customs;

(c)   an officer of the OFT;

(d)   a relevant officer; or

(e)   an officer of DETI acting for the purposes of its functions under these Regulations in relation to credit unions in Northern Ireland;

"recorded information" includes information recorded in any form and any document of any nature;

"relevant officer" means—

(a)   in Great Britain, an officer of a local weights and measures authority;

(b)   in Northern Ireland, an officer of DETI acting pursuant to arrangements made with the OFT for the purposes of these Regulations.

37   Power to require information from, and attendance of, relevant and connected persons

(1) An officer may, by notice to a relevant person or to a person connected with a relevant person, require the relevant person or the connected person, as the case may be—

(a)   to provide such information as may be specified in the notice;

(b)   to produce such recorded information as may be so specified; or

(c)   to attend before an officer at a time and place specified in the notice and answer questions.

APPENDIX 11

(2)   For the purposes of paragraph (1), a person is connected with a relevant person if he is, or has at any time been, in relation to the relevant person, a person listed in Schedule 4 to these Regulations.

(3)   An officer may exercise powers under this regulation only if the information sought to be obtained as a result is reasonably required in connection with the exercise by the designated authority for whom he acts of its functions under these Regulations.

(4)   Where an officer requires information to be provided or produced pursuant to paragraph (1)(a) or (b)—

> (a)   the notice must set out the reasons why the officer requires the information to be provided or produced; and
>
> (b)   such information must be provided or produced—
>
> > (i)   before the end of such reasonable period as may be specified in the notice; and
> >
> > (ii)   at such place as may be so specified.

(5)   In relation to information recorded otherwise than in legible form, the power to require production of it includes a power to require the production of a copy of it in legible form or in a form from which it can readily be produced in visible and legible form.

(6)   The production of a document does not affect any lien which a person has on the document.

(7)   A person may not be required under this regulation to provide or produce information or to answer questions which he would be entitled to refuse to provide, produce or answer on grounds of legal professional privilege in proceedings in the High Court, except that a lawyer may be required to provide the name and address of his client.

(8)   Subject to paragraphs (9) and (10), a statement made by a person in compliance with a requirement imposed on him under paragraph (1)(c) is admissible in evidence in any proceedings, so long as it also complies with any requirements governing the admissibility of evidence in the circumstances in question.

(9)   In criminal proceedings in which a person is charged with an offence to which this paragraph applies—

> (a)   no evidence relating to the statement may be adduced; and
>
> (b)   no question relating to it may be asked,

by or on behalf of the prosecution unless evidence relating to it is adduced, or a question relating to it is asked, in the proceedings by or on behalf of that person.

(10)   Paragraph (9) applies to any offence other than one under—

> (a)   section 5 of the Perjury Act 1911 (false statements without oath);
>
> (b)   section 44(2) of the Criminal Law (Consolidation) (Scotland) Act 1995 (false statements and declarations); or
>
> (c)   Article 10 of the Perjury (Northern Ireland) Order 1979 (false unsworn statements).

(11)   In the application of this regulation to Scotland, the reference in paragraph (7) to—

> (a)   proceedings in the High Court is to be read as a reference to legal proceedings generally; and
>
> (b)   an entitlement on grounds of legal professional privilege is to be read as a reference to an entitlement on the grounds of confidentiality of communications—
>
> > (i)   between a professional legal adviser and his client; or

(ii)   made in connection with or in contemplation of legal proceedings and for the purposes of those proceedings.

38   Entry, inspection without a warrant etc

(1)   Where an officer has reasonable cause to believe that any premises are being used by a relevant person in connection with his business or professional activities, he may on producing evidence of his authority at any reasonable time—

(a)   enter the premises;

(b)   inspect the premises;

(c)   observe the carrying on of business or professional activities by the relevant person;

(d)   inspect any recorded information found on the premises;

(e)   require any person on the premises to provide an explanation of any recorded information or to state where it may be found;

(f)   in the case of a money service business or a high value dealer, inspect any cash found on the premises.

(2)   An officer may take copies of, or make extracts from, any recorded information found under paragraph (1).

(3)   Paragraphs (1)(d) and (e) and (2) do not apply to recorded information which the relevant person would be entitled to refuse to disclose on grounds of legal professional privilege in proceedings in the High Court, except that a lawyer may be required to provide the name and address of his client and, for this purpose, regulation 37(11) applies to this paragraph as it applies to regulation 37(7).

(4)   An officer may exercise powers under this regulation only if the information sought to be obtained as a result is reasonably required in connection with the exercise by the designated authority for whom he acts of its functions under these Regulations.

(5)   In this regulation, "premises" means any premises other than premises used only as a dwelling.

39   Entry to premises under warrant

(1)   A justice may issue a warrant under this paragraph if satisfied on information on oath given by an officer that there are reasonable grounds for believing that the first, second or third set of conditions is satisfied.

(2)   The first set of conditions is—

(a)   that there is on the premises specified in the warrant recorded information in relation to which a requirement could be imposed under regulation 37(1)(b); and

(b)   that if such a requirement were to be imposed—

(i)   it would not be complied with; or

(ii)   the recorded information to which it relates would be removed, tampered with or destroyed.

(3)   The second set of conditions is—

(a)   that a person on whom a requirement has been imposed under regulation 37(1)(b) has failed (wholly or in part) to comply with it; and

(b)   that there is on the premises specified in the warrant recorded information which has been required to be produced.

(4)   The third set of conditions is—

APPENDIX 11

(a) that an officer has been obstructed in the exercise of a power under regulation 38; and

(b) that there is on the premises specified in the warrant recorded information or cash which could be inspected under regulation 38(1)(d) or (f).

(5) A justice may issue a warrant under this paragraph if satisfied on information on oath given by an officer that there are reasonable grounds for suspecting that—

(a) an offence under these Regulations has been, is being or is about to be committed by a relevant person; and

(b) there is on the premises specified in the warrant recorded information relevant to whether that offence has been, or is being or is about to be committed.

(6) A warrant issued under this regulation shall authorise an officer—

(a) to enter the premises specified in the warrant;

(b) to search the premises and take possession of any recorded information or anything appearing to be recorded information specified in the warrant or to take, in relation to any such recorded information, any other steps which may appear to be necessary for preserving it or preventing interference with it;

(c) to take copies of, or extracts from, any recorded information specified in the warrant;

(d) to require any person on the premises to provide an explanation of any recorded information appearing to be of the kind specified in the warrant or to state where it may be found;

(e) to use such force as may reasonably be necessary.

(7) Where a warrant is issued by a justice under paragraph (1) or (5) on the basis of information on oath given by an officer of the Authority, for "an officer" in paragraph (6) substitute "a constable".

(8) In paragraphs (1), (5) and (7), "justice" means—

(a) in relation to England and Wales, a justice of the peace;

(b) in relation to Scotland, a justice within the meaning of section 307 of the Criminal Procedure (Scotland) Act 1995 (interpretation);

(c) in relation to Northern Ireland, a lay magistrate.

(9) In the application of this regulation to Scotland, the references in paragraphs (1), (5) and (7) to information on oath are to be read as references to evidence on oath.

40 Failure to comply with information requirement

(1) If, on an application made by—

(a) a designated authority; or

(b) a local weights and measures authority or DETI pursuant to arrangements made with the OFT—

(i) by or on behalf of the authority; or

(ii) by DETI,

it appears to the court that a person (the "information defaulter") has failed to do something that he was required to do under regulation 37(1), the court may make an order under this regulation.

(2) An order under this regulation may require the information defaulter—

(a) to do the thing that he failed to do within such period as may be specified in the order;

(b) otherwise to take such steps to remedy the consequences of the failure as may be so specified.

(3) If the information defaulter is a body corporate, a partnership or an unincorporated body of persons which is not a partnership, the order may require any officer of the body corporate, partnership or body, who is (wholly or partly) responsible for the failure to meet such costs of the application as are specified in the order.

(4) In this regulation, "court" means—

(a) in England and Wales and Northern Ireland, the High Court or the county court;

(b) in Scotland, the Court of Session or the sheriff court.

41 Powers of relevant officers

(1) A relevant officer may only exercise powers under regulations 37 to 39 pursuant to arrangements made with the OFT—

(a) by or on behalf of the local weights and measures authority of which he is an officer ("his authority"); or

(b) by DETI.

(2) Anything done or omitted to be done by, or in relation to, a relevant officer in the exercise or purported exercise of a power in this Part shall be treated for all purposes as having been done or omitted to be done by, or in relation to, an officer of the OFT.

(3) Paragraph (2) does not apply for the purposes of any criminal proceedings brought against the relevant officer, his authority, DETI or the OFT, in respect of anything done or omitted to be done by the officer.

(4) A relevant officer shall not disclose to any person other than the OFT and his authority or, as the case may be, DETI information obtained by him in the exercise of such powers unless—

(a) he has the approval of the OFT to do so; or

(b) he is under a duty to make the disclosure.

Civil penalties, review and appeals

42 Power to impose civil penalties

(1) A designated authority may impose a penalty of such amount as it considers appropriate on a relevant person who fails to comply with any requirement in regulation 7(1), (2) or (3), 8(1) or (3), 9(2), 10(1), 11(1), 14(1), 15(1) or (2), 16(1), (2), (3) or (4), 19(1), (4), (5) or (6), 20(1), (4) or (5), 21, 26, 27(4) or 33 or a direction made under regulation 18 and, for this purpose, "appropriate" means effective, proportionate and dissuasive.

(2) The designated authority must not impose a penalty on a person under paragraph (1) where there are reasonable grounds for it to be satisfied that the person took all reasonable steps and exercised all due diligence to ensure that the requirement would be complied with.

(3) In deciding whether a person has failed to comply with a requirement of these Regulations, the designated authority must consider whether he followed any relevant guidance which was at the time—

(a) issued by a supervisory authority or any other appropriate body;

(b) approved by the Treasury; and

(c)   published in a manner approved by the Treasury as suitable in their opinion to bring the guidance to the attention of persons likely to be affected by it.

(4) In paragraph (3), an "appropriate body" means any body which regulates or is representative of any trade, profession, business or employment carried on by the person.

(5) Where the Commissioners decide to impose a penalty under this regulation, they must give the person notice of—

(a)   their decision to impose the penalty and its amount;

(b)   the reasons for imposing the penalty;

(c)   the right to a review under regulation 43; and

(d)   the right to appeal under regulation 44(1)(a).

(6) Where the Authority, the OFT or DETI proposes to impose a penalty under this regulation, it must give the person notice of—

(a)   its proposal to impose the penalty and the proposed amount;

(b)   the reasons for imposing the penalty; and

(c)   the right to make representations to it within a specified period (which may not be less than 28 days).

(7) The Authority, the OFT or DETI, as the case may be, must then decide, within a reasonable period, whether to impose a penalty under this regulation and it must give the person notice of—

(a)   its decision not to impose a penalty; or

(b)   the following matters—

    (i)   its decision to impose a penalty and the amount;

    (ii)   the reasons for its decision; and

    (iii)   the right to appeal under regulation 44(1)(b).

(8) A penalty imposed under this regulation is payable to the designated authority which imposes it.

43   Review procedure

(1)   This regulation applies to decisions of the Commissioners made under—

(a)   regulation 29, to refuse to register an applicant;

(b)   regulation 30, to cancel the registration of a registered person; and

(c)   regulation 42, to impose a penalty.

(2)   Any person who is the subject of a decision to which this regulation applies may by notice to the Commissioners require them to review that decision.

(3)   The Commissioners need not review any decision unless the notice requiring the review is given within 45 days beginning with the date on which they first gave notice of the decision to the person requiring the review.

(4)   Where the Commissioners are required under this regulation to review any decision they must either—

(a)   confirm the decision; or

(b)   withdraw or vary the decision and take such further steps (if any) in consequence of the withdrawal or variation as they consider appropriate.

(5)   Where the Commissioners do not, within 45 days beginning with the date on which the review was required by a person, give notice to that person of their determination of the review, they are to be taken for the purposes of these Regulations to have confirmed the decision.

44   Appeals

(1)   A person may appeal from a decision by—

    (a)   the Commissioners on a review under regulation 43; and

    (b)   the Authority, the OFT or DETI under regulation 34 or 42.

(2)   An appeal from a decision by—

    (a)   the Commissioners is to a VAT and duties tribunal;

    (b)   the Authority is to the Financial Services and Markets Tribunal;

    (c)   the OFT is to the Consumer Credit Appeals Tribunal; and

    (d)   DETI is to the High Court.

(3)   The provisions of Part 5 of the Value Added Tax Act 1994 (appeals), subject to the modifications set out in paragraph 1 of Schedule 5, apply in respect of appeals to a VAT and duties tribunal made under this regulation as they apply in respect of appeals made to such a tribunal under section 83 (appeals) of that Act.

(4)   The provisions of Part 9 of the 2000 Act (hearings and appeals), subject to the modifications set out in paragraph 2 of Schedule 5, apply in respect of appeals to the Financial Services and Markets Tribunal made under this regulation as they apply in respect of references made to that Tribunal under that Act.

(5)   Sections 40A (the Consumer Credit Appeals Tribunal), 41 (appeals to the Secretary of State under Part 3) and 41A (appeals from the Consumer Credit Appeals Tribunal) of the Consumer Credit Act 1974 apply in respect of appeals to the Consumer Credit Appeal Tribunal made under this regulation as they apply in respect of appeals made to that Tribunal under section 41 of that Act.

(6)   A VAT and duties tribunal hearing an appeal under paragraph (2) has the power to—

    (a)   quash or vary any decision of the supervisory authority, including the power to reduce any penalty to such amount (including nil) as they think proper; and

    (b)   substitute their own decision for any decision quashed on appeal.

(7)   Notwithstanding paragraph (2)(c), until the coming into force of section 55 of the Consumer Credit Act 2006 (the Consumer Credit Appeals Tribunal), an appeal from a decision by the OFT is to the Financial Services and Markets Tribunal and, for these purposes, the coming into force of that section shall not affect—

    (a)   the hearing and determination by the Financial Service and Markets Tribunal of an appeal commenced before the coming into force of that section ("the original appeal"); or

    (b)   any appeal against the decision of the Financial Services and Markets Tribunal with respect to the original appeal.

(8)   The modifications in Schedule 5 have effect for the purposes of appeals made under this regulation.

Criminal offences

45 Offences

(1) A person who fails to comply with any requirement in regulation 7(1), (2) or (3), 8(1) or (3), 9(2), 10(1), 11(1)(a), (b) or (c), 14(1), 15(1) or (2), 16(1), (2), (3) or (4), 19(1), (4), (5) or (6), 20(1), (4) or (5), 21, 26, 27(4) or 33, or a direction made under regulation 18, is guilty of an offence and liable—

    (a)   on summary conviction, to a fine not exceeding the statutory maximum;

    (b)   on conviction on indictment, to imprisonment for a term not exceeding two years, to a fine or to both.

(2) In deciding whether a person has committed an offence under paragraph (1), the court must consider whether he followed any relevant guidance which was at the time—

    (a)   issued by a supervisory authority or any other appropriate body;

    (b)   approved by the Treasury; and

    (c)   published in a manner approved by the Treasury as suitable in their opinion to bring the guidance to the attention of persons likely to be affected by it.

(3) In paragraph (2), an "appropriate body" means any body which regulates or is representative of any trade, profession, business or employment carried on by the alleged offender.

(4) A person is not guilty of an offence under this regulation if he took all reasonable steps and exercised all due diligence to avoid committing the offence.

(5) Where a person is convicted of an offence under this regulation, he shall not also be liable to a penalty under regulation 42.

46 Prosecution of offences

(1) Proceedings for an offence under regulation 45 may be instituted by—

    (a)   the Director of Revenue and Customs Prosecutions or by order of the Commissioners;

    (b)   the OFT;

    (c)   a local weights and measures authority;

    (d)   DETI;

    (e)   the Director of Public Prosecutions; or

    (f)   the Director of Public Prosecutions for Northern Ireland.

(2) Proceedings for an offence under regulation 45 may be instituted only against a relevant person or, where such a person is a body corporate, a partnership or an unincorporated association, against any person who is liable to be proceeded against under regulation 47.

(3) Where proceedings under paragraph (1) are instituted by order of the Commissioners, the proceedings must be brought in the name of an officer of Revenue and Customs.

(4) Where a local weights and measures authority in England or Wales proposes to institute proceedings for an offence under regulation 45 it must give the OFT notice of the intended proceedings, together with a summary of the facts on which the charges are to be founded.

(5) A local weights and measures authority must also notify the OFT of the outcome of the proceedings after they are finally determined.

(6)   A local weights and measures authority must, whenever the OFT requires, report in such form and with such particulars as the OFT requires on the exercise of its functions under these Regulations.

(7)   Where the Commissioners investigate, or propose to investigate, any matter with a view to determining—

(a)   whether there are grounds for believing that an offence under regulation 45 has been committed by any person; or

(b)   whether such a person should be prosecuted for such an offence,

that matter is to be treated as an assigned matter within the meaning of section 1(1) of the Customs and Excise Management Act 1979.

(8)   Paragraphs (1) and (3) to (6) do not extend to Scotland.

(9)   In its application to the Commissioners acting in Scotland, paragraph (7)(b) shall be read as referring to the Commissioners determining whether to refer the matter to the Crown Office and Procurator Fiscal Service with a view to the Procurator Fiscal determining whether a person should be prosecuted for such an offence.

47   Offences by bodies corporate etc

(1)   If an offence under regulation 45 committed by a body corporate is shown—

(a)   to have been committed with the consent or the connivance of an officer of the body corporate; or

(b)   to be attributable to any neglect on his part,

the officer as well as the body corporate is guilty of an offence and liable to be proceeded against and punished accordingly.

(2)   If an offence under regulation 45 committed by a partnership is shown—

(a)   to have been committed with the consent or the connivance of a partner; or

(b)   to be attributable to any neglect on his part,

the partner as well as the partnership is guilty of an offence and liable to be proceeded against and punished accordingly.

(3)   If an offence under regulation 45 committed by an unincorporated association (other than a partnership) is shown—

(a)   to have been committed with the consent or the connivance of an officer of the association; or

(b)   to be attributable to any neglect on his part,

that officer as well as the association is guilty of an offence and liable to be proceeded against and punished accordingly.

(4)   If the affairs of a body corporate are managed by its members, paragraph (1) applies in relation to the acts and defaults of a member in connection with his functions of management as if he were a director of the body.

(5)   Proceedings for an offence alleged to have been committed by a partnership or an unincorporated association must be brought in the name of the partnership or association (and not in that of its members).

(6)   A fine imposed on the partnership or association on its conviction of an offence is to be paid out of the funds of the partnership or association.

(7)   Rules of court relating to the service of documents are to have effect as if the partnership or association were a body corporate.

(8)   In proceedings for an offence brought against the partnership or association—

(a)   section 33 of the Criminal Justice Act 1925 (procedure on charge of offence against corporation) and Schedule 3 to the Magistrates' Courts Act 1980 (corporations) apply as they do in relation to a body corporate;

(b)   section 70 (proceedings against bodies corporate) of the Criminal Procedure (Scotland) Act 1995 applies as it does in relation to a body corporate;

(c)   section 18 of the Criminal Justice (Northern Ireland) Act 1945 (procedure on charge) and Schedule 4 to the Magistrates' Courts (Northern Ireland) Order 1981 (corporations) apply as they do in relation to a body corporate.

(9)   In this regulation—

"officer"—

(a)   in relation to a body corporate, means a director, manager, secretary, chief executive, member of the committee of management, or a person purporting to act in such a capacity; and

(b)   in relation to an unincorporated association, means any officer of the association or any member of its governing body, or a person purporting to act in such capacity; and

"partner" includes a person purporting to act as a partner.

PART 6
MISCELLANEOUS

48   Recovery of charges and penalties through the court

Any charge or penalty imposed on a person by a supervisory authority under regulation 35(1) or 42(1) is a debt due from that person to the authority, and is recoverable accordingly.

49   Obligations on public authorities

(1)   The following bodies and persons must, if they know or suspect or have reasonable grounds for knowing or suspecting that a person is or has engaged in money laundering or terrorist financing, as soon as reasonably practicable inform the Serious Organised Crime Agency—

(a)   the Auditor General for Scotland;

(b)   the Auditor General for Wales;

(c)   the Authority;

(d)   the Bank of England;

(e)   the Comptroller and Auditor General;

(f)   the Comptroller and Auditor General for Northern Ireland;

(g)   the Gambling Commission;

(h)   the OFT;

(i)   the Official Solicitor to the Supreme Court;

(j)   the Pensions Regulator;

(k)   the Public Trustee;

(l)   the Secretary of State, in the exercise of his functions under enactments relating to companies and insolvency;

(m)   the Treasury, in the exercise of their functions under the 2000 Act;

(n)   the Treasury Solicitor;

(o)   a designated professional body for the purposes of Part 20 of the 2000 Act (provision of financial services by members of the professions);

(p)   a person or inspector appointed under section 65 (investigations on behalf of Authority) or 66 (inspections and special meetings) of the Friendly Societies Act 1992;

(q)   an inspector appointed under section 49 of the Industrial and Provident Societies Act 1965 (appointment of inspectors) or section 18 of the Credit Unions Act 1979 (power to appoint inspector);

(r)   an inspector appointed under section 431 (investigation of a company on its own application), 432 (other company investigations), 442 (power to investigate company ownership) or 446 (investigation of share dealing) of the Companies Act 1985 or under Article 424, 425, 435 or 439 of the Companies (Northern Ireland) Order 1986;

(s)   a person or inspector appointed under section 55 (investigations on behalf of Authority) or 56 (inspections and special meetings) of the Building Societies Act 1986;

(t)   a person appointed under section 167 (appointment of persons to carry out investigations), 168(3) or (5) (appointment of persons to carry out investigations in particular cases), 169(1)(b) (investigations to support overseas regulator) or 284 (power to investigate affairs of a scheme) of the 2000 Act, or under regulations made under section 262(2)(k) (open-ended investment companies) of that Act, to conduct an investigation; and

(u)   a person authorised to require the production of documents under section 447 of the Companies Act 1985 (Secretary of State's power to require production of documents), Article 440 of the Companies (Northern Ireland) Order 1986 or section 84 of the Companies Act 1989 (exercise of powers by officer).

(2)   A disclosure made under paragraph (1) is not to be taken to breach any restriction on the disclosure of information however imposed.

50   Transitional provisions: requirement to be registered

(1)   Regulation 26 does not apply to an existing money service business, an existing trust or company service provider or an existing high value dealer until—

(a)   where it has applied in accordance with regulation 27 before the specified date for registration in a register maintained under regulation 25(1) (a "new register")—

   (i)   the date it is included in a new register following the determination of its application by the Commissioners; or

   (ii)   where the Commissioners give it notice under regulation 29(2)(b) of their decision not to register it, the date on which the Commissioners state that the decision takes effect or, where a statement is included in accordance with paragraph (3)(b), the time at which the Commissioners give it such notice;

(b)   in any other case, the specified date.

(2)   The specified date is—

(a)   in the case of an existing money service business, 1st February 2008;

(b)   in the case of an existing trust or company service provider, 1st April 2008;

(c)   in the case of an existing high value dealer, the first anniversary which falls on or after 1st January 2008 of the date of its registration in a register maintained under regulation 10 of the Money Laundering Regulations 2003.

(3)   In the case of an application for registration in a new register made before the specified date by an existing money service business, an existing trust or company service provider or an existing high value dealer, the Commissioners must include in a notice given to it under regulation 29(2)(b)—

(a)   the date on which their decision is to take effect; or

(b)   if the Commissioners consider that the interests of the public require their decision to have immediate effect, a statement to that effect and the reasons for it.

(4)   In the case of an application for registration in a new register made before the specified date by an existing money services business or an existing trust or company service provider, the Commissioners must give it a notice under regulation 29(2) by—

(a)   in the case of an existing money service business, 1st June 2008;

(b)   in the case of an existing trust or company service provider, 1st July 2008; or

(c)   where applicable, 45 days beginning with the date on which they receive any further information required under regulation 27(3).

(5)   In this regulation—

"existing money service business" and an "existing high value dealer" mean a money service business or a high value dealer which, immediately before 15th December 2007, was included in a register maintained under regulation 10 of the Money Laundering Regulations 2003;

"existing trust or company service provider" means a trust or company service provider carrying on business in the United Kingdom immediately before 15th December 2007.

51   Minor and consequential amendments

Schedule 6, which contains minor and consequential amendments to primary and secondary legislation, has effect.

Signatory text

Alan Campbell

Frank Roy

Two Lords Commissioners of Her Majesty's Treasury

24th July 2007

SCHEDULE 1
Activities Listed in Points 2 to 12 and 14 of Annex I to the Banking
Consolidation Directive

Regulation 3(3)(a)

2   Lending including, inter alia: consumer credit, mortgage credit, factoring, with or without recourse, financing of commercial transactions (including forfeiting).

3   Financial leasing.

4   Money transmission services.

5   Issuing and administering means of payment (eg credit cards, travellers' cheques and bankers' drafts).

6   Guarantees and commitments.

7   Trading for own account or for account of customers in:

(a)   money market instruments (cheques, bills, certificates of deposit, etc);

(b)   foreign exchange;

(c)   financial futures and options;

(d)   exchange and interest-rate instruments; or

(e)   transferable securities.

8   Participation in securities issues and the provision of services related to such issues.

9   Advice to undertakings on capital structure, industrial strategy and related questions and advice as well as services relating to mergers and the purchase of undertakings.

10   Money broking.

11   Portfolio management and advice.

12   Safekeeping and administration of securities.

14   Safe custody services.

SCHEDULE 2
Financial Activity, Simplified Due Diligence and Politically Exposed Persons

Regulations 4(1)(e) and (2),
13(6) and (8) and 14(5)

Financial activity on an occasional or very limited basis

1   For the purposes of regulation 4(1)(e) and (2), a person is to be considered as engaging in financial activity on an occasional or very limited basis if all the following conditions are fulfilled—

(a)   the person's total annual turnover in respect of the financial activity does not exceed £64,000;

(b)   the financial activity is limited in relation to any customer to no more than one transaction exceeding 1,000 euro, whether the transaction is carried out in a single operation, or a series of operations which appear to be linked;

(c)   the financial activity does not exceed 5% of the person's total annual turnover;

(d)   the financial activity is ancillary and directly related to the person's main activity;

(e)   the financial activity is not the transmission or remittance of money (or any representation of monetary value) by any means;

(f)   the person's main activity is not that of a person falling within regulation 3(1)(a) to (f) or (h);

(g)   the financial activity is provided only to customers of the person's main activity and is not offered to the public.

Simplified due diligence

2   For the purposes of regulation 13(6), the conditions are—

(a)   the authority has been entrusted with public functions pursuant to the Treaty on the European Union, the Treaties on the European Communities or Community secondary legislation;

(b)   the authority's identity is publicly available, transparent and certain;

(c)   the activities of the authority and its accounting practices are transparent;

(d)   either the authority is accountable to a Community institution or to the authorities of an EEA state, or otherwise appropriate check and balance procedures exist ensuring control of the authority's activity.

3   For the purposes of regulation 13(8), the conditions are—

(a)   the product has a written contractual base;

(b)   any related transaction is carried out through an account of the customer with a credit institution which is subject to the money laundering directive or with a credit institution situated in a non-EEA state which imposes requirements equivalent to those laid down in that directive;

(c)   the product or related transaction is not anonymous and its nature is such that it allows for the timely application of customer due diligence measures where there is a suspicion of money laundering or terrorist financing;

(d)   the product is within the following maximum threshold—

    (i)   in the case of insurance policies or savings products of a similar nature, the annual premium is no more than 1,000 euro or there is a single premium of no more than 2,500 euro;

    (ii)   in the case of products which are related to the financing of physical assets where the legal and beneficial title of the assets is not transferred to the customer until the termination of the contractual relationship (whether the transaction is carried out in a single operation or in several operations which appear to be linked), the annual payments do not exceed 15,000 euro;

    (iii)   in all other cases, the maximum threshold is 15,000 euro;

(e)   the benefits of the product or related transaction cannot be realised for the benefit of third parties, except in the case of death, disablement, survival to a predetermined advanced age, or similar events;

(f)   in the case of products or related transactions allowing for the investment of funds in financial assets or claims, including insurance or other kinds of contingent claims—

    (i)   the benefits of the product or related transaction are only realisable in the long term;

    (ii)   the product or related transaction cannot be used as collateral; and

    (iii)   during the contractual relationship, no accelerated payments are made, surrender clauses used or early termination takes place.

Politically exposed persons

4   (1)   For the purposes of regulation 14(5)—

(a)   individuals who are or have been entrusted with prominent public functions include the following—

    (i)   heads of state, heads of government, ministers and deputy or assistant ministers;

    (ii)   members of parliaments;

    (iii)   members of supreme courts, of constitutional courts or of other high-level judicial bodies whose decisions are not generally subject to further appeal, other than in exceptional circumstances;

(iv)   members of courts of auditors or of the boards of central banks;

(v)   ambassadors, chargés d'affaires and high-ranking officers in the armed forces; and

(vi)   members of the administrative, management or supervisory bodies of state-owned enterprises;

(b)   the categories set out in paragraphs (i) to (vi) of sub-paragraph (a) do not include middle-ranking or more junior officials;

(c)   immediate family members include the following—

(i)   a spouse;

(ii)   a partner;

(iii)   children and their spouses or partners; and

(iv)   parents;

(d)   persons known to be close associates include the following—

(i)   any individual who is known to have joint beneficial ownership of a legal entity or legal arrangement, or any other close business relations, with a person referred to in regulation 14(5)(a); and

(ii)   any individual who has sole beneficial ownership of a legal entity or legal arrangement which is known to have been set up for the benefit of a person referred to in regulation 14(5)(a).

(2) In paragraph (1)(c), "partner" means a person who is considered by his national law as equivalent to a spouse.

SCHEDULE 3
Professional Bodies

Regulations 17(2)(b), 23(1)(c) and 32(4)

PART 1

1   Association of Chartered Certified Accountants

2   Council for Licensed Conveyancers

3   Faculty of Advocates

4   General Council of the Bar

5   General Council of the Bar of Northern Ireland

6   Institute of Chartered Accountants in England and Wales

7   Institute of Chartered Accountants in Ireland

8   Institute of Chartered Accountants of Scotland

9   Law Society

10 Law Society of Scotland

11 Law Society of Northern Ireland

PART 2

12 Association of Accounting Technicians

13 Association of International Accountants

14 Association of Taxation Technicians

15 Chartered Institute of Management Accountants

16 Chartered Institute of Public Finance and Accountancy

17 Chartered Institute of Taxation

18 Faculty Office of the Archbishop of Canterbury

19 Insolvency Practitioners Association

20 Institute of Certified Bookkeepers

21 Institute of Financial Accountants

22 International Association of Book-keepers

SCHEDULE 4
Connected Persons

Regulation 37(2)

Corporate bodies

1 If the relevant person is a body corporate ("BC"), a person who is or has been—

(a)   an officer or manager of BC or of a parent undertaking of BC;

(b)   an employee of BC;

(c)   an agent of BC or of a parent undertaking of BC

Partnerships

2 If the relevant person is a partnership, a person who is or has been a member, manager, employee or agent of the partnership.

Unincorporated associations

3 If the relevant person is an unincorporated association of persons which is not a partnership, a person who is or has been an officer, manager, employee or agent of the association.

Individuals

4 If the relevant person is an individual, a person who is or has been an employee or agent of that individual.

SCHEDULE 5
Modifications in Relation to Appeals

Regulation 44(8)

PART 1
PRIMARY LEGISLATION

The Value Added Tax Act 1994 (c 23)

1   Part 5 of the Value Added Tax Act 1994 (appeals) is modified as follows—

(a)   omit section 84; and

(b)   in paragraphs (1)(a), (2)(a) and (3)(a) of section 87, omit ", or is recoverable as, VAT".

The Financial Services and Markets Act 2000 (c 8)

2   Part 9 of the 2000 Act (hearings and appeals) is modified as follows—

(a)   in the application of section 133 and Schedule 13 to any appeal commenced before the coming into force of section 55 of the Consumer Credit Act 2006, for all the references to "the Authority", substitute "the Authority or the OFT (as the case may be)";

(b)   in section 133(1)(a) for "decision notice or supervisory notice in question" substitute "notice under regulation 34(5) or (9) or 42(7) of the Money Laundering Regulations 2007";

(c)   in section 133 omit subsections (6), (7), (8) and (12); and

(d)   in section 133(9) for "decision notice" in both places where it occurs substitute "notice under regulation 34(5) or (9) or 42(7) of the Money Laundering Regulations 2007".

PART 2
SECONDARY LEGISLATION

The Financial Services and Markets Tribunal Rules 2001

3   In the application of the Financial Services and Markets Tribunal Rules 2001 to any appeal commenced before the coming into force of section 55 of the Consumer Credit Act 2006, for all the references to "the Authority" substitute "the Authority or the OFT (as the case may be)".

SCHEDULE 6
Minor and Consequential Amendments

Regulation 51

PART 1
PRIMARY LEGISLATION

The Value Added Tax Act 1994 (c 23)

1   In section 83 of the Value Added Tax Act 1994 (appeals), omit paragraph (zz).

The Northern Ireland Act 1998 (c 47)

2   In paragraph 25 of Schedule 3 to the Northern Ireland Act 1998 (reserved matters), for "2003" substitute "2007".

The Criminal Justice and Police Act 2001 (c 16)

3   In Part 1 of Schedule 1 to the Criminal Justice and Police Act 2001 (powers of seizure to which section 50 of the 2001 Act applies), after paragraph 73I insert—

"THE MONEY LAUNDERING REGULATIONS 2007

73J The power of seizure conferred by regulation 39(6) of the Money Laundering Regulations 2007 (entry to premises under warrant).".

PART 2
SECONDARY LEGISLATION

The Independent Qualified Conveyancers (Scotland) Regulations 1997

4   Regulation 28 of the Independent Qualified Conveyancers (Scotland) Regulations 1997 is revoked.

The Executry Practitioners (Scotland) Regulations 1997

5   Regulation 26 of the Executry Practitioners (Scotland) Regulations 1997 is revoked.

The Cross-Border Credit Transfers Regulations 1999

6   In regulation 12(2) of the Cross-Border Credit Transfers Regulations 1999, for "2003" substitute "2007".

The Terrorism Act 2000 (Crown Servants and Regulators) Regulations 2001

7   In regulation 2 of the Terrorism Act 2000 (Crown Servants and Regulators) Regulations 2001, in the definition of "relevant business", for "has the meaning given by regulation 2(2) of the Money Laundering Regulations 2003" substitute "means an activity carried on in the course of business by any of the persons listed in regulation 3(1)(a) to (h) of the Money Laundering Regulations 2007".

The Representation of the People (England and Wales) Regulations 2001

8   In regulation 114(3)(b) of the Representation of the People (England and Wales) Regulations 2001, for "2003" substitute "2007".

The Representation of the People (Scotland) Regulations 2001

9   In regulation 113(3)(b) of the Representation of the People (Scotland) Regulations 2001, for "2003" substitute "2007".

The Financial Services and Markets Act 2000 (Regulated Activities) Order 2001

10   In article 72E(9) of the Financial Services and Markets Act 2000 (Regulated Activities) Order 2001, for "2003" substitute "2007".

The Proceeds of Crime Act 2002 (Failure to Disclose Money Laundering: Specified Training) Order 2003

11   In article 2 of the Proceeds of Crime Act 2002 (Failure to Disclose Money Laundering: Specified Training) Order 2003, for "regulation 3(1)(c)(ii) of the Money Laundering Regulations 2003" substitute "regulation 21 of the Money Laundering Regulations 2007".

The Public Contracts (Scotland) Regulations 2006

12 In regulation 23(1)(f) of the Public Contracts (Scotland) Regulations 2006, for "2003" substitute "2007".

The Utilities Contracts (Scotland) Regulations 2006

13 In regulation 26(1)(f) of the Utilities Contracts (Scotland) Regulations 2006, for "2003" substitute "2007".

The Public Contracts Regulations 2006

14 In regulation 23(1)(e) of the Public Contracts Regulations 2006, for "2003" substitute "2007".

The Utilities Contracts Regulations 2006

15 In regulation 26(1)(e) of the Utilities Contracts Regulations 2006, for "2003" substitute "2007".

The SRA (Disciplinary Procedure) Rules 2010

[Law Society copyright. For the latest updates to the material, please see www.sra.org.uk.]

SRA (Disciplinary Procedure) Rules 2010

[Last updated 10 May 2010]

Contents

Rules dated 10 May 2010

commencing 1 June 2010

made by the Solicitors Regulation Authority Board, after consultation with the Solicitors Disciplinary Tribunal under sections 31, 44D, 79 and 80 of the Solicitors Act 1974, and section 9 of and paragraph 14B of Schedule 2 to the Administration of Justice Act 1985, with the approval of the Legal Services Board under paragraph 19 of Schedule 4 to the Legal Services Act 2007.

Part 1 – General

Rule 1 – Interpretation

In these rules, unless the context otherwise requires:

(1)   "adjudicator" means a person not involved in the investigation or preparation of a case who is authorised by the SRA to take disciplinary decisions;

(2)   "disciplinary decision" means a decision, following an SRA finding, to exercise one or more of the powers provided by section 44D(2) and (3) of the Solicitors Act 1974 or paragraph 14B(2) and (3) of Schedule 2 to the Administration of Justice Act 1985;

(3)   "discipline investigation" means an investigation by the SRA to determine whether a regulated person should be subject to an SRA finding, a disciplinary decision or an application to the Tribunal;

(4)   "LLP" means a limited liability partnership incorporated under the Limited Liability Partnerships Act 2000;

(5)   "manager" means:

(a)   a partner in a partnership;

(b)   a member of an LLP; or

(c)   a director of a company;

(6)   "recognised body" means a partnership, company or LLP recognised by the SRA under section 9 of the Administration of Justice Act 1985;

(7)   "registered European Lawyer" means a person registered by the SRA under regulation 17 of the European Communities (Lawyer's Practice) Regulations 2000;

(8)   "registered foreign lawyer" means a person registered by the SRA under section 89 of the Courts and Legal Services Act 1990;

(9)   "regulated person" means:

(a)   a solicitor;

(b)   a registered European lawyer;

(c)   a registered foreign lawyer;

(d)   a recognised body;

(e)   a manager of a recognised body; or

(f)   an employee of a recognised body, a solicitor or a registered European lawyer;

(10)   "SRA" means the Solicitors Regulation Authority, the independent regulatory body of the Law Society of England and Wales;

(11)   "SRA finding" is a decision that the SRA is satisfied in accordance with section 44D(1) of the Solicitors Act 1974 or paragraph 14B(1) of Schedule 2 to the Administration of Justice Act 1985 and for the avoidance of doubt does not include:

(a)   investigatory decisions such as to require the production of information or documents;

(b)   directions as to the provision or obtaining of further information or explanation;

(c)   decisions to stay or adjourn;

(d)   authorisation of the making of an application to the Tribunal;

(e)   authorisation of an intervention pursuant to the Solicitors Act 1974, the Administration of Justice Act 1985 or the Courts and Legal Services Act 1990;

(f)   a letter of advice from the SRA to the regulated person.

(12)   "the Tribunal" means the Solicitors Disciplinary Tribunal which is an independent statutory tribunal constituted under section 46 of the Solicitors Act 1974;

(13)   the singular includes the plural and vice versa.

Rule 2 – Scope

(1)   These rules govern the procedure for the SRA to:

(a)   exercise its powers pursuant to section 44D of the Solicitors Act 1974 or paragraph 14B of Schedule 2 to the Administration of Justice Act 1985; or

(b)   subject to rule 6(9), authorise an application to the Tribunal.

(2)   The powers referred to in sub-rule (1)(a) are to do one or a combination of the following:

(a)   give a regulated person a written rebuke;

(b)   direct a regulated person to pay a penalty not exceeding the maximum permitted by law;

(c)   publish details of a written rebuke or a direction to pay a penalty if the SRA considers it to be in the public interest to do so.

(3)   These rules shall not prevent, prohibit or restrict the exercise of any other powers or other action by the SRA.

Rule 3 – Disciplinary powers

(1)   The circumstances in which the SRA may make a disciplinary decision to give a regulated person a written rebuke or to direct a regulated person to pay a penalty are when the following three conditions are met:

(a)   the first condition is that the SRA is satisfied that the act or omission by the regulated person which gives rise to the SRA finding fulfils one or more of the following in that it:

(i)   was deliberate or reckless;

(ii)   caused or had the potential to cause loss or significant inconvenience to any other person;

(iii) was or was related to a failure or refusal to ascertain, recognise or comply with the regulated person's professional or regulatory obligations such as, but not limited to, compliance with requirements imposed by legislation or rules made pursuant to legislation, the SRA, the Law Society, the Legal Complaints Service, the Tribunal or the court;

(iv)   continued for an unreasonable period taking into account its seriousness;

(v)   persisted after the regulated person realised or should have realised that it was improper;

(vi)   misled or had the potential to mislead clients, the court or other persons, whether or not that was appreciated by the regulated person;

(vii) affected or had the potential to affect a vulnerable person or child;

(viii) affected or had the potential to affect a substantial, high-value or high-profile matter; or

(ix)   formed or forms part of a pattern of misconduct or other regulatory failure by the regulated person.

APPENDIX 12

(b)   the second condition is that a proportionate outcome in the public interest is one or both of the following:

    (i)   a written rebuke;

    (ii)   a direction to pay a penalty not exceeding the maximum permitted by law; and

(c)   the third condition is that the act or omission by the regulated person which gives rise to the SRA finding was neither trivial nor justifiably inadvertent.

(2)   The SRA may make a disciplinary decision to publish details of a written rebuke or a direction to pay a penalty when it considers it to be in the public interest to do so in accordance with the publication criteria in the appendix to these rules.

(3)   Nothing in this rule shall prevent the authorisation of an application to the Tribunal in accordance with rule 8.

Part 2 – Practice and Procedure

Rule 4 – Investigations

(1)   The parties to a discipline investigation are the SRA and the regulated person.

(2)   The SRA may exercise any investigative or other powers at any time including those arising from:

(a)   sections 44B, 44BA, 44BB of the Solicitors Act 1974;

(b)   rules made by the Law Society or the SRA for the production of documents, information or explanations.

(3)   Subject to sub-rule (4), the SRA may disclose any information or documents (including the outcome) arising from its discipline investigation:

(a)   to an informant;

(b)   to a regulated person who is under investigation;

(c)   to any person in order to facilitate its investigation and in particular to identify and obtain evidence, comments or information;

(d)   to other regulators, law enforcement agencies, or other persons in the public interest.

(4)   The SRA may restrict disclosure of information to protect another person's right of confidentiality or privilege.

Rule 5 – Seeking explanations

(1)   The SRA will give the regulated person the opportunity to provide an explanation of the regulated person's conduct.

(2)   When seeking an explanation from the regulated person as referred to in sub-rule (1) above, the SRA will warn the regulated person that:

(a)   failure to reply to the SRA may in itself lead to disciplinary action;

(b)   the reply and other information may be disclosed to other persons pursuant to rule 4(3); and

(c)   the reply may be used by the SRA for regulatory purposes including as evidence in any investigation, decision by the SRA, or proceedings brought by or against the SRA.

(3)   The regulated person must provide the explanation referred to in sub-rule (1) or any other information within a time period specified by the SRA, which shall be no less than 14 calendar days from the request for an explanation and where no explanation or information is received within the specified time, the SRA may proceed to decision in the absence of an explanation.

Rule 6 – Report stage

(1)   Before making a disciplinary decision, the SRA will prepare a report for disclosure to the regulated person.

(2)   Subject to sub-rule (7), the report will summarise the allegations against the regulated person, explain the supporting facts and evidence, and attach documentary evidence that the SRA considers to be relevant.

(3)   The report may also include evidence of the regulated person's propensity to particular behaviour and a summary of the regulatory and disciplinary history of the regulated person and of any other person that the SRA considers relevant.

(4)   The report will be provided to the regulated person for the regulated person to provide written comments upon it within a time period specified by the SRA, which shall be no less than 14 calendar days from the date on which the report has been sent to the regulated person.

(5)   The regulated person will also be invited to make submissions on whether any decision which is made by the SRA, in respect of the matters in the report, should be published. Any such submissions must be made within a time specified by the SRA, which shall be no less than 14 calendar days from the date on which the report has been sent to the regulated person.

(6)   The report may be disclosed by the SRA to any other person with a legitimate interest in the matter to enable that person to comment upon it. Any such comments shall be disclosed to the regulated person if they are to be included in the documents referred for adjudication.

(7)   The SRA may restrict disclosure of part of the report or all or part of the attached documents in the public interest or in the interests of efficiency and proportionality, such as:

(a)   by only providing to the regulated person or any other person documents that are not already in their possession;

(b)   by not providing to a person other than the regulated person whose conduct is to be considered the report or documents if they include information that is or might be subject to another person's right of confidentiality or privilege.

(8)   The SRA may recommend an outcome or advocate a particular position in the report or otherwise.

(9)   The report and comments received shall be referred for consideration within a reasonable time after receipt of any comments or the expiry of any time period specified for the provision of comments.

(10)   The SRA is not required to adopt the procedure in rules 5 and 6 in order to make an SRA finding or an application to the Tribunal under rule 8 below.

(11)   Where the SRA considers that it is just and in the public interest to do so the SRA may dispense with or vary the procedure and the time limits set out in rules 5 and 6.

(12)   Where the SRA dispenses with or varies the procedure or the time limits in accordance with sub-rule (11), the SRA shall, so far as practicable, notify the regulated person that it has done so.

Part 3 – Decisions and Referrals to the Tribunal

Rule 7 – Decisions

(1)   An SRA finding may be made by:

    (a)   agreement between the regulated person and the SRA;

    (b)   a person duly authorised by the SRA;

    (c)   a single adjudicator; or

    (d)   an adjudication panel.

(2)   A disciplinary decision may be made by:

    (a)   agreement between the regulated person and the SRA;

    (b)   a single adjudicator; or

    (c)   an adjudication panel.

(3)   An SRA finding which does not involve a consequential disciplinary decision may incorporate or be accompanied by:

    (a)   advice to the regulated person as to the regulated person's regulatory obligations;

    (b)   a warning to the regulated person as to the regulated person's future conduct.

(4)   A disciplinary decision may be made by a single adjudicator but the SRA may refer a matter to an adjudication panel for such a decision.

(5)   An adjudication panel shall be properly constituted if at least two members are present.

(6)   Where an adjudication panel is comprised of three or more members, a decision may be made by a majority.

(7)   The strict rules of evidence shall not apply to decisions of the SRA.

(8)   The standard of proof shall be the civil standard.

(9)   Decisions will normally be made on consideration of the report described in rule 6 but an adjudicator or adjudication panel may give directions as necessary as to the provision of evidence or representations whether oral or otherwise.

(10)   The decision shall be made when it is sent to the regulated person in writing. The decision will be accompanied with information in writing about any right of appeal within the SRA and any external right of appeal.

(11)   Where the SRA directs the regulated person to pay a penalty, such penalty shall be paid within a time and in the manner specified by the SRA but shall not become payable until:

    (a)   the end of the period during which an appeal may be made under rule 9 below, section 44E of the Solicitors Act 1974 or paragraph 14C of Schedule 2 to the Administration of Justice Act 1985; or

    (b)   if such an appeal is made, such time as the appeal is determined or withdrawn.

Rule 8 – Referrals to the Tribunal

(1)   The SRA may make an application to the Tribunal in respect of a regulated person at any time if the SRA is satisfied that:

    (a)   there is sufficient evidence to provide a realistic prospect that the application will be upheld by the Tribunal;

(b)   the allegation to be made against the regulated person either in itself or in the light of other allegations is sufficiently serious that the Tribunal is likely to order that the regulated person:

    (i)   be struck off;

    (ii)   be suspended;

    (iii)   be subject to an order revoking its recognition;

    (iv)   pay a penalty exceeding the maximum that can be imposed from time to time by the SRA; or

    (v)   be subject to any other order that the SRA is not empowered to make; and

(c)   it is in the public interest to make the application.

(2)   The SRA will apply sub-rule (1) in accordance with a code for referral to the Tribunal as promulgated by the SRA from time to time.

(3)   An application in respect of a regulated person to the Tribunal may be authorised by:

(a)   agreement between the regulated person and the SRA;

(b)   a person duly authorised by the SRA;

(c)   a single adjudicator; or

(d)   an adjudication panel.

(4)   There is no right of appeal against authorisation of an application to the Tribunal.

(5)   Subject to any contrary order of the Tribunal, the SRA may exercise any investigative or other powers at any time before a final hearing of an application at the Tribunal, including those arising from:

(a)   sections 44B, 44BA, 44BB of the Solicitors Act 1974;

(b)   rules made by the Law Society or the SRA for the production of documents, information or explanations.

Part 4 – Appeals and Reconsideration

Rule 9 – Internal appeals

(1)   A regulated person may appeal against all or any part of an SRA finding, a disciplinary decision or both.

(2)   There is no appeal under this rule against:

(a)   any decision other than an SRA finding or a disciplinary decision;

(b)   a decision on an appeal; or

(c)   an SRA finding or a disciplinary decision which has been made by agreement between the regulated person and the SRA.

(3)   An appeal by a regulated person must be made within 14 calendar days of the date of the letter or electronic communication informing the regulated person of the decision or within a longer time period specified by the SRA.

(4)   An appeal shall:

(a)   be in writing; and

(b)   provide reasoned arguments in support.

(5)   Appeals will be determined as follows:

(a)   where the decision was made by a person duly authorised by the SRA, the appeal will be decided by a single adjudicator;

(b)   where the decision was made by a single adjudicator, the appeal will be heard by an adjudication panel;

(c)   where the decision was made by an adjudication panel, the appeal will be decided by a differently constituted panel.

(6)   Appeals will be limited to a review of the decision which is being appealed, taking into account the reasoned arguments provided by the regulated person. Failure to provide reasoned arguments either at all or in sufficient or clear terms may result in summary dismissal of the appeal.

(7)   All powers available to the SRA on adjudication are exercisable on appeal and for the avoidance of doubt this means that an appeal decision may include findings or sanctions more severe than those made or applied in the decision being appealed.

(8)   Nothing in these rules shall affect a regulated person's right of appeal to the Tribunal under section 44E of the Solicitors Act 1974 or paragraph 14C of Schedule 2 to the Administration of Justice Act 1985.

(9)   Subject to any rule made by the Tribunal pursuant to section 46(9)(b) of the Solicitors Act 1974, an appeal to the Tribunal by a regulated person must be made within 21 calendar days of the date of the letter or electronic communication informing the regulated person of the decision or, if there has been an internal appeal, within 21 calendar days of the date of the letter or electronic communication informing the regulated person of that decision.

Rule 10 – Reconsideration

(1)   The SRA may reconsider or rescind any decision including an SRA finding, a disciplinary decision or authorisation of a referral to the Tribunal with the agreement of the regulated person.

(2)   In its absolute discretion the SRA may also reconsider any decision including an SRA finding, a disciplinary decision or authorisation of a referral to the Tribunal when it appears that the person or panel who made the decision:

(a)   was not provided with material evidence that was available to the SRA;

(b)   was materially misled by the regulated person or any other person;

(c)   failed to take proper account of material facts or evidence;

(d)   took into account immaterial facts or evidence;

(e)   made a material error of law;

(f)   made a decision which was otherwise irrational or procedurally unfair;

(g)   made a decision which was ultra vires; or

(h)   failed to give sufficient reasons.

(3)   Reconsideration pursuant to this rule may be directed by a duly authorised person who may also give directions for:

(a)   further investigations to be undertaken;

(b)   further information or explanation to be obtained from any person;

(c)   consideration of whether to authorise an application to the Tribunal;

(d)   the reconsideration of the decision to be undertaken by the original decision maker or adjudication panel or by a different decision maker or a differently constituted adjudication panel.

(4)   Nothing in these rules requires the SRA to commence or continue with any proceedings or prospective proceedings in the Tribunal or any other court or tribunal. A duly authorised person may rescind a decision to take proceedings in the Tribunal.

Part 5 – Publication and Commencement

Rule 11 – Publication of decisions

(1)   This rule governs the publication of details of a written rebuke or a direction to pay a penalty.

(2)   Subject to sub-rule (4), publication in accordance with this rule:

    (a)   will include a short statement of the disciplinary decision including brief details of its factual basis and the reasons for the decision;

    (b)   will identify the regulated person;

    (c)   will take reasonable steps to avoid the publication of information relating to other identifiable persons;

    (d)   will provide the practising details of the regulated person at the time of the matters giving rise to the decision and at the time of decision if different;

    (e)   will be in such form as the SRA may from time to time decide;

    (f)   may include provision of a copy of the publishable information upon request by any person;

    (g)   will be made promptly after the decision has been made, provided that the SRA may delay or withhold publication in the public interest.

(3)   The SRA may vary or dispense with any of the requirements in sub-rule (2) in the public interest.

(4)   The SRA may not publish details of a written rebuke or a direction to pay a penalty:

    (a)   during the period in which an appeal may be made under rule 9 above, section 44E of the Solicitors Act 1974 or paragraph 14C of Schedule 2 to the Administration of Justice Act 1985; or

    (b)   if such an appeal has been made, until such time as it is determined or withdrawn.

(5)   For the avoidance of doubt, the SRA may also publish information about other decisions or investigations.

Rule 12 – Commencement

These rules shall come into force on 1 June 2010 but shall not apply to any matters where the act or omission which gives rise to the SRA finding occurred wholly before these rules came into force.

Appendix – Publication Criteria (Rule 3(2))

1.   In deciding whether or not to publish a decision to give a regulated person a written rebuke or direct the regulated person to pay a penalty, the SRA will take into account all relevant circumstances including the following factors when relevant.

2.   Each case will be decided on its own merits.

APPENDIX 12

3.   The following support a decision to publish:

(a)   the circumstances leading to the rebuke or penalty, or the rebuke or penalty itself, are matters of legitimate public concern or interest;

(b)   the importance of transparency in the regulatory and disciplinary process;

(c)   the existence or details of the rebuke or penalty will or might be relevant to a client or prospective client of a regulated person in deciding whether to instruct or continue to instruct the regulated person, or as to the instructions to be given;

(d)   the existence or details of the rebuke or penalty will or might be relevant as to how any other person will deal with a regulated person;

(e)   the seriousness of the finding against the regulated person;

(f)   the rebuke or penalty has been given to a regulated person who has previously been the subject of disciplinary or regulatory decisions whether private or published;

(g)   the rebuke or penalty arises from facts that affected or may affect or have affected a number of clients or other persons;

(h)   the rebuke or penalty arises from facts that relate to the administration of justice.

(4)   The following support a decision not to publish:

(a)   publication would disclose a person's confidential or legally privileged information;

(b)   publication would disclose a regulated person's confidential medical condition or treatment;

(c)   publication may prejudice legal proceedings or legal, regulatory or disciplinary investigations;

(d)   publication would involve a significant risk of breaching a person's rights under Article 8 of the European Convention on Human Rights;

(e)   in all the circumstances the impact of publication on the individual or the firm would be disproportionate.

(5)   In deciding whether to publish, the SRA may also take into account:

(a)   the overall disciplinary and regulatory history of another regulated person when relevant;

(b)   whether any disciplinary or regulatory action by another body is being or has been taken against the regulated person.

(6)   The factors set out above are not exhaustive and do not prevent the SRA from taking into account other factors that it considers to be relevant.

(7)   The SRA will from time to time publish indicative guidance about the application of these criteria.

The SRA (Cost of Investigations) Regulations 2009

[Law Society copyright. For updates to the material, please see www.sra.org.uk.]

SRA (Cost of Investigations) Regulations 2009

[Last updated 31 March 2009]

Contents

SRA (Cost of investigations) Regulations 2009

Rules and regulations about charging for the costs of investigations carried out by the Solicitors Regulation Authority

dated 31 March 2009

commencing 31 March 2009

made by the Solicitors Regulation Authority Board under sections 31, 43, 44C, 79 and 80 of the Solicitors Act 1974 and section 9 of and paragraph 14A of Schedule 2 to the Administration of Justice Act 1985 with

- the concurrence of the Master of the Rolls under section 31 of the Solicitors Act 1974, paragraph 16 of Schedule 22 to the Legal Services Act 2007 and article 4 of the Legal Services Act 2007 (Commencement No. 4, Transitory and Transitional Provisions and Appointed Day) Order 2009; and

- the concurrence of the Lord Chancellor under paragraph 16 of Schedule 22 to the Legal Services Act 2007 and article 4 of the Legal Services Act 2007 (Commencement No. 4, Transitory and Transitional Provisions and Appointed Day) Order 2009.

Regulation 1 – Interpretation

In these regulations, unless the context otherwise requires:

(1) "adjudicator" means a person not involved in the investigation or preparation of a case who is authorised by the SRA to make an SRA finding;

(2) "discipline investigation" means an investigation by the SRA to determine whether a regulated person should be subject to an SRA finding or an application to the Tribunal;

(3) "LLP" means a limited liability partnership incorporated under the Limited Liability Partnerships Act 2000;

(4) "manager" means:

    (a)   a partner in a partnership;

    (b)   a member of an LLP; or

    (c)   a director of a company;

(5) "recognised body" means a partnership, company or LLP recognised by the SRA under section 9 of the Administration of Justice Act 1985;

(6) "registered European Lawyer" means a person registered by the SRA under regulation 17 of the European Communities (Lawyer's Practice) Regulations 2000;

(7) "registered foreign lawyer" means a person registered by the SRA under section 89 of the Courts and Legal Services Act 1990;

(8) "regulated person" means:

    (a)   a solicitor;

    (b)   a registered European lawyer;

    (c)   a registered foreign lawyer;

    (d)   a recognised body;

    (e)   a manager of a recognised body; or

    (f)   an employee of a recognised body, a solicitor or a registered European lawyer;

(9) "section 43 investigation" means an investigation by the SRA as to whether there are grounds for the SRA:

    (a)   to make an order under section 43(2) of the Solicitors Act 1974; or

    (b)   to make an application to the Tribunal for it to make such an order;

(10) "SRA" means the Solicitors Regulation Authority, the independent regulatory body of the Law Society of England and Wales;

(11) "SRA finding" is a decision that the SRA is satisfied in accordance with section 44D(1) of the Solicitors Act 1974 or paragraph 14B(1) of Schedule 2 to the Administration of Justice Act 1985;

(12) "the Tribunal" means the Solicitors Disciplinary Tribunal;

(13) the singular includes the plural and vice versa.

Regulation 2 – Scope

(1)   These regulations prescribe the charges to be paid to the SRA by:

    (a)   regulated persons who are the subject of a discipline investigation;

    (b)   persons who are the subject of a section 43 investigation.

(2)   These regulations shall not prevent, prohibit or restrict the exercise of any other powers or other action by the SRA.

Regulation 3 – Discipline investigations

(1)   A regulated person who is the subject of a discipline investigation may be required by the SRA to pay a charge in accordance with these regulations provided that there has been an SRA finding against the regulated person.

(2)   An SRA finding may be made by:

    (a)   agreement between the regulated person and the SRA;

    (b)   a person duly authorised by the SRA;

    (c)   a single adjudicator; or

    (d)   an adjudication panel.

Regulation 4 – Section 43 investigations

(1)   A person who is the subject of a section 43 investigation may be required by the SRA to pay a charge in accordance with these regulations provided that the SRA has made an order under section 43(2) of the Solicitors Act 1974.

(2)   An order under section 43(2) of the Solicitors Act 1974 may be made by:

    (a)   agreement between the person and the SRA;

    (b)   a single adjudicator; or

    (c)   an adjudication panel.

Regulation 5 – Decision to require payment of charges

(1)   The amount of charges payable by any person in the circumstances falling within regulation 3(1) or 4(1) above will be determined by the person, adjudicator or adjudication panel making the relevant SRA finding or decision to make an order under section 43(2) of the Solicitors Act 1974 or where such a finding or order is made by agreement, the person duly authorised by the SRA to enter into such an agreement.

(2)   Where a person is required to pay any charges under these regulations, such charges shall be paid within a time and in the manner specified by the SRA.

Regulation 6 – Basis of charges

(1)   Subject to regulation 6(2) below, the amount payable under regulation 5 will be determined in accordance with the schedule of charges in appendix 1 to these regulations.

(2)   In exceptional circumstances, the SRA may charge less than the amount that would be payable in accordance with the schedule of charges in appendix 1 to these regulations provided that it is considered by the SRA to be fair and reasonable to do so.

(3)   The SRA may require any person in the circumstances falling within regulation 3(1) or

APPENDIX 13

535

4(1) above to pay an additional charge where such person has made an unsuccessful appeal to the SRA against the SRA finding or the order made under section 43(2) of the Solicitors Act 1974.

(4)   The additional amount payable under regulation 6(3) shall be in accordance with the schedule of charges in appendix 1 to these regulations.

(5)   For the purposes of this regulation an appeal will be unsuccessful if, after the appeal has been heard, any SRA finding remains or the order made under section 43(2) of the Solicitors Act 1974 has not been quashed.

Regulation 7 – Recovery of charges

Any charge which a person is required to pay under these regulations is recoverable by the SRA as a debt due to the SRA from that person.

Regulation 8 – Commencement

(1)   These regulations shall come into force on 31 March 2009 but shall not apply to any decisions that were made before these regulations came into force.

(2)   Regulation 1(8)(c) does not come into force until 1 July 2009.

Appendix 1 – Schedule of Charges

1.   This Schedule of charges sets out the basis of calculating the amount of charges payable under regulations 5 and 6.

2.   The SRA will record the amount of time spent investigating and considering each case and the amount payable under the regulations will vary depending on the amount of time spent on that matter.

3.   The standard levels of charges are as follows:

Number of hours spent on matter	Standard Charge
Under 2 hours	£300.00
2 hours or more but under 8 hours	£600.00
8–16 hours	£1,350

4.   In addition to the fixed charge of £1,350, where investigations take more than 16 hours, an extra charge of £75 for every hour (£37.50 for every half hour) will be applied (rounded up or down to the nearest half hour).

.5.   For the purposes of regulations 6(3) and 6(4), the additional fixed charge for an appeal shall be £250.

SRA policy statement on publication of regulatory and disciplinary decisions

[31 July 2008]

Publication of regulatory and disciplinary decisions – Policy statement

Introduction

1.   The Solicitors Regulation Authority (SRA) will publish regulatory decisions when it considers it to be in the public interest to do so.

2.   In developing this policy we have had regard to the principles of good regulation:

- Proportionality
- Accountability
- Consistency
- Transparency
- Targeting

3.   We are convinced that publishing our regulatory decisions wherever possible is an important contribution to ensuring that what we do is transparent. It will inform users of legal services, and help others to hold us accountable by helping them to assess whether we are acting proportionately and consistently.

Decisions that may be published

4.   Regulatory decisions that may be published include:

- Findings pursuant to section 44D of the Solicitors Act 1974 (when in force) resulting in a rebuke or a direction to pay a penalty;

- The imposition of practising certificate conditions when they are first imposed or materially varied (and continuing the current policy of disclosing practising certificate conditions on enquiry);

- Decisions to prosecute at the Solicitors Disciplinary Tribunal (SDT) once the Tribunal has certified a prima facie case;

- Settlement Agreements[1] and Issue Agreements[2] unless otherwise stated in the Agreement;

- Intervention decisions[3] and the legal basis for the decision.

4A.   The nature of the decision to publish in the public interest will vary depending on the decision. Findings of misconduct pursuant to section 44D above require a statutory decision to publish and that will usually be part of the adjudication. In contrast, decisions to intervene have long been published as an essential part of informing clients that their solicitor's firm has been closed down. Similarly, a referral to the SDT, once a prima facie case has been certified, will lead to a public hearing, and conditions on practising certificates are already publicly available to telephone enquirers. Accordingly, whilst each decision in these circumstances by a staff member at caseworker level or equivalent in the relevant unit or at adjudication as appropriate will be taken on its own merits, it is expected that decisions will usually be published unless such a staff member considers that one or more of the factors at paragraph 8 below would make such publication inappropriate.

5.   Decisions will not generally be published when they are the subject of an outstanding internal appeal or appeal to the Master of the Rolls, High Court or SDT.

6.   Intervention decisions and the legal basis for the decision will generally be published even if there is an application to the High Court for the intervention notice to be withdrawn.

1.   Settlement Agreements record the outcome of an investigation agreed by the SRA and a solicitor.
2.   Issue Agreements record agreement on one or more issues in the course of a continuing investigation.
3.   An intervention involves the SRA taking possession of the money and documents in a solicitors' practice.

Criteria for publication

7.   Factors which support a decision to publish include:

- The importance of transparency in the SRA's decision-making processes;

- The importance of providing information about regulatory action against solicitors to enable, for example:

  - prospective clients to make informed choices about whom to instruct;

  - clients and others to decide whether behaviour of concern should be reported to the SRA;

- The need to maintain public confidence in the regulatory system by demonstrating what regulatory action is being or has been taken and why.

8.   Factors which support a decision to keep a decision confidential include:

- Potential damage to the underlying purpose of a Settlement or Issue Agreement, such as where substantial redress may be provided to clients or others but there is a risk of prejudicing the position of the solicitors or others in related litigation or potential claims;

- Inability to publish without:

  - disclosing a client's confidential or legally privileged information;

  - disclosing a solicitor's confidential medical condition or treatment;

  - prejudicing civil or criminal proceedings;

  - a significant risk of breaching a person's rights under Article 8 of the European Convention on Human Rights.

9.   Published information will usually be limited to a short statement of the decision with brief factual details such as the basis of a finding under section 44D of the Solicitors Act 1974 and the sanction imposed, the reasons for imposition of a practising certificate condition, or the basis of a referral to the SDT. The solicitor's name and practising details (at the time of the matters giving rise to the decision and at the time of publication) will usually be provided.

10.   Decisions will normally be published promptly but the SRA retains discretion to

publish them or parts of them at a later time. This may be necessary, for example, if an investigation or prosecution is sensitive, such as where there is a risk of prejudice to other proceedings or regulatory activity.

11. Other decisions or information may be published if the SRA considers it in the public interest to do so. For example, in relation to an investigation giving rise to significant public concern, it may be in the public interest to disclose how the investigation is progressing or that it has concluded without an adverse finding against the solicitor.

12. Information about internal decisions of the SRA which are not otherwise in the public domain will be removed from the SRA website three years after publication.

NOTES:

1. Reference to "solicitor" includes solicitors' practices and all persons who may be affected by the SRA's decisions such as Registered European Lawyers, Registered Foreign Lawyers, Recognised Bodies and unadmitted persons subjected to investigation or application pursuant to section 43 of the Solicitors Act 1974.

2. Reference to "investigation" includes all disciplinary and regulatory applications, investigations and prosecutions.

3. This policy applies to investigations commenced on or after 1 January 2008, save that decisions to refer a solicitor to the SDT may be published immediately upon adoption of this Statement (in accordance with paragraph 4). For the purposes of this policy the commencement of an investigation includes the sending of a letter requiring the production of documents or information pursuant to practice rules or a written request for a solicitor to provide information or an explanation of a matter.

4. The new approach established by this Statement supplements existing processes.

5. Reference to "the SRA" in this Statement includes those exercising delegated decision-making powers on its behalf.

The Solicitors (Keeping of the Roll) Regulations 1999

[For the latest updates to the material, please see www.sra.org.uk.]

[Last updated 1 July 2009]

Contents

Solicitors (Keeping of the Roll) Regulations 1999

1. Authority and date

These regulations, dated 22nd January 1999, are made and amended under section 28 of the Solicitors Act 1974 by the Master of the Rolls with the concurrence of the Lord Chancellor and the Lord Chief Justice, and since 19 August 2003 amended under that section by the Master of the Rolls with the concurrence of the Secretary of State and the Lord Chief Justice.

2. Commencement and repeal

As from 1st February 1999 these regulations replace the Solicitors (Keeping of the Roll) Regulations 1989.

2A. The roll

The Solicitors Regulation Authority (SRA) shall continue to keep a list of all solicitors of the Supreme Court, called "the roll".

2B. Mode of keeping the roll

The roll will be kept in electronic form.

2C. Content of the roll

In respect of entries made or altered as from 1 July 2009, the roll must contain, in respect of each solicitor, the following information:

(a)   full name, including title;

(b)   date of birth;

(c)   registration number;

(d)   date of admission;

(e)   principal place of business in the case of a practising solicitor;

(f)   address for correspondence in the case of a non-practising solicitor;

(g)   a note about any suspension of the solicitor from practice, or suspension of the solicitor's practising certificate, or suspension of the solicitor from practice as a sole practitioner, or suspension of the solicitor's authorisation as a recognised sole practitioner, or the termination of any such suspension;

(h)   a note of any order of the Solicitors Disciplinary Tribunal under section 47 of the Solicitors Act 1974 in respect of the solicitor (or former solicitor), and a note of any order of the High Court or the Court of Appeal striking the solicitor off the roll; and

(i)   any other reasonable information, necessary for carrying out the SRA's statutory objectives, from time to time prescribed by the SRA.

2D. Public access to information

(a)   Entries on the roll under (a), (c), (d), (e), (g) and (h) must be available for inspection by any member of the public during office hours without charge, except that the SRA may in exceptional circumstances, and if it considers that to do so would be in the public interest, withhold the address of a solicitor's principal place of business.

(b)   The date on which a solicitor's name was

        (i)   removed from or

(ii)   struck off

the roll must be made available to a member of the public on request.

3. Address for correspondence

When the SRA writes to any person under these regulations it shall write to the solicitor's last notified address.

4. Annual enquiry

The SRA shall once a year ask every solicitor without a practising certificate whether the solicitor wishes his or her name to remain on the roll.

5. Removal from the roll

The SRA may remove from the roll the name of any solicitor who:

(a)   replies, following an enquiry under regulation 4, that he or she does not wish to remain on the roll; or

(b)   fails to reply within eight weeks to an enquiry under regulation 4; or

(c)   fails, within eight weeks of an enquiry under regulation 4, to pay the fee prescribed by regulation 13(a) for remaining on the roll; or

(d)   applies to have his or her name removed from the roll; or

(e)   has died.

6. Application for restoration to the roll

(a)   A person whose name has been removed from the roll may apply to the SRA for his or her name to be restored to the roll.

(b)   This regulation does not apply if:

(i)   the Solicitors Disciplinary Tribunal has made an order prohibiting the restoration of the person's name to the roll except by order of the Tribunal; or

(ii)   the person's name has been struck off the roll.

7. Application for change of name on the roll

A solicitor whose name has changed may apply to the SRA to change his or her name on the roll.

8. Outstanding complaints

The SRA may refuse to remove from or restore to the roll the name of a solicitor or former solicitor against whom there is an outstanding complaint.

9. Disciplinary proceedings

The SRA shall not remove from or restore to the roll the name of any solicitor or former solicitor against whom disciplinary proceedings are pending before the Supreme Court or Tribunal.

10. Notice of intention to remove name

Where regulation 5(b) or (c) applies, the SRA shall not remove a solicitor's name from the roll until it has notified the solicitor in writing that it intends to remove his or her name.

11. Letter of confirmation or notice of refusal

The SRA shall write to a solicitor or former solicitor:

(a)   confirming that his or her name on the roll has been removed from, restored to or changed on the roll; or

(b)   giving notice that the SRA has refused to remove from, restore to or change his or her name on the roll.

12. Forms

The SRA may prescribe forms for replies or applications to the SRA and in the case of an application under regulation 7 may require such evidence as it sees fit.

13. Fees

(a)   Subject to paragraph (b) any reply, following an enquiry under regulation 4, that a solicitor wishes to remain on the roll must be accompanied by a fee of £20.

(b)   No fee is payable under regulation 4 by any solicitor whose name has been on the roll for 50 years or more or for such shorter period as the SRA may from time to time prescribe.

(c)   Any application under regulation 6 for restoration of a person's name to the roll shall be accompanied by such fee as the SRA may from time to time prescribe.

14. Appeals

(a)   Any person who is aggrieved because:

    (i)   the SRA has removed his or her name from the roll; or

    (ii)   the SRA refused to remove his or her name from the roll; or

    (iii)   the SRA refused to change his or her name on the roll

may appeal to the High Court under this regulation.

(b)   Any person aggrieved by the SRA's refusal to restore his or her name to the roll under regulation 6 may appeal to the High Court under section 8(4) of the Solicitors Act 1974.

(c)   A person must invoke the SRA's own appeals procedure before appealing to the High Court under this regulation, and has the option of invoking the SRA's own appeals procedure before appealing to the High Court under section 8(4) of the Solicitors Act 1974.

(d)   Appeals under the SRA's own appeals procedure must be commenced within 28 days of notification of the SRA's initial decision.

(e)   Unless otherwise provided in rules of Court, an appeal to the High Court must be commenced within 28 days of notification of the relevant decision, whether that is the SRA's initial decision or a decision under the SRA's own appeals procedure.

(f)   Under sections 8(4B) and 28(3F) of the Solicitors Act 1974 the decision of the High
        Court is final.

15. Amendment

With effect from the coming into force of section 59(1) of the Constitutional Reform
Act 2005, the reference to solicitors of the Supreme Court shall be replaced by a reference to
solicitors of the Senior Courts.

The Solicitors (Disciplinary Proceedings) Rules 2007 with Solicitors Disciplinary Tribunal practice directions and policy/practice note

[The practice directions are reproduced with the kind permission of the Solicitors Disciplinary Tribunal. For the latest updates to the material, please see www.solicitorstribunal.org.uk.]

Solicitors (Disciplinary Proceedings) Rules 2007

SI 2007/3588

Made 14th December 2007

Coming into force 14th January 2008

The Solicitors Disciplinary Tribunal in exercise of the powers conferred upon them by section 46 of the Solicitors Act 1974 hereby make the following Rules:

In accordance with section 46 of that Act the Master of the Rolls concurs with the making of these Rules.

PART 1
INTRODUCTION

1 Citation and Commencement

These Rules may be cited as the Solicitors (Disciplinary Proceedings) Rules 2007 and shall come into force on 14th January 2008.

2 Interpretation

(1) In these Rules—

"the Act" means the Solicitors Act 1974;

"applicant" means a person making an application;

"application" means an application made under these Rules;

"case to answer" means an arguable or prima facie case;

"clerk" means any clerk to the Tribunal appointed under Rule 3 (including the Clerk);

"the Clerk" means the clerk to the Tribunal who is in office at the date these Rules come into force, or the clerk subsequently appointed under Rule 3(5);

"Division" means a division of three members of the Tribunal appointed for the hearing of an application or any matter connected with an application;

"the Law Society" includes any duly constituted committee of the Law Society or any body or person exercising delegated powers of the Law Society;

"respondent" means any party to an application other than the applicant;

"recognised body" has the same meaning as in section 9 of the Administration of Justice Act 1985;

"the Roll" means the Roll of Solicitors kept by the Law Society under section 6 of the Act;

"solicitor members" and "lay members" have the same meanings as in section 46 of the Act;

"Statement" means a written statement (including a witness statement) containing a statement of truth;

"the Tribunal" means the Solicitors Disciplinary Tribunal and where a Division has been appointed for the hearing of an application or any matter connected with it, includes a Division.

(2)   References in these Rules to solicitors include, where appropriate, former solicitors.

(3)   References in these Rules to registered foreign lawyers are references to lawyers whose names are entered in the register of foreign lawyers maintained under section 89 of the Courts and Legal Services Act 1990 and include, where appropriate, those who have ceased to be registered in that register or whose registration has been suspended.

(4)   References in these Rules to registered European lawyers are references to lawyers whose names are entered in the register of registered European lawyers maintained by the Law Society under regulation 15 of the European Communities (Lawyer's Practice) Regulations 2000 and include, where appropriate, those who have ceased to be registered in that register or whose registration has been suspended.

PART 2
CONSTITUTION

3   President, Vice-Presidents and Clerk

(1)   The President of the Tribunal holding office immediately before the date on which these rules come into force shall continue to hold office until the Tribunal's annual general meeting next following 30th April 2009.

(2)   Subject to paragraph (1), the Tribunal, by a simple majority, shall appoint one of the solicitor members to be its President to hold office for a period of 3 years and the person so appointed may be re-appointed for a further period not exceeding 3 years.

(3)   The Tribunal, by a simple majority, shall appoint one solicitor member and one lay member to be its Vice-Presidents to hold office for such period or periods not exceeding 3 years as the Tribunal shall think fit and to exercise such functions as are exercisable under these rules by the President as he may direct.

(4)   The Tribunal shall meet not less than once in each calendar year and shall publish an annual report, a copy of which shall be delivered to the Master of the Rolls and the Law Society.

(5)   The Tribunal shall appoint a Clerk to the Tribunal.

(6)   The Tribunal may also appoint other clerks, including clerks appointed to deal with a particular case or cases.

(7)   A clerk appointed by the Tribunal under this rule shall be a solicitor or barrister of not less than 10 years standing.

(8)   A clerk shall vacate his office if—

(a)   in the Tribunal's opinion (with which the Master of the Rolls agrees) he is physically or mentally incapable of performing his duties; or

(b)   he retires; or

(c)   he is removed from office by a resolution of the Tribunal approved by the Master of the Rolls.

(9)   The Clerk shall be responsible to the Tribunal for the administration of the Tribunal in an efficient manner and, for so long as he shall be remunerated by the Law Society, shall be regarded as seconded to the Tribunal.

(10)   The services of a clerk may be provided to the Tribunal through a body independent of the Law Society and that body may employ him on such terms (including remuneration and pension provision) as the Tribunal shall think fit.

(11)   The Tribunal may prescribe the duties to be performed by the clerks or for which they shall be responsible and those duties shall include arrangements for—

(a)   the submission of applications for certification of a case to answer;

(b)   making pre-listing arrangements including directions of an administrative nature;

(c)   listing of and attendance at hearings;

(d)   securing a record of hearings (by tape recording or other means);

(e)   advising the Tribunal on matters of law or procedure as may be necessary or expedient;

(f)   preparing summaries of allegations, evidence and submissions for inclusion in the Tribunal's detailed findings;

(g)   drawing orders and findings and filing them with the Law Society;

(h)   the general supervision of other clerks and the Tribunal's administration and staff; and

(i)   maintaining records and collecting statistics required by the Tribunal.

4   Constitution of Divisions

Subject to rules 6(1) and 6(3), a Division shall be constituted for the hearing of any application or matter relating to an application. Two of the Division members shall be solicitor members and one shall be a lay member and (unless the President shall determine otherwise) a solicitor member shall act as Chairman.

PART 3
APPLICATIONS

5   Applications in respect of solicitors, recognised bodies, registered European lawyers and registered foreign lawyers

(1)   An application to the Tribunal in respect of any allegation or complaint made in respect of a solicitor, a recognised body, a registered European lawyer or a registered foreign lawyer shall be in the form of Form 1 in the Schedule to these Rules.

(2)   The application shall be supported by a Statement setting out the allegations and the facts and matters supporting the application and each allegation contained in it.

(3)   The application, the Statement and any documents exhibited with them shall be delivered to the Clerk together with 5 additional copies and a further copy for any second or further respondent.

6   Certification of a case to answer

(1)   An application made under Rule 5 shall be considered by a solicitor member, who shall certify whether there is a case to answer.

(2)   Paragraph (3) applies if—

   (a)   the solicitor member is minded not to certify that there is a case to answer; or

   (b)   in his opinion, the case is one of doubt or difficulty.

(3)   If this paragraph applies, the application shall be considered by a panel of three members of the Tribunal, at least one of whom shall be a solicitor member and one a Lay member.

(4)   If a solicitor member or a panel decides not to certify that a case to answer is established in accordance with this rule, the application shall be dismissed without formal order unless any party to the proceedings requires otherwise.

(5)   If it is certified that there is a case to answer, a clerk shall serve the application, the Statement and any documents exhibited with them on each respondent in accordance with rule 10.

7   Supplementary statements

(1)   The applicant may file supplementary Statements with the Clerk containing additional facts or matters on which the applicant seeks to rely or further allegations and facts or matters in support of the application. Any supplementary Statement containing further allegations against the respondent shall be treated as though it were an application for the purposes of rules 5(3) and 6(1), (2), (3) and (5).

(2)   Without prejudice to any further application which may be made, no supplementary Statement shall, unless by order of the Tribunal, be filed later than 12 months after the date of the Application or less than 30 days before the date fixed for the hearing of the application.

8   Applications by the Law Society against solicitors' employees

(1)   An application made by the Law Society for an order under section 43(2) of the Act shall be in the form of Form 2 in the Schedule to these rules.

(2)   In a case where the Law Society has applied to the Tribunal for an order under section 43(2) of the Act, the solicitor, recognised body, or registered European lawyer by or for whose benefit the respondent is employed or remunerated—

   (a)   may also be named or joined as a respondent to the application; and

   (b)   shall be joined as a respondent if the Tribunal so direct.

(3)   The provisions of rules 5(2) and (3) and 6(1) to (5) shall apply to every application made under section 43(2) of the Act.

(4)   An application for a review of an order made under section 43(3) of the Act shall be in the form of Form 3 in the Schedule to these Rules.

(5)   Every application under section 43(3) of the Act shall be served on the Law Society and the Law Society shall file with the Clerk a Statement setting out the facts and matters on which it relied in making the order under Section 43(2) of the Act.

9   Other Applications

(1)   This rule applies to applications made to the Tribunal under section 47 of the Act—

   (a)   by a former solicitor seeking restoration to the Roll;

   (b)   by a person seeking restoration to the register of European lawyers or the register of foreign lawyers if his name has been removed from either register;

(c)   by a solicitor, registered foreign lawyer or registered European lawyer seeking the termination of an indefinite period of suspension from practice imposed by the Tribunal.

(2)   An application to which this rule applies shall be made in the form of Form 4 in the Schedule to these Rules.

(3)   The Law Society shall be a respondent to every application to which this rule applies.

(4)   The applicant shall serve on the Law Society—

(a)   a copy of the application; and

(b)   a Statement in support of the application.

(5)   Every application to which this rule applies shall be advertised by the applicant once in the Law Society's Gazette and once in a newspaper circulating in the area of the applicant's former practice.

(6)   Any person may, no later than 10 days before the hearing date of an application to which this rule applies, serve on the Tribunal and the parties to the application notice of his intention to oppose the grant of the application and the Tribunal may allow that person to appear before the Tribunal at the hearing of the application, call evidence and make representations upon which the Tribunal may allow him to be cross-examined.

PART 4
PROCEDURE AND RULES OF EVIDENCE

10 Service of documents

(1)   Any application, Statement or other document required to be served under rules 6(5), 8(5) and 9(4) shall be served—

(a)   personally; or

(b)   by sending by guaranteed delivery post or other guaranteed and acknowledged delivery to the last known place of business or abode of the person to be served; and

(c)   in such other manner as the Tribunal may direct.

(2)   Any Statement, notice or document other than one which is required to be served in accordance with paragraph (1) may be served in accordance with that paragraph.

(3)   In the case of a solicitor, any Statement, notice or other document required to be served under these rules may be served—

(a)   by leaving it at the address shown as his place of business in the register kept by the Law Society under section 9 of the Act; or

(b)   by any of the methods mentioned in paragraphs (a) to (d) of rule 6.2(1) of the Civil Procedure Rules 1998 as they may be modified, amended or replaced.

(4)   Any application, Statement, notice or other document served in accordance with paragraph (1) shall be deemed served on the second working day following the day on which it is delivered, posted or transmitted.

(5)   An application, Statement, notice or other document delivered to the last known place of business or abode of the person to be served may be regarded by the Tribunal as duly served if it is satisfied that it is reasonable to expect that the application, Statement, notice or other document has been received by or brought to the attention of the person to be served.

(6)   If the Tribunal requires the advertisement of any proceedings under these Rules, it may regard that advertisement as service for the purposes of these Rules.

11 Directions

(1) A clerk may give any directions deemed necessary or appropriate for the hearing of any matter brought before the Tribunal.

(2) Without prejudice to paragraph (1), directions may be made about documentation, inspection, Statements, skeleton arguments and the place or time of any hearing.

(3) A clerk may appoint a time and place for the review of the progress of the matter and shall notify the parties of the date, time and place of any such review.

(4) A clerk may refer to the Tribunal any matter for a decision or directions and the Tribunal may itself or on the application of any party make an order on such terms as to the Tribunal shall appear just—

    (a) to give consent to the withdrawal of an application or allegation in respect of which a case to answer has been certified;

    (b) to adjourn any hearing listed for directions or for a substantive hearing;

    (c) to agree to the amendment of any application or allegation or the correction of any matter;

    (d) to make any directions which shall appear necessary or appropriate to secure the timely hearing of the matter.

(5) Any hearing under this rule shall be held in public unless rules 12(4) or (5) apply.

(6) No application or allegation in respect of which a case to answer has been certified may be withdrawn without the consent of the Tribunal.

12 Listing

(1) Unless the Tribunal has made directions in respect of the hearing, a clerk shall appoint a date for the hearing by the Tribunal and shall give notice of the date to the parties. The hearing shall not, unless all the parties have agreed or the Tribunal has so ordered, take place sooner than the expiry of a period of 42 days beginning with the date of service of the notice appointing the date of the hearing.

(2) A clerk shall arrange for the hearing date to be published in the Daily Cause List of the High Court.

(3) Subject to paragraphs (4) and (5) every hearing shall take place in public.

(4) Any party to an application and any person who claims to be affected by it may seek an order from the Tribunal that the hearing or part of it be conducted in private on the grounds of—

    (a) exceptional hardship; or

    (b) exceptional prejudice,

to a party, a witness or any person affected by the application.

(5) If it is satisfied that those grounds are met, the Tribunal shall conduct the hearing or part of it in private and make such order as shall appear to it to be just and proper.

(6) The Tribunal may, before or during a hearing, direct that the hearing or part of it be held in private if—

    (a) the Tribunal is satisfied that it would have granted an application under paragraph (4) had one been made; or

    (b) in the Tribunal's view a hearing in public would prejudice the interests of justice.

13   Evidence: general

(1)   Subject to the following provisions of this rule, the Civil Evidence Act 1968, and the Civil Evidence Act 1995 shall apply in relation to proceedings before the Tribunal in the same manner as they apply in relation to civil proceedings.

(2)   Any notice given under the provisions of the Acts mentioned in paragraph (1) shall be given no later than 21 days before the date fixed for the hearing of an application.

(3)   Any counter-notice shall be given no later than 10 days before the date fixed for the hearing.

(4)   No later than 28 days before the date fixed for the hearing of an application, the applicant may, by written notice, require any other party to the application to indicate to him, no later than the date on which the period of 14 days from the date of the giving of the notice expires, which of any facts set out in the Statement submitted in support of the application are in dispute.

(5)   Failure to reply to such a notice shall be material only in relation to the question of costs.

(6)   Any party to an application may, by written notice, not later than nine days before the date fixed for the hearing, request any other party to agree that any document may be admitted as evidence.

(7)   If any other party desires to challenge the authenticity of a document which is the subject of paragraph (6), he shall no later than the date on which the period of six days beginning with the date on which the notice was served, give notice that he does not agree to the admission of the document and that he requires that its authenticity be proved at the hearing.

(8)   If the recipient of a notice given under paragraph (6) does not give a notice in response within the period mentioned in paragraph (7), he shall be deemed to have admitted the document unless otherwise ordered by the Tribunal.

(9)   A party to an application may, pursuant to Section 46(11) of the Act, require the attendance at the hearing of any person or the production of any document relevant to the proceedings and any summons for that purpose shall be in the form of Form 5 in the Schedule to these Rules.

(10)   At the discretion of the Tribunal, the strict rules of evidence shall not apply at a hearing before the Tribunal.

14   Written evidence

(1)   The Tribunal may in its discretion, in respect of a whole case or of any particular fact or facts, proceed and act upon evidence given by Statement.

(2)   Every Statement upon which any party proposes to rely shall be filed with the Clerk and served on all other parties to the application in question no later than 21 days before the date fixed for the hearing of the application together with a notice in the form of Form 6 in the Schedule to these Rules.

(3)   Any party on whom a notice has been served under paragraph (2) and who requires the attendance, at the hearing, of the witness in question shall, no later than 9 days before the date of the hearing require, in writing, the other party to produce the witness at the hearing.

(4)   If no party requires the attendance of a witness in accordance with the provisions of this rule, the Tribunal may accept the Statement in question in evidence.

(5)   If a witness who has been required to attend a hearing in accordance with the provisions of this Rule fails to do so, the onus shall be on the party seeking to rely on the Statement of that witness to show why the Statement should be accepted in evidence.

(6)   If any party intends to call as a witness any person who has not produced a Statement, he must, no later than 10 days before the date fixed for the hearing, notify the Clerk and any

other party to the proceedings of his intention and forthwith serve a copy of a written proof of evidence on the other party and lodge five copies of the proof with the Clerk.

15 Previous findings of record

(1) In any proceedings before the Tribunal which relate to the decision of another court or tribunal, the following rules shall apply if it is proved that the decision relates to the relevant party to the application.

(2) A conviction for a criminal offence may be proved by the production of a certified copy of the certificate of conviction relating to the offence and proof of a conviction shall constitute evidence that the person in question was guilty of the offence. The findings of fact upon which that conviction was based shall be admissible as conclusive proof of those facts save in exceptional circumstances.

(3) The finding of and penalty imposed by any tribunal in or outside England and Wales exercising a professional disciplinary jurisdiction may be proved by producing a certified copy of the order, finding or note of penalty in question and the findings of fact upon which the finding in question was based shall be admissible as proof but not conclusive proof of the facts in question.

(4) The judgment of any civil court in any jurisdiction may be proved by producing a certified copy of the judgment and the findings of fact upon which that judgment was based shall be admissible as proof but not conclusive proof of those facts.

16 Hearings and Findings

(1) The hearing of an application shall take place at such time and place as shall be considered by the Tribunal to be appropriate and convenient.

(2) If the Tribunal is satisfied that notice of the hearing was served on the respondent in accordance with these Rules, the Tribunal shall have power to hear and determine an application notwithstanding that the Respondent fails to attend in person or is not represented at the hearing.

(3) At the conclusion of the hearing, the Tribunal shall make a finding as to whether any or all of the allegations in the application have been substantiated whereupon a clerk shall inform the Tribunal whether in any previous disciplinary proceedings before the Tribunal allegations were found to have been substantiated against the Respondent.

(4) The Respondent shall be entitled to make submissions by way of mitigation in respect of any sanction (including any order for costs) which the Tribunal may impose.

(5) The Tribunal may announce its decision and make an order at the conclusion of the hearing or may reserve its decision for announcement at a later date. In either case the announcement shall be made in public and in either case the Tribunal shall as soon as is practicable deliver to the applicant and to the respondent its detailed written findings which shall include its reasons and conclusions upon the evidence before it.

17 The Order

(1) An order made under rule 16(5) shall be signed by a member of the Tribunal upon the announcement of the decision and shall, subject to paragraph (2) be filed forthwith with the Law Society.

(2) The Tribunal may suspend the filing of the Order if it appears to the Tribunal that there is good reason to do so, in which event the Order shall not take effect (including any suspension from practice) until it is filed with the Law Society.

PART 5
MISCELLANEOUS

18   Costs

(1)   The Tribunal may make such order as to costs as the Tribunal shall think fit including an order—

    (a)   disallowing costs incurred unnecessarily; or

    (b)   that costs be paid by any party judged to be responsible for wasted or unnecessary costs, whether arising through non compliance with time limits or otherwise.

(2)   The Tribunal may order that any party bear the whole or a part or a proportion of the costs.

(3)   The amount of costs to be paid may either be fixed by the Tribunal or be subject to detailed assessment by a Costs Judge.

(4)   The Tribunal may also make an order as to costs under this Rule—

    (a)   where any application or allegation is withdrawn or amended;

    (b)   where no allegation of misconduct (including an application under Section 43 of the Solicitors Act) is proved against a respondent.

19   Re-hearing where respondent neither appears nor is represented

(1)   At any time before the filing of the Tribunal's Order with the Law Society under rule 17 or before the expiry of the period of 14 days beginning with the date of the filing of the order, the respondent may apply to the Tribunal for a re-hearing of an application if—

    (a)   he neither attended in person nor was represented at the hearing of the application in question; and

    (b)   the Tribunal determined the application in his absence.

(2)   An application for a re-hearing under this Rule shall be made in the form of Form 7 in the Schedule to these Rules and shall be supported by a Statement setting out the facts upon which the applicant wishes to rely.

(3)   If satisfied that it is just so to do, the Tribunal may grant the application upon such terms, including as to costs, as it thinks fit. The re-hearing shall be held before a Division of the Tribunal comprised of different members from those who heard the original application.

20   Adjournment for Law Society to investigate

In the case of an application by a person other than the Law Society, the Tribunal may, before or after certification of a case to answer, adjourn the matter for a period not exceeding 3 months to enable the Law Society to carry out its own investigations and—

    (a)   if it thinks fit, initiate its own application; or

    (b)   by agreement with the applicant, undertake the application.

21   Miscellaneous

(1)   Subject to the provisions of these Rules, the Tribunal may regulate its own procedure.

(2)   The Tribunal may dispense with any requirements of these Rules in respect of notices, Statements, witnesses, service or time in any case where it appears to the Tribunal to be just so to do.

(3)   The Tribunal (or a panel of Tribunal members consisting of not less than 5 members of whom not less than 2 shall be lay members) may give such notices or make such directions concerning the practices or procedures of the Tribunal as are consistent with these Rules and as shall seem appropriate.

APPENDIX 16

(4) The Tribunal shall promulgate notices or directions given or made under paragraph (3) under the authority of the President. Practice Directions in force prior to the date on which these Rules come into force shall remain in full force and effect after that date.

(5) Where the Tribunal has made a finding based solely upon the certificate of conviction for a criminal offence which is subsequently quashed the Tribunal may, on the application of the Law Society or the respondent to the application in respect of which the finding arose, revoke its finding and make such order as to costs as shall appear to be just in the circumstances.

22 Revocation

The Solicitors (Disciplinary Proceedings) Rules 1994 are revoked.

23 Transitional provision

These Rules shall not apply to proceedings in which an Application is made before the date on which these rules came into force and those proceedings shall be subject to the Solicitors (Disciplinary Proceedings) Rules 1994 as if they had not been revoked.

Signed by authority of the Solicitors' Disciplinary Tribunal and approved by the Master of the Rolls

Anthony Isaacs

President

Sir Anthony Clarke

Master of the Rolls

14th December 2007

SCHEDULE

FORM 1

Rule 5(1)

FORM OF APPLICATION in respect of existing and former Solicitors, Registered Foreign Lawyers, Registered European Lawyers, and Incorporated Solicitors Practices.

Number ....

IN THE MATTER of the Solicitors Act 1974 (as amended)

.... Applicant

.... Respondent

I, ... of ....

APPLY [on behalf of (1)] that (2)

of.. ....

be required to answer the allegations contained in the Statement which accompanies this Application and that such Order be made as the Tribunal shall think right.

SIGNED by the Applicant ....

whose address for service is

....

....

....

Dated

Notes:

1. Applicants making an application on behalf of a third party, e.g. the Law Society should so state.

2. Add the full names of the Respondent and his address or last known abode or last known place or places of business and his status as an existing or former Solicitor, registered European lawyer, registered foreign lawyer or Recognised Body (Incorporated Solicitors Practice).

3. An application may also be made in this form that a direction made by the Law Society in relation to inadequate professional services be made enforceable as if contained in an Order of the High Court.

FORM 2

Rule 8(1)

FORM OF APPLICATION in respect of a person who is or was employed or remunerated by a Solicitor, Registered European Lawyer or Recognised Body.

Number ....

IN THE MATTER OF The Solicitors Act 1974 and the Solicitors (Disciplinary Proceedings) Rules 2007

I ....

APPLY on behalf of The Law Society that an Order under Section 43 of the Solicitors Act 1974 (as amended) be made by the Tribunal directing that as from a date to be specified in such Order, no Solicitor, Recognised Body or registered European lawyer shall, employ or remunerate

....

who is or was employed or remunerated by .... ,

except in accordance with permission in writing granted by The Law Society or that such other Order might be made as the Tribunal should think right.

Dated ....

.... Applicant

Address of Applicant

FORM 3

Rule 8(4)

FORM of APPLICATION to review or revoke an Order made under Section 43 of the Solicitors Act 1974 (as amended) by The Law Society or the Tribunal with respect to a person who is or was employed or remunerated by a Solicitor, Recognised Body or Registered European lawyer.

Number ....

IN THE MATTER OF the Solicitors Act 1974 (as amended) and the Solicitors (Disciplinary Proceedings) Rules 2007

To: the Solicitors' Disciplinary Tribunal and to The Law Society

I, ... of ....

APPLY to the Tribunal for a [REVIEW][REVOCATION] of the Order made against me dated

(a copy of which is attached to this application)

Dated: ....

Signed: ....

Address: ....

....

....

Notes:

1. This Form should be used in respect of a person who is not a Solicitor or registered European lawyer and who has been made the subject of an Order under Section 43 of the Solicitors Act 1974 (as amended) by the Law Society and who (a) seeks a review of the Order or (b) seeks a revocation of the Order. It should be accompanied by a Statement setting out the grounds for such a review or revocation and attached to it should be a copy of the Order in question.

2. This Form should be served on the Tribunal and contemporaneously on The Law Society.

FORM 4

Rule 9(2)

FORM of APPLICATION for restoration to the Roll of Solicitors or Register of Foreign or European Lawyers; or

FORM of APPLICATION by a solicitor, Registered Foreign Lawyer or Registered European Lawyer who has been suspended from practice indefinitely by order of the Tribunal for an order to bring the suspension to an end

Number.. ....

IN THE MATTER OF the Solicitors Act 1974 (as amended) and the Solicitors (Disciplinary Proceedings) Rules 2007

I, ... of ....

was admitted as a Solicitor of the Supreme Court of Judicature★ registered as a registered European lawyer★/registered foreign lawyer

on

★ By an Order of the Solicitors Disciplinary Tribunal dated a true copy of which is attached to this application, I was struck off the Roll/Register of European/ Foreign Lawyers★ and—

(1) I APPLY that my name be restored to the Roll/Register★ of European/ Foreign Lawyers;

(2) I undertake to advertise this Application in accordance with the Rules.

★ By an Order of the Solicitors Disciplinary Tribunal dated a true copy of which is attached to this application, my right to practise was the subject of an order of suspension from practise for an indefinite period and I APPLY that a date be fixed for the ending of such indefinite period of suspension.:

★ delete as appropriate

Dated: ....

Signed ....

Note: This Form must be served on the Clerk to the Solicitors Disciplinary Tribunal and contemporaneously upon The Law Society accompanied by a Statement in support of the Application.

FORM 5

Rule 13(9)

WITNESS SUMMONS

Number.. ....

IN THE MATTER OF the Solicitors Act 1974

AND IN THE MATTER OF

....

To

```
┌────────────────────────────────────────────────────────────────────────┐
│                                                                          │
│                                                                          │
└────────────────────────────────────────────────────────────────────────┘
```

You are summoned to attend at the Solicitors' Disciplinary Tribunal at (Tribunal address)

on .... of .... at .. .. (am)(pm)

(and each following day of the hearing until the Tribunal tells you that you are no longer required.)

☐ to give evidence in respect of the above application

☐ to produce the following document(s) (*give details*)

The sum of £   is paid or offered to you with this summons. This is to cover your travelling expenses to and from the Tribunal and includes an amount by way of compensation for loss of time.

This summons was issued on the application of the applicant(respondent) or the applicant's (respondent's) solicitor whose name, address and reference number is:

Do not ignore this summons

If you were offered money for travel expenses and compensation for loss of time, at the time it was served on you, you must—

- attend the Tribunal on the date and time shown and/or produce documents as required by the summons; and

- take an oath or affirm as required for the purposes of answering questions about your evidence or the documents you have been asked to produce.

In the High Court, disobeyance of a witness summons is a contempt of court and you may be fined or imprisoned for contempt. You may also be liable to pay any wasted costs that arise because of your non-compliance.

If you wish to set aside or vary this witness summons, you make an application to the Tribunal.

APPENDIX 16

FORM 6

Rule 14(2)

FORM of NOTICE to accompany Statement of Evidence

Number ....

IN THE MATTER OF the Solicitors Act 1974 and the Solicitors Disciplinary Proceedings Rules 2007

AND IN THE MATTER OF

....

TAKE NOTICE that the applicant/respondent proposes to rely upon the statement(s) listed below, copies of which are served herewith.

If you wish any person who has made one of these statements to be required to attend the hearing as a witness you must, not less than 21 days before the date set down for the hearing of the application, notify me and the Clerk to the Tribunal to that effect. In the event of your failure to do so the Tribunal may accept the statement in question in evidence.

LIST

Date of Statement   Name of Person who made the Statement

1.

2.

3.

Date:

Signed:

Address:

FORM 7

Rule 19(2)

FORM of APPLICATION for a Rehearing

Number: ....

IN THE MATTER OF the Solicitors Act 1974 and the Solicitors Disciplinary Proceedings Rules 2007

AND IN THE MATTER OF

....

Number of Tribunal case in respect of which a rehearing is requested ....

I APPLY under Rule 19(2) of the Solicitors (Disciplinary Proceedings) Rules 2007 that the abovementioned case be reheard by the Tribunal. The facts upon which I rely in support of this application are set out below:

(*set out here full details of the facts on which the applicant for a rehearing relies and include the reasons why the person applying for the rehearing did not appear or was not represented before the Tribunal at the earlier hearing and set out all matters which he wishes to place before the Tribunal in mitigation or otherwise*).

Dated:

Signature:

Address:

Solicitors Disciplinary Tribunal practice directions

Practice Direction No 1

The Tribunal direct that generally pursuant to Rule 7(1)(iii) it will consider an Application and Statement or Affidavit pursuant to Rules 4 and 6 to have been properly served if an enquiry agent has established the address of the Respondent by enquiry and/or observation and leaves the appropriate papers at that address.

Practice Direction No 2

Dated: 25th February 1996

Amended: 27th November 2002

Re: Disclosure/Discovery

Where directions are sought as to disclosure or discovery of documents, the Tribunal will adopt the view that material should be disclosed which could be seen on a sensible appraisal by the Applicant:-

(i)   to be relevant or possibly relevant to an issue in the case;

(ii) to raise or possibly raise a new issue whose existence is not apparent from the evidence the Applicant proposes to use, and which would or might assist the Respondent in fully testing the Applicant's case or in adducing evidence in rebuttal;

(iii) to hold out a real (as opposed to a fanciful) prospect of providing a lead on evidence which goes to (i) or (ii).

There may be exceptional circumstances in which the Tribunal, balancing the interest in disclosure of a document against a competing public interest such as a specific and compelling need for confidentiality, may decide not to order disclosure of a document which falls within (i) (ii) or (iii) above.

Practice Direction No 3

An application for a rehearing made pursuant to Rule 25 of the Solicitors (Disciplinary Proceedings) Rules 1994 will normally be heard in public in open court before a division of the Tribunal of different constitution from that which heard the matter in respect of which a rehearing is sought. It will be only in exceptional circumstances that the Tribunal will exercise its discretion in favour of a private hearing.

Dated this 5th day of March 1998

On behalf of the Tribunal

(signed) G. B. Marsh

President

Practice Direction No 4

The Tribunal that direct that generally pursuant to Rule 7(1)(ii)(iii) it will consider an Application and Statement or Affidavit pursuant to Rules 4 and 6 to have been properly served if it has been sent using the Royal Mail's Special Delivery system in place of first class post with Recorded Delivery and Advice of Delivery.

APPENDIX 16

Dated this 29th day of January 2001

(signed) G. B. Marsh

President

Solicitors Disciplinary Tribunal policy/practice note

Adjournments

(1)   The following practice note is to give guidance to Applicants and Respondents who seek an adjournment of a hearing the date of which has been fixed.

(2)   Applications for an adjournment made more than 21 days before the hearing date should be made by letter to the Clerk. The letter should

    (a)   Indicate the full reasons why an adjournment is being sought

    (b)   Provide any documentary evidence in support e.g. medical reports

    (c)   State whether the other party to the proceedings supports or opposes the application for an adjournment

(3)   The Tribunal will be reluctant to agree to an adjournment unless the request is supported by both parties or, if it is not, the reasons appear to the Tribunal to be justifiable because not to grant an adjournment would result in injustice to the person seeking the adjournment.

(4)   The following reasons will NOT generally be regarded as providing justification for an adjournment:

    (a)   The Existence of Other Proceedings

    The existence or possibility of criminal proceedings unless the criminal proceedings relate to the same or substantially the same underlying facts as form the basis of the proceedings before the Tribunal AND there is a genuine risk that the proceedings before the Tribunal may 'muddy the waters of justice' so far as concerns the criminal proceedings. Proceedings which are not imminent will not usually meet this criterion. Civil proceedings are even less likely to do so.

    (b)   Lack of Readiness

    The lack of readiness on the part of either the Applicant or Respondent or any claimed inconvenience or clash of engagements whether professional or person.

    (c)   Ill-health

    The claimed medical condition of the Applicant or Respondent unless this is supported by a reasoned opinion of an appropriate medical adviser. A doctor's certificate issued for social security and statutory sick pay purposes only or other certificate merely indicating that the person is unable to attend for work is unlikely to be sufficient.

    (d)   Inability to Secure Representation

    The inability of the Respondent for financial or other reasons to secure the services of a representative at the hearing or financial reasons for the non attendance of the Respondent.

(5)   The Tribunal accepts that there may be reasons why an application for an adjournment needs to be made within a three week period before the date which has been fixed for the Hearing. Except for cases where the reason for the adjournment application has

genuinely arisen at a very late stage, the Tribunal will expect the Respondent to support a late application for adjournment with a statement of truth as to the reasons for the sought adjournment.

(6)   Where the guidance given in this Practice Note is not followed, Applicants and Respondents will appreciate that the Tribunal may, in its discretion and in appropriate cases, order costs to be paid by either or both parties regardless of the outcome of the substantive proceedings.

(7)   The Clerk to the Tribunal may agree to the adjournment of a matter if the application is made at least three weeks before the scheduled hearing date and she is satisfied that the adjournment is made in one of the circumstances referred to in this practice note. The Clerk may in any case where she considers it right either seek the approval of the Chairman of the Tribunal or list the matter for an adjournment hearing before a division of the Tribunal sitting in public. The Clerk will endeavour to list the adjournment hearing on a date before that fixed for the substantive hearing.

(8)   Those appearing before the Tribunal should be conscious of the need to ensure that cases are heard with reasonable expedition so that the interests of the Public as well as the Profession can be protected. The efficient and timely determination of cases before the Tribunal will usually be in the best interests of all concerned and the Tribunal will always need to be convinced that the interests of justice in any particular cases will be best served by agreeing to an adjournment. **The Tribunal can (and does, therefore, in appropriate cases) exercise its right under the Rules to reject an application for an adjournment and proceed with a substantive hearing on the date which has been previously fixed. The Rules provide that such a hearing may take place in the absence of the Respondent.**

(9)   Every application for adjournment will be considered on its own merits and this practice note is made to provide assistance as to matters which the Tribunal will regard as relevant to any such application, and to identify matters which in the experience of the Tribunal are frequently relied upon in support of applications but which, save in exceptional circumstances, the Tribunal does not currently regard, and would in the future be similarly unlikely to regard as persuasive in themselves.

Anthony Isaacs
President

Extracts from the Solicitors Act 1974

[With consolidated amendments to 1 January 2010]

Solicitors Act 1974

1974 CHAPTER 47

An Act to consolidate the Solicitors Acts 1957 to 1974 and certain other enactments relating to solicitors

[31st July 1974]

BE IT ENACTED by the Queen's most Excellent Majesty, by and with the advice and consent of the Lords Spiritual and Temporal, and Commons, in this present Parliament assembled, and by the authority of the same, as follows:—

PART I
RIGHT TO PRACTISE AS SOLICITOR

Qualifications and training

1 Qualifications for practising as solicitor

No person shall be qualified to act as a solicitor unless—

   (a)   he has been admitted as a solicitor, and

   (b)   his name is on the roll, and

   (c)   he has in force a certificate issued by the Society in accordance with the provisions of this Part authorising him to practise as a solicitor (in this Act referred to as a "practising certificate").

1A Practising certificates: employed solicitors

A person who has been admitted as a solicitor and whose name is on the roll shall, if he would not otherwise be taken to be acting as a solicitor, be taken for the purposes of this Act to be so acting if he is employed in connection with the provision of any legal services—

   (a)   by any person who is qualified to act as a solicitor;

   (b)   by any partnership at least one member of which is so qualified;

   (c)   by a body recognised ... under section 9 of the Administration of Justice Act 1985 (incorporated practices); or

   (d)   by any other person who, for the purposes of the Legal Services Act 2007, is an authorised person in relation to an activity which is a reserved legal activity (within the meaning of that Act).

1B Restriction on practice as sole solicitor

(1)   Rules under section 31 (rules as to professional practice etc) must provide that a solicitor may not practise as a sole solicitor unless he has in force—

(a)   a practising certificate, and

(b)   an endorsement of that certificate by the Society authorising him to practise as a sole solicitor (a "sole solicitor endorsement").

(2)   The rules may provide that, for the purposes of the rules and this Act, a solicitor is not to be regarded as practising as a sole solicitor in such circumstances as may be prescribed by the rules.

(3)   The rules must prescribe the circumstances in which a solicitor may be regarded by the Society as suitable to be authorised to practise as a sole solicitor.

13   Appeals etc in connection with the issue of practising certificates

(1)   A person who makes an application under section 9 may appeal to the High Court against—

(a)   a decision to refuse the application for a practising certificate,

(b)   if the application included an application for a sole solicitor endorsement, a decision to refuse the application for the endorsement, or

(c)   a decision to impose a condition on a practising certificate issued in consequence of the application.

(2)   A person who holds a practising certificate subject to a condition within section 10(4)(b) may appeal to the High Court against any decision by the Society to refuse to approve the taking of any step for the purposes of that condition.

(3)   The Society may make rules which provide, as respects any application under section 9 that is neither granted nor refused by the Society within such period as may be specified in the rules, for enabling an appeal to be brought under this section in relation to the application as if it had been refused by the Society.

(4)   On an appeal under subsection (1), the High Court may—

(a)   affirm the decision of the Society,

(b)   direct the Society to make a sole solicitor endorsement on the applicant's practising certificate and to issue that certificate subject to such conditions (if any) as the High Court may think fit,

(c)   direct the Society to issue a certificate to the applicant free from conditions or subject to such conditions as the High Court may think fit,

(d)   direct the Society not to issue a certificate,

(e)   if a certificate has been issued, by order suspend it,

(f)   if the certificate has been endorsed with a sole solicitor endorsement, by order suspend the endorsement, or

(g)   make such other order as the High Court thinks fit.

(5)   On an appeal under subsection (2), the High Court may—

(a)   affirm the decision of the Society,

(b)   direct the Society to approve the taking of one or more steps for the purposes of a condition within section 10(4)(b), or

(c)   make such other order as the High Court thinks fit.

(6)   In relation to an appeal under this section the High Court may make such order as it thinks fit as to payment of costs.

(7)   The decision of the High Court on an appeal under subsection (1) or (2) shall be final.

13ZA Application to practise as sole practitioner while practising certificate in force

(1) A solicitor whose practising certificate for the time being in force (his "current certificate") does not have a sole solicitor endorsement, may apply to the Society for such an endorsement.

(2) For the purposes of subsection (1) a practising certificate with a sole solicitor endorsement which is suspended is to be treated as having such an endorsement.

(3) A solicitor may not apply under subsection (1) if he is suspended from practice as a sole solicitor.

(4) An application must be—

  (a) made in accordance with regulations under section 28, and

  (b) accompanied by any fee payable under section 13ZB in respect of the endorsement applied for.

(5) Where a sole solicitor endorsement is granted to an applicant of a prescribed description, the applicant's practising certificate shall have effect subject to any conditions prescribed in relation to applicants of that description.

"Prescribed" means prescribed by regulations under section 28(3B)(f).

(6) A person who makes an application under this section may appeal to the High Court against—

  (a) a decision to refuse the application, or

  (b) a decision to impose a condition on a practising certificate in accordance with subsection (5).

(7) The Society may by rules make provision, as respects any application under this section that is neither granted nor refused by the Society within such period as may be specified in the rules, for enabling an appeal to be brought under this section in relation to the application as if it had been refused by the Society.

(8) On an appeal under this section the High Court may—

  (a) affirm the decision of the Society,

  (b) direct the Society to grant a sole solicitor endorsement,

  (c) direct that the applicant's practising certificate is to have effect subject to such conditions (if any) as the High Court thinks fit, or

  (d) make such other order as the High Court thinks fit.

(9) In relation to an appeal under this section the High Court may make such order as it thinks fit as to payment of costs.

(10) The decision of the High Court on an appeal under this section shall be final.

13ZB Fee payable on making of sole solicitor endorsement

(1) Before a sole solicitor endorsement is granted under section 13ZA, there must be paid to the Society in respect of the endorsement a fee of such amount as the Society may from time to time determine.

(2) Different fees may be specified for different categories of applicant and in different circumstances.

(3) If a fee payable under this section would not otherwise be a practising fee for the purposes of section 51 of the Legal Services Act 2007, it is to be treated for the purposes of that section as such a fee.

(4)   In subsection (3) "practising fee" has the meaning given by that section.

13A   Imposition of conditions while practising certificates are in force

(1)   Subject to the provisions of this section, the Society may in the case of any solicitor direct that his practising certificate for the time being in force (his "current certificate") shall have effect subject to such conditions as the Society may think fit.

(2)   The power conferred by subsection (1) is exercisable in relation to a solicitor at any time during the period for which the solicitor's current certificate is in force if—

(a)   under section 13ZA the Society grants a sole solicitor endorsement, or

(b)   it appears to the Society that the case is of a prescribed description.

(3)   "Prescribed" means prescribed by regulations under section 28.

(6)   A solicitor in whose case a direction is given under this section may appeal to the High Court against the decision of the Society.

(7)   On an appeal under subsection (6), the High Court may—

(a)   affirm the decision of the Society; or

(b)   direct that the appellant's current certificate shall have effect subject to such conditions as the High Court thinks fit; or

(c)   by order revoke the direction; or

(d)   make such other order as it thinks fit.

(7A)   The decision of the High Court on an appeal under subsection (6) shall be final.

(8)   Subsections (4) and (5) of section 10 apply for the purposes of subsection (1) of this section as they apply for the purposes of that section.

(9)   A solicitor who holds a practising certificate subject to a condition imposed under subsection (1) which prohibits that solicitor from taking any steps specified in the condition, except with the approval of the Society, may appeal to the High Court against any decision by the Society to refuse to approve the taking of any step for the purposes of that condition.

(10)   On an appeal under subsection (9), the High Court may—

(a)   affirm the decision of the Society,

(b)   direct the Society to approve the taking of one or more steps for the purposes of the condition, or

(c)   make such other order as the High Court thinks fit.

(11)   The decision of the High Court on an appeal under subsection (9) shall be final.

(12)   In relation to an appeal under this section the High Court may make such order as it thinks fit as to payment of costs.

13B   Suspension of practising certificates where solicitors convicted of fraud or serious crime

(1)   Where—

(a)   a solicitor has been convicted of—

(i)   an offence involving dishonesty or deception; or

(ii)   an indictable offence; and

(b)   the Society has made an application to the Tribunal under section 47 with respect to him, the Society may direct that any practising certificate or sole solicitor endorsement of his which is for the time being in force be suspended.

(2)   Any such suspension shall be for such period, not exceeding six months, as the Society shall specify in the direction.

(3)   If, before the specified period expires—

(a)   the Tribunal determines the Society's application;

(b)   the conviction is quashed or set aside; or

(c)   the Society withdraws its application to the Tribunal,

the suspension shall cease to have effect.

(4)   Where the specified period comes to an end without any of the events mentioned in subsection (3) having occurred, the Society may direct that the suspension be continued for such period, not exceeding six months, as it shall specify in the direction.

(5)   A suspension under this section may only be extended once under subsection (4).

(6)   Nothing in this section is to be taken as in any way affecting the Tribunal's power to suspend a solicitor from practice or from practice as a sole solicitor.

(7)   A solicitor in whose case a direction is given under subsection (1) or (4) may appeal to the High Court against the direction within one month of being notified of it.

(8)   In an appeal under subsection (7), the High Court may—

(a)   affirm the suspension;

(b)   direct that the appellant's certificate or sole solicitor endorsement shall not be suspended, but that the appellant's certificate shall have effect subject to such conditions as the High Court thinks fit;

(c)   by order revoke the direction; or

(d)   make such other order as it thinks fit.

(9)   In relation to an appeal under subsection (7) the High Court may make such order as it thinks fit as to payment of costs.

(10)   The decision of the High Court on an appeal under subsection (7) shall be final.

15   Suspension of practising certificates

(1)   The making by the Tribunal or by the court of an order suspending a solicitor from practice shall operate, and an adjudication in bankruptcy of a solicitor shall operate immediately, to suspend any practising certificate of that solicitor for the time being in force.

(1A)   Where the power conferred by paragraph 6(1), 6A(1) or 9(1) of Schedule 1 has been exercised in relation to a solicitor by virtue of paragraph 1(1)(a)(i), (aa), (c) (so far as it applies to rules made by virtue of section 31 or 32) or (e) of that Schedule, the exercise of that power shall operate immediately to suspend any practising certificate of that solicitor for the time being in force.

(1B)   Subsection (1A) does not apply if, at the time when the power referred to there is exercised, the Society directs that subsection (1A) is not to apply in relation to the solicitor concerned.

(1C)   If, at the time when the power referred to in subsection (1A) is exercised, the Society gives a direction to that effect, the solicitor concerned may continue to act in relation to any matter specified in the direction as if his practising certificate had not been suspended by virtue of subsection (1A), but subject to such conditions (if any) as the Society sees fit to impose.

(2) For the purposes of this Act, a practising certificate shall be deemed not to be in force at any time while it is suspended.

16 Duration of suspension of practising certificates

(1) Where a practising certificate is suspended, it expires on such date as may be prescribed by regulations under section 28.

(2) The suspension of a practising certificate by virtue of section 15(1) by reason of an adjudication in bankruptcy shall terminate if the adjudication is annulled and an office copy of the order annulling the adjudication is served on the Society.

(3) Where a solicitor's practising certificate is suspended—

(a) by an order under section 13(4); or

(b) by virtue of section 15(1) by reason of his adjudication in bankruptcy; or

(c) by virtue of section 15(1) by reason of his suspension from practice and the period of his suspension from practice expires before the date on which his certificate will expire,

(d) by virtue of section 15(1A)

the solicitor may at any time before the certificate expires (and, in the case of adjudication in bankruptcy, while the adjudication remains unannulled) apply to the Society to terminate the suspension.

(4) On an application under subsection (3), the Society may in its discretion—

(a) by order terminate the suspension either unconditionally or subject to such conditions as the Society may think fit; or

(b) refuse the application.

(5) If on an application by a solicitor under subsection (3) the Society refuses the application or terminates the suspension subject to conditions, the solicitor may appeal against the decision of the Society to the High Court, which may—

(a) affirm the decision; or

(b) terminate the suspension either unconditionally or subject to such conditions as it may think fit.

(6) In relation to an appeal under subsection (5) the High Court may make such order as it thinks fit as to payment of costs.

(7) The decision of the High Court on an appeal under subsection (5) shall be final.

17 Publicity in relation to suspension of practising certificates

(1) Where a solicitor's practising certificate is suspended by an order under section 13(4), or by virtue of section 15(1) by reason of his adjudication in bankruptcy, the Society shall forthwith cause notice of that suspension to be published ... and a note of it to be entered against the name of the solicitor on the roll.

(2) Where any such suspension of a practising certificate as is mentioned in subsection (1) is terminated under section 16(2), (4) or (5), the Society shall forthwith cause a note of that termination to be entered against the name of the solicitor on the roll and, if so requested in writing by the solicitor, a notice of it to be published ...

17A Suspension of sole solicitor endorsement

(1) The making by the Tribunal or by the court of an order suspending a solicitor from practice as a sole solicitor shall operate to suspend any sole solicitor endorsement of that solicitor for the time being in force.

(2)   For the purposes of this Act, a sole solicitor endorsement shall be deemed not to be in force at any time while it is suspended.

(3)   Subsection (2) is subject to section 13ZA(2).

17B   Duration and publicity of suspension of sole solicitor endorsement

(1)   Where a sole solicitor endorsement is suspended, it expires on such date as may be prescribed by regulations under section 28.

(2)   Where a solicitor's sole solicitor endorsement is suspended—

(a)   by an order under section 13(4), or

(b)   by virtue of section 17A(1) in circumstances where the period of that suspension expires before the date on which his endorsement will expire,

the solicitor may at any time before the endorsement expires apply to the Society to terminate the suspension.

(3)   Section 16(4) to (7) apply in relation to an application under subsection (2) as they apply in relation to an application under section 16(3).

(4)   Where a solicitor's sole solicitor endorsement is suspended by an order under section 13(4) or by virtue of section 17A(1), the Society shall forthwith cause notice of that suspension to be published and a note of it to be entered against the name of the solicitor on the roll.

(5)   Where any suspension is terminated by virtue of section 16(4) or (5), as applied by subsection (3) of this section, the Society shall forthwith cause a note of that termination to be entered against the name of the solicitor on the roll and, if so requested in writing by the solicitor, a notice of it to be published.

Supplementary

28   Regulations

(1)   The Society may make regulations about the following matters, namely—

(a)   admission as a solicitor;

(b)   the keeping of the roll;

(c)   practising certificates;

(ca)   sole solicitor endorsements and applications for them;

(d)   the keeping of the register under section 10A.

(3A)   Regulations about the keeping of the roll may (among other things)—

(za)   make provision about the form in which the roll is to be kept and the manner in which entries are to be made, altered and removed;

(a)   provide for the Society, at such intervals as may be specified in the regulations, to enquire of solicitors of any class so specified whether they wish to have their names retained on the roll;

(b)   require solicitors of any such class, at such intervals as aforesaid, to pay to the Society a fee in respect of the retention of their names on the roll of such amount as may be prescribed by the regulations;

(c)   authorise the Society to remove from the roll the name of any solicitor who—

(i)   fails to reply to any enquiry made in pursuance of paragraph (a) or to pay any fee payable by virtue of paragraph (b), or

        (ii)   replies to any such enquiry by indicating that he does not wish to have his name retained on the roll;

(d)   authorise the Society to remove from the roll the name of any solicitor who has died;

(e)   require the information on the roll to be made available to the public;

(f)   specify the manner in which information is to be made so available and require it to be made so available during office hours and without charge.

(3B) Regulations about practising certificates or sole solicitor endorsements may (among other things)—

(a)   prescribe the form and manner in which applications for, or relating to, practising certificates or sole solicitor endorsements are to be made;

(b)   prescribe information which must be included in or accompany such applications;

(c)   make provision about time limits for dealing with such applications, and confer on a person power to extend or bring forward such a time limit in prescribed circumstances;

(d)   prescribe the requirements which applicants for practising certificates must satisfy before they may be issued with a practising certificate;

(e)   prescribe descriptions of applicants, and conditions in relation to them, for the purposes of section 10(2) (circumstances in which practising certificates must be issued subject to prescribed conditions);

(f)   prescribe descriptions of applicants, and conditions in relation to them, for the purposes of section 13ZA(5) (circumstances in which a practising certificate endorsed with a sole solicitor endorsement after it was issued must be made subject to prescribed conditions);

(g)   prescribe circumstances for the purposes of section 10(3) (circumstances in which application may be refused etc in the public interest);

(h)   make provision about when conditions imposed on practising certificates take effect (including provision conferring power on the Society to direct that a condition is not to have effect until the conclusion of any appeal in relation to it);

(i)   make provision for the commencement, duration, replacement, withdrawal and expiry of practising certificates or sole solicitor endorsements;

(j)   prescribe circumstances for the purposes of section 13A(2) (circumstances in which conditions can be imposed during period of practising certificate);

(k)   require solicitors who hold practising certificates to notify the Society of such matters as may be prescribed, at such times, or in such circumstances as may be prescribed.

(3C) Regulations about the keeping of the register under section 10A may (among other things)—

(a)   make provision about the form in which the register is to be kept and the manner in which entries are to be made, altered and removed;

(b)   require information of a specified kind to be included in entries in the register;

(c)   require information (or information of a specified description) on the register to be made available to the public;

(d)   specify the manner in which it is to be made so available and require it to be made so available during office hours and without charge.

(3D)   Regulations under this section may make provision for appeals to the High Court against decisions made by the Society under the regulations.

(3E)   In relation to an appeal under regulations made by virtue of subsection (3D), the High Court may make such order as it thinks fit as to payment of costs.

(3F)   The decision of the High Court on such an appeal shall be final.

(3G)   Regulations under this section may—

(a)   provide for a person to exercise a discretion in dealing with any matter;

(b)   include incidental, supplementary and consequential provision;

(c)   make transitory or transitional provision and savings;

(d)   make provision generally or only in relation to specified cases or subject to specified exceptions;

(e)   make different provision for different cases.

PART II
PROFESSIONAL PRACTICE, CONDUCT AND DISCIPLINE OF SOLICITORS AND CLERKS

Practice rules

31   Rules as to professional practice, conduct and discipline

(1)   Without prejudice to any other provision of this Part the Society may make rules for regulating in respect of any matter the professional practice, conduct, fitness to practise and discipline of solicitors and for empowering the Society to take such action as may be appropriate to enable the Society to ascertain whether or not the provisions of rules made, or of any code or guidance issued, by the Society are being, or have been, complied with.

(1A)   The powers conferred on the Society by subsection (1) include power to make, in relation to solicitors, provision of a kind which the Society would be prohibited from making but for section 157(5)(c) of the Legal Services Act 2007 (exception from prohibition on approved regulators making provision for redress).

(2)   If any solicitor fails to comply with rules made under this section, any person may make a complaint in respect of that failure to the Tribunal.

Accounts etc

32   Accounts rules and trust accounts rules

(1)   The Society shall make rules—

(a)   as to the opening and keeping by solicitors of accounts at banks or with building societies for money within subsection (1A);

(aa)   as to the operation by solicitors of accounts kept by their clients or other persons at banks or with building societies or other financial institutions;

(b)   as to the keeping by solicitors of accounts containing information as to money received, held or paid by them for or on account of their clients or other persons (including money received, held or paid under a trust); and

(c)   empowering the Society to take such action as may be necessary to enable it to ascertain whether or not the rules are being, or have been, complied with;

(1A)   The money referred to in subsection (1) is money (including money held on trust) which is received, held or dealt with for clients or other persons.

(3)   If any solicitor fails to comply with rules made under this section, any person may make a complaint in respect of that failure to the Tribunal.

(4)   The Society shall be at liberty to disclose a report on or information about a solicitor's accounts obtained in the exercise of powers conferred by rules made under subsection (1) for use in investigating the possible commission of an offence by the solicitor or any of his employees and for use in connection with any prosecution of the solicitor or any of his employees consequent on the investigation.

(5)   Rules under this section may specify circumstances in which solicitors or any class of solicitors are exempt from the rules or a part of the rules.

33   Interest on clients' money

(1)   Rules under section 32 may require a solicitor to pay interest, or sums in lieu of and equivalent to interest, to a client, any other person or any trust, for whom the solicitor holds money.

(2)   The cases in which a solicitor may be required by the rules to act as mentioned in subsection (1) may be defined, among other things, by reference to the amount of any sum received or the period for which it is or is likely to be retained or both.

(3)   Except as provided by the rules, a solicitor is not liable to account to any client, other person or trust for interest received by the solicitor on money held at a bank or building society in an account which is for money received or held for, or on account of—

(a)   the solicitor's clients, other persons or trusts, generally, or

(b)   that client, person or trust, separately.

(4)   Rules under section 32 may—

(a)   prescribe the circumstances in which a solicitor may make arrangements to limit or exclude an obligation imposed on the solicitor by rules made by virtue of this section, and

(b)   prescribe the requirements to be met by and in relation to those arrangements.

33A   Inspection of practice bank accounts etc

(1)   The Society may make rules empowering the Society to require a solicitor to produce documents relating to any account kept by him at a bank or with a building society—

(a)   in connection with his practice; or

(b)   in connection with any trust of which he is or formerly was a trustee,

for inspection by a person appointed by the Society pursuant to the rules.

(2)   The Society shall be at liberty to disclose information obtained in exercise of the powers conferred by rules made under subsection (1) for use in investigating the possible commission of an offence by the solicitor and for use in connection with any prosecution of the solicitor consequent on the investigation.

34   Accountants' reports

(1)   The Society may make rules requiring solicitors to provide the Society with reports signed by an accountant (in this section referred to as an "accountant's report") at such times or in such circumstances as may be prescribed by the rules.

(2)   The rules may specify requirements to be met by, or in relation to, an accountant's report (including requirements relating to the accountant who signs the report).

(6)   If any solicitor fails to comply with the provisions of any rules made under this section, a complaint in respect of that failure may be made to the Tribunal by or on behalf of the Society.

(7) ...

(8) ...

(9) Where an accountant, during the course of preparing an accountant's report—

    (a)   discovers evidence of fraud or theft in relation to money held by a solicitor for a client or any other person (including money held on trust) or money held in an account of a client of a solicitor, or an account of another person, which is operated by the solicitor, or

    (b)   obtains information which the accountant has reasonable cause to believe is likely to be of material significance in determining whether a solicitor is a fit and proper person to hold money for clients or other persons (including money held on trust) or to operate an account of a client of the solicitor or an account of another person,

the accountant must immediately give a report of the matter to the Society.

(10) No duty to which an accountant is subject is to be regarded as contravened merely because of any information or opinion contained in a report under subsection (9).

Sole solicitors

34A Employees of solicitors

(1) Rules made by the Society may provide for any rules made under section 31, 32, 33A or 34 to have effect in relation to employees of solicitors with such additions, omissions or other modifications as appear to the Society to be necessary or expedient.

(2) If any employee of a solicitor fails to comply with rules made under section 31 or 32, as they have effect in relation to the employee by virtue of subsection (1), any person may make a complaint in respect of that failure to the Tribunal.

(3) If any employee of a solicitor fails to comply with rules made under section 34, as they have effect in relation to the employee by virtue of subsection (1), a complaint in respect of that failure may be made to the Tribunal by or on behalf of the Society.

34B Employees of solicitors: accounts rules etc

(1) Where rules made under section 32(1) have effect in relation to employees of solicitors by virtue of section 34A(1), section 85 applies in relation to an employee to whom the rules have effect who keeps an account with a bank or building society in pursuance of such rules as it applies in relation to a solicitor who keeps such an account in pursuance of rules under section 32.

(2) Subsection (3) applies where rules made under section 32—

    (a)   contain any such provision as is referred to in section 33(1), and

    (b)   have effect in relation to employees of solicitors by virtue of section 34A(1).

(3) Except as provided by the rules, an employee to whom the rules are applied is not liable to account to any client, other person or trust for interest received by the employee on money held at a bank or building society in an account which is for money received or held for, or on account of—

    (a)   clients of the solicitor, other persons or trusts, generally, or

    (b)   that client, person or trust, separately.

(4) Subsection (5) applies where rules made under section 33A(1) have effect in relation to employees of solicitors by virtue of section 34A(1).

(5) The Society may disclose a report on or information about the accounts of any employee of a solicitor obtained in pursuance of such rules for use—

(a)   in investigating the possible commission of an offence by the solicitor or any employees of the solicitor, and

(b)   in connection with any prosecution of the solicitor or any employees of the solicitor consequent on the investigation.

(6)   Where rules made under section 34 have effect in relation to employees of solicitors by virtue of section 34A(1), section 34(9) and (10) apply in relation to such an employee as they apply in relation to a solicitor.

Intervention in solicitor's practice, Compensation Fund and professional indemnity

35 Intervention in solicitor's practice

The powers conferred by Part II of Schedule 1 shall be exercisable in the circumstances specified in Part I of that Schedule.

Restrictions on employment of certain persons

41 Employment by solicitor of person struck off or suspended

(1)   No solicitor shall, except in accordance with a written permission granted under this section, employ or remunerate in connection with his practice as a solicitor any person who to his knowledge is disqualified from practising as a solicitor by reason of the fact that—

(a)   his name has been struck off the roll, or

(b)   he is suspended from practising as a solicitor, or

(c)   his practising certificate is suspended while he is an undischarged bankrupt.

(1A)   No solicitor shall, except in accordance with a written permission granted under this section, employ or remunerate in connection with his practice as a solicitor any person if, to his knowledge, there is a direction in force under section 47(2)(g) in relation to that person.

(1B)   Where—

(a)   a solicitor ("the employed solicitor") is employed by another solicitor in accordance with a written permission granted under this section, and

(b)   the employed solicitor is disqualified from practising as a solicitor by reason of a fact mentioned in subsection (1)(b) or (c),

section 20(1) does not apply in relation to anything done by the employed solicitor in the course of that employment.

(2)   The Society may grant a permission under this section for such period and subject to such conditions as the Society thinks fit.

(3)   A solicitor aggrieved by the refusal of the Society to grant a permission under subsection (2), or by any conditions attached by the Society to the grant of any such permission, may appeal to the High Court which may—

(a)   confirm the refusal or the conditions, as the case may be; or

(b)   grant a permission under this section for such period and subject to such conditions as it thinks fit.

(4)   If any solicitor acts in contravention of this section or of any conditions subject to which a permission has been granted under it, the Tribunal or, as the case may be, the High Court may—

(a)   order that his name be struck off the roll,

(b)   order that he be suspended from practice for such period as the Tribunal or court thinks fit, or

(c)   make such other order in the matter as it thinks fit.

(4A)   In relation to an appeal under subsection (3) the High Court may make such order as it thinks fit as to payment of costs.

(4B)   The decision of the High Court on an appeal under subsection (3) shall be final.

42   Failure to disclose fact of having been struck off or suspended

(1)   Any person who, while he is disqualified from practising as a solicitor by reason of the fact that—

(a)   his name has been struck off the roll, or

(b)   he is suspended from practising as a solicitor, or

(c)   his practising certificate is suspended while he is an undischarged bankrupt,

seeks or accepts employment by a solicitor in connection with that solicitor's practice without previously informing him that he is so disqualified shall be guilty of an offence and liable on summary conviction to a fine not exceeding level 3 on the standard scale.

(1A)   Any person—

(a)   with respect to whom a direction is in force under section 47(2)(g); and

(b)   who seeks or accepts employment by a solicitor in connection with that solicitor's practice without previously informing him of the direction,

shall be guilty of an offence and liable on summary conviction to a fine not exceeding level three on the standard scale.

(2)   Notwithstanding anything in the Magistrates' Courts Act 1980, proceedings under this section may be commenced at any time before the expiration of six months from the first discovery of the offence by the prosecutor, but no such proceedings shall be commenced except by, or with the consent of, the Attorney General.

43   Control of solicitors' employees and consultants

(1)   Where a person who is or was involved in a legal practice but is not a solicitor—

(a)   has been convicted of a criminal offence which is such that in the opinion of the Society it would be undesirable for the person to be involved in a legal practice in one or more of the ways mentioned in subsection (1A), or

(b)   has, in the opinion of the Society, occasioned or been a party to, with or without the connivance of a solicitor, an act or default in relation to a legal practice which involved conduct on his part of such a nature that in the opinion of the Society it would be undesirable for him to be involved in a legal practice in one or more of the ways mentioned in subsection (1A),

the Society may either make, or make an application to the Tribunal for it to make, an order under subsection (2) with respect to that person.

(1A)   A person is involved in a legal practice for the purposes of this section if the person—

(a)   is employed or remunerated by a solicitor in connection with the solicitor's practice;

(b)   is undertaking work in the name of, or under the direction or supervision of, a solicitor;

(c)   is employed or remunerated by a recognised body;

(d)   is employed or remunerated by a manager or employee of a recognised body in connection with that body's business;

(e)   is a manager of a recognised body;

(f)   has or intends to acquire an interest in such a body.

(2)   An order made by the Society or the Tribunal under this subsection is an order which states one or more of the following—

(a)   that as from the specified date—

  (i)   no solicitor shall employ or remunerate, in connection with his practice as a solicitor, the person with respect to whom the order is made,

  (ii)   no employee of a solicitor shall employ or remunerate, in connection with the solicitor's practice, the person with respect to whom the order is made,

  (iii) no recognised body shall employ or remunerate that person, and

  (iv)   no manager or employee of a recognised body shall employ or remunerate that person in connection with the business of that body,

  except in accordance with a Society permission;

(b)   that as from the specified date no recognised body or manager or employee of such a body shall, except in accordance with a Society permission, permit the person with respect to whom the order is made to be a manager of the body;

(c)   that as from the specified date no recognised body or manager or employee of such a body shall, except in accordance with a Society permission, permit the person with respect to whom the order is made to have an interest in the body.

(2A)   The Society may make regulations prescribing charges to be paid to the Society by persons who are the subject of an investigation by the Society as to whether there are grounds for the Society—

(a)   to make an order under subsection (2), or

(b)   to make an application to the Tribunal for it to make such an order.

(2B)   Regulations under subsection (2A) may—

(a)   make different provision for different cases or purposes;

(b)   provide for the whole or part of a charge payable under the regulations to be repaid in such circumstances as may be prescribed by the regulations.

(2C)   Any charge which a person is required to pay under regulations under subsection (2A) is recoverable by the Society as a debt due to the Society from the person.

(3)   Where an order has been made under subsection (2) with respect to a person by the Society or the Tribunal—

(a)   that person or the Society may make an application to the Tribunal for it to be reviewed, and

(b)   whichever of the Society and the Tribunal made it may at any time revoke it.

(3A)   On the review of an order under subsection (3) the Tribunal may order—

(a)   the quashing of the order;

(b)   the variation of the order; or

(c)   the confirmation of the order;

and where in the opinion of the Tribunal no prima facie case for quashing or varying the order is shown, the Tribunal may order its confirmation without hearing the applicant.

(4)   The Tribunal, on the hearing of any application under this section, may make an order as to the payment of costs by any party to the application.

(5)   Orders made under subsection (2) by the Society, or made, varied or confirmed under this section by the Tribunal and filed with the Society, may be inspected during office hours without payment.

(5A)   In this section—

"manager", in relation to a recognised body, has the same meaning as it has in relation to a body in the Legal Services Act 2007 (see section 207 of that Act);

"recognised body" means a body recognised under section 9 of the Administration of Justice Act 1985;

"specified date" means such date as may be specified in the order;

"Society permission" means permission in writing granted by the Society for such period and subject to such conditions as the Society may think fit to specify in the permission.

(5B)   A person has an interest in a recognised body for the purposes of this section if the person has an interest in that body within the meaning of Part 5 of the Legal Services Act 2007 (see sections 72 and 109 of that Act).

(6)   ...

(7)   For the purposes of this section an order discharging a person absolutely or conditionally in respect of an offence shall, notwithstanding anything in section 14 of the Powers of Criminal Courts (Sentencing) Act 2000, be deemed to be a conviction of the offence for which the order was made.

44   Offences in connection with orders under section 43(2)

(1)   It is an offence for a person in respect of whom there is in force an order under section 43(2) which contains provision within section 43(2)(a)—

(a)   to seek or accept any employment or remuneration from a solicitor, or an employee of a solicitor, in connection with the practice carried on by that solicitor without previously informing the solicitor or employee of the order;

(b)   to seek or accept any employment or remuneration from a recognised body, or a manager or employee of a recognised body, in connection with that body's business, without previously informing the body, or manager or employee, of the order.

(1A)   It is an offence for a person in respect of whom there is in force an order under section 43(2) which contains provision within section 43(2)(b) to seek or accept a position as a manager of a recognised body, without previously informing that body of the order.

(1B)   It is an offence for a person in respect of whom there is in force an order under section 43(2) which contains provision within section 43(2)(c) to seek or accept an interest in a recognised body from any person, without previously informing that person and (if different) the recognised body of the order.

(1C)   A person guilty of an offence under subsection (1), (1A) or (1B) is liable on summary conviction to a fine not exceeding level 3 on the standard scale.

(2)   Where an order under section 43(2) is in force in respect of a person, then, if any solicitor knowingly acts in contravention of that order or of any conditions subject to which permission for the taking of any action has been granted under it, a complaint in respect of that contravention may be made to the Tribunal by or on behalf of the Society.

(3)   Any document purporting to be an order under section 43(2) and to be duly signed in accordance with section 48(1) shall be received in evidence in any proceedings under this section and be deemed to be such an order without further proof unless the contrary is shown.

APPENDIX 17

(4) Notwithstanding anything in the Magistrates' Courts Act 1980, proceedings under subsection (1) may be commenced at any time before the expiration of six months from the first discovery of the offence by the prosecutor, but no such proceedings shall be commenced, except with the consent of the Director of Public Prosecutions, by any person other than the Society or a person acting on behalf of the Society.

(5) In this section—

"manager" has the same meaning as in section 43;

"recognised body" means a body recognised under section 9 of the Administration of Justice Act 1985;

and for the purposes of subsection (1B) a person seeks or accepts an interest in a recognised body if the person seeks or accepts an interest which if it were obtained by the person would result in the person having an interest in that body within the meaning of Part 5 of the Legal Services Act 2007 (see sections 72 and 109 of that Act).

Examination of files

44B Provision of information and documents by solicitors etc

(1) The Society may by notice require a person to whom this section applies—

(a) to provide information, or information of a description, specified in the notice, or

(b) produce documents, or documents of a description, specified in the notice.

(2) This section applies to—

(a) a solicitor;

(b) an employee of a solicitor;

(c) a recognised body;

(d) an employee or manager of, or a person with an interest in, a recognised body.

(3) The Society may give a notice under this section only if it is satisfied that it is necessary to do so for the purpose of investigating—

(a) whether there has been professional misconduct by a solicitor;

(b) whether a solicitor, or an employee of a solicitor, has failed to comply with any requirements imposed by or by virtue of this Act or any rules made by the Society;

(c) whether a recognised body, or any of its managers or employees has failed to comply with any requirement imposed by or by virtue of the Administration of Justice Act 1985 or any rules made by the Society and applicable to the body, manager or employee by virtue of section 9 of that Act;

(d) whether there are grounds for making, or making an application to the Tribunal for it to make, an order under section 43(2) with respect to a person who is or was involved in a legal practice (within the meaning of section 43(1A)).

(4) A notice under this section—

(a) may specify the time and place at which, and manner and form in which, the information is to be provided or document is to be produced;

(b) must specify the period within which the information is to be provided or the document produced;

(c) may require the information to be provided or document to be produced to the Society or to a person specified in the notice.

(5)   The Society may pay to any person such reasonable costs as may be incurred by that person in connection with the provision of any information, or production of any document, by that person pursuant to a notice under this section.

(6)   Paragraphs 9(3) and (4) and 13, 15 and 16 of Schedule 1 apply in relation to the powers to obtain information conferred by this section, but for this purpose—

(a)   paragraph 9 of that Schedule has effect as if—

(i)   in sub-paragraph (3) for "such documents" there were substituted "information to which a notice given to him under section 44B applies",

(ii)   in that sub-paragraph for "sub-paragraph (1)" there were substituted "the notice", and

(iii)   in sub-paragraph (4) for "produce" (in the first place) to the end there were substituted "provide information pursuant to a notice under section 44B to provide the information to any person appointed by the Society at such time and place as may be specified in the order.", and

(b)   the reference to the solicitor or his personal representative in paragraph 13 of that Schedule is to be construed as a reference to the person to whom the notice was given under this section.

(7)   Paragraphs 9 (other than sub-paragraphs (1) and (3)), 12, 13, 15 and 16 of Schedule 1 apply in relation to the powers to obtain documents conferred by this section as they apply in relation to the powers conferred by paragraph 9(1) of that Schedule, except that for this purpose—

(a)   any reference in paragraph 9 of that Schedule to a person appointed, or to a requirement, under sub-paragraph (1) of that paragraph is to be construed as a reference to a person appointed, or to a requirement to produce documents, under this section,

(b)   any reference in that paragraph to any such documents as are mentioned in paragraph 9(1) of that Schedule is to be construed as a reference to any documents to which a notice under this section applies,

(c)   the references to the solicitor or his firm in paragraph 9(5) and (6) of that Schedule, and the reference to the solicitor or personal representative in paragraph 9(7) of that Schedule, are to be construed as references to the person to whom the notice was given under this section, and

(d)   the reference in paragraph 9(12) of that Schedule to the Society is to be construed as including a reference to a person specified under subsection (4)(c).

(8)   Where powers conferred by Part 2 of Schedule 1 to the 1974 Act are exercisable in relation to a person within paragraph (a), (b), (c) or (d) of subsection (2), they continue to be so exercisable after the person has ceased to be a person within the paragraph in question.

(9)   In this section—

"manager" has the same meaning as in the Legal Services Act 2007 (see section 207 of that Act);

"recognised body" means a body recognised under section 9 of the Administration of Justice Act 1985;

and the reference to a person who has an interest in a recognised body is to be construed in accordance with sections 72 and 109 of the Legal Services Act 2007.

44BA Power to require explanation of document or information

(1) The Society may, by notice, require a person to whom a notice is given under section 44B (or a representative of the person) to attend at a time and place specified in the notice to provide an explanation of any information provided or document produced pursuant to the notice.

(2) The Society may pay to any person such reasonable costs as may be incurred by that person in connection with that person's compliance with a requirement imposed under subsection (1).

(3) Paragraphs 9(3) and (4) and 13, 15 and 16 of Schedule 1 apply in relation to a notice under this section, except that for this purpose—

> (a) paragraph 9 of that Schedule has effect as if—
>
> > (i) in sub-paragraph (3) for "having" to "sub-paragraph (1)" there were substituted "refuses, neglects or otherwise fails to comply with a requirement under section 44BA(1)", and
> >
> > (ii) in sub-paragraph (4) for "produce" (in the first place) to the end there were substituted "provide an explanation of any information provided or document produced pursuant to a notice under section 44B (or a representative of such a person) to attend at a time and place specified in the order to provide an explanation of any information so provided or document so produced.", and
>
> (b) the reference to the solicitor or his personal representative in paragraph 13 of that Schedule is to be construed as a reference to the person to whom the notice was given under this section.

44BB Provision of information and documents by other persons

(1) The High Court, on the application of the Society, may order a person to whom section 44B does not apply—

> (a) to provide information, or information of a description, specified in the notice, or
>
> (b) to produce documents, or documents of a description, specified in the notice.

(2) The High Court may make an order under this section only if it is satisfied—

> (a) that it is likely that the information or document is in the possession or custody of, or under the control of, the person, and
>
> (b) that there is reasonable cause to believe that the information or document is likely to be of material significance to an investigation into any of the matters mentioned in section 44B(3)(a) to (d).

(3) An order under this section may direct the Society to pay to a person specified in the order such reasonable costs as may be incurred by that person in connection with the provision of any information, or production of any document, by that person pursuant to the order.

(4) Section 44B(4) applies in relation to an order under this section as it applies in relation to a notice under section 44B.

(5) Paragraphs 9(5A) and (7) to (12), 12, 13, 15 and 16 of Schedule 1 apply in relation to an order under this section as they apply in relation to an order under paragraph 9(4) of that Schedule, except that for this purpose—

> (a) the reference to the solicitor or personal representative in paragraph 9(7) of that Schedule is to be construed as a reference to the person in respect of whom the order under this section is made,

(b) the reference in paragraph 9(12) of that Schedule to the Society is to be read as including a reference to a person specified under section 44B(4)(c) (as applied by subsection (4) of this section), and

(c) the reference to the solicitor or his personal representative in paragraph 13 of that Schedule is to be construed as a reference to the person to whom the notice was given under this section.

44BC Information offences

(1) It is an offence for a person who knows or suspects an investigation into any of the matters mentioned in section 44B(3)(a) to (d) is being or is likely to be conducted—

(a) to falsify, conceal, destroy or otherwise dispose of a document which the person knows or suspects is or would be relevant to the investigation, or

(b) to cause or permit the falsification, concealment, destruction or disposal of such a document.

(2) In proceedings for an offence under subsection (1) it is a defence for the accused to show that the accused had no intention of concealing facts disclosed by the documents from the person conducting the investigation.

(3) It is an offence for a person, in purported compliance with a requirement imposed on the person under section 44B, 44BA or 44BB—

(a) to provide information which the person knows to be false or misleading in a material particular, or

(b) recklessly to provide information which is false or misleading in a material particular.

(4) A person who is guilty of an offence under subsection (1) or (3) is liable—

(a) on summary conviction, to imprisonment for a term not exceeding 12 months or a fine not exceeding the statutory maximum, or both;

(b) on conviction on indictment, to imprisonment for a term not exceeding 2 years or a fine, or both.

(5) In relation to an offence under subsection (1) or (3) committed before the commencement of section 154(1) of the Criminal Justice Act 2003 the reference in subsection (4)(a) to 12 months is to be read as a reference to 6 months.

Costs of investigations

44C Power to charge for costs of investigations

(1) The Society may make regulations prescribing charges to be paid to the Society by solicitors who are the subject of a discipline investigation.

(2) A "discipline investigation" is an investigation carried out by the Society into—

(a) possible professional misconduct by a solicitor, or

(b) a failure or apprehended failure by a solicitor to comply with any requirement imposed by or by virtue of this Act or any rules made by the Society.

(3) Regulations under this section may—

(a) make different provision for different cases or purposes;

(b) provide for the whole or part of a charge payable under the regulations to be repaid in such circumstances as may be prescribed by the regulations.

(4)   Any charge which a solicitor is required to pay under regulations under this section is recoverable by the Society as a debt due to the Society from the solicitor.

(5)   This section (other than subsection (2)(a)) applies in relation to an employee of a solicitor as it applies in relation to a solicitor.

Disciplinary powers of the Society

44D   Disciplinary powers of the Society

(1)   This section applies where the Society is satisfied—

    (a)   that a solicitor or an employee of a solicitor has failed to comply with a requirement imposed by or by virtue of this Act or any rules made by the Society, or

    (b)   that there has been professional misconduct by a solicitor.

(2)   The Society may do one or both of the following—

    (a)   give the person a written rebuke;

    (b)   direct the person to pay a penalty not exceeding £2,000.

(3)   The Society may publish details of any action it has taken under subsection (2)(a) or (b), if it considers it to be in the public interest to do so.

(4)   Where the Society takes action against a person under subsection (2)(b), or decides to publish under subsection (3) details of any action taken under subsection (2)(a) or (b), it must notify the person in writing that it has done so.

(5)   A penalty imposed under subsection (2)(b) does not become payable until—

    (a)   the end of the period during which an appeal against the decision to impose the penalty, or the amount of the penalty, may be made under section 44E, or

    (b)   if such an appeal is made, such time as it is determined or withdrawn.

(6)   The Society may not publish under subsection (3) details of any action under subsection (2)(a) or (b)—

    (a)   during the period within which an appeal against—

        (i)   the decision to take the action,

        (ii)   in the case of action under subsection (2)(b), the amount of the penalty, or

        (iii)   the decision to publish the details,

        may be made under section 44E, or

    (b)   if such an appeal has been made, until such time as it is determined or withdrawn.

(7)   The Society must make rules—

    (a)   prescribing the circumstances in which the Society may decide to take action under subsection (2)(a) or (b);

    (b)   about the practice and procedure to be followed by the Society in relation to such action;

    (c)   governing the publication under subsection (3) of details of action taken under subsection (2)(a) or (b);

and the Society may make such other rules in connection with the exercise of its powers under this section as it considers appropriate.

(8)   Before making rules under subsection (7), the Society must consult the Tribunal.

(9)   A penalty payable under this section may be recovered as a debt due to the Society, and is to be forfeited to Her Majesty.

(10)   The Lord Chancellor may, by order, amend paragraph (b) of subsection (2) so as to substitute for the amount for the time being specified in that paragraph such other amount as may be specified in the order.

(11)   Before making an order under subsection (10), the Lord Chancellor must consult the Society.

(12)   An order under subsection (10) is to be made by statutory instrument subject to annulment in pursuance of a resolution of either House of Parliament.

(13)   This section is without prejudice to any power conferred on the Society or any other person to make an application or complaint to the Tribunal.

44E   Appeals against disciplinary action under section 44D

(1)   A person may appeal against—

(a)   a decision by the Society to rebuke that person under section 44D(2)(a) if a decision is also made to publish details of the rebuke;

(b)   a decision by the Society to impose a penalty on that person under section 44D(2)(b) or the amount of that penalty;

(c)   a decision by the Society to publish under section 44D(3) details of any action taken against that person under section 44D(2)(a) or (b).

(2)   Subsections (9)(b), (10)(a) and (b), (11) and (12) of section 46 (Tribunal rules about procedure for hearings etc) apply in relation to appeals under this section as they apply in relation to applications or complaints, except that subsection (11) of that section is to be read as if for "the applicant" to "application)" there were substituted "any party to the appeal".

(3)   Rules under section 46(9)(b) may, in particular, make provision about the period during which an appeal under this section may be made.

(4)   On an appeal under this section, the Tribunal has power to make such order as it thinks fit, and such an order may in particular—

(a)   affirm the decision of the Society;

(b)   revoke the decision of the Society;

(c)   in the case of a penalty imposed under section 44D(2)(b), vary the amount of the penalty;

(d)   in the case of a solicitor, contain provision for any of the matters mentioned in paragraphs (a) to (d) of section 47(2);

(e)   in the case of an employee of a solicitor, contain provision for any of the matters mentioned in section 47(2E);

(f)   make such provision as the Tribunal thinks fit as to payment of costs.

(5)   Where by virtue of subsection (4)(e) an order contains provision for any of the matters mentioned in section 47(2E)(c), section 47(2F) and (2G) apply as if the order had been made under section 47(2E)(c).

(6)   An appeal from the Tribunal shall lie to the High Court, at the instance of the Society or the person in respect of whom the order of the Tribunal was made.

(7)   The High Court shall have power to make such order on an appeal under this section as it may think fit.

(8)   Any decision of the High Court on an appeal under this section shall be final.

(9)   This section is without prejudice to any power conferred on the Tribunal in connection with an application or complaint made to it.

Disciplinary proceedings before Solicitors Disciplinary Tribunal

46   Solicitors Disciplinary Tribunal

(1)   Applications and complaints made by virtue of any provision of this Act shall be made, except so far as other provision is made by this Act or by any regulations under it, to the tribunal known as the "Solicitors Disciplinary Tribunal".

(2)   The Master of the Rolls shall appoint the members of the Tribunal.

(3)   The Tribunal shall consist—

(a)   of practising solicitors of not less than ten years' standing (in this section referred to as "solicitor members"); and

(b)   of persons who are neither solicitors nor barristers (in this section referred to as "lay members").

(4)   A member of the Tribunal shall hold and vacate his office in accordance with the terms of his appointment and shall, on ceasing to hold office, be eligible for re-appointment.

(5)   The Tribunal may pay its members such remuneration, fees or allowances as it may determine with the approval of the Legal Services Board.

(5A)   The Tribunal may do anything calculated to facilitate, or incidental or conducive to, the carrying out of any of its functions.

(6)   ...

(7)   ...

(8)   ...

(9)   The Tribunal may make rules—

(a)   empowering the Tribunal to elect a solicitor member to be its president; and

(b)   about the procedure and practice to be followed in relation to the making, hearing and determination of applications and complaints (including provision about the composition of the Tribunal).

(10)   Without prejudice to the generality of subsection (9)(b), rules made by virtue of that paragraph may in particular—

(a)   empower the president of the Tribunal to appoint a chairman for the hearing and determination of any application or complaint;

(b)   provide that, if the president does not appoint a chairman, a solicitor member shall act as chairman; and

(c)   provide, in relation to any application or complaint relating to a solicitor, that, where in the opinion of the Tribunal no prima facie case in favour of the applicant or complainant is shown in the application or complaint, the Tribunal may make an order refusing the application or dismissing the complaint without requiring the solicitor to whom it relates to answer the allegations and without hearing the applicant or complainant.

(11)   For the purposes of any application or complaint made to the Tribunal under this Act, the Tribunal may administer oaths, and the applicant or complainant and any person with respect to whom the application or complaint is made (or, in the case of an application under section 47(1)(b), any of the parties to the application) may issue writs of subpoena ad testificandum and duces tecum, but no person shall be compelled under any such writ to produce any document which he could not be compelled to produce on the trial of an action.

(12)   The power to make rules conferred by subsection (9) shall be exercisable by statutory instrument, and the Statutory Instruments Act 1946 shall apply to a statutory instrument containing such rules in like manner as if the rules had been made by a Minister of the Crown.

46A   Funding of the Tribunal

(1)   The Tribunal must submit to the Society in respect of each year a budget for the year approved by the Legal Services Board.

(2)   A budget for a year is a statement of the amount of money which the Tribunal estimates is required to enable it to meet all of its expenditure in that year (having regard to any amounts received but not spent in previous years).

(3)   Before approving a statement for the purposes of subsection (1) the Legal Services Board must consult the Society.

(4)   The budget for a year must be submitted to the Society under subsection (1) no later than the date in the preceding year specified by the Society for the purposes of this subsection.

(5)   Before specifying a date for this purpose the Society must consult the Tribunal.

(6)   The amount specified in a budget submitted under subsection (1) must be paid by the Society to the Tribunal—

(a)   in such instalments and at such times as may be agreed between the Society and the Tribunal, or

(b)   in the absence of such agreement, before the beginning of the year to which the budget relates.

(7)   The Society may pay the Tribunal such other amounts as the Society considers appropriate.

(8)   In this section "year" means a calendar year.

47   Jurisdiction and powers of Tribunal

(1)   Any application—

(a)   to strike the name of a solicitor off the roll;

(b)   to require a solicitor to answer allegations contained in an affidavit;

(c)   to require a former solicitor whose name has been removed from or struck off the roll to answer allegations contained in an affidavit relating to a time when he was a solicitor;

(d)   by a solicitor who has been suspended from practice for an unspecified period, by order of the Tribunal, for the termination of that suspension;

(e)   by a former solicitor whose name has been struck off the roll to have his name restored to the roll;

(ea)   by a solicitor who has been suspended from practice as a sole solicitor for an unspecified period, by order of the Tribunal, for the termination of that suspension;

(f)   by a former solicitor in respect of whom a direction has been given under subsection (2)(g) to have his name restored to the roll,

shall be made to the Tribunal; but nothing in this subsection shall affect any jurisdiction over solicitors exercisable by the Master of the Rolls, or by any judge of the High Court, by virtue of section 50.

(2)   Subject to subsections (2E) and (3) and to section 54, on the hearing of any application or complaint made to the Tribunal under this Act, other than an application under section 43,

the Tribunal shall have power to make such order as it may think fit, and any such order may in particular include provision for any of the following matters—

(a)   the striking off the roll of the name of the solicitor to whom the application or complaint relates;

(b)   the suspension of that solicitor from practice indefinitely or for a specified period;

(ba)   the revocation of that solicitor's sole solicitor endorsement (if any);

(bb)   the suspension of that solicitor from practice as a sole solicitor indefinitely or for a specified period;

(c)   the payment by that solicitor or former solicitor of a penalty, which shall be forfeit to Her Majesty;

(d)   in the circumstances referred to in subsection (2A), the exclusion of that solicitor from providing representation funded by the Legal Services Commission as part of the Criminal Defence Service (either permanently or for a specified period);

(e)   the termination of that solicitor's unspecified period of suspension from practice;

(ea)   the termination of that solicitor's unspecified period of suspension from practice as a sole solicitor;

(f)   the restoration to the roll of the name of a former solicitor whose name has been struck off the roll and to whom the application relates;

(g)   in the case of a former solicitor whose name has been removed from the roll, a direction prohibiting the restoration of his name to the roll except by order of the Tribunal;

(h)   in the case of an application under subsection (1)(f), the restoration of the applicant's name to the roll;

(i)   the payment by any party of costs or a contribution towards costs of such amount as the Tribunal may consider reasonable.

(2A)   An order of the Tribunal may make provision for the exclusion of a solicitor from providing representation as mentioned in subsection (2)(d) where the Tribunal determines that there is good reason for doing so arising out of—

(a)   his conduct, including conduct in the capacity of agent for another solicitor, in connection with the provision for any person of services funded by the Legal Services Commission as part of the Community Legal Service or Criminal Defence Service; or

(b)   his professional conduct generally.

(2B)   Where the Tribunal makes any such order as is referred to in subsection (2A) in the case of a solicitor who is a member of a firm of solicitors, the Tribunal may, if it thinks fit, order that any other person who is for the time being a member of the firm shall be excluded (either permanently or for a specified period) from providing representation funded by the Legal Services Commission as part of the Criminal Defence Service.

(2C)   The Tribunal shall not make an order under subsection (2B) unless an opportunity is given to him to show cause why the order should not be made.

(2D)   Any person excluded from providing representation funded by the Legal Services Commission as part of the Criminal Defence Service by an order under this section may make an application to the Tribunal for an order terminating his exclusion.

(2E)   On the hearing of any complaint made to the Tribunal by virtue of section 34A(2) or (3), the Tribunal shall have power to make one or more of the following—

(a)   an order directing the payment by the employee to whom the complaint relates of a penalty to be forfeited to Her Majesty;

(b)   an order requiring the Society to consider taking such steps as the Tribunal may specify in relation to that employee;

(c)   if that employee is not a solicitor, an order which states one or more of the matters mentioned in paragraphs (a) to (c) of section 43(2);

(d)   an order requiring the Society to refer to an appropriate regulator any matter relating to the conduct of that employee.

(2F)   Subsections (1) to (1C), (3) and (4) of section 44 apply in relation to an order under subsection (2E)(c) as they apply in relation to an order under section 43(2).

(2G)   Section 44(2), paragraph 16(1)(d) and (1A)(d) of Schedule 2 to the Administration of Justice Act 1985 and paragraph 15(3A) of Schedule 14 to the Courts and Legal Services Act 1990 apply in relation to an order under subsection (2E)(c) as they apply in relation to an order under section 43(2).

(2H)   For the purposes of subsection (2E)(d) an "appropriate regulator" in relation to an employee means—

(a)   if the employee is an authorised person in relation to a reserved legal activity (within the meaning of the Legal Services Act 2007), any relevant approved regulator (within the meaning of that Act) in relation to that employee, and

(b)   if the employee carries on activities which are not reserved legal activities (within the meaning of that Act), any body which regulates the carrying on of such activities by the employee.

(3)   On proof of the commission of an offence with respect to which express provision is made by any section of this Act, the Tribunal shall, without prejudice to its power of making an order as to costs, impose the punishment, or one of the punishments, specified in that section.

(3A)   Where, on the hearing of any application or complaint under this Act, the Tribunal is satisfied that more than one allegation is proved against the person to whom the application or complaint relates it may impose a separate penalty (by virtue of subsection (2)(c)) with respect to each such allegation.

(3B)   For the avoidance of doubt, nothing in this section permits the Tribunal to make an order requiring redress to be made in respect of any act or omission of any person.

(4)   ...

(5)   ...

(6)   ...

48   Orders of Tribunal

(1)   An order of the Tribunal shall be filed with the Society, and a statement of the Tribunal's findings, signed by the chairman or by some other member of the Tribunal authorised by him in that behalf, shall either be prefaced to the order or added to the file containing the order as soon as may be after the order has been made.

(2)   Where an order which has been filed includes provision for any of the matters referred to in paragraphs (a) to (i) of subsection (2) of section 47, or was made under subsection (2B) of that section, the Society—

(a)   shall cause a note of the effect of the order to be entered on the roll against the name of the solicitor or former solicitor with respect to whom the application or complaint was made; and

(b)   except where it only makes provision for matters referred to in paragraph (e), (ea), (f), (h) or (i) of section 47(2), shall forthwith upon filing the order cause a notice stating its effect to be published.

(3)   Any file kept by the Society under this section may be inspected during office hours without payment.

(4)   An order which has been filed shall be treated, for the purpose of enforcement, as if it had been made by the High Court.

(5)   In the case of orders of the Tribunal under section 44E, the reference in subsection (2)(a) to the application or complaint is to be read as a reference to the Tribunal's order.

49   Appeals from Tribunal

(1)   An appeal from the Tribunal shall lie to the High Court.

(2)   Subject to subsection (3) and to section 43(5) of the Administration of Justice Act 1985, an appeal shall lie at the instance of the applicant or complainant or of the person with respect to whom the application or complaint was made.

(3)   An appeal against an order under section 43(3A) shall lie only at the instance of the person with respect to whom the order was made, and an appeal against an order under section 47 excluding any person or persons from providing representation funded by the Legal Services Commission as part of the Criminal Defence Service shall lie only at the instance of any person so excluded.

(4)   The High Court shall have power to make such order on an appeal under this section as it may think fit.

(5)   Subject to any rules of court, on an appeal against an order made by virtue of rules under section 46(10)(c) without hearing the applicant or complainant, the court—

(a)   shall not be obliged to hear the appellant, and

(b)   may remit the matter to the Tribunal instead of dismissing the appeal.

(6)   Any decision of the High Court—

(a)   on an application under section 43(3) or 47(1)(d), (e), (ea) or (f), or

(b)   against an order under section 43(3A),

shall be final.

49A   Appeals to the Tribunal instead of the High Court

(1)   The Society may, with the approval of the Tribunal, make rules which provide that in such circumstances as may be prescribed by the rules an appeal under any of the provisions listed in subsection (2) lies to the Tribunal and not to the High Court.

(2)   Those provisions are—

(a)   section 8(4);

(b)   section 13A(6);

(c)   section 16(5);

(d)   section 28(3D);

(e)   section 41(3);

(f)   paragraph 14 of Schedule 14 to the Courts and Legal Services Act 1990 (foreign lawyers: appeals against conditions or refusals).

(3)   Any decision of the Tribunal on an appeal by virtue of rules made under this section shall be final.

Disciplinary proceedings before Senior Courts

50 Jurisdiction of Senior Courts over solicitors

(1) Any person duly admitted as a solicitor shall be an officer of the Senior Courts.

(2) Subject to the provisions of this Act, the High Court, the Crown Court and the Court of Appeal respectively, or any division or judge of those courts, may exercise the same jurisdiction in respect of solicitors as any one of the superior courts of law or equity from which the Senior Courts were constituted might have exercised immediately before the passing of the Supreme Court of Judicature Act 1873 in respect of any solicitor, attorney or proctor admitted to practise there.

(3) An appeal shall lie to the Court of Appeal from any order made against a solicitor by the High Court or the Crown Court in the exercise of its jurisdiction in respect of solicitors under subsection (2).

51 Procedure upon certain applications to High Court

(1) Where an application to strike the name of a solicitor off the roll or to require a solicitor to answer allegations contained in an affidavit is made to the High Court, then, subject to section 54, the following provisions of this section shall have effect in relation to that application.

(2) The court shall not entertain the application except on production of an affidavit proving that the applicant has served on the Society fourteen clear days' notice of his intention to make the application, together with copies of all affidavits intended to be used in support of the application.

(3) The Society may appear by counsel on the hearing of the application and any other proceedings arising out of or in reference to the application, and may apply to the court—

(a) to make absolute any order nisi which the court may have made on the application;

(b) to make an order that the name of the solicitor be struck off the roll; or

(c) to make such other order as the court may think fit.

(4) The court may order the costs of the Society of or relating to any of the matters mentioned in subsections (2) and (3) to be paid by the solicitor against whom, or by the person by whom, the application was made, or was intended to be made, or partly by one and partly by the other of them.

Disciplinary proceedings—general

54 Restrictions on powers to strike names off roll

(1) No solicitor shall be liable to have his name struck off the roll on account of any failure to comply with the requirements with respect to persons seeking admission as solicitors of any training regulations or on account of any defect in his admission and enrolment, unless—

(a) the application to strike his name off the roll is made within twelve months of the date of his enrolment; or

(b) fraud is proved to have been committed in connection with the failure or defect.

(2) No solicitor shall be liable to have his name struck off the roll by reason only—

(a) that a solicitor who undertook a training responsibility for him under training regulations neglected or omitted to take out a practising certificate; or

(b) that the name of a solicitor who undertook such a responsibility for a period has been removed from or struck off the roll after the end of that period.

55 Applications to require solicitor to answer allegations

For the avoidance of doubt it is hereby declared that an application by any person to require a solicitor to answer allegations contained in an affidavit, whether that application is made to the Tribunal or to the High Court, may be treated as an application to strike the name of that solicitor off the roll on the grounds of the matters alleged.

SCHEDULE 1
Intervention in Solicitor's Practice

Section 35

PART I
CIRCUMSTANCES IN WHICH SOCIETY MAY INTERVENE

1 (1) Subject to sub-paragraph (2), the powers conferred by Part II of this Schedule shall be exercisable where—

(a) the Society has reason to suspect dishonesty on the part of—

    (i) a solicitor, or

    (ii) an employee of a solicitor, or

    (iii) the personal representatives of a deceased solicitor,

    in connection with that solicitor's practice or former practice or in connection with any trust of which that solicitor is or formerly was a trustee or that employee is or was a trustee in his capacity as such an employee;

(aa) the Society has reason to suspect dishonesty on the part of a solicitor ("S") in connection with—

    (i) the business of any person of whom S is or was an employee, or of any body of which S is or was a manager, or

    (ii) any business which is or was carried on by S as a sole trader;

(b) the Society considers that there has been undue delay on the part of the personal representatives of a deceased solicitor who immediately before his death was practising as a sole solicitor in connection with that solicitor's practice or in connection with any trust;

(c) the Society is satisfied that a solicitor has failed to comply with rules made by virtue of section 31, 32 or 37(2)(c);

(d) a solicitor has been adjudged bankrupt or has made a composition or arrangement with his creditors;

(e) a solicitor has been committed to prison in any civil or criminal proceedings;

(ee) the Society is satisfied that a sole solicitor is incapacitated by illness, injury or accident to such an extent as to be unable to attend to his practice;

(f) a solicitor lacks capacity (within the meaning of the Mental Capacity Act 2005) to act as a solicitor and powers under sections 15 to 20 or section 48 of that Act are exercisable in relation to him; or

(g) the name of a solicitor has been removed from or struck off the roll or a solicitor has been suspended from practice;

(h) the Society is satisfied that a solicitor has abandoned his practice;

(i)   the Society is satisfied that a sole solicitor is incapacitated by age to such an extent as to be unable to attend to his practice;

(j)   any power conferred by this Schedule has been exercised in relation to a sole solicitor by virtue of sub-paragraph (1)(a) and he has acted as a sole solicitor within the period of eighteen months beginning with the date on which it was so exercised;

(k)   the Society is satisfied that a person has acted as a solicitor at a time when he did not have a practising certificate which was in force;

(l)   the Society is satisfied that a solicitor has failed to comply with any condition, subject to which his practising certificate was granted or otherwise has effect, to the effect that he may act as a solicitor only—

        (i)   in employment which is approved by the Society in connection with the imposition of that condition;

        (ii)   as a member of a partnership which is so approved;

        (iii)   as a manager of a body recognised by the Society under section 9 of the Administration of Justice Act 1985 and so approved; or

        (iv)   in any specified combination of those ways;

(m)   the Society is satisfied that it is necessary to exercise the powers conferred by Part 2 of this Schedule (or any of them) in relation to a solicitor to protect—

        (i)   the interests of clients (or former or potential clients) of the solicitor or his firm, or

        (ii)   the interests of the beneficiaries of any trust of which the solicitor is or was a trustee.

(1A) In sub-paragraph (1) "manager" has the same meaning as in the Legal Services Act 2007 (see section 207 of that Act).

2   On the death of a sole solicitor paragraphs 6 to 8 shall apply to the client accounts of his practice.

3   The powers conferred by Part II of this Schedule shall also be exercisable, subject to paragraphs 5(4) and 10(9), where—

(a)   the Society is satisfied that there has been undue delay—

        (i)   on the part of a solicitor in connection with any matter in which the solicitor or his firm is or was acting on behalf of a client or with any trust, or

        (ii)   on the part of an employee of a solicitor in connection with any trust of which the employee is or was a trustee in his capacity as such an employee; and

(b)   the Society by notice in writing invites the solicitor to give an explanation within a period of not less than 8 days specified in the notice; and

(c)   the solicitor fails within that period to give an explanation which the Society regards as satisfactory; and

(d)   the Society gives notice of the failure to the solicitor and (at the same or any later time) notice that the powers conferred by Part II of this Schedule are accordingly exercisable.

4   (1) Where the powers conferred by Part II of this Schedule are exercisable in relation to a solicitor, they shall continue to be exercisable after his death or after his name has been removed from or struck off the roll.

(2)   The references to the solicitor or his firm in paragraphs 5(1), 6(2) and (3), 6A, 8, 9(1), (5) and (6) and 10(2) and (7) include, in any case where the solicitor has died, references to his personal representatives.

PART II
POWERS EXERCISABLE ON INTERVENTION

Money

5   (1)   The High Court, on the application of the Society, may order that no payment shall be made without the leave of the court by any person (whether or not named in the order) of any money held by him (in whatever manner and whether it was received before or after the making of the order) on behalf of the solicitor or his firm.

(2)   No order under this paragraph shall take effect in relation to any person to whom it applies unless the Society has served a copy of the order on him (whether or not he is named in it) and, in the case of a bank or other financial institution, has indicated at which of its branches the Society believes that the money to which the order relates is held.

(3)   A person shall not be treated as having disobeyed an order under this paragraph by making a payment of money if he satisfies the court that he exercised due diligence to ascertain whether it was money to which the order related but nevertheless failed to ascertain that the order related to it.

(4)   This paragraph does not apply where the powers conferred by this Part of this Schedule are exercisable by virtue of paragraph 3.

6   (1)   Without prejudice to paragraph 5, if the Society passes a resolution to the effect that any sums of money to which this paragraph applies, and the right to recover or receive them, shall vest in the Society, all such sums shall vest accordingly (whether they were received by the person holding them before or after the Society's resolution) and shall be held by the Society on trust to exercise in relation to them the powers conferred by this Part of this Schedule and subject thereto and to rules under paragraph 6B upon trust for the persons beneficially entitled to them.

(2)   This paragraph applies—

  (a)   where the powers conferred by this paragraph are exercisable by virtue of paragraph 1, to all sums of money held by or on behalf of the solicitor or his firm in connection with:

    (i)   his practice or former practice,

    (ii)   any trust of which he is or formerly was a trustee, or

    (iii)   any trust of which a person who is or was an employee of the solicitor is or was a trustee in the person's capacity as such an employee;

  (b)   where they are exercisable by virtue of paragraph 2, to all sums of money in any client account; and

  (c)   where they are exercisable by virtue of paragraph 3, to all sums of money held by or on behalf of the solicitor or his firm in connection with the trust or other matter in connection with which the Society is satisfied there has been undue delay as mentioned in sub-paragraph (a) of that paragraph.

(3)   The Society shall serve on the solicitor or his firm and on any other person having possession of sums of money to which this paragraph applies a certified copy of the Council's resolution and a notice prohibiting the payment out of any such sums of money.

(4)   Within 8 days of the service of a notice under sub-paragraph (3), the person on whom it was served, on giving not less than 48 hours' notice in writing to the Society and (if the

notice gives the name of the solicitor instructed by the Society) to that solicitor, may apply to the High Court for an order directing the Society to withdraw the notice.

(5) If the court makes such an order, it shall have power also to make such other order with respect to the matter as it may think fit.

(6) If any person on whom a notice has been served under sub-paragraph (3) pays out sums of money at a time when such payment is prohibited by the notice, he shall be guilty of an offence and liable on summary conviction to a fine not exceeding level 3 on the standard scale.

6A (1) Without prejudice to paragraph 5, if the Society passes a resolution to the effect that any rights to which this paragraph applies shall vest in the Society, those rights shall vest accordingly.

(2) This paragraph applies to any right to recover or receive debts due to the solicitor or his firm in connection with his practice or former practice.

(3) Any sums recovered by the Society by virtue of the exercise of rights vested under sub-paragraph (1) shall vest in the Society and shall be held by it on trust to exercise in relation to them the powers conferred by this Part of this Schedule and, subject to those powers and to rules under paragraph 6B, upon trust for the persons beneficially entitled to them.

(4) The Society shall serve on the solicitor or his firm, and any person who owes a debt to which the order applies, a certified copy of the Society's resolution.

6B (1) The Society may make rules governing its treatment of sums vested in it under paragraph 6 or 6A(3).

(2) The rules may in particular make provision in respect of cases where the Society, having taken such steps to do so as are reasonable in all the circumstances of the case, is unable to trace the person or persons beneficially entitled to any sum vested in the Society under paragraph 6 or 6A(3) (including provision which requires amounts to be paid into or out of compensation funds (within the meaning of section 36A)).

7 (1) If the Society takes possession of any sum of money to which paragraph 6 or 6A(3) applies, the Society shall pay it into a special account in the name of the Society or of a person nominated on behalf of the Society, or into a client account of a solicitor nominated on behalf of the Society, and any such person or solicitor shall hold that sum on trust to permit the Society to exercise in relation to it the powers conferred by this Part of this Schedule and subject thereto and to rules under paragraph 6B on trust for the persons beneficially entitled to it.

(2) A bank or other financial institution at which a special account is kept shall be under no obligation to ascertain whether it is being dealt with properly.

8 Without prejudice to paragraphs 5 to 7, if the High Court is satisfied, on an application by the Society, that there is reason to suspect that any person

    (a)   holds money on behalf of the solicitor or his firm, or

    (b)   has information which is relevant to identifying any money held by or on behalf of the solicitor or his firm,

the court may require that person to give the Society information as to any such money and the accounts in which it is held.

Documents

9 (1) The Society may give notice to the solicitor or his firm requiring the production or delivery to any person appointed by the Society at a time and place to be fixed by the Society—

(a)   where the powers conferred by this Part of this Schedule are exercisable by virtue of paragraph 1, of all documents in the possession or under the control of the solicitor or his firm in connection with his practice or former practice or with any trust of which the solicitor is or was a trustee; and

(b)   where they are exercisable by virtue of paragraph 3, of all documents in the possession or under the control of the solicitor or his firm in connection with the trust or other matters of which the Society is satisfied (whether or not they relate also to other matters).

(2)   The person appointed by the Society may take possession of any such documents on behalf of the Society.

(3)   Except in a case where an application has been made to the High Court under sub-paragraph (4), if any person having possession or control of any such documents refuses, neglects or otherwise fails to comply with a requirement under sub-paragraph (1), he shall be guilty of an offence and liable on summary conviction to a fine not exceeding level 3 on the standard scale.

(4)   The High Court, on the application of the Society, may order a person required to produce or deliver documents under sub-paragraph (1) to produce or deliver them to any person appointed by the Society at such time and place as may be specified in the order, and authorise him to take possession of them on behalf of the Society.

(5)   If on an application by the Society the High Court is satisfied that there is reason to suspect that documents in relation to which the powers conferred by sub-paragraph (1) are exercisable have come into the possession or under the control of some person other than the solicitor or his firm, the court may order that person to produce or deliver the documents to any person appointed by the Society at such time and place as may be specified in the order and authorise him to take possession of them on behalf of the Society.

(5A)   In the case of a document which consists of information which is stored in electronic form, a requirement imposed by a notice under sub-paragraph (1) or an order under sub-paragraph (4) or (5), is a requirement to produce or deliver the information in a form in which it is legible or from which it can readily be produced in a legible form.

(6)   On making an order under this paragraph, or at any later time, the court, on the application of the Society, may authorise a person appointed by the Society to enter any premises (using such force as is reasonably necessary) to search for and take possession of—

(a)   any documents to which the order relates;

(b)   any property—

(i)   in the possession of or under the control of the solicitor or his firm, or

(ii)   in the case of an order under sub-paragraph (5), which was in the possession or under the control of such a person and has come into the possession or under the control of the person in respect of whom the order is made,

which the Society reasonably requires for the purpose of accessing information contained in such documents, and to use property obtained under paragraph (b) for that purpose.

(7)   The Society, on taking possession of any documents or other property under this paragraph, shall serve upon the solicitor or personal representatives and upon any other person from whom they were received on the Society's behalf or from whose premises they were taken a notice that possession has been taken on the date specified in the notice.

(8)   Subject to sub-paragraph (9) a person upon whom a notice under sub-paragraph (7) is served, on giving not less than 48 hours notice to the Society and (if the notice gives the name of the solicitor instructed by the Society) to that solicitor, may apply to the High Court for an order directing the Society to deliver the documents or other property to such person as the applicant may require.

(9)   A notice under sub-paragraph (8) shall be given within 8 days of the service of the Society's notice under sub-paragraph (7).

(10)   Without prejudice to the foregoing provisions of this Schedule, the Society may apply to the High Court for an order as to the disposal or destruction of any documents or other property in its possession by virtue of this paragraph or paragraph 10.

(11)   On an application under sub-paragraph (8) or (10), the Court may make such order as it thinks fit.

(12)   Except so far as its right to do so may be restricted by an order on an application under sub-paragraph (8) or (10), the Society may take copies of or extracts from any documents in its possession by virtue of this paragraph or paragraph 10 and require any person to whom it is proposed that such documents shall be delivered, as a condition precedent to delivery, to give a reasonable undertaking to supply copies or extracts to the Society.

Mail and other forms of communication

10   (1)   The High Court, on the application of the Society, may from time to time make a communications redirection order.

(2)   A communications redirection order is an order that specified communications to the solicitor or his firm are to be directed, in accordance with the order, to the Society or any person appointed by the Society.

(3)   For the purposes of this paragraph—

(a)   "specified communications" means communications of such description as are specified in the order;

(b)   the descriptions of communications which may be so specified include—

(i)   communications in the form of a postal packet;

(ii)   electronic communications;

(iii)   communications by telephone.

(4)   A communications redirection order has effect for such time not exceeding 18 months as is specified in the order.

(5)   Where a communications redirection order has effect, the Society or the person appointed by the Society may take possession or receipt of the communications redirected in accordance with the order.

(6)   Where a communications redirection order is made, the Society must pay to—

(a)   in the case of an order relating to postal packets, the postal operator concerned, and

(b)   in any other case, the person specified in the order,

the like charges (if any) as would have been payable for the redirection of the communications to which the order relates if the addressee had permanently ceased to occupy or use the premises or other destination of the communications and had applied to the postal operator or the specified person (as the case may be) to redirect the communications to him as mentioned in the order.

(7)   The High Court may, on the application of the Society, authorise the Society, or a person appointed by it, to take such steps as may be specified in the order in relation to any website purporting to be or have been maintained by or on behalf of the solicitor or his firm if the High Court is satisfied that the taking of those steps is necessary to protect the public interest or the interests of clients (or potential or former clients) of the solicitor or his firm.

(8)   In this paragraph "postal operator" and "postal packet" have the meaning section 125(1) of the Postal Services Act 2000.

(9)   This paragraph does not apply where the powers conferred by this Part of this Schedule are exercisable by virtue of paragraph 3.

Trusts

11   (1)   If the solicitor or his personal representative is a trustee of a trust, the Society may apply to the High Court for an order for the appointment of a new trustee in substitution for him.

(2)   The Trustee Act 1925 shall have effect in relation to an appointment of a new trustee under this paragraph as it has effect in relation to an appointment under section 41 of that Act.

General

12   The powers in relation to sums of money, documents and other property conferred by this Part of this Schedule shall be exercisable notwithstanding any lien on them or right to their possession.

13   Subject to any order for the payment of costs that may be made on an application to the court under this Schedule, any costs incurred by the Society for the purposes of this Schedule, including, without prejudice to the generality of this paragraph, the costs of any person exercising powers under this Part of this Schedule on behalf of the Society, shall be paid by the Solicitor or his personal representatives and shall be recoverable from him or them as a debt owing to the Society.

13A(1)   The High Court, on the application of the Society, may order a former partner of the solicitor to pay a specified proportion of the costs mentioned in paragraph 13.

(2)   The High Court may make an order under this paragraph only if it is satisfied that the conduct (or any part of the conduct) by reason of which the powers conferred by this Part were exercisable in relation to the solicitor was conduct carried on with the consent or connivance of, or was attributable to any neglect on the part of, the former partner.

(3)   In this paragraph "specified" means specified in the order made by the High Court.

14   Where an offence under this Schedule committed by a body corporate is proved to have been committed with the consent or connivance of, or to be attributable to any neglect on the part of, any director, manager, secretary or other similar officer of the body corporate or any person who was purporting to act in any such capacity, he, as well as the body corporate, shall be guilty of that offence and shall be liable to be proceeded against and punished accordingly.

15   Any application to the High Court under this Schedule may be disposed of in chambers.

16   The Society may do all things which are reasonably necessary for the purpose of facilitating the exercise of its powers under this Schedule.

Extracts from the Administration of Justice Act 1985

[With consolidated amendments to 6 October 2010 and prospective amendments shown in Schedule 2.]

Administration of Justice Act 1985

1985 CHAPTER 61

An Act to make further provision with respect to the administration of justice and matters connected therewith; to amend the Solicitors Act 1974; to regulate the provision of solicitors' services in the case of incorporated practices; to regulate the provision of conveyancing services by persons practising as licensed conveyancers; to make further provision with respect to complaints relating to the provision of legal aid services; to amend the law relating to time limits for actions for libel and slander; and to make further provision with respect to arbitrations and proceedings in connection with European patents

[30th October 1985]

BE IT ENACTED by the Queen's most Excellent Majesty, by and with the advice and consent of the Lords Spiritual and Temporal, and Commons, in this present Parliament assembled, and by the authority of the same, as follows:–

Incorporated practices

9 Incorporated practices

(1) The Society may make rules—

    (a)   making provision as to the management and control of legal services bodies;

    (b)   prescribing the circumstances in which such bodies may be recognised by the Society as being suitable bodies to undertake the provision of any solicitor services or other relevant legal services;

    (c)   prescribing the requirements which (subject to any exceptions provided by the rules) must at all times be satisfied by bodies so recognised if they are to remain so recognised; and

    (d)   regulating the conduct of the affairs of such bodies.

(1A) Where the Society makes rules under subsection (1), it must by rules under subsection (1)(c) prescribe the requirement that (subject to any exceptions provided by the rules) recognised bodies must not provide services other than—

    (a)   solicitor services, or

    (b)   solicitor services and other relevant legal services.

(1B) "Relevant legal services" means—

    (a)   solicitor services, and

    (b)   where authorised persons other than solicitors or registered European lawyers are managers or employees of, or have an interest in, a recognised body, services of the kind provided by individuals practising as such authorised persons (whether or not those services involve the carrying on of reserved legal activities within the meaning of the Legal Services Act 2007).

(1C) The Society may by rules under this section provide that services specified, or of a description specified, in the rules are not to be treated as solicitor services or other relevant legal services.

(2) Rules made by the Society may also make provision—

(a) for the manner and form in which applications for recognition under this section, or for the renewal of such recognition, are to be made, and requiring such applications to be accompanied by a fee of such amount as the Society may from time to time determine;

(aa) for the manner and form in which other applications under the rules are to be made, and requiring such applications to be accompanied by a fee of such amount as the Society may from time to time determine;

(b) for regulating the names that may be used by recognised bodies;

(c) about the time when any recognition, or renewal of recognition, takes effect and the period for which it is (subject to the provisions made by or under this Part) to remain in force;

(d) for the suspension or revocation of any such recognition, on such grounds and in such circumstances as may be prescribed by the rules;

(e) about the effect on the recognition of a partnership or other unincorporated body ("the existing body") of any change in the membership of the existing body, including provision for the existing body's recognition to be transferred where the existing body ceases to exist and another body succeeds to the whole or substantially the whole of its business;

(ea) for the keeping by the Society of a register containing the names and places of business of all bodies which are for the time being recognised under this section, and such other information relating to those bodies as may be specified in the rules;

(eb) for information (or information of a specified description) on such a register to be made available to the public, including provision about the manner in which, and times at which, information is to be made so available;

(f) for rules made under any provision of the 1974 Act to have effect in relation to recognised bodies with such additions, omissions or other modifications as appear to the Society to be necessary or expedient;

(fa) about the education and training requirements to be met by managers and employees of recognised bodies;

(fb) for rules made under any provision of the 1974 Act to have effect in relation to managers and employees of recognised bodies with such additions, omissions or other modifications as appear to the Society to be necessary or expedient;

(fc) requiring recognised bodies to appoint a person or persons to monitor compliance, by the recognised body, its managers and its employees, with requirements imposed on them by or by virtue of this Act or any rules applicable to them by virtue of this section;

(g) ...

(h) for the manner of service on recognised bodies of documents authorised or required to be served on such bodies under or by virtue of this Part.

(2A)   If rules under this section provide for the recognition of legal services bodies which have one or more managers who are not legally qualified, the rules must make provision—

(a)   for the recognition of such bodies to be suspended or revoked, on such grounds and in such circumstances as may be prescribed by the rules;

(b)   as to the criteria and procedure for the Society's approving, as suitable to be a manager of a recognised body, an individual who is not legally qualified (and for the Society's withdrawing such approval).

(2B)   Rules under this section may make provision for appeals to the High Court against decisions made by the Society under the rules—

(a)   to suspend or revoke the recognition of any body;

(b)   not to approve, as suitable to be the manager of a recognised body, an individual who is not legally qualified (or to withdraw such approval).

(2C)   The rules may provide for appeals against decisions within subsection (2B)(b) to be brought by the individual to whom the decision relates (as well as the body).

(2D)   In relation to an appeal under rules made by virtue of subsection (2B), the High Court may make such order as it thinks fit as to payment of costs.

(2E)   The decision of the High Court on such an appeal shall be final.

(2F)   Where the Society decides to recognise a body under this section it must grant that recognition subject to one or more conditions if—

(a)   the case is of a kind prescribed for the purposes of this section by rules made by the Society, and

(b)   the Society considers that it is in the public interest to do so.

(2G)   While a body is recognised under this section, the Society—

(a)   must direct that the body's recognition is to have effect subject to one or more conditions if—

(i)   the case is of a prescribed kind, and

(ii)   the Society considers that it is in the public interest to do so;

(b)   may, in such circumstances as may be prescribed, direct that the body's recognition is to have effect subject to such conditions as the Society may think fit.

"Prescribed" means prescribed by rules made by the Society.

(2H)   The conditions which may be imposed under subsection (2F) or (2G) include—

(a)   conditions requiring the body to take specified steps that will, in the opinion of the Society, be conducive to the carrying on by the body of an efficient business;

(b)   conditions which prohibit the body from taking any specified steps except with the approval of the Society;

(c)   if rules under this section provide for the recognition of legal services bodies which have one or more managers who are not legally qualified, a condition that all the managers of the body must be legally qualified.

"Specified" means specified in the condition.

(2I)   Rules made by the Society may make provision about when conditions imposed under this section take effect (including provision conferring power on the Society to direct that a condition is not to have effect until the conclusion of any appeal in relation to it).

(2J)   Section 86A of the 1974 Act applies to rules under this section as it applies to rules under that Act.

(2K)   Rules under this section may contain such incidental, supplemental, transitional or transitory provisions or savings as the Society considers necessary or expedient.

(3)   Despite section 24(2) of the 1974 Act, section 20 of that Act (prohibition on unqualified person acting as solicitor) does not apply to a recognised body; and nothing in section 24(1) of that Act applies in relation to such a body.

(4)   ...

(5)   A certificate signed by an officer of the Society and stating that any body is or is not, or was or was not at any time, a recognised body shall, unless the contrary is proved, be evidence of the facts stated in the certificate; and a certificate purporting to be so signed shall be taken to have been so signed unless the contrary is proved.

(6)   Schedule 2 (which makes provision with respect to the application of provisions of the 1974 Act to recognised bodies and with respect to other matters relating to such bodies) shall have effect.

(7)   Subject to the provisions of that Schedule, the Lord Chancellor may by order made by statutory instrument subject to annulment in pursuance of a resolution of either House of Parliament provide for any enactment or instrument passed or made before or in the same session as the Legal Services Act 2007 was passed and having effect in relation to solicitors to have effect in relation to recognised bodies with such additions, omissions or other modifications as appear to the Lord Chancellor to be necessary or expedient.

(8)   In this section—

"the 1974 Act" means the Solicitors Act 1974;

"authorised person" means an authorised person in relation to an activity which is a reserved legal activity (within the meaning of the Legal Services Act 2007);

"the Society" has the meaning given by section 87(1) of the 1974 Act;

"legally qualified" and "legal services body" have the meaning given by section 9A;

"manager", in relation to a body, has the same meaning as in the Legal Services Act 2007 (see section 207 of that Act);

"recognised body" means a body for the time being recognised under this section;

"registered European lawyer" means a person who is registered with the Law Society under regulation 17 of the European Communities (Lawyers' Practice) Regulations 2000;

"solicitor services" means professional services such as are provided by individuals practising as solicitors or lawyers of other jurisdictions;

and a person has an interest in a body if the person has an interest in the body within the meaning of Part 5 of the Legal Services Act 2007 (see sections 72 and 109 of that Act).

9A   Legal services bodies

(1)   For the purposes of section 9, a "legal services body" means a body (corporate or unincorporate) in respect of which—

(a)   the management and control condition, and

(b)   the relevant lawyer condition,

are satisfied.

(2)   The management and control condition is satisfied if—

(a)   at least 75% of the body's managers are legally qualified,

(b)   the proportion of shares in the body held by persons who are legally qualified is at least 75%,

(c)   the proportion of voting rights in the body which persons who are legally qualified are entitled to exercise, or control the exercise of, is at least 75%,

(d)   all the persons with an interest in the body who are not legally qualified are managers of the body, and

(e)   all the managers of the body who are not legally qualified are individuals approved by the Society as suitable to be managers of a recognised body.

(3)   The Society may by rules under section 9 provide that, in relation to specified kinds of bodies, subsection (2) applies as if the references to 75% were to such greater percentage as may be specified (and different percentages may be specified for different kinds of bodies).

(4)   The relevant lawyer condition is satisfied in relation to a body if at least one manager of the body is—

(a)   a solicitor,

(b)   a registered European lawyer, or

(c)   a qualifying body.

(5)   For that purpose a qualifying body is a body in respect of which—

(a)   the management and control condition is satisfied,

(b)   the relevant lawyer condition is satisfied by virtue of subsection (4)(a) or (b), and

(c)   the services condition is satisfied.

(6)   For the purposes of this section the following are legally qualified—

(a)   an authorised person who is an individual;

(b)   a registered foreign lawyer (within the meaning of section 89 of the Courts and Legal Services Act 1990 (c 41));

(c)   a person entitled to pursue professional activities under a professional title to which the Directive applies in a state to which the Directive applies (other than the title of barrister or solicitor in England and Wales);

(d)   an authorised person which is a body in respect of which—

(i)   the services condition is satisfied, and

(ii)   the management and control condition would be satisfied if the references in subsection (2) to persons who are legally qualified were to persons who are legally qualified by virtue of paragraphs (a) to (c);

(e)   a body which provides professional services such as are provided by individuals who are authorised persons or lawyers of other jurisdictions, and in respect of which the management and control condition would be satisfied if the references in subsection (2) to persons who are legally qualified were to persons who are legally qualified by virtue of paragraphs (a) to (c).

(f)   a legal partnership which—

(i)   was in existence immediately before the commencement of this paragraph,

(ii)   since that time has continued to be a partnership of the kind mentioned in rule 12.01(1)(b), 12.02(1)(b) or 12.04(1)(c)(i) of the pre-commencement conduct rules (framework of practice), and

    (iii) has not, since that time, had a body corporate (other than a body within paragraph (g)) as a member;

(g) a body corporate which—

    (i) was recognised under section 9 immediately before the commencement of this paragraph, and

    (ii) has since that time continued to satisfy the requirements of rule 14.03(1) and 14.04(1) to (3) or the requirements of rule 14.05(1) to (3) of the pre-commencement conduct rules (restrictions on directors, owners etc of incorporated practices);

(h) a body which—

    (i) is an authorised person and satisfies the services condition, or

    (ii) provides professional services such as are provided by individuals who are authorised persons or lawyers of other jurisdictions,

and which satisfies the requirements of rules under subsection (6C).

(6A) For the purposes of subsection (6)(f), a partnership is to be treated as the same partnership despite a change in membership, if any person who was a member before the change remains a member.

(6B) For the purposes of subsection (6)(f) and (g), the references in the pre-commencement conduct rules to a recognised body are to be construed as references to a body which was recognised under section 9 immediately before the commencement of subsection (6)(f) and (g).

(6C) The Society must make rules for the purposes of paragraph (h) of subsection (6) prescribing the requirements relating to management and control which must be satisfied by or in relation to a body for it to fall within that paragraph.

(7) For the purposes of this section, the services condition is satisfied in relation to a body if the body provides only services which may be provided by a recognised body (having regard to rules under section 9(1A) and (1C)).

(8) For the purposes of this section—

  "authorised person" has the same meaning as in section 9;

  "the Directive" means Directive 98/5/EC of the European Parliament and the Council, to facilitate practice of the profession of lawyer on a permanent basis in a Member State other than that in which the qualification was obtained;

  "legal partnership" means a partnership in which a solicitor, a registered European lawyer or a recognised body is permitted to practise by virtue of rules made under section 31 of the Solicitors Act 1974 (c 47), as those rules had effect immediately before the commencement of subsection (6)(f);

  "manager", in relation to a body, has the meaning given by section 9;

  "pre-commencement conduct rules" means rules under Part 2 of the Solicitors Act 1974 or section 9 of this Act, known as the Solicitors' Code of Conduct 2007, as those rules had effect immediately before the commencement of subsection (6)(f) and (g);

  "recognised body" has the same meaning as in section 9 (subject to subsection (6B) above);

  "registered European lawyer" has the same meaning as in section 9;

  "shares" has the same meaning as for the purposes of Part 5 of the Legal Services Act 2007 (see sections 72 and 109 of that Act);

  "the Society" has the meaning given by section 87(1) of the Solicitors Act 1974;

"specified" means specified in rules made by the Society;

and a person has an interest in a body if the person has an interest in the body for the purposes of section 9.

10 Penalty for pretending to be a body recognised under s 9

(1)   A body shall not describe itself or hold itself out as a body for the time being recognised under section 9 unless it is so recognised.

(2)   Any body which contravenes subsection (1) shall be guilty of an offence and liable on summary conviction to a fine not exceeding the fourth level on the standard scale.

(3)   Where an offence under this section committed by a body corporate is proved to have been committed with the consent or connivance of or to be attributable to any neglect on the part of an officer of the body corporate, that officer (as well as the body corporate) is guilty of the offence and is liable to be proceeded against and punished accordingly.

(4)   Where the affairs of a body corporate are managed by its members, subsection (3) applies in relation to the acts and defaults of a member in connection with the member's functions of management as it applies to an officer of the body corporate.

(5)   Proceedings for an offence under this section alleged to have been committed by an unincorporated body are to be brought in the name of that body (and not in that of any of its members) and, for the purposes of any such proceedings, any rules of court relating to the service of documents have effect as if that body were a corporation.

(6)   A fine imposed on an unincorporated body on its conviction of an offence under this section is to be paid out of the funds of that body.

(7)   If an unincorporated body is charged with an offence under this section, section 33 of the Criminal Justice Act 1925 (c 86) and Schedule 3 to the Magistrates' Courts Act 1980 (c 43) (procedure on charge of an offence against a corporation) have effect in like manner as in the case of a corporation so charged.

(8)   Where an offence under this section committed by an unincorporated body (other than a partnership) is proved to have been committed with the consent or connivance of, or to be attributable to any neglect on the part of, any officer of the body or any member of its governing body, that officer or member as well as the unincorporated body is guilty of the offence and liable to be proceeded against and punished accordingly.

(9)   Where an offence under this section committed by a partnership is proved to have been committed with the consent or connivance of, or to be attributable to any neglect on the part of, a partner, that partner as well as the partnership is guilty of the offence and liable to be proceeded against and punished accordingly.

(10)   In this section "officer", in relation to a body corporate, means—

(a)   any director, secretary or other similar officer of the body corporate, or

(b)   any person who was purporting to act in any such capacity.

SCHEDULE 2
Legal services practices: Supplementary Provisions

Section 9

Interpretation

1   (1)   Subject to sub-paragraph (2), references in this Schedule to a recognised body are references to a body for the time being recognised under section 9 of this Act.

(2)   References in this Schedule to a recognised body in relation to—

(a)   a complaint (other than such a complaint as is mentioned in paragraph 16(1)(a));

(b)   ...

include references to a body that was recognised under section 9 of this Act at the time when the conduct to which the complaint relates took place.

(2A)   References in this Schedule to a manager or employee of a recognised body, in relation to a complaint (other than such a complaint as is mentioned in paragraph 16(1A)(a)), include references to a person who was such a manager or employee at the time when the conduct to which the complaint relates took place.

(4)   In section 87(1) of the 1974 Act the definitions of "client", "contentious business" and "non-contentious business" shall apply for the purposes of—

(a)   this Schedule; and

(b)   any provision of the 1974 Act in so far as it has effect in relation to a recognised body by virtue of this Schedule,

as if for any reference to a solicitor there were substituted a reference to a recognised body.

(5)   Subject to sub-paragraphs (4) and (6), any expression used in this Schedule which is also used in the 1974 Act has the same meaning as in that Act.

(6)   In this Schedule—

"manager", in relation to a body, has the same meaning as in the Legal Services Act 2007 (see section 207 of that Act);

"registered European lawyer" has the same meaning as in section 9A;

"the 1974 Act" means the Solicitors Act 1974.

Appeal against refusal of Society to grant recognition etc

2   (1)   A body may appeal to the High Court against—

(a)   a decision to refuse an application by the body for recognition under section 9;

(b)   a decision to impose a condition under subsection (2F) of that section on the body's recognition under that section;

(c)   a decision to impose a condition under subsection (2G) of that section on the body's recognition under that section.

(2)   A recognised body whose recognition is subject to a condition within section 9(2H)(b) may appeal to the High Court against any decision by the Society to refuse to approve the taking of any step for the purposes of that condition.

(3)   Rules made by the Society may make provision, as respects any application for recognition that is neither granted nor refused by the Society within such period as may be specified in the rules, for enabling an appeal to be brought under this paragraph in relation to the application as if it had been refused by the Society.

(4)   On an appeal under sub-paragraph (1)(a) or (b), the High Court may—

(a)   affirm the decision of the Society,

(b)   direct the Society to grant the body recognition under section 9 free from conditions or subject to such conditions as the High Court may think fit,

(c)   direct the Society not to recognise the body,

(d)   if the Society has recognised the body, by order suspend the recognition, or

(e)   make such other order as the High Court thinks fit.

(5)   On an appeal under sub-paragraph (1)(c), the High Court may—

(a)   affirm the decision of the Society,

(b)   direct that the body's recognition under section 9 is to have effect subject to such conditions as the High Court may think fit,

(c)   by order revoke the direction given by the Society under section 9(2G), or

(d)   make such other order as the High Court thinks fit.

(6)   On an appeal under sub-paragraph (2), the High Court may—

(a)   affirm the decision of the Society,

(b)   direct the Society to approve the taking of one or more steps for the purposes of a condition within section 9(2H)(b), or

(c)   make such other order as the High Court thinks fit.

(7)   In relation to an appeal under this paragraph, the High Court may make such order as it thinks fit as to payment of costs.

(8)   The decision of the High Court on an appeal under this paragraph is final.

Accounts rules

3   (1)   This paragraph applies where rules made under section 32(1) of the 1974 Act are applied—

(a)   to recognised bodies in accordance with section 9(2)(f) of this Act, or

(b)   to managers or employees of such bodies in accordance with section 9(2)(fb) of this Act.

(2)   The Society may disclose a report on or information about the accounts of a recognised body, or a manager or employee of a recognised body, obtained in pursuance of such rules for use—

(a)   in investigating the possible commission of an offence by the body or any of its managers or employees, and

(b)   in connection with any prosecution of the body or any of its managers or employees consequent on the investigation.

Interest on client's money

4   (1)   Where rules made under section 32 of the 1974 Act and containing any such provision as is referred to in section 33(1) of that Act are applied to recognised bodies in accordance with section 9(2)(f) of this Act, then, except as provided by the rules, a recognised body is not liable to account to any client, other person or trust for interest received by the recognised body on money held at a bank or building society in an account which is for money received or held for, or on account of—

(a)   clients of the recognised body, other persons or trusts, generally, or

(b)   that client, person or trust separately.

4ZA   Where rules made under section 32 of the 1974 Act and containing any such provision as is referred to in section 33(1) of that Act are applied to managers or employees of recognised bodies in accordance with section 9(2)(fb), then, except as provided by the rules, a manager or employee to whom the rules are applied is not liable to account to any client, other person or trust for interest received by the manager or employee on money held at a bank or building society in an account which is for money received or held for, or on account of—

(a)   clients of the recognised body, other persons or trusts, generally, or

(b)   that client, person or trust, separately.

Inspection of bank accounts

4A (1)   This paragraph applies where rules made under section 33A(1) of the 1974 Act are applied—

(a)   to recognised bodies in accordance with section 9(2)(f) of this Act, or

(b)   to managers or employees of such bodies in accordance with section 9(2)(fb) of this Act.

(2)   The Society may disclose information about the accounts of a recognised body, or a manager or employee of a recognised body, obtained in pursuance of such rules for use—

(a)   in investigating the possible commission of an offence by the body or any of its managers or employees, and

(b)   in connection with any prosecution of the body or any of its managers or employees consequent on the investigation.

Accountant's reports

5   Where rules made under section 34 of the 1974 Act are applied to recognised bodies in accordance with section 9(2)(f), section 34(9) and (10) of that Act apply in relation to a recognised body as they apply in relation to a solicitor.

5A   Where rules made under section 34 of the 1974 Act are applied to managers or employees of recognised bodies in accordance with section 9(2)(fb), section 34(9) and (10) of that Act apply in relation to a manager or employee to which the rules are applied as they apply in relation to a solicitor.

Compensation Fund

6   (1)   Section 36 of the 1974 Act applies in relation to recognised bodies as if for paragraphs (a) and (b) of subsection (1) there were substituted—

"(a)   an act or omission of a recognised body or former recognised body;

(b)   an act or omission of a manager or employee, or former manager or employee, of a recognised body or former recognised body;

(2)   Section 36A(2) and (3) of the 1974 Act applies in relation to recognised bodies as it applies in relation to solicitors.

Solicitor who is justice of the peace not to act in certain proceedings

7   In section 38 of the 1974 Act references to any partner of a solicitor shall be construed, in relation to a solicitor who is a manager of a recognised body, as references to any other solicitor who is a manager of that body.

8   ...

Restriction on employment of person struck off roll or suspended

9   (1)   Section 41 of the 1974 Act (except subsection (4)) shall apply to a recognised body (and any manager or employee of it) and its business as such as it applies to a solicitor and his practice as such.

(2)   No recognised body (or manager or employee of such a body) may, except in accordance with a written permission granted by the Society under this paragraph, permit a person to whom sub-paragraph (3) applies to—

(a)   be a manager of the body, or

(b)   have an interest in the body;

and for this purpose a person has an interest in the body if he has an interest in the body within the meaning of Part 5 of the Legal Services Act 2007 (see sections 72 and 109 of that Act).

(3)   This sub-paragraph applies to a person who to the knowledge of the recognised body (or, as the case may be, the manager or employee) is a person—

(a)   who is disqualified from practising as a solicitor by reason of one of the facts mentioned in section 41(1)(a), (b) or (c) of the 1974 Act (name struck off the roll, suspension etc), or

(b)   in respect of whom there is a direction in force under section 47(2)(g) of that Act (prohibition on restoration to roll).

(4)   Permission granted for the purposes of sub-paragraph (2) may be granted for such period and subject to such conditions as the Society thinks fit.

(5)   A person aggrieved by the refusal of the Society to grant permission under sub-paragraph (4), or by any conditions attached by the Society to the grant of any such permission may appeal to the High Court which may—

(a)   confirm the refusal or the conditions, as the case may be, or

(b)   grant a permission under this paragraph for such period and subject to such conditions as it thinks fit.

(6)   In relation to an appeal under sub-paragraph (5) the High Court may make such order as it thinks fit as to payment of costs.

(7)   The decision of the High Court on an appeal under sub-paragraph (5) is final.

Failure to disclose fact of having been struck off or suspended

10   (1)   Section 42(1) and (1A) of the 1974 Act shall apply in relation to employment by a recognised body (or any manager or employee of such a body) in connection with its business as it applies in relation to employment by a solicitor in connection with his practice.

(2)   It is an offence for a person ("P") to whom sub-paragraph (3) applies—

(a)   to seek or accept from any person an interest in a recognised body, without previously informing that person (and, if different, the recognised body) that P is a person to whom that sub-paragraph applies, or

(b)   to seek or accept a position as a manager of a recognised body, without previously informing that body that P is such a person.

(3)   This sub-paragraph applies to a person—

(a)   who is disqualified from practising as a solicitor by reason of one of the facts mentioned in section 41(1)(a), (b) or (c) of the 1974 Act (name struck off the roll, suspension etc), or

(b)   in respect of whom there is a direction in force under section 47(2)(g) of that Act (prohibition on restoration to roll).

(4)   A person guilty of an offence under sub-paragraph (2) is liable on summary conviction to a fine not exceeding level 3 on the standard scale.

(5)   Subsection (2) of section 42 of the 1974 Act applies in relation to an offence under sub-paragraph (2) as it applies in relation to an offence under that section.

(6)   For the purposes of sub-paragraph (2)(a) a person seeks or accepts an interest in a recognised body if the person seeks or accepts an interest which if it were obtained by the person would result in the person having an interest in that body within the meaning of Part 5 of the Legal Services Act 2007 (see sections 72 and 109 of that Act).

11   ...

12   ...

13   ...

Information about suitability for recognition

14   (1)   The Society may give a notice under this paragraph if it is satisfied that it is necessary to do so for the purpose of investigating whether—

    (a)   a recognised body continues to be suitable to be recognised under section 9, or

    (b)   a manager of a recognised body who is not legally qualified (within the meaning of section 9A) continues to be suitable to be a manager of a recognised body.

(2)   A notice under this paragraph is a notice which requires a person within sub-paragraph (3)—

    (a)   to provide information, or information of a description, specified in the notice, or

    (b)   to produce documents, or documents of a description, specified in the notice.

(3)   The persons are—

    (a)   the recognised body;

    (b)   an employee or manager of the recognised body;

    (c)   a person who has an interest in the recognised body (within the meaning of the Legal Services Act 2007 (see sections 72 and 109 of that Act)).

(4)   For the purposes of this paragraph, section 44B(4) to (7) of the 1974 Act applies—

    (a)   in relation to a notice under this paragraph as if it were a notice under section 44B of that Act, and

    (b)   in relation to a person given a notice under this paragraph as if that person were a person given a notice under that section,

and references in subsections (6) and (7) of that section to powers conferred by that section are to be read as references to powers conferred by this paragraph.

(5)   Where powers conferred by Part 2 of Schedule 1 to the 1974 Act are exercisable in relation to a person within paragraph (a), (b) or (c) of sub-paragraph (3), they continue to be so exercisable after the person has ceased to be a person within the paragraph in question.

(6)   Section 44BA of the 1974 Act (power to require explanation of document or information) applies in relation to a notice under this paragraph and the person to whom such a notice is given as it applies in relation to a notice under section 44B of the 1974 Act and the person to whom such a notice is given.

(7)   Subsection (1) of section 44BC of that Act (falsification of documents etc) applies in relation to an investigation of the kind mentioned in sub-paragraph (1) as it applies in relation to the investigations mentioned in that subsection, and subsections (2), (4) and (5) of that section apply accordingly.

(8)   Subsection (3) of that section (provision of false information etc) applies in relation to a requirement imposed under this paragraph as it applies in relation to a requirement imposed by section 44B of that Act, and subsections (4) and (5) of that section apply accordingly.

Power to charge for costs of investigation

14A(1)   The Society may make regulations prescribing charges to be paid to the Society by recognised bodies who are the subject of a discipline investigation.

(2)   A discipline investigation is an investigation carried out by the Society into a failure or apprehended failure by a recognised body to comply with any requirement imposed by or by virtue of this Act or any rules applicable to it by virtue of section 9.

(3)   Regulations under this paragraph may—

(a)   make different provision for different cases or purposes;

(b)   provide for the whole or part of a charge payable under the regulations to be repaid in such circumstances as may be prescribed by the regulations.

(4)   Any charge which a recognised body is required to pay under regulations under this paragraph is recoverable by the Society as a debt due to the Society from the recognised body.

(5)   This paragraph applies in relation to a manager or employee of a recognised body as it applies in relation to a recognised body.

Disciplinary powers of the Society

14B(1)   This paragraph applies where the Society is satisfied that a recognised body, or a manager or employee of a recognised body, has failed to comply with a requirement imposed by or by virtue of this Act or any rules applicable to that person by virtue of section 9 of this Act.

(2)   The Society may do one or both of the following—

(a)   give the person a written rebuke;

(b)   direct the person to pay a penalty not exceeding £2,000.

(3)   The Society may publish details of any action it has taken under sub-paragraph (2)(a) or (b), if it considers it to be in the public interest to do so.

(4)   Where the Society takes action against a person under sub-paragraph (2)(b), or decides to publish under sub-paragraph (3) details of such action under sub-paragraph (2)(a) or (b), it must notify the person in writing that it has done so.

(5)   A penalty imposed under sub-paragraph (2)(b) does not become payable until—

(a)   the end of the period during which an appeal against the decision to impose the penalty, or the amount of the penalty, may be made under paragraph 14C, or

(b)   if such an appeal is made, such time as it is determined or withdrawn.

(6)   The Society may not publish under sub-paragraph (3) details of any action under sub-paragraph (2)(a) or (b)—

(a)   during the period within which an appeal against—

(i)   the decision to take the action,

(ii)   in the case of action under sub-paragraph (2)(b), the amount of the penalty, or

(iii)   the decision to publish the details,

may be made under paragraph 14C, or

611

(b)   if such an appeal has been made, until such time as it is determined or withdrawn.

(7)   The Society must make rules—

(a)   prescribing the circumstances in which the Society may decide to take action under sub-paragraph (2)(a) or (b);

(b)   about the practice and procedure to be followed by the Society in relation to such action;

(c)   governing the publication under sub-paragraph (3) of details of action taken under sub-paragraph (2)(a) or (b);

and the Society may make such other rules in connection with the exercise of its powers under this paragraph as it considers appropriate.

(8)   Before making rules under sub-paragraph (7), the Society must consult the Tribunal.

(9)   A penalty under this paragraph may be recovered as a debt due to the Society, and is to be forfeited to Her Majesty.

(10)   The Lord Chancellor may, by order, amend paragraph (b) of sub-paragraph (2) so as to substitute for the amount for the time being specified in that paragraph such other amount as may be specified in the order.

(11)   Before making an order under sub-paragraph (10), the Lord Chancellor must consult the Society.

(12)   An order under sub-paragraph (10) is to be made by statutory instrument subject to annulment in pursuance of a resolution of either House of Parliament.

(13)   This paragraph is without prejudice to any power conferred on the Society, or any other person, to make an application or complaint to the Tribunal.

14C(1)   A person may appeal against—

(a)   a decision by the Society to rebuke that person under paragraph 14B(2)(a) if a decision is also made to publish details of the rebuke;

(b)   a decision by the Society to impose a penalty on that person under paragraph 14B(2)(b) or the amount of that penalty;

(c)   a decision by the Society to publish under paragraph 14B(3) details of any action taken against that person under paragraph 14B(2)(a) or (b).

(2)   Subsections (9)(b), (10)(a) and (b), (11) and (12) of section 46 of the 1974 Act (Tribunal rules about procedure for hearings etc) apply in relation to appeals under this paragraph as they apply in relation to applications or complaints, except that subsection (11) of that section is to be read as if for "the applicant" to "application)" there were substituted "any party to the appeal".

(3)   Rules under section 46(9)(b) of the 1974 Act may, in particular, make provision about the period during which an appeal under this paragraph may be made.

(4)   On an appeal under this paragraph, the Tribunal has power to make an order which—

(a)   affirms the decision of the Society;

(b)   revokes the decision of the Society;

(c)   in the case of a penalty imposed under paragraph 14B(2)(b), varies the amount of the penalty;

(d)   in the case of a recognised body, contains provision for any of the matters mentioned in paragraph 18(2);

(e)   in the case of a manager or employee of a recognised body, contains provision for any of the matters mentioned in paragraph 18A(2);

(f)   makes such provision as the Tribunal thinks fit as to payment of costs.

(5) Where, by virtue of sub-paragraph (4)(e), an order contains provision for any of the matters mentioned in sub-paragraph (2)(c) of paragraph 18A, sub-paragraphs (5) and (6) of that paragraph apply as if the order had been made under sub-paragraph (2)(c) of that paragraph.

(6) An appeal from the Tribunal shall lie to the High Court, at the instance of the Society or the person in respect of whom the order of the Tribunal was made.

(7) The High Court shall have power to make such order on an appeal under this paragraph as it may think fit.

(8) Any decision of the High Court on an appeal under this section shall be final.

(9) This paragraph is without prejudice to any power conferred on the Tribunal in connection with an application or complaint made to it.

15   ...

Complaints to Tribunal with respect to recognised bodies

16 (1) The Tribunal shall have jurisdiction to hear and determine any of the following complaints made to it under this paragraph with respect to a recognised body, namely—

(a)   a complaint that the body has (while a recognised body) been convicted by any court of a criminal offence which renders it unsuitable to be recognised under section 9 of this Act;

(b)   a complaint that the body has failed to comply with any requirement imposed by or by virtue of this Act or with any rules applicable to it by virtue of section 9 of this Act;

(c)   a complaint that the body has acted in contravention of section 41 of the 1974 Act or paragraph 9(2) of this Schedule or of any conditions subject to which a permission has been granted under section 41 of that Act or that paragraph of this Schedule; or

(d)   a complaint that the body has knowingly acted in contravention of any such order as is mentioned in section 44(2) of the 1974 Act or of any conditions subject to which a permission has been granted under such an order.

(1A) The Tribunal shall have jurisdiction to hear and determine any of the following complaints made to it under this paragraph with respect to a manager or employee of a recognised body ("the relevant person")—

(a)   a complaint that the relevant person has been convicted by any court of a criminal offence which renders that person unsuitable to be a manager or employee (or both) of a recognised body;

(b)   a complaint that the relevant person has failed to comply with any requirement imposed by or by virtue of this Act or any rules applicable to the relevant person by virtue of section 9 of this Act;

(c)   a complaint that the relevant person has acted in contravention of section 41 of the 1974 Act or paragraph 9(2) of this Schedule or of any conditions subject to which a permission has been granted under that section or for the purposes of para-graph 9(2) of this Schedule;

(d)   a complaint that the relevant person has knowingly acted in contravention of an order under section 43(2) of the 1974 Act or of any conditions subject to which a permission has been granted under such an order.

(2)   A complaint may be made to the Tribunal under this paragraph by any person.

Procedure on applications and complaints

17   In subsections (9) to (11) of section 46 of the 1974 Act—

(a)   any reference to an application or complaint shall be construed as including a reference to any such application as is mentioned in paragraph 21(1) or any such complaint as is mentioned in paragraph 16(1) or (1A);

(b)   any reference to an application or complaint made under that Act shall be construed as including a reference to any such application or complaint as aforesaid made under this Schedule; and

(c)   in the case of subsection (10)(c), any reference to a solicitor shall be construed as including a reference to a recognised body or, in the case of such a complaint as is mentioned in paragraph 16(1A), to a manager or employee of such a body.

Powers of Tribunal with respect to recognised bodies

18   (1)   Where on the hearing of any complaint made to it under this Schedule (other than paragraph 16(1A)) the Tribunal is satisfied that a recognised body—

(a)   has been convicted as mentioned in paragraph (a) of paragraph 16(1); or

(b)   has failed to comply with any requirement imposed by or by virtue of this Act or with any such rules as are mentioned in paragraph (b) of paragraph 16(1); or

(c)   has acted as mentioned in paragraph (c) or (d) of that provision;

the Tribunal may, if it thinks fit, make one or more of the orders referred to in sub-paragraph (2).

(2)   Those orders are—

(a)   an order revoking the recognition under section 9 of this Act of the body to which the complaint relates;

(b)   an order directing the payment by that body of a penalty, to be forfeited to Her Majesty;

(c)   an order requiring that body to pay the costs incurred in bringing against it the proceedings before the Tribunal or a contribution towards those costs, being a contribution of such amount as the Tribunal considers reasonable.

(2A)   Where, on the hearing of any application or complaint made to it under this Schedule, the Tribunal is satisfied that more than one allegation is proved against the recognised body to whom the application or complaint relates, it may impose a separate penalty (by virtue of sub-paragraph (2)(b)) with respect to each such allegation.

18A(1)   Where, on the hearing of any complaint made to it under paragraph 16(1A) of this Schedule, the Tribunal is satisfied that a manager or employee of a recognised body—

(a)   has been convicted as mentioned in paragraph (a) of paragraph 16(1A),

(b)   has failed to comply with any requirement imposed by or by virtue of this Act or any rules applicable to the relevant person by virtue of section 9 of this Act, or

(c)   has acted as mentioned in paragraph (c) or (d) of paragraph 16(1A),

the Tribunal may, if it thinks fit, make one or more of the orders referred to in sub-paragraph (2).

(2)   Those orders are—

(a)   an order directing the payment by the relevant person of a penalty to be forfeited to Her Majesty;

(b)   an order requiring the Society to consider taking such steps as the Tribunal may specify in relation to the relevant person;

(c)   if the person is not a solicitor, an order which states one or more of the matters mentioned in sub-paragraph (3);

(d)   an order requiring the Society to refer to an appropriate regulator any matter relating to the conduct of the relevant person.

(3)   The matters referred to in sub-paragraph (2)(c) are—

(a)   that as from the specified date—

(i)   no solicitor or employee of a solicitor shall employ or remunerate, in connection with the practice carried on by that solicitor, the person with respect to whom the order is made, and

(ii)   no recognised body, or manager or employee of such a body, shall employ or remunerate that person, in connection with the business of the recognised body,

except in accordance with a Society permission;

(b)   that as from the specified date no recognised body or manager or employee of such a body shall, except in accordance with a Society permission, permit the person with respect to whom the order is made to be a manager of the body;

(c)   that as from the specified date no recognised body or manager or employee of such a body shall, except in accordance with a Society permission, permit the person with respect to whom the order is made to have an interest in the body.

(4)   For this purpose a person has an interest in a body if the person has an interest in the body within the meaning of Part 5 the Legal Services Act 2007 (see sections 72 and 109 of that Act).

(5)   Subsections (1) to (1C), (3) and (4) of section 44 of the 1974 Act (offences in connection with orders under section 43(2) of that Act) apply in relation to an order under sub-paragraph (2)(c) as they apply in relation to an order under section 43(2) of that Act, except that references in those subsections to provision within section 43(2)(a), (b) or (c) of that Act are to be read as references to provision within sub-paragraph (3)(a), (b) or (c).

(6)   Section 44(2) of the 1974 Act, paragraph 16(1)(d) and (1A)(d) of this Schedule and paragraph 15(3A) of Schedule 14 to the Courts and Legal Services Act 1990 apply in relation to an order under sub-paragraph (2)(c) as they apply in relation to an order under section 43(2) of the 1974 Act.

(7)   For the purposes of sub-paragraph (2)(d) an "appropriate regulator" in relation to the relevant person means—

(a)   if the person is an authorised person in relation to a reserved legal activity for the purposes of the Legal Services Act 2007, any relevant approved regulator (within the meaning of that Act) in relation to that person, and

(b)   if the person carries on activities which are not reserved legal activities, any body which regulates the carrying on of such activities by the person.

19   ...

Powers of Tribunal in respect of legal aid complaints

20 (1)   Where the Tribunal makes any such order as is referred to in subsection (2A) of section 47 of the 1974 Act in the case of a solicitor who is a manager or employee of a recognised body, the Tribunal may, if it thinks fit, order that any solicitor who is for the time being a manager of that body shall be excluded (either permanently or for a specified period) from providing representation funded by the Legal Services Commission as part of the Criminal Defence Service.

(2)   ...

Revocation of recognition by reason of default by director

21 (1)   Where—

(a)   any order is made by the Tribunal under section 47 of the 1974 Act in the case of a manager of a recognised body; or

(b)   an order is made by the High Court or the Court of Appeal that the name of a manager of a recognised body be struck off the roll or that such a manager be suspended from practice as a solicitor; or

(c)   any such order as is mentioned in paragraph (a) or (b) is made in the case of a person employed by a recognised body and the act or omission constituting the ground on which the order was made was instigated or connived at by a manager of the recognised body or, if the act or omission was a continuing act or omission, a manager of the body had or reasonably ought to have had knowledge of its continuance,

the Tribunal may, on an application made with respect to the recognised body by or on behalf of the Society, by order revoke its recognition under section 9 of this Act.

(2)   The Tribunal shall not take a case into consideration during any period within which proceedings by way of appeal may be brought which may result in sub-paragraph (1) being rendered inapplicable in that case, or while any such proceedings are pending.

(3)   Any reference to a manager of a recognised body in any of paragraphs (a) to (c) of sub-paragraph (1) includes a reference to a person who was a manager of the body at the time of the conduct leading to the making of the order referred to in that paragraph.

(4)   The reference in paragraph (c) of sub-paragraph (1) to a person employed by a recognised body includes a reference to a person who was so employed at the time of the conduct leading to the making of the order referred to in that paragraph.

Costs: general modification of provisions of Part III of 1974 Act

22 (1)   In the provisions to which this paragraph applies—

(a)   any reference to a solicitor or to a client of a solicitor shall be construed as including a reference to a recognised body or to a client of such a body; and

(b)   any reference to a client's solicitor shall be construed as including a reference to any recognised body acting for a client.

(2)   This paragraph applies to the following provisions of the 1974 Act (which relate to the remuneration of solicitors in respect of contentious and non-contentious business), namely—

section 56 (except subsections (1)(e) and (5));

sections 57 to 59;

section 60 (except subsection (5));

sections 61 and 62;

sections 64 and 65;

section 67;

section 69(1); and

sections 70 to 74.

Orders as to remuneration for non-contentious business

23 (1) In relation to an order under section 56 of the 1974 Act prescribing (by virtue of paragraph 22) general principles to be applied when determining the remuneration of recognised bodies in respect of non-contentious business, subsection (5) of that section shall have effect as if—

(a) in paragraph (a), for "the solicitor" there were substituted "the recognised body"; and

(b) in paragraph (d), the reference to the solicitor or any employee of the solicitor who is an authorised person were a reference to any manager or employee of the recognised body who is an authorised person.

(2) In this paragraph "authorised person" means a person who is an authorised person in relation to an activity which is a reserved legal activity, within the meaning of the Legal Services Act 2007 (see section 18 of that Act).

Effect of contentious business agreements

24 (1) This paragraph applies in relation to a contentious business agreement made between a recognised body and a client.

(2) A provision in the agreement that the body shall not be liable for the negligence of any of its managers or employees shall be void if the client is a natural person who, in entering that agreement, is acting for purposes which are outside his trade, business or profession.

(3) A provision in the agreement that the body shall be relieved from any responsibility to which it would otherwise be subject in the course of carrying on its business as a recognised body shall be void.

(4) A provision in the agreement that any manager of the body shall be relieved from any responsibility to which the manager would otherwise be subject in the course of the carrying on by the body of its business as a recognised body shall be void.

Effect on contentious business agreement of supervening incapacity of recognised body to act for client

25 (1) If, after some business has been done under a contentious business agreement made between a recognised body and a client but before the body has wholly performed it, the body ceases to be capable of wholly performing it by reason of one of the following events, namely—

(a) the body ceases (for any reason) to be a recognised body;

(b) a relevant insolvency event occurs in relation to the body; or

(c) the client terminates the retainer or employment of the body in favour of another recognised body or a solicitor (as, notwithstanding the agreement, he shall be entitled to do),

any party to, or the representative of any party to, the agreement may apply to the court, and the court shall have the same jurisdiction as to enforcing the agreement so far as it has been performed, or setting it aside, as the court would have had if the recognised body were still capable of wholly performing it.

(2)   The court, notwithstanding that it is of the opinion that the agreement is in all respects fair and reasonable, may order the amount due in respect of business under the agreement to be ascertained by assessment, and in that case—

(a)   the costs officer, in ascertaining that amount, shall have regard so far as may be to the terms of the agreement; and

(b)   payment of the amount found by him to be due may be enforced in the same manner as if the agreement had been wholly performed.

(3)   If in such a case as is mentioned in sub-paragraph (1)(c) an order is made for the assessment of the amount due to the recognised body in respect of the business done under the agreement, the court shall direct the costs officer to have regard to the circumstances under which the termination of the body's retainer or employment has taken place, and the costs officer, unless he is of the opinion that there has been no default, negligence, improper delay or other conduct on the part of any manager or employee of the body affording the client reasonable ground for terminating its retainer or employment, shall not allow to the body the full amount of the remuneration agreed to be paid to it.

(4)   For the purposes of this paragraph a relevant insolvency event occurs in relation to a recognised body if—

(a)   a resolution for a voluntary winding-up of the body is passed without a declaration of solvency under section 89 of the Insolvency Act 1986;

(b)   the body enters administration within the meaning of paragraph 1(2)(b) of Schedule B1 to that Act;

(c)   an administrative receiver within the meaning of section 251 of that Act is appointed;

(d)   a meeting of creditors is held in relation to the body under section 95 of that Act (creditors' meeting which has the effect of converting a members' voluntary winding up into a creditors' voluntary winding up);

(e)   an order for the winding up of the body is made.

Assessments with respect to contentious business

26   (1)   Subject to the provisions of any rules of court, on every assessment of costs in respect of any contentious business done by a recognised body, the costs officer may—

(a)   allow interest at such rate and from such time as he thinks just on money disbursed by the body for the client, and on money of the client in the possession of, and improperly retained by, the body or any manager or employee of the body; and

(b)   in determining the remuneration of the body, have regard to the skill, labour and responsibility on the part of any authorised person, being a manager or employee of the body, which the business involved.

(2)   In this paragraph "authorised person" means an authorised person, in relation to an activity which is a reserved legal activity, within the meaning of the Legal Services Act 2007.

Power of court to order delivery of bill of costs, etc.

27   Any jurisdiction—

(a)   of the High Court to make any such orders as are referred to in subsection (1) of section 68 of the 1974 Act in relation to a solicitor (whether or not business has been done by him in the High Court); or

(b)   of the county court to make any such orders as are referred to in subsection (2) of that section in relation to a solicitor, shall be exercisable in like manner in relation to a recognised body.

Power of court to order recognised body to pay over clients' money

28 Any jurisdiction of the High Court to make, in the case of a solicitor who is acting or has acted as such for a client, an order requiring the payment or delivery up of, or otherwise relating to, money or securities which the solicitor has in his possession or control on behalf of the client shall be exercisable in like manner in the case of a recognised body which is acting or has acted as such for a client or any manager or employee of such a body.

Actions to recover costs

29 (1) Subsection (2A) of section 69 of the 1974 Act shall have effect in relation to a bill of costs delivered by a recognised body as if for paragraphs (a) and (b) there were substituted—

"(a)   signed on behalf of the recognised body by any manager or employee of the body authorised by it to do so, or

(b)   enclosed in, or accompanied by, a letter which is so signed and refers to the bill.

(2)   Subsection (2E) of that section shall have effect in relation to such a bill as if for "the solicitor" there were substituted "the recognised body".

Power of Society to inspect files relating to certain proceedings

30 Section 83 of the 1974 Act shall apply in relation to proceedings which have been brought with respect to a recognised body for any of the following purposes, namely—

(a)   for the winding-up of the body;

(b)   for the appointment of an administrative receiver within the meaning of section 251 of the Insolvency Act 1986; or

(c)   for the appointment of an administrator under Schedule B1 to the Insolvency Act 1986,

as it applies in relation to proceedings in bankruptcy which have been taken against a solicitor.

Bank accounts

31 Where rules made under section 32(1) of the 1974 Act are applied to recognised bodies in accordance with section 9(2)(f) of this Act, section 85 of the 1974 Act shall apply in relation to a recognised body which keeps an account with a bank or building society in pursuance of any such rules as it applies in relation to a solicitor who keeps such an account in pursuance of rules under section 32.

31A Where rules made under section 32(1) of the 1974 Act are applied to managers or employees in accordance with section 9(2)(fb) of this Act, section 85 of the 1974 Act shall apply in relation to a manager or employee to whom the rules are applied who keeps an account with a bank or building society in pursuance of any such rules as it applies in relation to a solicitor who keeps such an account in pursuance of rules under section 32.

Intervention by Society

32 (1) Subject to sub-paragraph (2), where—

(a)   the Society is satisfied that a recognised body or a manager of such a body has failed to comply with any rules applicable to the body or manager by virtue of section 9 of this Act; or

(b)   a person has been appointed receiver or manager of property of a recognised body; or

(c)   a relevant insolvency event occurs in relation to a recognised body; or

(d)   the Society has reason to suspect dishonesty on the part of any manager or employee of a recognised body in connection with—

    (i)   that body's business,

    (ii)   any trust of which that body is or was a trustee,

    (iii)   any trust of which the manager or employee is or was a trustee in his capacity as such a manager or employee, or

    (iv)   the business of another body in which the manager or employee is or was a manager or employee or the practice (or former practice) of the manager or employee; or

(e)   the Society is satisfied that it is necessary to exercise the powers conferred by Part 2 of Schedule 1 to the 1974 Act (or any of them) in relation to a recognised body to protect—

    (i)   the interests of clients (or former or potential clients) of the recognised body,

    (ii)   the interests of the beneficiaries of any trust of which the recognised body is or was a trustee, or

    (iii)   the interests of the beneficiaries of any trust of which a person who is or was a manager or employee of the recognised body is or was a trustee in that person's capacity as such a manager or employee;

the powers conferred by Part II of Schedule 1 to the 1974 Act shall be exercisable in relation to the recognised body and its business in like manner as they are exercisable in relation to a solicitor and his practice.

(1A)   For the purposes of this paragraph a relevant insolvency event occurs in relation to a recognised body if—

(a)   a resolution for a voluntary winding-up of the body is passed without a declaration of solvency under section 89 of the Insolvency Act 1986;

(b)   the body enters administration within the meaning of paragraph 1(2)(b) of Schedule B1 to that Act;

(c)   an administrative receiver within the meaning of section 251 of that Act is appointed;

(d)   a meeting of creditors is held in relation to the body under section 95 of that Act (creditors' meeting which has the effect of converting a members' voluntary winding up into a creditors' voluntary winding up);

(e)   an order for the winding up of the body is made.

33 The powers conferred by Part II of Schedule 1 to the 1974 Act shall also be exercisable as mentioned in paragraph 32(1) of this Schedule where—

(a)   the Society is satisfied that there has been undue delay—

    (i)   on the part of a recognised body in connection with any matter in which it is or was acting on behalf of a client or with any trust of which it is or was a trustee, or

    (ii)   on the part of a person who is or was a manager or employee of a recognised body in connection with any trust of which the manager or employee is or was a trustee in his capacity as such a manager or employee;

(b) the Society by notice in writing invites the body to give an explanation within such period following the giving of the notice as may be specified in it, being a period of not less than eight days; and

(c) the body fails within that period to give an explanation which the Society regards as satisfactory; and

(d) the Society gives notice of the failure to the body and (at the same or any later time) notice that the powers conferred by Part II of Schedule 1 to the 1974 Act are accordingly exercisable in its case by virtue of this paragraph.

34 (1) Where the recognition of a body under section 9 of this Act—

(a) has been revoked in accordance with rules under that section or by an order of the Tribunal under this Schedule; or

(b) has expired and no further recognition of that body has been granted under that section,

the powers conferred by Part II of Schedule 1 to the 1974 Act shall be exercisable in relation to the body and its former business as a recognised body as they are exercisable in relation to a solicitor and his practice.

(2) Where the powers conferred by Part II of Schedule 1 to the 1974 Act are exercisable in relation to a recognised body in accordance with paragraph 32 or 33 of this Schedule they shall continue to be so exercisable after that body's recognition under section 9 of this Act has been revoked or has otherwise ceased to be in force.

35 In connection with the application of Part II of Schedule 1 to the 1974 Act for the purposes of this Schedule, in that Part of that Schedule—

(a) any reference to the solicitor or to his practice shall be construed as including a reference to the body in relation to which the powers conferred by that Part of that Schedule are exercisable by virtue of paragraph 32, 33 or 34(1) of this Schedule or to its business (or former business) as a recognised body;

(b) any reference to paragraph 1 of that Schedule shall be construed as including a reference to paragraph 32 or 34(1) of this Schedule;

(c) any reference to paragraph 3 of that Schedule shall be construed as including a reference to paragraph 33 of this Schedule;

(d) paragraph 6(2)(a) of that Schedule is to be construed as including a reference to sums of money held by or on behalf of the recognised body in connection with any trust of which a person who is or was a manager of the recognised body is or was a trustee in his capacity as such a manager;

(e) paragraph 9 of that Schedule is to be construed—

(i) as if sub-paragraph (1) included a reference to documents in the possession or under the control of the recognised body in connection with any trust of which a person who is or was a manager or employee of the recognised body is or was a trustee in his capacity as such a manager or employee, and

(ii) as applying to such a manager or employee and documents and property in his possession or under his control in connection with such a trust as it applies to a solicitor and documents and property in the possession or under the control of the solicitor;

(f) paragraph 11(1) of that Schedule is to be construed as including a power for the Society to apply to the High Court for an order for the appointment of a new trustee to a trust in substitution for a person who is a trustee, in his capacity as a manager or employee of the recognised body; and

(g)   paragraph 13A of that Schedule is to be read as if the references to a former partner were references—

   (i)   in the case of a recognised body which is a partnership, to a former partner in the partnership, and

   (ii)   in any other case to a manager or former manager of the recognised body.

Privilege from disclosure etc.

36   (1)   Where a recognised body acts as such for a client, any communication, document, material or information is privileged from disclosure in like manner as if the recognised body had at all material times been a solicitor acting for the client.

(2)   Any enactment or instrument making special provision in relation to a solicitor or other legal representative as to the disclosure of information, or as to the production, seizure or removal of documents, with respect to which a claim to professional privilege could be maintained shall, with any necessary modifications, have effect in relation to a recognised body as it has effect in relation to a solicitor.

(3)   In section 748(4), 749 and 771(5) and (6) of the Income Tax Act 2007 and section 832(5) and (6) of the Corporation Tax Act 2010 any reference to a solicitor's client shall, in relation to a solicitor who is a manager or employee of a recognised body, be construed as a reference to a client of that body.

(4)   This paragraph does not apply to a recognised body which holds a licence under Part 5 of the Legal Services Act 2007 (alternative business structures).

Modification of enactments relating to conveyancing etc.

37   In the following provisions, namely—

(a)   sections 10(2), 48 and 182 of the Law of Property Act 1925;

(b)   ...

(c)   section 12 of the Land Charges Act 1972;

(d)   section 13 of the Local Land Charges Act 1975;

any reference to a solicitor shall be construed as including a reference to a recognised body, and any reference to a person's solicitor shall be construed as including a reference to a recognised body acting for that person.

Extracts from the Courts and Legal Services Act 1990

[With consolidated amendments to 1 January 2010 and prospective amendments in section 89.]

Courts and Legal Services Act 1990

1990 CHAPTER 41

An Act to make provision with respect to the procedure in, and allocation of business between, the High Court and other courts; to make provision with respect to legal services; to establish a body to be known as the Lord Chancellor's Advisory Committee on Legal Education and Conduct and a body to be known as the Authorised Conveyancing Practitioners Board; to provide for the appointment of a Legal Services Ombudsman; to make provision for the establishment of a Conveyancing Ombudsman Scheme; to provide for the establishment of Conveyancing Appeal Tribunals; to amend the law relating to judicial and related pensions and judicial and other appointments; to make provision with respect to certain officers of the Supreme Court; to amend the Solicitors Act 1974; to amend the Arbitration Act 1950; to make provision with respect to certain loans in respect of residential property; to make provision with respect to the jurisdiction of the Parliamentary Commissioner for Administration in connection with the functions of court staff; to amend the Children Act 1989 and make further provision in connection with that Act; and for connected purposes

[1st November 1990]

BE IT ENACTED by the Queen's most Excellent Majesty, by and with the advice and consent of the Lords Spiritual and Temporal, and Commons, in this present Parliament assembled, and by the authority of the same, as follows:–

...

PART IV
SOLICITORS

89   Foreign lawyers: recognised bodies and partnerships with solicitors

(1)   The Law Society shall maintain a register of foreign lawyers for the purposes of this section.

(2)   A foreign lawyer who wishes to be registered under this section must apply to the Society in accordance with the requirements of Part I of Schedule 14.

(3)   The power to make rules under—

   (a)   the following provisions of the Solicitors Act 1974—

      (i)   section 31 (professional practice, conduct and discipline);

      (ii)   section 32 (accounts and trust accounts);

      (iii)   section 34 (accountants' reports);

   (iv) sections 36 and 36A (compensation grants); and

   (v) section 37 (professional indemnity); and

 (b) section 9 of the Administration of Justice Act 1985 (incorporated practices),

shall also be exercisable in relation to registered foreign lawyers.

(4) Subject to the provisions of Schedule 14, any such power may be exercised so as to make different provision with respect to registered foreign lawyers to the provision made with respect to solicitors.

(5) Subject to the provisions of Schedule 14, the Lord Chancellor may by order provide that any enactment or instrument—

 (a) passed or made before or in the same Session as the Legal Services Act 2007 was passed;

 (b) having effect in relation to solicitors; and

 (c) specified in the order,

shall have effect with respect to registered foreign lawyers as it has effect with respect to solicitors.

(6) An order under subsection (5) may provide for an enactment or instrument to have effect with respect to registered foreign lawyers subject to such additions, omissions or other modifications as the Lord Chancellor sees fit to specify in the order.

(7) Subject to the provisions of Schedule 14, the Lord Chancellor may by order provide that any enactment or instrument—

 (a) passed or made before or in the same Session as the Legal Services Act 2007 was passed;

 (b) having effect in relation to recognised bodies; and

 (c) specified in the order,

shall, in its application in relation to recognised bodies whose managers include one or more registered foreign lawyers, have effect with such additions, omissions or other modifications as the Lord Chancellor sees fit to specify in the order.

(8) Schedule 14 shall have effect for the purposes of supplementing this section.

(8A) Rules and regulations made by the Law Society under, or by virtue of, this section or Schedule 14 which are not regulatory arrangements within the meaning of the Legal Services Act 2007 are to be treated as such arrangements for the purposes of that Act.

(9) In this section and in Schedule 14—

 "foreign lawyer" means a person who is not a solicitor or barrister but who is a member, and entitled to practise as such, of a legal profession regulated within a jurisdiction outside England and Wales;

 "manager", in relation to a body, has the same meaning as in the Legal Services Act 2007 (see section 207 of that Act);

 "multi-national partnership" means a partnership whose members consist of one or more registered foreign lawyers and one or more solicitors;

 "recognised body" has the same meaning as in section 9 of the Administration of Justice Act 1985 (management and control by solicitors of incorporated practices); and

 "registered foreign lawyer" means a foreign lawyer who is registered under this section.

SCHEDULE 14
Foreign Lawyers: Partnerships and Recognised Bodies

Section 89

PART I
REGISTRATION

General

1   In this Schedule—

"the Act of 1974" means the Solicitors Act 1974;

"the register" means the register maintained by the Society under section 89;

"registration" means registration in that register;

"the Society" means the Law Society; and

"the Tribunal" means the Solicitors Disciplinary Tribunal.

Application for registration

2   (1)   An application for registration or for renewal of registration—

(a)   shall be made to the Society in such form as the Society may prescribe; and

(b)   shall be accompanied by such fee as the Society may, with the concurrence of the the Legal Services Board, prescribe.

(2)   Where such an application is duly made by a foreign lawyer, the Society may register the applicant if it is satisfied that the legal profession of which the applicant is a member is one which is so regulated as to make it appropriate for members of that profession to be managers of recognised bodies.

(3)   ...

(4)   The Society may make regulations, with the concurrence of the Legal Services Board, with respect to—

(a)   the keeping of the register (including the form of the register and the manner in which entries are to be made, altered or removed); and

(b)   applications for registration or renewal of registration; and

(c)   the making available to the public of the information contained in the register (including the manner in which, and hours during which, the information is to be made so available and whether the information is to be made available free of charge).

2A   (1)   The Society may direct that a foreign lawyer's registration is to have effect subject to such conditions as the Society thinks fit to impose.

(2)   A direction under sub-paragraph (1) may be given in respect of a foreign lawyer

(a)   at the time he is first registered, or

(b)   at any time when the registration has effect.

Duration of registration

3   (1)   Every registration shall have effect from the beginning of the day on which it is entered in the register.

(2)   The Society may make regulations—

(a)   prescribing the date ("the renewal date") by which each registered foreign lawyer must apply for his registration to be renewed; and

(b)   requiring every entry in the register to specify the renewal date applicable to that registration.

(3)   Any such regulations may—

(a)   provide different renewal dates for different categories of registered foreign lawyer or different circumstances;

(b)   provide for the Society to specify, in the case of individual registered foreign lawyers, different renewal dates to those prescribed by the regulations;

(c)   make such transitional, incidental and supplemental provision in connection with any provision for different renewal dates as the Society considers expedient.

(4)   Where a foreign lawyer is registered, the Society may cancel his registration if—

(a)   the renewal date for his registration has passed but he has not applied for it to be renewed; or

(b)   he has applied to the Society for it to be cancelled.

Evidence as to registration

4   Any certificate purporting to be signed by an officer of the Society and stating that a particular foreign lawyer—

(a)   is, or is not, registered; or

(b)   was registered during a period specified in the certificate,

shall, unless the contrary is proved, be evidence of that fact and be taken to have been so signed.

PART II
REGISTERED FOREIGN LAWYERS: SUPPLEMENTARY PROVISIONS

Intervention in practices

5   (1)   In this paragraph "the intervention powers" means the powers conferred by Part II of Schedule 1 to the Act of 1974 (intervention in solicitors' practices) as modified by this Schedule or under section 89.

(2)   Subject to sub-paragraphs (3) and (4), the intervention powers shall be exercisable in relation to a person who is or has been a registered foreign lawyer and the practice of the multi-national partnership of which he is or was a member as they are exercisable in relation to a solicitor and his practice.

(3)   The intervention powers are only exercisable where—

(a)   the Society has reason to suspect dishonesty on the part of the registered foreign lawyer, or on the part of an employee of the multi-national partnership, in connection with—

(i)   the practice of that partnership; or

(ii)   any trust of which the registered foreign lawyer is or was a trustee;

(b)   in the case of a registered foreign lawyer who has died, the Society has reason to suspect dishonesty on the part of his personal representative, in connection with—

(i)   the practice of the multi-national partnership; or

(ii)   any trust of which the registered foreign lawyer was a trustee;

(ba)   the Society has reason to suspect dishonesty on the part of the registered foreign lawyer ("L") in connection with—

(i)   the business of any person of whom L is or was an employee, or of any body of which L is or was a manager, or

(ii)   any business which is or was carried on by L as a sole trader;

(c)   the Society is satisfied that the registered foreign lawyer has failed to comply with rules made under section 32 or 37(2) of the Act of 1974;

(d)   a bankruptcy order (as defined in paragraph 10(3)) has been made against him or he has made a composition or arrangement with his creditors;

(e)   he has been committed to prison in any civil or criminal proceedings;

(ea)   the Society is satisfied that he has abandoned his practice;

(f)   he lacks capacity (within the meaning of the Mental Capacity Act 2005) to act as a registered foreign lawyer and powers under sections 15 to 20 or section 48 are exercisable in relation to him;

(g)   his name has been struck off the register or his registration has been suspended or cancelled;

(h)   he has purported to act as a member of a multi-national partnership at a time when he was not registered;

(i)   the Society is satisfied that he has failed to comply with any condition, subject to which he is registered, to the effect that—

(i)   he may only be a member of a partnership which is approved by the Society; or

(ii)   he may only be a manager of a recognised body which is so approved; or

(iii)   he may only be such a member or such a manager

(j)   the Society is satisfied that it is necessary to exercise the intervention powers (or any of them) in relation to the registered foreign lawyer to protect—

(i)   the interests of clients (or former or potential clients) of the registered foreign lawyer or the multi-national partnership, or

(ii)   the interests of the beneficiaries of any trust of which the registered foreign lawyer is or was a trustee.

(4) ...

(5) The intervention powers (other than those conferred by paragraphs 5 and 10 of Part II of Schedule 1 to the Act of 1974) shall also be exercisable where—

(a)   the Society is satisfied that there has been undue delay on the part of a registered foreign lawyer in connection with—

(i)   any matter in which he, or the multi-national partnership of which he is or was a member, was instructed on behalf of a client; or

(ii)   any trust;

(b)   the Society by notice invites the registered foreign lawyer to give an explanation within a period (of not less than 8 days) specified in the notice;

(c)   the registered foreign lawyer fails within that period to give an explanation which the Society regards as satisfactory; and

(d)   the Society gives notice of the failure to the registered foreign lawyer and notice that the intervention powers are accordingly exercisable.

(6)   Where the intervention powers are exercisable in relation to a registered foreign lawyer, they shall continue to be exercisable—

(a)   at any time when his registration is suspended;

(b)   after his name has been struck off the register or his registration has been cancelled; or

(c)   after his death.

(7)   Part II of Schedule 1 to the Act of 1974 shall have effect in relation to the intervention powers exercisable by virtue of this Schedule, subject to—

(a)   any express modifications made under section 89; and

(b)   any modifications necessary in the light of this paragraph.

(8)   For the purposes of this paragraph, Part II of Schedule 1 to the Act of 1974 shall be read with paragraph 4(2) of Part I of that Schedule.

(9)   The notices required to be given by this paragraph must be in writing but need not be given at the same time.

(10)   In this paragraph "manager", in relation to a recognised body, has the same meaning as in the Legal Services Act 2007 (see section 207 of that Act).

The Compensation Fund

6   Section 36 of the 1974 Act applies in relation to registered foreign lawyers as if for paragraphs (a) and (b) of subsection (1) there were substituted—

"(a)   an act or omission of a registered foreign lawyer or former registered foreign lawyer;

(b)   an act or omission of an employee or former employee of a registered foreign lawyer or former registered foreign lawyer;".

Contributions to the Fund

7   Section 36A(2) and (3) of the 1974 Act applies in relation to registered foreign lawyers as it applies in relation to solicitors.

Accountants' reports

8   Section 34 of the Act of 1974 applies in relation to registered foreign lawyers as it applies in relation to solicitors.

9   ...

Effect of bankruptcy

10 (1)   The registration of any foreign lawyer against whom a bankruptcy order is made shall be suspended on the making of that order.

(2)   The suspension of any registration by reason of a bankruptcy order shall terminate if the order is annulled and an office copy of the order annulling it is served on the Society.

(3) In sub-paragraph (1), "bankruptcy order" includes any order which is not a bankruptcy order but which has the same, or a similar, effect under the law in force in any territory outside England and Wales.

Effect of disciplinary action

11 (1) Where a registered foreign lawyer is struck off, or suspended from practice, his registration shall be suspended.

(2) In sub-paragraph (1) "struck off" and "suspended from practice" mean—

(a) any action taken within the jurisdiction by reference to which the registered foreign lawyer is qualified to be registered; or

(b) where the registered foreign lawyer is qualified to be registered by reference to more than one jurisdiction, any action taken within any one of those jurisdictions,

which is the equivalent, respectively, of a solicitor being struck off the roll or suspended from practice under the Act of 1974.

Re-instatement of disciplined foreign lawyer

12 (1) Where a person's registration has been suspended by virtue of paragraph 11, it shall be revived—

(a) if his right to practise in the jurisdiction in question is restored; and

(b) a copy of the instrument restoring his right, certified to be a true copy by an officer of the appropriate court in the jurisdiction in question, or the professional body concerned, is served on the Society.

(2) Where a person whose registration is suspended by virtue of paragraph 11 applies to the Society for the suspension to be terminated, the Society may terminate it subject to such conditions, if any, as it thinks fit to impose.

Effective date of revived registration

13 Where a foreign lawyer's registration is revived (whether as the result of the termination of its suspension, restoration by order of the Tribunal or for any other reason), that revival shall take effect on such date, and subject to such conditions, as the Society may direct.

Appeal against conditions or refusals

14 (1) Any foreign lawyer may appeal to the High Court against—

(a) the refusal of the Society to register him or to renew his registration;

(b) the refusal of the Society to terminate the suspension of his registration on an application made by him under paragraph 12;

(c) the failure of the Society to deal with any application by him for registration, renewal of registration or the termination (under paragraph 12(2)) of a suspension within a reasonable time; or

(d) any condition imposed by the Society under paragraph 2A, 12(2) or 13.

(2) ...

(3) On an appeal under this paragraph, the High Court may make such order as it thinks fit.

(4) In relation to an appeal under this paragraph the High Court may make such order as it thinks fit as to payment of costs.

(5) The decision of the High Court on an appeal under this paragraph shall be final.

Jurisdiction and powers of Disciplinary Tribunal

15 (1) Subject to paragraph 16, section 46 of the Act of 1974 (Solicitors Disciplinary Tribunal) shall apply, with the necessary modifications, in relation to applications and complaints made by virtue of any provision of this Schedule as it applies in relation to applications and complaints made by virtue of any provision of that Act.

(2) Any application—

    (a)   to strike the name of a foreign lawyer off the register;

    (b)   to require a registered foreign lawyer to answer allegations in an affidavit;

    (c)   to suspend the registration of a foreign lawyer for a specified or indefinite period;

    (d)   by a foreign lawyer whose name has been struck off the register by order of the Tribunal to have his name restored to the register;

    (e)   by a foreign lawyer whose registration has been suspended for an indefinite period by order of the Tribunal for the termination of that suspension,

shall be made to the Tribunal.

(3) Any person who alleges that a registered foreign lawyer has failed to comply with any rule made under section 31, 32, 34, or 37 of the Act of 1974 may make a complaint to the Tribunal.

(3A) Any person who alleges that a registered foreign lawyer has knowingly acted in contravention of any order under section 43(2) of the Act of 1974 or of any conditions subject to which a permission has been granted under such an order may make a complaint to the Tribunal.

(4) On the hearing of any application or complaint made to the Tribunal with respect to a foreign lawyer, the Tribunal shall have power to make such order as it may think fit, and any such order may in particular include provision for any of the following matters—

    (a)   the striking off the register of the name of the foreign lawyer to whom the application or complaint relates;

    (b)   the suspension of that foreign lawyer's registration indefinitely or for a specified period;

    (c)   the payment by that foreign lawyer of a penalty, which shall be forfeit to Her Majesty;

    (d)   the termination of that foreign lawyer's unspecified period of suspension from registration;

    (e)   the restoration to the register of the name of a foreign lawyer which has been struck off the register;

    (f)   the payment by any party of costs or a contribution towards costs of such amount as the Tribunal may consider reasonable.

Foreign lawyers assisting the Tribunal

16 (1) For the purposes of section 46 of the Act of 1974 (Solicitors Disciplinary Tribunal), the Tribunal may make rules providing for it to be assisted, in dealing with any application or complaint of a kind mentioned in paragraph 15, by a member of the legal profession in the jurisdiction by reference to which the foreign lawyer is or was qualified to be registered.

(2) Rules under sub-paragraph (1) shall not be made without the concurrence of the Legal Services Board.

(3)   Subsection (12) of section 46 of the Act of 1974 (rules to be made by statutory instrument etc) shall apply to rules made under this paragraph as it applies to rules made under subsection (9) of that section.

Appeals from Tribunal

17   (1)   An Appeal from the Tribunal shall lie to the High Court.

(2)   The High Court shall have power to make such order on an appeal under this paragraph as it may think fit.

(3)   Any decision of the High Court on an appeal in the case of an order on an application under paragraph 15(2)(d) or (e), or the refusal of any such application, shall be final.

Extracts from the Legal Services Act 2007

[Legislation appears as at Royal Assent on 30 October 2007.]

Legal Services Act 2007

2007 CHAPTER 29

An Act to make provision for the establishment of the Legal Services Board and in respect of its functions; to make provision for, and in connection with, the regulation of persons who carry on certain legal activities; to make provision for the establishment of the Office for Legal Complaints and for a scheme to consider and determine legal complaints; to make provision about claims management services and about immigration advice and immigration services; to make provision in respect of legal representation provided free of charge; to make provision about the application of the Legal Profession and Legal Aid (Scotland) Act 2007; to make provision about the Scottish legal services ombudsman; and for connected purposes.

[30th October 2007]

Be it enacted by the Queen's most Excellent Majesty, by and with the advice and consent of the Lords Spiritual and Temporal, and Commons, in this present Parliament assembled, and by the authority of the same, as follows:—

PART 1
THE REGULATORY OBJECTIVES

1 The regulatory objectives

(1)   In this Act a reference to "the regulatory objectives" is a reference to the objectives of—

(a)   protecting and promoting the public interest;

(b)   supporting the constitutional principle of the rule of law;

(c)   improving access to justice;

(d)   protecting and promoting the interests of consumers;

(e)   promoting competition in the provision of services within subsection (2);

(f)   encouraging an independent, strong, diverse and effective legal profession;

(g)   increasing public understanding of the citizen's legal rights and duties;

(h)   promoting and maintaining adherence to the professional principles.

(2)   The services within this subsection are services such as are provided by authorised persons (including services which do not involve the carrying on of activities which are reserved legal activities).

(3)   The "professional principles" are—

(a)   that authorised persons should act with independence and integrity,

(b)   that authorised persons should maintain proper standards of work,

(c)   that authorised persons should act in the best interests of their clients,

(d)   that persons who exercise before any court a right of audience, or conduct litigation in relation to proceedings in any court, by virtue of being authorised persons should comply with their duty to the court to act with independence in the interests of justice, and

(e)   that the affairs of clients should be kept confidential.

(4)   In this section "authorised persons" means authorised persons in relation to activities which are reserved legal activities.

...

PART 4
REGULATION OF APPROVED REGULATORS

Introductory

27 Regulatory and representative functions of approved regulators

(1)   In this Act references to the "regulatory functions" of an approved regulator are to any functions the approved regulator has—

(a)   under or in relation to its regulatory arrangements, or

(b)   in connection with the making or alteration of those arrangements.

(2)   In this Act references to the "representative functions" of an approved regulator are to any functions the approved regulator has in connection with the representation, or promotion, of the interests of persons regulated by it.

General duties of approved regulators

28 Approved regulator's duty to promote the regulatory objectives etc

(1)   In discharging its regulatory functions (whether in connection with a reserved legal activity or otherwise) an approved regulator must comply with the requirements of this section.

(2)   The approved regulator must, so far as is reasonably practicable, act in a way—

(a)   which is compatible with the regulatory objectives, and

(b)   which the approved regulator considers most appropriate for the purpose of meeting those objectives.

(3)   The approved regulator must have regard to—

(a)   the principles under which regulatory activities should be transparent, accountable, proportionate, consistent and targeted only at cases in which action is needed, and

(b)   any other principle appearing to it to represent the best regulatory practice.

...

Regulatory conflict

52 Regulatory conflict with approved regulators

(1) The regulatory arrangements of an approved regulator must make such provision as is reasonably practicable to prevent regulatory conflicts.

(2) For the purposes of this section and section 53, a regulatory conflict is a conflict between—

(a) a requirement of the approved regulator's regulatory arrangements, and

(b) a requirement of the regulatory arrangements of another approved regulator.

(3) Subsection (4) applies where a body is authorised by an approved regulator ("the entity regulator") to carry on an activity which is a reserved legal activity.

(4) If a conflict arises between—

(a) a requirement of the regulatory arrangements of the entity regulator, in relation to the body authorised by the entity regulator or an employee or manager of the body ("an entity requirement"), and

(b) a requirement of the regulatory arrangements of another approved regulator in relation to an employee or manager of the body who is authorised by it to carry on a reserved legal activity ("an individual requirement"),

the entity requirement prevails over the individual requirement.

…

PART 5
ALTERNATIVE BUSINESS STRUCTURES

Introductory

71 Carrying on of activities by licensed bodies

(1) The provisions of this Part have effect for the purpose of regulating the carrying on of reserved legal activities and other activities by licensed bodies.

(2) In this Act "licensed body" means a body which holds a licence in force under this Part.

72 "Licensable body"

(1) A body ("B") is a licensable body if a non-authorised person—

(a) is a manager of B, or

(b) has an interest in B.

(2) A body ("B") is also a licensable body if—

(a) another body ("A") is a manager of B, or has an interest in B, and

(b) non-authorised persons are entitled to exercise, or control the exercise of, at least 10% of the voting rights in A.

(3) For the purposes of this Act, a person has an interest in a body if—

(a) the person holds shares in the body, or

(b) the person is entitled to exercise, or control the exercise of, voting rights in the body.

(4) A body may be licensable by virtue of both subsection (1) and subsection (2).

(5)   For the purposes of this Act, a non-authorised person has an indirect interest in a licensable body if the body is licensable by virtue of subsection (2) and the non-authorised person is entitled to exercise, or control the exercise of, voting rights in A.

(6)   In this Act "shares" means—

(a)   in relation to a body with a share capital, allotted shares (within the meaning of the Companies Acts);

(b)   in relation to a body with capital but no share capital, rights to share in the capital of the body;

(c)   in relation to a body without capital, interests—

(i)   conferring any right to share in the profits, or liability to contribute to the losses, of the body, or

(ii)   giving rise to an obligation to contribute to the debts or expenses of the body in the event of a winding up;

and references to the holding of shares, or to a shareholding, are to be construed accordingly.

Licensing

84   Application for licence

(1)   A licensing authority other than the Board must determine any application for a licence which is made to it.

(2)   The Board (acting in its capacity as a licensing authority) may determine an application for a licence which is made to it only if the applicant is entitled to make the application by virtue of a decision of the Board (acting otherwise than in its capacity as a licensing authority) under Schedule 12.

(3)   A licensing authority may not grant an application for a licence unless it is satisfied that if the licence is granted the applicant will comply with its licensing rules.

(4)   If the licensing authority grants an application for a licence, it must issue the licence as soon as reasonably practicable.

(5)   The licence has effect from the date on which it is issued.

(6)   References in this section to an application for a licence are to an application for a licence which is—

(a)   made to a licensing authority by a licensable body, in accordance with the authority's licensing rules, and

(b)   accompanied by the required application fee (if any).

85   Terms of licence

(1)   A licence issued under section 84 must specify—

(a)   the activities which are reserved legal activities and which the licensed body is authorised to carry on by virtue of the licence, and

(b)   any conditions subject to which the licence is granted.

(2)   If an order under section 106 has been made in relation to the licensed body, the licence must also specify the terms of the order.

(3)   In the case of a licensing authority other than the Board, the licence may authorise the licensed body to carry on activities which are reserved legal activities only if the licensing authority is designated in relation to the reserved legal activities in question.

(4)   A licence must be granted subject to the condition that—

(a)   any obligation which may from time to time be imposed on the licensed body or a person within subsection (5) by or under the licensing authority's licensing rules is complied with, and

(b)   any other obligations imposed on the licensed body or a person within that subsection by or under this or any other enactment (whether passed before or after this Act) are complied with.

(5)   The persons mentioned in subsection (4) are the managers and employees of a licensed body, and non-authorised persons having an interest or an indirect interest, or holding a material interest, in the licensed body (in their capacity as such).

(6)   A licence may be granted subject to such other conditions as the licensing authority considers appropriate.

(7)   Those conditions may include conditions as to the non-reserved activities which the licensed body may or may not carry on.

(8)   In this Part references to the terms of the licence are to the matters listed in subsections (1) and (2).

86   Modification of licence

(1)   A licensing authority may modify the terms of a licence granted by it—

(a)   if the licensed body applies to the licensing authority, in accordance with its licensing rules, for it to do so;

(b)   in such other circumstances as may be specified in its licensing rules.

(2)   If a licensed body is a body to which section 106 applies, the licensing authority may modify the terms of its licence in accordance with sections 106 and 107.

(3)   A licensing authority modifies the terms of a licensed body's licence by giving the licensed body notice in writing of the modifications; and the modifications have effect from the time the licensing authority gives the licensed body the notice or such later time as may be specified in the notice.

(4)   The licensing authority's power under this section is subject to—

(a)   section 85(3) and (4), and

(b)   licensing rules made under paragraph 6 of Schedule 11.

…

Regulation of licensed bodies

…

93   Information

(1)   The relevant licensing authority in relation to a licensed body may by notice require a person within subsection (2)—

(a)   to provide information, or information of a description, specified in the notice, or

(b)   produce documents, or documents of a description, specified in the notice,

for the purpose of enabling the licensing authority to ascertain whether the terms of the licensed body's licence are being, or have been, complied with

(2)   The persons are—

(a)   the licensed body;

(b)   any manager or employee (or former manager or employee) of the licensed body;

(c)   any non-authorised person who has an interest or an indirect interest, or holds a material interest, in the licensed body.

(3) A notice under subsection (1)—

(a)   may specify the manner and form in which any information is to be provided;

(b)   must specify the period within which the information is to be provided or the document produced;

(c)   may require the information to be provided, or the document to be produced, to the licensing authority or to a person specified in the notice.

(4) The licensing authority may, by notice, require a person within subsection (2) (or a representative of such a person) to attend at a time and place specified in the notice to provide an explanation of any information provided or document produced under this section.

(5) The licensing authority may pay to any person such reasonable costs as may be incurred by that person in connection with—

(a)   the provision of any information, or production of any document, by that person pursuant to a notice under subsection (1), or

(b)   that person's compliance with a requirement imposed under subsection (4).

(6) The licensing authority, or a person specified under subsection (3)(c) in a notice, may take copies of or extracts from a document produced pursuant to a notice under subsection (1).

(7) For the purposes of this section and section 94, references to a licensed body include a body which was, but is no longer, a licensed body

94 Enforcement of notices under section 93

(1) Where a person is unable to comply with a notice given to the person under section 93, the person must give the licensing authority a notice to that effect stating the reasons why the person cannot comply.

(2) If a person refuses or otherwise fails to comply with a notice under section 93, the licensing authority may apply to the High Court for an order requiring the person to comply with the notice or with such directions for the like purpose as may be contained in the order.

95 Financial penalties

(1) A licensing authority may, in accordance with its licensing rules, impose on a licensed body, or a manager or employee of a licensed body, a penalty of such amount as it considers appropriate.

(2) The amount must not exceed the maximum amount prescribed under subsection (3).

(3) The Board must make rules prescribing the maximum amount of a penalty which may be imposed under this section.

(4) Rules may be made under subsection (3) only with the consent of the Lord Chancellor.

(5) A penalty under this section is payable to the licensing authority.

(6) For the purposes of this section—

(a)   references to a licensed body are to a body which was a licensed body at the time the act or omission in respect of which the penalty is imposed occurred, and

(b)   references to a manager or employee of a licensed body are to a person who was a manager or employee of a licensed body at that time,

(whether or not the body subsequently ceased to be a licensed body or the person subsequently ceased to be a manager or employee).

(7)   In sections 96 and 97 references to a "penalty" are to a penalty under this section.

96   Appeals against financial penalties

(1)   A person on whom a penalty is imposed under section 95 may, before the end of such period as may be prescribed by rules made by the Board, appeal to the relevant appellate body on one or more of the appeal grounds.

(2)   The appeal grounds are—

(a)   that the imposition of the penalty is unreasonable in all the circumstances of the case;

(b)   that the amount of the penalty is unreasonable;

(c)   that it is unreasonable of the licensing authority to require the penalty imposed or any portion of it to be paid by the time or times by which it was required to be paid.

(3)   On any such appeal, where the relevant appellate body considers it appropriate to do so in all the circumstances of the case and is satisfied of one or more of the appeal grounds, that body may—

(a)   quash the penalty,

(b)   substitute a penalty of such lesser amount as it considers appropriate, or

(c)   in the case of the appeal ground in subsection (2)(c), substitute for any time imposed by the licensing authority a different time or times.

(4)   Where the relevant appellate body substitutes a penalty of a lesser amount it may require the payment of interest on the substituted penalty at such rate, and from such time, as it considers just and equitable.

(5)   Where the relevant appellate body specifies as a time by which the penalty, or a portion of the penalty, is to be paid a time before the determination of the appeal under this section it may require the payment of interest on the penalty, or portion, from that time at such rate as it considers just and equitable.

(6)   A party to the appeal may appeal to the High Court on a point of law arising from the decision of the relevant appellate body, but only with the permission of the High Court.

(7)   The High Court may make such order as it thinks fit.

(8)   Except as provided by this section, the validity of a penalty is not to be questioned by any legal proceedings whatever.

97   Recovery of financial penalties

(1)   If the whole or any part of a penalty is not paid by the time by which, in accordance with licensing rules, it is required to be paid, the unpaid balance from time to time carries interest at the rate for the time being specified in section 17 of the Judgments Act 1838 (c. 110).

(2)   Where a penalty, or any portion of it, has not been paid by the time by which, in accordance with licensing rules, it is required to be paid and—

(a)   no appeal relating to the penalty has been made under section 96 during the period within which such an appeal can be made, or

(b)   an appeal has been made under that section and determined or withdrawn,

the licensing authority may recover from the person on whom the penalty was imposed, as a debt due to the licensing authority, any of the penalty and any interest which has not been paid.

(3)   A licensing authority must pay into the Consolidated Fund any sum received by it as a penalty (or as interest on a penalty).

98   Referral of employees etc to appropriate regulator

(1)   The relevant licensing authority may refer to an appropriate regulator any matter relating to the conduct of—

(a)   an employee or manager of a licensed body;

(b)   a person designated as a licensed body's Head of Legal Practice or Head of Finance and Administration.

(2)   The licensing authority may also refer any matter relating to the conduct of such a person to the Board.

(3)   Appropriate regulators are—

(a)   if the person is an authorised person in relation to a reserved legal activity, any relevant approved regulator in relation to that person, and

(b)   if the person carries on non-reserved activities, any person who exercises regulatory functions in relation to the carrying on of such activities by the person.

99   Disqualification

(1)   A licensing authority may in accordance with its licensing rules disqualify a person from one or more of the activities mentioned in subsection (2) if—

(a)   the disqualification condition is satisfied in relation to the person, and

(b)   the licensing authority is satisfied that it is undesirable for the person to engage in that activity or those activities.

(2)   The activities are—

(a)   acting as Head of Legal Practice of any licensed body,

(b)   acting as Head of Finance and Administration of any licensed body,

(c)   being a manager of any licensed body, or

(d)   being employed by any licensed body.

(3)   The disqualification condition is satisfied in relation to a person if, in relation to a licensed body licensed by the licensing authority, the person (intentionally or through neglect)—

(a)   breaches a relevant duty to which the person is subject, or

(b)   causes, or substantially contributes to, a significant breach of the terms of the licensed body's licence.

(4)   The relevant duties are—

(a)   the duties imposed on a Head of Legal Practice by section 91,

(b)   the duties imposed on a Head of Finance and Administration by section 92,

(c)   the duties imposed by section 176 on regulated persons (within the meaning of that section), and

(d)   the duty imposed on non-authorised persons by section 90.

100   Lists of disqualified persons

(1)   The Board must keep lists of persons who are disqualified from—

    (a)   acting as Head of Legal Practice of any licensed body,

    (b)   acting as Head of Finance and Administration of any licensed body,

    (c)   being a manager of any licensed body, or

    (d)   being employed by any licensed body.

(2)   A person is disqualified from acting in a way mentioned in subsection (1) if—

    (a)   the person has been disqualified from so acting by a licensing authority under section 99, and

    (b)   the disqualification continues in force.

(3)   The disqualification ceases to be in force if the appropriate licensing authority so determines, on a review or otherwise, in accordance with licensing rules made under paragraph 23 of Schedule 11.

(4)   The appropriate licensing authority is—

    (a)   the licensing authority which disqualified the person, or

    (b)   if the person was disqualified by an approved regulator which is no longer designated as a licensing authority, the successor licensing authority.

(5)   The successor licensing authority is—

    (a)   the licensing authority which licenses the body in relation to which the disqualification condition (within the meaning of section 99) was satisfied in respect of the person, or

    (b)   if there is no such licensing authority, the licensing authority designated by the Board on an application by the disqualified person.

(6)   The Board must publish the lists kept by it under subsection (1).

…

PART 6
LEGAL COMPLAINTS

Complaints procedures of authorised persons

112 Complaints procedures of authorised persons

(1)   The regulatory arrangements of an approved regulator must make provision requiring each relevant authorised person—

    (a)   to establish and maintain procedures for the resolution of relevant complaints, or

    (b)   to participate in, or make arrangements to be subject to, such procedures established and maintained by another person,

and provision for the enforcement of that requirement.

(2)   The provision made for the purposes of subsection (1) must satisfy such requirements as the Board may, from time to time, specify for the purposes of that subsection.

(3)   In this section—

    "relevant authorised person", in relation to an approved regulator, means a person in relation to whom the approved regulator is a relevant approved regulator;

    "relevant complaint", in relation to a relevant authorised person, means a complaint which—

      (a)   relates to an act or omission of that person, and

      (b)   may be made under the scheme provided for by this Part

(4)   The Board must publish any requirements specified by it for the purposes of subsection (2).

(5)   This section applies in relation to the licensing rules of the Board as it applies in relation to the regulatory arrangements of an approved regulator except that subsection (3) has effect as if for the definition of "relevant authorised person" there were substituted—

    "'relevant authorised person', in relation to the Board, means a person licensed by the Board under Part 5;".

Overview of the scheme

113 Overview of the scheme

(1)   This Part provides for a scheme under which complaints which—

      (a)   relate to an act or omission of a person ("the respondent") in carrying on an activity, and

      (b)   are within the jurisdiction of the scheme (see section 125),

may be resolved quickly and with minimum formality by an independent person.

(2)   Under the scheme—

      (a)   redress may be provided to the complainant, but

      (b)   no disciplinary action may be taken against the respondent.

(3)   Section 157 prevents provision relating to redress being included in the regulatory arrangements of an approved regulator, or licensing rules made by the Board in its capacity as a licensing authority.

(4)   But neither the scheme nor any provision made by this Part affects any power of an approved regulator, or the Board in its capacity as a licensing authority, to take disciplinary action.

(5)   "Disciplinary action" means the imposition of sanctions, in respect of a breach of conduct rules or discipline rules, on a person who is an authorised person in relation to an activity which is a reserved legal activity.

Jurisdiction and operation of the ombudsman scheme

125 Jurisdiction of the ombudsman scheme

(1)   A complaint which relates to an act or omission of a person ("the respondent") in carrying on an activity is within the jurisdiction of the ombudsman scheme if—

      (a)   the complaint is not excluded from the jurisdiction of the scheme by section 126, or by scheme rules made under section 127,

      (b)   the respondent is within section 128, and

      (c)   the complainant is within section 128 and wishes to have the complaint dealt with under the scheme.

(2)   In subsection (1) references to an act or omission include an act or omission which occurs before the coming into force of this section.

(3)   The right of a person to make a complaint under the ombudsman scheme, and the jurisdiction of an ombudsman to investigate, consider and determine a complaint, may not be limited or excluded by any contract term or by notice.

126 Complaints excluded because respondent's complaints procedures not used

(1) A complaint is excluded from the jurisdiction of the ombudsman scheme if the complainant has not first used the respondent's complaints procedures in relation to the complaint.

(2) The respondent's complaints procedures are the procedures established by the respondent, or which the respondent participates in or is subject to, in accordance with regulatory arrangements (or licensing rules of the Board) made in accordance with section 112.

(3) Scheme rules may provide that subsection (1) does not apply in specified circumstances.

127 Complaints excluded by scheme rules

(1) Scheme rules may make provision excluding complaints of a description specified in the rules from the jurisdiction of the ombudsman scheme.

(2) But they may not make provision excluding a complaint from the jurisdiction of the ombudsman scheme on the ground that it relates to a matter which has been or could be dealt with under the disciplinary arrangements of the respondent's relevant authorising body.

128 Parties

(1) The respondent is within this section if, at the relevant time, the respondent was an authorised person in relation to an activity which was a reserved legal activity (whether or not the act or omission relates to a reserved legal activity).

(2) The complainant ("C") is within this section if C—

(a) meets the first and second conditions, and

(b) is not excluded by subsection (5).

(3) The first condition is that C is—

(a) an individual, or

(b) a person (other than an individual) of a description prescribed by order made by the Lord Chancellor in accordance with a recommendation made under section 130.

(4) The second condition is that—

(a) the services to which the complaint relates were provided by the respondent to C;

(b) the services to which the complaint relates were provided by the respondent to an authorised person who procured them on C's behalf;

(c) the services to which the complaint relates were provided by the respondent—

(i) in the respondent's capacity as a personal representative or trustee, or

(ii) to a person acting as a personal representative or trustee,

and C is a beneficiary of the estate or trust in question; or

(d) C satisfies such other conditions, in relation to the services to which the complaint relates, as may be prescribed by order made by the Lord Chancellor in accordance with a recommendation made under section 130.

(5) C is excluded if, at the relevant time—

(a) C was an authorised person in relation to an activity which was a reserved legal activity and the services to which the complaint relates were procured by C on behalf of another person,

(b) C was a public body or was acting on behalf of such a body in relation to the services to which the complaint relates, or

(c)   C was a person prescribed, or of a description prescribed, as excluded by order made by the Lord Chancellor in accordance with a recommendation made under section 130.

(6)   In subsection (4)(b) "authorised person" means an authorised person in relation to any activity which is a reserved legal activity.

(7)   In this section—

"public body" means any government department, local authority or other body constituted for purposes of the public services, local government or the administration of justice;

"relevant time", in relation to a complaint, means the time when the act or omission to which the complaint relates took place.

129   Pre-commencement acts and omissions

(1)   For the purposes of section 128 a person is to be regarded as an authorised person in relation to an activity which is a reserved legal activity, at a time before section 125 comes into force, if the person was at that time—

(a)   a person of the kind mentioned in paragraph 2(4) of Schedule 15,

(b)   a body recognised under section 9 or 32 of the Administration of Justice Act 1985 (c. 61) (recognised bodies), or

(c)   a legal partnership, a conveyancing partnership, a patent attorney body or a trade mark attorney body.

(2)   In this section—

"conveyancing partnership" has the meaning given by paragraph 11(5) of Schedule 5;

"legal partnership" has the meaning given by paragraph 7(4) of that Schedule;

"patent attorney body" has the meaning given by paragraph 14(7) of that Schedule;

"trade mark attorney body" has the meaning given by paragraph 16(7) of that Schedule.

130   Orders under section 128

(1)   An interested body may, at any time, recommend to the Lord Chancellor that the Lord Chancellor make an order under section 128(3)(b), (4)(d) or (5)(c).

(2)   An interested body must, if requested to do so by the Lord Chancellor, consider whether or not it is appropriate to make a recommendation under subsection (1).

(3)   An interested body must, before making a recommendation under subsection (1)—

(a)   publish a draft of the proposed recommendation,

(b)   invite representations regarding the proposed recommendation, and

(c)   consider any such representations which are made.

(4)   Where the Lord Chancellor receives a recommendation under subsection (1), the Lord Chancellor must consider whether to follow the recommendation.

(5)   If the Lord Chancellor decides not to follow the recommendation, the Lord Chancellor must publish a notice to that effect which includes the Lord Chancellor's reasons for the decision.

(6)   In this section "interested body" means—

(a)   the OLC,

(b)   the Board, or

(c)   the Consumer Panel.

131 Acts and omissions by employees etc

(1) For the purposes of this Part and the ombudsman scheme, any act or omission by a person in the course of the person's employment is to be treated as also an act or omission by the person's employer, whether or not it was done with the employer's knowledge or approval.

(2) For the purposes of this Part and the ombudsman scheme, any act or omission by a partner in a partnership in the course of carrying on, in the usual way, business of the kind carried on by the partnership is to be treated as also an act or omission by the partnership.

(3) But subsection (2) does not apply if the partner had no authority to act for the partnership and the person purporting to rely on that subsection knew, at the time of the act or omission, that the partner had no such authority.

132 Continuity of complaints

(1) The ability of a person to make a complaint about an act or omission of a partnership or other unincorporated body is not affected by any change in the membership of the partnership or body.

(2) Scheme rules must make provision determining the circumstances in which, for the purposes of the ombudsman scheme, an act or omission of a person ("A") is, where A ceases to exist and another person ("B") succeeds to the whole or substantially the whole of the business of A, to be treated as an act or omission of B.

(3) Rules under subsection (2) must, in relation to cases where an act or omission of A is treated as an act or omission of B, make provision about the treatment of complaints under the ombudsman scheme which are outstanding against A at the time A ceases to exist.

(4) Scheme rules must make provision permitting such persons as may be specified in the rules to continue a complaint made by a person who has died or is otherwise unable to act; and for that purpose may modify references to the complainant in this Part and in scheme rules.

133 Operation of the ombudsman scheme

(1) Scheme rules must set out the procedure for—

(a)   the making of complaints under the ombudsman scheme, and

(b)   the investigation, consideration and determination of complaints by an ombudsman.

(2) Scheme rules—

(a)   must provide that a complaint is to be entertained under the ombudsman scheme only if the complainant has made the complaint under that scheme before the applicable time limit (determined in accordance with the scheme rules) has expired, and

(b)   may provide that an ombudsman may extend that time limit in specified circumstances.

(3) Scheme rules made under subsection (1) may (among other things) make provision—

(a)   for the whole or part of a complaint to be dismissed, in specified circumstances, without consideration of its merits;

(b)   for the reference of a complaint, in specified circumstances and with the consent of the complainant, to another body with a view to it being determined by that body instead of by an ombudsman;

(c)   for a person who, at the relevant time (within the meaning of section 128(7)) was an authorised person in relation to an activity to be treated in specified circumstances, for the purposes of the scheme and this Part, as if that person were a co-respondent in relation to a complaint;

(d) about the evidence which may be required or admitted and the extent to which it should be oral or written;

(e) for requiring parties to the complaint to attend to give evidence and produce documents, and for authorising the administration of oaths by ombudsmen;

(f) about the matters which are to be taken into account in determining whether an act or omission was fair and reasonable;

(g) for an ombudsman, in such circumstances as may be specified, to award expenses to persons in connection with attendance at a hearing before an ombudsman;

(h) for an ombudsman to award costs against the respondent in favour of the complainant;

(i) for an ombudsman to award costs against the complainant or the respondent in favour of the OLC for the purpose of providing a contribution to resources deployed in dealing with the complaint, if in the ombudsman's opinion that person acted so unreasonably in relation to the complaint that it is appropriate in all the circumstances of the case to make such an award;

(j) for the purpose of facilitating the settlement of a complaint with the agreement of the parties to it;

(k) for specified persons to be notified of complaints, determinations and directions under the ombudsman scheme.

(4) The circumstances specified under subsection (3)(a) may include the following—

(a) the ombudsman considers the complaint or part to be frivolous or vexatious or totally without merit;

(b) the ombudsman considers that the complaint or part would be better dealt with under another ombudsman scheme, by arbitration or by other legal proceedings;

(c) the ombudsman considers that there has been undue delay in the making of the complaint or part, or the provision of evidence to support it;

(d) the ombudsman is satisfied that the matter which is the subject of the complaint or part has previously been dealt with under another ombudsman scheme, by arbitration or by other legal proceedings;

(e) the ombudsman considers that there are other compelling reasons why it is inappropriate for the complaint or part to be dealt with under the ombudsman scheme.

(5) No person may be required by scheme rules—

(a) to provide any information or give any evidence which that person could not be compelled to provide or give in evidence in civil proceedings before the High Court, or

(b) to produce any document which that person could not be compelled to produce in such proceedings.

(6) Scheme rules may authorise an ombudsman making an award of costs in accordance with rules within subsection (3)(h) or (i) to order that the amount payable under the award bears interest, from a time specified in or determined in accordance with the order, at a rate specified in or determined in accordance with the rules.

(7)   An amount due under an award made in favour of a person by virtue of provision made under subsection (3)(g), (h) or (i) is recoverable as a debt due to that person.

(8)   In this section—

"party", in relation to a complaint, means—

(a)   the complainant,

(b)   the respondent, and

(c)   any other person who in accordance with scheme rules is to be regarded as a party to the complaint;

"specified" means specified in scheme rules.

134   Delegation of an ombudsman's functions

(1)   An ombudsman may delegate to a member of the OLC's staff appointed under paragraph 13 of Schedule 15—

(a)   any function of the ombudsman in relation to the making, investigation or consideration of a complaint;

(b)   any other function conferred on the ombudsman by or by virtue of this Part.

(2)   Nothing in subsection (1) applies to the following functions—

(a)   the function of determining a complaint;

(b)   the function of deciding that a complaint should be dismissed by virtue of rules under section 133(3)(a);

(c)   the Chief Ombudsman's power to consent to the appointment of an assistant ombudsman under section 122;

(d)   the duties imposed on the Chief Ombudsman by section 123 (Chief Ombudsman's report).

135   Notification requirements

(1)   This section applies where a complaint—

(a)   is excluded from the jurisdiction of the ombudsman scheme under section 126, or by virtue of scheme rules made under section 127;

(b)   is dismissed, or referred to another body, by virtue of scheme rules;

(c)   is settled, withdrawn or abandoned (or treated as withdrawn or abandoned by virtue of scheme rules).

(2)   The ombudsman must notify—

(a)   the complainant;

(b)   the respondent;

(c)   any relevant authorising body, in relation to the respondent, notified of the complaint in accordance with rules within section 133(3)(k),

and, in a case within subsection (1)(a) or (b), must give reasons for the exclusion, dismissal or referral.

136   Charges payable by respondents

(1)   Scheme rules must require respondents, in relation to complaints under the ombudsman scheme, to pay to the OLC such charges as may be specified in the rules.

(2)   The rules must provide for charges payable in relation to a complaint to be waived (or wholly refunded) where—

(a)   the complaint is determined or otherwise resolved in favour of the respondent, and

(b)   the ombudsman is satisfied that the respondent took all reasonable steps to try to resolve the complaint under the respondent's complaints procedures.

(3)   The rules may make provision as to—

(a)   the circumstances in which a complaint is to be treated as determined or otherwise resolved in favour of the respondent (which may include circumstances where a complaint is settled, withdrawn or abandoned (or treated as withdrawn or abandoned by virtue of scheme rules));

(b)   matters to be taken into account by the ombudsman for the purposes of subsection (2)(b).

(4)   The respondent's complaints procedures are the procedures established by the respondent, or which the respondent participates in or is subject to, in accordance with regulatory arrangements (or licensing rules of the Board) made in accordance with section 112.

(5)   The rules may, among other things—

(a)   provide for the OLC to reduce or waive a charge in such other circumstances as may be specified;

(b)   set different charges for different stages of the proceedings on a complaint;

(c)   provide for charges to be wholly or partly refunded in such other circumstances as may be specified;

(d)   provide that if the whole or any part of a charge is not paid by the time by which it is required to be paid under the rules, the unpaid balance from time to time carries interest at the rate specified in, or determined in accordance with, the rules.

(6)   Any charge which is owed to the OLC by virtue of rules made under this section may be recovered as a debt due to the OLC.

Determinations under the scheme

137 Determination of complaints

(1)   A complaint is to be determined under the ombudsman scheme by reference to what is, in the opinion of the ombudsman making the determination, fair and reasonable in all the circumstances of the case.

(2)   The determination may contain one or more of the following—

(a)   a direction that the respondent make an apology to the complainant;

(b)   a direction that—

(i)   the fees to which the respondent is entitled in respect of the services to which the complaint relates ("the fees") are limited to such amount as may be specified in the direction, and

(ii)   the respondent comply, or secure compliance, with such one or more of the permitted requirements as appear to the ombudsman to be necessary in order for effect to be given to the direction under sub-paragraph (i);

(c)   a direction that the respondent pay compensation to the complainant of such an amount as is specified in the direction in respect of any loss which has been suffered by, or any inconvenience or distress which has been caused to, the complainant as a result of any matter connected with the complaint;

(d)   a direction that the respondent secure the rectification, at the expense of the respondent, of any such error, omission or other deficiency arising in connection with the matter in question as the direction may specify;

(e)   a direction that the respondent take, at the expense of the respondent, such other action in the interests of the complainant as the direction may specify.

(3)   For the purposes of subsection (2)(b) "the permitted requirements" are—

(a)   that the whole or part of any amount already paid by or on behalf of the complainant in respect of the fees be refunded;

(b)   that the whole or part of the fees be remitted;

(c)   that the right to recover the fees be waived, whether wholly or to any specified extent.

(4)   Where—

(a)   a direction is made under subsection (2)(b) which requires that the whole or part of any amount already paid by or on behalf of the complainant in respect of the fees be refunded, or

(b)   a direction is made under subsection (2)(c),

the direction may also provide for the amount payable under the direction to carry interest from a time specified in or determined in accordance with the direction, at the rate specified in or determined in accordance with scheme rules.

(5)   The power of the ombudsman to make a direction under subsection (2) is not confined to cases where the complainant may have a cause of action against the respondent for negligence.

138   Limitation on value of directions under the ombudsman scheme

(1)   Where a determination is made under the ombudsman scheme in respect of a complaint, the total value of directions under section 137(2)(c) to (e) contained in the determination must not exceed £30,000.

(2)   For this purpose the total value of such directions is the aggregate of—

(a)   the amount of any compensation specified in a direction under subsection (2)(c) of section 137, and

(b)   the amount of any expenses reasonably incurred by the respondent when complying with a direction under subsection (2)(d) or (e) of that section.

(3)   For the purposes of determining that total value, any interest payable on an amount within subsection (2)(a) of this section, by virtue of section 137(4), is to be ignored.

139   Alteration of limit

(1)   The Lord Chancellor may by order amend section 138(1) in accordance with a recommendation made by an interested body under subsection (2).

(2)   An interested body may, at any time, recommend to the Lord Chancellor that section 138(1) should be amended so as to substitute the amount specified in the recommendation for the amount for the time being specified in that provision.

(3)   An interested body must, if requested to do so by the Lord Chancellor, consider whether or not it is appropriate to make a recommendation under subsection (2).

(4)   An interested body must, before making a recommendation under subsection (2)—

(a)   publish a draft of the proposed recommendation,

(b)   invite representations regarding the proposed recommendation, and

APPENDIX 20

(c)   consider any such representations which are made.

(5) Where the Lord Chancellor receives a recommendation under subsection (2), the Lord Chancellor must consider whether to follow the recommendation.

(6) If the Lord Chancellor decides not to follow the recommendation, the Lord Chancellor must publish a notice to that effect which includes the Lord Chancellor's reasons for the decision.

(7) In this section "interested body" means—

(a)   the OLC,

(b)   the Board, or

(c)   the Consumer Panel.

140 Acceptance or rejection of determination

(1) When an ombudsman has determined a complaint the ombudsman must prepare a written statement of the determination.

(2) The statement must—

(a)   give the ombudsman's reasons for the determination,

(b)   be signed by the ombudsman, and

(c)   require the complainant to notify the ombudsman, before a time specified in the statement ("the specified time"), whether the complainant accepts or rejects the determination.

(3) The ombudsman must give a copy of the statement to—

(a)   the complainant,

(b)   the respondent, and

(c)   any relevant authorising body in relation to the respondent.

(4) If the complainant notifies the ombudsman that the determination is accepted by the complainant, it is binding on the respondent and the complainant and is final.

(5) If, by the specified time, the complainant has not notified the ombudsman of the complainant's acceptance or rejection of the determination, the complainant is to be treated as having rejected it.

(6) But if—

(a)   the complainant notifies the ombudsman after the specified time that the determination is accepted by the complainant,

(b)   the complainant has not previously notified the ombudsman of the complainant's rejection of the determination, and

(c)   the ombudsman is satisfied that such conditions as may be prescribed by the scheme rules for the purposes of this subsection are satisfied,

the determination is treated as if it had never been rejected by virtue of subsection (5).

(7) The ombudsman must give notice of the outcome to—

(a)   the complainant,

(b)   the respondent, and

(c)   any relevant authorising body in relation to the respondent.

(8)   Where a determination is rejected by virtue of subsection (5), that notice must contain a general description of the effect of subsection (6).

(9)   A copy of the determination on which appears a certificate signed by an ombudsman is evidence that the determination was made under the scheme.

(10)   Such a certificate purporting to be signed by an ombudsman is to be taken to have been duly signed unless the contrary is shown.

(11)   Neither the complainant nor the respondent, in relation to a complaint, may institute or continue legal proceedings in respect of a matter which was the subject of a complaint, after the time when a determination by an ombudsman of the complaint becomes binding and final in accordance with this section.

141   Enforcement by complainant of directions under section 137

(1)   This section applies where—

  (a)   a determination is made in respect of a complaint under the ombudsman scheme,

  (b)   one or more directions are made under section 137(2), and

  (c)   the determination is final by virtue of section 140(4).

(2)   An amount payable in accordance with—

  (a)   a direction under subsection (2)(b) of section 137 which requires that the whole or part of any amount already paid by or on behalf of the complainant in respect of the fees be refunded, or

  (b)   a direction under subsection (2)(c) of that section,

including any interest payable by virtue of subsection (4) of that section, is recoverable, if a court so orders on the application of the complainant or an ombudsman, as if it were payable under an order of that court.

(3)   If the respondent fails to comply with any other direction under section 137(2), the complainant or an ombudsman may make an application to the court under this subsection.

(4)   If, on an application under subsection (3), the court decides that the respondent has failed to comply with the direction in question, it may order the respondent to take such steps as the court directs for securing that the direction is complied with.

(5)   An ombudsman may make an application under subsection (2) or (3) only in such circumstances as may be specified in scheme rules, and with the complainant's consent.

(6)   If the court makes an order under subsection (2) on the application of an ombudsman, the ombudsman may in such circumstances as may be specified in scheme rules and with the complainant's consent recover the amount mentioned in that subsection on behalf of the complainant.

(7)   In this section "court" means the High Court or a county court.

142   Reporting court orders made against authorised persons

(1)   Where a court makes an order under section 141, it must give the OLC notice to that effect.

(2)   Where the order is made against a person who is an authorised person in relation to any activity which is a reserved legal activity, the OLC must make arrangements to ensure that an ombudsman gives to each relevant authorising body, in relation to that person, a report which states that the order has been made.

(3)   A report under subsection (2) may require the relevant authorising body to report to the ombudsman the action which has been or is to be taken by it in response to the report under subsection (2) and the reasons for that action being taken.

(4)   If an ombudsman, having regard to any report produced by the relevant authorising body in compliance with a requirement imposed under subsection (3), or any failure to comply with such a requirement, considers—

(a)   that there has been a serious failure by the relevant authorising body to discharge its regulatory functions, or

(b)   if such a requirement has been imposed on the body on more than one occasion, that the relevant authorising body has persistently failed adequately to discharge its regulatory functions,

the ombudsman may make a report to that effect to the Board

Reporting misconduct

143   Reporting possible misconduct to approved regulators

(1)   This section applies where—

(a)   an ombudsman is dealing, or has dealt, with a complaint under the ombudsman scheme, and

(b)   the ombudsman is of the opinion that the conduct of the respondent or any other person in relation to any matter connected with the complaint is such that a relevant authorising body in relation to that person should consider whether to take action against that person.

(2)   The ombudsman must give the relevant authorising body a report which—

(a)   states that the ombudsman is of that opinion, and

(b)   gives details of that conduct.

(3)   The ombudsman must give the complainant a notice stating that a report under subsection (2) has been given to the relevant authorising body.

(4)   A report under subsection (2) may require the relevant authorising body to report to the ombudsman the action which has been or is to be taken by it in response to the report and the reasons for that action being taken.

(5)   The duty imposed by subsection (2) is not affected by the withdrawal or abandonment of the complaint.

(6)   If an ombudsman, having regard to any report produced by the relevant authorising body in compliance with a requirement imposed under subsection (4), or any failure to comply with such a requirement, considers—

(a)   that there has been a serious failure by the relevant authorising body to discharge its regulatory functions, or

(b)   if such a requirement has been imposed on the body on more than one occasion, that the relevant authorising body has persistently failed adequately to discharge its regulatory functions,

the ombudsman may make a report to that effect to the Board.

Co-operation with investigations

144   Duties to share information

(1)   Scheme rules must make provision requiring persons within subsection (3) to disclose to an approved regulator information of such description as may be specified in the rules, in such circumstances as may be so specified.

(2)   The regulatory arrangements of an approved regulator must make provision requiring the approved regulator to disclose to persons within subsection (3) information of such description as may be specified in the arrangements, in such circumstances as may be so specified.

(3)   The persons are—

(a)   the OLC;

(b)   an ombudsman;

(c)   a member of the OLC's staff appointed under paragraph 13 of Schedule 15.

(4)   Provision made under subsection (1) or (2) must satisfy such requirements as the Board may, from time to time, specify.

(5)   In specifying requirements under subsection (4) the Board must have regard to the need to ensure that, so far as reasonably practicable—

(a)   duplication of investigations is avoided;

(b)   the OLC assists approved regulators to carry out their regulatory functions, and approved regulators assist with the investigation, consideration and determination of complaints under the ombudsman scheme.

(6)   The Board must publish any requirements specified by it under subsection (4).

(7)   The OLC must—

(a)   before publishing under section 205(2) a draft of rules it proposes to make under subsection (1), consult each approved regulator to which the proposed rules apply, and

(b)   when seeking the Board's consent to such rules under section 155, identify any objections made by an approved regulator to the rules and not withdrawn.

(8)   An approved regulator must—

(a)   consult the OLC before making provisions in its regulatory arrangements of the kind mentioned in subsection (2), and

(b)   where an application is made for the Board's approval of such provisions, identify any objections made by the OLC to the provisions and not withdrawn.

(9)   This section applies to the Board in its capacity as a licensing authority and licensing rules made by the Board as it applies to an approved regulator and its regulatory arrangements; and for this purpose the reference in subsection (5)(b) to "regulatory functions" is to be read as a reference to the Board's functions under its licensing rules.

145   Duties of authorised persons to co-operate with investigations

(1)   The regulatory arrangements of an approved regulator, and licensing rules made by the Board in its capacity as a licensing authority, must make—

(a)   provision requiring each relevant authorised person to give ombudsmen all such assistance requested by them, in connection with the investigation, consideration or determination of complaints under the ombudsman scheme, as that person is reasonably able to give, and

(b)   provision for the enforcement of that requirement.

(2)   The provision made for the purposes of subsection (1) must satisfy such requirements as the Board may, from time to time, specify for the purposes of that subsection.

(3)   The Board must publish any requirements specified by it under subsection (2).

(4)   In this section "relevant authorised person"—

(a) in relation to an approved regulator, has the same meaning as in section 112, and

(b) in relation to the Board in its capacity as a licensing authority, means a person licensed by the Board under Part 5.

146 Reporting failures to co-operate with an investigation to approved regulators

(1) This section applies where an ombudsman is of the opinion that an authorised person has failed to give an ombudsman all such assistance requested by the ombudsman, in connection with the investigation, consideration or determination of a complaint under the ombudsman scheme, as that person is reasonably able to give.

(2) The ombudsman must give each relevant authorising body, in relation to that person, a report which—

(a) states that the ombudsman is of that opinion, and

(b) gives details of the failure.

(3) A report under subsection (2) may require the relevant authorising body to report to the ombudsman the action which has been or is to be taken by it in response to the report under that subsection and the reasons for that action being taken.

(4) The duty imposed by subsection (2) is not affected by the withdrawal or abandonment of the complaint.

(5) If an ombudsman, having regard to any report produced by the relevant authorising body in compliance with a requirement imposed under subsection (3), or any failure to comply with such a requirement, considers—

(a) that there has been a serious failure by the relevant authorising body to discharge its regulatory functions, or

(b) if such a requirement has been imposed on the body on more than one occasion, that the relevant authorising body has persistently failed adequately to discharge its regulatory functions,

the ombudsman may make a report to that effect to the Board.

(6) In this section "authorised person" means an authorised person in relation to any activity which is a reserved legal activity.

Information

147 Information and documents

(1) An ombudsman may, by notice, require a party to a complaint under the ombudsman scheme—

(a) to produce documents, or documents of a description, specified in the notice, or

(b) to provide information, or information of a description, specified in the notice.

(2) A notice under subsection (1) may require the information or documents to be provided or produced—

(a) before the end of such reasonable period as may be specified in the notice, and

(b) in the case of information, in such manner or form as may be so specified.

(3) This section applies only to information and documents the provision or production of which the ombudsman considers necessary for the determination of the complaint.

(4) An ombudsman may—

(a) take copies of or extracts from a document produced under this section, and

(b)   require the person producing the document to provide an explanation of it.

(5)   If a person who is required under this section to produce a document fails to do so, an ombudsman may require that person to state, to the best of that person's knowledge and belief, where the document is.

(6)   No person may be required under this section—

(a)   to provide any information which that person could not be compelled to provide or give in evidence in civil proceedings before the High Court, or

(b)   to produce any document which that person could not be compelled to produce in such proceedings.

(7)   In this section "party", in relation to a complaint, means—

(a)   the complainant;

(b)   the respondent;

(c)   any other person who in accordance with the scheme rules is to be regarded as a party to the complaint.

148 Reporting failures to provide information or produce documents

(1)   This section applies where an ombudsman is of the opinion that an authorised person has failed to comply with a requirement imposed under section 147(1).

(2)   The ombudsman must give each relevant authorising body, in relation to that person, a report which—

(a)   states that the ombudsman is of that opinion, and

(b)   gives details of the failure.

(3)   A report under subsection (2) may require the relevant authorising body to report to the ombudsman the action which has been or is to be taken by it in response to the report under that subsection and the reasons for that action being taken.

(4)   The duty imposed by subsection (2) is not affected by the withdrawal or abandonment of the complaint in relation to which the requirement was imposed under section 147(1).

(5)   If an ombudsman, having regard to any report produced by the relevant authorising body in compliance with a requirement imposed under subsection (3), or any failure to comply with such a requirement, considers—

(a)   that there has been a serious failure by the relevant authorising body to discharge its regulatory functions, or

(b)   if such a requirement has been imposed on the body on more than one occasion, that the relevant authorising body has persistently failed adequately to discharge its regulatory functions,

the ombudsman may make a report to that effect to the Board.

(6)   In this section "authorised person" means an authorised person in relation to any activity which is a reserved legal activity.

149 Enforcement of requirements to provide information or produce documents

(1)   This section applies where an ombudsman is of the opinion that a person ("the defaulter") has failed to comply with a requirement imposed under section 147(1).

(2)   The ombudsman may certify the defaulter's failure to comply with the requirement to the court.

(3)   Where an ombudsman certifies a failure to the court under subsection (2), the court may enquire into the case.

(4)   If the court is satisfied that the defaulter has failed without reasonable excuse to comply with the requirement, it may deal with—

(a)   the defaulter, and

(b)   in the case of a body, any manager of the body,

as if that person were in contempt.

(5)   Subsection (6) applies in a case where the defaulter is an authorised person in relation to any activity which is a reserved legal activity.

(6)   The ombudsman ("the enforcing ombudsman") may not certify the defaulter's failure to the court until a report by that or another ombudsman has been made as required by section 148(2) and the enforcing ombudsman is satisfied—

(a)   that each relevant authorising body to whom such a report was made has been given a reasonable opportunity to take action in respect of the defaulter's failure, and

(b)   that the defaulter has continued to fail to provide the information or produce the documents to which the requirement under section 147 related.

(7)   In this section "court" means the High Court.

150   Reports of investigations

(1)   The OLC may, if it considers it appropriate to do so in any particular case, publish a report of the investigation, consideration and determination of a complaint made under the ombudsman scheme.

(2)   A report under subsection (1) must not (unless the complainant consents)—

(a)   mention the name of the complainant, or

(b)   include any particulars which, in the opinion of the OLC, are likely to identify the complainant.

151   Restricted information

(1)   Except as provided by section 152, restricted information must not be disclosed—

(a)   by a restricted person, or

(b)   by any person who receives the information directly or indirectly from a restricted person.

(2)   In this section and section 152—

"restricted information" means information (other than excluded information) which is obtained by a restricted person in the course of, or for the purposes of, an investigation into a complaint made under the ombudsman scheme (including information obtained for the purposes of deciding whether to begin such an investigation or in connection with the settlement of a complaint);

"restricted person" means—

(a)   the OLC,

(b)   an ombudsman, or

(c)   a person who exercises functions delegated under paragraph 22 of Schedule 15.

(3)   For the purposes of subsection (2) "excluded information" means—

(a)   information which is in the form of a summary or collection of information so framed as not to enable information relating to any particular person to be ascertained from it;

(b)   information which at the time of the disclosure is or has already been made available to the public from other sources;

(c)   information which was obtained more than 70 years before the date of the disclosure.

152   Disclosure of restricted information

(1)   A restricted person may disclose restricted information to another restricted person.

(2)   Restricted information may be disclosed for the purposes of the investigation in the course of which, or for the purposes of which, it was obtained.

(3)   Section 151 also does not preclude the disclosure of restricted information—

     (a)   in a report made under—

         (i)   section 143(2) (report of possible misconduct to approved regulators),

         (ii)   section 146(2) (report of failure to co-operate with investigation),

         (iii)   section 148 (reporting failures to provide information or produce documents), or

         (iv)   section 150 (reports of investigations),

     (b)   for the purposes of enabling or assisting the Board to exercise any of its functions,

     (c)   to an approved regulator for the purposes of enabling or assisting the approved regulator to exercise any of its regulatory functions,

     (d)   with the consent of the person to whom it relates and (if different) the person from whom the restricted person obtained it,

     (e)   for the purposes of an inquiry with a view to the taking of any criminal proceedings or for the purposes of any such proceedings,

     (f)   where the disclosure is required by or by virtue of any provision made by or under this Act or any other enactment or other rule of law,

     (g)   to such persons (other than approved regulators) who exercise regulatory functions as may be prescribed by order made by the Lord Chancellor, for such purposes as may be so prescribed.

(4)   Subsections (2) and (3) are subject to subsection (5).

(5)   The Lord Chancellor may by order prevent the disclosure of restricted information by virtue of subsection (2) or (3) in such circumstances, or for such purposes, as may be prescribed in the order.

153   Data protection

In section 31 of the Data Protection Act 1998 (c. 29) (regulatory activity), after subsection (4B) (inserted by section 170) insert—

     "(4C)   Personal data processed for the purposes of the function of considering a complaint under the scheme established under Part 6 of the Legal Services Act 2007 (legal complaints) are exempt from the subject information provisions in any case to the extent to which the application of those provisions to the data would be likely to prejudice the proper discharge of the function."

Defamation

154 Protection from defamation claims

For the purposes of the law of defamation—

(a)   proceedings in relation to a complaint under the ombudsman scheme are to be treated as if they were proceedings before a court, and

(b)   the publication of any matter by the OLC under this Part is absolutely privileged.

PART 8
MISCELLANEOUS PROVISIONS ABOUT LAWYERS ETC

Duties of regulated persons

176 Duties of regulated persons

(1)   A person who is a regulated person in relation to an approved regulator has a duty to comply with the regulatory arrangements of the approved regulator as they apply to that person.

(2)   A person is a regulated person in relation to an approved regulator if the person—

(a)   is authorised by the approved regulator to carry on an activity which is a reserved legal activity, or

(b)   is not so authorised, but is a manager or employee of a person who is so authorised.

(3)   This section applies in relation to the Board in its capacity as a licensing authority and its licensing rules, as it applies in relation to an approved regulator and its regulatory arrangements.

The Solicitors' Code of Conduct 2007 (with **SRA** guidance)

[Law Society copyright. For the latest updates to the material, please see www.sra.org.uk.]

The Solicitors' Code of Conduct 2007

[Professional Ethics]

[Dated 10 March 2007 and commencing on 1 July 2007.]

[With amendments to 6 October 2010]

Contents

The Solicitors' Code of Conduct 2007

Preamble

Rules dated 10 March 2007 commencing 1 July 2007 made under Part II of the Solicitors Act 1974 and sections 9 and 9A of the Administration of Justice Act 1985 with the concurrence of the Master of the Rolls under sections 32 and 33A of the Solicitors Act 1974, section 9 of the Administration of Justice Act 1985 and paragraph 16 of Schedule 22 to the Legal Services Act 2007, the concurrence of the Lord Chancellor under paragraph 16 of Schedule 22 to the Legal Services Act 2007 and the approval of the Secretary of State under Schedule 4 to the Courts and Legal Services Act 1990, regulating the conduct of solicitors and their employees, registered European lawyers and their employees, registered foreign lawyers, and recognised bodies and their managers and employees.

The guidance and explanatory introductions issued with these rules are not mandatory and do not form part of the Solicitors' Code of Conduct. However, solicitors, and others subject to the rules, who do not follow the guidance may be required to demonstrate how they have nevertheless complied with the rule.

Rule 1 – Core duties

1.01 Justice and the rule of law

You must uphold the rule of law and the proper administration of justice.

1.02 Integrity

You must act with integrity.

1.03 Independence

You must not allow your independence to be compromised.

1.04 Best interests of clients

You must act in the best interests of each client.

1.05 Standard of service

You must provide a good standard of service to your clients.

1.06 Public confidence

You must not behave in a way that is likely to diminish the trust the public places in you or the legal profession.

Guidance to rule 1 – Core duties

General

1. A modern just society needs a legal profession which adopts high standards of integrity and professionalism. Lawyers, law firms and those who work in them serve both clients and society. In serving society, you uphold the rule of law and the proper administration of justice. In serving clients, you work in partnership with the client making the client's business your first concern. The core duties contained in rule 1 set the standards which will meet the needs of both clients and society. The core duties apply to solicitors, registered European lawyers (RELs), registered foreign lawyers (RFLs), recognised bodies, managers and employees of recognised bodies, and employees of recognised sole practitioners.

2. The core duties perform a number of functions:

    (a) They define the values which should shape your professional character and be displayed in your professional behaviour.

    (b) They form an overarching framework within which the more detailed and context-specific rules in the rest of the Code can be understood, thus illuminating the nature of those obligations and helping you to comply.

    (c) The core duties can help you to navigate your way through those situations not covered in the detailed rules, as no code can foresee or address every ethical dilemma which may arise in legal practice.

    (d) The core duties are fundamental rules. A breach may result in the imposition of sanctions.

3. Where two or more core duties come into conflict, the factor determining precedence must be the public interest, and especially the public interest in the administration of justice. Compliance with the core duties, as with all the rules, is subject to any overriding legal obligations.

4. It will be a breach of rule 1 if you permit another person to do anything on your behalf which would compromise or impair your ability to comply with any of the core duties.

Justice and the rule of law – 1.01

5. You have obligations not only to clients but also to the court and to third parties with whom you have dealings on your clients' behalf – see in particular rule 10 (Relations with third parties) and rule 11 (Litigation and advocacy).

Integrity – 1.02

6. Personal integrity is central to your role as the client's trusted adviser and must characterise all your professional dealings – with clients, the court, other lawyers and the public.

Independence – 1.03

7. "Independence" means your own and your firm's independence, and not merely your ability to give independent advice to a client. Examples of situations which might put your independence at risk include:

    (a) finance agreements/loans to your firm with particular strings attached;

    (b) finance arrangements which suggest dependency upon an outside body, such as could, at that body's discretion, effectively put your firm out of business;

    (c) contractual conditions in agreements with referrers of business or funders which effectively cede control of your firm to the outside body;

    (d) granting options to purchase your interest in your firm for nominal value;

    (e) allowing a third party access to confidential information concerning your clients;

    (f) a relationship with an outside body which is not at arm's length, and/or which suggests that your firm is more akin to a part of or subsidiary of that body, rather than an independent law firm;

    (g) fee sharing arrangements which go beyond what is allowed under rule 8.02;

    (h) any arrangement for a third party to fund legal actions which lays constraints on the conduct of the matter which go beyond the legitimate interests of a funder.

    See also rule 3 (Conflict of interests) and rule 9 (Referrals of business).

Best interests of clients – 1.04

8. You must always act in good faith and do your best for each of your clients. Most importantly, you must observe:

    (a) your duty of confidentiality to the client – see rule 4 (Confidentiality and disclosure);

    (b) your obligations with regard to conflicts of interests – see rule 3 (Conflict of interests); and

    (c) your obligation not to use your position to take unfair advantage of the client – see 10.01 (Not taking unfair advantage).

Standard of service – 1.05

9. You must provide a good standard of client care and of work, including the exercise of competence, skill and diligence. Disciplinary action will not always follow where breaches of this duty are minor and isolated.

Public confidence – 1.06

10. Members of the public must be able to place their trust in you. Any behaviour within or outside your professional practice which undermines this trust damages not only you but the ability of the legal profession as a whole to serve society.

Rule 2 – Client relations

Introduction

Rule 2 is designed to help both you and your clients understand each other's expectations and responsibilities. In particular, the purpose of 2.02 (Client care) and 2.03 (Information about the cost) is to ensure that clients are given the information necessary to enable them to make appropriate decisions about if and how their matter should proceed. Under rule 5 (Business management) a recognised body, a manager of a recognised body and a recognised sole practitioner must effect supervision and put in place management arrangements to provide for compliance with rule 2. The rule does not apply to your overseas practice but you must comply with 15.02.

Rule 2 – Client relations

2.01 Taking on clients

(1) You are generally free to decide whether or not to take on a particular client. However, you must refuse to act or cease acting for a client in the following circumstances:

    (a) when to act would involve you in a breach of the law or a breach of the rules of professional conduct;

    (b) where you have insufficient resources or lack the competence to deal with the matter;

    (c) where instructions are given by someone other than the client, or by only one client on behalf of others in a joint matter, you must not proceed without checking that all clients agree with the instructions given; or

    (d) where you know or have reasonable grounds for believing that the instructions are affected by duress or undue influence, you must not act on those instructions until you have satisfied yourself that they represent the client's wishes.

(2) You must not cease acting for a client except for good reason and on reasonable notice.

2.02 Client care

(1) You must:

    (a) identify clearly the client's objectives in relation to the work to be done for the client;

    (b) give the client a clear explanation of the issues involved and the options available to the client;

    (c) agree with the client the next steps to be taken; and

    (d) keep the client informed of progress, unless otherwise agreed.

(2) You must, both at the outset and, as necessary, during the course of the matter:

    (a) agree an appropriate level of service;

    (b) explain your responsibilities;

    (c) explain the client's responsibilities;

    (d) ensure that the client is given, in writing, the name and status of the person dealing with the matter and the name of the person responsible for its overall supervision; and

    (e) explain any limitations or conditions resulting from your relationship with a third party (for example a funder, fee sharer or introducer) which affect the steps you can take on the client's behalf.

(3)   If you can demonstrate that it was inappropriate in the circumstances to meet some or all of these requirements, you will not breach 2.02.

2.03 Information about the cost

(1)   You must give your client the best information possible about the likely overall cost of a matter both at the outset and, when appropriate, as the matter progresses. In particular you must:

    (a)   advise the client of the basis and terms of your charges;

    (b)   advise the client if charging rates are to be increased;

    (c)   advise the client of likely payments which you or your client may need to make to others;

    (d)   discuss with the client how the client will pay, in particular:

        (i)   whether the client may be eligible and should apply for public funding; and

        (ii)   whether the client's own costs are covered by insurance or may be paid by someone else such as an employer or trade union;

    (e)   advise the client that there are circumstances where you may be entitled to exercise a lien for unpaid costs;

    (f)   advise the client of their potential liability for any other party's costs; and

    (g)   discuss with the client whether their liability for another party's costs may be covered by existing insurance or whether specially purchased insurance may be obtained.

(2)   Where you are acting for the client under a conditional fee agreement, (including a collective conditional fee agreement) in addition to complying with 2.03(1) above and 2.03(5) and (6) below, you must explain the following, both at the outset and, when appropriate, as the matter progresses:

    (a)   the circumstances in which your client may be liable for your costs and whether you will seek payment of these from the client, if entitled to do so;

    (b)   if you intend to seek payment of any or all of your costs from your client, you must advise your client of their right to an assessment of those costs; and

    (c)   where applicable, the fact that you are obliged under a fee sharing agreement to pay to a charity any fees which you receive by way of costs from the client's opponent or other third party.

(3)   Where you are acting for a publicly funded client, in addition to complying with 2.03(1) above and 2.03(5) and (6) below, you must explain the following at the outset:

    (a)   the circumstances in which they may be liable for your costs;

    (b)   the effect of the statutory charge;

    (c)   the client's duty to pay any fixed or periodic contribution assessed and the consequence of failing to do so; and

    (d)   that even if your client is successful, the other party may not be ordered to pay costs or may not be in a position to pay them.

(4)   Where you agree to share your fees with a charity in accordance with 8.01(h) you must disclose to the client at the outset the name of the charity.

(5)   Any information about the cost must be clear and confirmed in writing.

(6)   You must discuss with your client whether the potential outcomes of any legal case will justify the expense or risk involved including, if relevant, the risk of having to pay an opponent's costs.

(7)   If you can demonstrate that it was inappropriate in the circumstances to meet some or all of the requirements in 2.03(1) and (5) above, you will not breach 2.03.

2.04 Contingency fees

(1)   You must not enter into an arrangement to receive a contingency fee for work done in prosecuting or defending any contentious proceedings before a court of England and Wales, a British court martial or an arbitrator where the seat of the arbitration is in England and Wales, except as permitted by statute or the common law.

(2)   You must not enter into an arrangement to receive a contingency fee for work done in prosecuting or defending any contentious proceedings before a court of an overseas jurisdiction or an arbitrator where the seat of the arbitration is overseas except to the extent that a lawyer of that jurisdiction would be permitted to do so.

2.05 Complaints handling

(1)   If you are a recognised body, a manager of a recognised body or a recognised sole practitioner, you must ensure:

    (a)   that the firm has a written complaints procedure and that complaints are handled promptly, fairly and effectively in accordance with it;

    (b)   that the client is told, in writing, at the outset (or in the case of existing clients, at the next appropriate opportunity):

        (i)   that, in the event of a problem, the client is entitled to complain; and

        (ii)   how and to whom the client should complain;

        (iii)   that this could include a complaint about the firm's bill;

        (iv)   that the firm has a complaints procedure, a copy of which is available on request;

        (v)   of their right to complain to the Legal Ombudsman at the conclusion of your complaint process, the timeframe for doing so and full details of how to contact the Legal Ombudsman;

        (vi)   that there may also be a right to object to the bill by applying to the court for an assessment of the bill under Part III of the Solicitors Act 1974; and

        (vii)   that if all or part of a bill remains unpaid the firm may be entitled to charge interest;

    (c)   that the client is given a copy of the complaints procedure on request; and

    (d)   that once a complaint has been made, the person complaining is told in writing:

        (i)   how the complaint will be handled; and

        (ii)   within what timescales they will be given an initial and/or substantive response.

    (e)   that at the conclusion of the firm's complaints process the client is told of their right to complain to the Legal Ombudsman, the timeframe for doing so and full details of how to contact the Legal Ombudsman.

(2)   If you can demonstrate that it was inappropriate in the circumstances to meet some or all of these requirements, you will not breach 2.05.

(3)   You must not charge your client for the cost of handling a complaint.

2.06 Commissions

If you are a recognised body, a manager of a recognised body or a recognised sole practitioner, you must ensure that your firm pays to your client commission received over £20 unless the client, having been told the amount, or if the precise amount is not known, an approximate amount or how the amount is to be calculated, has agreed that your firm may keep it.

2.07 Limitation of civil liability by contract

If you are a recognised body or a recognised sole practitioner, you must not exclude or attempt to exclude by contract all liability to your clients. However, you may limit your liability, provided that such limitation:

(a)   is not below the minimum level of cover required by the Solicitors' Indemnity Insurance Rules for a policy of qualifying insurance;

(b)   is brought to the client's attention; and

(c)   is in writing.

Guidance to rule 2 – Client relations

General

1.   The requirements of rule 2 do not exhaust your obligations to clients. As your client's trusted adviser, you must act in the client's best interests (see 1.04) and you must not abuse or exploit the relationship by taking advantage of a client's age, inexperience, ill health, lack of education or business experience, or emotional or other vulnerability.

2.   It is not envisaged or intended that a breach of 2.02, 2.03 or 2.05 should invariably render a retainer unenforceable. As noted in the introduction to this rule, the purpose of 2.02 and 2.03 is to ensure that clients are given the information necessary to enable them to make appropriate decisions about if and how their matter should proceed. These parts of the rule together with 2.05 require you to provide certain information to your client. Rules 2.02(3), 2.03(7) and 2.05(2) recognise that it is not always necessary to provide all this information to comply with the underlying purpose of the rule. Similarly, the information you are required to give to your client varies in importance both inherently and in relation to the individual client and the retainer. Consequently, the rule will be enforced in a manner which is proportionate to the seriousness of the breach. For example, if you were to fail to tell your client that they would be liable to pay another party's costs in breach of 2.03(1)(f), this is likely to be treated as a more serious breach than your failure to advise your client about your right to exercise a lien for unpaid costs in breach of 2.03(1)(e).

Taking on clients – 2.01

3.   Rule 2.01 identifies some situations where you must refuse to act for a client or, if already acting, must stop doing so.

The retainer is a contractual relationship and subject to legal considerations. You should be sure of your legal position as to who is your client if you contract to provide services to a third party. For example, if you agree to provide all or part of a Home Information Pack to an estate agent or Home Information Pack provider for the benefit of a seller, you should ensure there is an agreed understanding as to whether the estate agent/pack provider or the seller is your client.

4. Your right to decide not to accept instructions is subject to restrictions, including the following:

    (a) You must not refuse for a reason that would breach rule 6 (Equality and diversity).

    (b) Rule 11 (Litigation and advocacy), governing a solicitor or REL acting as an advocate, contains restrictions on when the solicitor or REL may refuse instructions.

    (c) Be aware of restrictions on when you can refuse to act or cease acting for a publicly funded client in a criminal matter.

5. If you are an in-house solicitor or in-house REL you are already in a contractual relationship with your employer who is, for the purpose of these rules, your client. You are not therefore usually as free as a solicitor or REL in a firm to refuse instructions, and will need to use your professional judgement in applying 2.01.

6. Rule 2.01 sets out situations in which you must refuse instructions or, where appropriate, cease acting. These might include the following:

    (a) *Breach of the law or rules*

        (i)   where there is a conflict of interests between you and your client or between two or more clients – see rule 3 (Conflict of interests);

        (ii) where money laundering is suspected, your freedom to cease acting is curtailed (see the Proceeds of Crime Act 2002, the Money Laundering Regulations 2007, other relevant law and directives, and guidance issued by the SRA Board on this subject); and

        (iii) where you may be dealing with a client who does not have mental capacity as defined in the Mental Capacity Act 2005 or where the client is a child special circumstances apply. You need to bear in mind that the question of capacity relates to the particular decision that needs to be made, and it is, for instance, entirely possible for someone to lack capacity to make certain decisions but have the capacity to instruct a solicitor on other matters. To ensure that you comply with the law you need to have regard to the provisions of that Act and its accompanying Code.

    (b) *Insufficient resources*

        Before taking on a new matter, you must consider whether your firm has the resources – including knowledge, qualifications, expertise, time, sufficient support staff and, where appropriate, access to external expertise such as agents and counsel – to provide the support required to represent the client properly. The obligation is a continuing one, and you must ensure that an appropriate or agreed level of service can be delivered even if circumstances change.

    (c) *Duress or undue influence*

        It is important to be satisfied that clients give their instructions freely. Some clients, such as the elderly, those with language or learning difficulties and those with disabilities are particularly vulnerable to pressure from others. If you suspect that a client's instructions are the result of undue influence you need to exercise your judgement as to whether you can proceed on the client's behalf. For example, if you suspect that a friend or relative who accompanies the client is exerting undue influence, you should arrange to see the client alone or if appropriate with an independent third party or interpreter. Where there is no actual evidence of undue influence but the client appears to want to act against their best interests, it may be sufficient simply to explain the consequences of the instructions the client has given and confirm that the client wishes to proceed. For evidential purposes, it would be sensible to get this confirmation in writing.

7.   As a matter of good practice you should not act for a client who has instructed another firm in the same matter unless the other firm agrees. If you are asked to provide a second opinion, you may do so but you should satisfy yourself that you have sufficient information to handle the matter properly.

Ceasing to act

8.   A client can end the retainer with you at any time and for any reason. You may only end the relationship with the client if there is a good reason and after giving reasonable notice. Examples of good reasons include where there is a breakdown in confidence between you and the client, and where you are unable to obtain proper instructions.

9.   If there is good reason to cease acting, you must give reasonable notice to the client. What amounts to reasonable notice will depend on the circumstances. For example, it would normally be unreasonable to stop acting for a client immediately before a court hearing where it is impossible for the client to find alternative representation. In such a case, if there is no alternative but to cease acting immediately, you should attend and explain the circumstances to the court – see rule 11 (Litigation and advocacy). There may be circumstances where it is reasonable to give no notice.

10.   The relationship between you and your client can also be ended automatically by law, for example by the client's bankruptcy or mental incapacity (see note 6(a)(iii) above).

11.   When you cease acting for a client, you will need to consider what should be done with the paperwork. You must hand over the client's files promptly on request subject to your right to exercise a lien in respect of outstanding costs. You should try to ensure the client's position is not prejudiced, and should also bear in mind his or her rights under the Data Protection Act 1998. Undertakings to secure the costs should be used as an alternative to the exercise of a lien if possible. There may be circumstances where it is unreasonable to exercise a lien, for example, where the amount of the outstanding costs is small and the value or importance of the matter is very great. In any dispute over the ownership of documents you should refer to the law. Further advice about the law of lien or the ownership of documents can be found in *Cordery on Solicitors* or other reference books on the subject.

Client care – 2.02

12.   The purpose of 2.02 is to set out the type of information that must normally be given to a client. This information must be provided in a clear and readily accessible form.

13.   Rule 2.02 is flexible about the extent of the information to be given in each individual case. Over-complex or lengthy terms of business letters may not be helpful.

14.   The "level of service" to be provided should be agreed at the outset. For example, the client may want regular written reports. Alternatively, the client may want to provide initial instructions then to hear no more until an agreed point has been reached. This will affect the projected costs of the matter.

15.   When considering the options available to the client (2.02(1)(b)), if the matter relates to a dispute between your client and a third party, you should discuss whether mediation or some other alternative dispute resolution (ADR) procedure may be more appropriate than litigation, arbitration or other formal processes. There may be costs sanctions if a party refuses ADR – see *Halsey v Milton Keynes NHS Trust and Steel and Joy* [2004] EWCA (Civ) 576. More information may be obtained from the Law Society's Practice Advice Service.

16.   Rule 2.02(2)(e) requires you to explain limitations or conditions on your acting arising from your relationship with a third party. Where such a relationship involves sharing any client information with a third party, you must inform the client and obtain their consent. Failure to do so would be a breach of client confidentiality (see rule 4 (Confidentiality and disclosure)) and possibly also a breach of the Data Protection Act 1998. Some arrangements with third parties, such as introducers under rule 9 (Referrals of business) or fee sharers under rule 8 (Fee sharing), may constrain the way in which you handle clients' matters.

17.   The constraints that such arrangements impose may fall into one of the following categories:

    (a)   Constraints which are proper and do not require disclosure to the client. These normally relate to service standards such as dealing with client enquiries within a specified time, the use of specified computer software, telecommunications systems, a particular advertising medium, or particular training provision.

    (b)   Constraints which are proper but require disclosure to the client. Some third parties may have a legitimate interest in the progress of the client's matter and the way it is dealt with – for instance, third parties who fund a client's matter, and insurers. Constraints that they impose, e.g. that you will not issue proceedings without the authority of the funder are proper provided they do not operate against the client's best interests, but should be disclosed to the client.

    (c)   Constraints which are improper cannot be remedied by disclosing them to the client. These are constraints which impair your independence and ability to act in the client's best interests. You cannot accept an arrangement which involves such constraints. They might include, for instance, requirements that you do not disclose information to the client to which the client is entitled, or give advice to the client which you know is contrary to the client's best interests, or with which you disagree, or that you act towards the court in a deceitful manner or lie to a third party.

18.   You must give the required information to the client as soon as possible after you have agreed to act. You must then keep the client up to date with the progress of the matter and any changes affecting the original agreement.

19.   The status of the person dealing with your client must be made absolutely clear, for legal and ethical reasons. For example, a person who is not a solicitor must not be described as one, either expressly or by implication. All staff having contact with clients, including reception, switchboard and secretarial staff, should be advised accordingly.

20.   All clients affected by a material alteration to the composition of the firm must be informed personally. Where the person having conduct of a matter leaves a firm, the client in question must be informed, preferably in advance, and told the name and status of the person who is to take over their matter.

21.   Rule 2.02(2)(d) refers to the person responsible for the overall supervision of a matter. Supervision requirements are dealt with in rule 5 (Business management) and guidance about who can supervise matters may be found there.

22.   There may be circumstances when it would be inappropriate to provide any or all of the information required by 2.02. It will be for you to justify why compliance was not appropriate in an individual matter. For example, where you are asked for one-off advice, or where you have a long-standing client who is familiar with your firm's terms of business and knows the status of the person dealing with the matter, this information may not need to be repeated. However, other aspects of 2.02 must be complied with and the client must be kept up to date and informed of changes.

23.   If you are an in-house solicitor or in-house REL much of 2.02 will be inappropriate when you are acting for your employer. However, it may be necessary for you to comply with aspects of 2.02 when you are acting for someone other than your employer in accordance with rule 13 (In-house practice).

APPENDIX 21

24. If you receive instructions from someone other than your client, you must still give the client the information required under 2.02. There are, however, exceptions to this. For example, where your client has an attorney appointed by an enduring power of attorney which has been registered with the Court of Protection, or a donee of a lasting power of attorney which has similarly been registered, or a deputy for financial affairs, the information required by 2.02 should be given to the attorney, donee or deputy. However, because the question of capacity relates to the particular decision that needs to be made (that is, just because a person lacks capacity as defined in the Mental Capacity Act 2005 to make certain decisions they do not necessarily lack the capacity to instruct a solicitor in other matters), you need to have regard to the provisions of that Act and its accompanying Code and must not assume that a person subject to the provisions of that Act lacks the capacity to instruct you in an area not covered by the power of attorney or the scope of the deputy's appointment.

25. In order to provide evidence of compliance with 2.02, you should consider giving the information in writing even though this is not a requirement.

26. Where you are, in effect, your firm's client – for example, as an executor administering a deceased's estate or a trustee of a trust – you should consider what information, if any, should be given to interested parties. There is no requirement, for example, that beneficiaries under a will or trust should be treated as though they were clients. It may, however, be good practice to provide some information – for example, about the type of work to be carried out and approximate timescales.

Information about the cost – 2.03

27. The purpose of 2.03 is to ensure that the client is given relevant costs information and that this is clearly expressed. Information about costs must be worded in a way that is appropriate for the client. All costs information must be given in writing and regularly updated.

28. Rule 2.03 recognises that there may be circumstances where it would be inappropriate to provide any or all of the information required. It will be for you to justify why compliance was not appropriate in an individual matter. For example, your firm may regularly do repeat work for the client on agreed terms and the client might not need the costs information repeated. However, the client should be informed, for example, of any changes in a firm's charging rates.

29. If you are an in-house solicitor or REL, much of 2.03 will be inappropriate if you are acting for your employer.

30. This guidance does not deal with the form a bill can take, final and interim bills, when they can be delivered and when and how a firm can sue on a bill. All these matters are governed by complex legal provisions, and there are many publications that provide help to firms and clients. Advice on some aspects of costs is available from the Law Society's Practice Advice Service.

31. You will usually be free to negotiate the cost and the method of payment with your clients. It will not normally be necessary for the client to be separately advised on the cost agreement. Different cost options may have different implications for the client – for example, where the choice is between a conditional fee agreement and an application for public funding. In those circumstances clients should be made aware of the implications of each option.

32. The rule requires you to advise the client of the circumstances in which you may be entitled to exercise a lien for unpaid costs. For more information see note 11 above.

33. Clients may be referred to you at a stage when they have already signed a contract for a funding arrangement – see also rule 9 (Referrals of business). You should explain the implications of any such arrangement fully including the extent to which the charges associated with such an arrangement may be recovered from another party to the proceedings.

34. There may be some unusual arrangements, however, where it should be suggested that the client considers separate advice on what is being proposed – for example, where you are to receive shares in a new company instead of costs. See also rule 3 (Conflict of interests) and 9.02(g) for details about your obligations to clients who have been referred to you.

35. Rule 2.03 does not cover all the different charging arrangements possible or the law governing them. However, it does require that the chosen option is explained as fully as possible to the client. It also requires that if you have agreed to pay all, or part, of your fees to a charity in accordance with rule 8 (Fee sharing) the client must be informed at the outset of the name of that charity.

36. It is often impossible to tell at the outset what the overall cost will be. Rule 2.03 allows for this and requires that you provide the client with as much information as possible at the start and that you keep the client updated. If a precise figure cannot be given at the outset, you should explain the reason to the client and agree a ceiling figure or review dates.

37. Particular information will be of relevance at particular stages of a client's matter. You should, for example, ensure that clients understand the costs implications of any offers of settlement. Where offers of settlement are made, clients must be fully informed of the amount to be deducted in respect of costs and how this figure is calculated. You should advise clients of their rights to assessment of your costs in such circumstances.

38. When a potential client contacts you with a view to giving you instructions you should always, when asked, try to be helpful in providing information on the likely costs of their matter.

Work under a conditional fee agreement or for a publicly funded client

39. Rules 2.03(2) and 2.03(3) set out additional information which must be explained to the client when work is done under a conditional fee agreement or on a publicly funded basis. Conditional fee agreements are subject to statutory requirements and all agreements must conform to these. Where you are acting under a conditional fee agreement and you are obliged under a fee sharing agreement to pay to a charity any fees which you receive by way of costs from the client's opponent or other third party, the client must be informed at the outset of the name of that charity.

Payments to others

40. You must explain at the outset to your client any likely payments they will have to make. These could include court fees, search fees, experts' fees and counsel's fees. Where possible, you should give details of the probable cost and if this is not possible you should agree with the client to review these expenses and the need for them nearer the time they are likely to be incurred.

Contingency fees – 2.04

41. A "contingency fee" is defined in rule 24 (Interpretation) as any sum (whether fixed, or calculated either as a percentage of the proceeds or otherwise) payable only in the event of success.

42. If you enter into an arrangement for a lawful contingency fee with a client, what amounts to "success" should be agreed between you and your client prior to entering into the arrangement.

43. Under rule 24 (Interpretation), "contentious proceedings" is to be construed in accordance with the definition of "contentious business" in section 87 of the Solicitors Act 1974.

44. Conditional fees are a form of contingency fees. In England and Wales a conditional fee agreement for certain types of litigation is permitted by statute. See section 58 of the Courts and Legal Services Act 1990 (as amended by section 27 of the Access to Justice Act 1999) and 2.03(2) above for more information.

45. It is acceptable to enter into a contingency fee arrangement for non-contentious matters (see section 87 of the Solicitors Act 1974 for the definition of "non-contentious business") but you should note that to be enforceable the arrangement must be contained in a non-contentious business agreement.

46. An otherwise contentious matter remains non-contentious up to the commencement of proceedings. Consequently, you may enter into a contingency fee arrangement for, for example, the receipt of commission for the successful collection of debts owed to a client, provided legal proceedings are not started.

Complaints handling – 2.05

47. The purpose of 2.05 is to ensure that clients know about their right to complain and how to do so; and that clients are confident that if they have a complaint it will be dealt with promptly, fairly, and effectively, in accordance with a procedure that provides clients with effective safeguards. The client's right to complain is an important public protection and it is not acceptable for the information required by the rule simply to be set out in your firm's terms and conditions; it will need to be drawn specifically to the client's attention.

48. The content of your firm's complaints handling procedure is a matter for the firm, but the procedure must be in writing and must enable your firm to deal with complaints promptly, fairly and effectively. In order to ensure complaints are dealt with fairly, the procedure should be clear and easy for clients to use, allowing complaints to be made by any reasonable means. (This is particularly important in relation to clients who may be vulnerable or have a disability). Any arrangements must also comply with rule 6 (Equality and diversity). Dealing with complaints effectively requires decisions to be based on a proper investigation of the circumstances leading to the complaint and offering an appropriate remedy or redress to the client where necessary. To ensure complaints are dealt with promptly your procedure should include timescales for the various stages of the procedure.

49. If a complaint is made to the Legal Ombudsman or the Solicitors Regulation Authority the firm will need to be able to demonstrate that is has dealt properly with the complaint with even if you do not consider the complaint to be justified. There are benefits to both your clients and your firm if complaints can be dealt with effectively at firm level, rather than being referred to the Legal Ombudsman. Therefore you should ensure that your complaints procedure is well publicised by, for example, including reference to it on your website or in other promotional literature.

50. Everyone in the firm will need to know about the firm's obligations under the rule and be familiar with the firm's complaints procedure.

51. The rule requires you to provide the client with information about the Legal Ombudsman, both at the outset and, if a complaint is made, at the conclusion of your firm's procedure. This information must include contact details of the Legal Ombudsman, and details of the time limits for making a complaint. These can be found at www.legalombudsman.org.uk.

52. Where your client is unhappy with your bill you should treat this like any other complaint about your service. In such circumstances it may be helpful, when responding to the complaint, to provide a detailed narrative of your bill so that your client can clearly understand how the costs were incurred. You may be required to provide the Legal Complaints Service Ombudsman with such a narrative where a complaint about your bill is referred to them. You should inform clients that the Legal Ombudsman may not deal with a complaint about a bill if the client has applied to the court for assessment of that bill.

53.   In some circumstances it will be appropriate for your firm to remind the client at a later stage whom they should approach under the firm's complaints handling procedure if they want to complain (or for your firm to inform the client of this at a later stage if the client has not been told at the outset). This will be appropriate if:

(a)   the client is particularly vulnerable;

(b)   the client is a private client and you are delivering a bill more than two years after the original information was given;

(c)   you are taking your costs from money held on client account, and have not previously supplied the information; or

(d)   you are suing on the bill, and have not previously supplied the information.

Where you or your firm are, in effect, the client – for example, as the executors administering a deceased's estate or as the trustees of a trust – you should consider whether information on complaining about a bill should be given to any person likely to be affected by the bill.

54.   Rule 2.05(3) prevents you charging your client for the cost of handling a complaint. Dealing properly with complaints is an integral part of any professional business. The associated costs are part of the firm's overheads, and complainants must not be charged separately.

55.   Rule 2.05(2) allows for situations where it may be inappropriate to give all the information required.

Commissions – 2.06

56.   Rule 2.06 reflects the legal position, preventing a solicitor making a secret profit arising from the solicitor–client relationship.

57.   A commission:

(a)   is a financial benefit you receive by reason of and in the course of the relationship of solicitor and client; and

(b)   arises in the context that you have put a third party and the client in touch with one another. (See *The Law Society v Mark Hedley Adcock and Neil Kenneth Mocroft* [2006] EWHC 3212 (Admin).)

58.   Examples of what amounts to a commission include payments received from a stockbroker on the purchase of stocks and shares, from an insurance company or an intermediary on the purchase or renewal of an insurance policy, and from a bank or building society on the opening of a bank account. Also, a payment made to you for introducing a client to a third party (unless the introduction was unconnected with any particular matter which you were currently or had been handling for the client) amounts to a commission.

59.   On the other hand, a discount on a product or a rebate on, for example, a search fee would not amount to a commission because it does not arise in the context of referring your client to a third party. Such payments are disbursements and the client must get the benefit of any discount or rebate.

60.   A client can give informed consent only if you:

(a)   provide details concerning the amount; and

(b)   make it clear that they can withhold their consent and, if so, the commission will belong to them when it is received by you.

61.   Commission received may be retained only if the conditions within 2.06 are complied with and the arrangement is in your client's best interests – either:

(a)   it is used to offset a bill of costs; or

(b)   you must be able to justify its retention – for example, the commission is retained in lieu of costs which you could have billed for work done in placing the business, but were not so billed.

62.   It cannot be in the best interests of the client for you to receive the commission as a gift. There must be proper and fair legal consideration, such as your agreement to undertake legal work. In consequence, except where the commission is to be offset against a bill of costs:

(a)   it is important that consent is obtained prior to the receipt of the commission (and preferably before you undertake the work leading to the paying of the commission);

(b)   for the purposes of complying with 2.06 you may not obtain your client's consent to retain the commission after you have received it. If consent is not given beforehand, there can be no legal consideration and so the money belongs to the client; and

(c)   if you have obtained consent but the amount actually received is materially in excess of the estimate given to your client, you cannot retrospectively obtain consent to retain the excess. The excess belongs to your client and should be handled accordingly.

63.   In order to minimise possible confusion and misunderstanding, and to protect both you and your client, it is recommended that the agreement containing the details about the commission be in writing.

64.   If it is your intention from the outset to use the commission to offset a bill of costs, it should be (subject to there being no specific instructions concerning the use of the commission):

(a)   paid into client account as money on account of costs, if received before the bill has been submitted; or

(b)   paid straight into office account if the bill has already been submitted.

65.   Where you intend to retain the commission in lieu of costs and your client has provided their consent in accordance with 2.06, the money may be paid into office account as soon as it is received. Where you have requested your client's consent and it has been refused, the commission will belong to the client on receipt and must be paid into client account. It may then be paid to the client or used to offset a bill subject to note 60 above. See the Solicitors' Accounts Rules 1998 for more information.

66.   Where you are a sole trustee or attorney or a joint trustee or attorney only with other solicitors, you cannot give proper consent to your retaining commission by purporting to switch capacities. Furthermore, you are very likely to be acting contrary to your fiduciary obligations at law.

67.   For further information about dealing with commission see the Solicitors' Financial Services (Scope) Rules 2001.

Limitation of civil liability by contract – 2.07

68.   For the qualifying insurance cover currently required see the Solicitors' Indemnity Insurance Rules.

69.   The details of any limitation must be in writing and brought to the attention of the client. Because such a limitation goes to the heart of the agreement between you and your client, you should ensure that your client knows about the limitation and, in your opinion, understands its effect. Consequently, it would not be appropriate to include the limitation within a "terms of business" letter without specifically drawing your client's attention to it.

70.   Where you are preparing a trust instrument for a client and that instrument includes a

term or terms which has or have the effect of excluding or limiting liability in negligence for a prospective trustee, you should take reasonable steps before the trust is created to ensure that your client is aware of the meaning and effect of the clause. Extra care will be needed if you are, or anyone in or associated with your firm is, or is likely later to become, a paid trustee of the trust.

71. Where you or another person in, or associated with, your firm is considering acting as a paid trustee you should not cause to be included a clause in a trust instrument which has the effect of excluding or limiting liability for negligence without taking reasonable steps before the trust is created to ensure that the settlor is aware of the meaning and effect of the clause.

It would be prudent to ensure both that:

(a) there is evidence that you have taken the appropriate steps; and

(b) that evidence is retained for as long as the trust exists and for a suitable period afterwards.

72. Rule 2.07 is subject to the position in law. The points which follow should be noted. The Solicitors Regulation Authority is entitled to expect you to undertake your own research and/or take appropriate advice as to the general law in this area. Relying upon this guidance alone may not be sufficient to ensure compliance with the law.

(a) Liability for fraud or reckless disregard of professional obligations cannot be limited.

(b) Existing legal restraints cannot be overridden. In particular, the courts will not enforce in your favour an unfair agreement with your client.

(c) Under section 60(5) of the Solicitors Act 1974 and paragraph 24 of Schedule 2 to the Administration of Justice Act 1985, a provision in a contentious business agreement that a firm shall not be liable for negligence, or shall be relieved from any responsibility which would otherwise apply is void.

(d) By section 2(2) of the Unfair Contract Terms Act 1977, a contract term which seeks to exclude liability for negligence is of no effect except insofar as it satisfies the requirement of reasonableness set out in section 11 of that Act. Section 11 specifies that the contract term must be fair and reasonable having regard to the circumstances which were or ought reasonably to have been known to, or in the contemplation of, the parties when the contract was made. Schedule 2 to the Act sets out guidelines as to the factors to be taken into account in considering whether the contract term meets the test of reasonableness.

(e) Section 11(4) of the Unfair Contract Terms Act 1977 provides that where a contractual term seeks to restrict liability to a specified sum of money, the question of whether the requirement of reasonableness has been satisfied must also take into account the resources available to you for the purpose of meeting the liability, and the extent to which insurance is available.

(f) The Unfair Terms in Consumer Contracts Regulations 1999 (SI 1999/2083) have a comparable effect to the Unfair Contract Terms Act 1977 as to limitation or exclusion of liability, where your client is a consumer and the term in question has not been individually negotiated. Regulation 3(1) of the 1999 Regulations defines a consumer as any natural person who, in contracts covered by those Regulations, is acting for purposes which are outside their trade, business or profession. Regulation 5(2) states that a term shall always be regarded as not having been individually negotiated where it has been drafted in advance and the consumer has therefore not been able to influence the substance of the term. Regulation 5(1) provides that a term is unfair if, contrary to the requirements of good faith, it causes a significant imbalance in the parties' rights and obligations. Schedule 2 to the Regulations contains an indicative, non-exhaustive list of contract terms which may be regarded as unfair. The test of fairness under these Regulations is not identical to the test of reasonableness under the Unfair Contract Terms Act 1977.

(g)   When the retainer may be affected by foreign law, such matters may need to be considered according to the law applicable to the contract.

73.   You should also note that if you want to limit your firm's liability to a figure above the minimum level for qualifying insurance but within your firm's top-up insurance cover, you will need to consider whether the top-up insurance will adequately cover a claim arising from the matter in question. For example:

(a)   If your firm agrees with a client that its liability will not exceed £4 million, and the top-up insurance is calculated on an aggregate yearly basis, there is no guarantee that the amount of the top-up cover would be sufficient where there have been multiple claims already.

(b)   Because insurance cover available to meet any particular claim is usually ascertained by reference to the year in which the claim itself is first made, or notice of circumstances which may give rise to a claim is first brought to the attention of insurers, the top-up cover when the claim is brought (or notice of circumstances given) may not be the same as it was when the contract was made.

74.   You will not breach 2.07 by agreeing with your client that liability will rest with your firm and not with any employee, director, member or shareowner who might otherwise be liable. However, any such agreement is subject to section 60(5) of the Solicitors Act 1974, the Unfair Contract Terms Act 1977 and the Unfair Terms in Consumer Contracts Regulations 1999.

75.   Rule 2.07 does not apply in relation to your overseas practice. However, if you are a principal or a recognised body 15.02(3) prohibits you from seeking to limit your civil liability below the minimum level of cover you would need in order to comply with 15.26 (Professional indemnity).

76.   You will not breach 2.07 by a term limiting or excluding any liability to persons who are not your client under the principle in *Hedley Byrne & Co Ltd v Heller & Partners Ltd* [1964] AC 465. However, any such term will be subject to section 60(5) of the Solicitors Act 1974, the Unfair Contract Terms Act 1977 and the Unfair Terms in Consumer Contracts Regulations 1999, where appropriate.

Rule 3 – Conflict of interests

Introduction

Rule 3 sets out provisions for dealing with conflicts of interests. Conflicts between the duty of confidentiality and duty of disclosure owed by an individual or a firm to two or more clients are dealt with in rule 4 (Confidentiality and disclosure).

Rules 3.01 to 3.03 deal with conflicts generally.

Rules 3.04 to 3.06 deal with conflicts in particular high risk situations – gifts from clients, public offices and appointments leading to conflict, and alternative dispute resolution (ADR).

Rules 3.07 to 3.22 deal with conflicts in conveyancing. Note the special meaning of "you" in 3.07 to 3.15 (acting for seller and buyer) and 3.16 to 3.22 (acting for lender and borrower). See also 18.03 which sets out additional requirements which apply to the provision of property selling services.

Rule 3.23 sets out that there is no power to waive 3.01 to 3.05.

Rules 3.07 to 3.22 do not apply to your overseas practice unless the land conveyed is situated in England and Wales.

Rule 3 – Conflict of interests

3.01 Duty not to act

(1)   You must not act if there is a conflict of interests (except in the limited circumstances dealt with in 3.02).

(2)   There is a conflict of interests if:

    (a)   you owe, or your firm owes, separate duties to act in the best interests of two or more clients in relation to the same or related matters, and those duties conflict, or there is a significant risk that those duties may conflict; or

    (b)   your duty to act in the best interests of any client in relation to a matter conflicts, or there is a significant risk that it may conflict, with your own interests in relation to that or a related matter.

(3)   For the purpose of 3.01(2), a related matter will always include any other matter which involves the same asset or liability.

3.02 Exceptions to duty not to act

(1)   You or your firm may act for two or more clients in relation to a matter in situations of conflict or possible conflict if:

    (a)   the different clients have a substantially common interest in relation to that matter or a particular aspect of it; and

    (b)   all the clients have given in writing their informed consent to you or your firm acting.

(2)   Your firm may act for two or more clients in relation to a matter in situations of conflict or possible conflict if:

    (a)   the clients are competing for the same asset which, if attained by one client, will make that asset unattainable to the other client(s);

    (b)   there is no other conflict, or significant risk of conflict, between the interests of any of the clients in relation to that matter;

    (c)   the clients have confirmed in writing that they want your firm to act in the knowledge that your firm acts, or may act, for one or more other clients who are competing for the same asset; and

    (d)   unless the clients specifically agree, no individual acts for, or is responsible for the supervision of, more than one of those clients.

(3)   When acting in accordance with 3.02(1) or (2) it must be reasonable in all the circumstances for you or your firm to act for all those clients.

(4)   If you are relying on the exceptions in 3.02(1) or (2), you must:

    (a)   draw all the relevant issues to the attention of the clients before agreeing to act or, where already acting, when the conflict arises or as soon as is reasonably practicable, and in such a way that the clients concerned can understand the issues and the risks involved;

    (b)   have a reasonable belief that the clients understand the relevant issues; and

    (c)   be reasonably satisfied that those clients are of full capacity.

3.03 Conflict when already acting

If you act, or your firm acts, for more than one client in a matter and, during the course of the conduct of that matter, a conflict arises between the interests of two or more of those clients, you, or your firm, may only continue to act for one of the clients (or a group of clients between whom there is no conflict) provided that the duty of confidentiality to the other client(s) is not put at risk.

3.04 Accepting gifts from clients

Where a client proposes to make a lifetime gift or a gift on death to, or for the benefit of:

    (a)   you;

    (b)   any manager, owner or employee of your firm;

    (c)   a family member of any of the above,

and the gift is of a significant amount, either in itself or having regard to the size of the client's estate and the reasonable expectations of the prospective beneficiaries, you must advise the client to take independent advice about the gift, unless the client is a member of the beneficiary's family. If the client refuses, you must stop acting for the client in relation to the gift.

3.05 Public office or appointment leading to conflict

You must decline to act where you, a member of your family, or a manager, owner or employee of your firm holds some public office or appointment as a result of which:

(a)   a conflict of interests, or a significant risk of a conflict, arises;

(b)   the public might reasonably conclude that you, or your firm, had been able to make use of the office or appointment for the advantage of the client; or

(c)   your ability to advise the client properly and impartially is inhibited.

3.06 Alternative dispute resolution (ADR)

If you provide ADR services you must not:

    (a)   advise or act for any party in respect of a dispute in which you or any person within your firm is acting, or has acted, as mediator;

    (b)   provide ADR services in connection with a matter in which you or any person within your firm has acted for any party; or

    (c)   provide ADR services where you or any person within your firm has acted for any of the parties in issues not relating to the mediation, unless that has been disclosed to the parties and they consent to your acting.

3.07 Acting for seller and buyer in conveyancing, property selling and mortgage related services

(1)   Rules 3.07 to 3.15 apply to the transfer of land for value, and the grant or assignment of a lease or some other interest in land for value. Both commercial and residential conveyancing transactions are covered. The terms "seller" and "buyer"

include a lessor and lessee. "You" is defined in 23.01, but is to be construed in 3.07 to 3.15 as including an associated firm (see rule 24 (Interpretation) for the meaning of "associated firms").

(2) You must not act for more than one party in conveyancing, property selling or mortgage related services other than as permitted by, and in accordance with, 3.08 to 3.15. "Property selling" means negotiating the sale for the seller. "Mortgage related services" means advising on or arranging a mortgage, or providing mortgage related financial services, for a buyer. "Mortgage" includes a remortgage.

3.08 Conveyancing transactions not at arm's length

Subject to the prohibition in 10.06(3) and 10.06(4), you may act for seller and buyer when the transaction between the parties is not at arm's length, provided there is no conflict or significant risk of conflict.

3.09 Conveyancing transactions at arm's length

Subject to the prohibition in 10.06(3) and (4), you may act for seller and buyer if the conditions set out in 3.10 below are satisfied and one of the following applies:

(a) both parties are established clients;

(b) the consideration is £10,000 or less and the transaction is not the grant of a lease; or

(c) seller and buyer are represented by two separate offices in different localities.

3.10 Conditions for acting under 3.09

In order to act for seller and buyer under 3.09 above, the following conditions must be met:

(a) the written consent of both parties must be obtained;

(b) no conflict of interests must exist or arise;

(c) the seller must not be selling or leasing as a builder or developer; and

(d) when the seller and buyer are represented by two separate offices in different localities:

(i) different individuals authorised to do the work, who normally work at each office, conduct or supervise the transaction for seller and buyer; and

(ii) no office of the firm (or an associated firm) referred either client to the office conducting the transactions.

3.11 Property selling and mortgage related services

Subject to the prohibition in 10.06(3) and (4), you may act for seller and buyer if the conditions set out in 3.13 below are satisfied and one of the following applies:

(a) the only way in which you are acting for the buyer is in providing mortgage related services; or

(b) the only way in which you are acting for the seller is in providing property selling services through a Solicitors' Estate Agency Limited (SEAL).

3.12 SEALs and participating firms

A SEAL means a recognised body which:

(a)   is a company;

(b)   does not undertake conveyancing;

(c)   is owned jointly by at least four participating firms which are not associated firms;

(d)   has no participating firm with majority control;

(e)   has at least one participating firm which is a recognised body or recognised sole practitioner; and

(f)   is conducted from accommodation physically divided from, and clearly differentiated from that of any participating firm.

A "participating firm" means a recognised sole practitioner, recognised body or authorised non-SRA firm which is a manager or owner of the SEAL, or one or more of whose managers or owners is a manager or owner of the SEAL.

3.13 Conditions for acting under 3.11

In order to act for seller and buyer under 3.11 above, the following conditions must be met:

(a)   the written consent of both parties must be obtained;

(b)   no conflict of interests must exist or arise;

(c)   the seller must not be selling or leasing as a builder or developer;

(d)   different individuals must conduct the work for the seller and the work for the buyer and, if these individuals need supervision, they must be supervised by different individuals who are authorised to do the work;

(e)   you must inform the seller in writing, before accepting instructions to deal with the property selling, of any services which might be offered to a buyer, whether through the same firm or any associated firm; and

(f)   you must explain to the buyer, before the buyer gives consent to the arrangement:

    (i)   the implications of a conflict of interests arising;

    (ii)   your financial interest in the sale going through; and

    (iii)   if you propose to provide mortgage related services to the buyer through a SEAL which is also acting for the seller, that you cannot advise the buyer on the merits of the purchase.

3.14 Special circumstances in property selling and conveyancing

If any of the circumstances set out in 3.09 apply (established clients; consideration of £10,000 or less; representation by two separate offices), you may sell the property, provide mortgage related services, and act for seller and buyer in the conveyancing, subject to the prohibition in 10.06(3) and (4) and compliance with the conditions set out in 3.10 and 3.13 as appropriate.

3.15 Conflict arising when acting for seller and buyer

If a conflict arises during the course of a transaction in which you are acting for more than one party, you may continue to act for one of the parties only if the duty of confidentiality to the other party is not at risk.

3.16 Acting for lender and borrower in conveyancing transactions

(1)   Rules 3.16 to 3.22 cover the grant of a mortgage of land and are intended to avoid conflicts of interests. "Mortgage" includes a remortgage. Both commercial and residential conveyancing transactions are covered. "You" is defined in 23.01, but is to be construed in 3.16 to 3.22 as including an associated firm (see rule 24 (Interpretation) for the meaning of "associated firms").

(2)   You must not act for both lender and borrower on the grant of a mortgage of land:

    (a)   if a conflict of interests exists or arises;

    (b)   on the grant of an individual mortgage of land at arm's length;

    (c)   if, in the case of a standard mortgage of property to be used as the borrower's private residence only, the lender's mortgage instructions extend beyond the limitations contained in 3.19 and 3.21, or do not permit the use of the certificate of title required by 3.20; or

    (d)   if, in the case of any other standard mortgage, the lender's mortgage instructions extend beyond the limitations contained in 3.19 and 3.21.

3.17 Standard and individual mortgages

(1)   A mortgage is a "standard mortgage" where:

    (a)   it is provided in the normal course of the lender's activities;

    (b)   a significant part of the lender's activities consists of lending; and

    (c)   the mortgage is on standard terms.

An "individual mortgage" is any other mortgage.

(2)   A mortgage will not be on standard terms if material terms in any of the documents relating to the mortgage transaction are negotiated between the lender's and borrower's lawyers contemporaneously with effecting the mortgage. In commercial transactions, the element of negotiation will often relate to the facility letter or facility agreement rather than the mortgage deed itself.

(3)   Provided there has been no contemporaneous negotiation of material terms between the parties' lawyers, a mortgage will be on standard terms where the lender uses a prescribed form of mortgage deed. Minor variations, such as the usual clause limiting the liability of trustee mortgagors, are not regarded as material and do not alter the nature of these terms as standard.

(4)   In addition to its normal standard terms, a lender may have a different set or sets of standard terms applicable to specialised types of borrower, such as registered social landlords. Provided these terms are applied by the lender to all equivalent specialist borrowers or have been agreed between the lender and a specialist borrower as applicable to all transactions between them, they will constitute standard terms for the purposes of 3.16 to 3.22.

(5)   The lender and the borrower must be separately represented on the grant of an individual mortgage at arm's length (see 3.16(2)(b)). Rules 3.16 to 3.22 are not then applicable.

(6) You may act for both lender and borrower in a standard mortgage (see 3.16(2)(c) to (d)), provided:

    (a)   there is no conflict of interests;

    (b)   the mortgage instructions do not go beyond the limits set out in 3.19; and

    (c)   in the case of a property to be used solely as the borrower's private residence, the approved certificate of title set out in the annex to rule 3 is used.

(7) The limitations of 3.19 also apply to a standard mortgage where the lender and the borrower are separately represented (see 3.22(1) which includes certificates of title). However, 3.22(2) allows the borrower's lawyer, in a transaction where the property is not to be used solely as the borrower's private residence, to give a certificate of title in any form recognised by the Solicitors Regulation Authority Board. You also remain free to give any other form of certificate which complies with this rule.

(8) There may be cases where the lapse of time between the mortgage offer and completion (for example, when new properties are added) results in use of an earlier edition of a recognised certificate. That is acceptable.

3.18 Notification of certain circumstances to lender

(1) If you wish to act for both lender and borrower on the grant of a standard mortgage of land, you must first inform the lender in writing of the circumstances if:

    (a)   the prospective borrower is:

        (i)   the firm or any of its managers or owners, or a member of their immediate family;

        (ii)   an associated firm, any of its managers or owners, or a member of their immediate family; and/or

        (iii)   the individual conducting or supervising the transaction, or a member of their immediate family; or

    (b)   you propose to act for seller, buyer and lender in the same transaction.

(2) "Immediate family" means spouse, children, parents, brothers and sisters.

3.19 Types of instruction which may be accepted

If acting for both lender and borrower in a standard mortgage, you and the individual conducting or supervising the transaction may only accept or act upon instructions from the lender which are limited to the following matters:

    (a)   (i)   taking reasonable steps to check the identity of the borrower (and anyone else required to sign the mortgage deed or other document connected with the mortgage) by reference to a document or documents, such as a passport, precisely specified in writing by the lender;

        (ii)   following the guidance given by the Law Society or the Solicitors Regulation Authority on property fraud and on money laundering;

        (iii)   checking that the seller's conveyancers (if unknown to you) appear in a current legal directory or hold practising certificates issued by their professional body; and

        (iv)   in the case of a lender with no branch office within reasonable proximity of the borrower, carrying out the money laundering checks precisely specified in writing by the lender;

(b) making appropriate searches relating to the property in public registers (for example, local searches, commons registration searches, mining searches), and reporting any results specified by the lender or which you consider may adversely affect the lender; or effecting search insurance;

(c) making enquiries on legal matters relating to the property reasonably specified by the lender, and reporting the replies;

(d) reporting the purchase price stated in the transfer and on how the borrower says that the purchase money (other than the mortgage advance) is to be provided; and reporting if you will not have control over the payment of all the purchase money (other than a deposit paid to an estate agent or a reservation fee paid to a builder or developer);

(e) reporting if the seller or the borrower (if the property is already owned by the borrower) has not owned or been the registered owner of the property for at least six months;

(f) if the lender does not arrange insurance, confirming receipt of satisfactory evidence that the buildings insurance is in place for at least the sum required by the lender and covers the risks specified by the lender; giving notice to the insurer of the lender's interest and requesting confirmation that the insurer will notify the lender if the policy is not renewed or is cancelled; and supplying particulars of the insurance and the last premium receipt to the lender;

(g) investigating title to the property and appurtenant rights; reporting any defects revealed, advising on the need for any consequential statutory declarations or indemnity insurance, and approving and effecting indemnity cover if required by the lender; and reporting if you are aware of any rights needed for the use or enjoyment of the property over other land;

(h) reporting on any financial charges (for example, improvement or repair grants or Housing Act discounts) secured on the property revealed by your searches and enquiries which will affect the property after completion of the mortgage;

(i) in the case of a leasehold property:

   (i) confirming that the lease contains the terms stipulated by the lender and does not include any terms specified by the lender as unacceptable;

   (ii) obtaining a suitable deed of variation or indemnity insurance if the terms of the lease are unsatisfactory;

   (iii) enquiring of the seller or the borrower (if the property is already owned by the borrower) as to any known breaches of covenant by the landlord or any superior landlord and reporting any such breaches to the lender;

   (iv) reporting if you become aware of the landlord's absence or insolvency;

   (v) making a company search and checking the last three years' published accounts of any management company with responsibilities under the lease;

   (vi) if the borrower is required to be a shareholder in the management company, obtaining the share certificate, a blank stock transfer form signed by the borrower and a copy of the memorandum and articles of association;

        (vii) obtaining any necessary consent to or prior approval of the assignment and mortgage;

        (viii) obtaining a clear receipt for the last payment of rent and service charge; and

        (ix) serving notice of the assignment and mortgage on the landlord;

(j)   in the case of a commonhold unit:

        (i) confirming receipt of satisfactory evidence that common parts insurance is in place for at least the sum required by the lender and covers the risks specified by the lender;

        (ii) confirming that the commonhold community statement contains the terms specified by the lender and does not include any restrictions on occupation or use specified by the lender as unacceptable;

        (iii) enquiring of the seller (or the borrower if the property is already owned by the borrower) and the commonhold association as to any known breaches of the commonhold community statement by the commonhold association or any unit-holder, and reporting any such breaches to the lender;

        (iv) making a company search to verify that the commonhold association is in existence and remains registered, and that there is no registered indication that it is to be wound up;

        (v) obtaining the last three years' published accounts of the commonhold association and reporting any apparent problems with the association to the lender;

        (vi) obtaining a commonhold unit information certificate; and

        (vii) serving notice of the transfer and mortgage of the commonhold unit on the commonhold association;

(k)   if the property is subject to a letting, checking that the type of letting and its terms comply with the lender's requirements;

(l)   making appropriate pre-completion searches, including a bankruptcy search against the borrower, any other person in whom the legal estate is vested and any guarantor;

(m)   receiving, releasing and transmitting the mortgage advance, including asking for any final inspection needed and dealing with any retentions and cashbacks;

(n)   procuring execution of the mortgage deed and form of guarantee as appropriate by the persons whose identities have been checked in accordance with any requirements of the lender under (a) above as those of the borrower, any other person in whom the legal estate is vested and any guarantor; obtaining their signatures to the forms of undertaking required by the lender in relation to the use, occupation or physical state of the property; and complying with the lender's requirements if any document is to be executed under a power of attorney;

(o)   asking the borrower for confirmation that the information about occupants given in the mortgage instructions or offer is correct; obtaining consents in the form required by the lender from existing or prospective occupiers of the property aged 17 or over specified by the lender, or of whom you are aware;

(p)   advising the borrower on the terms of any document required by the lender to be signed by the borrower;

(q) advising any other person required to sign any document on the terms of that document or, if there is a conflict of interests between that person and the borrower or the lender, advising that person on the need for separate legal advice and arranging for them to see an independent conveyancer;

(r) obtaining the legal transfer of the property to the mortgagor;

(s) procuring the redemption of:

    (i) existing mortgages on property the subject of any associated sale of which you are aware; and

    (ii) any other mortgages secured against a property located in England or Wales made by an identified lender where an identified account number or numbers or a property address has been given by the lender;

(t) ensuring the redemption or postponement of existing mortgages on the property, and registering the mortgage with the priority required by the lender;

(u) making administrative arrangements in relation to any collateral security, such as an endowment policy, or in relation to any collateral warranty or guarantee relating to the physical condition of the property, such as NHBC documentation;

(v) registering the transfer and mortgage;

(w) giving legal advice on any matters reported on under 3.19, suggesting courses of action open to the lender, and complying with the lender's instructions on the action to be taken;

(x) disclosing any relationship specified by the lender between you and the borrower;

(y) storing safely the title deeds and documents pending registration and delivery to or as directed by the lender; and

(z) retaining the information contained in your conveyancing file for at least six years from the date of the mortgage.

3.20 Using the approved certificate of title

In addition, if acting for both lender and borrower in a standard mortgage of property to be used as the borrower's private residence only:

(a) you must use the certificate of title set out in the annex to rule 3 (below) ("the approved certificate"); and

(b) unless the lender has certified that its mortgage instructions are subject to the limitations contained in 3.19 above and 3.21 below, you must notify the lender on receipt of instructions that the approved certificate will be used, and that your duties to the lender are limited to the matters contained in the approved certificate.

3.21 Terms of rule to prevail

The terms of 3.16 to 3.20 above will prevail in the event of any ambiguity in the lender's instructions, or discrepancy between the instructions and 3.19 above or the approved certificate.

3.22 Anti-avoidance

(1)   Subject to (2) below, if acting only for the borrower in a standard mortgage of property you must not accept or act upon any requirements by way of undertaking, warranty, guarantee or otherwise of the lender, the lender's lawyer or other agent which extend beyond the limitations contained in 3.19.

(2)   Provided the property is not to be used solely as the borrower's private residence, (1) above does not prevent you from giving any form of certificate of title recognised from time to time by the Solicitors Regulation Authority Board (a "recognised certificate"). Additions or amendments which arise from the individual transaction may be made to the text of a recognised certificate but, to the extent to which they create an increased or additional obligation, must not extend beyond the limitations contained in 3.19.

3.23 Waivers

In spite of 22.01(1) (Waivers), the Solicitors Regulation Authority Board shall not have power to waive any of the provisions of 3.01 to 3.05.

ANNEX

Certificate of title

Details box

TO: (Lender)

Lender's Reference or Account No:

The Borrower:

Property:

Title Number:

Mortgage Advance:

Price stated in transfer:

Completion Date:

Conveyancer's Name & Address:

Conveyancer's Reference:

Conveyancer's bank, sort code and account number:

Date of instructions:

WE THE CONVEYANCERS NAMED ABOVE CERTIFY as follows:

(1)   If so instructed, we have checked the identity of the Borrower (and anyone else required to sign the mortgage deed or other document connected with the mortgage) by reference to the document or documents precisely specified in writing by you.

(2)   Except as otherwise disclosed to you in writing:

   (i)   we have investigated the title to the Property, we are not aware of any other financial charges secured on the Property which will affect the Property after completion of the mortgage and, upon completion of the mortgage, both you and the mortgagor (whose identity has been checked in accordance with paragraph (1) above) will have a good and marketable title to the Property and to appurtenant rights free from prior mortgages or charges and from onerous encumbrances which title will be registered with absolute title;

   (ii)   we have compared the extent of the Property shown on any plan provided by you against relevant plans in the title deeds and/or the description of the Property in any valuation which you have supplied to us, and in our opinion there are no material discrepancies;

   (iii) the assumptions stated by the valuer about the title (its tenure, easements, boundaries and restrictions on use) in any valuation which you have supplied to us are correct;

   (iv)   if the Property is leasehold the terms of the lease accord with your instructions, including any requirements you have for covenants by the Landlord and/or a management company and/or by a deed of mutual covenant for the insurance, repair and maintenance of the structure, exterior and common parts of any building of which the Property forms part, and we have or will obtain on or before completion a clear receipt for the last payment of rent and service charge;

   (v)   if the Property is a commonhold unit, the commonhold community statement contains the terms specified by you and does not include any restrictions on occupation or use specified by you as unacceptable, and we have or will obtain on or before completion a commonhold unit information certificate;

   (vi)   we have received satisfactory evidence that the buildings insurance is in place, or will be on completion, for the sum and in the terms required by you;

   (vii) if the Property is to be purchased by the Borrower:

       (a)   the contract for sale provides for vacant possession on completion;

       (b)   the seller has owned or been the registered owner of the Property for not less than six months; and

       (c)   we are not acting on behalf of the seller;

   (viii) we are in possession of:

       (a)   either a local search or local search insurance; and

       (b)   such other searches or search insurance as are appropriate to the Property, the mortgagor and any guarantor, in each case in accordance with your instructions;

   (ix)   nothing has been revealed by our searches and enquiries which would prevent the Property being used by any occupant for residential purposes; and

   (x)   neither any principal nor any other individual in the firm giving this certificate nor any spouse, child, parent, brother or sister of such a person is interested in the Property (whether alone or jointly with any other) as mortgagor.

WE:

(a)   undertake, prior to use of the mortgage advance, to obtain in the form required by you the execution of a mortgage and a guarantee as appropriate by the persons whose identities have been checked in accordance with paragraph (1) above as those of the Borrower, any other person in whom the legal estate is vested and any guarantor; and, if required by you:

        (i)   to obtain their signatures to the forms of undertaking required by you in relation to the use, occupation or physical state of the Property;

        (ii)   to ask the Borrower for confirmation that the information about occupants given in your mortgage instructions or offer is correct; and

        (iii)   to obtain consents in the form required by you from any existing or prospective occupier(s) aged 17 or over of the Property specified by you or of whom we are aware;

(b)   have made or will make such Bankruptcy, Land Registry or Land Charges Searches as may be necessary to justify certificate no. (2)(i) above;

(c)   will within the period of protection afforded by the searches referred to in paragraph (b) above:

        (i)   complete the mortgage;

        (ii)   arrange for the issue of a stamp duty land tax certificate if appropriate;

        (iii)   deliver to the Land Registry the documents necessary to register the mortgage in your favour and any relevant prior dealings; and

        (iv)   effect any other registrations necessary to protect your interests as mortgagee;

(d)   will despatch to you such deeds and documents relating to the Property as you require with a list of them in the form prescribed by you within ten working days of receipt by us of the title information document from the Land Registry;

(e)   will not part with the mortgage advance (and will return it to you if required) if it shall come to our notice prior to completion that the Property will at completion be occupied in whole or in part otherwise than in accordance with your instructions;

(f)   will not accept instructions, except with your consent in writing, to prepare any lease or tenancy agreement relating to the Property or any part of it prior to despatch of the title information document to you;

(g)   will not use the mortgage advance until satisfied that, prior to or contemporaneously with the transfer of the Property to the mortgagor, there will be discharged:

        (i)   any existing mortgage on property the subject of an associated sale of which we are aware; and

        (ii)   any other mortgages made by a lender identified by you secured against a property located in England or Wales where you have given either an account number or numbers or a property address;

(h)   will notify you in writing if any matter comes to our attention before completion which would render the certificate given above untrue or inaccurate and, in those circumstances, will defer completion pending your authority to proceed and will return the mortgage advance to you if required; and

(i)   confirm that we have complied, or will comply, with your instructions in all other respects to the extent that they do not extend beyond the limitations contained in the Solicitors' Code of Conduct 2007, 3.19 (Conflict of interests – types of instruction which may be accepted).

OUR duties to you are limited to the matters set out in this certificate and we accept no further liability or responsibility whatsoever. The payment by you to us (by whatever means) of the mortgage advance or any part of it constitutes acceptance of this limitation and any assignment to you by the Borrower of any rights of action against us to which the Borrower may be entitled shall take effect subject to this limitation.

Signature box

SIGNED on behalf of
THE
CONVEYANCERS   ....

NAME of
Authorised Signatory   ....

QUALIFICATION
of Authorised
Signatory   ....

DATE of Signature   ....

Guidance to rule 3 – Conflict of interests

Conflict is defined – 3.01

1.   Conflict is defined as a conflict between the duties to act in the best interests of two or more different clients, or between your interests and those of a client. The definition appears in 3.01(2). This will encompass all situations where doing the best for one client in a matter will result in prejudice to another client in that matter or a related matter.

2.   The definition of conflict in 3.01(2) requires you to assess when two matters are "related". Rule 3.01(3) makes it clear that if the two matters concern the same asset or liability, then they are "related". Accordingly, if you act for one client which is negotiating with publishers for the publication of a novel, an instruction from another client alleging that the novel is plagiarised and breaches copyright would be a related matter.

3.   However, there would need to be some reasonable degree of relationship for a conflict to arise. If you act for a company on a dispute with a garage about the cost of repairs to a company car, your firm would not be prevented from acting for a potential bidder for the company, even though the car is a minor asset of the company and would be included in the purchase. If you act for a client selling a business, you might conclude that your firm could also act for a prospective purchaser on the creation of an employee share scheme which would cover all the entities in the purchaser's group, this work perhaps requiring the future inclusion of the target within the scheme and consideration as to whether this raised any particular issues.

4.   In each case, you will need to make a judgement on the facts. In making this judgement, you might want to consider the view of your existing client where you are professionally able to raise the issue with him or her. You should also take care to consider whether your firm holds any confidential information from your existing client which would be relevant to the new instructions and if so, to ensure that you comply with rule 4 (Confidentiality and disclosure).

You are or your firm is permitted to act with clients' consent in defined circumstances of conflict subject to suitable safeguards

5.   This reflects the fact that there may be circumstances in which, despite peripheral or

potential conflict, the clients' best interests are served by you, or your firm, being able to act for two or more clients who are able to give informed consent. The circumstances in which you could act despite a conflict are set out in 3.02.

6.   Two different situations are defined. These are in 3.02(1) and (2):

(a)   (i)   Rule 3.02(1) deals with the situation where the clients have a "common interest", they all want to continue to instruct you and it would be disproportionate, for example, in terms of cost and general disruption to their matter, to require them to instruct separate solicitors.

(ii)   For there to be a "common interest" there must be a clear common purpose and a strong consensus on how it is to be achieved. However, it will be for you to decide objectively on the facts in each case whether there is a "common interest" and it is appropriate to act. In making this decision, you should always consider whether the clients will be represented even-handedly with equal weight being given to the instructions from each.

(iii)   The "common interest" might arise, for example, where you are acting for several members of a family in relation to their affairs or acting for various individuals in the setting up of a company. Any areas of conflict must be substantially less important to all the clients than their common purpose and may, for example, relate to slightly different views on how the common purpose is to be achieved. It will be your duty to keep the differences under review with the clients and to decide if the point has been reached when it would be untenable to continue to represent all of them in a fair and open manner or without any of them being prejudiced.

(iv)   There exist some multi-party complex commercial transactions, where sophisticated users of legal services, who have a common purpose, may expect a firm to act for two or more parties, because this will facilitate efficient handling of the matter (taking into account amongst other things the desire to complete the transaction quickly, the availability of necessary experience/expertise and the overall costs). Indeed in many cases it may already be accepted business practice for firms to act in this manner. An example is acting for different tiers of lenders (for example senior lenders and mezzanine lenders) and/or different parties (for example arrangers/underwriters and bond/security trustees) in entering into a financing transaction where there is already an agreed or commonly understood structure with regard to the ranking of their respective claims, the content of their respective obligations and associated commercial issues.

(v)   While accepted business practice can be considered as a factor in determining whether an appropriate common purpose exists, you and your firm should always exercise caution when proposing to act in accordance with 3.02 and should be mindful of the residual test of reasonableness referred to in 3.02(3).

(vi)   In some situations it might be possible for you to consider whether the retainer could be limited to those areas where there is no conflict with the clients seeking separate advice on any areas of conflict. This could only be done where the conflict did not undermine the overriding common purpose (see below for further guidance on limiting retainers).

(vii)   In some circumstances it might be possible that, while a conflict would prevent you from acting for another party on all aspects of a matter, a mandate limited to a specific issue where there is common purpose might be accepted. For example, you may be retained by the owner of a company to advise on its disposal. In that case you would not generally be able to advise another party on the purchase of the company. However, in the hope and anticipation of a successful sale a seller client which is a sophisticated user of legal services might agree that you should also accept a limited retainer to provide competition law advice to the prospective purchaser regarding the filings for competition law purposes that would be required in the event that the two businesses were combined.

(viii)   When acting under this exception, especially in family situations, you need to consider the developing legal position. Courts are likely to make a presumption of undue influence where one of the parties who is considered vulnerable through age or other circumstances places trust and confidence in the other party. In any situation of doubt it may well be in the best interests of the clients that they are separately represented.

(b)   (i)   Rule 3.02(2) is intended to apply to specialised areas of legal services where the clients are sophisticated users of those services and conclude that rather than seek out new advisers they would rather use their usual advisers in the knowledge that those advisers might also act for competing interests. An "asset" is not necessarily physical, and can include a contract or a business opportunity. Examples where this exception might apply include:

(A) acting on insolvencies so that a firm can act for more than one creditor;

(B) acting for competing bidders, and/or for those involved with the funding of bidders, for a business being sold by auction; and

(C) acting for competing tenderers submitting tenders to perform a contract.

(ii)   The wording of 3.02(2) is sufficiently wide to permit other transactional work in the commercial field where clients can give consent. Solicitors and their firms should exercise considerable caution when proposing to act in accordance with 3.02(2) in categories of work where to do so is not already accepted business practice.

(iii)   Rule 3.02(2) should not be applied to disputes over assets other than in the context of corporate restructurings and insolvencies.

7.   Reasonableness is an important rider to 3.02. There may be situations where, despite compliance with 3.02, it would still not be reasonable to act. The apparent unequal bargaining position of the parties, concerns about the mental stability of one of the parties, a family arrangement where an elderly parent is providing security for their son's or daughter's business loan, and the importance of one of the clients to the firm may all be situations where instructions to act for both or all parties should be declined. Having accepted instructions you must be satisfied that you can act even-handedly for both or all clients and that, taking into account any limitations in a specific retainer, you do not favour one at the expense of the other(s).

8.   The criterion against which reasonableness will be judged is whether one client is at risk of prejudice because of the lack of separate representation. In relation to all situations where you are proposing to act for two or more clients under the provisions of 3.02, the onus will be on you to demonstrate why it was reasonable to act for all the clients at the time the instructions were accepted. Above all, you must be satisfied that unfettered advice can be given, without fear or favour, to the clients. You must also keep under review whether it remains reasonable to continue to act for them. You should also have regard to 1.04 (Best interests of clients) which requires you to act in the best interests of each of your clients.

9   (a)   Rule 3.02(4) places obligations on you to discuss with the clients the implications of you, or your firm, continuing to act for all of them. You must be satisfied that the clients understand the issues and that their consent is independently and freely given. You should consider setting out in your initial terms of business letter the issues discussed in relation to the conflict of interests and how that might affect your ability to represent both or all of the clients as the matter progresses. Extreme caution will be required where one of the clients is particularly vulnerable due to mental health, language or other problems affecting their understanding of the issues, although where a litigation friend acts for a person who lacks capacity they will be able to consent on that person's behalf. Similarly, you must always be alert to situations where a client might be consenting under duress or·undue influence and in those circumstances must insist on separate representation. For the avoidance of doubt, and for evidential purposes, you should always keep a written record of all discussions with the clients about the implications of your acting for them. You must always obtain all the clients' written consent on each occasion when acting under either of the exceptions.

     (b)   Where seeking informed consent under 3.02(1)(b) you should identify by name the other clients you or your firm propose(s) to act for, or be able to do so when their identities are known. Provided that you do this and comply with the requirements of 3.02(4), the obligation to obtain "informed" consent in 3.02(1)(b) will have been satisfied. Where consent is sought under 3.02(2), you need to comply with the requirements of 3.02(4) but you need not identify by name the other clients you or your firm propose(s) to act for.

10.   When acting for two or more clients on a matter, or a related matter, there may be circumstances where you will have to cease acting for one or both clients. This may be in circumstances where no conflict was apparent when accepting instructions but a conflict subsequently arose or when acting under one of the exceptions and it becomes impossible to fulfil the conditions set out in 3.02. In these circumstances it is important to try and limit the disruption that will inevitably be caused for the clients. One way of doing this is to discuss and agree with the clients at the outset what will happen if a conflict arises and agree which client the firm would continue to represent where this is possible.

11.   The rule does not specifically deal with potential or future conflict, although it does make clear that a significant risk of conflict should prevent a solicitor from acting. You should always be cautious, therefore, about accepting instructions where the possibility of future conflict is evident. The risks should be explained to the clients about the problems and expense which the requirement for future separate representation could bring.

Limited/defined retainers

12.   There may be situations where, when acting for two or more clients, it is appropriate to continue to advise them but necessary to make clear that there are defined areas of conflict on which you cannot advise, and one or more of them may need separate advice. Your retainer with your clients will, when these situations arise, need to be limited to exclude those areas of work or advice. Care must always be taken, however, to ensure that the clients understand:

     (a)   exactly what you are proposing to deal with on their behalf; and

     (b)   those contested areas which are to be excluded from the retainer.

13.   A limited retainer would be unlikely to be appropriate in any situation where one of the clients was disadvantaged in some way as against the other. This might be because of an unequal bargaining position or because one had some form of disability. In any

situation where you agree to act for two or more clients by limiting the retainer it is important that you keep all developments under review to ensure that it remains appropriate to continue to act.

Professional embarrassment

14. There may be some circumstances in which you should refuse instructions when, although there is no actual conflict of interests as defined in rule 3, you might feel unable to do your best for a client because of some form of professional embarrassment. It may be, for example, that if you have acted for a client in the past and accept instructions to act against that client you may feel inhibited in doing your best for the new client because of the past relationship with the former client. If so, the instructions from the new client should be refused as you would, otherwise, be in breach of core duties 1.03 (Independence) and 1.04 (Best interests of clients).

15. There may also be situations where you and your firm are asked to act with consent, using an information barrier in accordance with rule 4 (Confidentiality and disclosure), but the information you hold and which you cannot disclose to your client is of such a nature that it would cause severe embarrassment to your firm if, or when, it later came to light that your firm held such information. It may be, for example, that you are asked to act for a client on the acquisition of a business in circumstances where confidential information is held by your firm that the business has a serious problem with its accounts. Similarly, it may be that you are asked to prepare an employment contract for a company which is planning to recruit an individual who is known, confidentially, to be under investigation for fraud. In those circumstances you and your firm would be seriously embarrassed acting for a client who you knew was wasting legal fees on an outcome the client would not want to pursue if in possession of the knowledge held by your firm. It could be argued that you are not acting in the best interests of the client (see 1.04 (Best interests of clients)) or that you are damaging public confidence in the profession (see 1.06 (Public confidence)).

16. Where professional embarrassment is not a factor and the circumstances which would otherwise prevent you from acting in 4.03 (duty not to put confidentiality at risk by acting) do not arise, it will be a purely commercial decision as to whether you should act against the interests of another client or former client, provided there is no conflict as defined in 3.01 or 3.02.

In-house practice

17. If you are employed as an in-house lawyer your employer is your client. The nature of this relationship may cause problems because you do not have the same freedom as a firm would have to decline instructions. There may be occasions, for example, when you are asked to advise your employer in situations where conflict or potential conflict arises between your interests and the interests of your employer. These include:

    (a) where your personal interests as an employee may conflict with the interests of your employer who wants advice on a course of action which could be detrimental to you as an employee where, for example, a merger could lead to your redundancy;

    (b) where your employer asks you to do something which would place you in breach of your professional obligations, for example, to file a document with the court which you know contains false information; or

    (c) where your employer may act against your advice and, for example, engage in criminal activity which may require you to take action against your employer.

18. In relation to situations where your personal interests may conflict with a course of action proposed by your employer you need not necessarily be excluded from advising your employer. Your employer will usually be aware of exactly how you will be affected

by its proposals, and if you are able to give objective advice on the legal issues where your expertise is required you would normally be free to do so. There may, however, be situations where you are so affected by the advice you are asked to give that you feel your objectivity and independence are impaired and in those situations you would have to ask your employer to seek other advice, either internally or externally. What is important in these situations is that there is transparency about your interests. Beyond that, you will have to make a judgement about whether you feel you have the necessary objectivity to advise.

19.   If your employer was unaware of your interests – and, therefore, the potential for conflict – the position would be different. If, for example, you had a large shareholding in another company and your employer's proposed action could adversely affect the value of those shares then you would either have to disclose your interest or explain that a conflict prevented you from advising on that issue.

20.   In situations where you are asked to act contrary to your professional obligations then you should not compromise your position and you must refuse to carry out instructions which would have this result, even if ultimately this led to the loss of your job.

21.   There may be situations where there is a positive legal obligation on you to take action against your employer where, for example, your employer is engaging in money laundering or where there are "whistle blowing" obligations. Legal issues of this nature are beyond the remit of this guidance. They are situations where your relationship with your employer has reached the stage where you would need to consider the advisability of seeking legal advice on your own position.

22.   Finally, as an in-house lawyer you are, under rule 13 (In-house practice), able to act for a limited number of other bodies and individuals. For example, if employed by a company, you may act for a holding, associated or subsidiary company of that company employer. If you do so you must ensure that you do not act in any situation where there would be a conflict between the interests of your employer and the other company for whom you are also acting (see 13.01 and 13.03). Similarly, if employed in local government you may act, for example, for local councillors in certain circumstances, provided you can comply with rule 3.

Co-defendants

23.   In publicly funded cases, regulations require that one solicitor be appointed to act for all co-defendants in a legal aid case unless there is, or is likely to be, a conflict. The purpose of this is to ensure economy in the use of public funds by ensuring that a single solicitor represents co-defendants where it is proper to do so. The professional conduct obligations which deal with conflicts of interest have always prevented a solicitor or firm acting for two or more clients where there is a conflict or significant risk of a conflict arising between the interests of two or more clients. A solicitor can act, however, for co-defendants where conflict is not a factor. The difficulty often lies, however, in spotting potential conflict and deciding whether it is sufficiently real to refuse instructions.

24.   Your starting point should always be your fundamental professional obligation to act in each client's best interests. Can you discharge this obligation to each client? This means first asking each client if they are aware of any actual or potential conflict between them and then, if they indicate that there is no such conflict, asking yourself whether you feel there are any constraints on the advice you would want to give to one client, or on the action you would want to take on that client's behalf, which are likely to arise because you act for another co-defendant.

25.   A conflict of interest arises wherever there is a constraint of that sort, for example where it is in the best interests of client A:

(a)   to give evidence against client B;

(b)   to make a statement incriminating client B;

(c)   to implicate client B in a police interview;

(d)   to provide prejudicial information regarding client B to an investigator;

(e)   to cross-examine client B in such a manner as to call into question his or her credibility;

(f)   to rely upon confidential information given by client B without his or her consent; or

(g)   to adopt tactics in the course of the retainer which potentially or actually harm client B.

26.   If these obligations actually come into conflict when acting for two or more clients you will have to cease to act for one and often both. This can cause considerable disruption and expense, which is why the rules require that you should not accept instructions if there is a significant risk of this happening.

27.   Many criminal clients will, of course, have retained you at the police station prior to a police interview and are thus not at that stage defendants. The obligations referred to above apply at this early stage, and you must be satisfied that accepting instructions on behalf of a client prior to a police interview does not place you in conflict with another client who is also to be interviewed. In order to assess whether you can act for both clients it is important that you do not interview the clients together and that you get instructions which are as full as possible from the first client before any substantive contact with the second client. However, never let the police deter you from seeing the second client because they think there is a conflict – that decision must be yours.

28.   A further consideration when taking instructions at the police station, especially out of office hours when an immediate conflict check is not possible, is that the firm may already act for another defendant in that matter or information obtained at the police station may be relevant to another client on an unrelated matter. For example, the firm may be acting in divorce proceedings for a wife where violence is alleged and information that her husband has been charged with an offence involving violence would be relevant and may make it impossible to continue acting for the wife. This highlights the importance of carrying out a conflict check at the earliest opportunity.

29.   When considering accepting instructions from more than one client in the same matter you need to assess not only whether there is a conflict at the outset, but whether events are likely to arise which will prevent you from continuing to act for one or both at a later stage in the proceedings. In almost all cases there will be some possibility of differences in instructions between the clients but the rules do not prevent you acting unless the risk of conflict is significant. Assessing the risk is often not easy. It is also important that where you have accepted instructions from co-defendants you remain alert to the risk of conflict arising as the case progresses.

30.   When considering whether there is an actual conflict there are obvious indicators such as whether the clients have differing accounts of the important relevant circumstances of the alleged crime or where one seems likely to change his or her plea. There are also less obvious indicators. These would include situations where there is some clear inequality between the co-defendants which might, for example, suggest that one client is acting under the influence of the other rather than on his or her own initiative. If you are acting for both this may make it difficult for you to raise and discuss these issues equally with them. In trying to help one, you might be undermining the other. If you believe you are going to be unable to do your best for one without worrying about whether this might prejudice the other you should only accept instructions from one.

31.   The risk of future conflict can be an even more difficult issue to assess. It may be that you have two clients who are pleading not guilty and who are apparently in total agreement on the factual evidence. Should they both be found guilty, you need to consider at the outset whether you would be able to mitigate fully and freely on behalf of one client without in so doing harming the interests of the other. It may be that one has a long list of convictions and is considerably older than the other. If so, it may be

that the younger client with a comparatively clean record was led astray or pressurised into committing the crime and would want you to emphasise this in mitigation. If there is a significant risk of this happening you should not accept instructions from both.

32.   Even where care is taken when accepting instructions from more than one client in the same matter there will inevitably be situations where a conflict subsequently arises. This will commonly happen where one defendant changes his or her plea or evidence. A decision will then have to be taken as to whether it is proper to continue to represent one client or whether both will have to instruct new firms. In making this decision you need to consider whether in the changed circumstances your duty to disclose all relevant information to the retained client will place you in breach of your duty of confidentiality to the other client. In other words, you need to decide whether you hold confidential information about the departing client which is now relevant to the retained client. If you do have such information then you cannot act for either client.

33.   Following changes to regulations affecting publicly funded cases, some practitioners have reported pressure from some court clerks on solicitors to represent co-defendants even where there is a clear risk of conflict. Similar pressure has been applied by police at police stations prior to interviews. However, the professional rules of conduct preclude you acting for both clients in those circumstances, and the regulations are not intended to put solicitors in a position where they are asked to act contrary to their professional responsibilities. If asked by the court for your reasons why you cannot act for both defendants, you must not give information which would breach your duty of confidentiality to your client(s). This will normally mean that you can say no more than that it would be unprofessional for you to continue to act.

34.   For the avoidance of doubt, you cannot resolve a conflict by instructing another firm or counsel to undertake the advocacy on behalf of one client. Neither can you pass one of the clients to another member of your firm. The rules make it quite clear that your firm cannot act for clients whose interests conflict.

35.   Any decision to act, or not to act, for co-defendants should be recorded with a brief note of the reasons.

Mediation

36.   There is no objection to your acting as a conciliator and mediator between parties in a dispute. However, in so acting you should have regard to the appropriate codes of practice such as those issued by the Law Society from time to time. These codes provide detailed guidance on dealing with conflict when acting as mediators.

Local authority client

37.   If tendering for local authority work, your firm will need to consider how frequently the range of work is likely to give rise to conflicts between existing clients and the local authority, for example, in housing and custody matters where the firm acts against the local authority.

Insolvency practice

38.   If you are a licensed insolvency practitioner you must consider whether any relationship which you have, or your firm has, with clients or others might affect your independence and create a conflict preventing you accepting an appointment to administer an insolvent estate or bankruptcy. See also rule 17 (Insolvency practice).

Your interests conflicting with the client's — 3.01(2)(b)

39. There are no circumstances where you can act for a client whose interests conflict with your own interests. The situations outlined in 3.02 where you can act for two or more clients whose interests conflict have no application in this situation. This is because of the fiduciary relationship which exists between you and your client which prevents you taking advantage of the client or acting where there is a conflict or potential conflict of interests between you and your client. Examples appear below.

40. In conduct there is a conflict of interests where you in your personal capacity sell to, or buy from, or lend to, or borrow from, your client. In all these cases you should insist the client takes independent legal advice. If the client refuses you must not proceed with the transaction.

41. You should never enter into any arrangement or understanding with a client or prospective client prior to the conclusion of a matter under which you acquire an interest in the publication rights with respect to that matter. This applies equally to non-contentious business.

42. Whilst you are entitled to take security for costs you should be aware of the risk of the court finding undue influence. Before you do take a charge over a client's property it is advisable, therefore, to suggest the client consider seeking independent legal advice. Such advice would not normally be essential unless the terms of the proposed charge are particularly onerous or would give you some unusual benefit or profit. It is, however, important always to ensure that the client understands that a charge is being taken and the effect of such a charge.

43. You are not able to secure costs by a first legal charge over your client's property if this means that you are entering into a regulated mortgage contract as a lender. A regulated mortgage contract is an investment which is regulated by the Financial Services Authority (FSA). It arises where the lender provides credit to an individual or trustee, and it is secured by a first legal mortgage on land which is in the United Kingdom, and at least 40% of the land is, or is to be, used as a dwelling by the borrower or, where the borrower is a trustee, by a beneficiary of the trust or by a related person. You must be authorised by the FSA in order to secure your costs in this way. Detailed guidance on this is in the booklet "Financial Services and Solicitors" available from the Professional Ethics Guidance Team.

44. You must always disclose with complete frankness whenever you have, or might obtain, any personal interest or benefit in a transaction in which you are acting for the client. In such circumstances, you must insist that the client receives independent advice.

45. Independent advice means both legal advice and, where appropriate, competent advice from a member of another profession, e.g. a chartered surveyor.

46. Your interests referred to in this rule may be direct (for example, where you seek to sell to or buy property from the client or lend to, or borrow from, the client), or indirect (for example, where your business interests lead you to recommend the client to invest in a concern in which you are interested).

47. This rule applies, therefore, not only where you are personally interested in a transaction, but equally where another person working in your firm has an interest of which you are aware and it impairs your ability to give independent and impartial advice.

48. The interests envisaged by this rule are not restricted to those of a primarily economic nature only. For example, if you become involved in a sexual relationship with a client you must consider whether this may place your interests in conflict with those of the client or otherwise impair your ability to act in the best interests of the client.

49. If you are a director of a company for which you act, or own shares in the company, you must consider whether you are in a position of conflict when asked to advise the company upon steps it has taken or should take. It may sometimes be necessary to

resign from the board or for another solicitor (including a solicitor from the same firm if appropriate) to advise the company in a particular matter where your own interests conflict, or are likely to conflict. If acting for a company in which you have a personal interest you should always ensure that your ability to give independent and impartial advice is not, for that reason, impaired.

50. If you hold a power of attorney for a client you must not use that power to gain a benefit which, if acting as a professional adviser to that client, you would not be prepared to allow to an independent third party. This applies regardless of the legal position, for example, as to whether you could lend the donor's money to yourself.

51. You are free to negotiate your terms of business, including costs, with your clients. This includes negotiating conditional fees which are subject to statutory regulation. In all these negotiations you are not acting for the client. There may be situations, however, where the terms of business are particularly unusual and it would be prudent for you to suggest the client seeks independent advice. It would be advisable to do so if, for example, as part, or all, of your remuneration you are to receive shares in a company you are setting up on behalf of your client.

52. You need to consider whether the conditional fee agreement involves you in insurance mediation activities, such as arranging and/or advising on after the event insurance contracts, etc. Solicitors who carry on insurance mediation activities either need to be able to comply with the Solicitors' Financial Services (Scope) Rules 2001 or be authorised by the FSA. Detailed guidance is in the booklet *Financial Services and Solicitors* available from the Professional Ethics Guidance Team.

53. You must always be careful to ensure that any settlement achieved for a client, or any advice given in a non-contentious matter conducted on a contingency fee basis, is in the client's best interests and not made with a view to your obtaining your fee.

54. Where you discover an act or omission which would justify a claim against you, you must inform the client, and recommend they seek independent advice. You must also inform the client that independent advice should be sought in cases where the client makes a claim against you, or notifies an intention to do so. If the client refuses to seek independent advice, you should not continue to act unless you are satisfied that there is no conflict of interest. See 20.09 (Dealing with claims).

Accepting gifts from clients – 3.04

55. Rule 3.04 does not prevent you accepting a client's gift but does require the client to take independent advice where the gift is significant, or significant as compared with the client's likely estate and the reasonable expectations of prospective beneficiaries.

56. Rule 3.04 allows you to prepare a will for a family member under which you receive a significant gift without requiring the client to seek independent advice on that gift. However, extreme caution should always be exercised in these circumstances as your ability to give independent, dispassionate advice could easily be undermined by your relationship with others within, and outside, the family. The risk of conflict, therefore, is very high. If you are to receive a significant gift from the estate you need also to consider the reasonable expectations of the other prospective beneficiaries, who are likely to be your relatives. If, having taken these reasonable expectations into account, it appears that you are to receive a benefit which is in any way disproportionately large you should always ensure that the client is separately advised on that gift. "Prospective beneficiaries" in the context of this rule means others who would be reasonably expected to benefit because of their relationship to the client and their reasonable expectations would be dependent on the closeness of that relationship. An objective test would be applied in the event of a complaint.

57. There are other factors which should be taken into account when preparing a will for a family member under which you benefit. It may also be far easier for a close family member to talk through their proposals for their will with someone who has no

personal interest in its contents and who is unlikely to be offended by any suggestions they might wish to make. Finally, your relative's bequests are secure from allegations of undue influence if their will is drawn by someone totally independent and who does not take a benefit from it. "Family member" is not defined in 3.04 to allow a flexible approach to be taken. Co-habitants are not included in the exception to independent advice because their legal position is less secure than those related by blood, marriage or adoption.

58. A "significant amount" for the purposes of 3.04 cannot be quantified because the particular circumstances of the proposed gift must be taken into account. In general, however, anything more than a token gift will be considered significant. If, therefore, anything more than a token amount is accepted without the client having separate advice (other than where you are acting for a family member as permitted by 3.04) you may be exposed to allegations of misconduct.

59. When considering whether a gift is of a "significant amount" the date of preparation of the document is relevant when determining the size of the estate.

60. If more than one gift is made to members of a firm, for example, £1,000 to each of the partners in the firm, they should be amalgamated for the purpose of establishing whether the gift is "significant".

61. The implications of 3.04 need to be made clear to all members of your firm who take instructions from clients, whether solicitors or not. Supervision is important to ensure compliance.

62. Where you are given money or property to distribute for the benefit of others, such as in a secret trust, this is not considered to be a "gift" for the purposes of 3.04. However, care should be taken to ensure that records are kept confirming the arrangement and to ensure that the transaction is not one which could contain a potential for money laundering.

Public office or appointment leading to conflict – 3.05

63. Examples of the public offices and appointments which 3.05 covers are:

    (a)   local councillor;

    (b)   judicial appointments;

    (c)   justices and justices' clerks;

    (d)   the Gambling Commission;

    (e)   coroners;

    (f)   police authority;

    (g)   the Legal Services Commission's Regional Legal Services Committees; and

    (h)   Criminal Injuries Compensation Authority.

64. Where you hold (or a member of your firm or family holds) any of these, or similar, offices or appointments it will be up to you in every case to consider:

    (a)   whether any political or other interest which you may have in connection with the office or appointment may conflict with, or affect, your duty to act in the best interests of any of your clients (including your ability to advise impartially and independently);

    (b)   whether any duties which arise from your office or appointment conflict with, or affect, your duty to act in the best interests of your clients;

    (c)   whether the terms of appointment, or any statutory provisions, restrict your ability to act in any particular matter; and

(d)   whether there is likely to be a public perception that you have, or your firm has, been able to obtain an unfair advantage for your client(s) as a result of the office or appointment.

65.   Where you are aware that a member of your firm or family has accepted an appointment it is important for you to consider whether there is likely to be a public perception of your firm gaining an unfair advantage for your client(s).

ADR and conflict – 3.06

66.   You may provide ADR services as part of your practice or through a separate business. For more information on separate businesses see rule 21 (Separate businesses).

67.   Rule 3.06 also applies when you provide ADR services through a separate business.

68.   "ADR service" means the service provided by you when acting as an independent neutral, for example, as mediator, conciliator or arbitrator.

69.   The SRA Board recommends that those who offer ADR services comply with a code of practice such as the Law Society's Code of Practice for Civil and Commercial Mediation and Code of Practice for Family Mediation.

Acting for seller and buyer in conveyancing, property selling and mortgage related services

70.   Rules 3.07 to 3.15 set out the limited circumstances in which you may act for more than one party in conveyancing, property selling or mortgage related services. They apply to all types of conveyancing transaction, commercial and residential.

71.   The general rule is that separate representation is required because conveyancing is an area where the risk of a conflict arising between two parties is high and where any conflict may affect a conveyancing chain.

72.   When judging whether or not a transaction is "at arm's length", you need to look at the relationship between the parties and the context of the transaction. A transaction may be regarded as not "at arm's length", even if it is at market value or is stated to be on arm's length terms. A transaction would not usually be at arm's length, for example, if the parties are:

(a)   related by blood, adoption or marriage, or living together;

(b)   the settlor of a trust and the trustees;

(c)   the trustees of a trust and its beneficiary or the beneficiary's relative;

(d)   personal representatives and a beneficiary;

(e)   the trustees of separate trusts for the same family;

(f)   a sole trader or partners and a limited company set up to enable the business to be incorporated;

(g)   associated companies (i.e. where one is a holding company and the other is its subsidiary within the meaning of the Companies Act 1985, or two associated companies); or

(h)   a local authority and a company within the meaning of 13.08(c).

73.   Rules 10.06(3) and 10.06(4) deal with the prohibition on acting for more than one prospective buyer, or for seller and buyer where there is more than one prospective buyer. These provisions recognise the inevitable conflict of interests which makes it impossible to act for more than one prospective buyer, or for the seller and one of several prospective buyers. If you were already acting for seller and buyer (for example, both are established clients), you would be unable to continue acting for both if another

prospective buyer were introduced during the course of the transaction. There is a significant inherent conflict in these circumstances. It would be impossible, for example, to reconcile the interests of both clients if it were in the seller's best interests to exchange with the other prospective buyer.

74.   The test of whether a person is an "established client" is an objective one – is it reasonable to regard the person as an established client? A seller or buyer who instructs you for the first time is not an established client. A former client is not necessarily the same as an established client. There needs to be a degree of permanence in the solicitor–client relationship as exemplified by some continuity of instruction over time and the likelihood of future instruction. An individual related by blood, adoption or marriage to an established client, or who is living with an established client, counts as an established client. A person also counts as an established client if selling or buying jointly with an established client.

75.   The consideration will only count as £10,000 or less if the value of any property given in exchange or part exchange is taken into account.

76.   A builder or developer who acquires a property in part exchange, and sells it on without development, is not selling "as a builder or developer" within the meaning of 3.10(c) and 3.13(c).

77.   If acting for seller and buyer under the provisions of 3.07 to 3.15, you would have to stop acting for at least one of the clients if a conflict were to arise during the course of the transaction. Clients should be made aware of the consequent disruption and additional expense involved in such circumstances, and of the advantages of separate representation, before giving their written consent.

78.   An RFL cannot undertake conveyancing. RELs may undertake conveyancing only if they are entitled to do so under regulation 12 of the European Communities (Lawyer's Practice) Regulations 2000 (SI 2000/1119).

79.   The effect of 3.11 is as follows:

(a)   if providing mortgage related services to the buyer (either through your own firm or a SEAL – see 3.12 for the definition of a SEAL which allows participating authorised non-SRA firms but requires at least one participating firm to be a recognised body or recognised sole practitioner), you may also provide property selling services to the seller (either through your own firm or a SEAL) and do the seller's conveyancing; and

(b)   if providing property selling services to the seller through a SEAL (not your own firm), you may also provide mortgage related services to the buyer (either through your own firm or the SEAL) and do the buyer's conveyancing.

80.   A SEAL may act for the seller and provide mortgage related services to the buyer; one of the participating firms may do the seller's conveyancing, and another participating firm may do the buyer's conveyancing.

Acting for lender and borrower in conveyancing transactions

81.   There will be no breach of 3.16(2)(c) to (d) or 3.19 if the lender has certified that its mortgage instructions and documents sent pursuant to those instructions are subject to the limitations set out in 3.19 and 3.21, and certifies any subsequent instructions and documents in the same way. If there is no certification, when acting in a transaction involving the charge of property to be used solely as the borrower's private residence you must notify the lender that the approved certificate of title will be used and that your duties to the lender will be limited accordingly (see 3.20(b)). In other types of transaction, you should draw the lender's attention to the provisions of 3.19 and 3.21 and state that you cannot act on any instructions which extend beyond the matters contained in 3.19.

82. As an alternative to printing the approved certificate for each transaction, it is acceptable for a lender to use a short form certificate of title which incorporates the approved certificate by reference. The form must include, in the following order:

(a) the title "Certificate of Title";

(b) the contents of the details box in the order set out in the approved certificate (use of two columns is acceptable) but with details not required shaded out or stated not to be required; and

(c) the wording "We, the conveyancers named above, give the Certificate of Title set out in the annex to rule 3 of the Solicitors' Code of Conduct 2007 as if the same were set out in full, subject to the limitations contained in it."

Administrative details, such as a request for cheque, may follow the Certificate of Title.

83. The approved certificate is only required for a transaction where the property is to be used solely as the borrower's private residence. The approved certificate need not, therefore, be used for investment properties such as blocks of flats, business premises such as shops (even if living accommodation is attached), or "buy to let mortgages" on properties which are not intended for owner-occupation.

84. You must inform the lender of the circumstances, in accordance with 3.18, so that the lender can decide whether or not to instruct you.

85. A lender's instructions (see 3.19(x)) may require a wider disclosure of your circumstances than 3.18 requires; and you must assess whether the circumstances give rise to a conflict. For example, there will be a conflict between lender and borrower if you become involved in negotiations relating to the terms of the loan. A conflict might arise from the relationship you have or your firm has with the borrower – for example, if you are, or your firm is, the borrower's creditor or debtor or the borrower's business associate or co-habitant.

86. In relation to 3.22(2), the limitations contained in 3.19 will not apply to the insertion into a recognised certificate of any information required by that certificate. For example, where the recognised certificate requires details of the parties' repairing obligations under a lease of the property, you may provide a summary of the relevant terms of the lease despite the general limitation contained in 3.19(i). However, any additions or amendments to the text of a recognised certificate to suit a particular transaction must not, to the extent to which they create an increased or additional obligation, extend beyond the limitations contained in 3.19.

87. Many lenders require their lawyer or licensed conveyancer to check the vires of corporate borrowers and that the correct procedures have been followed to ensure the validity of the mortgage. Rule 3.19(n) enables lenders to impose duties on their lawyer or licensed conveyancer in relation to the execution of the mortgage and guarantee. Within this context it is perfectly proper for a lender to require you to obtain such information as the circumstances may require in relation to the capacity of, or execution of documents by, the borrower, third party mortgagor or guarantor; for instance, by way of certified copy minutes or an opinion from a lawyer of the relevant jurisdiction as to the validity and enforceability of the security or guarantee given by a foreign registered company. There is no reason why you should not assist corporate clients by drafting minutes or board resolutions. You should not, however, certify the validity or passing of resolutions unless you were present at the meeting and have verified that it was convened and held strictly in accordance with all relevant requirements.

88. Rule 3.19(u) allows you to accept instructions from a lender to carry out administrative arrangements in relation to any collateral security. This expression includes associated debentures, collateral warranties, second charges, rent assignments, charges over rent income and deeds of priority. The administrative arrangements necessarily include the preparation and execution of the relevant documents and subsequent registration.

Rule 4 – Confidentiality and disclosure

Introduction

Rule 4 sets out provisions for dealing with the protection of clients' confidential information and the duty of disclosure owed to clients.

Rule 4 – Confidentiality and disclosure

4.01 Duty of confidentiality

You and your firm must keep the affairs of clients and former clients confidential except where disclosure is required or permitted by law or by your client (or former client).

4.02 Duty of disclosure

If you are a lawyer or other fee earner you must disclose to a client for whom you are personally acting on a matter, whether individually or as one of a group, or whose matter you are personally supervising, all information of which you are aware which is material to that client's matter regardless of the source of the information, subject to:

(a) the duty of confidentiality in 4.01 above, which always overrides the duty to disclose; and

(b) the following where the duty does not apply:

    (i) where such disclosure is prohibited by law;

    (ii) where it is agreed expressly that no duty to disclose arises or a different standard of disclosure applies; or

    (iii) where you reasonably believe that serious physical or mental injury will be caused to any person if the information is disclosed to a client.

4.03 Duty not to put confidentiality at risk by acting

If you are a lawyer or other fee earner and you personally hold, or your firm holds, confidential information in relation to a client or former client, you must not risk breaching confidentiality by acting, or continuing to act, for another client on a matter where:

(a) that information might reasonably be expected to be material; and

(b) that client has an interest adverse to the first-mentioned client or former client,

except where proper arrangements can be made to protect that information in accordance with 4.04 and 4.05 below.

4.04 Exception to duty not to put confidentiality at risk by acting – with clients' consent

(1) You may act, or continue to act, in the circumstances otherwise prohibited by 4.03 above with the informed consent of both clients but only if:

(a) the client for whom you act or are proposing to act knows that your firm, or a lawyer or other fee earner of your firm, holds, or might hold, material information (in circumstances described in 4.03) in relation to their matter which you cannot disclose;

(b) you have a reasonable belief that both clients understand the relevant issues after these have been brought to their attention;

(c) both clients have agreed to the conditions under which you will be acting or continuing to act; and

(d) it is reasonable in all the circumstances to do so.

(2) "Both clients" in the context of 4.04(1) means:

(a) an existing or former client for whom your firm, or a lawyer or other fee earner of your firm, holds confidential information; and

(b) an existing or new client for whom you act or are proposing to act and to whom information held on behalf of the other client is material (in circumstances described in 4.03 above).

(3) If you, or you and your firm, have been acting for two or more clients in compliance with rule 3 (Conflict of interests) and can no longer fulfil its requirements you may continue to act for one client with the consent of the other client provided you comply with 4.04.

4.05 Exception to duty not to put confidentiality at risk by acting – without clients' consent

You may act, or continue to act, for a client in the circumstances otherwise prohibited by 4.03 above without the consent of the client for whom your firm, or a lawyer or other fee earner of your firm, holds, or might hold, confidential information which is material to your client (in circumstances described in 4.03) but only if:

(a) it is not possible to obtain informed consent under 4.04 above from the client for whom your firm, or a lawyer or other fee earner of your firm, holds, or might hold, material confidential information;

(b) your client has agreed to your acting in the knowledge that your firm, or a lawyer or other fee earner of your firm, holds, or might hold, information material to their matter which you cannot disclose;

(c) any safeguards which comply with the standards required by law at the time they are implemented are put in place; and

(d) it is reasonable in all the circumstances to do so.

4.06 Waivers

In spite of 22.01(1) (Waivers), the Solicitors Regulation Authority Board shall not have power to waive any of the provisions of this rule.

Guidance to rule 4 – Confidentiality and disclosure

Introduction

1. This rule draws together, and describes the interaction of, the obligations created by the

duties of confidentiality and disclosure. It also reinforces the common law duty whereby you and your firm must not put confidential information obtained from one client or former client at risk by acting adverse to the interests of that client or former client in a matter where the confidential information would be material. The rule also establishes that where a conflict between these duties arises the duty of confidentiality is paramount. The rule does recognise that confidential information can be protected by the use of information barriers with the consent of the client and, in very limited circumstances, without that consent.

2.   The rule should be read in conjunction with rule 3 (Conflict of interests) as there are important cross-references contained in both the rules and the guidance.

The duty of confidentiality – 4.01 – general

3.   Rule 4.01 sets out your fundamental duty to keep all clients' affairs confidential. It is important to bear in mind the distinction between this duty and the concept of law known as legal professional privilege. The duty of confidentiality extends to all confidential information about a client's affairs, irrespective of the source of the information, subject to the limited exceptions described below. Legal professional privilege protects certain communications between you and your client from being disclosed, even in court. However, not all communications are protected from disclosure and you should, if necessary, refer to an appropriate authority on the law of evidence.

4.   The duty of confidentiality continues after the end of the retainer. After the client dies the right to confidentiality passes to the personal representatives, but note that an administrator's power dates only from the grant of the letters of administration.

5.   Information received in the context of a joint retainer must be available between the clients. They must, however, all consent to any confidential information being disclosed to a third party. Information communicated to you when acting for one of the clients in relation to a separate matter must not be disclosed to the other client(s) without the consent of that client.

6.   If you obtain information in relation to a prospective client you may still be bound by a duty of confidentiality, even if that prospective client does not subsequently instruct your firm. There may be circumstances, however, where you receive information where there is no real or genuine interest in instructing your firm and that information is unlikely to be confidential.

Insolvency

7.   If a client becomes insolvent you will need to consider to whom you owe a duty of confidentiality. To some extent this will depend on whether your client is a company or an individual and you will need to refer to the relevant statutory authority, such as the Insolvency Act 1986. Where a statutory power overrides confidentiality you should consider carefully to what extent it is overridden. It may, for example, require you to disclose only certain categories of information or documents. You should ensure that any disclosure you make is strictly limited to what is required by the law.

Specific instances where confidentiality is required

8   (a)   You must not disclose the contents of a will, even after the death of the testator, other than to, or with the consent of, the executor(s), until probate has been obtained.

        (b)   You must not disclose the address of a client without the client's consent.

        (c)   Where a lender asks for a conveyancing file and you have kept a joint file for both borrower and lender clients, you cannot, without the consent of the borrower, send the whole file to the lender, unless the lender can show to your satisfaction that there is a prima facie case of fraud. If the client does not consent, you should send only those parts of the file which relate to work done for the lender.

(d) You cannot, without the consent of the relevant client (or, if applicable, its administrator or similar officeholder), sell book debts to a factoring company because of the confidential nature of your bill. If your firm grants, as security to a lender, a charge over your firm's book debts, you need to ensure that you protect clients' confidential information should the lender need to enforce the security. Further advice on this issue can be obtained from the Professional Ethics Guidance Team.

(e) You should only share office services with other businesses if confidentiality can be ensured.

(f) If you outsource services such as word processing, telephone call handling or photocopying you must be satisfied that the provider of those services is able to ensure the confidentiality of any information concerning your clients. This would normally require confidentiality undertakings from the provider and checks to ensure that the terms of the arrangements regarding confidentiality are being complied with. Whilst you might have implied consent to confidential information being passed to external service providers, it would be prudent to inform clients of any such services you propose to use in your terms of business or client care letters.

Disclosure of confidential information in exceptional circumstances

9. Despite your duty of confidentiality you may be required to disclose confidential information in certain circumstances. A number of statutes empower government and other bodies, for example HM Revenue and Customs, to require any person to disclose documents and/or information. In the absence of the client's specific consent, you should ask under which statutory power the information is sought, consider the relevant provisions and consider whether privileged information is protected from disclosure. You should only provide such information as you are strictly required by law to disclose.

10. There are reporting requirements in relation to money laundering which override the duty of confidentiality and these are set out in the Proceeds of Crime Act 2002, the terrorism legislation and the Money Laundering Regulations 2007. These often require difficult judgements to be made as to whether or not a situation has arisen which would require you to report information to the relevant authorities. You should, however, always be mindful of the importance of your duty of confidentiality to your client. If you are uncertain as to whether you should report confidential information you should consider seeking legal advice or contact the Professional Ethics Guidance Team for advice.

11. The Freedom of Information Act 2000 applies to the majority of public bodies and to local authorities. This Act establishes a right to know the content of records held by certain public bodies subject to certain exemptions such as legal professional privilege. The legal professional privilege exemption is conditional and can only be relied upon where the public interest in maintaining the exemption outweighs the public interest in disclosing the information. In some cases, disclosure of matters which are on legal files may be required by law under the Act. The Information Commissioner's website provides Awareness Guidance upon this area of the Act.

12. You may reveal confidential information to the extent that you believe necessary to prevent the client or a third party committing a criminal act that you reasonably believe is likely to result in serious bodily harm.

13. There may be exceptional circumstances involving children where you should consider

revealing confidential information to an appropriate authority. This may be where the child is the client and the child reveals information which indicates continuing sexual or other physical abuse but refuses to allow disclosure of such information. Similarly, there may be situations where an adult discloses abuse either by himself or herself or by another adult against a child but refuses to allow any disclosure. You must consider whether the threat to the child's life or health, both mental and physical, is sufficiently serious to justify a breach of the duty of confidentiality.

14. In proceedings under the Children Act 1989 you are under a duty to reveal experts' reports commissioned for the purposes of proceedings, as these reports are not privileged. The position in relation to voluntary disclosure of other documents or solicitor–client communications is uncertain. Under 11.01, an advocate is under a duty not to mislead the court. Therefore, if you are an advocate, and have certain knowledge which you realise is adverse to the client's case, you may be extremely limited in what you can state in the client's favour. In this situation, you should seek the client's agreement for full voluntary disclosure, for three reasons:

   (a) the matters the client wants to hide will probably emerge anyway;

   (b) you will be able to do a better job for the client if all the relevant information is presented to the court; and

   (c) if the information is not voluntarily disclosed, you may be severely criticised by the court.

   If the client refuses to give you authority to disclose the relevant information, you are entitled to refuse to continue to act for the client if to do so will place you in breach of your obligations to the court.

15. You should reveal matters which are otherwise subject to the duty to preserve confidentiality where a court orders that such matters are to be disclosed or where a warrant permits a police officer or other authority to seize confidential documents. If you believe that the documents are subject to legal privilege or that for some other reason the order or warrant ought not to have been made or issued, you should normally, without unlawfully obstructing its execution, discuss with the client the possibility of making an application to have the order or warrant set aside. Advice may be obtained from the Professional Ethics Guidance Team.

16. Occasionally you may be asked by the police or a third party to give information or to show them documents which you have obtained when acting for a client. Unless the client is prepared to waive confidentiality, or where you have strong prima facie evidence that you have been used by the client to perpetrate a fraud or other crime and the duty of confidence does not arise, you should insist upon receiving a witness summons or subpoena so that, where appropriate, privilege may be claimed and the court asked to decide the issue. If the request is made by the police under the Police and Criminal Evidence Act 1984 you should, where appropriate, leave the question of privilege to the court to decide on the particular circumstances. Advice may be obtained from the Professional Ethics Guidance Team.

17. Certain communications from a client are not confidential if they are a matter of public record. For example, the fact that you have been instructed by a named client in connection with contentious business for which that client's name is on the public record is not confidential, but the type of business involved will usually be confidential.

18. You may reveal confidential information concerning a client to the extent that it is reasonably necessary to establish a defence to a criminal charge or civil claim by your client against you, or where your conduct is under investigation by the SRA, or under consideration by the Solicitors Disciplinary Tribunal.

19. In the case of a publicly funded client, you may be under a duty to report to the Legal Services Commission information concerning the client which is confidential and privileged.

Duty to disclose information to a client – 4.02

20. You have a duty to disclose all information material to your client's matter. Your duty is limited to information of which you are aware (and does not extend to information of which others in your firm may be aware) but is not limited to information obtained while acting on the client's matter. You will not be liable, therefore, for failing to disclose material information held by others within your firm of which you were unaware. There are, however, some circumstances where you should not disclose material information because it is not in the best interests of your client to do so or because disclosure is prohibited by law. These include situations where:

    (a) disclosure may be harmful to the client because of the client's physical or mental condition;

    (b) the provisions in the money laundering legislation effectively prohibit you from passing information to clients;

    (c) it is obvious that privileged documents have been mistakenly disclosed to you; or

    (d) you come into possession of information relating to state security or intelligence matters to which the Official Secrets Act 1989 applies.

21. Rule 4.02 also prevents you from disclosing information where this would breach your firm's duty of confidentiality to another client. The duty of confidentiality will always override the duty of disclosure.

22. You cannot, however, excuse a failure to disclose material information because to do so would breach a separate duty of confidentiality. Unless the retainer with the client to which the information cannot be disclosed can be varied so that the inability to disclose is not a breach of duty (see note 25 below), you should refuse the instructions or, if already acting, immediately cease to act for that client. Any delay in ceasing to act is likely to increase the risk that you are liable for breach of duty.

23. You should not seek to pass the client to a colleague (who would not be bound by the same duty because he or she is personally unaware of the material information) unless the client agrees to this, knowing the reason for the transfer and, if you have already started to act for the client, agreeing that you are released from your duty to disclose up to the time when you personally cease to act for the client on that matter. Further, you should consider carefully whether, even if these conditions are satisfied, it is appropriate for any members of your firm to act. A firm which holds information which it cannot convey to a client but which, if known to that client, might affect the instructions to the firm in a material way will usually be in an invidious position and quite possibly unable to act in the best interests of the client – see rule 3 (Conflict of interests). See also note 15 of the guidance to rule 3.

24. The rule does not define "information which is material to that client's matter" but it must be information which is relevant to the specific retainer with the client and not just information which might be of general interest to the client. The information must also be more than of inconsequential interest to the client. It must, therefore, be information which might reasonably be expected to affect the client's decision making with regard to their matter in a way which is significant having regard to the matter as a whole.

25. The duty outlined above reflects and builds on the fiduciary duty which exists at common law. As 4.02(b)(ii) makes clear, however, you or your firm can expressly agree a different degree of duty. For example, a client might wish to instruct you because it knows that you act for other entities which operate in the same market and because it knows that you, therefore, understand the market. The client would not be surprised that you hold material market intelligence of a confidential nature from such other clients, and would not expect you to divulge it. The client might, therefore, agree that the usual duty to disclose would not apply.

Duties of confidentiality and disclosure conflicting – 4.03

26. Rule 4.03 sets out the duty not to put confidentiality at risk by acting for a client where to do so might put at risk the confidential information held by your firm for another client (or former client). The rule makes clear that the relevant circumstances of risk arise where:

    (a) the confidential information "might reasonably be expected to be material" to the client for whom you wish to act; and

    (b) the work for the client for whom you wish to act would be adverse to the interests of the client or former client to whom the duty of confidentiality is owed.

    The effect of note 26(b) is that you can act if the confidential information your firm holds is not reasonably expected to be material to your new client or is reasonably expected to be material to your new client but the interests of the clients are not adverse. The confidential information would, however, have to be protected and you and your firm would be answerable in law and conduct if it leaked.

27. The rule does not define adverse interest, but the intention is to mirror what is considered adverse for these purposes at common law (see *Bolkiah v KPMG* [1998] UKHL 52; [1999] 2 AC 222; [1999] 1 All ER 517; [1999] 2 WLR 215 and subsequent cases). Essentially, adversity arises where one party is, or is likely to become, the opposing party on a matter, whether in negotiations or some form of dispute resolution. For example, if your firm acted for a client in a criminal case in which the client was convicted of assault and the client's wife, unaware of the conviction, then wished you to represent her in divorce proceedings you would have to refuse the instructions. The confidential information held about the husband would be material to her case and, if so, her interests would be adverse to his.

28. In contrast, action which seeks to improve the new client's commercial position as against others generally within a particular sector would not be "adverse" to the interests of another client which is one such competitor. This should be the case even if there might be some risk that such a market competitor might seek to challenge the activities of the client before, for example, the competition authorities.

29. There may, however, be some circumstances where you are permitted to act under 4.03 but where other considerations will prevent you from doing so. It might be that you personally have confidential information from another client/former client which would be material to the new instruction but, since the instruction would not be adverse to the other client/former client, 4.03 does not bite. In this situation, the duty of confidentiality conflicts with your personal duty to disclose, and you should therefore not act, unless the new client has expressly agreed a lesser duty of disclosure (4.02(b)(ii)).

30. You may act, or continue to act, despite the prohibition in 4.03 if the confidential information can be protected through the use of appropriate safeguards in the circumstances set out in 4.04 and 4.05, and as more fully explained in the following guidance notes.

Acting with appropriate safeguards (information barriers) – 4.04 and 4.05

31. Rule 4.03 sets the basic standard that you should not normally act on a matter where material confidential information is held elsewhere in the firm and where the matter would be adverse to the interests of the client/former client to whom the duty of confidentiality is owed. To act in these circumstances might increase the risk that the confidential information could be put at risk. The firm can act if the confidential information is not material to the instructions. For guidance on the meaning of "material" see note 24 above.

32. Rules 4.04 and 4.05 set out two situations where you can act even when material confidential information is held by another member of the firm. Both recognise for the first time that it can be acceptable to use information barriers. The first situation is where the party to whom the duty of confidentiality is owed consents. The second situation is where you are already acting and consent has not been given or cannot be sought.

33. Where the client consents as envisaged by 4.04 there is scope for more flexibility in the arrangements for the information barrier as the safeguards can be discussed with, and agreed by, the client. It is important, nonetheless, that the safeguards are effective to avoid a real risk of disclosure. A firm will be liable if confidential information does leak in breach of that agreement.

34. Rule 4.04 requires "informed consent" and one of the difficulties with seeking such consent of the client is that it is often not possible to disclose sufficient information about the identity and business of the other client without risk of breaching that other client's confidentiality. You will have to decide in each case whether you are able to provide sufficient information for the client to be able to give "informed consent". Every situation will be different but generally it will be only sophisticated clients, for example, a corporate body with in-house legal advisers or other appropriate expertise, who will have the expertise and ability to weigh up the issues and the risks of giving consent on the basis of the information they have been given. If there is a risk of prejudicing the position of either client then consent should not be sought and you and your firm should not act. It may, however, be possible to give sufficient information to obtain informed consent even if the identity of the other client(s) and the nature of their particular interest(s) are not disclosed. Wherever possible you should try to ensure that the clients are advised of the potential risks arising from your firm acting before seeking their consent.

35. In the case of sophisticated clients (such as those referred to in note 34 above) only, it may be possible to seek consent to act in certain situations at the start of and as a condition of your retainer and to do so through standard terms of engagement. For example, a sophisticated client may give its consent in this way for a firm to act for a future bidder for that client if, when the bidder asks the firm to act, a common law compliant information barrier is put in place to protect any of the client's confidential information which is held by the firm and which would be material to a bidder.

36. Where the client does not consent or does not know about the arrangements, an extremely high standard in relation to the protection of confidential information must be satisfied. In this situation, as has been demonstrated in recent case law, the client can have the firm removed from acting with all the attendant disruption for the other client, if there is shown to be a real risk of confidential information being leaked.

37. Where your firm holds material confidential information you may act in circumstances where the party to whom the duty of confidentiality is owed refuses consent or cannot be asked (4.05). This may be because it cannot be contacted or because making the request would itself breach confidentiality. You should always seek consent when you can reasonably do so.

38. Where under 4.04 your firm has erected an information barrier without the consent of the party to whom the duty of confidentiality is owed, the firm should try to inform that party as soon as circumstances permit, and outline the steps which have been taken to ensure confidentiality is preserved. If some material points (such as the name of the client to whose matter the confidential information might be relevant, or the nature of that matter) still cannot be divulged for reasons of confidentiality and it is reasonably supposed that that party would be more concerned at news of your retention than if fuller details could be given, it might be appropriate to continue to wait before informing that party. There may be circumstances, however, where it is impossible to inform that party.

39. Where two or more firms amalgamate, or one firm takes over another, the new firm

needs to ensure that this does not result in any breach of confidentiality. If the firm holds confidential information that is material to a matter being handled for another client, the firm must be able to ensure that the confidential information is protected by ceasing to act for both clients, or ceasing to act for the client to whom the information is relevant, or by setting up adequate safeguards in accordance with either 4.04 or 4.05.

40. Confidential information may also be put at risk when partners or staff leave one firm and join another. This might happen where, for example, an individual joins a firm which is acting against one of the individual's former clients. An individual joining a new firm could not act personally for a client of the new firm where to do so would put at risk confidential information which he or she personally possesses about a client of the previous firm. In addition, the individual and the firm which the individual is joining must ensure that adequate safeguards are put in place in accordance with 4.04 or 4.05 to ensure that confidential information held by that individual is safeguarded.

Safeguards for information barriers

41. Rigid safeguards for information barriers have not been enshrined in the rules. Where 4.04 applies (i.e. consent has been given), it is for the firm to agree the appropriate safeguards, but it would normally be necessary to satisfy note 44(a) to (f). Some of note 44(g) to (n) may also be applicable. Where 4.05 applies, the firm must satisfy the requirements of common law and at least most, if not all, of note 44(a) to (n) might be essential.

42. If, at any stage after an information barrier has been established, it becomes impossible to comply with any of the terms, the firm may have to cease to act. The possibility of this happening should always be discussed when instructions are accepted so that the client is aware of this risk, or addressed with reasonable prominence in standard terms of engagement.

43. Firms will always need to consider whether it is appropriate in any case for an information barrier to be used, and also whether the size or structure of a firm means that it could not in any circumstances be appropriate. It is unlikely that, for example, safeguards could ever be considered adequate where:

    (a) a firm has only one principal and no other qualified staff;

    (b) the solicitor possessing, or likely to possess, the confidential information is supervised by a solicitor who acts for, or supervises another solicitor in the firm who acts for a client to whom the information is or may be relevant; or

    (c) the physical structure or layout of the firm is such that confidentiality would be difficult to preserve having regard to other safeguards which are in place.

44. The following note 44(a) to (f) would normally be appropriate to demonstrate the adequacy of an information barrier when you are proposing to act in circumstances set out in 4.04. It might also be appropriate to agree some or all of note 44(a) to (f) where you are acting with consent in accordance with 4.05:

    (a) that the client who or which might be interested in the confidential information acknowledges in writing that the information held by the firm will not be given to them;

    (b) that all members of the firm who hold the relevant confidential information ("the restricted group") are identified and have no involvement with or for the other client;

    (c) that no member of the restricted group is managed or supervised in relation to that matter by someone from outside the restricted group;

    (d) that all members of the restricted group confirm at the start of the engagement that they understand that they possess or might come to possess information which is confidential, and that they must not discuss it with any other member of the firm unless that person is, or becomes, a member of the restricted group, and that this obligation shall be regarded by everyone as an ongoing one;

(e)   that each member of the restricted group confirms when the barrier is established that they have not done anything which would amount to a breach of the information barrier; and

(f)   that only members of the restricted group have access to documents containing the confidential information.

The following arrangements may also be appropriate, and might in particular be necessary where acting in circumstances set out in 4.05:

(g)   that the restricted group is physically separated from those acting for the other client, for example, by being in a separate building, on a separate floor or in a segregated part of the offices, and that some form of "access restriction" be put in place to ensure physical segregation;

(h)   that confidential information on computer systems is protected by use of separate computer networks or through use of password protection or similar means;

(i)   that the firm issues a statement that it will treat any breach, even an inadvertent one, of the information barrier as a serious disciplinary offence;

(j)   that each member of the restricted group gives a written statement at the start of the engagement that they understand the terms of the information barrier and will comply with them;

(k)   that the firm undertakes that it will do nothing which would or might prevent or hinder any member of the restricted group from complying with the information barrier;

(l)   that the firm identifies a specific partner or other appropriate person within the restricted group with overall responsibility for the information barrier;

(m)   that the firm provides formal and regular training for members of the firm on duties of confidentiality and responsibility under information barriers or will ensure that such training is provided prior to the work being undertaken; and

(n)   that the firm implements a system for the opening of post, receipt of faxes and distribution of e-mail which will ensure that confidential information is not disclosed to anyone outside the restricted group.

"Member", in the context of this note, applies to principals and all staff members including secretaries, but does not apply to any staff member (not having any involvement on behalf of any relevant client) whose duties include the maintenance of computer systems or conflict/compliance procedures and who is subject to a general obligation of confidentiality in relation to all information to which he or she may have access in the course of his or her duties.

This guidance should not be read as a representation that compliance with note 44(a) to (n) above will necessarily be considered sufficient at common law.

45.   Where a firm proposes to erect an information barrier (whether under 4.04 or 4.05) it must first inform the client for whom it acts – or wishes to act – on the matter to which the confidential information might be material. The firm should not act – or continue to act – without that client's consent, with that client understanding that the firm holds information which might be material and which will not be communicated to it; see 4.04(1)(a) and 4.05(b). Although the rule does not require consent to be in writing, it is recommended that this be obtained for evidential purposes to protect both your client's position and your own position.

Rule 5 – Business management in England and Wales

Introduction

Rule 5 deals with the supervision and management of a firm or in-house practice, the maintenance of competence, and the internal business arrangements essential to the proper delivery of services to clients. "Supervision" and "management" refer, respectively, to the professional overseeing of staff and clients' matters; and to the overall direction and development of the firm or in-house practice and its day-to-day administration. The rule does not apply to your overseas practice but you must comply with 15.05.

Broadly, the rule aims to set out:

(a)   responsibility for the overall supervision and management framework of your firm or in-house practice;

(b)   the minimum requirements to be met in order to be "qualified to supervise";

(c)   the minimum standards applying to supervision of clients' matters; and

(d)   the minimum requirements in relation to those business arrangements considered to be essential to good practice and integral to compliance with supervision and other duties to clients.

Rule 5 – Business management in England and Wales

5.01 Supervision and management responsibilities

(1)   If you are a recognised body, a manager of a recognised body or a recognised sole practitioner, you must make arrangements for the effective management of the firm as a whole, and in particular provide for:

    (a)   compliance by the firm and its managers with the duties of a principal, in law and conduct, to exercise appropriate supervision over all staff, and ensure proper supervision and direction of clients' matters;

    (b)   compliance with the money laundering regulations, where applicable;

    (c)   compliance by the firm and individuals with key regulatory requirements such as certification, registration or recognition by the Solicitors Regulation Authority, compulsory professional indemnity cover, delivery of accountants' reports, and obligations to co-operate with and report information to the Authority;

    (d)   the identification of conflicts of interests;

    (e)   compliance with the requirements of rule 2 (Client relations) on client care, costs information and complaints handling;

    (f)   control of undertakings;

    (g)   the safekeeping of documents and assets entrusted to the firm;

    (h)   compliance with rule 6 (Equality and diversity);

    (i)   the training of individuals working in the firm to maintain a level of competence appropriate to their work and level of responsibility;

    (j)   financial control of budgets, expenditure and cashflow;

(k)   the continuation of the practice of the firm in the event of absences and emergencies, with the minimum interruption to clients' business; and

(l)   the management of risk.

(2)   If you are a solicitor or REL employed as the head of an in-house legal department, you must effect supervision and management arrangements within your department to provide for:

    (a)   adequate supervision and direction of those assisting in your in-house practice;

    (b)   control of undertakings; and

    (c)   identification of conflicts of interests.

5.02 Persons who must be "qualified to supervise"

(1)   The following persons must be "qualified to supervise":

    (a)   a recognised sole practitioner;

    (b)   one of the lawyer managers of a recognised body or of a body corporate which is a manager of the recognised body;

    (c)   one of the solicitors or RELs employed by a law centre; or

    (d)   one in-house solicitor or in-house REL in any department where solicitors and/or RELs, as part of that employment:

        (i)   do publicly funded work; or

        (ii)   do or supervise advocacy or the conduct of proceedings for members of the public before a court or immigration tribunal.

(2)   To be "qualified to supervise" under this paragraph a person:

    (a)   must have completed the training specified from time to time by the Solicitors Regulation Authority for this purpose; and

    (b)   must have been entitled to practise as a lawyer for at least 36 months within the last ten years; and must be able to demonstrate this if asked by the Solicitors Regulation Authority.

5.03 Supervision of work for clients and members of the public

(1)   If you are a recognised body, a manager of a recognised body or a recognised sole practitioner, you must ensure that your firm has in place a system for supervising clients' matters.

(2)   If you are an in-house solicitor or in-house REL and you are required to be "qualified to supervise" under 5.02(1)(c) or (d) above, you must ensure that your law centre or in-house legal department has in place a system for supervising work undertaken for members of the public.

(3)   The system for supervision under 5.03(1) and (2) must include appropriate and effective procedures under which the quality of work undertaken for clients and members of the public is checked with reasonable regularity by suitably experienced and competent persons within the firm, law centre or in-house legal department.

Guidance to rule 5 – Business management in England and Wales

Geographical scope of the rule

1.   Rule 5 applies only to practice from an office in England and Wales; but if you are a solicitor practising from an office outside England and Wales or an REL practising from an office in Scotland or Northern Ireland, you will need to comply with 15.05 in relation to that practice.

Guidance on 5.01 generally

2.   The term "arrangements" is used broadly in 5.01 to encompass all systems, procedures, processes and methods of organisation put in place to achieve the required outcome. There is no requirement that these take a particular form; the method of delivery is a matter for the firm. Evidence that appropriate arrangements are actually in place and are operating will be required to demonstrate compliance. It is anticipated that most well-run firms will already be complying.

3.   Factors to be taken into account in determining the appropriateness of a set of arrangements will include the size and complexity of the firm; the number, experience and qualifications of staff; and the nature of the work undertaken. Arrangements are unlikely to be considered appropriate unless they include a mechanism for periodic review of their effectiveness.

4.   The overarching responsibility for the management of the firm in the broadest sense – including, for example, practice development and business efficiency – rests with the recognised sole practitioner, or the managers of the recognised body and the recognised body itself.

5.   Firms will be expected to be able to produce evidence of a systematic and effective approach to management, and this may include the implementation by the firm of one or more of the following:

(a)   guidance issued from time to time by the SRA or the Law Society on the supervision and execution of particular types of work;

(b)   the firm's own properly documented standards and procedures;

(c)   the Lexcel standard or other practice management standards promoted from time to time by the Law Society;

(d)   the guidelines for accounting procedures and systems published as Appendix 3 to the Solicitors' Accounts Rules 1998;

(e)   external quality standards such as BS EN ISO 9000, Investors in People, or quality standards required by the Legal Services Commission in connection with undertaking publicly funded work; and

(f)   in the case of an in-house solicitor or in-house REL employed by a law centre, charitable or similar non-commercial advice service, management standards or procedures laid down by its management committee, the Law Centres Federation or equivalent "umbrella" organisation.

6.   The day-to-day management of a firm can be delegated to an employee who is suitably experienced and competent, and a fit and proper person to perform the role. Firms must be able to demonstrate this if required.

7.   Sections 41 to 44 of the Solicitors Act 1974 impose restrictions on the employment or remuneration of certain persons by a solicitor, REL or recognised body:

(a)   Under section 41 of that Act, permission must first be obtained from the SRA

APPENDIX 21

by any solicitor, REL or recognised body wishing to employ or remunerate a struck-off or suspended solicitor or REL. You can check with the SRA whether a solicitor or REL has been struck off or suspended.

(b)   Under section 43 of that Act, the Solicitors Disciplinary Tribunal or the SRA can order that a person who is or was involved in a legal practice may not be employed or remunerated in future by any solicitor, REL or recognised body without written permission. Such permission is given or withheld by the SRA. You can check with the SRA whether a section 43 order exists.

Compliance with duties in law and conduct, etc. – 5.01(1)(a)

8.   Principals are responsible in law and in conduct for their firms, including exercising proper control over their staff, and the rule lays these duties, as a matter of conduct, on a recognised body and its managers and on a recognised sole practitioner. For example, if certain work is to be done by unqualified staff it may only be done at the direction and/or under the supervision of persons who are allowed by law to do that work themselves. (See sections 22(2A) and 23(3) of the Solicitors Act 1974, section 9(4) of the Administration of Justice Act 1985, section 84(2)(e) of the Immigration and Asylum Act 1999 and paragraphs 1(7), 3(3) and 4(2) of Schedule 3 to the Legal Services Act 2007.) Recognised bodies, managers of a recognised body and recognised sole practitioners must therefore ensure that arrangements are in place to satisfy these statutory requirements. This would mean, for example, that conveyancing work could not be supervised by a manager who is:

(a)   an RFL, legal executive, patent agent, trade mark agent, law costs draftsman or non-lawyer; or

(b)   an REL who is not qualified to do the work under regulation 12 of the European Communities (Lawyer's Practice) Regulations 2000 (SI 2000/1119).

9.   Under the rule, recognised bodies, managers of a recognised body and recognised sole practitioners are responsible for the acts and omissions of all staff, admitted and unadmitted alike. The duty to supervise staff covers not only persons engaged under a contract of service, but also those engaged under a contract for services to carry out work on behalf of the firm, e.g. consultants, locums and outdoor clerks. You cannot avoid responsibility for work carried out by the firm by leaving it entirely to staff, however well qualified.

10.   Responsibility for the overall supervision framework rests with the recognised body and its managers, or the recognised sole practitioner. This includes, for example, matching staff expertise with relevant work so that work is supervised by the most appropriate individuals. More detailed requirements for the day-to-day supervision of work for clients and members of the public are set out in 5.03.

11.   Operationally, supervision can be delegated within an established framework of reporting and accountability. However, careful consideration should be given to the issues set out below.

12.   If a firm has more than one office, the recognised body and its managers, or the recognised sole practitioner, must be able to demonstrate the adequacy of their arrangements throughout the firm. This includes supervision and management of staff not working from a conventional office – for example, homeworkers, teleworkers, those visiting clients, attending court, at a police station, at a consulting room open only for a few hours a week, or staffing a stand at an exhibition.

13.   As a general guide, the lower the ratio of managers to offices and staff, or the greater the number of the offices and staff of a sole practice, the greater will be the onus on the recognised body and its managers, or the recognised sole practitioner, to demonstrate the adequacy of their supervision arrangements. For example, the more staff a

recognised sole practitioner employs, the higher the degree of personal involvement he or she may be expected to take in the supervision process, especially if those staff are inexperienced and/or unqualified.

Money laundering – 5.01(1)(b)

14. See the Money Laundering Regulations 2007 (SI 2007/2157) (and any subsequent regulations) and any guidance on compliance issued by the Law Society.

Compliance with key regulatory obligations – 5.01(1)(c)

15. The purpose of 5.01(1)(c) is to foster collective responsibility for the governance of the firm by requiring you to establish arrangements which provide for compliance with key regulatory obligations. These include arrangements to ensure that:

    (a) every solicitor in the firm holds a practising certificate (except in the rare case of a solicitor employee who is not required to hold a practising certificate – see 20.02) and that the practising certificate is renewed promptly when required;

    (b) every lawyer in the firm who is required to be registered in the UK under the Establishment Directive (see rule 24) and is not registered with another UK regulatory body for lawyers, is registered as an REL and that registration is renewed promptly when required;

    (c) every lawyer in the firm who is required under these rules to be an RFL (as a manager or shareowner of the firm) is registered as an RFL and that the registration is renewed promptly when required;

    (d) every lawyer manager or shareowner in the firm is eligible under these rules to undertake that role (see rule 14);

    (e) every manager in the firm who is entitled to be a manager only by virtue of approval under regulation 3 of the Recognised Bodies Regulations has received such approval;

    (f) every body corporate which is a manager or shareowner in the firm is entitled to undertake that role;

    (g) if the firm is a partnership or body corporate it has obtained recognition as a recognised body, its recognition is renewed promptly every year when required, and it complies with the requirements of rule 14 (Recognised bodies);

    (h) the firm complies with the Solicitors' Indemnity Insurance Rules;

    (i) an accountant's report is delivered in accordance with the Solicitors' Accounts Rules; and

    (j) the firm notifies the SRA of any change in the place or places of business of the solicitors, RELs and RFLs in the firm (they have a legal obligation to do this, under section 84 of the Solicitors Act 1974).

16. Some of these obligations mirror personal obligations of each solicitor, REL, RFL or recognised body (such as to renew a practising certificate or renew registration). The fact that 5.01(1)(c) is aimed at a recognised body and its managers or a recognised sole practitioner will not relieve an individual solicitor, REL or RFL of responsibility in this regard. The precise nature of the arrangements is for the firm to decide. See 20.02 (Practising certificates).

17. If you are a sole practitioner or a manager in a firm then you are personally responsible for complying with the Solicitors' Accounts Rules, including the delivery of an annual accountant's report. You will be liable to disciplinary action if there is a failure to comply with those rules, even if you have delegated book-keeping to someone else in the firm. The nature of the disciplinary action will depend on the seriousness of the

717

breach and the extent to which you knew or should have known of the breach. Similarly, in the case of a partnership or body corporate, the recognised body itself is directly responsible for complying with the Solicitors' Accounts Rules, including delivering an accountant's report, and is itself liable to disciplinary action.

18. If you are an in-house solicitor or in-house REL and you receive or hold client money you must comply with the Solicitors' Accounts Rules and must submit an accountant's report.

Identification of conflicts – 5.01(1)(d)

19. Firms must adopt a systematic approach to identifying and avoiding conflicts of interests, dealing with conflicts between the duties of confidentiality and disclosure, and maintaining client confidentiality. See also the guidance to rule 3 (Conflict of interests) and to rule 4 (Confidentiality and disclosure) for assistance in identifying the sort of issues your arrangements will need to address.

Compliance with the requirements of rule 2 on client care, costs information and complaints handling – 5.01(1)(e)

20. This provision is designed to ensure that compliance with 2.02, 2.03 and 2.05 is addressed at the level of the firm's systems and procedures. If you have appropriate arrangements for compliance but a member of staff fails to follow established procedures in a one-off case, you will nevertheless have satisfied 5.01(1)(e). However, a serious breach or repeated "minor" breaches of 2.02, 2.03 or 2.05 might indicate a failure to put in place effective arrangements, as required under 5.01(1)(e).

Control of undertakings – 5.01(1)(f)

21. See 10.05 (Undertakings) and the guidance to it for assistance in identifying the sort of issues your arrangements will need to address.

Safekeeping of documents and assets – 5.01(1)(g)

22. The terms "documents" and "assets" should be interpreted in a non-technical way to include, for example, client money, wills, deeds, investments and other property entrusted to the firm by clients and others.

23. The detail of the firm's arrangements will be a matter for you to decide in all the circumstances. However, as a minimum requirement you must be able to identify to whom documents and assets belong, and in connection with which matter.

Equality and diversity – 5.01(1)(h)

24. For guidance on equality and diversity and avoiding discrimination, see the guidance to rule 6 (Equality and diversity).

The training of individuals working in the firm to maintain a level of competence appropriate to their work and level of responsibility – 5.01(1)(i)

25. "Competence" is the ability to perform a task or role to a required standard by the application of essential knowledge, skill and understanding. The purpose of 5.01(1)(i) is to ensure that the competence of everyone in the firm involved in the provision of legal services is addressed systematically, at management level. Consequently, 5.01(1)(i)

focuses on effecting arrangements to "provide for" competence levels to be maintained, and leaves it to the firm to determine the best method of doing this. It is anticipated that most firms will already have such arrangements in place.

26. The nature of the arrangements will vary significantly depending on the work and level of responsibility of each individual. However, if a breach of 5.01(1)(i) is alleged, evidence may be required to demonstrate that issues of competence are addressed in the firm's procedures in relation to, for example, recruitment, ongoing work assessment and training.

   Firms will also need to consider which staff might need training in some or all of the rules of conduct. The rules apply to employees (see rule 23), but the impact will vary depending on the nature of the work and the responsibility of the employee concerned. All employees will need to be aware of the need to keep clients' matters confidential.

27. Training is an integral element of maintaining competence. Rule 5.01(1)(i) assumes that arrangements will include provision for training, but does not lay down any specific requirements. Training can be of any kind relevant to the work or responsibilities of the individual, and can be delivered by any appropriate method. For example, it could include on-the-job learning, mentoring schemes, in-house training, individual study, etc. It need not be accredited under the compulsory continuing professional development scheme (CPD) or involve attendance at courses.

28. Rule 5.01(1)(i) does not relieve an individual of the duty to decline to act when unable to provide a competent service, or allow an individual to escape obligations under the CPD scheme.

29. Rule 5.01(1)(i) is limited to effecting suitable arrangements. Therefore, an isolated case of incompetence would not normally indicate a breach. However, if you do not address issues of competence systematically, at management level, in your firm's arrangements for recruitment, ongoing work assessment and training, you would breach 5.01(1)(i).

30. It should be noted that training for the purpose of becoming "qualified to supervise" under 5.02 must be of a kind specified by the SRA from time to time (see note 44 below).

Financial control of budgets, expenditure and cashflow – 5.01(1)(j)

31. Client money is more likely to be at risk in a firm where the recognised body and its managers, or the recognised sole practitioner, do not exercise adequate oversight of the firm's own financial arrangements. The purpose of 5.01(1)(j) is to ensure this is addressed in the overall management framework – not to prescribe particular financial systems or to prevent you from delegating day-to-day financial operations to suitable staff. It may also help firms to ensure that they are looking forward when undertaking their financial management, so that they will know they will be able to cover their commitments and plan their resources properly. It should be noted, however, that some accounting and management information systems do not assist in this regard, as they tend to deal only with historic information.

Continuation of the practice of the firm in the event of absences and emergencies, etc. – 5.01(1)(k)

32. There is a continuing duty to ensure that the practice of your firm will be carried on with the minimum interruption to clients' business even if you are absent. Your supervision and management arrangements must therefore provide for the running of the firm during any period of absence (for example, holiday or sick leave). The arrangements must ensure that any duties to clients and others can be fully met. If you are a sole practitioner or sole director you should make adequate provision for the running of the practice, in the event that you die or become permanently disabled, by a solicitor (or REL) who is "qualified to supervise".

APPENDIX 21

33.   If you are away for a month or more, and you are the only person in the firm "qualified to supervise" under 5.02, the arrangements for complying with 5.01(1)(k) will normally need to include the provision of another person qualified to supervise.

34.   Rule 23 of the Solicitors' Accounts Rules requires that a withdrawal from a client account cannot be made without a specific authority. This rule cannot be complied with if blank cheques are left for completion by staff at a later date, as signing a blank cheque is not giving a specific authority.

35.   If you have not made adequate arrangements in advance to meet unforeseen circumstances, difficulties may arise in the conduct of clients' affairs and in the administration of your own business. For example, a client may attend the office asking for urgent assistance, an accountant's report must be submitted, a practising certificate must be applied for or indemnity cover must be obtained notwithstanding your absence. Consequently, if you are a sole practitioner or sole director, you should have an arrangement with another solicitor or REL (sufficiently experienced and entitled to practise) to supervise your firm until you return. You should notify your bank of these arrangements in advance, so that the solicitor or REL covering your absence can operate your client and office accounts.

36.   If you are a sole practitioner and your absence lasts beyond the period covered by your practising certificate, you may be able to obtain permission from the SRA for another solicitor to complete your application for a practising certificate. Your name can only remain on your professional stationery as sole practitioner if you continue to hold a practising certificate.

37.   If you are a sole practitioner and you are struck off or suspended, you must inform clients of the firm, your bank, insurers, and the SRA, and clients will need to be told how their matter will be affected. You will not be able to continue to practise. This means that, from the date of the striking off or suspension (at least until, for example, the suspension is lifted), your firm will need to be closed or otherwise disposed of, e.g. by being taken over by another solicitor or REL. It is not sufficient for another solicitor or REL to take over day-to-day management of the practice whilst you are suspended or struck off if you remain the proprietor of the firm because you will not be entitled to be a recognised sole practitioner. If the firm is taken over by another firm you cannot be employed or remunerated by that firm whilst suspended or struck off except with written permission from the SRA (see section 41 of the Solicitors Act 1974). Care will need to be taken in any correspondence relating to your former practice to ensure that your status is not misrepresented. For instance, if you are suspended you are a non-practising solicitor. If you are struck off you are no longer a solicitor.

38.   If you are a sole practitioner and you decide to stop practising, you must inform clients so that they may instruct another firm. Failure to inform clients could amount to misconduct, inadequate professional service and/or negligence. If you are considering retirement, guidance can be obtained from the Professional Ethics Guidance Team.

Management of risk – 5.01(1)(l)

39.   Firms should have arrangements in place for assessing the risks attaching to each area of their operation. The rule is aimed at ensuring risk is addressed in the firm's overall management framework. If a particular risk materialises which had not been foreseen in the firm's systems, this would not necessarily constitute a breach of 5.01(1)(l). Risk management arrangements are unlikely to be considered adequate unless they include periodic reviews of the firm's risk profile.

40.   Ideally the scope of the arrangements should not be confined to risks arising from professional negligence, but should extend to client-related and business-related risks of all sorts. A non-exhaustive list might include complaints (including a complaints log); client-related credit risks and exposure; claims under legislation relating to such matters as data protection; IT failures and abuses; and damage to offices.

In-house practice – 5.01(2)

41. As the head of an in-house legal department you do not have to institute all the arrangements required under 5.01(1). However, you must under 5.01(2) institute arrangements to ensure that:

   (a) work done for members of the public is adequately supervised, and if unqualified staff within the department undertake work reserved to solicitors, they are supervised by a person qualified to do that work, and the work is done in the name of that qualified person;

   (b) undertakings given by members of the department, whether or not they are solicitors or RELs, are given appropriately and can be fulfilled (you will be primarily responsible in conduct for fulfilling such undertakings); and

   (c) conflicts of interests are identified.

Qualified to supervise – 5.02

42. The purpose of 5.02 is to protect the public by ensuring that there is at least one person responsible for running the firm (or law centre or in-house legal practice falling within 5.02(1)(c) or (d)) who has the right kind of experience. The responsibilities involved relate to the management of the firm rather than the supervision of particular work, so the person "qualified to supervise" under 5.02 does not have to be personally entitled by law to supervise all work undertaken by the firm. However, an important part of that person's responsibilities would be to ensure that unqualified persons did not undertake reserved work except under the supervision of a suitably qualified person – see note 8 above.

43. Waivers may be granted in individual cases. An applicant must satisfy the SRA that the circumstances are sufficiently exceptional to justify a departure from the requirements of 5.02, bearing in mind its purpose. Applications should be made to the Professional Ethics Guidance Team.

44. The training presently specified by the SRA is attendance at or participation in any course(s), or programme(s) of learning, on management skills involving attendance or participation for a minimum of 12 hours. The courses or programmes do not have to be CPD accredited in order to satisfy the requirement. It is not normally necessary to check with the SRA before undertaking a course or programme unless the course is unusual and outside the mainstream of management training. Advice may be sought from the Professional Ethics Guidance Team.

Supervision of work for clients and members of the public – 5.03

45. Rule 5.03 is aimed firstly at a recognised body and its managers, or a recognised sole practitioner. Secondly, it applies to you if you are an in-house solicitor or in-house REL who acts for members of the public and fulfils the role of the person "qualified to supervise" under 5.02(1)(c) or (d).

46. A suitably experienced and competent person or persons must undertake the supervision required under 5.03. Such a person need not hold a particular qualification or have been in legal practice for a particular time; but in certain circumstances (for example, where a sole practitioner has more than one office) these may be relevant factors in determining compliance with 5.03.

47. Those supervising client matters under 5.03 would need to have sufficient legal knowledge and experience to be able to identify problems with the quality or conduct of the work; but might not need to be an expert in the area of work. The training, qualifications and experience of the member of staff whose matters are being checked under 5.03 will be relevant in assessing the level and type of expertise required by the person conducting the checks.

48.   Rule 5.03 requires that work for clients is supervised wherever staff happen to be working, including at home or from "virtual" offices.

49.   Supervision is an inherently internal function. The phrase "within the firm, law centre or in-house legal department" is included to ensure that supervision is not delegated outside your control but undertaken by someone who is genuinely part of the practice.

50.   If a complaint is made, you will have to demonstrate that the work-checking procedures are "appropriate", "effective", and undertaken with "reasonable regularity". Relevant factors will include the size and complexity of the firm, law centre or in-house department; the nature of the work; the experience of the individuals undertaking the work, and their level of responsibility.

51.   Rule 5.03 does not apply to business development and practice management work unrelated to work on client matters.

52.   Supervising "work for clients and members of the public" embraces all aspects of the work, including the handling of client money and compliance with rule 2 (Client relations).

Rule 6 – Equality and diversity

Introduction

Rule 6 is designed to prevent discrimination within your firm or in-house practice. The rule does not apply to overseas practice but solicitors practising overseas must comply with 15.06 (Equality and diversity) and 1.02 (Integrity). The duties contained in this rule are in addition to, and not in substitution for, your obligations to comply with anti-discrimination legislation.

Rule 6 – Equality and diversity

6.01 Duty not to discriminate

(1)   You must not in your professional dealings with the firm's managers and employees, other lawyers, clients or third parties discriminate, without lawful cause, against any person, nor victimise or harass them on the grounds of:

    (a)   race or racial group (including colour, nationality and ethnic or national origins);

    (b)   sex (including marital status, gender reassignment, pregnancy, maternity and paternity);

    (c)   sexual orientation (including civil partnership status);

    (d)   religion or belief;

    (e)   age; or

    (f)   disability.

(2)   You must take such steps, and make such adjustments, as are reasonable in all the circumstances in order to prevent any of your employees, partners, members, directors or clients who are disabled from being placed at a substantial disadvantage in comparison with those who are not disabled.

6.02 Evidence of breach

Where there has been a decision of a court or tribunal of the United Kingdom in proceedings to which you are a party, that you have committed, or are to be treated as having committed, an unlawful act of discrimination then that finding shall be treated as evidence of a breach of this rule.

6.03 Equality and diversity policy

If you are a recognised body, a manager of a recognised body or a recognised sole practitioner, you must adopt and implement an appropriate policy for preventing discrimination and harassment and promoting equality and diversity within your firm. You must take all reasonable steps to ensure that all employees, partners, members and directors are aware of, and act in compliance with, its provisions and that it is made available to clients, the Solicitors Regulation Authority and other relevant third parties where required.

6.04 In-house practice

If you have management responsibilities in in-house practice you must use all reasonable endeavours to secure the adoption and implementation of an appropriate policy for preventing discrimination and promoting equality and diversity within your department. You must take all reasonable steps to ensure that all staff within that department are aware of, and act in accordance with, its provisions.

6.05 Waivers

In spite of 22.01(1), the Solicitors Regulation Authority Board shall not have power to waive any of the provisions of this rule.

6.06 Meaning of terms

For the avoidance of doubt, unless otherwise defined in the rules, the terms used in this rule shall have the meanings assigned to them in law.

Guidance to rule 6 – Equality and diversity

1. The information which follows is by way of clarification and guidance. Those parts which deal with legal issues are intended only to provide an overview of the law and not an interpretative explanation or redefinition of it. This is to guide you and is not intended to lay down a binding course of action.

Duty not to discriminate – 6.01

The scope of the rule

2. You must, as a matter of general law, comply with the requirements set out in legislation in relation to discrimination and you should be aware that the provisions contained in this rule are in addition to, and not in substitution for, your legal duties.

3. This rule places two distinct requirements upon you:

(a)   not to discriminate against, without lawful cause, nor victimise or harass, in the course of your professional dealings, those groups of people, and in those circumstances, set out in 6.01(1); and

(b)   to make reasonable adjustments to prevent the firm's managers, employees or clients, or the clients of an in-house solicitor or REL, who are disabled from being at a disadvantage in comparison with those who are not disabled.

4.   You should be aware that, whilst the provisions contained in this rule are based upon legislative provisions, this rule goes beyond the scope of the legislation in a number of key areas and in particular in relation to age discrimination.

In particular you should note that it requires you to refrain from discriminating against all of those persons referred to in 6.01(1) in all of the circumstances referred to. There is no limitation in this requirement to discrimination occurring only in particular circumstances. Thus, for example, whilst the law dealing with age discrimination currently applies only in relation to employment and vocational training, this rule applies to all of your professional dealings with barristers, other lawyers, clients or third parties.

Please note, however, that the provisions relating to reasonable adjustment for disability set out in 6.01(2) are limited to an adjustment for clients, employees and the firm's managers.

5.   The following points should be noted:

(a)   Discrimination based on age is now included in this rule, as are requirements not to discriminate on the basis of civil partnership status, gender reassignment, pregnancy, maternity and paternity.

(b)   This rule does not address, but you should nevertheless be aware of, discrimination-related employment issues such as those which relate to fixed-term and part-time workers, the requirements for flexible working, and provisions relating to participation in, or abstention from, trade union activities.

(c)   Although this rule does not address issues set out in the Human Rights Act 1998 you should be aware of these, especially if you are working in the public sector.

(d)   Whilst this rule does not apply to overseas practice, nevertheless you should be aware of the provisions set out in regulation 11 of the Employment Equality (Sex Discrimination) Regulations 2005 (SI 2005/2467) in relation to employment wholly or partly outside Great Britain and its applicability to sex discrimination and equal pay.

(e)   Although they are not specifically dealt with in this rule, nevertheless you should be aware of the provisions of the Racial and Religious Hatred Act 2006 in so far as they affect your practice.

(f)   The terms "employer" and "employment" in this guidance are used in their normal everyday sense and not as defined in rule 24 (Interpretation).

(g)   The term "without lawful cause" means that the discrimination has taken place in circumstances which are not dealt with in notes 11, 12 and 13 below where there is a permitted exception within the law or where circumstances are such that it is possible to justify why the discrimination has taken place.

What is discrimination?

6.   Discrimination occurs when one person is treated less favourably than another is treated, or would be treated, in the same or similar circumstances without legitimate reason.

7.   The grounds upon which a person must not be discriminated against are:

(a)   race or racial group (including colour, nationality and ethnic or national origin);

(b)   sex (including marital status, gender reassignment, pregnancy, maternity and paternity);

(c)   sexual orientation (including civil partnership status);

(d)   religion or belief;

(e)   age; or

(f)   disability.

These terms have the same meaning in this rule as they have in law.

8.   In particular you should note that:

(a)   discrimination on the grounds of race or racial group includes discrimination on the basis of colour, nationality and national or ethnic origin;

(b)   sex discrimination includes discrimination against:

      (i)   a married person on the grounds of their marital status;

      (ii)   a person who is about to undergo, is undergoing or has undergone gender reassignment;

      (iii)   a woman on the grounds of pregnancy or maternity; and

      (iv)   a man on the grounds of paternity;

(c)   you are subject to the provisions of the Equal Pay Act 1970;

(d)   sexual orientation applies equally to those who are heterosexual as it does to those who are lesbian, gay or bisexual; discrimination based on sexual orientation includes discrimination against a person because they are in a civil partnership; it should also be noted that discrimination can be on the grounds of perceived sexual orientation as well as actual sexual orientation;

(e)   disability is widely defined and includes stress related illnesses (which do not need to be "clinically well-recognised" to be capable of founding a claim), progressive illnesses (such as HIV and cancer) from the time of diagnosis, illnesses which would be substantial if not controlled by drugs (such as insulin-dependent diabetes) and conditions such as learning disabilities or dyslexia which restrict a person's ability to interact or communicate;

(f)   religion or belief includes philosophical beliefs similar to a religion (for example humanism); and

(g)   age means any age, not just old age and can include discrimination based on the age of others, e.g. a person's spouse. It should also be noted that discrimination can be on the grounds of perceived age as well as actual age.

9.   Discrimination can take a variety of forms including direct discrimination, indirect discrimination, harassment, victimisation, less favourable treatment and failure to make an adjustment. A brief summary of each of these is set out below although you should rely upon the meanings assigned to them by law when interpreting your duties under this rule.

10   (a)   Direct discrimination occurs where one person treats another less favourably by reason of:

      (i)   race or racial group (including colour, nationality and ethnic or national origins);

      (ii)   their sex (including marital status, gender reassignment, pregnancy, maternity and paternity);

      (iii)   sexual orientation (including their civil partnership status);

      (iv)   religion or belief;

(v)   age; or

(vi)   disability,

and, in respect of age discrimination only, it cannot be shown that the treatment in question was justified.

To treat a person less favourably for other reasons, for example because they have not performed adequately, will not generally be regarded as discrimination amounting to professional misconduct unless the true reason for the treatment is, or includes, one of the matters referred to above.

(b)   Indirect discrimination occurs where a provision, criterion, practice, requirement or condition (as appropriate) which is applied to everyone, has the effect of placing at a disadvantage a particular person, or group of people, by reason of:

    (i)   race or racial group (including colour, nationality and ethnic or national origins);

    (ii)   sex (including marital status, gender reassignment, pregnancy, maternity and paternity);

    (iii)   sexual orientation (including civil partnership status);

    (iv)   religion or belief; and

    (v)   age,

and it cannot be shown that to apply that provision, criterion, practice, requirement or condition in that way is a proportionate means for achieving a legitimate aim.

Note that the provisions relating to indirect discrimination are not applicable to discrimination on the grounds of disability.

Indirect discrimination can occur whether or not the person applying the provision, criterion, practice, requirement or condition intended to discriminate against the person or group of people affected.

(c)   Harassment occurs when one person subjects another to "unwanted conduct that has the purpose or effect ... of creating an intimidating, hostile, degrading, humiliating or offensive environment" (section 4A(1) of the Sex Discrimination Act 1975, as amended by the Employment Equality (Sex Discrimination) Regulations 2005 (SI 2005/2467)), in other words threatening, abusive or insulting behaviour, words or actions which violate the other person's dignity or create a humiliating, intimidating or hostile environment. Harassment may involve physical acts or verbal and non-verbal communications and gestures. Harassment can also occur where it has the defined effect upon the victim, notwithstanding the harasser's intention – it is the effect which the harassment has upon the victim that is important. For example, remarks made humorously or without malicious intent can still constitute harassment if that is the effect which they had upon the person being harassed.

In determining whether harassment has occurred you should be aware that a series of minor acts or comments can constitute harassment as can a one-off act of sufficient severity. However, the acts complained of must be capable of amounting to harassment.

You should also be aware of the provisions of section 4A(1)(b) of the Sex Discrimination Act 1975 in respect of sexual harassment.

(d)   Victimisation occurs when a person is treated less favourably because he or she:

    (i)   has asserted a right not to be discriminated against on one of the prohibited grounds set out in 6.01;

(ii)   has assisted another to assert a right not to be discriminated against on one of the prohibited grounds set out in 6.01; or

(iii)   has given evidence in a tribunal or court relating to the assertion of such a right.

The protection applies only to assertions made in good faith.

(e)   Less favourable treatment, as used in relation to disability discrimination, occurs when a person with a disability is treated in a detrimental way in circumstances when a person without that disability would not be so treated. Thus, for example, charging more to a disabled client than a client without a disability because their disability means that more time is required to obtain instructions could constitute less favourable treatment, as could offering less favourable terms or refusing to act.

(f)   Failure to make reasonable adjustment is another concept used in relation to disability discrimination. You are under a duty to take such steps (adjustments) as are reasonable in all the circumstances to ensure that employment arrangements, arrangements for partners, members, directors and clients, the premises from which your business is undertaken and the service provided, do not put at a substantial disadvantage a person with a disability when compared with a person without that disability, without justification.

The following points should be borne in mind when making a reasonable adjustment:

(i)   the duty to make the adjustment stands alone and requires no other form of less favourable treatment or intention to discriminate;

(ii)   the duty is a positive one – it requires that you take active steps to ensure that a person with a disability can access employment opportunities or services as if they did not have that disability;

(iii)   the cost of making the adjustment is one which must be absorbed by you, where it is reasonable to do so, and not passed on to the disabled client by way of a disbursement, additional charge or less comprehensive service;

(iv)   the duty is to make a reasonable adjustment – if the adjustment is not reasonable then you may not be under a duty to make it;

(v)   the fact that the cost of the adjustment exceeds the charges or profits from the matter in question does not of itself make the adjustment unreasonable. A more relevant factor is the resources of the firm;

(vi)   an adjustment does not have to be a physical adjustment – it may simply be a change to working practices such as visiting a client at home if they are unable to access your premises; and

(vii)   an adjustment is not always a one-off action – it may need to be made on numerous occasions, for example employing the services of a British Sign Language Interpreter when advising a client with profound hearing loss. So long as the adjustment continues to be reasonable, its cost must be absorbed by you.

Permitted exceptions and justifiable discrimination

11.   There are situations in which it is permitted to discriminate without breach of the legislation or this rule. In some instances this will be by way of specific exceptions to the legislation, whilst in others it will depend upon the nature of the discrimination and the extent to which it can be justified. Although a brief explanation is given below, in both cases you should rely upon the meanings assigned to them by law when interpreting your duties under this rule.

12. There are permitted exceptions to the legislation variously referred to as Genuine Occupational Qualifications (GOQs) and Genuine Occupational Requirements (GORs). These apply in relation to discrimination on the basis of race, sex, sexual orientation, religion or belief, and age. The exception to the concept of GOQs and GORs is discrimination on the grounds of disability. This relies upon whether it can be shown that the discrimination in question was reasonable.

13. In certain circumstances you may be able to justify discriminating against a person even though it is on one of the prohibited grounds set out in 6.01.

   (a) Direct discrimination cannot be justified other than in relation to age discrimination (where it must be a proportionate means of achieving a legitimate aim).

   (b) With regard to indirect discrimination, it may be possible for you to show that a provision, criterion, practice, requirement or condition which is applied to everyone, but which places a person or group of people at a disadvantage, is justified. To do so, you would need to show, amongst other things, that:

      (i) it was imposed other than for the purposes of discriminating;

      (ii) it was appropriate and necessary to achieve the required aim; and

      (iii) the means of achieving that legitimate aim were appropriate and necessary.

Dealing with clients and third parties

14. You are generally free to decide whether to accept instructions from any client provided that your refusal to act is not based upon any of the grounds in 6.01. You should also note 11.04 (Refusing instructions to act as advocate) which limits the circumstances in which you can refuse to act as an advocate and 2.01 (Taking on clients) which deals with taking on clients.

15. You should instruct barristers on the basis of their skill, experience and ability and it is unlawful to instruct them, or avoid instructing them, on the basis of any of the grounds in 6.01, or to request or encourage a barrister's clerk to do so.

16. You should normally comply with a client's request to instruct a named barrister (subject to your duty to discuss the suitability of that barrister for a particular type of work). Where a client's instructions as to the choice of barrister are based on any of the grounds in 6.01, you should encourage the client to modify their instructions. If they refuse to do so, you should cease to act for them as aiding an unlawful act is prohibited.

17. In relation to the instruction of a barrister, in addition to the requirements of this rule, you are subject to provisions relating to the giving, withholding or acceptance of instructions contained in:

   (a) section 26A(3) of the Race Relations Act 1976;

   (b) section 35A(3) of the Sex Discrimination Act 1975;

   (c) section 7A(3) of the Disability Discrimination Act 1995;

   (d) regulation 12(4) of the Employment Equality (Religion or Belief) Regulations 2003 (SI 2003/1660);

   (e) regulation 12(4) of the Employment Equality (Sexual Orientation) Regulations 2003 (SI 2003/1661); and

   (f) regulation 15(4) of the Employment Equality (Age) Regulations 2006 (SI 2006/1031).

18. If you maintain lists or databases of contractors, agents and other third parties who are regarded as suitable to be instructed by others within the firm, you should ensure that those lists or databases:

(a)   are compiled on the basis only of their ability to undertake work of a particular type; and

(b)   do not contain any discriminatory bias based on any of the grounds in 6.01.

Partners and partnerships

19.   In relation to a position as partner in a firm, you should not discriminate against partners or potential partners. In addition to the provisions of this rule, you should note that you are subject to provisions as to discrimination in relation to a position as partner contained in:

(a)   section 10 of the Race Relations Act 1976;

(b)   section 11 of the Sex Discrimination Act 1975 as amended by section 1(3) of the Sex Discrimination Act 1986;

(c)   sections 6A, 6B and 6C of the Disability Discrimination Act 1995;

(d)   regulation 14 of the Employment Equality (Religion or Belief) Regulations 2003 (SI 2003/1660);

(e)   regulation 14 of the Employment Equality (Sexual Orientation) Regulations 2003 (SI 2003/1661);

(f)   regulation 14 of the Employment Equality (Sex Discrimination) Regulations 2005 (SI 2005/2467); and

(g)   regulation 17 of the Employment Equality (Age) Regulations 2006 (SI 2006/1031).

20.   You should also comply with the various provisions which prohibit discrimination after the end of a professional relationship and which apply to both staff and managers. This means, for example, that you should exercise care when giving a reference for someone so as to ensure that you do not permit that reference to be in any way discriminatory or to appear to have been influenced by issues of a discriminatory nature.

Evidence of breach – 6.02

21.   Whilst decisions of unlawful discrimination by an employment tribunal are not binding on the SRA or the Solicitors Disciplinary Tribunal in determining whether an allegation of misconduct involving discrimination is well founded, such decisions are admissible in evidence in disciplinary proceedings. The SRA or the Tribunal must determine whether an allegation or decision of discrimination against you amounts to misconduct. The starting point for this will be that the decision represents a strong indication that misconduct has taken place and it will be for you to show why, despite the decision, there has not been misconduct.

Equality and diversity policy – 6.03

22   (a)   In order to encourage you to abide by the provisions of this rule, and to assist you in ensuring that managers and employees do so too, it is a requirement that your firm adopts and implements an appropriate written policy for promoting equality, preventing discrimination and dealing with any instances of discrimination which might arise.

(b)   To be appropriate the policy must:

(i)   be in writing;

(ii)   include such provisions as are relevant to your firm (having regard to its nature and size);

      (iii)   as a minimum, deal with the following core items:

          (A) how the firm plans to implement, communicate, monitor, evaluate and update the policy;

          (B) how the firm intends to ensure equality in relation to employees, managers, clients and third parties and the means by which it will monitor, evaluate and update any procedures and policies in relation to this;

          (C) how complaints and disciplinary issues are to be dealt with;

          (D) a requirement that all employees and managers comply with the provisions set out in 6.01; and

          (E) a commitment to the principles of equality and diversity and to observing legislative requirements;

      (iv)   not contain any additional items which would conflict with the core items.

  (c)   In adopting and implementing that policy you should be aware that:

      (i)   account must be taken of the size and nature of your firm and any policy which you adopt and implement should contain provisions which are relevant to your firm;

      (ii)   you must ensure that all managers and employees are aware of, and act in compliance with, the provisions contained in the policy. A policy which is not brought to their attention will not be an appropriate policy.

          In order to demonstrate that the policy has been brought to the attention of managers and employees in an effective manner, you may wish to give consideration to providing staff with training and information about complying with equality and diversity requirements. Where a client, the SRA or other relevant third party requests a copy of the policy to be provided to them, you must do so within a reasonable period of time; and

      (iii)   since the equality and diversity needs of your practice may change from time to time, you should monitor the continuing appropriateness of your policy and make such changes as are necessary.

In-house practice – 6.04

23.   If you are a solicitor or REL with management responsibilities in in-house practice then it is likely that you will not have the same opportunity to formulate, adopt and implement measures for preventing discrimination and promoting equality and diversity, as a sole practitioner or manager in a firm. You may, however, have an opportunity to influence those measures which are implemented, especially within your own department.

24.   If you are practising in-house then you are required to use your best endeavours to secure the adoption and implementation of an appropriate policy for preventing discrimination and promoting equality and diversity within your department. You should also ensure, so far as you are able, that employees within your department are aware of, and act in compliance with, its provisions. However, where you are unable to do so, no burden of professional misconduct will be placed upon you.

25.   If there is an allegation of misconduct based upon discrimination on any of the grounds listed in 6.01, and you have management responsibility, you will be required to show good reason why you were unable to secure the operation of an appropriate policy.

26.   In all other respects you will be required to abide by the terms of this rule to the same extent as a solicitor in private practice.

Rule 7 – Publicity

Introduction

You are generally free to publicise your firm or practice, subject to the requirements of this rule. The rule as it applies to your overseas practice is modified by 15.07.

Rule 7 – Publicity

7.01 Misleading or inaccurate publicity

Publicity must not be misleading or inaccurate.

7.02 Clarity as to charges

Any publicity relating to your, or your firm's, charges must be clearly expressed. In relation to practice from an office in England and Wales it must be clear whether disbursements and VAT are included.

7.03 Unsolicited approaches in person or by telephone

(1)   You must not publicise your firm or practice by making unsolicited approaches in person or by telephone to a member of the public.

(2)   "Member of the public" does not include:

(a)   a current or former client;

(b)   another firm or its manager;

(c)   an existing or potential professional or business connection; or

(d)   a commercial organisation or public body.

7.04 International aspects of publicity

Publicity intended for a jurisdiction outside England and Wales must comply with:

(a)   the provisions of rule 7 (and 15.07, if applicable); and

(b)   the rules in force in that jurisdiction concerning lawyers' publicity.

Publicity intended for a jurisdiction where it is permitted will not breach 7.04 through being incidentally received in a jurisdiction where it is not permitted.

7.05 Responsibility for publicity

You must not authorise any other person to conduct publicity for your firm or practice in a way which would be contrary to rule 7 (and 15.07, if applicable).

7.06 Application

(1)   Rule 7 applies to any publicity you or your firm conduct(s) or authorise(s) in the course of setting up or carrying on the practice in relation to:

    (a)   the firm or your practice;

    (b)   any other business or activity carried on by you or your firm; or

    (c)   any other business or activity carried on by others.

(2)   Rules 7.01 to 7.05 apply to all forms of publicity including the name or description of your firm, stationery, advertisements, brochures, websites, directory entries, media appearances, promotional press releases, and direct approaches to potential clients and other persons, and whether conducted in person, in writing, or in electronic form.

7.07 Letterhead, website and e-mails

(1)   The letterhead, website and e-mails of a recognised body or recognised sole practitioner must show the words "regulated by the Solicitors Regulation Authority", and either

    (a)   the firm's registered name and number if it is an LLP or company, or

    (b)   if the firm is a partnership or sole practitioner, the name under which it is recognised by the Solicitors Regulation Authority, and the number allocated to it by the Authority.

(2)   (a)   The letterhead of a recognised sole practitioner must include the name of the sole practitioner.

    (b)   The letterhead of a recognised body which is a partnership of 20 or fewer partners, must include a list of the partners.

    (c)   The letterhead of a recognised body which is a partnership of more than 20 partners, must include either

        (i)   a list of the partners; or

        (ii)   a statement that a list of the partners is open to inspection at the office.

    (d)   The letterhead of a recognised body which is an LLP must include either

        (i)   a list of the members, identified as members; or

        (ii)   a statement that a list of the members is open to inspection at the office.

    (e)   The letterhead of a recognised body which is a company with a sole director must include the name of the director, identified as director.

    (f)   The letterhead of a recognised body which is a company with more than one director must include either

        (i)   a list of the directors, identified as directors; or

        (ii)   a statement that a list of the directors is open to inspection at the office.

(3)   In a recognised body, if the managers include persons other than solicitors, any list referred to in this rule must:

    (a)   identify any solicitor as a solicitor;

> (b)   in the case of any lawyer or notary of an Establishment Directive state other than the UK:
>
>   (i)   identify the jurisdiction(s) – local or national as appropriate – under whose professional title the lawyer or notary is practising;
>
>   (ii)   give the professional title(s), expressed in an official language of the Establishment Directive state(s) concerned; and
>
>   (iii) if the lawyer is an REL, refer to that lawyer's registration with the Solicitors Regulation Authority;
>
> (c)   indicate the professional qualification(s) of any other lawyer and the country or jurisdiction of qualification of any RFL not included in (b) above;
>
> (d)   identify any individual non-lawyer as a non-lawyer; and
>
> (e)   identify the nature of any body corporate, if this is not clear from its name.
>
> (4) Whenever an REL is named on the letterhead used by any firm or in-house practice, there must be compliance with 7.07(3)(b).
>
> (5) In 7.07 "letterhead" includes a fax heading.

Guidance to rule 7 – Publicity

Geographical scope of the rule

1   (a)   Rule 7 applies to publicity in connection with practice from any office, whether in England and Wales or overseas – but the provisions are amended by 15.07 for publicity in connection with overseas practice.

     (b)   Rule 7 does not apply to the website, e-mails, text messages or similar electronic communications of any practice you conduct from an office in an EU state other than the UK (see 15.07(2)).

     (c)   Rule 7.07 (Letterhead, website and e-mails) does not apply to a solicitor's practice conducted from an office outside England and Wales or to an REL's practice conducted from an office in Scotland or Northern Ireland. However, you must comply with 15.07(3).

General

2.   In the delivery of professional services, there is an imbalance of knowledge between clients and the public on the one hand, and the service provider on the other. Rule 7 addresses this in a number of ways – for example, by ensuring that clients and the public have appropriate information about you, your firm and the way you are regulated; and by prohibiting misleading publicity and inappropriate approaches for business.

Local law society involvement in dealing with minor breaches

3.   In the case of breaches of the rule which are not serious, the SRA encourages local law societies to bring the breaches to the attention of the practitioners concerned. Serious or persistent cases should be reported to the SRA.

Identifying your firm

4.   Rule 7.07(1), as amended on 31 March 2009, applies to the letterhead, fax heading, website and e-mails of a recognised body or recognised sole practitioner. The effect of the rule is that:

(a) a sole practitioner must state his or her SRA number and the name under which he or she is recognised;

(b) a partnership must state its SRA number and the name under which it is recognised; and

(c) an LLP or company must state its registered number from Companies House and its corporate name.

Statutory requirements and voluntary codes

5. You must comply with the general law on advertising, including:

(a) any regulations made under the Consumer Credit Act 1974, concerning the content of advertisements;

(b) sections 20 and 21 of the Consumer Protection Act 1987, regarding misleading price indications;

(c) the Business Names Act 1985, concerning lists of partners and an address for service on stationery, etc.;

(d) the Companies (Trading Disclosures) Regulations 2008 (SI 2008/495) regarding the appearance of the company name and other particulars on stationery, etc.;

(e) the Consumer Credit (Advertisements) Regulations 1989 (SI 1989/1125), in relation to advertisements to arrange mortgages;

(f) the Control of Misleading Advertisements (Amendment) Regulations 2000 (SI 2000/914), in relation to comparative advertising;

(g) the Data Protection Act 1998;

(h) E-Commerce Directive 2000/31/EC and the Electronic Commerce (EC Directive) Regulations 2002 (SI 2002/2013); and

(i) the Privacy and Electronic Communications (EC Directive) Regulations 2003 (SI 2003/2426).

6. You should also have regard to the British Code of Advertising, Sales Promotion and Direct Marketing ("the Advertising Code"). The main principle of the Advertising Code is that media advertisements be legal, decent, honest and truthful. For further information see the website of the Advertising Standards Authority.

7. A breach of a statutory provision or the Advertising Code may also entail a breach of rule 7 or another rule of conduct, but would not necessarily do so. For example, an advert adjudged by the Advertising Standards Authority to be untruthful under the Advertising Code might also, in the context of a complaint, be found by the SRA to breach 7.01 (which requires that publicity is not misleading or inaccurate).

Responsibility for publicity – 7.05

8. Where you become aware of breaches of rule 7 in publicity conducted on your or your firm's behalf, you should take reasonable steps to have the publicity changed or withdrawn.

Clarity as to charges – 7.02

9. Publicity relating to charges must not be misleading or inaccurate, and must be clearly expressed. The following examples in notes 10 to 12 below will assist in complying.

10. Particular care should be taken when quoting fees which are intended to be net fees, i.e. fees which are reduced by the availability of commission (such as that on an endowment policy). Any fee quoted in these circumstances should be the gross fee.

11.   The following are examples of publicity which would breach 7.01 and/or 7.02:

   (a)   publicity which includes an estimated fee pitched at an unrealistically low level;

   (b)   publicity which refers to an estimated or fixed fee plus disbursements, if expenses which are in the nature of overheads (such as normal postage and telephone calls) are then charged as disbursements; and

   (c)   publicity which includes an estimated or fixed fee for conveyancing services, if you then make an additional charge for work on a related mortgage loan or repayment, including work done for a lender – unless the publicity makes it clear that any such additional charge may be payable (e.g. by the use of a phrase like "excluding VAT, disbursements, mortgage related charges and fees for work done for a lender").

12.   Offers of discounts could be misleading if there are no clear rates of charges included. Similarly, if you publicise a service or services as being "free", this should genuinely be the case and should not be conditional upon some other factor (e.g. receiving further instructions or some other benefit). If you publicise work as being done on a pro bono basis there must be no fees charged to the client, except where a conditional fee agreement is used and the only fees charged are those which the firm receives by way of costs from the client's opponent or other third party and which are paid to a charity under a fee sharing agreement.

Agreeing to donate fees to charity

13.   If you publicise that you will donate all, or a percentage, of the firm's fees in respect of certain matters to charity, it would be misleading not to do so. The same applies if you agree to pay to a charity fees received by way of costs from your client's opponent or other third party where you act under a conditional fee agreement.

Name of firm

14.   It would be misleading for a name or description to include the word "solicitor(s)", if none of the managers are solicitors.

15.   It would be misleading for a sole principal to use "and partners" or "and associates" in a firm name unless the firm did formerly have more than one principal.

E-commerce, e-mail and websites

16.   The E-Commerce Directive 2000/31/EC covers cross-border e-commerce within the EU, including e-mails and websites. It affects any firm with a website, because a website can be accessed from other member states.

17.   The Electronic Commerce (EC Directive) Regulations 2002 (SI 2002/2013) implementing the Directive require you to give certain information to persons visiting your firm's website or receiving e-mails from the firm (other than certain activities outside the scope of the Directive, e.g. litigation). The information you will need to give includes:

   (a)   details of the professional body with which the firm is registered – see note 18;

   (b)   your professional title and the member state where it was granted – it is recommended that you either state that the partners/members/directors of the firm are solicitors of England and Wales (if that is the case) or list the professional title and jurisdiction of qualification (or state "non-lawyer") for each of the partners/members/directors; and

   (c)   a reference to the professional rules applicable to the firm in the member state where you are established and the means to access them – see note 18.

18.   If you are "established" in the UK (i.e. your office is in the UK), it is appropriate to say that the firm is regulated by the SRA. For the rules, you are recommended to provide a link to the SRA's website on **www.sra.org.uk/solicitors/code-of-conduct.page**. If you are "established" in another Establishment Directive state, the professional body will be the bar or law society with which you are registered under the Establishment Directive, and the applicable rules will be their rules. Of course, your firm may be "established" in more than one Establishment Directive state.

19.   Any promotional material is publicity. E-mails sent to individuals, companies or organisations with the intention of promoting your practice are advertisements and therefore publicity. Any promotional material in a business e-mail – such as the name and description of the firm – will also be publicity. In these cases 7.01 to 7.07 will apply.

20.   Rule 7.07(1) applies to the letterhead, fax heading, website and e-mails of a recognised body or recognised sole practitioner.

21.   Rule 7.07(2)–(4), which applies only to letterheads and fax headings, reflects some of the provisions of the Business Names Act 1985 and the Companies (Trading Disclosures) Regulations 2008, which apply to "business letters". It is for the courts to determine whether or to what extent these Acts may apply to e-mails. However, the SRA's guess is that e-mails will only be "business letters" when they are formally set out as such and not when they are used as an alternative to a telephone call, telegram or telex. It would be prudent for you to ensure that third parties with whom you deal by e-mail are given your practising address at an early stage, together with the details which would normally appear on the firm's letterhead.

22.   Rule 7.03 prohibits unsolicited approaches in person or by telephone to members of the public. E-mails do not fall within this prohibition. However, you should check the terms of your agreement with your internet service provider as to the use of unsolicited e-mail, and in some jurisdictions the law prohibits unsolicited e-mail. See also note 33 below on data protection.

23.   Websites are publicity and should comply with 7.01 to 7.07. See also notes 24 to 28 below.

24.   If your website or e-mails are to include any financial promotion as defined in the Financial Services and Markets Act 2000, your firm will need to be authorised by the Financial Services Authority. See also notes 31 and 32 below.

International aspects of publicity – 7.04

25.   The effect of the E-Commerce Directive is that there are two different regimes governing international e-publicity:

(a)   cross-border e-publicity within the EU; and

(b)   other cross-border e-publicity, i.e. the e-publicity of law firms established outside the EU, wherever it is accessed or received; and the e-publicity of law firms established in the EU, if it is accessed or received outside the EU.

26.   Cross-border e-publicity within the EU is governed by the E-Commerce Directive and national implementing legislation. Other cross-border e-publicity is not. However, as a website can be accessed from anywhere, your firm's website will have to comply with the E-Commerce Directive and the relevant implementing legislation if your firm is established anywhere within the EU.

27.   Rule 7.04 provides that publicity intended for a jurisdiction outside England and Wales must comply with rule 7 (or, in the case of overseas practice, 15.07) and with the rules in force in that jurisdiction concerning lawyers' publicity. Publicity intended for a jurisdiction where it is permitted will not breach this provision through being incidentally received in a jurisdiction where it is not permitted.

28. Websites can, of course, be accessed worldwide. The relevant factor is the jurisdiction or jurisdictions at which a website is targeted. For example, a website aimed at Australia must comply with rule 7 (if the solicitor's office is in England and Wales) or 15.07 (if the office is elsewhere), and any other restrictions in force in Australia concerning lawyers' publicity.

Mailshots

29. Unsolicited mailshots may be sent and may be targeted. However, you should note the data protection considerations discussed in note 33 below.

"Cold calling"

30. Rule 7.03(1) prohibits you from making unsolicited approaches, either in person or by telephone, to a "member of the public". This is intended to protect the public from the intrusiveness and pressure of unsolicited telephone calls and approaches in person. This rule, therefore, bans what is often termed "cold calling" and prohibits, for example, knocking on doors, approaching people newly arrived at ports of entry, approaching someone in the street, in a hospital or at the scene of an accident, or handing out leaflets in the street. The rule also prohibits approaching a member of the public (either in person, e.g. in the street, or by telephone) to conduct a survey which involves the collection of contact details of potential clients, or otherwise promotes your firm's practice.

A combination of 7.03, 7.05 (Responsibility for publicity) and 9.02 (Financial arrangements with introducers) means that you must not have a financial arrangement with an introducer in respect of business which has been obtained (either by that introducer or through an intermediary) by way of unsolicited face-to-face or telephone "cold calling".

This means that, if a member of the public has indicated in a general consumer survey that they may have a claim, you cannot contact them in person or by telephone unless:

(a) they have explicitly agreed to be contacted about making a claim; and

(b) their response to the questionnaire was not obtained as a result of an unsolicited approach, in person or by telephone, by your firm, or by any party authorised by your firm, or by any other party if your firm has a financial arrangement with the introducer.

Financial promotions

31. Under section 21 of the Financial Services and Markets Act 2000 an unsolicited communication which invites or induces a person to enter into an investment activity is a financial promotion, and cannot be made by an unauthorised person.

32. If you intend to make any form of unsolicited contact allowed under 7.03, where it relates to an investment activity you must consider carefully whether you are authorised to carry out the activity, and also consider whether your contact constitutes a financial promotion and whether you are authorised to make such an approach. Breach of the Act is a criminal offence.

Data protection

33. Rule 7.03(2)(a) permits unsolicited visits or telephone calls to a current or former client. Before contacting clients or former clients in order to publicise your firm you should consider the requirements of the Data Protection Act 1998. It is advisable to give all clients the opportunity to refuse to receive direct marketing correspondence or

contact – for example, in a terms of business letter. This applies to unsolicited mailshots to current or former clients as well as unsolicited approaches in person or by telephone. Under the Privacy and Electronic Communications (EC Directive) Regulations 2003 (SI 2003/2426), prior opt-in consent is needed for direct marketing by e-mail.

Naming non-partners

34.   If non-partners are named on a partnership's letterhead, their status should be made clear. A printed line is not sufficient in itself to distinguish partners from non-partners in a list. A similar standard applies to a company or an LLP's letterhead.

Salaried partners

35.   A manager who is held out on the letterhead of an unincorporated firm as a partner – even if separately designated as a "salaried" or "associate" partner – is treated by the SRA as a full partner and manager, and therefore must comply with the Solicitors' Accounts Rules and the Solicitors' Indemnity Insurance Rules. Holding out as a partner someone who is not entitled under rule 14 to be a partner will put you and your firm in breach both of rule 7 and rule 14.

"Partners" in an LLP

36.   In the context of an LLP, it is permitted, if desired, to refer to members of the LLP as "partners", provided the firm complies with the provisions of the Companies Act 1985, the Companies Act 2006, the Business Names Act 1985 and 7.07(2) as regards the items that must appear on the firm's notepaper, including use of the word "members" in heading up or referring to the list of members.

37.   Some firms may also wish to designate some non-members of the LLP as "partners". This is potentially misleading, so if a firm wishes to go down this path care must be taken to ensure that:

(a)   no non-member is designated as a "partner" unless he or she:

    (i)   is a consultant or employee of the LLP with equivalent standing to a member; and

    (ii)   is a practising lawyer, and would be entitled under rule 14 to become a member of the LLP;

(b)   appropriate explanatory wording (see note 38 below) appears on:

    (i)   the firm's notepaper, faxes, e-mails, brochures and websites; and

    (ii)   any bill on which the word "partner" appears;

(c)   proper distinction is made between a member of the LLP and a person who is not a member but who is referred to as a "partner":

    (i)   in any agreement, terms of business letter or client care letter in which the word "partner" appears;

    (ii)   when addressing any client or third party who is not in receipt of a letter, fax or e-mail; and

    (iii)   in any formal context such as an affidavit, a statement to a court, or a communication with the Legal Services Commission.

38.   Appropriate explanatory wording for a firm's notepaper, faxes, e-mails, brochures, websites or bills would be to the effect that:

"We use the word 'partner' to refer to a member of the LLP, or an employee or consultant who is a lawyer with equivalent standing and qualifications."

If a firm wishes to refer to a list of "partners" as well as the statutory list of members, it is suggested that this might be done by way of some such wording as:

"A list of the members of the LLP is displayed at the above address, together with a list of those non-members who are designated as partners."

39. Notes 36 to 38 above deal only with what is or is not professionally proper. They do not deal with any legal consequences for individuals or the firm if members or non-members are held out as "partners".

"Partners" in a company

40. In the context of practice carried on by way of a company, it may be desired to designate some participants in the practice as "partners". This is potentially misleading, so if you wish to go down this path care must be taken to ensure that:

(a) the company complies with the provisions of the Companies Act 1985, the Companies Act 2006, the Business Names Act 1985 and 7.07(2) as regards the items that must appear on the firm's notepaper, including use of the word "directors" in heading up or referring to the list of directors;

(b) no person is designated as a "partner" unless he or she:

(i) is a shareowner or director of the company, or a consultant in or employee of the company with equivalent standing; and

(ii) is a practising lawyer, and would be entitled under rule 14 to own shares in the company;

(c) appropriate explanatory wording (see note 41 below) appears on:

(i) the company's notepaper, faxes, e-mails, brochures and websites; and

(ii) any bill on which the word "partner" appears; and

(d) no misunderstanding arises as to the status of a "partner":

(i) in any agreement, terms of business letter or client care letter in which the word "partner" appears;

(ii) when addressing any client or third party who is not in receipt of a letter, fax or e-mail; or

(iii) in any formal context such as an affidavit, a statement to a court, or a communication with the Legal Services Commission.

41. Appropriate explanatory wording for a company's notepaper, faxes, e-mails, brochures, websites or bills would be to the effect that:

"We use the word 'partner' to refer to a shareowner or director of the company, or an employee or consultant who is a lawyer with equivalent standing and qualifications."

If you wish to refer to a list of "partners" as well as the statutory list of directors, it is suggested that this might be done by way of some such wording as:

"A list of the directors is displayed at the above address, together with a list of those persons who are designated as partners."

42. Notes 40 and 41 above deal only with what is or is not professionally proper. They do not deal with any legal consequences if shareowners or other participants are held out as "partners".

Identifying the qualifications of managers (and RELs)

43. Rule 7.07(3) and (4) sets out the requirements to be followed when an REL, an RFL, any other lawyer, a non-lawyer manager or a body corporate is named as a manager on

a recognised body's letterhead, and whenever an REL is named in any capacity on a letterhead used by a firm or in-house practice. The following example illustrates how to comply:

"Paul van den Hoek, advocaat (Brussels), registered with the Solicitors Regulation Authority".

Naming staff

44.   You may name staff on your letterhead. However, it would be misleading (and could involve a criminal offence) to use the word "solicitor" to refer to an individual who is not a solicitor of the Supreme Court of England and Wales.

45.   A lawyer whose professional title is "solicitor" in another jurisdiction but who is not a solicitor of England and Wales can only be referred to in publicity as "solicitor" if the word is suitably qualified, for example by the name of that lawyer's jurisdiction of qualification.

Naming clients

46.   The fact that you have acted for a client and details of the client's transactions are subject to the duty of confidentiality – see rule 4 (Confidentiality and disclosure) – and you will therefore normally need the client's consent before disclosing such information in any publicity.

Fee earner leaving a firm

47.   It is not in itself misconduct for you to write to clients of a firm after leaving that firm, inviting their instructions. However, this cannot absolve you from any legal obligations arising out of your former contract of employment or partnership agreement.

Rule 8 – Fee sharing

Introduction

Rule 8 restricts the persons and businesses with whom or with which you can share your professional fees. Broadly, you may not share fees with a non-lawyer unless the fee sharing is with a non-lawyer employee or manager in your firm, or in the strictly defined circumstances set out in this rule. Its purpose is to protect your independence and professional judgement in these situations for the ultimate public benefit.

In relation to European cross-border practice the restrictions on fee sharing are more stringent and you will need to refer to rule 16.

Rule 8 – Fee sharing

8.01   Fee sharing with lawyers and colleagues

Except as permitted under 8.02 below, you may only share or agree to share your professional fees with the following persons:

(a)   practising lawyers, and businesses carrying on the practice of lawyers;

(b)   non-lawyer managers or owners within your firm;

(c)   a retired manager, member, owner or predecessor, or the dependants or personal representatives of a deceased manager, member, owner or predecessor;

(d)   your genuine employee (this does not allow you to disguise as "employment" what is in fact a partnership which rule 12 prohibits);

(e)   your non-lawyer employer, if you are practising in-house and acting in accordance with rule 13 (In-house practice, etc.) or 15.13 (In-house practice overseas);

(f)   a law centre or advice service operated by a charitable or similar non-commercial organisation if you are working as a volunteer and receive fees or costs from public funds or recovered from a third party;

(g)   an estate agent who is your sub-agent for the sale of a property; or

(h)   a charity (as defined in rule 24 (Interpretation)), provided:

   (i)   you remain in compliance with 1.02 (Integrity), 1.03 (Independence) and 1.04 (Best interests of clients);

   (ii)   if requested by the Solicitors Regulation Authority to do so, you supply details of all agreements to share fees with a charity;

   (iii) the operation of any such agreement does not result in a partnership;

   (iv)   any such agreement does not involve a breach of rule 9 (Referrals of business); and

   (v)   if you are employed in-house, you remain in compliance with 13.04 (Pro bono work).

8.02 Fee sharing with other non-lawyers

(1)   You may share your professional fees with another person or business ("the fee sharer") if:

(a)   the purpose of the fee sharing arrangement is solely to facilitate the introduction of capital and/or the provision of services to your firm;

(b)   neither the fee sharing agreement nor the extent of the fees shared permits any fee sharer to influence or constrain your professional judgement in relation to the advice which you give to any client;

(c)   the operation of the agreement does not result in a partnership prohibited by rule 12 (Framework of practice);

(d)   if requested by the Solicitors Regulation Authority to do so, you supply details of all agreements which you have made with fee sharers and the percentage of your firm's annual gross fees which has been paid to each fee sharer; and

(e)   your fee sharing agreement does not involve a breach of rule 9 (Referrals of business) or 15.09 (Overseas practice – referrals of business).

(2)   "Fee sharer" means a person or business who or which shares your fees in reliance on (1) above and the expression includes any person or business connected to or associated with the fee sharer.

Guidance to rule 8 – Fee sharing

What is fee sharing?

1. Fee sharing is not defined in rule 8. It can have a variety of forms and includes relationships where you make a payment within a firm or to a third party by reference to a percentage of the fees charged to a client in respect of a particular case, or a percentage of your gross or net fees, or your profits.

Fee sharing with lawyers and colleagues

2. Sharing your fees within a firm, or with other lawyers or in the other circumstances listed in 8.01, does not represent a serious risk to your independence and is therefore permitted.

3. Rule 8.01 allows you to share fees with a business carrying on the practice of lawyers. This allows you to share fees with a legal disciplinary practice, or with a multi-disciplinary practice outside England and Wales.

Fee sharing with charities and other non-lawyers

4. Rule 8.01(h) permits you to share fees with a charity. This rule applies to charitable giving where you have agreed with your client or a charity that you will share all, or some, of your fees in respect of a particular matter or matters with a charity. This will include situations where you use a conditional fee agreement and agree to pay to a charity fees you receive by way of costs from your client's opponent or other third party. By contrast, where you decide to make a donation to a charity without any binding commitment to do so, this will not constitute fee sharing and is permitted.

5. If you act in accordance with a pro bono conditional fee agreement and you advance disbursements on behalf of your client, and these disbursements are received by way of costs from your client's opponent or from another third party, you may retain from the costs which are received the element which covers such disbursements. The terms of this arrangement will need to be set out in the conditional fee agreement.

6. You may share your fees with other third party non-lawyers in the strictly defined circumstances set out in 8.02. The aim of 8.02 is to give practitioners greater freedom of choice as to the methods available to fund their firms or to pay for services provided to their firms, subject to safeguards designed to protect the public interest. Rule 8.02 allows you to enter into agreements with third party non-lawyers which provide that, in return for the third party making available capital and/or a service to you, you make payment to the third party by reference to a percentage of your fees.

7. You must take account of the requirements of rule 1 (Core duties), specifically of the requirements of independence, integrity, and your duty to act in the best interests of the client. This means that although a fee sharer may properly require you to, for example, observe certain service delivery standards, it would be improper for the fee sharer to interfere with your professional judgement in relation to the advice given to clients.

8. If the fee sharing relationship involves referrals between you and the fee sharer, you must also comply with rule 9 (Referrals of business) or 15.09 (which relates to referrals of business overseas).

9. You must also comply with rule 12 (Framework of practice), which sets out the types of business through which solicitors, RELs, RFLs and recognised bodies may practise. Solicitors who do share fees in accordance with 8.02 should take care that they do not, even inadvertently, enter into an unauthorised partnership with the fee sharer.

10. You must comply with rule 3 (Conflict of interests) to ensure that there is no conflict between the interests of the client and your own interests by virtue of your agreement

with the fee sharer. Should a fee sharer become your client, you should be particularly conscious of the need to ensure that conflicts of interests do not arise, and that the wish to avoid offending the fee sharer does not colour the actions taken and advice given in respect of other clients.

11.   Rule 8.02 allows you to share fees with a non-lawyer third party, but only in return for the fee sharer providing capital and/or services to your firm. The rule does not permit the fee sharer to provide services to your client as part of the fee sharing agreement.

12.   Examples of the kind of arrangements which 8.02 permits include:

(a)   A bank may provide a loan to your firm in return for a sum, in whole or part, calculated as a percentage of the gross fees of your firm. The fact that some clients of your firm are also customers of the bank would not, of itself, prevent the bank from sharing your fees.

(b)   A supplier of information and communications technology may provide computer hardware, software, back-up and training to your firm in return for a share of the firm's gross fees.

(c)   You may pay a supplier of an interactive web based will-writing package on the basis of a percentage of the fee for each will.

13.   Although 8.02 does not specify any cap or limit on the amount of fees which you may share with third parties, you must ensure that the extent of the fees shared does not put at risk your duties to act independently and in clients' best interests – see rule 1 (Core duties). Firms should carry out an assessment of any risk to these core duties that could be created by any fee sharing arrangement, and take action to limit or manage that risk. In assessing whether a firm may have been in breach of these duties, particularly where the percentage of all fees shared is higher than 15% of gross fees, the SRA may ask for evidence of this risk assessment.

14.   If you have a fee sharing relationship with a third party non-lawyer in accordance with 8.02, you may need to disclose the existence and nature of the fee sharing relationship to any client whose affairs are significantly and directly connected to it. Service delivery standards agreed with a fee sharer need not normally be disclosed. See also 2.02(2)(e) and notes 16 and 17 of the guidance to rule 2 (Client relations).

15.   There would, for example, be no obligation to disclose to clients that the firm has a fee sharing relationship with a bank which has supplied a loan to the firm, even to those clients who obtain banking services from that same bank.

16.   Rule 8.02 states that you must, if asked to do so, make available to the SRA details of any fee sharing agreement. This may, for example, include the percentage of gross fees which has been passed to the fee sharer(s) pursuant to an agreement made under 8.02.

17.   The SRA will respect the commercial sensitivity of any information supplied to it.

18.   You are not allowed to share fees with a non-lawyer "fee sharer" under 8.02 in your European cross-border activities, because it is prohibited by rule 16 (European cross-border practice). The following are prohibited by rule 16:

(a)   solicitors (wherever practising) sharing fees with a non-lawyer fee sharer situated in a CCBE state other than the UK; and

(b)   solicitors practising in a CCBE state other than the UK sharing fees with a non-lawyer fee sharer (wherever situated).

Further information can be found in rule 16 (European cross-border practice) and notes 6 and 7 of the guidance to that rule.

Rule 9 – Referrals of business

Introduction

Rule 9 applies when you receive referrals of business from, or make referrals to, third parties. Its purpose is to protect your independence. Additional provisions apply when you have a financial arrangement with an introducer. In relation to European cross-border practice the restrictions on financial arrangements with introducers are more stringent and you will need to refer to rule 16. The rule does not apply to your overseas practice but you must comply with 15.09.

Rule 9 – Referrals of business

9.01 General

(1) When making or receiving referrals of clients to or from third parties you must do nothing which would compromise your independence or your ability to act and advise in the best interests of your clients.

(2) You must draw the attention of potential introducers to this rule and to the relevant provisions of rule 7 (Publicity).

(3) This rule does not apply to referrals between lawyers (including businesses carrying on the practice of lawyers).

(4) You must not, in respect of any claim arising as a result of death or personal injury, either:

(a) enter into an arrangement for the referral of clients with; or

(b) act in association with,

any person whose business, or any part of whose business, is to make, support or prosecute (whether by action or otherwise, and whether by a solicitor or agent or otherwise) claims arising as a result of death or personal injury, and who, in the course of such business, solicits or receives contingency fees in respect of such claims.

(5) The prohibition in 9.01(4) shall not apply to an arrangement or association with a person who solicits or receives contingency fees only in respect of proceedings in a country outside England and Wales, to the extent that a local lawyer would be permitted to receive a contingency fee in respect of such proceedings.

(6) In 9.01(4) and (5) "contingency fee" means any sum (whether fixed, or calculated either as a percentage of the proceeds or otherwise howsoever) payable only in the event of success in the prosecution or defence of any action, suit or other contentious proceedings.

9.02 Financial arrangements with introducers

The following additional requirements apply when you enter into a financial arrangement with an introducer:

(a) The agreement must be in writing and be available for inspection by the Solicitors Regulation Authority.

(b) The introducer must undertake, as part of the agreement, to comply with the provisions of this rule.

(c)   You must be satisfied that clients referred by the introducer have not been acquired as a result of marketing or publicity or other activities which, if done by a person regulated by the Solicitors Regulation Authority, would be in breach of any of these rules.

(d)   The agreement must not include any provision which would:

    (i)   compromise, infringe or impair any of the duties set out in these rules; or

    (ii)   allow the introducer to influence or constrain your professional judgement in relation to the advice given to the client.

(e)   The agreement must provide that before making a referral the introducer must give the client all relevant information concerning the referral, in particular:

    (i)   the fact that the introducer has a financial arrangement with you; and

    (ii)   the amount of any payment to the introducer which is calculated by reference to that referral; or

    (iii)   where the introducer is paying you to provide services to the introducer's customers:

        (A)   the amount the introducer is paying you to provide those services; and

        (B)   the amount the client is required to pay the introducer.

(f)   If you have reason to believe that the introducer is breaching any of the terms of the agreement required by this rule, you must take all reasonable steps to ensure that the breach is remedied. If the introducer continues to breach it you must terminate the agreement.

(g)   Before accepting instructions to act for a client referred under 9.02 you must, in addition to the requirements contained in 2.02 (Client care), 2.03 (Information about the cost) or 2.05 (Complaints handling), give the client, in writing, all relevant information concerning the referral, in particular:

    (i)   the fact that you have a financial arrangement with the introducer;

    (ii)   the amount of any payment to the introducer which is calculated by reference to that referral; or

    (iii)   where the introducer is paying you to provide services to the introducer's customers:

        (A)   the amount the introducer is paying you to provide those services; and

        (B)   the amount the client is required to pay the introducer;

    (iv)   a statement that any advice you give will be independent and that the client is free to raise questions on all aspects of the transaction; and

    (v)   confirmation that information disclosed to you by the client will not be disclosed to the introducer unless the client consents; but that where you are also acting for the introducer in the same matter and a conflict of interests arises, you might be obliged to cease acting.

(h)   You must not enter into a financial arrangement with an introducer for the referral of clients in respect of criminal proceedings or any matter in which you will act for the client with the benefit of public funding.

(i)   For the purpose of this rule:

(i)   "financial arrangement" includes:

   (A)   any payment to a third party in respect of referrals; and

   (B)   any agreement to be paid by a third party introducer to provide services to the third party's customers; and

(ii)   "payment" includes any other consideration but does not include normal hospitality, proper disbursements or normal business expenses.

9.03 Referrals to third parties

(1)   If you recommend that a client use a particular firm, agency or business, you must do so in good faith, judging what is in the client's best interests.

(2)   You must not enter into any agreement or association which would restrict your freedom to recommend any particular firm, agency or business.

(3)   Paragrah (2) above does not apply to arrangements in connection with any of the following types of contracts:

   (a)   regulated mortgage contracts;

   (b)   general insurance contracts; or

   (c)   pure protection contracts.

(4)   The terms "regulated mortgage contracts", "general insurance contracts" and "pure protection contracts" in (3) above have the meanings given in 19.01(4).

(5)   Where you refer a client to a firm, agency or business that can only offer products from one source, you must notify the client in writing of this limitation.

(6)   If a client is likely to need an endowment policy, or similar life insurance with an investment element, you must refer them only to an independent intermediary authorised to give investment advice.

Guidance to rule 9 – Referrals of business

General

1.   You should not enter into a referral arrangement with an introducer whose overall scheme or arrangement will not be in the best interests of the clients referred to you.

2.   You must ensure that your arrangement with an introducer (including your wish to avoid offending the introducer and your interest in continuing to receive work) does not compromise your duties to act in the best interests of your client, to be independent and to provide a good standard of service (rule 1). You will therefore need to consider carefully any proposed referral arrangement (even if no financial arrangement is in place) before accepting work from an introducer. It is also recommended that your firm conducts regular reviews of your referral arrangements to ensure that they remain compliant.

3.   If a client is entering into or has already entered into a scheme or arrangement with an introducer which is not in their best interests then you must advise the client accordingly. Schemes or arrangements which involve the client paying unnecessary or unreasonable fees will not normally be in the client's best interests.

4.   In addition to the core duties (rule 1), whenever you review a proposed or existing referral arrangement you should also consider:

(a) whether the arrangement enables you to comply with the provisions of rule 9;

(b) whether the arrangement involves confidential client information being disclosed to an introducer (see rule 4.01) and what authority you should seek from your client;

(c) whether your introducer's publicity is appropriate – see guidance note 14 below;

(d) whether your advice to the client includes the relevant information regarding the arrangements with an introducer in respect of any limitations placed upon you (see rule 2.02(2)(e)) and if the outcome sought justifies the costs involved (see rule 2.03(6));

(e) whether you retain control of the work you do for clients. No arrangement with an introducer should affect your duty to communicate directly with the client to obtain or confirm instructions, in the process of providing advice and at all appropriate stages of the transaction.

5. If you own an interest in, or provide services through a separate business which is an introducer, you must ensure that you comply with rule 21 (Separate businesses).

Financial arrangements with introducers

6. Rule 9 permits you to pay for referrals, and to be paid by an introducer to provide services to the introducer's customers, subject to conditions. These conditions apply whenever you make a payment, or give other consideration, to a third party who refers clients to you, unless you can show that the payment is wholly unconnected with the referral of any client to you. The conditions also apply regardless of how the payment (or other consideration) is described. For example, the conditions would apply to the payment of administrative or marketing fees, payments described as "disbursements" which are not proper disbursements, and panel membership fees. Placing an advert in a publication operated by a third party and receiving business direct (so not via any third party) as a result would not constitute a financial arrangement with an introducer. However, paying a fee to a third party to recommend your firm would constitute a financial arrangement with an introducer.

7. Equally, you will not be able to avoid the requirements of the rule by, for example, making the payment to an intermediary who, in turn, has an arrangement with the introducer. When investigating complaints the SRA will consider the substance of any relationship rather than the mere form.

8. "Other consideration" might include, for example, the provision of services and secondment of staff to the introducer, or an agreement to purchase services or products from the introducer (where such a purchase is a condition of referrals being made). The payment or consideration does not have to be specifically identified as relating to the referrals of business – it could include a much broader relationship if the referrals take place as a result of that relationship.

Disclosure – by you

9. Where a payment is made to an introducer in relation to each client referred by the introducer, either as a fixed amount or as a proportion of the fee charged to the client, the amount of the payment must be disclosed to each client. Where a payment to an introducer is more general in nature (for example, it may be a fixed, annual or monthly fee), clients referred by the introducer should be informed that you are making a payment and of the nature of the financial arrangement (or other consideration given). If the client asks for more information about the overall amount of payments made, you should supply the client with the best information that you reasonably can. In any case where it is reasonably possible for you to calculate how much of the payment to an introducer relates to a particular client, you must disclose the amount.

10   Where you are being paid by an introducer to provide services to the introducer's customers, both you and the introducer are required to disclose both the amount the introducer is paying you to provide services to the client and the amount the introducer is charging the client for your services. This will enable the client to ascertain whether, and if so how much, the introducer is charging for making the referral and to make an informed decision whether to accept the referral on that basis.

11.   In addition to disclosing information about fees paid in respect of referrals and the other specific disclosures listed in 9.02(g), you must disclose any other "relevant information" concerning the referral. This would include a summary of your overall relationship with an introducer if this involves consideration other than the payment of specific fees. For example, if you provide legal services to an introducer free of charge on the understanding that the introducer refers clients to you, then the client should be informed of this relationship

12   The requirement that you should make disclosure before accepting instructions will normally mean that you should write to the client as soon as you are asked to act for the client, rather than waiting until the first interview with the client. If time does not permit this, disclosure should be made at the beginning of the interview and confirmed in writing.

Disclosure – by the introducer

13.   Rule 9.02(e) requires the introducer to provide the client with all information concerning the referral. It will therefore be necessary for you to agree the nature of this information with the introducer. See note 9 above on disclosure of payments. It is recommended that you check any standard letters or scripts which an introducer uses when providing this information and that you ask referred clients on a regular basis what information the introducer has provided about the referral arrangement. It is recommended that you keep written records of checks made with clients for evidential purposes.

Publicity

14.   Rule 9.02(c) requires you to be satisfied that the introducer has not acquired the client as a consequence of marketing, publicity or other activities which, if done by a person regulated by the SRA, would have been in breach of these rules (particularly rule 7 (Publicity)). Three requirements of rule 7 are particularly important for you to bear in mind in the context of payments for referrals:

     (a)   the general ban on misleading or inaccurate publicity;

     (b)   the prohibition of unsolicited approaches in person or by telephone to a "member of the public" (see 7.03); and

     (c)   the requirement that you must not authorise a third party to publicise your firm in a way which would be contrary to rule 7.

Duty to monitor/terminate referral agreements

15.   Whilst rule 9.02(c) does not place a specific obligation upon you to investigate your introducer's marketing methods and material at the outset and periodically thereafter, it is likely that this will be necessary in practice in order to ensure that you comply with the rule. If the client was referred to your introducer by another third party, then you should also consider the publicity of that third party wherever practicable.

16.   If you become aware of possible breaches of rule 9 or rule 7 (Publicity), you must bring these to the attention of introducers, and if necessary must terminate a referral agreement.

Improper constraints and referrals to third parties

17. Rule 9.02(d)(ii) aims to prevent the introducer from influencing or constraining your professional judgement in respect of advice given to clients. Any referral by you to a third party will be subject to rule 1 (Core duties) and 9.01, as well as 9.03. In order to ensure that you can act in accordance with the core duties you must not enter into an arrangement which limits or restricts your ability to give advice to your clients. This would include an agreement with an introducer which requires you to refrain from issuing court proceedings or to only act in future matters for a referred client with the original introducer's consent or to refer a client to a particular expert, search provider or advocate.

18. However, you would not be prevented from acting on your client's instructions to conduct their matter in accordance with the terms and conditions of a "before the event" insurance policy.

19. You would also not be prevented from making use of an introducer's preferred supplier of certain services but you should not enter into a binding agreement to use that supplier. In every case the use of that supplier must also be in the best interests of the client (see rule 9.03).

20. Any agreement you enter into in respect of regulated mortgage contracts, general insurance contracts (including after the event insurance contracts) or pure protection contracts should provide that referrals will only be made where this is in the best interests of the particular client and the contract is suitable for the needs of that client.

Excepted work

21. Rule 9.02(h) prohibits you having a financial arrangement with an introducer in respect of criminal proceedings, or in any matter in which you will act for the client with the benefit of public funding. You would, however, not be prohibited from continuing to act for a referred client if there was a subsequent unanticipated need to obtain public funding or to represent the client in criminal proceedings. In this situation you should retain evidence as to how those circumstances had arisen.

"Normal hospitality"

22. What amounts to "normal hospitality" (see 9.02(i)(ii)) will depend on the circumstances in every case. For example, corporate entertainment, dinners or lunches are acceptable and would not amount to payment for a referral, provided these are proportionate to the relationship with a business contact/introducer.

"Normal business expenses"

23. "Normal business expenses" (see 9.02(i)(ii)) are payments for services provided to your firm which are totally unrelated to the referral of any client. So, for example, you would not be prevented from accepting referrals from the company with which you place your firm's indemnity or buildings insurance, or from the accountant who prepares your annual report or tax return.

24. Rule 19 (Financial services) deals with referrals in relation to financial services.

25. Rule 2.06 (Commissions) applies in relation to commission received for the introduction of clients.

European cross-border practice

26. Rule 16 (European cross-border practice) prohibits you from making payments for referrals to non-lawyers when undertaking cross-border activities (see 16.06 and notes 12 and 13 of the guidance to rule 16).

Rule 10 – Relations with third parties

Introduction

Rule 10 draws together a variety of obligations linked by the need to deal with third parties in a proper manner. The rule as it applies to your overseas practice is modified by 15.10.

Rule 10 – Relations with third parties

10.01 Not taking unfair advantage

You must not use your position to take unfair advantage of anyone either for your own benefit or for another person's benefit.

10.02 Agreeing costs with another party

When negotiating the payment of your client's costs by another firm's client or a third party, you must give sufficient time and information for the amount of your costs to be agreed or assessed.

10.03 Administering oaths

You can administer oaths or affirmations or take declarations if you are authorised to do so. You must not do so where you or your firm is acting for any party in the matter.

10.04 Contacting other party to a matter

You must not communicate with any other party who to your knowledge has retained a lawyer, or a business carrying on the practice of lawyers, to act in a matter, except:

    (a)   to request the name and address of the other party's lawyer;

    (b)   where it would be reasonable to conclude that the other party's lawyer has refused or failed for no adequate reason either to pass on messages to their client or to reply to correspondence, and has been warned of your intention to contact their client direct;

    (c)   with that lawyer's consent; or

    (d)   in exceptional circumstances.

10.05 Undertakings

(1)   You must fulfil an undertaking which is given in circumstances where:

    (a)   you give the undertaking in the course of practice;

    (b)   you are a recognised body, a manager of a recognised body or a recognised sole practitioner, and any person within the firm gives the undertaking in the course of practice;

    (c)   you give the undertaking outside the course of practice, but as a solicitor; or

(d)   you are an REL based at an office in England and Wales, and you give the undertaking within the UK, as a lawyer of an Establishment Directive profession, but outside your practice as an REL.

(2)   You must fulfil an undertaking within a reasonable time.

(3)   If you give an undertaking which is dependent upon the happening of a future event, you must notify the recipient immediately if it becomes clear that the event will not occur.

(4)   When you give an undertaking to pay another's costs, the undertaking will be discharged if the matter does not proceed unless there is an express agreement that the costs are payable in any event.

10.06 Dealing with more than one prospective buyer in a conveyancing transaction

(1)   Each time a seller of land, other than in a sale by auction or tender, either:

(a)   instructs you to deal with more than one prospective buyer; or

(b)   to your knowledge:

(i)   deals directly with another prospective buyer (or their conveyancer); or

(ii)   instructs another conveyancer to deal with another prospective buyer;

you must, with the client's consent, immediately inform the conveyancer of each prospective buyer, or the prospective buyer if acting in person.

(2)   If the seller refuses to agree to such disclosure, you must immediately stop acting in the matter.

(3)   You must not act for both the seller and any of the prospective buyers.

(4)   You must not act for more than one of the prospective buyers.

10.07 Fees of lawyers of other jurisdictions

(1)   If in the course of practice you instruct a lawyer of another jurisdiction you must, as a matter of professional conduct, pay the lawyer's proper fees unless the lawyer is practising as a lawyer of England and Wales; or

(a)   you have expressly disclaimed that responsibility at the outset, or at a later date you have expressly disclaimed responsibility for any fees incurred after that date;

(b)   the lawyer is an REL or is registered with the Bar of England and Wales under the Establishment Directive; or

(c)   the lawyer is an RFL based in England and Wales and practising in a firm.

(2)   If in the course of practice you instruct a business carrying on the practice of a lawyer of another jurisdiction you must, as a matter of professional conduct, pay the proper fees for the work that lawyer does, unless:

(a)   you have expressly disclaimed that responsibility at the outset, or at a later date you have expressly disclaimed responsibility for any fees incurred after that date; or

(b)   the business is a firm.

Guidance to rule 10 – Relations with third parties

Not taking unfair advantage – 10.01

1. Rule 10.01 does not only apply to your actions which arise out of acting for a client. For example, if you are personally involved in a road accident and use your position as a solicitor unfairly to harass or intimidate the other motorist, you would breach 10.01.

2. Particular care should be taken when you are dealing with a person who does not have legal representation. You need to find a balance between fulfilling your obligations to your client and not taking unfair advantage of another person. To an extent, therefore, 10.01 limits your duty to act in the best interests of your client. For example, your duty may be limited where an unrepresented opponent provides badly drawn documentation. In the circumstances you should suggest the opponent finds legal representation. If the opponent does not do so, you need to ensure that a balance is maintained between doing your best for the client and not taking unfair advantage of the opponent's lack of legal knowledge and drafting skills.

3. You should take care, when dealing with an unrepresented third party, that any help given does not inadvertently create a contractual relationship with that party. For further information see *Cordery on Solicitors*. See also note 3 of the guidance to rule 2 (Client relations). You should also be careful, when dealing with unqualified persons, that you are not involved in possible breaches of the Solicitors Act 1974, in terms of the prohibitions relating to reserved work. For further details see 20.01 (Reserved work and immigration work) and the guidance to that rule.

4. There may be situations where it is inappropriate for you to use your professional title in advancing your personal interests. You should consider public confidence in the profession – see 1.06 (Public confidence).

5. It would be unfair to demand anything that is not recoverable through the proper legal process. This would include a letter of claim and any other communication with another party to the action. For instance, where you are instructed to collect a simple debt, you should not demand from the debtor the cost of the letter of claim, since it cannot be said at that stage that such a cost is legally recoverable.

6. The following are some further examples of how you should act in order to ensure you comply with 10.01 and core duty 1.02 (Integrity):

   (a) If a person sends you documents or money subject to an express condition, you should return the documents or money if you are unwilling or unable to comply with the condition.

   (b) If you are sent documents or money on condition that they are held to the sender's order, you should return the documents or money to the sender on demand.

   (c) If you ask anyone to supply copies of documents, you should expect to pay a proper charge for them.

Agreeing costs with another party – 10.02

7. Rule 10.02 applies to all types of work. Its application is clear in litigation matters but will also commonly be relevant to other matters, such as where a landlord's solicitor's costs for dealing with a request for a licence to assign a lease are to be paid by the tenant.

8. You should expect to supply information about the basis of charging (for example an hourly rate or an estimate of the total amount) together with an indication of the nature of the elements of the work done or to be done.

Administering oaths – 10.03

9.   You may administer oaths if you are:

    (a)   a solicitor with a current practising certificate – see section 81(1) of the Solicitors Act 1974; or

    (b)   an REL, under the Establishment Directive.

10.   When administering oaths or affirmations or taking declarations, you must ensure the giver:

    (a)   is present;

    (b)   signs the document in your presence or, if the document is already signed, confirms that the signature is their own and that any attachments are correct; and

    (c)   appears to understand what they are doing and that the purpose is to confirm that the contents of the document and any attachments are true.

11.   You are not responsible for the contents of the document, but if you have a good reason to believe that the contents may be false, you should not proceed.

12.   You must not administer an oath where you or your firm are acting for a party in the matter or where you or your firm are otherwise interested in it. This prohibition can be found in section 81(2) of the Solicitors Act 1974 and other related legislation. The effect of these provisions would, for example, prevent you from administering an oath for your spouse where it arises out of a personal matter.

13.   When the document has already been signed, it is sufficient for you to accept the giver's word that it is their signature, unless there is clear evidence to the contrary.

Contacting other party to a matter – 10.04

14.   Rule 10.04 requires that you do not contact another party to a matter, subject to exceptions, if that party is represented by a lawyer or a business carrying on the practice of a lawyer. It is not intended to prevent you from dealing with other types of representative, if appropriate. If you are asked to deal with such a representative you should ensure that you are not involved in possible breaches of the Solicitors Act 1974 (see note 3 above) and that to do so is in your client's best interest. For example, where the other party is disabled and vulnerable you may well think it appropriate to deal with a representative from a specialist advice organisation or a disability charity. To do so, may mean that the matter is dealt with more efficiently and that you derive some protection from an allegation that you are acting in breach of 10.01 (Not taking unfair advantage). On the other hand, you would be unlikely to want to deal with a person purporting to represent another party who clearly does not have the relevant knowledge or skill.

15.   Where an enquiry agent has been instructed, the agent may serve documents direct where the other party's lawyer has refused to accept service, but should not take a statement or in any other way communicate with the other party.

16.   Care should be taken if you are instructed in a dual capacity. For example, if you are additionally instructed as an estate agent for the seller, you may contact the buyer, but solely about estate agency matters.

17.   The other party's lawyer may consent explicitly to your contacting their client, or this may be implied, such as when a protocol is being followed or where it has been agreed that certain documents be sent to all parties.

18.   It is not always easy to establish why another lawyer involved in a matter is not responding to correspondence. If you reasonably consider that the other lawyer may be refusing or failing to take instructions from their client, or may be refusing or failing to communicate your requests or correspondence to their client, then a warning should

give them the opportunity to object if an incorrect conclusion has been drawn. If there is no valid objection, then you should be able to advance the matter by directly contacting the other client.

19. It is recommended that any communications permitted by 10.04 between you and another lawyer's client be in writing.

20. Rule 10.04 extends to your contact with the in-house lawyers of organisations. For example, if you are acting for a client in a matter concerning a local authority, and you have express or implied notice that the authority's solicitor has been instructed to act in the matter, you must not discuss that matter directly with another officer of the authority, the relevant lead member, any individual councillor or any political group on the authority. You can be involved in political lobbying of a relevant officer or lead member, individual councillors or a political group on the local authority on behalf of a client, even if you know that the authority's solicitor has been instructed to deal with the legal issues.

21. Where the other party is an organisation, you will not breach 10.04 by contacting employees who are not responsible for the giving of instructions because they are not regarded as the client for the purpose of 10.04. However, you should have regard to any contractual obligations employees may have to their employer. It may be appropriate to notify the employer or its lawyer of your intention to contact the employee. This would enable the employee to be advised as to the appropriate response.

22. Lawyers employed by organisations such as the SRA or the Land Registry may properly deal with represented clients when carrying out a statutory function.

23. There may be other situations where it becomes necessary to communicate directly with a represented client. Rule 10.04(d) refers to these as "exceptional circumstances". Such circumstances would include where you are contacted by the client of another lawyer. Care should be taken to avoid taking unfair advantage of this situation but it is acceptable for you to deal with that client's request, if appropriate, and explain that in future they should contact you through their own lawyer.

Undertakings – 10.05

24. An undertaking is any statement, made by you or your firm, that you or your firm will do something or cause something to be done, or refrain from doing something, given to someone who reasonably relies upon it (see rule 24 (Interpretation)). It can be given orally or in writing and need not include the word "undertake". However, it is recommended that oral undertakings be confirmed or recorded in writing for evidential purposes.

25. An agreement to pay a trading debt such as your electricity bill is not normally an undertaking. Once an undertaking is given and the recipient has relied upon it, it can only be withdrawn by agreement.

26. You are not obliged to give or accept undertakings.

27. In 10.05(1)(b) "person within the firm" includes anyone held out by the firm as representing the firm, as well as locums, agents, consultants and other employees.

28. It is important that there be a time frame within which an undertaking should be fulfilled. In the event that no specific time is referred to when the undertaking is given, fulfilment "within a reasonable time" will be expected. What amounts to a "reasonable time" will depend on the circumstances but the onus is on the giver to ensure that the recipient is kept informed of the likely timescale and any delays to it.

29. Failure to fulfil an undertaking may result in disciplinary action.

30. If an undertaking requires the recipient to take certain steps and the recipient fails to do so, the giver may ask the SRA to give notice to the recipient that unless these steps are taken within a period of time it will not then consider a complaint.

31. All undertakings given by solicitors and RELs can be enforced by the court. (See court rules for the appropriate procedure to be followed.) The SRA will not investigate complaints of breaches of undertakings given to the court unless the court makes a complaint to the SRA.

32. Where you undertake to pay the costs of another party or a professional agent's costs, unless a specific amount is agreed, the term "costs" will mean "proper costs". This allows you to request an assessment of the costs by the court.

33. If a complaint is made to the SRA concerning an alleged breach of an undertaking and it is found that the undertaking was procured by fraud, deceit or, in certain circumstances, innocent misrepresentation, the SRA is unlikely to take any action in respect of the alleged breach.

34. The SRA will generally interpret an ambiguous undertaking in favour of the recipient.

35. If you give an undertaking "on behalf" of a client it will usually fall within the definition of an undertaking (see rule 24 (Interpretation)) and its performance would, therefore, be your responsibility. If this is not what you intend, you should ensure that liability is disclaimed or it is made clear that you are simply informing the other party about your client's intentions.

36. A promise to give an undertaking is normally treated as an undertaking and will be binding.

37. Where an undertaking has been breached, the aggrieved party may seek compensation. Your firm's insurance as required by the Solicitors' Indemnity Insurance Rules should cover valid claims. If you are in in-house practice, you should consider whether your employer has appropriate insurance. You will remain personally liable in conduct, and may also be financially liable, regardless of whether you have adequate insurance.

38. An undertaking is binding even if it is to do something outside your control. For example, if you undertake to make a payment out of the proceeds of sale of an asset, unless you clearly state to the contrary, you will be expected to make the payment even if the fund (gross or net) is insufficient.

39. If you have received written instructions from your client that are expressed as irrevocable, they are nonetheless revocable, until you have acted on them in such a way as to change your personal position.

40. Certain areas of work, particularly conveyancing, involve the use of standard undertakings. Care should be taken when using standard undertakings to ensure that they suit the specific circumstances. For further details, please refer to a specialist publication.

41. Guidance on undertakings can be obtained from the Professional Ethics Guidance Team.

Dealing with more than one prospective buyer in a conveyancing transaction – 10.06

42. When you are acting for a seller and are asked to "deal" with more than one prospective buyer you must comply with 10.06. "Deal" means any communication you have with any of the relevant parties intended to progress the matter – for example, the sending of a draft contract or a plan of the property. Communicating information of an estate agency nature, such as sending out particulars of sale or showing prospective buyers around a property, would not amount to "dealing" for the purposes of 10.06. If you provide information for an estate agent or Home Information Pack provider only as part of the creation of a Home Information Pack, you will not have "dealt" with prospective buyers for the purpose of 10.06. However, providing additional information to buyers, either direct or through the estate agent or Home Information Pack provider, will normally amount to "dealing".

43. This requirement is sometimes known as the "contract races" rule. This has created the impression that when a transaction is proceeding under such terms, whichever party presents their contract ready for exchanging first is the "winner". In fact, the terms of the arrangement are entirely at the discretion of the parties and speed may or may not be a factor. You should be careful to agree the terms of the arrangement.

44. If you are required to inform another conveyancer of your intention to proceed with two or more prospective buyers, you should do so immediately by the most suitable means. If the information is given in person or on the telephone, there is no requirement that the details be confirmed in writing but this is advisable.

45. Special care should be taken when dealing with unqualified conveyancers or unrepresented buyers. See notes 2 and 3 above.

Fees of lawyers of other jurisdictions – 10.07

46. Rule 10.07 does not apply when you merely introduce or refer a client to a lawyer of another jurisdiction. However, when you instruct such a lawyer, you will be accepting the liability to pay the lawyer's proper fees unless one of the exceptions in 10.07 applies. For example, if you do not hold money on account and your client is declared bankrupt, you may have to pay the lawyer's proper fee out of your own funds.

47. The fees of a lawyer of another jurisdiction may be regulated by a scale approved by the relevant bar association or law society. You can contact the International Unit of the Law Society for advice.

48. In the event that a dispute arises concerning the payment of the fees of a lawyer of a CCBE state, 16.07 and note 14 of the guidance to rule 16 (European cross-border practice) should be consulted and the necessary action taken before starting any proceedings.

Rule 11 – Litigation and advocacy

Introduction

Rule 11 imposes additional duties on you if you are a firm or lawyer when exercising a right to conduct litigation or act as an advocate. "Court" in this rule has a wide meaning – see rule 24 (Interpretation). References to appearing or acting as an advocate apply when you are exercising rights of audience before any court, not just if you have been granted rights of audience in the higher courts. The rule only applies in a modified form to overseas practice – see 15.11.

Rule 11 – Litigation and advocacy

11.01 Deceiving or misleading the court

(1) You must never deceive or knowingly or recklessly mislead the court or knowingly allow the court to be misled.

(2) You must draw to the court's attention:

   (a) relevant cases and statutory provisions;

   (b) any material procedural irregularity.

(3)   You must not construct facts supporting your client's case or draft any documents relating to any proceedings containing:

(a)   any contention which you do not consider to be properly arguable; or

(b)   any allegation of fraud unless you are instructed to do so and you have material which you reasonably believe establishes, on the face of it, a case of fraud.

11.02 Obeying court orders

You must comply with any court order requiring you or your firm to take, or refrain from taking, a particular course of action.

11.03 Contempt of court

You must not become in contempt of court.

11.04 Refusing instructions to act as advocate

(1)   You must not refuse to act as an advocate for any person on any of the following grounds:

(a)   that the nature of the case is objectionable to you or to any section of the public;

(b)   that the conduct, opinions or beliefs of the prospective client are unacceptable to you or to any section of the public; or

(c)   that the source of any financial support which may properly be given to the prospective client for the proceedings is unacceptable to you.

(2)   You are not required to act as an advocate:

(a)   under a conditional fee agreement; or

(b)   if you reasonably consider that you are not being offered a proper fee having regard to:

(i)   the circumstances of the case;

(ii)   the nature of your practice; or

(iii)   your experience and standing.

11.05 Appearing as an advocate

If you are appearing as an advocate:

(a)   you must not say anything which is merely scandalous or intended only to insult a witness or any other person;

(b)   you must avoid naming in open court any third party whose character would thereby be called into question, unless it is necessary for the proper conduct of the case;

(c)   you must not call into question the character of a witness you have cross-examined unless the witness has had the opportunity to answer the allegations during cross-examination; and

(d)   you must not suggest that any person is guilty of a crime, fraud or misconduct unless such allegations:

   (i)   go to a matter in issue which is material to your client's case; and

   (ii)   appear to you to be supported by reasonable grounds.

11.06 Appearing as a witness

You must not appear as an advocate at a trial or act in the litigation if it is clear that you, or anyone within your firm, will be called as a witness, unless you are satisfied that this will not prejudice your independence as an advocate, or litigator, or the interests of your client or the interests of justice.

11.07 Payments to witnesses

You must not make, or offer to make, payments to a witness dependent upon the nature of the evidence given or upon the outcome of the case.

11.08 Recordings of child witnesses' evidence

If you are acting in the defence or prosecution of an accused and you have in your possession a copy of an audio or video recording of a child witness which has been identified as having been prepared to be admitted in evidence at a criminal trial in accordance with the relevant provisions of the Criminal Justice Act 1991 or the Youth Justice and Criminal Evidence Act 1999, you must:

(a)   not make or permit any person to make a copy of the recording;

(b)   not release the recording to the accused;

(c)   not make or permit any disclosure of the recording or its contents to any person except when, in your opinion, it is necessary in the course of preparing the prosecution, defence or appeal against conviction and/or sentence;

(d)   ensure that the recording is always kept in a locked, secure container when not in use; and

(e)   return the recording when you are no longer instructed in the matter.

Guidance to rule 11 – Litigation and advocacy

General

1.   If you are a solicitor you are entitled to conduct litigation in any court. You are also entitled to exercise any right of audience which solicitors had immediately before 7 December 1989, provided that your exercise of that right is in compliance with these rules. You are entitled to exercise additional rights of audience in the higher courts if you have obtained a relevant higher courts advocacy qualification under the Higher Courts Qualification Regulations 2000, or if you had already acquired a relevant higher courts qualification from another regulator before becoming a solicitor.

2.   If you are an REL you can conduct litigation or appear as an advocate provided you are instructed in conjunction with a solicitor or barrister who is entitled to perform that

service. The role of the solicitor or barrister is not to supervise you or take responsibility for your work, but to assist the court in the event of a problem arising. You can appear as an advocate in those courts and cases in which all solicitors can exercise a right of audience. Like solicitors, you are eligible to acquire extended rights of audience by obtaining one of the solicitors' higher courts qualifications – or you may exercise a relevant higher courts qualification acquired from another regulator before registering with the SRA as an REL.

3. If you are an RFL you do not have any rights of audience or right to conduct litigation (or the right to supervise or assume responsibility for the exercise of any such right) other than those rights which are not reserved by law to any category of persons but are open to any individual. The only exception to this is that you have litigation and advocacy rights before Asylum Support Adjudicators and the Asylum and Immigration Tribunal, or in a tribunal hearing an appeal from one of these, but only if you do the work as a manager or employee of a recognised body or as the employee of a recognised sole practitioner. See also 12.03 and notes 21–29 of the guidance to rule 12 (Framework of practice).

4. If you are a barrister, legal executive, patent agent, trade mark agent or a law costs draftsman you may also be entitled to exercise rights of audience or conduct litigation. When doing so you must comply with any professional obligations arising from such qualification and act within the limitations set by law, in addition to your obligations under these rules.

5. When acting for a client requiring advocacy services you should always consider whether the interests of the client would be best served by you, another lawyer from the same firm or another advocate providing these services. Factors to be taken into consideration include the nature and complexity of the case, your experience and ability, the cost of the advocacy service and the nature of your practice. See rule 2 (Client relations) and the guidance to it for fuller information on issues which you should discuss with your client when accepting instructions.

6. If you are a solicitor you are an officer of the court and you should take all reasonable steps to assist in the smooth running of the court but only insofar as this is consistent with your duties to your client. Difficulties are likely to arise, for example, where the defendant client absconds in a criminal case. If the client does fail to attend:

   (a) in relation to your duty of confidentiality you may properly state that you are without instructions, but may not disclose information about the client's whereabouts; and

   (b) in relation to your duty to act in the client's best interests, you may consider it appropriate to withdraw from the hearing where, having regard to the client's best interests, you believe you cannot properly represent the client. There may be cases where you would be able to proceed in the absence of your client, for example, where you may infer that the defendant expects you to continue to represent them, or where a legal point can be taken which would defeat the prosecution case.

   If you are an REL you are treated as if you were an officer of the court – see paragraph 21 of Schedule 4 to the Establishment Directive Regulations. Even if you are not a solicitor or REL, a similar standard of conduct is required of you in relation to litigation or advocacy as a manager or employee of a recognised body or as an employee of a recognised sole practitioner.

7. You should be cautious about communicating with judges outside the courtroom, in respect of matters in which you are appearing before them, unless you are invited to do so in the presence of the solicitor or counsel for the other side or party.

8. You should not agree to stand bail for your client except in very rare circumstances. By standing bail you risk becoming too closely involved with your client's situation and

this may affect your ability to act independently. It is unlawful for you, or any other person, to be party to a bargain to indemnify a surety for bail.

Attending advocates at court

9. Whenever you instruct an advocate you will need to decide whether it is in the interests of your client and the interests of justice for you, or a responsible representative of your firm, to attend the proceedings. In reaching this decision you will need to consider what is necessary for the proper conduct of the case, taking into account the nature and complexity of the case and the capacity of the client to understand the proceedings. For example, you, or your representative, should normally attend:

   (a) where the client is charged with an offence classified pursuant to section 75(2) of the Supreme Court Act 1981 as class 1 or 2 (such as murder, manslaughter or rape);

   (b) in cases of complex or serious fraud;

   (c) where the client may have difficulty in giving or receiving instructions or in understanding the proceedings, for example if the client is a child, has inadequate knowledge of English, or has a mental illness or some other disability;

   (d) where the client is likely to disrupt proceedings if the advocate appears alone;

   (e) where the advocate is representing more than one party to the hearing;

   (f) where there are a substantial number of defence documents at a trial;

   (g) where there are a large number of witnesses in the case;

   (h) on the day on which the client is to be sentenced, particularly where the client is likely to receive a custodial sentence; or

   (i) where issues are likely to arise which question the client's character or your conduct of the case.

10. Where you decide that an advocate should not be attended you should inform the advocate and deliver a full and detailed brief sufficiently early for the advocate to consider the papers and to decide whether it would be appropriate for the advocate to attend alone. You should also inform the client that the advocate will be unattended and how instructions may be given.

Statements to the media

11. You should exercise your professional judgement as to whether it is appropriate to make a statement to the media about your client's case and, if you do make a statement, about its content. In making these decisions you should consider:

   (a) whether it is in the client's best interests to do so;

   (b) whether the client has consented to this course of action; and

   (c) the legal position and, for example whether anything you say might be in contempt of court (see 11.03 and note 21).

Deceiving or misleading the court – 11.01

12. Rule 11.01 makes a distinction between deceiving the court, where knowledge is assumed, and misleading the court, which could happen inadvertently. You would not normally be guilty of misconduct if you inadvertently misled the court. However, if during the course of proceedings you become aware that you have inadvertently misled the court, you must, with your client's consent, immediately inform the court. If the client does not consent you must stop acting. Rule 11.01 includes attempting to deceive or mislead the court.

13. You might deceive or mislead the court by, for example:

    (a)   submitting inaccurate information or allowing another person to do so;

    (b)   indicating agreement with information that another person puts forward which you know is false;

    (c)   calling a witness whose evidence you know is untrue;

    (d)   not immediately disclosing a document you have become aware of during the course of a case, which should have been, but was not, disclosed;

    (e)   attempting to influence a witness, when taking a statement from that witness, with regard to the contents of their statement; and

    (f)   tampering with evidence or seeking to persuade a witness to change their evidence. To avoid such allegations it would be wise, when seeking to interview a witness for the other side, to offer to interview them in the presence of the other side's representative.

14. Whilst a person may call themselves by whatever name they choose, you must (in the context of court proceedings) be satisfied that the client is not adopting a different name or date of birth to avoid previous convictions becoming known to the court, or to deceive the court in any other way.

15. If you are acting for a defendant, you need not correct information given to the court by the prosecution or any other party which you know may allow the court to make incorrect assumptions about the client or the case, provided you do not indicate agreement with that information.

16. Where a client admits to having committed perjury or having misled the court in any material matter relating to ongoing proceedings, you must not act further in those proceedings unless the client agrees to disclose the truth to the court.

17. If, either before or during the course of proceedings, the client makes statements to you which are inconsistent, this is not of itself a ground for you to stop acting. Only where it is clear that the client is attempting to put forward false evidence to the court should you stop acting. In other circumstances it would be for the court, and not for you, to assess the truth or otherwise of the client's statement.

18. There are some types of information which you are obliged to disclose to the court, whether or not it is in the best interests of the client to do so. Failure to disclose such information could amount to a breach of 11.01. For example:

    (a)   The advocates on both sides must advise the court of relevant cases and statutory provisions. If one of them omits a case or provision or makes an incorrect reference to a case or provision, it is the duty of the other to draw attention to it even if it assists the opponent's case.

    (b)   Except when acting or appearing for the prosecution, if you know of facts which, or of a witness who, would assist the adversary you are not under any duty to inform the adversary, or the court, of this to the prejudice of your own client.

19. You are permitted, even when acting as an advocate, to interview and take statements from any witness or prospective witness at any stage in the proceedings, whether or not that witness has been interviewed or called as a witness by another party. (However, see note 13(e) and (f) above.)

Obeying court orders – 11.02

20. You have a responsibility to ensure that you comply with any court order made against you. Similarly, you must advise your clients to comply with court orders made against them. If you are the recipient of a court order which you believe to be defective you are obliged under 11.02 to comply with it unless it is revoked by the court, or unless an

application for a stay is pending. If your client is the recipient of an order you believe to be defective you must discuss with the client the possibility of challenging it and explain to the client the client's obligation to comply if the order is not overturned.

Contempt of court – 11.03

21.   You could, for example, become in contempt of court by making a statement to the press which is calculated to interfere with the fair trial of a case which has not been concluded.

Refusing instructions to act as advocate – 11.04

22.   In addition to complying with 11.04 you must comply with rule 6 (Equality and diversity) in your dealings with clients, staff, other lawyers and third parties.

23.   Rule 11.04(2)(b) states that you may refuse to act if you are not being offered a proper fee. In the case of publicly funded matters this means that if the fee likely to be received from the Legal Services Commission is lower than your normal charging rate, you may decline to act.

Appearing as an advocate – 11.05

24.   Rule 11.05 sets out a number of issues relating to the way in which you conduct yourself in court. There may be other restrictions, such as rules of court, which affect the way a case may be presented in court and you should familiarise yourself with these.

25.   It is not the intention of 11.05 to prevent you robustly defending your client's position.

Appearing as a witness – 11.06

26.   The circumstances in which it will be proper for you to appear as an advocate at a trial or act in litigation when you are also a witness will be extremely rare. Factors you will need to consider include:

(a)   the nature of the evidence you are being asked to give, its importance to the case and in particular whether it is likely to be contested or is purely formal;

(b)   whether the situation would give rise to a conflict between you or your firm and your client. For example, it would not be appropriate for you to give evidence for another party (or, in a criminal case, the prosecution); and

(c)   how your client would be affected if, having already accepted instructions to act, you were to stop acting.

27.   Provided the evidence is unlikely to be contested on a factual basis, it will normally be acceptable for you to act as an advocate if a member of your firm is to give evidence. For example, if an employee of your firm has advised a client at a police station, and is required to give evidence as to the reasons for advising the client to exercise the right to silence, it would not be improper for you to act as an advocate in the case.

28.   You will need to consider your client's interests when asked to act in a matter in which there is a significant risk that you, or a member of your firm, will be called as a witness in the case. You should not accept instructions to act for a client in circumstances where you could not act if you had already been called – for example, if you had witnessed events which were material to the issue being tried. On the other hand there is always a degree of risk that events you witnessed at a police station, such as the client exercising the right to silence or an identity parade, will become an issue at the trial. However this would not normally prevent you appearing as an advocate.

29.   Rule 11.06 would not normally prevent you giving evidence at a pre-trial hearing, for example by making a witness statement which is purely concerned with procedural issues, provided your evidence is unlikely to be contested at the trial.

Payments to witnesses – 11.07

30.   There is no objection to your paying reasonable expenses to witnesses and reasonable compensation for loss of time attending court.

Recording of child witnesses' evidence – 11.08

31.   The SRA recommends that you use the following form of undertaking in order to comply with 11.08:

"I/We acknowledge receipt of the recording marked 'evidence of ...'.

I/We undertake that whilst the recording is in my/our possession I/we shall:

(a)   not make or permit any other person to make a copy of the recording;

(b)   not release the recording to [*name of the accused*];

(c)   not make or permit any disclosure of the recording or its contents to any person except when in my/our opinion it is necessary in the course of preparing the prosecution, defence, or appeal against conviction and/or sentence;

(d)   ensure that the recording is always kept in a locked, secure container when not in use; and

(e)   return the recording to you when I am/we are no longer instructed in the matter."

32.   Recordings should preferably be delivered to third parties by hand but where this is not possible the recording should be sent by recorded delivery. To avoid the risk of theft the contents of the package should not be apparent from the outside. If you personally collect, or a member of staff personally collects, a recording, you or they should be able to produce a proper form of identification.

33.   Although 11.08 does not specifically define "locked, secure container" a locked car cannot be considered as such and a recording should never be left unattended in a car.

34.   You may be asked to give an undertaking in the form recommended by the Home Office, which is similar to that recommended by the SRA. As with the giving of any undertaking, you should first ensure that you can comply with its terms.

Rule 12 – Framework of practice

Introduction

This rule sets out the types of business through which solicitors, RELs, RFLs and recognised bodies may practise. The rule restricts the types of business available in order to reflect statutory provisions and to ensure that clients and the public have the protections provided for by statute.

Rule 12 – Framework of practice

12.01 Solicitors

Practice from an office in England and Wales

(1) You may practise as a solicitor from an office in England and Wales in the following ways only:

    (a) as a recognised sole practitioner or the employee of a recognised sole practitioner;

    (b) as a solicitor exempted under 20.03(2) from the obligation to be a recognised sole practitioner;

    (c) as a manager, employee, member or owner of:

        (i) a recognised body; or

        (ii) a body corporate which is a manager, member or owner of a recognised body;

    (d) as a manager, employee, member or owner of:

        (i) an authorised non–SRA firm; or

        (ii) a body corporate which is a manager, member or owner of an authorised non–SRA firm,

    provided that all work you do is either of a sort authorised by the firm's approved regulator, or done for the firm itself, or within 13.02 (Work colleagues), 13.03 (Related bodies) or 13.04 (Pro bono work);

    (e) as the employee of another person, business or organisation, provided that you undertake work only for your employer, or as permitted by rule 13 (In-house practice, etc.).

Practice from an office outside England and Wales

(2) You may practise as a solicitor from an office outside England and Wales in the following ways only:

    (a) as a sole practitioner (including a recognised sole practitioner);

    (b) as the employee of a sole principal who is a lawyer;

    (c) as a manager, employee, member or owner of a recognised body, provided that if any of the body's managers or owners are non-lawyers and the office is in an Establishment Directive state other than the UK, the rules for local lawyers would permit a local lawyer to practise through a business of that composition and structure;

    (d) as a manager, employee, member or owner of a business which has no office in England and Wales and meets all the following conditions:

        (i) the business carries on the practice of law;

        (ii) a controlling majority of the managers and the owners are lawyers and/or bodies corporate in which lawyers constitute a controlling majority of the managers and owners;

(iii) if any of the business's managers or owners are non-lawyers and any manager or owner is subject to the rules for local lawyers, the composition and structure of the business complies with those rules; and

(iv) if any of the business's managers or owners are non-lawyers and the office is in an Establishment Directive state, the rules for local lawyers would permit a local lawyer to practise through a business of that composition and structure;

(e) as the employee of another person, business or organisation, provided that you undertake work only for your employer, or as permitted by 15.13 (In-house practice overseas).

12.02 RELs

If you are an REL:

Practice from an office in England and Wales

(1) You may practise as an REL from an office in England and Wales in the following ways only:

(a) as a recognised sole practitioner or the employee of a recognised sole practitioner;

(b) as an REL exempted under 20.03(2) from the obligation to be a recognised sole practitioner;

(c) as a manager, employee, member or owner of:

(i) a recognised body; or

(ii) a body corporate which is a manager, member or owner of a recognised body;

(d) as a manager, employee, member or owner of:

(i) an authorised non-SRA firm; or

(ii) a body corporate which is a manager, member or owner of an authorised non-SRA firm,

provided that all work you do is either of a sort authorised by the firm's approved regulator, or done for the firm itself, or within 13.02 (Work colleagues), 13.03 (Related bodies) or 13.04 (Pro bono work);

(e) as the employee of another person, business or organisation, provided that you undertake work only for your employer, or as permitted by rule 13 (In-house practice, etc.).

Practice from an office in Scotland or Northern Ireland

(2) You may practise as an REL from an office in Scotland or Northern Ireland in the following ways only:

(a) as a sole practitioner (including a recognised sole practitioner);

(b) as the employee of a sole principal who is a lawyer;

(c) as a manager, employee, member or owner of a recognised body;

(d)   as a manager, employee, member or owner of a business which has no office in England and Wales and meets all the following conditions:

         (i)   the business carries on the practice of law;

         (ii)   a controlling majority of the managers and the owners are lawyers and/or bodies corporate in which lawyers constitute a controlling majority of the managers and owners; and

         (iii)   if any of the business's managers or owners are non-lawyers, the professional rules governing a solicitor of that jurisdiction would allow such a solicitor to practise through a business of that composition and structure;

(e)   as the employee of another person, business or organisation, provided that you undertake work only for your employer, or as permitted by 15.13 (In-house practice overseas).

12.03 RFLs

Practice in the capacity of an RFL

(1)   Your practice as a foreign lawyer in the capacity of an RFL is confined to practice as:

(a)   the employee of a recognised sole practitioner;

(b)   a manager, employee, member or owner of:

         (i)   a recognised body; or

         (ii)   a body corporate which is a manager, member or owner of a recognised body;

(c)   a manager, employee, member or owner of:

         (i)   an authorised non-SRA firm; or

         (ii)   a body corporate which is a manager, member or owner of an authorised non-SRA firm,

in which case all the work you do must be of a sort authorised by the firm's approved regulator, or done for the firm itself, or within 13.02 (Work colleagues), 13.03 (Related bodies) or 13.04 (Pro bono work).

Practice in another capacity than as an RFL

(2)   If you provide services as a foreign lawyer in any of the following ways in England and Wales or elsewhere, you will not be practising in the capacity of an RFL and you must not be held out or described in that context as an RFL, or as regulated by or registered with the Law Society or the Solicitors Regulation Authority:

(a)   as a sole principal; or

(b)   as a manager, member or owner of any business or organisation other than a recognised body or an authorised non-SRA firm; or

(c)   as a manager, member or owner of a body corporate which is a manager, member or owner of any business or organisation other than a recognised body or an authorised non-SRA firm; or

(d)   as the employee of any business or organisation other than a recognised sole practitioner, a recognised body or an authorised non-SRA firm.

(3)   If you have a practice under (1) above, and another business under (2) above, the latter is a "separate business" for the purpose of these rules and you must therefore comply with rule 21 (Separate businesses).

Scope of practice

(4)   Whether or not you are practising in the capacity of an RFL you must not:

(a)   be held out in any way which suggests that you are, or are entitled to practise as, a lawyer of England and Wales;

(b)   undertake the following reserved work in England and Wales:

(i)   advocacy in open court;

(ii)   the conduct of court litigation;

(iii) the administration of oaths and statutory declarations;

(c)   undertake advocacy in chambers in England and Wales, except under instructions given by a person qualified to direct reserved work;

(d)   undertake the following reserved work in England and Wales, except at the direction and under the supervision of a person qualified to direct reserved work:

(i)   the preparation of court documents;

(ii)   the preparation of instruments and the lodging of documents relating to the transfer or charge of land;

(iii) the preparation of papers on which to found or oppose a grant of probate or a grant of letters of administration;

(iv)   the preparation of trust deeds disposing of capital,

unless you also have an appropriate legal qualification as a lawyer of England and Wales.

(5)   If you are not practising in the capacity of an RFL you must not give immigration advice or provide immigration services in the UK unless:

(a)   you are entitled under the Immigration and Asylum Act 1999 to do that work in your own right; or

(b)   you do the work under the supervision of a person who is not a solicitor, an REL or an RFL but is entitled under the Immigration and Asylum Act 1999 to do that work.

12.04 Recognised bodies

Practice from an office in England and Wales

(1)   A recognised body may practise from an office in England and Wales in the following ways only:

(a)   as a stand-alone firm;

(b)   as a manager, member or owner of another recognised body; or

(c)   as a manager, member or owner of an authorised non-SRA firm, in which case the services you provide must all fall within the scope of the firm's authorisation;

(d)   as an executor, trustee or nominee company, or a company providing company secretarial services, owned and operated by another recognised body or by a recognised sole practitioner.

Practice from an office outside England and Wales

(2)   A recognised body may practise from an office outside England and Wales in the following ways only:

(a)   as a stand-alone firm, provided that if any of the body's managers or owners are non-lawyers and the office is in an Establishment Directive state other than the UK, the rules for local lawyers would permit a local lawyer to practise through a business of that composition and structure;

(b)   as a manager, member or owner of a business which has no office in England and Wales and meets all the following conditions:

(i)   the business carries on the practice of law;

(ii)   a controlling majority of the managers and the owners are lawyers and/or bodies corporate in which lawyers constitute a controlling majority of the managers and owners;

(iii)   if any of the business's managers or owners are non-lawyers and any manager or owner is subject to the rules for local lawyers, the composition and structure of the business complies with those rules; and

(iv)   if any of the business's managers or owners are non-lawyers and the office is in an Establishment Directive state other than the UK, the rules for local lawyers would permit a local lawyer to practise through a business of that composition and structure;

(c)   as an executor, trustee or nominee company, or a company providing company secretarial services, owned and operated by another recognised body or by a recognised sole practitioner.

12.05 Managers and employees authorised by another approved regulator

(1)   If you are a manager or employee of a recognised body or an employee of a recognised sole practitioner and you are not a solicitor but you are authorised by an approved regulator other than the SRA, you must not:

(a)   be held out in any way which suggests that you are, or are entitled to practise as, a solicitor;

(b)   undertake the following reserved work in England and Wales, unless authorised by your approved regulator to do so:

(i)   advocacy in open court;

(ii)   the conduct of court litigation;

(iii)   the administration of oaths and statutory declarations;

(c)   undertake advocacy in chambers in England and Wales, unless authorised by your approved regulator or acting under instructions given by a person qualified to direct reserved work;

(d)   undertake the following reserved work in England and Wales, unless authorised by your approved regulator or acting under the supervision of a person qualified to direct reserved work:

      (i)   the preparation of court documents;

      (ii)   the preparation of instruments and the lodging of documents relating to the transfer or charge of land;

      (iii) the preparation of papers on which to found or oppose a grant of probate or a grant of letters of administration;

      (iv) the preparation of trust deeds disposing of capital;

(e)   (i)   undertake the conduct of immigration tribunal proceedings in the UK or advocacy before an immigration tribunal in the UK unless you are authorised by your approved regulator or the Immigration Services Commissioner to do that work;

      (ii)   prepare documents in the UK for immigration tribunal proceedings unless you are authorised by your approved regulator or the Immigration Services Commissioner to do that work or acting under the supervision of a person qualified to direct reserved work; or

(f)   give immigration advice or undertake immigration services in the UK which are not within (b) to (e) above, unless you are authorised by your approved regulator or the Immigration Services Commissioner to do that work, or acting under the supervision of an individual working in the firm who is authorised under statute to do that work.

12.06 Managers and employees who are not lawyers

(1)   If you are a manager or employee of a recognised body or an employee of a recognised sole practitioner and you are not a lawyer of England and Wales, an RFL, or a lawyer of an Establishment Directive profession, you must not:

(a)   be held out in any way which suggests that you are, or are entitled to practise as, a lawyer of England and Wales;

(b)   undertake the following reserved work in England and Wales:

      (i)   advocacy in open court;

      (ii)   the conduct of court litigation;

      (iii) the administration of oaths and statutory declarations;

(c)   undertake advocacy in chambers in England and Wales, except under instructions given by a person qualified to direct reserved work;

(d)   undertake the following reserved work in England and Wales, except at the direction and under the supervision of a person qualified to direct reserved work:

      (i)   the preparation of court documents;

      (ii)   the preparation of instruments and the lodging of documents relating to the transfer or charge of land;

      (iii) the preparation of papers on which to found or oppose a grant of probate or a grant of letters of administration;

      (iv) the preparation of trust deeds disposing of capital;

(e)   (i)   undertake the conduct of immigration tribunal proceedings in the UK or advocacy before an immigration tribunal in the UK unless you are authorised by the Immigration Services Commissioner to do that work;

      (ii)   prepare documents in the UK for immigration tribunal proceedings unless you are authorised by the Immigration Services Commissioner to do that work, or acting under the supervision of a person qualified to direct reserved work; or

(f)   give immigration advice or undertake immigration services in the UK which are not within (b) to (e) above, unless you are authorised by the Immigration Services Commissioner to do that work or you do the work under the supervision of an individual working in the firm who is authorised under statute to do that work.

Guidance to rule 12 – Framework of practice

1.   The Legal Services Act 2007 (the LSA) provided for significant changes to the regulation of lawyers, and the ways in which they can practise, to increase competition and facilitate access to justice for the public. The framework established by the LSA enables the SRA (as well as other regulators) to update and improve its regulation, and solicitors and RELs to increase the scope of their practice, by allowing:

(a)   the SRA

    (i)   to permit and regulate legal disciplinary practices (LDPs),

    (ii)   to approve non-lawyers as managers of firms,

    (iii)   to apply firm-based regulation to all practices;

(b)   solicitors and RELs

    (i)   to practise through an LDP with lawyers regulated by another approved regulator and/or with non-lawyers,

    (ii)   to practise through an LDP regulated by another approved regulator.

2.   The lawyers of England and Wales (other than solicitors) who can practise in an LDP, and their approved regulators for the purposes of the LSA, are:

barrister	Bar Council (through the Bar Standards Board)
legal executive	Institute of Legal Executives (through ILEX Professional Standards Ltd)
licensed conveyancer	Council for Licensed Conveyancers
patent agent	Chartered Institute of Patent Attorneys (through the Intellectual Property Regulation Board)
trade mark agent	Institute of Trade Mark Attorneys (through the Intellectual Property Regulation Board)
law costs draftsman	Association of Law Costs Draftsmen
notary public	Faculty Office of the Archbishop of Canterbury.

Firms regulated by one of the other approved regulators are referred to in the rules as authorised non-SRA firms.

3.   A non-lawyer must be approved by the SRA under regulation 3 of the Recognised Bodies Regulations to be a manager of a recognised body.

4.   Rules 12, 13, 14 and 20 make up the framework rules which set out the ways in which individuals and bodies subject to the SRA's rules can practise, and restrictions upon those individuals and bodies. Rule 12 imposes restrictions on the type of firm through which you may practise if you are a solicitor, an REL, an RFL or a recognised body. It also sets out the restrictions on you if you are a manager or employee of a firm

regulated by the SRA and you are a lawyer regulated by another approved regulator or are a non-lawyer. The ability to impose such restrictions on any individual or body in a firm providing legal services and, if necessary, enforce them enables the SRA to protect clients and the public interest as anticipated by the LSA.

5. Rule 12 governs the types of business through which you may practise, but disgraceful conduct outside of practice may put you in breach of 1.06 (Public confidence) if you are a solicitor, an REL or an RFL, and 10.01 (Not taking unfair advantage) if you are a solicitor or an REL. Rule 10.05(1)(c) and (d), (2) and (3) (undertakings given outside the course of practice) apply to you if you are a solicitor or REL.

6. The SRA's approach to regulation is primarily firm-based. The LSA facilitates this to ensure proper regulation of practices that can involve a variety of lawyers and non-lawyers. This approach does not prevent the SRA taking regulatory action against individuals, as well as firms, in appropriate cases. This could include action against anyone in the firm including non-lawyer managers and employees, as the requirements in the Code apply to all recognised bodies and their managers and employees, as well as to solicitor and REL sole practitioners and their employees (23.01(1)).

Solicitors – 12.01

England and Wales

7. The rule requires every private practice firm providing legal services to the public in England and Wales under the SRA's regulation to be a recognised body or a recognised sole practitioner. A solicitor can be a manager, employee, member or owner of a recognised body, or of a body corporate which is a manager, member or owner of a recognised body. "Manager" is the term used in the LSA to refer to a partner in a partnership, a member of an LLP or a director of a company. Owner is included, in addition to manager, as you may be a share-owner in a company but not hold a directorship. Member is included, in addition to owner, because holding a share (as member of the company) is not the same as owning the share – you could, for example, be holding the share as nominee.

8. A recognised body must be at least 75% owned and controlled by lawyers. Rule 14 does not prohibit layers of ownership of recognised bodies, but a body corporate with an ownership interest in a recognised body must itself be a recognised body, an authorised non-SRA firm with at least 75% ownership by lawyers, or a European corporate practice (as defined in rule 24) with similar ownership restrictions.

9. New partnerships, companies and LLPs must apply to the SRA for recognition of the firm before being able to practise (rule 14 deals with the composition, structure and services of recognised bodies and the Recognised Bodies Regulations set out the procedural and administrative requirements).

10. If you wish to practise on your own account, you must be authorised as a recognised sole practitioner by the SRA endorsing your practising certificate, before you can establish your firm (see 20.03 and the SRA Practising Regulations). There are limited exceptions in 20.03(2) permitting sole practice without such an endorsement, for example when practising entirely outside England and Wales, as a locum or when providing services to family and friends free of charge.

11. If you are practising as a manager, employee, member or owner of an authorised non-SRA firm, what you can do will depend on the type of work you want to do, and for whom you want to do it.

(a)   The services you can provide to the public are limited to those which are regulated by the firm's approved regulator. For example, as a partner in a firm regulated by the Council for Licensed Conveyancers (CLC) you could not carry out litigation on behalf of clients of the firm, as the CLC is not authorised to regulate this work. When you are providing services of a type regulated by the firm's approved regulator (whether to the public or to the firm itself), you will primarily be regulated by the firm's regulator, and you will in general be complying with that regulator's rules rather than the SRA's rules – see 23.01(2).

(b)   Under rule 12.01(1)(d) you could also, however, provide services that are not regulated by the firm's approved regulator. As a partner in the CLC-regulated firm you could provide, say, litigation services to the firm itself or, subject to the limitations in rule 13, to colleagues, or to related bodies of the firm, or to clients on a pro bono basis. When providing services which are not regulated by the firm's approved regulator, you will be subject to all the SRA's rules.

12.   Rule 13 (In-house practice, etc.) sets out the limited circumstances in which, if you are an in-house solicitor in England and Wales, you can provide services to persons other than your employer.

Outside England and Wales

13.   If you are a sole practitioner and practise only from an office outside England and Wales, you will not need to be (and will not be able to be) a recognised sole practitioner. However, if your sole practice also has an office in England and Wales, you will need to be a recognised sole practitioner.

14.   A solicitor may practise with other lawyers from an office outside England and Wales in almost any kind of partnership or body corporate, including, for example, through an overseas partnership with a separate legal identity. You can practise as a manager, employee, member or owner of such a firm, which may be an overseas legal practice or a recognised body.

15.   If the firm is an overseas legal practice (i.e. it is practising entirely outside England and Wales):

(a)   a controlling majority (i.e. more than 50%) of the managers *and* owners must be lawyers;

(b)   if any of the managers or owners are non-lawyers, and the firm has an office in an Establishment Directive state, the composition and structure of the firm must comply with rules for local lawyers (even if there are no local lawyers in the firm);

(c)   if any of the managers or owners are non-lawyers, and the firm has an office in any other jurisdiction, compliance with local rules with regard to the composition and structure of the firm is only necessary if any of the firm's managers are subject to those rules (either because they are local lawyers, or because the local law applies local rules to the firm).

16.   If the firm is a recognised body (i.e. it also has an office or offices in England and Wales), *and* it has any non-lawyer managers or owners, *and* it has an office in any Establishment Directive state other than the UK, the composition and structure of the firm must comply with rules for local lawyers (even if there are no local lawyers in the firm).

17.   You may practise as an in-house solicitor outside England and Wales, within the limits set by 15.13 (In-house practice overseas).

Registered European lawyers (RELs) – 12.02

England and Wales

18. An REL is subject to the same restrictions as a solicitor in relation to practice from an office in England and Wales.

19. If you wish to practise on your own account, you must be authorised as a recognised sole practitioner by the SRA endorsing your certificate of registration, before you can establish your firm.

Outside England and Wales

20. The overseas provisions for an REL are the same as for a solicitor except that they apply only in Scotland and Northern Ireland. You are not subject to rule 12 in relation to practice from an office outside the UK.

Registered foreign lawyers (RFLs) – 12.03

England and Wales

21. Any foreign lawyer (whether based in England and Wales or elsewhere) must be registered with the SRA as an RFL to be a manager, member or owner of a recognised body, with the following exceptions:

     (a) a foreign lawyer who is also qualified as a lawyer of England and Wales does not have to be an RFL;

     (b) a member of an Establishment Directive profession – except that if the lawyer is *not* a national of an Establishment Directive state and will be based, or partly based, in England and Wales, he or she *does* have to be an RFL in order to be a manager, member or owner of a recognised body.

     Additional guidance on RFLs and multi-national practice can be found on our website.

22. There is no requirement to register as an RFL in order to be employed by a recognised body or a recognised sole practitioner but, if you are registered, you will be subject to SRA regulation in this capacity when working for an SRA regulated firm or an authorised non-SRA firm.

23. An RFL is subject to the same restrictions as a solicitor or REL in relation to practice from an office in England and Wales with two exceptions. Your registration as an RFL does not entitle you to practise:

     (a) as an RFL sole practitioner; or

     (b) as an in-house RFL.

24. Registration as an RFL is portable to the extent that it will enable you to be a manager, employee, member or owner of an authorised non-SRA firm, although your ability to work within such a firm will depend on the framework of practice requirements of the relevant approved regulator. You will be able to undertake work authorised by the firm's approved regulator (subject to any statutory limitations or requirements). Additionally you will be able to function as an in-house lawyer under rule 13, doing other work for the employer, related bodies, work colleagues and pro bono clients under the SRA's rules. For example, you might be an Australian solicitor employed to do conveyancing work for the clients of a firm authorised by the Council for Licensed Conveyancers. Under the SRA's authorisation of RFLs you could advise the firm and fellow employees on immigration issues, but would need to comply with rule 13 and all other SRA rules.

APPENDIX 21

25.   Rule 12.03(2) specifies the activities that will constitute practice in a capacity other than as an RFL. In effect, your registration as an RFL will not be relevant in the role of owner or employee of a business in England and Wales which is not regulated by the SRA or one of the other approved regulators. The SRA does not regulate any practice you might have outside the framework established under the LSA, so there must be no implication in such a context that you are an RFL, or that you or the business are regulated by or registered with the SRA or the Law Society. As your work in such a role is not regulated by the SRA, any implication that it is could, for example, lead to removal from the register of RFLs.

26.   If you are practising as an RFL in an SRA regulated firm or in an authorised non-SRA firm, and at the same time you are involved in a separate legal practice as a foreign lawyer, this will be a separate business and you must comply with the requirements of 21.05.

27.   Rules 12.03(4) and 12.03(5) set out a number of prohibitions relating to RFLs. For example:

(a)   whether or not you are practising as an RFL you cannot be held out or described in any way that suggests you are a lawyer of England and Wales, unless you have an appropriate additional qualification;

(b)   whether or not you are practising as an RFL you must not provide any reserved legal services unless you have an appropriate additional qualification or do the work under appropriate supervision;

(c)   if you are not practising as an RFL you must not give immigration advice or provide (non-reserved) immigration services unless you have an appropriate additional qualification or authorisation or do the work under appropriate supervision.

28.   Where, in order to satisfy statutory requirements, there is a need for an RFL doing reserved work to be supervised or directed by someone in the firm, this can only be undertaken by a person of equivalent or higher status. For example, it would not be appropriate for the work of an RFL manager to purport to be supervised or directed by an employee.

Outside England and Wales

29.   The rules in general do not apply to an RFL in relation to practice outside England and Wales. However 15.01 makes clear that 1.06 (Public confidence) applies to an RFL's activities outside England and Wales, whether as a lawyer or in some other business or private capacity. Rule 15.01(1)(b)(iv) states that 12.03(2), (3), (4)(a) and (5) also apply to an RFL's activities outside England and Wales. Rule 12.03(2) applies to prohibit an RFL from being held out or described as an RFL or as regulated by or registered with the Law Society or the SRA when participating outside England and Wales in a legal practice which is not authorised by the SRA or any other approved regulator, or in an in-house practice. Rule 12.03(3) provides that when an RFL participates in England and Wales in a legal practice which is authorised by the SRA or another approved regulator, and also participates in a separate practice or business outside England and Wales, he or she must comply with 21.05 (Separate businesses). Rule 12.03(4)(a) provides that an RFL must not be held out outside England and Wales as a lawyer of England and Wales (unless of course the RFL does have such a qualification). Rule 12.03(5) applies in Scotland and Northern Ireland and provides that an RFL who is not practising in that capacity is subject to the prohibitions in note 27(c) above.

Recognised bodies – 12.04

England and Wales

30.   A recognised body must have at least one office in England and Wales (see rule 14 for the composition and structure requirements for recognised bodies) and may be:

    (a)   a stand-alone firm which itself provides legal services to the public;

    (b)   a manager, member or owner of another recognised body or of an authorised non-SRA firm (but see below for the services you can provide);

    (c)   an executor, trustee or nominee company, or a company providing company secretarial services, which is owned and operated by another recognised body or recognised sole practitioner and is providing services in conjunction with that firm.

31.   If the recognised body is a manager, member or owner of an authorised non-SRA firm it may only provide services through that firm which the firm is authorised to provide.

32.   Recognised bodies can have a complex structure, involving multi-layered ownership by other legally qualified bodies (see rule 24). But note that a partnership cannot be a partner in another partnership which is a recognised body (although, as an exception, an overseas partnership with separate legal identity could be a partner in a partnership which is a recognised body). Non-lawyer participation in all recognised bodies is restricted to 25% as measured by three different indicators:

    (a)   numbers of managers;

    (b)   proportion of shares or other ownership rights;

    (c)   proportion of voting rights exercised or controlled.

Outside England and Wales

33.   If a firm practises only from an office or offices outside England and Wales, it will not need to be (and will not be able to be) a recognised body. However, if the firm also has at least one office in England and Wales it must be a recognised body and can practise as such outside England and Wales.

34.   Outside England and Wales the rules apply to a "solicitor-controlled recognised body" (and also to an "REL-controlled recognised body" in Scotland or Northern Ireland) – see the definitions in rule 24, and further details in 15.01(2) and 15.27.

35.   A recognised body can practise outside England and Wales as a stand-alone firm or as a manager, member or owner of an overseas legal practice (i.e. one that practises entirely outside England and Wales). It may also of course practise as a manager, member or owner of another recognised body with an overseas office.

36.   If the recognised body has any non-lawyer managers or owners, and it has an office in any Establishment Directive state other than the UK, see note 16 above.

37.   If the recognised body is a manager, member or owner of an overseas legal practice which does not have an office in England and Wales, see note 15 above.

Managers and employees authorised by an approved regulator other than the SRA – 12.05

England and Wales

38.   Rule 14 permits lawyers and firms authorised by another approved regulator to be

owners and managers of a recognised body. Rule 12 sets out the ways in which such persons authorised by other approved regulators can and cannot practise as a manager or employee of a recognised body or as the employee of a recognised sole practitioner. The Code applies to such a manager or employee.

39.   An individual authorised by another approved regulator cannot practise as a recognised sole practitioner regulated by the SRA as the SRA can only authorise and regulate sole solicitors and RELs. Likewise the SRA can only grant recognised body status to a firm with at least one solicitor or REL manager (or at least one manager which is a legally qualified body with a solicitor or REL manager) so, for example, a firm made up solely of licensed conveyancers or a mix of lawyers approved by other approved regulators cannot become a recognised body.

40.   The restrictions in 12.05 establish that the following legal prohibitions on non-solicitors, which include those authorised by another approved regulator, will be treated as breaches of the Code:

(a)   you cannot be held out or described in any way that suggests you are, or are entitled to practise as, a solicitor; and

(b)   you must not provide any reserved legal services, unless, for example, authorised by your own approved regulator; or under the supervision and direction of a person qualified to direct such work; or are authorised by another regulator, such as the Office of the Immigration Services Commissioner, to do the work.

41.   Where, in order to satisfy statutory requirements, there is a need for an individual doing reserved work to be supervised or directed by someone in the firm, this can only be undertaken by a person of equivalent or higher status. For example, it would not be appropriate for the work of a manager to purport to be supervised or directed by an employee.

Outside England and Wales

42.   A lawyer of England and Wales who is an individual authorised by another approved regulator is subject to the rules in relation to practice outside England and Wales if he or she is a manager of a solicitor-controlled recognised body (and also if he or she is a manager of an REL-controlled recognised body in Scotland or Northern Ireland).

Non-lawyers – 12.06

England and Wales

43.   From March 2009, non-lawyers can be owners and managers, as well as employees, of SRA-regulated firms. Rule 12 permits a non-lawyer to become a manager or employee of one of the practice vehicles permitted to solicitors, RELs and so on.

44.   The position of non-lawyer employees changed in 2009 in that the SRA has direct powers of regulation over all employees and not just over solicitors and RELs. The guidance to rules 5 and 23 provides some more detail on this.

45.   The purpose of rule 12.06 is to establish that the following legal prohibitions on non-lawyers will be treated as breaches of the Code. For example:

(a)   you cannot be held out or described in any way that suggests you are, or are entitled to practise as, a lawyer of England and Wales; and

(b)   you must not provide any reserved legal services, unless, for example, acting under the supervision and direction of a person qualified to direct such work (see also note 41 above), or are authorised by a regulator, such as the Office of the Immigration Services Commissioner, to do the work.

46.   The LSA requires that any non-lawyer owners of practices must be approved by the SRA, and must also be managers. This means that a non-lawyer could only be a shareowner in a company (whether beneficially or as nominee) if he or she is also a director of the company (subject to a limited exception in 14.01(3)(e)).

Outside England and Wales

47.   A non-lawyer manager is subject to the rules in relation to practice outside England and Wales if he or she is a manager of a solicitor-controlled recognised body (and also if he or she is a manager of an REL-controlled recognised body in Scotland or Northern Ireland). Non-lawyer employees, employed outside England and Wales, are not subject to the rules.

Rule 13 – In-house practice, etc.

Introduction

Rule 12 (Framework of practice) allows a solicitor or an REL to practise in-house from an office in England and Wales as the employee of a business which is not a recognised sole practitioner, recognised body or authorised non-SRA firm, but subject to restrictions. The solicitor or REL may act only for the employer or in the circumstances set out in rule 13.

Rule 12 also provides that a solicitor, REL or RFL in an authorised non-SRA firm may do work which falls outside the firm's authorisation, but only if acting for the firm or within 13.02 (Work colleagues), 13.03 (Related bodies) or 13.04 (Pro bono work). The rule, except for 13.04, does not apply to your overseas practice, but you must comply with 15.13 (In-house practice overseas).

Rule 13 – In-house practice, etc.

13.01 Conditions applying at all times

(1)   (a)   You must not, as an in-house solicitor or REL, act for a client other than your employer under 13.02 to 13.12 if to do so would compromise:

        (i)   your professional independence or integrity;

        (ii)   your duty to act in the best interests of that client;

        (iii)   your duty to comply with rule 3 (Conflict of interests);

        (iv)   your duty to keep information about that client's affairs confidential from your employer (unless the other client consents to disclosure, or you are acting under 13.11 as the employee of a foreign law firm); or

        (v)   your ability to discharge any other duty owed to that client under these rules.

    (b)   (i)   In order to act for a client other than your employer under 13.04, 13.07, 13.09 and 13.11, you must have professional indemnity insurance cover.

        (ii)   In all other cases you must consider whether your employer has appropriate indemnity insurance or funds to meet any award made as a result of a claim in professional negligence against you, for which your employer might be vicariously liable. If not, you must inform the client in writing that you are not covered by the compulsory insurance scheme.

(2)   If you are a solicitor, REL or RFL in an authorised non-SRA firm, you must comply with this rule as if you were an in-house solicitor or REL when, as:

(a)   a manager or employee; or

(b)   a manager or employee of a body which is a manager of the firm,

you do work of a type which is outside the scope of the firm's authorisation in accordance with rule 12, either for the firm itself or within 13.02 (Work colleagues), 13.03 (Related bodies) or 13.04 (Pro bono work).

13.02 Work colleagues

(1)   Subject to the provisos in 13.02(2) below, you may act for a person who is, or was formerly:

(a)   an employee, a manager, the company secretary, a board member or a trustee of the employer or authorised non-SRA firm;

(b)   an employee, a manager, the company secretary, a board member or a trustee of a related body (within the meaning of 13.03(1) or 13.08(c) below) of the employer or authorised non-SRA firm; or

(c)   a contributor to a programme or periodical publication, broadcast or published by the employer (or by a related body within the meaning of 13.03(1) or 13.08(c) below), but only where the contributor is a defendant or potential defendant in a defamation case.

(2)   You may act under (1) above only if:

(a)   the matter relates to or arises out of the work of the employee, manager, company secretary, board member, trustee or contributor in that capacity;

(b)   the matter does not relate to a claim arising as a result of a personal injury to the employee, manager, company secretary, board member, trustee or contributor;

(c)   you are satisfied that the employee, manager, company secretary, board member, trustee or contributor does not wish to instruct some other lawyer; and

(d)   no charge is made for your work unless those costs are recoverable from another source.

(3)   Where acting in a conveyancing transaction under (1)(a) or (b) above you may also act for a joint owner/buyer and for a mortgagee.

13.03 Related bodies

(1)   You may act for:

(a)   the employer's, or authorised non-SRA firm's, holding, associated or subsidiary company;

(b)   a partnership, syndicate, LLP or company by way of joint venture in which the employer, or authorised non-SRA firm, and others have an interest;

(c)   a trade association of which the employer or authorised non-SRA firm, is a member; or

    (d)   a club, association, pension fund or other scheme operated for the benefit of employees of the employer, or the employees or managers of the authorised non-SRA firm.

(2)   If you are employed in local government, (1)(a) and (b) above do not apply.

(3)   For the purpose of 13.04 to 13.07 references to your employer or authorised non-SRA firm include related bodies of the employer or authorised non-SRA firm as set out in (1) above, and "employment" and "employed" must be construed accordingly.

13.04 Pro bono work

(1)   You may, in the course of your practice, conduct work on a pro bono basis for a client other than your employer or authorised non-SRA firm provided:

    (a)   the work is covered by an indemnity reasonably equivalent to that required under the Solicitors' Indemnity Insurance Rules; and

    (b)   either:

        (i)   no fees are charged; or

        (ii)   a conditional fee agreement is used and the only fees charged are those which you receive by way of costs from your client's opponent or other third party and pay to a charity under a fee sharing agreement.

(2)   Paragraph (1) above does not permit you to conduct work on a pro bono basis in conjunction with services provided by your employer under 13.05 (Associations), 13.06 (Insurers), 13.07 (Commercial legal advice services) or 13.11 (Foreign law firms).

13.05 Associations

If you are employed by an association you may act for a member provided:

    (a)   the membership of the association is limited to persons engaged or concerned in a particular trade, occupation or activity or otherwise having a community of interest;

    (b)   the association is one formed bona fide for the benefit of its members and not formed directly or indirectly for your benefit or primarily for securing assistance in legal proceedings; and

    (c)   there is no charge to the member in non-contentious matters, and in contentious matters the association indemnifies the member in relation to your costs and disbursements insofar as they are not recoverable from any other source.

13.06 Insurers

(1)   If you are employed by an insurer subrogated to the rights of an insured in respect of any matter you may act on behalf of the insurer in relation to that matter in the name of the insured, and also:

    (a)   act on behalf of the insured in relation to uninsured losses in respect of the matter;

    (b)   act in proceedings both for the insured and for a defendant covered by another insurer where the insurers have agreed an apportionment of liability; and/or

(c)   act in the matter on behalf of the employer and another insurer in the joint prosecution of a claim.

(2)   If you are employed by a legal expenses insurer you may, provided that the insured has given specific consent, act for an insured in any proceedings which are covered by the legal expenses insurance policy, provided that the proceedings do not include:

         (a)   a personal injury claim (whether made by or for the insured); or

         (b)   a civil claim for damages which:

                 (i)   exceeds the small claims limit from time to time in operation in the county court; and/or

                 (ii)   is allocated or re-allocated to the fast track or the multi-track.

13.07 Commercial legal advice services

If you are employed by a commercial organisation providing a telephone legal advice service you may advise enquirers, provided:

         (a)   the advice comprises telephone advice only, together with a follow up letter to the enquirer when necessary; and

         (b)   you are satisfied that there is indemnity cover reasonably equivalent to that required under the Solicitors' Indemnity Insurance Rules.

13.08 Local government

If you are employed in local government you may act:

         (a)   for another organisation or person to which or to whom the employer is statutorily empowered to provide legal services, subject to the conditions in (b) to (g) below;

         (b)   for a member or former member of the local authority, provided that:

                 (i)   the matter relates to or arises out of the work of the member in that capacity;

                 (ii)   the matter does not relate to a claim arising as a result of a personal injury to the member;

                 (iii)   you are satisfied that the member does not wish to instruct some other lawyer; and

                 (iv)   no charge is made for your work unless those costs are recoverable from some other source;

         (c)   for a company limited by shares or guarantee of which:

                 (i)   the employer or nominee of the employer is a shareholder or guarantor; or

                 (ii)   you are, or an officer of the employer is, appointed by the employer as an officer of the company,

         provided the employer is acting in pursuance of its statutory powers;

         (d)   for lenders in connection with new mortgages arising from the redemption of mortgages to the local authority, provided:

                 (i)   neither you nor any other employee acts on behalf of the borrowers; and

(ii)   the borrowers are given the opportunity to be independently advised by a qualified conveyancer of their choice;

(e)   for a charity or voluntary organisation whose objects relate wholly or partly to the employer's area, provided that there is no charge to the charity or voluntary organisation in non-contentious matters, and in contentious matters the employer indemnifies the charity or voluntary organisation in relation to your costs insofar as they are not recoverable from any other source;

(f)   for a patient who is the subject of a Court of Protection Order where you are acting for a work colleague (under 13.02 above) who is appointed as receiver for the patient; or

(g)   for a child or young person subject to a Care Order in favour of the employer on an application to the Criminal Injuries Compensation Authority.

13.09 Law centres, charities and other non-commercial advice services

(1)   If you are employed by a law centre or advice service operated by a charitable or similar non-commercial organisation you may give advice to and otherwise act for members of the public, provided:

(a)   no funding agent has majority representation on the body responsible for the management of the service, and that body remains independent of central and local government;

(b)   no fees are charged save:

(i)   where the client is publicly funded; or

(ii)   where the organisation indemnifies the client in relation to your costs insofar as they are not recoverable from any other source;

(c)   all fees you earn and costs you recover are paid to the organisation for furthering the provision of the organisation's services;

(d)   the organisation is not described as a law centre unless it is a member of the Law Centres Federation; and

(e)   the organisation effects indemnity cover reasonably equivalent to that required under the Solicitors' Indemnity Insurance Rules.

(2)   Paragraph (1) above does not apply to an association formed for the benefit of its members.

13.10 The Crown, non-departmental public bodies, and the Legal Services Commission

If you are employed by the Crown, a non-departmental public body, or the Legal Services Commission (or any body established or maintained by the Legal Services Commission), you may give legal advice to, and act for, other persons if in doing so you are carrying out the lawful functions of the employer.

13.11 Foreign law firms

(1)   You may provide legal services to your employer's clients, subject to the conditions set out in (2) below, if you are a solicitor or an REL employed by:

    (a)   a practising lawyer of another jurisdiction who:

        (i)   is not struck off or suspended from the register of foreign lawyers or the register of European lawyers; and

        (ii)   is not practising in that context as a solicitor or as an REL; or

    (b)   a business whose managers and owners are all practising through that business as lawyers of jurisdictions other than England and Wales, and do not include any person who:

        (i)   is struck off or suspended from the register of foreign lawyers or the register of European lawyers; or

        (ii)   is practising through or in the context of that business as a solicitor or as an REL.

(2)   You must meet the following conditions if acting for anyone other than your employer.

    (a)   Even if you are qualified to do such work for your employer, you must not do, or supervise or assume responsibility for doing any of the following:

        (i)   drawing or preparing any instrument or papers, or making any application or lodging any document relating to litigation reserved to qualified persons by the Solicitors Act 1974;

        (ii)   exercising any right of audience, or right to conduct litigation before a court or immigration tribunal; or

        (iii)   providing any immigration advice or immigration services, unless the employer, or a senior fellow employee, is registered with the Immigration Services Commissioner.

    (b)   You must ensure that the work is covered by professional indemnity insurance reasonably equivalent to that required under the Solicitors' Indemnity Insurance Rules.

    (c)   You must inform your client that your employer is not regulated by the Solicitors Regulation Authority and that the Authority's compulsory insurance scheme does not apply; and either give or confirm this information in writing, if you are a solicitor, and you are held out to a client as a solicitor (or as an English or Welsh lawyer) in connection with work you are doing for that client.

    (d)   You must ensure that if you are identified on the notepaper as a solicitor (or as an English or Welsh lawyer) the notepaper also states that your employer is not regulated by the Solicitors Regulation Authority.

(3)   Paragraph (2)(c) and (d) above should also be read as referring to an REL being held out or identified as a lawyer, or under the REL's home title.

13.12 Regulatory bodies

If you are employed by a regulatory body you may in carrying out the function of the employer give legal advice to other persons and in the case of statutory functions may act generally for such persons.

Guidance to rule 13 – In-house practice, etc.

1. If you are a solicitor working in-house (whether in or outside England and Wales) you must comply with 20.02 (Practising certificates). Examples of situations where you will be practising as a solicitor, and will therefore need a practising certificate, include:

   (a) you are employed as a solicitor;

   (b) you are held out, on stationery or otherwise, as a solicitor for your employer;

   (c) you administer oaths;

   (d) you appear before a court or tribunal in reliance upon your qualification as a solicitor;

   (e) you instruct counsel;

   (f) you undertake work which is prohibited to unqualified persons by the Solicitors Act 1974 and under the forthcoming provisions of Part 3 of the Legal Services Act 2007, unless you are supervised by, and acting in the name of, a solicitor with a practising certificate or another qualified person;

   (g) your only qualification as a lawyer is that you are a solicitor, and:

       (i) you are employed or held out as a lawyer;

       (ii) you undertake work in another jurisdiction which is reserved to lawyers;

       (iii) you are registered in a state other than the UK under the Establishment Directive; or

       (iv) you are a registered foreign legal consultant in another jurisdiction.

2. In England and Wales a number of statutory exceptions apply to qualify this. Certain in-house government solicitors are allowed to practise as solicitors without practising certificates. Some reserved work can be undertaken by non-solicitors working for local government, and therefore by non-practising solicitors working for local government. See also rule 20 (Rights and obligations of practice) and the guidance to it.

3. A solicitor acting only as a justices' clerk in England and Wales is not practising as a solicitor and can instruct counsel without a practising certificate.

4. Although the guidance to this rule will generally apply to practice in and outside England and Wales unless otherwise stated, the only provision of rule 13 which applies to practice outside England and Wales is 13.04 (Pro bono work). However, you must also comply with the provisions of 15.13 (which relates to in-house practice overseas) in relation to your in-house practice, if you are employed at an office outside England and Wales (or if you are an REL, employed at an office in Scotland or Northern Ireland).

5. If you are an in-house solicitor or in-house REL you are personally bound by undertakings given in the course of your professional duties – see 10.05 (Undertakings) (or, if you practise overseas, 15.10(2)).

6. When you act in your capacity as an in-house solicitor or in-house REL you should not communicate with third parties who you know are represented by another lawyer, except with that lawyer's consent. Any communication should be made through the lawyer acting for the third party.

7. You may use the stationery of, or stationery including the name of, your employer for professional work, provided:

   (a) the letterhead or the signature makes it clear that the stationery is being used by an in-house solicitor or in-house REL on legal professional business and that person is responsible for the contents of the letter; and

(b)   the stationery is being used for the business of the non-lawyer employer or for third parties in circumstances permitted by rule 13 or 15.13 (which relates to in-house practice overseas).

8.   You may, as an in-house solicitor or in-house REL, use a style of stationery or description which appears to hold you out as a principal in a firm. However, if you are held out as a principal on notepaper and you hold or receive clients' money, you will be required to pay the full contribution to the Compensation Fund. Note that you should be careful not to hold out a non-existent entity as if it were regulated by the SRA. There is no objection to your stating "John Smith, solicitor, is regulated by the Solicitors Regulation Authority".

9.   If you are an in-house solicitor the address of your employer's legal department is the place (or one of the places) where you practise and must therefore be notified to the SRA.

Accounts rules and accountants' reports

10.   If you are an in-house solicitor or in-house REL employed in England and Wales, and you receive or hold clients' money, you must comply with the Solicitors' Accounts Rules 1998. If you pay in or endorse over a cheque made out in your favour, you receive clients' money and must deal with it in accordance with the relevant rules (see note (viii) to rule 35 of the Solicitors' Accounts Rules 1998). For the name of a client account, see rule 14(3) of the Solicitors' Accounts Rules 1998. Even if a cheque is simply endorsed over to your employer, you will need to keep a record (see rule 32 of the Solicitors' Accounts Rules 1998), submit an accountant's report, and pay the full contribution to the Compensation Fund. If you receive only your employer's money you can try to ensure that all cheques are made payable to the employer. If you are an in-house solicitor or in-house REL employed overseas, the Solicitors' Accounts Rules do not apply but you must comply with similar requirements which are set out in 15.27.

11.   An in-house accountant (working for the same employer) may not prepare an accountant's report for an in-house solicitor or in-house REL (see rule 37(2)(a) of the Solicitors' Accounts Rules 1998).

12.   If you only undertake a small number of transactions or handle a small volume of clients' money in a year, you can apply to the Caseworking and Applications department of the SRA for a dispensation from the obligation to deliver an accountant's report. However, dispensations are not given as a matter of course.

13.   If you are:

(a)   a solicitor or REL practising as an employee of:

(i)   a local authority;

(ii)   statutory undertakers;

(iii)   a body whose accounts are audited by the Comptroller and Auditor General;

(iv)   the Duchy of Lancaster;

(v)   the Duchy of Cornwall; or

(vi)   the Church Commissioners;

(b)   a solicitor practising as the Solicitor of the City of London; or

(c)   a solicitor or REL carrying out the functions of:

(i)   a coroner or other judicial office; or

(ii)   a sheriff or under-sheriff,

you need not comply with the Solicitors' Accounts Rules 1998 (see rule 5 of those rules) or submit an accountant's report. However, if you hold or receive client money, you must pay the full Compensation Fund contribution, but this will not apply if you come within note 13(c) and are not practising as a solicitor.

Separate practice through a firm

14. If you are an in-house solicitor or in-house REL you can also be a manager in a firm. However, you must effect indemnity insurance for the firm in accordance with the Solicitors' Indemnity Insurance Rules, and notify the SRA of the address of the firm.

15. The firm must not act for a private client where there is any conflict between the interests of that client and the interests of your employer.

16. For details regarding arrangements for the referral of clients, see rule 9 (Referrals of business).

17. If you hold or receive client money as a manager in a firm in England and Wales you must comply with the Solicitors' Accounts Rules 1998.

18. You may agree to reimburse your employer for that proportion of your salary and of the employer's other overhead expenses which is attributable to any work carried out in the employer's time for your firm, on the employer's premises and/or with the assistance of staff and materials provided by the employer. You must make sure that this allowance for overheads is properly calculated, otherwise there could be a breach of rule 8 (Fee sharing).

Industrial action by in-house solicitors or in-house RELs

19. It is not professional misconduct for you to strike or take other industrial action, but you must have regard to your duties to the court and third parties. Before deciding to take such action you must:

    (a) ensure that no client for whom you act is prejudiced by the action in any crucial way, e.g. by missing a time limit;

    (b) ensure that steps are taken to cover all court engagements;

    (c) ensure compliance with your professional undertakings; and

    (d) promptly arrange to notify persons who may be affected by the proposed action.

Costs recovered from third parties

20. When you put forward a claim for costs against a third party, you must, as an in-house solicitor or in-house REL, have regard to the proper indemnity basis for costs.

21. Where you act for your employer, there is no presumption that it is any cheaper to employ an in-house lawyer than to retain a firm. The court will, therefore, normally regard it as proper for your bill to be drawn on the usual principles applicable to firms. There may, however, be special cases where it is clear that a bill drawn on this basis would improperly remunerate the employer and should therefore be disallowed (see *Henderson v Merthyr Tydfil UDC* [1900] 1 QB 434 and *Re Eastwood (deceased)* [1975] Ch 112). There seems no reason in principle why such an approach should not also be applicable to non-contentious business, or to matters where you act for someone other than the employer.

22. Under certain circumstances rule 13 allows you to act for someone other than your employer, as part of your employment. In such cases there will be no breach of rule 8 (Fee sharing) when you account to your employer for costs paid either by the client, the client's opponent or another third party (see rule 8). Similarly, there will be no

breach of rule 8 if you conduct work on a pro bono basis in accordance with 13.04(1)(b)(ii) and fees received by way of costs from your client's opponent or other third party are paid to a charity under a fee sharing agreement.

Direct access to client

23. If you are the senior legal adviser of a company or a local authority you should have direct access to the board or to the council and its committees, and should try to ensure that your terms of employment provide for such access. "Direct access" does not mean that all instructions and advice must pass directly to and from the council, committee or board, but you must have direct access where necessary.

Insurers and commercial legal advice services

24. If you are employed as a solicitor or REL by an insurer which runs a commercial legal telephone advice service, the restrictions in 13.07 will not apply to prevent you acting for an insured under a legal expenses insurance policy in accordance with 13.06.

Law centres, charities and other non-commercial advice services

25. If you are employed as a solicitor or REL by a law centre or advice service operated by a charitable or similar non-commercial organisation, you can advise and act for members of the public provided you comply with 13.09. This contains important provisions relating to (for example) professional indemnity, the charging of fees, and the independence of the body responsible for the management of the service. A solicitor or REL who works as a volunteer for such an advice service must comply with the Solicitors' Indemnity Insurance Rules unless exempted by a waiver.

Foreign law firms

26. In-house practice in England and Wales includes any employment by a business which is not authorised by the SRA or some other approved regulator. As the in-house employee of a foreign law firm, you are not as free to act for your employer's clients as you would be if you were employed in England and Wales by a solicitor, an REL or a recognised body. Under 13.11 you may not do reserved work for clients, or (unless your employer is separately authorised) immigration work. You must also comply with special requirements as to insurance and "health warnings". Note also, that if you are employed by a foreign law firm and a principal, owner or director of the firm is a solicitor, 13.11 will not apply unless the solicitor is dually qualified and is practising only as a lawyer of another jurisdiction in the context of that business.

27. By contrast, employment *overseas* by a foreign law firm will not usually fall within the definition of in-house practice in rule 24 (Interpretation) if your employer is a lawyer or a law firm.

Practice as a manager or employee of an authorised non-SRA firm

28. If you are a solicitor, REL or RFL practising as a manager, employee, member or owner of an authorised non-SRA firm, neither rule 13, nor the bulk of the other rules in the Code, nor the Accounts Rules, will be relevant to you when you do work of a type which is within the scope of the firm's authorisation. See 23.01(2).

29. If you are a solicitor, REL or RFL practising as a manager, employee, member or owner of an authorised non-SRA firm, you must comply with rule 13, and all the other rules in the Code, and with the Accounts Rules, as if you were an in-house solicitor or REL when you do work of a type which is outside the scope of the firm's

authorisation – see 13.01(2). Rule 12.01(1)(d) allows you to do such work for the firm itself, or if the work would come within 13.02 (Work colleagues), 13.03 (Related bodies) or 13.04 (Pro bono work).

30. Note that if you are a solicitor, REL or RFL and you are a manager, member or owner of an authorised non-SRA firm, or employed in such a firm in connection with the provision of any legal services, it must be:

(a) in your capacity as a solicitor, REL or RFL, or

(b) in the capacity of an individual authorised by an approved regulator other than the SRA, if you are so authorised, or

(c) in both such capacities;

except that if you are a solicitor who is a director of an authorised non-SRA firm or employed in such a firm in connection with the provision of any legal services, you must be practising in your capacity as a solicitor, even if also in some other capacity. See 20.04(2) and (3), as well as section 1A(d) of the Solicitors Act 1974.

Rule 14 – Recognised bodies

Introduction

Under rule 12 (Framework of practice) solicitors and RELs must not provide services to the public in England and Wales except through a firm which is a recognised body or a recognised sole practitioner (both regulated by the Solicitors Regulation Authority) or through an authorised non-SRA firm (regulated by another approved regulator). Rule 14 governs the composition and structure of a recognised body and the services a recognised body may provide, and is to a large extent based on the requirements of sections 9 and 9A of the Administration of Justice Act 1985.

Rule 14 – Recognised bodies

14.01 Fundamental requirements for all recognised bodies

Services requirement

(1) The business of a recognised body may consist only of the provision of:

(a) professional services of the sort provided by individuals practising as solicitors and/or lawyers of other jurisdictions; and

(b) professional services of the sort provided by notaries public, but only if a notary public is a manager or employee of a recognised body,

but this does not prevent a recognised body providing services within 21.03, or having an ownership interest in a company which is a separate business.

Relevant lawyer requirement

(2) (a) At all times at least one manager of a recognised body must be:

(i) a solicitor with a current practising certificate;

(ii) an REL; or

(iii)   (in the case of a partnership or LLP) a body corporate which is a legally qualified body with at least one manager who is a solicitor with a current practising certificate or an REL.

(b)   If an event which could not reasonably have been foreseen would put a recognised body in breach of the relevant lawyer requirement but within 28 days the situation is remedied, the recognised body will be deemed to have remained in compliance with the relevant lawyer requirement and to that extent will not be liable to have its recognition revoked under regulation 9.1(b) of the Recognised Bodies Regulations.

(c)   If the only, or last remaining, solicitor or REL whose role in the body ensures compliance with the relevant lawyer requirement:

    (i)   is committed to prison in civil or criminal proceedings;

    (ii)   becomes and continues to be unable to attend to the practice of the body because of incapacity caused by illness, accident or age;

    (iii)   becomes and continues to be a person who lacks capacity under Part 1 of the Mental Capacity Act 2005;

    (iv)   abandons the practice of the body; or

    (v)   is made subject to a condition on his or her practising certificate or registration which would be breached by continuing to fulfil the role of relevant lawyer within the body,

the body must inform the Solicitors Regulation Authority within seven days and must within 28 days either ensure that the body can fulfil the relevant lawyer requirement without reference to that person, or cease to practise.

Management and control requirement

(3)   (a)   At least 75% of the body's managers must be:

    (i)   individuals who are, and are entitled to practise as, lawyers of England and Wales, lawyers of Establishment Directive professions or RFLs; or

    (ii)   bodies corporate which are legally qualified bodies;

although a legally qualified body cannot be a director of a recognised body which is a company, as under 14.06(1) all the directors must be individuals.

(b)   Individuals who are, and are entitled to practise as, lawyers of England and Wales, lawyers of Establishment Directive professions or RFLs must make up at least 75% of the ultimate beneficial ownership of the recognised body.

(c)   Individuals who are, and are entitled to practise as, lawyers of England and Wales, lawyers of Establishment Directive professions or RFLs, and/or legally qualified bodies, must:

    (i)   exercise or control the exercise of at least 75% of the voting rights in the recognised body; and

    (ii)   if the recognised body is a company with shares, hold (as registered members of the company) at least 75% of the shares.

(d)   Every owner of the recognised body, and every person who exercises or controls the exercise of any voting rights in the body, must be:

    (i)   an individual who is, and is entitled to practise as, a lawyer of England and Wales, a lawyer of an Establishment Directive profession or an RFL;

    (ii)   a legally qualified body; or

(iii) an individual who is approved under regulation 3 of the Recognised Bodies Regulations and, subject to (e) below, is a manager of the body.

(e) An individual who is not entitled under (d)(i) above may be an owner of a recognised body without being a manager of the body if:

    (i) the recognised body is a company which is wholly or partly owned by a partnership or LLP which is a legally qualified body;

    (ii) the individual is approved under regulation 3 of the Recognised Bodies Regulations and is a manager of the partnership or LLP; and

    (iii) the individual is precluded under the partnership agreement or members' agreement from exercising or authorising any vote in relation to the company.

(f) If an event which could not reasonably have been foreseen would put a recognised body in breach of the management and control requirement but within 28 days the situation is remedied, the recognised body will be deemed to have remained in compliance with the management and control requirement and to that extent will not be liable to have its recognition revoked under regulation 9.1(b) of the Recognised Bodies Regulations.

(g) If the only or last remaining lawyer of England and Wales, lawyer of an Establishment Directive profession or RFL whose role in the body ensures compliance with the management and control requirement:

    (i) is committed to prison in civil or criminal proceedings;

    (ii) becomes and continues to be unable to attend to the practice of the body because of incapacity caused by illness, accident or age;

    (iii) becomes and continues to be a person who lacks capacity under Part 1 of the Mental Capacity Act 2005;

    (iv) abandons the practice of the body; or

    (v) is made subject to a condition on his or her practising certificate or registration which would be breached by continuing to fulfil that role,

the body must inform the Solicitors Regulation Authority within seven days and must within 28 days either ensure that the body can fulfil the management and control requirement without reference to that person, or cease to practise.

14.02 Duties in relation to compliance

(1) (a) A recognised body and its managers and employees must comply with rule 14.

    (b) A recognised body must so far as possible ensure that its managers, members and owners comply with rule 14.

    (c) A recognised body must not take on a new manager without first being satisfied of that manager's eligibility, by:

        (i) checking that any solicitor has a practising certificate, that any REL or RFL is registered with the Solicitors Regulation Authority, and that the practising certificate or registration is not subject to a condition which would preclude that person becoming a manager;

        (ii) obtaining (and retaining, for production to the Solicitors Regulation Authority if required), in respect of any lawyer authorised by an approved regulator but not by the SRA, written confirmation from the approved regulator to the effect that the lawyer is authorised by that approved regulator, entitled to practise and not subject to a condition or other restriction which would preclude that person becoming a manager;

(iii) obtaining (and retaining, for production to the Solicitors Regulation Authority if required), in respect of any individual who is entitled to be a manager only by virtue of approval under regulation 3 of the Recognised Bodies Regulations, written confirmation:

(A) from the Authority that the individual concerned is approved under regulation 3; and

(B) from the individual concerned, details of any event which the body will have to declare when next renewing its recognition, which has occurred in relation to that individual since he or she was last a manager of a recognised body renewing its recognition; and

(iv) in relation to any body corporate, making checks and obtaining (and retaining, for production to the Solicitors Regulation Authority if required) confirmations under (i) to (iii) above in respect of every individual who is a manager of or who has an interest in that body corporate.

(2) A manager of a recognised body:

(a) must so far as possible ensure that the body complies with rule 14;

(b) must ensure that the body complies with any condition imposed on its recognition; and

(c) must not cause, instigate or connive at any breach of these rules by the recognised body or any of its managers or employees.

(3) A solicitor, REL or RFL who is a member of, or the owner of a share in, a recognised body which is a company must not cause, instigate or connive at any breach of these rules by the recognised body or any of its managers or employees.

(4) A person employed to work in the practice of a recognised body must not cause, instigate or connive at any breach of these rules.

(5) The partners in a recognised body which is a partnership are responsible not only as managers but also, jointly and severally, as the recognised body.

14.03 Formation, office in England and Wales and registered office

Law of formation

(1) (a) A recognised body which is a partnership may be formed under the law of any country and may be a legal person.

(b) A recognised body which is an LLP must be incorporated and registered in England and Wales, Scotland or Northern Ireland under the Limited Liability Partnerships Act 2000.

(c) A recognised body which is a company must be:

(i) incorporated and registered in England and Wales, Scotland or Northern Ireland under Parts I and II of the Companies Act 2006;

(ii) incorporated in an Establishment Directive state and registered as an overseas company under Part 34 of the Companies Act 2006; or

(iii)   incorporated and registered in an Establishment Directive state as a societas Europaea.

Practising address in England and Wales

(2)   A recognised body must have at least one practising address in England and Wales.

Registered office of a company or LLP

(3)   A recognised body must have its registered office at a practising address in England and Wales if the recognised body is registered in England and Wales:

(a)   under Parts 1 and 2 of the Companies Act 2006;

(b)   under the Limited Liability Partnerships Act 2000; or

(c)   as a societas Europaea.

14.04 Recognised bodies which are partnerships

Who may be a partner

(1)   Provided that the fundamental requirements for all recognised bodies set out in 14.01 are met, a recognised body which is a partnership may have all or any of the following as a partner:

(a)   a lawyer of England and Wales (including a solicitor with a current practising certificate);

(b)   an REL;

(c)   an RFL;

(d)   an exempt European lawyer;

(e)   an individual approved under regulation 3 of the Recognised Bodies Regulations;

(f)   a body corporate which is a legally qualified body.

Change to the composition of the partnership

(2)   Recognition may continue despite a change in the composition of a recognised body which is a partnership, subject to (3) to (5) below.

(3)   (a)   A recognised body which is a partnership must cease to practise from the date of any failure to comply with 14.01(2)(a) or (b) (relevant lawyer requirement), and with 14.01(3)(a)–(e) or (f) (management and control requirement) which results from the change.

(b)   A recognised body which is a partnership must cease to practise from the date of any change which results in there being no remaining partner who was a partner before the change; the 28 day period under 14.01(2)(b) and 14.01(3)(f) does not apply.

(4)   If a partnership change results in there being only one remaining principal who or which needs to be recognised as a recognised sole practitioner but could not reasonably have commenced an application in advance of the change, the firm need not cease to practise if the remaining principal:

      (a)   is a solicitor or REL;

      (b)   notifies the Solicitors Regulation Authority within seven days;

      (c)   is granted temporary emergency recognition.

(5)   (a)   Temporary emergency recognition may be granted for an initial period of 28 days and may be extended in response to a reasonable request by the applicant.

      (b)   During the initial 28 day period, or such extended period as the Solicitors Regulation Authority may allow, the remaining principal must:

           (i)   cease to practise, and notify the Solicitors Regulation Authority; or

           (ii) commence a substantive application for recognition as a recognised sole practitioner (or, if the remaining principal has taken on a new partner, as a recognised body) by submitting a completed application form, together with the prescribed fee and any Compensation Fund contribution required.

      (c)   Subject to (d) below, if an application has been commenced under (b)(ii) above, temporary emergency recognition must be extended pending determination of the application.

      (d)   In exceptional circumstances and for reasonable cause the Solicitors Regulation Authority may revoke a temporary emergency recognition at any time.

      (e)   The grant or extension of a temporary emergency recognition is without prejudice to the discretion of the Solicitors Regulation Authority to refuse a substantive application made under (b)(ii) above.

Partnership splitting into two or more firms

(6)   Subject to (7) to (9) below, if a recognised body which is a partnership splits so that the recognised body will continue but one or more of the former partners intend to carry on as a separate firm, the separate firm must, before commencing practice, obtain recognition as a recognised body or a recognised sole practitioner.

(7)   Following such a partnership split, the Solicitors Regulation Authority will if necessary decide which of the groups of former partners will continue to be covered by the existing recognition and which must apply for a new recognition, and may apportion recognition fees and Compensation Fund contributions between the groups. Any such decision will be without prejudice to the outcome of any legal dispute between the former partners.

(8)   If the principal(s) in the new firm could not reasonably have commenced an application for recognition in advance of the change, the new firm may practise from the date of the split provided that the following conditions are met:

      (a)   the new firm is:

           (i)   a partnership which complies with rule 14 of the Solicitors' Code of Conduct in its formation, composition and structure; or

           (ii) a solicitor or REL sole practitioner;

      and complies with the Solicitors' Indemnity Insurance Rules;

      (b)   the new firm notifies the Solicitors Regulation Authority within seven days; and

      (c)   the Solicitors Regulation Authority grants the firm temporary emergency recognition.

(9)   (a)   Temporary emergency recognition may be granted for an initial period of 28 days and may be extended in response to a reasonable request by the applicant.

       (b)   During the initial 28 day period, or such extended period as the Solicitors Regulation Authority may allow, the new firm must:

            (i)   cease to practise, and notify the Solicitors Regulation Authority; or

            (ii)   commence a substantive application for recognition as a recognised body or recognised sole practitioner by submitting a completed application form, together with the prescribed fee and any Compensation Fund contribution required.

       (c)   Subject to (d) below, if an application has been commenced under (b)(ii) above, temporary emergency recognition must be extended pending determination of the application.

       (d)   In exceptional circumstances and for reasonable cause the Solicitors Regulation Authority may revoke a temporary emergency recognition at any time.

       (e)   The grant or extension of a temporary emergency recognition is without prejudice to the discretion of the Solicitors Regulation Authority to refuse a substantive application made under (b)(ii) above.

Only one active partner remaining

(10)   If a partner in a partnership which is a recognised body:

       (a)   is committed to prison in civil or criminal proceedings;

       (b)   becomes and continues to be unable to attend to the practice of the body because of incapacity caused by illness, accident or age;

       (c)   becomes and continues to be a person who lacks capacity under Part 1 of the Mental Capacity Act 2005;

       (d)   abandons the practice of the body; or

       (e)   is made subject to a condition on his or her practising certificate or registration which would be breached by continuing as a partner;

and this results in there being only one active partner, that partner must inform the Solicitors Regulation Authority within seven days.

Prohibition on creating third party interests

(11)   A partner in a partnership must not create any charge or other third party interest over his or her interest in the partnership.

14.05 Recognised bodies which are LLPs

Who may be a member

(1)   Provided that the fundamental requirements for all recognised bodies set out in 14.01 are met, a recognised body which is an LLP may have all or any of the following as a member:

       (a)   a lawyer of England and Wales (including a solicitor with a current practising certificate);

APPENDIX 21

    (b)   an REL;

    (c)   an RFL;

    (d)   an exempt European lawyer;

    (e)   an individual approved under regulation 3 of the Recognised Bodies Regulations;

    (f)   a body corporate which is a legally qualified body.

Minimum number of members

(2)   (a)   A recognised body which is an LLP must have at least two members.

    (b)   If an event which could not reasonably have been foreseen results in an LLP having fewer than two members, but within six months the situation is remedied, the LLP will be deemed to have remained in compliance with (a) above and to that extent will not be liable to have its recognition revoked under regulation 9.1(b) of the Recognised Bodies Regulations.

Prohibition on creating third party interests

(3)   A member must not create any charge or other third party interest over the member's interest in the LLP.

14.06 Recognised bodies which are companies

Who may be a director

(1)   Provided that the fundamental requirements for all recognised bodies set out in 14.01 are met, a recognised body which is a company may have all or any of the following as a director:

    (a)   a lawyer of England and Wales (including a solicitor with a current practising certificate);

    (b)   an REL;

    (c)   an RFL;

    (d)   an exempt European lawyer;

    (e)   an individual approved under regulation 3 of the Recognised Bodies Regulations.

Who may be a member or shareowner

(2)   Provided that the fundamental requirements for all recognised bodies set out in 14.01 are met, a recognised body which is a company may have all or any of the following as a member or shareowner:

    (a)   a lawyer of England and Wales (including a solicitor with a current practising certificate);

    (b)   an REL;

    (c)   an RFL;

    (d)   an exempt European lawyer;

(e) an individual approved under regulation 3 of the Recognised Bodies Regulations, who is also a director of the company;

(f) a legally qualified body.

Prohibition on creating third party interests

(3) A member or shareowner must not create any charge or other third party interest over his or her interest in the company, except by holding a share as nominee for a non-member shareowner who is eligible to be a member or shareowner under (2) above.

Record of non-member shareowners

(4) (a) A recognised body which is a company with shares must keep a record of any non-member shareowners, and retain the record for at least three years after their ownership ceases; and

(b) a member who holds a share as nominee for a non-member shareowner must keep the recognised body informed of all facts necessary to keep an accurate and up-to-date record.

Death of member or shareowner of a company

(5) (a) If a recognised body is a company with shares and a member or shareowner dies and is eligible to be a member or shareowner at the date of death, then, whether or not the personal representatives are themselves eligible to be members or shareowners, the personal representatives may replace the deceased member or shareowner in their capacity as personal representatives, provided that:

    (i) no vote may be exercised by or on behalf of a personal representative (and no such vote may be accepted) unless all the personal representatives are eligible to be members or shareowners;

    (ii) no personal representative may hold or own a share in that capacity for longer than 12 months from the date of death;

    (iii) within 12 months of the death the recognised body must cancel or acquire the shares or ensure that they are held and owned by persons eligible to be members or shareowners, but without this resulting in RFLs being the only shareowners; and

    (iv) no vote may be exercised by or on behalf of any personal representative (and no such vote may be accepted) after the 12 month period has expired.

(b) If, following the death of a member or shareowner, a company meets the requirements of (a) above the company will be deemed to have remained in compliance with (2) above as to membership and share ownership, and to that extent will not be liable to have its recognition revoked under regulation 9.1(b) of the Recognised Bodies Regulations.

Member or shareowner ceasing to be eligible to be a member or shareowner

(6) (a) If a recognised body is a company with shares and a member or shareowner ceases to be eligible to be a member or shareowner, or ceases to exist as a body corporate, then:

(i)   no vote may be exercised or accepted on the shares held by or on behalf of that member or shareowner;

(ii)   in the case of a member or shareowner becoming ineligible, a trustee in bankruptcy or liquidator may (whether or not eligible to be a member or shareowner) replace that member or shareowner in the capacity of trustee or liquidator for a period which must not exceed six months from the date the member or shareowner became ineligible; and

(iii)   the company must cancel or acquire the shares within six months, or within that time ensure that the shares are held and owned by persons eligible to be members or shareowners, but without this resulting in breach of the relevant lawyer requirement or the management and control requirement in 14.01(2) or (3).

(b)   If (a) above applies and a company meets its requirements, the company will be deemed to have remained in compliance with (2) above as to membership and share ownership, and to that extent will not be liable to have its recognition revoked under regulation 9.1(b) of the Recognised Bodies Regulations.

Member or shareowner becoming insolvent but not ineligible

(7)   (a)   If a recognised body is a company with shares and a member or shareowner becomes insolvent but remains eligible to be a member or shareowner, then the trustee in bankruptcy or liquidator (whether eligible or not) may replace the insolvent member or shareowner in the capacity of trustee in bankruptcy or liquidator, provided that:

(i)   no vote may be exercised by or on behalf of a trustee in bankruptcy or liquidator (and no such vote may be accepted) unless the trustee or liquidator is eligible to be a member or shareowner;

(ii)   no trustee in bankruptcy or liquidator may hold or own a share in that capacity for longer than six months from the date of the insolvency;

(iii)   within six months of the insolvency the company must cancel or acquire the shares or ensure that they are held and owned by persons eligible to be members or shareowners, but without this resulting in breach of the relevant lawyer requirement or the management and control requirement in 14.01(2) or (3); and

(iv)   no vote may be exercised by or on behalf of any trustee in bankruptcy or liquidator (and no such vote may be accepted) after the six month period has expired.

(b)   If (a) above applies and a company meets its requirements, the company will be deemed to have remained in compliance with (2) above as to membership and share ownership, and to that extent will not be liable to have its recognition revoked under regulation 9.1(b) of the Recognised Bodies Regulations.

Court of Protection deputy

(8)   (a)   A Court of Protection deputy appointed under section 19 of the Mental Capacity Act 2005 may be a member or shareowner in that capacity, without breach of these rules, provided that:

(i)   the person in respect of whom the deputy has been appointed remains eligible to be a member or shareowner; and

        (ii)   if the deputy is not eligible to be a member or shareowner, no vote is exercised or accepted on the shares.

(b)   If (a) above applies and a company meets its requirements, the company will be deemed to have remained in compliance with (2) above as to membership and share ownership, and to that extent will not be liable to have its recognition revoked under regulation 9.1(b) of the Recognised Bodies Regulations.

14.07 Information and documentation

(1)   A recognised body must supply any information and documentation relating to its composition and structure or to any of its managers, employees, members or owners, as and when requested to do so by the Solicitors Regulation Authority.

(2)   A recognised body must notify the Solicitors Regulation Authority within seven days of any change to:

    (a)   its name;

    (b)   its registered office and/or any of its practising addresses;

    (c)   its managers; or

    (d)   its members and/or shareowners if it is a company.

(3)   A recognised body must notify the Solicitors Regulation Authority within seven days if it is an unlimited company and it is re-registered as limited under the Companies Act 2006.

(4)   If a relevant insolvency event within the meaning of paragraph 32(1A) of Schedule 2 to the Administration of Justice Act 1985 occurs in relation to a recognised body its managers must notify the Solicitors Regulation Authority within seven days.

(5)   If a recognised body which is an overseas company or a societas Europaea registered outside the United Kingdom is subject to an event in its country of incorporation analogous to a winding-up order, an administration order under Part II of the Insolvency Act 1986, a resolution for voluntary winding-up, or the appointment of an administrative receiver, the directors must notify the Solicitors Regulation Authority within seven days.

14.08 Mental Health Act equivalents

In this rule:

    (a)   references to a person who lacks capacity under Part 1 of the Mental Capacity Act 2005 include a "patient" as defined by section 94 of the Mental Health Act 1983 and a person made the subject of emergency powers under that Act, and equivalents in other Establishment Directive states; and

    (b)   references to a Court of Protection deputy appointed under section 19 of the Mental Capacity Act 2005 include a Court of Protection receiver appointed under the Mental Health Act 1983, and equivalents in other Establishment Directive states.

Guidance to rule 14 – Recognised bodies

The legal and regulatory framework

1.   A recognised body is a partnership, LLP or company recognised by the SRA under section 9 of the Administration of Justice Act 1985 and regulation 2 of the SRA Recognised Bodies Regulations 2009.

2.   Rule 12 (Framework of practice) states that solicitors and RELs must not provide services to the public in England and Wales except through a firm which is a recognised body or a recognised sole practitioner (both regulated by the SRA) or through an authorised non-SRA firm, or as permitted under rule 13 (In-house practice, etc.) in respect of law centres, advice centres, etc. Rule 14 governs the composition and structure of a recognised body and the services a recognised body may provide. The rule is largely based on the requirements of section 9A of the Administration of Justice Act 1985.

3.   A recognised body, and a "manager" or employee of a recognised body, are subject to the Code and other SRA rules, subject to regulation by the SRA, and subject to disciplinary sanctions of the SRA and the Solicitors Disciplinary Tribunal.

4.   In this guidance the term "manager" has a special meaning, as in rule 14 and in the Recognised Bodies Regulations. It means:

    (a)   a partner, or a person held out as a partner, in an unincorporated firm;

    (b)   a member of an LLP; or

    (c)   a director of a company.

In other words the "manager" as an individual does not necessarily have to perform any particular management function – although the "manager" will be subject to the rules him- or herself, and in many circumstances will also be responsible under the rules and in law for the conduct of the recognised body.

The three fundamental requirements

5.   The fundamental requirements which must be fulfilled for recognised body status are:

    (a)   the services requirement,

    (b)   the relevant lawyer requirement,

    (c)   the management and control requirement.

These are explained in more detail below.

The services requirement

6.   Rule 14.01(1) sets out the type of services which a recognised body is permitted to provide – legal services and "man (or woman) of affairs" services as provided by solicitors, services as provided by foreign lawyers, and notarial services (if the firm has a "manager" or employee who is a notary).

7.   A recognised body is not prohibited from owning a "separate business" – i.e. a business which provides "man (or woman) of affairs" services but not as a legal practice – so long as there is compliance with rule 21 (Separate businesses).

The relevant lawyer requirement

8.   Rule 14.01(2)(a) states that at least one "manager" of a recognised body must be:

    (a)   a solicitor with a current practising certificate;

    (b)   an REL; or

    (c)   (in the case of a recognised body which is a partnership or LLP) a "legally qualified body" with at least one "manager" who is a solicitor with a current practising certificate or an REL.

9.   A "legally qualified body" is defined as:

    (a)   a recognised body,

(b)   an authorised non–SRA firm, or

(c)   a European corporate practice (as defined in rule 24),

of which lawyers must make up at least 75% of the ultimate beneficial ownership.

The management and control requirement

10.   The management and control requirement is set out in rule 14.01(3), and is aimed at ensuring that every recognised body is at least 75% owned and managed by lawyers.

11.   More specifically, the management and control requirement is made up of the following six tests, which deal with various markers of management, ownership and the holding of shares:

(a)   at least 75% of a recognised body's "managers" must be lawyers or "legally qualified bodies";

(b)   lawyers must make up at least 75% of the ultimate beneficial ownership of the recognised body;

(c)   lawyers and/or "legally qualified bodies" must exercise or control the exercise of at least 75% of the voting rights in the recognised body;

(d)   if the recognised body is a company with shares, lawyers and/or "legally qualified bodies" must hold (as registered members of the company) at least 75% of the shares;

(e)   every owner of the recognised body must be a lawyer, a "legally qualified body" or an individual non-lawyer who is approved by the SRA under regulation 3 of the Recognised Bodies Regulations; and

(f)   every non-lawyer owner of the recognised body must be a "manager" of the body unless:

(i)   the recognised body is a company which is wholly or partly owned by a partnership or LLP which is a "legally qualified body";

(ii)   the non-lawyer owner is a "manager" of the partnership or LLP; and

(iii)   the non-lawyer owner is precluded under the partnership agreement or members' agreement from exercising or authorising any vote in relation to the company.

12.   "Lawyers" in the context of the management and control requirement means practising lawyers – solicitors, barristers, notaries, legal executives, licensed conveyancers, patent agents, trade mark agents, law costs draftsmen, European lawyers of Establishment Directive professions, and RFLs.

Some regulatory provisions

13.   Recognition is granted on an annual basis, and an application for renewal has to be made by 31 October in each year. There is an annual recognition fee and an annual contribution to the Compensation Fund. Applications for initial recognition, and for renewal of recognition, are made under regulation 2 of the Recognised Bodies Regulations.

14.   The "relevant lawyer requirement" basically provides that there must be at least one solicitor or REL "manager". The "management and control requirement" basically provides that at least 75% of the management and ownership must be in the hands of lawyers.

15.   In addition, rule 14 provides that the partners in a recognised body which is a partnership, the members of a recognised body which is an LLP, and the members and shareowners of a recognised body which is a company must comprise some combination of the following:

(a)   practising lawyers of England and Wales (solicitors, barristers, notaries, legal executives, licensed conveyancers, patent agents, trade mark agents, law costs draftsmen);

(b)   practising European lawyers of Establishment Directive professions;

(c)   RFLs;

(d)   individuals approved by the SRA under regulation 3 of the Recognised Bodies Regulations as suitable to be a "manager" of a recognised body – such individuals fall into one of three categories:

    (i)   non-lawyers;

    (ii)   lawyers of foreign legal professions whose members are not eligible to become RFLs;

    (iii)   non-practising barristers or non-practising foreign lawyers, whose professional rules or training regulations prevent them from changing status so as to be able to practise through the recognised body as practising lawyers;

an application for SRA approval of an individual as suitable to be a "manager" must be made under regulation 3 of the Recognised Bodies Regulations by the recognised body or prospective recognised body concerned;

(e)   "legally qualified bodies" – recognised bodies, authorised non-SRA firms, or European corporate practices.

16.   In relation to the directors of a recognised body which is a company, the "relevant lawyer requirement" has the effect that at least one director must be a solicitor or REL. The "management and control requirement" has the effect that at least 75% of the directors must be lawyers. Rule 14 further provides that the directors must comprise some combination of the following:

(a)   practising lawyers of England and Wales (solicitors, barristers, notaries, legal executives, licensed conveyancers, patent agents, trade mark agents, law costs draftsmen);

(b)   practising European lawyers of Establishment Directive professions;

(c)   RFLs;

(d)   individuals approved by the SRA under regulation 3 of the Recognised Bodies Regulations.

17.   A solicitor must have a current practising certificate in order to be a partner, a director, a member or a shareowner in a recognised body. Under section 1A of the Solicitors Act 1974, a solicitor must have a current practising certificate in order to be employed in a recognised body in England and Wales in connection with the provision of any legal services.

18.   Every recognised body must have at least one practising address in England and Wales. A recognised body incorporated in England and Wales as an LLP or company must have its registered office in England or in Wales, and must practise from that office. These requirements as to the registered office do not apply to a recognised body incorporated outside England and Wales – whether it is an LLP incorporated in Scotland, or a company incorporated in Scotland, Northern Ireland or some other Establishment Directive state.

Note that the fact that a firm has been recognised as a recognised body under Scottish law does not exempt it from having to be recognised as a recognised body by the SRA.

19.   A recognised body may practise as a firm in its own right (a partnership, LLP or company), or it may wholly or partly own another recognised body, or be wholly or partly owned by another recognised body. A recognised body which is a company or

LLP can be a partner together with solicitors, RELs, RFLs and/or other recognised bodies in a partnership which is itself a recognised body; or it can be a member together with solicitors, RELs, RFLs and/or other recognised bodies in an LLP which is itself a recognised body.

20. A recognised body may practise outside England and Wales in addition to practising in England and Wales.

21. If your firm practises overseas through an associated firm which has no office in England and Wales it does not have to be a recognised body – and indeed cannot be a recognised body because a recognised body has to have at least one practising address in England and Wales.

Compliance with rules

22. In addition to these rules, a recognised body must comply with the Solicitors' Indemnity Insurance Rules, the Solicitors' Accounts Rules and (unless authorised by the FSA) with the Solicitors' Financial Services (Scope) Rules and the Solicitors' Financial Services (Conduct of Business) Rules.

(a) *Indemnity insurance*

23. The Solicitors' Indemnity Insurance Rules require a recognised body to have "qualifying insurance" from a "qualifying insurer" (with some limited scope for exemptions in respect of RELs' participation in recognised bodies). The basic minimum level of cover is £2 million for any one claim. A recognised body with limited liability (i.e. an LLP, a limited company, or a partnership one or more of whose partners is an LLP or a limited company) is required to have minimum cover of £3 million for any one claim. Some recognised bodies which are nominee companies escape the requirement for an extra £1 million cover – see note 28(d) below. A recognised body may also have additional "top-up" cover, from any insurer.

(b) *Accountants' reports*

24. If a recognised body holds or receives client money, it will in due course have to deliver an accountant's report to the SRA. This obligation also extends to the "managers" of the recognised body. The names of the current "managers" along with the name of the recognised body must appear on the accountant's report, as well as the name of any employee or "manager" who or which has held or received client money, and any individual employee or "manager" who has operated a client's own account as signatory.

Charging a member's interest in a recognised body – 14.04(11), 14.05(3) and 14.06(3)

25. A partner in a recognised body which is a partnership, or a member of a recognised body which is an LLP, or a member or shareowner of a recognised body which is a company, must not create any charge or other third party interest over his or her interest in the body, except, in the case of a company, that a member may hold a share as nominee for a person who is eligible under the rules to own a share. The purpose is to ensure that control of the recognised body remains solely in the hands of persons who are eligible to be members, and that there is no breach of the management and control condition.

Steps to be taken to deal with certain emergencies

26. Rule 14 contains a number of provisions setting out what must be done if certain events befall a recognised body and its members, directors or shareowners. It is essential to deal with these situations in accordance with the rules:

   (a) an unforeseeable event which would put the body in breach of the relevant lawyer requirement – see 14.01(2)(b);

   (b) certain specified events (e.g. imprisonment, or incapacity caused by illness) which demonstrate that the last solicitor or REL whose role ensures compliance with the relevant lawyer requirement is no longer suitable to fulfil that role – see 14.01(2)(c);

   (c) an unforeseeable event which would put the body in breach of the management and control requirement – see 14.01(3)(f);

   (d) certain specified events (e.g. imprisonment, or incapacity caused by illness) which demonstrate that the last lawyer whose role ensures compliance with the management and control requirement is no longer suitable to fulfil that role – see 14.01(3)(g);

   (e) a foreseeable event which causes a partnership to be in breach of the relevant lawyer requirement or the management and control requirement – see 14.04(3)(a);

   (f) an event in relation to a partnership which results in there being no remaining partner – see 14.04(3)(b);

   (g) a partnership change which results in there being only one remaining solicitor or REL principal who could not reasonably have made prior arrangements – see 14.04(4);

   (h) a partnership split, where the new firm was in a position to make prior arrangements – see 14.04(6) and (7);

   (i) a partnership split, where the new firm could not reasonably have made prior arrangements – see 14.04(7) and (8);

   (j) certain specified events (e.g. imprisonment, or incapacity caused by illness) which demonstrate that a partner is no longer suitable to fulfil that role, and which leave only one partner who is not subject to such an event – see 14.04(10);

   (k) death of a member or shareowner of a company – see 14.06(5)(a) and (b);

   (l) member or shareowner of a company ceases to be eligible to be a member or shareowner – see 14.06(6)(a) and (b);

   (m) member or shareowner of a company becomes insolvent but remains eligible to be a member or shareowner – see 14.06(7)(a) and (b);

   (n) Court of Protection deputy appointed in respect of a member or shareowner of a company – see 14.06(8)(a) and (b).

Executor, trustee and nominee companies

27. If you wish to operate an executor, trustee or nominee company in conjunction with your main practice you should bear the following matters in mind:

   (a) An English executor, trustee or nominee company itself provides the executor, trustee or nominee service. If run in conjunction with your practice it is a "business" for the purpose of rule 21 (Separate businesses), whether or not it is dormant for Companies Act purposes and whether or not a charge is made for its services. The company must therefore be a recognised body, or you will breach rule 21 – see 21.02(1)(g) and note 11 of the guidance to rule 21.

(b) An overseas executor, trustee or nominee company cannot be a recognised body. It can be run in accordance with rule 12 (Framework of practice), as an overseas practice. Alternatively, it can be operated as a "separate business" provided that you comply with rule 21 (Separate businesses) in relation to the company. See also note 12 of the guidance to rule 21.

28. In relation to an English executor, trustee or nominee company, you should also note that:

(a) a recognised body, when holding money or receiving dividends as nominee, holds client money, and it must have its own client account, in its own name;

(b) a single set of accounting records may be used for the company and the main practice and a single accountant's report can be delivered for both, if the relevant accounting periods are the same, and provided the accountant deals with the accounts for each separately;

(c) a wholly owned executor, trustee or nominee company can be covered by the same policy of qualifying insurance as your main practice, but only if the company is named on the policy and certificate of insurance as a separate insured; and

(d) a nominee company may be exempt from the requirement to have an extra £1 million qualifying insurance if it can show that:

(i) it is a nominee company only;

(ii) all the directors of the company are partners or members in your main practice;

(iii) it holds assets only for clients of your main practice;

(iv) it can act only as agent for your main practice; and

(v) all fees accrue to the benefit of your main practice.

Companies providing company secretarial services

29. Your firm may own a company whose purpose is to provide company secretarial services to clients of the firm. Such a company may either be operated as a legal practice (and must therefore be a recognised body), or it may be operated as a "separate business" (and must therefore be operated in compliance with rule 21 and may also need to be separately regulated by HMRC under the anti-money laundering legislation).

Service companies

30. A firm may have a wholly owned service company which has no face to the public and provides no services to the public but carries out administrative functions concerned with the running of the firm, such as the employment of staff, the hiring of premises, furniture and equipment and general maintenance. Such a company does not need to be a recognised body and is not a "separate business". The books of the company must be made available if the SRA requires an inspection of accounts. See also notes 14 and 15 of the guidance to rule 21 (Separate businesses).

Rule 15 – Overseas practice

Introduction

Rule 15 is specific to overseas practice, which is defined in rule 24 (Interpretation) and means practice from an office outside England and Wales, except in the case of an REL, where it means practice from an office in Scotland or Northern Ireland.

Rule 15 applies the provisions of these rules to your overseas practice. Sometimes rule 15 disapplies one of these rules, or a provision in one of the rules, and in some cases substitutes alternative provisions.

Rule 15 also makes specific provisions in relation to accounts, deposit interest and professional indemnity, because the equivalent domestic rules do not apply to your overseas practice.

The purpose of applying different provisions to overseas practice is to ensure similar protection for clients but by way of rules which are more adaptable to conditions in other jurisdictions.

Rule 15 – Overseas practice

15.01   Core duties (rule 1) application, and conflicts of rules

The core duties

(1)   (a)   Rule 1 (Core duties) applies to your overseas practice.

(b)   In relation to activities outside England and Wales which fall outside the scope of practice as defined by rule 24, whether undertaken as a lawyer or in some other business or private capacity:

(i)   rule 1.06 (Public confidence) applies to you if you are a solicitor, an REL or an RFL;

(ii)   rule 10.01 (Not taking unfair advantage) applies to you if you are a solicitor; and within the UK if you are an REL;

(iii)   rule 15.10(2)(a)(ii) and (iii), (b) and (c) (undertakings given outside the course of practice) apply to you if you are a solicitor, and within the UK if you are an REL;

(iv)   rules 12.03(2) and (3) (practice in another capacity than as an RFL) and 12.03(4)(a) (holding out as a lawyer of England and Wales) apply to you if you are an RFL, and 12.03(5) (wrongfully doing immigration work) applies to your activities in Scotland or Northern Ireland.

General application of these rules to overseas practice

(2)   (a)   Subject to (3) and (4) below, these rules apply, in relation to practice from an office outside the UK:

(i)   to a solicitor as an individual, whether or not the solicitor's firm or employer is subject to these rules;

(ii)   to a solicitor-controlled recognised body (as defined in rule 24); and

(iii)   to a lawyer of England and Wales other than a solicitor, and to a non-lawyer, in relation to practice as a manager of a solicitor-controlled recognised body,

and notwithstanding the application of the rules to its solicitor managers and solicitor employees, a recognised body which is not a solicitor-controlled recognised body is not itself subject to these rules in relation to practice from such an office.

(b)   Subject to (3) and (4) below, these rules apply, in relation to practice from an office in Scotland or Northern Ireland:

(i)   to a solicitor or REL as an individual, whether or not the solicitor's or REL's firm or employer is subject to these rules;

(ii)   to a solicitor-controlled recognised body;

(iii)   to an REL-controlled recognised body (as defined in rule 24);

(iv)   to a lawyer of England and Wales other than a solicitor, to a European lawyer registered with the Bar Standards Board and to a non-lawyer, in relation to practice as a manager of a solicitor-controlled recognised body or an REL-controlled recognised body; and

(v)   a solicitor who was formerly an REL, when practising as a lawyer of an Establishment Directive profession,

and notwithstanding the application of the rules to its solicitor and REL managers and its solicitor and REL employees, a recognised body which is not a solicitor-controlled recognised body or an REL-controlled recognised body is not itself subject to these rules in relation to practice from such an office.

Modification of these rules in relation to overseas practice

(3)   If this rule states that a rule or a provision of these rules does not apply to your overseas practice, you may disregard that rule or provision in relation to your overseas practice, but you must comply with any alternative provision which is substituted by this rule.

(4)   If compliance with any applicable provision of these rules would result in your breaching local law, you may disregard that provision to the extent necessary to comply with that local law.

15.02 Client relations (rule 2)

(1)   Rule 2 (Client relations) does not apply to your overseas practice but you must comply with (2) to (4) below.

(2)   (a)   You must pay to the client any commission received, unless:

        (i)   the client, having been told the amount of the commission (or an approximate amount if the precise amount is not known) has agreed that you or your firm may keep the commission; or

        (ii)   in all the circumstances it is not reasonable to pay the commission to the client.

    (b)   In deciding whether it is reasonable to pay a commission to a client you must have regard to all the circumstances, including the law governing the retainer and the prevailing custom of lawyers in the jurisdiction in which you are practising.

(3)   If you are a sole practitioner, a partner in a partnership, or a recognised body to which this rule applies, you must not exclude or attempt to exclude by contract all liability to a client. However, you may limit your liability, provided that such limitation:

    (a)   is not below the minimum level of cover you would need in order to comply with 15.26 below;

    (b)   is brought to the client's attention; and

    (c)   is in writing.

(4)   (a)   (i)   You must not enter into an arrangement to receive a contingency fee

for work done in prosecuting or defending any contentious proceedings before a court of England and Wales, a British court martial or an arbitrator where the seat of the arbitration is in England and Wales, except as permitted by statute or the common law.

(ii) If you enter into a conditional fee agreement with a client in relation to such proceedings, you must explain, both at the outset and, where appropriate, as the matter progresses:

(A) the circumstances in which the client may be liable for your costs, and whether you will seek payment of these from the client, if entitled to do so; and

(B) if you intend to seek payment of any or all of your costs from the client, you must advise the client of their right to an assessment of those costs.

(b) You must not enter into an arrangement to receive a contingency fee for work done in prosecuting or defending any contentious proceedings before a court of an overseas jurisdiction or an arbitrator where the seat of the arbitration is overseas except to the extent that a lawyer of that jurisdiction would be permitted to do so.

15.03 Conflict of interests (rule 3)

Rule 3 (Conflict of interests) applies to your overseas practice, except that you do not have to comply with 3.07 to 3.22 (provisions relating to conveyancing of land) if the land in question is situated outside England and Wales.

15.04 Confidentiality (rule 4)

Rule 4 (Confidentiality and disclosure) applies to your overseas practice.

15.05 Business management (rule 5)

(1) Rule 5 (Business management in England and Wales) does not apply to your overseas practice but you must comply with (2) to (4) below.

(2) You must not set up as a solicitor sole practitioner outside England and Wales, or as an REL sole practitioner in Scotland or Northern Ireland, unless you have been entitled to practise as a lawyer for a minimum of 36 months within the last 10 years.

(3) You must ensure that your firm has at least one manager who has been entitled to practise as a lawyer for a minimum of 36 months within the last 10 years, if you are:

(a) a solicitor manager of a firm which is not a recognised body, and solicitors control the firm, either directly as partners, members or owners, or indirectly by their ownership of bodies corporate which are partners, members or owners, or

(b) a solicitor or REL manager of a firm which is not a recognised body and which is practising from an office in Scotland or Northern Ireland, and solicitors and/or RELs control the firm, either directly as partners, members or owners, or indirectly by their ownership of bodies corporate which are partners, members or owners.

(4) If you are:

(a)   a solicitor sole practitioner practising from an office outside England and Wales, or an REL sole practitioner practising from an office in Scotland or Northern Ireland;

(b)   a solicitor or REL manager within (3)(a) or (b) above;

(c)   in relation to an office outside the UK, a solicitor-controlled recognised body or a manager of a solicitor-controlled recognised body who is a lawyer of England and Wales or a non-lawyer; or

(d)   in relation to an office in Scotland or Northern Ireland, a solicitor, an REL, a solicitor-controlled recognised body or a manager of a solicitor-controlled recognised body who is a lawyer of England and Wales or a non-lawyer, an REL-controlled recognised body or a manager of an REL-controlled recognised body who is a lawyer of England and Wales or a non-lawyer,

you must ensure that the firm is managed and supervised with a view to ensuring that its affairs are properly conducted at all times; and that clients' matters receive proper attention, and are supervised so as to ensure that the quality of the work is checked with reasonable regularity by suitably experienced and competent persons within the firm.

15.06 Equality and diversity (rule 6)

Rule 6 (Equality and diversity) does not apply to your overseas practice, but rule 1 (Core duties) will always apply.

15.07 Publicity (rule 7)

(1)   Rule 7 (Publicity) applies to your overseas practice, except as set out in (2) and (3) below.

(2)   Rule 7 does not apply to the website, e-mails, text messages or similar electronic communications of any practice you conduct from an office in an EU state other than the UK.

(3)   Rule 7.07 (Letterhead, website and e-mails) does not apply, but:

(a)   if an REL is named on the letterhead (including a fax heading) of an office in Scotland or Northern Ireland, the letterhead must also identify:

(i)   the European jurisdiction(s) – local or national as appropriate – under whose professional title the REL is practising;

(ii)   the REL's professional title(s), expressed in an official language of the European state concerned; and

(iii) the fact that the REL is registered with the Solicitors Regulation Authority of England and Wales; and

(b)   you must make clear on your firm's letterhead (including a fax heading) that it is the letterhead of a law firm, if you are:

(i)   a solicitor sole practitioner practising from an office outside England and Wales, or an REL sole practitioner practising from an office in Scotland or Northern Ireland; or

(ii)   a solicitor manager of a firm which is practising from an office outside England and Wales, and solicitors control the firm, either directly as partners, members or owners, or indirectly by their ownership of bodies corporate which are partners, members or owners; or

(iii)   a solicitor or REL manager of a firm which is practising from an office in Scotland or Northern Ireland, and solicitors and/or RELs control the firm, either directly as partners, members or owners, or indirectly by their ownership of bodies corporate which are partners, members or owners.

15.08 Fee sharing (rule 8)

Rule 8 (Fee sharing) applies to your overseas practice.

15.09 Referrals of business (rule 9)

(1)   Rule 9 (Referrals of business) does not apply to your overseas practice, but you must comply with (2) below.

(2)   When you accept referrals of business from other persons and when you refer business to other persons, you must ensure that there is no breach of rule 1 (Core duties) or any other applicable provision of these rules.

15.10 Relations with third parties (rule 10)

(1)   Rule 10 (Relations with third parties) applies to your overseas practice except as provided in (2) and (3) below.

(2)   Rule 10.05 (Undertakings) does not apply, but:

(a)   you must fulfil an undertaking which you give:

(i)   in the course of practice;

(ii)   outside the course of practice, but as a "solicitor"; or

(iii)   if you are an REL based at an office in Scotland or Northern Ireland, and you give the undertaking within the UK, outside your practice as an REL, but as a lawyer of an Establishment Directive profession;

(b)   you must fulfil an undertaking within a reasonable time; and

(c)   if you give an undertaking which is dependent upon the happening of a future event, you must notify the recipient immediately if it becomes clear that the event will not occur.

(3)   Rule 10.06 (Dealing with more than one prospective buyer in a conveyancing transaction) applies only if the land in question is situated in England and Wales.

15.11 Litigation and advocacy (rule 11)

Rule 11 (Litigation and advocacy) applies to your overseas practice in relation to litigation or advocacy conducted before a court, tribunal or inquiry in England and Wales or a British court martial. Rule 11 does not apply to your overseas practice in relation to litigation or advocacy conducted before a court or tribunal of another jurisdiction, but rule 1 (Core duties) will always apply.

15.12 Framework of practice (rule 12)

Rule 12 (Framework of practice) applies to your overseas practice.

15.13 In-house practice overseas (rule 13)

(1) Rule 13.04 (Pro bono work) applies to your overseas practice. The other provisions of rule 13 (In-house practice, etc.) do not apply to your overseas practice, but you must comply with (2) below.

(2) (a) Subject to (b) below, you may act as an in-house lawyer, but only for:

    (i) your employer;

    (ii) a company or organisation controlled by your employer or in which your employer has a substantial measure of control;

    (iii) a company in the same group as your employer;

    (iv) a company which controls your employer; or

    (v) an employee (including a director or a company secretary) of a company or organisation under (i) to (iv) above, provided that the matter relates to or arises out of the work of that company or organisation, does not relate to a claim arising as a result of a personal injury to the employee, and no charge is made for your work unless those costs are recoverable from another source.

    (b) If you are a solicitor registered in another state under the Establishment Directive with the professional body for a local legal profession you may practise in-house to the extent that a member of that legal profession is permitted to do so.

15.14 Recognised bodies (rule 14)

(1) Rule 14 (Recognised bodies) applies to a recognised body in relation to the recognised body's overseas practice.

(2) Rule 14 applies to your overseas practice as:

    (a) a manager of a recognised body, if you are a lawyer of England and Wales or an individual non-lawyer;

    (b) a member of, or the owner of a share in, a recognised body which is a company, if you are a solicitor or (in relation to practice from an office in Scotland or Northern Ireland) an REL,

except that 14.02(2)(c), (3) and (4) apply only to the extent that a rule applies to the recognised body, manager or employee by virtue of this rule or rule 23.

(3) If you are a solicitor or an REL you are not required to comply with rule 14 in order to practise through a firm which has no office in England and Wales, but you must comply with 12.01(2) or 12.02(2).

15.15 Deposit interest

(1) You must comply with (2) below, if you are:

    (a) a solicitor sole practitioner practising from an office outside England and Wales, or an REL sole practitioner practising from an office in Scotland or Northern Ireland;

    (b) a solicitor-controlled recognised body or (in relation to practice from an office in Scotland or Northern Ireland) a solicitor-controlled recognised body or an REL-controlled recognised body;

    (c) a solicitor manager of a firm which is practising from an office outside the

UK, and solicitors control the firm, either directly as partners, members or owners, or indirectly by their ownership of bodies corporate which are partners, members or owners; or

(d)   a solicitor or REL manager of a firm which is practising from an office in Scotland or Northern Ireland, and solicitors and/or RELs control the firm, either directly as partners, members or owners, or indirectly by their ownership of bodies corporate which are partners, members or owners.

(2)   If interest ought, in fairness, to be earned for the client on client money held under (1) above, you must ensure that:

(a)   the client money is dealt with so that proper interest is earned upon it, and that the interest is paid to the client;

(b)   the client is paid a sum equivalent to the interest that would have been earned if the client money had earned proper interest; or

(c)   any alternative written agreement with the client setting out arrangements regarding the payment of interest on that money is carried out.

(3)   In deciding whether interest ought, in fairness, to be earned for a client on client money, you must have regard to all the circumstances, including:

(a)   the amount of the money;

(b)   the length of time for which you are likely to hold the money; and

(c)   the law and prevailing custom of lawyers practising in the jurisdiction in which you are practising.

15.16   European cross-border practice (rule 16)

Rule 16 (European cross-border practice) applies to your overseas practice, to the extent that such practice is European cross-border practice as defined in 16.01(1).

15.17   Insolvency practice (rule 17)

Rule 17 (Insolvency practice) does not apply to your overseas practice except in relation to appointments appertaining to orders made in the courts of England and Wales.

15.18   Property selling (rule 18)

Rule 18 (Property selling) applies to your practice from offices in Scotland or Northern Ireland but not to your practice from offices outside the UK.

15.19   Financial services (rule 19)

(1)   Rule 19 (Financial services) does not apply to your overseas practice except as provided in (2) below.

(2)   Rule 19 applies to regulated activities you conduct:

(a)   from an office in Scotland or Northern Ireland; or

(b)   into the UK from an office outside the UK.

15.20   Rights and obligations of practice (rule 20)

Rule 20 (Rights and obligations of practice) applies to your overseas practice.

15.21 Separate businesses (rule 21)

(1)   (a)   Rule 21 (Separate businesses) applies to you if you practise from an office in England and Wales and you have a separate business, wherever the separate business is situated.

        (b)   If you do not practise from an office in England and Wales but you practise from an office outside England and Wales and you have a separate business, rule 21 does not apply but you must comply with (2) below, wherever the separate business is situated.

(2)   In relation to your separate business:

        (a)   you must do nothing in the course of practice, or in the course of making referrals to the business or accepting referrals from the business, which would contravene rule 1 (Core duties);

        (b)   you must not allow the separate business to be held out or described in such a way as to suggest that it is carrying on the practice of a lawyer regulated by the Solicitors Regulation Authority;

        (c)   you must ensure that all paperwork, documents, records or files relating to the separate business and its customers are kept separate from those of any firm or in-house practice, even where a customer of the separate business is also a client of the firm or in-house practice;

        (d)   you must not allow the client account of your firm or in-house practice to be used to hold money for the separate business, or for customers of the separate business in their capacity as such; and

        (e)   you must ensure that if you or your firm refer(s) a client to the separate business, the client is first informed of your interest in the separate business, that the separate business is not regulated by the Solicitors Regulation Authority of England and Wales, and that the statutory protections attaching to clients of a lawyer regulated by the Authority are not available to clients of the separate business.

15.22 Waivers (rule 22)

Rule 22 (Waivers) applies to your overseas practice.

15.23 Application of these rules (rule 23)

Rule 23 (Application of these rules), with the exception of 23.01(3), does not apply to your overseas practice.

15.24 Interpretation (rule 24)

Rule 24 (Interpretation) applies to your overseas practice.

15.25 Commencement and repeals (rule 25)

Rule 25 (Commencement and repeals) applies to your overseas practice.

15.26 Professional indemnity

(1)   You must comply with (2) below in relation to your overseas practice, unless you are practising only in-house in compliance with 15.13.

(2)   (a)   You must ensure that in relation to your overseas practice you are at all times covered by insurance or other indemnity against professional liabilities.

       (b)   The extent and amount of the insurance or other indemnity need not exceed the current requirements of the Solicitors' Indemnity Insurance Rules or any other current rules made under section 37 of the Solicitors Act 1974 but must be reasonable having regard to:

            (i)   the nature and extent of the risks you incur in your overseas practice;

            (ii)   the local conditions in the jurisdiction in which you are practising; and

            (iii)   the terms upon which insurance or other indemnity is available.

15.27 Accounts

Practice from an office outside the UK

(1)   You must comply with (3) and (4) below in relation to practice from an office outside the UK if you are:

       (a)   a solicitor sole practitioner who has held or received client money;

       (b)   a solicitor-controlled recognised body which has held or received client money as a firm;

       (c)   a lawyer of England and Wales, or a non-lawyer, who is a manager of a solicitor-controlled recognised body which holds or receives client money;

       (d)   a solicitor manager of any other firm which is controlled by solicitors, either directly as partners, members or owners, or indirectly by their ownership of bodies corporate which are partners, members or owners, if the firm holds or receives client money;

       (e)   a solicitor who holds or receives client money as a named trustee;

       (f)   a lawyer of England and Wales, or a non-lawyer, who is a manager of a solicitor-controlled recognised body and who holds or receives client money as a named trustee.

Practice from an office in Scotland or Northern Ireland

(2)   You must comply with (3) and (4) below in relation to practice from an office in Scotland or Northern Ireland if you are:

       (a)   a solicitor or REL sole practitioner who has held or received client money;

       (b)   a solicitor-controlled recognised body or an REL-controlled recognised body which has held or received client money as a firm;

       (c)   a lawyer of England and Wales, an REL, a European lawyer registered with the Bar Standards Board or a non-lawyer, who is a manager of a solicitor-controlled recognised body, or an REL-controlled recognised body, which holds or receives client money;

       (d)   a solicitor or REL manager of any other firm which is controlled by solicitors and/or RELs, either directly as partners, members or owners, or indirectly by their ownership of bodies corporate which are partners, members or owners, if the firm holds or receives client money;

       (e)   a solicitor or REL who holds or receives client money as a named trustee;

(f)   a lawyer of England and Wales, a European lawyer registered with the Bar Standards Board or a non-lawyer, who is a manager of a solicitor-controlled recognised body or an REL-controlled recognised body and who holds or receives client money as a named trustee.

Dealings with client money

(3)   In all dealings with client money, you must ensure that:

(a)   it is kept in a client account separate from money which is not client money;

(b)   on receipt, it is paid without delay into a client account and kept there, unless the client has expressly or by implication agreed that the money shall be dealt with otherwise or you pay it straight over to a third party in the execution of a trust under which it is held;

(c)   it is not paid or withdrawn from a client account except:

(i)   on the specific authority of the client;

(ii)   where the payment or withdrawal is properly required:

(A)   for a payment to or on behalf of the client;

(B)   for or towards payment of a debt due to the firm from the client or in reimbursement of money expended by the firm on behalf of the client; or

(C)   for or towards payment of costs due to the firm from the client, provided that a bill of costs or other written intimation of the amount of the costs incurred has been delivered to the client and it has thereby (or otherwise in writing) been made clear to the client that the money held will be applied in payment of the costs due; or

(iii)   in proper execution of a trust under which it is held;

(d)   accounts are kept at all times, whether by written, electronic, mechanical or other means, to:

(i)   record all dealings with client money in any client account;

(ii)   show all client money received, held or paid, distinct from any other money, and separately in respect of each client or trust; and

(iii)   ensure that the firm is able at all times to account, without delay, to each and every client or trust for all money received, held or paid on behalf of that client or trust; and

(e)   all accounts, books, ledgers and records kept in relation to the firm's client account(s) are preserved for at least six years from the date of the last entry therein.

Accountants' reports

(4)   (a)   You must deliver an accountant's report in respect of any period during which you or your firm have held or received client money and you were subject to (3) above.

(b)   The accountant's report must be signed by the reporting accountant, who must be an accountant qualified in England and Wales or in the overseas jurisdiction where your office is based, or by such other person as the Solicitors Regulation Authority may think fit. The Authority may for reasonable cause disqualify a person from signing accountants' reports.

(c)   The accountant's report must be based on a sufficient examination of the relevant documents to give the reporting accountant a reasonable indication whether or not you have complied with (3) above during the period covered by the report, and must include the following:

      (i)   your name, practising address(es) and practising style and the name(s) of the firm's managers;

      (ii)   the name, address and qualification of the reporting accountant;

      (iii)   an indication of the nature and extent of the examination the reporting accountant has made of the relevant documents;

      (iv)   a statement of the total amount of money held at banks or similar institutions on behalf of clients and trusts, and of the total liabilities to clients and trusts, on any date selected by the reporting accountant (including the last day), falling within the period under review; and an explanation of any difference between the total amount of money held for clients and trusts and the total liabilities to clients and trusts;

      (v)   if the reporting accountant is satisfied that (so far as may be ascertained from the examination) you have complied with (3) above during the period covered by the report, except for trivial breaches, or situations where you have been bound by a local rule not to comply, a statement to that effect; and

      (vi)   if the reporting accountant is not sufficiently satisfied to give a statement under (v) above, details of any matters in respect of which it appears to the reporting accountant that you have not complied with (3) above.

Guidance to rule 15 – Overseas practice

How these rules apply to overseas practice

1.   These rules apply, in different ways, to the following in respect of their overseas practice:

    (a)   solicitors;

    (b)   RELs;

    (c)   recognised bodies;

    (d)   non-lawyers who are managers of recognised bodies; and

    (e)   other lawyers of England and Wales and European lawyers registered with the Bar Standards Board, who are managers of recognised bodies.

2.   Because of the lighter touch regulation in respect of overseas practice, the rules regulate, in essence, the practice of individual solicitors and RELs in respect of their overseas practice (outside England and Wales for solicitors, and in Scotland and Northern Ireland for RELs), and the practice of recognised bodies. They also regulate individual non-solicitor lawyer and non-lawyer managers of recognised bodies. In some situations, the rules apply only to certain types of recognised body or solicitors involved in certain types of practice.

3.   The situation, in more detail, is as follows:

    (a)   A solicitor, as an individual, is subject to these rules in relation to practice from an office outside England and Wales, whether or not the solicitor's firm or employer is subject to the rules.

(b)   An REL, as an individual, is subject to these rules in relation to practice from an office in Scotland or Northern Ireland (but not in relation to practice from an office outside the UK) whether or not the REL's firm or employer is subject to the rules.

(c)   A "solicitor-controlled recognised body" (in which English lawyers form the dominant, or equal largest, group of lawyers – see rule 24) is subject to the rules in relation to practice from an office outside England and Wales;

(d)   An "REL-controlled recognised body" (in which RELs and English lawyers together form the dominant, or equal largest, group of lawyers – see rule 24) is subject to the rules in relation to practice from an office in Scotland or Northern Ireland;

(e)   A lawyer of England and Wales other than a solicitor is subject to the rules in relation to practice as a manager of a "solicitor-controlled recognised body" from an office outside England and Wales;

(f)   A lawyer of England and Wales other than a solicitor is subject to the rules in relation to practice as a manager of an "REL-controlled recognised body" from an office in Scotland or Northern Ireland;

(g)   A European lawyer registered with the Bar Standards Board is subject to the rules in relation to practice as a manager of a "solicitor-controlled recognised body" or an "REL-controlled recognised body" from an office in Scotland or Northern Ireland;

(h)   A non-lawyer is subject to the rules in relation to practice as a manager of a "solicitor-controlled recognised body" from an office outside England and Wales;

(i)   A non-lawyer is subject to the rules in relation to practice as a manager of an "REL-controlled recognised body" from an office in Scotland or Northern Ireland.

4.   A recognised body which is not a "solicitor-controlled recognised body" or an "REL-controlled recognised body" will not itself have to comply with the rules. However, individual solicitors who are managers or employees will still be subject to the rules (and so will individual RELs in Scotland or Northern Ireland).

5.   Non-lawyer employees of a recognised body or a recognised sole practitioner are not subject to the rules in respect of overseas practice.

6.   RFLs are not subject to the rules in respect of overseas practice.

Core duties – 15.01(1)

7.   Rule 1 (Core duties) applies to your overseas practice because these duties are fundamental to the legal profession. However, although lawyers' professional cultures are usually similar, legal and professional requirements vary from jurisdiction to jurisdiction, and therefore the specific expectations of clients, local lawyers and the courts will be different. It may be necessary to clarify in advance what rules you are bound by in relation to your dealings with your client, the opposing party and the opposing party's lawyer, and in particular it may be necessary to clarify in advance the rules by which the opposing party's lawyer is bound.

In some jurisdictions all communications between lawyers (written or by word of mouth) are automatically regarded as not to be produced in court and as not to be disclosed to others, even the lawyers' clients. In other jurisdictions such communications must be marked "confidential" before they are to be regarded in this way. On the other hand, in some jurisdictions (as will normally be the case for an English solicitor) the lawyer has to keep the client fully informed of all relevant communications from the lawyer acting for another party, and marking a letter "confidential" is no more than a reminder to the recipient that it is not to be disclosed to anyone but the other lawyer's client. In some jurisdictions, if a lawyer wishes to indicate that a letter is sent in an attempt to settle a dispute, and is not to be produced in court, the lawyer should mark the letter as "without prejudice".

These national differences give rise to many misunderstandings, so you need to be careful in conducting cross-border correspondence. Rule 16.05 lays down specific requirements in relation to cross-border correspondence in Europe.

Conflicts of rules – 15.01(4)

8.   A conflict of rules can arise when you are required to comply with two sets of rules, but if you comply with one you will breach the other. This situation can arise when:

(a)   you are practising in another jurisdiction and you are required by local or EU legislation to comply with the rules of the local legal profession – for instance, you are a solicitor registered in another jurisdiction under the Establishment Directive, and there is a conflict between one of the local rules and one of the solicitors' rules; or

(b)   you are practising under dual title, e.g. as a solicitor and as a New York attorney, and a rule of the New York Bar conflicts with one of the solicitors' rules.

9.   If a local rule applies, you cannot choose to comply only with that rule, if you can also comply with the solicitors' rule. You must comply with both, which will mean meeting the stricter standard. However, 15.01(4) addresses the possibility of a conflict of rules by disapplying any provisions of the solicitors' rules to the extent (and no more) that it conflicts with an applicable local rule. In a situation where compliance with both rules might be possible but perhaps create a bizarre result, application can be made to the SRA for a waiver.

10.   Rule 15 modifies the provisions of other rules to allow for adaptation to the legal and professional framework of the jurisdiction in which you are practising. Sometimes more general provisions are substituted, in recognition of the fact that legal and market conditions may be very different in other jurisdictions.

11.   Where a rule relates closely to the legal or regulatory framework in England and Wales it may be disapplied by rule 15 without a substitute. If a rule applies in part – for example rule 3 (Conflict of interests) – or in full – for example rule 4 (Confidentiality and disclosure), you will need to refer to that rule and its guidance, as well as the provisions in rule 15 and this guidance. Even if rule 15 has completely replaced the provisions of another rule, the guidance on the corresponding rule may help you to understand how you are expected to act.

Client relations – 15.02

12.   This provision embodies three general principles.

(a)   You must account to your client for any commission or secret profit, unless your client agrees otherwise in full knowledge of the amount or approximate amount involved. However, the requirement does not apply if, in all the circumstances, it is not reasonable to pay the commission to the client, taking account of the wide differences in conditions outside England and Wales. For example, the general custom, or the custom in legal practice in that jurisdiction might make it reasonable to deal with commissions in a different way.

(b)   You must not attempt to exclude all liability to your client. For more information on limitation of liability, see the guidance to 2.07 where appropriate to your overseas practice.

(c)   You must not enter into an unlawful contingency fee arrangement (see also the guidance to 2.04).

Equality and diversity – 15.06

13. Because rule 6 (Equality and diversity) largely reflects UK statutes its detailed requirements are unsuitable for application outside the jurisdiction. However rule 1 (Core duties) applies to your overseas practice. Rule 1.01 (Justice and the rule of law) requires that "You must uphold the rule of law and the proper administration of justice". This would normally include compliance with the equality and diversity provisions of the jurisdiction(s) in which you practise.

Publicity – 15.07

14. The requirements of rule 7 (Publicity) on publicity apply except as regards the e-mails, websites, etc. of an office in an EU state other than the UK, and the requirements of 7.07 (Letterhead, website and e-mails) which are replaced by 15.07(3) in relation to your overseas practice. When considering your publicity in relation to the guidance to rule 7 you should bear in mind that the law of the jurisdiction in which your overseas office is based will apply rather than the law of England and Wales; and that you may also be directly subject to local rules. You should therefore interpret the guidance to rule 7 in the light of the following:

    (a) Publicity intended for a jurisdiction outside England and Wales must comply with:

        (i) any applicable law or rules regarding lawyers' publicity in the jurisdiction in which your office is based;

        (ii) the applicable provisions of rule 7 and 15.07; and

        (iii) if the publicity is intended for a third jurisdiction, the rules in force in the "target" jurisdiction governing lawyers' publicity.

    (b) Your publicity will not breach rule 7 through being incidentally received in a jurisdiction where it is not permitted (this is important in relation to a website, which can be accessed worldwide).

    (c) Your website must comply with the E-Commerce Directive 2000/31/EC and, if you are established anywhere within the EU, with the relevant implementing legislation and the rules which apply to you by virtue of your establishment in an EU state other than the UK.

Fee sharing – 15.08

15. In general, you must not share your professional fees except with other lawyers or law firms, or with non-lawyer managers or owners within your firm, or with your employee, or with a retired manager, member, owner or predecessor, or the dependants or personal representatives of a deceased manager, member, owner or predecessor. You may, however, share your professional fees with a non-lawyer business for the purpose of facilitating the introduction of capital and/or the provision of services to your firm, though not in relation to European cross-border practice – see rule 8 (Fee sharing) and rule 16 (European cross-border practice) and the attached guidance.

Undertakings – 15.10(2)

16. Rule 15.10(2)(a)(i) (undertakings given in the course of practice) applies to undertakings given by:

    (a) a solicitor, however practising;

    (b) an REL, however practising, practising in Scotland or Northern Ireland;

    (c) a "solicitor-controlled recognised body" practising outside the UK or any of its managers who is a lawyer of England and Wales or a non-lawyer;

(d)   a "solicitor-controlled recognised body" or an "REL-controlled recognised body" practising in Scotland or Northern Ireland or any of its managers who is a lawyer of England and Wales, a European lawyer registered with the Bar Standards Board or a non-lawyer.

This guidance is derived from rule 15.01(2) and the definition of "practice" in rule 24.

Framework of practice – 15.12

17.   An overseas firm – that is, a firm which has no office in England and Wales – may have lawyer principals, directors and owners who are not registered with the SRA but would need to be registered if the firm had an office in England and Wales. An overseas firm may also have non-lawyer managers and/or owners, provided there is majority control by lawyers and no breach of applicable local rules, or rules applying in an Establishment Directive state.

A recognised body which has non-lawyer managers or owners cannot have an office in an Establishment Directive state other than the UK unless the rules for local lawyers would permit a local lawyer to practise through a business of that composition and structure.

In-house practice overseas – 15.13

18.   If you are employed at an office outside England and Wales (or in Scotland or Northern Ireland if you are an REL) 15.13 replaces rule 13 (In-house practice, etc.) with more general requirements. If your employer is structured in a way which would allow a solicitor (or an REL) to be a manager or owner under 12.01(2) and 12.02(2) you will be practising in a firm as defined in rule 24 and will not be practising in-house.

19.   Note also that if you are registered with another regulatory body under the Establishment Directive rule 15.13(2)(b) allows you to practise in-house to the extent allowed to the profession governed by that regulatory body. This may be more or less restrictive than the requirements of these rules.

Deposit interest – 15.15

20.   In relation to overseas practice, you are not bound by the interest requirements in the Solicitors' Accounts Rules 1998, but by those in 15.15. You must ensure that a client gets proper interest – but this is subject to the proviso that the circumstances must be such that interest ought, in fairness, to be earned for the client. This might not be so if the interest is or would be negligible, or it is customary in that jurisdiction to deal with interest in a different way. It is also open to you to enter into a written agreement with the client regarding the payment of interest.

European cross-border practice – 15.16

21.   The requirements of rule 16 (European cross-border practice) are applied in full. European cross-border practice is:

(a)   any professional activity in a CCBE state other than the UK, whether or not you are physically present in that CCBE state; and

(b)   any professional contact with a lawyer of a CCBE state other than the UK.

"CCBE state" is defined in rule 24 (Interpretation). A list of the CCBE states and the legal professions covered by the CCBE Code appears in note 1 of the guidance to rule 16 (European cross-border practice).

22.   For the purpose of rule 16 (European cross-border practice), "professional contacts" and "professional activities" taking place within a firm or in-house practice do not constitute European cross-border practice.

Separate businesses – 15.21

23. Rule 21 (Separate businesses) and 15.21 do not regulate your separate business, but regulate the interface between a firm or an in-house practice and a business which is not regulated by the SRA, wherever the separate business is situated or carries on business. Therefore, if you have a separate business but have no office in England and Wales only 15.21 will apply. However, if you also practise from an office in England and Wales, the more detailed provisions of rule 21 will apply.

24. Rule 15.21 completely replaces the provisions of rule 21 (Separate businesses) if you practise wholly outside England and Wales. It applies a lighter regime than rule 21. The requirements of 15.21 are mainly designed to ensure that:

    (a) your compliance with rule 1 (Core duties) as a person regulated by the SRA is not compromised by your involvement with the separate business;

    (b) you keep the separate business truly separate from any firm or in-house practice; and

    (c) you ensure that people who obtain services from the separate business know it is not carrying on the practice of a lawyer regulated by the SRA.

Professional indemnity – 15.26

25. In relation to overseas practice, you are not bound by the Solicitors' Indemnity Insurance Rules but by 15.26, which requires that you must be covered by insurance if you are a manager or employee of a firm. The insurance must be reasonable, and it is not "reasonable" insurance to have none at all. The extent and amount of the insurance under 15.26 need not exceed the minimum requirements for practice from an office in England and Wales, but local law may apply more onerous requirements.

Accounts – 15.27

26. In relation to overseas practice, you are not bound by the Solicitors' Accounts Rules 1998 but by 15.27, which imposes similar but more general provisions. If an applicable local rule conflicts with a provision of 15.27, you will still be expected to comply with any other provisions of 15.27 that do not conflict.

27. Although the Solicitors' Accounts Rules 1998 do not apply, they may provide useful information about keeping accounts, the kind of checks an accountant might make, and the preparation of accountants' reports. Also, if your firm has offices in and outside England and Wales, a single accountant's report may be submitted covering your practice from offices both in, and outside, England and Wales – such a report must cover compliance both with the Solicitors' Accounts Rules 1998 and rule 15.27(3) of the Solicitors' Code of Conduct 2007.

28. The accounting requirements and the obligation to deliver an accountant's report in 15.27 are designed to apply to you in relation to money held or received by your firm unless it is primarily the practice of lawyers of other jurisdictions. The fact that they do not apply in certain cases is not intended to allow a lower standard of care in the handling of client money – simply to prevent the Solicitors' Accounts Rules 1998 applying "by the back door" in a disproportionate or inappropriate way.

Rule 16 – European cross-border practice

Introduction

The purpose of rule 16 is to apply the provisions of the CCBE Code to European cross-border practice. This is necessary to provide a system of mutual professional understanding for professional relations between lawyers of different CCBE states. Although the CCBE

Code contains a large number of requirements, rule 16 contains only those requirements which are not replicated elsewhere in these rules.

Rule 16 – European cross-border practice

16.01 Definition and application

Definition

(1)   (a)   European cross-border practice is:

        (i)   any professional activity in a CCBE state other than the UK, whether or not you are physically present in that CCBE state; and

        (ii)   any professional contact with a lawyer of a CCBE state other than the UK.

     (b)   For the purposes of this rule professional contacts and professional activities taking place within a firm or in-house legal department are not European cross-border practice.

Application of this rule

(2)   (a)   If you are a solicitor this rule applies to your European cross-border practice from an office in, or outside, England and Wales.

     (b)   If you are an REL this rule applies to your European cross-border practice from an office within the UK.

     (c)   If you are an RFL and you are a manager or employee of a recognised body or the employee of a recognised sole practitioner, this rule applies to your European cross-border practice from an office in England and Wales.

     (d)   This rule applies to a recognised body as follows:

        (i)   A solicitor-controlled recognised body is subject to the rule in relation to its European cross-border practice from any of its offices, wherever situated.

        (ii)   An REL-controlled recognised body is subject to the rule in relation to its European cross-border practice from any of its offices in the UK.

        (iii)   A recognised body which is not within (i) or (ii) is subject to the rule in relation to its European cross-border practice from any of its offices in England and Wales.

     (e)   If you are a manager of a recognised body and you are not a solicitor but you are a lawyer of England and Wales or a non-lawyer, this rule applies to you to the extent that the rule applies to the body itself under (d) above.

     (f)   If you are a manager of a recognised body and you are registered with the Bar Standards Board under the Establishment Directive, this rule applies to your European cross-border practice from an office of the recognised body in the UK to the extent that the rule applies to the body itself under (d) above.

16.02 Occupations considered incompatible with legal practice

(1)   If you act in legal proceedings or proceedings before public authorities in a CCBE

state other than the UK, you must, in that state, comply with any rules regarding occupations incompatible with the practice of law, as if you were a lawyer of that state, whether or not you are based at an office in that state.

(2) If you are a solicitor based at an office in a CCBE state other than the UK, you must respect any rules regarding participation in commercial or other activities not connected with the practice of law, as they are applied to lawyers of that state.

16.03 Fee sharing with non-lawyers

(1) You must not share your professional fees with a non-lawyer situated in a CCBE state other than the UK except:

    (a)   within a firm which is permitted under rule 12 (Framework of practice); or

    (b)   with a retired manager, member, owner or predecessor of the firm, or the dependants or personal representatives of a deceased manager, member, owner or predecessor.

(2) If you are practising from an office in a CCBE state other than the UK, whether or not you are actually present at that office, you must not share your professional fees from that practice with a non-lawyer, except:

    (a)   within a firm which is permitted under rule 12 (Framework of practice); or

    (b)   with a retired manager, member, owner or predecessor of the firm, or the dependants or personal representatives of a deceased manager, member, owner or predecessor.

16.04 Co-operation between lawyers of different CCBE states

(1) If you are approached by a lawyer of a CCBE state other than the UK to undertake work which you are not competent to undertake, you must assist that lawyer to obtain the information necessary to find and instruct a lawyer capable of providing the service asked for.

(2) When co-operating with a lawyer of a CCBE state other than the UK you must take into account the differences which may exist between your respective legal systems and the professional organisations, competencies and obligations of lawyers in your respective states.

16.05 Correspondence between lawyers in different CCBE states

(1) If you are practising from an office in a CCBE state and you want to send to a lawyer in a different CCBE state (with the exception of the UK) a communication which you wish to remain "confidential" or "without prejudice", you must, before sending the communication, clearly express your intention in order to avoid misunderstanding, and ask if the lawyer is able to accept the communication on that basis. When you send the communication you must express your intention clearly at the head of the communication or in a covering letter.

(2) If you are the intended recipient of a communication from a lawyer in another CCBE state which is stated to be "confidential" or "without prejudice", but which you are unable to accept on the basis intended by that lawyer, you must inform the sender accordingly without delay. If the communication has already been sent you must return it unread without revealing the contents to others. If you have already read the communication and you are under a professional duty to reveal it to your client you must inform the sender of this immediately.

16.06 Paying referral fees to non-lawyers

You must not pay a fee, commission or any other compensation to a non-lawyer as a consideration for referring a client to you:

- (a) if the non-lawyer is situated in a CCBE state other than the UK; or

- (b) if you are practising from an office in a CCBE state other than the UK, whether or not you are physically present at that office.

16.07 Disputes between lawyers in different member states

- (1) If you consider that a lawyer in a CCBE state other than the UK has acted in breach of a rule of professional conduct you must draw the breach to the other lawyer's attention.

- (2) Before commencing any form of proceedings against the other lawyer, you must inform the Law Society and the other lawyer's bar or law society in order to allow them an opportunity to assist in resolving the matter.

Guidance to rule 16 – European cross-border practice

1. Since 1990 the CCBE Code, interpreted in the light of article 1 of the CCBE Code and the CCBE's Explanatory Memorandum, has been binding upon solicitors in relation to their European cross-border practice. The current version of the CCBE Code applies in relation to all the CCBE states and their legal professions, which are as follows.

Albania	avukat
Armenia	pastaban
Austria	Rechtsanwalt
Belgium	avocat/advocaat/Rechtsanwalt
Bulgaria	advokat
Croatia	odvjetnik
Cyprus	dikegóros
Czech Republic	advokát
Denmark	advokat
Estonia	vandeadvokaat
Finland	asianajaja/advokat
FYRO Macedonia	advokat
France	avocat
Georgia	advokati
Germany	Rechtsanwalt
Greece	dikegóros
Hungary	ügyvéd
Iceland	lögmaður
Ireland	solicitor; barrister
Italy	avvocato
Latvia	zvērināts advokāts

Liechtenstein	Rechtsanwalt
Lithuania	advokatas
Luxembourg	avocat/Rechtsanwalt
Malta	avukat; prokuratur legali
Moldova	avocet
Montenegro	advokat
Netherlands	advocaat
Norway	advokat
Poland	adwokat; radca prawny
Portugal	advogado
Romania	avocat
Serbia	advokat
Slovakia	advokát/advokátka
Slovenia	odvetnik/odvetnica
Spain	abogado/advocat/abokatu/avogado
Sweden	advokat
Switzerland	Rechtsanwalt/Anwalt/Fürsprecher/Fürsprech/avocat/avvocato/advokat
Turkey	avukat
Ukraine	advokat
United Kingdom	solicitor; barrister/advocate

2.   If you comply with these rules in relation to your practice generally, and with rule 16 in relation to European cross-border practice, you will also comply with the requirements of the CCBE Code, as interpreted in the light of article 1 of the CCBE Code and the CCBE's Explanatory Memorandum.

Incompatible occupations – 16.02

3.   Rule 16.02(1) prohibits you from pursuing any occupation prohibited to local lawyers as incompatible with the practice of law, in another CCBE state in which you act in legal proceedings or proceedings before a public authority. This does not prevent you from pursuing such an occupation in the UK if it is permitted under these rules, or in another CCBE state where it is allowed.

4.   Rule 16.02(2) requires you to "respect" the rules regarding incompatible occupations in a CCBE state where you are established. If you are registered under the Establishment Directive any such local rule will apply to you directly. If you are established in a CCBE state, but you are not subject to the Establishment Directive, you may not be subject to the host state rule but rule 16 will apply. "Respect" for a rule is not the same as an obligation to comply with that rule, but the SRA Board would expect you to comply with the spirit of such a rule where it is not unreasonable to do so.

Fee sharing – 16.03

5.   Rule 16.03 permits fee sharing in European cross-border practice within a law firm, and between law firms. Fee sharing is permitted, for instance, with an overseas practice which includes non-lawyers, provided a controlling majority of the owners and managers are lawyers.

6.   Although 8.02 (Fee sharing with other non-lawyers) allows you to share fees with a non-lawyer "fee sharer" in some circumstances, this is prohibited by 16.03 in respect of European cross-border practice.

APPENDIX 21

7.   Interpreting how this prohibition applies to a firm sharing fees with a non-lawyer fee sharer operating in more than one state, and how it applies to a firm practising in more than one state, may be complex. For example:

(a)   rule 16.03 would prohibit your firm, wherever it is practising, from sharing fees with a non-lawyer company whose principal place of business is in a CCBE state other than the UK, or with a non-lawyer company's branch establishment in a CCBE state other than the UK; and

(b)   if your firm has its main office in the UK and a branch office in another CCBE state, the fees of the branch office cannot be shared with a non-lawyer company wherever situated, so the firm cannot share a percentage of its fees as a whole with a non-lawyer company. However, the firm could share a percentage of the fees of its UK office, and of any office in a state which is not a CCBE state, with a non-lawyer company, provided:

(i)   the non-lawyer company is situated in the UK or in a state which is not a CCBE state; and

(ii)   the requirements of 8.02 are met.

Correspondence between lawyers in different CCBE states – 16.05

8.   Rule 16.05 reflects the requirements of article 5.3 of the CCBE Code. Differences between the ways in which client business is conducted in different states can give rise to misunderstandings between lawyers, and this provision is designed to help avoid such misunderstandings. Terms such as "confidential" and "without prejudice" are not of universal application.

(a)   *"Confidential"*

In some states all communications between lawyers (written or by word of mouth) are automatically regarded as not to be produced in court and as not to be disclosed to others, even the lawyers' clients. In other states such communications must be marked "confidential" before they are to be regarded in this way.

On the other hand, in some states, including the UK, the lawyer has to keep the client fully informed of all relevant communications from the lawyer acting for another party, and marking a letter "confidential" is no more than a reminder to the recipient that it is not to be disclosed to anyone but the other lawyer's client.

(b)   *"Without prejudice"*

In some states, if a lawyer wishes to indicate that a letter is sent in an attempt to settle a dispute, and is not to be produced in court, the lawyer should mark the letter as "without prejudice".

These important national differences give rise to many misunderstandings, so you need to be careful in conducting cross-border correspondence.

9.   Where 16.05 applies, you must ask in advance whether your communication can be accepted on the basis you intend, and you must express your intention clearly at the head of your communication or in a covering letter.

10.   If 16.05 applies and you are informed that a communication is to be sent to you on a basis which you are not able to respect – for example, that it must not be disclosed to your client – you must inform the other lawyer immediately so that the communication is not sent. If it has already been sent you must return it to the sender unread and without revealing its contents or referring to it in any way. It can happen that, as a result of misunderstanding between sender and recipient, the recipient has already read the communication. If this happens to you, you may be under a professional duty to reveal the contents to your client, either under these rules or under rules of an Establishment Directive state in which you are registered. If so you must tell the sender immediately.

Referral fees – 16.06

11. Rule 16.06 permits, in European cross-border practice, the payment of a referral fee or commission to another law firm. It is permitted, for instance, to pay a referral fee to an overseas practice which includes non-lawyers, provided a controlling majority of the owners and managers are lawyers.

12. Rule 9 (Referrals of business), which refers to practice from an office in England and Wales, allows you to have an arrangement with a non-lawyer for the referral of clients, and, subject to disclosure, to pay the introducer. However, such payments are prohibited by 16.06 in respect of European cross-border practice whether from an office in England and Wales or from an overseas office.

13. As with the prohibition on fee sharing with a non-lawyer, there are complexities involved in interpreting how the prohibition applies to a firm practising in more than one state, and to an arrangement with a non-lawyer introducer operating in more than one state. For example:

    (a)   if your firm has its main office in the UK and a branch office in another CCBE state, the branch office cannot pay a referral fee to a non-lawyer company wherever situated, but the UK office, and any office in a state which is not a CCBE state, could do so provided that:

        (i)   the non-lawyer company is situated in the UK or in a state which is not a CCBE state; and

        (ii)   in respect of payments from an office in England and Wales the requirements of rule 9 are met, or in respect of payments from an overseas office the requirements of 15.09(2) are met; and

    (b)   rule 16.06 would prohibit your firm, wherever it is practising, from paying a referral fee to a non-lawyer company whose principal place of business is in a CCBE state other than the UK, or to a non-lawyer company's branch establishment in a CCBE state other than the UK.

Disputes between lawyers in different CCBE states – 16.07

14. If a professional dispute arises between you and a lawyer in a CCBE state other than the UK, it is desirable that the dispute be settled in a friendly way, and this is the purpose of the requirements of 16.07. Under 16.07(2) you will need to contact the Law Society's International Unit.

Rule 17 – Insolvency practice

Introduction

If you are a solicitor or an REL, and an insolvency practitioner in a firm, rule 17 applies to you when you accept appointments and act as an appointment holder. Rule 17 should be read in conjunction with the Code of Ethics produced by the Joint Insolvency Committee and adopted by all recognised professional bodies (RPBs) including the Solicitors Regulation Authority. The purpose of the the Joint Insolvency Committee's Code of Ethics is to ensure your independence and objectivity when acting as an appointment holder and that you can identify and avoid conflicts of interest. The rule does not apply to your overseas practice except in relation to appointments appertaining to orders made in the courts of England and Wales.

Rule 17 – Insolvency practice

17.01

If you are a solicitor or an REL you must, when accepting an appointment or acting as an appointment holder as an insolvency practitioner, comply with the Code of Ethics produced by the Joint Insolvency Committee and adopted by the Solicitors Regulation Authority Board.

Guidance to rule 17 – Insolvency practice

1. You must comply with the requirements of the Insolvency Act 1986 and other relevant legislation in relation to accepting appointments and acting as an appointment holder.
2. You should have regard to the other guidance and best practice promulgated from time to time by the SRA as an RPB on all issues relating to appointment holding, including professional independence.

Rule 18 – Property selling

Introduction

This rule sets out requirements for providing property selling services through your firm. Requirements for providing property selling services through a separate business are dealt with under rule 21 (Separate businesses).

The seller is your client, and any property selling work you do is, in addition to this rule, subject to the same law and professional rules binding on you in relation to your other work.

The rule applies to your overseas practice from offices in Scotland or Northern Ireland but not to your overseas practice from offices outside the UK.

Rule 18 – Property selling

18.01 Standards of property selling services

(1) When providing property selling services through your firm, you must:

    (a) ensure that you, or the relevant staff, are competent to carry out the work;

    (b) not seek from any prospective buyer a pre-contract deposit in excess of any prescribed limit; and

    (c) promptly send to your client written accurate details of any offer you have received from a prospective buyer in respect of an interest in the property (other than those of a description which your client has indicated in writing that they do not want to receive).

(2) If you are the person who is responsible for marketing a residential property you must comply with any Home Information Packs Regulations made under the Housing Act 2004.

(3)   (a)   In 18.01(1) above:

        (i)   "competent" includes meeting any standards of competence set by the Secretary of State under section 22 of the Estate Agents Act 1979; and

        (ii)   "prescribed limit" means any limit prescribed by the Secretary of State under section 19 of the Estate Agents Act 1979.

      (b)   In 18.01(2) "the person who is responsible for marketing a residential property" has the meaning used in sections 151–153 of the Housing Act 2004.

18.02 Statement on the cost

(1)   When accepting instructions to act in the sale of a property, you must, at the outset of communication between you and the client, or as soon as is reasonably practicable, and before the client is committed to any liability towards you, give the client a written statement setting out your agreement as to:

      (a)   the identity of the property;

      (b)   the interest to be sold;

      (c)   the price to be sought;

      (d)   the amount of your fee or the method of its calculation;

      (e)   the circumstances in which your fee is to become payable;

      (f)   regarding any payments to be made to others, and charged separately:

        (i)   the amount, or the method by which they will be calculated; and

        (ii)   the circumstances in which they may be incurred; and

      (g)   the incidence of VAT.

(2)   You must also, within the written statement:

      (a)   state whether or not you are to have "sole agency" or "sole selling rights". The statement must also include a clear explanation of the intention and effect of those terms, or any similar terms used; and

      (b)   if the statement refers to a "ready, willing and able" buyer (or similar term), include a clear explanation of the term.

18.03 Conflict of interests

(1)   In addition to your duties under rule 3 (Conflict of interests), when selling property you must comply with the following requirements.

      (a)   If you or any connected person has, or is seeking to acquire, a beneficial interest in the property or in the proceeds of sale of any interest in the property, you must promptly inform your client in writing.

      (b)   If you act in the sale of property, even if not in the conveyancing, you must not act for the buyer in the negotiations.

      (c)   If a prospective buyer makes an offer for a client's property, you must promptly inform the client in writing if, to your knowledge, you or any connected person has been instructed, or is to be instructed by the buyer to sell an interest in land, and that sale is necessary to enable the buyer to buy from the client or results from that prospective purchase.

(d)   If you have, or to your knowledge any connected person has, a beneficial interest in a property or in the proceeds of sale of any interest in it, you must promptly inform in writing any person negotiating to acquire or dispose of any interest in that property. You must make this disclosure before entering into any negotiations with a prospective buyer.

(e)   You must not discriminate against a prospective buyer because they are unlikely to instruct you to sell an interest in land, which sale is necessary to enable the buyer to buy from your client or results from that prospective purchase.

(f)   When acting for a seller, you must restrict communication with the buyer to your property selling function. In particular:

   (i)   you must communicate about legal matters so far as possible only through the buyer's solicitor; and

   (ii)   you must not lead the buyer to believe that they are receiving legal advice from you.

(g)   When acting for a seller, if you arrange for a mortgage to be available on the property in order to facilitate the sale, you may inform prospective buyers of the availability of the mortgage (subject to the buyer's status) but, unless exempted by rule 3 (Conflict of interests) you must also inform prospective buyers in writing:

   (i)   that you cannot advise or act for the prospective buyer in respect of the mortgage;

   (ii)   that the mortgage may not be the only one available; and

   (iii) that the prospective buyer should consult their own lawyer.

(2) In 18.03(1) above:

(a)   "connected person" means:

   (i)   spouse, former spouse, reputed spouse, brother, sister, uncle, aunt, nephew, niece, direct descendant, parent or other direct ancestor;

   (ii)   any employee of your firm, and any member of your employee's family;

   (iii) any owner or employee of an associated firm defined in rule 24 (Interpretation) or any member of their families;

   (iv)   any company of which you are a director or employee, or any LLP of which you are a member or employee, or any company in which you, either alone or with any other connected person or persons are entitled to exercise, or control the exercise of, one-third or more of the voting power at any general meeting;

   (v)   any company of which any of the persons mentioned in (i) to (iii) above is a director or employee, or any LLP of which any of them is a member or employee, or any company in which any of them, either alone or with any other connected person or persons, is entitled to exercise, or control the exercise of, one-third or more of the voting power at any general meeting; and

   (vi)   any other "associate" as defined in section 32 of the Estate Agents Act 1979; and

(b)   "you" includes anyone with whom you carry on a joint property selling practice, and owners of an associated firm as defined in rule 24 (Interpretation).

18.04 Waivers

In spite of 22.01(1) (Waivers), the Solicitors Regulation Authority Board shall not have power to waive any of the provisions of this rule.

Guidance to rule 18 – Property selling

General – business structures and property selling

1. You may sell property through a separate business – see notes 8 and 9 below and rule 21 (Separate businesses) – or as part of the general work of your firm, or through a firm formed especially for that purpose, either alone or with other firms. If you form a property selling firm with solicitors from other firms, it will be a distinct firm for all purposes.

2. A jointly owned property selling firm may be incorporated as a SEAL (Solicitors' Estate Agency Limited). A SEAL is defined in 3.12. See rule 3 (Conflict of interests) for the position of a SEAL regarding conflicts of interests.

3. A further alternative for firms wishing to co-operate in selling property is a joint Property Display Centre (PDC), where the principal activity carried on is publicising properties in the sale of which an individual participating firm is instructed. It is also possible for a single firm to establish its own PDC. A PDC:

    (a) is not itself a firm, and is not a separate entity; it is an administrative extension of the practices of the participating firms, and its address should be notified to the Information Directorate of the SRA;

    (b) can have no clients; it may merely carry out certain activities on behalf of the participating firms (only individual participating firms may be instructed in the sale of a property);

    (c) is a place where the principal activity carried on is the display and dissemination of information about properties which the individual participating firms have for sale; and

    (d) cannot carry on any part of your professional practice. In particular no negotiations may be conducted at the PDC; prospective buyers must be referred to the individual participating firm instructed in the sale of the property in question. Instructions to sell a property may only be accepted at offices of participating firms. To avoid problems with rule 3 (Conflict of interests), the participating firms must operate totally independently so far as their professional business, including property selling, is concerned.

4. You and the other participating firms may wish to establish a joint service company to carry out support functions connected with the running of the PDC, e.g. hiring premises and equipment. The service company (as with a service company established by an individual firm of solicitors) cannot carry on any legal practice or have any dealings with the property selling or property buying public.

5. As no part of the professional practice of the participating firms is carried out at the PDC, rule 5 (Business management in England and Wales) does not apply. Nor would rule 5 apply to a PDC established by a single firm. The participating firms, or the single firm, would nevertheless be responsible for the activities of the PDC staff and would have a duty to supervise them.

6. If you sell property you may share your professional fees with an estate agent who is your sub-agent for a sale – see 8.01(g).

7. You may properly provide structural surveys and formal valuations of property through your firm. You must ensure that you, or relevant staff, have the appropriate level of competence.

8. You may provide property selling services through a separate business – see 21.04(1)(c). If so, you must comply with the safeguards in 21.05. Note also that a separate business will not fall within the exemption in section 1 of the Estate Agents Act 1979 (see note 10 below). The effect of this is that your separate business providing property selling services will be subject to all the provisions of the Estate Agents Act 1979.

9. If you are selling a property through a separate business, your firm may do the seller's conveyancing, but may not normally do the buyer's conveyancing unless you comply with 21.05(2)(f), and:

   (a) your firm is not doing the seller's conveyancing; or

   (b) your firm is allowed to act for both buyer and seller under rule 3 (Conflict of interests).

   Your separate business may, however, provide mortgage related services to the buyer even if your firm is doing the seller's conveyancing.

Standards of property selling services – 18.01

10. Section 1(2)(a) of the Estate Agents Act 1979 exempts from that Act "things done in the course of his profession by a practising solicitor or a person employed by him." This exemption is on the basis that certain standards, set out in the Act, are already required of you under the rules of professional conduct. These standards are contained in rule 18 and in other rules of professional conduct, all of which remain applicable when you are selling property.

11. These standards are:

   (a) a requirement of competence, imposed by 18.01(1)(a);

   (b) a prohibition on making false statements as set out in section 1 of the Property Misdescriptions Act 1991 – "a false or misleading statement about a prescribed matter" (section 1(1)). A prescribed matter is "any matter relating to land which is specified in an order made by the Secretary of State" (section 1(5)). A statement can be made by pictures as well as words. Any false statement will be a breach of 1.02 (Integrity);

   (c) a prohibition on seeking a pre-contract deposit in excess of the prescribed limit, imposed by 18.01(1)(b);

   (d) requirements for the holding of clients' money and the keeping of client accounts, which are imposed on you under the Solicitors' Accounts Rules 1998;

   (e) requirements relating to the provision of information to clients, imposed on you by 18.01(1)(c) and 18.02; this also reflects rule 2 (Client relations);

   (f) requirements relating to conflict of interests. Some of these are imposed on you by 18.03, and some by rule 3 (Conflict of interests). In addition to the general provisions on conflict of interests (3.01 to 3.06), you should also have regard to the provisions specifically on conveyancing, property selling and mortgage related services (3.07 to 3.22). Note that there are also special conflict provisions where you sell property through a separate business – see notes 8 and 9 above and 21.05(2)(f); and

   (g) requirements relating to home information packs resulting from the Housing Act 2004 and the Home Information Pack Regulations (No. 2) 2007 (SI 2007/1667). These are imposed on you by 18.01(2).

Statement on the cost – 18.02

12. If you are acting for a seller in marketing a property, you have a duty to have a home information pack for the property under the Housing Act 2004. The Home Information Pack Regulations (No. 2) 2007 set out the requirements in relation to home information packs.

13. Under the Housing Act, enforcement of the Regulations in respect of non-solicitor estate agents is carried out by the Office of Fair Trading. Because of the exemption of solicitors' services from the provisions of the Estate Agents Act 1979, enforcement of the requirements of the Regulations in respect of solicitors is carried out by the SRA. Similarly, the redress scheme operated by the Ombudsman for Estate Agents does not apply to solicitors: redress is provided by the Legal Complaints Service.

14. Notes 15 to 18 below set out the detailed information requirements to help you comply with 18.02. These requirements correspond to those in the Estate Agents (Provision of Information) Regulations 1991 (SI 1991/859) and the Schedule to those Regulations.

15. A clear explanation of the intention and effect of the terms sole agency/sole selling rights or similar terms, given to clients will take the following form.

   "Sole agency

   You will be liable to pay a fee to us, in addition to any other costs or charges agreed, if unconditional contracts for the sale of the property are exchanged at any time:

   with a buyer introduced by us with whom we had negotiations about the property in the period during which we have sole agency; or

   with a buyer introduced by another agent during the period of our sole agency.

   Sole selling rights

   You will be liable to pay a fee to us, in addition to any other costs or charges agreed, in each of the following circumstances:

   if unconditional contracts for the sale of the property are exchanged in the period during which we have sole selling rights, even if the buyer was not found by us but by another agent or by any other person, including yourself; or

   if unconditional contracts for the sale of the property are exchanged after the expiry of the period during which we have sole selling rights but to a buyer who was introduced to you during that period or with whom we had negotiations about the property during that period."

16. A clear explanation of the term "ready, willing and able" given to clients will take the following form.

   "A buyer is a 'ready, willing and able' buyer if he or she is prepared and is able to exchange unconditional contracts for the purchase of your property. You will be liable to pay a fee to us, in addition to any other costs or charges agreed, if such a buyer is introduced by us in accordance with your instructions and this must be paid even if you subsequently withdraw and unconditional contracts for sale are not exchanged, irrespective of your reasons."

17. If, by reason of the provisions of the statement in which any of the terms referred to above appear, any of the prescribed explanations is in any way misleading, you should alter the content of the explanation so as accurately to describe the liability of the client to pay a fee in accordance with those provisions. Subject to this requirement, you should reproduce the explanations prominently, clearly and legibly without any material alterations or additions. They should be given no less prominence than that given to any other information in the statement apart from the heading, firm names, names of the parties, numbers or lettering subsequently inserted.

18.   You may quote or publicise a composite fee for property selling and conveyancing, but should be prepared to quote separate fees if asked. The separate fees may total more than the composite fee.

Conflict of interests – 18.03

19.   The requirements of 18.03 are similar to those imposed on estate agents by the Estate Agents (Undesirable Practices) (No.2) Order 1991 (SI 1991/1032).

20.   It is important to read the requirements of 18.03 in close conjunction with rule 3 (Conflict of interests).

Waivers – 18.04

21.   The exemption from the Estate Agents Act 1979, explained in note 10 above, is on the basis that the standards in rule 18 are complied with in all circumstances. For this reason there is no power to waive rule 18.

Rule 19 – Financial services

Introduction

This rule sets out the requirements for ensuring that your independence is preserved when acting in connection with the provision of financial services for clients, both through your firm and through a separate business.

The rule applies to your overseas practice in relation to regulated activities you conduct from an office in Scotland or Northern Ireland and to regulated activities you conduct into the UK from an office outside the UK.

Rule 19 – Financial services

19.01 Independence

(1)   You must not, in connection with any regulated activity:

(a)   be an appointed representative; or

(b)   have any arrangement with other persons under which you could be constrained to recommend to clients or effect for them (or refrain from doing so) transactions:

(i)   in some investments but not others;

(ii)   with some persons but not others; or

(iii)   through the agency of some persons but not others; or

(c)   have any arrangement with other persons under which you could be constrained to introduce or refer clients or other persons with whom you deal to some persons but not others.

(2)   You must not have any active involvement in a separate business which is an appointed representative, unless it is the appointed representative of an independent financial adviser.

(3)   Paragraph (1)(b) and (c) above shall not apply to arrangements in connection with any of the following types of investments:

    (a)   regulated mortgage contracts;

    (b)   general insurance contracts; or

    (c)   pure protection contracts.

(4)   In this rule:

    (a)   "appointed representative" has the meaning given in the Financial Services and Markets Act 2000;

    (b)   "general insurance contract" is any contract of insurance within Part 1 of Schedule 1 to the Financial Services and Markets Act 2000 (Regulated Activities) Order 2001 (SI 2001/544);

    (c)   "investment" means any of the investments specified in Part III of the Financial Services and Markets Act 2000 (Regulated Activities) Order 2001 (SI 2001/544);

    (d)   "pure protection contract" has the meaning given in rule 8(1) of the Solicitors' Financial Services (Scope) Rules 2001;

    (e)   "regulated activity" means an activity which is specified in the Financial Services and Markets Act 2000 (Regulated Activities) Order 2001 (SI 2001/544); and

    (f)   "regulated mortgage contract" has the meaning given by article 61(3) of the Financial Services and Markets Act 2000 (Regulated Activities) Order 2001 (SI 2001/544).

Guidance to rule 19 – Financial services

1.   Independence is a core duty (1.03). However rule 19 sets out the exact scope of this duty when carrying on regulated activities.

2.   Note that under the Financial Services and Markets Act 2000 the Financial Services Authority (FSA) is the single statutory regulator of financial services business. Under the Financial Services and Markets Act 2000, if you carry on "regulated activities" you will need either to be regulated by the FSA or to rely on the Part XX exemption.

3.   The SRA is not therefore able to authorise you to conduct investment business. However, Part XX of the Financial Services and Markets Act 2000 makes special provision for professional firms which do not carry on mainstream investment business but which may carry on regulated activities in the course of other work such as conveyancing, corporate, matrimonial, probate and trust work. Part XX enables firms regulated by the SRA which meet certain conditions to be treated as exempt professional firms and to carry on activities known as exempt regulated activities. These firms will not need to be regulated by the FSA but will be able to carry on exempt regulated activities under the supervision of and regulation by the SRA. This exemption does not apply to an authorised non-SRA firm simply by virtue of that firm having a solicitor as a manager, owner or employee. If you are a solicitor practising in an authorised non-SRA firm, neither you nor the firm will be exempt under Part XX simply because you are a solicitor. However, the firm may benefit from an exemption relating to its own regulator under Part XX.

4.   In carrying out the functions of a designated professional body, the SRA is required to make rules governing the carrying on of regulated activities by its members. In accordance with this requirement, the Solicitors' Financial Services (Scope) Rules 2001 set out the scope of the activities which may be undertaken by firms under the Part XX

exemption in the Financial Services and Markets Act 2000. You should refer to these rules and the Solicitors' Financial Services (Conduct of Business) Rules 2001 regarding the carrying on of regulated activities.

5. This rule applies specifically in connection with regulated activities. It prohibits you from being an appointed representative (i.e. a tied agent) or from being actively involved in a separate business which is an appointed representative unless the separate business is the appointed representative of an independent financial adviser.

6. It also prevents you from entering into any restrictive arrangements in connection with regulated activities that could constrain the advice you give to clients or the referrals that you make. However, it would not prevent you from regularly introducing clients to a particular broker, provided that you have not entered into any arrangement which could constrain you to use that broker.

7. The prohibition on entering into restrictive arrangements does not apply to arrangements in connection with:

    (a) regulated mortgage contracts;

    (b) general insurance contracts, for example after the event insurance; or

    (c) pure protection contracts, for example term assurance.

    This means that you would not be prevented from having an arrangement under which an introducer stipulates that you might only sell one particular insurance policy – for example, if there is a conditional fee agreement, provided that it is suitable for the client's needs and you have informed the client of the constraint. Although the prohibition in rule 19 does not apply to arrangements in connection with particular types of investments, you must still comply with 1.03 (Independence) and rule 9 (Referrals of business).

Rule 20 – Rights and obligations of practice

Introduction

Rule 20 sets out the requirements for certification and provision of information to the Solicitors Regulation Authority, and authorises solicitors, RELs and RFLs to do certain reserved work and immigration work.

Rule 20 – Rights and obligations of practice

20.01 Reserved work and immigration work

Solicitors

(1) As a solicitor, provided that you comply with 20.02(1) you are authorised by the Solicitors Regulation Authority:

    (a) to undertake the following reserved work:

        (i) the exercise of any right of audience which solicitors had immediately before 7 December 1989;

        (ii) the exercise of any additional right of audience if you have a relevant higher courts advocacy qualification awarded by the SRA or another approved regulator;

       (iii)   the conduct of, and the preparation of documents in, court and immigration tribunal proceedings;

       (iv)   the preparation of instruments and the lodging of documents relating to the transfer or charge of land;

       (v)   the preparation of trust deeds disposing of capital;

       (vi)   the preparation of papers on which to found or oppose a grant of probate or a grant of letters of administration;

       (vii)   the administration of oaths and statutory declarations; and

(b)   to undertake immigration services not included under (a) above, and to provide immigration advice.

RELs

(2)   As an REL, you are authorised by the Solicitors Regulation Authority:

    (a)   to undertake the following reserved work:

       (i)   the exercise of any right of audience which solicitors had immediately before 7 December 1989;

       (ii)   the exercise of any additional right of audience provided that you have a relevant higher courts advocacy qualification awarded by the SRA or another approved regulator;

       (iii)   the conduct of, and the preparation of documents in, court and immigration tribunal proceedings;

       (iv)   the preparation of instruments and the lodging of documents relating to the transfer or charge of land, provided you are a member of a profession listed under regulation 12 of the European Communities (Lawyer's Practice) Regulations 2000;

       (v)   the preparation of trust deeds disposing of capital;

       (vi)   the preparation of papers on which to found or oppose a grant of probate or a grant of letters of administration, provided you are a member of a profession listed under regulation 13 of the European Communities (Lawyer's Practice) Regulations 2000;

       (vii)   the administration of oaths and statutory declarations;

    (b)   to undertake immigration services not included under (a) above, and to provide immigration advice.

(3)   When as an REL you exercise a right of audience before a court under (2)(a)(i) or (ii), conduct court litigation under (2)(a)(iii) or prepare court documents under (2)(a)(iii) you must act in conjunction with a solicitor or barrister authorised to do that work.

RFLs

(4)   As an RFL working within 12.03(1) you are authorised by the Solicitors Regulation Authority:

    (a)   to undertake the following reserved work:

       (i)   advocacy before immigration tribunals; and

       (ii)   the conduct of, and the preparation of documents in, immigration tribunal proceedings;

(b)   to undertake immigration services which are not reserved work and are not included under (a) above, and to provide immigration advice.

Recognised bodies

(5)   (a)   A recognised body is authorised by the Solicitors Regulation Authority to undertake the following reserved work:

      (i)   advocacy before a court or immigration tribunal provided the manager or employee exercising the right of audience is authorised by the Solicitors Regulation Authority, or otherwise entitled, to do so;

      (ii)   the conduct of proceedings in a court or immigration tribunal;

      (iii)   the preparation of documents in proceedings before a court or immigration tribunal;

      (iv)   the preparation of instruments and the lodging of documents relating to the transfer or charge of land, provided the body has a manager who is an individual authorised to do that work, or a body corporate with a manager who is authorised to do that work;

      (v)   the preparation of trust deeds disposing of capital;

      (vi)   the preparation of papers on which to found or oppose a grant of probate or a grant of letters of administration, provided the body has a manager who is an individual authorised to do that work, or a body corporate with a manager who is authorised to do that work;

      (vii)   the administration of oaths and statutory declarations.

(b)   A recognised body is authorised to undertake immigration services which are not within (a) above, and to provide immigration advice.

(c)   A recognised body which has an individual working in the practice who is authorised by the Master of the Faculties to do the work is authorised to provide notarial services within paragraph 7 of Schedule 2 to the Legal Services Act 2007.

Recognised sole practitioners

(6)   (a)   A recognised sole practitioner who is a solicitor is authorised by the Solicitors Regulation Authority:

      (i)   to provide any reserved work which the solicitor is authorised to provide under (1)(a) above, and any other advocacy service to the extent that an employee of the firm exercising a right of audience is authorised by the Solicitors Regulation Authority, or otherwise entitled, to do so;

      (ii)   to undertake immigration services which are not within (i) above, and provide immigration advice; and

      (iii)   to provide notarial services within paragraph 7 of Schedule 2 to the Legal Services Act 2007, if the sole practitioner or an employee of the firm is authorised by the Master of the Faculties to do the work.

(b)   A recognised sole practitioner who is an REL is authorised by the Solicitors Regulation Authority:

      (i)   to provide any reserved work which the REL is authorised to provide under (2)(a) above, and any other advocacy service to the extent that an employee of the firm exercising a right of audience is authorised by the Solicitors Regulation Authority, or otherwise entitled, to do so;

(ii) to undertake immigration services which are not within (i) above, and provide immigration advice; and

(iii) to provide notarial services within paragraph 7 of Schedule 2 to the Legal Services Act 2007, if the sole practitioner or an employee of the firm is authorised by the Master of the Faculties to do the work.

20.02 Practising certificates

(1) If you are practising as a solicitor you must, whether practising in a firm or in-house:

(a) have in force a practising certificate issued by the Solicitors Regulation Authority; or

(b) be exempt under section 88 of the Solicitors Act 1974 from holding a practising certificate.

(2) You will be practising as a solicitor if you are involved in legal practice and:

(a) your involvement in the firm or the work depends on your being a solicitor;

(b) you are held out explicitly or implicitly as a practising solicitor;

(c) you are employed explicitly or implicitly as a solicitor; or

(d) you are deemed by section 1A of the Solicitors Act 1974 to be acting as a solicitor.

(3) In (2) above "legal practice" includes not only the practice of law but also the provision of other services such as are provided by solicitors.

(4) If you are a solicitor who was formerly an REL, and you are practising from an office in the UK as a lawyer of an Establishment Directive profession, you must have in force a practising certificate issued by the Solicitors Regulation Authority, even if you are not practising as a solicitor.

20.03 Sole practitioners

(1) If you are a solicitor or REL you must not practise as a sole practitioner unless:

(a) the Solicitors Regulation Authority has first authorised you as a recognised sole practitioner by endorsing your practising certificate or certificate of registration to that effect; or

(b) your practice falls within (2) below and you are therefore exempt from the obligation to be a recognised sole practitioner.

(2) For the purpose of (1) above and section 1B of the Solicitors Act 1974 you are deemed not to be practising as a sole practitioner if:

(a) your practice is conducted entirely from an office or offices outside England and Wales;

(b) your practice consists entirely of work as a temporary or permanent employee and any firm which employs you takes full responsibility for you as an employee; or

(c) your practice consists entirely of:

(i) providing professional services without remuneration for friends, relatives, companies wholly owned by you or your family, or registered charities;

      (ii)   administering oaths and statutory declarations; and/or

      (iii)   activities which could constitute practice but are done in the course of discharging the functions of any of the offices or appointments listed in paragraph (b) of the definition of "Private Practice" in rule 3.1 of the Solicitors' Indemnity Insurance Rules.

(3)   (a)   Within 28 days of the death of a recognised sole practitioner, an emergency application may be made for recognition as a recognised sole practitioner by a solicitor or an REL who is:

      (i)   the sole practitioner's executor;

      (ii)   a practice manager appointed by the sole practitioner's personal representatives; or

      (iii) an employee of the firm;

and if the application is granted, recognition will be deemed to run from the date of death.

    (b)   Recognition in the capacity of personal representative, practice manager or employee will not be renewed for any period after the winding up of the estate or 12 months from the date of death, whichever is the earlier.

20.04 Participation in legal practice

(1)   If you are a solicitor, REL or RFL and you are:

    (a)   a manager, member or owner of:

      (i)   a recognised body; or

      (ii)   a body corporate which is a manager of a recognised body; or

    (b)   employed in England and Wales in connection with the provision of legal services by:

      (i)   a recognised sole practitioner;

      (ii)   a recognised body; or

      (iii) a body corporate which is a manager of a recognised body;

it must be in your capacity as a solicitor, REL or RFL. This does not prevent you practising also as an individual authorised by an approved regulator other than the Solicitors Regulation Authority or providing services as a member of a non-lawyer profession.

(2)   Subject to (3) below, if you are a solicitor, REL or RFL and you are:

    (a)   a manager, member or owner of:

      (i)   an authorised non-SRA firm; or

      (ii)   a body corporate which is a manager of an authorised non-SRA firm; or

    (b)   employed in England and Wales in connection with the provision of legal services by:

      (i)   an authorised non-SRA firm; or

      (ii)   a body corporate which is a manager of an authorised non-SRA firm,

it must be in your capacity as a solicitor, REL or RFL or as an individual authorised by an approved regulator other than the Solicitors Regulation Authority. This does not prevent you practising in both capacities or providing services as a member of a non-lawyer profession in addition to practising as a lawyer.

(3)   If you are a solicitor who is employed by, or is a director of, an authorised non-SRA firm, section 1A of the Solicitors Act 1974 will require you to practise through that firm in the capacity of solicitor, even if also practising in some other capacity.

20.05 Duty to co-operate with the Solicitors Regulation Authority, the Legal Ombudsman and the Legal Complaints Service

(1)   You must deal with the Solicitors Regulation Authority, the Legal Ombudsman and the Legal Complaints Service in an open, prompt and co-operative way.

(2)   You must:

    (a)   provide the Solicitors Regulation Authority with information necessary in order to issue you with a practising certificate, or deal with renewal of registration or renewal of recognition, as appropriate; and

    (b)   during the period your practising certificate, registration or recognition is in force, notify the Authority of any changes to relevant information about you, or your firm or in-house practice.

(3)   As a solicitor, REL, RFL or recognised body you must act promptly to:

    (a)   investigate whether any person may have a claim for redress resulting from an act or omission of yours;

    (b)   provide the Solicitors Regulation Authority with a report on the outcome of such an investigation, identifying persons who may have such a claim;

    (c)   notify such persons that they may have a right of redress against you, providing them with information as to the nature of the possible claim, about the firm's complaints procedures and about the Legal Ombudsman;

    (d)   where you have identified a person who may have a claim for redress, ensure that the matter is dealt with under the firm's complaints procedures as if that person had made a complaint,

if required by the Solicitors Regulation Authority in relation to a matter specified by the Authority.

20.06 Reporting serious misconduct and serious financial difficulty

You must (subject, where necessary, to your client's consent) report to the Solicitors Regulation Authority if:

    (a)   you become aware of serious misconduct by a solicitor, an REL, an RFL, a recognised body, a manager of a recognised body, or an employee of a recognised body or recognised sole practitioner;

    (b)   you have reason to doubt the integrity of a solicitor, an REL or an RFL, a manager of a recognised body or an employee of a recognised body or recognised sole practitioner; or

    (c)   you have reason to believe that a solicitor, an REL, an RFL, a recognised body, a manager of a recognised body, or a firm is in serious financial difficulty which could put the public at risk.

20.07 Obstructing complaints

(1)   You must not try to hinder or prevent a person who wishes to report your conduct to the Solicitors Regulation Authority or the Legal Ombudsman from doing so.

(2)   You must not victimise a person for reporting your conduct to the Solicitors Regulation Authority, the Legal Complaints Service or the Legal Ombudsman.

(3)   You must not on your own or on your clients' behalf enter into an agreement which would attempt to preclude the Solicitors Regulation Authority, the Legal Complaints Service or the Legal Ombudsman from investigating any actual or potential allegation of professional misconduct.

(4)   Unless you can properly allege malice, you must not issue defamation proceedings in respect of a complaint to the Solicitors Regulation Authority, the Legal Complaints Service or the Legal Ombudsman.

20.08 Production of documents, information and explanations

(1)   You must promptly comply with:

(a)   a written notice from the Solicitors Regulation Authority that you must produce for inspection by the appointee of the Solicitors Regulation Authority all documents held by you or held under your control and all information and explanations requested:

(i)   in connection with your practice; or

(ii)   in connection with any trust of which you are, or formerly were, a trustee;

for the purpose of ascertaining whether any person subject to these rules is complying with or has complied with any provision of these or any other rules, codes or mandatory guidance made or issued by the Solicitors Regulation Authority; and

(b)   a notice given by the Solicitors Regulation Authority in accordance with section 44B or 44BA of the Solicitors Act 1974 for the provision of documents, information or explanations.

(2)   You must provide any necessary permissions for information to be given so as to enable the appointee of the Solicitors Regulation Authority to:

(a)   prepare a report on the documents produced under (1) above; and

(b)   seek verification from clients, staff and the banks, building societies or other financial institutions used by you.

(3)   You must comply with all requests from the Solicitors Regulation Authority or its appointee as to:

(a)   the form in which you produce any documents you hold electronically; and

(b)   photocopies of any documents to take away.

(4)   A notice under this rule is deemed to be duly served:

(a)   on the date on which it is delivered to or left at your address;

(b)   on the date on which it is sent electronically to your e-mail or fax address; or

(c)   seven days after it has been sent by post or document exchange to your last notified practising address.

20.09 Dealing with claims

(1)   If you are a sole practitioner or a manager of a firm and you discover an act or omission which could give rise to a claim, you must inform the client.

(2)   If a client makes a claim against you, or notifies an intention to do so, or if you discover an act or omission which could give rise to a claim, you must:

(a) inform the client that independent advice should be sought (unless the client's loss, if any, is trivial and you promptly remedy that loss);

(b) consider whether a conflict of interests has arisen, and if so not act further for the client in the matter giving rise to the claim; and

(c) notify your compulsory professional indemnity insurer under the Solicitors' Indemnity Insurance Rules or 15.26 or, if appropriate, the Solicitors Indemnity Fund Ltd.

20.10 Compliance with conditions

If you are a solicitor, REL, RFL or recognised body you must comply with any condition which the Solicitors Regulation Authority (or previously the Law Society) has imposed on your practising certificate, registration or recognition.

Guidance to rule 20 – Rights and obligations of practice

Scope of rule 20

1. In summary, rule 20:

(a) formally authorises solicitors, RELs, RFLs, recognised bodies and recognised sole practitioners to do specific types of reserved work and immigration work;

(b) requires practising solicitors to have a practising certificate unless they are exempt under section 88 of the Solicitors Act 1974;

(c) sets out the requirement that a solicitor or REL who wishes to practise as a sole practitioner must be authorised as a recognised sole practitioner;

(d) requires that a solicitor's, REL's or RFL's participation in a law firm must be as a practising lawyer;

(e) requires co-operation with regulators in providing information;

(f) requires reporting of serious misconduct;

(g) requires fair dealing with clients in relation to claims and complaints;

(h) requires compliance with conditions imposed by the SRA.

Reserved work and immigration work – 20.01

Solicitors

2. Provided you hold a practising certificate or are exempt under section 88 of the Solicitors Act, rule 20.01 authorises you to conduct advocacy (but note that for advocacy in the higher courts you will need to have obtained a qualification to exercise a right of audience), litigation, reserved instrument activities, probate activities, immigration work and to administer oaths.

RELs

3. If you are an REL 20.01 authorises you to do the same work as solicitors, but note that:

(a) you can only exercise higher rights of audience if you have a higher courts advocacy qualification;

(b) if you are undertaking advocacy or litigation or drawing court documents you must act in conjunction with a solicitor and/or barrister authorised to do that work;

(c) only an REL from certain jurisdictions can do reserved instrument activities relating to conveyancing or probate:

   (i) under regulation 12 of the European Communities (Lawyer's Practice) Regulations 2000 (SI 2000/1119), only RELs qualified in Cyprus, the Czech Republic, Denmark, Finland, Hungary, Iceland, the Irish Republic, Liechtenstein, Norway, Slovakia and Sweden are entitled to do reserved conveyancing work in England and Wales; and

   (ii) under regulation 13 of those regulations, only RELs qualified in Austria, Cyprus, Denmark, Finland, Germany, Iceland, the Irish Republic, Liechtenstein, Norway, Slovakia and Sweden are entitled to do reserved probate work in England and Wales.

RFLs

4. If you are an RFL you are authorised:

(a) to do advocacy before immigration tribunals;

(b) to conduct, and prepare documents in, immigration tribunal proceedings;

(c) to do all other immigration work which is not reserved work.

Note that RFLs are not authorised to do immigration work before the courts.

Recognised bodies

5. Recognised bodies are authorised to do the same reserved work as solicitors, but note that a recognised body can only:

(a) undertake higher court advocacy work if it has a manager or employee entitled to do that work;

(b) reserved instrument activities relating to conveyancing, or probate activities if it has a manager who is an individual entitled to do that work, or which is a body corporate with a manager who is entitled to do that work;

(c) notarial work if it has an individual working in the practice who is authorised to do the work.

Recognised sole practitioners

6. Recognised sole practitioners are authorised to:

(a) undertake the reserved work the solicitor or REL sole practitioner is authorised to do as an individual;

(b) exercise advocacy rights additional to those the solicitor or REL sole practitioner is authorised to exercise as an individual if an employee exercising the right is authorised by the SRA or otherwise entitled to do so;

(c) undertake notarial work if the sole practitioner or an employee is authorised by the Master of Faculties to do the work.

Reserved work

7. Reserved work is work that is defined in Schedule 2 to the Legal Services Act 2007 as

a "reserved legal activity". Certain categories of reserved work (rights of audience in chambers, reserved instrument activities and probate activities) can be done by an unqualified person under the supervision of a manager or fellow employee qualified to do that work – see Schedule 3 to the Legal Services Act.

Immigration work

8.   Immigration work (immigration advice and immigration services) is restricted to certain persons under the Immigration and Asylum Act 1999. Immigration services relating to courts or immigration tribunals are reserved work – advocacy, the conduct of cases, and the preparation of papers. The court work is subject to the normal restriction on court work. Immigration Tribunal work can be done by RFLs who are practising as such. Other immigration work is not reserved work, but can only be done by an authorised person such as a solicitor, a barrister, a legal executive, a member of an Establishment Directive profession, or an RFL practising as such, or under the supervision of an authorised person, or under an exemption given by the Office of the Immigration Services Commissioner.

Financial services

9.   The Financial Services and Markets Act 2000 reserves the provision of "regulated activities" to persons authorised by the Financial Services Authority (FSA). Certain "regulated activities", ancillary to the provision of a professional service, are exempt from regulation by the FSA when carried out by solicitors' or RELs' firms – see the Solicitors' Financial Services (Scope) Rules. Note that the firm must be a recognised body or recognised sole practitioner to rely on this exemption. For the definition of "regulated activity" see 19.01(4).

Practising certificates – 20.02

10.   Rule 20.02 includes, in rule form, the requirements of section 1 of the Solicitors Act 1974. The section reads:

"No person shall be qualified to act as a solicitor unless –

(a)   he has been admitted as a solicitor, and

(b)   his name is on the roll, and

(c)   he has in force a certificate issued by the Society in accordance with the provisions of this Part authorising him to practise as a solicitor (in this Act referred to as a 'practising certificate')."

The issuing of practising certificates under Part II of the Act is the responsibility of the SRA.

11.   Under section 1A of the Solicitors Act, a solicitor is always deemed to be acting as a solicitor if he or she is employed, in connection with the provision of any legal services, by a solicitor with a practising certificate, any partnership with at least one member who is a solicitor with a practising certificate, a recognised body, or an individual or firm authorised by any approved regulator under the Legal Services Act 2007.

12.   If you practise as a solicitor, whether in a firm or in-house, without having a practising certificate, you will commit a criminal offence, as well as a breach of the rules, unless you are entitled to rely on the exemption in section 88 of the Solicitors Act.

13.   Section 88 of the Solicitors Act 1974 exempts from the requirement to hold a practising certificate the solicitor to certain public authorities, and a solicitor who is the "clerk" to such a solicitor. The section reads:

"(1)   Nothing in this Act shall prejudice or affect any rights or privileges of the solicitor to the Treasury, any other public department, the Church Commissioners or the Duchy of Cornwall, or require any such officer or any clerk or officer appointed to act for him to be admitted or enrolled or to hold a practising certificate in any case where it would not have been necessary for him to be admitted or enrolled or to hold such a certificate if this Act had not been passed.

(1A)   The exemption from the requirement to hold a practising certificate conferred by subsection (1) above shall not apply to solicitors who are Crown Prosecutors.

(2)   Sections 31 and 32(1) shall not apply to, and nothing in this Act shall prejudice or affect any rights or privileges which immediately before the commencement of this Act attached to the office of the Solicitor of the City of London."

14.   Although section 88 of the Solicitors Act 1974 preserves certain pre-existing rights, privileges and exemptions, it does not say what these are. They are to be found in a number of statutory provisions of some age, each conferring different rights, privileges or exemptions on different persons. Some of the older provisions do not fit easily into modern conditions and it is not possible to provide a full list of exemptions. The view of the SRA Board is as follows.

(a)   A solicitor is exempt who holds office as the solicitor (i.e. the principal solicitor) to:

    (i)   the Treasury;

    (ii)   any other public department;

    (iii)   the Church Commissioners; and

    (iv)   the Duchy of Cornwall; or

    (v)   a solicitor who is a clerk or officer appointed to act for one of the above.

(b)   The exemption relates to the capacity and employment of the solicitor. Thus, for instance, a solicitor who holds office as the principal solicitor to a public department, but in a different capacity or employment administers oaths, cannot rely on the section 88 exemption in respect of that other capacity or employment.

(c)   There is no definition of "public department" in the Solicitors Act. In the absence of a definition, the SRA Board takes the view that "any other public department" would include any department of central government in the UK, the National Assembly of Wales and any "non-ministerial department", but would not include other agencies or "non-departmental public bodies".

Assistance in determining whether a department or agency is a "non-ministerial department" or a "non-departmental public body" can be found on the Civil Service website – **www.civilservice.gov.uk**.

(d)   Section 88(1A) of the Solicitors Act requires a solicitor who is a Crown Prosecutor to hold a practising certificate.

Being held out as a practising solicitor – 20.02(2)(b)

15.   Being described on your firm's notepaper or website as a member of the Law Society is an example of being held out "implicitly" as a solicitor.

16.   There is a presumption that you are practising as a solicitor if you are held out (explicitly or implicitly) as a solicitor whilst providing lawyer-like services. The same presumption arises if you are described as a lawyer in such a context, if you have no other legal qualification to justify that description. It is possible in some circumstances to rebut the presumption by ensuring that some such words as "non-practising" are used whenever you are held out as a solicitor or lawyer. However, you cannot rebut the presumption if you rely on being a solicitor in the context of legal practice – for example in order:

(a)   to be a partner in a firm of lawyers;

(b)   to be employed as a solicitor or lawyer;

(c)   to do work in England and Wales which is reserved to solicitors;

(d)   to do work in another jurisdiction which is reserved to lawyers;

(e)   to be a registered foreign legal consultant in another jurisdiction; or

(f)   to be a registered lawyer in another European profession under the Establishment Directive.

Instructing counsel is not restricted to any particular category of person by statute. However, barristers only accept instructions made professionally on behalf of clients from solicitors and limited categories of non-solicitors – see the Bar Standards Board's website for details – **www.barstandardsboard.org.uk**. If you instruct counsel as a solicitor, you will be practising as a solicitor and must have a practising certificate.

17.   If you are dually qualified you may be practising as a member of both professions simultaneously, either through a single combined practice, or through two separate practices. In the latter case you would need separate notepaper, etc., to distinguish the two practices.

18.   The context of a description can make a real difference as to whether you are held out as a practising solicitor or not. For example:

(a)   if you are running a web-based or telephone advice service, and describe yourself as a solicitor (without qualifying the description with words such as "non-practising"), you will need a practising certificate; and

(b)   if your only work is as an academic and writer, and you have written a legal textbook in which you are described as a solicitor or as a lawyer on the title page, you will not need a practising certificate. This is because there is no context of services normally provided by practising solicitors.

Retirement from practice

19.   You may continue to need a practising certificate after you retire, depending on how complete your retirement is. If you have closed your firm, but will continue to hold money for clients only while you submit bills of costs and close your practice accounts, you will still be subject to the Solicitors' Accounts Rules 1998. However, if that is all you are doing you will not need a practising certificate, provided that a solicitor with a practising certificate authorises any withdrawals from your client account.

20.   If you have retired but continue to do some work, you may need a practising certificate. For example:

(a)   you must have a practising certificate if you continue to work in a firm in connection with the provision of legal services. This would include being a consultant or supervising fee earners, even if you only help out on an occasional basis or cover a professional colleague's holiday absences; or

(b)   you must have a practising certificate if you continue to undertake any reserved work.

21.   If you are completely retired from all legal work you may still need a practising certificate if, for example:

(a)   you continue to be held out as a solicitor or lawyer by your former firm; or

(b)   your name appears on your firm's notepaper as a "consultant", unless it is made clear on the notepaper that you are not practising.

APPENDIX 21

Sole practitioners – 20.03

22.   From 1 July 2009, rule 20.03 prohibits a solicitor or REL from practising as a sole practitioner in England and Wales unless authorised by the SRA as a recognised sole practitioner or exempt under the rule. Existing sole practitioners who qualify for recognition will be "passported" to recognition as of 1 July 2009. If you wish to set up in sole practice on or after that date you will need to apply to the SRA for your practising certificate (in the case of a solicitor) or your certificate of registration (in the case of an REL) to be endorsed to that effect.

23.   The rule exempts solicitors and RELs from this requirement whose practice:

   (a)   is conducted entirely overseas;

   (b)   consists entirely of work for firms which employ and take full responsibility for them (e.g. consultants and locums);

   (c)   consists entirely of providing free professional services to friends, relatives, wholly owned companies or registered charities, administering oaths and statutory declarations;

   (d)   consists entirely of activities done in the course of discharging the functions of certain offices or appointments.

24.   The rule allows a period of 28 days from the death of a recognised sole practitioner to make an emergency application for recognition as a recognised sole practitioner by a solicitor or REL who is:

   (a)   the sole practitioner's executor;

   (b)   a practice manager appointed by the sole practitioner's personal representatives; or

   (c)   an employee of the firm.

   If the application is granted, recognition is deemed to run from the date of death.

25.   Recognition in the capacity of personal representative, practice manager or employee will not be renewed for any period after the winding up of the estate or 12 months from the date of death, whichever is the earlier.

Participation in legal practice – 20.04

26.   Rule 20.04 provides that a solicitor, REL or RFL who is a manager, member or owner of a recognised body, or who is employed in England and Wales in connection with the provision of legal services by a recognised body, a recognised sole practitioner or an authorised non-SRA firm must participate as a solicitor, REL or RFL (even if also in some other capacity as well).

Duty to co-operate with the Solicitors Regulation Authority and the Legal Complaints Service – 20.05

27.   Rule 20.05 requires you to deal with any communication from the SRA or the Legal Complaints Service properly. This means that you will need to respond promptly and substantively to communications when appropriate – for example, to a letter referring to a complaint made against you or a member of your firm.

28.   The duty imposed by 20.05 may be limited by your legal obligations to your clients or others, for example your obligation to protect clients' confidentiality and privilege.

29.   You should note that failure to comply with a request for an explanation of any matter in relation to your conduct may result in the imposition of conditions on a recognised body's recognition, a solicitor's practising certificate or an REL's or RFL's registration, or even refusal by the SRA to issue a practising certificate or renew a registration.

30. Rules 1.02 (Integrity) and 1.06 (Public confidence) require you to act with integrity and to refrain from behaviour likely to diminish the trust the public places in you or the profession. You should therefore, unless there is good reason to the contrary, comply with binding orders or requests for information from the Legal Services Ombudsman. Similarly, it may be appropriate, subject to any overriding duties, to assist the Bar Council or other regulatory body when they are investigating the conduct of a member of their profession. If you are an individual authorised by an approved regulator other than the SRA, you must comply with that regulator's requirements.

31. Abusive communications and unreasonable attempts to delay an investigation or enquiry are inconsistent with the co-operation required by 20.05.

32. Rule 20.05(3) requires solicitors, RELs, RFLs and recognised bodies to take prompt action to comply with an SRA requirement in relation to a specified matter:

    (a) to investigate whether anyone may have a claim for redress;

    (b) to provide the SRA with a report identifying those who may have a claim for redress;

    (c) notify those who may have a claim for redress, providing them with relevant information concerning the complaints process;

    (d) deal with the matter under your firm's complaints procedures as if the person with a claim had made a complaint.

Reporting serious misconduct and serious financial difficulty – 20.06

33. The purpose of 20.06 is to protect the public and the integrity of the profession. Often, professional colleagues will be aware of serious misconduct and/or risk arising from a firm's financial problems before any complaint has been made, and if the SRA is notified it can take timely action. The SRA's Fraud and Confidential Intelligence Bureau will consider information of this nature on an anonymous basis if requested.

34. Unless you are required by law to report a matter, 20.06 does not apply to confidential and/or privileged information another lawyer discloses to you:

    (a) as your client or the client of your firm; or

    (b) when seeking advice from a confidential helpline, such as the Solicitors' Assistance Scheme or Lawcare.

35. You will not breach 20.06 if you take no action because you know that someone else has already reported a matter of which you are aware.

36. Whether or not "misconduct" can be considered "serious", and whether or not a firm's financial difficulties could put the public at risk, will depend on the circumstances. In general, any conduct involving dishonesty or deception or a serious criminal offence would amount to "serious misconduct". If in your judgement a firm's financial difficulties present a risk to its clients or to others, you should report the matter, and can do so on a confidential basis if you wish.

37. If reporting misconduct which has taken place within your own firm and which may give rise to a claim, you should also consider your obligations to your insurers. See also note 54 of the guidance to rule 3 (Conflict of interests).

38. If making a report about another lawyer or firm would involve disclosing confidential information, you should obtain your client's consent before proceeding.

39. You should exercise care where there may be evidence of money laundering activities (see the Proceeds of Crime Act 2002, other relevant statutes and regulations, and guidance issued by the Law Society and the SRA on this subject).

APPENDIX 21

Obstructing complaints – 20.07

40.   No agreement, whether with a client or a third party, can affect the rights of the SRA or the Legal Complaints Service to investigate misconduct or to consider complaints. To attempt to make such an agreement is a breach of 20.07. Examples of situations that would breach 20.07 are:

(a)   accepting instructions to act for a client which involve any agreement preventing the SRA or the Legal Complaints Service from investigating your conduct or the conduct of a member of your firm;

(b)   improperly demanding, offering or accepting payment in return for not reporting alleged misconduct;

(c)   harassing or bringing improper pressure to bear on a complainant or potential complainant; and

(d)   issuing proceedings for defamation against a client or former client in relation to material contained in a complaint to the SRA or the Legal Complaints Service, unless you are alleging malice.

41.   The following, however, would not breach 20.07:

(a)   proper attempts to persuade the client that the client's complaint is unfounded; and

(b)   in a case of inadequate professional services, genuine attempts to propose an agreement to compensate the aggrieved client.

Production of documents, information and explanations – 20.08

42.   The SRA will only exercise its powers under 20.08 in accordance with the law, in pursuit of a legitimate aim and proportionate to that aim.

43.   The SRA may use or disclose any information obtained under 20.08 and the report prepared by its appointee:

(a)   in proceedings before the Solicitors Disciplinary Tribunal;

(b)   to the police, the Crown Prosecution Service or the Serious Fraud Office for use in investigating the matter and in any subsequent prosecution, if it appears that you or any manager, employee, member or owner of your firm may have committed a serious criminal offence;

(c)   to your regulatory body in your home state or states if you are an REL or RFL;

(d)   to the regulatory body with which you are registered, if you are a solicitor registered under the Establishment Directive;

(e)   to the regulatory body of any manager or employee of your firm; and/or

(f)   to the professional body of which the accountant who has signed the firm's accountant's report is a member, or by which the accountant is regulated (and the information and report may also be taken into account by the SRA in relation to a possible disqualification of that person from signing an accountant's report in future).

44.   Note that sections 44B and 44BA of the Solicitors Act 1974 give the SRA power to require the production of documents, give information and to provide explanations for the purpose of investigation whether there has been professional misconduct or regulatory non-compliance.

Dealing with claims – 20.09

45. The aim of 20.09 is to ensure that a claim or a potential claim is dealt with fairly and efficiently. In particular, the client should be advised at the earliest possible opportunity of an act or omission which could give rise to a claim. "Claim" has the meaning given in the Solicitors' Indemnity Insurance Rules (Minimum Terms and Conditions).

46. You must consider whether a conflict of interests has arisen between your interests and your client's. It will be rare for there to be no conflict. Where there is, you must refuse to act further in the matter.

47. Under 2.05 firms must operate a complaints handling procedure. Complaints should be dealt with under that procedure, where appropriate, rather than as claims. For example, if your client makes a complaint purely relating to poor service, it would rarely be appropriate to treat that complaint as a claim.

48. In order that a claim can be dealt with efficiently, you should consult the qualifying insurer or ARP Manager in accordance with the policy terms. In some circumstances, you may need to take limited steps to preserve your client's position.

49. There is no general duty for you to keep under review work which has been concluded. However, if you discover an act or omission which could give rise to a claim relating to a former client, you should notify your compulsory professional indemnity insurer (or, if appropriate, SIF) and seek their advice as to what further steps to take.

50. Under the Solicitors' Indemnity Insurance Rules a firm must provide details of its insurer to a person who asserts a claim against the firm. The details are the name and address of the qualifying insurer and the policy number. It is good practice for you also to provide these details to a potential claimant if you discover an act or omission which could give rise to a claim. The SRA may disclose information regarding a firm's qualifying insurer where it considers it appropriate to do so to any person asserting a claim against the firm.

51. You and your insurers should also comply with the terms of the professional negligence pre-action protocol (available from the website of the Ministry of Justice).

52. The aim of the protocol is to establish a framework in which there is an early exchange of information between the parties so that a claim can be fully investigated and, if possible, resolved without the need for litigation. This includes:

    (a) ensuring that the parties are on an equal footing;

    (b) saving expense;

    (c) dealing with the dispute in ways which are proportionate:

        (i) to the amount of money involved;

        (ii) to the importance of the case;

        (iii) to the complexity of the issues; and

        (iv) to the financial position of each party; and

    (d) ensuring that the claim is dealt with expeditiously and fairly.

53. The court can make an order for costs against a party for failure to comply with the protocol. While normally it would be a matter for the insurer to ensure that the protocol is complied with, you should be aware of it when asked to provide information to the insurer, and in the occasional circumstances where an insurer may agree to you handling the claim.

Compliance with conditions – 20.10

54.   The SRA has powers to impose conditions on your practising certificate, registration as an RFL or REL, on your recognition as a recognised body, or on the practising certificate or registration of a recognised sole practitioner. You must comply with any condition.

In-house solicitors

55.   If you are an in-house solicitor, you do not have to hold a practising certificate unless:

   (a)   you are held out or employed explicitly as a solicitor, or held out or employed implicitly as a solicitor by using a description or title such as "lawyer" or "counsel";

   (b)   you do reserved work (other than at the direction and under the supervision of a fellow employee as provided in the Solicitors Act 1974 or under Schedule 3 to the Legal Services Act 2007);

   (c)   you rely on your qualification as a solicitor in order to instruct counsel;

   (d)   you fulfil the role of a "person qualified to supervise" in the limited circumstances set out in 5.02(1)(c) (law centres), (d)(i) (legal aid) or (d)(ii) (litigation or advocacy for members of the public); or

   (e)   you authorise the withdrawal of money from a client account, under rule 23(1)(a) of the Solicitors' Accounts Rules 1998.

56.   Solicitors employed by authorised non-SRA firms (such as a firm of licensed conveyancers or patent agents) are not treated as in-house solicitors for the purposes of the rules. They can do work, within the scope of the firm's authorisation, for clients of the firm as well as for the firm itself. They can also do a wider range of work for the firm itself, related bodies, work colleagues or pro bono. See 12.01(1)(d).

Rule 21 – Separate businesses

Introduction

A "separate business" is a business which is not a recognised body, a recognised sole practitioner, an authorised non-SRA firm or a firm within 12.01(2)(a)–(d) or 12.02(2)(a)–(d) but which offers a service or services that could properly be offered by a recognised body. Rule 21 regulates the interface between the practice of a solicitor and the operation of a solicitor's separate business:

●   to ensure that members of the public are not confused or misled into believing that a business carried on by a solicitor, REL or RFL is regulated by the Solicitors Regulation Authority or another approved regulator when it is not;

●   to ensure that the protections afforded to the clients of practising lawyers are in place in relation to certain mainstream legal services; and

●   to prevent a solicitor severing part of a case or matter in such a way that the client loses statutory protections.

The rule as it applies to your overseas practice is modified by 15.21.

Rule 21 – Separate businesses

21.01 General

(1) If you are practising from an office in England and Wales as a solicitor, REL, RFL or recognised body, or if you are a manager or employee of a recognised body, or an employee of a recognised sole practitioner, you must comply with the provisions of this rule in relation to:

    (a) services which may not be provided through a separate business;

    (b) services which may be provided through a separate business or (subject to these rules) through a firm or in-house practice; and

    (c) services which fall outside the scope of a solicitor's practice but which may be provided in conjunction with a firm or in-house practice.

(2) This rule applies to your involvement in any separate business whether the separate business is in England and Wales or outside the jurisdiction.

(3) For the avoidance of doubt, in this rule "practising" includes practising as an in-house solicitor or an in-house REL.

21.02 Services which may not be provided through a separate business

(1) Subject to (2) below, you must not provide any of the following services through a separate business:

    (a) the conduct of any matter which could come before a court, tribunal or inquiry, whether or not proceedings are started;

    (b) advocacy before a court, tribunal or inquiry;

    (c) instructing counsel in any part of the UK;

    (d) immigration advice or immigration services;

    (e) any activity in relation to conveyancing, applications for probate or letters of administration, or drawing trust deeds or court documents, which is reserved to solicitors and others under the Solicitors Act 1974;

    (f) drafting wills;

    (g) acting as nominee, trustee or executor in England and Wales;

    (h) legal advice not included above; or

    (i) drafting legal documents not included above.

Exceptions

(2) The provisions of (1) above do not apply to prohibit you from providing services through a separate business:

    (a) which carries on your practice as a lawyer of another jurisdiction;

    (b) which carries on your business as a parliamentary agent;

    (c) which is a wholly owned nominee company operated as a subsidiary but necessary part of the work of a separate business providing financial services; or

(d)   which provides legal advice and/or drafts legal documents within (1)(h) and/or (i) above, as a subsidiary but necessary part of some other service which is one of the main services of the separate business.

However, you must comply with the requirements of 21.05 in relation to any such separate business.

21.03 Services which may be provided in conjunction with a firm or in-house practice

(1)   The following services extend beyond, or fall outside, the scope of a solicitor's practice but you may provide such services in conjunction with a firm or in-house practice:

(a)   educational and training activities; and

(b)   authorship, journalism and publishing.

(2)   Such services are not provided through a separate business for the purpose of this rule.

21.04 Services which may be provided (subject to these rules) either through a firm or in-house practice, or through a separate business

(1)   You may provide the following services either (subject to these rules) through a firm or in-house practice, or through a separate business:

(a)   alternative dispute resolution;

(b)   financial services (except those that cannot form part of a solicitor's practice);

(c)   estate agency;

(d)   management consultancy;

(e)   company secretarial services;

(f)   acting as a parliamentary agent;

(g)   practising as a lawyer of another jurisdiction;

(h)   acting as a bailiff;

(i)   acting as nominee, trustee or executor outside England and Wales; or

(j)   providing any other business, advisory or agency service which could be provided (subject to these rules) through a firm or in-house practice but is not included in 21.02.

(2)   If you provide any service listed in (1) above through a separate business you must comply with 21.05.

21.05 Safeguards in relation to a separate business

(1)   If you provide services through a separate business you must do nothing in the course of practice, or in the course of making referrals to the business or accepting referrals from the business, which would breach rule 1 (Core duties).

(2)   You must ensure that the following safeguards are in place in relation to a separate business which offers or provides any of the services listed in 21.04(1):

(a)   the separate business must not be held out or described in such a way as to suggest that the separate business is carrying on a practice regulated by the Solicitors Regulation Authority or another approved regulator, or that any lawyer connected with your firm is providing services through the separate business as a practising lawyer regulated by the Solicitors Regulation Authority or another approved regulator;

(b)   all paperwork, documents, records or files relating to the separate business and its customers must be kept separate from those of any firm or in-house practice, even where a customer of the separate business is also a client of the firm or in-house practice;

(c)   the client account or other account used to hold money for the clients of any firm or in-house practice must not be used to hold money for the separate business, or for customers of the separate business in their capacity as such;

(d)   if the separate business shares premises, office accommodation or reception staff with any firm or in-house practice:

   (i)   the areas used by the firm or in-house practice must be clearly differentiated from the areas used by the separate business; and

   (ii)   all customers of the separate business must be informed that it is not regulated by the Solicitors Regulation Authority and that the statutory protections attaching to clients of a lawyer regulated by the Authority are not available to them as customers of that business;

(e)   if you or your firm refer a client to the separate business, the client must first be informed of your interest in the separate business, that the separate business is not regulated by the Solicitors Regulation Authority, and that the statutory protections attaching to clients of a lawyer regulated by the Authority are not available to them as customers of the separate business; and

(f)   if the separate business is an estate agency, then without prejudice to the provisions of these rules regarding conflicts of interests, neither you nor any firm through which you practise may act in the conveyance for the buyer of any property sold through the estate agency unless:

   (i)   the firm shares ownership of the estate agency with at least one other business in which neither you nor the firm have any financial interest;

   (ii)   neither you nor anyone else in the firm is dealing with or has dealt with the sale of the seller's property for the separate business; and

   (iii) the buyer has given written consent to you or the firm acting, after your financial interest in the sale going through has been explained to the buyer.

Guidance to rule 21 – Separate businesses

1.   A separate business is a business which is not a firm (recognised body, recognised sole practitioner, authorised non-SRA firm or overseas law firm) or an in-house practice but which offers a service or services that could properly be offered by a firm or in-house practice – for instance, title checks, searches, etc. for the provision of Home Information Packs.

2.   Providing a service through a separate business means having any active involvement in a separate business which provides that service – see the definitions of "separate business" and "providing a service through a separate business" in rule 24 (Interpretation). You are not providing services through a separate business solely by virtue of being a non-executive director of, or having an insignificant shareholding in, a company which provides, for example, financial services.

3.   In England and Wales there is no legal impediment to a non-lawyer giving legal advice,

APPENDIX 21

drafting wills or administering estates, or running a business which provides such services. However, the client of a firm or an in-house practice has the protections afforded by these rules, the SRA's regulatory powers, the Compensation Fund and (if a recognised body or recognised sole practitioner provides the service) indemnity insurance under the SRA's compulsory indemnity scheme. The customers of a business which is not a firm or an in-house practice will not have the same protections.

4.   Rule 21 applies to you if you are a solicitor, REL or RFL practising from an office in England and Wales, or a recognised body, a manager of a recognised body, or an employee of a recognised body or recognised sole practitioner, practising in England and Wales. The rule does two things:

   (a)   it prohibits you from "hiving off" the kind of services a member of the public would expect you to provide as a lawyer regulated by the SRA or another approved regulator (i.e. core legal services) to a business which is not so regulated; and

   (b)   it requires you to institute safeguards in relation to other services which you are allowed to "hive off" (the kind of services a member of the public would not necessarily expect to be provided only by a lawyer regulated by the SRA but which are "solicitor-like" services).

   The above applies even if the separate business is overseas.

5.   The purposes of the rule are:

   (a)   to ensure that members of the public are not confused or misled into believing that a business is regulated by the SRA or another approved regulator when it is not;

   (b)   to ensure that the protections afforded to the clients of a practising lawyer or firm are in place in relation to core legal services; and

   (c)   to prevent a practising lawyer or firm severing part of a case or matter in such a way that the client loses statutory protections.

6.   If you are practising wholly outside England and Wales, the provisions of this rule do not apply to you but you must comply with 15.21(2) in relation to your involvement in any separate business.

7.   If you are an in-house solicitor, and you have a separate business in addition to your in-house practice you must comply with rule 21 or, if you are employed outside England and Wales, with 15.21(2).

Business as a professional not regulated by the SRA – 21.02(2)(a) and (b)

8.   Although you may not in general provide core legal services through a separate business, you may have a separate business as a parliamentary agent, or as a lawyer of another jurisdiction. Such a business may undertake some of the activities listed in 21.02(1), and 21.02(2) states that you are not prohibited from having such a business. The safeguards for a separate business as set out in 21.05 are intended to make it clear that the business is governed by a different legal and regulatory regime from that governing services provided by solicitors.

9.   Note that a solicitor who was formerly an REL, when practising in the UK as a lawyer of an Establishment Directive profession, is subject to the rules of professional conduct and the SRA's regulatory procedures as if he or she were practising as a solicitor, and such a practice would not therefore be regarded as a separate business – see 15.01(2)(b)(v), 20.02(4) and 23.01(1)(e), and regulation 36 of the Establishment Directive Regulations.

Legal advice as a necessary and subsidiary part of another service

10. The prohibitions on providing legal advice and drafting legal documents through separate businesses do not apply when the advice or drafting is a necessary but subsidiary part of another service which you are allowed to provide through a separate business. An example would be a management consultancy business giving ancillary advice on obligations under the Data Protection Act 1998.

Executor, trustee and nominee companies

11. You are not allowed to provide executor, trustee or nominee services in England and Wales through a separate business. An executor, trustee or nominee company operated in conjunction with the practice of a firm must be a recognised body, because:

    (a) a company has a separate legal identity, so if a firm owns a company, and the company provides a service to the firm's clients, it is the company and not the firm that provides the service; and

    (b) a company providing a service for clients of a firm will constitute a "business" for the purpose of rule 21, even if the company is dormant for Companies Acts purposes, and even if no charge is made to clients for its services.

12. You are allowed to have a separate business which provides executor, trustee and nominee services outside England and Wales. If you do, you must put in place the safeguards required. You can, on the other hand, run an executor, trustee or nominee company which provides services only outside England and Wales as an overseas corporate firm within rule 12 (Framework of practice).

Companies providing company secretarial services

13. Your firm may own a company whose purpose is to provide company secretarial services to clients of the firm. Such a company may either be operated as a legal practice (and must therefore be a recognised body), or it may be operated as a "separate business" (and must therefore be operated in compliance with rule 21 and may also need to be separately regulated by HMRC under the anti-money laundering legislation).

Service companies

14. A service company operated for the purpose of providing services only to carry out administrative functions concerned with the running of the firm which wholly owns it, such as the employment of staff, the hiring of premises, furniture and equipment and general maintenance, is not a separate business, and does not require to be a recognised body because it is not regarded as practising.

15. A company incorporated by an individual solicitor to provide that solicitor's services to a firm or in-house practice is not a separate business. If the circumstances of the individual and the company fulfil the requirements of paragraph (c)(iii) of the definition of an "employee" in rule 24, such a company will not be regarded as practising and so will not be required to become a recognised body.

Marketing and description of a separate business

16. Under 21.05(2)(a) your separate business must not be held out or described in such a way as to suggest that the separate business is carrying on a practice regulated by the SRA or another approved regulator, or that any lawyer connected with your firm is providing services through the separate business as a practising lawyer regulated by the SRA or another approved regulator. Unlike the more specific safeguards in 21.05(2)(b)

to (f), this prohibition has a wide application and amounts to an absolute requirement to take all necessary steps to ensure that customers and third parties dealing with the separate business are not misled. However, it is not intended to prohibit you from running a separate business in association with your firm or mentioning your firm, or the fact that you are a lawyer, in connection with your separate business. The provision will have the following implications:

(a) You could not properly carry on your separate business under the same name as your firm, because that would create too strong a suggestion that the business, like the firm, is regulated by the SRA or other approved regulator. On the other hand, 21.05(2)(a) does not prohibit you from running your separate business in association with your firm, or using a similar or related name or "brand". However, in order to comply with 21.05(2)(a) you would need to differentiate properly the separate business from your firm and make it clear on the face of any notepaper or other publicity of the separate business using a similar or related name that the services of the separate business are not the services of practising lawyers.

(b) You could not properly market your separate business to potential customers on the basis that it is owned and run by practising solicitors and/or RELs, because that would create too strong a suggestion that the services of the separate business are provided by practising lawyers regulated by the SRA or other approved regulator. On the other hand, 21.05(2)(a) does not prohibit you from marketing your separate business on the basis that it is run and owned by persons who are qualified as lawyers – provided you make it clear that no lawyer involved in the separate business is practising as such through the separate business.

(c) Rule 21.05(2)(a) does not prohibit the use of the word "solicitor", "lawyer" or "attorney" in connection with your separate business. However, it would be a breach of 21.05(2)(a) if such a reference suggested that lawyers regulated by the SRA or other approved regulator practise through the separate business – so any such reference must be appropriately qualified so as to make it clear that the services of the separate business are not the services of practising lawyers. If the reference is in a letterhead or other publicity that statement should be in the same document.

Financial services

17. Examples of financial services which cannot form part of a solicitor's practice (and which will not be covered by qualifying insurance under the Solicitors' Indemnity Insurance Rules) include banking, stockbroking and insurance underwriting.

Rule 22 – Waivers

22.01

(1) In any particular case or cases the Solicitors Regulation Authority Board shall have power to waive in writing the provisions of these rules for a particular purpose or purposes expressed in such waiver, to place conditions on and to revoke such waiver.

(2) In spite of (1) above, the Solicitors Regulation Authority Board shall not have power to waive any of the provisions of the following rules:

(a) rule 1 (Core duties);

(b) rules 3.01 to 3.05 (conflict of interests, excluding provisions relating to alternative dispute resolution, conveyancing and property selling);

(c)   rule 4 (Confidentiality and disclosure);

(d)   rule 6 (Equality and diversity);

(e)   rules 15.01, 15.03, 15.04, 15.18, 15.22, 15.23 and 15.24 (overseas practice provisions which apply provisions that cannot be waived for practice in England and Wales);

(f)   rule 18 (Property selling);

(g)   rule 22 (Waivers);

(h)   rule 23 (Application of these rules); and

(i)   rule 24 (Interpretation).

Guidance to rule 22 – Waivers

1.   If you apply for a waiver, you will need to show that your circumstances are exceptional in order for it to be granted. Advice may be obtained from the Professional Ethics Guidance Team. We would normally expect an application in respect of an individual working in the practice of a recognised body to be made by the recognised body itself.

2.   The list in 22.01(2) should not be taken as an indication that any other rule may be waived in any circumstances. A waiver cannot be granted where to do so would run counter to the overall purpose of the rule. For example, it is difficult to foresee circumstances in which many of the provisions of rule 2 (Client relations) would be waived.

3.   The SRA Board has confirmed that every existing waiver of the Solicitors' Practice Rules 1990, the Solicitors' Overseas Practice Rules 1990 or the Solicitors' Incorporated Practice Rules 2004 would be extended as a like waiver of the Solicitors' Code of Conduct 2007 for a period of two years from 1 July 2007, or until the date of expiry specified in the waiver if earlier. Every such waiver will expire at the end of the two-year extension period, or earlier if an earlier date of expiry is specified in the waiver. Any firms still holding over on such waivers should consider whether they need to apply for a new waiver and, if so, should contact the Professional Ethics Guidance Team to apply forthwith.

Rule 23 – Application of these rules

23.01

These rules apply to you (and "you" must be construed accordingly) in the following circumstances.

Application in relation to practice from an office in England and Wales

(1)   Subject to (2) below, rules 1 to 14 and 16 to 25 of these rules apply to your practice from an office in England and Wales if you are:

(a)   a solicitor or REL (including a recognised sole practitioner);

(b)   a recognised body;

(c)   an RFL who is:

(i)   the employee of a recognised sole practitioner;

        (ii)   a manager, employee, member or owner of a recognised body;

        (iii)   a manager, member or owner of a body corporate which is a manager, member or owner of a recognised body; or

        (iv)   practising through or employed by an authorised non-SRA firm;

    (d)   any other person who is a manager or employee of a recognised body or the employee of a recognised sole practitioner; or

    (e)   a solicitor who was formerly an REL, when practising as a lawyer of an Establishment Directive profession.

(2)   (a)   Only this rule and rules 1, 12, 20, 21 and 24 apply to you if you are a solicitor, REL or RFL practising through or employed by an authorised non-SRA firm when doing work of a sort authorised by the firm's approved regulator.

    (b)   "Practising through" an authorised non-SRA firm includes:

        (i)   being a partner if the firm is a partnership;

        (ii)   being a member if the firm is an LLP; and

        (iii) being a director or having an ownership interest if the body is a company,

    even if you undertake no work for your firm's clients.

Application in relation to practice from an office outside England and Wales

(3)   These rules apply to your practice from an office outside England and Wales to the extent specified in rule 15.

23.02

In relation to activities in England and Wales which fall outside the scope of practice as defined by rule 24, whether undertaken as a lawyer or in some other business or private capacity:

    (a)   rule 1.06 (Public confidence) applies to you if you are a solicitor, an REL or an RFL;

    (b)   rule 10.01 (Not taking unfair advantage) applies to you if you are a solicitor or REL;

    (c)   rules 10.05(1)(c) and (d), (2) and (3), (undertakings given outside the course of practice) apply to you if you are a solicitor or REL; and

    (d)   rules 12.03(2) to (5) (practice in another capacity than as an RFL, holding out as a lawyer of England and Wales, and wrongfully doing reserved or immigration work) apply to you if you are an RFL.

23.03

In relation to acting for seller and buyer "you" must be interpreted in accordance with 3.07(1), and in relation to acting for lender and borrower "you" must be interpreted in accordance with 3.16(1).

Guidance to rule 23 – Application of these rules

1.   Rule 23 applies all these rules, except rule 15, to your practice from an office in

England and Wales if you are a solicitor, an REL, a recognised body, or any other person who is a manager or employee of a recognised body or an employee of a recognised sole practitioner. The application of the rules to RFLs is dealt with in note 4.

2.	These rules are also applied to your practice from an office outside England and Wales but only to the extent specified in rule 15. The key to the application of a rule is, therefore, whether a matter relates to practice from an office in England and Wales, or to practice from an office outside England and Wales. This does not mean that different rules apply at different times during a cross-jurisdictional transaction. For example, if a client gives instructions for a transaction to your London office, then that transaction will fall into the category of practice from an office in England and Wales.

3.	These rules (as from 31 March 2009) now apply to employees of recognised bodies and recognised sole practitioners. Such employees, as well as managers of recognised bodies, are subject to new powers given to the SRA to impose a rebuke or a fine of up to £2,000 for a breach of these rules. Some rules, by virtue of their wording or their subject matter, will have no or limited application to employees. For example 5.01(1) (Supervision and management responsibilities) is applicable only to managers and to firms. Rule 4.01 (Duty of confidentiality) is a prime example of a rule which will apply to all employees, breach of which would make an employee individually culpable – without prejudice to any culpability on the part of the firm. The rules do not apply to non-solicitor employees employed outside England and Wales (except for REL employees employed elsewhere in the UK).

4.	The rules apply to an RFL who is a manager or employee of a recognised body or an employee of a recognised sole practitioner, in relation to practice from an office in England and Wales. An RFL who is a manager or employee of an authorised non-SRA firm is subject to the rules in the way set out in note 5. An RFL is not subject to any of the rules in relation to any other form of practice, or outside practice, or in relation to practice from an office outside England and Wales, except as set out in note 6.

5.	If you are a solicitor, an REL or an RFL practising as a manager or employee of an authorised non-SRA firm, when doing work of a sort authorised by the firm's approved regulator, rule 1 will apply to you but most of the remainder of these rules, as well as the Accounts Rules, are disapplied – for details see 23.01(2)(a). You will, however, be subject to the rules of the authorised non-SRA firm's regulator and any serious breach of those rules could also be a breach of rule 1. If you do work of a sort which is outside the scope of the firm's authorisation you will be subject to these rules, and to the Accounts Rules, in full. These rules would allow you to do such work for the firm itself, or for related bodies or work colleagues, or pro bono – see also 13.01(2).

6.	Certain rules also apply in relation to other forms of practice, and outside practice:

(a)	Under 1.06 (Public confidence), if you are a solicitor, REL or RFL you must not behave in a way that is likely to diminish the trust the public places in you or the legal profession. Rule 1.06 applies to your conduct both in your practice as a solicitor, REL or RFL and outside it, and in England and Wales or anywhere else in the world.

(b)	Under 10.01 (Not taking unfair advantage), if you are a solicitor (anywhere in the world) or an REL (in the UK) you must not, whether in the course of practice or outside it, take unfair advantage of your position.

(c)	Under 10.05(1)(c) and (d), (2) and (3), and 15.10(2)(a)(ii) and (iii), (b) and (c) you must fulfil an undertaking even if it is given outside the course of your practice as a solicitor or as an REL, if you give the undertaking as a solicitor or as a lawyer of another Establishment Directive state, and this applies to a solicitor anywhere in the world and to an REL anywhere in the UK.

(d)	Under 12.03(2) and (3), if you are an RFL you must not be held out as an RFL, or as regulated by or registered with the Law Society or the SRA, except in the context of practice as a manager or employee of a recognised body or as an employee of a recognised sole practitioner. Under 12.03(4)(a) you are prohibited from being held out as a solicitor or barrister (or as any other category of lawyer of England and Wales unless you have that qualification). All these provisions apply outside England and Wales as well as in England and Wales. Under 12.03(4)(b)–(d) you must not do reserved work in England and Wales – whether or not you are practising as an RFL – unless you have a separate qualification which allows you to do that work. Under 12.03(5), if you are not practising as an RFL you must not do any immigration work anywhere in the UK unless you are authorised to do so in your own right, or working under the supervision of someone (not a solicitor, REL or RFL) who is so authorised.

Rule 24 – Interpretation

24.01

In these rules, unless the context otherwise requires, all references to legislation include existing and future amendments to that legislation and:

"approved regulator"	means a body listed in paragraph 1 of Schedule 4 to the Legal Services Act 2007 (whether or not that paragraph has been brought into force), or designated as an approved regulator by an order under paragraph 17 of that Schedule, and reference to the Solicitors Regulation Authority as an approved regulator means the Solicitors Regulation Authority carrying out regulatory functions assigned to the Law Society as an approved regulator;
"arrangement"	in relation to financial services, fee sharing and the introduction of clients, means any express or tacit agreement between you and another person, whether contractually binding or not;
"associated companies"	means two companies which are subsidiary companies of the same holding company;
"associated firms"	means two or more partnerships with at least one partner in common; two or more companies without shares with at least one member in common; two or more LLPs with at least one member in common; two or more companies with shares with at least one owner in common, or any combination of these;
"authorised non-SRA firm"	means a sole practitioner, partnership, LLP or company authorised to practise by another approved regulator and not by the Solicitors Regulation Authority;
"body corporate"	means:
	(a) a company;
	(b) an LLP; or
	(c) a partnership which is a legal person in its own right;
"British Court martial"	means the Summary Appeal Court, the Court Martial, the Court Martial Appeal Court or the Service Civilian Court;
"CCBE"	means the Council of the Bars and Law Societies of Europe;
"CCBE Code"	means the CCBE's Code of Conduct for European Lawyers;
"CCBE state"	means any state whose legal profession is a full member, an associate member or an observer member of the CCBE;

"charity"	has the same meaning as in section 96(1) of the Charities Act 1993;
"claim for redress"	in rule 20.05(3), has the same meaning as in section 158 of the Legal Services Act 2007;
"client account"	in rule 15 (Overseas practice), means an account at a bank or similar institution, subject to supervision by a public authority, which is used only for the purpose of holding client money and/or trust money, and the title or designation of which indicates that the funds in the account belong to the client or clients of a solicitor or REL or are held subject to a trust; (for the definition of "client account" in relation to practice from an office in England and Wales, see the Solicitors' Accounts Rules 1998);
"client money"	in rule 15 (Overseas practice), means money you receive or hold for or on behalf of a client or trust; (for the definition of "client money" in relation to practice from an office in England and Wales, see the Solicitors' Accounts Rules 1998);
"company"	in rule 14 (Recognised bodies), means a company registered under Parts 1 and 2 of the Companies Act 2006, an overseas company incorporated in an Establishment Directive state and registered under Part 34 of the Companies Act 2006, or a societas Europaea;
"contentious proceedings"	is to be construed in accordance with the definition of "contentious business" in section 87 of the Solicitors Act 1974;
"contingency fee"	except in 9.01(4) to (6), means any sum (whether fixed, or calculated either as a percentage of the proceeds or otherwise) payable only in the event of success;
"court"	in rule 11 (Litigation and advocacy) means any court, tribunal or enquiry of England and Wales, or a British court martial, or any court of another jurisdiction;
"director"	means a director of a company, and includes the director of a recognised body which is a company; and in relation to a societas Europaea includes:
	(a) in a two-tier system, a member of the management organ and a member of the supervisory organ; and
	(b) in a one-tier system, a member of the administrative organ;
"documents"	in rule 20 (Rights and obligations of practice) includes documents, whether written or electronic, relating to the solicitor's client and office accounts;
"eligible to be a member or shareowner"	in rule 14 (Recognised bodies), mean a person who falls within one of the following categories:
	(a) a solicitor with a practising certificate;
	(b) a registered European lawyer;
	(c) a registered foreign lawyer;
	(d) a lawyer of an Establishment Directive profession (including the UK);
	(e) a lawyer of England and Wales;

	(f) an individual approved under regulation 3 of the Recognised Bodies Regulations as suitable to be a manager of a recognised body;
	(g) a legally qualified body,
	and "ineligible" must be construed accordingly;
"employee"	except in rule 6 (Equality and diversity) includes an individual who is:
	(a) employed as a director of a company;
	(b) engaged under a contract of service (for example, as an assistant solicitor) by a firm or its wholly owned service company; or
	(c) engaged under a contract for services (for example, as a consultant or a locum), made between a firm or organisation and:
	(i) that individual;
	(ii) an employment agency; or
	(iii) a company which is not held out to the public as providing legal services and is wholly owned and directed by that individual,
	under which the firm or organisation has exclusive control over the individual's time for all or part of the individual's working week; or in relation to which the firm or organisation has designated the individual as a fee earner in accordance with arrangements between the firm or organisation and the Legal Services Commission pursuant to the Access to Justice Act 1999;
	and "employer" and "employment" must be construed accordingly;
"Establishment Directive"	means the Establishment of Lawyers Directive 98/5/EC;
"Establishment Directive profession"	means any profession listed in Article 1.2(a) of the Establishment Directive, including a solicitor, barrister or advocate of the UK;
"Establishment Directive Regulations"	means the European Communities (Lawyer's Practice) Regulations 2000 (SI 2000/1119);
"Establishment Directive state"	means a state to which the Establishment of Lawyers Directive 98/5/EC applies – currently all the states of the EU plus Iceland, Liechtenstein, Norway and Switzerland;
"EU"	means the European Union;
"European corporate practice"	means a lawyers' practice which is a body incorporated in an Establishment Directive state, or a partnership with separate legal identity formed under the law of an Establishment Directive state:
	(a) which has an office in an Establishment Directive state but does not have an office in England and Wales;

	(b)	whose ultimate beneficial owners include at least one individual who is not a lawyer of England and Wales but is, and is entitled to practise as, a lawyer of an Establishment Directive profession;
	(c)	whose managers include at least one such individual, or at least one body corporate whose managers include at least one such individual;
	(d)	75% of whose ultimate beneficial ownership is in the hands of individuals who are, and are entitled to practise as, lawyers of Establishment Directive professions, lawyers of England and Wales, and/or RFLs; and
	(e)	75% of whose managers comprise such individuals, and/or bodies corporate 75% of whose managers comprise such individuals;
"European cross-border practice"		has the meaning assigned by 16.01(1);
"exempt European lawyer"		means a member of an Establishment Directive profession:
	(a)	registered with the Bar Standards Board; or
	(b)	based entirely at an office or offices outside England and Wales,
		who is not a lawyer of England and Wales (whether entitled to practise as such or not);
"firm"		means any business through which a solicitor or REL carries on practice other than in-house practice;
"foreign lawyer"		means a person who is not a solicitor or barrister of England and Wales, but who is a member, and entitled to practise as such, of a legal profession regulated within a jurisdiction outside England and Wales;
"holding company"		has the meaning assigned by the Companies Act 2006;
"immigration tribunal"		means:
	(a)	the Asylum Support Tribunal;
	(b)	the Asylum and Immigration Tribunal; and
	(c)	a tribunal hearing an appeal from (a) or (b);
"in-house practice"		means a solicitor's practice within 12.01(1)(e) or 12.01(2)(e), or an REL's practice within 12.02(1)(e) or 12.02(2)(e);
"lawyer"		means a member of one of the following professions, entitled to practise as such:
	(a)	the profession of solicitor, barrister or advocate of the UK;
	(b)	a profession whose members are authorised to practise by an approved regulator other than the Solicitors Regulation Authority;
	(c)	an Establishment Directive profession other than a UK profession;
	(d)	a legal profession which has been approved by the Solicitors Regulation Authority for the purpose of recognised bodies in England and Wales; or

	(e)	any other regulated legal profession which is recognised as such by the Solicitors Regulation Authority;
"lawyer of England and Wales"		means a solicitor with a current practising certificate or an individual who is authorised to practise in England and Wales by an approved regulator other than the Solicitors Regulation Authority, but excludes a member of an Establishment Directive profession registered with the Bar Standards Board under the Establishment Directive;
"legal profession"		means a profession whose members are lawyers as defined in this rule;
"legally qualified body"		for the purposes of these rules and for the purposes of section 9A(6)(h) and (6C) of the Administration of Justice Act 1985 means a body which would meet the services requirement in 14.01(1) and is:
	(a)	a recognised body;
	(b)	an authorised non-SRA firm of which individuals who are, and are entitled to practise as, lawyers of England and Wales, lawyers of Establishment Directive professions or RFLs make up at least 75% of the ultimate beneficial ownership; or
	(c)	a European corporate practice;
"LLP"		means a limited liability partnership formed by being incorporated under the Limited Liability Partnerships Act 2000;
"manager"		means:
	(a)	a partner in a partnership;
	(b)	a member of an LLP; or
	(c)	a director of a company;
"member"		in relation to a recognised body, means:
	(a)	a person who has agreed to be a member of a company and whose name is entered in the company's register of members; or
	(b)	a member of an LLP;
"non-lawyer"		means:
	(a)	an individual who is not a lawyer practising as such; or
	(b)	a body corporate or partnership which is not:
		(i) a recognised body;
		(ii) an authorised non-SRA firm; or
		(iii) a business, carrying on the practice of lawyers from an office or offices outside England and Wales, in which a controlling majority of the owners and managers are lawyers;
"notary public"		means a duly certificated notary authorised to practise by the Master of Faculties;
"officer"		in relation to a company, means a director or the company secretary;
"overseas"		means in or of a jurisdiction other than England and Wales;

"overseas practice"	means:	
	(a)	the practice from an office outside England and Wales of:
		(i) a solicitor;
		(ii) a recognised body;
		(iii) a manager of a recognised body who is a lawyer of England and Wales;
	(b)	the activities of an individual non-lawyer as a manager of a recognised body practising from an office outside England and Wales;
	(c)	the activities of a body corporate as a manager of a recognised body practising from an office outside England and Wales; and
	(d)	the practice of an REL from an office in Scotland or Northern Ireland;
"owner"	in relation to a body, means a person with any ownership interest in the body;	
"partner"	means a person who is or is held out as a partner in an unincorporated firm;	
"partnership"	means an unincorporated partnership, and includes any unincorporated firm in which persons are or are held out as partners, but does not include an LLP;	
"person"	includes an individual and a body corporate;	
"person qualified to direct reserved work"	means an individual who is qualified under statute to do the relevant reserved work and who is:	
	(a)	a fellow-manager; or
	(b)	the employer, a manager of the firm or a fellow-employee, if the person doing the work is not a manager;
"practice"	means:	
	(a)	the activities of a solicitor, in that capacity;
	(b)	(i) the activities of an REL in the capacity of lawyer of an Establishment Directive profession, from an office or offices within the UK;
		(ii) the activities of a member of an Establishment Directive profession registered with the Bar Standards Board under the Establishment Directive, in that capacity, from an office or offices in the UK;
	(c)	the activities of an RFL from an office or offices in England and Wales as:
		(i) the employee of a recognised sole practitioner;
		(ii) a manager, employee, member or owner of a recognised body or of an authorised non-SRA firm;

	(iii)	a manager, member or owner of a body corporate which is a manager, member or owner of a recognised body or of an authorised non-SRA firm;
(d)		the activities of a recognised body;
(e)		the activities of an individual non-lawyer:
	(i)	as a manager of a recognised body; or
	(ii)	employed in England and Wales by a recognised body or recognised sole practitioner;
(f)		the activities of a body corporate as a manager of a recognised body;
(g)		the activities of a lawyer of England and Wales, in that capacity; and
(h)		the activities of an authorised non-SRA firm,

and "practise" and "practising" should be construed accordingly;

"practice from an office"	includes practice carried on:

(a)	from an office at which you are based; or
(b)	from an office of a firm in which you are the sole principal, or a manager, or in which you have an ownership interest, even if you are not based there,

and "practising from an office in England and Wales", etc. should be construed accordingly;

"practice through a body"	includes having an ownership interest in a body and being a director if the body is a company, even if you yourself undertake no work for the body's clients, and "practising through an authorised non-SRA firm" should be construed accordingly;
"principal"	means a sole practitioner or a partner in a partnership;
"providing a service through a separate business"	means having any active involvement in a separate business which provides that service, and includes:

(a)	any substantial ownership in the business;
(b)	any direct control over the business, and any indirect control through another person such as a spouse; and
(c)	any active participation in the business or the provision of its services to customers;

(being a non-executive director or providing services under rule 13 (In-house practice, etc.) or 15.13 (In-house practice overseas) does not, on its own, constitute active involvement);

"publicity"	includes all promotional material and activity, including the name or description of your firm, stationery, advertisements, brochures, websites, directory entries, media appearances, promotional press releases, and direct approaches to potential clients and other persons, whether conducted in person, in writing, or in electronic form, but does not include press releases prepared on behalf of a client;
"Recognised Bodies Regulations"	means the SRA Recognised Bodies Regulations 2009;

"recognised body"	means a partnership, company or LLP for the time being recognised by the Solicitors Regulation Authority under section 9 of the Administration of Justice Act 1985 and the Recognised Bodies Regulations;
"recognised sole practitioner"	means a solicitor or REL authorised by the Solicitors Regulation Authority under section 1B of the Solicitors Act 1974 to practise as a sole practitioner;
"register of European lawyers"	means the register of European lawyers maintained by the Solicitors Regulation Authority under regulation 15 of the Establishment Directive Regulations;
"register of foreign lawyers"	means the register of foreign lawyers maintained by the Solicitors Regulation Authority under the Courts and Legal Services Act 1990;
"REL (registered European lawyer)"	means an individual registered with the Solicitors Regulation Authority under regulation 17 of the Establishment Directive Regulations;
"REL-controlled recognised body"	means a recognised body in which RELs, or RELs together with lawyers of England and Wales and/or European lawyers registered with the Bar Standards Board, constitute the national group of lawyers with the largest (or equal largest) share of control of the recognised body either as individual managers or by their share in the control of bodies which are managers, and for this purpose RELs and European lawyers registered with the Bar Standards Board belong to the national group of England and Wales;
"reserved work"	means the following activities:

(a) advocacy before a court or immigration tribunal;

(b) the conduct of proceedings in a court or immigration tribunal;

(c) the preparation of documents in proceedings before a court or immigration tribunal;

(d) the preparation of instruments and the lodging of documents relating to the transfer or charge of land, and the preparation of trust deeds disposing of capital, within paragraph 5 of Schedule 2 to the Legal Services Act 2007, and the preparation of any other instrument coming within sub-paragraph (1)(c) of that paragraph;

(e) the preparation of papers on which to found or oppose a grant of probate or a grant of letters of administration;

(f) the administration of oaths and statutory declarations;

(g) notarial activities within paragraph 7 of Schedule 2 to the Legal Services Act 2007;

"RFL (registered foreign lawyer)"	means an individual registered with the Solicitors Regulation Authority under section 89 of the Courts and Legal Services Act 1990;
"separate business"	means a business which is not a recognised body, a recognised sole practitioner, an authorised non-SRA firm or a firm within 12.01(2)(a)–(d) or 12.02(2)(a)–(d) but which offers a service or services that could properly be offered by a recognised body;

"shareowner"	means:
	(a) a member of a recognised body which is a company with a share capital, who owns a share in the body; or
	(b) a person who is not a member of a company with a share capital, but owns a share in the body, which is held by a member as nominee;
"societas Europaea"	means a European public limited liability company within the meaning of article 1 of Council Regulation 2157/2001/EC;
"sole practitioner"	means a solicitor or REL practising as a sole principal, and does not include a solicitor or REL practising in-house;
"solicitor-controlled recognised body"	means a recognised body in which lawyers of England and Wales constitute the national group of lawyers with the largest (or equal largest) share of control of the recognised body either as individual managers or by their share in the control of bodies which are managers;
"subsidiary company"	has the meaning assigned by the Companies Act 2006;
"UK"	means United Kingdom;
"ultimate beneficial owners"	in relation to a body means all those individuals who together beneficially own the body, whether:
	(a) directly, as partners in a partnership, members of an LLP or shareholders in a company, or
	(b) indirectly:
	(i) as beneficial owners of shares held by nominees or trustees, or
	(ii) by way of an ownership interest in one or more intermediate bodies corporate, or
	(iii) by way of some combination of (i) and (ii) above;
	and "ultimate beneficial ownership" should be construed accordingly;
"undertaking"	in 10.05 and 15.10, means a statement made by you or your firm to someone who reasonably relies upon it, that you or your firm will do something or cause something to be done, or refrain from doing something. The undertaking can be given orally or in writing and need not include the words "undertake" or "undertaking".
"voting rights"	in a body includes the right to vote in a partners', members', directors' or shareholders' meeting or otherwise in relation to the body, and "control the exercise of voting rights" shall be interpreted as including de facto as well as legal control over such rights.

Rule 25 – Commencement and repeals

25.01

(1) These rules, together with the Solicitors' Recognised Bodies Regulations 2007, shall come into force on 1 July 2007.

(2)   The following provisions are repealed by these rules:

(a)   the Solicitors' Practice Rules 1990;

(b)   the Solicitors' Publicity Code 2001;

(c)   the Solicitors' Introduction and Referral Code 1990;

(d)   the Employed Solicitors Code 1990;

(e)   the Solicitors' Separate Business Code 1994;

(f)   the Solicitors' Costs Information and Client Care Code 1999;

(g)   the Law Society's Code for Advocacy;

(h)   the Solicitors' Anti-Discrimination Rules 2004;

(i)   the Solicitors' Overseas Practice Rules 1990; and

(j)   the Solicitors' Incorporated Practice Rules 2004.

(3)   These rules also replace the conduct obligations imposed by virtue of *The Guide to the Professional Conduct of Solicitors* (1999) and Guide Online.

(4)   For the avoidance of doubt, the following will remain in force after the coming into force of these rules:

(a)   the Solicitors' Accounts Rules;

(b)   the Solicitors' Indemnity Insurance Rules;

(c)   the Solicitors' Indemnity (Enactment) Rules;

(d)   the Solicitors' Financial Services (Scope) Rules;

(e)   the Solicitors' Financial Services (Conduct of Business) Rules;

(f)   the Solicitors' Compensation Fund Rules; and

(g)   the Solicitors' Compensation Fund (Foreign Lawyers' Contributions) Rules.

(5)   As of 31 March 2009:

(a)   the Solicitors' Recognised Bodies Regulations 2007 are replaced by the SRA Recognised Bodies Regulations 2009, and

(b)   the Solicitors' Compensation Fund (Foreign Lawyers' Contributions) Rules are repealed.

(6)   Until 1 July 2009:

(a)   there is no requirement for a solicitor or REL practising in England and Wales as a sole practitioner to be a recognised sole practitioner; and

(b)   rules which apply to a recognised sole practitioner are to be interpreted as applying to a solicitor or REL practising in England and Wales as a sole practitioner.

(7)   The provisions of rule 7.07(1) requiring

(a)   a partnership to have on its website and e-mails the words "regulated by the Solicitors Regulation Authority", and to have on its letterhead, fax heading, website and e-mails the name under which the partnership is recognised and the number allocated to it by the Authority, shall not apply until 1 October 2009;

(b)   an LLP or company to have on its website and e-mails the words "regulated by the Solicitors Regulation Authority" shall not apply until 1 October 2009;

(c)   a sole practice to have on its website and e-mails the words "regulated by the

Solicitors Regulation Authority", and to have on its letterhead, fax heading, website and e-mails the name under which the sole practice is recognised and the number allocated to it by the Authority, shall not apply until 1 January 2010.

Guidance to rule 25 – Commencement and repeals

1. See note 3 of the guidance to rule 22 (Waivers) regarding commencement of the Solicitors' Code of Conduct 2007 and waivers of repealed rules.

Draft SRA Code of Conduct

[Law Society copyright. For the latest updates to the material, please see www.sra.org.uk.]

Draft SRA Code of Conduct (Annex C)

[Professional Ethics]

[With amendments to 21 October 2010.]

Introduction to the SRA Code of Conduct

Overview

Outcomes-focused regulation concentrates on providing positive outcomes which when achieved will benefit and protect *clients* and the public. The SRA Code of Conduct (the Code) sets out our outcomes-focused conduct requirements. These requirements encourage you to consider what are the right outcomes for your *client* taking into account the way that your *firm* works and its client base. The Code is underpinned by effective, risk-based supervision and enforcement.

Those involved in providing legal advice and representation have long held the role of trusted adviser. There are fiduciary duties arising from this role and obligations owed to others, especially the *court*. No code can foresee or address every issue or ethical dilemma which may arise. You must strive to uphold the spirit of the Code as well as the letter.

The Principles

The Code forms part of the Handbook, in which the 10 mandatory *Principles* are all-pervasive. They apply to all those we regulate and to all aspects of *practice*. They define the fundamental ethical and professional standards that we expect of all *firms* and individuals (including *owners* who may not be *lawyers*) when providing legal services. You should always have regard to the *Principles* and use them as your starting point when faced with an ethical dilemma.

Where two or more *Principles* come into conflict the one which takes precedence is the one which best serves the public interest in the particular circumstances, especially the public interest in the proper administration of justice. Compliance with the *Principles* is also subject to any overriding legal obligations.

You must:

1   uphold the rule of law and the proper administration of justice;

2   act with integrity;

3   not allow your independence to be compromised;

4   act in the best interests of each client;

5   provide a proper standard of service to your clients;

6   behave in a way that maintains the trust the public places in you and in the provision of legal services;

7   comply with your legal and regulatory obligations and deal with your regulators and ombudsmen in an open, timely and co-operative manner;

8   run your business or carry out your role in the business effectively and in accordance with proper governance and sound financial and risk management principles;

9   run your business or carry out your role in the business in a way that encourages equality of opportunity and respect for diversity;

10   protect client money and assets.

Structure of the Code

The Code is divided into 5 sections:

*   You and your client

*   You and your business

*   You and your regulator

*   You and others

*   Application, waivers and interpretation

Each section is divided into chapters dealing with particular regulatory issues, for example: client care, *conflicts of interests*, and *publicity*.

These chapters show how the *Principles* apply in certain contexts through mandatory and non-mandatory provisions.

Mandatory provisions

The following provisions are mandatory:

*   the outcomes;

*   the application and waivers provisions in chapter 13;

*   the interpretations in chapter 14; and

*   the commencement, repeal and transitional provisions in chapter 15.

The outcomes describe what *firms* and individuals are expected to achieve in order to comply with the relevant *Principles* in the context of the relevant chapter. Judgement will need to be exercised to decide if the outcome is relevant to your *practice*. You will need to bear in mind:

*   some of the outcomes do not apply to *overseas practice*;

*   outcomes may be different when applied to *in-house practice* and/or where services are provided only to your employer.

In each of these cases we have explained at the end of the chapter how the outcomes apply.

The outcomes contained in each chapter are not an exhaustive list of the application of all the *Principles*. We have tried to make them as helpful as possible.

Non-mandatory provisions

The following provisions are non-mandatory:

- indicative behaviours;
- notes.

The outcomes are supplemented by indicative behaviours. The indicative behaviours specify, but do not constitute an exhaustive list of, the kind of behaviour which may establish compliance with, or contravention of the *Principles*. These are not mandatory but they may help us to decide whether an outcome has been achieved in compliance with the *Principles*.

We recognise that there may be other ways of achieving the outcomes. Where you have chosen a different method from those we have described as indicative behaviours, we might require you to demonstrate how you have nevertheless achieved the outcome. We encourage *firms* to consider how they can best achieve the outcomes, taking into account the nature of the *firm*, the particular circumstances of the matter and, crucially, the needs of their particular *clients*.

Waivers

Due to the flexibility of approach this structure allows, we do not anticipate receiving many applications for waivers from the mandatory outcomes. The SRA, nonetheless, reserves power to waive a provision in exceptional circumstances.

Definitions

For the definition of words in italics, see chapter 14 – Interpretation.

Sources of help

You can access the Code and other elements of the Handbook and find information on particular issues on our Freedom in Practice pages. You can also seek guidance on professional conduct from our Professional Ethics Guidance Team.

List of contents of the Code

1st section – You and your client

Chapter 1 Client care

Chapter 2 Equality and diversity

Chapter 3 Conflicts of interests

Chapter 4 Confidentiality and disclosure

Chapter 5 Your client and the court

Chapter 6 Your client and introductions to third parties

2nd section – You and your business

Chapter 7 Management of your business

Chapter 8 Publicity

Chapter 9 Fee sharing and referrals

3rd section – You and your regulator

Chapter 10 You and your regulator

4th section – You and others

Chapter 11 Relations with third parties

Chapter 12 Separate businesses

5th section – Application, waivers and interpretation

Chapter 13 Application and waivers provisions

Chapter 14 Interpretation

Chapter 15 Commencement, repeals and transitional provisions

1st Section – You and your client

Chapter 1 – Client care

This chapter is about providing a proper standard of service, which takes into account the individual needs and circumstances of each *client*. This includes providing *clients* with the information they need to make informed decisions about the services they need, how these will be delivered and how much they will cost. This will enable you and your *client* to understand each others' expectations and responsibilities. This chapter is also about ensuring that if *clients* are not happy with the service they have received they know how to make a *complaint* and that all *complaints* are dealt with promptly and fairly.

Your relationship with your *client* is a contractual one which carries with it legal, as well as conduct, obligations. This chapter focuses on your obligations in conduct.

You are generally free to decide whether or not to accept instructions in any matter, provided you do not discriminate unlawfully (see Chapter 2).

The outcomes in this chapter show how the *Principles* apply in the context of client care.

Outcomes

You must achieve these outcomes:

O(1) you treat your *clients* fairly;

O(2) you provide services to your *clients* in a manner which protects their interests in their matter, subject to the proper administration of justice;

O(3) when deciding whether to act, or terminate your instructions, you comply with the law and the Code;

O(4) you have the resources, skills and procedures to carry out your *clients*' instructions;

O(5) the service you provide to *clients* is competent , delivered in a timely manner and takes account of your *clients*' needs and circumstances;

O(6) you only enter into fee agreements that are legal, and which you consider are suitable for the *client's* needs and take account of the *client's* best interests;

O(7) you inform *clients* whether the services you provide are regulated and by whom;

O(8) *clients* have the benefit of your *compulsory professional indemnity insurance* and you do not exclude or attempt to exclude liability below the minimum level of cover required by the SRA Indemnity Insurance Rules;

O(9) *clients* are informed in writing at the outset of their matter of their right to complain and how *complaints* can be made;

O(10) *clients* are informed in writing both at the outset of their matter and if appropriate at the conclusion of your *complaints* procedure, of their right to complain to the *Legal Ombudsman*, the time frame for doing so and full details of how to contact the *Legal Ombudsman*;

O(11) *clients' complaints* are dealt with promptly, fairly, openly and effectively;

O(12) *clients* are in a position to make informed decisions about the services they need, how their matter will be handled and the options available to them;

O(13) *clients* receive the best possible information, both at the outset and when appropriate as their matter progresses, about the likely overall cost of their matter;

O(14) *clients* are informed of their right to challenge or complain about your bill and the circumstances in which they may be liable to pay interest on an unpaid bill;

O(15) you properly account to *clients* for any *financial benefit* you receive as a result of your instructions;

O(16) you inform *clients* of any act or omission which could give rise to a claim by them against you.

Indicative behaviours

Acting in the following way(s) may tend to show that you have achieved these outcomes and therefore complied with the *Principles*:

Dealing with the client's matter

IB(1) agreeing an appropriate level of service with your *client*, for example the type and frequency of communications;

IB(2) explaining your responsibilities and those of the *client*;

IB(3) ensuring that the *client* is told, in writing, the name and status of the person(s) dealing with the matter and the name of the person responsible for its overall supervision;

IB(4) explaining any *arrangements*, such as fee sharing or *referral arrangements*, which are relevant to the *client's* instructions;

IB(5) explaining any limitations or conditions on what you can do for the *client*, for example, because of the way the *client's* matter is funded;

IB(6) in taking instructions and during the course of the retainer, having proper regard to your *client's* mental capacity or other vulnerability, such as incapacity or duress;

IB(7) considering whether you should decline to act because you cannot act in the *client's* best interests;

IB(8) if you seek to limit your liability to your *client* to a level above the minimum required by the SRA Indemnity Insurance Rules, you ensure that you have the *client's* informed consent;

IB(9) refusing to act where your *client* proposes to make a gift of significant value to you or a member of your family, or a member of your *firm* or their family, unless the *client* takes independent legal advice;

Fee arrangements with your client

IB(10) discussing whether the potential outcomes of the *client's* case are likely to justify the expense or risk involved including any risk of having to pay someone else's legal fees;

IB(11) clearly explaining your fees and if and when they are likely to change;

IB(12) warning about any other payments for which the *client* may be responsible;

IB(13) discussing how the *client* will pay, including whether public funding may be available, whether the *client* has insurance that might cover the fees, and whether the fees may be paid by someone else such as a trade union;

IB(14) where you are acting for a *client* under a fee arrangement governed by statute such as a conditional fee agreement, giving the *client* all relevant information relating to that arrangement;

IB(15) where you are acting for a publicly funded *client*, explaining the impact on costs of their publicly funded status;

IB(16) providing the information in a clear and accessible form which is appropriate to the needs and circumstances of the *client*;

IB(17) where you receive a *financial benefit* as a result of acting for a *client*, either:

- paying it to the *client*;

- offsetting it against your fees; or

- keeping it only where you can justify keeping it, you have told the *client* the amount of the benefit (or an approximation if you do not know the exact amount) and the *client* has agreed that you can keep it;

IB(18) ensuring that *disbursements* included in your bill reflect the actual amount spent or to be spent on behalf of the *client*;

Complaints handling

IB(19) having a written *complaints* procedure which:

- is brought to *clients'* attention at the outset of the matter;

- is easy for *clients* to use and understand, allowing for *complaints* to be made by any reasonable means;

- is responsive to the needs of individual *clients*, especially those who are vulnerable;

- enables *complaints* to be dealt with promptly and fairly, with decisions based on a sufficient investigation of the circumstances;

- provides for appropriate remedies; and

- does not involve any charges to *clients* for handling their *complaints*;

IB(20) providing the *client* with a copy of the *firm's complaints* procedure on request;

IB(21) in the event that a *client* makes a *complaint*, providing them with all necessary information concerning the handling of the *complaint*.

Acting in the following way(s) may tend to show that you have not achieved these outcomes and therefore not complied with the *Principles*:

Accepting and refusing instructions

IB(22) acting for a *client* when instructions are given by someone else, or by only one *client* when you act jointly for others unless you are satisfied that the *client* providing the instructions has the authority to do so on behalf of all of the *clients*;

IB(23) ceasing to act for a *client* without good reason and without providing reasonable notice;

IB(24) entering into unlawful fee arrangements such as an unlawful contingency fee;

IB(25) acting for a *client* when there are reasonable grounds for believing that the instructions are affected by duress or undue influence without satisfying yourself that they represent the *client's* wishes.

In-house practice

Outcomes 3,4,6,7, 9 to 11, 13, 14, and 16 apply to your *in-house practice*. Outcomes 1, 2, 5, 12, and 15 also apply where you act for a *client* other than your *employer*. Instead of outcome 8, you must achieve the following outcome:

IHP(1) you comply with the SRA Practice Framework Rules in relation to professional indemnity insurance.

Overseas practice

The outcomes in this chapter do not apply to your *overseas practice*. Instead you must achieve the following outcomes:

OP(1) you properly account to your *clients* for any *financial benefit* you receive as a result of your instructions unless it is the prevailing custom of your local jurisdiction to deal with *financial benefits* in a different way;

OP(2) *clients* have the benefit of insurance or other indemnity in relation to professional liabilities which takes account of:

(i) the nature and extent of the risks you incur in your *overseas practice*;

(ii) the local conditions in the jurisdiction in which you are *practising*;

(iii) the terms upon which insurance is available;

and you have not attempted to exclude liability below the minimum level required for practice in the local jurisdiction;

OP(3) you do not enter into unlawful contingency fee arrangements.

Notes

1   The information you give to *clients* will vary according to the needs and circumstances of the individual *client* and the type of work you are doing for them, for example an

individual instructing you on a conveyancing matter is unlikely to need the same information as a sophisticated commercial *client* who instructs you on a regular basis.

2   Information about the *Legal Ombudsman*, including the scheme rules, contact details and time limits, can be found at legalombudsman.org.uk.

Chapter 2 – Equality and diversity

This chapter is about encouraging equality of opportunity and respect for diversity and preventing unlawful discrimination, in your relationship with your *clients* and others. The requirements apply in relation to age, disability, gender reassignment, marriage and civil partnership, pregnancy and maternity, race, religion or belief, and sex or sexual orientation.

Everyone can contribute to compliance with these requirements, for example by treating each other, and *clients*, fairly and with respect, by embedding such values in the workplace and by challenging inappropriate behaviour and processes. Your role in embedding these values will vary depending on your role in the *firm* or business.

As a matter of general law you must comply with requirements set out in legislation – including the Equality Act 2010 – as well as the conduct duties contained in this chapter.

The outcomes in this chapter show how the *Principles* apply in the context of equality and diversity.

Outcomes

You must achieve these outcomes:

O(1)   you have a policy for encouraging equality of opportunity and respect for diversity, and preventing discrimination and harassment within your *firm*;

O(2)   you actively monitor and respond to issues identified by your policy and review and update your policy wherever necessary;

O(3)   your policy is made available to the SRA, *clients* and other relevant third parties upon request;

O(4)   You do not discriminate unlawfully or victimise or harass anyone in the course of your professional dealings.

Indicative behaviours

Acting in the following way(s) may tend to show that you have achieved these outcomes and therefore complied with the *Principles*:

IB(1)   having an equality and diversity policy which includes the following features:

● provisions which are appropriate to the nature and the size of your *firm*;

● provisions to encompass your recruitment and interview processes;

● details of how the *firm* intends to implement, communicate, monitor, evaluate and update the policy;

● details of how the *firm* intends to ensure equality in relation to the treatment of *employees*, *managers*, *clients* and third parties instructed in connection with *clients'* matters and the means by which it will monitor, evaluate and update any procedures and policies in relation to this;

- details of how *complaints* and disciplinary issues are to be dealt with;

- a requirement that all *employees* and *managers* comply with the outcomes;

- a commitment to the principles of equality and diversity and to observing legislative requirements;

IB(2) *employees* and *managers* are provided with training and information about complying with equality and diversity requirements;

IB(3) making reasonable adjustments to ensure that disabled *clients*, *employees* or *managers* are not placed at a substantial disadvantage compared to those who are not disabled, and you do not pass on the costs of these adjustments to your disabled *clients*, *employees* or *managers*;

IB(4) complaints of discrimination are investigated in an appropriate manner.

Acting in the following way(s) may tend to show that you have not achieved these outcomes and therefore not complied with the *Principles*:

IB(5) being subject to any decision of a *court* or tribunal of the *UK* , that you have committed, or are to be treated as having committed, an unlawful act of discrimination;

IB(6) discriminating unlawfully when accepting or refusing instructions to act for a *client*.

In-house practice

Outcome 4 applies to your *in-house practice*. Instead of outcomes 1–3 you must achieve the following outcomes:

IHP(1) If you are a *manager* of an in-house legal department, you take all reasonable steps to secure the adoption and implementation of a policy for encouraging equality of opportunity and respect for diversity, and preventing discrimination and harassment, within your place of work,

Overseas practice

The outcomes in this chapter do not apply to your *overseas practice*. Instead you must achieve the following outcome:

OP(1) You do not discriminate unlawfully according to the jurisdiction in which you are *practising*.

Notes

1   The obligations in this chapter closely mirror your legal obligations. You can obtain further information from the Equality and Human Rights Commission, www.equali-tyhumanrights.com.

2   See also Chapter 7 (Management of your business) for your obligation to have in place appropriate systems and controls for complying with the outcomes in this chapter.

Chapter 3 – Conflicts of interests

This chapter deals with the proper handling of *conflicts of interests*, which is a critical public protection. It is important to have in place systems that enable you to identify and deal with potential conflicts. The indicative behaviours should help you in assessing whether there is a conflict and whether you should refuse instructions.

Conflicts of interests can arise between:

(a)   one or more current *clients* ("*client conflict*"- see definition in Chapter 14); and

(b)   you and current *clients* ("*own interest conflict*"-see definition in Chapter 14).

You can never act where there is a conflict between you and your *client*, but there are limited circumstances in which you can act where there is a conflict between two or more current *clients*. (See outcomes 4 and 5.) In deciding whether to act in these circumstances, the overriding consideration will be the best interests of each of the *clients* concerned and, in particular, whether the benefits of you acting for all or both of the *clients* outweigh the risks.

You should also bear in mind that *conflicts of interests* may affect your duties of confidentiality and disclosure which are dealt with in Chapter 4.

The outcomes in this chapter show how the *Principles* apply in the context of *conflicts of interests*.

Outcomes

You must achieve these outcomes:

O(1)   you have effective systems and controls in place to enable you to identify and assess potential *conflicts of interests*;

O(2)   you do not act where there is an *own interest conflict*;

O(3)   you do not act if there is a *client conflict* unless the circumstances set out in outcomes 4 or 5 apply;

O(4)   where there is a *client conflict* and the clients have a *substantially common interest* in relation to a matter or a particular aspect of it, you only act if:

(a)   you have explained the relevant issues and risks to the *clients* and you have a reasonable belief that they understand those issues and risks;

(b)   all the *clients* have given informed consent in writing to you acting;

(c)   you are satisfied that it is reasonable for you to act for all the *clients*; and

(d)   the sole purpose of the transaction is not the *conveyance of land*;

O(5)   where there is a *client conflict* and the *clients* are *competing for the same objective*, you only act if:

(a)   you have explained the relevant issues and risks to the *clients* and you have a reasonable belief that they understand those issues and risks;

(b)   the *clients* have confirmed in writing that they want you to act, in the knowledge that you act, or may act, for one or more other *clients* who are *competing for the same objective*;

(c)   there is no other *client conflict* in relation to that matter;

(d)   unless the *clients* specifically agree, no individual acts for, or is responsible for the supervision of work done for, more than one of the *clients* in that matter;

(e)   you are satisfied that it is reasonable for you to act for all the *clients*; and

(f)   the sole purpose of the transaction is not the *conveyance of land*.

Indicative behaviours

Acting in the following way(s) may tend to show that you have achieved these outcomes and therefore complied with the *Principles*:

IB(1) your system for identifying *client conflicts* is appropriate to the size and complexity of the *firm* and the nature of the work undertaken, and enables you to assess all relevant circumstances, including whether:

- the *clients'* interests are different;
- your ability to give independent advice to the *clients* may be fettered;
- there is a need to negotiate between the *clients*;
- there is an imbalance in bargaining power between the *clients*;
- any *client* is vulnerable;

IB(2) your system for identifying *own interest conflicts* is appropriate to the size and complexity of the *firm* and the nature of the work undertaken, and enables you to assess all the relevant circumstances, including whether your ability as an individual, or that of anyone within your *firm*, to act in the best interests of the *client(s)*, is impaired by:

- any financial interest;
- a personal relationship;
- the appointment of you, or a member of your *firm* or family to public office;
- commercial relationships;
- your employment.

In-house practice

The outcomes in this chapter also apply to your *in-house practice*.

Overseas practice

The outcomes in this chapter also apply to your *overseas practice*.

Notes

1. The following areas may give rise to a high risk of *conflicts of interests*:

   - conveyancing;
   - litigation.

2. In assessing whether it is reasonable to act in the circumstances set out in outcome 5, you may need to consider whether it is appropriate to act for anyone other than sophisticated users of legal services.

Chapter 4 – Confidentiality and disclosure

This chapter is about the protection of *clients'* confidential information and the disclosure of material information to *clients*.

Protection of confidential information is a fundamental feature of your relationship with *clients*. It exists as a concept both as a matter of law and as a matter of conduct. This duty continues despite the end of the retainer and even after the death of the *client*.

It is important to distinguish the conduct duties from the concept of law known as legal professional privilege. This is a separate legal issue.

Bear in mind that all members of the *firm*, including support staff, consultants and locums, owe a duty of confidentiality to *clients* of the *firm*.

The duty of confidentiality to all *clients* must be reconciled with the duty of disclosure to *clients*. This duty of disclosure is limited to information of which you are aware which is material to your *client's* matter. Where you cannot reconcile these two duties, then the protection of confidential information is paramount. You should not continue to act for a *client* for whom you cannot disclose material information, except in very limited circumstances, where safeguards are in place. Such situations often also give rise to a *conflict of interests* which is discussed in Chapter 3.

The outcomes in this chapter show how the *Principles* apply in the context of confidentiality and disclosure.

Outcomes

You must achieve these outcomes:

O(1) the affairs of *clients* are kept confidential by you and your *firm* unless disclosure is required or permitted by law or the *client* consents;

O(2) any individual within your *firm* who is advising a *client* makes that *client* aware of all information material to that retainer of which the individual has personal knowledge;

O(3) you ensure that where your duty of confidentiality to one *client* comes into conflict with your duty of disclosure to another *client*, your duty of confidentiality takes precedence;

O(4) you do not act for A in a matter where A has an interest adverse to B and B is a *client* for whom you hold confidential information which is material to A in that matter, unless the confidential information can be protected by the use of safeguards and:

    (a)   you reasonably believe that A is aware of, and understands, the relevant issues and gives informed consent;

    (b)   B either gives informed consent or you are unable to trace B;

    (c)   where B can be traced you agree effective safeguards, including information barriers, with B or, where this is not possible, you put in place effective safeguards including information barriers which comply with the common law;

    (d)   it is reasonable in all the circumstances to act for A with such safeguards in place;

O(5) you have effective systems and controls in place to enable you to identify risks to *client* confidentiality and to mitigate those risks.

Indicative behaviours

Acting in the following way(s) may tend to show that you have achieved these outcomes and therefore complied with the *Principles*:

IB(1) your system for identifying risks to *client* confidentiality is appropriate to the size and complexity of the *firm* and the nature of the work undertaken, and enables you to assess all the relevant circumstances;

IB(2) you comply with the law in respect of your fiduciary duties in relation to confidentiality and disclosure;

IB(3) you only outsource services, such as word processing and photocopying, when you are satisfied that the provider has taken all appropriate steps to ensure that your *clients'* confidential information will be protected;

IB(4) where an individual has responsibility for acting for a *client* or supervising a *client's* matter they disclose to the *client* all information material to the *client's* matter of which they are personally aware except when:

- the *client* gives specific informed consent to non-disclosure or a different standard of disclosure arises;

- there is evidence that serious physical or mental injury will be caused to a person(s) or *persons* if the information is disclosed to the *client*;

- legal restrictions effectively prohibit you from passing the information to the *client*, such as the provisions in the money-laundering and anti-terrorism legislation;

- it is obvious that privileged documents have been mistakenly disclosed to you;

- you come into possession of information relating to state security or intelligence matters to which the Official Secrets Act 1989 applies;

IB(5) not acting for A where B is a *client* for whom you hold confidential information which is material to A unless the confidential information can be protected.

Acting in the following way(s) may tend to show that you have not achieved these outcomes and therefore not complied with the *Principles*:

IB(6) disclosing the content of a will on the death of a *client* unless consent has been provided by the personal representatives for the content to be released;

IB(7) disclosing details of bills sent to *clients* to third parties, such as debt factoring companies in relation to the collection of book debts, unless the *client* has consented.

In-house practice

The outcomes listed above apply to your *in-house practice*.

Overseas practice

The outcomes listed above also apply to your *overseas practice*.

Notes

1. The protection of confidential information may be at particular risk where:

   - two or more *firms* merge,

   - when you leave one *firm* and join another, such as if you join a *firm* acting against one of your former *clients*.

2. The following circumstances may make it difficult to implement effective safeguards and information barriers:

   - you are a small *firm*;

   - the physical structure or layout of the *firm* means that it will be difficult to preserve confidentiality; and

   - the *clients* are not sophisticated users of legal services.

APPENDIX 22

Chapter 5 – Your client and the court

This chapter is about your duties to your *client* and to the *court* if you are exercising a right to conduct litigation or acting as an advocate. The outcomes apply to both litigation and advocacy but there are some indicative behaviours which may be relevant only when you are acting as an advocate.

"*Court*" has a wide meaning – see Chapter 14.

The outcomes in this chapter show how the *Principles* apply in the context of your *client* and the *court*.

Outcomes

You must achieve these outcomes:

O(1) you do not attempt to deceive or mislead, or knowingly allow another person(s) to deceive or mislead, or recklessly deceive or mislead, the *court*;

O(2) you comply with *court* orders which place obligations on you;

O(3) you do not place yourself in contempt of *court*;

O(4) where relevant, *clients* are informed of the circumstances in which your duties to the *court* outweigh your obligations to your *client*;

O(5) you comply with your duties to the *court*;

O(6) you ensure that evidence relating to sensitive issues is not misused;

O(7) you do not make or offer to make payments to witnesses dependent upon their evidence or the outcome of the case.

Indicative behaviours

Acting in the following way(s) may tend to show that you have achieved these outcomes and therefore complied with the *Principles*:

IB(1) advising your *clients* to comply with *court* orders made against them, and advising them of the consequences of failing to comply;

IB(2) drawing the *court's* attention to relevant cases and statutory provisions, and any material procedural irregularity;

IB(3) ensuring child witness evidence is kept securely and not released to *clients* or third parties;

IB(4) immediately informing the *court*, with your *client's* consent, if during the course of proceedings you become aware that you have inadvertently misled the *court*, or ceasing to act if the *client* does not consent to you informing the *court*;

IB(5) refusing to continue acting for a *client* if you become aware they have committed perjury or misled the *court* or attempted to mislead the *court* in any material matter unless the *client* agrees to disclose the truth to the *court*;

IB(6) not appearing as an advocate, or acting in litigation, if it is clear that you, or anyone within your *firm*, will be called as a witness in the matter unless you are satisfied that this will not prejudice your independence as an advocate, or litigator, or the interests of your *clients* or the interests of justice.

Acting in the following way(s) may tend to show that you have not achieved these outcomes and therefore not complied with the *Principles*:

IB(7)   constructing facts supporting your *client's* case or drafting any documents relating to any proceedings containing:

- any contention which you do not consider to be properly arguable;
- any allegation of fraud unless you are instructed to do so and you have material which you reasonably believe shows, on the face of it, a case of fraud;

IB(8)   suggesting that any *person* is guilty of a crime, fraud or misconduct unless such allegations:

(a)   go to a matter in issue which is material to your own *client's* case, and

(b)   appear to you to be supported by reasonable grounds;

IB(9)   calling a witness whose evidence you know is untrue;

IB(10)   attempting to influence a witness, when taking a statement from that witness, with regard to the contents of their statement;

IB(11)   tampering with evidence or seeking to persuade a witness to change their evidence;

IB(12)   when acting as an advocate, naming in open *court* any third party whose character would thereby be called into question, unless it is necessary for the proper conduct of the case;

IB(13)   when acting as an advocate, calling into question the character of a witness you have cross-examined unless the witness has had the opportunity to answer the allegations during cross-examination.

In-house practice

The outcomes in this chapter also apply to your *in-house practice*.

Overseas practice

The outcomes in this chapter also apply to your *overseas practice* in relation to litigation or advocacy conducted before a *court*, tribunal or enquiry in England and Wales or a British court martial.

Notes

1.   If you are a litigator or an advocate there may be occasions when your obligation to act in the best interests of a *client* may conflict with your duty to the *court*. In such situations you may need to consider whether the public interest is best served by the proper administration of justice and should take precedence over the interests of your *client*.

Chapter 6 – Your client and introductions to third parties

There may be circumstances in which you wish to refer your *clients* to third parties, perhaps to another *lawyer* or a financial services provider. This chapter describes the conduct duties which arise in respect of such introductions. It is important that you retain your independence when recommending third parties to your *client* and that you act in the *client's* best interests.

The outcomes in this chapter show how the *Principles* apply in the context of your *client* and introductions to third parties.

Outcomes

You must achieve these outcomes:

O(1) whenever you recommend that a *client* uses a particular *person* or business, your recommendation is in the best interests of the *client* and does not compromise your independence;

O(2) *clients* are fully informed of any financial or other interest which you have in referring the *client* to another *person* or business.

Indicative behaviours

Acting in the following way(s) may tend to show that you have achieved these outcomes and therefore complied with the *Principles*:

IB(1) if a *client* is likely to need advice on *investments,* such as life insurance with an investment element, pension policies and endowment policies, you refer them only to an *independent intermediary*;

IB(2) any *arrangement* you enter into in respect of *regulated mortgage contracts*, general insurance *contracts* (including after the event insurance) or *pure protection contracts* provides that referrals will only be made where this is in the best interests of the particular *client* and the contract is suitable for the needs of that *client*.

IB(3) any *referral* in respect of *regulated mortgage contracts, general insurance contracts* and *pure protection contracts* to a third party that can only offer products from one source, is made only after the *client* has been informed of this limitation.

Acting in the following way(s) may tend to show that you have not achieved these outcomes and therefore not complied with the *Principles*:

IB(4) entering into any *arrangement* which restricts your freedom to recommend any particular business, except in respect of *regulated mortgage* contracts, *general insurance contracts* or *pure protection contracts*;

IB(5) being an *appointed representative*.

In-house practice

The outcomes in this chapter also apply to your *in-house practice*.

Overseas practice

The outcomes in this chapter also apply to your *overseas practice*.

Notes

1   See outcome 15 in Chapter 1, in relation to *financial benefits* that you may receive in respect of introductions to third parties.

2   If the introduction is in connection with the provision of financial services, and your *firm* is not authorised by the Financial Services Authority, you will need to comply with the SRA Financial Services (Scope) Rules 2001 and the SRA Financial Services (Conduct of Business) Rules 2001. Where an introduction is not a regulated activity because you can rely on an exclusion in the *Regulated Activities Order*, you will need nevertheless to consider the outcome 15 in Chapter 1.

3   This chapter should be read in conjunction with Chapter 12 (Separate businesses).

2nd Section – You and your business

Chapter 7 – Management of your business

This chapter is about the management and supervision of your *firm* or *in-house practice*.

Everyone has a role to play in the efficient running of a business, although of course that role will depend on the individual's position within the organisation. However, overarching responsibility for the management of the business in the broadest sense rests with the *manager(s)* of the firm. The *manager(s)* should determine what arrangements are appropriate to meet the outcomes. Factors to be taken into account will include the size and complexity of the *firm*; the number, experience and qualifications of the *employees*; the number of offices; and the nature of the work undertaken.

The outcomes in this chapter show how the *Principles* apply in the context of the management of your business.

Outcomes

You must achieve these outcomes:

O(1) you have a clear and effective governance structure and reporting lines;

O(2) you have effective systems and controls in place to achieve and comply with all the *Principles*, rules and outcomes and other requirements of the Handbook, where applicable;

O(3) you identify, monitor and manage risks to compliance with all the *Principles*, rules and outcomes and other requirements of the Handbook if applicable to you and take steps to address issues identified;

O(4) you maintain systems and controls for monitoring the financial stability of your *firm* and risks to money and *assets* entrusted to you by *clients* and others, and you take steps to address issues identified;

O(5) you comply with legislation applicable to your business, including anti-money laundering and data protection legislation;

O(6) you train individuals working in the *firm* to maintain a level of competence appropriate to their work and level of responsibility;

O(7) you comply with the statutory requirements for the direction and supervision of *reserved legal activities* and *immigration work*;

O(8) you have a system for supervising *clients'* matters, to include the regular checking of the quality of work by suitably competent and experienced people;

O(9) where you outsource *legal activities* or operational functions you ensure such outsourcing:

   (a)   does not adversely affect your ability to comply with, or the *SRA's* ability to monitor your compliance with, your obligations in the Handbook; and.

   (b)   is subject to contractual arrangements that enable the SRA to obtain information from, inspect the records of, or enter the premises of the third party, in relation to the outsourced activities or functions.

Indicative behaviours

Acting in the following way(s) may tend to show that you have achieved these outcomes and therefore complied with the *Principles*:

IB(1) safekeeping of documents and *assets* entrusted to the *firm*;

IB(2) controlling budgets, expenditure and cash flow;

IB(3) identifying and monitoring business continuity risks including *complaints*, credit risks and exposure, claims under legislation relating to matters such as data protection, IT failures and abuses, and damage to offices;

IB(4) making arrangements for the continuation of the *practice* of your *firm* in the event of absences and emergencies, for example holiday or sick leave, with the minimum interruption to *clients'* business.

In-house practice

Outcomes 1–3, 5, and 7–9 apply to your *in-house practice*. Outcomes 6 and 8 apply to you only if you are the *manager* of an in-house legal department.

Overseas practice

The outcomes in this chapter also apply to your *overseas practice*.

Notes

1   All of the chapters in the Code will be relevant to the management of your business, in particular those which require you to have systems and controls in place. For example chapter 1 requires you to have a *complaints* handling procedure and chapter 2 requires you to have an equality and diversity policy.

2   This chapter should also be read with the *SRA Authorisation Rules*, the SRA Financial Services (Conduct of Business) Rules 2001 and the SRA Indemnity Insurance Rules.

Chapter 8 – Publicity

This chapter is about the manner in which you publicise your *firm* or *practice* or any other business. The overriding concern is that *publicity* is not misleading and is sufficiently informative to ensure that *clients* and others can make informed choices.

In your *publicity*, you must comply with statutory requirements and take account of any voluntary codes that may be relevant.

The outcomes in this chapter show how the *Principles* apply in the context of *publicity*.

Outcomes

You must achieve these outcomes:

O(1) your *publicity* in relation to your *firm* or *practice* or for any other business is accurate and not misleading, and is not likely to diminish the trust the public places in you and in the provision of legal services;

O(2) your *publicity* relating to charges is clearly expressed and identifies whether VAT and *disbursements* are included;

O(3) you do not make unsolicited approaches in person or by telephone to *members of the public* in order to publicise your *firm* or *practice* or another business;

O(4) *clients* and the public have appropriate information about you, your *firm* and how you are regulated;

O(5) your letterhead, website and e-mails show the words "authorised and regulated by the Solicitors Regulation Authority" and either the *firm*'s registered name and number if it is an *LLP* or *company* or, if the *firm* is a *partnership* or *sole practitioner*, the name under which it is licensed/authorised by the SRA and the number allocated to it by the SRA.

Indicative behaviours

Acting in the following way(s) may tend to show that you have achieved these outcomes and therefore complied with the *Principles*:

IB(1) where you conduct other regulated activities your publicity discloses the manner in which you are regulated in relation to those activities;

IB(2) where your *firm* is a multi-disciplinary *practice*, any *publicity* in relation to that *practice* makes clear which services are regulated legal services and which are not;

IB(3) any *publicity* intended for a jurisdiction outside England and Wales complies the *Principles* and with the rules in force in that jurisdiction concerning *publicity*;

IB(4) where you and another business jointly market services, the nature of the services provided by each business is clear.

Acting in the following way(s) may tend to show that you have not achieved these outcomes and therefore not complied with the *Principles*:

IB(5) approaching people in the street, at ports of entry, in hospital or at the scene of an accident; including approaching people to conduct a survey which involves collecting contact details of potential *clients*, or otherwise promotes your *firm* or *practice*;

IB(6) allowing any other *person* to conduct *publicity* for your *firm* in a way that would breach the *Principles*;

IB(7) advertising an estimated fee which is pitched at an unrealistically low level;

IB(8) describing overheads of your *firm* (such a normal postage and telephone calls and charges arising in respect of client due diligence under the Money Laundering Regulations 2007) as *disbursements* in your advertisements ;

IB(9) advertising an estimated or fixed fee without making it clear that additional charges may be payable, if that is the case;

IB(10) using a name or description of your *firm* or *practice* that includes the word "solicitor(s)" if none of the *managers* are *solicitors;*

IB(11) advertising your *firm* in a way that suggests that services provided by another business are provided by your *firm;*

IB(12) producing misleading information concerning the professional status of any *manager* or *employee* of your *firm*.

In-house practice

Outcomes 1–4 also apply to your *in-house practice*.

Overseas practice

Outcomes 1 and 4 above apply to your overseas practice. In addition you must comply with the following outcome:

OP(1) *publicity* intended for a jurisdiction outside England and Wales must comply with

    (a)   any applicable law or rules regarding *lawyers' publicity* in the jurisdiction in which your office is based and the jurisdiction in which the publicity is received.

Notes

This chapter should be read in conjunction with Chapters 1 and 9.

Chapter 9 – Fee sharing and referrals

This chapter is about protecting *clients'* interests where you have *arrangements* with third parties who introduce business to you and/or with whom you share your fees. The relationship between *clients* and *firms* should be built on trust, and any arrangement should not jeopardise that trust by, for example, compromising your independence or professional judgement.

The outcomes in this chapter show how the *Principles* apply in the context of fee sharing and *referrals*.

Outcomes

You must achieve these outcomes:

O(1)   your independence and your professional judgement are not prejudiced by virtue of any *arrangement* with another *person*;

O(2)   your *clients'* interests are protected regardless of the interests of an *introducer* or *fee sharer* or your interest in receiving *referrals*;

O(3)   *clients* are in a position to make informed decisions about how to pursue their matter;

O(4)   *clients* are informed of any financial or other interest which an *introducer* has in referring the *client* to you;

O(5)   *clients* are informed of any fee sharing *arrangement* that is relevant to their matter;

O(6)   you do not make payments to an *introducer* in respect of *clients* who are the subject of criminal proceedings or who have the benefit of public funding.

Indicative behaviours

Acting in the following way(s) may tend to show that you have achieved these outcomes and therefore complied with the *Principles*:

IB(1)   only entering into *arrangements* with reputable third parties and monitoring the outcome of those *arrangements* to ensure that *clients* are treated fairly;

IB(2)   in any case where a *client* has entered into, or is proposing to enter into, an *arrangement* with an *introducer* in connection with their matter, which is not in their best interests, advising the *client* that this is the case;

IB(3)   terminating any *arrangement* with an *introducer* or *fee sharer* which is causing you to breach any requirements of the Code;

IB(4)   being satisfied that any *client* referred by an *introducer* has not been acquired as a result of marketing or other activities which, if done by a *person* regulated by the SRA, would be contrary to the *Principles*;

IB(5) drawing the *client's* attention to any payments you make, or other consideration you provide in connection with any *referral*;

IB(6) where information needs to be given to *clients*, ensuring the information is clear and in writing.

Acting in the following way(s) may tend to show that you have not achieved these outcomes and therefore not complied with the *Principles*:

IB(7) entering into any type of business relationship with a third party, such as an unauthorised *partnership*, which places you in breach of the *SRA Authorisation Rules* or any other regulatory requirements in the Handbook;

IB(8) allowing an *introducer* or *fee sharer* to influence the advice you give to *clients*;

IB(9) accepting *referrals* where you have reason to believe that *clients* have been pressurised or misled into instructing you.

In-house practice

The outcomes in this chapter also apply to your *in-house practice*.

Overseas practice

The outcomes in this chapter also apply to your *overseas practice*, except where they conflict with the SRA European Cross-Border Practice Rules which will prevail in any conflict.

Notes

1.   This chapter should be read in conjunction with:

- Chapter 1 (Client care)

- Chapter 4 (Confidentiality and disclosure)

- Chapter 8 (Publicity)

- The *SRA Authorisation Rules*

- The SRA European Cross-Border Practice Rules

3rd Section – You and your regulator

Chapter 10 – You and your regulator

This chapter is about co-operation with your regulators and ombudsmen, primarily the SRA and the *Legal Ombudsman*.

The information which we are requesting from *firms* will help us understand any risks to *clients*, and the public interest more generally.

The outcomes in this chapter show how the *Principles* apply in the context of you and your regulator.

Outcomes

You must achieve these outcomes:

O(1) you ensure that you comply with all the reporting and notification requirements in the Handbook;

O(2) you provide the SRA with relevant information to enable the SRA to decide upon any application you make, such as for a practising certificate, registration, recognition or a licence and whether any conditions should apply;

O(3) you notify the SRA promptly of any changes to relevant information about you including serious financial difficulty, action taken against you by another regulator and serious failure to comply with or achieve the *Principles*, rules, outcomes and other requirements of the Handbook;

O(4) you report to the SRA promptly, serious misconduct by any person or *firm* authorised by the SRA, or any *employee, manager* or *owner* of any such *firm* (taking into account, where necessary, your duty of confidentiality to your *client*);

O(5) you ensure that the SRA is in a position to assess whether any persons requiring prior approval are fit and proper at the point of approval and remain so;

O(6) you co-operate fully with the SRA and the *Legal Ombudsman* at all times including in relation to any investigation about a *claim for redress* against you;

O(7) you do not attempt to prevent anyone from providing information to the SRA or the *Legal Ombudsman*;

O(8) you comply promptly with any written notice from the SRA;

O(9) you produce for inspection by the SRA all *documents* held by you, or held under your control, and all information and explanations requested, in connection with your *practice* or in connection with any trust of which you are, or formerly were, a trustee; and you comply with all requests from the SRA as to:

(a) the form in which you produce any *documents* you hold electronically; and

(b) photocopies of any *documents* to take away;

O(10) you provide any necessary permissions for information to be given, so as to enable the SRA to:

(a) prepare a report on any *documents* produced; and

(b) seek verification from *clients*, staff and the banks, building societies or other financial institutions used by you;

O(11) When required by the SRA in relation to a matter specified by the SRA, you:

(a) act promptly to investigate whether any *person* may have a *claim for redress* against you;

(b) provide the SRA with a report on the outcome of such an investigation, identifying *persons* who may have such a claim;

(c) notify *persons* that they may have a right of redress against you, providing them with information as to the nature of the possible claim, about the *firm's complaints* procedure and about the *Legal Ombudsman*; and

(d) where you have identified a *person* who may have a *claim for redress*, ensuring the matter is dealt with under the *firm's complaints* procedure as if that *person* had made a *complaint*;

O(12) you do not attempt to abrogate to any third party your regulatory responsibilities in the Handbook, including the role of *Compliance Officer for Legal Practice* (*COLP*) or *Compliance Officer for Finance and Administration* (*COFA*);

O(13) once you are aware that your *firm* will cease to *practise*, you effect the orderly and transparent wind-down of activities, including informing the SRA before the firm closes.

Indicative behaviours

Acting in the following way(s) may tend to show that you have achieved these outcomes and therefore complied with the *Principles*:

IB(1) actively monitoring your achievement of the outcomes in order to improve standards and identify non-achievement of the outcomes;

IB(2) actively monitoring your financial stability and viability in order to identify and mitigate any risks to the public;

IB(3) notifying the SRA promptly of any indicators of serious financial difficulty, such as inability to pay your professional indemnity insurance premium, or rent or salaries, or breach of bank covenants;

IB(4) notifying the SRA promptly when you become aware that your business may not be financially viable to continue trading as a going concern, for example because of difficult trading conditions, poor cash flow, increasing overheads, loss of *managers* or *employees* and/or loss of sources of revenue;

IB(5) notifying the SRA of any serious issues identified as a result of monitoring referred to in **IB(1)** and **IB(2)** above, and producing a plan for remedying issues that have been identified;

IB(6) responding appropriately to any serious issues identified concerning competence and fitness and propriety of your *employees*, *managers* and *owners*;

IB(7) if a *client* makes a claim against you, or notifies an intention to do so, or if you discover an act or omission which could give rise to a claim:

    (a) informing the *client* that independent advice should be sought (unless the *client's* loss, if any, is trivial and you promptly remedy that loss);

    (b) considering whether a *conflict of interests* has arisen, and if so not acting further for the *client* in the matter giving rise to the claim; and

    (c) notifying your compulsory professional indemnity insurer under the SRA Indemnity Insurance Rules or, if appropriate, the Solicitors Indemnity Fund Ltd.

IB(8) reporting disciplinary action taken against you by another regulator;

IB(9) informing the SRA promptly when you become aware of a significant change to your *firm*, for example:

- key personnel, such as a *manager*, *CoLP* or *CoFA*, joining or leaving the *firm*;
- a merger with, or an acquisition by or of, another *firm*;

IB(10) having appropriate arrangements for the orderly transfer of *clients'* property to another *authorised body* if your *firm* closes.

Acting in the following way(s) may tend to show that you have not achieved these outcomes and therefore not complied with the *Principles*:

IB(11) entering into an agreement which would attempt to preclude the SRA or the *Legal Ombudsman* from investigating any actual or potential *complaint* or allegation of professional misconduct;

IB(12) unless you can properly allege malice, issuing defamation proceedings in respect of a *complaint* to the SRA.

In-house practice

Outcomes 1–12 in this chapter also apply to your *in-house practice*.

893

Overseas practice

The outcomes in this chapter also apply to your *overseas practice*.

Notes

1. A notice under this chapter is deemed to be duly served:

    (a) on the date on which it is delivered to or left at your last notified *practising* address;

    (b) on the date on which it is sent electronically to your e-mail or fax address; or

    (c) seven days after it has been sent by post or document exchange to your last notified *practising* address.

2. The outcomes in this chapter should be considered in conjunction with the following:

    *   Chapter 7 (Management of your business) – requirements for risk management procedures;

    *   Rule 8.7 of the *SRA Authorisation Rules* – annual reporting requirements for authorised bodies and requirement for the COFA to report breaches of the SRA Accounts Rules;

    *   Rule 18 of the SRA Practice Framework Rules – requirements for *authorised bodies* to supply information to the SRA on composition and structure, changes in composition, changes in status from unlimited to limited *company* and insolvency.

4th Section – You and others

Chapter 11 – Relations with third parties

This chapter is about ensuring you do not take unfair advantage of those you deal with and that you act in a manner which promotes the proper operation of the legal system.

This includes your conduct in relation to *undertakings*; there is no obligation to give or receive an *undertaking* on behalf of a *client* but, if you do, you must ensure that you achieve the outcomes listed in this chapter.

The conduct requirements in this area extend beyond professional and business matters. They apply in any circumstances in which you may use your professional title to advance your personal interests.

The outcomes in this chapter show how the *Principles* apply in the context of your relations with third parties.

Outcomes

You must achieve these outcomes:

O(1) you do not take unfair advantage of third parties in either your professional or personal capacity;

O(2) you perform all *undertakings* given by you within an agreed timescale or within a reasonable amount of time;

O(3) where you act for a seller of land, you inform all buyers immediately of the seller's intention to deal with more than one buyer;

O(4) you properly administer oaths, affirmations or declarations where you are authorised to do so.

Indicative behaviours

Acting in the following way(s) may tend to show that you have achieved these outcomes and therefore complied with the *Principles*:

IB(1) providing sufficient time and information to enable the costs in any matter to be agreed;

IB(2) returning documents or money sent subject to an express condition if you are unable to comply with that condition;

IB(3) returning documents or money on demand if they are sent on condition that they are held to the sender's order;

IB(4) ensuring that you do not communicate with another party when you are aware that the other party has retained a *lawyer* in a matter, except:

- to request the name and address of the other party's *lawyer*; or

- the other party's *lawyer* consents to you communicating with the *client*; or

- where there are exceptional circumstances;

IB(5) maintaining an effective system which records when *undertakings* have been given and when they have been discharged;

IB(6) where an *undertaking* is given which is dependent upon the happening of a future event and it becomes apparent the future event will not occur, notifying the recipient of this.

Acting in the following way(s) may tend to show that you have not achieved these outcomes and therefore not complied with the *Principles*:

IB(7) taking unfair advantage of an opposing party's lack of legal knowledge where they have not instructed a *lawyer*;

IB(8) demanding anything for yourself or on behalf of your *client*, that is not legally recoverable , such as when you are instructed to collect a simple debt, demanding from the debtor the cost of the letter of claim since it cannot be said at that stage that such a cost is legally recoverable;

IB(9) using your professional status or qualification to take unfair advantage of another *person* in order to advance your personal interests;

IB(10) taking unfair advantage of a public office held by you, or a member of your family, or a member of your *firm* or their family.

In-house practice

The outcomes in this chapter also apply to your *in-house practice*.

Overseas practice

The outcomes in this chapter also apply to your *overseas practice*, except that outcome 3 only applies if the land in question is situated in England and Wales.

Notes

1.   This chapter should be read in conjunction with chapter 7 (Management of your business) in relation to the system you will need to have in place to control *undertakings*.

Chapter 12 – Separate businesses

The purpose of this chapter is to ensure *clients* are protected when they obtain mainstream legal services from a *firm* regulated by the SRA. This is accomplished by restricting the services that can be provided through a *separate business* that is not authorised by the SRA or another *approved regulator*.

This chapter addresses two kinds of services:

(a)   those which you cannot offer through a *separate business* ("*prohibited separate business activities*" – see definition in Chapter 14). These are "mainstream" legal services which members of the public would expect you to offer as a *lawyer* regulated by the SRA or another *approved regulator*; and

(b)   those which you can offer either through a *separate business* ("a *permitted separate business*" – see definition in Chapter 14), or through an *authorised body*. These are the kind of services a member of the public would not necessarily expect to be provided only by a *lawyer* regulated by the SRA or another *approved regulator*, but which are "solicitor-like" services.

Clients of a *permitted separate business* will not have the same statutory protections as *clients* of an *authorised body* and it is important that this is clear to *clients* of the *separate business*, particularly where they are being referred from one business to the other.

This chapter does not address services which cannot be, or would not normally be, offered through an *authorised body*.

The outcomes in this chapter show how the *Principles* apply in the context of separate businesses.

Outcomes

You must achieve these outcomes:

O(1)   you do not:

(a)   *own*,

(b)   have a significant interest in, or

(c)   *actively participate in*,

a *separate business* which conducts *prohibited separate business activities*.

O(2)   if you are a *firm*:

(a)   you are not *owned by*, or

(b)   *connected with*,

a *separate business* which conducts *prohibited separate business activities*.

O(3)   where you:

(a)   have a significant interest in,

(b)   *actively participate in,*

(c)   *own* or

(d)   are a *firm* and *owned by* or *connected with,*

a *permitted separate business,* you have safeguards in place to ensure that *clients* are not misled about the extent to which the services that you and the *separate business* are offering are regulated;

O(4)   you do not represent any *permitted separate business* as being regulated by the SRA or any of its activities as being provided by an individual who is regulated by the SRA;

O(5)   you are only *connected with* reputable *separate businesses;*

O(6)   you are only *connected with* a *permitted separate business* which is an *appointed representative* if it is an *appointed representative* of an independent financial adviser.

Indicative behaviours

Acting in the following way(s) may tend to show that *you* have achieved these outcomes and therefore complied with the *Principles*:

IB(1)   ensuring that *client* information and records are not disclosed to the *permitted separate business,* without the express consent of the *client;*

IB(2)   complying with the SRA Accounts Rules and not allowing the *client account* to be used to hold money for the *permitted separate business;*

IB(3)   where you are referring a *client* to a *permitted separate business,* informing *clients* of your interest in the *separate business;*

IB(4)   terminating any connection with a *permitted separate business* where you have reason to doubt the integrity or competence of that *separate business.*

In-house practice

Outcomes 1 and 3–6 in this chapter apply to your *in-house practice.*

Overseas practice

Notes

1.   It is important that *clients* are not misled or confused about the regulatory status of a *permitted separate business,* the services it provides and the people working within it. Particular care needs to be taken regarding:

- the name or branding of the *separate business;*
- misleading *publicity;* and
- the proximity of the permitted *separate business* to your *firm,* particularly if you share premises.

2.   This chapter should be read in conjunction with:

- Chapter 3 (Conflicts of interests)
- Chapter 6 (Your client and introductions to third parties); and
- Chapter 8 (Publicity).

5th section – Application, waivers and interpretation

Chapter 13 – Application and waivers

The SRA Code of Conduct applies to you in the following circumstances (and "you" must be construed accordingly):

Application of the SRA Code of Conduct in relation to practice from an office in England and Wales

1. Subject to paragraphs 2 to 9 and any other provisions in the Code, the Code applies to you if you are:

    (a) a *solicitor* or a *REL* who is:

        (i)   a *sole practitioner*;

        (ii) a *manager* of an *authorised body*, or of a body which is a *manager* of an *authorised body*, or of a body which should be a *recognised body* but has not been recognised by the SRA;

        (iii) an *employee* (including as an assistant, associate, professional support *lawyer*, consultant, locum or otherwise employed in the practice) of an *authorised body*, *recognised sole practitioner*, or of a body which should be a *recognised body* but has not been recognised by the SRA, or of a *sole practitioner* who should be a *recognised sole practitioner* but has not been authorised by the *SRA*;

        (iv) a *manager* or *employee* of an *authorised non-SRA firm*, or a *manager* of a body which is a *manager* of an *authorised non-SRA firm*, when doing work authorised by the *SRA* as an in-house *lawyer*;

        (v)   employed as an in-house *lawyer*;

        (vi) an *owner* of an *authorised body*, or of a body which should be a *recognised body* but has not been recognised by the SRA, even if the *owner* undertakes no work for the body's *clients*;

    (b) a *RFL* who is:

        (i)   a *manager* of an *authorised body*, or of a body which is a *manager* of an *authorised body*, or of a body which should be a *recognised body* but has not been recognised by the SRA;

        (ii) an *employee* (including an assistant, associate, professional support *lawyer*, consultant, locum or otherwise employed in the *practice*) of an *authorised body*, *recognised sole practitioner*, a body which should be a *recognised body* but has not been recognised by the SRA, or of a *sole practitioner* who should be a *recognised sole practitioner* but has not been recognised by the SRA;

        (iii) a *manager* or *employee* of an *authorised non-SRA firm*, or a *manager* of a body which is a *manager* of an *authorised non-SRA firm*, when doing work authorised by the SRA as an in-house *lawyer*;

        (iv) an *owner* of an *authorised body*, or a body which should be a *recognised body* but has not been recognised by the SRA even if the *owner* undertakes no work for the body's *clients*;

    (c) an *authorised body*, or a body which should be a *recognised body* but has not been recognised by the SRA;

(d)   a *manager* or *employee* of an *authorised body*, or of a body which should be a *recognised body* but has not been recognised by the SRA;

(e)   an *employee* of a *recognised sole practitioner*, or of a *sole practitioner* who should be a *recognised sole practitioner* but has not been recognised by the SRA;

and "you" includes "your" as appropriate.

2.   Chapters 10, 12, 13 and 14 of the Code apply to you if you are a *solicitor, REL* or *RFL*:

(a)   practising as a *manager* or *employee* of an *authorised non-SRA firm* when doing work of a sort authorised by the *authorised non-SRA firm*'s approved regulator, or

(b)   *owner* of an *authorised non-SRA firm* even if you undertake no work for the body's clients.

Application of the SRA Code of Conduct in relation to practice from an office outside England and Wales

3.   Subject to 5 and 6 below, the Code applies, in relation to *practice from an office* outside the *UK* to:

(a)   a *solicitor* as an individual, whether or not the *solicitor's firm* or *employer* is subject to this Code;

(b)   a *lawyer-controlled body*;

(c)   a *lawyer of England and Wales* other than a *solicitor*, and a non-lawyer, in relation to *practice* as a *manager* of an *authorised body*.

4.   Subject to 5 and 6 below the Code applies, in relation to *practice from an office* in Scotland or Northern Ireland to:

(a)   a *solicitor* or *REL* as an individual, whether or not the *solicitor* or *REL's firm* or *employer* is subject to this Code;

(b)   a *lawyer-controlled body*;

(c)   a *REL-controlled body*;

(d)   a *lawyer of England and Wales* other than a *solicitor*, a European *lawyer* registered with the Bar Standards Board and to a non-lawyer, in relation to *practice* as a *manager* of an *authorised body*; and

(e)   a *solicitor* who was formerly a *REL*, when *practising* as a *lawyer* of an *Establishment Directive profession*.

5.   If any outcome in the Code does not apply to your *overseas practice*, you may disregard that outcome in relation to your *overseas practice*, but you must comply with any alternative provision substituted for *overseas practice*.

6.   If compliance with any outcome in the Code would result in your breaching local law, you may disregard that outcome to the extent necessary to comply with that local law.

Application of the SRA Code of Conduct outside practice

7.   In relation to activities which fall outside *practice*, as defined in chapter 14 (Interpretation), whether undertaken as a *lawyer* or in some other business or private capacity, the following apply to you if you are a *solicitor* or *REL*:

(a)   outcome 1 of chapter 11; and

(b)   outcome 2 of chapter 11.

General Provisions

8.   The extent to which you are expected to implement the requirements of the Code will

depend on your role in the *firm*, or your way of *practising*. For example, those who are managing the business will be expected to have more influence on how the *firm* or business is run than those *practising* in-house but not managing a legal department, or those *practising* as *employees* of a *firm*.

9.   You must deliver all outcomes which are relevant to you and your situation.

10.   Where in accordance with this chapter, the requirements of the Code apply to a *licensed body*, this extends to the *reserved legal activities*, and other activities regulated by the SRA, carried on by the body.

Waivers

In any particular case or cases the SRA Board shall have the power, in exceptional circumstances, to waive in writing the provisions of these outcomes for a particular purpose or purposes expressed in such waiver, to place conditions on and to revoke such a waiver.

Chapter 14 – Interpretation

"*AJA*" means the Administration of Justice Act 1985;

"*actively participate in*" means, in relation to a *separate business*, having any active involvement in the *separate business*, and includes:

(a)   any direct control over the business, and any indirect control through another person such as a spouse; and

(b)   any active participation in the business or the provision of its services to customers;

"*appointed representative*" has the meaning given in the Financial Services and Markets Act 2000;

"*approved regulator*" means any body listed as an *approved regulator* in paragraph 1 of Schedule 4 to the *LSA* or designated as an *approved regulator* by an order under paragraph 17 of that Schedule;

"*arrangement*" in relation to financial services, fee sharing and *referrals*, in chapters 1, 6 and 9, means any express or tacit agreement between you and another *person*, whether contractually binding or not;

"*assets*" includes, for example, money, documents, wills, deeds, investments and other property;

"*authorised body*" means a body that has been authorised by the *SRA*, to *practise* as a *licensed body* or a *recognised body*;

"*authorised non-SRA firm*" means a firm which is authorised to carry on *legal activities* by an *approved regulator* other than the *SRA*;

"*body corporate*" means a *company*, an *LLP*, or a *partnership* which is a legal *person* in its own right;

"*claim for redress*" has the same meaning as in section 158 of the *LSA*;

"*client*" where the context permits, includes prospective and former *clients*;

"*client account*" has the meaning given in the SRA Accounts Rules

"*client conflict*" for the purposes of Chapter 3, means any situation where you owe separate duties to act in the best interests of two or more *clients* in relation to the same or related matters, and those duties conflict, or there is a significant risk that those duties may conflict;

"*client money*" has the meaning given in the SRA Accounts Rules

"*COFA or Compliance Officer for Finance and Administration*" shall be construed in accordance with rule 8.5 of the *SRA Authorisation Rules* and in relation to a *licensable body* is a reference to its Head of Finance and Administration within the meaning of the *LSA*;

"*COLP or Compliance Officer for Legal Practice*" shall be construed in accordance with rule 8.5 of the *SRA Authorisation Rules* and in relation to a *licensable body* is a reference to its Head of Legal Practice within the meaning of the *LSA*;

"*Companies Acts*" means the Companies Act 1985 and the Companies Act 2006;

"*company*" means a *company* registered under the *Companies Acts*, an overseas company incorporated in an *Establishment Directive* state and registered under the Companies Act 1985 and/or the Companies Act 2006 or a *societas Europaea*;

"*competing for the same objective*" for the purposes of Chapter 3 means any situation in which one or more clients are competing for an *objective* which, if attained by one client will make that *objective* unattainable to the other *client* or *clients* and "*objective*" means, for the purposes of Chapter 3, an asset, contract or business opportunity which one or more *clients* are seeking to acquire or recover through a liquidation (or some other form of insolvency process) or by means of an auction or tender process or a bid or offer which is not public;

"*commercial arrangement*" means an arrangement under which you receive referrals of business from, and/or share your fees with, another person, business or organisation, including not-for-profit organisations;

"*complaint*" means an oral or written expression of dissatisfaction which alleges that the complainant has suffered (or may suffer) financial loss, distress, inconvenience or other detriment;

"*compulsory professional indemnity insurance*" means the insurance you are required to have in place under the SRA Indemnity Insurance Rules;

"*conflict of interests*" means any situation where:

    (a)   you owe separate duties to act in the best interests of two or more *clients* in relation to the same or related matters, and those duties conflict, or there is a significant risk that those duties may conflict (a "*client conflict*"); or

    (b)   your duty to act in the best interests of any *client* in relation to a matter conflicts, or there is a significant risk that it may conflict, with your own interests in relation to that or a related matter (an "*own interest conflict*");

"*connected with*" means in relation to a *separate business* for the purpose of Chapter 12:

    (a)   having one or more *partner(s)*, *owner(s)*, *director(s)* or *member(s)* in common with the separate business;

    (b)   being a *subsidiary company* of the same holding company as the *separate business*; or

    (c)   being a *subsidiary company* of the separate business;

"*conveyance of land*" means, for the purposes of Chapter 3, the transfer of land for value, and the grant or assignment of a lease or some other interest in land for value;

"*court*" means any *court*, tribunal or enquiry of England and Wales, or a British court martial, or any *court* of another jurisdiction;

"*director*" means a *director* of a *company*; and in relation to a *societas Europaea* includes:

    (a)   in a two-tier system, a member of the management organ and a member of the supervisory organ; and

    (b)   in a one-tier system, a member of the administrative organ;

"*disbursement*" means any sum spent or to be spent on behalf of a *client* or trust (including any VAT element);

"*document*" in Chapter 10, includes documents, whether written or electronic, relating to the *firm*'s *client accounts* and *office accounts*;

"*employee*" includes an individual who is:

(a) employed as a *director* of a *company*;

(b) engaged under a contract of service (for example, as an assistant *solicitor*) by a *firm* or its wholly owned service *company*; or

(c) engaged under a contract for services (for example, as a consultant or a locum), made between a *firm* or organisation and:

   (i) that individual;

   (ii) an employment agency; or

   (iii) a *company* which is not held out to the public as providing legal services and is wholly owned and directed by that individual,

   under which the *firm* or organisation has exclusive control over the individual's time for all or part of the individual's working week; or in relation to which the *firm* or organisation has designated the individual as a fee earner in accordance with arrangements between the *firm* or organisation and the Legal Services Commission pursuant to the Access to Justice Act 1999;

and "***employer***" is to be construed accordingly;

"*Establishment Directive*" means the Establishment of Lawyers Directive 98/5/EC;

"*Establishment Directive profession*" means any profession listed in Article 1.2(a) of the *Establishment Directive*, including a *solicitor*, barrister or advocate of the *UK*;

"*Establishment Directive state*" means a state to which the *Establishment Directive* applies;

"*fee sharer*" means another *person* or business who or which shares your fees;

"*financial benefit*" includes, for example, any commission, discount or rebate, but does not include your fees or interest earned on any *client account*;

"*firm*" means an *authorised body* or any business through which a *solicitor* or *REL practises* other than *in-house practice*;

"*general insurance contract*" means any contract of insurance within Part I of Schedule 1 to the Financial Services and Markets Act 2000 (Regulated Activities) Order 2001 (SI 2001/544);

"*holding company*" has the meaning given in the Companies Act 2006;

"*immigration work*" means the provision of immigration advice and immigration services, as defined in section 82 of the Immigration and Asylum Act 1999;

"*independent intermediary*" in chapter 6, means an independent financial adviser who is able to advise on investment products from across the whole of the market and offers consumers the option of paying fees rather than receiving payment through commission;

"*introducer*" means any *person*, business or organisation who or that introduces or refers potential *clients* to your business, or recommends your business to *clients* or otherwise puts you and *clients* in touch with each other;

"*investment*" for the purposes of chapter 6, has the meaning given in the SRA Financial Services (Scope) Rules 2001;

"*in-house practice*" means *practice* as a *solicitor*, *REL* or *RFL* (as appropriate) in accordance with Rules 1.1(c)(B), 1.1(d)(B), 1.1(e), 1.2(f), 2.1(c)(B), 2.1(d)(B), 2.1(e), 2.2(f), 3.1(b)(B) or 3.1(c)(B) of the SRA Practice Framework Rules [2011];

"*lawyer*" means a member of one of the following professions, entitled to practise as such:

(a) the profession of *solicitor*, barrister or advocate of the *UK*;

(b)   a profession whose members are authorised to carry on *legal activities* by an *approved regulator* other than the *SRA*;

(c)   an *Establishment Directive profession* other than a *UK* profession;

(d)   a legal profession which has been approved by the *SRA* for the purpose of *recognised bodies* in England and Wales; and

(e)   any other regulated legal profession specified by the *SRA* for the purpose of this definition;

"*lawyer-controlled body*" means an *authorised body* in which *lawyers of England and Wales* constitute the national group of *lawyers* with the largest (or equal largest) share of control of the body either as individual *managers* or by their share in the control of bodies which are *managers*;

"*lawyer of England and Wales*" means:

(a)   a *solicitor*; or

(b)   an individual who is authorised to carry on *legal activities* in England and Wales by an *approved regulator* other than the *SRA*, but excludes a member of an *Establishment Directive profession* registered with the Bar Standards Board under the *Establishment Directive*;

"*legal activity*" has the meaning given in section 12 of the *LSA* and includes any *reserved legal activity* and any other activity which consists of the provision of legal advice or assistance, or representation in connection with the application of the law or resolution of legal disputes;

"*Legal Ombudsman*" means the scheme administered by the Office for Legal Complaints under Part 6 of the *LSA*;

"*licensable body*" means a body which meets the criteria in rule 14 (eligibility criteria for licensable bodies) of the SRA Practice Framework Rules 2011;

"*licensed body*" means a body licensed by the *SRA* under Part 5 of the *LSA*;

"*LLP*" means a limited liability partnership incorporated under the Limited Liability Partnerships Act 2000;

"*LSA*" means the Legal Services Act 2007;

"*manager*" means:

(a)   a *member* of an *LLP*;

(b)   a *director* of a *company*;

(c)   a *partner* in a *partnership*; or

(d)   in relation to any other body, a member of its governing body;

"*member*" means:

(a)   in relation to a *company* a *person* who has agreed to be a *member* of the *company* and whose name is entered in the *company's* register of *members*; and

(b)   in relation to an *LLP*, a member of that *LLP*;

"*members of the public*" for the purposes of Chapter 8 does not include:

(a)   a current or former *client*;

(b)   another *firm* or its *manager*;

(c)   an existing or potential professional or business connection; or

(d)   a commercial organisation or public body;

"*office account*" has the meaning given in the SRA Accounts Rules;

"*overseas practice*" means *practice from an office* outside England and Wales, except in the case of an *REL*, where it means *practice from an office* in Scotland or Northern Ireland;

"*own*" means having a *substantial ownership interest* in and "*owner*" and "*owned by*" shall be construed accordingly;

"*own interest conflict*" for the purpose of Chapter 3, means any situation where your duty to act in the best interests of any *client* in relation to a matter conflicts, or there is a significant risk that it may conflict, with your own interests in relation to that or a related matter;

"*partner*" means a *person* who is or is held out as a partner in a *partnership*;

"*partnership*" means an unincorporated body in which *persons* are or are held out as *partners* and does not include a body incorporated as an *LLP*;

"*permitted separate business*" means, for the purpose of Chapter 12, a *separate business* offering any of the following services:

(a)   alternative dispute resolution;

(b)   financial services;

(c)   estate agency;

(d)   management consultancy;

(e)   company secretarial services;

(f)   acting as a parliamentary agent;

(g)   practising as a *lawyer* of another jurisdiction;

(h)   acting as a bailiff;

(i)   acting as nominee, trustee or executor outside England and Wales;

(j)   acting as a nominee, trustee or executor in England and Wales where such activity is provided as a subsidiary but necessary part of a *separate business* providing financial services;

(k)   providing legal advice or drafting legal documents not included in (a) to (j) above, where such activity is provided as a subsidiary but necessary part of some other service which is one of the main services of the *separate business*; and

(l)   providing any other business, advisory or agency service which could be provided through a *firm* or *in-house practice* but is not a *prohibited separate business activity*;

"*person*" includes a *body corporate*, *partnership* and other unincorporated association or body of persons;

"*practice*" means the activities, in that capacity, of:

(a)   a *solicitor*;

(b)   a *REL*, from an office or offices within the *UK*;

(c)   a member of an *Establishment Directive profession* registered with the Bar Standards Board under the *Establishment Directive*, carried out from an office or offices in England and Wales;

(d)   a *RFL*, from an office or offices in England and Wales as:

    (i)   an *employee* of a *recognised sole practitioner*;

    (ii)   a *manager*, *employee* or *owner* of an *authorised body* or of an *authorised non-SRA firm*; or

    (iii)   a *manager*, *employee* or *owner* of a body which is a *manager* or *owner* of an *authorised body* or of an *authorised non-SRA firm*;

(e)   an *authorised body*;

(f)   a *manager* of an *authorised body*;

(g)   a *person employed* in England and Wales by an *authorised body* or *recognised sole practitioner*;

(h)   a lawyer of England and Wales; or

(i)   an *authorised non-SRA firm*;

but does not include providing professional services without remuneration for friends, relatives or *companies* wholly owned by the *solicitor* or *REL's* family, or registered charities; and *"practise"* and *"practising"* should be construed accordingly;

"practice from an office" includes practice carried on:

(a)   from an office at which you are based; or

(b)   from an office of a *firm* in which you are the sole practitioner, or a *manager*, or in which you have an ownership interest, even if you are not based there;

"Principles" means the *Principles* in the SRA Handbook;

"prohibited separate business activities" means for the purpose of Chapter 12:

(a)   the conduct of any matter which could come before a *court*, tribunal or enquiry, whether or not proceedings are started;

(b)   advocacy before a *court*, tribunal or enquiry;

(c)   instructing counsel in any part of the *UK*;

(d)   *immigration work*;

(e)   any activity in relation to conveyancing, applications for probate or letters of administration, or drawing trust deeds or *court* documents, which is reserved to *solicitors* and others under the *LSA*;

(f)   drafting wills;

(g)   acting as nominee, trustee or executor in England and Wales, where such activity is not provided as a subsidiary but necessary part of a *separate business* providing financial services; and

(h)   providing legal advice or drafting legal documents not included in (a) to (g) above where such activity is not provided as a subsidiary but necessary part of some other service which is one of the main services of the *separate business*;

"publicity" includes all promotional material and activity, including the name or description of your *firm*, stationery, advertisements, brochures, websites, directory entries, media appearances, promotional press releases, and direct approaches to potential *clients* and other *persons*, whether conducted in person, in writing, or in electronic form, but does not include press releases prepared on behalf of a *client*;

"pure protection contract" has the meaning given in rule 8(1) of the SRA's Financial Services (Scope) Rules 2001;

"recognised body" means a body recognised by the *SRA* under section 9 of the *AJA*;

"recognised sole practitioner" means a *solicitor* or *REL* authorised by the *SRA* under section 1B of the Solicitors Act 1974 to practise as a *sole practitioner*;

"referrals" includes any situation in which another *person*, business or organisation introduces or refers a *client* to your business, recommends your business to a *client* or otherwise puts you and a *client* in touch with each other;

"REL" or *"registered European lawyer"* means an individual registered with the *SRA* under regulation 17 of the European Communities (Lawyer's Practice) Regulations 2000 (SI 2000/1119);

"*REL-controlled body*" means an *authorised body* in which *RELs* or *RELs* together with *lawyers* of England and Wales and or/European *lawyers* registered with the Bar Standards Board, constitute the national group of lawyers with the largest (or equal largest) share of control of the body, either as individual *managers* of by their share in the control of bodies which are *managers*, and for this purpose *RELs* and European *lawyers* registered with the Bar Standards Board belong to the national group of England and Wales;

"*Regulated Activities Order*" means the Financial Services and Markets Act 2000 (Regulated Activities) Order 2001 (SI 2001/554);

"*regulated mortgage contract*" has the meaning given by the *Regulated Activities Order*;

"*reserved legal activity*" has the meaning given in section 12 of the *LSA*, and includes the exercise of a right of audience, the conduct of litigation, reserved instrument activities, probate activities, notarial activities and the administration of oaths, as defined in Schedule 2 of the *LSA*;

"*RFL*" or "*registered foreign lawyer*" means an individual registered with the *SRA* under section 89 of the Courts and Legal Services Act 1990;

"*separate business*" means a business which is not an *authorised body*, a *recognised sole practitioner*, an *authorised non-SRA firm* or an *in-house practice* and includes businesses situated overseas;

"*shares*" means:

(a) in relation to a body with a share capital, allotted shares (within the meaning of the Companies Acts);

(b) in relation to a body with capital but no share capital, rights to share in the capital of the body;

(c) in relation to a body without capital, interests:

(i) conferring any right to share in the profits, or liability to contribute to the losses, of the body; or

(ii) giving rise to an obligation to contribute to the debts or expenses of the body in the event of a winding up;

"*societas Europaea*" means a European public limited liability *company* within the meaning of article 1 of Council Regulation 2157/2001/EC;

"*sole practitioner*" means a *solicitor* or *REL* practising as a sole principal, and does not include a *solicitor* or *REL practising* in-house;

"*solicitor*" means an individual who is a *solicitor* of the Senior Courts of England and Wales;

"*SRA*" means the Solicitors Regulation Authority, and reference to the *SRA* as an *approved regulator* or *licensing authority* means the *SRA* carrying out regulatory functions assigned to the Law Society as an *approved regulator* or *licensing authority*;

"*SRA Authorisation Rules*" means the SRA Authorisation Rules for Legal Services Bodies and Licensable Bodies 2011;

"*subsidiary company*" has the meaning given in the Companies Act 2006;

"*substantial ownership interest*" in a *firm* ("A") means:

(a) owning at least 10% of the *shares* in A;

(b) owning at least 10% of the *shares* in apparent *undertaking* of A;

(c) being entitled to exercise, or control the exercise of, at least 10% of the voting rights in A; or

(d) being entitled to exercise, or control the exercise of, at least 10% of the voting rights of a *parent undertaking* of A;

and for the purpose of this definition, *"parent undertaking"* has the meaning given in the Financial Services and Markets Act 2000;

"Substantially common interest" for the purposes of Chapter 3, means a situation:

(a)   where there is a clear common purpose in relation to any matter or a particular aspect of it between the *clients* and a strong consensus on how it is to be achieved and the *client conflict* is peripheral to this common purpose; and

(b)   which does not involve a transfer of land or the grant or assignment of a lease or some other interest in land.

"UK" means United Kingdom;

"undertaking" means a statement, given orally or in writing, whether or not it includes the word "undertake" or *"undertaking"*, made by or on behalf of you or your *firm*, to someone who reasonably places reliance on it, that you or your *firm* will do something or cause something to be done, or refrain from doing something;

"voting rights" in relation to a body which does not have general meetings at which matters are decided by the exercise of *voting rights*, means the right under the constitution of the body to direct the overall policy of the body or alter the terms of its constitution.

Chapter 15 – Commencement, repeals and transitional provisions

1.   The SRA Code of Conduct shall come into force:

(a)   on [10 August 2011], in respect of *licensable bodies*;

(b)   for all other purposes on [6 October 2011], on which date the following provisions of the Solicitors' Code of Conduct 2007 shall be repealed:

(i)   Rules 2 to 4;

(ii)   Rules 5.01 and 5.03;

(iii)   Rules 6 to 11;

(iv)   Rules 17 and 19;

(v)   Rules 20.05 to 20.10; and

(vi)   Rules 21 to 25.

2.   For the avoidance of doubt, where a breach of any provision of the Solicitors' Code of Conduct 2007 comes to the attention of the *SRA* after 6 October 2011, this shall be subject to action by the *SRA* notwithstanding any repeal of the relevant provision.

3.   From 31 March 2012, Chapter 13 shall have effect subject to the following amendments:

(a)   paragraph 1(a)(i) and 1(e) shall be omitted;

(b)   in paragraph 1(a)(iii), 1(b)(ii) and 1(e), the words *"recognised sole practitioner"* shall be omitted;

(c)   in paragraph 1(a)(iii) and 1(b)(ii), the words "or of a *sole practitioner* who should be but has not been authorised by the SRA" shall be omitted; and

(d)   in paragraph 1(b)(i) the words "other than a *sole practitioner*" shall be inserted after the words *"authorised body"*.

4.   From 31 March 2012, Chapter 14 shall have effect subject to the following amendments:

(a)   in the definition of *authorised body*, the words ", and include a sole practitioner authorised by the SRA" shall be inserted after *"recognised body"*;

(b)   in the definition of *"manager"* the words "(ai) a *sole practitioner;*" shall be inserted before the words "(a) a *member* of a *LLP;*";

(c)   in the definition of *practice*, sub-paragraph (d)(i) and, in sub-paragraph (g) the words "or *recognised sole practitioner*" shall be omitted;

(d)   in the definition of separate business, the words *"recognised sole practitioner"* shall be omitted;

(e)   the following shall be substituted for the definition of *recognised body*:

"means a legal services body recognised by the *SRA* under section 9 of the *AJA*, and includes a *sole practitioner* authorised by the *SRA;*";

(f)   the definition of *recognised sole practitioner* shall be omitted and the following definition inserted after the definition of *"sole practitioner"*:

"sole practitioner authorised by the SRA" means a *solicitor* or *REL* authorised by the *SRA* under section 1B of the Solicitors Act 1974 or section 9 of the *AJA* to practise as a *sole practitioner;*".

Useful addresses

LawCare Ltd.
Health Support and Advice for Lawyers

LawCare is a registered charity providing free and entirely confidential support and assistance to lawyers, their families and staff, on health issues such as stress, depression, addiction to alcohol or drugs, eating disorders etc. LawCare also offers free (except for expenses) CPD accredited presentations and workshops about stress recognition and management and related issues.
Freephone helpline: 0800 279 6888. Open 9–7.30 weekdays, 10–4 weekends and public holidays.
www.lawcare.org.uk.

The Law Society

The Law Society's Practice Advice Service is a dedicated support line for solicitors, trainees and employees of law firms. It is staffed by a team of experienced solicitors who deal with enquiries on all areas of law using their own knowledge and a variety of information sources as well as the experience of other specialists within the Law Society.
Telephone: 0870 606 2522. Open 9–5 weekdays.
www.lawsociety.org.uk.

The Solicitors' Assistance Scheme helps solicitors, their families and staff by putting them in contact with a fellow practitioner who will listen and, where appropriate, provide advice and assistance. SAS members are experts in their fields and happy to provide up to an hour's free advice on a wide range of matters including disciplinary, employment, financial and business related issues as well as dealing with personal and emotional problems. For assistance please contact one of the members listed on the website (www.thesas.org.uk) email help@thesas.org.uk or telephone the helpline on 020 7117 8811.

SBA

The Solicitors Benevolent Association is a registered charity which aims to assist solicitors; those who are or have been on the roll, and their dependants. The SBA helps those suffering ill-health (typical examples are debilitating diseases such as multiple sclerosis, and mental conditions such as bipolar disorder and schizophrenia), accident victims, and those without work – for whatever reason. Most applicants are in receipt of state benefits.
Telephone: 020 8675 6440.
www.sba.org.uk.

Index